Lecture Notes in Computer Science 10016

Commenced Publication in 1973
Founding and Former Series Editors:
Gerhard Goos, Juris Hartmanis, and Jan van Leeuwen

More information about this series at http://www.springer.com/series/7412

Jacques Blanc-Talon · Cosimo Distante
Wilfried Philips · Dan Popescu
Paul Scheunders (Eds.)

Advanced Concepts for Intelligent Vision Systems

17th International Conference, ACIVS 2016
Lecce, Italy, October 24–27, 2016
Proceedings

 Springer

Editors
Jacques Blanc-Talon
DGA
Paris
France

Dan Popescu
CSIRO, Data 61
Canberra, ACT
Australia

Cosimo Distante
University of Salento
Lecce
Italy

Paul Scheunders
University of Antwerp
Wilrijk
Belgium

Wilfried Philips
Ghent University
Ghent
Belgium

ISSN 0302-9743   ISSN 1611-3349   (electronic)
Lecture Notes in Computer Science
ISBN 978-3-319-48679-6   ISBN 978-3-319-48680-2   (eBook)
DOI 10.1007/978-3-319-48680-2

Library of Congress Control Number: 2016954946

LNCS Sublibrary: SL6 – Image Processing, Computer Vision, Pattern Recognition, and Graphics

Printed on acid-free paper

This Springer imprint is published by Springer Nature
The registered company is Springer International Publishing AG
The registered company address is: Gewerbestrasse 11, 6330 Cham, Switzerland

Preface

These proceedings gather the selected papers of the Advanced Concepts for Intelligent Vision Systems (ACIVS) conference which was held in Lecce, Italy, during October 24–27, 2016.

This event was the 17th ACIVS. Since the first event in Germany in 1999, ACIVS has become a larger and independent scientific conference. However, the seminal distinctive governance rules have been maintained:

- To update the conference scope on a yearly basis. While keeping a technical backbone (the classic low-level image processing techniques), we have introduced topics of interest such as – chronologically – image and video compression, 3D, security and forensics, and evaluation methodologies, in order to fit the conference scope to our scientific community's needs. In addition, speakers usually give invited talks on hot issues.
- To remain a single-track conference in order to promote scientific exchanges among the audience.
- To grant oral presentations a duration of 25 minutes and published papers a length of 12 pages, which is significantly different from most other conferences.

The second and third items entail a complex management of the conference; in particular, the number of time slots is rather small. Although the selection between the two presentation formats is primarily determined by the need to compose a well-balanced program, papers presented during plenary and poster sessions enjoy the same importance and publication format.

The first item is strengthened by the notoriety of ACIVS, which has been growing over the years: official Springer records show a cumulated number of downloads on July 1, 2016, of more than 440,000 (for ACIVS 2005–2015 only).

The regular sessions also included a couple of invited talks by Professor Andrea Cavallaro (Queen Mary University of London, UK), Professor Thomas B. Moeslund (Aalborg University, Denmark), Professor François Brémond (Inria, France), and Professor Sebastiano Battiato (Catania University, Italy). We would like to thank all of them for enhancing the technical program with their presentations.

ACIVS attracted submissions from many different countries, mostly from Europe, but also from the rest of the world: Algeria, Australia, Austria, Brazil, Belgium, Canada, China, Cyprus, Czech Republic, Denmark, Ecuador, France, Finland, Germany, Hungary, India, Israel, Italy, Korea, Mexico, The Netherlands, Poland, Romania, Russia, Switzerland, Taiwan, Tunisia, Turkey, the Ukraine, United Arab Emirates, the UK, and the USA.

From 137 submissions, 36 were selected for oral presentation and 28 as posters. The paper submission and review procedure was carried out electronically and a minimum of three reviewers were assigned to each paper. A large and energetic Program Committee (87 people), helped by additional reviewers (95 people in total), as listed on the following pages, completed the long and demanding reviewing process. We would like to thank all of them for their timely and high-quality reviews, achieved in quite a short time and during the summer holidays.

Also, we would like to thank our sponsors (in alphabetical order) Antwerp University, Commonwealth Scientific and Industrial Research Organization (CSIRO), Ghent University, Institute of Applied Sciences and Intelligent Systems (ISASI), and the National Research Council (CNR) of Italy for their valuable support.

Finally, we would like to thank all the participants who trusted in our ability to organize this conference for the 17th time. We hope they attended a different and stimulating scientific event and that they enjoyed the atmosphere of the ACIVS social events in the city of Lecce.

As mentioned, a conference like ACIVS would not be feasible without the concerted effort of many people and the support of various institutions. We are indebted to the local organizers Marco Leo, Pier Luigi Mazzeo, Paolo Spagnolo, Pierluigi Carcagní, and Marco Del Coco, for having smoothed all the harsh practical details of an event venue, and we hope to welcome them in the near future.

July 2016

Jacques Blanc-Talon
Cosimo Distante
Wilfried Philips
Dan Popescu
Paul Scheunders

Organization

Acivs 2016 was organized by the University of Salento, located in Lecce, Italy.

Steering Committee

Jacques Blanc-Talon	DGA, France
Cosimo Distante	CNR, University of Salento, Italy
Wilfried Philips	Ghent University/iMinds, Belgium
Dan Popescu	CSIRO, Australia
Paul Scheunders	University of Antwerp, Belgium

Organizing Committee

Pier Luigi Carcagni	Consiglio Nazionale delle Ricerche, Italy
Marco Del Coco	CNR, Italy
Marco Leo	Consiglio Nazionale delle Ricerche, Italy
Pier Luigi Mazzeo	Consiglio Nazionale delle Ricerche, Italy
Paolo Spagnolo	Consiglio Nazionale delle Ricerche, Italy

Program Committee

Alin Achim	University of Bristol, UK
Sos Agaian	The University of Texas, USA
Hamid Aghajan	Stanford University, USA
Edoardo Ardizzone	University of Palermo, Italy
Atilla Baskurt	INSA, France
Sebastiano Battiato	University of Catania, Italy
Fabio Bellavia	Università degli Studi di Palermo, Italy
Jenny Benois-Pineau	Université Bordeaux 1, France
Bir Bhanu	University of California, USA
Philippe Bolon	University of Savoie, France
Egor Bondarev	Technische Universiteit Eindhoven, The Netherlands
Salah Bourennane	Ecole Centrale de Marseille, France
Catarina Brites	Instituto Superior Técnico, Portugal
Alfred M. Bruckstein	Technion IIT, Israel
Vittoria Bruni	University of Rome La Sapienza, Italy
Dumitru Dan Burdescu	University of Craiova, Romania
Tiago Carvalho	Instituto Federal de São Paulo, Campinas, Brazil
Giuseppe Cattaneo	University of Salerno, Italy
Andrea Cavallaro	Queen Mary University of London, UK
Emre Celebi	Louisiana State University, USA
Jocelyn Chanussot	Université de Grenoble Alpes, France
Eric Debreuve	CNRS, France

Raimondo Schettini	University of Milano Bicocca, Italy
Ivan Selesnick	NYU Polytechnic School of Engineering, USA
Andrzej Sluzek	Khalifa University, United Arab Emirates
Zhan Song	Shenzhen Institutes of Advanced Technology, China
Concetto Spampinato	University of Catania, Italy
Changming Sun	CSIRO, Australia
Hugues Talbot	ESIEE, France
Yuliya Tarabalka	Inria, France
Domenico Tegolo	University of Palermo, Italy, Italy
Jean-Philippe Thiran	EPFL, Switzerland
Nadège Thirion-Moreau	SeaTech, Université de Toulon, France
Frederic Truchetet	Université de Bourgogne, France
Sotirios Tsaftaris	University of Edinburgh, UK
Marc Van Droogenbroeck	University of Liège, Belgium
Peter Veelaert	Ghent University/iMinds, Belgium
Nicole Vincent	Université Paris Descartes, France
Domenico Vitulano	IAC CNR, Italy
Toshihiko Yamasaki	The University of Tokyo, Japan
Shin Yoshizawa	RIKEN, Japan
Titus Zaharia	Télécom SudParis, France
Pavel Zemcik	Brno University of Technology, Czech Republic
Djemel Ziou	Sherbrooke University, Canada

Additional Reviewers

Alin Achim	University of Bristol, UK
Jan Aelterman	Ghent University, Belgium
Hamid Aghajan	Stanford University, USA
Edoardo Ardizzone	University of Palermo, Italy
Fabio Bellavia	Università degli Studi di Palermo, Italy
Jenny Benois-Pineau	Université Bordeaux 1, France
Jacques Blanc-Talon	DGA, France
Nyan Bo Bo	Gent University/iMinds, Belgium
Philippe Bolon	University of Savoie, France
Egor Bondarev	Technische Universiteit Eindhoven, The Netherlands
Salah Bourennane	Ecole Centrale de Marseille, France
Catarina Brites	Instituto Superior Técnico, Portugal
Alfred M. Bruckstein	Technion IIT, Israel
Vittoria Bruni	University of Rome La Sapienza, Italy
Dumitru Dan Burdescu	University of Craiova, Romania
Pier Luigi Carcagni	Consiglio Nazionale delle Ricerche, Italy
Tiago Carvalho	Instituto Federal de São Paulo, Campinas, Brazil
Giuseppe Cattaneo	University of Salerno, Italy
Jocelyn Chanussot	Université de Grenoble Alpes, France
Francis Deboeverie	Ghent University, Belgium

Ljiljana Platisa	Ghent University/iMinds, Belgium
Dan Popescu	University Politehnica of Bucharest, Romania
Dan Popescu	CSIRO, Australia
Giovanni Ramponi	University of Trieste, Italy
Patrice Rondao Alface	Nokia Bell Labs, Belgium
Florence Rossant	ISEP, France
Luis Salgado Alvarez de Sotomayor	Universidad Politécnica de Madrid, Spain
Carlo Sansone	Università degli Studi di Napoli Federico II, Italy
Raimondo Schettini	University of Milano Bicocca, Italy
Paul Scheunders	University of Antwerp, Belgium
Adam Schmidt	University of Rouen, France
Ivan Selesnick	NYU Polytechnic School of Engineering, USA
Vasileios Sevetlidis	University of Edinburgh, UK
Andrzej Sluzek	Khalifa University, United Arab Emirates
Paolo Spagnolo	National Research Council, Italy
Changming Sun	CSIRO, Australia
Hugues Talbot	ESIEE, France
Yuliya Tarabalka	Inria, France
Nadège Thirion-Moreau	SeaTech, Université de Toulon, France
Frederic Truchetet	Université de Bourgogne, France
Marc Van Droogenbroeck	University of Liège, Belgium
Peter Veelaert	Ghent University/iMinds, Belgium
Nicole Vincent	Université Paris Descartes, France
Domenico Vitulano	IAC CNR, Italy
Michiel Vlaminck	Ghent University, Belgium
Xingzhe Xie	Ghent University, Belgium
Shin Yoshizawa	RIKEN, Japan
Pavel Zemcik	Brno University of Technology, Czech Republic
Djemel Ziou	Sherbrooke University, Canada
Witold Zorski	Military University of Technology, Poland

Contents

Gradients versus Grey Values for Sparse Image Reconstruction and Inpainting-Based Compression

Markus Schneider[1], Pascal Peter[1(✉)], Sebastian Hoffmann[1],
Joachim Weickert[1], and Enric Meinhardt-Llopis[2]

[1] Mathematical Image Analysis Group, Faculty of Mathematics and Computer
Science, Saarland University, Campus E1.7, 66041 Saarbrücken, Germany
{schneider,peter,hoffmann,weickert}@mia.uni-saarland.de
[2] École Normale de Supérieure de Cachan,
61, Avenue du Président Wilson, 94235 Cachan, France
enric.meinhardt@cmla.ens-cachan.fr

Abstract. Interpolation methods that rely on partial differential equations can reconstruct images with high quality from a few prescribed pixels. A whole class of compression codecs exploits this concept to store images in terms of a sparse grey value representation. Recently, Brinkmann et al. (2015) have suggested an alternative approach: They propose to store gradient data instead of grey values. However, this idea has not been evaluated and its potential remains unknown. In our paper, we compare gradient and grey value data for homogeneous diffusion inpainting w.r.t. two different aspects: First, we evaluate the reconstruction quality, given a comparable amount of data of both kinds. Second, we assess how well these sparse representations can be stored in compression applications. To this end, we establish a framework for optimising and encoding the known data. It allows a fair comparison of both the grey value and the gradient approach. Our evaluation shows that gradient-based reconstructions avoid visually distracting singularities involved in the reconstructions from grey values, thus improving the visual fidelity. Surprisingly, this advantage does not carry over to compression due to the high sensitivity to quantisation.

Keywords: Partial differential equations (pdes) · Laplace interpolation · Poisson equation · Inpainting · Image compression · Derivatives

1 Introduction

Interpolation methods based on partial differential equations (PDEs) have been successfully used for image restoration [2, 4, 12]: So-called inpainting approaches propagate known data into missing or damaged image areas. If the known data can be freely selected from the original image, PDE-based inpainting even allows reconstructions with high quality from much sparser grey value data [8, 11, 16].

© Springer International Publishing AG 2016
J. Blanc-Talon et al. (Eds.): ACIVS 2016, LNCS 10016, pp. 1–13, 2016.
DOI: 10.1007/978-3-319-48680-2_1

PDE-based compression codecs such as [4,7,17] use this fact and only store the locations and grey values of a few pixels.

Many approaches rely on homogeneous diffusion inpainting due to its simplicity and the availability of efficient solvers [4,8,11,14,16]. However, this simple differential equation has a drawback: The inpainting solution can be expressed as a superposition of Green's functions which have singularities [13]. This behaviour often leads to unpleasant artifacts that spoil the visual perception of the reconstructions. Several existing codecs [7,17] avoid these artifacts by using anisotropic PDEs at the price of a higher complexity and computational cost.

However, using different known data than grey values might be an alternative to circumvent the drawbacks of homogeneous diffusion inpainting: Brinkmann et al. [3] have suggested that gradient data could be useful for sparse image representations and compression. So far, this idea has not been implemented, and the potential of gradient data for PDE-based is yet to be explored.

Our Contribution. We fill this gap with a comparative evaluation of grey value and gradient data. First, we investigate the advantages and drawbacks of both kinds of data for sparse image representations with homogeneous diffusion inpainting. To enable a fair comparison, we embed both approaches into a common framework that provides probabilistic algorithms to optimise the known data. In particular, we examine if gradient data can avoid reconstruction artifacts that are common for homogeneous grey value inpainting. Secondly, we analyse the impact of widely used compression techniques such as quantisation and entropy coding on grey values and derivatives. With our experiments on well-known test images, we evaluate their overall compression quality, and also compare to JPEG.

Outline. Section 2 recaps PDE-based reconstructions from grey values and shows an image reconstruction approach from sparse gradients. The following sections also review existing concepts based on grey values, and continue with their adaption to a gradient-based setting. The data optimisation is covered in Sect. 3. We combine these optimisation strategies with compression techniques to form a complete codec in Sect. 4. We evaluate the grey value-based methods and their gradient-based counterparts in Sect. 5, firstly for image reconstructions from sparse data, and secondly in a compression context as proposed by Brinkmann et al. [3]. Finally, we conclude with a summary in Sect. 6.

2   PDE-Based Reconstructions from Sparse Data

2.1   Reconstructions from Grey Values

The goal of PDE-based inpainting is to fill in missing areas in an image $f : \Omega \to \mathbb{R}$ with image domain $\Omega \subset \mathbb{R}^2$. A binary image $c : \Omega \to \{0,1\}$, the so-called *mask*, characterises each pixel $\boldsymbol{x}$ of f as known ($c(\boldsymbol{x}) = 1$) or unknown ($c(\boldsymbol{x}) = 0$).

A homogeneous diffusion inpainting propagates the known data equally in all directions. The steady state solves the inpainting equation

$$c(\boldsymbol{x}) \cdot (u(\boldsymbol{x}) - f(\boldsymbol{x})) - (1 - c(\boldsymbol{x})) \cdot \Delta u(\boldsymbol{x}) = 0 \quad \forall \boldsymbol{x} \in \Omega \tag{1}$$

for u under reflecting boundary conditions. For the unknown pixels, the Laplace equation $\Delta u = 0$ imposes a smoothness constraint. In addition, the known data stays fixed and determines the inpainting result in terms of Dirichlet boundary conditions. A discretisation of (1) leads to a linear system of equations that we solve efficiently with multigrid methods [10].

2.2 Reconstructions from Gradients

Let us now describe how to reconstruct an image from a few known gradients.

Given two masks c_x and c_y representing the locations of the stored x- and y-derivatives, we denote the values for the x- and y-derivatives at these positions by p and q. Because one of the two derivatives might have much more structure than the other in a certain image region or in the whole image, it makes sense to use separate masks. This allows a direct adaption of the masks to the local image structure.

The first reconstruction step performs a componentwise homogeneous diffusion inpainting of the derivatives: We apply an inpainting as given in (1) once to inpaint the x-derivative on a mask c_x, and once to inpaint the y-derivative on c_y. Together, both yield an approximation $\boldsymbol{v}$ of the original gradient field ∇f.

The second step is a numerical integration, that eliminates the singularities the inpainting suffers from. In general, the dense vector field $\boldsymbol{v}$ will be non-integrable, because there is not necessarily an image u whose gradient field is $\boldsymbol{v}$. Therefore, we integrate $\boldsymbol{v}$ numerically by minimising the Poisson functional

$$E(u) = \int_{\Omega} |\nabla u - \boldsymbol{v}|^2 \, d\boldsymbol{x} . \tag{2}$$

This process searches for a differentiable image reconstruction u whose gradient field is closest to the given vector field $\boldsymbol{v}$ in terms of the squared Euclidean distance. Its minimiser u has to satisfy the Poisson equation $\Delta u = \operatorname{div} \boldsymbol{v}$ with reflecting boundary conditions and is determined up to an additive constant. Requiring u to have the same mean μ as the original image, the minimiser becomes unique. Thus, we additionally need the original mean μ in the reconstruction step.

Altogether, the reconstruction procedure consists of the following three steps:

1. Inpaint the x-derivative by solving $c_x(v_1 - p) - (1 - c_x)\Delta v_1 = 0$ for v_1.
2. Inpaint the y-derivative by solving $c_y(v_2 - q) - (1 - c_y)\Delta v_2 = 0$ for v_2.
3. Minimise (2), under the constraint that u has mean μ.

Efficient Algorithmic Realisation. We discretise the first derivatives by forward differences and the Laplacian by its standard discretisation. Consequently, the first derivatives are given on a shifted grid. Discretising the divergence by backward differences finally ensures a discretisation with second order of consistency.

We compute both inpaintings in parallel, as they are independent of each other. To solve the Poisson equation, we apply the discrete Fourier transform and solve the corresponding equation in the Fourier domain [6]. Hereby, the Fourier coefficient $\mathcal{F}[u]_{0,0}$ in the origin is set to the scaled mean μ. In summary, this yields an efficient solver, if the Fast Fourier Transform is used.

3   Data Optimisation for PDE-Based Reconstructions

To find a compact image representation we optimise both the *locations* of the stored grey values/gradients (*spatial optimisation*), and the grey / gradient *values* themselves at these positions (*tonal optimisation*). We consider both aspects for grey values in Sect. 3.1 and for gradients in Sect. 3.2.

3.1   Optimisation Algorithms for Grey Values

Spatial Optimisation. We first aim at finding an optimal image representation without caring about how efficiently it can be stored later on. We call the resulting masks *exact masks*, since they allow to place known data freely and with pixel accuracy. Belhachmi et al. [1] proved that one should choose the mask pixels as an increasing function of the Laplacian magnitude. An optimal control approach of Hoeltgen et al. [8] minimises the trade-off between reconstruction error and sparsity of the known data. Another approach was introduced by Mainberger et al. [11]: Starting with a full mask, they successively remove a certain fraction of randomly chosen mask pixels which have the smallest error. They call this process probabilistic sparsification. Since a pixel is never put back into the mask, the algorithm typically runs into a local minimum. Therefore, they post-optimise the resulting mask by a nonlocal pixel exchange allowing randomised swaps between mask and non-mask pixels. This is the approach we later adapt for gradients.

Tonal Optimisation. For the optimisation of the grey values, we assume the mask to be fixed. We now switch to a discrete setting by reordering all the pixels of an image u row-wise into a vector $\boldsymbol{u}$. Given the grey values at a few locations, collected in a sparse vector $\boldsymbol{g}$, one can express the inpainting in matrix-vector notation as $\boldsymbol{u} = \boldsymbol{M}\boldsymbol{g}$ [10]. It computes the inpainting solution $\boldsymbol{u}$ from the grey values $\boldsymbol{g}$. The matrix $\boldsymbol{M}$ implicitly contains the mask.

To find the best grey values to store we minimise the reconstruction error

$$\underset{\boldsymbol{g}}{\operatorname{argmin}} |\boldsymbol{M}\boldsymbol{g} - \boldsymbol{f}|^2 \ . \tag{3}$$

This least squares problem leads to a linear system of equations. We use an algorithm introduced by Mainberger et al. [11], which is based on so-called inpainting echoes. An inpainting echo is the reconstruction Me_i on the i-th unit vector e_i. This allows to express the final reconstruction u as a linear combination of the inpainting echoes. The flexibility of this approach allows an adaption to the gradient-based setting.

3.2   Optimisation Algorithms for Gradients

Spatial Optimisation. Since we aim at a fair comparison, we optimise both the grey values and the gradients using the probabilistic approach of Mainberger et al. [11]. We apply their algorithm on the x-derivative and on the y-derivative of the original image to generate two masks containing the positions for x- and y-derivatives. Our modified version of their nonlocal pixel exchange minimises the mean squared error in the final reconstruction u after the integration step, and the pixel exchange step allows the mask pixels to swap from one mask into the other. We thereby automatically adapt the number of mask pixels of ∂_x- and ∂_y-mask to the proportion of structures in horizontal and vertical direction in the original image. This modified nonlocal pixel exchange converges towards the global optimum. This allows us to assess the true potential of gradient data for image reconstructions.

In Fig. 1, we show three pairs of exact masks for the standard test images *trui*, *walter* and *peppers*. As expected, we observe that the ∂_x- and the ∂_y-mask prefer locations with structures in horizontal and vertical direction, respectively. The resulting ∂_x- and ∂_y-masks roughly have the same density, as the structures in our test images are more orc less balanced between both derivative directions.

Tonal Optimisation. Given a mask pair (c_x, c_y) and the sparse stored gradients $d = (p, q)$ at these locations, we can express the reconstruction procedure in matrix-vector notation as $u = Ld + \mu$. It computes the reconstructed image u from the stored gradients d, which includes the inpaintings and the integration. L implicitly contains the masks c_x and c_y. We define L to return an image with zero mean. The vector μ represents the mean correction by an additive shift.

The minimisation problem to find the best gradients values to store reads:

$$\underset{d}{\operatorname{argmin}} \left| (Ld + \mu) - f \right|^2 \tag{4}$$

To solve this problem, we extend the idea of inpainting echoes [11] to our setting. For this purpose, we define the *reconstruction echo* $r_i := Le_i$ for the i-th stored data point as the overall reconstruction with zero mean on the i-th unit vector e_i. Thereby, the reconstruction can be expressed as a linear combination of the reconstruction echoes followed by the mean correction:

$$u = Ld + \mu = L\sum_{i \in K} d_i e_i + \mu = \sum_{i \in K} d_i(Le_i) + \mu = \sum_{i \in K} d_i r_i + \mu \tag{5}$$

Hereby, K denotes the set of all mask pixels of the ∂_x- and the ∂_y-mask. That is, if a stored gradients value d_i is changed by some value α, (5) directly specifies how the reconstruction changes, namely by αr_i. This connection enables the adaption of the iterative algorithm of Mainberger et al. [11].

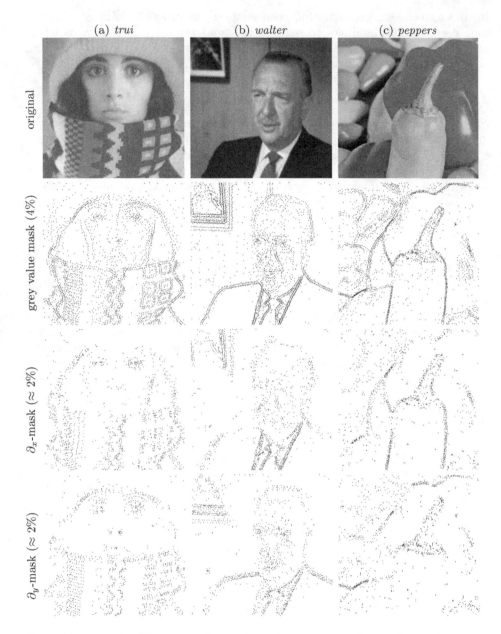

Fig. 1. Exact masks. **First row:** Original test images *trui*, *walter* and zoom into *peppers*. **Second row:** Masks for 4 % grey values from the probabilistic approach by Mainberger et al. [11]. **Third and fourth row:** ∂_x- and ∂_y-mask from the gradient-based approach for 4 % derivatives in total. The density of each derivative mask can slightly differ from 2 % since we allow a flexible adaption of this proportion. Each mask pair of ∂_x- and ∂_y-mask, however, contains exactly 4 % of all pixels.

4 Encoding Framework

4.1 Encoding of Grey Value Data

The previously mentioned methods for exact masks [5,8,11] yield sparse image representations in the spatial domain, which can also be useful for image compression. However, this optimal data might be expensive to store, even if we use efficient coding techniques such as a block coding scheme to encode exact masks [19]. In the following, we discuss an alternative approach that incorporates a trade-off between reconstruction quality and memory cost.

Subdivision Trees. Galić et al. [7] restricted the allowed positions to triangular subdivisions, which can be efficiently encoded by a binary tree. Thereby, nodes efficiently encode mask positions. Such a tree describes a subdivision of the image into regions. In areas which are difficult to reconstruct, it allows a local refinement of the mask. This concept was improved by Schmaltz et al. [17], who used rectangular subdivisions, and was adapted to a probabilistic approach by Peter et al. [16]. They transfer the probabilistic approach for exact masks to binary trees, where tree nodes play the role of pixels. This is the approach that we choose and adapt to gradients.

Quantisation and Encoding. To store the grey values, we have to quantise them. An equidistant quantisation, where successive quantisation levels have the same distance, is sufficient. For both exact and tree-based masks, we write the data into a single file and apply the lossless entropy coder PAQ of Mahoney [9], which is a context mixing scheme and well-suited for heterogeneous data.

4.2 Encoding of Gradient Data

Just as for grey values, we adapt the tree-based approach to the gradient setting. We would like to generate one tree for each gradient component.

Subdivision Trees. In order to adapt the stochastic tree densification of Peter et al. [16], we consider the node sets of both trees together. This automatically tailors the proportion between the size of ∂_x- and ∂_y-tree to the image: For images with more structures in x-direction, the algorithm will put more mask pixels into the ∂_x-mask than into the ∂_y-mask. We post-optimise the resulting pair of trees by an adapted version of the nonlocal node exchange [16]. Similar to the nonlocal pixel exchange for exact masks [11], it prevents the densification from getting trapped in local minima. Besides the fact that we build all the node sets over both trees, another modification is that we consider the final reconstruction error after the integration step whenever the algorithm has to decide if a node swap is kept or not. Just as the nonlocal pixel exchange, this global nonlocal node exchange converges to the global optimum, now with respect to the restriction to the rectangular subdivisions. Figure 2 (c) and (d) show an example for our tree-based masks in comparison to a corresponding exact mask pair for *trui*.

(a) exact ∂_x-mask   (b) exact ∂_y-mask   (c) tree ∂_x-mask   (d) tree ∂_y-mask

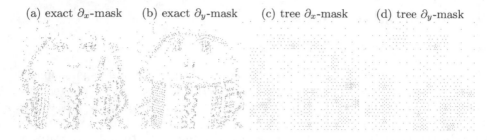

Fig. 2. Exact mask pair and tree-based mask pair for the test image *trui* (shown in Fig. 3) with approximately 2 % x-derivatives and 2 % y-derivatives.

Quantisation of the Gradient Data. The optimised gradients d in (4) are not constrained to integer values, but given in floating point precision. However, in order to store them efficiently, they must be quantised. We use the same equidistant quantisation for x- and y-derivatives. The remaining freedom is to choose the number of quantised values q and their range, yielding two quantisation parameters.

We optimise the quantisation parameters in a direct search during the tonal optimisation and store both in the encoded image file. Within each iteration, we optimise the gradient values w.r.t. the current quantisation.

5   Evaluation of Gradients Versus Grey Values

5.1   PDE-Based Image Reconstruction

For a fair comparison of gradient-based reconstructions and homogeneous grey value inpaintings, we use the optimisation strategies from Sect. 3 to select the same amount of data points for each method. Figure 3 shows three exemplary reconstructions from exact masks. We evaluate the reconstruction quality not only in terms of the mean squared error (MSE), but also in terms of the *mean squared Sobolev error* (MSSE)

$$\mathrm{MSSE}(u, f) = \frac{1}{|\Omega|} \int_{\Omega} \left((u - f)^2 + (u_x - f_x)^2 + (u_y - f_y)^2 \right) \mathrm{d}\boldsymbol{x} , \qquad (6)$$

which rewards a faithful approximation of the gradient. Pure gradient-based reconstructions often achieve a better MSE than homogeneous inpainting on grey values. In terms of MSSE, the gradient-based reconstructions even yield a better error on all the three test images. Moreover, a closer look at the zoomed sections reveals that they indeed avoid the unpleasant singularities (see zooms in Fig. 3). This improves the perceived quality considerably. For instance, around the textured scarf in *trui*, the improvement becomes obvious.

(a) original	(b) grey values	(c) gradients

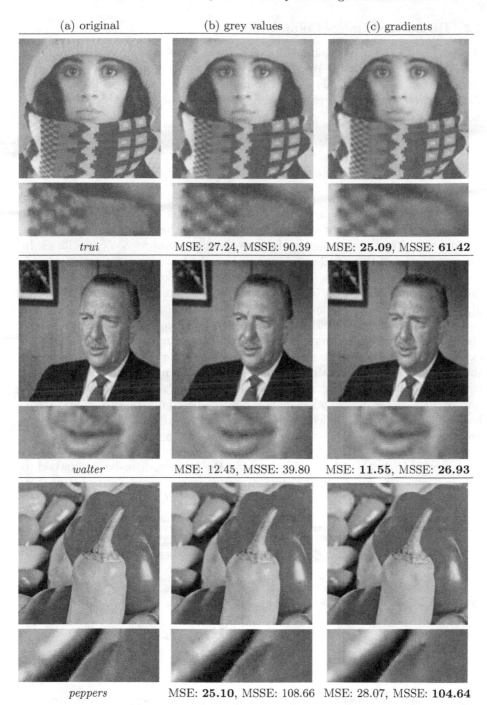

trui	MSE: 27.24, MSSE: 90.39	MSE: **25.09**, MSSE: **61.42**
walter	MSE: 12.45, MSSE: 39.80	MSE: **11.55**, MSSE: **26.93**
peppers	MSE: **25.10**, MSSE: 108.66	MSE: 28.07, MSSE: **104.64**

Fig. 3. First column: Test image. **Second column:** Reconstruction on exact masks with homogeneous grey value inpainting on 4 % grey values. **Third column:** Our gradient-based result on 2 % x- and 2 % y-derivatives. The corresponding exact masks are shown in Fig. 1. Zoomed sections below. The best results are highlighted in bold.

5.2 PDE-Based Image Compression

Comparing the reconstruction quality of grey value-based compared to gradient-based methods on the same amount of stored data points neglects how efficiently this data can be stored. This section evaluates the proposal of Brinkmann et al. [3] to use gradient data for compression. Thereby, we focus on three questions:

- Should one store x- and y-derivatives at different positions, or can we perform better with joint positions, saving the memory costs of a second mask?
- Does it pay off to use exact masks or should we restrict the allowed positions to the structure given by efficiently storable subdivision trees [16,17]?
- How can we quantise the gradient data efficiently?

To answer the first two questions, we compare joint masks to an individual selection of known data for each derivative, and do this for exact and for tree-based masks. Finally, we compare the corresponding compression capabilities. In the second part of this section, we have a closer look at the quantisation effects.

Mask Generation. Figure 4 (a) shows the compression results for four variants of the gradient-based approach: For exact or for tree-based masks, we consider one joint mask or separated masks, respectively. Generating two exact masks and encoding them performs the worst, because storing two exact masks is too expensive: The proportion between the storage costs for two encoded masks and the derivative values typically is about 4:1 for exact masks, but about 1:8 for tree-based masks. One joint mask ($c_x = c_y$) does not allow to get a significant improvement in the overall performance. For tree-based masks, two separate tree-based masks perform significantly better: It pays off to allow different positions for x- and y-derivatives, since these masks are fairly inexpensive to store.

Quantisation Effects. Figure 4 (b) compares the best gradient-based method to existing codecs. Surprisingly, the grey value inpainting now performs better than

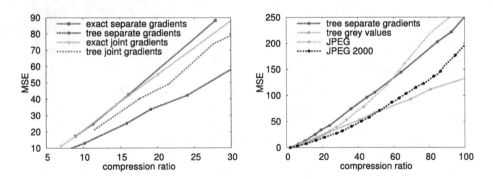

Fig. 4. Compression results. **(a) Left:** Comparison of two separate masks (c_x, c_y) versus one joint mask ($c_x = c_y$), and exact versus tree-based masks. **(b) Right:** Comparison of the best gradient-based method (two separate tree-based masks) against existing codecs for *trui*, including JPEG [15] and JPEG 2000 [18].

Table 1. Comparison of the MSE in dependence on the quantisation for test image *trui* with 4 % data points in total. **First row:** The optimal data in float precision subsequently is quantised to different quantisations. We allow q different values in the range $[0, 255]$ for the grey values, and q different values in the range $[-255, 255]$ for the gradient data. **Second row:** After optimisation w.r.t. the discrete quantisation.

	Float precision	$q = 256$	$q = 128$	$q = 64$
Grey values	27.24	27.26	27.31	27.50
Optimised for discrete levels	–	27.25	27.29	27.42
Gradients	25.09	56.69	80.84	209.36
Optimised for discrete levels	–	26.11	27.50	37.17

the gradient-based approach, even though its reconstruction quality was worse before. The main reason for this behaviour is the high sensitivity of gradient data to quantisation: In regions with few mask points a small error in known derivative values propagates into its neighbourhood by the inpainting and is amplified further by the integration step. Table 1 illustrates this behaviour by showing the effect of a coarser quantisation. For grey value inpainting, we see that restricting the number of quantised values does not significantly degrade the reconstruction. For gradients, however, already small restrictions in the number of quantised values introduce large errors. Optimising the gradient values w.r.t. the discrete quantisation levels attenuates these effects again. Thus, the optimisation tailored to the discrete quantisation levels is crucial for gradient-based compression.

The gradient-based codec is capable of beating JPEG for high compression ratios. However, the limitations imposed by lossy compression steps like quantisation seem too severe to achieve better results with purely gradient-based techniques. This shows that the proposal of Brinkmann et al. [3] has severe drawbacks for image compression, even though it allows for a compact representation of an image in the gradient domain and avoids artifacts in the reconstruction.

6   Conclusions

We have established an evaluation framework which allows to explore the potential of gradient-based image reconstructions compared to grey value-based methods. Derivatives allow for a sparse image representation in gradient domain: Considering the same amount of known data points, gradients typically provide a better quality in both a quantitative and a perceptual sense. In contrast to grey value-based methods, they avoid unpleasant artifacts, have a higher smoothness, and preserve the average grey value.

However, if one employs this approach for image compression as proposed by Brinkmann et al. [3], it turns out that one has to pay a high price for these benefits: Compared to grey value-based methods, the data optimisation becomes more challenging. Furthermore, the gradient data reveals a much higher sensitivity to its quantisation, which is the main reason why a pure gradient-based model in the sense of Brinkmann et al. [3] is not promising for compression. In our future work, we concentrate on models that *combine* gradient data and grey value data in order to unify the advantages of both.

References

1. Belhachmi, Z., Bucur, D., Burgeth, B., Weickert, J.: How to choose interpolation data in images. SIAM J. Appl. Math. **70**(1), 333–352 (2009)
2. Bertalmío, M., Sapiro, G., Caselles, V., Ballester, C.: Image inpainting. In: Proceedings of the SIGGRAPH 2000, New Orleans, LI, pp. 417–424, July 2000
3. Brinkmann, E.-M., Burger, M., Grah, J.: Regularization with sparse vector fields: from image compression to TV-type reconstruction. In: Aujol, J.-F., Nikolova, M., Papadakis, N. (eds.) SSVM 2015. LNCS, vol. 9087, pp. 191–202. Springer, Heidelberg (2015). doi:10.1007/978-3-319-18461-6_16
4. Carlsson, S.: Sketch based coding of grey level images. Sig. Process. **15**(1), 57–83 (1988)
5. Chen, Y., Ranftl, R., Pock, T.: A bi-level view of inpainting-based imagecompression. In: Proceedings of the 19th Computer Vision Winter Workshop, Křtiny, Czech Republic, pp. 19–26, Feb 2014
6. Frankot, R.T., Chellappa, R.: A method for enforcing integrability in shapefrom shading algorithms. IEEE Trans. Pattern Anal. Mach. Intell. **10**(4), 439–451 (1988)
7. Galić, I., Weickert, J., Welk, M., Bruhn, A., Belyaev, A., Seidel, H.P.: Image compression with anisotropic diffusion. J. Math. Imaging Vis. **31**(2–3), 255–269 (2008)
8. Hoeltgen, L., Setzer, S., Weickert, J.: An optimal control approach to find sparse data for laplace interpolation. In: Heyden, A., Kahl, F., Olsson, C., Oskarsson, M., Tai, X.-C. (eds.) EMMCVPR 2013. LNCS, vol. 8081, pp. 151–164. Springer, Heidelberg (2013). doi:10.1007/978-3-642-40395-8_12
9. Mahoney, M.: Adaptive weighing of context models for lossless data compression. Technical report, CS-2005-16, Florida Institute of Technology, Melbourne, FL, December 2005
10. Mainberger, M., Bruhn, A., Weickert, J., Forchhammer, S.: Edge-basedcompression of cartoon-like images with homogeneous diffusion. Pattern Recogn. **44**(9), 1859–1873 (2011)
11. Mainberger, M., Hoffmann, S., Weickert, J., Tang, C.H., Johannsen, D., Neumann, F., Doerr, B.: Optimising spatial and tonal data for homogeneous diffusion inpainting. In: Bruckstein, A.M., Haar Romeny, B.M., Bronstein, A.M., Bronstein, M.M. (eds.) SSVM 2011. LNCS, vol. 6667, pp. 26–37. Springer, Heidelberg (2012). doi:10.1007/978-3-642-24785-9_3
12. Masnou, S., Morel, J.M.: Level lines based disocclusion. In: Proceedings of the 1998 IEEE International Conference on Image Processing, Chicago, IL, vol. 3, pp. 259–263, October 1998
13. Melnikov, Y.A., Melnikov, M.Y.: Green's Functions: Construction and Applications. De Gruyter, Berlin (2012)
14. Ochs, P., Chen, Y., Brox, T., Pock, T.: iPiano: inertial proximal algorithm for nonconvex optimization. SIAM J. Appl. Math. **7**(2), 1388–1419 (2014)
15. Pennebaker, W.B., Mitchell, J.L.: JPEG: Still Image Data Compression Standard. Springer, New York (1992)
16. Peter, P., Hoffmann, S., Nedwed, F., Hoeltgen, L., Weickert, J.: Evaluating the true potential of diffusion-based inpainting in a compression context. Sig. Process. Image Commun. **46**, 40–53 (2016)

17. Schmaltz, C., Peter, P., Mainberger, M., Ebel, F., Weickert, J., Bruhn, A.: Understanding, optimising, and extending data compression with anisotropic diffusion. Int. J. Comput. Vis. **108**(3), 222–240 (2014)
18. Taubman, D.S., Marcellin, M.W. (eds.): JPEG 2000: Image Compression Fundamentals, Standards and Practice. Kluwer, Boston (2002)
19. Zeng, G., Ahmed, N.: A block coding technique for encoding sparse binary patterns. IEEE Trans. Acoust. Speech Sig. Process. **37**(5), 778–780 (1989)

Global Bilateral Symmetry Detection Using Multiscale Mirror Histograms

Mohamed Elawady[1(✉)], Cécile Barat[1], Christophe Ducottet[1],
and Philippe Colantoni[2]

[1] Universite Jean Monnet, CNRS, UMR 5516, Laboratoire Hubert Curien,
42000 Saint-Étienne, France
mohamed.elawady@univ-st-etienne.fr
[2] Université Jean Monnet, Centre Interdisciplinaire d'Etudes et de Recherches sur
l'Expression Contemporaine n° 3068, Saint-Étienne, France

Abstract. In recent years, there has been renewed interest in bilateral symmetry detection in images. It consists in detecting the main bilateral symmetry axis inside artificial or natural images. State-of-the-art methods combine feature point detection, pairwise comparison and voting in Hough-like space. In spite of their good performance, they fail to give reliable results over challenging real-world and artistic images. In this paper, we propose a novel symmetry detection method using multi-scale edge features combined with local orientation histograms. An experimental evaluation is conducted on public datasets plus a new aesthetic-oriented dataset. The results show that our approach outperforms all other concurrent methods.

Keywords: Symmetry detection · Reflection symmetry · Edge features · Pairwise similarity · Symmetry histogram

1 Introduction

Symmetry is a very important measure in some computer vision applications such as aesthetic analysis [21], object detection and segmentation [18], depth estimation [20], or medical image processing [2]. This paper focuses on detecting a single bilateral symmetry axis by exploring the similarity between regions which are mirror reflected around an image axis.

Bilateral symmetry detection has been improved over decades since 1930's [9]. In particular, Loy and Eklundh [11] approach was a great milestone in the domain, thanks to the use of SIFT descriptor [10], an appropriate pairwise comparison, and Hough-voting scheme [6]. Since then, many methods [3,4,7,12,14,16] proposed some improvements and refinements of Loy's method, but still, they fail in cases where SIFT is not adapted (uniform texture, scale variation, etc.). Our idea is to exploit another type of local features, edges, which are the most important visual cues used by the human visual system to detect symmetry. Only few attempts have been done in this direction [1,5,13,19].

© Springer International Publishing AG 2016
J. Blanc-Talon et al. (Eds.): ACIVS 2016, LNCS 10016, pp. 14–24, 2016.
DOI: 10.1007/978-3-319-48680-2_2

The general framework for symmetry detection proposed by [5] provides promising results, but only edge fragments are used and it fails to account for texture information.

We propose a novel method for symmetry detection preserving the shape and texture information inside an image. This work contributes with: (1) introducing a local edge orientation histogram, (2) utilizing multi-scale edge extraction to exploit the full resolution image. In addition, we introduce groundtruth of a global symmetry axis inside images extracted from the large-scale Aesthetic Visual Analysis (AVA) dataset [15]. This dataset is composed of artistic photographs which involved in on-line professional photography competitions.

In Sect. 2, we analyze related work of symmetry detection. Then we describe the details of the proposed algorithm in Sect. 3. We present the experimental results on PSU and AVA datasets in Sect. 4 and the conclusion in the last section.

2   Related Work

The baseline algorithm to detect a global bilateral symmetry axis was introduced by Loy and Eklundh [11]. The general scheme is as follows: (1) extraction of local-feature points using Lowe's SIFT [10], (2) matching of pairs of those keypoints based on the similarity of corresponding mirror SIFT descriptors, and (3) use of the pairs in Hough-voting space to find the best symmetrical candidate. Many attempts proposed refinements to Loy's general scheme, especially Mo and Draper [14] in selecting all symmetry candidate pairs instead of finding closest matches at each point, and using less complex hough voting scheme. The improvement produced more particles than [11] for the symmetry axis, to elongate the output axis according to the global texture information of an image. These intensity-based methods depend mainly on the properties of SIFT features, and their capabilities for symmetry matching with respect to intensity and orientation in the neighboring pixels. In the presence of smooth objects with noisy background, the global symmetry information is lost due to a small number of extracted feature points inside an image.

Cicconet et al. [5] approach exploits the idea of using edge detection in a symmetry measure based on edge orientations. The method can be summarized in the following steps. First, a regular set of feature points with local edge amplitude and orientation is extracted. Second, given any pair of points, a symmetry axis candidate is defined (parametrized by angle and displacement variables) and a symmetry coefficient is associated with this axis. Third, a symmetry voting image is defined as the sum of the weighted contribution of all pairs of points for a given axis. Finally, the best candidate is extracted as the maximum over this voting image. This approach lacks neighborhood's texture information inside the feature representation, and it is totally dependable on the scale parameter of the edge detector. Because of these drawbacks, some local symmetric characteristics are neglected.

Our method investigates Cicconet's edge features [5] within Loy's scheme [11] by adding neighboring-pixel information resulting a better symmetry representation in the voting space. Additionally, it overcomes the scale limitations by adding multi-scale information.

3   Algorithm Details

The main steps of the proposed symmetry detection algorithm is: (1) dense edge extraction, (2) multi-scale edge description with a local orientation histogram h_p as a texture feature, (3) edge triangulation to find symmetry pairs, and (4) voting based on weighted pairs to detect a global bilateral axis.

3.1   Local Orientation Histogram

Given an image I to analyze, feature points are sampled along a regular grid (stride and cell size are computed with respect to image size). A feature point p and its local edge characteristics (J_p, τ_p) are extracted within each cell using a Morlet wavelet $\psi_{k,\sigma}$ of constant scale σ and varying orientation $\{\tau_k, k = 1 \ldots n\}$. The wavelet parameters are set to detect edges: the wavelength is 4σ, and the elongation along the main orientation is half value of its orthogonal. Formally, The mother Morlet wavelet at point $p = (p_x, p_y)$ is defined as:

$$\psi(p) = e^{jk_0 p^T} e^{-\frac{1}{2}|Ap|^2} \tag{1}$$

where $k_0 = (\frac{\pi}{2}, 0)$ and $A = diag(1, \frac{1}{2})$. The wavelet function of scale σ and orientation τ_k is:

$$\psi_{k,\sigma}(p) = \frac{1}{\sigma}\psi(\frac{\Omega_k p}{\sigma}) \tag{2}$$

$$\Omega_k = \begin{pmatrix} \cos(\phi_k) & \sin(\phi_k) \\ -\sin(\phi_k) & \cos(\phi_k) \end{pmatrix} \tag{3}$$

where ϕ_k is the angle associated with τ_k.

If $J_k(p)$ denote the modulus of wavelet coefficients at point p, local edge characteristics J_p and τ_p are obtained by seeking the maximum wavelet response and orientation over all orientations. Formally:

$$J_k(p) = |I * \psi_{k,\sigma}|(p) \tag{4}$$

$$k_p = \arg \max_k J_k(p) \tag{5}$$

$$J_p = J_{k_p}(p) \tag{6}$$

$$\tau_p = \tau_{k_p} \tag{7}$$

where $*$ denotes the 2D convolution operation.

Although local edge orientation is important to detect symmetry, the surrounding texture around an edge segment is also an important feature especially for natural images. Thus, we introduce a local orientation histogram h_p as the

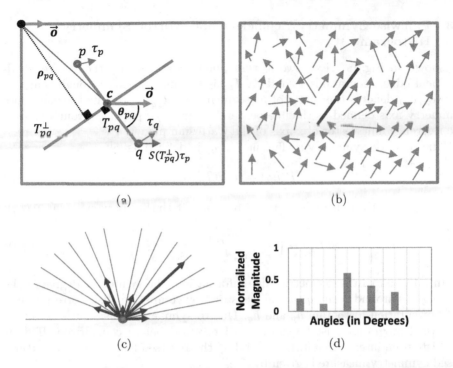

Fig. 1. Pairwise mirror symmetry and local orientation histogram. (a) Pairwise mirror symmetry. (b) Edge segment distribution within a cell. (c) Angular distribution of edge segments for 16 main orientations over 180°. (d) Normalized local orientation histogram. Best seen in screen.

weighted directional contribution of all neighboring points r in the corresponding grid cell. As described in Fig. 1(b-d), the histogram count at a given orientation τ_k is:

$$h_p(k) = \sum_{r \in N(p)} J_r \delta_{\phi_k - \phi_r} \tag{8}$$

where ϕ_k and ϕ_r are angles associated with τ_k and τ_r, J_r and τ_r are defined the same way as for p (Eqs. (5)-(7)) and δ_x is the Kronecker delta. h_p is subsequently $\ell 1$ normalized and circular shifted so as the first bin corresponds to τ_p.

3.2   Multi-scale Information

In most images, relevant information about the visual content may appear at different scales. To consider this information, we propose to detect the feature points at multiple scales. For that purpose, we consider a set of regular grids at different scales and a corresponding set of wavelet scales $\{\sigma_l, l = 1..m\}$. The whole set of feature points is augmented by extracting wavelet local maxima at each scale and by computing their corresponding local characteristics.

3.3   Pairwise Symmetry Coefficient and Mirror Symmetry Histogram

As shown in Fig. 1a, given two feature points p and q and their corresponding local edge orientations τ_p and τ_q, T_{pq} is the line passing through p and q, $c = (c_x, c_y)$ denotes the center of pq segment and $T_{pq}^\perp$ represents the candidate symmetry axis defined as the line perpendicular to pq passing through c. $\vec{o}$ is the reference unit vector of x-axis of the Cartesian plane.

The pairwise symmetry coefficient $f(p,q)$ is defined as [5]:

$$f(p,q) = |\tau_q S(T_{pq}^\perp)\tau_p| \tag{9}$$

where $S(T_{pq}^\perp)$ is the reflection matrix with respect to the line perpendicular to (pq):

$$S(T_{pq}^\perp) = \begin{pmatrix} -\cos(2\theta_{pq}) & -\sin(2\theta_{pq}) \\ -\sin(2\theta_{pq}) & \cos(2\theta_{pq}) \end{pmatrix} \tag{10}$$

In addition to the geometric edge information, the symmetry degree of the two regions around p and q can be measured by comparing their corresponding local orientation histogram h_p and h_q. Due to symmetry considerations, one of the two histograms must be shifted and reversed before comparison. If d_I is the histogram intersection distance, and h_q^* the reversed histogram, the texture-based symmetry measure is given by:

$$d_I(h_p, h_q^*) = \sum_{k=1}^{n} \min(h_p(k), h_q^*(k)) \tag{11}$$

Given a pair of feature points (p, q), the candidate axis $T_{pq}^\perp$ perpendicular to (pq) is parametrized by the orientation of its normal θ_{pq} and its distance to the origin $\rho_{pq} = c_x \cos\theta_{pq} + c_y \sin\theta_{pq}$ where (c_x, c_y) are the coordinates of point c located at the middle of (p, q) segment (see Fig. 1a). A mirror symmetry histogram $H_S(\rho, \theta)$ is defined as the sum of the contribution of all pairs of feature points such as:

$$H(c_x, c_y, \theta) = \sum_{\substack{p,q \\ p \neq q}} J_p J_q f(p,q) d_I(h_p, h_q) \delta_{(c_x,c_y) - \frac{p+q}{2}} \delta_{\theta - \theta_{pq}} \tag{12}$$

$$H_S(\rho, \theta) = \sum_{c_x, c_y} H(c_x, c_y, \theta) \delta_{\rho - \rho_{pq}} \tag{13}$$

The best bilateral symmetry axis inside the image is detected by searching for the global maximum of the mirror symmetry histogram H_S. For that purpose, we solve the orientation discontinuity problem by extending the voting space in a circular way. The spatial extension of this axis can be determined as the convex hull of the set of feature points contributing to this axis. Figures 2(a-d) show the symmetry detection for some example in terms of two voting histograms. The first H presents one major axis (A3 - red color) in the middle surrounded by four

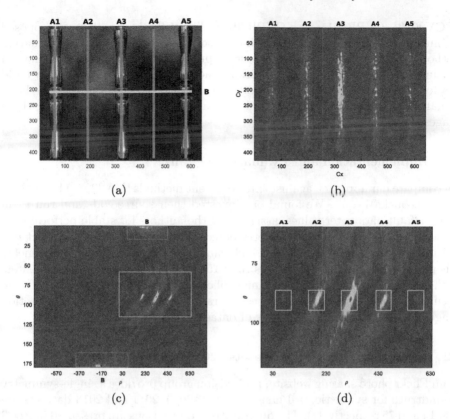

Fig. 2. Symmetry detection process: (a) Input image with local symmetry axis candidates indicated with red and green lines. (b) The output of the voting histogram $H(c_x, c_y)$ marginalized over the orientation variable θ and the corresponding symmetry axis IDs. (c) The output of the voting histogram $H_S(\rho, \theta)$. And (d) the zoomed-in region inside the red rectangle. Local maxima correspond to candidate symmetry axes (framed in red and green). (Color figure online)

minor axes (A1, A2, A4, A5 - red color) vertically in Fig. 2b. In H_S histogram (Fig. 2c) and its zoom-in version (Fig. 2d), these axes are represented by 5 local maxima aligned along the line of orientation $\theta = 90°$. Additionally, a horizontal axis (B - green color) appears near the boundaries of θ axis, it describes another symmetry detection (the top half of steel and its mirror in the bottom side). The main axis is the vertical one (A3 - red color) located in the center.

4   Experiments and Discussions

The aim of this part is to evaluate the results of our method and to compare it to concurrent methods from the state-of-the-art. The evaluation of symmetry detection had received re-surging interest in the main computer vision conferences. Indeed, symmetry detection challenges [8,17] were successively proposed with

ECCV2010[1], CVPR2011[2] and CVPR2013[3]. They all rely on a dataset proposed by Liu's group publicly available with an associated groundtruth and evaluation method. We then use these three general purpose datasets for our evaluation and in addition, we provide an additional aesthetic-oriented dataset. To build this fourth dataset, we extracted some symmetrical images from the Aesthetic Visual Analysis (AVA) collection and generated axis groundtruth among those images.

4.1   Implementation and Evaluation Details

We compare our approach against three different methods (Loy2006 [11], Mo2011 [14], Cicconet2014 [5]). We found or requested their source code and ran them using default parameter values, assigned by the authors for stable performance. As described in [8], a global symmetry detection is considered to be correct if it satisfies the following conditions: (1) The angle between the detected symmetry axis and the groundtruth axis is less than 15°. (2) The distance between centers of these two axes is less than 0.2 multiplied by minimum length of the axes. Accuracy represents the correct detection rate (the number of correct detection images divided by the total number of dataset images).

4.2   Comparison on PSU Datasets (2010, 2011 and 2013)

From Flickr photo sharing website, Liu's vision group provides a single-symmetry groundtruth for synthetic/real images (size of 2010, 2011 and 2013 datasets are 134, 14 and 75 respectively). The quantitative comparisons are presented in Fig. 3 with respect to each version of PSU dataset. Our method is ranked first for all PSU version with a difference of more than 10 % among the nearest competent Loy2006 [11], which achieves the best detection accuracy among 2011 and 2013 symmetry challenges [8,17]. Cic2014 [5] approach has ranked third due to the absence of local neighborhood information in the mirror symmetry histogram for candidate selection.

Figures 4(a-f) gives some detection examples[4] to present the superior performance of the proposed algorithm over others. In Fig. 4(a,d), our method correctly detects the symmetry axis of the bird with an extra line fitting on axis endpoints. However, [11] finds very few SIFT features generating a tiny non-meaningful detection, and [5,14] output misalignment axes representing different components within an image. Figure 4b shows a valid axis detection by our method, while [5,11] attempt to find an inaccurate global axis due to presence of the non-exact shapes inside the centered object. Inside Fig. 4c with different changes in environment illumination, our method perfectly aligned with the full symmetry

---

[1] http://vision.cse.psu.edu/research/symmetryCompetition/index.shtml.
[2] http://vision.cse.psu.edu/research/symmComp/index.shtml.
[3] http://vision.cse.psu.edu/research/symComp13/content.html.
[4] All PSU output with detected symmetry axes can be found in: http://perso. univ-st-etienne.fr/em68594h/SupplementalFilesPSU.zip.

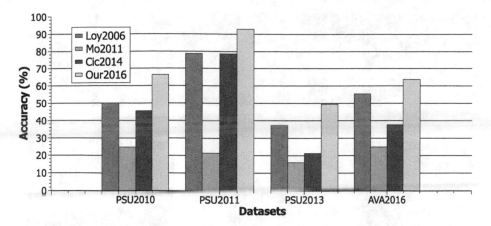

Fig. 3. Comparison of accuracy rates for our method "Our2016" against the baseline algorithm "Loy2006" [11], its improvement "Mo2011" [14] and one of the recent algorithms "Cic2014" [5]. The used datasets are: different versions of PSU (2010, 2011, 2013) with provided groundtruth [8, 17] and AVA with our groundtruth.

axis and [11,14] select different secondary global axes due to surface's mirror effect of the glass. A synthetic butterfly of Fig. 4e represents an easy detection of all methods except [14]. Our method has the most accurate axis output compared to the axis groundtruth. With a camera flash-on, facial Fig. 4f results a challenging axis detection, in which [11] shortly aligns over the groundtruth according to insufficient SIFT features. But our method gives the most appropriate axis output with a horizontal shift, such that it covers all human parts (including frontal face, neck, and hair). In all figures except Fig. 4e, [5] is very sensitive to noise in limited contrast environments and in high-texture foreground/background objects.

4.3   Comparison on AVA Dataset

From DPChallenge photo contest website, Murray et al. [15] introduces different annotations[5] (aesthetic, semantic and photographic style) for more than 250,000 images for Aesthetic Visual Analysis "AVA". From the following photography challenges, we labeled global-axis symmetry groundtruth[6] for 253 out of 878 images: (1) five challenges of "Reflections Without Mirrors": images containing bilateral representation without using mirror, (2) three challenges of "Symmetry": photographs composing symmetrical balance. These images are selected to neglect unclear instances of ambiguity symmetry, and to represent many comparison cases (non-centering viewpoint, perspective view, blurring reflection, etc.)

---

[5] http://www.lucamarchesotti.com/.

[6] Source code to generate AVA images and their symmetry labels: http://perso. univ-st-etienne.fr/em68594h/SymAVA.zip.

Fig. 4. Some images in (a-f) PSU datasets and (g-n) our labeled AVA dataset with groundtruth (blue), where our method (cyan) produces better or similar results over Loy2006 [11] (green), Mo2011 [14] (magenta) and Cic2014 [5] (yellow). Each axis is shown in a straight line with squared endpoints and a starred midpoint. Best seen on screen. (Color figure online)

for detection algorithms. Figure 3 shows that our approach has better performance over other methods.

Figures 4(g-n) presents some experimental results[7] representing different types of artistic scene. Natural landscapes in Fig. 4(g,k) illustrate that [5] behaves

---

[7] All AVA output with the detected symmetry axes can be found in: http://perso.univ-st-etienne.fr/em68594h/SupplementalFilesAVA.zip.

abnormally with perspective view conditions, and [11,14] act incomplete with high shape occlusions. Abstract Figs. 4(h,l) demonstrate the superior performance of [5] compared to [11], in order to fit the global symmetry axis. [14] works better among less texture objects with clear contours. In Figs. 4(i,j), our method easily detects global symmetry axis, while [11,14] stuck with the local ones if exists. Our method only finds a clear symmetry detection in Fig. 4m with a high-reflected object with non-homogeneous background. Contour-based approaches, as ours and [5] ones, execute successfully within the non-exact symmetry Fig. 4n. In summary, our method and [5] ones align better in figures containing objects with clear edges, [11] locally detects shapes with smooth background, and [14] provides incorrect and unclear symmetry over the most visual cases.

5   Conclusion

This paper introduces multi-scale edge features combined with local orientation histograms, in order to develop a reliable global symmetry detection among variants of visual cues. Quantitative and qualitative comparisons show a substantial advantage for our proposed method on different types of public datasets. Our model can be improved to handle complex images with non-centered viewpoints and large degrees of perspective view. It can be extended to solve the over-fitting of axis endpoints. The future work is to introduce a stable balance measure; describing the existence and degree of global axes in terms of both geometrical and symmetrical properties inside an image, and to integrate this measure within existing retrieval systems of visual arts.

References

1. Atadjanov, I., Lee, S.: Bilateral symmetry detection based on scale invariant structure feature. In: 2015 IEEE International Conference on Image Processing (ICIP), pp. 3447–3451. IEEE (2015)
2. Bairagi, V.: Symmetry-based biomedical image compression. J. Digital Imaging 28, 718–726 (2015)
3. Cai, D., Li, P., Su, F., Zhao, Z.: An adaptive symmetry detection algorithm based on local features. In: 2014 IEEE Visual Communications and Image Processing Conference, pp. 478–481. IEEE (2014)
4. Cho, M., Lee, K.M.: Bilateral symmetry detection via symmetry-growing. In: BMVC, pp. 1–11. Citeseer (2009)
5. Cicconet, M., Geiger, D., Gunsalus, K.C., Werman, M.: Mirror symmetry histograms for capturing geometric properties in images. In: 2014 IEEE Conference on Computer Vision and Pattern Recognition (CVPR), pp. 2981–2986. IEEE (2014)
6. Duda, R.O., Hart, P.E.: Use of the hough transformation to detect lines and curves in pictures. Commun. ACM 15(1), 11–15 (1972)
7. Kondra, S., Petrosino, A., Iodice, S.: Multi-scale kernel operators for reflection and rotation symmetry: further achievements. In: 2013 IEEE Conference on Computer Vision and Pattern Recognition Workshops (CVPRW), pp. 217–222. IEEE (2013)

8. Liu, J., Slota, G., Zheng, G., Wu, Z., Park, M., Lee, S., Rauschert, I., Liu, Y.: Symmetry detection from realworld images competition 2013: summary and results. In: 2013 IEEE Conference on Computer Vision and Pattern Recognition Workshops (CVPRW), pp. 200–205. IEEE (2013)

9. Liu, Y., Hel-Or, H., Kaplan, C.S.: Computational Symmetry in Computer Vision and Computer Graphics. Now Publishers Inc., Boston (2010)

10. Lowe, D.G.: Distinctive image features from scale-invariant keypoints. Int. J. Comput. Vis. **60**(2), 91–110 (2004)

11. Loy, G., Eklundh, J.-O.: Detecting symmetry and symmetric constellations of features. In: Leonardis, A., Bischof, H., Pinz, A. (eds.) ECCV 2006. LNCS, vol. 3952, pp. 508–521. Springer, Heidelberg (2006). doi:10.1007/11744047_39

12. Michaelsen, E., Muench, D., Arens, M.: Recognition of symmetry structure by use of gestalt algebra. In: 2013 IEEE Conference on Computer Vision and Pattern Recognition Workshops (CVPRW), pp. 206–210. IEEE (2013)

13. Ming, Y., Li, H., He, X.: Symmetry detection via contour grouping. In: 2013 20th IEEE International Conference on Image Processing (ICIP), pp. 4259–4263. IEEE (2013)

14. Mo, Q., Draper, B.: Detecting bilateral symmetry with feature mirroring. In: CVPR 2011 Workshop on Symmetry Detection from Real World Images (2011)

15. Murray, N., Marchesotti, L., Perronnin, F.: AVA: a large-scale database for aesthetic visual analysis. In: 2012 IEEE Conference on Computer Vision and Pattern Recognition (CVPR), pp. 2408–2415. IEEE (2012)

16. Patraucean, V., von Gioi, R.G., Ovsjanikov, M.: Detection of mirror-symmetric image patches. In: 2013 IEEE Conference on Computer Vision and Pattern Recognition Workshops (CVPRW), pp. 211–216. IEEE (2013)

17. Rauschert, I., Brocklehurst, K., Kashyap, S., Liu, J., Liu, Y.: First symmetry detection competition: summary and results. Technical report CSE11-012, Department of Computer Science and Engineering, The Pennsylvania State University (2011)

18. Teo, C.L., Fermuller, C., Aloimonos, Y.: Detection and segmentation of 2D curved reflection symmetric structures. In: Proceedings of the IEEE International Conference on Computer Vision, pp. 1644–1652 (2015)

19. Wang, Z., Tang, Z., Zhang, X.: Reflection symmetry detection using locally affine invariant edge correspondence. IEEE Trans. Image Process. **24**(4), 1297–1301 (2015)

20. Yang, L., Liu, J., Tang, X.: Depth from water reflection. IEEE Trans. Image Process. **24**(4), 1235–1243 (2015)

21. Zhao, S., Gao, Y., Jiang, X., Yao, H., Chua, T.S., Sun, X.: Exploring principles-of-art features for image emotion recognition. In: Proceedings of the ACM International Conference on Multimedia, pp. 47–56. ACM (2014)

Neural Network Boundary Detection for 3D Vessel Segmentation

Robert Ieuan Palmer and Xianghua Xie[✉]

Department of Computer Science, Swansea University, Swansea, UK
x.xie@swansea.ac.uk

Abstract. Conventionally, hand-crafted features are used to train machine learning algorithms, however choosing useful features is not a trivial task as they are very much data-dependent. Given raw image intensities as inputs, supervised neural networks (NNs) essentially learn useful features by adjusting the weights of its nodes using the *back-propagation* algorithm. In this paper we investigate the performance of NN architectures for the purpose of boundary detection, before integrating a chosen architecture in a data-driven deformable modelling framework for full segmentation. Boundary detection performed well, with boundary sensitivity of >88 % and specificity of >85 % for highly obscured and diffused lymphatic vessel walls. In addition, the vast majority of all boundary-classified pixels were in the immediate vicinity of the ground truth boundary. When integrated into a 3D deformable modelling framework it produced an area overlap with the ground truth of >98 %, and both point-to-mesh and Hausdorff distance errors were less than other approaches. To this end it has been shown that NNs are suitable for boundary detection in deformable modelling, where object boundaries are obscured, diffused and low in contrast.

1 Introduction

Deformable models are popular techniques for both image segmentation [5,6, 12–14,18–20] and tracking [1], and have also been used specifically for vessel segmentation [2–4,7,9,21]. Typically, an initial model is aligned with a test image before being deformed to fit the object boundary. By using bottom-up data-driven constraints as well as top-down prior shape knowledge, they have the ability to overcome appearance inconsistencies which are often present in images from numerous modalities.

To avoid contour entanglement, search paths are regularly defined along the surface normal direction for each of the initial contour points. The search path coordinates with the strongest boundary responses are then taken as the contour points' new position. Learning-based boundary detectors are therefore often necessary in order to drive the initial model towards the object boundary, and have been used in medical image deformable modelling [11,12,15]. Often, these studies consist of hand-picking useful features to distinguish between boundary and non-boundary pixels, e.g. Haar features [15], and gradient steerable features [11]. However, choosing appropriate features to use is not a trivial task as

© Springer International Publishing AG 2016
J. Blanc-Talon et al. (Eds.): ACIVS 2016, LNCS 10016, pp. 25–36, 2016.
DOI: 10.1007/978-3-319-48680-2_3

useful features are very much data-dependent, with object type, image modality and image contrast all effecting the usefulness of a feature. In addition, highly abstract features may be very useful for boundary detection, therefore by using hand-crafted features it is possible to miss out on some additional, potentially useful information.

Multilayer NNs are composed of multiple processing layers which are themselves composed of multiple nodes that are interconnected by weighted connections. An error is computed by comparing the *forward-propagation* of the inputs through the network with the desired output, and the *back-propagation* algorithm is implemented to adjust the weights. The network therefore fits a function to a supervised output given the input values and output prediction, essentially learning abstract representations of the input data. As a result, the weight of each node is essentially an individual feature, meaning the network is capable of learning useful features. For these reasons NNs are popular learning systems for image recognition, and have been used specifically for edge detection [10, 16].

Due to the nature of the imaging modality, slices tend to have a highly prominent boundary appearance on the left hand side of the vessel, whereas they are extremely obscure to the right hand side. This makes choosing features capable of identifying all boundary pixels very challenging. We propose inputting raw intensity values into a neural network to be used as a learning-based boundary detector for deformable model-based segmentation. We perform experiments on ex-vivo confocal microscopy images of the lymphatic vessel, where vessel walls are very low in contrast with many weak edges. Pixels are classified as being on the vessel's outer wall or not, and mesh regularisation is used for complete 3D segmentation.

2   Method

The proposed framework consists of an initial segmentation based on a simple intensity filter on each individual image slice, which is used to generate an initial mesh model. Following this, an iterative deformable modelling process is implemented which deforms the initial mesh towards the lymphatic vessel wall. An overview of the proposed framework is shown in Fig. 1. For full vessel segmentation, the segmentation framework is implemented twice; once for the outer wall and once for the inner wall; so that segmentation of both walls are carried out independently.

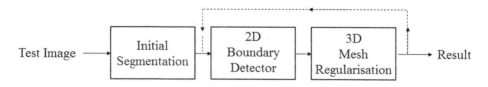

Fig. 1. Overview of the proposed lymphatic vessel segmentation at the testing stage.

The initial meshes are generated by first carrying out an initial segmentation on each individual image slice. These segmentation contours have the same number of points, making it possible to define edges between slices to generate a face-vertex mesh.

The deformable modelling process is iterative and stops when the maximum number of iterations is reached. This process consists of two components. Firstly a 2D boundary detector is carried out on each individual slice, where search paths are defined along the normal direction of each mesh vertex. A neural network is used for boundary detection in order to learn useful features, rather than spending time hand crafting them. Finally, 3D mesh regularisation is implemented on the entire mesh, using a B-spline-based method. This ensures a smooth surface not only on each 2D contour, but also between contours in the third dimension.

On every iteration the boundary detector's search path decreases in order to reach convergence, and the degrees of freedom associated with the mesh regularisation increases to allow the mesh to deform to areas of high curvature. As a result, the deformable modelling process can be thought of as an iterative refinement process.

2.1   Initial Segmentation

Before deformable modelling, an initial mesh model must be defined. This section describes an initial 2D intensity-based segmentation on a slice-by-slice basis, before combining the estimated 2D contours to generate a simple 3D mesh structure.

It is assumed that the pixel intensities within the lymphatic vessel walls are significantly higher than the remaining pixels, therefore it is assumed that the pixels with highest local gradient are on the boundary. To this end, a simple 2-rectangle Haar-like filter [17] is employed to highlight the pixels of high gradient. For every pixel in the image a filter response is computed as follows;

$$f = \sum_{k=0}^{N} \mu_1^k - \sum_{k=0}^{N} \mu_2^k \tag{1}$$

where μ_1^k is the intensity of pixel k in rectangle 1, μ_2^k is the intensity of pixel k in rectangle 2, and N is the number of pixels in each rectangle.

The filter is applied to the image in polar coordinates, and for each column in the polar image the pixel with the optimal filter response is identified. As the appearance of the outer and inner walls are opposite each other, so too will the filter response. Therefore the maximum value of Eq. 1 is used to identify pixels on the inner wall, and the minimum value is used to identify outer wall pixels. A filter size of 1×21 is centred at the test pixel, where $N = 10$ pixels are summed in rectangle 1, and $N = 10$ pixels are also summed in rectangle 2. The contour in polar coordinates is then converted back to cartesian coordinates, and is smoothed by fitting the contour to an ellipse. This is done by optimising the conic equation for an ellipse using the least-squares algorithm.

This process is repeated for every slice in the 3D image. However, it is also assumed that the boundary walls do not significantly change between adjacent slices, therefore the smoothed contour from the previous slice is used to help estimate the contour on the next slice. This is done by restricting the search space for finding the optimal filter response in each polar image column. A contour point in column j in the polar image of slice $i + 1$ must be within ± 10 of the contour point in column j in slice i.

Given that each slice was converted to polar images of the same size, the number of contour points on each slice is also equal. Therefore contour point j of slice i is correspondent to contour point j in slice $i + 1$. This makes generating the mesh a simple task by simply defining mesh edges between corresponding contour points in adjacent slices.

2.2   Neural Network Boundary Detection

Search paths are defined along the inward and outward normals of each vertex of the initial mesh. The normal directions can be straightforwardly computed given the vertices' neighbours. Each search path coordinate is tested to get a boundary probability score, and the coordinate with the highest score on each path is considered the new vertex position.

Raw intensity values from a local patch are inputted into a NN for each search path coordinate. Layers of nodes are connected by weights, and each node is treated as a perceptron. Their activations are then calculated by passing their weighted sum of inputs through an activation function. Given a supervised output the weights are optimised using the *back-propagation* and *Levenberg-Marquardt* algorithms.

To ensure that the appearance of the boundary pixels' local patches are rotationally invariant, the local patch is aligned with the search path. This comes at no extra computational cost as the normal directions have already been computed in order to define the search paths. Local patches are down-sampled to reduce the number of network inputs, which subsequently speeds up the training process. *Max-pooling* is used for this purpose. The process involves sliding a non-overlapping pooling window across the image and extracting the maximum intensity value in each window. While this is an effective down-sampling technique, it also creates position invariance over larger local regions. The size of the pooling window and its stride are chosen to ensure a 10×5 output, in all cases. The fully-connected neural network architecture is constructed in the conventional manner, with the 50 pixels of the local patch being represented by an input layer of 50 nodes. The output layer consists of 2 nodes representing boundary and non-boundary, essentially making this a binary classification problem. All nodes in adjacent layers are fully connected. A schematic diagram of the local patch extraction, and an example of a neural network architecture with 2 hidden layers are shown in Fig. 2.

An additional smoothing process follows boundary detection. Given the assumption that both the inner and outer vessel walls are tubular in shape, any distant outliers from an ellipse-like shape on any slice are discarded, and are

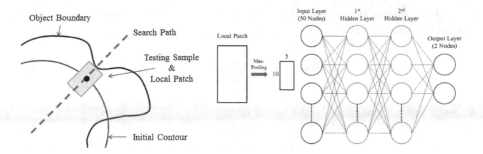

Fig. 2. Left: Schematic diagram of local patch intensity extraction. Right: Example NN architecture with 2 hidden layers.

replaced by "interpolated" contour points. Given a 2D contour V containing n points after boundary detection, an ellipse is fitted which yields a new contour of n points, V_e. Outliers in V are identified if the distance to V_e is above threshold $t = 25$ pixels. Any outliers in V are then replaced by their nearest neighbour in V_e. This small step becomes important especially when detecting the boundary of the inner wall, where a valve-like structure is seen at the centre of the vessel. This avoids vertices converging near the valve instead of the inner vessel wall.

2.3   Segmentation with B-Spline Mesh Regularisation

Before boundary detection, there is an original set of mesh vertices V, and after boundary detection there is now a new set of mesh vertices V'. As there is no shape restrictions in these components (apart from the length of the boundary detector search path itself), an additional process is needed to preserve the mesh's smooth surface. We use B-spline based mesh regularisation, where a local transformation $T(x, y, z)$ between V and V' is estimated with 3D B-splines. The transformation is then performed on V using free-form-deformation, so that it fits as close as possible to V'. As a result, the smoothness of the transformed mesh is a function of the number of B-spline degrees of freedom.

The FFD is estimated by warping an underlying voxel lattice controlled by a set of control points. The control points are defined as $\phi_{i,j,k}^h$ of size $n_x \times n_y \times n_z$, which are separated by δ, and the FFD is formulated as follows;

$$T(x, y, z) = \sum_{l=0}^{3} \sum_{m=0}^{3} \sum_{n=0}^{3} B_l(u) B_m(v) B_n(w) \phi_{i+l, j+m, k+n} \qquad (2)$$

where B_l represents the lth basis function of the B-spline. The voxel lattice positions are $i = \lfloor x/n_x \rfloor - 1$, $j = \lfloor y/n_y \rfloor - 1$, and $k = \lfloor z/n_z \rfloor - 1$. $u = x/n_x - \lfloor x/n_x \rfloor$, $v = y/n_y - \lfloor y/n_y \rfloor$, and $w = z/n_z - \lfloor z/n_z \rfloor$ are the fractional positions along the lattice [8]. In addition, the non-rigid transformation is estimated in a multi-resolution procedure which is expressed as a summation of FFDs at multiple resolutions H [8].

$$T^H(x, y, z) = \sum_{h=1}^{H} T^h(x, y, z) \tag{3}$$

At each mesh resolution h, the voxel lattice is warped by moving the set of control points $\phi_{i,j,k}^h$ which is consequential of δ_h, and computed as $\delta_h = \delta_0/2^h$, where δ_0 is the original control point spacing and h is the resolution level. The B-spline parameters $\phi_{i,j,k}^h$, are optimised by minimising the following energy function with gradient descent;

$$E(\phi) = E_s(V', V) + \lambda E_r(T), \tag{4}$$

where E_r is a smoothness cost and λ is a constant that defines the contribution of the smoothness term. E_s, is a similarity metric, which is a sum-of-squared-difference (SSD) metric between V and V'.

A high δ yields less control points that are sparsely separated, yielding less degrees of freedom. A low δ increases the number of control points, making interpolation distances shorter, yielding more degrees of freedom. A balance is found to allow V to deform as close to the boundary positions as possible (V'), while resulting in a sufficiently smooth surface. Two parameters are changed on every iteration in order to achieve such a trade-off. Firstly the boundary detector's search path decreases on every iteration, allowing the system to reach convergence more quickly. Secondly, as the amount of possible deformation is reduced at each iteration, it is less likely that the mesh surface will get tangled. Therefore on every iteration, the value of δ is also reduced.

3   Application and Results

The lymphatic vessel was labelled on six $512 \times 512 \times 512$ *ex-vivo* confocal microscopic volumes. For each volume the vessel's inner and outer wall were labelled on every tenth slice, and ground truth meshes were then generated by manually defining mesh edge connections. Inner and outer wall ground truths were obtained independently, and so all experimental results are also evaluated independently. Gaussian smoothing was applied to the image volumes in an attempt to remove noise, and all experiments were performed with leave-one-out cross-validation.

3.1   Boundary Detection Results

Before obtaining full segmentation, initial classification tests were carried out on several neural network architectures for boundary detection. The effect of the number of nodes in the network's first hidden layer, the total number of hidden layers, and the local patch size were analysed before deciding on an architecture for segmentation. In all cases 50,000 sample pixels were used for training, 50 % of which were boundary (positive) and 50 % non-boundary (negative). Search paths were defined for all ground truth vertices with a length of 30 pixels at either side. Non-boundary samples were randomly selected from these search paths. At the testing stage a search path of 30 pixels was also used, resulting in 61 path pixels for each point. All of the search path coordinates at this stage were classified as boundary or non-boundary.

Inner wall classification sensitivity and specificity from all initial tests ranged between 87 %–92 %, and 74 %–85 %, respectively, while outer wall sensitivity and specificity ranged between 87 %–92 % and 77 %–87 %. This indicates that at first attempt NNs can produce acceptable results for obscured lymphatic vessel boundary detection. The detectors' sensitivity values are significantly higher and have lower variance than their specificity, which is to be expected as the boundary region is highly diffused. Given this, it is important to find an architecture which produces the highest specificity results as possible to accurately classify non-boundary pixels close to the boundary.

Architectures with 1, 2, 5, 15, 40 and 100 nodes were tested. These tests showed little variance in the inner and outer wall's sensitivity (2 % and 3 % respectively), however the specificity variance was significant larger (11 % and 10 %). Furthermore the specificity for both walls increased with increasing nodes, and plateaued at 40 nodes with 85 % and 87 %. This suggests that a sufficient number of nodes is necessary to discriminate between boundary and non-boundary pixels. Architectures with 1, 2 and 3 layers were also tested, however increasing the layers had a marginal detrimental effect on the specificity of both walls (~2 %), possibly due to overfitting. Given that the boundary area is diffused, highly abstract and complex features may be too specific for good generalisation, suggesting that a simple NN architecture of one hidden layer is sufficient for boundary detection. Networks were trained by extracting patch sizes of 20×10, 40×20 and 80×40 were also extracted, which showed that there was little difference between extracting larger patch sizes ($<1\%$). However, there was a drop of 3 % in the specificity of inner wall classification for the smallest patch, suggesting that a relatively large patch is needed to incorporate useful boundary features.

Based on these results a NN architecture was chosen for full segmentation. For simplicity the same architecture is used for both inner and outer walls. An architecture with 40 nodes in the first hidden layer is sufficient, and larger patches of 40×20 or 80×40 should be extracted due to their higher specificity for the vessel's inner wall. For simplicity and to reduce computation, the smaller of the two was chosen. Finally a simple architecture of one hidden layer produced the best specificity results. To this end, the NN boundary detector used for segmentation has a single hidden layer of 40 nodes with local patch extraction of size 40×20. This architecture produced boundary sensitivities of $88 \pm 2\%$ and $91 \pm 4\%$ for the inner and outer walls receptively, and specificities of $85 \pm 3\%$ and $87 \pm 1\%$. Furthermore, the vast majority of incorrectly classified non-boundary pixels were in the immediate vicinity of the ground truth boundary. Given that the appearance of the vessel is diffused, classification errors would be expected in this small region.

3.2   Segmentation Results

The proposed method was compared to two alternative approaches, as well as our initial segmentation method. For fair comparison our results were only compared to other methods working on the same dataset. To our knowledge, Essa et al. [3] are the only others to do this, and so we compared our results to their *minimum s-excess* graph segmentation. This involved formulating a graph to segment both inner and outer walls simultaneously in polar coordinates, and a hidden Markov model was used to track the vessel walls between the columns. Secondly, a simple intensity-based approach was implemented using Haar-like filtering. This was the same filtering used in Sect. 2.1, but without contour smoothing in the cartesian coordinate system. For the remainder of this paper this approach is referred to as *intensity-based* segmentation. In doing this we have allowed comparison with a purely data-driven approach which had no shape regularisation, and to a completely different segmentation approach. Evaluation was performed on a 2D slice-by-slice basis in polar coordinates. The point-to-mesh distance (PMD),

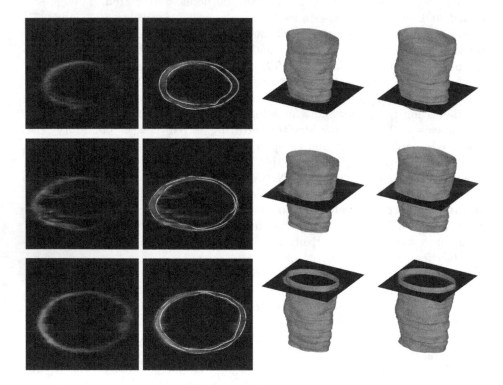

Fig. 3. Example segmentation results. From left to right; 1st column: Image slices. 2nd column: Inner and outer wall segmentation results. Green contours are the ground truth and blue contours are the result. 3rd column: Resulting inner wall mesh with corresponding slices. 4th column: Resulting outer wall mesh with corresponding slices. (Color figure online)

Hausdorff distance (HD), area overlap (AO), and foreground and background specificity and sensitivity were the metrics used.

Figure 3 shows an example segmentation of the proposed method, which shows close correlation with the ground truth. Smooth resulting mesh surfaces are also shown, with no tangled or extremely faceted mesh faces. Tables 1 and 2 show that the proposed method produced the lowest PMD and HD, and the highest AO, specificity and sensitivity results. Figures 4 and 5 compare the qualitative slice segmentations and mesh results for the inner and outer walls of the data-driven approaches.

It is immediately noticeable that the simplistic intensity-based segmentation produced significantly worse quantitative results, and large regions of both walls deviated significantly from the ground truth. Noticeably, the boundary detector has caused inner wall vertices to converge at the valve at the centre of the vessel, as its appearance is similar to the wall itself. The lack of any shape regularisation is therefore unsuitable for such data where the vessel walls are not always prominent. The initial segmentation results are significantly better. By fitting each slice contour to an ellipse the majority of *correctly* deviated vertices have forced the *incorrectly* placed vertices nearer the boundary walls. This simple shape regularisation approach has had dramatic effects on the smoothness of the mesh surface, however it does not allow enough degrees of freedom to reach boundary areas of high curvature. The results from the proposed method show that the additional deformable modelling process is necessary after initial segmentation. The iterative boundary detector allows deformation towards areas of high curvature, which is represented by both the low PMD and HD errors. Meanwhile the iterative mesh regularisation maintains the mesh's smooth surface, which can be seen in Fig. 5.

Table 1. Inner wall quantitative results comparison.

Method	PMD (vox)	HD2 (vox)	AO (%)	Sens. (%)	Spec. (%)
S-Excess Graph [3]	3.1 ± 1.9	9.8 ± 4.3	95.5 ± 3.2	96.9 ± 3.1	99.2 ± 0.8
Intensity-based	5.9 ± 0.8	48.5 ± 7.1	92.4 ± 1.5	93.0 ± 1.4	99.1 ± 0.1
Initial Seg.	2.9 ± 0.4	9.3 ± 0.9	96.4 ± 0.4	97.0 ± 0.4	**99.6 ± 0.1**
Proposed	**1.6 ± 0.1**	**5.8 ± 0.5**	**98.0 ± 0.4**	**99.1 ± 0.4**	99.2 ± 0.2

Table 2. Outer wall quantitative results comparison.

Method	PMD (vox)	HD2 (vox)	AO (%)	Sens. (%)	Spec. (%)
S-Excess Graph [3]	2.0 ± 0.8	7.4 ± 3.1	97.6 ± 1.0	98.7 ± 1.1	99.1 ± 0.6
Intensity-based	4.5 ± 1.4	46.9 ± 8.1	95.0 ± 1.8	96.9 ± 1.4	98.3 ± 0.8
Initial Seg.	1.7 ± 0.2	5.7 ± 0.3	98.2 ± 0.1	99.2 ± 0.1	99.0 ± 0.3
Proposed	**1.5 ± 0.1**	**5.4 ± 0.4**	**98.4 ± 0.1**	**99.2 ± 0.2**	**99.2 ± 0.03**

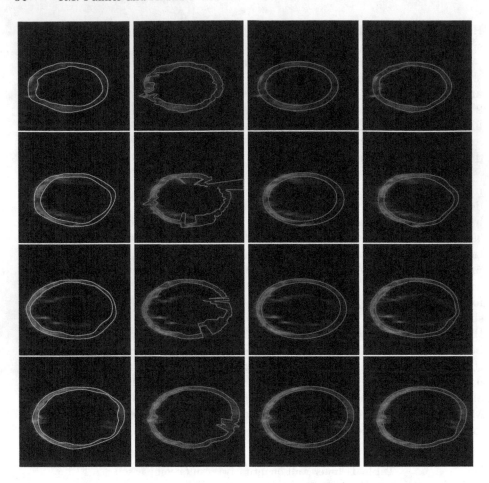

Fig. 4. Comparison results on image slices. From left to right; 1ˢᵗ column: Ground truth. 2ⁿᵈ column: Intensity-based segmentation. 3ʳᵈ column: Initial segmentation. 4ᵗʰ column: Proposed framework.

Compared to the minimum s-excess graph method, the proposed method still produced better segmentation results. The tracking-based method produced PMD and HD metrics that were higher for the outer wall, and almost double that of the proposed method for the inner wall. This is also reflected in the AO, specificity and sensitivity metrics. This may be a result of the tracking model, however a likely cause is the hand-crafted edge features used for emission probability. This being the case it would show that using learned features from algorithms such as NN has an advantage for edge detection in such data.

Fig. 5. Comparison mesh results. The top row shows the inner vessel wall mesh and the bottom row shows the outer wall mesh. From left to right; 1st column: Ground truth. 2nd column: Intensity-based segmentation. 3rd column: Initial segmentation. 4th column: Proposed framework.

4   Conclusion

A fully automatic deformable modelling method has been presented for the segmentation of 3D lymphatic vessels in confocal microscopy images. A bottom-up, data-driven framework was used, which included a learning-based boundary detector and mesh regularisation for shape preservation. A simple intensity-based initial segmentation was first adopted which was followed by a deformable modelling system. A neural network was used for boundary detection, which allowed suitable features to be learned instead of hand-crafting them. This proved particularly useful, as choosing features for edges with varying degrees of contrast is not a trivial task. It was also shown that this type of boundary detection was able to accurately detect both vessel walls, proving it was capable of detecting edges of highly varying contrasts. Mesh regularisation was also necessary in order to obtain smooth vessel surfaces.

References

1. Chiverton, J., Xie, X., Mirmehdi, M.: Automatic bootstrapping and tracking of object contours. IEEE T-IP **21**(3), 1231–1245 (2012)
2. Espona, L., Carreira, M., Penedo, M., Ortega, M.: Retinal vessel tree segmentation using a deformable contour model. In: ICPR, pp. 2128–2131 (2008)
3. Essa, E., Xie, X., Jones, J.-L.: Minimum s-excess graph for segmenting and tracking multiple borders with HMM. In: Navab, N., Hornegger, J., Wells, W.M., Frangi, A.F. (eds.) MICCAI 2015. LNCS, vol. 9350, pp. 28–35. Springer, Heidelberg (2015). doi:10.1007/978-3-319-24571-3_4

4. Hu, Y., Rogers, W., Coast, D., Kramer, C., Reichek, N.: Vessel boundary extraction based on a global and local deformable physical model with variable stiffness. MRI **16**, 943–951 (1998)
5. Jones, J.-L., Essa, E., Xie, X., Smith, D.: Interactive segmentation of media-adventitia border in IVUS. In: Wilson, R., Hancock, E., Bors, A., Smith, W. (eds.) CAIP 2013. LNCS, vol. 8048, pp. 466–474. Springer, Heidelberg (2013). doi:10.1007/978-3-642-40246-3_58
6. Jones, J., Xie, X., Essa, E.: Combining region-based and imprecise boundary-based cues for interactive medical image segmentation. J. Numer. Methods Biomed. Eng. **30**(12), 1649–1666 (2014)
7. Kirbas, C., Quek, F.: A review of vessel extraction techniques and algorithms. ACM Comput. Surv. (CSUR) **36**(2), 81–121 (2004)
8. Lee, S., Wolberg, G., Shin, S.Y.: Scattered data interpolation with multilevel b-splines. Trans. Vis. Comput. Graph. **3**, 228–244 (1997)
9. Lesage, D., Angelini, E.D., Bloch, I., Funka-Lea, G.: A review of 3D vessel lumen segmentation techniques: models, features and extraction schemes. Med. Image Anal. **13**(6), 819–845 (2009)
10. Lu, D., Yu, X., Jin, X., Li, B., Chen, Q., Zhu, J.: Neural network based edge detection for automated medical diagnosis. In: IEEE ICIA, pp. 343–348 (2011)
11. Ma, J., Lu, L., Zhan, Y., Zhou, X., Salganicoff, M., Krishnan, A.: Hierarchical segmentation and identification of thoracic vertebra using learning-based edge detection and coarse-to-fine deformable model. In: Jiang, T., Navab, N., Pluim, J.P.W., Viergever, M.A. (eds.) MICCAI 2010. LNCS, vol. 6361, pp. 19–27. Springer, Heidelberg (2010). doi:10.1007/978-3-642-15705-9_3
12. McInerney, T., Terzopoulos, D.: Deformable models in medical image analysis: a survey. MIA **1**(2), 91–108 (1996)
13. Mesejo, P., Ibáñez, O., Cordón, O., Cagnoni, S.: A survey on image segmentation using metaheuristic-based deformable models: state of the art and critical analysis. Appl. Soft Comput. **44**, 1–29 (2016)
14. Paiement, A., Mirmehdi, M., Xie, X., Hamilton, M.: Integrated segmentation and interpolation of sparse data. IEEE T-IP **23**(11), 3902–3914 (2014)
15. Palmer, R., Xie, X., Tam, G.: Automatic aortic root segmentation with shape constraints and mesh regularisation. In: BMVC (2015)
16. Senthilkumaran, N., Rajesh, R.: Edge detection techniques for image segmentation-a survey of soft computing approaches. IJRTE **1**(2), 250–254 (2009)
17. Viola, P., Jones, M.: Rapid object detection using a boosted cascade of simple features. In: Proceedings of the Conference on Computer Vision and Pattern Recognition, pp. 511–518 (2001)
18. Xie, X., Mirmehdi, M.: Magnetostatic field for the active contour model: a study in convergence. In: BMVC, pp. 127–136 (2006)
19. Xie, X., Mirmehdi, M.: Implicit active model using radial basis function interpolated level sets. In: BMVC, pp. 1–10 (2007)
20. Yeo, S., Xie, X., Sazonov, I., Nithiarasu, P.: Level set segmentation with robust image gradient energy and statistical shape prior. In: IEEE ICIP (2011)
21. Yim, P., Cebral, R., Mullick, R., Choyle, P.: Vessel surface reconstruction with a tubular deformable model. IEEE T-MI **20**, 1411–1421 (2001)

A Simple Human Activity Recognition
Technique Using DCT

Aziz Khelalef[1], Fakhreddine Ababsa[2($\boxtimes$)], and Nabil Benoudjit[1]

[1] Laboratoire d'Automatique Avancée et d'Analyse des Systèmes (LAAAS),
Université Batna-2-, Fesdis, Algeria
Khelalef_aziz@yahoo.fr, nbenoudjit@gmail.com
[2] Laboratoire Informatique, Biologie Integrative et Systèmes
Complexes (IBISC), Université d'Evry Val d'Essonne, Évry, France
ababsa@iup.univ-evry.fr

Abstract. In this paper, we present a simple new human activity recognition method using discrete cosine transform (DCT). The scheme uses the DCT coefficients extracted from silhouettes as descriptors (features) and performs frame-by-frame recognition, which make it simple and suitable for real time applications. We carried out several tests using radial basis neural network (RBF) for classification, a comparative study against stat-of-the-art methods shows that our technique is faster, simple and gives higher accuracy performance comparing to discrete transform based techniques and other methods proposed in literature.

Keywords: Human activity recognition · DCT transform · Neural network · Features extraction · Classification

1 Introduction

Human activity recognition is one of the most important subjects in computer vision research because of its various applications; it is used in surveillance, human-machine interaction, monitoring systems, virtual reality and more.

Human activity recognition algorithms must recognize various activities efficiently and in real time, and by using less machine resources. In general, we can divide human activity methods into two parts:

The first part is features extraction. Indeed, in this area, it is important to extract features that can separate each activity from the others efficiently. Various features extraction approaches where proposed and can be classified into four categories [1]:

1- Space-time volume (STV) features use the relationship between time and space to create a volume for each video sequence. In [2], Blank et al. used the silhouettes to construction a space-time volume from which space-time saliency, shape structure and orientation are extracted. In [3] Dollar et al. used the space-temporal volume to find local region of interest used as descriptors to separate the different actions.

2- Discrete Transform (DT) features use discrete transform (DT) of each frame to form distinctive features, in [4] Kumari and Mitra use discrete Fourier transforms (DFTs) of small image blocks as features for activity recognition, in [5], Tasweer et al.

© Springer International Publishing AG 2016
J. Blanc-Talon et al. (Eds.): ACIVS 2016, LNCS 10016, pp. 37–46, 2016.
DOI: 10.1007/978-3-319-48680-2_4

used a blocked based truncated discrete cosine transform from motion history image (MHI) to form features for activity recognition. In [18] Hafiz et al. extracted spectral features from frames using DFT and (principal component analysis) PCA to reduce the features dimension. Generally STV and DT features are also known as global features.

3- Local features are widely used in human activity recognition, in [6, 7] Lowe introduced the scale invariant feature transform (SIFT) which are invariant features to image scaling, translation and rotation. In [8], Dalal and al. proposed the oriented gradient descriptors (HOG) for human activity recognition, in [9] Lu and Little proposed an improved HOG based technique using (principal component analysis) PCA, the result PCA-HOG descriptors are invariant to the variation of illumination, pose and viewpoint. In [10], Timo Ojala, Matti Pietikäinen et al. introduced Local Binary Patterns (LBP) for texture classification, in [11] Zhao and Pietikäinen used the LBP-TOP, which is formed by calculating the LBP features from the planes and concentrating the histograms. In [12], Lin et al. proposed a nonparametric weighted feature extraction (NWFE) to build histogram vector for human activity recognition.

4- The last category of human activity features extraction is Body modeling type, here the human body is modeled to be tracked, and pose estimation. In [13] Nakazawa et al. represent the human body using an ellipse, in [13] Iwasawa et al. resemble the human skeleton by using stick-figures to represent human structure information. In [14] Huo et al. proposed to construct a head-shoulder-upper-body model to track and detect human body, in [15] Sedai et al. use a 3D human body model with orientation of 10 body parts (torso, head, arms, and legs).

The second part of a human activity recognition technique is activities classification, various algorithms were used in literature [1]: 1- generative model techniques such as HMM (hidden Markov model) used in [29, 30], 2- discriminative models based techniques using SVM (Support Vector Machine) [18, 25, 26], ANN [27, 28], or by using other techniques like Kalman filter [32] or KNN [5].

In this paper, we present a new human activity recognition method using discrete cosine transform; we use the Discrete Cosine Transform (DCT) of the extracted silhouettes as features, and (ANN) artificial neural network (RBF) for classification.

Against other methods in literature, our technique is simple to implement, after training it recognize actions instantly, fast and suitable for real-time applications.

This paper is organized as follow, in Sect. 2 we give a brief introduction to DCT transform. Next, we present the proposed method in Sect. 3. Experimental results will be given in the fourth Section. Finally, section five contains concluding remarks and perspectives.

2 Discrete Cosine Transform (DCT)

The discrete cosine transform (DCT) is a very popular transform function used in signal processing. It transforms the signal from spatial to frequency domain [16]. It allows the concentration of the signal energy in few coefficients. DCT has been used in data compression, image denoising, image watermarking and so on. In this section, we give a brief presentation of the DCT.

The 1-D DCT transform of length N is described by [17]:

$$C(u) = \alpha(u) \sum_{x=0}^{N-1} f(x)\cos\left[\frac{\pi(2x+1)u}{2N}\right],$$ (1)

For u $= 0, 1, 2, \ldots, N - 1$. Similarly, the inverse transformation is defined as

$$f(x) = \sum_{u=0}^{N-1} \alpha(u)C(u)\cos\left[\frac{\pi(2x+1)u}{2N}\right],$$ (2)

For x $= 0, 1, 2, \ldots, N - 1$. In both Eqs. (1) and (2) $\alpha(u)$ is defined as

$$\alpha(u) = \begin{cases} \frac{1}{\sqrt{N}}, & u = 0 \\ \sqrt{\frac{2}{N}}, & u \neq 0. \end{cases}$$ (3)

DCT transform outcome are the DC coefficient, which represent highest energy concentration of the signal, and the AC coefficients.

The 2-D DCT transform is extended from the 1D DCT and it is given by [17]:

$$C(u,v) = \alpha(u)\alpha(v) \sum_{x=0}^{N-1}\sum_{y=0}^{N-1} f(x,y)\cos\left[\frac{\pi(2x+1)u}{2N}\right]\cos\left[\frac{\pi(2y+1)v}{2N}\right],$$ (4)

For u, v $= 0, 1, 2, \ldots, N - 1$ and $\alpha(u)$ and $\alpha(v)$ are defined in (3), the inverse transform is defined as

$$f(x,y) = \sum_{u=0}^{N-1}\sum_{v=0}^{N-1} \alpha(u)\alpha(v)C(u,v)\cos\left[\frac{\pi(2x+1)u}{2N}\right]\cos\left[\frac{\pi(2y+1)v}{2N}\right],$$ (5)

For x, y $= 0, 1, 2, \ldots, N - 1$.

(a)   (b)

Fig. 1. Example of DCT applied on Cameraman image: (a) original, (b) DCT.

An example of discrete cosine transform is presented in Fig. 1, in (a) we present a grey scale original image, and (b) is the DCT of that image where the maximum energy is concentrated in few coefficients in the upper left corner of the image.

3 DCT Based Human Activity Recognition Method

Our proposed method is a simple discrete cosine transform based technique. DCT is one of the most used transforms in computer vision fields, because it shows interesting proprieties, for example it allows the concentration of the signal information (energy) in few coefficients, we tried to use this propriety to describe human activities from silhouettes.

We extract feature descriptors by applying the DCT transform on the extracted silhouettes, and by using a supervised Radial basis functions neural network (RBF) we classify the human activities:

Step I: Features extraction

- Extract silhouettes from each frame of the input video stream;
- Apply the 2D DCT for the extracted silhouette;
- Use the NxM window coefficients as shown in Fig. 2 to create distinctive features used to recognise each action in the next classification step;

Step II: Action classification and recognition

- Classify and recognise instantly each frame by using the optimum neural network RBF model obtained after training and validation processes using representative samples.

The recognition algorithm is as follow:

```
For f = 1 to Nbr_frame
Silhouette (f) = op (frame (f));
C = DCT (Silhouette (f));
Features = {C (k, l) / k = 1 to M, l = 1 to N};
Class = RBF_model (Features);
End
```

Where:

Nbr_frame:	The number of frames in the video feed
Op:	Silhouette extraction operation
Silhouette:	Silhouette extracted from the frame
C:	DCT coefficients of the silhouette
Features:	The features vector
RBF_model:	The RBF model used in the classification after the learning phase

Steps I and II are repeated instantly for each frame of the video stream, which makes this method suitable for real time applications.

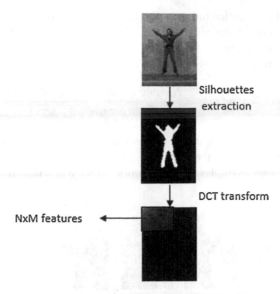

Fig. 2. Features extraction.

For each frame of the video stream, we propose to perform a DCT transform on silhouettes extracted from the video frame. The features are the MxN DCT coefficients in the window as presented in Fig. 2.

In the recognition step, we use radial bases neural network (RBF) to classify each activity frame by frame.

4 Experimental Results

To evaluate the performance of the proposed method, we created and run Matlab codes on a laptop using a core 2 due processor and 4 GB of RAM, we carried out several tests using Weizmann [19] database because it allows to directly compare our results to the state-of-the-art methods. Weizmann database provides extracted silhouettes consists of 10 activities performed by nine persons i.e. 90 actions, using a simple background and a fixed camera. The Table 1 below shows the training, validation and test sets using an ANN classification.

Table 1. Different sets used in classification step.

	Number of frames in database (images)	Training set	Validation set	Test set
RBF	100 %	40 %	30 %	30 %
	5528	2212	1658	1658

The database used in the radial basis neural network (RBF) classification step is divided into training, validation and test sets as follow: 40 % of frames for training set, and 30 % for validation and test sets each.

The input of the classification step are features extracted by using DCT of sil-houettes at each frame of the video stream, the output of the RBF classifier in the assigned class of each frame.

The classification rate used is defined by:

$$classification\ rate = \frac{Number\ of\ good\ classified\ frames}{Total\ Number\ of\ frames} \tag{6}$$

Achieved results show that the best classification rate was found by using 400 neurons in the hidden layer of the RBF classifier.

Figure 3, shows an examples of some action from Weizmann database and their extracted silhouettes.

Fig. 3. Samples from Weizmann database before and after silhouettes extraction.

Table 2. Classification rate using different DCT window size.

DCT window size	Best identification rate
3 × 3	71.4113 %
4 × 4	83.2931 %
5 × 5	92.1592 %
6 × 6	94.0290 %
7 × 7	97.8287 %
8 × 8	**99.0350 %**

Table 2 shows the classification accuracy by using different window's size of the DCT coefficients. Simulation results show that the best windows size used for the feature selection is 8×8.

Table 3, shows that our technique achieved a success rate of 99.03 %, compared to other state-of-the-art techniques. The obtained results shows that our proposed method gives a better classification rate than the most transform based techniques cited in [4, 5], and clearly outperform the other methods even by using 10 activities in the Weizmann database.

The confusion matrix below (Fig. 4) shows that the proposed method achieved 100 % classification rate for almost all the actions, and the most classification's errors are related to the skipping action (in [20,24], authors used the Weizmann dataset

Table 3. Human activity recognition rates obtained in the literature and in our approach.

Method	Accuracy
Boiman and Irani 2006 [20]	97.5 % (9 actions)
Scovanner et al. 2007 [21]	82.6 % (10 actions)
Wang and Suter 2007 [22]	97.8 % (10 actions)
Kellokumpu et al. 2008 [23]	97.8 % (10 actions)
Kellokumpu et al. 2009 [24]	98.7 % (9 actions)
Hafiz Imtiaz et al. 2015 (DFT based) [18]	100 % (10 actions)
Tasweer et al. 2015 (DCT based) [5]	92.25 % (10 actions)
Our approach	**99.03 % (10 actions)**

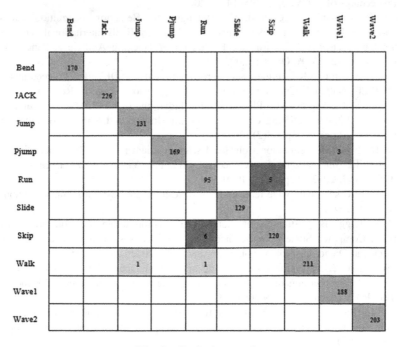

Fig. 4. Confusion matrix.

without the skipping action) which shows the robustness and the superiority of our technique against stat-of-the-art schemes.

5 Conclusion

In this paper, we presented a new frame-by-frame human activity recognition technique based on DCT transform applied on the extracted silhouettes. We used radial basis neural network (RBF) to classify the activities.

The method gives highest classification accuracy compared to transform based techniques and other state-of-the-art schemes.

The proposed method is simple, efficient, fast to implement and can be used in real time application because it does not need many hardware resources.

In future work, we plan to combine the principal component analysis (PCA) and the discrete cosine transform in order to develop new DCT-PCA descriptors and to use SVM in the classification step.

References

1. Ke, S.-R., Thuc, L.H.L., Lee, Y.-J., Hwang, J.-N., Yoo, J.-H., Choi, K.-H.: A review on video-based human activity recognition. Computers 2(2), 88–131 (2013)
2. Blank, M., Gorelick, L., Shechtman, E., Irani, M., Basri, R.: Actions as space-time shapes. In: Proceedings of ICCV, pp. 1395–1402 (2005)
3. Dollár, P., Rabaud, V., Cottrell, G., Belongie, S.: Behavior recognition via sparse spatio-temporal features. In: Proceedings of the 2nd Joint IEEE International Workshop on Visual Surveillance and Performance Evaluation of Tracking And Surveillance, Beijing, China, pp. 65–72, 15–16 October 2005
4. Kumari, S., Mitra, S.K.: Human action recognition using DFT. In: Proceedings of the Third IEEE National Conference on Computer Vision, Pattern Recognition, Image Processing and Graphics (NCVPRIPG), Hubli, India, pp. 239–242, 15–17 December 2011
5. Ahmad, T., Rafique, J.: Using discrete cosine transform based features for human action recognition. J. Image Graph. 3(2) (2015)
6. Lowe, D.G.: Object recognition from local scale-invariant features. In: Proceedings of the Seventh IEEE International Conference on Computer Vision, Kerkyra, Greece, vol. 2, pp. 1150–1157, 20–25 September 1999
7. Lowe, D.G.: Distinctive image features from scale-invariant keypoints. Int. J. Comput. Vis. 60, 91–110 (2004)
8. Dalal, N., Triggs, B.: Histograms of oriented gradients for human detection. In: Proceedings of IEEE Computer Society Conference on Computer Vision and Pattern Recognition (CVPR), San Diego, CA, USA, vol. 1, pp. 886–893, 20–26 June 2005
9. Lu, W., Little, J.J.: Simultaneous tracking and action recognition using the PCA-HOG descriptor. In: Proceedings of the 3rd Canadian Conference on Computer and Robot Vision, Quebec, PQ, Canada, p. 6, 7–9 June 2006
10. Ojala, T., Pjetikainen, M.: Multiresolution grey-scale and rotation invariant texture classification with local binary patterns. IEEE Trans. Pattern Anal. Mach. Intell. 24, 971–987 (2002)

11. Zhao, G., Pietikäinen, M.: Dynamic texture recognition using local binary patterns with an application to facial expressions. PAMI **29**(6), 915–928 (2007)
12. Lin, C., Hsu, F., Lin, W.: Recognizing human actions using NWFE-based histogram vectors. EURASIP J. Adv. Sig. Process. **2010**, 9 (2010)
13. Nakazawa, A., Kato, H., Inokuchi, S.: Human tracking using distributed vision systems. In: Proceedings of IEEE Fourteenth International Conference on Pattern Recognition, Brisbane, QLD, Australia, vol. 1, pp. 593–596, 20 August 1998
14. Huo, F., Hendriks, E., Paclik, P., Oomes, A.H.J.: Markerless human motion capture and pose recognition. In: Proceedings of the 10th IEEE Workshop on Image Analysis for Multimedia Interactive Services (WIAMIS), London, UK, pp. 13–16, 6–8 May 2009
15. Sedai, S., Bennamoun, M., Huynh, D.: Context-based appearance descriptor for 3D human pose estimation from monocular images. In: Proceedings of IEEE Digital Image Computing: Techniques and Applications (DICTA), Melbourne, VIC, Australia, pp. 484–491, 1–3 December 2009
16. Abdrhman, A., Ukasha, M.: Contour compression of image watermarking using DCT transform & ramer method. In: 2nd International Conference on Mechanical, Electronics and Mechatronics Engineering (ICMEME 2013), London, UK, pp, 147–151, 17–18 June 2013
17. Zhao, R.M., Lian, H., Pang, H.W., Hu, B.N.: A watermarking algorithm by modifying AC coefficies in DCT domain. In: International Symposium on Information Science and Engineering, pp. 159–162. IEEE (2008)
18. Imtiaz, H., et al.: Human action recognition based on spectral domain features. In: 19th Annual Conference KES-2015, Singapore
19. Gorelick, L., Blank, M., Shechtman, E., Irani, M., Basri, R.: Weizmann database (2007). http://www.wisdom.weizmann.ac.il/~vision/SpaceTimeActions.html
20. Boiman, O., Irani, M.: Similarity by composition. In: Proceedings of Neural Information Processing Systems (NIPS)
21. Scovanner, P., Ali, S., Shah, M.: A 3-dimensional SIFT descriptor and its application to action recognition. In: Proceedings of ACM Multimedia, pp. 357–360 (2007)
22. Wang, L., Suter, D.: Recognizing human activities from silhouettes: motion subspace and factorial discriminative graphical model. In: Proceedings of CVPR, p. 8 (2007)
23. Kellokumpu, V., Zhao, G., Pietikäinen, M.: Texture based description of movements for activity analysis. In: Proceedings of VISAPP, vol. 1, pp. 206–213 (2008)
24. Kellokumpu, V., Zhao, G., Pietikäinen, M.: Human activity recognition using a dynamic texture based method. In: Proceedings of BMVC, p. 10 (2008)
25. Schuldt, C., Laptev, I., Caputo, B.: Recognizing human actions: a local SVM approach. In: Proceedings of the 17th IEEE International Conference on Pattern Recognition (ICPR), Cambridge, UK, vol. 3, pp. 32–36, 23–26 August 2004
26. Laptev, I., Marszalek, M., Schmid, C., Rozenfeld, B.: Learning realistic human actions from movies. In: Proceedings of the IEEE Conference on Computer Vision and Pattern Recognition (CVPR), Anchorage, AK, USA, pp. 1–8, 23–28 June 2008
27. Foroughi, H., Naseri, A., Saberi, A., Yazdi, H.S.: An eigenspace-based approach for human fall detection using integrated time motion image and neural network. In: Proceedings of IEEE 9th International Conference on Signal Processing, pp. 1499–1503 (2008)
28. Fiaz, M.K., Ijaz, B.: Vision based human activity tracking using artificial neural networks. In: Proceedings of IEEE International Conference on Intelligent and Advanced Systems (ICIAS), Kuala Lumpur, Malaysia, pp. 1–5, 15–17 June 2010

29. Duong, T.V., Bui, H.H., Phung, D.Q., Venkatesh, S.: Activity recognition and abnormality detection with the switching hidden semi-markov model. In: Proceedings of the IEEE Computer Society Conference on Computer Vision and Pattern Recognition (CVPR), San Diego, CA, USA, vol. 1, pp. 838–845, 20–25 June 2005
30. Yamato, J., Ohya, J., Ishii, K.: Recognizing human action in time-sequential images using Hidden Markov Model. In: Proceedings of the IEEE Computer Society Conference on Computer Vision and Pattern Recognition (CVPR), Champaign, IL, USA, pp. 379–385, 15–18 June 1992

Hand Gesture Recognition Using Infrared Imagery Provided by Leap Motion Controller

Tomás Mantecón$^{(\boxtimes)}$, Carlos R. del-Blanco, Fernando Jaureguizar, and Narciso García

Grupo de Tratamiento de Imágenes, E.T.S.I. de Telecomunicación,
Universidad Politécnica de Madrid, Madrid, Spain
{tmv,cda,fjn,narciso}@gti.ssr.upm.es

Abstract. Hand gestures are one of the main alternatives for Human-Computer Interaction. For this reason, a hand gesture recognition system using near-infrared imagery acquired by a Leap Motion sensor is proposed. The recognition system directly characterizes the hand gesture by computing a global image descriptor, called Depth Spatiograms of Quantized Patterns, without any hand segmentation stage. To deal with the high dimensionality of the image descriptor, a Compressive Sensing framework is applied, obtaining a manageable image feature vector that almost preserves the original information. Finally, the resulting reduced image descriptors are analyzed by a set of Support Vectors Machines to identify the performed gesture independently of the precise hand location in the image. Promising results have been achieved using a new hand-based near-infrared database.

Keywords: Feature extraction · Gesture recognition · Random projections · Image classification · Near-infrared imaging

1 Introduction

The number of works in the field of gesture recognition have increased considerably during the last years, boosting the Human-Machine Interaction (HMI). This is due to the advent of low-cost sensors that are able to obtain multimodal information from the scene. This is the case of Kinect 2 that provides depth, color, and skeletal information; Senz3D that can acquire depth and color information; Intel Realsense that provides depth, color, and skeletal information; and Leap Motion that can capture near-infrared and skeletal information. Some works have employed this kind of sensors to improve the interaction between a human and a robot. For example, the work presented in [7] controls the motion of a robot by vision. In [22] the payload is managed, while in [19] a robot is operated by using a remote connection for rescue situations. In other cases, the recognition system can be used to allow a car driver to interact with the radio [10], or to be able to answer phone calls while driving [11]. It can be also used for rehabilitation purposes by reproducing the arm movement [6].

© Springer International Publishing AG 2016
J. Blanc-Talon et al. (Eds.): ACIVS 2016, LNCS 10016, pp. 47–57, 2016.
DOI: 10.1007/978-3-319-48680-2_5

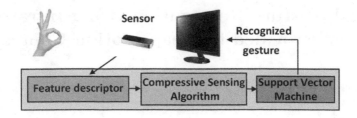

Fig. 1. General system of the proposed solution.

In comparison with other hand-based HMI sensors, Leap Motion controller has been scarcely exploited for HMI. Possibly, the two main reasons are: (1) it is a close range sensor that can only sense the hands, but not the human body; (2) it is strongly oriented to process hand-skeletal information, discarding raw imagery data. This last issue can be further attributed to two factors. The first one is that the Leap Motion Software Development Kit is oriented to provide high level hand information, such as fingertip position and velocity, palm orientation, etc. But, there is a lack of functionalities to process the near-infrared raw imagery, such as hand detection or segmentation. Moreover, the second factor is related to the two cameras embedded in the Leap Motion sensor which have a very wide field of view that introduces strong image distortions, which complicates even more their processing.

Due to the aforementioned factors, the researcher activity with the Leap Motion sensor has been mainly limited to the use of the hand skeleton information. In [23], they propose to use the palm trajectory (information given by the skeleton) to recognize on-air written numbers by means of a Support Vector Machine (SVM) classifier. In [17], the signature of a person is proposed to check his identity by processing skeleton-derived trajectories. For this purpose, a combination of 3D Histogram of Oriented Optical Flow (HOOF) and Histogram of Oriented Trajectories (HOT) are used as input feature vectors to an SVM classification stage. Multiple Leap Motion sensors have also been proposed in [9] to process the acquired hand skeletons using a framework based on Hidden Markov Models (HMM).

Alternatively, some works use the skeletal information of the Leap Motion with the color or depth imagery provided by other HMI sensors, mainly to avoid to process the highly geometrically distorted infrared images. For example, [15] that uses color imagery acquired by Kinect sensor to complement the hand skeleton provided by the Leap Motion. In [24], a Leap Motion skeleton is combined with the information provided by the accelerometers of a wearable watch, which is also used to give some feedback via vibration signals.

Although there are no works addressing the hand gesture recognition task using directly the geometrically distorted infrared images of the Leap Motion (as far as the authors' knowledge), the use of color and depth information for hand gesture recognition has been quite investigated. Based on machine learning approaches, different descriptors have been used with different classification techniques and probabilistic/Bayesian frameworks. For example, in [2], they propose a recognition solution based on the hand shape and its motion combined with a Hidden Markov Model (HMM) to control a robot. Other solutions make use of Fourier descriptors with Recurrent Neural Networks (RNN) [16]. In [4], they use a combination of Gabor features with SVM classifiers to perform hand gesture recognition under varying illumination scenes. Many other solutions have adopted popular object feature descriptors such as the Scale Invariant Feature Transform (SIFT) [21], the Histogram of Oriented Gradients (HOG) [12], the Local Binary Patterns (LBP) [8], and different LBP variations [13].

In this paper, a novel algorithm for hand gesture recognition using just the near-infrared imagery of the Leap Motion controller is presented. This paper considers that the aforementioned drawbacks of the Leap Motion sensor can be considered as strong advantages from other point of view. More precisely, the close range of the Leap Motion is ideal for reducing the background clutter, allowing to directly focus on the hand patterns. On the other hand, a specific machine learning framework is proposed, whose performance is not deteriorated by the geometrical distortions introduced by the Leap Motion cameras. Within this framework, there is no detection process as the feature descriptor is computed over the whole image, so no preprocessing is needed and the final computational cost is not incremented. Figure 1 shows the stages of the entire gesture recognition system: (1) computation of a DSQP based feature vector, (2) dimensionality reduction based on Compressive Sensing, and (3) classification based on a bank of SVMs.

The organization of the paper is as follows. Section 2 describes the feature extraction algorithm. Section 3 describes the Compressive Sensing (CS) algorithm. In Sect. 4, the classification process is presented. Section 5 describes the Leap Motion controller. Section 6 summarizes the obtained results with the proposed algorithm. Finally, conclusions are drawn in Sect. 7.

2   DSQP-Based Feature Description

To achieve the characterization of the hand gesture information in near-infrared imagery, some modifications have been made over the Depth Spatiograms of Quantized Patterns (DSQP) feature descriptor presented in [14], that is an evolution of the LBP algorithm [18]. There are two main differences between the original LBP and the DSQP descriptor. One is related to the relationship among pixels in a neighborhood. Instead of computing differences between the central pixel and each pixel in the neighborhood (LBP), the DSQP descriptor computes differences between each pair of pixels within the neighborhood, as it can be seen in Fig. 2, where $N_{neig} = 8$ pixels is chosen. Only one of the two possible difference values between two pixels is considered, obtaining the following total number of differences:

$$N_{diff} = \frac{(N_{neig} + 1)^2 - (N_{neig} + 1)}{2} \tag{1}$$

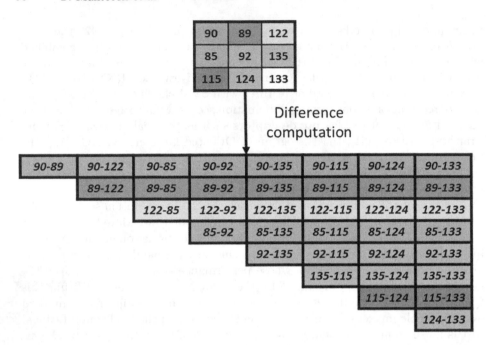

Fig. 2. Difference computation for the DSQP descriptor, specifying the differences that are taken into account.

The second difference affects the quantization process of each difference value. Instead of using a thresholding process in which the difference is represented by just 1 bit (encoding the sign), the DSQP algorithm uses $N_b = 3$ bits for the quantization of the difference following a non-uniform scheme, which results in 8 intervals of quantization. Since the DSQP descriptor is typically used with depth imagery, an adaptation is performed for infrared images, where the decision values are tuned to acquire the range of infrared difference values. The reason is that the nature and depth resolution of the infrared imagery is fundamentally different from the depth imagery (it is not directly related to the 3D hand structure).

Likewise LBP, DSQP also uses a bag of features approach. Each set of neighborhood differences are encoded into a decimal number, which contributes to a histogram that compactly represents all the decimal codes of an image region. Taking into account the previous configuration, the resulting dimension of the histogram is $2^{N_{diff} \times N_b} = 2^{108}$, which is clearly prohibitive for both, computational cost and memory requirements. To obtain a more tractable histogram, an alternative approach has been considered. It consists in dividing the long binary word into binary sub-words of $N_{div} = 6$ bits, computing then a histogram for every set of sub-words. As can be seen in Fig. 3, this result have the following number of histograms:

$$N_h = \frac{N_{diff} \times N_b}{N_{div}} = \frac{36 \times 3}{6} = 18 \tag{2}$$

Which are composed of the following number of bins:

$$2^{N_{div}} = 2^6 = 64 \tag{3}$$

The last step consists in dividing the image into $N_s \times N_s$ non-overlapping blocks, and computing a DSQP descriptor for each image block. This strategy adds more spatial information to the resulting descriptor. For the considered resolution images, a value of $N_s = 6$ has been fixed, which experimentally has achieved good recognition results. The performed block division is higher than the original DSQP configuration because only one descriptor is used to encode the whole image, independently of the exact hand location within the image, and therefore additional spatial information is desirable.

The final DSQP-based image descriptor is obtained as a concatenation of all DSQP descriptors coming from the different image blocks. Considering this configuration, the final length of the image descriptor is:

$$N_{T\_DSQP} = N_s \times N_s \times N_h \times 2^{N_{div}} = 41472 \tag{4}$$

Although the length of the final vector has been considerably reduced by spitting the binary words into sub-words, it is still too long to be efficiently used as the input of an SVM classifier. For this reason, a CS-based dimensionality reduction algorithm is considered in the next section.

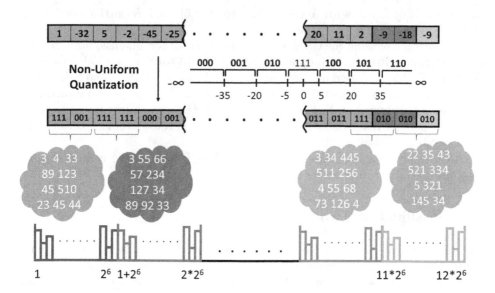

Fig. 3. Computation of the DSQP descriptor for an image region.

3   Compressive Sensing

As the dimension of the DSQP feature vector is quite high, a solution based on the CS framework is used to reduce its dimensionality, but preserving almost all the intrinsic information. Based on the CS paradigm, as the original vector of dimension N is sparese in some domain, it is possible to obtain a much lower dimensionality vector of dimension M. The vector of reduced dimensionality y is obtained by projecting the original vector x in a subspace by means of a matrix ϕ of dimensions $M \times N$, usually called measurement matrix. One of the keys of the CS algorithm is the design of the ϕ matrix as the distance between the original vectors and the reduced ones needs to be preserved. This is the reason why that matrix must satisfy the Restricted Isometry Property (RIP) [1], which can be expressed as follows:

$$(1 - \delta_k) \|x\|_2^2 \leq \|\phi x\|_2^2 \leq (1 + \delta_k) \|x\|_2^2 \tag{5}$$

where $\|x\|_2$ is the euclidean norm of the original vector x, $\|\phi x\|_2$ is the euclidean norm of the reduced vector ϕx, and $\delta_k \in (0, 1)$ is the error in the vector distances after the projection ϕ.

Although the RIP theorem does not say how to obtain such a ϕ matrix, it has been proven in the literature that random matrices satisfy the RIP condition. More specifically, a matrix which elements are random realizations of a Bernoulli distribution is used in the present implementation, where the RIP is satisfied if:

$$M \geq c \times K \times \log(N/K) \tag{6}$$

where c is a constant with a value close to 0.3 [5], and K is the number of non-zero elements of x.

The decision of using the CS algorithm, instead of other dimensionality reduction algorithms (Principal Component Analysis (PCA) or Singular Value Decomposition (SVD)) was based on the computational cost. Both PCA and SVD algorithms needs to make expensive operations using all features of all gestures. In the case of CS algorithm, just a multiplication between each feature vector and the measurement matrix ϕ, whose number of rows is considerable less than the total number of features.

After applying the CS framework to the DSQP vectors the computational cost and memory requirements are decreased.

4   Classification Process

For the classification process, an SVM solution based on the SVM Pegasos algorithm [20] is proposed. For the purpose of multiple gesture recognition, a one-vs.-all strategy is used, where one SVM classifier is trained for each gesture. The main objective is to be able to distinguish between different hand gestures in the dataset, and therefore each SVM is trained using as positive samples those containing the considered gesture, and as negative samples the other gestures samples. A non-linear Hellinger kernel, more commonly known as Battacharyya coefficient [3], is used to improve the recognition score

$$k(h, h') = \sum_i \sqrt{h(i)h'(i)} \tag{7}$$

where h and h' are the test and train feature descriptors respectively.

Regarding the training and evaluation procedure, the database images have been divided into training and testing sets, 50 % for training and 50 % for testing process.

5   Leap Motion Controller

The Leap Motion controller is a small USB peripheral device designed for HMI that supports hand and finger tracking without physical contact. As it can be seen in Fig. 4, the sensor has its own LEDs that emit infrared light, and two wide-angle monochromatic infrared cameras that receive the light reflected by the objects close to the Leap Motion. The Leap Motion SDK computes the 3D position of some hand key elements by a proprietary algorithm that uses a stereo-matching technique over the infrared images and a predefined hand skeleton model. Thus, the Leap Motion SDK is able to describe hands, fingers, palm, wrist, arms, and tools (similar to fingers but thinner). Regarding the characteristics of the infrared images, they have a resolution of 640 × 240 and a frame rate of 60 frames per second and per camera. Figure 5 shows some examples of captured infrared images.

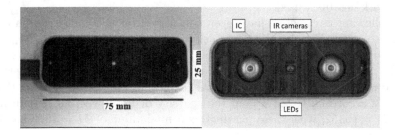

Fig. 4. Leap Motion controller showing where the LEDs and infrared cameras are placed.

6   Results

As far as the authors' knowledge, there is no hand database using the infrared information provided by the Leap Motion. This is the reason for which some samples of different hand poses have been acquired using a Leap Motion sensor placed over a table, the subjects sat close to it, and moved their right hand over the sensor at a distance between 10 and 15 cm in front of it. A group of 10

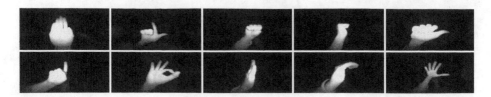

Fig. 5. Dataset samples.

different gestures that were performed by 10 different subjects (5 women and 5 men) have been acquired. A total number of 200 frames have been recorded for each gesture and subject. In Fig. 5, a sample of each hand gestures performed by different subjects is shown. In the first row from left to right, there are an open palm parallel to the sensor (Palm), a closed palm with the thumb and index fingers extended (L), a palm closed (Fist), a fist perpendicular to the sensor (Fist_m), and a palm closed with the thumb extended (Thumb). In the second row from left to right, there are a palm closed with the index extended (Index), an open palm with the index and thumb making a circle (OK), an open palm perpendicular to the sensor (Palm_m), a semi close palm in a shape like a 'C' (C), and an open palm with all its fingers separate (Palm_d).

To test those recorded images, the proposed hand gesture recognition system has been compared with the one proposed by Huang in [4]. This solution has three main stages: the first one is a segmentation stage to determine where the hand is placed in the image; a second stage computes image descriptors using a bank of Gabor filters; and the final stage also uses SVM classification algorithm for the recognition. For the comparison, the same parameters proposed by the original work has been used.

The following parameters have been considered for the configuration of the proposed solution. For the DSQP descriptor, $N_{neigh} = 8$, $N_b = 3$, $N_{div} = 6$, and $N_s = 6$ have been selected. For the CS algorithm, the parameter M has been selected according to Eq. 6. Two additional parameters related with the input data are needed to obtain M, the length of the DSQP vector that is $N = 41472$ according to Eq. 4, and the sparsity of input vectors that in mean value is $K = 15352$; with these parameters a final value of $M = 4579$ has been obtained.

To obtain quantitative results, the confusion matrix (CM) has been used. As the aim of this work is to recognize different gestures independently of the subject, each column of the CM represents the percentage of gestures that belongs to each class, and each row represents the number of gestures, positive and negative, recognized to each class. From CM matrix two measurements can be directly observed, the precision and the recall, which can be expressed as follows:

$$\text{Precision} = 100 \times \frac{\text{true positives}}{\text{true positives} + \text{false positives}} \tag{8}$$

Table 1. Confusion Matrix with result for the proposed system.

	Palm	L	Fist	Fist_m	Thumb	Index	OK	Palm_m	C	Palm_d
Palm	100	0	0	0	0	0	0	0	0	0
L	0	99,9	0	0	0	0	0	0	0	0
Fist	0	0	99,8	0	0	0	0,3	0	0	0
Fist_m	0	0	0	100	0	0	0	0	0	0
Thumb	0	0,1	0,2	0	100	0	0	0	0	0
Index	0	0	0	0	0	100	0	0	0	0
OK	0	0	0	0	0	0	99,7	0	0	0
Palm_m	0	0	0	0	0	0	0	100	0	0
C	0	0	0	0	0	0	0	0	100	0
Palm_d	0	0	0	0	0	0	0	0	0	100

$$\text{Recall} = 100 \times \frac{\text{true positives}}{\text{true positives} + \text{false negatives}} \tag{9}$$

In Table 1, the CM results obtained by using the proposed algorithm. As it can be seen, for all the gestures the precision, elements of the main diagonal, are over 99 % and just a small percentage of samples are detected as belonging to other gestures, but an amount less than 0.5 %. This indicates that our algorithm is quite accurate in both measurements, precision and recall.

Along with the CM values, the F-Score measure is also used to compare the results of both solutions. This measure is obtained as follows:

Table 2. Accuracy results for the proposed system and [4].

Gest.	Alg.	
	Proposed	[4]
Palm	**1**	0,95
L	0,99	**1**
Fist	**0,99**	0,87
Fist_m	**1**	**1**
Thumb	**0,99**	0,95
Index	**1**	**1**
OK	**0,99**	0,87
Palm_m	**1**	0,95
C	**1**	0,87
Palm_d	**1**	0,87
Mean	**0,99**	0,94

$$F\text{-Score} = 2 \times \frac{\text{Precision} \times \text{Recall}}{\text{Precision} + \text{Recall}}. \tag{10}$$

Table 2 shows the accuracy results of the proposed solution and the one proposed by Huang in [4]. The proposed solution is the one that achieves better results. In addition, the presented solution does not need a segmentation stage as the one used by Huang, decreasing significantly the complexity. This comparison also allows us to notice that a segmentation stage is not so important within this database.

7   Conclusions

A hand gesture recognition system for near-infrared images acquired by the Leap Motion has been presented. The system computes a DSQP-based image descriptor directly, without any hand segmentation stage. The resulting image descriptor is reduced in dimension by applying a CS framework. Finally, the obtained reduced vectors are delivered to a bank of SVMs that perform the gesture recognition. The promising obtained recognition scores prove the efficiency of the presented recognition framework, and claim a higher prominence of the Leap Motion sensor for future HMI applications.

Acknowledgements. This work has been partially supported by the Ministerio de Economía y Competitividad of the Spanish Government under project TEC2013-48453 (MR-UHDTV), and by AIRBUS Defense and Space under project SAVIER.

References

1. Achlioptas, D.: Database-friendly random projections: Johnson-Lindenstrauss with binary coins. J. Comput. Syst. Sci. **66**(4), 671–687 (2003)
2. Aditya, R., Namrata, V., Santanu, C., Subhashis, B.: Recognition of dynamic hand gestures. Pattern Recogn. **36**(9), 2069–2081 (2003)
3. Choi, E., Lee, C.: Feature extraction based on the Bhattacharyya distance. Pattern Recogn. **36**(8), 1703–1709 (2003)
4. Deng-Yuan, H., Wu-Chih, H., Sung-Hsiang, C.: Gabor filter-based hand-pose angle estimation for hand gesture recognition under varying illumination. Expert Syst. Appl. **38**(5), 6031–6042 (2011)
5. Eldar, Y.C., Kutyniok, G.: Compressed Sensing: Theory and Applications. Cambridge University Press, Cambridge (2012)
6. Gieser, S.N., Boiselle, A., Makedon, F.: Real-time static gesture recognition for upper extremity rehabilitation using the leap motion. In: Duffy, V.G. (ed.) DHM 2015. LNCS, vol. 9185, pp. 144–154. Springer, Heidelberg (2015). doi:10.1007/978-3-319-21070-4_15
7. Tran, T.T.H.: How can human communicate with robot by hand gesture? In: International Conference on Computing, Management and Telecommunications, pp. 235–240, January 2013
8. Jiang, F., Wang, C., Gao, Y., Wu, S., Zhao, D.: Discriminating features learning in hand gesture classification. IET Comput. Vis. **9**(5), 673–680 (2015)

9. Kai-Yin, F., Ganganath, N., Chi-Tsun, C., Tse, C.: A real-time ASL recognition system using Leap Motion sensors. In: International Conference on Cyber-Enabled Distributed Computing and Knowledge Discovery, pp. 411–414, September 2015
10. Kim, J., Ryu, J., Han, T.: Multimodal interface based on novel HMI UI/UX for in-vehicle infotainment system. ETRI J. **37**(4), 793–803 (2015)
11. Kopinski, T., Geisler, S., Handmann, U.: Gesture-based human-machine interaction for assistance systems. In: IEEE International Conference on Information and Automation, pp. 510–517, August 2015
12. Kuizhi, M., Lu, X., Boliang, L., Bin, L., Fang, W.: A real-time hand detection system based on multi-feature. Neurocomputing **158**, 184–193 (2015)
13. Mantecon, T., del Blanco, C.R., Jaureguizar, F., Garcia, N.: New generation of human machine interfaces for controlling UAV through depth-based gesture recognition. In: Proceedings of the SPIE, vol. 9084, May 2014
14. Mantecon, T., Mantecon, A., del Blanco, C., Jaureguizar, F., Garcia, N.: Enhanced gesture-based human-computer interaction through a compressive sensing reduction scheme of very large and efficient depth feature descriptors. In: IEEE International Conference on Advanced Video and Signal Based Surveillance, pp. 1–6, August 2015
15. Marin, G., Dominio, F., Zanuttigh, P.: Hand gesture recognition with Leap Motion and Kinect devices. In: IEEE International Conference on Image Processing, pp. 1565–1569, October 2014
16. Ng, C.W., Ranganath, S.: Real-time gesture recognition system and application. Image Vis. Comput. **20**(1314), 993–1007 (2002)
17. Nigam, I., Vatsa, M., Singh, R.: Leap signature recognition using HOOF and HOT features. In: IEEE International Conference on Image Processing, pp. 5012–5016, October 2014
18. Ojala, T., Pietikinen, M., Harwood, D.: A comparative study of texture measures with classification based on featured distributions. Pattern Recogn. **29**(1), 51–59 (1996)
19. Shang, W., Cao, X., Ma, H., Zang, H., Wei, P.: Kinect-based vision system of mine rescue robot for low illuminous environment. J. Sens. **2016**, 1–9 (2016)
20. Singer, Y., Srebro, N.: Pegasos: primal estimated sub-gradient solver for SVM. In: ICML, pp. 807–814, October 2007
21. Sykora, P., Kamencay, P., Hudec, R.: Comparison of SIFT and SURF methods for use on hand gesture recognition based on depth map. In: AASRI Conference on Circuit and Signal Processing, vol. 9, pp. 19–24, September 2014
22. Tornow, M., Al-Hamadi, A., Borrmann, V.: Gestic-based human machine interface for robot control. In: IEEE International Conference on Systems, Man, and Cybernetics, pp. 2706–2711, October 2013
23. Yuanrong, X., Qianqian, W., Xiao, B., Yen-Lun, C., Xinyu, W.: A novel feature extracting method for dynamic gesture recognition based on support vector machine. In: IEEE International Conference on Information and Automation, pp. 437–441, Jul 2014
24. Zhang, P., Li, B., Du, G., Liu, X.: A wearable-based and markerless human-manipulator interface with feedback mechanism and kalman filters. Int. J. Adv. Robot Syst. **12**, 164–170 (2015)

Horizon Line Detection from Fisheye Images Using Color Local Image Region Descriptors and Bhattacharyya Coefficient-Based Distance

Youssef El merabet[1]([✉]), Yassine Ruichek[2], Saman Ghaffarian[3], Zineb Samir[1], Tarik Boujiha[1], Raja Touahni[1], and Rochdi Messoussi[1]

[1] Laboratoire LASTID, Département de Physique, Faculté des Sciences, Université Ibn Tofail, B.P 133, 14000 Kenitra, Morocco
y.el-merabet@univ-ibntofail.ac.ma

[2] Laboratoire IRTES-SeT, Université de Technologie de Belfort-Montbéliard, 13 rue Ernest Thierry-Mieg, 90010 Belfort, France
yassine.ruichek@utbm.fr

[3] Faculty of Geo-Information Science and Earth Observation (ITC), University of Twente, 7500 AE Enschede, The Netherlands

Abstract. Several solutions allowing to compensate the lack of performance of GNSS (Global Navigation Satellites Systems) occurring when operating in constrained environments (dense urbain areas) have emerged in recent years. Characterizing the environment of reception of GNSS signals using a fisheye camera oriented to the sky is one of these relevant solutions. The idea consists in determining LOS (Line-Of-Sight) satellites and NLOS (Nonline-Of-Sight) satellites by classifying the content of acquired images into two regions (sky and not-sky). In this paper, aimed to make this approach more effective, we propose a region-based image classification technique through Bhattacharyya coefficient-based distance and local image region descriptors. The proposed procedure is composed of four major steps: (i) A simplification step that consists in simplifying the acquired image with an appropriate couple of colorimetric invariant and exponential transform. (ii) The second step consists in segmenting the simplified image in different regions of interest using Statistical Region Merging segmentation method. (iii) In the third step, the segmented regions are characterized with a number of local color image region descriptors. (iv) The fourth step introduces the supervised $\mathcal{MSRC}$ (Maximal Similarity Based Region Classification) method by using Bhattacharyya coefficient-based distance to classify the characterized regions into sky and non sky regions. Experimental results prove the robustness and performance of the proposed procedure according to the proposed group of color local image region descriptors.

Keywords: GNSS · Region classification · Image segmentation · Fisheye · Color invariance · Maximal similarity · Bhattacharyya coefficient

© Springer International Publishing AG 2016
J. Blanc-Talon et al. (Eds.): ACIVS 2016, LNCS 10016, pp. 58–70, 2016.
DOI: 10.1007/978-3-319-48680-2_6

1 Introduction

Obtaining an accurate localization is very useful for many transport market applications such as monitoring of containers, fleet management, etc. As known, there are several GNSS systems, such as European GALILEO, GPS, COMPASS and GLONASS that give satisfying accuracy in terms of positioning in Intelligent Transport Systems (ITS). Unfortunately, these GNSS systems remain incapable to avoid propagation problems caused by multi-path phenomena of GNSS signals (occurring mainly in constraint environments such as urban zones). Figure 1 illustrates an example of dense environments where signals can be direct, shadowed (signal received after reflections without any direct ray) and blocked (no signal received). Obviously, the evaluation of estimated position reliability become difficult in presence of these constraints. Are not concerned by these drawbacks, certain applications like flot management, containers monitoring, etc., not requiring high availability, integrity and accuracy of the positioning system, but this is a real challenge for specific applications such as safety-related applications (automatic guidance or control), requiring more stringent performances. In this context, several solutions for localization performance enhancement have been proposed in the literature. One can cite multi-sensor-based approaches allowing to compensate the lack of performance of GNSS by adding other sensors (Inertial Measurement Unit, odometer, etc.) that increase the system complexity [1,2]. Marais et al. [3] within the CAPLOC project, have recently proposed a solution that consists in using complementarity between computer vision and localization systems to characterize the environment of reception of satellites. Their workaround permits to enhance localization accuracy by analyzing the structure of the environment traveled by a vehicle using a single camera delivering visible range to overcome problems like lack of precision of 3D models, time computation, etc. The wide-angle camera (fisheye camera with a large field of view of 180°), mounted near to a GPS receiver on the roof of the mobile and oriented to the sky, acquires fisheye images when the vehicle is traveling. Once an image is acquired, two major steps are sequentially applied. The first one concerns image analysis to detect the visible sky and the others objects present in the image. For that, both image simplification and classification are employed. First, the acquired image is simplified using a geodesic reconstruction with an optimal contrast parameter. Second, the simplified image is classified into two classes (sky and not-sky). For that, a set of supervised (Bayes, KNN and SVM) and unsupervised (KMlocal, Fuzzy C-means, Fisher and Statistical Region Merging) clustering algorithms are compared in order to define the best classifier in terms of good classification rate. The second step consists of repositioning satellites in classified images to identify GNSS signals with direct path (resp. blocked/reflected signals) i.e. located in sky region of the image (resp. located in not-sky region). More details of this repositioning step can be found in [3]. It might be worth to mention that the reliability of the proposed system depend greatly on the classification results. The work presented in this paper tries to make the framework proposed in [3] more effective in terms of image classification results. Figure 2 illustrates the flowchart of the image analysis-based

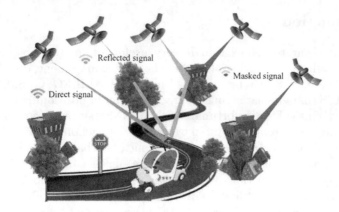

Fig. 1. Illustration of the multipath phenomenon in urban areas.

method for localization. The proposed method incorporates two major stages: image analysis and localization. Our contribution is concerned with the image analysis stage. The method we propose is composed of several sub-steps: 1/ image simplification, 2/ image segmentation, 3/ region features extraction and 4/ region classification.

The rest of the paper is organized as follows. Section 2 presents the image simplification step of the proposed approach. Section 3 describes briefly the Statistical Region Merging algorithm used to obtain the preliminary fisheye image

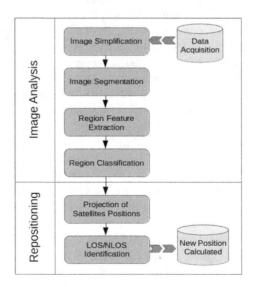

Fig. 2. Flowchart of the image analysis-based method for localization.

segmentation. In Sect. 4, we introduce the implemented local color RGB and local color invariance histograms as region descriptors. Section 5 describes the proposed $\mathcal{MSRC}$ algorithm for region classification. Experimental results and discussions are given in Sect. 6. Section 7 concludes the paper and presents future works.

2 Image Simplification

Before performing image segmentation, an image pre-processing step is employed in order to suppress undesired details (noise and unimportant fine-scale details) present in the acquired images. Indeed, in order to obtain efficient attenuation of over-segmentation problem and reach a more precise segmentation that is faithful to the desired real objects, we propose to simplify the fisheye images by an appropriate couple of colorimetric invariant and exponential transform.

2.1 Colorimetric Invariants (CI)

For specific applications, such as sky recognition in fisheye images acquired in mobility with a mobile platform (instrumented vehicle), the non utilization of any pre-processing step makes the segmentation task delicate and difficult to perform. Indeed, in our application, the camera mounted on the roof of the moving vehicle acquires the sky in the presence of clouds and sun rays with high brightness (see Fig. 5). Therefore, applying any segmentation algorithm directly on the images without any pre-processing step yields to segmented images which are over-segmented caused by insignificant structures or noise affecting the acquired images. To alleviate this problem, we adopt a common strategy consisting of simplifying the input image with a suitable CI [7–10]. In this paper, we used and tested the 16 CI summarized in Table 1.

Table 1. The 16 tested colorimetric invariants.

CI	Acronym	CI	Acronym
- Greyworld normalization [13]	Greyworld	- RGB-rank [14]	-
- MaxRGB normalization [14]	MaxRGB	- A1A2A3 [6]	-
- Affine normalization [4]	Affine	- c1c2c3 [5]	-
- Standard L_2 [6]	L2	- l4l5l6 [16]	-
- Intensity normalization [14]	Chromaticity	- l1l2l3 [5]	-
- Comprehensive color normalization [13]	Comprehensive	- m1m2m3 [5]	-
- Maximum-intensity normalization [15]	Mintensity	-hsl	-

2.2   Exponential Transform (ET)

This second pre-processing step, assured by the ET (cf. Eq. 1), is another effective technique that we have used to improve the robustness of image simplification step. The effect of ET is to approximate the exponential correction factor of grayscale images which maximizes the contrast of the images in the class of exponential intensity mapping functions. In other words, ET enhances detail in high-value regions of the image (bright) whilst decreasing the dynamic range (defined as the difference between the smallest and largest pixel values within the image, i.e. $I_{max} - I_{min}$) in low-value regions (dark).

$$\begin{cases} I'_{ij} = exp(\chi/\xi) - 1 + I'_{min} \\ \chi = I_{ij} - I_{min} \\ \xi = (I_{max} - I_{min})/(log(I'_{max} - I'_{min} + 1)) \end{cases} \tag{1}$$

where I_{ij} is the intensity of the pixel at position (i,j), I_{max} and I_{min} are the highest and lowest intensities of the image I, respectively and ξ is a normalization factor for stretching output values between the new lowest I'_{min} and highest I'_{max} intensities of the resultant image I'.

Note that, the ET and CI operations are sequentially applied. Then, the simplification result is significantly influenced by the colorimetric invariant used. For that, several tests were performed in order to study the influence of the simplified image on the segmentation results obtained by the SRM algorithm, and, thus, to define the optimal couple of CI/ET for our application (see Sect. 6.1).

3   Initial Segmentation Using Statistical Region Merging

As the proposed method is a region based image classification, the next step of our approach consists of segmenting the fisheye images into different regions of interest. Since region analysis is based on regions as defined by the segmentation step, no robust classification is possible without a satisfactory segmentation method. Indeed, the method to choose should be able to extract all significant regions where boundaries coincide as closely as possible with the significant edges present in the image. In this paper, we have used SRM algorithm [11], which generally provides satisfactory results compared to other implemented segmentation techniques. In fact, SRM algorithm has several advantages: (1) it dispenses dynamical maintenance of region adjacency graph (RAG); (2) it allows defining a hierarchy of partitions and (3) it runs in linear-time by using bucket sorting algorithm while transversing the RAG.

4   Region Feature Extraction

Image segmentation permits to identify different regions present in the images. Classification requires the extraction of features to discriminate between them. Indeed, after segmenting fisheye images using SRM algorithm, no information estimation on the content of the segmented regions, which is necessary for the classification process, is yet available. For that, we rejoin the strategy adopted by many authors by characterizing the segmented regions using suitable descriptors [12]. In this research, we investigate the performance of color information. For that, an evaluation of a proposed comprehensive set of 17 local color histograms (rgb color histogram and 16 local color invariance histograms) descriptors is performed. The descriptors we have chosen for the tests are explained below.

4.1 Local Color RGB Histograms

RGB color histogram is an important descriptor for image representation [20]. In this work, in order to calculate the RGB color histograms, we proceed as follows: first we uniformly quantize each RGB color channel into l levels; afterwards, the color histogram of each region is calculated in the feature space of $z = l \times l \times l$ bins. Given an image I containing N pixels quantized in $z = 16 \times 16 \times 16 = 4096$ color bins, the RGB color histogram of a segmented region $\mathcal{R}$ is represented as

$$\mathcal{H}ist^{RGB}(\mathcal{R}) = [\mathcal{H}ist_{\mathcal{R}}^1, \mathcal{H}ist_{\mathcal{R}}^2, ..., \mathcal{H}ist_{\mathcal{R}}^z] \tag{2}$$

where

$$\mathcal{H}ist_{\mathcal{R}}^i = \sqrt{(\frac{\sum_{j=1}^{N} p_{i|j}}{\tau})}; j \in \mathcal{R} \text{ and } 0 \leqslant i \leqslant z. \tag{3}$$

$\mathcal{H}ist_{\mathcal{R}}^i$ is the ith normalized histogram bin and $\tau = \mathrm{card}(\mathcal{R})$ is the number of pixels in the region $\mathcal{R}$. $p_{i|j}$ is the conditional probability of the selected jth pixel belonging to the ith color bin. It is expressed as follows:

$$p_{i|j} = \begin{cases} 1, & \text{if the } j\text{th pixel is quantized into the } i\text{th color bin} \\ 0, & \text{otherwise.} \end{cases} \tag{4}$$

4.2 Local Color Invariance Histograms

In order to obtain invariant signatures, i.e. descriptors invariants with different kinds of illumination changes (shadows, brightness, etc.), we have proposed to extend the RGB color histogram to colorimetric invariants. Indeed, using CI to produce color histogram permits to increase the photometric invariance properties and enhance the discriminative performance. Using the 16 CI summarized in Table 1, and by following the same way as for RGB color histogram, we create 16 new local color invariance histograms ($\mathcal{H}ist^{L_2}$, $\mathcal{H}ist^{Greyworld}$, $\mathcal{H}ist^{c1c2c3}$, etc.).

5   Maximal Similarity Based Region Classification

At this stage of our approach, we dispose of segmented regions $\mathcal{M}_{\mathbf{SRM}}$, obtained via SRM algorithm and characterized with some descriptors. The next step consists in calculating similarity between the regions of $\mathcal{M}_{\mathbf{SRM}}$ and those of two learning databases $\mathcal{B}_{\mathbf{obj}}$ and $\mathcal{B}_{\mathbf{back}}$ that are constructed respectively with m

distinctive textures of sky regions and n distinctive textures of non-sky regions such as building, road, tree, etc. For this purpose, a similarity measure ϱ is needed to calculate similarity $\varrho(\mathcal{R}, \mathcal{Q})$ between two regions $\mathcal{R}$ and $\mathcal{Q}$ basing on their descriptors. In order to measure the similarities between image region features, the similarity measures consider these image region features as points in the vector space and calculate close degree of two points. Several well-known goodness-of-fit statistical metrics exist in the literature. One can cite histogram intersection method [17], log-likelihood ratio statistic [19], Bhattacharyya coefficient [18], etc. Denote by $\mathcal{H}ist_{\mathcal{R}}^i$ the normalized histogram of a region $\mathcal{R}$, the superscript i represents its ith element. $z = l \times l \times l = 4096$ represents the feature space. In this work, we adopted Bhattacharyya coefficient (cf. Eq. 5), which represents the cosine of angle between the unit vectors representing the two regions to be compared: $(\sqrt{\mathcal{H}ist_{\mathcal{R}}^1}, ..., \sqrt{\mathcal{H}ist_{\mathcal{R}}^z})^T$ and $(\sqrt{\mathcal{H}ist_{\mathcal{Q}}^1}, ..., \sqrt{\mathcal{H}ist_{\mathcal{Q}}^z})^T$.

The higher the Bhattacharyya coefficient $\varrho(\mathcal{R}, \mathcal{Q})$ between regions $\mathcal{R}$ and $\mathcal{Q}$ is, the higher the similarity between them is. That is to say that the angle between the two histogram vectors is very small involving that their histograms are very similar. Certainly, two similar histograms do not necessarily involve that the two corresponding regions are perceptually similar. Nevertheless, coupled with the proposed $\mathcal{MSRC}$ algorithm summarized in Algorithm 1, Bhattacharyya similarity works well in the proposed approach.

$$\varrho(\mathcal{R}, \mathcal{Q}) = \sum_{i=1}^{z} \sqrt{\mathcal{H}ist_{\mathcal{R}}^i . \mathcal{H}ist_{\mathcal{Q}}^i} \tag{5}$$

Algorithm 1. Maximal similarity based region classification

Require: $I \leftarrow$ The set $\mathcal{M}_{\mathbf{SRM}}$ of segmented regions.
$\qquad \mathcal{B}_{\mathbf{obj}} \leftarrow$ learning database of objects of interest (sky regions).
$\qquad \mathcal{B}_{\mathbf{back}} \leftarrow$ learning database of background (building, road, tree, etc.).
1: Calculate the local image region descriptor for all regions of $\mathcal{M}_{\mathbf{SRM}}$ and for those composing the two constructed learning databases $\mathcal{B}_{\mathbf{obj}}$ and $\mathcal{B}_{\mathbf{back}}$.
2: **for** each candidate region $\mathcal{R} \in \mathcal{M}_{\mathbf{SRM}}$ **do**
3: $\qquad$ Calculate the similarity vector $V_{obj}^{\mathcal{R}} = \{\varrho(\mathcal{R}, \mathcal{Q}_i); (\mathcal{Q}_i)_{i=1..m} \in \mathcal{B}_{\mathbf{obj}}\}$ between $\mathcal{R}$ and $\mathcal{B}_{\mathbf{obj}}$. $\varrho(\mathcal{R}, \mathcal{Q}_i)$ is the similarity between $\mathcal{R}$ and the region $\mathcal{Q}_i \in \mathcal{B}_{\mathbf{obj}}$.
4: $\qquad$ Calculate the similarity vector $V_{back}^{\mathcal{R}} = \{\varrho(\mathcal{R}, \mathcal{Q}_j); (\mathcal{Q}_j)_{j=1..n} \in \mathcal{B}_{\mathbf{back}}\}$ between $\mathcal{R}$ and $\mathcal{B}_{\mathbf{back}}$. $\varrho(\mathcal{R}, \mathcal{Q}_j)$ is the similarity between $\mathcal{R}$ and the region $\mathcal{Q}_j \in \mathcal{B}_{\mathbf{back}}$.
5: $\qquad$ Get the order of $V_{obj}^{\mathcal{R}}$ and $V_{back}^{\mathcal{R}}$ by decreasing sorting;
6: $\qquad$ Calculate $\mu_{obj}^{\mathcal{R}} = \frac{\sum_{i=1}^{K} \varrho(\mathcal{R}, \mathcal{Q}_i)}{K}$, $K \leq m$, the mean of the K first elements of $V_{obj}^{\mathcal{R}}$.
7: $\qquad$ Calculate $\mu_{back}^{\mathcal{R}} = \frac{\sum_{j=1}^{K} \varrho(\mathcal{R}, \mathcal{Q}_j)}{K}$, $K \leq n$, the mean of the K first elements of $V_{back}^{\mathcal{R}}$.
8: $\qquad$ **if** $(\mu_{obj}^{\mathcal{R}} \geq \mu_{back}^{\mathcal{R}})$ **then**
9: $\qquad\qquad$ The region $\mathcal{R}$ has the maximal similarity with $\mathcal{B}_{\mathbf{obj}}$, it is then classified as a part of sky regions.
10: $\qquad$ **else**
11: $\qquad\qquad$ The region $\mathcal{R}$ has the maximal similarity with $\mathcal{B}_{\mathbf{back}}$, it is then classified as a part of background.
12: $\qquad$ **end if**
13: **end for**
14: **return** The final segmentation map.

The key decision rule of the proposed $\mathcal{MSRC}$ algorithm consists in assigning an unknown region R to the class C_n, if the average of the K first high similarity measures calculated between the region R and the regions of the learning database corresponding to the class C_n is maximal, i.e.,

$$C(\mathcal{R}) = \arg\max_{C_n \in C} \frac{1}{K} \sum_{i=1}^{K} \varrho(\mathcal{R}, \mathcal{Q}_i),\ \mathcal{Q}_i \in B_n \tag{6}$$

where $B_1, B_2, ..., B_j$ are the learning databases corresponding to the classes $C_1, C_2, ..., C_j$, $\mathcal{R}$ is a query, and ϱ is the similarity measure.

6 Results and Discussion

In this section, we study the ability of the proposed $\mathcal{MSRC}$ method and the proposed group of local color region descriptors to classify the regions of interest in fisheye images into sky and non-sky regions. For that, an extensive experimental study and a comparison with the method in [3] were carried out to show the improvement that our method provides. We point out that the image database, acquired in the framework of the CAPLOC project and containing 150 images exhibiting various complex situations (urban canyon, vegetation abundance, overexposure, brightness changes, etc.), was used to validate the proposed nky detection/extraction procedure.

6.1 Choice of the Appropriate Couple of CI/ET

As indicated in Sect. 2, the first step of the proposed approach consists of simplifying the input image with the optimal couple of CI/ET optimized for the application, with the objective to limit illumination changes and thus reduce over-segmentation problem. Figure 3 illustrates the impact of different CI and the ET used conjointly to attenuate the over-segmentation problem. Each bar represents the mean value of the number of segmented regions calculated on all images of the test database according to the couple CI/ET tested. It appears from this figure that the most tested CI when used conjointly with the ET, permit to reduce considerably the number of segmented regions. Basing on the region reduction rate, we can rank the best couples as follows: RedCoord/ET (reduction rate of 84.65 %), Affine/ET (reduction rate of 73.46 %), o1o2/ET (reduction rate of 72.62 %), etc. Nevertheless, if we consider the evaluation of classification results (cf. Table 2), we notice that the couple Affine/ET appears to be a good compromise between attenuation of over-segmentation and proper restitution of sky regions. Indeed, the use of the couple RedCoord/ET allows reducing over-segmentation of the images (providing in average 5.8467 regions per image), however the classification accuracy measure (cf. Table 2) indicates that it is not suitable for obtaining the preliminary fisheye image segmentation. This may be explained by the fact that the use of the couple RedCoord/ET produces an under-segmentation of the image, i.e. presence of regions that contain

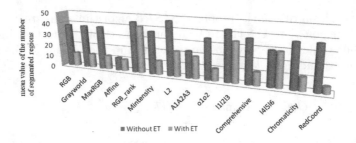

Fig. 3. Attenuation of over-segmentation problem according to the use of the couple CI/ET.

Table 2. Impact of different CI used without/with ET on classification performance of the $\mathcal{MSRC}$ method based on local color RGB histograms.

Tested CI	Accuracy (%)	Tested CI	Accuracy (%)
RGB	99.00	Affine	98.98
RGB+ET	99.17	Affine+ET	99.13
RedCoord	94.29	o1o2	99.12
RedCoord+ET	96.34	o1o2+ET	99.20
MaxRGB	99.00	RGB-rank	96.94
MaxRGB+ET	99.17	RGB-rank+ET	98.77

pixels belonging to different classes in the corresponding segmentation results. Consequently, the classifier, independently to the descriptor and the classifier being used, will affect the same label to the whole pixels belonging to any mixed segmented region, leading thus to some errors. Even if the couple Affine/ET leads to a number of segmented regions, which is relatively higher (in average 10,43 regions per image) in comparison with the couple RedCoord/ET, it provides good classification results where the produced classified images are most close the corresponding ground truth. In conclusion, we opted to use Affine normalization/ET as an appropriate couple for image simplification purpose.

6.2 $\mathcal{MSRC}$ and Descriptors Performance

In this section, we present the performance of the proposed $\mathcal{MSRC}$ method and the proposed local color descriptors to classify the segmented regions into sky and non-sky regions. Table 3 shows the evaluation results according to the $\mathcal{MSRC}$ procedure and the local color RGB and color invariance histograms used. As can be seen, all of the tested local color descriptors allow obtaining good classification results with a small increase when using certain local color invariance histograms. It is worthy to notice that the local color invariance histograms Greyworld,

Table 3. Classification results according to the local color invariance histograms used.

Descriptors	Accuracy (%)	Descriptors	Accuracy (%)
RGB	99.13	A1A2A3	98.33
A1A2A3	99.17	o1o2	99.10
Affine	99.05	hsl	99.03
RedCoord	99.16	L2	99.18
Greyworld	99.26	MaxRGB	99.26
l1l2l3	99.02	Mintensity	99.26
l4l5l6	98.97	m1m2m3	99.00

Maximum intensity and MaxRGB are the most promising because they give the maximum classification rates compared to the other tested descriptors.

6.3 Comparative Evaluation and Discussion

As indicated in Sect. 1, the work presented in this paper is aimed at improving the framework introduced in [3] within the CAPLOC project in terms of classification of the content of fisheye images into two class (sky, not sky). In this framework, the authors have compared the performance of their method used with different well known clustering algorithms often used for image classification purposes. Several supervised (Bayes, KNN, SVM) and unsupervised (Fisher, KMlocal, Fuzzy-Cmeans, SRM) classifiers are tested [3]. The objective here is to compare our approach with the method of [3] used with all these clustering algorithms. Figure 4 illustrates the classification results for each tested method. One can state clearly that the proposed approach behaves better than all of the tested classifiers. Indeed, the proposed procedure maximizes the accuracy measure compared to other supervised and unsupervised tested classifiers, i.e. the proposed approach gives the classification rate of 99.26 % vs 97,71 % with

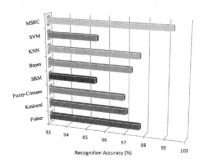

Fig. 4. Classification results according to the method and classifiers used in the CAPLOC project [3] and according to our proposed method.

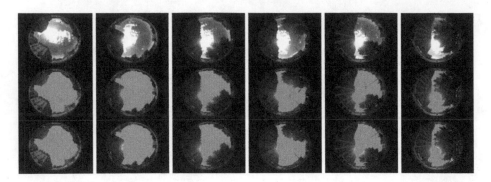

Fig. 5. Visual comparison of region classification results. From left to right: acquired image, classified image into two classes (sky and non-sky) obtained by the best classifier defined in [3] and classification result obtained by the proposed $\mathcal{MSRC}$ approach.

Fisher vs 97.67 % with KNN, etc. Figure 5 illustrates some visual comparison results for a set of images of the test database. It appears from this figure that the proposed approach allowed obtaining good classification results. Indeed, for all of the images in the first column of Fig. 5, the produced classification results agree most closely with the corresponding ground truth where the majority of the sky regions are detected with good boundary delineation.

7   Conclusion

In this paper, we presented a region based classification method for horizon line detection from fisheye images using an group of local color image region descriptors and Bhattacharyya coefficient-based distance. The procedure we proposed starts by simplifying the input images using an optimal couple of colorimetric invariant and exponential transform, optimized for the application, in order to limit illumination changes (shadows, brightness, etc.) affecting the images. Then, we have introduced several new local color descriptors for image region description based on color invariance. 17 local color histograms (RGB color histogram and 16 local color invariance histograms) based descriptors have been proposed. Finally, from regions obtained with the SRM algorithm, a Maximal Similarity Based Region Classification using Bhattacharyya coefficient-based distance has been proposed in order to classify the characterized regions into two classes (sky and non-sky regions). According to the results and their analysis, the proposed approach allowed obtaining good classification results with better extraction of the sky regions. Comparison of our method with the method of [3] with several unsupervised (KMlocal, Fisher, fuzzy C-means and SRM) and supervised (Bayes, KNN and SVM) classifiers showed that the proposed method provides the best performance. For future works, we plan to extend the proposed supervised $\mathcal{MSRC}$ algorithm and the proposed local color descriptors to other data sets related to applications dealing with automatic objects recognition.

References

1. Wang, J.-H., Gao, Y.: High-sensitivity GPS data classification based on signal degradation conditions. IEEE Trans. Veh. Technol. **56**(2), 566–574 (2007)
2. Lentmaier, M., Krach, B., Robertson, P.: Bayesian time delay estimation of GNSS signals in dynamic multipath environments. Int. J. Navig. Obser. **2008**, 11 (2008). Hindawi Publishing Corporation
3. Marais, J., Meurie, C., Attia, D., Ruichek, Y., Flancquart, A.: Toward accurate localization in guided transport: combining GNSS data and imaging information. Trans. Res. Part C Emerg. Technol. **43**, 188–197 (2013)
4. Fusiello, A., Trucco, E., Tommasini, T., Roberto, V.: Improving feature tracking with robust statistics. Pattern Anal. Appl. **2**, 312–320 (1999)
5. Gevers, T., Smeulders, A.: Colour based object recognition. Pattern Recogn. **32**, 453–464 (1999)
6. Gouiffés, M.: Apports de la Couleur et des Modéles de Rèflexion pour l'Extraction et le Suivi de Primitives. Ph.D. thesis, Université de Poitiers, Poitiers, France, Décembre 2005
7. Merabet, Y., Meurie, C., Ruichek, Y., Sbihi, A., Touahni, R.: Orthophotoplan segmentation and colorimetric invariants for roof detection. In: Maino, G., Foresti, G.L. (eds.) ICIAP 2011. LNCS, vol. 6979, pp. 394–403. Springer, Heidelberg (2011). doi:10.1007/978-3-642-24088-1_41
8. Cong, T., Khoudour, L., Achard, C., Meurie, C., Lezoray, O.: People re-identification by spectral classification of silhouettes. Signal Process. **90**, 2362–2374 (2010)
9. El merabet, Y., Meurie, C., Ruichek, Y., Sbihi, A., Touahni, R.: Segmentation d'images aériennes par coopération LPE-régions et LPE-contours. Application á la caractérisation de toitures. Revue Francaise de Photogrammetrie et de Teledetection 2014, no 206, pp. 29–44 (2014)
10. El merabet, Y., Meurie, C., Ruichek, Y., Sbihi, A., Touahni, R.: Building roof segmentation from aerial images using a line and region-based watershed segmentation technique. In: Sensors 2015, vol. 15, pp. 3172–3203 (2015)
11. Nock, R., Nielsen, F.: Statistical region merging. IEEE Trans. Pattern Anal. Mach. Intell. **26**, 1452–1458 (2004)
12. Dornaika, F., Moujahid, A., El merabet, Y., Ruichek, Y.: Building detection from orthophotos using a machine learning approach: an empirical study on image segmentation and descriptors. Expert Syst. Appl. **58**, 130–142 (2016)
13. Schaefer, G.: How useful are colour invariants for image retrieval. In: Second International Conference, Computer Vision and Graphics, Poland, pp. 381–386 (2004)
14. Finlayson, G., Hordley, D., Schaefer, G., Tian, G.: Illuminant and device invariant colour using histogram equalization. Pattern Recogn. **38**, 179–190 (2005)
15. Dargham, J.: Lip detection by the use of neural networks. Artif. Life Robot. **12**(1–2), 301–306 (2008)
16. Latecki, L., Rajagopal, V., Gross, A.: Image retrieval and reversible illumination normalization. In: IS&T/SPIE. Internet Imaging VI, San Jose (2005)

17. Swain, M.J., Ballard, D.H.: Color indexing. Int. J. Comput. Vis. **7**, 11–32 (2002)
18. Kailath, T.: The divergence and Bhattacharyya distance measures in signal selection. IEEE Trans. Commun. Technol. **15**, 52–60 (1967)
19. Fukunaga, K.: Introduction to Statistical Pattern Recognition, 2nd edn. Academic Press, New York (1990)
20. Shahbahrami, A., Juurlink, D.B.B.: Comparison between color and texture features for image retrieval. In: 19th Annual Workshop on Circuits Systems and Signal Processing 2008, Veldhoven, Netherlands

Joint Segmentation of Myocardium on Rest and Stress Spect Images

Marc Filippi[1], Michel Desvignes[1(⊠)], Anastasia Bozok[1],
Gilles Barone-Rochette[2], Daniel Fagret[2], Laurent Riou[2],
and Catherine Ghezzi[2]

[1] GIPSA-LAB, University Grenoble-Alpes, G INP, Grenoble, France
michel.desvignes@gipsa-lab.grenoble-inp.fr
[2] University Grenoble-Alpes, INSERM1039, Grenoble, France

Abstract. This paper presents a level set segmentation of the myocardium, endocardium and epicardium surfaces of the heart from 2D SPECT rest and stress perfusion images of the same patient to compute a heterogeneity index. Cardiac SPECT images have low resolution, low signal to noise ratio and lack of anatomical information. So accurate segmentation is difficult. The proposed method adds joint constraints of shape, parallelism and intensity in a level-set framework to simultaneously extract myocardium from rest and stress images. Results are compared to classical level-set segmentation.

Keywords: Segmentation · SPECT · Left Ventricle · Myocardium · Levet Set · Constraints · Spatial relations

1 Introduction

Coronary macrovessel stenosis has long been considered as the main cause of ischemic heart disease. However, coronary microvascular dysfunction (CMD) has recently been demonstrated to play a major role as well in the occurrence of myocardial ischemia leading to major cardiovascular events or death. It results in patchy coronary microvessel constriction and subsequent myocardial perfusion heterogeneity throughout the myocardium without overt ischemia [2]. Perfusion heterogeneity is also observed at advanced stages in superimposition with the so-called macrovessel obstruction caused by coronary atherosclerotic plaque development. To quantify perfusion heterogeneity, two images of the same patient are acquired and segmented separately: one at rest state, another at stress state. The segmentation of the left ventricle (LV) allows quantitative analysis of perfusion defects and cardiac function by computing a heterogeneity index on the segmented surface [12].

However, no links exist between the 2 segmented surfaces on which the index is computed, since they represent the same organ.

And unfortunately, if a perfusion defect is present, a lost of signal is present in the stress and/or rest images (Fig. 1, top line) and the segmentation sometimes fails (Fig. 1, middle line). So, the computed heterogeneity index is false.

© Springer International Publishing AG 2016
J. Blanc-Talon et al. (Eds.): ACIVS 2016, LNCS 10016, pp. 71–80, 2016.
DOI: 10.1007/978-3-319-48680-2_7

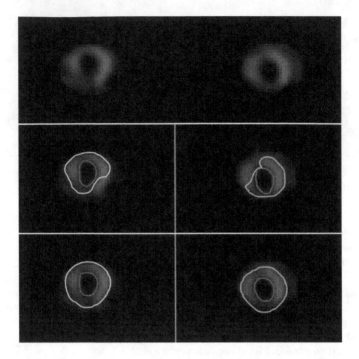

Fig. 1. Top line: Rest and Stress images, with lack of information on the left/bottom part. Middle line: independent segmentation without constraints. Bottom line: joint segmentation with constraints

In fact, several constraints can be added to the segmentation process: epi-cardium and endocardium contours have circular or elliptical shape, with nearly constant thickness and a hight intensity value. Both stress and rest images are representation of the same heart and should be jointly processed for a better result (Fig. 1, bottom line). So, our problem is to add these constraints in a joint segmentation framework.

Main challenges of segmentation of LV from SPECT are due to artifacts, low-contrast, noise, small resolution and inhomogeneities of images. In addition, SPECT images provide a physiological representation of the heart, and not an anatomical one. Moreover, the image data often contains bright structures in the proximity of the LV.

Many image segmentation techniques [5,7,9,12,15,17] have been used for LV detection, including threshold, edge and region based methods, deformable models, graph-based algorithms [6,11]. Classical denoising method and segmen-tation fail to extract the myocardium. Among those, deformable models provide a robust segmentation approach utilizing bottom-up image fidelity term and top-down prior knowledge terms [1]. The basic idea is to evolve a curve, an interface, subject to those terms embedded in an energy function to minimize.

Level-set framework is often used with the region-based active contour models in contrast to edge-based models. It uses region intensity information and has better performances for images with weak boundaries. The classical Chan and Vese (CV) model utilizes global intensity information and assumes that an image consists of statistically homogeneous regions [19]. The major drawback of this model is that it usually fails to detect inhomogeneous objects.

To solve this problem, various models consider local region properties, in particular the local binary fitting (LBF) model [8]. However, many local minimums of the energy functional exist and the result is dependent on the initialization of the contour.

To cope with a-priori knowledge, most of the recent works are based on the classical Chan and Vese model [10, 16].

[18] proposed to model the cerebral cortex as a ribbon structure with nearly constant thickness by incorporating this a-priory information as a constraint condition. However, the main drawback of this method is the assumption that the distance is constant and is known for all the images.

[16] suggested to use an implicit dual shape prior to detect left ventricle in cardiac MRI images based on the anatomical shape similarity between endocardium and epicardium, without any training set. This constraint was added to the classical Chan and Vese model. Their model is built on the assumption that the shapes of two level set functions ϕ_1 and ϕ_2, representing the boundaries of endocardium and epicardium, respectively, are similar under scaling transformation.

There are multiple other ways to define a shape prior for the segmentation problem as a distance or dissimilarity measure for two shapes encoded by the level-set functions [3]. Most of them seek for transformations that best match the level set representation of the shapes of the training set [14] or a statistical shape model to represent inter-subject variability [4].

There are fews works on joint segmentation. [13] suggested to perform a coupled segmentation for both images, in which the information gained in the evolving segmentation of one image is a dynamic prior for the other. The obvious drawback is that errors are easily propagated from the first image segmentation.

So, we proposed to include a distance constraint, a shape constraint in a joint, multi-phase, local binary level set framework to evolve simultaneously the pair of curves modeling the interaction between them. These constraints are embedded in a unique energy function to segment rest and stress images simultaneously. The initialization is provided by our coarse segmentation [12].

2   Segmentation

2.1   Three Phase Local Binary Fitting Model

The method proposed in the current work is based on the local binary fitting model, as this model has good noise-resistance performance and efficiently uses local region intensity information. Therefore, the classical local binary fitting

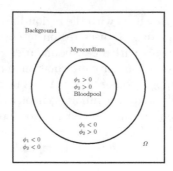

Fig. 2. 2 curves $\{\phi_1 = 0\} \cup \{\phi_2 = 0\}$ partition the domain into 3 regions: $\{\phi_1 > 0, \phi_2 > 0\}$ - bloodpool, $\{\phi_1 < 0, \phi_2 > 0\}$ - myocardium, $\{\phi_1 < 0, \phi_2 < 0\}$ - background.

model is modified to the three phases model by adding the second level set function (the partition corresponds to the Fig. 2).

The energy for n = 3 phases or classes (using m = 2 level set functions) is written as

$$E^{\mathrm{LBF3}}(f, \Phi) = F^{\mathrm{LBF3}}(f, \Phi) + L(\Phi) + P(\Phi), \tag{1}$$

where $\Phi = (\phi_1, \phi_2)$ - the vector of level set functions, $f = (f_1, f_2, f_3)$ - the vector of fitting intensity values functions.

The first term F^{LBF3} is the data fidelity term, $L(\Phi)$ and $P(\Phi)$ are the regularization terms defined as:

$$
\begin{aligned}
F^{\mathrm{LBF3}}(f, \Phi) &= \int_\Omega \sum_{i=3}^{3} \lambda_i M_i(\Phi) e_i(f) dx, \\
M_1 &= H(\phi_1(x)); \\
M_2 &= (1 - H(\phi_1(x))) H(\phi_2(x)); \\
M_3 &= 1 - H(\phi_2(x)) \\
e_i(f) &= \int_\Omega K_\sigma(x - y) |I(y) - f_i(x)|^2 dy
\end{aligned}
\tag{2}
$$

$$L(\Phi) = \nu_1 \int_\Omega |\nabla H(\phi_1)| dx + \nu_2 \int_\Omega |\nabla H(\phi_2)| dx$$

$$P(\Phi) = \rho \int_\Omega \frac{1}{2}(|\nabla \phi_1(x)| - 1)^2 dx + \rho \int_\Omega \frac{1}{2}(|\nabla \phi_2(x)| - 1)^2 dx.$$

$H(x)$ is the Heaviside function and $K_\sigma(x)$ is a gaussian kernel.

The functions $f_1(x)$, $f_2(x)$ and $f_3(x)$ that minimize the energy functional for a fixed ϕ_1 and ϕ_2 are found by calculating variations similar to the two-phase case:

$$f_i(x) = \frac{\int K_\sigma(x - y) I(y) M_i(\phi_1(y), \phi_2(y)) dy}{\int K_\sigma(x - y) M_i(\phi_1(y), \phi_2(y)) dy} \tag{3}$$

The following gradient descent flow equations achieve the minimization of the energy E^{LBF3} (similarly for ϕ_2):

$$\frac{\partial \phi_1}{\partial t} = -\delta_\varepsilon(\phi_1)\left(\lambda_1 e_1 - \lambda_2 e_2 H(\phi_2)\right) \tag{4}$$

$$+ \nu_1 \delta_\varepsilon(\phi_1) \operatorname{div}\left(\frac{\nabla \phi_1}{|\nabla \phi_1|}\right)$$

$$+ \rho\left(\nabla^2 \phi_1 - \operatorname{div}\left(\frac{\nabla \phi_1}{|\nabla \phi_1|}\right)\right)$$

$$e_1(x) = \int K_\sigma(y - x)\,|I(x) - f_1(y)|^2\,dy$$

$$e_2(x) = \int K_\sigma(y - x)\,|I(x) - f_2(y)|^2\,dy$$

2.2 Parallelism and Distance Constraint

The endocardium and epicardium are parallel surfaces and the thickness values of the myocardium are in the range $[d \quad D]$. Then, endocardium ϕ_1 should be interior to epicardium ϕ_2 and ϕ_1 should fall between the level sets of $\phi_2 = d$ and $\phi_2 = D$. We define this constraint, assuming parallelism and distance as a new distance term ($F^{\text{dist}}(\phi_1)$ is similar):

$$F^{\text{dist}}(\phi_2) = \frac{\alpha}{2} \int_\Omega \left[1 - (H(\phi_1 + D) - H(\phi_1 + d))\right] \tag{5}$$

$$\cdot \left[(H(\phi_1 + d) - H(\phi_2))^2 + (H(\phi_1 + D) - H(\phi_2))^2\right] dx$$

The first term is a constant which equals to zero when the distance falls into the range $[d \quad D]$ and equals to one when the distance is out of the preferred range. Hence, the minimization will only take place when this term is equal to one, i.e. only when the thickness is out of range. The second term restrains the level set function ϕ_2 to move towards the acceptable range between the level sets $\phi_1 = -d$ and $\phi_1 = -D$. If the thickness of the detected myocardium is smaller than d, then the distance energy forces ϕ_2 to go away from ϕ_1. If the distance between the level sets is larger than D, then the constraint forces ϕ_2 to decrease that distance by getting closer to ϕ_1.

The distance energy functional F^{dist} is added to the three phase LBF model:

$$E = E^{\text{LBF3}}(\phi_1, \phi_2) + F^{\text{dist}}(\phi_1) + F^{\text{dist}}(\phi_2) \tag{6}$$

And the functions ϕ_1 and ϕ_2 are now given by the following gradient descent flow:

$$\frac{\partial \phi_1}{\partial t} = -\frac{\partial E^{\text{LBF3}}}{\partial \phi_1} - \frac{\partial F^{\text{dist}}(\phi_1)}{\partial \phi_1} \tag{7}$$

$$\frac{\partial F^{\text{dist}}(\phi_1)}{\partial \phi_1} = \alpha\delta(\phi_1)\left[1 - (H(\phi_2 - d) - H(\phi_2 - D))\right]$$

$$\times \left[2H(\phi_1) - H(\phi_2 - d) - H(\phi_2 - D)\right]$$

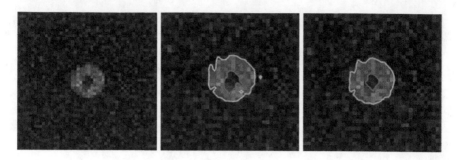

Fig. 3. Initial Image, 3 Phase-LBF, Distance constraint

This constraint is helpful in performing segmentation on images with low SNR (see Fig. 3) as it ensures the consistency of segmented myocardium.

2.3   Shape Constraint

The geometrical constraint on the segmentation energy is based on the functional proposed by [16].

$$F^{\text{shape}}(\phi_i) = \gamma_i \int_\Omega \frac{(|\phi_i - \phi_i^M| - \eta_i)^2}{2\sigma_s^2} \tag{8}$$
$$\cdot ((1 - H(\phi_i))H(\phi_i^M) + (1 - H(\phi_i^M))H(\phi_i))dx$$

where ϕ_i^M denotes the reference shape for the level set function ϕ_i. σ_s is a parameter based on the deformation properties of the region to segment. The higher σ_s value is, the more the two shapes can differ.

The gradient descent flow for the shape term is:

$$\frac{\partial F^{\text{shape}}}{\partial \phi_i} = \gamma_i \delta(\phi_i)(1 - 2H(\phi_i^M))\frac{(|\phi_i - \phi_i^M| - \eta_i)^2}{2\sigma_s^2} \tag{9}$$
$$+ \frac{\gamma_i}{\sigma_s^2}(|\phi_i - \phi_i^M| - \eta_i)$$

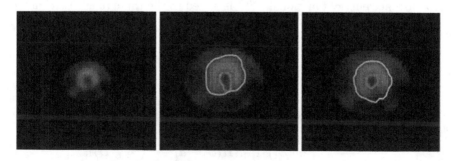

Fig. 4. Initial image, 3 Phase-LBF, shape constraint

$$.(2\delta(\phi_i - \phi_i^M)(\phi_i - \phi_i^M) + 2H(\phi_i - \phi_i^M) - 1)$$
$$\times ((1 - H(\phi_i))H(\phi_i^M) + (1 - H(\phi_i^M))H(\phi_i))$$

This constraint can be seen as a shape prior when a reference shape or a statistical model is available. In our case, the model is a circle inferred from the coarse segmentation. Future work will use a statistical model.

An example of segmentation by posing the shape constraint is shown on the Fig. 4.

2.4 Joint Segmentation

As the anatomical content is the same in the rest and stress images, we define 2 pairs of level set functions, ϕ_1/ϕ_2 on the rest image and ϕ_3/ϕ_4 ont the stress image.

To guide the curve evolution of the pair of two interfaces ϕ_1/ϕ_3 and ϕ_2/ϕ_4, the shape dissimilarity measures $F^{\text{Coupling}}(\phi_1), F^{\text{Coupling}}(\phi_2)$ are defined by (similarly for $F^{\text{Coupling}}(\phi_3), F^{\text{Coupling}}(\phi_4)$):

$$F^{\text{Coupling}}(\phi_1) = \beta \int_{\Omega_1} (H(\phi_1(x + \mu_{\phi_1})) - H(\phi_3(x - \mu_{\phi_3})))^2 dx,$$

$$F^{\text{Coupling}}(\phi_2) = \beta \int_{\Omega_1} (H(\phi_2(x + \mu_{\phi_2})) - H(\phi_4(x - \mu_{\phi_4})))^2 dx,$$

μ_{ϕ_i} is the center of gravity of the function ϕ_i and it is given as:

$$\mu_{\phi_i} = \frac{\int_{\Omega} x H(\phi_i) dx}{\int_{\Omega} H(\phi_i) dx} \text{ for } i = 1, 2, 3, 4. \tag{10}$$

The term $\phi_3(x - \mu_{\phi_3})$ in the energy functional $E_{\text{Coupling}}(\phi_1)$ plays a role of the reference shape for ϕ_1 and reciprocally.

The final gradient descent flow has the following form:

$$\frac{\partial \phi_i}{\partial t} = -\frac{\partial F^{\text{LBF3}}}{\partial \phi_i} - \frac{\partial L}{\partial \phi_i} - \frac{\partial P}{\partial \phi_i} - \frac{\partial F^{\text{dist}}(\phi_i)}{\partial \phi_i}$$
$$- \frac{\partial F^{\text{shape}}}{\partial \phi_i} - \frac{\partial F^{\text{coupling}}}{\partial \phi_i} \tag{11}$$

$$\frac{\partial F^{\text{Cou}}(\phi_1)}{\partial \phi_1} = 2\beta\delta(\phi_1(x)) \tag{12}$$
$$\times [(H(\phi_1(x)) - H(\phi_3(x - \mu_{\phi_1} - \mu_{\phi_3})))$$
$$+ \frac{(x - \mu_{\phi_1}))^T}{\int_{\Omega} H(\phi_1(x)) dx} \times$$
$$\int_{\Omega} (H(\phi_1(x')) - H(\phi_3(x' - \mu_{\phi_1} - \mu_{\phi_3})))$$

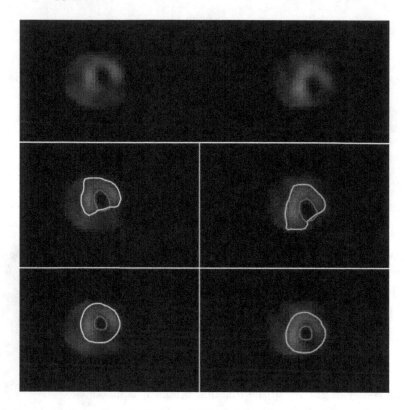

Fig. 5. Rest and Stress images, 3 phase LBF model without constraints, Segmentation with joint constraint term

$$\delta(\phi_1(x')\nabla\phi_1(x')dx']$$

where the term $H(\phi_3(x - \mu_{\phi_1} - \mu_{\phi_3})$ defines a reference shape from the second image aligned to the center of gravity of the shape $H(\phi_1(x))$ to cope with the translation (and reciprocally).

Unlike 2 single perfusion SPECT segmentations, the proposed coupled approach combines the information of both images to enhance the segmentation (Fig. 5).

3   Results and Conclusion

We compare our method with the classical Chen and Vese level-set method.

Tests are performed on a set of 30 pairs of images of different patients. The SPECT images are $64 \times 64 \times H$ (H<64) short-axis images (not gated), voxel size is $6,77\,\text{mm} \times 6,77\,\text{mm} \times 6,77\,\text{mm}$, Field of View is $433.28\,\text{mm} \times 433.28\,\text{mm} \times H*0.1477\,\text{mm}$.

On 3D images, the segmentation is computed slice by slice. One expert draws manual segmentation on images for quantitative evaluation and also gives a qualitative evaluation (acceptable or not). The same parameters were used for all the SPECT images. The average thickness of the myocardium is set to be $d_{ave} = 4$ pixels. The radius of the bloodpool (the inner circle) is $r = 1.4$. The time steps for the level set functions ϕ_1 (the inner contour) and ϕ_2 (the outer contour) are $\Delta t_1 = 0.005$ and $\Delta t_2 = 0.01$, respectively. The space steps $\Delta x = \Delta y = 1$, and $\varepsilon = 0.5$. The parameters chosen are: $\lambda_1 = \lambda_2 = \lambda_3 = 1$, $\rho = 10$, $\nu_1 = 0$ (in practice, there is generally no need to restrict the length of the inner contour), $\nu_2 = 0.02 * 255 * 255 = 1300$, $\alpha = 1500$, $\gamma_1 = 15000$, $\gamma_2 = 750$, $\sigma_s = 3$, $\beta = 600$. The initial state of the interfaces are given by the segmentation of [12].

3.1   Qualitative Evaluation

We have computed the ratio of not accepted image segmentations to the number of image pairs. If the segmentation has failed at least on one image in a pair, the pair is not accepted. If the results of segmentation cannot be used for the quantitative perfusion analysis, for example, if the geometry of the left ventricle is not conserved, the results are not accepted.

With the classical level-set method, 11 of 30 pairs of images has shown unacceptable segmentation, with only 63 % of success rate. With the joint constraint level-set method, 3 image pairs failed the segmentation process completely, yelling the 90 % success rate.

3.2   Quantitative Evaluation

We have also computed the DICE index for the 2 methods. The classical level-set method has a DICE index of 0.853 while the constrained level-set has a DICE index of 0.912. The joint constraint approach outperforms the classical CV level set method as well as out previous dynamic programming approach.

3.3   Conclusion

In conclusion, we have proposed a method to simultaneously 2 perfusion SPECT images. New priors in the local binary level set model as well as the joint evolution of the 2 pairs of interfaces on the 2 images enhance the accuracy of the segmentation.

Future works include the development of this method on 3D images and tests on a large database.

References

1. Becker, M., Magnenat-Thalmann, N.: Deformable models in medical image segmentation. In: Magnenat-Thalmann, N., Ratib, O., Choi, H.F. (eds.) 3D Multiscale Physiological Human, pp. 81–106. Springer, London (2014)
2. Camici, P.G., d'Amati, G., Rimoldi, O.: Coronary microvascular dysfunction: mechanisms and functional assessment. Nat. Rev. Cardiol. **12**(1), 48–62 (2015). http://dx.doi.org/10.1038/nrcardio.2014.160

3. Cremers, D., Osher, S.J., Soatto, S.: Kernel density estimation and intrinsic alignment for shape priors in level set segmentation. Int. J. Comput. Vis. **69**(3), 335–351 (2006)
4. Grosgeorge, D., Petitjean, C., Dacher, J.N., Ruan, S.: Graph cut segmentation with a statistical shape model in cardiac MRI. Comput. Vis. Image Underst. **117**(9), 1027–1035 (2013)
5. Kang, D., Woo, J., Slomka, P.J., Dey, D., Germano, G., Jay Kuo, C.C.: Heart chambers and whole heart segmentation techniques: review. J. Electron. Imaging **21**(1), 010901-1–010901-16 (2012)
6. Khan, M.W.: A survey: image segmentation techniques. Int. J. Future Comput. Commun. **3**(2), 89 (2014)
7. Kohlberger, T., Funka-Lea, G., Desh, V.: Soft level set coupling for LV segmentation in gated perfusion SPECT. In: Ayache, N., Ourselin, S., Maeder, A. (eds.) MICCAI 2007. LNCS, vol. 4791, pp. 327–334. Springer, Heidelberg (2007). doi:10. 1007/978-3-540-75757-3_40
8. Li, C., Kao, C.Y., Gore, J., Ding, Z.: Implicit active contours driven by local binary fitting energy. In: IEEE Conference on Computer Vision and Pattern Recognition, CVPR 2007, pp. 1–7, June 2007
9. Paragios, N.: A level set approach for shape-driven segmentation and tracking of the left ventricle. IEEE Trans. Med. Imaging **22**(6), 773–776 (2003)
10. Paragios, N.: Curve propagation, level set methods and grouping. In: Paragios, N., Chen, Y., Faugeras, O. (eds.) Handbook of Mathematical Models in Computer Vision, pp. 145–159. Springer, New York (2006)
11. Pham, D.L., Xu, C., Prince, J.L.: Current methods in medical image segmentation 1. Ann. Rev. Biomed. Eng. **2**(1), 315–337 (2000)
12. Poujol, J., Desvignes, M., Broisat, A., Barone-Rochette, G., Vanzetto, G., Fagret, D., Riou, L., Ghezzi, C.: Myocardium segmentation on 3d spect images. In: 2015 IEEE International Conference on Image Processing, ICIP 2015, pp. 4788–4792 (2015)
13. Riklin-Raviv, T., Sochen, N., Kiryati, N.: Shape-based mutual segmentation. Int. J. Comput. Vis. **79**(3), 231–245 (2008)
14. Rousson, M., Paragios, N.: Shape priors for level set representations. In: Heyden, A., Sparr, G., Nielsen, M., Johansen, P. (eds.) ECCV 2002. LNCS, vol. 2351, pp. 78–92. Springer, Heidelberg (2002). doi:10.1007/3-540-47967-8_6
15. Soneson, H., Ubachs, J.F., Ugander, M., Arheden, H., Heiberg, E.: An improved method for automatic segmentation of the left ventricle in myocardial perfusion spect. J. Nucl. Med. **50**(2), 205–213 (2009)
16. Woo, J., Slomka, P.J., Kuo, C.C.J., Hong, B.W.: Multiphase segmentation using an implicit dual shape prior: application to detection of left ventricle in cardiac mri. Comput. Vis. Image Underst. **117**(9), 1084–1094 (2013)
17. Yang, R., Mirmehdi, M., Xie, X., Hall, D.J.: Shape and appearance based spatiotemporal constraint for LV segmentation in 4D cardiac SPECT. In: CI2BM09 - MICCAI Workshop on Cardiovascular Interventional Imaging and Biophysical Modelling, London, United Kingdom, p. 10, September 2009
18. Yu, Z.Q., Zhu, Y., Yang, J., Zhu, Y.M.: A hybrid region-boundary model for cerebral cortical segmentation in mri. Comput. Med. Imaging Graph. **30**(3), 197–208 (2006). http://dx.doi.org/10.1016/j.compmedimag.2006.03.006
19. Zhao, Y.Q., Wang, X.F., Shih, F.Y., Yu, G.: A level-set method based on global and local regions for image segmentation. Int. J. Pattern Recogn. Artif. Intell. **26**(01), 1255004 (2012)

Parallel Hough Space Image Generation Method for Real-Time Lane Detection

Hee-Soo Kim[✉], Seung-Hae Beak, and Soon-Yong Park

School of Computer Science and Engineering, Kyungpook National University,
Daegu, Republic of Korea
heesoo91124@gmail.com, eardrops@naver.com, sypark@knu.ac.kr

Abstract. This paper proposes a new parallelization method to generate Hough space images for real-time lane detection, using the new NVIDIA Jetson TK1 board. The computation cost in Standard Hough Transform is relatively high due to its higher amount of unnecessary operations. Therefore, in this paper, we introduce an enhanced Hough image generation method to reduce computation time for real-time lane detection purposes, and reduce all the unnecessary operations exist in the Standard method. We implemented our proposed method in both CPU and GPU based platforms and compared the processing speeds with the Standard method. The experiment results induce that the proposed method runs 10 times faster than the existing method in CPU platform, whereas 60 times faster in the GPU platform.

Keywords: Hough space image · Lane detection · Lane Departure Warning System(LDWS) · CUDA · Advance Driver Assistant System(ADAS)

1 Introduction

Providing convenience to, and assuring the safety of a driver is one of the main interests in Advanced Driver Assistant System (ADAS). Much related work has been actively carried out throughout the past few years; mainly in many autonomous vehicle systems. ADAS has many features such as CNS (Car Navigation System) [1] which updates traffic conditions around the vehicle in real-time, LDWS (Lane Departure Warning System) [2], and IPAS (Intelligent Parking Assist System) [3] for automatic parking using rear and front sensors, and voice commands. In among these, LDWS is extensively studied, because of its capability to warn drivers when the vehicle moves away from its current driving lane and to prevent accidents caused due to drowsiness.

LDWS technology requires higher accuracy and fast processing speeds. In general, many lane detection techniques exist that use laser scanners [4], Lidar sensors [5], and vision sensors. B-Snake method [6], methods that use color information [7, 8] and edge information [9, 10] are examples for some of the techniques that use vision sensors. These vision sensor based techniques use Hough space images for lane detection with higher recognition rates.

The standard Hough transformation method has been widely used to generate Hough space images within the range of 0°~180° considering all straight lines, but the total

© Springer International Publishing AG 2016
J. Blanc-Talon et al. (Eds.): ACIVS 2016, LNCS 10016, pp. 81–91, 2016.
DOI: 10.1007/978-3-319-48680-2_8

computation time is high due to several unnecessary operations. The main motivation of this paper is to propose a new idea to reduce the computation cost it takes to generate Hough space images, and to detect lanes in real-time with a fewer number of operations.

In this approach, we implement a parallelism method to generate Hough space images quickly using a CUDA based NVIDIA Jetson TK1 board. In our approach, we first extract feature points of the lane based on two constraints, the lane is brighter than the road surface, and the width of the lane is constant in the bird's eye view. Next, we use these extracted feature points to generate the Hough space image.

One of the conventional real-time lane detection methods proposed in [12] describes a method to reduce the computation cost by using the ideas of ROI (Region of Interest) and RHT (Randomized Hough Transform). The ROI in the current frame is first calculated with relative to the detected lanes in the prior frame, which is then treated with RHT for path tracking. A full performance analysis between this method and our proposed method is mentioned in Sect. 3.

The structure of this paper is as follows. Section 2.1 describes how feature points of the lane are extracted. Sections 2.2 and 2.3 describe how these extracted feature points are used in the Hough space image transformation along with the method we used to reduce the computation time. Section 2 compares the proposed method with the standard Hough transformation method in both CPU and GPU platforms, using images obtained from a camera that is parallel to the driving lane and installed in the vehicle.

Also, this section compares some of the existing lane detection methods with our proposed method. Section 4 consists of conclusions.

2   Lane Detection System

Figure 1 depicts the overall flow of the proposed lane detection method. First, we assign the Block and Threads for feature point extraction in parallel. We followed a robust, Kyungpook National University illumination invariant feature point extraction method

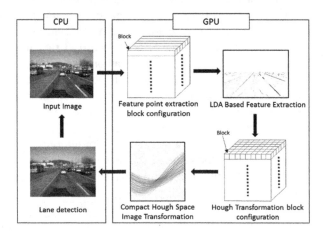

Fig. 1. Lane detection system configuration

as mentioned in [8]. After allocating the Block and Threads for Hough transformation, we then generate the Hough space image based on parallel computation. Finally, we detect two driving lanes from this generated Hough space image.

2.1 Lane Feature Point Extraction

Feature point extraction is one of the primary modules that affects lane detection results in LDWS. Color [7, 8] and edge [9, 10] based methods are highly sensitive to shadows and obstacles around; hence erroneous feature point detection rate is considerably high. Therefore, we, in this paper use an already studied illumination-invariant feature extraction method [11] to reduce these erroneously detected features.

Figure 2 depicts an example of lane feature extraction performed using this robust method. Figure 2(a) is the original input image and, (b) is the feature point detected image. In this image, we only considered the area below the vanishing point to reduce the total computation time.

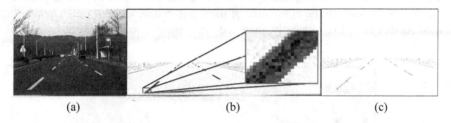

| (a) | (b) | (c) |

Fig. 2. Lane feature point, (a) Original image, (b) Feature extraction, (c) Noise removal result

Fig. 3. Block configuration for feature point extraction

Figure 2(b), the intensity values increase from the edge towards the center of the lane. As it is shown in Fig. 2(c), the final output result is generated by first finding the center points of the lane and removing noise.

In general, the computation time depends on the configuration of the Blocks and the number of Threads used. Figure 3 depicts the Block configuration we used to extract feature points in parallel.

2.2 Standard Hough Transform

Point P_f in Fig. 4 represents one of the arbitrarily selected feature points, which we extracted in Sect. 2.1, and $l_0 \sim l_3$ represent straight lines (in among multiple lines) that pass this point. In traditional Hough transformation method, the distance from the origin to these straight lines is calculated by changing the angle between X-axis and the line connecting the origin within $0 \sim 180°$ range. Assuming the angle between X-axis is θ, and distance from origin is ρ, we first create the relevant Hough space image and then detect straight lines in the original input image. Standard Hough transform performs lane detection throughout the entire area of the input image, without only considering the road surface area. Consequently, there are many unnecessary operations.

Fig. 4. The relationship between the origin and a line that passed a particular feature point

2.3 Compact Hough Transform

The camera mounted inside the vehicle is used to capture perspective images of the road surface. All road lines meet at a single vanishing point as depicted in Fig. 5. One special characteristic of these lanes is that the driving and neighboring lanes pass adjacent to the vanishing point of the previous image plane.

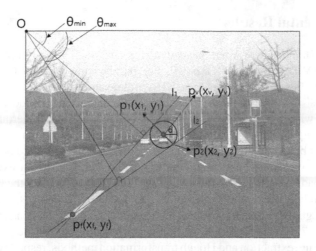

Fig. 5. New idea of reducing the search area to Hough space image transformation

In among the multiple straight lines extracted from the Hough space image, the line that passes adjacent to the vanishing point is considered as the lane candidate in the standard Hough line transformation method. However, some unnecessary operations occur as the search area of this standard method ranges from $0\sim180°$.

However, it is possible to detect the lane candidates by reducing this search area based on the assumption that the driving lane and its adjacent lanes pass through the same vanishing point.

$$\theta_{min} = (\pi/2) - tan^{-1}(g_{min}) - sin^{-1}(\overline{\mathbf{p_1p_v}}/\overline{\mathbf{p_fp_v}}) \tag{1}$$

$$\theta_{max} = (\pi/2) - tan^{-1}(g_{max}) + sin^{-1}(\overline{\mathbf{p_2p_v}}/\overline{\mathbf{p_fp_v}}) \tag{2}$$

$$g_{min} = (y_1 - y_f)/(x_1 - x_f) \tag{3}$$

$$g_{max} = (y_2 - y_f)/(x_2 - x_f) \tag{4}$$

Figure 5 demonstrates how we can reduce the search range in Hough space image transformation. Here, p_f and p_v represent one of the detected feature points and the vanishing point, respectively. Two straight lines – l_1 and l_2 - can be drawn from p_f such that the distance from p_v is d. p_1, p_2 represent the intersection points between the perpendicular lines from p_v and l_1, l_2.

Since the driving lane and its adjacent lanes pass through the same vanishing point, the lane candidates can be easily detected by $\theta_{min} \sim \theta_{max}$ values in Fig. 5. These angle values can be derived from (1) and (2) where g_{min}, g_{max} values represent the gradient values and can be calculated using (3) and (4). Unnecessary computations in lane detection can be easily removed by generating the Hough space image for these two θ values.

3 Experimental Results

The proposed Hough transformation method for lane detection is implemented in a Linux based NVIDIA Jetson TK1 board. For parallelism, we used CUDA 6.5 and OpenCV 2.4.10. Figure 7 describes the CUDA architecture we used. The Host calls the device that consists of a Grid. Furthermore, this Grid contains many blocks and memory configurations within. A block has its own shared memory and numerous threads. In general, the computation time in parallelism varies based on memory allocation and configuration of blocks and threads. The application speed of the shared memory is fast, but in contrast, consists of a low memory capacity. As a result, in our experiment, we decided to upload input images in the Global memory. Figure 3 shows the Block configuration we used in feature point extraction, which has 640×2 Threads. Figure 6 shows the Block configuration for Hough space image generation, which consists of 16×16 threads. In Fig. 7, F_B, H_B represent the number of threads used at the grid side while performing feature extraction and Hough transformation methods, respectively, whereas F_T, H_T represent the number of threads used within a single Block.

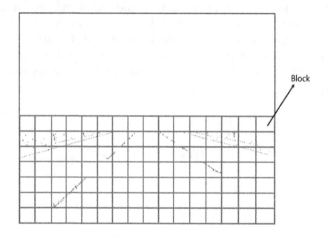

Fig. 6. Block configuration used to generate Hough space image

We performed the experiments on images (640×480) obtained from a camera mounted on a vehicle and evaluated the performance of our proposed method.

Figures 8 and 9 depict the generated Hough space images using standard Hough transformation and the proposed method, respectively. Figures 8(a) and 9(a) represent the generated Hough space images when d is 400 pixels, whereas Figs. 8(b) and 9(b) represent the generated Hough space images when d is 20 pixels.

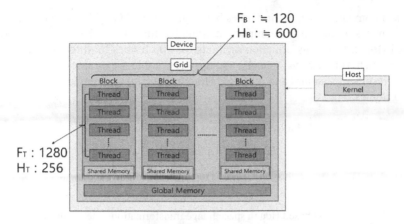

Fig. 7. CUDA architecture

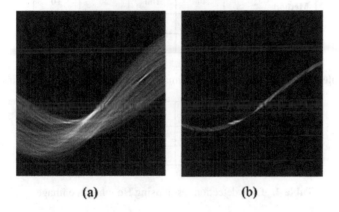

Fig. 8. Proposed Hough space image, (a) d = 400, (b) d = 20

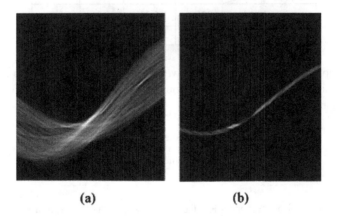

Fig. 9. Standard Hough space image, (a) d = 400, (b) d = 20

Table 1 compares computation times between CPU and GPU for feature extraction. Tables 2 and 3 summarize and compare computation time results between standard and proposed Hough line transformation methods for 300 frames in different environment conditions such as highways, tunnels, and flyovers. Table 4 expresses the ratio of lane detection results of standard and proposed Hough space image transformation methods for 1000 frames.

Table 1. Feature Point detection time (ms)

Platform	Time consumed
CPU	15.4
GPU	2.4

Table 2. CPU based Hough space image transformation time result (ms)

d (pixel) Method	400	100	20	10
Standard	148.4	150.2	151.3	150.9
Proposed	147.2	78.6	20.2	14.4

Table 3. GPU based Hough space image transformation time result (ms)

d (pixel) Method	400	100	20	10
Standard	7.9	7.2	7.1	7.5
Proposed	7.6	5.5	3.1	2.5

Table 4. Lane detection result using Hough space image

d (pixel) Method	400	100	20	10
Standard	97.9%	98.2%	96.5%	95.1%
Proposed	97.8%	98.1%	96.7%	94.7%

Table 5 depicts comparison results between the method mentioned in [12] and our proposed method. The results affirm that our proposed lane detection method runs 4 times faster than the previous method.

Table 5. Lane detection time (ms)

	Existing method	Proposed method
Time consumed	150	34

This previous method performs RHT using two apriori-detected lanes, which sometimes could be difficult. The main drawback lies in the difficulty in detecting these apriori lanes when dotted lines exist. Consequently, the detection rate is low due to a high number of incorrectly detected lanes. Another drawback of this edge information based lane detection method is that the detection rate becomes lower when white vehicles appear inside the ROI. However, the proposed method is not sensitive to any white vehicles with-in the concerned ROI region, and the accuracy of the detection rate is higher when the initial recognition rate is high.

Table 2 depicts results when the methods are implemented on the CPU of Jetson TK1. As it is mentioned in Table 3, the standard Hough line transformation method required 150 ms in the Hough space image transformation, while the proposed method performed 10 times faster. Table 4 depicts the results when they are implemented on the GPU of Jetson TK1. When d is 10 pixels, the proposed method generated the Hough space image within 2.5 ms, which is 60 times faster, compared to the CPU-based standard Hough transformation method. In consequent, the proposed method generates Hough space image at a faster rate when d value is reduced. The final lane detection results are depicted in Fig. 10.

Fig. 10. Lane detection results using a compact Hough transform

4 Conclusions

In this paper, we proposed a new parallelism method to generate Hough space images quickly for real-time lane detection situations. The proposed parallelism method was implemented on the new NVIDIA Jetson TK1 board. The current driving lane and its adjacent lanes pass through an identical vanishing point, and we used this characteristic to calculate the reduced search area within the input image. Unlike in Standard Hough transformation method, we only considered this search range to generate the Hough space image, which allowed reducing the total computation time and number of operations used. We implemented this method on both CPU and GPU-based platforms and compared with the standard Hough transformation method. The experiment results affirmed that our proposed method runs 10 times faster than the standard method in CPU-based implementation, and 60 times faster in GPU-based implementations.

Next, we performed lane detection using Hough space images, and compared experiment results with an already existing lane detection algorithm. Experiment results affirmed that our proposed method runs 6 times faster compared to the previous method.

Acknowledgment. This research was supported by the MSIP(Ministry of Science, ICT and Future Planning), Korea, under the ITRC(Information Technology Research Center) (IITP-2016-H8601-16-1002) supervised by the IITP(Institute for Information & communications Technology Promotion).

References

1. Kim, S., Kim, J.H.: Adaptive fuzzy-network-based C-measure map-matching algorithm for car navigation system. IEEE Trans. Indus. Electron. **48**(2), 432–441 (2011)
2. Suzuki, K., Jansson, H.: An analysis of driver's steering behaviour during auditory or haptic warnings for the designing of lane departure warning system. JSAE Rev. **24**(1), 65–70 (2003)
3. Jung, H.G., Kim, D.S., Yoon, P.J., Kim, J.: Parking slot markings recognition for automatic parking assist system. In: IEEE Intelligent Vehicles Symposium, pp. 106–113 (2006)
4. Sparbert, J., Dietmayer, K., Streller, D.: Lane detection and street type classification using laser range images. IEEE Intelligent Transportation System Conference, pp. 454–459 (2001)
5. Lindner, P., Richter, E., Wanielik, G., Takagi, K., Isogai, A.: Multi-channel lidar processing for lane detection and estimation. IEEE Conference on Intelligent Transportation, pp. 1–6 (2009)
6. Wang, Y., Teoh, E.K., Shen, D.: Lane detection and tracking using B-Snake. Image Vis. Comput. **22**(4), 269–280 (2004)
7. Lee, S.G., Choi, G.H., Bae J.G., Lee, H.J., Choi, S.Y., Hyun, S.H., Han, D.S.: A study on awareness method of lane color using HSV color model for lane departure warning system. In: Proceedings of Symposium of the Korean Institute of Communications and Information Sciences, pp. 291–293 (2014)
8. He, Y., Wang, H., Zhang, B.: Color-based road detection in urban traffic scenes. IEEE Trans. Intell. Transp. Syst. **5**(4), 309–318 (2004)
9. Lin, Q., Han, Y., Hahn, H.: Real-time lane departure detection based on extended edge-linking algorithm. In: International Conference on Computer Research and Development, pp. 725–730 (2010)
10. Hardzeyeu, V., Klefenz, F.: On using the hough transform for driving assistance applications. In: International Conference on Intelligent Computer Communication and Processing, pp. 91–98 (2008)

11. Jang, H.J., Baek, S.H., Park, S.Y.: Lane marking detection in various lighting conditions using robust feature extraction. In: International Conference in Central Europe on Computer Graphics, pp. 83–88 (2014)
12. Wang, J., Wu, Y., Liang, Z., Xi, Y.: Lane detection based on random hough transform on region of interesting. In: IEEE International Conference in Information and Automation, pp. 1735–1740 (2010)

A Novel Decentralised System Architecture for Multi-camera Target Tracking

Gaetano Di Caterina, Trushali Doshi[(✉)], John J. Soraghan,
and Lykourgos Petropoulakis

Department of Electronic and Electrical Engineering,
University of Strathclyde, 204 George Street, Glasgow G1 1XW, UK
trushali.doshi@strath.ac.uk

Abstract. Target tracking in a multi-camera system is an active and challenging research that in many systems requires video synchronisation and knowledge of the camera set-up and layout. In this paper a highly flexible, modular and decentralised system architecture is presented for multi-camera target tracking with relaxed synchronisation constraints among camera views. Moreover, the system does not rely on positional information to handle camera hand-off events. As a practical application, the system itself can, at any time, automatically select the best target view available, to implicitly solve occlusion. Further, to validate the proposed architecture, an extension to a multi-camera environment of the colour-based IMS-SWAD tracker is used. The experimental results show that the tracker can successfully track a chosen target in multiple views, in both indoor and outdoor environments, with non-overlapping and overlapping camera views.

Keywords: Video Analytics · Multi-camera · Decentralised · Tracking

1 Introduction

The need for automatic analysis of video data on computer systems has led to the development of image and video processing techniques usually referred to as Video Analytics (VA), to extract relevant information from surveillance camera feeds. Central to many smart surveillance systems is the detection and identification of a target object in consecutive frames, i.e. target tracking [1].

In the context of multi-camera systems, information extracted from a set of semantically clustered cameras can be fused together and exploited, to achieve a better understanding of the environment surrounding the cameras [2] and monitor areas wider than a single camera field of view (FOV). Each sensor can be associated with VA processing tasks [3,4], to distribute the surveillance workload among cameras and decentralise it towards the edges of the network. This approach produces a collaborative, or co-operative, network of smart surveillance sensors [5,6]. To fully exploit the information gathered by a sensor network,

© Springer International Publishing AG 2016
J. Blanc-Talon et al. (Eds.): ACIVS 2016, LNCS 10016, pp. 92–104, 2016.
DOI: 10.1007/978-3-319-48680-2_9

both topological and geographical layouts of the network can be used. While the former defines which cameras have overlapping FOVs, the latter specifies the position in space of each sensor, with respect to a common coordinate frame.

From the network topology only, it is possible, at any time, to know which other cameras should be seeing a specific target in their FOV. If overlapping cameras can simultaneously detect the same target, information from multiple FOVs can be merged to obtain a better understanding of the target. Such a smart surveillance system can automatically select, from a set of views, the one that gives the best visualisation of the target, and camera overlapping can be exploited to overcome target occlusion [7]. Many algorithms have been proposed in literature for multi-camera system calibration [8,9].

In this paper a complete, highly flexible, modular system architecture is proposed for decentralised multi-view target tracking, where synchronisation constraints among processes can be relaxed. Unlike the approaches in [10,11], the presented novel architecture does not rely on geographical layout, to initialise the trackers or handle camera handoff events. Tracking in separate camera views is performed solely on the visible characteristics of the target, reducing the system setup phase to a minimum. For this purpose, only the knowledge of the topological layout of the network is required at initialisation step. This system architecture is complete, because it also includes initial target detection upon occurrence of events of interests; it is also modular because the specific algorithms implemented in its components can be changed and new features can easily be added to the system, without affecting how the proposed architecture works.

In the context of multi-view systems, colour as a discriminant feature is ideal for target tracking, as it requires minimal computation and it is very resilient against geometric transformations. To validate the effectiveness of the proposed architecture, a modified version of our colour-based IMS-SWAD tracker described in [12] is used as a tracking algorithm in each camera view. In practice any tracking algorithm could be adopted. However, the IMS-SWAD tracker has been chosen because it is easy to appreciate how its operation in each view does not rely on any positional information extracted from other views. Indeed, algorithmic parameters are automatically set in separate views, with respect to the colour characteristics of the target only.

The remainder of the paper is organised as follows. Section 2 describes in detail the proposed architecture and its components. Section 3 describes the improved IMS-SWAD tracker and its incorporation into the architecture. Experimental results are reported in Sect. 4, while Sect. 5 concludes the paper.

2   Decentralised Multi-camera Tracking System

From a conceptual point of view, multi-camera target tracking system can be divided into four tasks:

1. initial target detection upon occurrence of an event of interest;
2. target status storage and broadcasting;

3. target tracking in each separate camera view;
4. data collection from all the trackers and collation.

Such tasks can be mapped into separate processes, which share information with each other for target tracking across multiple views. Therefore four types of processing entities are defined, (i) a detection agent (DA) symbolised as D, (ii) a tracking agent (TA) symbolised as T, (iii) a status server (SS) and (iv) a data server (DS). Figure 1a shows the layout of an implementation of the system.

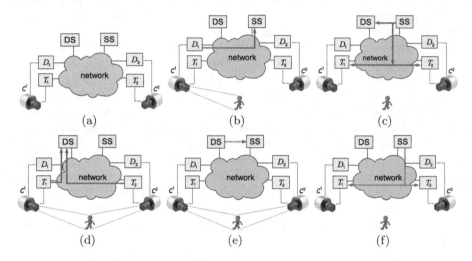

Fig. 1. System implementation with two cameras $\mathcal{C}^1$ and $\mathcal{C}^2$ (a). The DA D_1 detects a target and sends data to the SS (b). The SS broadcasts target information to both TAs T_1 and T_2 (c). The TAs track the target and send their results to the DS (d). The DS merges the TA results and sends the new target representation to the SS (e). The SS broadcasts the new target representation to all the TAs (f).

A separate TA and DA must be associated with each camera in the system, to track a target in a single camera view and to be able to detect events of interest in each camera view respectively. Conversely, it is reasonable to have a single SS acting as a central hub that receives detections from single DAs and broadcasts these to all the TAs. Concerning data collection, a single DS can act as a sink for the tracking information produced by all the TAs.

In general, for a multi-camera tracking system with N cameras, tracking agent T_n and detection agent D_n are associated with the nth camera $\mathcal{C}^n$ with $n \in [1, N]$, and $\mathbf{F}_i^n$ is the ith frame in the nth camera view. For all the agents, a single SS and DS are available. As shown in Fig. 1b, target information is first sent by a DA (D_1) to the SS, upon occurrence of an event of interest. The SS broadcasts this information to T_1 and T_2 (Fig. 1c). The TAs send their tracking results to the DS (Fig. 1d), which merges them in an attempt to resolve possible inconsistencies and produce a unique multi-camera track of the target. Also, the

DS can produce a better representation of the target using information from different TAs; that can then be transmitted from the DS to the SS (Fig. 1e), which can then broadcast it again to all the TAs (Fig. 1f). This cycle allows for a refinement of the target model, by exploiting characteristics of the target in the different views available in the system.

All agents and servers are loosely coupled, as they share their information through simple messages over the network. The system architecture is therefore highly flexible and multiple configurations are possible to deploy the processing entities on physical processing units. For example: (a) all entities can run on the same machine; (b) SS and DS can run on the same machine, while each set of TA and DA associated with the same camera runs on a different machine; (c) each entity runs on a dedicated machine.

2.1 DA – Target Detection

Any DA in the system can select a target within its FOV, upon occurrence of a predefined event of interest. The detection algorithm implemented in the DA is application-dependent and one could either manually select the target, or apply the automatic event detection algorithms [13,14]. In the current system, our adaptive algorithm for the detection of abandoned and removed objects presented in [15] has been implemented in the DAs. However, differently from [15], the algorithm in the DA D_n sends to the SS only the camera number n and the portion of frame $\mathbf{F}_i^n$ corresponding to the selected target (Fig. 2). The reason for this transmission is to further decouple the DAs from the TAs: the TAs can extract from the "image" of the target the features required for their tracking algorithm, without the DAs needing to know what these features and algorithms are. Moreover, separate TAs can implement different tracking algorithms, so they may need to extract different features, such as colour, texture, shape, and so on.

2.2 SS – Target Information Storage

The SS receives data from a DA, i.e. the portion of frame $\mathbf{F}_i^n$ representing the detected object (Fig. 2) and stores it along with a timestamp, the camera number n and a unique identification number ξ for the target.

The SS acts as a sink for all the DA detections, while it follows a publisher-subscriber pattern with respect to the TAs. More specifically, the SS is always running and the TAs subscribe to it at their setup time. When the SS receives target data from a DA, it broadcasts such information to all its subscribers, i.e. TAs, and also to the DS, so that the DS knows what target, with identification number ξ, is under tracking within the system. The TAs can then look for the new target in their FOVs, and track it if present. The role of the SS is to store and forward data between DAs and TAs, and between DAs and DS.

2.3 TA – Single View Target Tracking

The TAs perform target tracking in single views, independently of each other. After receiving target information from the SS, a TA is initialised in the current

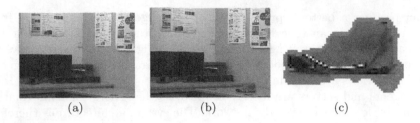

| (a) | (b) | (c) |

Fig. 2. DA target detection: (a) background image; (b) new frame $\mathbf{F}_i^n$ with the selected target in it; (c) close-up of the portion of $\mathbf{F}_i^n$ sent to the SS.

frame when the data from the SS is received. Then the TA performs a loop in which a single step of the selected tracking algorithm is executed on the next frame. If the target has been found, a message with relevant information is sent to the DS. Otherwise, the TA proceeds directly to the next frame. In the rest of the paper, the case where the target has been found by the tracker in the current frame is referred to as "tracking hit".

Any algorithm can be adopted in the TAs. However, the chosen algorithm must be able to extract discriminative features of the target from the data received from the SS, in order to overcome the problem of different target appearance across multiple FOVs in a multi-camera system. In the current implementation of the system, a modified version of the colour-based IMS-SWAD tracker introduced in [12] is adopted, as described in more detail in Sect. 3.

2.4   DS – Data Collation and Multi-view Tracking

The DS collects tracking results from all the TAs and collates them, to remove inconsistencies and create a unique coherent multi-view track of the target.

In a multi-camera tracking system it is possible to synchronise multiple machines using the Network Time Protocol (NTP), to be able to reliably collate target tracks from different views. However, it is difficult to ensure temporal synchronisation at a frame level among multiple trackers. Therefore the presented system adopts a notion of temporal synchronisation in terms of tracking hits falling in the same time interval defined by the DS. This means that the DS defines a time line of consecutive time slots t_s^{DS} of given temporal length Δt^{DS}. The TAs run at their own specific pace and regularly send their tracking results to the DS. Tracking hits flagged by different TAs and received by the DS within the same time slot t_s^{DS} are considered to be synchronous.

Similarly, each TA defines a time line of consecutive time slots t_s^{TA} of temporal length Δt^{TA}, and tracking hits in separate frames falling within the same time slot t_s^{TA} are accounted for as a unique tracking hit. At the end of each time slot t_s^{TA}, the TA sends its tracking results to the DS if a target was found in such a time interval; otherwise no transmission takes place. The information sent by the nth TA includes the camera number n, the target number ξ, a timestamp and the value of the highest match λ_n^ξ, for all the tracking hits in time slot t_s^{TA}.

The reason behind defining also a time slot t_s^{TA} for the TAs is to avoid the need to transmit possible tracking hits for every frame processed by a TA.

Having defined time slots for both DS and TAs, timing constraints for the overall system are relaxed and Δt^{DS} and Δt^{TA} can be set to accommodate the application requirements. As a guideline, assuming the worst case where the DS processes TA notifications sequentially, the lengths of Δt^{DS} and Δt^{TA} can be set according to:

$$\Delta t^{DS} > N\Delta t^{TX} + \Delta t^{TA}$$
$$\Delta t^{TA} > \Delta t^{TX} \tag{1}$$
$$\Delta t^{TA} \geq \frac{1}{fps^{TA}}$$

where N is the number of TAs sending information to the DS, Δt^{TX} is the transmission time from TA to DS and fps^{TA} is the TA processing rate. The "frame rate" of the DS is $1/\Delta t^{DS}$.

At the end of each time slot t_s^{DS}, the DS knows which TAs have found the target ξ in their FOV and which have not. Moreover it can use the match value λ_n^{ξ} of each tracking hit as a level of confidence for it. When any two TAs, T_n and T_m, send their tracking hits to the DS for the same target ξ, in the same time slot t_s^{DS}, the DS selects as best view for the time slot Δt^{DS} the view associated with the tracker that returned the highest match value; therefore the DS can generate a single continuous video stream made up of the portions of video feeds coming from the selected best views, at each Δt^{DS}. Such a strategy is also useful in overlapping cameras, to be able to select the best view of the target in case of occlusion.

Moreover, as the DS gathers all the tracking hits and collates them, it can be argued that it indirectly performs target tracking across multiple camera views as oppose to a single view in the TAs. Also, the DS can use the gathered data to update the current model of target ξ; the updated model can then be forwarded to the SS, for a new broadcast to all the TAs.

3   Multi-view IMS-SWAD Tracking Algorithm

The effectiveness of the proposed architecture for multi-camera target tracking is validated using the colour-based IMS-SWAD tracker described in [12]. This colour-based tracker is selected to highlight the fact that the proposed architecture does not require any position information of the target or of the cameras. The only required information is whether or not cameras have overlapping FOV. The only modification required in our IMS-SWAD [12] to be integrated within a multi-camera environment is in the initialisation step. After that, the algorithm running in each TA processes its own camera view independently from the others and therefore it is ideal for a parallel implementation in the context of a decentralised tracking system, as the one described in this paper.

For multi-view colour tracking, colour calibration among all the cameras is required. Therefore the Gray World Assumption [16] is used to colour-normalise all camera views. Such a normalisation is applied to both TAs and DAs. Further, to make the algorithm more resilient to different lighting conditions in separate views, the YCbCr colour space is adopted, but the luminance component Y is removed and only the red and blue chrominance Cb and Cr are used to compute colour distributions.

Knowledge of the camera topology is required for a correct setup of the instance of the algorithm in each view. For this purpose the tracking algorithm only needs to know which cameras have overlapping FOVs. Therefore, the required information can be easily encoded with a look-up table (LUT) stating whether two camera views overlap or not. Such an LUT can be provided to each tracker instance, i.e. TA, at setup time. In the context of the decentralised architecture (Sect. 2), for a target ξ selected in camera $\mathcal{C}^n$, the initialisation of the tracker T_n is same as the one described in [12]. For the other $N-1$ trackers T_m with $m \neq n$, their initialisation depends on whether the FOVs of cameras $\mathcal{C}^n$ and $\mathcal{C}^m$ overlap or not.

3.1   Non-overlapping Camera Views

If cameras $\mathcal{C}^n$ and $\mathcal{C}^m$ do not overlap, target ξ selected at a given time instant in $\mathcal{C}^n$ is certainly not present in $\mathcal{C}^m$. Clearly the position in $\mathcal{C}^m$ of the best match for the given target model $\mathbf{Q}$ refers to an object which is not the target. Therefore the threshold τ_m for tracker T_m is computed as:

$$\tau_m = \operatorname*{arg\,min}_{\mathbf{o}_l^m} \left[d(\mathbf{o}_l^m) \right] \tag{2}$$

where $\mathbf{o}_l^m$ are the candidate points selected as in the tracker initialisation step in [12], but with no spatial constraints on their position in the initial frame $\mathbf{F}_0^m$.

After initialisation, tracker T_m proceeds to the failure recovery step, as by definition target ξ was not present in $\mathbf{F}_0^m$, so the initial target position in $\mathbf{F}_1^m$ is undefined. Here it is assumed that, when the target ξ enters the FOV of camera $\mathcal{C}^m$, its colour distribution will have a distance $d(\cdot)$ from the target model $\mathbf{Q}$ smaller than any other object in the frame $\mathbf{F}_0^m$ and therefore smaller than τ_m. So the tracker T_m can successfully start to track the correct target ξ in $\mathcal{C}^m$.

3.2   Overlapping Camera Views

If cameras $\mathcal{C}^n$ and $\mathcal{C}^m$ have overlapping FOVs, it means that target ξ should be present in both $\mathbf{F}_0^m$ and $\mathbf{F}_0^n$. The failure recovery procedure applied to $\mathbf{F}_0^m$ gives the position of the best match for $\mathbf{Q}$ in the frame. This best match should be the correct target ξ, assuming that its distribution minimises the distance $d(\cdot)$ from $\mathbf{Q}$. So tracker T_m finds the correct target ξ in $\mathbf{F}_0^m$ and then proceeds to the next frame $\mathbf{F}_1^m$.

If the target ξ is hidden or not visible in $\mathbf{F}_0^m$, the best match found in the frame by the failure recovery procedure will refer to an incorrect target ξ'. This incorrect tracking hit is automatically corrected by the tracker as soon as target ξ is visible again in camera $\mathcal{C}^m$, as ξ gives a higher match than ξ' and therefore

ξ is selected as target to track. However, an initial value for the threshold τ_m is computed anyway and it is updated by the tracker T_m in the next frames of C^m.

This approach allows an initial value of the threshold for each camera view to be defined. Such threshold values are soon tuned by the trackers, so potential initial incorrect hits are confined to a small number of frames. Moreover possible tracking inconsistencies across different views can be resolved by the DS at data collation time as explained in Sect. 2.4.

4   Experimental Results

The purpose of the following experiments is to visually and numerically evaluate the proposed architecture and the IMS-SWAD tracker implemented in the TAs. In the current system software, the tracking block of the TA components is implemented in Matlab and the communication blocks, the SS and the DS are implemented in Java. The computer used to run the experiments is an Intel Core 2 Quad CPU at 3 GHz, with 3 GB of RAM. The cameras used to record the indoor sequences are three 1.3 megapixel IP cameras from Arecont Vision.

4.1   Tracking Performance

The tracking performance of the system is numerically evaluated in terms of precision, recall, specificity and accuracy [1]. In all the experiments in this paper, the ground truth is manually annotated by putting a bounding box around the main colour of the chosen target.

As a first experiment, two multi-camera indoor video sequences have been recorded, respectively one with three non-overlapping views and one with three overlapping views (Fig. 3). In this experiment, the target (a pink cap), which is manually moved from view to view, has been automatically detected by the algorithm implemented in the DAs, in one of the views and then tracked by the TAs in the other two views (Fig. 3). This is repeated for all views to obtain a total of six tests (1–6) for both cases. After target detection in the DA, the portion of frame corresponding to the selected target is sent to the SS (Sect. 2.1). As it is difficult to make sure that pre-recorded sequences are re-run synchronously during testing, the TA activity is simulated by launching one TA per sequence at the time. Each TA initially subscribes with the already running SS, which in turns sends to the TA the target information previously stored. The TA computes the target model needed and tries to track the target in its corresponding video sequence. In this way the target is then tracked in all six tests.

Numerical values of such tests compared with the manually labelled ground truth in Fig. 4 show that the system has high precision, recall, specificity and accuracy, i.e. more than 85 % in all 12 tests. In the overlapping case in particular, neither False Positives nor False Negatives have been detected (Fig. 4b). These results indicate that the system and in particular its current implementation, has good tracking performance in an indoor environment.

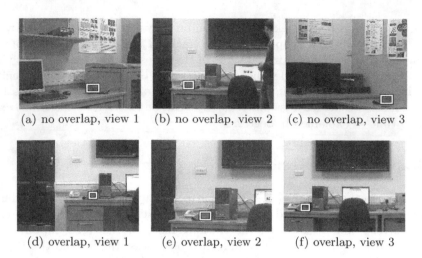

(a) no overlap, view 1   (b) no overlap, view 2   (c) no overlap, view 3

(d) overlap, view 1   (e) overlap, view 2   (f) overlap, view 3

Fig. 3. Indoor testing: non-overlapping (top row) and overlapping (bottom row) views (Color figure online).

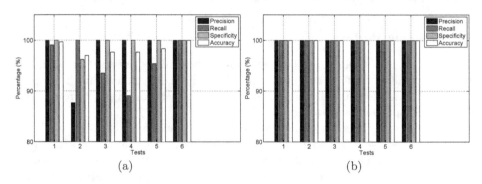

Fig. 4. Results for indoor testing with (a) non-overlapping views (b) overlapping views.

As a second experiment, six entire video sequences (1–6) from the PETS2009 [17] dataset have been used. Since the focus of this experiment is not on the DA, the target (the woman in the red jacket (Fig. 5)), is manually selected in frame #72 of sequence 2. The target image is then sent to the SS and from there to the TA for each of the six PETS2009 sequences. The target is therefore tracked in all sequences as it moves across camera views. Of these video sequences, the sequences 1, 2 and 3 and sequences 4, 5 and 6 are synchronised with each other, which means that the nth frame in each sequence refers to the same instant in time and it has a counterpart in the other two sequences (Fig. 5). It can be observed from Fig. 5 how the target may not be visible at times in some of the views (e.g. Fig. 5e), while it can still be tracked at the same time instant, i.e. same frame number, in other views (e.g. Fig. 5b and h). This aspect is fundamental for selecting the best view of a target, at any time.

Further, from numerical values in Fig. 6, it can be seen that the system has high precision and specificity also in an outdoor setup, with only 4 False Positives erroneously detected in all six sequences. In general, recall and accuracy are also high ($> 90\%$), apart from sequence 6, where the lower value of recall (83%) is due to the fact that in this sequence the target walks away from the camera and its size decreases to less than half of the original. In this case, the histogram of the target changes significantly, resulting in a poor match and therefore a high number of False Negatives. This second experiment indicates the effectiveness of the proposed architecture, in terms of communication between SS and TAs, also in an uncontrolled environment, such as outdoor sequences.

(a) sequence 4, frame #479   (b) sequence 4, frame #507   (c) sequence 4, frame #716

(d) sequence 5, frame #479   (e) sequence 5, frame #507   (f) sequence 5, frame #716

(g) sequence 6, frame #479   (h) sequence 6, frame #507   (i) sequence 6, frame #716

Fig. 5. Synchronised images from PETS2009 sequences 4 (S2-L1-12.34-05), 5 (S2-L1-12.34-06) and 6 (S2-L1-12.34-07) with correct target highlighted by tracking algorithm. (Color figure online)

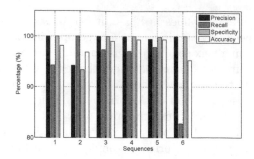

Fig. 6. Precision, recall, specificity and accuracy for six PETS2009 sequences.

4.2   Best View Selection and Occlusion Handling

In the proposed system, the DS receives information on tracking hits, i.e. camera number n, target number ξ and match value λ_n^ξ, from each TA which has found the target in its FOV, and from this data it can select the best view of the target. Therefore, it can produce a continuous video stream from multiple views, when the selected target appears in the different FOVs of non-overlapping cameras (Fig. 7). The current system implementation uses three IP cameras and for testing purposes only, the DS shows the best view of the target, at the top of its video output, and also the current feeds from the three cameras, at the bottom (Fig. 7). In the three sets of camera feed subimages in Fig. 7, it can be seen that the target (person in yellow) is sequentially detected in camera 1 (Fig. 7a), camera 3 (Fig. 7b) and camera 2 (Fig. 7c).

Moreover, the DS can use the tracking results from the TAs associated with overlapping cameras, to select at any time the view with the highest TA match λ_n^ξ. Therefore the DS is able to easily solve the occlusion problem in overlapping cameras, when the target is occluded in one of the views. As illustrated in Fig. 8,

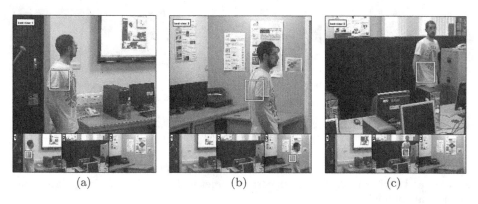

(a)   (b)   (c)

Fig. 7. Three images from the DS: the system is able to switch between camera views wherein the target is detected, to create a continuous video stream of the target (Color figure online).

Fig. 8. DS with best view selection: the target is occluded in view 3; partially occluded in view 2; completely visible in view 1.

the target is correctly tracked in views 1 ($\lambda_1^\xi = 76.4\,\%$) and 2 ($\lambda_2^\xi = 44.5\,\%$). As view 1 gives higher λ_n^ξ value, it is selected as best view among the three available ones, and occlusion is implicitly solved.

5   Conclusion

In this paper a novel decentralised multi-camera tracking system architecture has been presented. The proposed architecture is highly flexible and synchronisation constraints on software and hardware can be relaxed. No positional information is used to localise the target in multiple views, while only the knowledge of occurrence of overlapping between views is required to initialise the trackers. The colour-based IMS-SWAD tracking algorithm adopted in the current implementation demonstrate the effectiveness of the overall system in both indoor and outdoor environments, in tracking a target over multiple overlapping and non-overlapping views. It is expected that the presence of multiple objects with colour similar to the chosen target may lead to wrong detection by the DA, and therefore possible tracking loss. However, the IMS-SWAD itself can be expanded to include other features, such as texture, which should help differentiate between correct target and such other objects with similar colour. Nonetheless, the proposed multi-camera architecture would not require any modification. The system is ideal in situations where video synchronisation and detailed knowledge of cameras' setup is not available.

References

1. Smeulders, A., Chu, D., Cucchiara, R., Calderara, S., Dehghan, A., Shah, M.: Visual tracking: an experimental survey. IEEE Trans. Pattern Anal. Mach. Intell. **36**(7), 1442–1468 (2014)
2. Wang, X.: Intelligent multi-camera video surveillance: a review. Pattern Recogn. Lett. **34**(1), 3–19 (2013)

3. Collins, R.T., Lipton, A.J., Fujiyoshi, H., Kanade, T.: Algorithms for cooperative multisensor surveillance. Proc. IEEE **89**(10), 1456–1477 (2001)
4. Tron, R., Vidal, R.: Distributed computer vision algorithms. IEEE Sig. Process. Mag. **28**(3), 32–45 (2011)
5. Remagnino, P., Shihab, A.I., Jones, G.A.: Distributed intelligence for multi-camera visual surveillance. Pattern Recogn. **37**(4), 675–689 (2004). Elsevier
6. Taj, M., Cavallaro, A.: Distributed and decentralized multicamera tracking. IEEE Sig. Process. Mag. **28**(3), 46–58 (2011)
7. Ercan, A., Gamal, A., Guibas, L.: Object tracking in the presence of occlusions using multiple cameras: a sensor network approach. ACM Trans. Sen. Netw. **9**(2), 16:1–16:36 (2013)
8. Javed, O., Shafique, K., Rasheed, Z., Shah, M.: Modeling intercamera spacetime and appearance relationships for tracking across nonoverlapping views. Comput. Vis. Image Underst. **109**(2), 146–162 (2008)
9. Lobaton, E., Vasudevan, R., Bajcsy, R., Sastry, S.: A distributed topological camera network representation for tracking applications. IEEE Trans. Image process. **19**(10), 2516–2529 (2010)
10. Porikli, F., Divakaran, A.: Multi-camera calibration, object tracking and query generation. In: International Conference on Multimedia and Expo I, pp. 653–656 (2003)
11. Moller, B., Plotz, T., Fink, G.A.: Calibration-free camera handover for fast and reliable person tracking in multi-camera setups. In: International Conference on Pattern Recognition, pp. 1–4 (2008)
12. Di Caterina, G., Soraghan, J.: A robust, precise and flexible tracking algorithm based on IMS and SWAD. In: IEEE International Conference on Acoustics, Speech and Signal Processing, pp. 6588–6592 (2014)
13. Adam, A., Rivlin, E., Shimshoni, I., Reinitz, D.: Robust real-time unusual event detection using multiple fixed-location monitors. IEEE Trans. Pattern Anal. Mach. Intell. **30**(3), 555–560 (2008)
14. D'Orazio, T., Guaragnella, C.: A survey of automatic event detection in multi-camera third generation surveillance systems. Int. J. Pattern Recogn. Artif. Intell. **29**(1), 1–29 (2015). 1555001
15. Di Caterina, G., Soraghan, J.J.: An abandoned and removed object detection algorithm in a reactive smart surveillance system. In: International Conference on Digital Signal Processing, pp. 1–6 (2011)
16. Buchsbaum, G.: A spatial processor model for object colour perception. J. Franklin Inst. **310**(1), 1–26 (1980)
17. PETS2009: Benchmark data. http://www.cvg.reading.ac.uk/PETS2009/a.html. Accessed 14 May 2016

Intramolecular FRET Efficiency Measures for Time-Lapse Fluorescence Microscopy Images

Mark Holden$^{(\boxtimes)}$

Graduate School of Informatics, Kyoto University, Kyoto, Japan
mark_holden@i.kyoto-u.ac.jp

Abstract. Here we investigate quantitative measures of Förster resonance energy transfer (FRET) efficiency that can be used to quantify protein-protein interactions using fluorescence microscopy images of living cells. We adopt a joint intensity space approach and develop a parametric shot noise model to estimate the uncertainty of FRET efficiency on a per pixel basis. We evaluate our metrics rigorously by simulating photon emission events corresponding to typical conditions and demonstrate advantages of our metrics over the conventional ratiometric one. In particular, our measure is linear, normalised and has greater tolerance to low SNR characteristic of FRET fluorescence microscopy images.

1 Introduction

The understanding of cellular processes is at the frontier of bio-medical research [11]. The conventional optical microscope has been the key observational instrument for microbiology for centuries, however its resolution is diffraction limited to around 200 nm, whereas many cellular processes occur at molecular scales of just a few nm. This limitation has recently motivated several decades of research on imaging methods able to detect objects smaller than the optical diffraction limit. One of the most successful approaches is fluorescence microscopy which makes use of fluorophores (fluorescent proteins) that were originally discovered in the jellyfish *Aequorea victoria* by Shimomura *et al.* [15]. Fluorophores can be excited with a narrow band of photons and emit photons of similar wavelengths. They can be bound to biologically active molecules and used to probe the dynamics of many molecular processes in living organisms. Many fluorescence microscopy methods have emerged to determine fluorophore motion, see the recent review [8]. A widely used one is known as Förster resonance energy transfer (FRET) [5]. FRET has several advantages compared with other methods: (a) it can detect fluorophore separation distances of just a few nm, ideal for studying sub-cellular molecular processes; (b) it can be targeted to specific protein-protein interactions; (c) it can be applied *in-vivo*. FRET imaging is based on a pair of fluorophores that interact by electric dipole-dipole coupling. The efficiency of this dipole interaction, denoted $E(r)$ where r is the separation distance, was found by Förster [5] to be $E(r) = \frac{1}{1+\frac{r^6}{r_0^6}}$ where r_0 is known as the Förster distance. Because of the rapid decrease in efficiency with r dipoles only

© Springer International Publishing AG 2016
J. Blanc-Talon et al. (Eds.): ACIVS 2016, LNCS 10016, pp. 105–116, 2016.
DOI: 10.1007/978-3-319-48680-2_10

interact significantly when $r \approx r_0$, which typically corresponds to $r < 10$ nm. The fluorophore pair is chosen so that the two fluorophores are excited by, and emit, photons of slightly different frequencies so that filters can be applied to separate the two signals. When energy is transferred during this interaction one fluorophore (donor) loses energy while the other (acceptor) gains energy. This results in a corresponding decrease in donor, and increase in acceptor emission. Recently there have been several advances in fluorescence microscopy hardware which has led to its increasing use by bio-medical researchers. Despite these advances many researchers assess images qualitatively. Quantitative image processing methods are potentially of enormous benefit. However, conventional methods often do not perform well. For instance, a recent evaluation study of methods to detect isolated fluorophores [16] found that the performance of state-of-the-art object detection methods was significantly compromised due to the low SNR. This is because the relatively small number of fluorescent molecules result in a much smaller number of photons detected for fluorescence images when compared to typical optical images. Typically, as few as ten fluorescent photons are detected per pixel. As a consequence, fluorescent microscopy images are characterized by Poisson, rather than Gaussian, distributed noise (shot noise) and have low SNR. Furthermore, many biological researchers are interested in dynamical processes and use time-lapse microscopy which decreases exposure time and leads to very low SNR, typically in the range 2 to 3.

There are three main imaging methods for measuring E: intensity based FRET, Fluorescence lifetime and anisotropy imaging, see [9,19]. Fluorescence lifetime methods rely on fluorescence-decay histograms to accurately fit decay curves. This requires a relatively greater number of photons and so reduces spatio-temporal resolution. Anisotropy methods rely on polarization which reduces the number of photons collected. The advantages and disadvantages of these imaging methods for the living cell is discussed in [13]. In summary, intensity based FRET is used in most laboratories [19]. The standard method of measuring FRET for intensity based images is to calculate the ratio of the acceptor:donor intensity, see [9]. However, this has the disadvantage of not being linear in E. Linearity can be achieved by using the donor only FRET signal as proposed by Birtwistle *et al.* [2]. Image noise impacts the measurement of E, however, there is very little existing work in this area. Recently we introduced a measure of E for FRET imaging in general [7] that is linear and has the advantage of using both donor and acceptor FRET signals. Here we extend this work and specifically focus on measuring E using intra-molecular FRET biosensors with a fixed one-one stoichiometry. We establish a quantitative imaging model and derive the $(1 - E)^{-1}$ dependence of the standard ratio measure based on Gordon *et al.* [6]. We investigate the accuracy of a Poisson noise model and use this to derive a new fractional uncertainty FRET measure. We test the measures by simulation of photon emission with shot noise and demonstrate that our measures are unbiased. Finally we apply our measures to real-world clinical atherosclerosis data and demonstrate structure consistent with biological expectation.

2 Quantitative FRET Imaging Model

Intramolecular FRET biosensors are designed to target particular proteins within a molecular pathway to measure the level of activation of that pathway. The biosensor is typically genetically encoded and is expressed by every targeted cell. Figure 1 shows a schematic illustration of the architecture of an intramolecular FRET biosensor designed to measure EGF signalling. There are several similar architectures, see [1] for further details. The key component is a pair of fluorophores which fluoresce at slightly different wavelengths and interact through electric dipole coupling (FRET). These fluorophores are attached to specific proteins in the pathway and the conformational change causes a change in the separation distance r that can be detected by FRET. In the example of Fig. 1, the donor and acceptor are attached to SH3 (sensor) and SH2 (ligand) protein sub-domains respectively. When a epidermal growth factor (EGF) signalling molecule binds to its receptor (EGFR) it induces the phosphorylation of CrkII on tyrosine 221, which produces a residue that binds to SH2 [14]. As a consequence the protein complex changes from an open to a closed conformational state. The donor and acceptor fluorophores are continuously excited by photons at rates γ_d^* and γ_a^* (not shown) and emit photons at rates γ_d and γ_a. In the open state, shown left, r is much greater than the Förster distance r_0, a few nm, and their electric dipoles do not interact. In the closed state, shown right, $r \approx r_0$ and so their dipoles interact and energy is transferred from donor to acceptor. This results in a decrease in the donor, and a increase in the acceptor photon emission rates γ_d and γ_a. So, in summary, the donor and acceptor fluorophores emit photons at rates γ_{d0}, γ_{d0} when $r \gg r_0$ and at rates γ_{d1}, γ_{a1} when $r \lesssim r_0$. The photons emitted by the donor and acceptor fluorophores are filtered into two channels and converted by the microscope into two electrical signals. These signals are amplified independently and sampled to produce two digital images, one for the set of donor I_d fluorophores and one for the set of acceptor I_a. The pixel intensity, for a fluorophore image, I, is linearly related to the number of photons detected for that pixel, γ such that: $I = \alpha\gamma$. Here α denotes the gain factor which depends on how the photon signal is filtered, amplified and sampled to a pixel intensity. Accordingly, when the fluorophore separation distance r is such that $r \gg r_0$, the fluorophores do not interact and since their relative concentration is fixed the donor and acceptor image intensities I_d and I_a are linearly related, as follows:

$$I_{a0} = g_0 I_{d0} \tag{1}$$

where the zero subscript denotes negligible dipole interaction (no FRET). The constant of proportionality g_0 is related to the efficiency of the fluorophores and the gains α_d and α_a. When r decreases so that $r \lesssim r_0$ energy is transferred from the donor to acceptor fluorophore. Hence I_d decreases while I_a increases, so the change in intensities $\Delta I_d(r)$ and $\Delta I_a(r)$ can be written as:

$$\begin{aligned}
\Delta I_d(r) &= I_{d0} - I_{d1}(r) \geq 0 \\
\Delta I_a(r) &= I_{a1}(r) - I_{a0} \geq 0
\end{aligned} \tag{2}$$

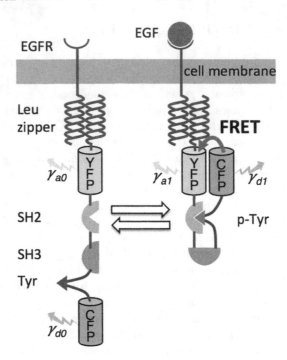

Fig. 1. Schematic illustration of imaging method with a intramolecular FRET biosensor. Two fluorophores, donor (CFP) and acceptor (YFP), are attached to the SH2 and SH3 protein domains. When epidermal growth factor (EGF) binds to the receptor (EGFR) it stimulates Tyrosine (Tyr) phosphorylation (p-Tyr) which binds to the SH2 protein domain. This causes a conformational change in the protein complex which reduces the donor-acceptor separation distance that is detected by FRET.

Here the subscript one denotes dipole interaction and zero denotes no interaction. In [6] the changes in intensity associated with the dipole interaction are related linearly to $E(r)$ and the free donor intensity I_{d0} as follows:

$$\left. \begin{array}{l} \Delta I_d(r) = E(r)I_{d0} \\ \Delta I_a(r) = g_1 E(r)I_{d0} \end{array} \right\} \Rightarrow \frac{\Delta I_a}{\Delta I_d} = g_1 \tag{3}$$

Here the constant of proportionality denoted by g_1, G in [6], depends on the ratio of the quantum yields, $\frac{\#\text{photons emitted}}{\#\text{photons absorbed}}$, of the donor and acceptor fluorophores and the filter efficiencies [6]. So the fluorophore image intensities I_d, I_a are related by two linear Eqs. (2) and (3). In summary, Gordon *et al.* [6] provide a imaging model where changes fluorophore image intensities are linearly related to E, but the model ignores: (a) image noise; (b) diffraction effects; (c) inhomogeneous FRET states within a single pixel.

3   Measuring FRET Efficiency

First we analyse the standard ratio metric $\frac{I_a}{I_d}$. Its dependence on the efficiency $E(r)$ can be derived from Eqs. (1), (2), (3) as follows:

$$
\frac{I_{a1}}{I_{d1}} = \frac{I_{a0} + g_1 I_{d0} E}{(1-E)I_{d0}}
$$

$$
= \frac{g_0 + g_1 E}{(1-E)} \tag{4}
$$

$$
- \frac{g_0 + g_1}{(1-E)} - g_1
$$

Equation (4) indicates that it is linear in $(1-E)^{-1}$. Figure 2 shows a plot of the relationship. Since the photons emitted by biosensors within a pixel add linearly we require a measure that preserves this property. We argue that a non-linear measure cannot achieve this and so is unsuitable as a quantitative measure of FRET efficiency. Therefore we require to determine a more suitable one.

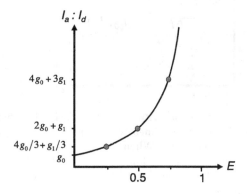

Fig. 2. Non-linear relationship between the intensity ratio $\frac{I_a}{I_d}$ and E.

We can gain insight into the problem by placing the imaging model equations in the joint donor and acceptor intensity space $I_d \times I_a$ as shown in Fig. 3. We can see that the two linear equations are represented by the blue line, $I_a = g_0 I_d$, and the red line, corresponding to the intensity transition due to FRET. The position on the blue line $I_a = g_0 I_d$ depends on the concentration of fluorophores. The greater the concentration, the more photons are emitted so the larger are both I_d and I_a. The length of the red line depends on the amount of energy transferred or efficiency of FRET. We therefore propose that the length of the red line is a 'natural' measure of the amount of FRET. This length is just the Euclidean norm of intensity change ΔI_d and ΔI_a. Since both ΔI_d and ΔI_a are linear in E by Eq. (3) then so is the Euclidean norm d_f, which we refer to as JIN (Joint Intensity Norm), we can write:

$$d_f = \sqrt{\Delta I_d{}^2 + \Delta I_a{}^2}$$
$$= \sqrt{1 + g_1{}^2} E(r) I_{d0}$$

(5)

It is straightforward to determine the normalised measure d_{fn}. Simply by dividing the maximal value of d_f, $d_f(E = 1) = \sqrt{1 + g_1{}^2} I_{d0}$. This is the length of the g_1 line from the intercept with the y-axis, $I_d = 0$, corresponding to $E = 1$, to (I_{d0}, I_{d0}). This gives $d_{fn} = \frac{d_f}{(\sqrt{1+g_1^2}) I_{d0}}$.

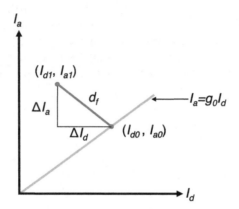

Fig. 3. Donor and acceptor intensities with and without FRET. When there is no dipole interaction (no FRET) I_a and I_d are linearly dependent on the intra-pixel biosensor concentration, shown by the blue line. When dipoles interact FRET occurs and there is a transition from a point on this blue line (I_{d0}, I_{a0}) in the direction g_1 to the point (I_{d1}, I_{a1}), shown by the red line. The length of the red line d_f is a linear measure of the FRET efficiency. (Color figure online)

4   Uncertainty of FRET Efficiency Measure

We aim to determine a quantitative noise model and use it to predict the uncertainty of our measure of FRET efficiency. First we recognize that fluorescence photons are emitted randomly as probabilistic quantum events. These events constitute a counting experiment and so conform to Poisson statistics. Because of the small photon count, photomultipliers are often the preferred detectors. A photomultiplier is a multi-stage amplifier. The first stage, photocathode, converts photons into electrons by the photoelectric effect. The second and subsequent stages, dynodes, amplify the electrons by secondary emission. Both of these stages involve quantum mechanical processes which have Poisson statistics. A photomultiplier can be considered as a cascade of Poisson processes which is itself a Poisson process [4]. If solid state devices are used then they are likely to contribute to signal independent Gaussian distributed noise. Hence, in general, the observed signal I has two components, a signal dependent Poisson noise component Q and signal independent Gaussian noise component W, s.t. $I = \alpha Q + W$ where α is the gain, see [10]. Q and W can be modelled as random variables. Q has a single parameter, emission rate, λ discrete Poisson probability density function given by: $P(y = x|\lambda) = \frac{e^{-\lambda}\lambda^x}{x!}$, where $x \in \mathbb{N}_0$. Note that for a Poisson random variable y, the mean $\bar{y}$ equals the variance $\sigma^2(y)$ and the uncertainty of y equals its standard deviation so $\delta y = \sigma(y) = \sqrt{\bar{y}}$, see [17] Chap. 11. W has a normal probability density function given by: $P(x|\mu, \sigma^2) = \frac{1}{\sqrt{2\pi\sigma^2}}e^{-\frac{(\mu-x)^2}{2\sigma^2}}$ where μ is the mean and σ^2 the variance. The shot noise component Q can be reduced by increasing the photon count while the noise component W can be reduced by using low noise components or by cooling. We investigated the noise characteristics of our microscope images experimentally. We used time lapse images and manually defined two rectangular ROIs for each of the donor and acceptor image sequences. One ROI for background samples, uniform minimal intensity, the other in the foreground samples, uniform maximal intensity, likely to correspond to FRET events. We selected a series of frames for which the signal was uniform so that we had over 10^5 intensity samples. Then we compensated for amplifier gain and fitted a Poisson distribution to the rescaled signal using poissfit (matlab, Mathworks, MA, USA). The results are shown in Fig. 4. These clearly show that the distributions for both ROIs, for both (a) donor and (b) acceptor, can be accurately modelled as Poisson distributions. This result suggests that noise (uncertainty) is predominantly shot noise and the signal independent Gaussian component is a lot smaller. Hence for our time lapse sequence we use a pure shot noise model and neglect the signal independent W term. We make use of this result and use a shot noise model to estimate the uncertainty of d_f in Fig. 3. d_f is a distance between two joint intensity samples (I_{d0}, I_{a0}) and

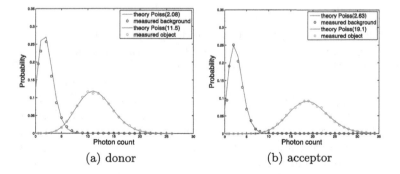

(a) donor   (b) acceptor

Fig. 4. Poisson fit to rescaled pixel intensities of background (blue circles) and foreground (green circles). (a) donor image, (b) acceptor image. The best fits are shown as solid red curves. The means of the distributions is given in the legends. (Color figure online)

(I_{d1}, I_{a1}) in the direction g_1. The samples (I_{d0}, I_{a0}) lie on the g_0 line which can be determined precisely since we have many samples of this, so we may ignore its uncertainty and we need only consider the point (I_{d1}, I_{a1}). In the joint intensity space noise can be represented as an uncertainty ellipse where the axes correspond to the uncertainty of the donor and acceptor intensity which we denote as σ_d and σ_a. We need a scalar value of uncertainty which we refer to as σ_f, this can be obtained by projecting this uncertainty ellipse onto the red line. By geometrical argument $\sigma_f = \sqrt{\dfrac{1+g_1^2}{\frac{1}{\sigma_d^2}+\frac{g_1^2}{\sigma_a^2}}}$. Now we need obtain estimates for σ_d and σ_a.

Since photon emission is a Poisson process, its uncertainty σ is the square root of the mean photon count rate. Furthermore, since pixel intensity is the mean count rate multiplied by the gain α, the fractional uncertainty of intensity equals that of the photon count, [17] page 54. Hence we may estimate the uncertainty of intensity σ_I in terms of the mean intensity and gain as follows: $\sigma_I = \sqrt{\alpha \bar{I}}$. We therefore can predict the uncertainty of d_f. To determine a fractional uncertainty d_{fu} we divide this uncertainty by the best estimate of d_f which gives: $d_{fu} = \frac{\sigma_f}{d_f}$.

5   Evaluation

We have developed d_f, a measure of E, and d_{fu} an estimate of the fractional uncertainty of d_f. In this section we evaluate the accuracy of these measures and compare them with the standard one. Ideally we would have ground truth FRET images with known separation distances and uncertainties. However, it is very difficult and costly to produce such data. So instead, our evaluation strategy is based on simulation of the photon emission events corresponding to realistic FRET experiments which gives quantitative results, and qualitative evaluation of results for clinical images. We argue that this is a robust evaluation strategy.

Implementation

There are four important parameters needed to determine d_f, d_{fn} and d_{fu}, namely: g_0, g_1, α_d, α_a. If we assume shot noise then g_0, α_d and α_a can be estimated from the mean and variance of intensity sample in a ROI. The g_1 parameter is probably the most difficult one to estimate. Because it is needed to compare results across different platforms there are a number of existing imaging methods. For example, Zal and Gascoigne [18] estimate g_1 using donor recovery after acceptor photobleaching. Our implementation provides a pixelwise measure of d_f etc. Given an input intensity sample (I_d, I_a) it first determines whether the sample lies in a valid half space, compared to $I_a = g_0 I_d$. Then it finds the point of intersection (I_{d0}, I_{a0}) with the line $I_a = g_0 I_d$ and determines d_f by calculating the Euclidean norm. The intercept $(0, I_a)$ of the g_1 line is used to determine d_{fn}. The uncertainty of the sample (I_{d1}, I_{a1}) is estimated using the gain and intensity value and the projected uncertainty σ_f is calculated from the equation derived in the previous section which gives d_{fu}.

Accuracy

We estimated the accuracy of the proposed measures d_f, d_{fn} and d_{fu} as a function of the FRET efficiency $E(r)$ and SNR and included the standard $\frac{I_a}{I_d}$ ratio measure for comparison. To assess the measures quantitatively we developed a strategy of modeling the photon count γ as a Poisson distributed random variable using the imnoise function of Matlab. We used four independent random variables to generate: γ_{d0}, γ_{a0}, γ_{d1} and γ_{a1}. We used realistic values for these and α_d, α_a and g_1 based on the experimental results. We assumed linear signal amplification and the free donor Eq. (1) to calculate I_{d0} and I_{a0}. The intensities I_{d1} and I_{a1} are functions of the FRET efficiency E. We calculate these using the FRET efficiency Eqs. (2) and (3). We varied E over the range 0 to 0.8 in 0.01 steps. For each value of E, we generated 100 instances of the photon count random variables γ_{d0}, γ_{a0}, γ_{d1} and γ_{a1} and used these to generate the intensities I_{d0}, I_{a0}, I_{d1}, I_{a1} and the FRET measures d_f, d_{fu} and ratio for each instance. Figure 5 shows the average values, of 100 instances, of d_f, d_{fu} and $\frac{I_a}{I_d}$. The theoretical model is also shown to assess bias. Figure 5 (a) and (b) indicate that d_f is a linear measure of $E(r)$ while $\frac{I_a}{I_d}$ is not. The accuracy of the model was

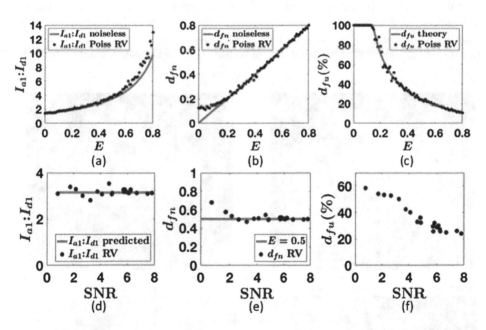

Fig. 5. (a)-(c) $\frac{I_a}{I_d}$, d_{fn}, d_{fu} FRET efficiency measures as a function of E. (a) The standard $\frac{I_a}{I_d}$ ratio measure predicted (red) and mean value for random variable (black). (b) d_{fn} normalised FRET measure theoretical (red) and mean value for random variable (black). (c) d_{fu} fractional uncertainty estimate theory (red) and median value for random variable (black), values clipped at 100 %. (d)-(f) $\frac{I_a}{I_d}$, d_{fn}, d_{fu} measures respectively as a function of SNR with $E = 0.5$ with the true values in red. (Color figure online)

assessed by taking the theoretical model as ground truth x_{true} and calculating the fractional error: $\frac{\sigma(x-x_{true})}{|\bar{x}_{true}|}$. The fractional error for d_{fn} was 0.29 which is comparable to 0.25 for I_{d1} and 0.11 for I_{a1}, i.e. the noise level. The difference between the d_{fn} and the theoretical model in the region $E < 0.2$ is thought to be because of the non-symmetry of the Poisson distribution. Figure 5 (c) shows the median value of d_{fu} as a function of E. We used the median, because the mean was affected by outliers for low E. Values greater than 100 % have been clipped to facilitate presentation. Figure 5 (d)-(f) are plots of (d) ratio, d_{fn} and (b) d_{fu} measures as a function of SNR for $E = 0.5$ solid line (red). The corresponding mean fractional error, over the SNR range, for d_{fn} and the ratio were 0.38 and 0.51 respectively, indicating that d_{fn} is more robust over typical SNR levels compared to the ratio measure. Figure 5 (f) shows the d_{fu} correlates highly with decreasing SNR, correlation coefficient $r = -0.95$.

Application to clinical images

We used a FRET timelapse sequence from a clinical atherosclerosis study which applied extracellular-signal-regulated kinase (ERK) FRET biosensors to detect signalling during thrombus formation. These images had very low SNR, between 2.4 and 3.1. Furthermore the joint intensity distribution in high signal regions was highly dispersed. We decided to address this using the denoising algorithm of Luisier [12] because of its capability of reducing mixed noise. Although, for this

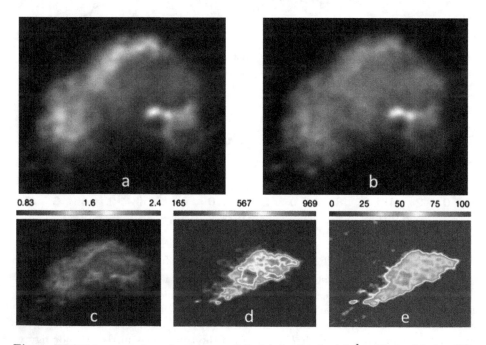

Fig. 6. FRET image pair and measures of E: (a) I_d, (b) I_a, (c) $\frac{I_a}{I_d}$, (d) d_f, (e) d_{fu} (%).

data we could have used a Poisson denoiser such as [3]. Any bias in the denoiser would lead to systematic error in our measures so we tested it thoroughly on a high signal region and noted: a large reduction in dispersion; small changes in local mean ($< 2\%$) and in the shape of the PDF; a doubling of SNR and no obvious artifacts. Figure 6 (a) and (b) show a donor (CFP) and acceptor (YFP) image frame during FRET. Note the lower intensity of the central part of the donor image. Figure 6 (c) shows the ratio image in intensity-modulated display IMD format. For IMD the ratio is linearly mapped to colour space and $\frac{I_a + I_d}{2}$ is mapped to gray scale. The colorbar indicates the upper and lower limits and values less than the lower limit are shown as black. Figure 6 (d) shows d_f and (e) shows d_{fu} fractional uncertainty. Signalling is thought to occur uniformly throughout the body of platelets so FRET efficiency should reflect their shape. During thrombosis platelets change shape and become blob or roughly hemispherical shaped with extruding filapods. We can see that the structure in (d) better matches this than in (c), indicating that d_f is more sensitive to FRET. Furthermore, the regions of lower uncertainty Fig. 6 (e) correspond to those more likely to be involved in thrombus formation, demonstrating the plausibility of our d_{fu} uncertainty estimate.

6   Conclusion

We have approached the problem of FRET measurement from the perspective of the joint intensity space and used the fundamental equations of FRET imaging to derive a linear measure of FRET d_f, in contrast to the standard ratio metric which has a $(1 - E)^{-1}$ dependence. We have demonstrated experimentally that the intensity distributions for our fluorescence microscopy images are consistent with a Poisson distributed shot noise model. We have used this to quantitatively model the intensity uncertainty with Poisson distributed random variables in the joint intensity space. We have combined this uncertainty measure with the FRET measure d_f to construct a new measure of the fractional uncertainty of FRET events d_{fu}. We have evaluated our measures by simulating the photon emission during FRET events as Poisson distributed random variables and real-world data. Our results have demonstrated: the linearity of our JIN d_f measure; that d_f is unbiased under typical noise conditions, and that the error in d_f is comparable to the intrinsic photon noise level. When applied to real-world data our d_f measure appears to produce image structure that is more consistent with biological expectation. Furthermore, the d_{fu} measure predicts the lowest uncertainty in regions thought likely to have signalling events during thrombosis.

Acknowledgements. Supported by Platform for Dynamic Approaches to Living Systems from MEXT Japan.

References

1. Aoki, K., Kiyokawa, E., Nakamura, T., Matsuda, M.: Visualization of growth signal transduction cascades in living cells with genetically encoded probes based on Förster resonance energy transfer. Philos. Trans. R. Soc. Lond. B. Biol. Sci. **363**(1500), 2143–2151 (2008)

2. Birtwistle, M.R., von Kriegsheim, A., Kida, K., Schwarz, J.P., Anderson, K.I., Kolch, W.: Linear approaches to intramolecular Förster resonance energy transfer probe measurements for quantitative modeling. PloS one **6**(11), e27823 (2011)
3. Boulanger, J., Kervrann, C., Bouthemy, P., Elbau, P., Sibarita, J.B., Salamero, J.: Patch-based nonlocal functional for denoising fluorescence microscopy image sequences. IEEE Trans. Med. Imag. **29**(2), 442–454 (2010)
4. Foord, R., Jones, R., Oliver, C.J., Pike, E.D.: The use of photomultiplier tubes for photon counting. Appl. Opt. **8**(10), 1975–1989 (1969)
5. Förster, T.: Intermolecular energy migration and fluorescence. Ann. Phys. **2**, 55–75 (1948)
6. Gordon, G.W., Berry, G., Liang, X.H., Levine, B., Herman, B.: Quantitative fluorescence resonance energy transfer measurements using fluorescence microscopy. Biophys. J. **74**, 2702–2713 (1998)
7. Holden, M.: A linear measure of Förster resonant energy transfer (FRET) efficiency incorporating a shot noise uncertainty model for fluorescence microscopy intensity images. In: Proceedings of 13th IEEE International Symposium on Biomedical Imaging (ISBI), pp. 672–675. IEEE (2016)
8. Ishikawa-Ankerhold, H.C., Ankerhold, R., Drummen, G.P.C.: Advanced fluorescence microscopy techniques FRAP, FLIP, FLAP, FRET and FLIM. Molecules **17**(4), 4047–4132 (2012)
9. Jares-Erijman, E.A., Jovin, T.M.: FRET imaging. Nat. Biotechnol. **21**(11), 1387–1395 (2003)
10. Jezierska, A., Talbot, H., Chaux, C., Pesquet, J.C., Engler, G.: Poisson-Gaussian noise parameter estimation in fluorescence microscopy imaging. In: Proceedings of 9th IEEE International Symposium on Biomedical Imaging (ISBI), pp. 1663–1666. IEEE (2012)
11. Lodish, H., Berk, A., Kaiser, C.A., Krieger, M., Bretscher, A., Ploegh, H., Amon, A., Scott, M.P.: Molecular Cell Biology. Freeman W. H., New York (2012)
12. Luisier, F., Blu, T., Unser, M.: Image denoising in mixed poisson-gaussian noise. IEEE Trans. Image Process. **20**(3), 696–708 (2011)
13. Padilla-Parra, S., Tramier, M.: FRET microscopy in the living cell: Different approaches, strengths and weaknesses. BioEssays **34**(5), 369–376 (2012)
14. Rosen, M.K., Yamazaki, T., Gish, G.D., Kay, C.M., Pawson, T., Kay, L.E.: Direct demonstration of an intramolecular sh2-phosphotyrosine interaction in the crk protein. Nature **374**, 477–479 (1995)
15. Shimomura, O., Johnson, F.H., Saiga, Y.: Extraction, purification and properties of aequorin, a bioluminescent protein from the luminous hydromedusan, aequorea. J. Cell. Comput. Physiol. **59**, 223–239 (1962)
16. Smal, I., Loog, M., Niessen, W., Meijering, E.: Quantitative comparison of spot detection methods in fluorescence microscopy. IEEE Trans. Med. Imaging **29**(2), 282–301 (2010)
17. Taylor, J.R.: An Introduction to Error Analysis. University Science Books, Herndon (1997)
18. Zal, T., Gascoigne, N.R.J.: Photobleaching-corrected FRET efficiency imaging of live cells. Biophys. J. **86**(6), 3923–3939 (2004)
19. Zeug, A., Woehler, A., Neher, E., Ponimaskin, E.G.: Quantitative intensity-based FRET approaches a comparative snapshot. Biophys. J. **103**(9), 1821–1827 (2012)

Predicting Image Aesthetics with Deep Learning

Simone Bianco, Luigi Celona, Paolo Napoletano$^{(\boxtimes)}$, and Raimondo Schettini

Department of Informatics, Systems and Communication,
University of Milano-Bicocca, viale Sarca, 336, 20126 Milan, Italy
{bianco,luigi.celona,napoletano,schettini}@disco.unimib.it

Abstract. In this paper we investigate the use of a deep Convolutional Neural Network (CNN) to predict image aesthetics. To this end we fine-tune a canonical CNN architecture, originally trained to classify objects and scenes, by casting the image aesthetic prediction as a regression problem. We also investigate whether image aesthetic is a global or local attribute, and the role played by bottom-up and top-down salient regions to the prediction of the global image aesthetic. Experimental results on the canonical Aesthetic Visual Analysis (AVA) dataset show the robustness of the solution proposed, which outperforms the best solution in the state of the art by almost 17 % in terms of Mean Residual Sum of Squares Error (MRSSE).

1 Introduction

The automatic assessment of image aesthetic is a novel challenge for the computer vision community that has wide applications, e.g. image retrieval, photo management, photo enhancement, image cropping, etc. [13,20]. Because of the subjectivity of humans' aesthetic evaluation, in recent years, many research efforts have been made and various approaches have been proposed [5,19,24,26,29]. According to the way the problem is formulated, computational approaches can be divided into two groups: aesthetic classification and aesthetic regression. The first group of methods treats aesthetic quality assessment as a binary classification problem, i.e. distinguish between aesthetic and unaesthetic images. Most of these methods have focused on designing features able to replicate the way people perceive the aesthetic quality of images. For example, Datta et al. [12] design special visual features (colorfulness, the rule of thirds, low depth of field indicators, etc. [3,4,7]) and use the Support Vector Machine (SVM) and Decision Tree (DT) to discriminate between aesthetic and unaesthetic images. Nishiyama et al. [28] propose an approach based on color harmony and bags of color patterns to characterize color variations in local regions. Marchesotti et al. [25] demonstrate that generic image descriptors, such as GIST, Bag-of-Visual-words (BOV) encoded from Scale-Invariant Feature Transform (SIFT) information, and Fisher Vector (FV) encoded from SIFT information, are able to capture a wealth of statistics useful for aesthetic evaluation of photographs. Simon et al. [29] show that aesthetic quality depends on context since they obtain more accurate predictions by selecting features for specific image categories. Methods able to learn effective aesthetic features directly from images

© Springer International Publishing AG 2016
J. Blanc-Talon et al. (Eds.): ACIVS 2016, LNCS 10016, pp. 117–125, 2016.
DOI: 10.1007/978-3-319-48680-2_11

have been proposed. Lu et al. [24] present the RAting PIctorical aesthetics using Deep learning (RAPID) system, which adopts a Convolutional Neural Network (CNN) approach to automatically learn features for aesthetic quality categorization. Kao et al. [19] train a linear SVM using the features extracted from a CNN pre-trained on ImageNet classification task.

The second group of approaches considers aesthetic quality assessment as a regression problem, i.e. they predict an aesthetic rating or score of the images. Datta et al. [12] propose the use of Linear Regression (LR) with polynomial terms of the features to predict the aesthetic score. Bhattacharya et al. [2] propose to use a saliency map and a high-level semantic segmentation technique for extracting aesthetic features subsequently used for training a Support Vector Regression (SVR) machine. Wu et al. [30] design a new algorithm called Support Vector Distribution Regression (SVDR) in order to use a distribution of user ratings instead of a scalar for model learning. More recently, Kao et al. [19] propose a regression model based on CNNs, which achieves the state-of-the-art results on aesthetic quality assessment.

In this paper we investigate the use of a deep CNN to predict image aesthetic scores. To this end we fine-tune [1,31] a canonical CNN architecture, originally trained to classify both objects and scenes, by casting the image aesthetic prediction as a regression problem. We also investigate whether image aesthetic is a global or local attribute, and the role played by bottom-up and top-down salient regions [16,18] to the prediction of the global image aesthetic. For the evaluation we use the AVA dataset [26], because it is actually the largest dataset available and the only one providing aesthetic ratings instead of binary classification of aesthetic quality (e.g. "high" or "low"). Experimental results show the robustness of the solution proposed, which outperforms the best solution in the state of the art by almost 17 % in terms of Mean Residual Sum of Squares Error (MRSSE).

The rest of the paper is organized as follows: Sect. 2 describes the data and the evaluation metric; Sect. 3 describes the proposed approach; Sect. 4 analyzes the experimental results; finally, Sect. 5 presents our final considerations.

2   Database and Evaluation Criterions

In this work we use the Aesthetic Visual Analysis (AVA) dataset [26], that is a large-scale collection of images and meta-data obtained from the on-line community of photography amateurs and covering a wide variety of subjects on almost 1,000 challenges derived from www.dbchallenge.com. Figure 1 shows some samples from the AVA dataset. It contains over 255,000 images, both in RGB and grayscale with three types of annotations: aesthetic ratings ranging from 1 to 10; semantic annotations consisting in 66 textual tags describing the semantics of the images; photographic style annotations corresponding to 14 photographic techniques.

For the experiments we follow the same experimental procedure as in [19]. We discard the images whose longest dimension is three times more than the smallest

Fig. 1. Sample images from the Aesthetic Visual Analysis (AVA) database sorted by their aesthetic score (decreasing from left to right).

dimension, resulting in a total of 255,099 images. Among them, 250,129 images are selected for train and 4,970 for test. The average score of user ratings is taken as the images aesthetic quality ground truth. For performance evaluation, we use the Mean Residual Sum of Squares Error (MRSSE), that is defined as follows:

$$MRSSE = \frac{1}{n} \sum_{i=1}^{n} (y_i - \hat{y}_i)^2$$

where $\hat{y}_i$ is the predicted aesthetic score and y_i is the ground truth of image i.

3   Proposed Approach for Image Aesthetic Assessment

Deep CNNs have demonstrated to be very effective in many image domains [22]. CNNs consist in a stack of layers involving linear, non-linear and spatial operators and are usually trained using back-propagation [23]. Most of the methods, due to the lack of very large datasets, take a CNN that is pre-trained for a different task (e.g. ImageNet competition [15]) and then use it as an initialization for a transfer learning process, known as fine-tuning [1,31]. In this work, we modify and fine-tune the Caffe network architecture [17] (inspired by the AlexNet architecture [21]) to model image aesthetic. We replace the last fully connected layer with a single-neuron layer in order to produce, given an input image, a predicted aesthetic score as a real number ranging between 1 and 10. We evaluate the effect of several design choices for pre-processing including the use of cropping and visual attention models for salient regions masking [6,8,27].

3.1   DeepIA: A CNN for Image Aesthetic Assessment

In this paper, we treat the aesthetic quality assessment as a regression problem, because it is closer to the human photo rating process [14]. Thus, the output of our CNN is a single-real value indicating the predicted aesthetic score.

Image aesthetic may depend on both the scenes and objects depicted. To this end we have chosen to fine-tune a pre-trained CNN as generic as possible to predict the aesthetic of an unseen image. The network used is the Hybrid-CNN [32], originally trained by merging the scene categories from Places dataset [32] and the object categories from ImageNet [15] for a total of 1,183 different classes. The proposed CNN is obtained by fine-tuning the Hybrid-CNN after replacing the last fully connected with a single-neuron layer and using the Euclidean loss layer instead of the Softmax loss layer:

$$\min \sum_{i=1}^{n} \|y_i - \hat{y}_i\|_2^2$$

where y_i is the ground truth of image i, $\hat{y}_i$ is the predicted aesthetic score and n is the number of images. We call our final CNN *DeepIA*.

We fine-tune our CNN using Stochastic Gradient Descent (SGD) by chopping and retraining the last fully connected and by slightly updating the weights for the other layers. We use a batch size of 256, momentum set to 0.9, and a weight decay parameter of 0.0005. Then, we initialize the learning rate to a value of 0.001, and drop it every 20,000 iterations. We fine-tune for a total of 50,000 iterations. In all the experiments we use the Caffe open-source framework [17] for both the CNN training and prediction processes. During the training process, the original images are resized to 256×256 pixels without preserving the aspect ratio and then a random region of 227×227 pixels is extracted from the resized image. This approach increases the training set size in order to avoid overfitting. The mean-pixel values calculated across the training set images is the subtracted from the resized images.

At test time, we resize the original images to fixed dimensions and then we evaluate different design choices:

- we resize the images to 256×256 pixels and we use the 227×227 pixels central crop for image aesthetic prediction.
- we resize the images to 256×256 pixels and we average the prediction of multiple 227×227 pixels sub- regions (i.e. crops) of the input the image. We consider 10 crops corresponding to the four corners, the center region and their horizontal reflections.
- we resize the input image to 314×314 pixels and extract 10 crops with size 227×227 pixels.
- we weight the image pixels on the basis of their saliency using both a top-down and a bottom-up saliency models. To this end, the saliency map values have been scaled to fit the range $[0, 1]$. We use two different algorithms for estimating salient regions: the Itti et al. [16], which is built upon a biologically plausible computational model of focal bottom-up attention, and the Judd et al. [18], integrating a set of low, mid and high-level image features. In Fig. 2, we show the saliency maps predicted by the two considered algorithms.

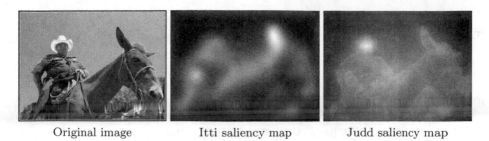

Original image   Itti saliency map   Judd saliency map

Fig. 2. Saliency maps predicted using the Itti et al. [16] and the Judd et al. [18] algorithms on an image of the Aesthetic Visual Analysis (AVA) dataset [26].

Table 1. Performances of aesthetic quality assessment on the AVA dataset.

Method	Image size	#crops	MRSSE
DeepIA+Itti saliency map	256	1	0.5822
DeepIA+Itti saliency map	256	10	0.5766
DeepIA+Judd saliency map	256	1	0.4900
DeepIA+Judd saliency map	256	10	0.4829
DeepIA	314	10	0.4034
DeepIA	256	1	0.3866
DeepIA	256	10	**0.3727**

4   Experimental Results

The MRSSE obtained on the AVA dataset by our DeepIA for the different design choices outlined in Sect. 3, is reported in Table 1. The best results are obtained using the average prediction over 10 crops of size 227×227 extracted from the 256×256 image. The second best result is obtained by considering only the central 227×227 crop extracted from the image of size 256×256. The use of relatively smaller crops (i.e. 227×227 from 314×314 images) is not able to improve the results, giving a hint that image aesthetic is a global rather than a local attribute. The use of both top-down and bottom-up saliency models to filter out not-salient image content does not help to improve the accuracy of the prediction. In Table 2 we compare our best solution with different methods in the state of the art. As a reference, we also report the performance that could be achieved by always predicting an average score of 5. From the results it is possible to see that our DeepIA outperforms all the methods considered, with a reduction of MRSSE by almost 17 % with respect to the best method in the state of the art.

We report in Fig. 3 the five test images with the smallest MRSSE between ground truth and predicted aestetic scores. Figure 4 reports the ten test images

Table 2. Performance comparison of aesthetic quality assessment on the AVA dataset.

Method	MRSSE
Always predicting 5 as aesthetic score	0.5700
BOV-SIFT+rbfSVR ([25] adapted in [19])	0.5513
BOV-SIFT+linSVR ([25] adapted in [19])	0.5401
GIST+rbfSVR ([25] adapted in [19])	0.5307
GIST+linSVR ([25] adapted in [19])	0.5222
Aest-CNN [19]	0.4501
DeepIA	**0.3727**

Fig. 3. Top 5 test images with the lowest error between ground truth (GT) and predicted (PR) aesthetic score.

Fig. 4. Top 10 test images with the highest error between ground truth (GT) and predicted (PR) aesthetic score. Test images for which the predicted aesthetic score is overestimated (first row), and images whose predictions are underestimated (second row).

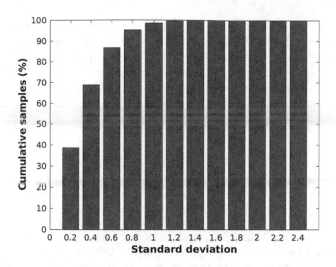

Fig. 5. Number of samples (%) with respect to the ratio between absolute estimation error and standard deviations (σ) of human scores.

with the largest errors: in the first row we report the top five overestimation errors, while in the second row the top five underestimation errors. The highest errors reported in Fig. 4 show that sometimes bad predictions reflect a lack of information consisting in the already defined *aesthetic gap* [14], defined as follows: *The aesthetics gap is the lack of coincidence between the information that one can extract from low-level visual data (i.e., pixels in digital images) and the interpretation of emotions that the visual data may arouse in a particular user in a given situation.*

Finally, since human aesthetic scores are noisy, we investigate how close is the score predicted by our DeepIA with the whole distribution of scores given by the humans to each image. To this end, for each image, we measure the ratio between our estimation error and the standard deviation of human scores. The cumulative histogram is reported in Fig. 5. From the plot it is possible to see that almost 99 % of the predictions have an error smaller or equal to a standard deviation value of 1.

5   Conclusions

We have investigated the use of a deep Convolutional Neural Network (CNN) to predict image aesthetics. Our approach consists in fine-tuning a canonical CNN architecture, originally trained to classify both objects and scenes, by casting the image aesthetic prediction as a regression problem. Experimental results on the canonical Aesthetic Visual Analysis (AVA) dataset show the robustness of the solution proposed, which outperforms the best solution in the state of the art by almost 17 % in terms of Mean Residual Sum of Squares Error (MRSSE). We also investigated whether image aesthetic is a global or local attribute, and the role played by bottom-up and top-down salient regions to the prediction of the global image aesthetic. Experimental results indicate that image aesthetic is a global attribute, and that the use of a saliency map to filter out not salient regions in the prediction stage does not help to achieve more accurate aesthetic score predictions. As a future work we plan to further investigate how can we exploit additional textual information, such as user comments or tagging, to predict image aesthetics [9–11].

References

1. Bengio, Y.: Deep learning of representations for unsupervised and transfer learning. Unsupervised Transf. Learn. Challenges Mach. Learn. **7**, 19 (2012)
2. Bhattacharya, S., Sukthankar, R., Shah, M.: A framework for photo-quality assessment and enhancement based on visual aesthetics. In: Proceedings of the 18th ACM International Conference on Multimedia, pp. 271–280. ACM (2010)
3. Bianco, S.: Reflectance spectra recovery from tristimulus values by adaptive estimation with metameric shape correction. JOSA A **27**(8), 1868–1877 (2010)
4. Bianco, S., Bruna, A.R., Naccari, F., Schettini, R.: Color correction pipeline optimization for digital cameras. J. Electron. Imaging **22**(2), 023014–023014 (2013)
5. Bianco, S., Ciocca, G., Marini, F., Schettini, R.: Image quality assessment by preprocessing and full reference model combination. In: IS&T/SPIE Electronic Imaging, p. 72420O. International Society for Optics and Photonics (2009)
6. Bianco, S., Ciocca, G., Napoletano, P., Schettini, R.: An interactive tool for manual, semi-automatic and automatic video annotation. Comput. Vis. Image Underst. **131**, 88–99 (2015)
7. Bianco, S., Schettini, R.: Adaptive color constancy using faces. IEEE Trans. Pattern Anal. Mach. Intell. **36**(8), 1505–1518 (2014)
8. Cagli, R.C., Coraggio, P., Napoletano, P., Boccignone, G.: What the draughtsman's hand tells the draughtsman's eye: a sensorimotor account of drawing. Int. J. Pattern Recogn. Artif. Intell. **22**(05), 1015–1029 (2008)
9. Colace, F., De Santo, M., Greco, L., Napoletano, P.: A query expansion method based on a weighted word pairs approach. In: Proceedings of the 3rd Italian Information Retrieval (IIR) vol. 964, pp. 17–28 (2013)
10. Colace, F., De Santo, M., Greco, L., Napoletano, P.: Weighted word pairs for query expansion. Inf. Process. Manag. **51**(1), 179–193 (2015)
11. Cusano, C., Napoletano, P., Schettini, R.: Evaluating color texture descriptors under large variations of controlled lighting conditions. JOSA A **33**(1), 17–30 (2016)
12. Datta, R., Joshi, D., Li, J., Wang, J.Z.: Studying aesthetics in photographic images using a computational approach. In: Leonardis, A., Bischof, H., Pinz, A. (eds.) ECCV 2006. LNCS, vol. 3953, pp. 288–301. Springer, Heidelberg (2006). doi:10.1007/11744078_23
13. Datta, R., Li, J., Wang, J.Z.: Learning the consensus on visual quality for next-generation image management. In: Proceedings of the 15th International Conference on Multimedia, pp. 533–536. ACM (2007)
14. Datta, R., Li, J., Wang, J.Z.: Algorithmic inferencing of aesthetics and emotion in natural images: an exposition. In: 15th IEEE International Conference on Image Processing, ICIP 2008, pp. 105–108. IEEE (2008)

15. Deng, J., Berg, A., Satheesh, S., Su, H., Khosla, A., Fei-Fei, L.: Imagenet large Scale Visual Recognition Competition (ILSVRC 2012) (2012)
16. Itti, L., Koch, C.: Computational modelling of visual attention. Nat. Rev. Neurosci. **2**(3), 194–203 (2001)
17. Jia, Y., Shelhamer, E., Donahue, J., Karayev, S., Long, J., Girshick, R., Guadarrama, S., Darrell, T.: Caffe: convolutional architecture for fast feature embedding. In: Proceedings of the ACM International Conference on Multimedia, pp. 675–678. ACM (2014)
18. Judd, T., Ehinger, K., Durand, F., Torralba, A.: Learning to predict where humans look. In: IEEE International Conference on Computer Vision (ICCV) (2009)
19. Kao, Y., Wang, C., Huang, K.: Visual aesthetic quality assessment with a regression model. In: 2015 IEEE International Conference on Image Processing (ICIP), pp. 1583–1587. IEEE (2015)
20. Ke, Y., Tang, X., Jing, F.: The design of high-level features for photo quality assessment. In: Computer Vision and Pattern Recognition, 2006 IEEE Computer Society Conference on. vol. 1, pp. 419–426. IEEE (2006)
21. Krizhevsky, A., Sutskever, I., Hinton, G.E.: Imagenet classification with deep convolutional neural networks. In: Proceedings of Advances in Neural Information Processing Systems, pp. 1097–1105 (2012)
22. LeCun, Y., Bengio, Y., Hinton, G.: Deep learning. Nature **521**(7553), 436–444 (2015)
23. LeCun, Y., Bottou, L., Orr, G.B., Müller, K.-R.: Efficient backprop. In: Orr, G.B., Müller, K.-R. (eds.) Neural Networks: Tricks of the Trade. LNCS, vol. 1524, pp. 9–50. Springer, Heidelberg (1998). doi:10.1007/3-540-49430-8_3
24. Lu, X., Lin, Z., Jin, H., Yang, J., Wang, J.Z.: Rapid: rating pictorial aesthetics using deep learning. In: Proceedings of the ACM International Conference on Multimedia, pp. 457–466. ACM (2014)
25. Marchesotti, L., Perronnin, F., Larlus, D., Csurka, G.: Assessing the aesthetic quality of photographs using generic image descriptors. In: 2011 IEEE International Conference on Computer Vision (ICCV), pp. 1784–1791. IEEE (2011)
26. Murray, N., Marchesotti, L., Perronnin, F.: Ava: a large-scale database for aesthetic visual analysis. In: 2012 IEEE Conference on Computer Vision and Pattern Recognition (CVPR), pp. 2408–2415. IEEE (2012)
27. Napoletano, P., Boccignone, G., Tisato, F.: Attentive monitoring of multiple video streams driven by a Bayesian foraging strategy. IEEE Trans. Image Process. **24**(11), 3266–3281 (2015)
28. Nishiyama, M., Okabe, T., Sato, I., Sato, Y.: Aesthetic quality classification of photographs based on color harmony. In: 2011 IEEE Conference on Computer Vision and Pattern Recognition (CVPR), pp. 33–40. IEEE (2011)
29. Simond, F., Arvanitopoulos Darginis, N., Süsstrunk, S.: Image aesthetics depends on context. In: International Conference on Image Processing, vol. 1 (2015)
30. Wu, O., Hu, W., Gao, J.: Learning to predict the perceived visual quality of photos. In: 2011 IEEE International Conference on Computer Vision (ICCV), pp. 225–232. IEEE (2011)
31. Yosinski, J., Clune, J., Bengio, Y., Lipson, H.: How transferable are features in deep neural networks? In: Proceedings of Advances in Neural Information Processing Systems, pp. 3320–3328 (2014)
32. Zhou, B., Lapedriza, A., Xiao, J., Torralba, A., Oliva, A.: Learning deep features for scene recognition using places database. In: Proceedings of Advances in Neural Information Processing Systems, pp. 487–495 (2014)

Automatic Image Splicing Detection Based on Noise Density Analysis in Raw Images

Thibault Julliand[1]([✉]), Vincent Nozick[2], and Hugues Talbot[1]

[1] Université Paris-Est, LIGM (UMR 8049), CNRS, ENPC, ESIEE Paris, UPEM, 93162 Noisy-le-Grand, France
{thibault.julliand,hugues.talbot}@esiee.fr
[2] Université Paris-Est, LIGM (UMR 8049), CNRS, ENPC, ESIEE Paris, UPEM, 77454 Marne-la-Vallée, France
vincent.nozick@u-pem.fr

Abstract. Image splicing is a common manipulation which consists in copying part of an image in a second image. In this paper, we exploit the variation in noise characteristics in spliced images, caused by the difference in camera and lighting conditions during the image acquisition. The proposed method automatically gives a probability of alteration for any area of the image, using a local analysis of noise density. We consider both Gaussian and Poisson noise components to modelize the noise in the image. The efficiency and robustness of our method is demonstrated on a large set of images generated with an automated splicing.

Keywords: Image forgery · Noise · Raw image

1 Introduction

The number of digital images has hugely increased over the last decades. Their sources have diversified with the arrival of smartphones and tablets, and they form the majority of the pictures we see nowadays. The number of falsified images has increased accordingly, both in number and sophistication, with tools more and more efficient to do so. Farid [4] explains the rise of digital forensics to combat this trend.

In this paper, we show a new method to detect a common falsification called splicing. Splicing is one of the more common forms of image alteration. It consists in inserting part of an image in a second, different image. Our method is based on exploiting the noise density of an image. We focus here on raw images, with the assumption that the noise is unaltered. Although raw images are harder to tamper with than more common image formats, it is still possible, especially with the DNG open file format [9].

1.1 Image Splicing Detection

Various ways to detect splicing already exist, however most of them cannot be used on raw images: Farid bases his on JPEG ghosting [5] or on an analysis of

© Springer International Publishing AG 2016
J. Blanc-Talon et al. (Eds.): ACIVS 2016, LNCS 10016, pp. 126–134, 2016.
DOI: 10.1007/978-3-319-48680-2_12

Color Filter Array perturbations with Popescu [18]. Lin et al. [11], He et al. [8], and Popescu et al. [17] exploit the quantization in JPEG images. Some other methods are either very high-level or have hard to meet prerequisites. Lukas et al. [12] present a method based on the camera fingerprint, but this method requires some unaltered images taken by the camera, or access to the camera itself. Machine learning is also a possibility, such as presented by Bayram et al. [2] or Fu et al. [7]: a classifier of image features learned from training sets of authentic and forged images can be used to detect spliced regions in an image.

1.2 Splicing Detection from Image Noise

Noise is a perturbation that can be found in all images captured by a digital sensor. Although this noise may be reduced by the camera internal pipeline or with post-processing, the noise in a single image will have the same parameters throughout the image. These parameters will vary according to the camera model and the light exposition during the image capture. Thus, observing a variation in noise parameters in a specific zone of an image will often be a strong indicator of falsification. Consequently, some methods use image noise to detect splicing regions. In most noise estimation methods used in digital forensics, noise is simplified as Gaussian. This approach ignores the Poisson component in raw images, which tends to be dominant in high-intensity zones.

Mahdian and Saic [14] use a block-based inconsistency detection relying on the homogeneity of the standard deviation of the Gaussian noise. This approach, however, relies on the assumption that the noise standard deviation is homogeneous over an image. This is not always true, especially in raw images where the noise also includes a Poisson component. Pan et al. [15,16] also propose a block-based approach. Their method uses an analysis of kurtosis values in an image. Although this method is very efficient at detecting noise inconsistencies, it less efficient on images including textures and low noise values, increasing the difficulty of splicing detection in natural images. Popescu and Farid [17] also use noise estimation to detect splicing with excellent results, but their method needs preliminary informations about the noise of the original image, which can not be done in the case of a blind analysis. Finally, Julliand et al. [10] offer an approach which takes into account the Poisson component, but their method lacks precision in the localisation of the altered region.

Some methods are a combination of various approach. For example, Mahdian and Saic [13] combine resampling detection and noise analysis to highlight suspicious areas.

2   Noise Density Contribution Tables

2.1 Principles and Definitions

Noise in digital images can come from a wide variety of sources. In a raw image, noise follows a Poisson-Gauss probability distribution, with the standard deviation varying with the intensity of each pixel. A noise density table is the representation of this probability distribution. For each pixel, we consider its denoised value v_d and its noised value v_n. To each pixel of the image corresponds a value pair (v_d, v_n), which are accumulated in the table. This way, the table can be seen as a 2D histogram, as depicted in Fig. 1. The exact function defining the Poisson-Gauss probability density table is shown in Eq. 1, where σ is the standard deviation of the Gaussian portion of the function and α a scaling parameter applied to the Poisson portion:

$$f(v_d, v_n) = \frac{\alpha}{\sigma\sqrt{2\pi}} \sum_{x=0}^{\infty} \frac{(\alpha v_d)^{\alpha x} e^{-\alpha v_d}}{(\alpha x)!} \exp\left(\frac{-(v_n - x)^2}{2\sigma^2}\right) \qquad (1)$$

In practice, the value of the table at any point (i, j) is the number of value pairs where $(v_d, v_n) = (i, j)$. For numerical purposes, we normalize the table on each row (denoised values) to offset potential intensity imbalances in the image. Indeed, the table of an image with a high proportion of high (or low) intensity pixels would have very high values in the corresponding areas. This would reduce the usability of the table. The normalization suppresses this problem, as shown in Fig. 1.

A cross-section of the table along a single denoised value follows a Poisson-Gauss probability distribution (see dark line in Fig. 1). However, in the case of a spliced image, the noise density will be the sum of two different noise probability functions: one for the original image, and one for the spliced element (Fig. 2). The objective of our method is to differentiate these two contributions, and to identify the parts of the image that participate in each contribution.

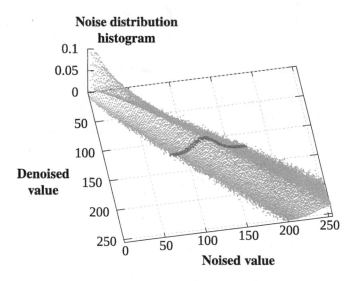

Fig. 1. Poisson-Gauss density map. The dark line is a cross-section along a single denoised value.

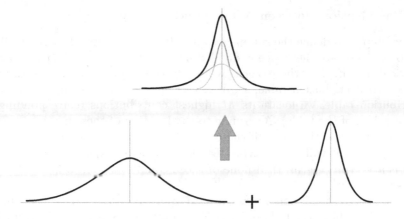

Fig. 2. Density map is an addition of two curves.

A naive approach would be to try to fit a model, such as the one in Eq. 1, based on the overall noise characteristics over the noise density table, to try and see which parts can be considered as outliers. However, this proves to be ill adapted for two reasons: first, unless the spliced area represents a significant portion of the original image, the impact on the noise density table will not be noticeable. Second, the normalization process will flatten any major and noticeable difference.

2.2 Noise Density Contribution Table

A noise density contribution table (referred to as "contribution table" from here on) represents the contribution percentage of any subimage of an image to the noise density table of the full image − more specifically, its contribution to each of the (v_d, v_n) value pair presented before. Basically, a contribution table C_{sub} is the noise density table D_{sub} of a subimage divided by the noise density table D_{im} of the whole image. A contribution can never be more than 1, 1 meaning that all the pixels contributing to a pair are included in the subimage. More formally, we get:

$$C_{sub}(v_d, v_n) = \frac{D_{sub}(v_d, v_n)}{D_{im}(v_d, v_n)}, \quad \forall(v_d, v_n)$$

As a consequence of the overall noise being the sum of two different noises, two shapes of contribution tables in a spliced image will appear. This is due to the impact of each type of noise on the global one: as we can see on Fig. 2, each curve will have a zone with higher participation. The first will have higher contributions on the identity axis, and the second higher contributions outside of the identity axis, respectively referred to as ∧ type and ∨ type.

2.3   Classification Between ∧ Type and ∨ Type

The next step is to define the subimages and identify the type of their contribution tables. To do so, the image is divided into a high number of square blocks of identical size. Each of these blocks will be considered as a subimage, and will have its own contribution table, see Fig. 3(a) and (b). To identify the type of a contribution table, we locate its M highest contributions (corresponding to the M maxima of the table). According to the location of these maxima, a type will be attributed to the block: if there is a clear majority of them on, or near, the identity axis, it will be a ∧ type. If there is a clear majority outside of this axis, it is a ∨ type (Fig. 3(c)). If none of those conditions are fulfilled, the type remains undefined.

   To make the method more robust, a good approach is to increase the number of pixels in the subimages. Indeed, contribution tables are easier to identify when they are built from more pixels. However, increasing the size of our blocks would greatly reduce the spatial precision of our detection. To increase the robustness while keeping the same precision, we create overlapping square cells, each containing a moderate number of blocks. The contribution table of a cell is the sum of the contribution tables of the blocks it contains. This results in contribution tables which are easier to identify, thanks to the higher amounts of pixels used in each cell. The type of each block then corresponds to the type in majority present in the cells containing it. If there is no clear majority, the block type is undefined and it will be changed in the seed expansion phase (see Fig. 4, middle column).

3   Seed Expansion

Once every block has been assigned a primary type (be it ∧, ∨, or undefined), we begin the expansion to find which of the two main categories each undefined block is more likely to belong to. This expansion is based on the similarity between blocks and the assumption that two similar blocks will probably belong to the same type ∧ or ∨. The similarity s between two contribution tables $C_1(v_d, v_n)$ and $C_2(v_d, v_n)$ is simply a sum of term by term absolute difference, but only in the rows where both tables have non-zero values:

$$s = \sum_{i \in \mathcal{D}} \sum_{j=0}^{v_n^{max}} |C_1(i,j) - C_2(i,j)|$$

where

$$\mathcal{D} = \left\{ i \mid \sum_{j=0}^{v_n^{max}} C_1(i,j) \neq 0 \text{ and } \sum_{j=0}^{v_n^{max}} C_2(i,j) \neq 0 \right\}$$

For a higher accuracy, we assign to each undefined block a probability p to belong to the ∧ shape group, and thus a probability $1 - p$ to belong to the ∨ shape group. These probabilities are computed with an iterative scheme with an initial

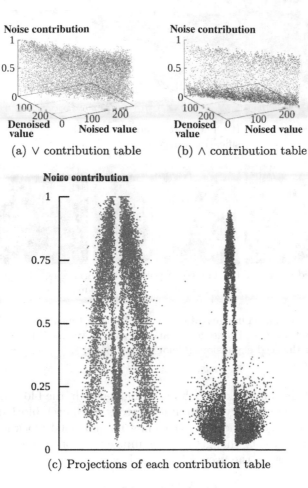

(c) Projections of each contribution table

Fig. 3. The two types of contribution tables. (a) and (b) show their overall appearance, (c) shows their projection on a plane orthogonal to the identity axis.

value set to 0.5. Then, each undefined block probability is iteratively set as the weighted average probability of the N blocks whose contribution table is the most similar to that of the current block, with higher similarities giving a higher weight. At an iteration k, the probability p_b^k of an undefined block b is:

$$p_b^k = \frac{\displaystyle\sum_{n=1}^{N} \frac{p_n^{k-1}}{n}}{\displaystyle\sum_{n=1}^{N} \frac{1}{n}}$$

This process is iterated on all undefined blocks until convergence, or until a set amount of iterations have been reached. Convergence can be reached in two

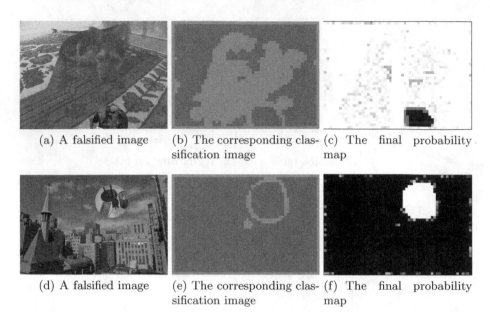

(a) A falsified image

(b) The corresponding classification image

(c) The final probability map

(d) A falsified image

(e) The corresponding classification image

(f) The final probability map

Fig. 4. Left column: spliced images. Middle column: block types after the initial classification. Blue zones are ∧, red zones are ∨, and grey zones are undefined. Right column: Final result after the seed expansion. (Color figure online)

different ways: first, if a block probability is high enough, the block is considered as being fully in said category. Computation stops when each block of the image is fully in one category or the other (meaning no undefined block left). Second, when the total probability changes δ in the image from one iteration to another is under a value ϵ set by the user. δ is defined as:

$$\delta = \sum_{b \in \mathcal{B}} |p_b^k - p_b^{k-1}|$$

where $\mathcal{B}$ is the ensemble containing all blocks of the image. The result can be seen in Fig. 4, right column.

4   Multichannel

In order to improve our results, we apply the whole process - denoising, noise density table, contribution tables, classification, and expansion - to each channel of the input image (R, G_1, B, G_2). Although the grey world assumption [6] can be applied on a multi-channel image, each channel can contain drastically different information − a clear sky, for example, will appear with a much higher intensity on the blue channel. As each channel can give a more precise information on various parts of the image, the multi-channel approach grants a higher precision and more robustness in the final result. To do so, the probability map of each channel are averaged, with each map having an equal weight. As we work with raw images, we have 4 channels to work with − including two green channels. No bias towards one particular channel was observed in our experiments.

5 Implementation and Results

The raw images are loaded using LibRaw [1]. The denoising process is performed by BM3D using the Matlab code provided by [3]. Not taking the denoising time into account, which we have little control over, the multi-channel version of the code runs in around a minute for a 2000 × 2000 pixels image on consumer-grade hardware.

The choice of the code handling the denoising part is a crucial part of the method: indeed, our method is extremely dependent on the quality of the denoising. Although the procedure we used [3] is state-of-the-art for Poisson-Gauss denoising, it tends to produce relatively poor results on dark textured areas. Even though our method has no theoretical weakness on such areas, due to this, our output quality drops similarly on images containing this kind of elements.

For our experiments, we used a base of 290 spliced images and 27 authentic images. Those images come from a wide variety of cameras: Canon (2 models), Leica (4 models), Nikon (1 model), Panasonic (9 models), Pentax (3 models), and Sony (3 models). The results are exposed in Table 1. However, those results do not take into account images containing dark textured areas (respectively 73 spliced and 7 authentic). If those images are considered, the splicing localization rate drops to 51.7 %, and the authentic detection rate to 58 %. The splicing detection rate remains at 100 %.

Our method's effectiveness is likely to increase in accordance to the efficacy of upcoming denoising methods.

Table 1. The detection rate on spliced and unspliced images.

Image type	falsified/authentic correctly identified	Splicing localization correct
Spliced	100 %	68.6 %
Authentic	86 %	na

6 Conclusion

We present a new method to automatically detect splicing in raw images. This method is based on the discrimination of contributions in the noise density of the image, when the image contains a spliced element. By looking at the locations where the contribution to the noise is different, we show that it is possible to pinpoint a spliced area in an image. The robustness of the approach is increased by replicating it over all the channels of the image. Further research will aim to adapt this method for JPEG images.

References

1. LibRaw-0.17: Image decoder library (2015). www.libraw.org
2. Bayram, S., Avcibas, I., Sankur, B., Memon, N.D.: Image manipulation detection. Electron. Imaging **15**(4), 1–17 (2006)
3. Dabov, K., Foi, A., Katkovnik, V., Egiazarian, K.: Image denoising by sparse 3D transform-domain collaborative filtering. IEEE Trans. Image Process. **16**(8), 2080–2095 (2007)
4. Farid, H.: A survey of image forgery detection. IEEE Signal Process. Mag. **26**(2), 16–25 (2009)
5. Farid, H.: Exposing digital forgeries from JPEG ghosts. IEEE Trans. Inf. Forensics Secur. **4**(1), 154–160 (2009)
6. Finlayson, G., Shiele, B., Crowley, J.: Comprehensive colour normalization. In: Proceedings European Conference on Computer Vison, vol. I, pp. 475–490 (1998)
7. Fu, D., Shi, Y.Q., Su, W.: Image splicing detection using 2D phase congruency and statistical moments of characteristic function. In: Proceedings of SPIE Security, Steganography, and Watermarking of Multimedia Contents IX (2007)
8. He, J., Lin, Z., Wang, L., Tang, X.: Detecting doctored JPEG images via DCT coefficient analysis. In: Leonardis, A., Bischof, H., Pinz, A. (eds.) ECCV 2006. LNCS, vol. 3953, pp. 423–435. Springer, Heidelberg (2006). doi:10.1007/11744078_33
9. Adobe Systems Incorporated: Digital negative (DNG) specification, version 1.4.0.0 (2012)
10. Julliand, T., Nozick, V., Talbot, H.: Automated image splicing detection from noise estimation in raw images. In: Imaging for Crime Prevention and Detection, pp. 1–6 (2015)
11. Lin, Z., He, J., Tang, X., Tang, C.: Fast, automatic and fine-grained tampered JPEG images detection via DCT coefficient analysis. Pattern Recogn. **42**(11), 2492–2501 (2009)
12. Lukáš, J., Fridrich, J., Goljan, M.: Detecting digital image forgeries using sensor pattern noise. In: Proceedings SPIE, Electronic Imaging, Security, Steganography, and Watermarking of Multimedia Contents VIII, vol. 6072, pp. 0Y1-0Y11 (2006)
13. Mahdian, B., Saic, S.: Detection of resampling supplemented with noise inconsistencies analysis for image forensics. In: International Conference on Computational Sciences and its Applications, pp. 546–556, July 2008
14. Mahdian, B., Saic, S.: Using noise inconsistencies for blind image forensics. Image Vis. Comput. **27**, 1497–1503 (2009)
15. Pan, X., Zhang, X., Lyu, S.: Exposing image forgery with blind noise estimation. In: The 13th ACM Workshop on Multimedia and Security, Buffalo, NY (2011)
16. Pan, X., Zhang, X., Lyu, S.: Exposing image splicing with inconsistent local noise variances. In: International Conference on Computation Photography (ICCP), pp. 1–10, April 2012
17. Popescu, A.C., Farid, H.: Statistical tools for digital forensics. In: 6th International Workshop on Information Hiding (2004)
18. Popescu, C., Farid, H.: Exposing digital forgeries in color filter array interpolated images. IEEE Trans. Signal Process. **53**(10), 1948–3959 (2005)

Breast Shape Parametrization
Through Planar Projections

Giovanni Gallo[1], Dario Allegra[1](✉), Yaser Gholizade Atani[2],
Filippo L.M. Milotta[1], Filippo Stanco[1], and Giuseppe Catanuto[3]

[1] Department of Mathematics and Computer Science,
University of Catania, Catania, Italy
{gallo,allegra,milotta,fstanco}@dmi.unict.it
[2] Department of Applied Mathematics,
Azarbaijan Shahid Madani University, Tabriz, Iran
y.gholizade@azaruniv.ac.ir
[3] Multidisciplinary Breast Unit, Azienda Ospedaliera Cannizzaro, Catania, Italy
giuseppecatanuto@gmail.com

Abstract. In the last years, 3D scanning has replaced the low tech
approach to acquire direct anthropometric measurements. These new
methodologies provide a detailed digital model of the body and allow
analysis of more complex information like volume, shape, curvature, and
so on. The possibility to acquire the shape of soft tissues, such as the
female human breast, has attracted the interest breast surgery specialists. The main aim of this work is to propose an innovative strategy to
automatically analyze 3D breast shape in order to describe them within
a quantitative well defined framework. In particular we propose a scanning procedure for a proper acquisition of breast surfaces by using the
handheld scanner Structure Sensor, as well as a framework to process 3D
digital data to extract the shape information. The proposed method consists in two main parts: firstly, the acquired digital 3D surfaces are projected in a 2D space and a set of 17 geometrical landmarks are extracted;
then by exploiting Thin Plate Splines and Principal Components Analysis the original data are summarised and the breast shape is described
by a small set of numerical parameters.

Keywords: Breast · Medical · 3D model · Principal component analysis · Thin plate splines

1 Introduction

Attempts to define a set of numerical parameters that could represent the human
shape have a long tradition: they are documented since the Renaissance, thanks
to the great work of famous artists like Leonardo da Vinci or Albrecht Durer.
More recently the need to define ergonometric standards has given a new impulse
to this kind of studies. A turning point has been attained when a reasonable 3D
body scanning methodology has been introduced. Nowadays 3D scanning has

© Springer International Publishing AG 2016
J. Blanc-Talon et al. (Eds.): ACIVS 2016, LNCS 10016, pp. 135–146, 2016.
DOI: 10.1007/978-3-319-48680-2_13

replaced the obsolete low tech approach to take a set of measurement of distances between skeletal human landmarks. This new methodology may provide a detailed digital copy of the body of a subject and allows the measurement of volume, shape, curvature, etc. The new possibility to acquire the shape of soft tissues, like the female human breast, has attracted the interest of the medical specialist in breast reconstructive surgery.

The joint European and America project "CAESAR" has created a massive database of a greatly variety of human body shapes [1]. Facing this kind of complex data, Principal Component Analysis (PCA) represents a valuable approach to reduce the high dimensionality of the datasets and capture just some significant features. PCA has already been used for parametrization of the human body shapes [2] and also for the breast parametrization purpose [3]. There are few studies about human breast parametrization at present, distinguishable from the point of view of industrial and clothing applications [4–6], and from the medical studies [7–10]. Old laser scanning devices (e.g., Microsoft Kinect $v1.0$, Asus Xtion Pro, . . .) although sufficiently accurate were not practical for medical purposes: typically they required a long scanning time and patient's breathing or involuntary micro-movements lead to excessive noise in the final acquired data. The newest handheld laser scanners (e.g., Structure Sensor, Scanify Fuel 3D, Google Project Tango, Artec Spider, . . .) overcome these problems and give the opportunity to acquire data of a sufficiently high quality to further process the final mesh. The high portability of handheld scanners allows the operator to use them without annoying (and potentially dangerous) wires in the acquisition room. Despite the higher acquisition quality, some parts of the breast frequently remain occluded to the optical laser: missing parts can be reconstructed with proper filling techniques [11].

This paper presents an innovative way to analyze and classify the breast shape using the data acquired with one of such handheld scanner devices: Structure [12]. This handy device allowed us to collect a quite large database of shapes with a relatively economical effort. In particular during a one month acquisition campaign we have collected data of about 41 female subjects of ages between 25 and 65 years. The paper focuses on some promising analytical techniques but it is part of a larger project whose aim is to introduce the reference to digitalized breast shapes into common clinical practice. Research in this direction is ongoing and here we restrict our presentation only on the data standardization and summarization procedures. We process the 3D mesh data of a breast and convert them into a 2D representation applying a quite standardized planar projection. We propose a novel method for breast parametrization, based on thin-plate spline (TPS) deformation. We show how selecting a small set of landmarks on breast planar projections and exploiting TPS principal warps [13] and principal component analysis (PCA) is possible to find two main principal components to parameterize most of the breast shape variability.

The rest of the paper is organized as follows: in Sect. 2 we recall the Thin-Plate Spline (TPS) method applied in biological and biomedical research field. A comprehensive description of the dataset construction and the proposed method is given in Sect. 3. Details on the hardware employed for 3D model acquisition, the pose that the patient assumes during scan phase and the data cleaning procedure are reviewed. Secondarily, the strategy to process breast 3D models and to describe their shape is explained. Experimental results are reported in Sect. 4 while the final considerations are given in the conclusion of the paper.

2   Thin-Plate Spline in Biomedical Investigations

In many biological and biomedical investigations, the most effective way to analyze the forms of whole biological organs or organisms is by recording geometric locations of landmark points. Methods of geometric morphometry, based on the analysis of landmark configurations, allow further in-depth investigation of morphological processes [14, 15]. The most widely applied method for landmark-based nonrigid registration is based on Thin-Plate Spline (TPS). TPS provides a mathematical framework to decompose into affine and non-affine components the matching between shapes while minimizing a bending energy based on the second derivative of the mapping. This approach has been introduced into medical image registration by Bookstein [16] and has been widely applied since then in biological, medical and other applications. The method of TPS, allows a quantitative shape analysis by means of taking into account a specific series of morphological variables, the so-called "principal warps". At the first step, the mean configuration of landmarks is calculated as a reference shape. Then, the mean shape is morphed into the other landmark sets by using TPS. This transformation may be factorized in two parts namely the affine part that includes rotation, scaling and translation and a nonlinear part which can be obtained as a linear combination of a radial basis function $U(r)$. Function $U(r)$ depends on the dimension of the space where landmarks have been obtained. In 2D $U(r) = -r^2 lg(r)$, while in 3D $U(r) = |r|$. In Reference [13] Bookstein suggested to extract from the linear weights that define the deformation in terms of $U(r)$'s functions, a special basis, that he has named "Principal Warps Basis". This basis provides a useful principled way to understand the nonlinear warping on a given landmark configuration. Researchers have used the space of Principal Warps as a direct parameter space. Usually, dimension reduction of the Principal Warps space is achieved by using Principal Component Analysis (PCA), hence we have taken this course in our approach.

3   Materials and Methods

3.1   Dataset Acquisition

Our study mainly focuses on the digital shape analysis through a low-cost device, in order to test if it could be of clinical value to assist breast specialists for surgery or diagnostic purposes. The 3D meshes of the female volunteers have been obtained with the hand-held scanner Structure Sensor (Fig. 1(a)). It is a small sensor which uses structured infrared light to produce a depth map of

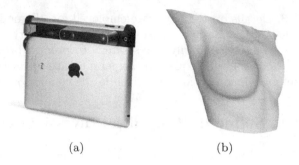

(a)   (b)

Fig. 1. (a) Structure Sensor used to acquire breasts 3D models. (b) A sample not post-processed 3D model acquired with Structure Sensor.

the scanned area. The scanner is able to acquire objects up to 12 m, although it is recommended a distance in the range 0.4 and 3.5 m. Its max accuracy is 0.5 mm, but it gets worse when the volume of scanned area is increased. Since this scanner exploits infrared ray, it is recommended for indoor usages only. The sensor is not able to acquire RGB color information, however it is possible to clip it onto an iPad and exploits the tablet camera to this purpose.

To acquire a breast model, we propose a clinical procedure where the women volunteers hold the hands behind and above head, so that the operator can turn around the breast with the Structure Sensor (clipped onto the iPad). Although texture information could be acquired, this has not been used for the present investigation. An example of the model acquired with Structure Sensor is shown in Fig. 1(b); we select this specific device after a technical comparison with other 3D scanner currently on the market [17]. After the acquisition, the model are automatically cleaned through 3D processing software (e.g., Meshlab [18]), by removing noise and isolated vertices or faces.

To complete the cleaning, meshes are manually cropped to preserve only the region of interest (ROI) that contains the breast. ROI extraction is a critical part of the suggested procedure. To make it more robust it is one of the open problems of our project. Here we adopt a simple approach that has been proved to be replicable and reasonable precise. We select the ROI by four anatomical reperees suggested by the breast specialist. Figure 2 illustrates the four landmarks used for cropping. We have acquired both left and right breasts but all the breasts have been, when needed, vertically mirrored in order to make the dataset right-left side invariant, as shown in Fig. 2. The dataset, built by following the aforementioned steps, contains 41 breast 3D models. Each of the models is stored in the standard OBJ format, which describes the information on vertices, faces and face normals. Furthermore we have built another dataset of 40 for a proper test of our method. Specifically, we used the mathematical model obtained by the first 41 models to represent the new ones.

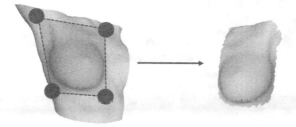

Fig. 2. The four anatomical reperees (in red) delimit the highlighted region of interest. After the cropping is performed, the right breasts are vertically mirrored. (Color figure online)

3.2   Standard Projection of the Breast Shape

In this subsection we present our method to process the 3D breast surfaces in order to standardize the description of its shape. The proposed algorithm is aimed to extract two main characterizing parameters for every 3D mesh in the dataset. As first step, all the meshes into the dataset have to be oriented along the same direction and translate to the center of a standard cartesian coordinate system. Then, the 3D mesh is projected to a 2D space along the Z axis of the coordinate system. This leads to a grayscale depth-map representation. Each breast depth-map is quantized to extract seventeen landmarks which are hence used as reference points to apply the TPS algorithm. Finally, the transformation matrix obtained by TPS is subject to principal component analysis (PCA) to identify the most significant warps. The three main steps are detailed as follows.

Breast Alignment and Projection. Automatic breast model alignment has been performed by exploiting face normals orientations. For each 3D mesh, the average normal to its surface is computed and it is aligned to a predefined unit vector. To perform the 3D rotation, we have employed Rodrigues's rotation formula [19]. Given two vectors v_1 and v_2, the formula allows to compute the rotation matrix to align v_1 to v_2. The predefined reference unit vector is $(0, 0, 1)$ in order to orientate the average normal along the Z axis. Moreover, each mesh is translated into the origin of the coordinate system, using their average vertex as pivot. Successively, vertices coordinates are linearly normalized in $[0, 1]$ exploiting the global minimum (minimum coordinates among all the models) and the global maximum for both the components X and Y. In this way the scale variability along X and Y axes for our models is preserved. The Z component is also normalized in $[0, 1]$: in this case local minimum of the Z component for each model is translated to 0 and the global maximum is mapped to 1. This guarantees that the at least a vertex for each mesh has coordinate value $Z = 0$. The alignment process is graphically summarized in Fig. 3.

After the alignment and the normalization have been performed, the model is quantized and the mesh is projected on the X-Y plane (frontal view). In our

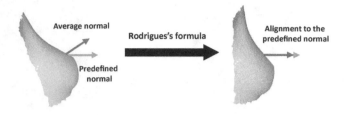

Fig. 3. Alignment process using Rodrigues's formula.

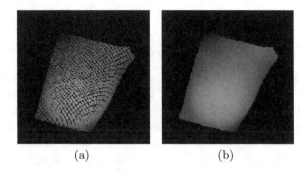

| (a) | (b) |

Fig. 4. (a) The projected 3D mesh. The empty regions in (x, y) point indicates that no vertices have been found there. (b) The depth-map (a) after the closure morphological operator has been applied.

work, we quantized X and Y into 150 levels, in order to obtain depth-maps with a 150×150 resolution. For each point in X-Y the depth value is the Z component. Since folds may happen or more than 2 measured points may fall above the same quantized X-Y point. The maximum Z value is chosen. In general, gap may arise (see Fig. 4(a)). Hence, as a last step, grayscale morphological closure is performed to fill the empty regions inside the breast area (Fig. 4(b)). We used a circle with a diameter equals to 5 pixels as structural element for grayscale morphological closure, and then we applied a Gaussian smoothing with a kernel of size 3×3 pixels and standard deviation equals to 1 to regularize the data.

Landmarks Extraction. TPS is able to compute a non-linear transformation to fit a set of landmarks to a reference set. Our idea is to use TPS to estimate the deformation to applay yo a "standard" breast to morph it into another one. To successfully apply TPS we need to extract a fixed number of landmarks for each of the 3D models, and to fix a set of landmarks for a reference breast shape.

Landmarks extraction is performed by linearly normalizing each of the depth-map in $[0, 1]$ and quantizing the Z value into 3 levels. The landmarks are extracted as follows: the first landmark is the maximum value of the original depth-map. Please notice that this point may or may not correspond to the

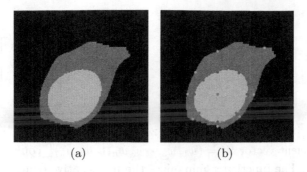

(a)   (b)

Fig. 5. (a) The 3-levels quantized depth-map of Fig. 4(b). (b) The landmarks extracted from depth-map of Fig. 4(b); red landmark is the maximum value of the original depth-map, blue and green landmarks are respectively the landmarks related to the first and the second quantized levels. (Color figure online)

nipple. We consider the 8 lines which pass for the first landmark along 8 fixed directions $(0°, 45°, ..., 315°)$. The second set of 8 landmarks is identified by the crossing between the same 8 lines and the highest quantization level boundary. Finally, the last 8 landmarks are chosen accordingly with the previous strategy, but considering the second quantization level. Eventually, 17 landmarks are extracted. An example of landmarks extraction is shown in Fig. 5.

The set of reference landmarks is learnt by computing the average of the 41 sets of 17 landmarks.

Thin Plate Spline (TPS). In this subsection we quickly recall the mathematical theory of TPS as introduced by Bookstein [13]. Let $P = \{p_i = (x_i, y_i), i = 1, 2, \ldots, n\}$ and $Q = \{q_i = (x'_i, y'_i), i = 1, 2, \ldots, n\}$ be two sets of points in the plane. We are looking for a transformation $F : R^2 \rightarrow R^2$ such that $F(p_i) = q_i$ for $i = 1, 2, \ldots, n$. This problem can be broken down into two interpolation problems $f_x(p_i) = x'_i$ and $f_y(p_i) = y'_i$ in x and y directions, respectively. The TPS model for one direction interpolation function is

$$f(x, y) = a_0 + a_x x + a_y y + \sum_{i=1}^{n} w_i U(|p_i - (x, y)|) \tag{1}$$

where $U(r) = -r^2 \log(r)$ with $r = \sqrt{x^2 + y^2}$ is the basis function, $A = (a, a_x, a_y)$ defines the affine part and $W = (w_1, w_2, \cdots, w_n)$ describes an additional non-linear deformation.

Now, let

$$L = \left[\begin{array}{c|c} K & P \\ \hline P^T & O \end{array} \right],$$

where

$$K = \begin{bmatrix} 0 & U(r_{12}) & \cdots & U(r_{1n}) \\ U(r_{12}) & 0 & \cdots & U(r_{2n}) \\ \vdots & \vdots & \vdots & \vdots \\ U(r_{1n}) & U(r_{2n}) & \cdots & 0 \end{bmatrix} \qquad P = \begin{bmatrix} 1 & x_1 & y_1 \\ 1 & x_2 & y_2 \\ \vdots & \vdots & \vdots \\ 1 & x_N & y_N \end{bmatrix}$$

$r_{ij} = \sqrt{|p_i - p_j|}$ and O is 3×3 matrix of zeros. Let $V = (x'_1, x'_2, \cdots, x'_n, 0, 0, 0)^T$, then the coefficient vector $\widetilde{W} = (w_1, w_2, \cdots, w_n, a, a_x, a_y)^T$ could be calculated by $\widetilde{W} = L^{-1}V$. The function f minimizes the nonnegative quantity

$$I_f = \int \int \left(\left(\frac{\partial^2 f}{\partial x^2} \right)^2 + \left(\frac{\partial^2 f}{\partial x \partial y} \right)^2 + \left(\frac{\partial^2 f}{\partial y^2} \right)^2 \right) dx dy$$

which is called "bending energy". Deformation through the Y direction could be achieved similarly.

In our algorithm TPS has been employed to compute non-linear transformation of a set of 17 landmarks into the set of reference ones. This allows to estimate the shape of a breast 3D model, by using the transformation matrix as descriptor. The description of the transformation takes into account issues about the scale and rotations. For the clinical application scale is a relevant parameter that is taken hence into account. The principal aim of this paper, however, is not concerned with size or volume, but wishes to address the shape variability of the female breast independently from the scale. For this reason the successive analysis uses only the coefficients of the non linear shape warping.

Principal Warps. Bookstein in [13] suggests that a more meaningful analysis can be done using not the w_i's from Eq. 1, but their combination along the "Principal Warps" that could be found as $P = WS$ where $W = (w_1, w_2, \cdots, w_n)$ and S is a $n \times n$ matrix that contains eigenvectors of matrix $L_n^{-1}KL_n^{-1}$ and L_n^{-1} is the upper left $n \times n$ subblock matrix of L^{-1} in Eq. 1. Moreover, since W is a $2 \times n$ matrix then P results into a $2 \times n$ matrix.

The principal warps formalism allows to read the original data in term of a result of a set of relevant principal deformations along directions that are prescribed by the intrinsic geometry of the reference landmarks set. Unfortunately, the dimension of the principal warps is equal to the dimension of the original data. So, it may not useful for clinicians when the original data has a high dimension. In our case, the dimension would be $2 \times 17 = 34$. Since it is not easy to analyse the high dimension data, we reduce their dimension applying the principal component analysis, as it is explained in the next subsection.

Principal Component Analysis (PCA). Dimension reduction to the main independent component is especially attractive when one wishes to identify the main characteristics of a complex shape like the human breast. For this reason

PCA is performed. PCA is a statistical procedure that analyzes a data set in which observations are described by several inter-correlated quantitative dependent variables. Its goal is to extract the important information from the data set, to represent it as a set of new orthogonal variables called "Principal Component" and compress the size of the data set, by reducing the number of dimensions, to highlight their similarities and differences, [20].

We apply PCA on Principal Warps of our dataset which counts $m = 41$ observations (breasts) and $n = 34$ dimensions. The two first principal components which have largest variances can be easily extracted by seeking the largest eigenvalues. The amount of variance retained using only two principal components is 93 %. In particular the first one accounts for 78 % and the second one for 15 %.

4 Results

After the PCA application on the Principal Warps we obtain two principal components, so that each breast can be identified by two coordinates. We plot each breast in a 2D space for a proper visual analysis (Fig. 6(a)). The breast specialist has carefully assessed the meaning of this parametrization, and come to the following asserts: the second principal component, plotted along X axis, seems not particularly meaningful, whilst the first one (along Y axis) captures the size and ptosis variability of the breast. Smaller breasts with low level of ptosis tend to have lower Y values, similarly larger breasts with high level of ptosis assume

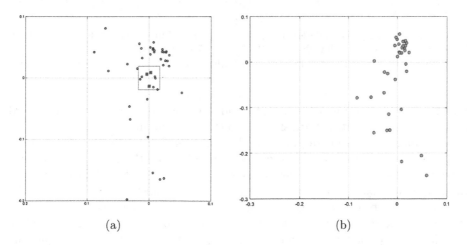

(a)   (b)

Fig. 6. (a) Breasts landmark 2D representation. Axis are the two first principal components of principal warps. Yellow circle markers are the 41 observations of our dataset, while the blue square markers are the representation of the inter operator test.(b) Breasts landmark 2D representation of the second dataset. Yellow circle markers are the 40 observations of the second dataset. (Color figure online)

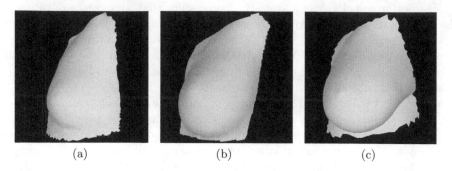

(a)   (b)   (c)

Fig. 7. Results related to the plot in Fig. 6(a). (a) Breast mesh related to the minimum Y value (very low ptosis level), $y = -0.198$. (b) An intermediate breast, $y = -0.047$. (c) Breast mesh related to the maximum Y value (very high ptosis level), $y = 0.081$.

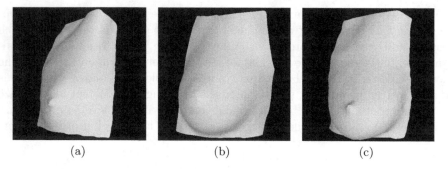

(a)   (b)   (c)

Fig. 8. Results related to the plot in Fig. 6(b). (a) Breast mesh related to the minimum Y value (very low ptosis level), $y = -0.249$. (b) An intermediate breast, $y = -0.067$. (c) Breast mesh related to the maximum Y value (very high ptosis level), $y = 0.061$.

the higher values. In Fig. 7 the breasts landmark visualization for minimum and maximum Y value (ptosis) are shown together with an intermediate one.

To validate the framework we conduct also an inter operator experiment: three different operators have acquired the breast of the same patient. Our expectation is that the three new meshes will be represented close together in the parameter space to demonstrate the small inter operator-invariance of the descriptors. We projected the 3D meshes in 2D by using the proposed breast projection method described in Sect. 3.2. In the normalization step along Z axis we exploit the global maximum computed on proposed dataset. Then, we extract the principal components of these acquisitions accordingly to the PCA model previously built. Results are shown in Fig. 6(a), where the blue square are the three meshes of the same volunteer: although the landmark representations are not exactly the same due to noise introduced by involuntary micro-movements and cropping, the final representation in the 2D space is quite similar, as expected.

To further confirm the proposed method we have acquired a second dataset with 40 new breasts models and we have processed them by using the model learnt with the first dataset. Results of this experiment are shown in Fig. 6(b). Moreover, in Fig. 8 three examples of the second dataset are reported. In according to the result achieved with the first dataset, a low value for Y is correlated to a low level of ptosis and viceversa. This has confirmed the goodness of the model produced by learning by the first 41 meshes.

5   Conclusions

In this paper we presented a novel method of analysis and parametrization of a breast 3D mesh acquired with the handheld 3D scanner Structure. We collected a quite large database of 41 female volunteers of ages between 25 and 65 years. We processed the 3D mesh data of a breast and convert them into a 2D representation applying a planar projection. Exploiting TPS principal warps [13] we developed a novel method for breast parametrization. Finally, applying the principal component analysis (PCA) we found two main principal components to parameterize breast shape variability. Breast specialist assessed that the first principal component computed in this way is a meaningful parametrization of shape and ptosis level. We have also conducted an inter operator test to further validate the soundness of our proposed approach. As future work we planned to investigate the TPS approach with a larger number of landmarks, to better capture the breast shape variability. We expect that an improved TPS approach could be useful to obtain an higher number of meaningful principal components and, hence, of parameters for the practical clinical usage of the proposed method.

Acknowledgment. The authors would like to thank the "Azienda Ospedaliera Cannizzaro", the "Associazione Santantonese per la lotta ai tumori (ASLT)" and the female volunteers for their contribution as models.

References

1. Robinette, K.M., Daanen, H., Paquet, E.: The Caesar project: a 3-D surface anthropometry survey. In: Second International Conference on 3-D Digital Imaging and Modeling, pp. 380–386 (1999)
2. Allen, B., Curless, B., Popovi, Z.: The space of human body shapes: reconstruction and parameterization from range scans. In: International Conference on Computer Graphics and Interactive Techniques, pp. 587–594 (2003)
3. Gallo, G., Guarnera, G.C., Catanuto, G.: Human breast shape analysis using PCA. In: BIOSIGNALS 2010 - Proceedings of the Third International Conference on Bioinspired Systems and Signal Processing (2010)
4. Lee, H.-Y., Hong, K., Kim, E.A.: Measurement protocol of womens nude breasts using a 3D scanning technique. Appl. Ergon. **35**, 353–360 (2004)
5. Olaru, S., Filipescu, E., Filipescu, E., Niculescu, C., Salistean, A.: 3D fit garment simulation based on 3D body scanner anthropometric data. In: 8th International DAAAM Baltic Conference on Industrial Engineering (2012)

6. Zhang, X., Liu, F., Ying, B., Bai, Y.: Parameterized design of female chest shape based on UG-platform. J. Fiber Bioeng. Inf. **4**(3), 221–233 (2011)
7. Catanuto, G., Gallo, G., Farinella, G.M., Impoco, G., Nava, M.B., Pennati, A., Spano, A.: Breast shape analysis on three-dimensional models. In: Third European Conference on Plastic and Reconstructive Surgery of the Breast (2005)
8. Catanuto, G., Spano, A., Pennati, A., Riggio, E., Farinella, G.M., Impoco, G., Spoto, S., Gallo, G., Nava, R.B.: Experimental methodology for digital breast shape analysis and objective surgical outcome evaluation. J. Plast. Reconstr. Aesthetic Surg. **61**(3), 314–318 (2008)
9. Farinella, G.M., Impoco, G., Gallo, G., Spoto, S., Catanuto, G., Nava, M.B.: Objective outcome evaluation of breast surgery. In: Larsen, R., Nielsen, M., Sporring, J. (eds.) MICCAI 2006. LNCS, vol. 4190, pp. 776–783. Springer, Heidelberg (2006). doi:10.1007/11866565_95
10. Chen, D.T., Kakadiaris, I.A., Miller, M.J., Loftin, R.B., Patrick, C.: Modeling for plastic and reconstructive breast surgery. In: Delp, S.L., DiGoia, A.M., Jaramaz, B. (eds.) MICCAI 2000. LNCS, vol. 1935, pp. 1040–1050. Springer, Heidelberg (2000). doi:10.1007/978-3-540-40899-4_108
11. Farinella, G.M., Impoco, G., Gallo, G., Spoto, S., Catanuto, G.: Unambiguous analysis of woman breast breast shape for plastic surgery outcome evaluation. In: 4th Conference Eurographics Italian Chapter (2006)
12. Structure Sensor Website. http://structure.io/. Accessed May 2016
13. Bookstein, F.L.: Principal warps: thin-plate splines and the decomposition of deformations. IEEE Trans. Pattern Anal. Mach. Intell. **11**(6), 567–585 (1989)
14. Bookstein, F.L.: Thin-plate splines and the atlas problem for biomedical images. In: Colchester, A.C.F., Hawkes, D.J. (eds.) IPMI 1991. LNCS, vol. 511, pp. 326–342. Springer, Heidelberg (1991). doi:10.1007/BFb0033763
15. Rosas, A., Bastir, M.: Thin-plate spline analysis of allometry and sexual dimorphism in the human craniofacial complex. Am. J. Phys. Anthropol. **117**(3), 236–245 (2002)
16. Bookstein, F.L.: Morphometric Tools for Landmark Data: Geometry and Biology. Cambridge University Press, Cambridge (1997)
17. Allegra, D., Gallo, G., Inzerillo, L., Lombardo, M., Milotta, F.L.M., Santagati, C., Stanco, F.: Low cost hand held 3D scanning for cultural heritage: experimenting low cost structure sensor scan. In: Handbook of Research on Emerging Technologies for Cultural Heritage (2015)
18. Cignoni, P., Callieri, M., Corsini, M., Dellepiane, M., Ganovelli, F., Ranzuglia, G.: Meshlab: an open-source mesh processing tool. In: Eurographics Italian Chapter Conference 2008, pp. 129–136 (2008)
19. Weisstein, E., Formula, Rodrigues' Rotation : http://mathworld.wolfram.com/rodriguesrotationformula.html, Last visited., May 2016
20. Pearson, K.: On lines and planes of closest fit to systems of points in space. Phil. Mag. **2**(6), 559–572 (1901)

Decreasing Time Consumption of Microscopy Image Segmentation Through Parallel Processing on the GPU

Joris Roels[1,2(✉)], Jonas De Vylder[1], Yvan Saeys[2], Bart Goossens[1], and Wilfried Philips[1]

[1] Department of Telecommunications and Information Processing, Ghent University, Sint-Pietersnieuwstraat 41, 9000 Ghent, Belgium
Joris.Roels@telin.ugent.be
[2] Inflammation Research Center, Flanders Institute for Biotechnology, Technologiepark 927, Zwijnaarde, 9052 Ghent, Belgium

Abstract. The computational performance of graphical processing units (GPUs) has improved significantly. Achieving speedup factors of more than 50x compared to single-threaded CPU execution are not uncommon due to parallel processing. This makes their use for high throughput microscopy image analysis very appealing. Unfortunately, GPU programming is not straightforward and requires a lot of programming skills and effort. Additionally, the attainable speedup factor is hard to predict, since it depends on the type of algorithm, input data and the way in which the algorithm is implemented. In this paper, we identify the characteristic algorithm and data-dependent properties that significantly relate to the achievable GPU speedup. We find that the overall GPU speedup depends on three major factors: (1) the coarse-grained parallelism of the algorithm, (2) the size of the data and (3) the computation/memory transfer ratio. This is illustrated on two types of well-known segmentation methods that are extensively used in microscopy image analysis: SLIC superpixels and high-level geometric active contours. In particular, we find that our used geometric active contour segmentation algorithm is very suitable for parallel processing, resulting in acceleration factors of 50x for 0.1 megapixel images and 100x for 10 megapixel images.

Keywords: Microscopy · Image segmentation · GPGPU computing

1 Introduction

High throughput and resolution microscopy imaging has gained a lot of interest due to advanced acquisition development. Consequently, image analysis algorithms should be able to keep up with the increasing data stream. In practice, this seems to be a stumbling block, especially in the case of microscopy image segmentation: higher complexity algorithms typically yield more accurate results,

© Springer International Publishing AG 2016
J. Blanc-Talon et al. (Eds.): ACIVS 2016, LNCS 10016, pp. 147–159, 2016.
DOI: 10.1007/978-3-319-48680-2_14

but because of the increasing amount of data, they become less usable. A second issue results from the increasing interest in more complex (ultra)structural content. This requires more advanced segmentation algorithms that incorporate prior knowledge such as shape and texture characteristics, typically resulting into higher computational complexity. In some cases, inaccurate automated segmentation algorithms or challenging data sets force researchers to perform segmentation completely manual. For example, in [8], a team of 224 people annotated 950 thin neuron structures in a 1 million μm^3 electron microscopy (EM) dataset at nanometer resolution, leading to more than 20000 annotator hours.

On the one hand, it is possible to use computationally cheap segmentation algorithms, typically requiring a substantial amount of manual post-processing. On the other hand, higher quality algorithms exist that typically require more computational resources. The latter is a common reason why some segmentation algorithms are not used in practice, even if they guarantee high-quality results. A popular approach to mitigate this, is the use of hardware accelerators such as graphical processing units (GPUs). These devices allow us to exploit massive parallelism resulting in significant speedup factors of more than 50x and even real-time performance in microscopy applications [5,17].

However, GPU acceleration is not straightforward: it requires extreme care and programming expertise and the achievable speedup depends on the granularity and memory requirements of the algorithm, input data dimensions, hardware characteristics, etc. In this paper, we discuss how microscopy image segmentation algorithms can be accelerated through GPU processing and how the algorithm properties and input data influence the achievable speedup. We point out that the algorithm needs to exhibit coarse-grained parallelism, the processed data size needs to be sufficiently large to benefit from GPU parallelization and the computation/transfer ratio needs to sufficiently large so that the computational cost outweigh the memory transfer cost. In Sect. 2 we will discuss the conceptual idea of GPU processing compared to traditional CPU processing. Two different segmentation algorithms are described in Sect. 3: basic superpixel segmentation and high-level active contours. Next, we identify the key properties of the algorithm and input data in order to attain a higher speedup in Sect. 4. The paper is concluded in Sect. 5.

2   CPU-GPU Parallel Processing

Traditionally, algorithm implementations are serially executed on the central processing unit (CPU). Using the GPU it is possible to exploit massive parallelism in algorithms resulting in significant speedups. However, there are several caveats linked to GPU processing:

- GPU programming in low-level programming approaches like CUDA/OpenCL requires specific knowledge on the GPU hardware architecture. One has to be aware of memory allocation, memory transfer between the CPU and GPU, memory type (local, global, shared, texture), thread synchronization, choosing GPU block sizes, etc. To alleviate these problems, recently several high-level libraries have been developed (e.g. Thrust, HSA-Bolt, Vector, etc.) to be used from, e.g. C/C++. Alternatively, the GPU can be accessed from high-level languages like Python/Matlab. However, the program then needs to be specifically designed to run on (or take advantage of) a GPU, by using existing library functions that have been accelerated on the GPU. In many of these approaches, the programmer is still required to revert to low-level GPU programming for functionality that does not exist within these libraries.

– The GPU contains a large number of processing cores (called streaming processors) that are designed and optimized for parallel numerical computations. To take advantage of the processing abilities and memory architecture of the GPU, a relatively large number of cores (typically more than 256) needs to perform the same operation in parallel.

– The type of algorithm influences the achievable speedup using the GPU as well. Algorithms with the property that a large number of numerical operations can be performed independently, with limited dynamic control flow and limited recursion are more likely to have higher speedup factors. Memory accesses either need to be optimized for locality (shared/texture memory) or coalescing (global memory).

– Additionally, the type of data to process influences the achievable speedup using the GPU. Copying data from CPU to GPU memory and back requires time and introduces an overhead. For small data dimensions, the GPU will be scarcely occupied and acceleration due to parallel processing may not be as high as was hoped for. In these cases, parallel processing using the CPU might be more efficient (assuming the CPU is multi-core).

Recent programming languages such as Halide [15], Rust [9] and Quasar [6] (which we have used for our experiments) address the first issue by allowing the algorithm to be specified on a high level, automatic memory transfer, load balancing, scheduling, etc. The remaining points are more related to the algorithmic and data-depending influence on the attainable speedup. This is addressed in more detail in the following sections.

3   Microscopy Image Segmentation

One of the most fundamental and challenging image processing problems in microscopic imaging is segmentation. Typically, one defines this as isolating objects of interest in a given input image. In the next sections, we will describe two popular microscopy image segmentation approaches that are distinctive in terms of computational complexity and coarse-grained parallelism. We note that it is not within the scope of this manuscript to provide a detailed discussion of the techniques, for this we refer to the respective references.

3.1   Notations

We will describe a gray scale image as a function $f : \Omega \mapsto \mathbb{R}$, such that $f(\mathbf{x})$ corresponds with the pixel intensity of the image at spatial position $\mathbf{x} \in \Omega$. A multichannel image is represented by a vector function $\mathbf{f} : \Omega \mapsto \mathbb{R}^C$ that consists of C gray scale images, one for each channel, e.g. $\mathbf{f}(\mathbf{x}) = [f_R(\mathbf{x}), f_G(\mathbf{x}), f_B(\mathbf{x})]$ for an RGB image.

A segmentation result involving K classes is defined by a classification function $u : \Omega \mapsto \mathcal{L}$ (where $\mathcal{L} = \{0, 1, \ldots, K - 1\}$ denotes the set of K class labels) such that $u(\mathbf{x}) = i$ if the pixel located at position $\mathbf{x} \in \Omega$ belongs to segment class i. In the case of binary segmentation, this means that $u(\mathbf{x})$ will be a binary function evaluating to 1 if the pixel positioned at $\mathbf{x}$ belongs to the foreground segment and 0 otherwise. For the matter of readability, in the following, we will discard the spatial information unless this could lead to confusing expressions.

3.2   Superpixel Segmentation

Superpixel segmentation methods are essentially segmentation algorithms applied in over-segmentation mode. The obtained segments (or superpixels) should be connected regions of pixels with similar (intensity and/or texture) characteristics. Typically, they are used as a pre-processing step for complex image processing algorithms that are impractical on large data sets. As a result, superpixel techniques should require minimal computation time in order to avoid overhead. Superpixels have been applied intensively in electron microscopy applications because of its typical large-scale data sets [11,13,18].

A popular superpixel segmentation technique is the Simple Linear Iterative Clustering (SLIC) algorithm [1]. SLIC superpixels are generated by applying the K-nearest neighboring algorithm on a multidimensional space incorporating intensity and spatial information (where K is the desired number of superpixels). Originally, it was described for color images. The multidimensional space would then correspond to the span of the CIELAB color space (because of its perceptual meaningfulness) and the 2D spatial domain (i.e. a 5-dimensional space). However, for general multichannel images, any kind of intensity space can be used. The distance d between two points of the joint $(C+2)$-dimensional space $[\mathbf{f}(\mathbf{x}), \mathbf{x}]$ and $[\mathbf{f}(\mathbf{x}'), \mathbf{x}']$, corresponding to spatial positions $\mathbf{x}$ and $\mathbf{x}'$, is then defined as a linear combination of the Euclidean color distance and spatial distance:

$$d = \|\mathbf{f}(\mathbf{x}) - \mathbf{f}(\mathbf{x}')\|_2 + \frac{m}{S} \|\mathbf{x} - \mathbf{x}'\|_2 , \qquad (1)$$

where $\| \cdot \|_2$ denotes the Euclidean norm, m is a compactness parameter that allows a trade-off between the intensity and normalized spatial distance and $S = \lfloor \sqrt{N/K} \rfloor$ is the approximate superpixel size (where N is the number of pixels in the image). Note that we have discarded vector dependencies for notational simplicity. To enforce connectivity, all disjoint clusters are reassigned to their largest neighboring cluster at then end of the algorithm. The pseudocode of this technique is shown in Algorithm 1 and Fig. 1 shows the result of SLIC superpixels computed on an electron micrograph.

As superpixels are typically generated on large-scale data sets and their computing time should be minimized to avoid overhead, GPU acceleration would be helpful.

Algorithm 1. SLIC superpixels

1: Input: an image $\mathbf{f}(\mathbf{x})$, compactness parameter m, preferred superpixel size S, number of iterations $niter$

2: Output: a labeled image $u(\mathbf{x})$ where pixels with the same label belong to the same superpixel

3: Lines starting with '#' indicate comments

4:

5: # Initialize seeds

6: $\mathbf{c}_k = [\mathbf{f}(\mathbf{x}_{r_k}), \mathbf{x}_{r_k}]$ (cluster centers and corresponding intensities across a regular grid r_k)

7: $pixelDistances(\mathbf{x}) = +\infty$

8: $X_k = \emptyset$

9: **for** $i = 0 \ldots niter - 1$ **do**

10:     # Reassign pixels

11:     **for all** $\mathbf{c}_k$ **do**

12:         **for all** $\mathbf{x}$ in a $2S \times 2S$ region around $\mathbf{c}_k$ **do**

13:             $dist = d([\mathbf{f}(\mathbf{x}), \mathbf{x}], \mathbf{c}_k)$

14:             **if** $dist < pixelDistances(\mathbf{x})$ **then**

15:                 $pixelDistances(\mathbf{x}) = dist$

16:                 $u(\mathbf{x}) = k$

17:             **end if**

18:         **end for**

19:     **end for**

20:     # Recompute cluster centers

21:     **for all** $\mathbf{c}_k$ **do**

22:         $X_k = \{\mathbf{x} \in \Omega | u(\mathbf{x}) = k\}$

23:         $\mathbf{c}_k = \frac{1}{|X_k|} \sum_{\mathbf{x} \in X_k} [\mathbf{f}(\mathbf{x}), \mathbf{x}]$ ($|X|$ represents the cardinality of a set X)

24:     **end for**

25: **end for**

26: # Enforce connectivity

27: **for all** disjoint clusters Y_l of connected pixels with the same label l **do**

28:     $X_k =$ largest neighbouring cluster of Y_l

29:     $u(\mathbf{x}) = k$ for all $\mathbf{x} \in Y_l$

30: **end for**

3.3   Active Contour Segmentation

Model-based approaches such as active contours isolate objects of interest by using stronger prior knowledge, i.e. by modeling motion, appearance, shape characteristics, etc. A specific energy function is minimized by moving and deforming an initial contour. This energy function should be minimal when the contour is delineating the object of interest. Active contours have been applied extensively in a broad range of microscopy applications such as phase contrast [10], confocal [14] and EM [12] due to the possibility of designing very application-specific energy functions.

A popular class of active contours, so-called geometric active contours, that benefits from a convex optimization problem represents the contour implicitly

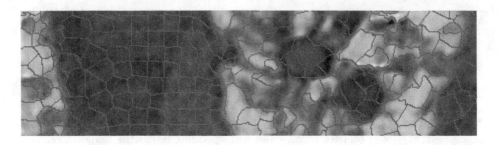

Fig. 1. SLIC superpixels computed on an electron microscopy image.

using a characteristic function $u : \Omega \mapsto [0, 1]$. This evaluates to 0 if the pixel does not belong to the segment, 1 elsewhere. We will focus on the segmentation method proposed in [4] where the contour is assumed to be smooth and forced to an intensity-based data-fit:

$$r(\mathbf{x}) = (\mu_1 - f(\mathbf{x}))^2 - (\mu_2 - f(\mathbf{x}))^2 \tag{2}$$

where μ_1 (respectively, μ_2) is the expected intensity inside (respectively, outside) of the contour. A gradient-based smoothness constraint suggests the following energy function that should be minimized:

$$E[u] = |\nabla u| + \beta \langle u, r \rangle + b(u), \tag{3}$$

where ∇ is the gradient operator, $|(w_1, w_2)| = \sqrt{\sum_{\mathbf{x}} w_1(\mathbf{x})^2 + w_2(\mathbf{x})^2}$ for images w_i, β a weighting parameter used to tune the influence of the data-fit term in relation to the total variation regularization and $\langle w, w' \rangle = \sum_{\mathbf{x}} w(\mathbf{x}) w'(\mathbf{x})$ for an image w. The function b is a convex potential function in order to constrain the minimal solution of Eq. 3 to the interval $[0, 1]$. In our experiments, we used:

$$b(x) = \min \left(\max \left(x, 0 \right), 1 \right). \tag{4}$$

The energy function in Eq. 3 can be efficiently minimized by introducing an additional variable v and computing the following iteration scheme [3]:

$$u^{(k+1)} = v^{(k)} - \frac{1}{\lambda} \nabla \cdot p \tag{5}$$

$$v^{(k+1)} = \min \left(\max \left(u^{(k+1)} - \frac{\beta}{\lambda} r, 0 \right), 1 \right), \tag{6}$$

where $\nabla \cdot$ denotes the divergence operator, $p(\mathbf{x})$ can be efficiently calculated using the following fixed point algorithm [2]:

$$p^{(0)} = (0, 0) \tag{7}$$

$$p^{(l+1)} = \frac{p^{(l)} + \delta t \, \nabla (\nabla \cdot p^{(l)} - \lambda v^{(k)})}{1 + \delta t \, \left| \nabla (\nabla \cdot p^{(l)} - \lambda v^{(k)}) \right|}, \tag{8}$$

Algorithm 2. Geometric active contours

1: Input: a grayscale image $f(\mathbf{x})$, expected foreground and background intensities μ_1
    and μ_2, regularization parameters λ and β

2: Output: a binary image $u(\mathbf{x})$ representing the segmentation

3: Lines starting with '#' indicate comments

4:

5: # Initialization

6: $u(\mathbf{x}) = 0$, $v(\mathbf{x}) = 0$

7: $r(\mathbf{x}) = (\mu_1 - f(\mathbf{x}))^2 - (\mu_2 - f(\mathbf{x}))^2$

8: **repeat**

9:    # Estimate p

10:    $p(\mathbf{x}) = 0$

11:    **repeat**

12:        $divp(\mathbf{x}) = \nabla \cdot p(\mathbf{x})$

13:        $graddivp(\mathbf{x}) = \nabla(divp(\mathbf{x}) - \lambda v(\mathbf{x}))$

14:        $p(\mathbf{x}) = \dfrac{p(\mathbf{x}) + \delta t\, graddivp(\mathbf{x})}{1 + \delta t\, |graddivp(\mathbf{x})|}$

15:    **until** convergence criterium for $p(\mathbf{x})$ is satisfied

16:    # Update u

17:    $u(\mathbf{x}) = v(\mathbf{x}) - \frac{1}{\lambda} divp(\mathbf{x})$

18:    # Update v

19:    $v(\mathbf{x}) = b\left(u(\mathbf{x}) - \frac{\beta}{\lambda} r(\mathbf{x})\right)$

20: **until** convergence criterium for $u(\mathbf{x})$ is satisfied

21: # Binarization

22: $u(\mathbf{x}) = u(\mathbf{x}) > 0.5$

---

where δt is the step size. The pseudocode of this technique is shown in Algorithm 2 and Fig. 2 shows the result of geometric active contours applied on a fluorescence microscopy image.

Active contours are a more complex segmentation method and, due to the iterative implementation, significantly more computationally intensive.

Fig. 2. Active contour segmentation result on the blue channel of a fluorescence micrograph. (Color figure online)

However, because of the high amount of pixel-wise image operations, parallel computing seems computationally interesting.

4   Accelerating Programs Using the GPU

Accelerating SLIC superpixel segmentation and active contour algorithms using the GPU has been studied in literature [7, 16]. We stress that, in this paper, it is our goal to identify the general algorithmic and data-dependent properties that give rise to a higher potential speedup, such that GPU porting can be performed whenever it is likely to escribe. Firstly, it is worth noticing we can distinguish between two types of programs that have different acceleration properties as more computing resources are provided to the system: strongly and weakly scaled programs.

4.1   Strong and Weak Scaling

Intuitively, more computing resources result in faster computation, for programs assuming the workload remains constant (the program will not benefit in performance by increasing the workload). This type of programs is typically called *strongly* scaled, e.g. matrix operations such as addition, multiplication, etc. More specifically, the theoretically achievable speedup s by providing n times more computing resources to a subprogram that is responsible for a fraction q of the total (original) execution time is then given by Amdahl's law:

$$s = \frac{1}{1 - q + \frac{q}{n}}. \tag{9}$$

As $n \to +\infty$, the achievable speedup will be maximized to $\frac{1}{1-q}$. However, even in this case, a subprogram that requires a relatively small fraction of computing time ($q \to 0$) will still result in an insignificant global speedup. Clearly, in order to guarantee a high potential speedup, it is important to initially detect the subprograms that are responsible for the largest fraction q of computing time and focus on these parts of the program for parallelization.

Alternatively, increasing the workload may benefit the performance of an algorithm. This type of programs is also called *weakly* scaled, e.g. training-based algorithms. The fixed workload assumption is invalid and the theoretically achievable speedup s by providing n times more computing resources to a subprogram that is responsible for a fraction q of the total (original) execution time is then given by Gustafson's law:

$$s = 1 + (n - 1)q. \tag{10}$$

In this case, the achievable speedup is linearly related to the amount of computing resources and subprogram execution time fraction.

In general a program neither exhibits strong nor weak scalability, but rather a combination of both. The key message in the context of GPU processing is

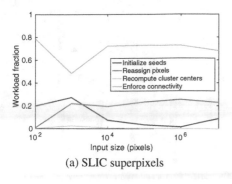 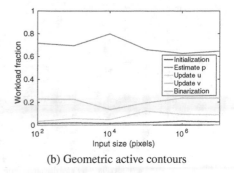

(a) SLIC superpixels   (b) Geometric active contours

Fig. 3. Execution time percentage of parts of the (a) SLIC superpixel and (b) active contour algorithm for variable input sizes (note that this axis is logarithmically scaled). The indicated subprograms are shown in comment in their corresponding pseudocode (Algorithms 1 and 2, respectively).

to parallelize the subprograms that are responsible for the largest fraction of computing time.

Algorithms 1 and 2 show the pseudocode of the discussed SLIC superpixel and geometric active contour algorithm, respectively. We have separated the algorithms in subprograms, indicated by the commented lines. Figure 3 shows the workload fraction of each part of the algorithms for variable input sizes. The most interesting function to parallelize in the SLIC algorithm is the connectivity enforcement. In this example, we have chosen for 10 iterations in the algorithm (which typically suffices). Obviously, a higher number of iterations will result into relatively more computing time reassigning the pixels and recomputing the cluster centers. The active contours algorithm spends most of the computing time in the estimation of p (fortunately, we typically have convergence after 1 iteration). As a consequence, this part of the algorithm is essential to parallelize in order to guarantee a higher speedup.

4.2 Estimating the Achievable Speedup

Figure 4 illustrates the achieved speedup by GPU acceleration of SLIC superpixel and active contour segmentation applied on a 0.001, 0.1 and 10 megapixel 8-bit grayscale image using Quasar. An important notice is that Quasar is designed for program execution on heterogeneous hardware and will decide at runtime whether to run a function on the host CPU or another specific device (usually a GPU) according to its own heuristics. The experiments were performed using an Intel Core i7 4720 2.60 GHz CPU and GeForce GTX 960M GPU.

Once the most time-requiring functions are detected, it is important to analyze their characteristics and the type of data that they will have to process. We provide a (non-exhaustive) list of properties that, according to our experiences, significantly impact the achievable speedup and illustrate them with examples of subprograms of the accelerated segmentation algorithms (see Fig. 4):

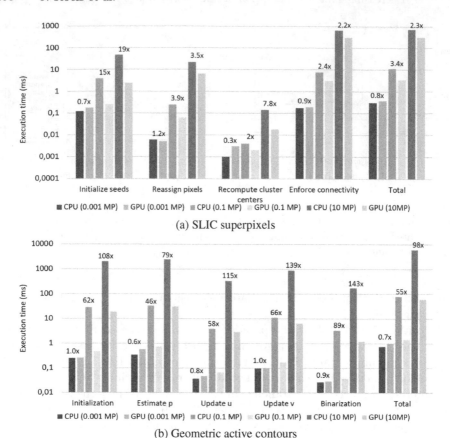

(a) SLIC superpixels

(b) Geometric active contours

Fig. 4. Execution timing distribution (in ms) of the (a) SLIC superpixel and (b) geometric active contours algorithm applied on 0.001, 0.1 and 10 megapixel 8-bit images using multi threaded CPU and GPU processing. For each part of the program, the achieved speedup is indicated on top of the bars. Note that the execution time axis is logarithmically scaled.

- **Coarse-grained parallelism of the function:** Functions that consist of many computations that are mutually independent are typically called functions with coarse-grained parallelism. This naturally translates to parallel computing and is therefore an indicator for a high or low potential speedup. For example, all the functions in the active contour algorithm are pixel-wise image operations resulting in significant speedups.
- **Size of the data to process:** This is a consequence of concealing memory latency while accessing it. Larger amounts of data typically allow more operations to be performed in parallel, resulting in higher speedups, compared to small amounts of data. For example, we establish higher speedups in the initialization of the seeds and the cluster center recomputing of the SLIC algorithm. However, since the amount of superpixels is usually much smaller compared to

the number of pixels, and the pixel reassigning and cluster center recomputation iterate over the cluster centers, their corresponding speedup is relatively smaller. The active contours computation requires sufficiently enough input data in order to efficiently execute a number of iterations and conceal memory latency. This can be seen by the attained speedups as the input data size increases.

- **Computational complexity:** The operational complexity should justify the cost of transferring data to and from the device, i.e. maximize the computation/memory transfer ratio. Note that in many cases, data remains on the GPU memory: in this case global memory reads/writes should be used in order to compute the computation/transfer ratio. As an example, assume two $N \times N$ matrices have to be added using the GPU: this requires N^2 operations and $3N^2$ data reads/writes to global memory, resulting in a computation/transfer ratio of $\frac{1}{3}$. Alternatively, the case of matrix multiplication would require N^3 operations and $3N^2$ elements to be transferred, resulting in a computation/transfer ratio of $\frac{N}{3}$. In this case, the algorithm would benefit from larger matrix sizes. Similarly, we denote in the parts of the active contour algorithm where u and v are being updated, that the update for v is computationally (slightly) more intense than the update on u. Hence, the corresponding speedups are increasing faster as the input data size increases.

In practice, the achievable speedup is determined by a combination of the previous and other functional and data-dependent properties. Even under perfect function and data circumstances, the achievable speedup may still rely on implementation-dependent factors such as memory transfer, data type and alignment, thread divergence, etc. Nevertheless, the coarse-grained parallelism, data size and computation/memory transfer ratio give a good indication whether an algorithm is suitable to GPU acceleration.

5 Conclusion

Image segmentation remains one of the most challenging problems in microscopy analysis. Typically, the user is obligated to find an optimal balance between algorithm complexity on the one hand, which is heavily correlated with computational complexity, and manual post-processing on the other hand. High computational costs are a common reason for the impracticality of many high-quality segmentation algorithms and can be mitigated through recent developments in GPU accelerated computing. However, accelerating algorithms using the GPU is a costly operation because of the required programming expertise. Additionally, predicting the attainable speedup is difficult in practice because of the large amount of influencing factors. In this paper, we identify which algorithm and data characteristics significantly relate to the achievable GPU speedup. In particular, we have found that (1) the algorithm needs to exhibit coarse-grained parallelism, (2) the data size needs to be sufficiently large to benefit from GPU parallelization and (3) the computation/memory transfer ratio needs to sufficiently large so that the computational cost outweigh the memory transfer cost.

158   J. Roels et al.

This is illustrated on two types of well-known segmentation methods that are extensively used in microscopy image analysis: superpixels and active contours.

References

1. Achanta, R., Shaji, A., Smith, K., Lucchi, A.: SLIC superpixels compared to state-of-the-art superpixel methods. IEEE Trans. Pattern Anal. Mach. Intell. **34**(11), 2274–2281 (2012)
2. Aujol, J.F., Chambolle, A.: Dual norms and image decomposition models. Int. J. Comput. Vision **63**(1), 85–104 (2005)
3. Bresson, X., Esedoglu, S., Vandergheynst, P., Thiran, J.P., Osher, S.: Fast global minimization of the active contour/snake model. J. Math. Imaging Vision **28**(2), 151–167 (2007)
4. Chan, T.F., Esedoglu, S., Nikolova, M.: Algorithms for finding global minimizers of image segmentation and denoising models. SIAM J. Appl. Math. **66**(5), 1632–1648 (2006)
5. Crookes, D., Miller, P., Gribben, H., Gillan, C., McCaughey, D.: GPU Implementation of MAP-MRF for microscopy imagery segmentation. In: Proceedings - 2009 IEEE International Symposium on Biomedical Imaging: From Nano to Macro, ISBI 2009, pp. 526–529 (2009)
6. Goossens, B., De Vylder, J., Philips, W.: Quasar: a new heterogeneous programming framework for image and video processing algorithms on CPU and GPU. In: Proceedings of the IEEE International Conference on Image Processing, pp. 2183–2185 (2014)
7. He, Z., Kuester, F.: GPU-based active contour segmentation using gradient vector flow. In: Bebis, G., et al. (eds.) ISVC 2006. LNCS, vol. 4291, pp. 191–201. Springer, Heidelberg (2006). doi:10.1007/11919476_20
8. Helmstaedter, M., Briggman, K.L., Turaga, S.C., Jain, V., Seung, H.S., Denk, W.: Connectomic reconstruction of the inner plexiform layer in the mouse retina. Nature **500**(7461), 168–174 (2013). http://www.ncbi.nlm.nih.gov/pubmed/23925239
9. Holk, E., Pathirage, M., Chauhan, A., Lumsdaine, A., Matsakis, N.D.: GPU programming in rust: implementing high-level abstractions in a systems-level language. In: Proceedings - IEEE 27th International Parallel and Distributed Processing Symposium Workshops and PhD Forum, IPDPSW 2013, pp. 315–324 (2013)
10. Huang, Y., Liu, Z.: Segmentation and tracking of lymphocytes based on modified active contour models in phase contrast microscopy images. Comput. Math. Methods Med. **2015**, 1–9 (2015)
11. Jain, V., Turaga, S.C., Briggman, K.L., Helmstaedter, M.N., Denk, W., Seung, H.S.: Learning to agglomerate superpixel hierarchies. In: Advances in Neural Information Processing Systems, pp. 1–9 (2011)
12. Jorstad, A., Fua, P.: Refining mitochondria segmentation in electron microscopy imagery with active surfaces. In: Agapito, L., Bronstein, M.M., Rother, C. (eds.) ECCV 2014. LNCS, vol. 8928, pp. 367–379. Springer, Heidelberg (2015). doi:10.1007/978-3-319-16220-1_26
13. Lucchi, A., Smith, K., Achanta, R., Knott, G., Fua, P.: Supervoxel-based segmentation of mitochondria in EM image stacks with learned shape features. IEEE Trans. Med. Imaging **31**, 474–486 (2012)

14. Meziou, L., Histace, A., Precioso, F., Matuszewski, B.J., Murphy, M.F.: Confocal microscopy segmentation using active contour based on alpha (α)-divergence. In: Proceedings of the International Conference on Image Processing, pp. 3077–3080 (2011)
15. Ragan-Kelley, J., Adams, A., Paris, S., Durand, F., Barnes, C., Amarasinghe, S.: Halide: a language and compiler for optimizing parallelism, locality, and recomputation in image processing pipelines. In: Proceedings of the 34th ACM SIGPLAN Conference on Programming Language Design and Implementation, pp. 519–530 (2013)
16. Ren, C.Y., Reid, I.: gSLIC: a real-time implementation of SLIC superpixel segmentation. University of Oxford, Department of Engineering Science, pp. 1–6 (2011)
17. Stegmaier, J., Amat, F., Lemon, W.C., McDole, K., Wan, Y., Teodoro, G., Mikut, R., Keller, P.J.: Real-time three-dimensional cell segmentation in large-scale microscopy data of developing embryos. Dev. Cell **36**(2), 225–240 (2016)
18. Wang, S., Cao, G., Wei, B., Yin, Y., Yang, G., Li, C.: Hierarchical level features based trainable segmentation for electron microscopy images. Bio-Med. Eng. OnLine **12**, 59 (2013). http://www.biomedical-engineering-online.com/content/12/1/59

Coral Reef Fish Detection and Recognition in Underwater Videos by Supervised Machine Learning: Comparison Between Deep Learning and HOG+SVM Methods

Sébastien Villon[1]([✉]), Marc Chaumont[1,2], Gérard Subsol[2], Sébastien Villéger[3], Thomas Claverie[3], and David Mouillot[3]

[1] LIRMM, University of Montpellier/CNRS, Montpellier, France
villon@lirmm.fr
[2] University of Nîmes, Nîmes, France
[3] MARBEC, IRD/Ifremer/University of Montpellier/CNRS, Montpellier, France

Abstract. In this paper, we present two supervised machine learning methods to automatically detect and recognize coral reef fishes in underwater HD videos. The first method relies on a traditional two-step approach: extraction of HOG features and use of a SVM classifier. The second method is based on Deep Learning. We compare the results of the two methods on real data and discuss their strengths and weaknesses.

1 Introduction

Quantifying human impact on fish biodiversity in order to propose solutions to preserve submarine ecosystems is an important line of research for marine ecology. This quantification requires in situ sampling of the fish community. Measurements based on extraction-fishing give only limited data, and could lead to misinterpretation [1]. Moreover, the use of fishing, even for survey purposes, impacts the studied biodiversity.

Another standard method consists in two divers who note visual observations of fishes under water. This kind of survey is expensive in both time and money, and results are greatly impacted by divers' experience and fish behavior. Moreover, data acquisition remains limited by the human physical capacities [1].

A more recent method consists in acquiring underwater images or videos [3], with either a moving or a fixed camera. An expert will then be asked to detect, count and recognize fishes on a screen offline. At the moment, this task is performed entirely manually, and the amount of data is often too large to be completely analyzed on screen. Moreover, the latest technical improvements of HD camera allow recording fish communities for a long time at a very low cost. Significant examples of a huge amount of underwater HD images/videos, that have been collected for assessing fish biodiversity, are the 115 terabytes of the European project Fish4Knowledge [3], or the XL Catlin Seaview Survey Initiative[1].

---

[1] http://catlinseaviewsurvey.com/.

© Springer International Publishing AG 2016
J. Blanc-Talon et al. (Eds.): ACIVS 2016, LNCS 10016, pp. 160–171, 2016.
DOI: 10.1007/978-3-319-48680-2_15

Fig. 1. Left, a 640 × 480 highly compressed frame extracted from the SeaClef database. Right, a 1280 × 720 HD frame from the MARBEC laboratory database.

The research community in image processing has been asked to propose algorithms in order to assist, and recently even automatize the detection/identification of fishes in images or videos. Recently, a challenge called Coral Reef Species Recognition has been proposed in the evaluation campaign SeaClef[2], which is based indeed on Fish4Knowledge data. Unfortunately, in this task, the video quality remains quite limited (640 × 480 pixels) whereas current acquisitions are in High Definition or even in 4K (see Fig. 1). This offers much more details for image processing but increases the processing time.

Among the issues and difficulties of detecting and recognizing fish in underwater videos, there are color variations due to the depth, lighting variations from one frame to another, the sediments and dirt which degrades the videos quality, or the seaweed which makes the background changing and moving [4]. The classification itself encounters other issues such as the variation of shape or color within the same species and moreover the variation of size and orientation due to the fish position. We chose not to avoid these issues, and to take into account all these problems as we work on videos acquired in natural conditions instead of controlled acquisitions [5]. We chose for this study to focus on the processing of each frame and not on the video.

Many methods to detect and recognize fishes in underwater videos were proposed these last years [3]. In general, the first step consists in selecting features based on the shape, color, context, specifics landmarks or texture [6]. Some algorithms use specific feature vectors computed at some landmarks. Other use more complex features such as SIFT [8–10] or *shape context* (SC) [5]. But in [11], the authors conclude that the Histogram Of Oriented Gradients feature leads to better results than both SIFT and SC.

In the 2015 SeaClef contest [23], the best results have shown that Deep Learning can achieve a better classification for fish detection than SVM or other classical methods. This may be due to the fact that in Deep Learning, features are automatically built by the classifier itself, in an optimal way. The winner of the SeaClef contest used several Deep classifiers and fused the results to obtain the definitive scores. Unfortunately, we will not be able to compare our approach

---

[2] http://www.imageclef.org/lifeclef/2016/sea.

with his as the databases are different (we have a higher definition and mobile cameras).

In this paper, we propose also to explore the performances of fish detection and classification by Deep Learning. In particular, we assess the results with respect to a more classical method based on a combination of HOG feature extraction and SVM classification. For this, we will use High Definition videos acquired for an actual marine ecology study. In Sect. 2, we briefly present Deep-learning and SVM+HOG methods. In Sect. 3, we detail the implementation in particular the multi-resolution approach and data preprocessing. In Sect. 4 we present the results and compare both methods. In Sect. 5, we present some future work.

2   Presentation of the Methods

2.1   Histogram of Oriented Gradients + Support Vector Machine

The Histogram of Oriented Gradients [12] characterizes an object in an image based on its contours by using the distribution of the orientations of local gradients. As shown in [13], HOG features may lead to better results even in a complex classification task as ours, where a fish can be hidden in coral reefs or occluded by another fish.

The Support Vector Machine (SVM) [7] is a supervised method to classify feature vectors. SVM method represents each vector in a high dimensional space, mapped so that the samples of the different classes are separated by a clear gap that is as wide as possible. Support vector machines have been used in a lot of applications and have shown good overall results [14–17].

2.2   Deep Learning

Since the 2012 ImageNet competition, and new computational power accessible through latest GPU, Neural Network came back as a strong possibility for classification tasks [18]. Moreover, by integrating convolutional layers, Deep Neural Networks (DNN) are able to both create features vectors and classify them.

Neural network is a mathematical model which tries to mimic human brains [19]. Like SVM, neural networks may classify feature vectors after a training phase. A neural network is composed of interconnected nodes called neurons and each neuron of each layer receives a signal from the neurons of the previous layer. This signal is modified according to an activation function and transferred to the neurons of the next layer.

We can define for the neuron n, the first operation $\alpha^{(n)}$ as:

$$\alpha^{(n)}(\mathbf{x}^{(n)}) = \sum_{i=1}^{c} w_i^{(n)} x_i^{(n)} \tag{1}$$

where $\mathbf{x}$ is the input vector, a given neuron, c the number of connections of this neuron, $w_i^{(n)}$ the weight of rank i of a neuron n, and $x_i^{(n)}$ the input of rank i of a neuron n.

We can then define the output of a neuron n as $\sigma^{(n)}$ with $f^{(n)}$ the activation function:

$$\sigma^{(n)}(\mathbf{x}^{(n)}) = f^{(n)}(\alpha^{(n)}(\mathbf{x}^{(n)})) \tag{2}$$

Each layer of a neural network except the first one which receive the feature vector and the last one are called hidden layers. During the learning process, the network will have its parameters modified in order to optimize its classification rate of learning.

We will use the back-propagation. Given a feature vector representing an object from class $k \in \{1, K\}$ as network input, we compare the expected value (100 % of probability to belong to class k) to the results obtained by the network, and we compute the error of the output layer. Then, the error is back-propagated from the layer j to the neurons of the layer $j-1$. Finally, the weight of each neuron is updated according to a gradient-based descent in order to get a computed value closer to the expected value [20].

To make a network able to build its own feature, we move from a simple network to a Convolutional Neural Network (CNN). One or more convolutional layers are connected between the input layer and the hidden layers. Each convolutional layer transforms the signal sent from the previous layer using convolutional kernels, an activation function breaking the linearity and a pooling phase which reduces the image and strengthens the learning by selecting significant pixels (the highest value from a region for instance). The last convolutional layer eventually concatenates all the information in one feature vector and sends it to another layer or to a classifier.

For the training phase, a CNN is given a database consisting of couples $(I^i, l^i)_{i=1}^{i=N}$ with I^i, the image $i \in \{1, ..., N\}$ and l^i its label. Basically, in our application, the label $l^i \in \{1, ..., L\}$ is the fish species.

3   Practical Implementation

3.1   Data Preprocessing

The choice of learning data is a crucial point. We worked with biology experts of the MARBEC laboratory to label many videos. We cropped some frames of the videos and created a training database composed of 13000 fish thumbnails. The thumbnail size varies from a minimum of 20×40 pixels to a maximum of 150×200 pixels. Each thumbnail contains only one labeled-fish as shown on Fig. 2.

We decided to keep only the species with more than 450 thumbnails. We also widen the database by applying rotations and symmetries in order to capture all the possible position of the fishes. Table 1 lists the retained species.

Due to the highly textured natural background, we also added a class for the background. This class is constituted with *random* thumbnails of the background which were randomly selected in frames and *specific* background thumbnails which were taken around the fish thumbnails.

Fig. 2. Some training thumbnails from the MARBEC database

Table 1. Fish species in the learning database

Species	Thumbnails	Rotations and symmetries
Acanthurus lineatus	493	2465
Acanthurus nigrofuscus	1455	3923
Chromis ternatensis	951	4755
Chromis viridis/Chromis atripectoralis	523	2619
Pomacentrus sulfureus	766	3830
Pseudanthias squamipinnis	1180	5900
Zebrasoma scopas	488	2400
Ctenochatus striatus	1400	4000

To be able to do multi-resolution classification, all the background thumbnails were taken with random dimensions, from 40×60 pixels to 400×500 pixels.

Finally, in order to improve the localization accuracy, we decided to create another class called *part of fish*, to ensure that the network does not focus on a distinctive part of a fish as a stripe, a fin, the head, but processes the fish as a whole. We also created a class *fish* which contains some unknown fishes to make the method able to recognize any fish even though it is not in the learning database. However, this class must contain less samples in order to be sure that a fish will most likely be labeled by its specific class rather than the generic class *fish*. Finally, we added 3 classes to our initial thumbnail database as listed in Table 2.

Table 2. Classes added to the species database

Class Label	Samples
Random/specific background	116,820/91,247
Part of Fish	55,848
Fish	970

3.2   Detection/Recognition Pipeline

The HOG+SVM and the Deep Learning methods process the video frames through the same pipeline (see Fig. 3). We chose for this study to process each frame independently without introducing any object tracking algorithm. First, we pass a multi-resolution sliding window through the frame. For each position of the window, the method gives a probability score for each class. We also compute a motion probability score based on the comparison of the current and the previous frame. We then compare the probability scores given by the classifier to some predefined thresholds. If the scores are over the thresholds, we output a bounding box corresponding to the window position. At the end, for each position, we will fuse all the bounding boxes found at different resolutions.

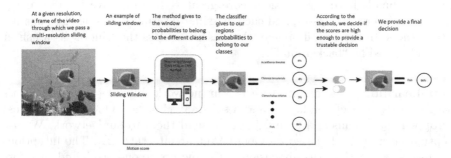

Fig. 3. Detection/Recognition pipeline

Multi-resolution Sliding Window. In order to deal with multi-resolution detection, the size of the sliding window varies from 1/18 of the frame at least, and 1/1 at most. This allows to recognizes fishes with a minimum of 60 pixel length and 40 pixel width, and a maximum equal to the full size of the frame. The sliding window is displaced by a stride equals to a third of the window width.

HOG + SVM. We divide each thumbnail in 10 zones (one zone is the complete thumbnail, and the 9 others are the thumbnail divided in 9 even parts). For each zone, we compute a HOG feature over 8 direction axes, and we concatenate all these HOG features in a unique feature vector. For each fish species, we fed a SVM with all the corresponding thumbnail features as a class, and all the other thumbnails features (other species and background) in order to obtain a specific classifier.

The SVM we used non-linear SVR (Support Vector Machine for regression) implemented using the library libsvm[3] with a Gaussian radial basis function kernel. We obtained a clean separation for the training database (over 85 % of

---

[3] https://www.csie.ntu.edu.tw/~cjlin/libsvm/.

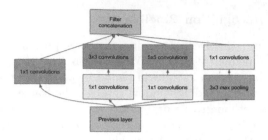

Fig. 4. An inception module, as presented in Szegedy et al. [22]

backgrounds thumbnails have a regression score lesser than 0.5, and 85 % of fishes thumbnails have a regression score greater than 0.5) We built as many classifiers as there are classes, and each classifier discriminates one class against all the others. In the end, if none of the classifiers class the window as a fish, it will be classified as "background".

Deep Learning. The architecture of our network follows the GoogLeNet's with 27 layers, 9 inception layers, and a soft-max classifier. Once we have a list of cropped thumbnails and their labels, we send them to our network. We use inception layers (Fig. 4) based on GoogLeNet architecture [22]. The inceptions here allows us to reduce the dimension of the picture to one pixel, and therefore not to be dependent of the dimensional impact. We adapted some parameters such as the size of the strides and the first convolutions adapted to the size of our thumbnails, which allowed us to achieve better results than a classic architecture (e.g. [18]).

3.3 Post-processing and Bounding Box Fusion

For each sliding window, we define a motion score by computing the average absolute difference with the window at the same position in the previous frame. Based on the hypothesis that most of the fishes are moving, we use this score for the final detection decision.

After processing all the resolutions of a frame, we obtain a list of bounding boxes, and for each bounding box a probability of belonging to a class. Yet the classification remains ambiguous if there is more than one bounding box corresponding to the same potential fish (see Fig. 5).

To suppress the redundant bounding boxes, we first keep the boxes whose probabilities are above a given probability threshold T (T = 98 %) in the case of Fig. 5. So if the motion score is greater than our motion threshold and the probabilities to belong to a class of fish is greater than 98 %, we keep the box. Then, we fuse the remaining boxes following based on the following properties:

Fig. 5. Results of the detection before (left) and after (right) post-processing. Note that two fishes in the center are not displayed because they do not belong to one of the species which have been learned.

if two bounding boxes are labeled with the same species, and their overlap ratio is greater than 30 %[4], we suppress the bounding box with the lower probability.

4 Results, Comparison and Discussion

We used 4 test videos (which are different from the training videos) to experiment our complete process. The 4 videos were taken on coral reefs, and the diver was holding the camera which then slightly moves. The video acquisition were not deep, and therefore we had a lot of colors on both the fishes and the background but the light is moving with the waves, bringing many distortions. The videos are very different in terms of fish species, background texture, colors, fish density, etc. Biology experts from MARBEC selected 400 frames all over the videos and defined ground-truth bounding boxes of all the visible fishes in the frame.

To determine if a detected bounding box is correct, we compute its overlap ratio with the ground truth bounding box. If this value is over a threshold λ, then the detection is considered as true positive, otherwise it is labeled as false positive. On the opposite, if a ground truth bounding box has no over the threshold overlap with any detected bounding box, it counts as a true negative. We chose to put the value 0.5 to λ.

Results (recall, precision and F-Measure) of the entire detection/recognition process with Deep-Learning method is given in Table 3 with T = 98 %.

We also show on Fig. 6 the relation between recall and precision with respect to the threshold T. The differences come mostly from the texture of the background, but also from the species, as some fishes are easier to detect (bright colors, stripes...).

We can now compare in Table 4 the results of the two methods, for the same threshold. It seems that the discrimination of the HOG+SVM is less efficient

---

[4] The overlap ratio is defined as $OA = IS/US$ with IS the intersection surface and US the union surface.

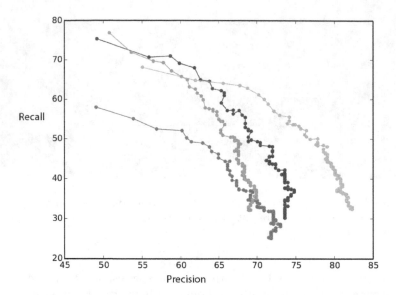

Fig. 6. ROC Curves of the Deep Learning method on the four test videos, with the threshold T as parameter. (Color figure online)

Table 3. Results with the Deep Learning method (T = 98 %)

Video	Precision	Recall	F-measure
1655	0.58	0.69	0.62
1654	0.68	0.63	0.65
1547	0.77	0.64	0.70
1546	0.60	0.52	0.55

Table 4. F-measure of the two methods with the same parameter

Video	F-measure from HOG+SVM	F-measure Deep Learning
1655	0.28	0.62
1654	0.24	0.65
1547	0.49	0.64
1546	0.14	0.55

than the CNN's. Indeed, the F-measure of the HOG+SVM is always below 49 % whereas it is always above 55 % for the CNN.

As we can observe in Fig. 7, the Deep Learning method approach efficiently recognizes fishes on different resolutions even when there is a strongly textured background and is able to distinguishes fishes which are close.

Fig. 7. The Deep Learning method succeeds in detecting fishes partially occluded by coral (bottom left)

Fig. 8. A rock detected as a fish. On the left, the ground truth, on the right, the results of our processing

On the other hand, parts of the coral can be misclassified. In Fig. 8, we were able to detect the three fishes we were supposed to, but we also detected a part of the coral reef which presents features we can also find on fishes such as an enlighten top and a darker bottom, an oval shape, etc.

5   Future Work

In this paper, we have presented two methods to detect and recognize fishes in underwater videos.

When we apply the Deep Learning method directly on test thumbnails, which consists in recognizing if a thumbnail belong to a class, we reach a F-score of 98 %. We believe that the results can not really be improved as long as we keep the same network architecture. According to this, we focused our work on the post and pre-processing. The reduction of performance on a frame, in most case, comes from fishes which overlap or occlude and from confusion with the background. We tried to improve the method by adding three more classes and also through the use of a well chosen overlap decision.

At the moment, the Deep Learning method gives quite good results. A possible way to treat errors is to integrate the temporal aspect in a more advanced way by implementing a fish tracking algorithm.

Acknowledgement. This work has been carried out thanks to the support of the LabEx NUMEV project (n° ANR-10-LABX-20) funded by the "Investissements d'Avenir" French Government program, managed by the French National Research Agency (ANR). We thank very much Jérôme Pasquet and Lionel Pibre for scientific discussions.

References

1. Mallet, D., Pelletier, D.: Underwater video techniques for observing coastal marine biodiversity: a review of sixty years of publications (1952–2012). Fish. Res. **154**, 44–62 (2014)
2. Boom, B.J., Huang, P.X., Beyan, C., et al.: Long-term underwater camera surveillance for monitoring and analysis of fish populations. In: VAIB12 (2012)
3. Fisher, R.B., Chen-Burger, Y.-H., Giordano, D., Hardman, L., Lin, F.-P. (eds.): Fish4Knowledge: Collecting and Analyzing Massive Coral Reef Fish Video Data. ISRL, vol. 104. Springer, Heidelberg (2016)
4. Alsmadi, M.K.S., Omar, K.B., Noah, S.A., et al.: Fish recognition based on the combination between robust feature selection, image segmentation and geometrical parameter techniques using Artificial Neural Network and Decision Tree. J. Comput. Sci. **6**(10), 1088–1094 (2010)
5. Rova, A., Mori, G., Dill, L.M.: One fish, two fish, butterfish, trumpeter: recognizing fish in underwater video. In: Machine Vision Applications, pp. 404–407 (2007)
6. Spampinato, C., Giordano, D., Di Salvo, R.: Automatic fish classification for underwater species behavior understanding. In: Proceedings of the First ACM International Workshop on Analysis and Retrieval of Tracked Events and Motion in Imagery Streams, pp. 45–50 (2010)
7. Hearst, M.A., Dumais, S.T., Osman, E., et al.: Support vector machines. IEEE Intell. Syst. Appl. **13**(4), 18–28 (1998). MLA
8. Matai, J., Kastner, R., Cutter Jr., G.R.: Automated techniques for detection, recognition of fishes using computer vision algorithms. In: Williams, K., Rooper, C., Harms, J. (eds.) NOAA Technical Memorandum NMFS-F/SPO-121, Report of the National Marine Fisheries Service Automated Image Processing Workshop, 4–7 September 2010, Seattle, Washington (2010)
9. Shiau, Y.-H., Lin, S.-I., Chen, Y.-H., et al.: Fish observation, detection, recognition, verification in the real world. In: Proceedings of the International Conference on Image Processing, Computer Vision, and Pattern Recognition (IPCV), p. 1 (2012)
10. Blanc, K., Lingrand, D., Precioso, F.: Fish species recognition from video using SVM classifier. In: Proceedings of the 3rd ACM International Workshop on Multimedia Analysis for Ecological Data, pp. 1–6. ACM (2014)
11. Zhu, Q., Yeh, M.-C., Cheng, K.-T., et al.: Fast human detection using a cascade of histograms of oriented gradients. In: 2006 IEEE Computer Society Conference on Computer Vision and Pattern Recognition, pp. 1491–1498. IEEE (2006)
12. Dalal, N., Triggs, B.: Histograms of oriented gradients for human detection. In: 2005 IEEE Computer Society Conference on Computer Vision and Pattern Recognition, CVPR 2005, pp. 886–893. IEEE (2005)

13. Pasquet, J., Chaumont, M., Subsol, G.: Comparaison de la segmentation pixel et segmentation objet pour la détection d'objets multiples et variables dans des images. In: CORESA: COmpression et REprésentation des Signaux Audiovisuels, Reims (2014). (in French)
14. Das, S., Mirnalinee, T.T., Varghese, K.: Use of salient features for the design of a multistage framework to extract roads from high-resolution multispectral satellite images. IEEE Trans. Geosci. Remote Sens. **49**(10), 3906–3931 (2011)
15. Sun, X., Wang, H., Fu, K.: Automatic detection of geospatial objects using taxonomic semantics. IEEE Geosci. Remote Sens. Lett. **7**(1), 23–27 (2010)
16. Zhang, W., Sun, X., Fu, K., et al.: Object detection in high-resolution remote sensing images using rotation invariant parts based model. IEEE Geosci. Remote Sens. Lett. **11**(1), 74–78 (2014)
17. Zhang, W., Sun, X., Wang, H., et al.: A generic discriminative part-based model for geospatial object detection in optical remote sensing images. ISPRS J. Photogrammetry Remote Sens. **99**, 30–44 (2015)
18. Krizhevsky, A., Sutskever, I., Hinton, G.E.: ImageNet classification with deep convolutional neural networks. In: Advances in Neural Information Processing Systems, pp. 1097–1105 (2012)
19. Atkinson, P.M., Tatnall, A.R.L.: Introduction neural networks in remote sensing. Int. J. Remote Sens. **18**(4), 699–709 (1997)
20. Schmidhuber, J.: Deep learning in neural networks: an overview. Neural Netw. **61**, 85–117 (2015)
21. Lecun, Y., Bottou, L., Bengio, Y., et al.: Gradient-based learning applied to document recognition. Proc. IEEE **86**(11), 2278–2324 (1998)
22. Szegedy, C., Liu, W., Jia, Y.: Going deeper with convolutions. In: Proceedings of the IEEE Conference on Computer Vision and Pattern Recognition, pp. 1–9 (2015)
23. Joly, A., et al.: LifeCLEF 2015: multimedia life species identification challenges. In: Mothe, J., Savoy, J., Kamps, J., Pinel-Sauvagnat, K., Jones, G.J.F., SanJuan, E., Cappellato, L., Ferro, N. (eds.) CLEF 2015. LNCS, vol. 9283, pp. 462–483. Springer, Heidelberg (2015). doi:10.1007/978-3-319-24027-5_46

A Real-Time Eye Gesture Recognition System Based on Fuzzy Inference System for Mobile Devices Monitoring

Hanene Elleuch[1]([✉]), Ali Wali[1], Anis Samet[2], and Adel M. Alimi[1]

[1] REGIM: REsearch Groups in Intelligent Machines, University of Sfax,
National Engineering School of Sfax (ENIS), BP 1173, 3038 Sfax, Tunisia
{hanene.elleuch,ali.wali@ieee.org,adel.alimi}@ieee.org
[2] SiFAST: Software and Computing Services Company, 3003 Sfax, Tunisia

Abstract. In this paper, we proposed a new system of mobile human-computer interaction based on eye gestures. This system aims to control and command mobile devices through the eyes for the purpose of providing an intuitive communication with these devices and a flexible usage with all contexts that a user can be situated. This system is based on a real-time streaming video captured from the front-facing camera without needing any additional equipment. The algorithm aims in the first time to detect user's face and their eyes in the second time. The eyes gesture recognition is based on fuzzy inference system. We deployed this algorithm on an android-based tablet and we asked 8 volunteers to test it. The obtained results proved that this system has promising and competitive results.

Keywords: Eye gesture recognition · Face detection · Eye tracking · Fuzzy inference system · Mobile device · Mobile human computer interaction

1 Introduction

Eyes are the important way to communicate with our surrounding environment. It can in the same time receive information about the exterior environment and give information about the expressive state of the human. The position and movement of the eyes hold a key role in gaze-based monitoring that is applied in many fields. Mobile human-computer interaction is one of the most important domains which exploits this technique. In fact, the widely use of these devices manifests the limits of the current mode of interaction; it is not adaptable to all contexts that a user can be situated. So, gaze gestures can be an alternative potential way of interaction. Many products are available in the market provide high-level precision of eye-gaze estimation, but they are high-priced and intrusive; they require specific hardware like active infrared illumination, lenses, glasses and electrodes [1]. Despite the robustness of these products, they cannot

© Springer International Publishing AG 2016
J. Blanc-Talon et al. (Eds.): ACIVS 2016, LNCS 10016, pp. 172–180, 2016.
DOI: 10.1007/978-3-319-48680-2_16

be popular because of their intrusiveness that makes the daily use of these solutions discomfortable. For this reason, many research works are interested in eye-gaze detection and estimation focused on image-based solutions. This approach confronts many challenges for the localization and recognition of eye gestures. Indeed, the face and eyes are in continuous movement in the time, therefore, making the difference between the natural and intentional movements is indispensable in this case. The lightness condition, head pose, wearing glasses have an important influence on the result mainly when we deal with a low resolution camera like the case of mobile devices camera.

In this paper, a real-time system of gaze gesture recognition for mobile devices is presented. This system aims to detect, track and recognize the eye-gaze in the purpose of providing an alternative way of interaction. This paper is organized as follow: In Sect. 2, a literature review in the field of eye-gaze recognition is cited. Section 3 presented an overview of the proposed system and detailed each step. The experiment setup and the results obtained are presented in Sect. 4. In Sect. 5, we concluded the paper.

2 Related Work

Several algorithms of eyes localisation and tracking and gaze gesture recognition are proposed in the literature. Few of these works interested by the deployment of this modalities in mobile devices. In fact, the gaze gesture recognition comprises tow types: the movement of the pupils and the movement of eyelids and eyebrows like blink, wink, etc. In the both cases, two modules are indispensable before this step: eye detection and eye tracking.

We can divided the algorithms of eyes detection in appearance-based methods and feature-based methods.

The appearance-based methods use the intensity distribution of the eyes and it surrounding to detect the eyes. These methods require a large of training eye's images taken in different conditions and face orientation. To this end, many classifiers have been employed.

Pino and Kavasidis [2] presented a non-intrusive eye tracking system for mobile devices. From the front-facing camera of the device, the system aims to detect and track eyes and then provides and interaction way of communication for the device based on user's gaze. The eye's detection of this system is assured by Haar classifier based on Haar-like features.

Vaitukaitis and Bulling [3] proposed an eye gesture-based system for mobile devices. Their system aims to control the hand-held devices through eyes gesture captured from the camera of the device. The eye detector is based on Viola and Jones algorithm [4].

These methods have a high accuracy in eyes detection and they are computational speed, however they have many limits in the variation of pose and illumination conditions.

The feature-based methods extracts the characteristics of the eyes like shape, color, symmetry, etc. in the purpose of determination the eyes' features.

Miluzzo et al. [5] proposed a human-phone interaction system based on eyes tracking and blink detection to control mobile application. Eyes detection is assured by the determination of eyes contours in consecutive frames.

Wood and Bulling [6] proposed a model-based approach for binocular gaze estimation designed for unmodified tablet: EyeTab. This system based on real-time gaze estimation algorithms that can detect gaze direction and estimate the point of regard on the screen using eye rough and limbal ellipse fitting to estimate the gaze.

Skodras and Fakotakis [7], proposed an eye system based on the color information that derives a novel eye map. This map enhances the iris area and a radial symmetry transform. The experiment results proved the robustness of this approach mainly in the difficult cases where there is many variation in the pose and lightness conditions.

Although these methods achieved a high accuracy, they required a high resolution image and they are high computational demanding.

For the eye tracking, several algorithms are used in the previous works, such as template-matching [3,5] and CamSHIFT [2].

Only few work developed an eye gesture recognition system for mobile device. Vaitukaitis and Bulling [3] analysed a sequence of eyes gesture using template matching. An initialization step is necessary in the evaluation for each user. The authors consider the eye gestures as the movement of the eyelids and the motion of pupils is precise directions. This system achieve an accuracy about 60 % when it is deployed on an android device.

Drewes et al. [8] studied the feasibility of using eyes gestures recognition system to interact with mobile devices. They proposed as well a sequence of eye gesture as a mode of communication.

3   Proposed System

The architecture of our proposed system is composed by many modules that each one is responsible for executing a specific function like shows Fig. 1.

- The principal input of this system is a real-time video capturing from the front-facing camera. Each frame captured is converted to gray scale to be processed by the next modules.
- A face and eyes detectors are on charge of localizing the face of the user and their eyes. Once the eyes are detected, a pupils detector searches and localizes the pupils.
- A tracking module tracks the pupils and extracts their positions that a classification module recognize the gaze gestures.

3.1   Face and Pupils Detection

In the first step, our proposed system aims to detect the user's face. This step is carried out using the face detector proposed by Viola and Jones [4] applied on

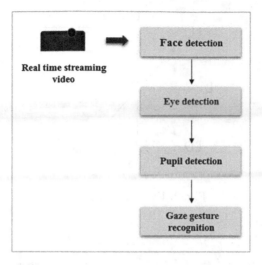

Fig. 1. System overview

the input image. This detector based on boosted cascade classifiers and Haar-like features, is known in the literature as a reference in the face detection field thanks to its robustness and its rapid response time. These two reasons facilitate the deployment of this algorithm in mobile devices and in real-time context. Once the face is detected, an eye detector is launching in the purpose of the detection of the two eyes. The region of interest is the image of the detected face using the same algorithm of the face detector. The eye detector provides an image of the eyes region that is composed by the pupils, iris, sclera, eyelid and all the zone around it. A pupil detector is launched lo localize the eye's center. In fact, the pupil is the darkest circle in the eye. Once the pupil is detected, a tracking module based on template-matching is launched to track the eyes and the pupils [9].

3.2 Eye Gesture Recognition

Once the pupils are detected and the tracking module tracks the pupils positions a recognition module is charged to classify the eye-gaze gesture. We proposed to recognize the motion of the eyes in one direction: *right, right up, up, up left, left, left down, down* and *down right* like shows Fig. 2, because these motions are simple and does not tired the eyes. However, the determination of these gestures is ambiguous and cannot be distinguished with high precision. There is not a precise limit that can separates *right* from *right up* for example. To cope with this issue, we proposed a fuzzy-based recognition module that aims to classify the eye-gaze gestures from the pupils positions.

Fuzzy Inference System. Fuzzy logic introduced by Zadeh [10], is considering as a revolutionary tool in the artificial intelligence. It is inspiring from vagueness

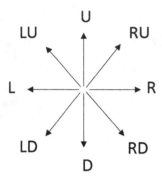

Fig. 2. Eye gaze gestures

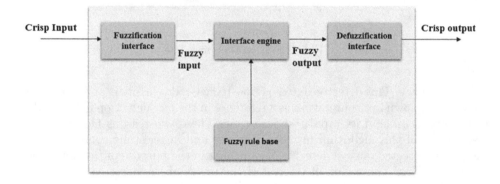

Fig. 3. Standard fuzzy inference system

in our daily life to provide approximated means for complex systems that is difficult to be represented with precise mathematical statements. Fuzzy systems can be helpful for resolving classification problems applied on several fields like control systems, robotics, etc.

Figure 3 presents the architecture of a common fuzzy system. The fuzzification interface is responsible of the conversion of the crisp values of inputs variable to fuzzy inputs. The fuzzy rule base contains all the inference rules that match the linguistic variables input (fuzzy inputs) to linguistic values outputs (fuzzy outputs). The interface engine search the correspondent rule for the current input and apply it to have the fuzzy output. Finally, the defuzzification interface gives the crisp output from the fuzzy output.

To determine the eye-gaze motion, our system receives for each frame the position of the pupils. The coordinates of the 2 consecutive frames give us informations about the direction of the pupils. The system computes the difference between two positions of the pupils in two consecutive frames. d_x and d_y are the distance between 2 points P_1 and P_2 in the x and y axis respectively like show the Eqs. 1 and 2.

$$d_x = P_2(x) - P_1(x) \tag{1}$$

$$d_y = P_2(y) - P_1(y) \tag{2}$$

The values of d_x and d_y may have a positive, negative or zero value. As it is a little bit difficult for a human to move it eyes in specific direction with high precision, we define threshold values $Val_{Thresold}$ for each d_x and d_y to take in consideration the eye movement. The following pseudo code details this step.

```
if ( dx > ValThresold) then
|   dx ← POSITIVE
else
    if ( dx < −ValThresold) then
    |   dx ← NEGATIVE
    else
    |   dx ← ZERO
    end
end
```

The fuzzy-based recognition module classify the eye-gaze gestures by applying the following fuzzy rules.

- Rule 1: if d_x is POSITIVE and d_y is ZERO then Gesture is RIGHT
- Rule 2: if d_x is POSITIVE and d_y is POSITIVE then Gesture is RIGHT UP
- Rule 3: if d_x is ZERO and d_y is POSITIVE then Gesture is UP
- Rule 4: if d_x is NEGATIVE and d_y is POSITIVE then Gesture is LEFT UP
- Rule 5: if d_x is NEGATIVE and d_y is ZERO then Gesture is LEFT
- Rule 6: if d_x is NEGATIVE and d_y is NEGATIVE then Gesture is LEFT DOWN
- Rule 7: if d_x is ZERO and d_y is NEGATIVE then Gesture is DOWN
- Rule 8: if d_x is POSITIVE and d_y is NEGATIVE then Gesture is RIGHT DOWN

Figures 4, 5 and 6 show the fuzzification of the linguistic variables: d_x, d_y and Gesture.

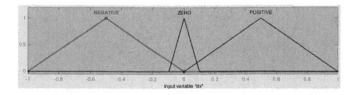

Fig. 4. Fuzzification of the linguistic variable d_x

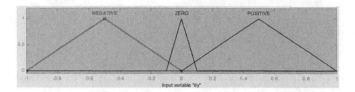

Fig. 5. Fuzzification of the linguistic variable d_y

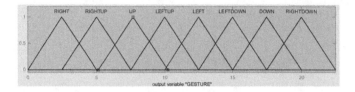

Fig. 6. Fuzzification of the linguistic variables gestures

4   Experiment Result

For validation of the proposed system, we deployed the proposed system on an android-based tablet with NVIDIA Tegra 3 Quad-Core, 32 Go of RAM and front-facing camera with 2 Mega pixels resolution. Two library have been used to assure the image processing and fuzzy system modules that they are respectively OpenCV [11] and FuzzyLite libraries [12]. We conducted a study on 8 volunteers aged between 25 and 31 years. They are never used before any system based on eyes gesture modality. We asked each of them to take the tablet in a distance between 25 cm and 40 cm to be sure that all the face is captured correctly by the camera. Then, we demand from each participant to move their eyes in the 8 directions.

During this evaluation step, we compute the sensitivity, the false positive rate and the accuracy based on the following equations:

$$Sensitivity = \frac{TP}{TP + FN} \tag{3}$$

$$FPR = \frac{FP}{FP + TN} \tag{4}$$

$$Accuracy = \frac{TP + TN}{TP + FP + FN + TN} \tag{5}$$

Where TP is the true positive, TN is the true negative, FN is the false negative and FP is the false positive. These values are counted like follow:

- A TP was counted if a correct gesture was detected.
- A FN was counted if none or an incorrect gesture was recognised.
- A FP was counted in the case of a gesture recognition but in reality no gesture.

– A TN is counted if non gesture is detected when we asked the user to not move his eyes.

The result of this experimental and a comparison with the most closed work are presented in the following table.

	Sensitivity [%]	FPR [%]	Accuracy [%]
Our system	85	27	76.53
[3]	28.3	17.6	60.0

This test proves that our system has promising results comparing to other works; we obtain 76.53 % of accuracy while [3] achieved 60 %. We note that the recognition rate of some gestures like down lower than the other gestures. In fact, this difference is due to the confusion with the closed eyes when the user looks down.

In the other hand, we tested system measurement based on the computation of RAM and CPU consumption and number of frame per second. In the next table, we present each of these measures.

	CPU	RAM	FPS
Our system	40 %	90 %	24
[5]	65.4	56.51	-

Our proposed system consumes 40 % CPU and 90 % RAM. Comparing to [5], we found that our system required high memory but less CPU. However, this system can be running be achieving 24 FPS. This value proved that our system can run is real-time conditions in contrary of others similar system [3, 7] which achieved a FPS number less than 15.

5   Conclusion

In this paper, we presented a new system of eye-gaze gesture recognition for mobile devices. This system based on the real-time video streaming captured from the front facing camera without any additional equipment. Several modules are responsible of the face and eyes detection. A eye-gaze recognition system based on fuzzy inference system is developed to classify eye gestures based on the pupils coordinates. This algorithm is running entirely on an android tablet, that we asked 8 participants to test it. The experiments proved that our system achieved promising and competitive results.

Acknowledgments. The authors would like to acknowledge the financial support of this work by grants from General Direction of Scientific Research - (DGRST), Tunisia, under the ARUB program. The research and innovation are performed in the framework of a thesis MOBIDOC financed by the EU under the program PASRI.

References

1. Bulling, A., Gellersen, H.: Toward mobile eye-based human-computer interaction. IEEE Pervasive Comput. **9**, 8–12 (2010)
2. Pino, C., Kavasidis, I.: Improving mobile device interaction by eye tracking analysis. In: Federated Conference on Computer Science and Information Systems, pp. 1199–1202, Wroclaw (2012)
3. Vaitukaitis, V., Bulling, A.: Eye gesture recognition on portable devices. In: Proceedings of ACM Conference on Ubiquitous Computing, pp. 711–714, United States (2012)
4. Viola, P., Jones, M.J.: Robust real-time face detection. Int. J. Comput. Vis. **57**, 137–154 (2004)
5. Miluzzo, E., Wang, T., Campbell, A.T.: EyePhone: activating mobile phones with your eyes. In: Proceedings of the Second ACM SIGCOMM Workshop on Networking, Systems, and Applications on Mobile Handhelds, pp. 15–20, India (2010)
6. Wood, E., Bulling, A.: EyeTab: model-based gaze estimation on unmodified tablet computers. In: Proceedings of the Symposium on Eye Tracking Research and Applications, pp. 207–210, USA (2014)
7. Skodras, E., Fakotakis, N.: Precise localization of eye centers in low resolution color images. J. Image Vis. Comput. **36**, 51–60 (2015)
8. Drewes, H., De Luca, A., Schmidt, A.: Eye-Gaze interaction for mobile phones. In: International Conference on Mobile Technology, Applications and Systems, pp. 364–371, Singapore (2007)
9. Elleuch, H., Wali, A., Alimi, A.M.: Smart tablet monitoring by a real-time head movement, eye gestures recognition system. In: International Conference on Future Internet of Things and Cloud, pp. 393–398, Spain (2014)
10. Zadeh, L.A.: Fuzzy sets. Inf. Control **8**(3), 338–353 (1965)
11. OpenCV library. http://opencv.org/platforms/android.html
12. FuzzyLite. http://www.fuzzylite.com/

Spatially Varying Weighting Function-Based Global and Local Statistical Active Contours. Application to X-Ray Images

Aicha Baya Goumeidane[1]([✉]) and Nafaa Nacereddine[1,2]

[1] Research Center in Industrial Technologies CRTI ex-CSC,
P.O.Box 64, 16014 Algiers, Algeria
{a.goumeidane,n.nacereddine}@crti.dz, ab_goumeidane@yahoo.fr
[2] Lab. des Math. et leurs Interactions, Centre Universitaire de Mila, Mila, Algeria

Abstract. Image segmentation is a crucial task in the image processing field. This paper presents a new region-based active contour which handles global information as well as local one, both based on the pixels intensities. The trade-off between these information is achieved by a spatially varying function computed for each contour node location. The application preliminary results of this method on computed tomography and X-ray images show outstanding and efficient object extraction.

Keywords: Image segmentation · Active contour · Averaged Shifted Histogram · Pressure forces · Statistics · Spatially varying function

1 Introduction

Image segmentation is a fundamental problem in the fields of computer vision, image processing and pattern recognition. It is the crucial task aiming at separating the domain of interest from the background to change the representation of the image into something that is more meaningful and easier to analyze by the next higher analysis stages. Hence, its outcomes have indisputably a direct effect on the analysis issue. For delicate applications such as processing radiographic images in both fields of industry and medicine, an accurate segmentation is more than ever required, since a bad interpretation or a false diagnosis lead, sometimes, to irreparable harm to the human patient and the industrial plant in question [1]. In the applications which involve X-ray images, the distinction of the region of interest structure is complicated by inherent noise, artifacts and intensity inhomogeneity. Image segmentations in such cases is not easy for numerous reasons: Firstly, partitioning the image into non overlapping regions and extracting regions of interest require a tradeoff between the computational efficiency of the involved algorithm, its degree of automation and the accuracy of its outcomes. Secondly, image noise, intensity inhomogeneity linked to the image acquisition, and poor contrast are very difficult to reckon with in segmentation algorithms without the user interacting [2]. Due to the causes previously evoked, designing a

© Springer International Publishing AG 2016
J. Blanc-Talon et al. (Eds.): ACIVS 2016, LNCS 10016, pp. 181–192, 2016.
DOI: 10.1007/978-3-319-48680-2_17

robust and efficient segmentation method is still a difficult problem in practical applications. To overcome these difficulties, segmentation with deformable models or active contours seems to be quite suitable to extract complex structures with complex texture, inhomogeneity and complex shapes. The most important reason for this is the fact that the active contours can incorporate global and local view of image segmentation by assessing continuity and curvature combined with the local edge strength and/or the region information [3]. Furthermore, by considering the boundary as a whole, a structure is imposed to the solution. As a result, the overall structure shape to be extracted is recovered by means of one smooth curve located as close as possible to the real boundary. Moreover, such boundary description can be readily used by subsequent applications [3]. Since they were proposed, active contours have gained researchers interest and have been widely applied in the computer vision field with promising results. The central idea of active contour models is to evolve a curve under some constraints from a given image to detect the desired objects. Based on the nature of constraints and image features, the existing active contour models can be roughly categorized into two classes: edge-driven and region-driven. Edge-driven are called so because the information used to drive the curves to the edges is strictly along the boundaries. Edge-driven models show satisfactory results when segmenting images with distinct edges. Nevertheless, these models are sensitive to noise and initial conditions and sometimes are with severe boundary leakage problems. With the region-driven ones [4], the inner and the outer region defined by the model are considered, making this model class well-adapted to situations for which it is difficult to extract boundaries from the target and is less sensitive to noise and to the initial position of the curve.

The present paper deals with object extraction from images by means of a region-based active contour that uses global and local statistical pressures forces controlled by an adaptive weighting function. The remainder of the paper is organized as follows: In Sect. 2, we introduce the mathematical foundation of active contours. In Sect. 3, we present our method for object extraction. Section 4 is dedicated to experimental results. We draw the main conclusions in Sect. 5.

2   Background

2.1   Active Contours

The active contour models for image segmentation, known as snakes, are characterized by a curve $\mathbf{c}(s) = [x(s), y(s)]', s = [0\ 1]$ which evolves towards certain image features under forces to minimize the energy [5]

$$E(\mathbf{c}) = \int_0^1 (E^{int}(\mathbf{c}(s)) + E^{ext}(\mathbf{c}(s)))ds \tag{1}$$

where s is the curvilinear abscissa, E^{int} the internal energy of the contour which maintains a certain degree of smoothness and controls the snake nodes spacing along the contour and E^{ext} the image energy responsible for driving the contour toward edges and computed from the image data. The minimization of Eq. (1) leads to an iterative solution that governs the model evolution as given in [5].

$$\begin{cases} x_t = (A + \gamma I_d)^{-1}(\gamma x_{t-1} + \nabla E_x^{ext}(x_{t-1}, y_{t-1})) \\ y_t = (A + \gamma I_d)^{-1}(\gamma y_{t-1} + \nabla E_y^{ext}(x_{t-1}, y_{t-1})) \end{cases} \qquad (2)$$

If the model is made of N nodes, then, A is a $N * N$ matrix, I_d an identity matrix sized as A, γ an evolution coefficient, x_t and y_t are the model nodes coordinates at the iteration t. $\nabla E_x^{ext}(x_t, y_t)$ and $\nabla E_y^{ext}(x_t, y_t)$ are the external forces of the input image at the model nodes locations in the x and y direction respectively.

2.2 External Forces

In addition to the standard external force proposed in [5], a variety of external forces have been proposed to improve the performance of snakes. The external forces can be generally classified as dynamic forces and static forces [6]. The dynamic forces are those that depend on the snake and, as a result, change as the snake deforms. In turn, the static forces are those that are calculated from the image only, and remain unchanged as the snake deforms [6]. The pressure force given in Eq. (3) also called the balloon force [7] which is a useful dynamic force, is the inflation/deflation force that pushes the curve outward or inward. By introducing a pressure weight k for individual nodes as in [2,4,8–10], the model, regarding to the initialization issue, is strengthened since it can inflate and deflate independently and at the same time. The pressure force may be released to various forms. Indeed, diverse region information can be used to modulate the pressure weight and sign, so that the contour part shrinks when placed outside the object of interest and expands when placed inside.

$$F_B(\mathbf{c}(s^*)) = k.\mathbf{n}(\mathbf{c}(s^*)) \qquad (3)$$

$\mathbf{n}(\mathbf{c}(s^*))$ is the normal unit vector to the curve at $\mathbf{c}(s^*)$ and k the pressure weight. An example of this individual pressure weight is proposed in [11], where k was introduced as

$$k = p(z_{s^*}/O) - p(z_{s^*}/B) \qquad (4)$$

where z_{s^*} is the gray value of the pixel falling on the snake node $\mathbf{c}(s^*)$, whereas $p(z_{s^*}/O)$ and $p(z_{s^*}/B)$ are, respectively, the conditional probability density functions of the object (O) and the background (B). The model does not make assumptions on the probability density function (pdf) of the object features. The problem is reduced, then, to an accurate estimation of the pdf of both object and background pixels gray-values, particularly in the case of non-simple gray-levels distributions [11].

3   The Proposed Model

Region-driven active contours can get more robust and global segmentation results when using global information, but mostly the object is distinguished by local variations. Thus, a compromise between global and local features is needed [12]. Furthermore, in image segmentation, both of object boundaries and fine structures can be detected accurately by incorporating the local neighbor region information. Meanwhile, to lessen the impact of noise and the possibility of getting stuck in local minima, the global region information plays an important role and particularly decreases the sensitivity to the contour initialization [10]. In this work, the averaged shifted histogram (ASH) method is used to model the gray levels *pdf* inside and outside the model curve and is exploited as global region information. Moreover, the local information is also taken into consideration to refine detection accuracy, however in a novel way. In fact, we combine, here, the advantages of global and local information where the contour evolution is held by these two kinds of information. On one hand, the global intensity allows the model expansion while incorporating global image information which improves the model robustness against noise and initial position. On the other hand, the local intensity information which is dominant near boundaries because of its sensitivity to the region transition, is integrated to operate near the object boundaries and then attract the model to them.

3.1   Progressing the Model Curve

To exploit the Bayesian weight of Eq. (4), one should have a good estimation of the *pdf* of the image data model. The simplest way to estimate the *pdf* of the pixels gray levels, is to compute the intensity histogram of the image, which is the tonal distribution in a digital image. Indeed, it shows the appearance frequency of gray levels and when normalized, it can roughly assess the density function of the gray-values. In fact, the histogram is a classical nonparametric density estimator probably dating back to the seventeenth century [13]. Nowadays, histogram remains an important statistical tool for summarizing data. Computing an image histogram is a trivial operation, but results for noisy images could be unusable for density estimation without some processing. Smooth versions of histogram have been proposed in the literature. Among them, we can cite the averaged shifted histogram ASH, which has been employed in the scope of *pdf* estimation to drive the active contour to the boundaries in [14]. Indeed, ASH has desirable properties and numerous advantages as we will see later.

Averaged Shifted Histogram ASH. The averaged shifted histogram [15] is a nonparametric probability density estimator derived from a collection of histograms. The ASH enjoys several advantages compared to a single histogram and a more complex non-parametric histogram-based *pdf* estimators like kernels estimators. As advantages, we can cite better visual interpretation, better approximation, and nearly the same computational efficiency in regards to the former [15,16] and computation speed and the same efficiency compared to the latter.

Indeed, the *ASH* provides a bridge between the histogram and advanced kernel methods, which are more computationally intensive. *ASH* method combines a set of m histograms generated with a certain shift into the bin borders [16]. It can be shown that when the number of histograms tends to infinity, the *ASH* approximates the kernel estimator [15]. In practice, *ASH* is implemented by generating an histogram with smaller bin width, and computing the discrete convolution with a triangular window. If $X_1, \ldots, X_n$ are samples of random variables with density f, the *pdf* estimation, with m histograms, of all samples X being in the finer interval B_k, using the *ASH* gives

$$\hat{f}(X)_{ASH} = \frac{1}{n.h} \sum_{i=1-m}^{m-1} \left(1 - \frac{|i|}{m}\right) v_{k+i} \qquad \forall x \in B_k \qquad (5)$$

where h, n and v_k are, respectively, the bin width of the averaged histograms, the total number of samples and the number of observations falling in the sub-bin B_k. *ASH* strongly depends on the band width h. If we suppose that the underlying density is Gaussian, then, it can be shown that an optimal choice for h is [13]

$$h_{opt} = 3.5\hat{\sigma}.n^{-1/3} \qquad (6)$$

where $\hat{\sigma}$ is a standard deviation estimate.

Therefore, the global force is a pressure one, whose weight is called here k_{Global} and computed using Eq. (4) where the *pdf* is determined with the *ASH* method.

Deviation from the Central Pixel Gray-Level. By adding another pressure force to make the contour model progress, also, regarding to the local properties of the image, the contour can detect significant changes in the local neighborhood of the overall model nodes, like region transitions. Let call k_{Local} this new pressure force weight which is computed as the central pixel gray level deviation from the pixels gray levels within a circular window centered at the current model node. As shown in Fig. 1, this window and the model curve, split jointly, the local neighborhood of the model node into local interior and local exterior.

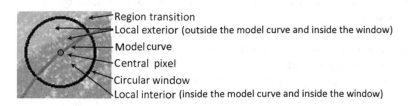

Fig. 1. Local window

k_{Local} is the deviation from the central pixel gray level and is computed as

$$k_{Local} = \sqrt{\sum_{i=1}^{N^{in}} \tau(c(s^*)), x_i^{in})(z_{s^*} - z_{x_i^{in}})^2} - \sqrt{\sum_{j=1}^{N^{out}} \tau(c(s^*)), x_j^{out})(z_{s^*} - z_{x_j^{out}})^2}$$

(7)

where $c(s^*)$ is the center of the circular neighborhood, $z_{x^{in}}$ the gray level of the ith pixel x_i^{in} in the interior local neighborhood, $z_{x_j^{out}}$ the gray level of the jth pixel x_j^{out} in the exterior local neighborhood. N^{in} (N^{out}) is the pixels number in the local interior (local exterior). We call τ a weighting function related to the distance between the central pixel and the other ones in the circular window, so that the sum of the weights in the interior/exterior local neighborhood equals to one '1'. τ can be chosen as a gaussian kernel function as done in [3], for example, to handel inhomogeneities. The values of k_{Local} are normalized so that they belong to $[-1\ 1]$. When a snake node is in a homogeneous local region, this weight moves towards zero since the intensities are quite similar and then global information only controls the model progression for this node. However, when the node is near a region boundary as in Fig. 1 where the local interior is homogeneous and the local exterior is not, the first term of Eq. (7) tends to zero whereas the second term does not. This produces a negative weight and the model will expand at this node location (positive normal vectors point inward by convention here). The iterative evolution equation of the model is given by

$$\begin{cases} x_t = (A + \gamma I_d)^{-1}(\gamma x_{t-1} + [\omega k_{Local} + (1 - \omega)k_{Global}]N_x) \\ y_t = (A + \gamma I_d)^{-1}(\gamma y_{t-1} + [\omega k_{Local} + (1 - \omega)k_{Global}]N_y) \end{cases}$$

(8)

where N_x and N_y are, respectively, the normal unit vector components in the x and the y direction and ω the spatially adaptive trade-off function between the local and global force.

The Spatially Varying Function ω. The global and the local pressures forces, in this work, are encouraged to be complementary rather than competitive. So, the ω function is designed to remove the two forces competition. When the model is far away from object boundaries, the global forces should have the decisive effect on the contour evolution. Furthermore, near the boundaries, the evolution should be taken over by the local forces. The choice of ω is done by the following observation: when a local neighborhood of a node is made up of a homogeneous part or a part with a slightly variable intensity between the local interior and the local exterior, then, this neighborhood is very likely within the object or within the background. Moreover, when the intensity vary too much between the mentioned local neighborhoods, then the latter is probably in a transition region. This can be supported by Fig. 2. If μ_{loc}^{in} and μ_{loc}^{out} ($\sigma_{loc}^{in}, \sigma_{loc}^{out}$) are the mean (the standard deviation) of the local interior and the local exterior, respectively, then, ω is empirically computed for each node as

$$\omega = 1 \text{ if } |\mu_{loc}^{in} - \mu_{loc}^{out}| > \sigma_{loc}^{in} + \sigma_{loc}^{out}, \qquad \omega = 0 \text{ otherwise}$$

(9)

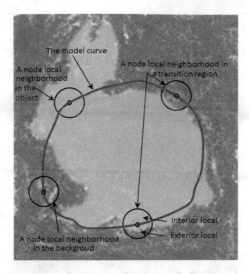

Fig. 2. Local neighborhoods centered at different nodes of the snake model

4   Experiments

In the proposed active contour model, the *pdf* estimation is of a major importance. Usually, kernels-based estimators are employed in the scope of deformable
models evolution using a non-parametric *pdf* estimation. As the global statistical pressure forces computed by the mean of *pdf* estimation, have in charge the
model expansion, we begin our experiments by showing an example of an image
histogram and estimated *pdfs* using the *ASH* and the kernels-based (Parzen
window) methods. Figure 3 shows an X-ray image of a crater crack, while are
depicted in Fig. 4 its histogram, its *ASH* and kernels-based *pdfs* estimations. We
can note that the various histogram modes, for the *ASH*-based estimation, are
quite visible, whereas they are over smoothed for the kernels-based one. However,
to make the latter better in terms of histogram fitting, the kernel bandwidth h
[17] should be refined accordingly, instead of computing it just by the rule of
thumb [18]. Consequently, a supplementary running-time will be required.

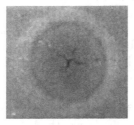

Fig. 3. X-ray image of a crater crack

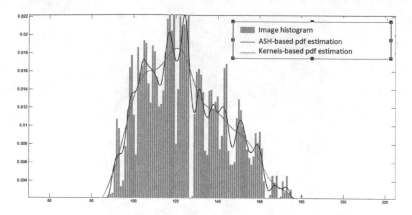

Fig. 4. Histogram, ASH and Kernels-based *pdf* estimations

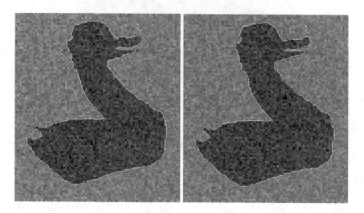

Fig. 5. *ASH* (left) and kernels-based (right) active contours results beginning from the same initialization

We continue these tests by using global pressure forces alone to drive the active contour model in a synthetic image, illustrated in Fig. 5, to show the results of the *ASH* and kernels-based active contours in terms of object segmentation and progression time. Since the segmentation accuracy, in the presented method, is achieved by the local forces, these preliminary results ascertain the opportunity to use *ASH*-based *pdf* estimation in order to speed up the contour progression in comparison to kernels-based *pdf* estimation. Indeed, the running time takes 3.5 s for the *ASH*-based active contour instead of 9 s for the kernels-based one. This shows that the *ASH* method could be a good alternative for histogram-based *pdf* estimation for active contours instead of more sophisticated and time-consuming methods.

In the next experiments, we show the active contour progression with only the local forces. Far from the boundaries, the local forces based model does not progress, since local forces can operate, as explained before, exclusively at the

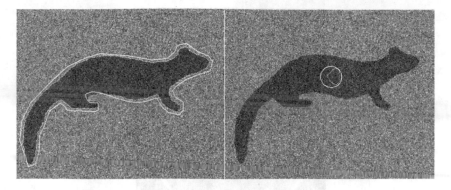

Fig. 6. Left: Initialization near the boundaries (solid line) and the local forces-based model final contour (in dashed line). Right: Initialization far from the boundaries (solid line) and the local forces-based model final contour (in dashed line).

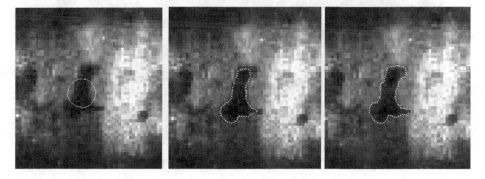

Fig. 7. From Left to right: Initialization, final contour without local forces, and final contour of the proposed model.

model nodes neighborhood. Whereas, when placed near the boundaries, these forces could push the model curve to them as shown by the Fig. 6. For this example, the neighborhood is chosen to have a radius of 3.

The following tests are carried out on real X-ray-based images. The image shown in Fig. 7 represents a region of interest (ROI) of X-ray image of a welded joint subjected to segmentation. In this case, the task is to extract the weld defect indications from the ROI. In this example, the opportunity of using local forces is highlighted. Indeed, when the model is faced to blurred edges, local forces bring more precision to the weld defect extraction as shown by this figure. Furthermore, leakage problems could happen when edges are weak or in presence of inhomogeneities when using only global information, as shown in Fig. 8, which represents a brain computed tomography (CT) image. In this case, the challenge is to exact, as accurately as possible, the shape of the lesion from healthy tissues, for surgery purpose, for example, which is successfully done with our model.

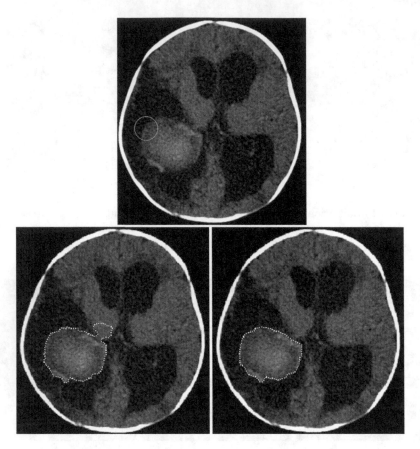

Fig. 8. Contour initialization in the top. Down:(left) Final contour without local forces with a leakage problem, (right) Final contour of the proposed model.

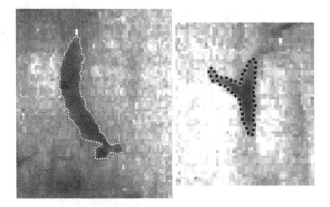

Fig. 9. Final contours of the proposed model on two radiographic images.

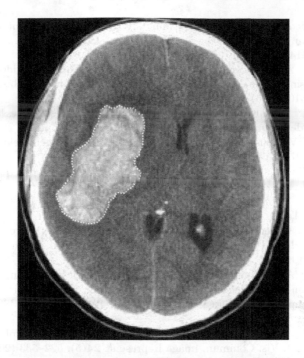

Fig. 10. Final contour on a computed tomography brain image.

To finish this section, we give some other results of applying the proposed active contour on weld X-ray and CT images shown in Figs. 9 and 10. It is to note that the local window radii for X-ray images and for CT images have been empirically chosen equal to 5 and 20, respectively.

5   Conclusion

In the present paper, we have proposed a method to extract objects from X-ray images based on local and global information and a spatially varying trade-off function that removes the competition between them. Results seem to be very promising since the model avoids leakage problem, when the boundaries are weak, and performs better segmentation than a model based on global information used alone.

References

1. Nacereddine, N., Ziou, D.: Asymmetric generalized Gaussian mixtures for radiographic image segmentation. In: Burduk, R., Jackowski, K., Kurzyński, M., Woźniak, M., Żołnierek, A. (eds.) Proceedings of the 9th International Conference on Computer Recognition Systems CORES 2015. AISC, vol. 403, pp. 521–532. Springer, Heidelberg (2016). doi:10.1007/978-3-319-26227-7_49

2. Akram, F., Jeong, H.K., Lim, H.U., Nam, C.K.: Segmentation of intensity inhomogeneous brain MR images using active contourss. Comput. Math. Methods Med., pp. 1–14 (2014)
3. Goumeidane, A.B., Nacereddine, N., Kahamdja, M.: Computer aided weld defect delination using active contours in radiographic inspection. J. X-Ray Sci. Technol. 23(3), 289–310 (2015)
4. Goumeidane, A.B., Khamadja, M., Naceredine, N.: Bayesian pressure snake for weld defect detection. In: Blanc-Talon, J., Philips, W., Popescu, D., Scheunders, P. (eds.) ACIVS 2009. LNCS, vol. 5807, pp. 309–319. Springer, Heidelberg (2009). doi:10.1007/978-3-642-04697-1_29
5. Kass, M., Witkin, A., Terzopoulos, A.D.: Snakes: active contour models. Int. J. Comput. Vis. 1, 321–331 (1988)
6. Li, B., Acton, S.T.: Automatic active model initialization via Poisson inverse gradient. IEEE Trans. Image Process. 17(8), 1406–1420 (2008)
7. Cohen, L.D., Cohen, I.: Finite-element methods for active contour models and balloons for 2D and 3D images. IEEE Trans. Pattern Anal. Mach. Intell. 15(11), 1131–1147 (1993)
8. Goumeidane, A.B., Khamadja, M., Odet, C.: Parametric active contour for boundary estimation of weld defects in radiographic testing. In: Proceedings of the International Symposium on Signal Processing and Its Application ISSPA, pp. 1–4 (2007)
9. Li, D., Li, W., Liao, Q.: Active contours driven by local and global probability distributions. J. Vis. Commun. Image Represent. 24(5), 522–533 (2013)
10. Wang, H., Huang, T.Z.: An adaptive weighting parameter estimation between local and global intensity fitting energy for image segmentation. Commun. Nonlinear Sci. Numer. Simul. 19, 3098–3105 (2014)
11. Abd-Almageed, W., Ramadan, S., Smith, C.E.: Kernel snakes: non-parametric active contour models. In: IEEE International Conference on Systems, Man and Cybernetics, Washington, pp. 1131–1147 (2003)
12. Liu, W., Shang, Y., Yang, X.: Active contour model driven by local histogram fitting energy. Pattern Recogn. Lett. 34, 655–662 (2013)
13. Scott, D.W.: On optimal and data-based histograms. Biometrika 66, 605–610 (1979)
14. Goumeidane, A.B., Boukahel, L., Djen Salah, I.: Histogram-based CT Brain Lesions Image segmentation using active contours. In: 2015 4th International Conference on Electrical Engineering (ICEE), pp. 1–5 (2015)
15. Scott, D.W.: Averaged shifted histogram: effective non parametric density estimators in several dimensions. Ann. Statist. 13(3), 1024–1040 (1985)
16. Bourel, M., Fraiman, R., Ghattas, B.: Random average shifted histogram. Comput. Stat. Data Anal. 79, 149–164 (2014)
17. Parzen, E.: On the estimation of a probability density function and the mode. Ann. Math. Stat. 33, 1065–1076 (1962)
18. Silverman, B.W.: Density Estimation for Statistics and Data Analysis. Monographs on Statistics and Applied Probability, vol. 26. Chapman and Hall, London (1986)

Vegetation Segmentation in Cornfield Images Using Bag of Words

Yerania Campos[1]([⊠]), Erik Rodner[2], Joachim Denzler[2], Humberto Sossa[3], and Gonzalo Pajares[1]

[1] Department of Software Engineering and Artificial Intelligence, Faculty of Informatics, Complutense University, 28040 Madrid, Spain
yeraniac@ucm.es
[2] Computer Vision Group, Friedrich Schiller University Jena, 07743 Jena, Germany
[3] Instituto Politécnico Nacional-CIC, Av. Juan de Dios Batis, S/N, Col. Nva. Industrial Vallejo, 07738 Mexico D.F., Mexico

Abstract. We provide an alternative methodology for vegetation segmentation in cornfield images. The process includes two main steps, which makes the main contribution of this approach: (a) a low-level segmentation and (b) a class label assignment using Bag of Words (BoW) representation in conjunction with a supervised learning framework. The experimental results show our proposal is adequate to extract green plants in images of maize fields. The accuracy for classification is 95.3 % which is comparable to values in current literature.

Keywords: Bag-of-Words · Machine learning · Colour Vegetation Indices · Green detection

1 Introduction

Advances in electronics, artificial intelligence, machine vision and other technologies have been integrated in the design and development of autonomous agricultural vehicles (AAV). Vehicles are equipped with vision-based sensors, which provide all the data needed to develop activities of localization, mapping, path planning and obstacle avoidance. In a AAV, segmentation of vegetation is a critical step towards the development of different activities in the crop field such as counting plants, detecting weeds, or nutrient application. Segmentation is usually performed from images acquired by the vision system and must therefore be considered in the design of agricultural vehicles. In short, a good algorithm to split an image into foreground (maize/plants) and background (soil) is highly demanded to improve the performance of the activities carried out by the AAV.

In this paper, we provide a method for vegetation segmentation in agricultural images (AI). The procedure includes a low level segmentation process to get regions of interest (ROIs), these are subsequently evaluated using a classifier model to determine which ROIs are vegetation. Additionally, we provide a dataset composed of maize field images and their corresponding labelled images

© Springer International Publishing AG 2016
J. Blanc-Talon et al. (Eds.): ACIVS 2016, LNCS 10016, pp. 193–204, 2016.
DOI: 10.1007/978-3-319-48680-2_18

Table 1. The current state-of-the-art in vegetation detection for agricultural applications.

Reference	Application	Methodology	Performance/Remarks
*Haug et al. [4]	Plant classification crop/weed in carrot farm images.	Segmentation of vegetation from soil is obtained from NDVI. To discriminate between crops and weeds machine learning is applied.	Classification accuracy 93.8%.
Hlaing and Khaing [5]	Weed and crop segmentation and classification.	Segmentation is achieved combining ExG and area thresholding algorithms.	Error rate 33.3% for misclassified plants.
Tewari et al. [6]	Herbicide applicator for weed control.	The weed percentage in an image (total number of green pixels / size image) is computed to determine the herbicide amount.	Efficiency 90%
Choi et al. [7]	Line extraction in paddy fields.	Preocess includes: NIR imge, gray colour, median filter, Otsu and blob noise elimination.	Green segmentation is not evaluated.
*+Torres et al. [8]	Vegetation detection in herbaceous crops.	Automatic thresholding algorithm based on Otsus method, susceptible to segmentation shape and compactness.	Error< 10%
Yang [9]	Greenness identification in cornfield	Segmentation is achieved from Hue components in HSV colour space and ExG metric.	Accuracy 95%, sensible to change illumination
*Jiang et al. [10]	Crop row detection	Rows detection from binary image obtained from Gray$_1$ metric.	Crop row detection accuracy 93%.
Meng et al. [11]	System to Inter-row weeding in maize crop field.	H component (HIS colour space) is segmented considering Hue values in the range of [120,160]. From segmentation a scanning method is applied for crop lines detection.	Avg. error below 2.7 cm.
*Guijarro et al. [12]	Greenness segmentation.	Combining vegetation indices (greenness) and wavelets (texture).	Useful when the quality of imaging greenness is low. Precision 92.09%.
Ananthi el at. [13]	Segment incomplete nutrient-deficient crop images	Fuzzy C-means colour clustering	Accuracy over 90% in extraction of deficiency region.
*Kazmi et al. [14]	Thistle detection in sugar beet fields.	Detection based on CVI, Mahalanobis distance and Linear discriminant analysis (LDA).	Accuracy up to 97%.
*Kazmi et al. [15]	Weed detection sugar beet and creeping thistle images.	BoW scheme with KNN and SVM classifiers to analyze scanned leaf images.	Accuracy 99%.
Ye et al. [16]	Crop segmentation	Adoption of Markov random field to provide belief information from crop extraction.	92.29% accuracy, it support strong illumination changes.
Cheng et al. [17]	Rice and weed discrimination.	Harris corner detection and machine learning (decision tree).	Precision of 98.8% to distinguish weeds from rice plants.
Moorthy et al. [18]	Vegetation segmentation in sugar beet and maize plants.	Naive Bayesian model using features from RGB and HSV colour spaces.	Accuracy 87%.
Santos et al. [19]	3D plant modelling for plant phenotyping (stereo vision)	3D Point cloud segmented by spectral clustering.	Unsuccessful in corn plants.
Lonescu et al. [20]	Biomass type identification.	Texture features, local texton dissimilarity and BoW representation.	Accuracy 90%. Available for mobile devices.

* Otsu as threshold strategy.
+ Unmanned aerial vehicle (UAV). The normalized difference vegetation index (NDVI) value is obtained from a multi-spectral camera.

which were made by inspection and carefully hand painted. Images were captured with a single camera mounted on board a tractor, which is part of the fleet in the RHEA project [1].

This paper is organized as follow: Sect. 2 provides a revision of the state of the art, Sect. 3 explains our work, Sect. 4 shows the testing we conducted to prove its efficiency, and Sect. 5 gives the conclusions.

2   Literature Review

The first attempts to develop AAV were reported in the 1960s, new proposals have been introduced to increase the effectiveness of the navigation systems in agricultural vehicles [2,3]. This work is limited to dealing with outdoor scenes where vegetation segmentation is the first step within a complex process. In this context, Table 1 provides an overview of recent research, abbreviations in this table are defined in Table 2, they refer to the colour vegetation indices (CVIs).

3   Proposed Methodology

Bag of Words was initially introduced for text analysis [27] and subsequently adopted in applications of computer vision, where; a *visual word* is a sparse

Table 2. Colour channels and colour vegetation indices.

Abbreviation	Expression
Normalization	$R_n = R^*/(R^* + G^* + B^*)$, $G_n = G^*/(R^* + G^* + B^*)$, $B_n = B^*/(R^* + G^* + B^*)$, $R^* = R/max(R)$, $G^* = G/max(G)$, $B^* = B/max(B)$
Gray	$0.2898 * R_n + 0.5870 * G_n + 0.1140 * B_n$
Gray$_1$ [10]	$1.262 * G_n - 0.884 * R_n - 0.311 * B_n$
ExG [21]	$2 * G_n - R_n - B_n$
ExR [22]	$1.4 * R_n - G_n$
CIVE [23]	$0.441 R_n - 0.811 G_n + 0.385 B_n - 18.78$
ExGR [24]	$ExG - ExR$
NDI [25]	$(G_n - B_n)/(G_n + B_n)$
GB [21]	$G_n - B_n$
RBI [26]	$(R_n - B_n)/(R_n + B_n)$
ERI [26]	$(R_n - G_n) * (R_n - B_n)$
EGI [26]	$(G_n - R_n) * (G_n - B_n)$
EBI [26]	$(B_n - G_n) * (B_n - R_n)$
VEG	$G_n * R_n^a * B_n^{(a-1)}$

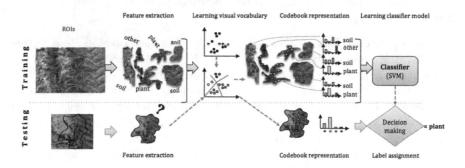

Fig. 1. Bag of Words scheme for agricultural images.

vector of occurrence counts of a *visual vocabulary* of local image features [14,20]. The process consists of two stages: training and testing, Fig. 1. On the first, a classifier model for three classes is built with features extracted from ROIs. The model is used to predict the label of a new ROI into the second stage. The three classes involved are; vegetation (v), soil (s) and one more identified as others (o). The last class includes elements that did not identify with the two predominant classes. The feature selection plays an important role in the performance of the classifier function [28]. Our work focuses on finding an appropriate set of features for vegetation characterization. Because of this, local and colour

Table 3. CVI descriptors proposed by Kazim et al. [15].

	Colour vegetation indices
CVI_2	ExG, GB
CVI_4	ExG, CIVE, GB, ERI
CVI_9	ExR, ExGR, NDI, GB, RBI, ERI, EGI, R_n, G_n
CVI_{14}	ExG, CIVE, ExR, ExGR, NDI, GB, RBI, ERI, EGI, EBI, R_n, G_n, B_n, Gray

descriptors were considered for analysis: SIFT [29], SURF [30], COM [31] and $CVI_{2,4,9,14}$ (Table 3).

3.1   Classification Model

Consider N-interest regions $R = \{R_1, ..., R_N\}$, where R_i has m-pixels, m is different in each region. Also, the labels associated to each region $L = \{l_1, ..., l_N\}, l_i \in \{v, s, o\}$ are given. R is split into two complementary sets: R_A and R_B ($R_A \cap R_B, \oslash$), $\mid R_A \mid = a$ and $\mid R_B \mid = b$. Similarly with L: L_A and L_B ($L_A \cap L_B, \oslash$), $\mid L_A \mid = a$ and $\mid L_B \mid = b$. R_A and L_A are used for training the model while R_B and L_B for parameter estimation.

Training Process. Input: R_A, L_A and the vocabulary size K. Output: classification function Ψ.

1. Feature extraction: Consider a region $R_i \in R_A$. For each pixel in R_i, a feature descriptor is computed: $F_i = F_i^1, ..., F_i^m$, $F_i^j \in \Re^z$. Repeat for all of the elements in R_A, getting as a result a set of descriptors: $F_A = \{F_1, ..., F_a\}$.
2. Visual vocabulary: Set F_A is used to train a clustering method to obtain K-centres [32]. Each centre represents a visual word. The set of K-visual words is the visual vocabulary: $W = \{w_1, ..., w_K\}$, $w_k \in \Re^z$. Also, from clustering, each descriptor in F has associated the label of the nearest centre, e.g., F_i is represented for $D_i = \{D_i^1, ..., D_i^m\}$, $D_i^j \in \{1, ..., K\}$. Then, the set of labels associated to F_A is $D_A = \{D_1, ..., D_a\}$.
3. Codebook: For each element in D_A, the frequency of each visual word is computed and the vector of counts is divided by the number of pixels in the ROI. The normalized vectors are the codebooks: $CB_A = \{H_1, ..., H_a\}$.
4. Classification function: CB_A and L_A are processed during the learning process to get Ψ. The decision function chosen for classification is the one provided by support vector machines (SVM) with parameter c which tells the SVM optimization how much misclassifying is allowed at each training [33].

Testing Process. Input: R_B, L_B, W and Ψ. Output: Performance model.

5. Feature extraction: Apply Step 1 to get descriptors in R_B: $F_B = \{F_1, ..., F_b\}$.
6. Visual words: At each descriptor in F_B is associated the label of the nearest cluster in W: $D_B = \{D_1, ..., D_b\}$.

Table 4. Statistical measures for performance evaluation [34]; n_{TP}, n_{TN}, n_{FP} and n_{FN} represent the number of true positives, true negatives, false positives and false negative respectively.

ID	Description	Expression
OSR	Overall success rate	$(n_{TP} + n_{TN})/(n_{TP} + n_{TN} + n_{FP} + n_{FN})$
TPR	True positive rate	$n_{TP}/(n_{TP} + n_{FN})$
TNR	True negative rate	$n_{TN}/(n_{TN} + n_{FP})$
PPV	Positive predictive value	$n_{TP}/(n_{TP} + n_{FP})$
NPV	Negative predictive value	$n_{TN}/(n_{TN} + n_{FN})$
F	F-measure	$(2 * n_{TP})/(2 * n_{TP} + n_{FN} + n_{FP})$

7. Codebook: Apply step 3 to get the codebooks in D_B: CB_B.
8. Class assignment: Use Ψ to get the labels in CB_B: $L_B^* = \{l_1^*, ..., l_b^*\}$.
9. Performance model: The true labels (L_B) and the predicted labels (L_B^*) are processed with the first expression in Table 4 to get the accuracy value.

3.2 Image Vegetation Segmentation

Image to Interest Regions. Without knowledge of the image structure, the first step is to find nearly uniform regions - ROIs. The principle is that pixels in small regions tend to contain elements of the same class. Ideally, each ROI would contain a single class of elements; vegetation, soil or other. However, improvement of the labelling process, using the BoW and the learning strategy together, is not guaranteed. In short, each image pixel is assigned to a unique region: $IR = \{IR_1, ..., IR_p\}$, p is the number of ROIs in the image. To group pixels into multiple ROIs four algorithms were tested: K-means (KM) [32], Self-organization maps (SOM) [35], Fuzzy C-means (FCM) [36] and Over-segmentation (OS) [37].

Interest Regions to Vegetation Segmentation. IR is processed following steps 5 through 8 above to get the region labels: $L_{IR}^* = \{l_1^*, ..., l_p^*\}, l_i^* \in \{v, s, o\}$. At each pixel in I_{rgb} is assigned the label of the IR at which it belongs: $I_{lab}(x, y) = l_i^*$ if $I_{rgb}(x, y) \in IR_i$. Finally, segmentation is achieved with the expression 1.

$$I_{bin}(x, y) = \begin{cases} 1 & \text{if } I_{lab}(x, y) = v, \\ 0 & \text{otherwise.} \end{cases} \quad (1)$$

4 Experimental Results

$\Omega = 168$ images, which were acquired under different illumination conditions and different plant growth state, were selected and manually segmented. Unique pixels only contain a main component (vegetation, soil or perhaps other unidentified component), so no mixed information can be considered as relevant in this

Table 5. First row: RGB images. Second row: hand-labelled images (v, s and o). Third row: Binary image, foreground (v) and background (joint s and o).

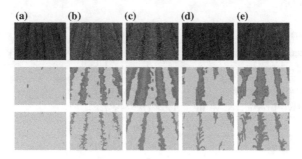

regard. From Ω, $\Omega_1 = 26$ images were used for building the classifier function and the remaining $\Omega_2 = 142$ for measuring the success in the segmentation process. Table 5 displays some representative colour images (first row) and their corresponding hand-labelled images (second row). The labelled images have three different colour labels; green for vegetation (v), light-brown for soil (s), and dark-brown for elements on the border between green plants and soil or any different item on the image (o). Manual segmentation on the vegetation borders is even difficult to carry out under the supervision of an expert. Moreover, we noted that the vegetation detection accuracy using a model with three classes (v, s, o) is greater than the accuracy achieved with a binary classifier (v, s). Under this scenario, the inclusion of the third class in the classifier design is justified.

Classifier Function Estimation. Ω_1 is divided into two sets: 20 images for training and 6 images for accuracy evaluation. 1005 regions in the first set (346-v, 171-s, 488-o) and 739 regions in the second set (399-v, 166-s, 174-o). Two models were considered; linear and nonlinear. In both cases, the parameter c was selected from the range [0.1:0.5:22]. For the nonlinear model, a radial base function (RBF) with parameter γ was used as kernel. The searching consists on testing with pairwise (c, γ) and the one with the best cross-validation accuracy is picked - γ takes the same range values than c. This process was repeated several times changing the vocabulary size $K \in [50 : 50 : 2000]$. The best values were achieved with the descriptors proposed by Kazim et al. [15]. They reported an accuracy of 97 % with CVI_{14} to detect creeping thistle. We have similar performance for maize images; 95.31 % with CVI_4, (c, γ) = (21.6, 20.6) and $K = 1970$, Table 6.

Extraction of ROIs. The quality segmentation of 50 images, selected from Ω_2, was used as criteria to select the partitioning method. The evaluation was made with a linear classifier with COM as feature descriptor, see Table 7; the average values of OSR and TPR are similar in all cases. The parameter selection was made as follow: For KM and FCM, the number of clusters was chosen from

Table 6. Accuracy (%) of the classifier models, z is the dimension of the descriptor.

Descriptor		SVM-Linear			SVM-RBF		
Abbr.	z	W	c	$OSR(\%)$	W	(c, γ)	$OSR(\%)$
COM	1	1790	16.6	85.17	590	21.1, 6.6	91.50
CVI_2	2	2000	13.6	80.25	1490	19.6, 21.1	93.83
CVI_4	4	1400	9.6	78.49	1970	21.6, 20.6	95.31
CVI_9	9	1900	17.6	82.31	1670	14.1, 21.6	94.65
CVI_{14}	14	1950	17.1	81.20	1490	17.1, 20.6	94.84
SIFT	128	1550	21.6	68.12	1650	19.1, 21.0	90.99
SURF	64	1650	21.1	66.68	1950	18.1, 18.1	90.38

$\{5, 10, 20, 30, 40, 50, 60\}$, KM has shown good performance with 30 clusters, while FCM works better with 10. For SOM, matlab default parameters were used. In the case of OS, we set $(k, \sigma, min) = (0.1, 300, 100)$ to get small regions. Visual results for a single image are displayed in Table 8. In conclusion, SOM was chosen as partitioning method due to its TPR value is the highest in Table 7.

Table 7. Performance evaluation of different partitioning methods.

Case	Measure	KM	SOM	FCM	OS
Average	OSR(%)	86.3	86.45	81.47	85.9
	TPR(%)	65.47	68.79	35.92	62.59
Best	OSR(%)	91.1	88.1	86.7	87.8
	TPR(%)	89.3	96.7	84.7	77.2
Worst	OSR(%)	74.8	80.8	61.1	68
	TPR(%)	50	60.9	37.61	42.8

4.1   Comparative Analysis

We compare our algorithm with methodologies proposed in precision agriculture and computer vision. A brief description of these methods is given now.

(i) Vegetation indices: Green pixels are detected by thresholding, the CVIs values are used as threshold [5,9,10,14,31]. The resulting image is filtered to remove noise. For analysis we use; ExG, ExGR, Gray$_1$, CIVE, VEG, and COM indices and a 5×5 median filter for noise remotion [14].

(ii) Yang el at. [9]: The RGB image is transformed to HSV space. From Hue, the smallest (h_1) and largest (h_2) values are extracted. RGB channels are processed separately with the expression 2. The new $R^*G^*B^*$ image is segmented as described in (i) with ExG as threshold.

$$A^*(x, y) = \begin{cases} 0 & \text{if } h_2 < H(x, y) < h_1, \text{ H is the colour channel} \\ A(x, y) & \text{otherwise.} \end{cases} \tag{2}$$

Table 8. First row: RGB image split into multiples regions with different algorithms. Second row: True labelled image followed by the segmentation results with their performance values ($TPR\%, OSR\%$).

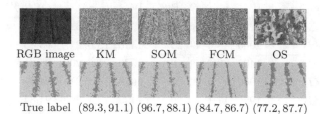

RGB image   KM   SOM   FCM   OS

True label $(89.3, 91.1)$ $(96.7, 88.1)$ $(84.7, 86.7)$ $(77.2, 87.7)$

Table 9. Performance evaluation for vegetation segmentation including our proposal. Metrics into rows, and methods into columns.

ID	ExG	ExGR	CIVE	VEG	COM	Gray$_1$	Yang	Hlaing	Tewari	ICF	CN24	BoW
OSR	86.95	85.83	83.76	85.72	75.95	87.71	79.40	70.64	87.34	75.29	82.64	86.11
TPR	71.67	83.51	74.02	67.27	53.22	74.16	60.25	13.65	75.59	53.90	71.43	73.24
TNR	89.58	85.20	85.14	88.35	90.58	89.40	84.08	76.60	89.84	82.04	84.89	90.39
PPV	66.38	40.17	44.25	60.16	73.36	63.32	44.28	4.23	60.31	54.16	39.71	58.60
NPV	93.00	97.47	95.74	92.99	78.61	94.00	91.08	90.44	92.49	83.95	93.72	89.51
F	67.10	53.05	50.27	61.29	55.59	67.67	44.94	3.24	64.96	52.35	43.32	61.60

(iii) Hlaing and Khaing [5]: For each pixel, the absolute values of green minus red and green minus blue are calculated. If both of these distance values are greater than the threshold ($T = 20$), the pixel is classified as plant. If none or only one is greater than T, the pixel is classified as background.

(iv) Tewari et al. [6]: For each pixel, when G colour intensity is greater than R and B colour intensity values simultaneously, the pixel is assumed to be green pixel. Otherwise, the pixel is assumed to be background.

(v) Brust et al. [38]. A semantic segmentation is carried out by using convolutional patch networks (CN), they provide an open source library (CN24) which includes a pre-trained model able to identify multiple classes in urban scenes. In our dataset, different CN architectures were tested, however, the best results were achieved with the pre-trained model.

(vi) Fröhlich et al. [39]. The semantic segmentation approach is based on the massive use of random decision forests (RDF) and the computation of several basic as well as high-level contextual features during learning (ICF).

Images in Ω_2 were processed with methods above described. The segmentation performance is provided in Table 9, the best value is achieved with Tewari; 87.34% and 75.59% of OSR and TPR respectively. For a single image, the vegetation segmentation obtained with methods in Table 9 are shown in Table 10.

The results reported by Yang et al. and Hlaing and Khaing were computed with a dataset where plants are well defined (usually, one plant per image). On the first paper, an accuracy of 95% is reported, in the second case, authors do

Table 10. Segmentation of an image with methodologies in Table 9. In brackets, the performance values $(TPR\%, OSR\%)$.

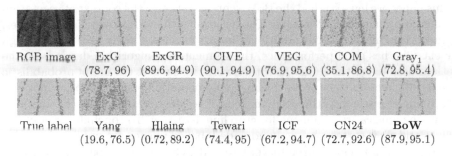

RGB image	ExG	ExGR	CIVE	VEG	COM	Gray$_1$
	$(78.7, 96)$	$(89.6, 94.9)$	$(90.1, 94.9)$	$(76.9, 95.6)$	$(35.1, 86.8)$	$(72.8, 95.4)$
True label	Yang	Hlaing	Tewari	ICF	CN24	**BoW**
	$(19.6, 76.5)$	$(0.72, 89.2)$	$(74.4, 95)$	$(67.2, 94.7)$	$(72.7, 92.6)$	$(87.9, 95.1)$

Table 11. Segmentation results under differents scenarios. In Table 5, the RGB images and their corresponding true labelled image (image per column). Performance values in brackets $(TPR\%, OSR\%)$.

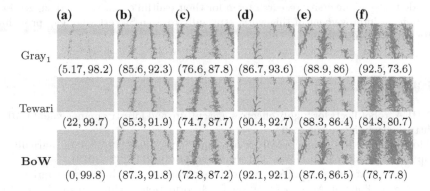

	(a)	**(b)**	**(c)**	**(d)**	**(e)**	**(f)**
Gray$_1$	$(5.17, 98.2)$	$(85.6, 92.3)$	$(76.6, 87.8)$	$(86.7, 93.6)$	$(88.9, 86)$	$(92.5, 73.6)$
Tewari	$(22, 99.7)$	$(85.3, 91.9)$	$(74.7, 87.7)$	$(90.4, 92.7)$	$(88.3, 86.4)$	$(84.8, 80.7)$
BoW	$(0, 99.8)$	$(87.3, 91.8)$	$(72.8, 87.2)$	$(92.1, 92.1)$	$(87.6, 86.5)$	$(78, 77.8)$

not provide vegetation segmentation results. In our dataset (many plants per image), the performance of these two proposals is poor, below 80 %.

It is well known from the literature that CNs have been shown high performance in segmentation tasks. In our case, we tested different architectures with CN24 framework in our dataset and we could not find a configuration able to increase the performance value. ICF shows similar performance than CN24, it is important to mention that although ICF has low performance in vegetation detection, results can be relevant in the context of crop lines detection given that vegetation on the crop line is preserved and well limited. Finally, BoW representation has a OSR of 86.11 % with a percentage of vegetation correctly identified of 73.24 %. The rate of elements well classified is 90.39 %, however the overlapping between green plants and background is 61.6 %, similar values as such obtained with the other proposals.

In addition to the results above displayed, images in Table 5 were processed with; Gray$_1$, Tewari et al. and BoW, they have the best performance in Table 9, see Table 11. Lastly, results were computed using the Image Processing Toolbox MATLAB 2013a for 64 bits under Windows 7.

5   Conclusions

In this paper, we have studied the BoW representation in the context of vegetation segmentation in cornfield images. The accuracy achieved is over 95 %; however, segmentation method needs additional improvements. This is because although the classifier has good performance, the segmentation algorithm depends on the method used to get the ROIs. As future work, we suggest the use of probabilistic models [40] in order to improve the image segmentation results. Another possible future line of research is the deep analysis of results obtained with IFC method, segmented images are promising for crop line detection. To conclude, a set of 168 images and their corresponding handmade-labelled images are publicly available (https://www.fdi.ucm.es/profesor/pajares/ACIVS/), they are part of the contributions of this work.

Acknowledgments. H. Sossa thanks CONACyT under call: Frontiers of Science (grant number 65) for the economic support. We would like to express our sincere gratitude to Jena University research team for their fruitful comments and suggestions for significant improvement of this work, especially to Sven Sickert who help providing results with ICF algorithm.

References

1. RHEA: robot fleets for highly effective agriculture and forestry management (2016). http://www.rhea-project.eu/
2. Mousazadeh, H.: A technical review on navigation systems of agricultural autonomous off-road vehicles. J. Terramech. **50**(3), 211–232 (2013)
3. Saxena, L., Armstrong, L.: A survey of image processing techniques for agriculture. In: Proceedings of Asian Federation for Information Technology in Agriculture (2014)
4. Haug, S., Michaels, A., Biber, P., Ostermann, J.: Plant classification system for crop/weed discrimination without segmentation. In: IEEE Winter Conference on Applications of Computer Vision, pp. 1142–1149, March 2014
5. Hlaing, S.H., Khaing, A.S.: Weed and crop segmentation and classification using area thresholding. J. Res. Eng. Technol. **3**, 375 (2014)
6. Tewari, V., Kumar, A.A., Nare, B., Prakash, S., Tyagi, A.: Microcontroller based roller contact type herbicide applicator for weed control under row crops. Comput. Electron. Agric. **104**, 40–45 (2014)
7. Choi, K.H., Han, S.K., Han, S.H., Park, K.H., Kim, K.S., Kim, S.: Morphology-based guidance line extraction for an autonomous weeding robot in paddy fields. Comput. Electron. Agric. **113**, 266–274 (2015)
8. Torres-Snchez, J., Lpez-Granados, F., Pea, J.: An automatic object-based method for optimal thresholding in UAV images: application for vegetation detection in herbaceous crops. Comput. Electron. Agric. **114**, 43–52 (2015)
9. Yang, W., Zhao, X., Wang, S., Chen, L., Chen, X., Lu, S.: A new approach for greenness identification from maize images. In: Huang, D.-S., Bevilacqua, V., Prashan, P. (eds.) ICIC 2015. LNCS, vol. 9225, pp. 339–347. Springer, Heidelberg (2015). doi:10.1007/978-3-319-22180-9_33

10. Jiang, G., Wang, Z., Liu, H.: Automatic detection of crop rows based on multi-rois. Expert Syst. Appl. **42**(5), 2429–2441 (2015)
11. Meng, Q., Qiu, R., He, J., Zhang, M., Ma, X., Liu, G.: Development of agricultural implement system based on machine vision and fuzzy control. Comput. Electron. Agric. **112**, 128–138 (2015). Precision Agriculture
12. Guijarro, M., Riomoros, I., Pajares, G., Zitinski, P.: Discrete wavelets transform for improving greenness image segmentation in agricultural images. Comput. Electron. Agric. **118**, 396–407 (2015)
13. Balasubramaniam, P., Ananthi, V.P.: Segmentation of nutrient deficiency in incomplete crop images using intuitionistic fuzzy c-means clustering algorithm. Nonlinear Dyn. **83**(1), 849–866 (2015)
14. Kazmi, W., Garcia-Ruiz, F.J., Nielsen, J., Rasmussen, J., Andersen, H.J.: Detecting creeping thistle in sugar beet fields using vegetation indices. Comput. Electron. Agric. **112**, 10–19 (2015). Precision Agriculture
15. Kazmi, W., Garcia-Ruiz, F., Nielsen, J., Rasmussen, J., Andersen, H.J.: Exploiting affine invariant regions and leaf edge shapes for weed detection. Comput. Electron. Agric. **118**, 290–299 (2015)
16. Ye, M., Cao, Z., Yu, Z., Bai, X.: Crop feature extraction from images with probabilistic superpixel Markov random field. Comput. Electron. Agric. **114**, 247–260 (2015)
17. Cheng, B., Matson, E.T.: A feature-based machine learning agent for automatic rice and weed discrimination. In: Rutkowski, L., Korytkowski, M., Scherer, R., Tadeusiewicz, R., Zadeh, L.A., Zurada, J.M. (eds.) ICAISC 2015. LNCS (LNAI), vol. 9119, pp. 517–527. Springer, Heidelberg (2015). doi:10.1007/978-3-319-19324-3_46
18. Moorthy, S., Boigelot, B., Mercatoris, B.: Effective segmentation of green vegetation for resource-constrained real-time applications. In: Proceedings of Precision Agriculture (2015)
19. Santos, T.T., Koenigkan, L.V., Barbedo, J.G.A., Rodrigues, G.C.: 3D plant modeling: localization, mapping and segmentation for plant phenotyping using a single hand-held camera. In: Agapito, L., Bronstein, M.M., Rother, C. (eds.) ECCV 2014. LNCS, vol. 8928, pp. 247–263. Springer, Heidelberg (2015). doi:10.1007/978-3-319-16220-1_18
20. Ionescu, R.T., Popescu, A.L., Popescu, M., Popescu, D.: Biomassid: a biomass type identification system for mobile devices. Comput. Electron. Agric. **113**, 244–253 (2015)
21. Woebbecke, D., Meyer, G., Von Bargen, K., Mortensen, D.: Color indices for weed identification under various soil, residue, and lighting conditions. Trans. ASAE **38**(1), 259–269 (1995)
22. Meyer, G., Mehta, T., Kocher, M., Mortensen, D., Samal, A.: Textural imaging and discriminant analysis for distinguishing weeds for spot spraying. Trans. ASAE **41**(4), 1189 (1998)
23. Kataoka, T., Kaneko, T., Okamoto, H., et al.: Crop growth estimation system using machine vision. In: Proceedings of 2003 IEEE/ASME International Conference on Advanced Intelligent Mechatronics, AIM 2003, vol. 2, pp. b1079–b1083. IEEE (2003)
24. Meyer, G.E., Neto, J.C.: Verification of color vegetation indices for automated crop imaging applications. Comput. Electron. Agric. **63**(2), 282 (2008)

25. Woebbecke, D.M., Meyer, G.E., Von Bargen, K., Mortensen, D.A.: Plant species identification, size, and enumeration using machine vision techniques on near-binary images. In: Proceedings of Applications in Optical Science and Engineering, International Society for Optics and Photonics, pp. 208–219 (1993)

26. Golzarian, M.R., Frick, R.A.: Classification of images of wheat, ryegrass and brome grass species at early growth stages using principal component analysis. Plant Methods **7**(1), 1–11 (2011)

27. Salton, G., Mcgill, M.J.: Introduction to Modern Information Retrieval. McGraw-Hill Inc., New York (1986)

28. Bishop, C.M.: Pattern Recognition and Machine Learning (Information Science and Statistics). Springer, New York (2006)

29. Lowe, D.G.: Distinctive image features from scale-invariant keypoints. Int. J. Comput. Vis. **60**(2), 91–110 (2004)

30. Bay, H., Ess, A., Tuytelaars, T., Gool, L.V.: Speeded-up robust features (SURF). Comput. Vis. Image Underst. **110**(3), 346–359 (2008). Similarity Matching in Computer Vision and Multimedia

31. Guijarro, M., Pajares, G., Riomoros, I., Herrera, P., Burgos-Artizzu, X., Ribeiro, A.: Automatic segmentation of relevant textures in agricultural images. Comput. Electron. Agric. **75**(1), 75–83 (2011)

32. MacQueen, J.: Some methods for classification and analysis of multivariate observations. In: Proceedings of the Fifth Berkeley Symposium on Mathematical Statistics and Probability, pp. 281–297. University of California Press, Berkeley (1967)

33. Chang, C.C., Lin, C.J.: LIBSVM: a library for support vector machines. ACM Trans. Intell. Syst. Technol. **2**, 27:1–27:27 (2011)

34. Labatut, V., Cherifi, H.: Accuracy measures for the comparison of classifiers. CoRR abs/1207.3790 (2012)

35. Kohonen, T. (ed.): Self-organizing Maps. Springer, New York (1997)

36. Dunn, J.C.: A fuzzy relative of the isodata process and its use in detecting compact well-separated clusters. J. Cybern. **3**(3), 32–57 (1973)

37. Felzenszwalb, P.F., Huttenlocher, D.P.: Efficient graph-based image segmentation. Int. J. Comput. Vis. **59**(2), 167–181 (2004)

38. Brust, C., Sickert, S., Simon, M., Rodner, E., Denzler, J.: Convolutional patch networks with spatial prior for road detection and urban scene understanding. CoRR abs/1502.06344 (2015)

39. Fröhlich, B., Rodner, E., Denzler, J.: Semantic segmentation with millions of features: integrating multiple cues in a combined random forest approach. In: Lee, K.M., Matsushita, Y., Rehg, J.M., Hu, Z. (eds.) ACCV 2012. LNCS, vol. 7724, pp. 218–231. Springer, Heidelberg (2013). doi:10.1007/978-3-642-37331-2_17

40. Larlus, D., Verbeek, J., Jurie, F.: Category level object segmentation by combining bag-of-words models with dirichlet processes and random fields. Int. J. Comput. Vis. **88**(2), 238–253 (2010)

Fast Traffic Sign Recognition Using Color Segmentation and Deep Convolutional Networks

Ali Youssef, Dario Albani$^{(\boxtimes)}$, Daniele Nardi, and Domenico Daniele Bloisi

Department of Computer, Control, and Management Engineering,
Sapienza University of Rome, via Ariosto 25, 00185 Rome, Italy
{youssef,albani,nardi,bloisi}@dis.uniroma1.it

Abstract. The use of Computer Vision techniques for the automatic recognition of road signs is fundamental for the development of intelligent vehicles and advanced driver assistance systems. In this paper, we describe a procedure based on color segmentation, Histogram of Oriented Gradients (HOG), and Convolutional Neural Networks (CNN) for detecting and classifying road signs. Detection is speeded up by a preprocessing step to reduce the search space, while classification is carried out by using a Deep Learning technique. A quantitative evaluation of the proposed approach has been conducted on the well-known German Traffic Sign data set and on the novel Data set of Italian Traffic Signs (DITS), which is publicly available and contains challenging sequences captured in adverse weather conditions and in an urban scenario at night-time. Experimental results demonstrate the effectiveness of the proposed approach in terms of both classification accuracy and computational speed.

1 Introduction

The increasing interest towards autonomous vehicles and advanced driver assistance systems is demonstrated by the prototypes developed by Google, Volvo, Tesla, and other manufacturers. In this paper, we focus on the use of visual information for traffic sign recognition, which is fundamental for achieving autonomous driving in real world applications. In recent years, many methods for traffic sign detection (TSD) and recognition (TSR) based on Computer Vision techniques have been proposed. Since road signs have bright fixed colors (for aiding human detection), some approaches are based on color segmentation to locate the signs in the input images. Sliding windows approaches have also been proposed, relying mostly on the use of Histogram of Oriented Gradients (HOG), Integral Channel Features (ICF) and its modifications [11] to extract discriminative visual features from the images. Our method aims at combining the speed of the color segmentation techniques with the accuracy of the sliding windows approaches, in particular HOG. Color information from high resolution images in input are used to select a set of regions of interest (ROIs), thus reducing the search space. Then, visual features are extracted from each ROI

A. Youssef and D. Albani—These two authors contributed equally to the work.

© Springer International Publishing AG 2016
J. Blanc-Talon et al. (Eds.): ACIVS 2016, LNCS 10016, pp. 205–216, 2016.
DOI: 10.1007/978-3-319-48680-2_19

and compared with a Support Vector Machine (SVM) model for detecting road signs. Finally, a Convolutional Neural Network (CNN) is used for the recognition of the traffic signs. Different architectures for the network are proposed, starting from the ones presented in [9,13]. For the implementation of the net, we rely on TensorFlow[1], a recent open source framework released by Google. Quantitative experimental results have been carried out on the publicly available German Traffic Sign Data set (GTSRB) in order to allow a comparison with other approaches. Moreover, we have created a novel publicly available data set, called the Data set of Italian Traffic Signs (DITS), containing Italian traffic signs captured in challenging conditions (i.e., nigh-time, fog, and complex urban scenarios). The results demonstrate that our method achieves good results in terms of accuracy, requiring only 200 ms for processing an HD image. The contributions of this paper are threefold: *(i)* A new approach for speeding up the traffic sign detection process is proposed. *(ii)* A complete pipeline, including sign detection and recognition, is described. *(iii)* A novel challenging data set, called DITS, has been created and made publicly available. The rest of the paper is organized as follows. Section 2 provides a brief overview of the state-of-the-art methods for traffic signs detection and classification in single images. Our method is presented in Sect. 3. The newly created DITS data set is described in Sect. 4, while the experimental results, carried out both on DITS and on GTSRB, are presented in Sect. 5. Finally, conclusions are drawn in Sect. 6.

2 Related Work

The problem of automatically recognizing road signals from cameras mounted on cars is gaining more and more interest with the advent of advanced driver assisted systems to help the driver in avoiding potentially dangerous situations. According to the different tasks in image recognition pointed out by Perona in [12], the problem of recognizing traffic signs in single images can be divided into two sub-problems, namely detection and classification.

Detection. Given an image, the goal is to decide if a sign is located somewhere in the scene and to provide position information about it, i.e., the image patch containing the sign. Detection can be carried out by analysing images from single or multiple views. Although traditional systems count on the single view approach (e.g., [1]), today's cars are often equipped with multiple cameras, thus multi-view data are often available. Since existing work on multi-view recognition consists of single-view sign detection followed by a multi-view fusing step [15], we will discuss here single-view approaches with the consideration that they can be conveniently adapted when multiple views are available. Mathias et al. published a recent review on the current state-of-the-art for single-view methods [10]. Top performance can be reached by using approaches designed for pedestrian (i.e., HOG features) and face (i.e., Haar-like features) detection.

---

[1] http://www.tensorflow.org.

Another widely used technique in traffic sign detection, which has been originally developed for pedestrian detection, is based on Integral Channel Features
[4]: multiple registered image channels are computed by using linear and non-
linear transformations of the input image. Features (e.g., Haar-like wavelets and
local histograms) are extracted from each channel along with integral images.
Variants of the Integral Channel Feature detector (e.g., [2, 5]) have demonstrated
to reach high speed (i.e., 50 frames per second) maintaining accurate detection.

Classification. Given the image patch extracted in the detection phase, the classification problem consists in deciding if it contains a signal among the possible signal categories. A common pipeline for classification [10] is made of three
stages: *(i)* Feature Extraction, *(ii)* Dimensionality Reduction, and *(iii)* Labeling.
Extracting visual features from the image at hand is the first step for classification. Since traffic signs are designed for colour-blind people, visual features
like shape and inner pattern are more descriptive than color attributes. This
is demonstrated by Mathias et al. [10] in their experiments, where no gain is
obtained by using color-dependent features for classification in place of grayscale
features. Dimensionality reduction plays an important role on classification.
Timofte et al. in [16] present a technique called Locality Preserving Projections (LPP) that represent an alternative to the classical Principal Component
Analysis (PCA). A LPP variant is the Iterative Nearest Neighbours based Linear
Projection (INNLP) presented in [17]. It uses iterative nearest neighbours instead
of sparse representations in the graph construction. The labeling step is the last
phase in the pipeline. The competition[2] on the German Traffic Sign Recognition
Benchmark (GTSRB) has allowed to test and compare different solutions for
road sign classification. Among those, Deep Learning based methods obtained
great results. In particular, Ciresan et al. [3] won the final phase of the competition using a GPU implementation of a Deep Neural Network (DNN), further
improved in a Multi-Column DNN that makes the system robust to variations
in contrast and illumination. Sermanet et al. [13] use a Multi-Scale Convolutional Neural Network, obtaining results above the average human performance.
Extreme Learning Machine classifier fed with CNN features is proposed by Zeng
et al. in [20], obtaining competitive results with a limited computational cost.

3 Proposed Approach

The functional architecture of the proposed approach is shown in Fig. 1. At the
beginning, a color segmentation step is used for reducing the search space. The
regions of the input image having color attributes similar to the road sign models
are selected, creating an initial set of regions of interest (ROIs). Then, features
are extracted from each ROI and represented as HOG descriptors. After that,
a multi-scale detection process, based on a trained SVM model, takes place.
Information about the position and the size of each possible sign are stored for
being used later. At the same time, each detection is passed to the CNN based

---

[2] http://benchmark.ini.rub.de.

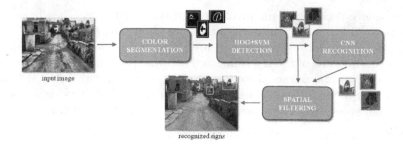

Fig. 1. The proposed pipeline for automatic traffic sign detection and recognition. Image best viewed in color (Color figure online).

recognition module: If a sign is successfully assigned to a class, it is sent to the final stage of the procedure, otherwise it is processed by using a probabilistic spatial filtering, whose probabilities are computed among adjacent ROIs. The ROIs that passed all the processing phases are labeled as recognized signs.

Traffic Sign Detection. We use a combination of color and shape-based methods for detecting the signs. The shape-based method includes normalizing operations in addition to multi-scale image processing, in order to handle the challenges presented in a typical street scene. Since the pixels belonging to traffic signs usually represents a small percentage of all the pixels in input, it is desirable to reduce the initial search space. According to [6], we assume that traffic signs have bright and saturated colors, in contrast with the surrounding environment, to be recognized easily by drivers. This assumption helps in covering with the detection windows only a small subset of the patches extracted from the original image. The extraction of the ROIs is carried out by utilizing the Improved Hue, Saturation, and Luminance (IHSL) color space [8], which is useful for taking into account lighting changes since the chromatic and achromatic components are independent in IHSL. The original image is transformed from RGB to IHSL by applying the following thresholding operation:

$$
IHSL(x,y) = \begin{cases} 0, \text{ if } Max(I_R(x,y), I_G(x,y), I_B(x,y)) = I_G(x,y) \quad \vee \\ \quad (|I_R(x,y) - I_G(x,y)| < \zeta \wedge |I_B(x,y) - I_G(x,y)| < \gamma) \\ \\ F_{ihsl}(I_R(x,y), I_G(x,y), I_B(x,y)), \text{ otherwise} \end{cases}
$$

(1)

where $IHSL(x,y)$ is the IHSL color space value for the pixel in position (x,y), having I_R, I_G, and I_B RGB values. The function $F_{ihsl}(.)$ represents the usual conversion $RGB_{colorspace} \rightarrow IHSL_{colorspace}$ as described in [7]. It is worth noting that RGB pixels with a considerable percentage of green (e.g., representing vegetation) are discarded. The ζ and γ thresholds play a significant role in filtering out further pixels (e.g., belonging to road and sky), thus reducing the computational time for the IHSL conversion and the subsequent detection steps.

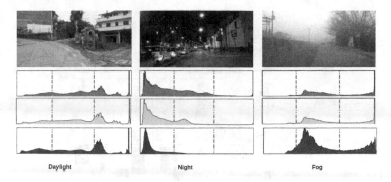

Fig. 2. The color histogram of the three types of scenes. The dashed lines represents the three different areas considered over each histogram. This image is best viewed in color (Color figure online).

The values for ζ and γ are set based on the lighting conditions in the scene: the color distribution represented by the RGB histogram is used to detect the illumination conditions (see Fig. 2). Each RGB histogram is divided into three equal areas. This division helps to determine where the color information is condensed and to locate the peak value in each histogram. In daylight conditions, the color information distribution is located in the right area of the histogram, with peak values at the most right side. Night-time scenes have a higher number of pixels located within the left area, while in foggy conditions the greater number of pixels is distributed over the middle and right areas. More formally, the color distribution over each histogram area is computed as:

$$\epsilon_n = \frac{\sum_n H(i), \quad if \quad H(i) \geq \alpha}{\sum_{\forall_n} H(i)} \tag{2}$$

where ϵ_n represents the distribution of each RGB color channel over one of the three areas ($n \in \{1, 2, 3\}$), $H(i)$ is the number of pixels with color value i, where $i \in [0, 255]$, and α is set to $0.3 * max(H(i)), \forall i$. The maximum ϵ_n is used to detect the lighting condition of the scene and to adapt the values of γ and ζ according to it. The final binary image is computed by applying the approach described in [18], where the Normalized Hue-Saturation (NHS) method and post-processing steps are used to find the potential pixels belonging to road signs. Erosion and dilation morphological operators are applied on the binary image for noise removal. The remaining pixels are grouped into contours, which in turns are filtered according to their size. The bounding box of each extracted contour is computed and clustered into spatial-classes according to the distances and the overlapping of each bounding box. This procedure is useful for handling partially occluded, with multiple colors, or damaged road signs. Figure 3 shows the color segmentation along with the contour extraction procedure that led to the extraction of the patches (highlighted in the last row of the figure). Visual descriptors are then computed over the extracted patches. For HOG, we use a 40×40 detection window with 10×10 block size and 2×2 striding. Three rounds

Fig. 3. Color segmentation and contour extraction. Original images are in the first row. The second row shows the results of the RGB thresholding, while the third row contains the contour extraction. In the first column $\zeta = 15$ and $\gamma = 25$ are used, in the second $\zeta = 40$ and $\gamma = 25$ and in the third $\zeta = 15$ and $\gamma = 20$ (Color figure online).

of training are performed in total, adding hard negatives to the training images in every round. For the first round, we used GTSRB positives samples along with custom negatives: around 2000 samples were added. In the second round, the same procedure has been applied to DITS data. Positives samples from both GTSRB and DITS together with all the collected hard negatives from the previous steps are used for the last round of training. The color segmentation stage helps in decreasing the false positive detection and to accelerate the overall procedure.

Traffic Sign Recognition. Our recognition module is based on CNN and built over the Deep Learning framework TensorFlow. All images are down-sampled to 28×28. For both DITS and GTSRB, also jitter (augmented) samples are used. Images are randomly rotated, scaled and translated. Max values for the perturbations are $[-15, 15]$ for rotation, $[-4, 4]$ for translation and a factor $[0.8, 1.2]$ for scaling. The augmented data set is four times bigger than the original. The Deep Learning approach has two different architectures (see Fig. 4), a Single-Scale Convolutional Neural Network and a modified version of the Multi-Scale architecture proposed by Sermanet et al. for the GTSRB competition. The single-scale architecture presents two convolutional layers, each one followed by a pooling layer, and two sequential fully connected layer with rectification. The last layer is a softmax linear classifier. The multi-scale CNN is based on both the work by Sermanet and LeCun [13] and the single-scale architecture above described. The model presents two stages of convolutional layers, two local fully connected layer with rectified linear activation and a softmax classifier. As for the single-scale case, each convolutional layer presents pooling layer. The output of the first convolutional stage has two ramifications, one feeds the next stage in a feed-forward fashion, while the other serves as part of the input for the first of the fully

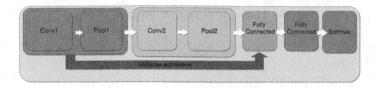

Fig. 4. Proposed architecture for CNN. In case of multiscale architecture, the output of the first convolutional layer feeds both the second convolutional layer and the first fully connected one.

connected layer. The input of such layer is built from the output of the first stage and the output of the second stage.

Spatial Neighbourhood Filtering. The last module of our pipeline is in charge of fusing information from the detection module and the classification one. Algorithm 1 contains the details about this last step. A probability based on their position and on their neighbour patches is assigned to the patches that are not recognized as a specific traffic sign. A thresholding process is further applied over the final probabilities to filter out untrusted patches from the final list. It is worth noting that in real applications, such as driver assistance systems, the driver should not be warned due to false detections. Indeed, although the proposed solution helps to increase the accuracy by 1–2 % depending on the data set, it strongly relies on the recognition sub-systems, adding a small probability to discard correct detections. The output of the classification module is divided into *classified detections* (i.e., the detections successfully assigned to a class by the CNN) and *not-classified* ones. For every element in the not-classified detection set, we define a search range around it and compute, for every sample in the classified set that lies within the range, the following two metrics: *(i)* the similarity between the size of the not-classified and the classified element and *(ii)* the distance between the center of the two elements. If the sum of the two above listed comparison metrics is below a given threshold, then the not-classified detection is definitively discarded, otherwise it is accepted.

Algorithm 1. Spatial Neighbourhood Filtering

Input   : unrecognised detections α, recognized detections β.
Output: Accepted detection
1 **for** $\forall d$: $d \in \beta$ **do**
2   1: M ←**maximum range** for **d**;
3   2: **for** $\forall c$: $c \in \alpha \land c$ *in range M* **do**
4   i: p_d ← **compareSize** (**d,c**);
5   ii: p_d ← **compareDistance** (**d,c**);
6   **end**
7   3: **if** $p_d > threshold$ **then**
8   accept **d**;
9   **else**
10   discard **d**;
11   **end**
12 **end**

---

4   The Data Set of Italian Traffic Signs

Since the release of the German Traffic Sign Data set (GTSRB) in 2011, no other challenging data sets have been released. According to Mathias et al. [10], the GTSD have been saturated and there is the need of novel public and more complex data sets. Here, we present the Data set on Italian Traffic Signs (DITS), which is a novel data set, generated in part from HD videos (1280 × 720 frame size recorded at 10 fps) taken from a commercial web-cam and different smart phones. DITS data can be downloaded at: http://www.dis.uniroma1.it/~bloisi/ds/dits.html.

The aim of DITS is to provide more challenging images than its predecessors. First, not all the used sensors are intended for outdoor shooting and the quality of the images is lower if compared with the one in GTSRB. As suggested in [10], we have increased the difficulty by adding images captured at night time and in presence of fog (see Fig. 5). A big part of the samples contains complex urban environments that can increase the presence of false positives. Finally, DITS presents a new challenging class of traffic signs, named Indication, that include square-like traffic signs. Both detection and classification training and test sets are present. The detection subset offers 1,416 images for training and 471 for testing, while the classification subset contains 8,048 samples for training and 1,206 for testing. Currently, DITS is at an early stage and our plan is to improve it in the next few months.

DITS has been originally generated from 43,289 images extracted from more than 14 h of videos recorded in different places around Italy. Images are then down-sampled to fullfill the following requirements. All the images in the data set are enclosed in classes. In particular, training images for both detection and classification are organized in folders, where each folder represent a single superclass or sub-class. Annotated images are available for testing and text files with more accurate information and annotations are provided.

About the detection subset, we decided to define three shape-based super-classes, namely circle, square, and triangle, obtaining the Prohibitive, Indication, and Warning classes. The bottom threshold for the width and the height of the samples present is set to 40 pixels for both; images are not necessarily squared. The classification data set presents 58 classes of signs: each class presents a variable number of tracks where the concept of track collide with the one previously

Fig. 5. Two annotated images from the DITS data set captured at night time (left) and with fog conditions (right). Annotations are shown in green (Color figure online).

Fig. 6. Images from the classification sub set of the DITS data set. DITS contains 58 different classes.

used in GTSRB [14]. The difference with the GTSRB is on the number of images present in each track (15) and mainly dictated by the lower frame rate offered by the sensor used. Tracks presenting a higher number of images are downsized by equidistant samples; tracks with less than 15 samples are discarded. Images in the track have different size and, as for the detection subset, they may vary in aspect ratio. Figure 6 shows some samples coming from the classification test set.

5   Experimental Results

The approach proposed in this paper have been tested on two different publicly available data sets, the German Traffic Sign Data set (GTSRB) and the Data set of Italian Traffic Signs (DITS). We have evaluated the proposed approach for detection on 300 images coming from GTSRB and 471 from DITS.

The two data sets present some differences: *(i)* only the Danger superclass has a direct correspondence; *(ii)* the Mandatory and Prohibitive superclasses of GTSRB are merged into the Prohibitive superclass for DITS; *(iii)* DITS has a new Indication superclass (i.e., square signs).

For both the German and the Italian data sets, we have tuned the parameters according to the different settings of the sensors. Most of the images in GTSRB present a saturated blue sky and low saturation on the red, translating into a slightly higher value on γ, while DITS data present a less saturated sky in daylight conditions, while night time images present alterations over the red and blue channels. Night time images present also a lower accuracy of the color segmentation process, thus lowering the performance in subsequent phases. Common street lamps have a color temperature that ranges between 2000 and 3000 K and this reduces the area discarded by the red-based threshold. Moreover, car headlights cause a sudden change in brightness that blur the image. In this case, we have used $\zeta = 40$ and $\gamma = 25$. Fog affects the segmentation process, slightly increasing the false negative rate. For fog images, we have used $\zeta = 5$ and $\gamma = 5$.

After the tuning, results show that we are able to discard, on average, 82 % of the pixels for the images in DITS and 69 % for GTSRB data. This strong

Table 1. Comparison results on the GTSRB data set of our approach with and without activating the color segmentation (ColSeg).

Method	Prohibitive		Danger		Mandatory	
	AUC	∼ Time(ms)	AUC	∼ Time(ms)	AUC	∼ Time(ms)
HOG	96.33%	693	**96.12%**	693	89.18%	693
ColSeg+HOG	**98.67%**	**231**	96.01%	**234**	**90.43%**	**243**

Table 2. Results on the DITS data set with and without color segmentation (ColSeg).

Method	Prohibitive		Danger		Indication	
	AUC	∼ Time(ms)	AUC	∼ Time(ms)	AUC	∼ Time(ms)
HOG	96.63%	615	98.00%	615	81.06%	615
ColSeg+HOG	**97.87%**	**198**	**98.12%**	**197**	**89.71%**	**200**

Table 3. Recognition results with single scale (sc) and multi scale (ms) CNN.

Method	DITS	Jit. DITS	GTSRB	Jit. GTSRB
sc CNN	-	93.1%	-	97.2%
ms CNN	88.4%	**95.0%**	95.1%	**98.2%**

reduction allows the next stage of the detection sub-system to process a smaller portion of the original image, speeding up the analysis up to 5 times. Table 1 and Table 2 show the improvements in accuracy and computational time that can be obtained by using a pre-classification step based on color segmentation. Our method obtains comparable results with others existing methods (see [19] for results obtained by other approaches on GTSDB). Experimental results on DITS show even higher speed than those obtained on GTSRB. The lower accuracy when dealing with the new Indication superclass is due to the high presence of false positive in urban environment (e.g., square-like object as windows).

Classification results are shown in Table 3. Results for DITS data are completely new and not comparable. On the GTSRB we reached good results if compared with those previously published on the German Traffic Sign Recognition Benchmark page (http://benchmark.ini.rub.de).

The accuracy of the proposed pipeline (detection+classification+spatial filtering) has been evaluated on DITS data. For the detection process, we started from an overall accuracy of 95.23%, while the recognition subsystem consist in the single-scale Convolutional Neural Network trained on the jittered data set. From 347 outputs from the detection, 93% samples have been successfully assigned to a class. The remaining 7% is processed by our Spatial Neighborhood Filter to mitigate the error of the classifier. Results show that 1.2% samples are confirmed, while the other are discarded as false positives. Among the confirmed samples, only the 0.2% resulted in false positives.

6   Conclusions

In this paper, we have described a fast and accurate pipeline for road sign recognition. The proposed approach merge different state-of-the-art methods obtaining competitive results on both detection and classification of traffic signs. Particular attention has been given to the detection phase, where color segmentation is used to reduce the portion of the image to process, thus reducing the computational time. Quantitative experimental results show an 82 % average reduction of the search space, which speed up the process without affecting the detection accuracy. The CNN architecture allows to further discard false positives by combining the outputs from the detection and the recognition modules. Moreover, we have presented a novel data set, called the Data set of Italian Traffic Signs (DITS), which presents some innovations over existing data sets, such as night-time and complex urban scenes. Since available data sets already reached saturation (over 99 % accuracy), we believe that the development of a novel data set with more challenging data is an important contribution of this work. As future directions, we intend to extend DITS with additional images, captured under adverse weather conditions (e.g., rain and snow).

References

1. Barnes, N., Zelinsky, A.: Real-time radial symmetry for speed sign detection. In: Intelligent Vehicles Symposium, pp. 566–571 (2004)
2. Benenson, R., Mathias, M., Timofte, R., Van Gool, L.: Pedestrian detection at 100 frames per second. In: CVPR, pp. 2903–2910 (2012)
3. Ciresan, D.C., Meier, U., Masci, J., Schmidhuber, J.: Multi-column deep neural network for traffic sign classification. Neural Netw. **32**, 333–338 (2012)
4. Dollár, P., Tu, Z., Perona, P., Belongie, S.: Integral channel features. In: BMVC (2009)
5. Dollr, P., Appel, R., Kienzle, W.: Crosstalk cascades for frame-rate pedestrian detection. In: Fitzgibbon, A., Lazebnik, S., Perona, P., Sato, Y., Schmid, C. (eds.) ECCV 2012. Lecture Notes in Computer Science, vol. 7573, pp. 645–659. Springer, Heidelberg (2012). doi:10.1007/978-3-642-33709-3_46
6. Doman, K., Deguchi, D., Takahashi, T., Mekada, Y., Ide, I., Murase, H., Sakai, U.: Estimation of traffic sign visibility considering local and global features in a driving environment. In: Intelligent Vehicles Symposium, pp. 202–207 (2014)
7. Fleyeh, H.: Color detection and segmentation for road and traffic signs. In: 2004 IEEE Conference on Cybernetics and Intelligent Systems, pp. 809–814 (2004)
8. Hanbury, A.: A 3D-polar coordinate colour representation well adapted to image analysis. In: Bigun, J., Gustavsson, T. (eds.) SCIA 2003. LNCS, vol. 2749, pp. 804–811. Springer, Heidelberg (2003). doi:10.1007/3-540-45103-X_107
9. Krizhevsky, A., Sutskever, I., Hinton, G.E.: Imagenet classification with deep convolutional neural networks. In: Proceedings of Advances in neural information processing systems, pp. 1097–1105 (2012)
10. Mathias, M., Timofte, R., Benenson, R., Van-Gool, L.: Traffic sign recognition how far are we from the solution? In: IJCNN, pp. 1–8 (2013)

11. Overett, G., Tychsen-Smith, L., Petersson, L., Pettersson, N., Andersson, L.: Creating robust high-throughput traffic sign detectors using centre-surround hog statistics. Mach. Vis. Appl. **25**, 713–726 (2014)
12. Perona, P.: Visual recognition, Circa 2007. In: Object Categorization Computer and Human Vision Perspectives, pp. 55–68. Cambridge University Press (2009)
13. Sermanet, P., LeCun, Y.: Traffic sign recognition with multi-scale convolutional networks. In: IJCNN, pp. 2809–2813 (2011)
14. Stallkamp, J., Schlipsing, M., Salmen, J., Igel, C.: Man vs. computer: benchmarking machine learning algorithms for traffic sign recognition. Neural Netw. **32**, 323–332 (2012)
15. Tan, M., Wang, B., Wu, Z., Wang, J., Pan, G.: Weakly supervised metric learning for traffic sign recognition in a LIDAR-equipped vehicle. IEEE Trans. Intell. Transp. Syst. **17**(5), 1415–1427 (2016)
16. Timofte, R., van Gool, L.: Sparse representation based projections. In: BMVC, pp. 61.1–61.12 (2011)
17. Timofte, R., van Gool, L.: Iterative nearest neighbors for classification and dimensionality reduction. In: CVPR, pp. 2456–2463 (2012)
18. Vega, V., Sidibé, D., Fougerolle, Y.: Road signs detection and reconstruction using gielis curves. In: International Conference on Computer Vision Theory and Applications, pp. 393–396 (2012)
19. Wang, D., Yue, S., Xu, J., Hou, X., Liu, C.-L.: A saliency-based cascade method for fast traffic sign detection. In: Intelligent Vehicles Symposium, pp. 180–185 (2015)
20. Zeng, Y., Xu, X., Fang, Y., Zhao, K.: Traffic sign recognition using deep convolutional networks and extreme learning machine. In: IScIDE, pp. 272–280 (2015)

The Orlando Project: A 28 nm FD-SOI Low Memory Embedded Neural Network ASIC

Giuseppe Desoli[1], Valeria Tomaselli[2], Emanuele Plebani[3]([✉]), Giulio Urlini[3],
Danilo Pau[0], Viviana D'Alto[3], Tommaso Majo[1], Fabio De Ambroggi[3],
Thomas Boesch[1], Surinder-pal Singh[4], Elio Guidetti[1], and Nitin Chawla[4]

[1] STMicroelectronics, Cornaredo, Italy
[2] STMicroelectronics, Catania, Italy
[3] STMicroelectronics, Agrate Brianza, Italy
emanuele.plebani1@st.com
[4] STMicroelectronics, Greater Noida, India

Abstract. The recent success of neural networks in various computer
vision tasks open the possibility to add visual intelligence to mobile and
wearable devices; however, the stringent power requirements are unsuitable for networks run on embedded CPUs or GPUs. To address such challenges, STMicroelectronics developed the Orlando Project, a new and low
power architecture for convolutional neural network acceleration suited
for wearable devices. An important contribution to the energy usage is
the storage and access to the neural network parameters. In this paper,
we show that with adequate model compression schemes based on weight
quantization and pruning, a whole AlexNet network can fit in the local
memory of an embedded processor, thus avoiding additional system complexity and energy usage, with no or low impact on the accuracy of the
network. Moreover, the compression methods work well across different
tasks, e.g. image classification and object detection.

Keywords: Convolutional neural networks · Hardware acceleration

1 Introduction

In the last few years, the representation paradigm of data in Computer Vision,
Speech Recognition and Signal Processing in general, has drastically changed.
Before 2012, the signal representation problem was addressed by the design
of ad-hoc and hand-crafted features, followed by task-driven machine learning
approaches. Features with different discrimination power and increasing complexity have been designed over the years for different kinds of signals (images,
videos, audio, etc.); moreover, features codifying different characteristics have
often been integrated together to improve representation capabilities, and hence
increasing the recognition accuracy on 1D and 2D signals.

Thanks to the advances in both hardware capabilities and neural network
training, today it is possible to rethink the representation paradigms, both supervised and unsupervised, by taking into consideration the algorithms developed

© Springer International Publishing AG 2016
J. Blanc-Talon et al. (Eds.): ACIVS 2016, LNCS 10016, pp. 217–227, 2016.
DOI: 10.1007/978-3-319-48680-2_20

in the field of deep learning. In 2012 the ImageNet Large Scale Visual Recognition Challenge [1], consisting in the classification of 1000 different object classes, was won by the University of Toronto with a huge performance gap with respect to competing approaches, by exploiting a deep Convolutional Neural Network (CNN) [2], later called *AlexNet*.

Now the most successful and accurate approaches in object classification and detection are based on convolutional neural networks, which significantly outperform all the other approaches. In order to exploit this technology in everyday life and make it pervasive in mobile and wearable devices, an hardware accelerator with the ability to work in real time with very limited power consumption and with embedded memory is required. For this reason the Orlando processor was developed.

The rest of this paper is organized as follows. In Sect. 2 a review of hardware acceleration approaches for neural networks is offered. Section 3 gives a brief description of the Orlando processor and Sect. 4 illustrates a model compression scheme required to fit the existing networks in Orlando's limited embedded memory. In Sect. 5 the results of compressed models on classification and detection are presented and discussed. Finally, in Sect. 6 the conclusions are drawn.

2   Overview of the State of the Art

Right after the introduction of CNNs, their good performances but high computational complexity encouraged to the first attempts to accelerate neural networks in hardware. The ANNA processor [3], proposed in 1991, implements a network for hand-written digit recognition using internally an analog representation to save transistors, achieving up to 1000 classifications per second.

The recent revival in neural networks is based mostly on the availability of cheap and powerful GPUs, first used to train AlexNet [2] with hand-coded CUDA kernels; however, the ever increasing size and expressiveness of modern neural networks create demand for even more efficient architectures. One of the first examples is the Neuflow processor [4], which includes a number of Processing Elements (PE) with dedicated convolution accelerators; already on Field Programmable Gate Arrays (FPGAs), the performances per Watt were competitive with GPUs and mobile CPUs in 2011. An evolution of the architecture is the *nn-X* processor [5] proposed by the startup Teradeep; a similar layout in PEs and memory accesses, but with compression of memory transfers, is implemented in the Eyeriss architecture [6].

An architecture proposed by [7] and implemented in FPGA, reduces complexity by aggressively quantizing activations and weights to 4/8 bits, achieving 137 Giga Operations Per Second (GOPS) at 150 MHz. The DianNiao [8] series of processors (DaDianNao [9] and ShinDianNao [10]) are ASICs specifically developed to accelerate neural networks by using an array of multiply-add units; they achieve gains in power efficiency up to an order of magnitude compared to a K20 GPU, but the power consumption is still dominated by memory accesses. As the memory accesses are an important factor in energy efficiency, the EIE processor

[11] combines low precision arithmetics with a set of network compression strategies [12] in order to fit the model in the local SRAM and reduce the number of operations involved; it can reach 10 k frames per second on the fully connected layers of AlexNet at 0.6 W, but no specific acceleration has been implemented for the convolutional layers.

Neuromorphic processor have also been used to approximate and accelerate CNNs. In [13], a neuromorphic unit performs tracking with a CNN over the output of an event camera; in [14], the chip TrueNorth [15] developed by IBM runs a CNN by converting weights and activations to binary values and achieves a power footprint of 50 mW.

3   Orlando System-On-a-Chip

"Orlando", code name for a STMicroelectronics System On Chip (SoC) R&D prototype, is a hardware platform combining ultra-high computational performances with ultra-low power consumption suitable for IoT, wearable and smart sensing applications. The processors include programmable heterogeneous hardware. The SoC has been designed to be scalable, allowing the use of all processors and accelerators or only a fraction, in order to achieve different trade-offs between computational power and energy consumption, thus supporting different computer vision applications.

Orlando can accelerate different computer vision and image processing tasks, including the large number of convolutions and dot products in a typical state-of-the-art feed-forward neural network; however, the flexibility of its architecture allows the acceleration of a wide range of network architectures, including Recurrent Neural Networks (RNN) and the recently proposed Residual Networks [16].

The test chip is currently under fabrication and will be ready by the end of the third quarter of 2016; in the meantime, an implementation running on a Xilinx Zynq FPGA emulator has been demonstrated running an image classification network and an object detector. In order to fit the limited memory available on the FPGA platform, the models have been compressed using the methods described in the following sections.

Orlando's software environment is integrated with the deep learning platform *Caffe* [17], enabling access to the training infrastructure implemented in the toolbox and to the large number of pre-trained neural networks. A set of tools converts the weights and the network architecture in Orlando's internal representation.

4   Model Compression

One of the most challenging aspects of the integration of a CNN into an embedded system is the memory usage. The successful AlexNet requires 60 million parameters (217 MB in single precision floating point), and the more recent *VGG16* network [18] can require more than 500 MB. Such amount of data cannot be integrated into a single chip without the adoption of aggressive memory reduction methods with low impact on the model accuracy. Moreover, if a reduced model can fit on the embedded memory of a processor, huge energy savings can be achieved, as the power consumption of SRAM cache accesses and the power consumption of external LPDDR2 DRAM accesses are separated by two orders of magnitude, from 640 pJ in DRAM to 5 pJ in SRAM at 45 nm [12]. This motivates developing a fully embedded implementation of a neural network fitting the small memory budget of an embedded platform such as Orlando, and thus estimating the memory required by networks used for real-world applications.

Our effort is devoted to the compression of weights of both convolutional and fully-connected layers. Moreover, we have performed a deep analysis of weights compression in two different use cases, both based on an AlexNet architecture: classification of 1000 object categories and pedestrian/car detection. The impact of compression in the classification task has been evaluated on a pre-trained AlexNet model available from the MatConv Matlab toolbox [19], whereas compression in the detection task has been evaluated on an optimized pedestrian detection pipeline [20], dubbed *DeepPed*.

4.1   Compression Strategy

We have tested different compression strategies with the goal of reducing the CNN model size with minimal accuracy loss. We tried scalar quantization up to 1 bit per weight and then we pruned the CNN connections based on the absolute value of the connection weights. Quantization and pruning are then applied together to check their mutual dependence and build a final compressed model. The strategies follow closely the approach outlined in *Deep Compression* [12], with the difference that in our best detector model quantization and pruning are applied in reverse (first quantization, then pruning).

The strategies are implemented as follows:

Scalar Quantization: each CNN layer is compressed individually. The layer weights are clustered using k-means, where the number of centroids is computed as a function of the desired compression factor assuming that the uncompressed weights are represented in single precision floating point:

$$n_{centroids} = 2^{\frac{32}{f_{compr}}} \tag{1}$$

Pruning: each CNN layer is compressed individually. All the layer weights below a threshold are zeroed-out, and the threshold is decided based on the desired compression factor:

$$w_{ij} = \begin{cases} 0, & \text{if } |w_{ij}| < threshold \\ w_{ij}, & \text{otherwise} \end{cases} \tag{2}$$

In the case a hardware designer is able to specify the connections between neurons individually on an ASIC or an FPGA, the pruned weights simply translate in missing connections. Since power consumption increases linearly with wire capacity loads, the pruned connections reduce power, space and storage usage. However, a binary map coding the non-null neurons connections is necessary for a software implementation, increasing the required memory.

Quantization and Pruning: The combination of both quantization and pruning lets the strengths of one method compensate the weaknesses of the other. The accuracy obtained by the combination of the two methods outperforms both of them at a fixed compression factor, and conversely, at a given accuracy target, the best compression factor is obtained by combining the two approaches.

When comparing individually scalar quantization and pruning, the former outperforms the latter in the two main scenarios that have been evaluated:

- compressing the convolutional layers
- compressing the fully connected layers

in classification and detection. Regardless of the method used to compress the weights, we noticed that, due to the strong correlation between weights belonging to different layers, better results are achieved when compressing both convolutional and fully connected layers.

While in this work we only apply compression on pre-trained networks, it should be noted that the compressed network can be further retrained to compensate for the impact of quantization and pruning and thus achieving even higher accuracy for a given level of compression, as shown in [12]. However, retraining requires the full access to the training infrastructure (dataset and algorithms).

5 Experiments

5.1 Classification

In order to evaluate the best compression strategy in classification, a pre-trained AlexNet model, downloaded from [19] has been used as starting point. The model is trained on the ImageNet dataset on 1000 different object classes. As aforementioned, AlexNet requires up to 217 MB in single precision, of which 208 MB are required by the fully connected layers; for this reason, compression was applied first to the fully connected layers and only after on convolutional layers.

As discussed in Sect. 4.1, the fully connected layers have been quantized using k-means; in addition, the centroids have been converted to a fixed point format to assess the accuracy drop related to the floating to fixed-point conversion. In a second set of analyses, the weights below a certain threshold have been pruned. Finally, both strategies (quantization and pruning) have been combined together. In order to measure the accuracy drop with respect to the original model, the compressed models have been tested on the ImageNet validation set, composed by 50000 images from 1000 object classes. In the test phase, the algorithm needs to produce 5 class labels $l_j, j = 1..5$ in decreasing order of confidence. The ground

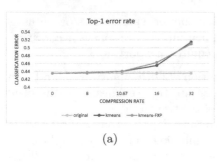
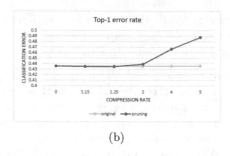

(a)   (b)

Fig. 1. Results of compression: classification error (top-1) vs compression rate. In (a) weights quantization; in (b) weight pruning. (Color figure online)

truth labels for the image are g_k, $k = 1, ..., n$ with n labeled object classes. The error of the algorithm for a single image is:

$$e = \frac{1}{n} \sum_k \min_j d\left(l_j, g_k\right) \quad \text{where} \quad d(x, y) = \begin{cases} 1, & \text{if } x = y \\ 0, & \text{otherwise} \end{cases} \quad (3)$$

and the overall error score is the average error over all test images. More specifically, 2 error rates are measured: top-1 and top-5 error rates, which are the error rates in making 1 guess or 5 guesses about the label, respectively.

To assess the impact of weights quantization on the classification error rate, the weights of each fully connected layer have been separately quantized in a specified number of centroids. We chose codebook with power of 2 sizes because the centroids can be represented with an integer number of bits. We tested centroids with $\{1, 2, 3, 4\}$ bits; as the compression rate when using floats (32 bit per value) is $\frac{32}{b}$, where b is the number of bits for the compressed representation, the corresponding compression rates are $\{32, 16, 10.67, 8\}$. Moreover, to evaluate the impact of floating to fixed-point conversion, the centroids have been converted to fixed point before the evaluation.

The plot in Fig. 1(a) shows in blue the baseline error rate (top-1: 43.56 %); a compression rate up to 10.67× (8 centroids) is reached without significant impact on accuracy, while a larger compression factor leads to an exponential growth in the error rate. Moreover, fixed-point conversion does not increase the error significantly. The same behavior has been observed in top-5 error rate.

To assess the impact of pruning on classification error rate, we have zeroed out the weights of each fully connected layer below a certain threshold, set differently for each layer. The thresholds have been decided by calculating a set of percentiles (13th, 20th, 50th, 75th, 80th) of the weights, which then correspond to compression rates of 1.15, 1.25, 2, 4 and 5 times, respectively.

In Fig. 1(b) the error rate rapidly increases with the compression rate; in particular, pruning rates larger than 2× highly compromise the accuracy and pruning alone performs worse than scalar quantization alone at the same level of compression.

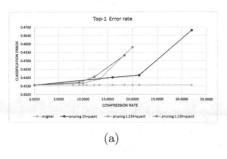
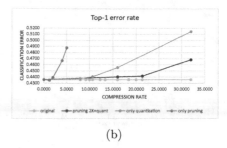

(a)   (b)

Fig. 2. Combining quantization and weight pruning (a) and the best results achieved for each compression strategy (b).

The two compression strategies (quantization and pruning) have been finally tested together to investigate their complementarity. In particular, we tested pruning (1.15, 1.25 and 2 times) followed by quantization (16, 8, 4 centroids); results are reported in Fig. 2(a).

The best compromise between compression and accuracy has been achieved by pruning half of the connections (pruning 2×) and then quantizing the remaining weights using 8 centroids (global compression rate of 21.34) or 16 centroids (global compression rate of 16), with a top-1 error rate increase of 0.6 % and 0.4 %, respectively.

We also tested the operations in inverted order, by firstly quantizing weights with 16 centroids and then pruning them with the aforementioned compression rates; however, results were much worse than in the former approach. To have a better understanding of the best compression strategy, Fig. 2(b) shows a summary plot, comparing all the best performing strategies we evaluated.

From Fig. 2(b) it is quite evident that pruning alone is the worst approach; quantization alone achieves a 10.67× compression rate with a 0.5 % error increase; pruning 2× followed by quantization achieves a compression of around 21× with a 0.6 % error rate increase. We have demonstrated that pruning and quantization are complementary strategies, and hence they can be beneficially combined to achieve higher compression rates, but the order of the two operations is important.

Convolutional layers have also been quantized; in a first test, all the weights of the convolutional layers have been compressed using the same codebook of 256 centroids, but top-1 error rate increased of about 4 %; afterwards, weights have been quantized using a different codebook of size 256 per layer; with this strategy, the top-1 error rate increased by only 0.3 %.

5.2   Detection

The evaluation of compression on object detection is based on the DeepPed model [20]. DeepPed is a Regions with CNN (R-CNN) detector [21] following [22] in using an efficient pedestrian detector as proposal method; in particular,

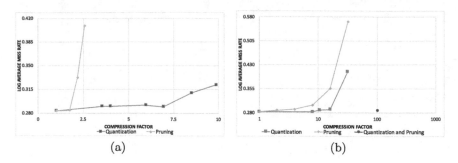

Fig. 3. DeepPed results. In (a), comparison between compression by scalar quantization and by pruning in convolutional layers: the pruning method has a dramatic impact on the information content. In (b), comparison between compression by scalar quantization and by pruning in fully connected layers.

the Aggregated Channel Features (ACF) detector [23] is used. The CNN is an AlexNet without the softmax layer, trained on ImageNet and then fine-tuned on the Caltech training dataset [24]. The features from the last CNN layer are extracted from the regions proposed by ACF and used as input to a first Support Vector Machine (SVM) to extract a confidence score; then, the ACF and the CNN scores are fed to a second SVM classifier giving a final score for the region. The details of the algorithm are discussed in [20].

We use the *Log Average Miss Rate* (LAMR) evaluation metrics proposed by Dollár *et al.* [24] on the Caltech Pedestrian dataset and we evaluate the compression performances in terms of trade-off between the *compression factor* (CF) and LAMR measured on the Caltech test set. In this case, the effects of compression have been analyzed on both the convolutional and fully connected layers.

Figure 3(b) shows the results of scalar quantization and weight pruning on the fully connected layers. Both scalar quantization and pruning give a significant size reduction, but, as in the case of classification, the best results are achieved with quantization.

Figure 3(a) shows the result of compressing the convolutional layers. The first layer is especially sensitive to corruption and thus compressed with a low factor (9 bit/weight) and never pruned. Conversely, the convolutional layers 3, 4 and 5 are compressed with higher factors. The blue curve, representing the effect of scalar quantization, shows that the error increases almost linearly with the compression factor. The gray curve, representing the effect of pruning, shows that throwing away small coefficients is not desirable in convolutional layers, since their effect greatly influences the next layers and thus the final accuracy.

5.3   Compressed Models

Tables 1 and 2 summarize the best mix of weight quantization and pruning for the convolutional layers alone, the fully connected layers alone and for both sets

Table 1. Performances of compressed classification.

Layers	Compression		Size (MB)		Top-1 error
	quant.	pruning	original	compr.	
conv1-5	4×	–	8.9	2.23	43.86 % (+0.3 %)
fc6-7	10.67×	2×	208.04	9.75	44.16 % (+0.6 %)
Total	18.1×		216.94	11.98	44.56 % (+0.9 %)

Table 2. Performances of compressed detection.

Layers	Compression		Size (MB)		LAMR
	quant.	pruning	original	compr.	
conv1-5	5.94×		8.9	1.5	29.2 % (+0.9 %)
fc6-7	102×		208.04	2.04	28.6 % (+0.3 %)
Total	61.35×		216.93	3.54	28.7 % (+0.4 %)

of layers. The best results are achieved by compressing the network as a whole; in the detection case the compression of the fully connected (*fc*) layers even improve performances, because they act as a regularizer for the SVM trained on top of them.

The detection network is the only network we tested that reached the 4 MB target without significant loss in accuracy; however, even if the classification network requires an external memory, its access cost is still reduced by 20×. Additional tricks could improve the power consumption ever more, e.g. using a larger internal memory in a smaller technological node (e.g. 7 nm) or by using a classification layer with a smaller memory footprint (e.g. the recently proposed tensor layer [25]).

6   Conclusions

We presented a set of compression strategies for neural networks suitable for embedded hardware accelerators and we evaluated them in the context of a real processor, Orlando, which is being developed by STMicroelectronics. We show that the power savings achieved by Orlando with respect to general purpose CPUs and GPUs are further enhanced by the compression of the network parameters. Energy-intensive accesses to external DRAM are reduced or, in the case of our best detector model, completely avoided as the network fits into the local memory of a small embedded processor with a negligible loss in performance. We thus show that the size of the network parameters is not a limiting constraint.

Of the two approaches we tested, weight quantization and weight pruning, the former gives the best results in both classification and detection. However, the two approaches are complimentary and the best results, compression of 20 times for classification and 100 times for detection, are achieved by combining the two methods, while the loss in accuracy is kept below 1 % in both cases. An additional advantage of the proposed methods is that they do not require a new network architecture, new types of layers or the retraining of the model and thus they can easily be applied on existing networks with minimal changes in the deployment pipeline, improving the applicability of embedded hardware accelerators such as Orlando.

References

1. Russakovsky, O., Deng, J., Su, H., Krause, J., et al.: ImageNet large scale visual recognition challenge. Arxiv, p. 37, September 2014
2. Krizhevsky, A., Sutskever, I., Hinton, G.: ImageNet classification with deep convolutional neural networks. In: NIPS, Lake Tahoe, pp. 1097–1105 (2012)
3. Boser, B., Sackinger, E., Bromley, J., LeCun, Y., et al.: An analog neural network processor and its application to high-speed character recognition. In: International Joint Conference on Neural Networks, Seattle, vol. i, pp. 415–420 (1991)
4. Farabet, C., Martini, B., Corda, B., Akselrod, P., et al.: NeuFlow: a runtime reconfigurable dataflow processor for vision. In: IEEE Computer Society Conference on Computer Vision and Pattern Recognition Workshops (2011)
5. Gokhale, V., Jin, J., Dundar, A., Martini, B., et al.: A 240 G-ops/s mobile coprocessor for deep neural networks. In: CVPR (2014)
6. Chen, Y.H., Krishna, T., Emer, J., Sze, V.: Eyeriss: an energy-efficient reconfigurable accelerator for deep convolutional neural networks. In: Proceedings of ISSCC (2016)
7. Qiu, J., Song, S., Wang, Y., Yang, H., et al.: Going deeper with embedded FPGA platform for convolutional neural network. In: Proceedings of the 2016 ACM/SIGDA International Symposium on Field-Programmable Gate Arrays, pp. 26–35. ACM, New York, February 2016
8. Chen, T., Du, Z., Sun, N., Wang, J., et al.: DianNao: a small-footprint high-throughput accelerator for ubiquitous machine-learning. In: International Conference on Architectural Support for Programming Languages and Operating Systems - ASPLOS, pp. 269–283 (2014)
9. Chen, Y., Luo, T., Liu, S., Zhang, S., et al.: DaDianNao: a machine-learning supercomputer. In: 2014 47th Annual IEEE/ACM International Symposium on Microarchitecture, pp. 609–622. IEEE. December 2014
10. Du, Z., Fasthuber, R., Chen, T., Ienne, P., et al.: ShiDianNao: shifting vision processing closer to the sensor. In: ISCA, pp. 92–104 (2015)
11. Han, S., Liu, X., Mao, H., Pu, J., et al.: EIE: Efficient Inference Engine on compressed deep neural network. In: ISCA, February 2016
12. Han, S., Mao, H., Dally, W.J.: Deep compression: compressing deep neural networks with pruning, trained quantization and Huffman Coding. In: ICLR, San Juan, October 2016
13. Serrano-Gotarredona, R., Oster, M., Lichtsteiner, P., Linares-Barranco, A., et al.: CAVIAR: A 45k neuron, 5M synapse, 12G connects/s AER hardware sensory-processing-learning-actuating system for high-speed visual object recognition and tracking. IEEE Trans. Neural Netw. **20**, 1417–1438 (2009)
14. Esser, S.K., Merolla, P.A., Arthur, J.V., Cassidy, A.S., et al.: Convolutional networks for fast, energy-efficient neuromorphic computing. Arxiv, p. 7, March 2016

15. Merolla, P.A., Arthur, J.V., Alvarez-Icaza, R., Cassidy, A.S., et al.: A million spiking-neuron integrated circuit with a scalable communication network and interface. Science **345**(6197), 668–673 (2014)
16. He, K., Zhang, X., Ren, S., Sun, J.: Deep residual learning for image recognition. Technical report, Microsoft Research, December 2015
17. Jia, Y., Shelhamer, E., Donahue, J., Karayev, S., Long, J., Girshick, R., Guadarrama, S., Darrell, T.: Caffe: convolutional architecture for fast feature embedding. Technical report, Berkeley Vision and Learning Center, June 2014
18. Simonyan, K., Zisserman, A.: Very Deep convolutional networks for large-scale image recognition. Technical report, Google Research, September 2014
19. Vedaldi, A., Lenc, K.: MatConvNet - convolutional neural networks for MATLAB. Arxiv, December 2014
20. Tomè, D., Monti, F., Baroffio, L., Bondi, L., et al.: Deep convolutional neural networks for pedestrian detection. Technical report, Politecnico di Milano, October 2015
21. Girshick, R., Donahue, J., Darrell, T., Malik, J.: Rich feature hierarchies for accurate object detection and semantic segmentation. In: CVPR, Columbus, November 2014
22. Hosang, J., Omran, M., Benenson, R., Schiele, B.: Taking a deeper look at pedestrians. In: CVPR, Boston, January 2015
23. Dollar, P., Appel, R., Belongie, S., Perona, P.: Fast feature pyramids for object detection. IEEE Trans. Pattern Anal. Mach. Intell. **36**(8), 1532–1545 (2014)
24. Dollár, P., Wojek, C., Schiele, B., Perona, P.: Pedestrian detection: an evaluation of the state of the art. Pattern Anal. Mach. Intell. **34**(4), 743–761 (2012)
25. Novikov, A., Podoprikhin, D., Osokin, A., Vetrov, D.: Tensorizing neural networks. In: NIPS. Montreal, September 2015

Factor Analysis of Dynamic Sequence with Spatial Prior for 2D Cardiac Spect Sequences Analysis

Marc Filippi[1]([envelope]), Michel Desvignes[1], Eric Moisan[1], Catherine Ghezzi[1], Pascale Perret[1], and Daniel Fagret[2]

[1] University Grenoble-Alpes, GIPSA-LAB, Saint-Martin-d'Hères, France
marc.filippi@gipsa-lab.fr
[2] University Grenoble-Alpes, INSERM1039, Saint-Martin-d'Hères, France

Abstract. Unmixing is often a necessary step to analyze 2D SPECT image sequence. However, factor analysis of dynamic sequences (FADS), the commonly used method for unmixing SPECT sequences, suffers from non-uniqueness issue. Optimization-based methods were developed to overcome this issue. These methods are effective but need improvement when the mixing is important or with very low SNR. In this paper, a new objective function using soft spatial prior knowledge is developed. Comparison with previous methods, efficiency and robustness to the choice of priors are illustrated with tests on synthetic dataset. Results on 2D SPECT sequences with high level of noise are also presented and compared.

Keywords: Source separation · SPECT · Factor Analysis · Spatial priors · Penalized least squares

1 Introduction

Insulin resistance is the desensitization of cells to insulin. It can lead to type 2 diabete and cardiovascular disease. Knowledge of the insulin resistance index is of great interest in order to prevent these diseases. However, actual methods are rather invasive and can't be used in clinical routines. A new and easier method has been proposed [1]. It uses a tracer of glucose transport (6-DIG), injected to a patient. The activity of the tracer is dynamically acquired with a gamma camera which produces a 2D SPECT images sequence. Because of the collimator, a very few number of radiations are counted and these images suffer from a high Poisson noise with a very low Signal-to-Noise Ratio (Fig. 1).

To compute the insulin resistance index [1], the dynamic activity of the tracer in the myocardium, and in the left and right ventricles (LV and RV) have to be determined. As images are the 2D projections of the 3D organs, spatial overlaps are present in these 2D images, particularly in the cardiac area between the myocardium and the ventricles. Then, to obtain the pure time-activity curve (TAC) of each organ, methods based on region of interest (ROI) give poor results.

© Springer International Publishing AG 2016
J. Blanc-Talon et al. (Eds.): ACIVS 2016, LNCS 10016, pp. 228–237, 2016.
DOI: 10.1007/978-3-319-48680-2_21

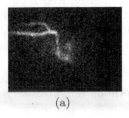
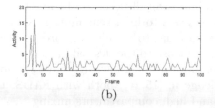

(a)   (b)

Fig. 1. 6-DIG SPECT dataset (a) 3rd image of a sequence - Tracer reaching right ventricle (b) Activity of a pixel located on the right ventricle on the first 100 frames.

Because of the spatial overlaps, the activity on these ROIs is composed of a mixture of pure organs TAC. Therefore, the tracer activity in each physiological compartments have to be unmixed in order to be further analyzed.

It is a common issue in medical imaging, particularly in scintigraphy. Data are assumed to be a mixing of physiological compartments activity and are represented with a linear mixing model (1). Each compartment has its own temporal signature (factor or TAC) and its own spatial signature (factor image).

$$Y = A \times F + \epsilon \qquad (1)$$

The dynamic data are represented in the $N \times P$ matrix Y, where N is the number of pixels (vectorized) and P is the number of images. The $N \times K$ matrix A contains the factor images and the $K \times P$ matrix F contains the factors, where K is the number of physiological compartments. The activity in each pixel is then a linear combination of several factors F. The coefficients of this linear combination are contained in the matrix A. The matrix ϵ of size $N \times P$ contains the noise.

The matrix A represents the quantity of each organ on each pixel, and the matrix F represents the number of gamma photons detected on a pixel during a short time span. Then coefficients of matrix A and F must be non-negative. Two classes of methods [2] have been typically used to find A and F with non-negative coefficients by solving Eq. (1): spectral-type methods [3] and Factor Analysis of Dynamic Structures (FADS) methods [4].

In spectral methods, F is a combination of chosen basis functions such as splines. In general, these methods produce too smooth solutions.

FADS, introduced by Barber [5], shares the same foundation than some Independent Component Analysis (ICA) or Non-Negative Matrix Factorization methods, widely used in hyperspectral unmixing [6–10]. FADS has a great geometrical interpretation and proceeds in two steps, an orthogonal analysis followed by an oblique analysis. The first step is used to reduce noise and project data into a low dimension space. The second step uses oblique rotation of factors in order to find factors and factor images with positive coefficients.

FADS has been improved and adapted to scintigraphy [11]. In order to face high Poisson noise an optimal metric has been found [12], and a regularized factor analysis has been proposed [13]. However finding A and F in Eq. (1) with positive constraints is an ill-posed problem, the solution is not mathematically unique, and this leads to high remaining mixture in factors obtained. Prior knowledge on the data has to be added in order to perform the right unmixing and obtain a solution close to the desired one.

Temporal prior knowledge have already been used in [14] and spatial prior knowledge in [15,16], both with FADS, but these methods fail with very low SNR and high compartments mixing.

In order to overcome non-uniqueness issue of FADS, a penalized least squares objective function has been proposed in [17]. This optimization-based method gives good results when the mixing in the data is low, but results can be improved when the mixing is higher, because solutions with overlaps are penalized in the objective function.

We propose here to exploit soft spatial prior knowledge on the data to improve unmixing in an optimization-based method, by constructing a new objective function. Our method is described in Sect. 2, algorithm and implementation details are given in Sect. 3 and results are shown in Sect. 4.

2   Methods

We propose a new objective function to minimise defined as:

$$f = f_{LS}(\hat{A}, \hat{F}) + a \times f_{UNI}(\hat{A}) + b \times f_{PRIOR}(\hat{A}) \tag{2}$$

and under the following constraints:

$$\forall (i,t,k)\hat{A}_{i,k} \geq 0 \quad and \quad \hat{F}_{k,t} \geq 0 \tag{3}$$

where a and b are penalty constants. f_{LS} corresponds to the least squares objective. This term measures the distance between the data and the factor model, and ensures data fidelity. This function is not convex in $(\hat{A}, \hat{F})$ but is convex in both $\hat{A}$ and $\hat{F}$, so that we can use an alternate minimization gradient method.

$$f_{LS}(\hat{A}, \hat{F}) = \sum_{i=1}^{N} \sum_{t=1}^{P} (Y_{i,t} - \sum_{k=1}^{K} \hat{A}_{i,k} \times \hat{F}_{k,t})^2 \tag{4}$$

f_{UNI} penalizes solutions with high correlation between factor images [17] to reduce amount of mixing and favors the separation of factor images with no intersections. It can be seen as a sparsity promoting criterion.

$$f_{UNI}(\hat{A}) = \sum_{k=1}^{K} \sum_{h=k+1}^{P} \sum_{i=1}^{N} \frac{\hat{A}_{i,k}}{\sqrt{\sum_{j=1}^{N} \hat{A}_{j,k}^2}} \frac{\hat{A}_{i,h}}{\sqrt{\sum_{j=1}^{N} \hat{A}_{j,h}^2}} \tag{5}$$

f_{PRIOR} is a new penalization term. This criterion ensures fidelity to spatial prior knowledge. The idea behind this criterion is to penalize solutions whose compartments are too far from their expected locations. In Cardiac SPECT exams, the ventricles can be easily coarsely located. So, the new term exploits this information to obtain a solution which respect the expected positions of the ventricles.

$$f_{PRIOR}(\hat{A}) = \sum_{k=1}^{K} \sum_{i=1}^{N} dist_{W_k}(i)^2 \times \hat{A}_{i,k}^2 \tag{6}$$

W_K is a patch containing a set of pixels where the kth physiological compartment is likely to be located. This patch represents prior knowledge and is the coarse spatial location of the kth physiological compartment. $dist_{W_k}(i)$ is the Euclidean distance between the ith pixel and the kth patch (i.e. to the closest pixel in the patch). This criterion has the advantage to be convex and computation is fast. Prior knowledge contained in this criterion is also very soft. In most of scintigraphic studies, spatial positions of physiological compartments are easily available thanks to the perfusion. This criterion ensures fidelity with prior knowledge by penalizing factor images far from their expected position. This fidelity is essential in hard unmixing problem to obtain physically meaningful solutions, and overcome non-uniqueness issue.

3   Algorithm and Implementation Details

Before minimizing the objective function, the number of physiological compartments K, the patches W and an initialization of $\hat{A}$ and $\hat{F}$ had to be chosen.

K can be chosen manually with prior knowledge on data, or can be computed with an analysis of singular values given by a singular value decomposition applied on Y.

Spatial prior knowledge or patches W can be chosen manually, or automatically with a first segmentation method. In our problem, a first factor analysis gives a first coarse location of LV and RV. Factor images are thresholded and skeletonization creates patches W_k containing spatial prior knowledge. When no spatial prior knowledge on a physiological compartment exists, the associated patch contains all the pixels because there are no constraints. Matrix of factor images $\hat{A}$ is initialized by a constant. $\hat{F}$ is initialized with a mean on appropriate ROI for each factor. These ROI can be those used to build the patches W_k. For the purpose of speeding-up the optimization process, $\hat{F}$ was multiplied by a constant to have the same order of magnitude on Y and $\hat{A} \times \hat{F}$.

As f_{LS} is convex in $\hat{A}$ and convex in $\hat{F}$, but not in $(\hat{A}, \hat{F})$, an alternating minimization method was used. Depending on the alternation, a gradient of the objective function f is calculated analytically according to $\hat{A}$ or $\hat{F}$.

For each alternation, a nonlinear conjugate gradient method is used, with Polak-Ribière method to choose descent direction. The minimum of the objective function in this direction is computed thanks to the Brent method. In order to speed-up the algorithm, the number of iterations for each alternation is limited to 8 and the alternation is stopped if the relative change in the objective function in one iteration is less than 10^{-6}.

To satisfy the positivity constraints in (3), the negative coefficients of A and F are forced to zero after each iteration. Each factor image is also re-scaled in order to have their maximum to one after each iteration. Each factors are re-scaled by the reciprocal, in order for (1) to hold.

The optimization process is stopped when the relative change in the objective function between two groups of two alternations is less than 10^{-6}. We have no proofs of convergence, but in all our tests, the algorithm has always converged in less than 500 alternations.

4   Results

4.1   Synthetic Data

First, this method is tested on synthetic data set inspired from [17] and representing cardiac area. Dataset is a sequence of 400 images of 30-by-30 pixels. Three physiological compartments are present: right ventricle (RV), left ventricle (LV) and myocardium. Some overlaps are added, in order to have myocardium softly present in the right and left ventricles, as in SPECT sequences.

Poisson noise is added to this data set, with different SNR.

Patches W_k are chosen manually, to show robustness of the method to the choice of the prior. The robustness is shown in this example in three ways. Firstly, no prior is selected for the myocardium. Secondly, instead of taking all pixels of the organ (which lead to better results), prior for right and left ventricles are a very thin skeleton of their respective organ. Thirdly, these skeletons are slightly shifted and not exactly located at their right places. These priors are shown on Fig. 2. Penalty constants a and b are chosen empirically, a variation of 30 % of these constants does not change significantly the results.

Our algorithm F_{Global} is compared to the optimization-based method F_{PLS} [17] and the regularized FADS method F_{REG} [13]. F_{REG} is the method previously used for the 6-DIG SPECT data. To compare these algorithms, the errors A_{error} and F_{error} are computed. Noise was measured with the formula in (9).

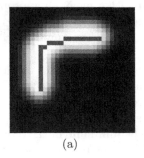
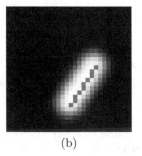

(a)   (b)

Fig. 2. Prior used for synthetic data set. (a) Right ventricle in white, and its prior in blue. (b) Left ventricle in white and its prior in red. (Color figure online)

$$A_{error} = \frac{\sum_{i=1}^{N} \sum_{k=1}^{K} |A_{i,k} - \hat{A}_{i,k}|}{\sum_{i=1}^{N} \sum_{k=1}^{K} A_{i,k}} \tag{7}$$

$$F_{error} = \frac{\sum_{k=1}^{K} \sum_{t=1}^{P} |F_{k,t} - \hat{F}_{k,t}|}{\sum_{k=1}^{K} \sum_{t=1}^{P} F_{k,t}} \tag{8}$$

$$SNR = 20 * log(\frac{\sum_{i=1}^{N} \sum_{t=1}^{P} |Y_{i,t}|^2}{\sum_{i=1}^{N} \sum_{t=1}^{P} |\epsilon_{i,t}|^2}) \tag{9}$$

Results on synthetic data with different noise levels are detailed in Table 1. For F_{PLS} and F_{Global}, penalty constants were first chosen adequately for each noise level. Examples of factors and image factors obtained with synthetic data with a SNR of 10 are shown respectively in Figs. 3 and 4, with $a = 150000$ for F_{PLS} and $a = 80000$ and $b = 300$ for F_{Global}.)

Table 1. Comparison of measures A_{error} and F_{error}, with different methods and noise levels. Each measure is a mean of 20 tests.

SNR		F_{REG}	F_{PLS}	F_{Global}
6	A_{error}	0.298	0.225	0.169
	F_{error}	0.254	0.120	0.112
8	A_{error}	0.237	0.172	0.135
	F_{error}	0.166	0.085	0.077
10	A_{error}	0.206	0.142	0.109
	F_{error}	0.140	0.068	0.059
12	A_{error}	0.184	0.110	0.088
	F_{error}	0.109	0.055	0.049

Table 1 shows that unmixing is better performed by optimization-based methods (F_{PLS} and F_{Global}) than FADS method (F_{REG}), for every noise levels and for both estimation of factors and factor images.

Even if the added priors are very soft (just a skeleton) and not perfectly located, the new criterion f_{PRIOR} greatly improves the unmixing, especially on factor images. This new criterion penalizes the factor image corresponding to LV when having high coefficients in the RV area, because the distance to the prior is high. Furthermore, this criterion doesn't penalize myocardium factor image and this myocardium factor image has positive coefficients on the LV or RV area because there is really a superimposition of these organs on the 2D images. At the contrary, the f_{UNI} criterion penalizes overlaps between factor images and can't cope with this problem, and so myocardium is underestimated on the ventricles area with F_{PLS}. The improvement on factor image estimation with F_{Global} leads to a better estimation of factor curves (Fig. 4).

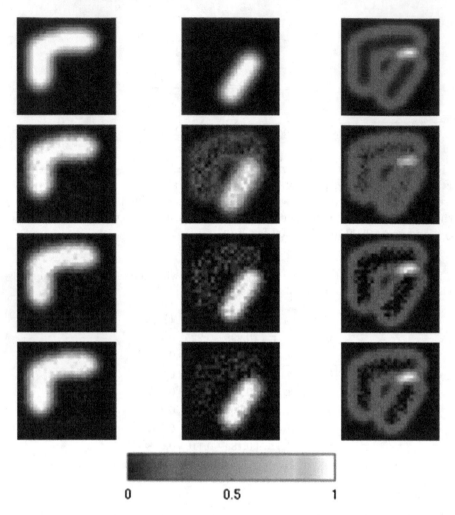

Fig. 3. Comparison of algorithms on synthetic data with a SNR of 10. First row correspond to ground truth. Row 2, 3 and 4 correspond to factor images obtained respectively with $F_{REG}, F_{PLS}, F_{Global}$. Column 1, 2 and 3 correspond respectively to RV, LV and myocardium.

4.2   6-DIG SPECT Sequence

The second data set is a 6-DIG SPECT sequence of a patient (see Fig. 1), and contains a sequence of 450 images of 128-by-128 pixels. A zoom is performed in order to focus on the cardiac area. Priors chosen are illustrated in Fig. 5 and factor images obtained are in Fig. 6.

Method f_{PLS} does not have a coherent factor image for the myocardium, this is due to the dimness of the myocardium signal. With f_{Global}, the myocardium is

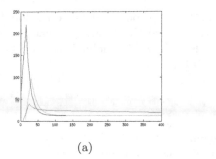
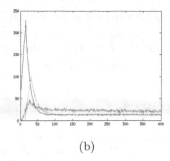

(a)   (b)

Fig. 4. Comparison of factors obtained with F_{Global} on synthetic data with a SNR of 10. (a) Ground Truth (b) Factor obtained with F_{Global}. The blue curves correspond to RV, the red curves to Myocardium, and the green curves to LV. (Color figure online)

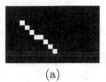
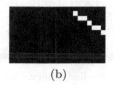
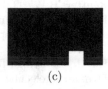

(a)   (b)   (c)

Fig. 5. Prior used for 6-DIG SPECT data set. Set of pixel W_k is represented in white. (a) Prior of RV. (b) Prior of LV. (c) Prior of myocardium.

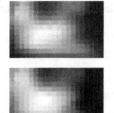

Fig. 6. Factor images obtained when unmixing of 6-DIG dataset. First row: with f_{PLS}. Second row: with f_{Global}. Columns 1, 2 and 3 represent respectively RV, LV and myocardium.

realistic thanks to the prior located on the cardiac apex, and has been validated by a cardiologist.

5   Conclusion

In this paper, we have presented a new spatial prior that can be defined coarsely to improve dynamic sequence analysis. This prior is a convex term and is embedded in an objective function to minimize by an alternate gradient method. This prior can be automatically defined because the method is robust to the location and shape of the prior. Tests on synthetic and SPECT dataset show the efficiency and the potential of this method. Future works include tests on larger database and quantitative analysis of the robustness.

References

1. Perret, P., Slimani, L., Briat, A., Villemain, D., Halimi, S., Demongeot, J., Fagret, D., Ghezzi, C.: Assessment of insulin resistance in fructose-fed rats with 125i-6-deoxy-6-iodo-d-glucose, a new tracer of glucose transport. Eur. J. Nuclear Med. Mol. Imaging **34**(5), 734–744 (2007)
2. Gullberg, G.T., Reutter, B.W., Sitek, A., Maltz, J.S., Budinger, T.F.: Dynamic single photon emission computed tomography-basic principles and cardiac applications. Phys. Med. Biol. **55**(20), R111 (2010)
3. Reutter, B.W., Gullberg, G.T., Boutchko, R., Balakrishnan, K., Botvinick, E.H., Huesman, R.H.: Fully 4-D dynamic cardiac spect image reconstruction using spatiotemporal B-spline voxelization. In: Nuclear Science Symposium Conference Record, 2007. NSS 2007, vol. 6, pp. 4217–4221. IEEE (2007)
4. Hu, J., Boutchko, R., Sitek, A., Reutter, B.W., Huesman, R.H., Gullberg, G.T.: Dynamic molecular imaging of cardiac innervation using a dual head pinhole spect system, Lawrence Berkeley National Laboratory (2008)
5. Barber, D.C.: The use of principal components in the quantitative analysis of gamma camera dynamic studies. Phys. Med. Biol. **25**(2), 283 (1980)
6. Moussaoui, S., Hauksdottir, H., Schmidt, F., Jutten, C., Chanussot, J., Brie, D., Douté, S., Benediktsson, J.A.: On the decomposition of mars hyperspectral data by ICA and Bayesian positive source separation. Neurocomputing **71**(10), 2194–2208 (2008)
7. Dobigeon, N., Moussaoui, S., Tourneret, J.-Y., Carteret, C.: Bayesian separation of spectral sources under non-negativity and full additivity constraints. Signal Process. **89**(12), 2657–2669 (2009)
8. Jia, S., Qian, Y.: Constrained nonnegative matrix factorization for hyperspectral unmixing. IEEE Trans. Geosci. Remote Sens. **47**(1), 161–173 (2009)
9. Huck, A., Guillaume, M., Blanc-Talon, J.: Minimum dispersion constrained nonnegative matrix factorization to unmix hyperspectral data. IEEE Trans. Geosci. Remote Sens. **48**(6), 2590–2602 (2010)
10. Bioucas-Dias, J.M., Plaza, A., Dobigeon, N., Parente, M., Qian, D., Gader, P., Chanussot, J.: Hyperspectral unmixing overview: geometrical, statistical, and sparse regression-based approaches. IEEE J. Sel. Topics Appl. Earth Obs. Remote Sens. **5**(2), 354–379 (2012)
11. Di Paola, R., Bazin, J.P., Aubry, F., Aurengo, A., Cavailloles, F., Herry, J.Y., Kahn, E.: Handling of dynamic sequences in nuclear medicine. IEEE Trans. Nuclear Sci. **29**(4), 1310–1321 (1982)
12. Benali, H., Buvat, I., Frouin, F., Bazin, J.P., Di Paola, R.: A statistical model for the determination of the optimal metric in factor analysis of medical image sequences (FAMIS). Phys. Med. Biol. **38**(8), 1065 (1993)
13. Frouin, F., De Cesare, A., Bouchareb, Y., Todd-Pokropek, A., Herment, A.: Spatial regularization applied to factor analysis of medical image sequences (FAMIS). Phys. Med. Biol. **44**(9), 2289 (1999)

14. Buvat, J., Benali, H., Frouin, F., Basin, J.P., Di Paola, R.: Target apex-seeking in factor analysis of medical image sequences. Phys. Med. Biol. **38**(1), 123 (1993)
15. Sitek, A., Di Bella, E.V.R., Gullberg, G.T.: Factor analysis with a priori knowledge-application in dynamic cardiac spect. Phys. Med. Biol. **45**(9), 2619 (2000)
16. Filippi, M., Desvignes, M., Moisan, E., Ghezzi, C., Perret, P., Fagret D.: A priori spatiaux et analyse factorielle de séquences scintigraphiques. In: GRETSI (2015)
17. Sitek, A., Gullberg, G.T., Huesman, R.H.: Correction for ambiguous solutions in factor analysis using a penalized least squares objective. IEEE Trans. Med. Imaging **21**(3), 216–225 (2002)

Soccer Player Detection with only Color Features Selected Using Informed Haar-like Features

Ryusuke Miyamoto[1(✉)] and Takuro Oki[2]

[1] Department of Computer Science, School of Science and Technology,
Meiji University, Kanagawa 2148571, Japan
miya@cs.meiji.ac.jp
[2] Department of Fundamental Science and Technology, Graduate School of Science
and Technology, Meiji University, Kanagawa 2148571, Japan
o_tkr@cs.meiji.ac.jp
http://www.ip.cs.meiji.ac.jp

Abstract. Player detection is important for tactical analysis, sports science, and video broadcasting, which is one of the practical applications of human detection. For human detection, filtered channel features shows better accuracy than methods based on deep learning. Considering the results on human detection, we constructed a detector having good balance between accuracy and computational speed for soccer players and using only color features to train a strong classifier. Experimental results using the PETS2003 dataset show that the proposed method can achieve about a 1.28 % miss rate at 0.1 FPPI, which is extremely good accuracy.

Keywords: Player detection · Color features · Informed Haar-like features

1 Introduction

Image-based object detection is one of the most challenging problems in the field of image processing. In particular, human detection is very significant, and several methods have been proposed to solve it because accurate detection is necessary to achieve autonomous navigation and intelligent security. One of the authors also has tackled this problem to improve detection speed [7,8,17] and accuracy [12]. Deep learning has shown impressive results in several research fields [6,14] using machine learning, but quite different results have been found in the field of human detection: a state-of-the-art method using gradient histograms [20] has shown better accuracy than deep learning.

The most important problem in human detection is how to find object boundaries of humans from generic scenes, where several kinds of objects exist. HOG, one of the most well-known methods since this research field began, tried to model such object boundaries using gradient orientation, and moderate accuracy for the INRIA dataset was achieved with a support vector machine.

© Springer International Publishing AG 2016
J. Blanc-Talon et al. (Eds.): ACIVS 2016, LNCS 10016, pp. 238–249, 2016.
DOI: 10.1007/978-3-319-48680-2_22

After that, several derivatives from HOG have been proposed for object detection and recognition: part-based models using HOG features for local feature descriptors [4] and higher-order feature descriptors based on gradient orientation [2,16]. Their viewpoints are not the same, but they have a common property: they can appropriately model object boundaries using machine learning.

One human detection method that focuses on extracting object boundaries to improve detection accuracy: informed Haar-like features [19]. This method is a straightforward extension of Viola-Jones' method [15] and integral channel features [2] but has a special process to create feature pools suitable for human detection on the basis of an edgemap. In addition to this process, the feature detector used in the method is extended from binary to ternary. In the original Haar-like features, rectangular regions are divided into two categories corresponding to "+1" and "−1," but the informed Haar-like features use three kinds of regions corresponding to "+1," "−1," and "0." This scheme have shown excellent accuracy for human detection and filtered channel features [20], which have more features in a pool in addition to informed Haar-like features show much better accuracy than deep learning.

One of the most significant applications of human detection is automatic player localization in sports videos [3,9–11], and the visualization of statistics of players' motion during TV broadcasting has been achieved in soccer [1]. However, the current detection and tracking systems used for this application are very large and expensive, so they are equipped only at large stadiums, though these systems are strongly required by club teams. To achieve compact but accurate detection systems, we try to construct an accurate detection method that does not require special cameras and huge computing resources. In this paper, soccer player detection with only color features is proposed, enabling accurate detection if feature selection is performed appropriately.

This paper is organized as follows. Section 2 introduces informed Haar-like features that are used in our method for feature selection. Section 3 details our human detector constructed only with color features, and an evaluation using the PETS2003 dataset is shown in Sect. 4. Finally, Sect. 5 concludes this paper.

2   Informed Haar-like Features for Human Detection

Informed Haar-like features [19], proposed by Zhang et al. enables accurate human detection with not many features owing to its well-designed feature pool generated before construction of a classifier. To design such feature pools, statistical patterns included in detection targets are analyzed in detail. Feature pools are designed for human detection on the basis that human shapes have strong patterns, and in particular regions near the head and shoulders are unique to humans. For this analysis, an edgemap is generated as shown in Fig. 1 using several sample images. In [19], a human body can be roughly classified into three parts: a head, an upper body, and a lower body. The procedure of the feature pool generation can be summarized as follows:

1. edgemap generation as shown in Fig. 1,
2. cell division as shown in Fig. 2,
3. labeling considering object shapes as shown in the left side of Fig. 3, and
4. template generation as shown in the right side of Fig. 3.

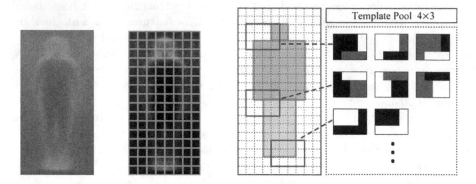

Fig. 1. Edgemap.   **Fig. 2.** Divided cells.   **Fig. 3.** Template generation.

Here, we explain how to generate a template using the labeled cells in Fig. 3. As you can see, the generated feature, called a template, consists of several cells divided in the 2nd process. A feature includes three kinds of regions corresponding to properties of divided cells. For example, templates in the first row are divided into three regions corresponding to the head, upper body, and background in the same way. Differences between these three templates are only the color allocation. The color allocation means how a feature value is obtained from a template. In [19], ternary computation is applied, where "−1," "0," and "+1" are assigned as coefficients to these three regions, respectively. In addition to the ternary templates, binary templates compute feature value the same as the well-known Haar-like features proposed by Viola and Jones [15]. In Fig. 3, the third row shows binary templates.

With the aforementioned feature extraction, very accurate classifier for human detection can be constructed by boosting, and the detection accuracy has been shown to outperform recent schemes based on deep learning if a feature pool is extended [20].

In this paper, we show that the idea of informed Haar-like features enables us to construct a classifier with sufficient accuracy for practical applications that does not require huge computational costs if feature selection is performed well.

3   Soccer Player Detection with only Color Features Selected Using Informed Haar-like Features

This section explains how to construct an accurate classifier for soccer player detection with only color features and without gradient orientation; these are considered as the most significant visual cues for object detection.

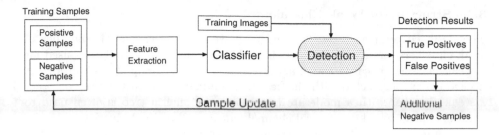

Fig. 4. Training flow.

3.1   Dataset Used in Our Method

To apply informed Haar-like features for feature selection, a dataset needs to be prepared before a classifier is constructed. Therefore, first, we explain the dataset used in this paper. In this study, we used the PETS2003 dataset, which includes video sequences of a soccer game and annotations about player positions as ground truth.

3.2   Design of Templates

Figures 5 and 6 show an edgemap and assigned labels for some positive samples included in the PETS dataset, respectively. In this process, the authors do not consider detailed properties on targets such as the team name or whether the humans are player or referees, so all humans included in the annotation file are treated as positive samples. As you can see, the human silhouette represented by the edgemap in this case is inclined because the video sequences were captured from a corner and all players seem to be inclined from this view point. Templates for this classification target were designed as shown in Fig. 7.

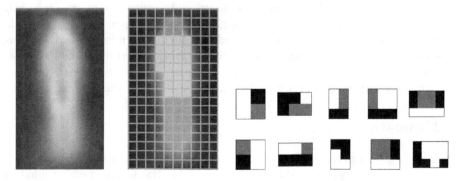

Fig. 5. Edgemap for PETS samples.

Fig. 6. Labeling for PETS samples.

Fig. 7. Templates used to construct a classifier for players in the PETS2003 dataset.

3.3   Structure of Weak Classifiers

The designed templates can be used as a weak classifier but the number of weak classifiers for strong classifiers must become huge if a template is used for a weak classifier because the expressiveness of only a template is too low. A decision tree constructed with the designed templates was utilized to construct a weak classifier with a moderate expressiveness; such a tree is often used to train classifiers based on integral channel features [2] or its derivatives.

Computation speed becomes very low if a strong classifier is constructed with a boosting algorithm using decision trees as weak classifiers without any effort to reduce computational cost. To construct a computationally effective classifier, we constructed a softcascade structure using multiple instance pruning [18] during training.

3.4   Update of Training Samples and Construction of a Strong Classifier

Selecting appropriate training samples is important because the proposed scheme does not use gradient orientation, one of the most powerful feature descriptors in the existing methods. Therefore, we constructed a strong classifier, shown in Fig. 4. In the first step, positive samples and negative samples were prepared from the PETS2003 dataset. Here, positive samples were randomly selected from training images using annotation, and negative samples were selected from training images so as not to have intersections between positive samples. The number of positive and negative samples extracted from 2000 images in the dataset was 30,000 and 60,000, respectively. After preparation of training samples, a strong classifier was constructed using the boosting algorithm with feature extraction including templates designed as in the aforementioned subsection.

Then, classification was performed with the constructed classifier for training samples, where an exhaustive search was applied. In this step, some subwindows may have been classified incorrectly. If many subwindows were misclassified, written as false positives in Fig. 4, a strong classifier was reconstructed. For this reconstruction, training samples were updated including misclassified subwindows as negative samples. Using this iterative training, the number of subwindows that were difficult to classify in an exhaustive search could be reduced. A final strong classifier was obtained after some iterations of the training loop.

4   Evaluation

This section presents our evaluation of accuracy of a classifier constructed using the aforementioned procedure. In the experiments, 100 images not included in training samples were randomly selected from the PETS2003 dataset and used as test images and miss rate vs false positive per image was measured as a detection error tradeoff (shortly DET) curve to compare the classification accuracy between several methods and conditions. For this evaluation, an exhaustive search based on the sliding window detection was applied to test images.

4.1   Image Resolution and Window Size for Detection

The image resolution of the PETS dataset was only 720 × 576, and the smallest size of the target players annotated as positive samples was about 10 × 28. This seems too small for the informed Haar-like features, so we decided to resize the video sequences to 2160 × 1728, i.e., three times larger for both horizontal and vertical directions. For the size of the detection window, we tried three sizes: 40 × 80, 50 × 100, and 60 × 120. 60 × 120 and 50 × 100 are the window sizes used in the original informed Haar-like features [19] and integral channel features [2], respectively. In addition, 40 × 80 was selected to evaluate the detection accuracy using smaller window size.

4.2   Comparison About Color Spaces

The first experiments compared the classification accuracy between three kinds of classifiers constructed with different color spaces: LUV, RGB, and HSV. Figures 8, 10, and 12 show DET curves corresponding to these three color spaces used for training; their window sizes were 40 × 80, 50 × 100, and 60 × 120, respectively. According to the results, LUV had the best accuracy among the three color spaces when the size of the detection window was 50 × 100 and 60 × 120. HSV had the second best, though the HSV color space was reported as a good cue for detection and tracking of players on the field in [13], and the accuracy of the RGB was the worst in this experiment for these sizes.

However, when the size of the detection window was 40 × 80, the accuracy using LUV features became worse, so determining which is best one is quite difficult. In addition, we found another interesting point in these results: HSV color space became the worst for these three color spaces at this window size.

The detection results for these three window sizes show quite different tendencies regarding detection accuracy when color spaces for feature extraction changed. These results were very interesting, but the detection accuracy itself became better as the size of the detection window increased. The following subsection describes our evaluation of the detection accuracy for several conditions.

The miss rate of the classifier with only LUV features was about 2.76 % at 0.1 FPPI. This was good accuracy considering that the dataset used in the experiments consisted of images including some targets that are not correctly annotated as positive or negative samples per frame.

4.3   Influence of the Number of Training Iterations and Depth of the Weak Classifier on Accuracy

Figures 9, 11, and 13 show DET curves corresponding to several classifiers constructed with several training iterations and depth of weak classifiers. Here, the size of the detection window was 40 × 80, 50 × 100, and 60 × 120 for Figs. 9, 11, and 13 respectively. In these figures, "round" means the number of updates of training examples. By the results, two was the best for training iterations. The iteration number was also adopted for training of the other classifiers.

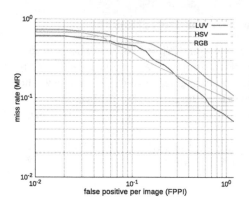

Fig. 8. DET curves for several color spaces. (Color figure online)

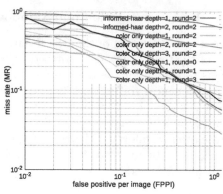

Fig. 9. DET curves for several conditions.

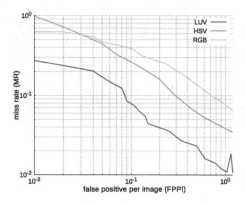

Fig. 10. DET curves for several color spaces. (Color figure online)

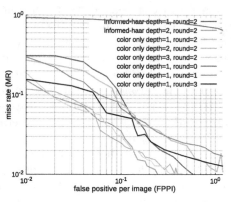

Fig. 11. DET curves for several conditions.

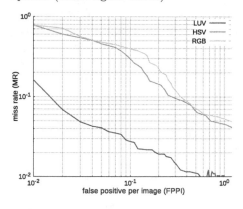

Fig. 12. DET curves for several color spaces. (Color figure online)

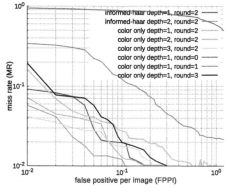

Fig. 13. DET curves for several conditions.

First, the results when the window size was 60×120 are detailed. The results show that the best miss rate for our implementation was about 1.28 % at 0.1 FPPI when the depth was two, which is excellent accuracy, and good accuracy could be achieved even using a classifier with a depth of one and three training iterations, where the miss rate was about 2.00 % at 0.1 FPPI. As you can see, the original method of informed Haar-like features using gradient orientations, one of the state-of-the-art, showed the best accuracy when the depth was two; it had about 1.22 % miss rate at 0.1 FPPI. However, the difference in the miss rate between the informed Haar-like features and our method was only about 0.06 % at this FPPI.

The same tendency can be seen in Figs. 9 and 11, which show DET curves by detection with the 40×80 and 50×100 detection windows, respectively. However, the detection accuracy itself decreased if the size of the detection window decreased.

4.4 Processing Speed

Next, the processing speed of the classifier constructed with only LUV features was measured. In this evaluation, we used required time to execute an exhaustive search with the classifier for 100 images in the PETS2003 dataset. This experiment was performed on a Linux PC with an Intel Corei7 4790K CPU with 16 GB memory. A classifier using only color features and a classifier using gradient orientations required 74.21 and 219.63 s, respectively, when the depth of both classifiers was two and the size of the detection window was 60×120. When the size became 50×100, the required times were 73.16 and 213.93 s using a classifier with only color features and with gradient orientations, respectively, and they became 70.93 and 208.91 s for the 40×80 detection window, respectively. Table 1 summarizes these results.

Table 1. Processing speed

The window size	40×80	50×100	60×120
LUV only	70.93	73.16	74.21
w grad orientation	208.91	213.93	219.63

According to these results, the computational time was reduced to 33.79 % of the original informed Haar-like features when the size of the detection window was 60×120. Considering that the difference of miss rate at 0.1 FPPI was only about 0.06 %, the constructed classifier using only color features was well balanced between the computational speed and the accuracy. The processing speed became slightly faster if the size of the detection window decreased, but the accuracy also decreased according to the window size. In this application, 60×120 was the best window size considering the detection accuracy.

Fig. 14. Detection results.

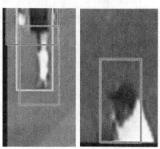

Fig. 15. False positives. Here, green and red rectangles represent ground truth and falsely detected targets, respectively. (Color figure online)

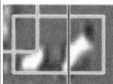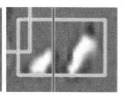

Fig. 16. Heavily occluded samples. Here, green rectangles mean ground truth and blue rectangles show detection results. (Color figure online)

Fig. 17. Samples with difficult poses.

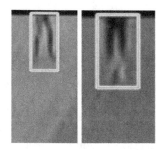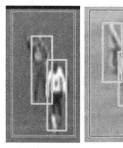

Fig. 18. Positive samples including only legs.

Fig. 19. False detections owing to failure of pairwise max suppression.

4.5 Detection Examples and Discussion

Finally, some detection results are shown in Fig. 14. In this figure, perfect detection was achieved. However, this evaluation had some false positives, as shown in Fig. 15. Some false positives were caused by the insufficient performance of the constructed classifier, but some detection results were counted as false because some humans were not annotated as positive samples. Some false negatives also occurred due to the similar reason: only leg parts of the target player were annotated as positive samples, but detecting them correctly by human detectors was difficult. Some of these false negatives are shown in Fig. 18. In actual applications, such false detections could be counted as correct. Therefore, the actual accuracy in practical applications could be considered much better. In addition, heavily occluded targets as shown in Fig. 16 were not detected, and they were counted as false negatives. As you can see, localizing their positions by only detection was difficult. In this case, object tracking using inter-frame information should be applied to improve localization accuracy, but it is beyond the scope of this research.

However, other kinds of false negatives also were found in this experiment, as shown in Fig. 17. In this case, quite different poses from the edgemap obtained from averaging could not be adequately treated by the filters designed by us. Such targets may be detected if the filters are designed to consider their appearance or if multi-class classification that can handle different poses is used. In addition, window merging by pairwise max suppression [5] does not work well in some cases, as shown in Fig. 19. These kinds of falses also degrade the detection accuracy because both the number of false positives and miss detection must increase: large detection results are counted as false positives, and detection targets included in these rectangles are regarded as false negatives. Our future work is to improve the detection accuracy considering these problems.

5 Conclusion

This paper proposed a soccer player detector using only color features, and it achieves excellent accuracy with moderate computational cost. Using the proposed method, the detection accuracy of a classifier became comparable to a classifier constructed with gradient orientation—in addition to LUV features—even when only LUV features were used for the classifier. This study evaluated RGB and HSV color spaces in addition to an LUV color space. It was shown that LUV features can achieve more accurate detection than RGB and HSV features, though HSV features was reported as a good visual cues for detection and tracking in [13] when the size of the detection window was 60×120. 40×80 and 50×100 were tested as the size of the detection window, but the accuracy decreased if it became smaller. Moreover, we found that sufficient accuracy for practical applications could be achieved even when the depth of is reduced to one, i.e., a weak classifier constructed with only a designed feature extractor. In this case, the miss rate was 2.00 % at 0.1 FPPI. The miss rate was improved to 1.28 % at the same FPPI if the depth of the classifier became two. For computational speed, a classifier constructed with only LUV features was about 3.0 times faster than a classifier using gradient orientation features.

Recently, several schemes based on deep learning have shown remarkable accuracy than other kinds of schemes. However, deep learning is not the best for all applications. For example, Filtered Channel Features shows better performance than deep learning in the field of pedestrian detection. Especially, to construct a classifier for practical applications, accuracy and processing speed must be balanced. This paper has shown a case study about how to construct a well-balanced classifier to detect field players in a soccer sequence. The results can be applied for field player not limited to soccer and, moreover, it may be also applied for surveillance applications where background images are not so complicated. In the future, we will try to evaluate the classification accuracy of our proposal using actual data obtained from such practical applications. Furthermore, we would like to implement the proposed scheme on FPGA-based systems because simple features without gradient orientations are very suitable for hardware-based acceleration.

Acknowledgments. The research results have been achieved by "Research and development of Innovative Network Technologies to Create the Future", the Commissioned Research of National Institute of Information and Communications Technology (NICT), JAPAN.

References

1. ChyronHego: Tracab optical tracking (2003). http://chyronhego.com/sportsdata/tracab
2. Dollár, P., Tu, Z., Perona, P., Belongie, S.: Integral channel features. In: Proceedings of the British Machine Vision (2009)
3. D'Orazio, T., Leo, M., Spagnolo, P., Mazzeo, P., Mosca, N., Nitti, M., Distante, A.: An investigation into the feasibility of real-time soccer offside detection from a multiple camera system. IEEE Trans. Circuits Syst. Video Technol. **19**(12), 1804–1818 (2009)
4. Felzenszwalb, P., Girshick, R., McAllester, D., Ramanan, D.: Object detection with discriminatively trained part based models. IEEE Trans. Pattern Anal. Mach. Intell. **32**(9), 1627–1645 (2010)
5. Felzenszwalb, P., McAllester, D., Ramanan, D.: A discriminatively trained, multiscale, deformable part model. In: Proceedings of IEEE Conference on Computer Vision and Pattern Recognition (2008)
6. He, K., Zhang, X., Ren, S., Sun, J.: Deep residual learning for image recognition. In: Proceedings of IEEE Conference on Computer Vision and Pattern Recognition, pp. 770–778 (2016)
7. Hiromoto, M., Miyamoto, R.: Hardware architecture for high-accuracy real-time pedestrian detection with CoHOG features. In: Proceedings of IEEE International Conference on Computer Vision Workshops, pp. 894–899 (2009)
8. Hiromoto, M., Sugano, H., Miyamoto, R.: Partially parallel architecture for AdaBoost-based detection with Haar-like features. IEEE Trans. Circuits Syst. Video Technol. **19**(1), 41–52 (2009)

9. Kayumbi, G., Mazzeo, P., Spagnolo, P., Taj, M., Cavallaro, A.: Distributed visual sensing for virtual top-view trajectory generation in football videos. In: Proceedings of International Conference on Content-Based Image and Video Retrieval, pp. 535–542 (2008)
10. Leo, M., Mosca, N., Spagnolo, P., Mazzeo, P., D'Orazio, T., Distante, A.: Real-time multiview analysis of soccer matches for understanding interactions between ball and players. In: Proceedings of International Conference on Content-Based Image and Video Retrieval, pp. 525–534 (2008)
11. Mazzeo, P., Spagnolo, P., Leo, M., D'Orazio, T.: Visual players detection and tracking in soccer matches. In: Proceedings of IEEE International Conference on Advanced Video and Signal Based Surveillance, pp. 326–333 (2008)
12. Miyamoto, R., Jaehoon, Y., Onoye, T.: Normalized channel features for accurate pedestrian detection. In: Proceedings of IEEE ISCCSP, pp. 582–585 (2014)
13. Okuma, K., Taleghani, A., de Freitas, N., Little, J.J., Lowe, D.G.: A boosted particle filter: multitarget detection and tracking. In: Proceedings of European Conference on Computer Vision, pp. 28–39 (2004)
14. Taigman, Y., Yang, M., Ranzato, M., Wolf, L.: Deepface: Closing the gap to human-level performance in face verification. In: Proceedings of IEEE Conference on Computer Vision and Pattern Recognition, pp. 1701–1708 (2014)
15. Viola, P., Jones, M.: Rapid object detection using a boosted cascade of simple features. In: Proceedings of IEEE Conference on Computer Vision and Pattern Recognition, vol. 1, pp. 511–518 (2001)
16. Watanabe, T., Ito, S., Yokoi, K.: Co-occurrence histograms of oriented gradients for pedestrian detection. In: Proceedings of IEEE Pacific-Rim Symposium on Image and Video Technology, pp. 37–47 (2009)
17. Yu, J., Miyamoto, R., Onoye, T.: Fast pedestrian detection using a soft-cascade of the CoHOG-based classifier: how to speed-up SVM classifiers based on multiple-instance pruning. IEEE Trans. Image Process. 22(12), 4752–4761 (2013)
18. Zhang, C., Viola, P.: Multiple-instance pruning for learning efficient cascade detectors. In: Proceedings of Advances in Neural Information Processing Systems (2007)
19. Zhang, S., Bauckhage, C., Cremers, A.: Informed Haar-like features improve pedestrian detection. In: Proceedings of IEEE Conference on Computer Vision and Pattern Recognition, pp. 947–954 (2014)
20. Zhang, S., Benenson, R., Schiele, B.: Filtered channel features for pedestrian detection. In: Proceedings of IEEE Conference on Computer Vision and Pattern Recognition, pp. 1751–1760 (2015)

Person Re-identification in Frontal Gait Sequences via Histogram of Optic Flow Energy Image

Athira Nambiar[✉], Jacinto C. Nascimento, Alexandre Bernardino, and José Santos-Victor

Institute for Systems and Robotics, Instituto Superior Técnico, Universidade de Lisboa, 1049-001 Lisbon, Portugal
anambiar@isr.ist.utl.pt

Abstract. In this work, we propose a novel methodology of re-identifying people in frontal video sequences, based on a spatio-temporal representation of the gait based on optic flow features, which we call Histogram Of Flow Energy Image (**HOFEI**). Optic Flow based methods do not require the silhouette computation thus avoiding image segmentation issues and enabling online re-identification (Re-ID) tasks. Not many works addressed Re-ID with optic flow features in frontal gait. Here, we conduct an extensive study on CASIA dataset, as well as its application in a realistic surveillance scenario- HDA Person dataset. Results show, for the first time, the feasibility of gait re-identification in frontal sequences, without the need for image segmentation.

Keywords: Gait analysis · Optic flow · Histogram of Flow · Gait Energy Image

1 Introduction

Over the past few years, human gait, has been receiving unprecedented attention from pattern recognition and computer vision communities, as a rich behavioural soft-biometric cue. A plethora of studies have been conducted on the visual analysis of human motion and automated person Re-identification/Recognition. The cognitive and psychological studies have proclaimed that humans are able to identify his peers by their distinct gait signature [1]. Human gait, which includes both the body appearance and the dynamics of walking [2], is considered to be quite pertinent in visual surveillance scenario. This is because gait analysis is unobtrusive, does not require explicit user cooperation, is perceivable from a distance, and is unique for each individual.

During the last decade, a number of gait analysis techniques have been proposed towards Person Re-identification/Recognition. Re-identification (Re-ID) is the process of identifying the same individual in different time instances either in the same camera or in different cameras. Re-identification is associated with

© Springer International Publishing AG 2016
J. Blanc-Talon et al. (Eds.): ACIVS 2016, LNCS 10016, pp. 250–262, 2016.
DOI: 10.1007/978-3-319-48680-2_23

change in appearance (carrying bags and different clothings etc.) and uncontrolled conditions (changes in illumination, pose and background). Recognition is a special case of Re-ID, where there is no apparent change in the appearance of the subject and the operator has much control on the conditions (same camera, no change in pose/background/illumination etc.).

The gait analysis techniques are broadly categorised as model based and model free approaches. The former leverage explicit either structural or motion gait models, whose parameters are estimated using the underlying kinematics of human motion in a sequence of images [3], whereas the latter category operate directly on the gait image sequences without fitting any underlying structure [4–6]. Although the model based approach is less susceptible to the changes in viewing angle or clothing, the inaccurate model fitting (mainly due to noisy data) may lead to the poor recognition performance. Instead, the model free approaches provide better performance by using information directly from the temporal evolution of the gait image sequences.

In classical gait analysis, the most commonly used views are lateral and frontal views. Most of the state-of-the-art techniques address the lateral case, in which the gait can be better observed. Lateral views have the advantage of minimizing perspective distortion and the amount of self occlusion, however, they cannot be applied in narrow passages, since very few gait cycles are observed in those conditions. Hence, in many real world scenarios like indoor narrow corridors and confined spaces, systems that rely on frontal gait analysis are preferred due to the convenience to be installed in confined spaces, as well as the capability to capture longer video sequences, at the same time impose more challenges in terms of perspective and occlusions.

In this paper, we propose a novel framework for model-free and frontal gait analysis for person Re-ID, by amalgamating the Histogram of Flow (HOF) [7] into the framework of Gait Energy Image (GEI) [4], and building upon the advantages of both representations. First, the HOF represents the dynamic gait characteristics by encoding the pattern of apparent motion of the subject in a visual scene. Second, GEI enables to average the energy information over a gait cycle to obtain the spatio-temporal gait signature. Our major contributions are:

- A new technique (termed as **HOFEI**) for person Re-ID in frontal videos leveraging optic flow features.
- Our proposal does not require binary silhouettes, instead computes global dense motion descriptors directly from raw images. This not only bypasses the segmentation and binarization phases, but also facilitates online Re-ID.
- Proposal of a new gait period estimation directly from the temporal evolution of the HOF computed at the lower limbs.
- The demonstration of an optic flow-based method to frontal gait recognition, which, to the best of our knowledge, is absent in the literature.

The pipeline of our proposed algorithm is shown in Fig. 1, which will be detailed in the forthcoming sections. The rest of the paper is structured as follows. Section 2 discusses related works in the area. Section 3 presents our proposed method, with a detailed description of HOF computation and the gait

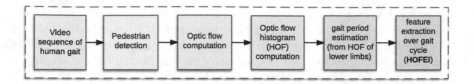

Fig. 1. Proposed pipeline of the gait analysis.

feature extraction. Section 4 presents the experimental results to demonstrate the effectiveness of the proposed algorithm. Finally, Sect. 5 concludes this work.

2　Related Work

One of the most acclaimed research in model free gait recognition viz., Gait Energy Image (GEI) by Han et al. [4], presented the idea of generating spatio-temporal description by averaging the normalized binary silhouette over gait cycle. Inspired by the same, many other energy image improvements were carried out e.g., active energy image [10], gait entropy image [12], gradient histogram energy image [11] to quote a few.

The idea of HOF was adopted from Histogram of Oriented Gradients (HOG) [13], which divide the image into cells and compile a histogram of gradient directions, weighed by its magnitude for the pixels within each cell. The same approach has been extended to the optic flow and the spatial derivatives of its components [7,15]. Optic flow and their histograms have also been proposed for gait analysis such as in [16] by using motion intensity and direction from optical flow field, while in [8] a silhouette based gait representation has been used to generate gait flow image. In the field of optic flow based gait recognition also some energy image concepts were proposed in the recent works by [8,9]. However, both of those works were reasonably insufficient to convey the motion information of the whole human body since their optic flow measurements are on the binary silhouette edges. Much inspired from the aforementioned literature studies, here we propose a novel spatio-temporal gait representation termed as Histogram Of Flow Energy Image (**HOFEI**), which is a dense descriptor computed over the entire body parts.

Different from the aforementioned literature on optic flow based gait recognition conducted in the lateral view, we demonstrate the potential of our proposal in the front view (in HDA and CASIA dataset), for which no similar state-of-the-art using optic flow has been reported. However, there have been some works in CASIA dataset frontal sequences, leveraging the binary silhouettes for gait recognition. Chen et al. [19] demonstrated the performance of various gait features including Gait Energy Image (GEI), Gait History Image (GHI), Gait Moment Image (GMI), Frame Difference Energy Image (FDEI) etc. in each view angle, from frontal to rear view. We will show that our proposed method is competitive with this state-of-the-art, while using an optic-flow method, which does not require silhouette segmentation.

3   Methodology

In this section, the target representation strategy via HOF, gait period estimation and the generation of gait signature **HOFEI** are explained in detail.

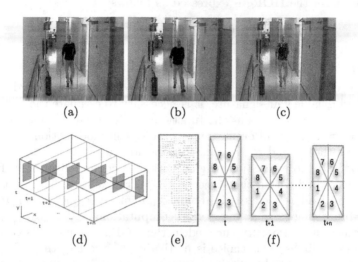

(a)   (b)   (c)

(d)   (e)   (f)

Fig. 2. Optic flow computation (*top*) and polar sampling scheme for the computation of Histogram of Optic Flow (HOF) (*bottom*); (a) and (b) show the adjacent video frames of gait. (c) shows the optic flow of the person computed. (d) The cuboid represents a slice of the video sequence spanning a gait cycle (n frames). The shaded regions are the Bounding Box (BB) of the person detected in each frame. (e) A sample of person's optic flow inside the BB. (f) Polar sampling of histogram of flow HOF in each of the images during a gait cycle, whose average results in the **HOFEI** gait signature.

Histogram of flow: We leverage the HOG encoding scheme mentioned in [13] on the human detection bounding boxes (BB). We provide 2 choices for the human detection BB: either by using the *'Ground truth'* annotations provided, or by using the *'Optic flow'* features to detect the moving section in the image. In this work, we use the default *'Ground truth'* BB. Then, the relative motion distributions of the peripheral human body parts - heads, arms and legs - are described within this BB. In contrast to the original HOG encoding scheme using grid of rectangular cells which overlap, here we use polar cells which better represent the spatial locations of limbs and head along time. Figure 2(a)–(c) show the optic flow computation over a continuous walking sequence of frontal gait and Fig. 2(d)–(f) illustrate the sampling scheme of HOF.

When an optic flow image is provided, the first step is to divide it into cells according to the polar sampling strategy mentioned above, followed by the computation of histogram of flow orientation weighed by its magnitude. Let nR be the number of angular regions (i.e. cells) and nB be the number of bins that define each cell. Hence, the HOF features are parameterised as follows:

$$\mathbf{HOF^t} = \left[HOF^t_1 \cdots HOF^t_i \cdots HOF^t_{nR} \right] \in \mathbb{R}^{nR \times nB} \tag{1}$$

where $HOF^t{}_i$ denotes the normalized HOF computed at cell i at frame t. Figure 2 illustrates this, where a polar sampling scheme with 8 angular cells is shown (see Fig. 2(f)). $\mathbf{HOF^t}$ is of dimension 64 with $nR = 8$ and $nB = 8$. We compute the $\mathbf{HOF^t}$ for each frame throughout the video sequence S and the representation for the $\mathbf{HOF_S}$ is expressed as follows:

$$\mathbf{HOF_S} = \left[\mathbf{HOF^t} \mid \cdots \mid \mathbf{HOF^{t+\tau}}\right]^{\top} \in \mathbb{R}^{\tau \times nR \times nB}. \tag{2}$$

where τ denotes the number of frames in the video sequence.

Gait cycle estimation: Humans walk in a periodic fashion. In order to have coherent and reliable gait signature, it is necessary to estimate the gait features over a gait cycle, which acts as the functional unit of gait. A gait cycle is the time period or sequence of events/movements during locomotion in which one foot contacts the ground to when that same foot again contacts the ground. In our proposal, the estimation of gait period is computed directly from the optic flow measured within the subjects' BB in raw images. This bypasses the computational load related to the traditional image segmentation and other image pre-processing steps in gait period computation.

We extract the periodicity encoded in the HOF sampling cells corresponding to the lower limbs. This choice is motivated by the fact that, the periodic information can reliably be obtained using the dynamic motion cues from the legs. The periodicity of right and left legs induces a similar periodic pattern in its corresponding optic flow. For instance, in a frontal gait sequence, as shown in Fig. 3(a) and (b), the polar sampling of cells 2 and 3, correspond to the location of legs in the image. More specifically, cell 2 and cell 3 correspond to the right and left leg, respectively.

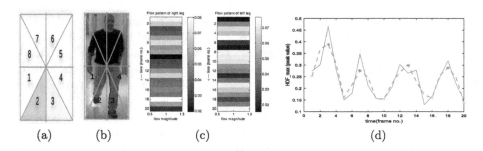

(a)   (b)   (c)   (d)

Fig. 3. (a) Cells 2 and 3 represent sampling cells corresponding to the lower limbs. (b) Person's BB under polar sampling scheme depicts that the major area of motion pattern is described by the lower limbs cells. (c) Magnitude of the highest peak of the histogram of the right and left legs (cell 2 and 3) during a walking sequence. It is worth mentioning that the minimum value corresponding to the *stance* phase in one leg is accompanied with the maximum value corresponding to the *swing* phase in the other leg. (d) Estimation of gait period. The frames within two adjacent peaks (in *Magenta* markers) denote a gait cycle. (see online version for colours).

In order to estimate the gait period, we leverage the subset of histogram bins corresponding to cells 2 and 3, i.e., HOF^t_2 and HOF^t_3, which represents the lower limbs motion patterns, whose amplitude provides a good signal-to-noise ratio for detection. Then, we compute $\textbf{HOF}^\textbf{t}$ throughout the video sequence corresponding to either HOF^t_2 or HOF^t_3 (since both are complementary). We can notice that this evolution undergoes a periodic pattern as depicted in Fig. 3(c), (d). Figure 3(d) shows a periodic sinusoidal curve generated by plotting the HOF peaks of a single leg against the frame (as a function of time). A moving average filter is employed to smooth the obtained curve measurements (see green dashed curve), and the peaks of the filtered gait waveform allow us to identify the gait cycles. The frames between two consecutive peak points represent a gait cycle. Figure 3(c) visualizes the simultaneous evolution of the HOF pattern peaks of both legs i.e., the amplitude of the highest peak in the histogram of each corresponding leg over time, are complementary since stride phase in one leg is accompanied by the stance phase in the other and vice versa.

Histogram of flow Energy Image: Based on the gait period estimation as well as the HOF features over video sequences, we compute HOF Energy Image (**HOFEI**), which is used as the key descriptor of each person. Inspired by the GEI scheme, HOF energy image is obtained by averaging the $\textbf{HOF}^\textbf{t}$ representations over a full gait cycle, as follows:

$$\textbf{HOFEI} = \frac{1}{t_2 - t_1} \sum_{t=t_1}^{t_2} \textbf{HOF}^\textbf{t} \tag{3}$$

where t_1 and t_2 are the beginning and ending frame indices of a gait cycle and $\textbf{HOF}^\textbf{t}$ is the histogram of flow of the person at time instant t, as defined in Eq. (1). More intuitively, the **HOFEI** gait signature provides the relative motion of each body part with respect to the other, over a complete gait cycle.

4 Experimental Results

Experiments are conducted in two scenarios: Re-ID in controlled scenario vs Re-ID in uncontrolled (busy office) scenario. For the former, we use CASIA dataset B [14] which contains multiple videos of subjects including normal and apparel change (*bag, overcoat*) conditions, which makes it suitable for Re-ID scenario. Nevertheless, there is much control over the pose, illumination and background. Hence, it is also suitable to study the recognition of the subject under similar conditions. Hence, we conduct an extensive study on both the re-identification as well as recognition analysis in CASIA dataset. After this feasibility analysis, we apply our algorithm on a more realistic dataset (HDA Person dataset [17]) which is used for benchmarking video surveillance algorithms. In contrast to the CASIA dataset, HDA provides uncontrolled environment conditions (change in illumination, pose changes and occlusions) as well as lower frame rate (5 fps) similar to a real world video surveillance system, which enables to conduct a Re-ID task in realistic scenario.

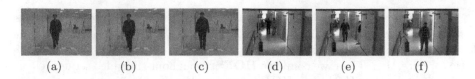

(a)   (b)   (c)   (d)   (e)   (f)

Fig. 4. Some sample images from CASIA database and HDA database. (a)–(c) show various appearance (*'normal walk'*, *'carrying bag'*, *'wearing coat'*) conditions of subjects in CASIA dataset B. (d)–(e) depict the position of subjects in HDA dataset, at various distances D_{far}, D_{middle} and D_{near} respectively.

4.1   Re-ID in Controlled Scenario: CASIA Dataset

CASIA is one of the largest databases available for gait recognition and related research[1]. Among the available four different datasets, we used Dataset B for our experiments. Dataset B [14] is a large multiview gait dataset collected indoors with 124 subjects and 13640 samples from 11 different views ranging from 0 to 180°. In our experiments, we consider only the frontal walks (0°), i.e., walking towards the camera. Database B contains three variations, namely view angle, clothing and carrying condition changes, and also presents the human silhouettes for each case. For each person, it contains 10 different video sequences (6 *'normal'* walk, 2 *'bag carrying'* walk and 2 *'overcoat wearing'* walk). Please refer to Fig. 4(a)–(c) for samples from CASIA dataset.

In order to evaluate the performance of our system towards long term re-identification, we conducted experiments not only under normal scenario, but also in the apparel change situations. For each of these experiments we considered 105 subjects, out of all the available 124 subjects. Videos in which the optical flow information can not be successfully extracted are excluded. For each of these available 1050 videos, we could get at least 3 gait cycles, in order to have enough data for training and testing. Then, for each gait cycle, the corresponding **HOFEI** is extracted. Regarding the dense optical flow computation, we use Stefan's implementation[2], which provides robust flow estimation by various methods of which, we select the Lucas- Kanade method [18].

Three main experiments are carried out in this dataset: The first is to verify the recognition performance under the same appearance and similar conditions. The second experiment is the Re-ID test conducted in order to verify performance under different appearance conditions. The third experiment is to test the influence of the distance of the subject in the performance of our system.

Experiment (1) Recognition in regular conditions: In this experiment, we only consider the *'normal'* type videos. The first four sequences are used for training and the last two are placed into the probe set. Then for each person's probe sequences, we compute the minimal Euclidean distance between any of

---

[1] http://www.cbsr.ia.ac.cn/english/Gait%20Databases.asp.

[2] http://www.mathworks.com/matlabcentral/fileexchange/44400-tutorial-and-tool box-on-real-time-optical-flow.

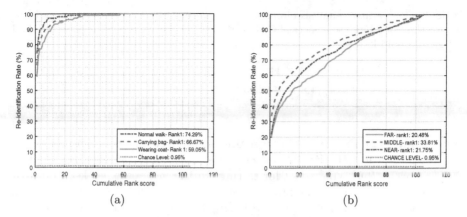

(a)   (b)

Fig. 5. Re-ID results: (a) presents the CMC curves obtained for Experiment 1 and 2 for different probe cases viz., *normal* case, *bag* carrying case and *coat* wearing case. A chance level of 0.95 % is also denoted in *magenta*. The Rank1 recognition achieved for normal, bag and overcoat are 74.29 % (78 times the chance level), 66.67 % (70 times the chance level), 59.05 % (62 times the chance level) respectively. (b) depicts the CMC curves obtained for Experiment 3 at various distance probes viz., D_{far}, D_{middle} and D_{near}. Middle case outperforms the others. (see online version for colours).

the HOFEI descriptors in the probe and those of each person on the gallery. The minimal distance (most similar) gallery sequence is selected as the best matching and sets the identity of the recognized person. The distances to the other persons in the gallery are used to provide a ranked list of identifications, for evaluation. Blue dotted curve in Fig. 5(a) shows the Correct Classification Rate (CCR) of this experiment, in terms of Cumulative Matching Characteristic (CMC) Curve. CMC curve shows, how often on average, the correct person ID is included in the best K matches against the training set for each probe. We could observe that a high CCR rate of 74.29 % (78 times the chance level), has been achieved under the regular '*normal* walking' conditions.

A similar evaluation strategy, but using silhouette-based approach, had been carried out in [19] in all the view angles in CASIA dataset '*normal*' sequences. In order to conduct a reasonable comparison with our approach, we select the frontal view results they obtained by using various gait features (GEI, GHI, GMI, FDEI). Table 1 shows the comparison results of our strategy (HOFEI) against them in the ascending order. We can observe that CCR of our approach lies in between the others. The higher performance of FDEI and GEI could be attributed to their usage of segmented binary silhouettes and a more powerful classification method (HMM), whereas we use more flexible optic flow based features and a simpler classification method (Euclidean distance). Therefore, we consider the proposed feature competitive with the state-of-the-art, while more versatile. Since it does not require any pre-segmentation phase, it is easier to use in automatic RE-ID systems.

Table 1. Comparative analysis of our method against silhouette-based approaches in [19], for the frontal gait sequences of CASIA dataset B. The proposed method (HOFEI) is shown in bold letters.

GMI	GHI	**HOFEI**	GEI	FDEI
68.5%	71.8%	**74.3%**	91.1%	95.2%/100%

Experiment (2) Re-identification under change in appearance: In this experiment, we use all the 6 *'normal'* type videos for training, and *'wearing coat'/'carrying bag'* type videos for testing. In the *'bag'* case, we keep both the bag carrying sequences as the probe whereas all the 6 *'normal'* video sequences as the training set. A similar method is employed for *overcoat* scenario as well. Classification is similar to Experiment 1 (NN classifier+ Euclidean distance). The recognition results obtained are presented in Fig. 5(a). The apparel change recognition rates for bag (*red curve*) and coat (*green curve*) scenarios are 66.67% (70 times the chance level) and 59.05% (62 times the chance level) respectively. The lower CCR of *overcoat* condition could be ascribable to the global change in the flow features, whereas the *bag* either influence only a local flow change, or being occluded in some cases (occluded by hand, as in Fig. 4(b) or occluded while wearing as a backpack). No similar results in the appearance change conditions have been encountered in [19] for comparative evaluation.

Experiment (3) Variable distance to camera: Here, we are testing the robustness of the system when the subject is at different distance to the camera. In frontal sequences, the variability of the gait features with distance may have a significant impact on performance. Here we study the ability of the method in recognizing persons at a distance for which there are no gallery examples. We consider the *'normal'* type of videos for this experiment. In order to verify the impact of different distances, we conduct 3 case studies. In contrast to the previous experiments carried out on sets of videos, here we are conducting the analysis on each gait cycle instance. Performance will be lower than in the previous experiments, that used all gait cycles in the sequence for the classification. However, in this experiment we are not comparing absolute performance, but relative performance according to camera distance.

There are minimum of 3 gait cycles in each video sequence. In the first case study we keep all the *'normal'* gait cycle snippets seen at far distance D_{far} as the probe. The training set in this case is the *'normal'* D_{middle} and *'normal'* D_{near}. Hence per person, we have 6 D_{far} probe and 12 training set (D_{middle} and D_{near}). Then, in the second case study, the D_{middle} is considered as the probe and D_{far} and D_{near} are kept as the training sets. Similarly, in the third case study, D_{near} videos are the probe and the others are kept as the training set. The Re-ID results are shown in Fig. 5(b). We can observe an expected drop in the CCR rate while conducting Re-ID with each gait cycle as the probe in this Experiment 3, rather than sets of videos as the probe in Experiment 1 & 2. D_{middle} case outperforms the other two cases, with 33.81% rate (35 times the chance level) whereas the far and near cases have recognition rates 20.48 % (21 times the chance level) and 21.75 % (22 times the chance level) respectively. In the case of $\mathbf{D_{middle}}$ as the probe, higher recognition rate could be attributed to the fact that, trained on the extreme ranges the classifier performs an interpolation when predicting values for the middle range, whereas in the other two $\mathbf{D_{far}}$ and $\mathbf{D_{near}}$ cases it has to extrapolate to one of the extremes, which is often an ill-posed operation.

4.2   Re-ID in Uncontrolled Scenario: HDA Person Dataset

HDA dataset [17][3], is a labelled image sequence data set for research on high-definition surveillance. The dataset was acquired from 13 indoor cameras distributed over three floors of one building, recording simultaneously for 30 min during a busy noon hour inside a University building. Among the 13, we select only a single camera recording (Camera19), containing frontal gait sequences. The camera has the VGA resolution of 640×480, with a frame rate of $5fps$. In this experiment we considered 12 people that crossed the whole corridor, and for which we could get at least 3 gait cycles in order to have enough data for training and testing. We collect each subject's walking frames, and from them we extract minimum three gait cycles and their corresponding **HOFEI**. Unlike the CASIA dataset, HDA is uncontrolled scenario since it contains varying illumination conditions during the walk, changing backgrounds, break points in between the walks (entry/exit in the room along the way), occlusions by other person/wall/image boundary as well as self occlusions, also slight changes in the pose and limb movements during the walks.

Due to the limitation of larger video sequences as well as varying appearance conditions per person, we exclude the CASIA counterpart Experiment 1 and Experiment 2 in HDA dataset. Here we only conduct Experiment 3, quite similar to the one carried out in CASIA dataset. We consider three cases in which we compute the **HOFEI** descriptor: far ($\mathbf{D_{far}}$), middle ($\mathbf{D_{middle}}$) and near ($\mathbf{D_{near}}$) sequences, as depicted in Fig. 4(d)–(f). Under this set of descriptors, we perform a leave-one-out evaluation where one set is kept as the probe and the other two sets as the gallery (i.e., a total of three trials). Thus, in each trial we have 24 training descriptors in the Gallery and we test against 12 test probes. Then, each test sample will search for the minimal Euclidean distance between itself and the gallery descriptors, under the nearest neighbor classification method. Figure 6 demonstrates the recognition results in terms of Cumulative Matching Characteristic (CMC) curve as well as confusion matrix. The highest Rank-1 recognition rate of 75 % (9 times the chance level) is achieved while using $\mathbf{D_{middle}}$ as the testing data. At the same time, the Rank-1 accuracy achieved by the test sets $\mathbf{D_{far}}$ and $\mathbf{D_{near}}$ are 50 % and 58.33 %, respectively.

Referring to the CMC curve, another interesting observation is that the cumulative recognition rate improves drastically for both $\mathbf{D_{middle}}$ as well as $\mathbf{D_{far}}$ cases in comparison with $\mathbf{D_{near}}$, with the number of trials. This accentuates that gait sequences are better observed in far sequences than the closer ones

---

[3] http://vislab.isr.ist.utl.pt/hda-dataset/.

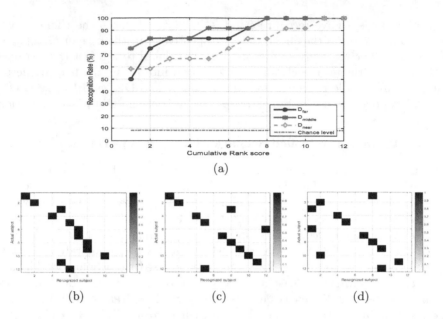

Fig. 6. Recognition results: (a) presents the CMC curves obtained on 3 different probe cases viz., D_{far}, D_{middle} and D_{near}. A chance level of 8.333 % is also denoted in *magenta*. The Rank1 recognition achieved for D_{far}, D_{middle} and D_{near} are 50 % (6 times the chance level), 75 % (9 times the chance level), 58.33 % (7 times the chance level) respectively. (b)-(d) show the confusion matrices for the 3 probe cases D_{far}, D_{middle} and D_{near} respectively. (Color figure online)

since video frames close to the camera may undergo occlusions and thus result in poor encoding of the body flow features.

5   Conclusions and Future Work

We analysed the potential of exploiting histogram of optic flow for frontal human gait analysis for Person re-identification. The main advantage of such a methodology is that no silhouette segmentation is required and thus can be facilitated towards online Re-ID system. A novel idea of flow based gait period estimation as well as a novel Histogram of Optic flow Energy Image (**HOFEI**) over the entire body are proposed in this work. We experimented the proposed framework upon a controlled benchmarking gait dataset (CASIA dataset) and a more unconstrained, thus harder, benchmarking video surveillance dataset (HDA Person dataset). We verified the effectiveness of the proposed method in both cases, under very different background clutter and sampling rates (25 Hz in CASIA vs 5 Hz in HDA). Extensive studies were conducted in CASIA dataset, i.e., regular case, change in appearance and influence of variable distance. Promising results were reported in each experiment, showing a Re-ID rate of 74.29 % (78 times the chance level) in the *normal* scenario. In HDA dataset person Re-ID also a good performance rate of 75 % (9 times the chance level) was reported, under different camera distance conditions. In future work, we plan to extrapolate this work towards pose invariant person re-identification scenario.

Acknowledgements. This work was supported by the FCT projects [UID/EEA/ 50009/2013], AHA CMUP-ERI/HCI/0046/2013 and FCT doctoral grant [SFRH/ BD/97258/2013].

References

1. Stevenage, S.V., Nixon, M.S., Vince, K.: Visual analysis of gait as a cue to identity. Appl. Cogn. Psychol. **13**, 513–526 (1999)
2. Lee, L., Grimson, W.: Gait Analysis for Recognition and Classification. In: Proceedings of IEEE International Conference on Automatic Face and Gesture Recognition (2002)
3. Cunado, D., Nixon, M., Carter, J.: Automatic extraction and description of human gait models for recognition purposes. Comput. Vis. Image Underst. **90**, 1–41 (2003)
4. Han, J., Bhanu, B.: Individual recognition using gait energy image. Pattern Anal. Mach. Intell. **28**, 316–322 (2006)
5. Chen, S., Gao, Y.: An invariant appearance model for gait recognition. In: Proceedings of IEEE Conference on Multimedia and Expo, pp. 1375–1378 (2007)
6. Goffredo, M., Carter, J., Nixon, M.: Front-view gait recognition. In: International Conference on Biometrics: Theory, Applications and Systems, pp. 1–6 (2008)
7. Dalal, N., Triggs, B., Schmid, C.: Human detection using oriented histograms of flow and appearance. In: Leonardis, A., Bischof, H., Pinz, A. (eds.) ECCV 2006. LNCS, vol. 3952, pp. 428–441. Springer, Heidelberg (2006). doi:10.1007/ 11744047_33
8. Lam, T.H.W., Cheung, K.H., Liu, J.N.K.: Gait flow image: a silhouette-based gait representation for human identification. Pattern Recognit. **44**, 973–987 (2011)
9. Yang, Y., Tu, D., Li, G.: Gait recognition using flow histogram energy image. In: International Conference on Pattern Recognition, pp. 444–449 (2014)
10. Zhang, E., Zhao, Y., Xiong, W.: Active energy image plus 2DLPP for gait recognition. Signal Process. **90**, 2295–2302 (2010)
11. Hofmann, M., Rigoll, G.: Improved gait recognition using gradient histogram energy image. In: ICIP, pp. 1389–1392 (2012)
12. Bashir, K., Xiang, T., Gong, S.: Gait recognition without subject cooperation. Pattern Recognit. Lett. **31**, 2052–2060 (2010)
13. Dalal, N., Triggs, B.: Histograms of oriented gradients for human detection. Comput. Vis. Pattern Recognit. **1**, 886–893 (2005)
14. Yu, S., Tan, D., Tan, T.: A framework for evaluating the effect of view angle, clothing and carrying condition on gait recognition. In: International Conference on Pattern Recognition, pp. 441–444 (2006)
15. Moreno, P., Figueira, D., Bernardino, A., Victor, J.S.: People and mobile robot classification through spatio-temporal analysis of optical flow. Int. J. Pattern Recognit. Artif. Intell. **29** (2015)
16. Bashir, K., Xiang, T., Gong, S.: Gait representation using flow fields. In: British Machine Vision Conference (BMVC) (2009)
17. Nambiar, A., Taiana, M., Figueira, D., Nascimento, J.C., Bernardino, A.: A multi-camera video dataset for research on high-definition surveillance. Int. J. Mach. Intell. Sens. Signal Process. **1**, 267–286 (2014)

18. Lucas, B.D., Kanade, T.: An iterative image registration technique with an application to stereo vision. In: Proceedings of Imaging Understanding Workshop, pp. 674–679 (1981)
19. Chen, C., Liang, J., Zhao, H., Hu, H., Tian, J.: Frame difference energy image for gait recognition with incomplete silhouettes. Pattern Recognit. Lett. **30**, 977–984 (2009)

A Bayesian Approach to Linear Unmixing in the Presence of Highly Mixed Spectra

Bruno Figliuzzi$^{(\boxtimes)}$, Santiago Velasco-Forero, Michel Bilodeau, and Jesus Angulo

Center for Mathematical Morphology, Mines ParisTech, PSL Research University, Fontainebleau, France
bruno.figliuzzi@mines-paristech.fr

Abstract. In this article, we present a Bayesian algorithm for endmember extraction and abundance estimation in situations where prior information is available for the abundances. The algorithm is considered within the framework of the linear mixing model. The novelty of this work lies in the introduction of bound parameters which allow us to introduce prior information on the abundances. The estimation of these bound parameters is performed using a simulated annealing algorithm. The algorithm is illustrated by simulations conducted on synthetic AVIRIS spectra and on the SAMSON dataset.

1 Introduction

Spectra measured by hypersensors often mix the contributions of several sources or *endmembers*. Given a set of measured spectra, the problem of identifying the endmembers and of quantifying their respective *abundances* is classically referred to as spectral unmixing. This problem is usually considered in the framework of the linear mixing model, which is based upon the assumption that the observed pixel spectrum is a linear combination of the endmembers spectra.

In numbers of situations, the number R of endmembers is significantly smaller than the dimension L of the spectra. Hence, the data lie in a subspace of dimension $R - 1$ of the vector space $\mathbb{R}^L$. In addition, since the abundances of all endmembers must sum to one and be non-negative, it can easily be shown that the observed spectra are embedded in a $R - 1$-simplex of $\mathbb{R}^L$.

As reviewed by Bioucas-Dias *et al.* [Bi], several methods have been developed for endmembers identification that work by estimating the data simplex using geometrical approaches. Classical geometrical methods include the pixel purity index (PPI) algorithm [Bo], N-FINDR [Wi], vertex component analysis (VCA) [Na] or the simplex growing algorithm (SGA) [Cha]. A common assumption behind most geometrical methods is that there is at least one pure pixel per endmember in the data. In practical situations, it is however common that the measurements yield highly mixed spectra, hence invalidating this assumption.

In presence of highly mixed data, statistical methods come as good alternatives to geometrical approaches. Bayesian approaches to spectral unmixing have been

© Springer International Publishing AG 2016
J. Blanc-Talon et al. (Eds.): ACIVS 2016, LNCS 10016, pp. 263–274, 2016.
DOI: 10.1007/978-3-319-48680-2_24

proposed by Moussaoui *et al.* in 2008 [Mou] and by Dobigeon *et al.* [Dob] in 2009. These approaches have been further developed in subsequent articles [Tho, Hal]. A major interest of statistical methods is their ability to account for endmembers variability [Zar, Som]. An other advantage is that the Bayesian approach provides a solid mathematical framework to incorporate prior knowledge in the problem. In this article, we present an extension of the Bayesian algorithm first described in [Dob] to cases where informative priors are readily available for the endmembers abundances. More precisely, the novelty of this work lies in the introduction of bound parameters which allow us to introduce qualitative prior information on the abundances. The estimation of these bound parameters is performed using a simulated annealing algorithm.

The development of the method is motivated by the problem of unmixing Raman spectra measured on B-lymphocytes cells. Due to the limited spatial resolution of the acquisition, the Raman spectra typically mix elements of the nucleus, of the cytoplasm and of the membrane of the cell. However, we know that the contribution of the membrane and of the cytoplasm to the measured spectra remains limited, with abundances around 0.2 or 0.3 at most.

The outline of the article is as follows. In Sect. 2, we present the Bayesian approach used to perform the endmembers identification and the abundances determination. The model is simulated and validated on synthetic and on real data in Sect. 3. Conclusions are finally drawn in Sect. 4.

2   Mathematical Model

In this section, we consider N independant spectra of (typically high) dimension L. Our aim is twofold: 1/ identifying the endmembers, also referred to as sources, which constitute the spectra and 2/ quantifying the respective abundances of the endmembers in each spectrum. In this section, we present a Bayesian approach to jointly performs both tasks, derived from the algorithm proposed by Dobigeon *et al.* in [Dob].

2.1   Linear Mixing Model

We rely on the classical linear mixing model to describe the spectra $\{\mathbf{y}_n, 1 \leq n \leq N\}$ as linear combinations of R endmembers. For all integer n with $1 \leq n \leq N$, the nth spectrum is given by

$$\mathbf{y_n} = \sum_{r=1}^{R} \mathbf{m_r} a_{r,n} + \mathbf{w_n}. \tag{1}$$

In Eq. (1), $\mathbf{m_r} = [m_{r,1}, .., m_{r,L}]^T$ is the rth endmember and $a_{r,n}$ is the abundance of the rth endmember in the nth spectrum vector. $\mathbf{w_n}$ is an additive noise. We assume that the elements of the sequence $\{\mathbf{w}_n, 1 \leq n \leq N\}$ are independent and identically distributed according to a zero-mean Gaussian distribution with covariance matrix $\mathbf{\Sigma}_n = \sigma^2 \mathbf{I}_L$.

The model is completed by constraints satisfied by the abundances, namely the inequalities

$$l_r \leq a_{r,n} \leq s_r \qquad (2)$$

and the sum-to-one constraint

$$\sum_{r=1}^{R} a_{r,n} = 1. \qquad (3)$$

Obviously, relations (2) and (3) can only be satisfied simultaneously if the following conditions are fullfilled:

$$\sum_{r=1}^{R} l_r < 1, \quad \sum_{r=1}^{R} s_r > 1. \qquad (4)$$

In relation (2), we have introduced bounds on the abundances. Typically, these bounds reflect prior available information. In many practical situations, we know for instance that the abundance of some endmember cannot exceed a given value, or on the contrary that an endmember is always present in the spectra in some proportion. To reflect the uncertainties on this prior information, we will consider the quantites $\{l_r, s_r\}_{1 \leq r \leq R}$ to be random variables.

To keep simple notations, we introduce the quantities $\mathbf{s} = [s_1, \ldots, s_R]^T$ and $\mathbf{l} = [l_1, \ldots, l_R]^T$. Similarly, it is of interest to reformulate the model in matricial form. Equation (1) becomes

$$\mathbf{Y} = \mathbf{Ma} + \mathbf{W}, \qquad (5)$$

where $\mathbf{Y} = [\mathbf{y_1}, ..., \mathbf{y_N}] \in \mathbb{R}^{L \times N}$, $\mathbf{M} = [\mathbf{m_1}, ..., \mathbf{m_R}] \in \mathbb{R}^{L \times R}$ is classically referred to as the mixing matrix and $\mathbf{a} = [\mathbf{a_1}, ..., \mathbf{a_N}] \in \mathbb{R}^{R \times N}$ as the abundance matrix. Starting from the data matrix $\mathbf{Y}$, our aim is to estimate the mixing matrix and the abundances. To reduce dimensionality, the data are classicaly projected in a lower-dimensional space. We can indeed observe that the set

$$\{\mathbf{x} \in \mathbb{R}^L | \mathbf{x} = \sum_{r=1}^{R} \mathbf{m}_r p_r, \quad \sum_{r=0}^{R} p_r = 1, \quad p_r \geq 0\} \qquad (6)$$

is a $(R-1)$-dimensional convex polytope in $\mathbb{R}^L$. Geometrical methods to endmember extraction exploit the geometrical properties of the data in the reduced dimension space to identify a particular simplex enclosing the data points. In this study, our aim is to introduce prior information on the form of the simplex. Bayesian approaches to inversion therefore appear to be particularly well adapted.

2.2   Bayesian Formulation

Our method for endmembers identification is derived from the Bayesian approach developed by Dobigeon *et al.* [Dob]. We recall here the main steps of the method and we refer the readers to the original article [Dob] for a more detailed description. The algorithm works in the reduced dimension space. To reduce dimensionality, we perform a principal components analysis (PCA) on the data. We only keep the $R-1$ first principal directions, R being the number of sources, assumed to be known. Next, we apply the N-FINDR algorithm to identify candidates $\{e_r, 1 \le r \le R\}$ for the projected endmembers $\{t_r, 1 \le r \le R\}$ in the reduced dimensionality space. The algorithm works by growing a simplex inside the data, beginning with a random set of pixels. The endmembers $\mathbf{m_r}$ can be recovered from the projected endmembers t_r using relation

$$\mathbf{m}_r = \mathbf{U}t_r + \bar{\mathbf{y}}, \tag{7}$$

where $\mathbf{U}$ is the pseudo-inverse of the projection matrix projecting the data in the dimensionality reduced space and $\bar{\mathbf{y}}$ the average of the spectral vectors. The linear mixing model can be recasted in probabilistic terms to yield

$$p(\mathbf{Y}|\mathbf{M}, \mathbf{a}, \sigma^2, \mathbf{l}, \mathbf{s}) = \mathcal{N}(\mathbf{Ma}, \sigma^2 \mathbf{I}_L). \tag{8}$$

Making use of Bayes formula, we can express the density function as

$$f(\mathbf{M}, \mathbf{a}, \sigma^2, \mathbf{l}, \mathbf{s}|\mathbf{Y}) \propto f(\mathbf{Y}|\mathbf{M}, \mathbf{a}, \sigma^2, \mathbf{l}, \mathbf{s}) f(\mathbf{M}) f(\mathbf{a}|\mathbf{l}, \mathbf{s}) f(\sigma^2). \tag{9}$$

In this expression, the likehood function is given by Eq. (8). Following Dobigeon et al., we consider the prior $p(\mathbf{m_r})$ for each endmember to be a Gaussian distribution of fixed variance d_r^2 centered at the point $\mathbf{e_r}$ identified as a candidate endmember by the N-FINDR algorithm. Similarly, we consider the abundances to be uniformly distributed over the subset $\mathcal{T}_R$ of $\mathbb{R}^{R-1}$ defined by

$$\mathcal{T}_R = \{\mathbf{a} \in \mathbb{R}^{R-1} | \forall k, 1 \le k \le R, l_k \le a_k \le s_k\} \tag{10}$$

conditionally to $\mathbf{l}$ and $\mathbf{s}$. We select a conjugate prior for the noise variance σ^2, given by the inverse Gamma law

$$p(\sigma^2|\gamma) \sim \mathcal{IG}(1, \frac{\gamma}{2}). \tag{11}$$

In this relation, γ is a random hyperparameter sampled from the non informative Jeffrey's prior

$$f(\gamma) \propto \frac{1}{\gamma} \mathbf{1}_{\mathbb{R}^+}(\gamma). \tag{12}$$

This choice of prior accounts for the lack of information on γ.

2.3 Gibbs Sampling Algorithm

We draw samples from the posterior distribution (9) by relying on a Gibbs sampler [Rob, And]. Gibbs sampling is a Markov Chain Monte Carlo (MCMC) method which generates samples conditionally to the posterior distribution of the other parameters.

Abundances Sampling. Let a_n be the vector of abundances for the nth spectrum. We can split a_n in two parts to yield

$$\mathbf{a}_n = \begin{pmatrix} \mathbf{c}_n \\ a_{R,n} \end{pmatrix}, \text{ with } \mathbf{c}_n = \begin{pmatrix} a_{1,n} \\ \vdots \\ a_{R-1,n} \end{pmatrix}. \tag{13}$$

The sum-to-one constraint reads

$$a_{R,n} = 1 - \sum_{r=0}^{R-1} c_{r,n}. \tag{14}$$

If we inject this relation into the bound constraints, we find, for all k such that $1 \le k \le R-1$,

$$\hat{l}_k \equiv \max(l_k, 1 - s_R + \sum_{j=0, j\neq k}^{R-1} c_j) \le c_k \le \hat{s}_k \equiv \min(s_k, 1 - l_R + \sum_{j=0, j\neq k}^{R-1} c_j). \tag{15}$$

According to Bayes formula, we have

$$f(\mathbf{c}|\mathbf{Y}, \mathbf{M}, \sigma^2, \mathbf{l}, \mathbf{s}) \propto f(\mathbf{Y}|\mathbf{c}, \mathbf{M}, \sigma^2) f(\mathbf{c}|\mathbf{l}, \mathbf{s}). \tag{16}$$

The likehood is given by Eq. (8), while the prior distribution is uniform on the subset $\mathcal{T}_R$. Hence, after some algebra, we can show that

$$f(\mathbf{c}_n|\mathbf{Y}, \mathbf{M}, \sigma^2, \mathbf{l}, \mathbf{s}) \propto \exp\left[- \frac{(\mathbf{c}_n - \mathbf{v}_n)^T \boldsymbol{\Sigma}_n^{-1}(\mathbf{c}_n - \mathbf{v}_n)}{2} \right] \mathbf{1}_{\mathcal{T}_R}(\mathbf{c}_n). \tag{17}$$

Each vector of abundances is distributed according to a Gaussian law of mean $\mathbf{v}_n$ and of covariance matrix $\boldsymbol{\Sigma}_n$ truncated on the subset $\mathcal{T}_R$. The parameters $\mathbf{v}_n$ and $\boldsymbol{\Sigma}_n$ are given by

$$\begin{cases} \boldsymbol{\Sigma}_n = [(\mathbf{M}_{-R} - \mathbf{m}_R \mathbf{1}_{R-1}^T)^T \frac{1}{\sigma^2} \mathbf{I}_L (\mathbf{M}_{-R} - \mathbf{m}_R \mathbf{1}_{R-1}^T)]^{-1} \\ \mathbf{v}_n = \boldsymbol{\Sigma}_n [(\mathbf{M}_{-R} - \mathbf{m}_R \mathbf{1}_{R-1}^T)^T \frac{1}{\sigma^2} \mathbf{I}_L (\mathbf{y}_n - \mathbf{m}_R)]. \end{cases} \tag{18}$$

In these expressions, $\mathbf{M}_{-R}$ is the mixing matrix $\mathbf{M}$ whose Rth column has been removed, and $\mathbf{m}_R$ is the Rth endmember.

Endmember Sampling. By applying Bayes formula, we find that the posterior distribution of $\mathbf{T} = [\mathbf{t_1}, \dots, \mathbf{t_R}]$ is

$$f(\mathbf{t}_r|\mathbf{T}_{-r}, \mathbf{c}_r, \sigma^2, \mathbf{Y}) \propto \exp\left[- \frac{(\mathbf{t}_r - \tau_r)^T \boldsymbol{\Lambda}_r^{-1}(\mathbf{t}_r - \tau_r)}{2} \right], \tag{19}$$

where

$$\begin{cases} \boldsymbol{\Lambda}_r = [\sum_{n=1}^N a_{r,n}^2 \mathbf{U}^T \frac{1}{\sigma^2} \mathbf{I}_L \mathbf{U} + \frac{1}{d_r^2} \mathbf{I}_K]^{-1} \\ \tau_r = \boldsymbol{\Lambda}_r [\sum_{n=1}^N a_{r,n}^2 \mathbf{U}^T \frac{1}{\sigma^2} \mathbf{I}_L \epsilon_{r,n} + \frac{1}{d_r^2} \mathbf{e}_r]. \end{cases} \tag{20}$$

In this expression, the quantity $\epsilon_{r,n}$ is given by

$$\epsilon_{r,n} = \mathbf{y}_n - a_{r,n}\hat{\mathbf{y}} - \sum_{j \neq r} a_{j,p}\mathbf{m}_j. \tag{21}$$

A more detailed derivation of these results can be found in Ref. [Dob].

Noise Sampling. The conditional distribution of the noise variance with respect to other parameters is easily determined from Baye's formula to be

$$f(\sigma^2|\mathbf{c}, \mathbf{M}, \mathbf{Y}) \propto \left(\frac{1}{\sigma^2}\right)^{\frac{NL}{2}+1} \exp\left(-\frac{\sum_{n=1}^{N}(\mathbf{y}_n - \mathbf{M}a_n)^2}{2\sigma^2}\right) \tag{22}$$

The projected endmembers are estimated to be, for all k with $1 \leq k \leq R$,

$$\hat{\mathbf{t}}_k \simeq \frac{1}{M - M_b} \sum_{m=M_b+1}^{M} \mathbf{t}_k^{(m)}, \tag{23}$$

where M is the number of iteration of the Gibbs sampler algorithm, M_b the number of burn-in iterations and $\mathbf{t}_k^{(m)}$ the kth projected endmember as sampled at iteration m of the Gibbs sampler. The endmembers $\{\mathbf{m}_k, 1 \leq k \leq R\}$ can be estimated from $\{\hat{\mathbf{t}}_k, 1 \leq k \leq R\}$ using Eq. (7).

2.4 Simulated Annealing for Bounds Estimation

At this step, we are left with the estimation of the bounds $\{s_k, l_k, 1 \leq k \leq K\}$. We rely on the simulated annealing algorithm to optimize these bounds, by iteratively 1/ estimating the mixing matrix $\mathbf{M}$, the abundances $\mathbf{a}$ and the noise σ^2 for fixed bounds vector $\mathbf{s}$ and $\mathbf{l}$ with the Gibbs sampling algorithm described in the previous section and 2/ proposing new values for one of the parameters $\{l_k, s_k, 1 \leq k \leq R\}$ and accepting/rejecting it with respect to some cost function.

We can define a cost function $J(\mathbf{s}, \mathbf{l})$ after each run m of the Gibbs sampling procedure by considering the quantity

$$J^{(m)}(\mathbf{s}, \mathbf{l}) = \sum_{n=1}^{N} ||\hat{\mathbf{M}}\hat{\mathbf{a}} - Y||^2, \tag{24}$$

where $\hat{\mathbf{M}}$ and $\hat{\mathbf{a}}$ are the estimated mixing matrix and abundances, respectively. At each iteration of the simulated annealing algorithm, we sample a new value for a randomly chosen parameter among $\{l_k, s_k, 1 \leq k \leq R\}$, and we recompute an estimate of the cost function $J^{(m+1)}$ with the Gibbs sampler algorithm. We denote by $\Delta J^{(m)}$ the quantity $J^{(m+1)} - J^{(m)}$. If $\Delta J^{(m)} < 0$, we accept the proposed parameter with probability 1. If $\Delta J^{(m)} \geq 0$, we accept the proposed parameter with probability $\exp(-\Delta J^{(m)}/T^{(m)})$, where $T^{(m)}$ is the temperature associated to the simulated annealing algorithm at iteration m. The temperature is classically modified stage by stage using a geometrical law of parameter α:

$$T^{(m+1)} = \alpha T^{(m)}. \tag{25}$$

3   Results on Synthetic and Real Data

We first validate the proposed approach on simulated data. To construct the data, we selected $R = 3$ endmembers from the AVIRIS database (see Fig. 1) obtained from Ref. [Na]. Then, we sampled abundances uniformly on the set

$$\mathcal{T}_R = \{ \mathbf{a} \in \mathbb{R}^{R-1} | \forall k, 1 \leq k \leq R, l_k \leq a_k \leq s_k \}. \qquad (26)$$

The actual bounds $\{ s_k, l_k, 1 \leq k \leq R \}$ selected for generating the spectra are specified in the caption of Tables 1 and 2.

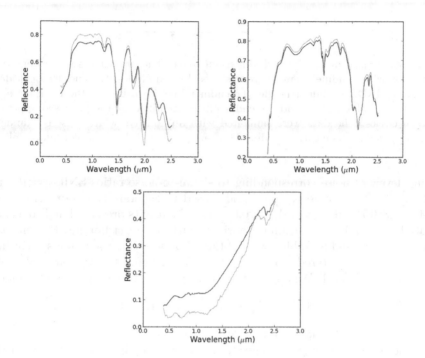

Fig. 1. Reflectance spectra selected from the AVIRIS database (in blue). The spectra estimated by our method are represented in red, for the simulation in Table 2 with $\text{SNR}_{db} = 10$. (Color figure online)

Each run of the Gibbs sampling algorithm is constituted of 500 iterations. The burn-in number is 100. The temperature of the simulated annealing algorithm is initially set to $T = 1$. It is changed after 12 iterations according to a geometrical sequence of coefficient $\alpha = 0.8$. The algorithm is stopped when the temperature falls below 0.4. We compared the results of our algorithm to the ones obtained with N-FINDR and with the Bayesian approach [Dob]. The results are presented in Tables 1 and 2. The estimated endmembers spectra are plotted in Fig. 2. A scatter plot of the endmembers and of the projected data is shown in Fig. 2. For each simulation, we generated $N = 150$ synthetic spectra with two

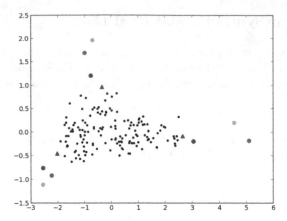

Fig. 2. Scatter plot in the reduced dimension space. The projected spectra appear in black. The actual endmembers are represented by red circles, the endmembers identified by N-FINDR by blue triangle, the endmembers identified by the Bayesian approach [Dob] by blue circles, and the endmembers identified by the proposed approach by green circles. The data were simulated with an additive white noise of standard deviation $\sigma = 0.22$. The corresponding MSE are given in Table 2. (Color figure online)

distinct levels of noise corresponding to signal-to-noise ratios $\mathrm{SNR}_{db} = 10$ and $\mathrm{SNR}_{db} = 20$. The bound vectors **l** and **s** used to generate the data were set to $\mathbf{s} = [0.6, 0.8, 0.7]^T$ and $\mathbf{l} = [0.1, 0.2, 0.0]^T$. For the results presented in Table 1, we initiated the simulated annealing algorithm with the exact bounds. By contrast, the results presented in Table 2 were obtained by selecting the bounds according to a Gaussian law centered around $\mathbf{l} = [0.1, 0.1, 0.1]^T$ and $\mathbf{s} = [0.8, 0.8, 0.8]^T$ with standard deviation 0.1. We rely on the mean square errors between endmembers

$$\mathrm{MSE}_r^2 = ||\hat{\mathbf{m}}_r - \mathbf{m}_r||^2, \quad r = 1, \ldots R, \qquad (27)$$

to compare the performance of the algorithms.

We note that the proposed algorithm performs significantly better than the Bayesian approach [Dob]. This is easily explained by the greater amount of prior information introduced in the algorithm. In [Dob], the prior for the abundances is simply the simplex

Table 1. MSE obtained with the proposed algorithm, compared with the Bayesian method [Dob] and the N-FINDR algorithm. In these simulations, the simulated annealing algorithm was initialized with the exact bounds **l** and **s**.

$\mathrm{SNR}_{db} = 20$	ALG	[Dob]	N-FINDR
End #1	0.441	0.578	1.213
End #2	0.579	0.550	0.564
End #3	1.676	4.867	6.560
Mean	0.899	1.998	2.779

$\mathrm{SNR}_{db} = 10$	ALG	[Dob]	N-FINDR
End #1	0.661	0.279	1.09
End #2	0.057	0.047	0.851
End #3	0.835	6.339	5.531
Mean	0.518	2.222	2.49

Table 2. MSE obtained with the proposed algorithm, compared with the Bayesian method [Dob] and the N-FINDR algorithm.

$SNR_{db} = 20$	ALG	[Dob]	N-FINDR	$SNR_{db} = 10$	ALG	[Dob]	N-FINDR
End #1	0.899	0.806	1.175	End #1	1.034	0.897	1.436
End #2	1.388	2.579	0.750	End #2	0.868	0.484	0.885
End #3	0.239	1.763	6.60	End #3	2.972	5.786	6.970
Mean	0.842	1.716	2.842	Mean	1.625	2.389	3.097

$$T_R = \{\mathbf{a} \in \mathbb{R}^{R-1} | \forall k, 1 \leq k \leq R, 0 \leq a_k \leq 1\}, \tag{28}$$

so that the algorithm selects the smallest polytope embedding the data set. When the abundances are such that no data points are included in the facets of the polytope, then the problem is under-determined and prior information has to be introduced in the description of the problem. By relying on the simulated annealing algorithm, we can account for the uncertainties on this prior information by conducting an optimization procedure that adjust the prior information to match the geometric characteristics of the dataset.

To illustrate a case with realistic noise and abundances, we test the proposed algorithm on the SAMSON dataset [Fyz]. The image in the SAMSON dataset is a 952×952 pixels image, where each pixel corresponds to 156 channels covering wavelengths ranging from 401 to 889 nm. Each spectrum combine 3 sources, corresponding to soil, tree and water. In this study, we consider a sub-image of size 95×95 pixels. A ground truth is available for the endmembers and abundances. The purpose of our algorithm is to estimate the endmembers in the presence of highly mixed spectra. Therefore, we selected one endmember and removed all spectra for which the corresponding abundance is below 0.2. Similarly, we removed all spectra for which the abundances of the remaining endmembers are greater than 0.7. The remaining spectra are represented in Fig. 3 in the projection space of dimension 3.

For the extraction, we run the Gibbs sampling algorithm with 500 iterations, with a burn-in number of 100. We set the initial temperature of the simulated annealing algorithm to $T = 10$, which roughly corresponds to the typical cost variation between two successive runs. The temperature is changed after 12 iterations according to a geometrical sequence of coefficient $\alpha = 0.8$. The algorithm is stopped when the temperature falls below 4.0. The simulated annealing algorithm is initialized with the lower and upper bounds set to $\mathbf{l} = [0.1, 0.1, 0.1]^T$ and $\mathbf{l} = [1.0, 1.0, 1.0]^T$ respectively.

A scatter plot of the endmembers found with NFINDR and the Bayesian algorithm is shown in Fig. 3. We can note that the endmembers found by the Bayesian approach are significantly closer from the actual endmembers than the one found with NFINDR algorithm. Again, this is explained by the prior information introduced in the problem parametrization (Table 3).

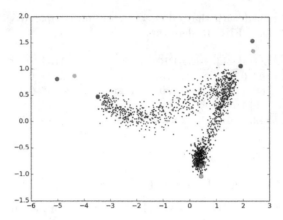

Fig. 3. Scatter plot in the reduced dimension space for the SAMSON dataset. The projected spectra appear in black. The actual endmembers are represented by red circles, the endmembers identified by N-FINDR by blue circles, and the endmembers identified by the proposed approach by green circles. (Color figure online)

Table 3. MSE obtained with the proposed algorithm, compared with the N-FINDR algorithm.

	ALG	N-FINDR
End #1	3.643	4.918
End #2	3.031	4.133
End #3	0.175	0.177
Mean	2.283	3.076

4   Conclusion

In this article, we proposed an approach to spectral unmixing derived from the Bayesian method in [Dob]. Our methodology is adapted to situations where prior information is available on the abundances. The Bayesian framework allows us to incorporate this prior information into the problem's description in a rigorous manner. The prior parameters are then adapted to the intrinsic geometrical characteristics of the data using an optimization procedure based upon the simulated annealing algorithm. Our approach was illustrated on synthetic data obtained by mixing sources from the AVIRIS database with additive Gaussian noise and on real data from the SAMSON dataset, and compared with a geometrical method [Wi] and the Bayesian method [Dob]. The introduction of additional prior information allows us to slightly improve the results when compared to both methods. However, the simultaneous use of Gibb's sampling and simulated annealing requires a significant calculation time.

The development of the method is motivated by the problem of unmixing Raman spectra measured on B-lymphocytes cells. Due to the limited spatial resolution of the acquisition, the Raman spectra typically mix elements of the nucleus, of the cytoplasm and of the membrane of the cell. However, the acquisition is usually focused on the nucleus. Hence, we know that the contribution of the membrane and of the cytoplasm to the measured spectra remains limited, with abundances around 0.2 at most. The application of the proposed method to Raman spectra unmixing and the interpretation of the results is a topic of our current work. Finally, interesting questions arise regarding the use of principal component analysis to perform the dimensionality reduction. Using maximum noise fraction (MNF) [Bi] or learning based methods [Moh, Cas] could potentially constitute interesting alternatives.

Acknowledgements. This work has been supported by the European Commission project M3S (Molecular Signature Detection with Multi-modal Microscopy Scanner) under the ICT PSP Call (Contract no. 621152). The authors would like to thank MEDyC team from Reims University for providing Raman spectra used in the experimental part. Special thanks also go to Jacques Klossa (TRIBVN) for discussion.

References

[Bi] Bioucas-Dias, J.M., Plaza, A., Dobigeon, N., Parente, M., Du, Q., Gader, P., Chanussot, J.: Hyperspectral unmixing overview: geometrical, statistical, and sparse regression-based approaches. IEEE J. Sel. Top. Appl. Earth Observations Remote Sens. **5**(2), 354–379 (2012)

[Bo] Boardman, J.W., Kruse, F.A., Green, R.O.: Mapping target signatures via partial unmixing of AVIRIS data (1995)

[Wi] Winter, M.E.: N-FINDR: an algorithm for fast autonomous spectral endmember determination in hyperspectral data. In: SPIE's International Symposium on Optical Science, Engineering, and Instrumentation. International Society for Optics and Photonics (1999)

[Na] Nascimento, J.M.P., Bioucas Dias, J.M.: Vertex component analysis: a fast algorithm to unmix hyperspectral data. IEEE Trans. Geosci. Remote Sens. **43**(4), 898–910 (2005)

[Cha] Chang, C.-I., et al.: A new growing method for simplex-based endmember extraction algorithm. IEEE Trans. Geosci. Remote Sens. **44**(10), 2804–2819 (2006)

[Dob] Dobigeon, N., et al.: Joint Bayesian endmember extraction and linear unmixing for hyperspectral imagery. IEEE Trans. Sig. Proc. **57**(11), 4355–4368 (2009)

[Tho] Thouvenin, P.-A., Dobigeon, N., Tourneret, J.-Y.: Hyperspectral unmixing with spectral variability using a perturbed linear mixing model. IEEE Trans. Sig. Proc. **64**(2), 525–538 (2016)

[Hal] Halimi, A., Dobigeon, N., Tourneret, J.-Y.: Unsupervised unmixing of hyperspectral images accounting for endmember variability. IEEE Trans. Image Proc. **24**(12), 4904–4917 (2015)

[Zar] Zare, A., Ho, K.C.: Endmember variability in hyperspectral analysis: addressing spectral variability during spectral unmixing. IEEE Sig. Proc. Mag. **31**(1), 95–104 (2014)

[Som] Somers, B., et al.: Endmember variability in spectral mixture analysis: a review. Remote Sens. Environ. **115**(7), 1603–1616 (2011)

[Rob] Robert, C., George, C.: Monte Carlo statistical methods. Springer Science and Business Media, New York (2013)

[And] Andrieu, C., et al.: An introduction to MCMC for machine learning. Mach. Learn. **50**(1–2), 5–43 (2003)

[Fyz] Feiyn, Z., et al.: Structured sparse method for hyperspectral unmixing. ISPRS J. Photogrammetry Remote Sens. **88**, 101–118 (2014)

[Mou] Moussaoui, S., et al.: On the decomposition of Mars hyperspectral data by ICA and Bayesian positive source separation. Neurocomputing **71**(10), 2194–2208 (2008)

[Moh] Mohan, A., Sapiro, G., Bosch, E.: Spatially coherent nonlinear dimensionality reduction and segmentation of hyperspectral images. IEEE Geosci. Remote Sens. Lett. **4**(2), 206–210 (2007)

[Cas] Castrodad, A., et al.: Learning discriminative sparse representations for modeling, source separation, and mapping of hyperspectral imagery. IEEE Trans. Geosci. Remote Sens. **49**(11), 4263–4281 (2011)

Key Frames Extraction Based on Local Features for Efficient Video Summarization

Hana Gharbi[(✉)], Mohamed Massaoudi, Sahbi Bahroun,
and Ezzeddine Zagrouba

Research Team Systèmes Intelligents en Imagerie et Vision Artificielle
SIIVA– RIADI Laboratory ISI,
2 Rue Abou Rayhane Bayrouni, 2080 Ariana, Tunisia
hanagharbi@yahoo.fr, Sahbi.Bahroun@isi.rnu.tn,
ezzeddine.zagrouba@fsm.rnu.tn

Abstract. Key frames are the most representative images of a video. They are used in different areas in video processing, such as indexing, retrieval and summarization. In this paper we propose a novel approach for key frames extraction based on local feature description. This approach will be used to summarize the salient visual content of videos. First, we start by generating a set of candidate keyframes. Then we detect interest points for all these candidate frames. After that we will compute repeatability between them and stock the repeatability values in a matrix. Finally we will model repeatability table by an oriented graph and the selection of keframe is inspired from shortest path algorithm A*. Realized experiments on challenging videos show the efficiency of the proposed method: it demonstrates that it is able to prevent the redundancy of the extracted key frames and maintain minimum requirements in terms of memory space.

Keywords: Key frame extraction · Interest points · Local features · Repeatability

1 Introduction

Compared with text, audio and image, videos become the main source of information due to its abundant amount of information and intuitive experience. With rapid progress of computer and network technologies, millions of videos are daily being uploaded on Internet consisting of news, tutorials, sports clips, lectures contents and many others. Content based retrieval of video has emerged as a growing challenge and therefore, automatic keyframes extraction; the main step for the efficient retrieval, video classification and story retrieval; has become so important and vital.

A successful video summarization process aims to obtain a compact representation, which should be used to properly characterize videos. Key frames are a subset of still frames extracted from different video shots, and can be theoretically defined as the most representative and informative frames that maintain the salient content of the video. According to the definition, the purpose of key frame extraction algorithm is to extract correct and proper key frames from each video, which can perfectly represent the whole visual contents of the shot while eliminating all redundancy.

© Springer International Publishing AG 2016
J. Blanc-Talon et al. (Eds.): ACIVS 2016, LNCS 10016, pp. 275–285, 2016.
DOI: 10.1007/978-3-319-48680-2_25

In this paper, we propose a novel keyframe extraction method based on local features. Local features have being applied successfully in the image retrieval domain, mainly due their capabilities of providing robust descriptors against different transformation types (rotation, viewpoint changes,…) [1–3]. However, in spite of their importance, local features have been poorly explored in the video keyframe extraction field.

In Sect. 2, we present some recent approaches of key frame extraction for video summary and retrieval. In Sect. 3 we describe the key frame proposed approach. The results and observations of the new key frame extraction method comparing with other recent works are discussed in Sect. 4. We conclude in Sect. 5.

2   Related Works

While we are faced to a huge volume of video content, video summarization plays an important role in efficient storage, quick browsing, and retrieval of large collection of video data without losing important resources like time, man power and storage [4]. The video can be seen as a combination of frames that is called GOP (groups of pictures). The key frame extraction is an important technique for video summarization. We can summarize the traditional key frame extraction for video summarization methods in five categories:

Shot boundary based methods [5, 6] suppose that the semantic and visual contents in one shot are mainly stable and change softly, only three frames which are: the first, the last and the middle frames in each shot are selected as the key frames, which is certainly not robust to majority of videos.

Motion analysis-based methods [7–9]: key frames are selected in local minimum through the computation of optical-flow. However, the computational cost is huge and the results aren't always accurate.

Clustering based methods and visual content based methods [10, 11]: they use the difference between adjacent frames to select key frames, and these two methods can be easily affected by noise and motion.

Event/object based methods [12, 13]: These algorithms jointly consider key-frame extraction and object/event detection in order to ensure that the extracted key-frames contain information about objects or events. Calic and Thomas [14] use the positions of regions obtained using frame segmentation to extract key-frames where objects merge. The merit of the object/event-based algorithms is that the extracted key-frames are semantically important, reflecting objects or the motion patterns of objects. The limitation of these algorithms is that object/event detection strongly relies on heuristic rules specified according to the application.

Trajectory based methods [15]: These algorithms represent each frame in a shot as a point in the feature space. The points are linked in the sequential order to form a trajectory curve and then searched to find a set of points which best represent the shape of the curve. Calic et al. [15] generate the frame difference metrics by analyzing statistics of the macro block features extracted from the MPEG compressed stream. The merit of the curve simplification-based algorithms is that the sequential information is kept during the key-frame extraction. Their limitation is that optimization of the best representation of the curve has a high computational complexity.

In this work, we will focus in particular in feature based methods to extract key frames. We will try to present some novel key frame extraction methods based on local description. Liu, et al. [16] proposed a method based on Maximum a Posteriori (MAP) to estimate the positions of key frames. Ejaz, et al. [17] proposed an aggregation mechanism to combine the visual features extracted from the correlation of RGB color channels, the color histogram and the moments of inertia to extract key frames. Xu, et al. [18] developed a Jensen–Shannon divergence, Jensen–Rényi divergence and Jensen–Tsallis divergence-based approach to measure the difference between neighboring frames and extract key frames. Lai, et al. [19] used a saliency-based visual attention model and selected the frames with maximum saliency value as key frames. Kumar, et al. [20] analyzed the spatio-temporal information of the video by sparse representation and used a normalized clustering method to generate clusters; the middle frame in each temporal order-sorted cluster was selected as a key frame. Sargent et al. [28] proposes a novel scalable summary generation approach based on the On-Line Analytical Processing data cube. Such a structure integrates tools like the drill down operation allowing to browse efficiently multiple descriptions of a dataset according to increased levels of detail.

Despite that many methods have been presented in the literature, key frame extraction remains a challenging and difficult problem due to the complexity and diversity of video content. Most of the feature extraction techniques are based on global feature extraction from each shot in the key frame. Local features can give an accurate solution for these problems. Chergui et al. [21] adopted a strategy that select a single keyframe to represent each shot. But this key frame extraction method is not robust. They consider that the key frame is the relevant image that contains richest visual details. Thus, they defined the key frame as the frame with the highest number of points of interest in the shot. Despite using images content, it is not possible to guarantee that the frame with the highest number of points of interest is the most representative one in all cases. Besides, one image may not be enough to describe the diverse content of some shots and important information can be lost. This method is also more computationally demanding, because the selection step involves processing all shot frames. Tapu et al. [22] developed an approach to extract a variable number of keyframes from each shot. Using a window size parameter N, the first frame is selected N frames after a detected shot transition. Next, they analyze images located at integer multipliers of the window size N. These images are compared with the existing keyframes set already extracted. If the visual dissimilarity (defined as the chi-square distance of HSV color histograms) between them is significant (above a pre-established threshold), the current image is added to the keyframes set. Then, they discard irrelevant frames, computing points of interest with SIFT descriptor. If the number of keypoints is zero, the image is removed. After that, the keyframes are described by SIFT features. This keyframe extraction method has the advantage that not all shot frames are processed. However, many parameters need to be set (window size N, dissimilarity threshold, histograms quantization), what can influence the quality of the shot representation. Gharbi et al. proposed [25] an approach which is based on interest points description and repeatability measurement. Before key frame extraction, the video is segmented into shots. Then, for each shot, detect interest points in all images. After that, calculate repeatability matrix for each shot. Finally, apply PCA and HAC to extract key frames.

This approach shows good results in comparison with state of the art methods but it suffers from some problems like the loss of information by using PCA and redundancy since it treats separately shots, so each shot will have necessary at least one keyframe.

After this study of the related work of key frame extraction, we can see that different methods are either too naïve or too complex. The most simple of these techniques sorely compromise the key frames extracted quality and the most sophisticated ones are computationally very expensive. Also, some of these methods give us key frames with approximately the same content.

As we can see also, the related work using local features can be good alternative for keyframe representations. However, as discussed, the current approaches present problems of representativeness and, sometimes, computational costs leading to high processing times. Our proposed work gives a good agreement between local features, quality and complexity of results and this will be proved in experimental results.

3 Proposed Approach

3.1 Candidates Frames Generation

In order to select the best frames to be the keyframes, we initially select some frames into a Candidates Set (CS). The first frame to be included in the CS is defined as the first video frame. Then the next frames to be included in the CS follow a windowing rule. We defined a window of size n and the frames at positions n + 1, 2n + 1, 3n + 1, and so on, are selected for later analysis. We set the fps (frame per seconds) value for n because within 1 s there is no significant variation in consecutive frames content.

3.2 SURF Detector

The next step is to extract SURF [23] features from the frames in the CS. The result is a number of feature vectors representing each frame, each one is of 64 dimensions. SURF features matching is faster compared to other descriptors such as SIFT [3]. The exact number of vectors varies according to the frames content but it is generally high. This is another reason to adopt the windowing rule mentioned in Sect. 3.1 instead of to use all frames in the shot.

3.3 Build the Repeatability Table

After detecting interest points in each frame of (CS) in the video shots, we will compute the repeatability matrix using the SURF matching results. Repeatability is a criterion which proves the stability of the interest point detector. It is the average number of corresponding interest points detected in images under noise or changes undergone by the image [24]. This matrix is built from all images belonging to (CS). We must compute repeatability between each two part of the (CS) frames.

```
Inputs:
  M: matrix with N x N dimension
  N: number of (CS) in the video
Outputs:
  M: matrix filled with the repeatability values
Begin
M[i][j]= M[N][ N]
for (int i = 0; i < N ; i++)
  for (int i = 0; i < N ; i++)
  // apply matching algorithm for the two images
  // compute the repeatability between I and J frames
  M[i][j]=Repeatability i,j
  End
End
End
```

Our goal now is to detect the keyframes from this repeatability table and in order to reduce time and complexity we will resort to model this table into an oriented graph.

3.4   Keyframe Selection Using Shortest Path Algorithm

In this part we will consider the repeatability table as an adjacency matrix and we will model it by oriented graph: Frames are considered as vertices and the edges are weighted by repeatability values. Our method is inspired from shortest path algorithm A* which is a best-first search, meaning that it solves problems by searching among all possible paths to the goal for the one that incurs the smallest cost. In our case the smallest cost is the repeatability values. The path is directed and requires that consecutive vertices be connected by an appropriate directed edge since repeatability values are ordered in chronological sense. After founding the first occurrence of the minimum value (min-value) of the repeatability table we do the algorithm explained below:

```
Inputs
M: matrix filled with the repeatability values
KS= Ø ;          // Keyframes set
Nb_Lign= Nb_Col=N; // number of (CS) in the shot;
i=j=0;
Outputs:
KS: Keyframes set
Begin
While  (j<N) do
  While (i<N) do
     If T[i][j]==minvalue
           Add j to KS;
           j=i;
     else i++;
     End if
  End while
  j++; i=j;
End while
End
```

The use of shortest path algorithm to select relevant key frames help us to eliminate redundancy and to enhance accuracy with best time cost and complexity.

4 Experimental Results

To evaluate the efficiency of our proposed key frame extraction method, we did experimental tests on some videos (news, cartoons, games,...). These video illustrate different challenges (camera motion, background-foreground similar appearance, dynamic background,...). Experimental results proved that our method can extract efficiently key frames resuming the salient content of a video with no redundancy.

To verify the robustness of the key frame extraction proposed method we use qualitative and quantitative evaluation of the extracted key frames in order to enhance the proof of the effectiveness of our proposed approach.

In experimental setup, the experiments were done on movies from YUV Video sequences (http://trace.eas.asu.edu/yuv/) and some other standard test videos with different sizes and contents. The shot detection is based on the $\chi 2$ histogram matching [27]. Table 1 shows the number of frames and shots for the 6 movies:

Table 1. The video characteristics

Movie	Nb frames	Nb shots
Filinstone.mpg	510	10
Foreman.avi	297	5
Mov1.mpg	377	6
HallMonitor.mpg	299	4
MrBean.avi	2377	8
Coast-guard.mpg	299	2

4.1 Validity Mesures

Fidelity. The fidelity measure is based on semi-Hausdorff distance to compare each key frame in the summary with the other frames in the video sequence. Let $V_{seq} = \{F_1,$ $F_2,... F_N\}$ the frames of the input video sequence and let KF all key frames extracted KF = $\{F_{K1}, F_{K2},...., F_{KM}...\}$. The distance between the set of key frames and F belonging to V_{seq} is defined as follows:

$$DIST(F, KF) = Min\left\{(Diff(F, F_{Kj})\right\}, j = 1\, to\, M \tag{1}$$

Diff() is a suitable frame difference. This difference is calculated from their histograms: a combination of color histogram intersection and edge histogram-based dissimilarity measure [13]. The distance between the set of key frames KF and the video sequence V_{seq} is defined as follows:

$$DIST(V_{seq}, KF) = Max\{DIST(F_i, KF)\}, \; i = 1, .., N \qquad (2)$$

So we can define the fidelity as follows:

$$FIDELITY(V_{seq}, KF) = MaxDiff - DIST(V_{seq}, KF) \qquad (3)$$

MaxDiff is the largest value that can take the difference between two frames Diff (). High Fidelity values indicate that the result of extracted key frames from the video sequence provides good global description of the visual content of the sequence.

Compression Rate. Keyframe extraction result should not contain many key frames in order to avoid redunduncy. That's why we should evaluate the compactness of the summary. The compression ratio is computed by dividing the number of key frames in the summary by the length of the video sequence. For a given video sequence, the compression rate is computed as follows:

$$CR = 1 - \frac{card\{(Keyframes)\}}{card\{(frames)\}} \qquad (4)$$

Where card(keyframes) is the number of extracted key frames from the video. Card (frames) is the number of frames in the video

Signal to noise ratio. We calculate also the signal to noise ratio (PSNR) for each couple (Fu, Fv) of selected key frames with size (N * M), we compute the PSNR between them and the mean value is considered for each video.

$$PSNR(F_u, F_v) = 10.\log\left(\frac{N.M.255^2}{\sum_{x=1}^{N}\sum_{y=1}^{M}(F_u(x, y) - F_v(x, y))^2}\right) \qquad (5)$$

4.2 Key Frame Extraction Results

In Fig. 3 we show a comparison between our proposed approach (PA) and two state of the art methods in terms of compression rate. As the CR value is high as we have different key frames. As we can see that our proposed approach (PA) reduced considerably the number of extracted key frames.

In Fig. 4, we show a comparison between our proposed approach (PA) and two state of the art methods in terms of PSNR. As the PSNR is low as we have different key frames. So, from Fig. 4 we can see that our proposed approach gives the lowest values

Table 2. Key frame extraction by the proposed method from somes standard videos "news. mpg"

Movie	Number of key frames
Filinstone.mpg	13
Foreman.avi	4
Mov1.mpg	3
HallMonitor.mpg	4
MrBean.avi	7
Coast-guard.mpg	2

Fig. 1. Key frame extraction by the proposed method from the standard video "foreman.mpg"

Fig. 2. Key frame extraction by the proposed method from the standard video "flinstone.mpg"

for PSNR. So, we can conclude, that it gives lowest redundancy in key frames according to CR and PSNR values.

All these results demonstrate the feasibility and efficiency of the proposed method. Our method can offer us a video summary with a no redundant key frames since our

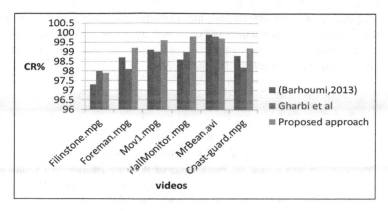

Fig. 3. Comparison of the quality of the extracted key frames in term of compression rate (CR)

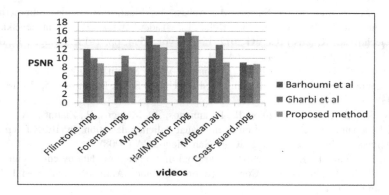

Fig. 4. Comparison of the quality of the produced results in term of PSNR values

approach is based on oriented graphs. All similar images will be presented by one key frame. Also, our approach is with low computational cost since it is based on shortest path algorithm (Figs. 1 and 2, Table 2).

5 Conclusions

In this paper, we have proposed a simple and effective technique for keyframe extraction based on SURF local features and using the repeatability matrix method. Firstly, candidate frames are selected adaptively using a leap extraction method. Each candidate frame is described by SURF local features vectors. Secondly, we will build the repeatability table and model it by an oriented graph. The selection of keyframes was inspired from the shortest path algorithm A*. The proposed approach proved to have superior effectiveness to others successful state of the art works, i.e., gives a set of image that covers all significant events in the standard video while minimizing information redundancy in keyframes.

As a perspective, we consider developing a complete system for still image-based face based on visual summary which is composed by faces from the extracted key-frames. The user can initiate his visual query by selecting one face and the system respond with videos which contains that face.

References

1. Baber, J., Satoh, S., Afzulpurkar, N. and Keatmanee, C.: Bag of visual words model for videos segmentation into scenes. In: Proceedings of the Fifth International Conference on Internet Multimedia Computing and Service, New York, NY, USA, pp. 191–194 (2013)
2. Blanken, H.M., Vries, A.P., Blok, H.E., Feng, L.: Multimedia Retrieval. Springer, Heidelberg (2010)
3. Lowe, D.G.: Distinctive image features from scale-invariant keypoints. Int. J. Comput. Vis. **60**(2), 91–110 (2004)
4. Ajmal, M., Ashraf, M.H., Shakir, M., Abbas, Y., Shah, F.A.: Video summarization: techniques and classification. In: Bolc, L., Tadeusiewicz, R., Chmielewski, L.J., Wojciechowski, K. (eds.) ICCVG 2012. LNCS, vol. 7594, pp. 1–13. Springer, Heidelberg (2012). doi:10.1007/978-3-642-33564-8_1
5. Uchihachi, S., Foote, J., Wilcox, L.: Automatic Video Summarization Using a Meaure of Shot Importance and a Frame Packing Method. United States Patent 6, 535,639, March 18 (2003)
6. Evangelopoulos, G., Rapantzikos, K., Potamianos, A., Maragos, P., Zlatintsi, A., Avrithis, Y.: Movie summarization based on audio-visual valiency detection. In: IEEE International Conference on Image Processing (ICIP), San Diego, CA (2008)
7. Bulut, E., Capin, T.: Key frame extraction from motion capture data by curve saliency. In: Proceedings of 20th Annual Conference on Computer Animation and Social Agents, Belgium (2007)
8. Peyrard, N., Bouthemy, P.: Motion-based selection of relevant video segments for video summarization. Multimedia Tools Appl. **26**(3), 259–276 (2005)
9. Li, C., Wu, Y.T., Yu, S.S., Chen, T.: Motion-focusing key frame extraction and video summarization for lane surveillance system. In: 16th IEEE International Conference on Image Processing (ICIP), pp. 7–10 (2009)
10. Chheng, T.: Video Summarization Using Clustering. Department of Computer Science University of California, Irvine (2007)
11. Damnjanovic, U., Fernandez, V., Izquierdo, E.: Event detection and clustering for surveillance video summarization. In: Proceedings of the Ninth International Workshop on Image Analysis for Multimedia Interactive Services. IEEE Computer Society, Washington (2008)
12. Liu, D., Chen, T., Hua, G.: A hierarchical visual model for video object summarization. IEEE Trans. Pattern Anal. Mach. Intell. **32**, 2178–2190 (2010)
13. Lee, Y.J., Ghosh, J., Grauman, K.: Discovering important people and objects for egocentric video summarization. In: Proceedings of the IEEE Conference on Computer Vision and Pattern Recognition, CVPR (2012)
14. Calic, J., Thomas, B.: Spatial analysis in key-frame extraction using video segmentation. In: Proceedings of Workshop Image Analysis of Multimedia Interactive Services Lisbon, Portugal (2004)

15. Calic, J., Izquierdo, E.: Efficient key-frame extraction and video analysis. In: Proceedings of International Conference on Information Technology: Coding and Computing, pp. 28–33 (2002)
16. Liu, X., Song, M.L., Zhang, L.M., Wang, S.L.: Joint shot boundary detection and key frame extraction. In: Proceedings of the 21st International Conference on Pattern Recognition (ICPR 2012), pp. 2565–2568 (2012)
17. Ejaz, N., Tariq, T.B., Baik, S.W.: Adaptive key frame extraction for video summarization using an aggregation mechanism. J. Vis. Commun. Image Represent. **23**, 1031–1040 (2012)
18. Xu, Q., Liu, Y., Li, X., Yang, Z., Wang, J., Sbert, M., Scopigno, R.: Browsing and exploration of video sequences: a new scheme for key frame extraction and 3D visualization using entropy based Jensen divergence. Inf. Sci. **278**, 736–756 (2014)
19. Lai, J.L., Yi, Y.: Key frame extraction based on visual attention model. J. Vis. Commun. Image Represent. **23**, 114–125 (2012)
20. Kumar, M., Loui, A.C.: Key frame extraction from consumer videos using sparse representation. In: Proceedings of the 18th IEEE International Conference on Image Processing (ICIP 2011), pp. 2437–2440, (2011)
21. Chergui, A., Bekkhoucha, A., Sabbar, W.: Video scene segmentation using the shot transition detection by local characterization of the points of interest. In: 2012 6th International Conference on Sciences of Electronics, Technologies of Information and Telecommunications (SETIT), pp. 404–411 (2012)
22. Tapu, R., Zaharia, T.: A complete framework for temporal video segmentation. In: 2011 IEEE International Conference on Consumer Electronics-Berlin (ICCE-Berlin), pp. 156–160 (2011)
23. Bay, H., Ess, A., Tuytelaars, T., Van Gool, L.: Speeded-up robust features (surf). Comput. Vis. Image Underst. **110**(3), 346–359 (2008)
24. Schmid, C., Mohr, R., Bauckhage, C.: Evaluation of interest point detectors. Int. J. Comput. Vis. **37**, 151–172 (2000)
25. Gharbi, H., Bahroun, S., Zagrouba, E.: A novel key frame extraction approach for video summarization. In: International Joint Conference on Computer Vision Theory and Applications, Rome (2016)
26. Barhoumi, W., Zagrouba, E.: On-the-fly extraction of key frames for efficient video summarization. In: AASRI Conference on Intelligent Systems and Control (2013)
27. Bo, C., Lu, Z., Dong-ru, Z.: A study of video scenes clustering based on shot key frames. Wuhan Univ. J. Nat. Sci. **10**, 966–970 (2005). Series Core Journal of Wuhan University (English)
28. Sargent, G., Perez-Daniel, K.R., Stoian, A., Benois-Pineau, J., Maabout, S.: A scalable summary generation method based on cross-modal consensus clustering and OLAP cube modeling. Multimedia Tools Appl. **75**, 1–22 (2016)

A Simple Evaluation Procedure for Range Camera Measurement Quality

Boris Bogaerts[1]([✉]), Rudi Penne[1,2], Seppe Sels[1], Bart Ribbens[1],
and Steve Vanlanduit[1]

[1] Faculty of Applied Engineering, University of Antwerp,
Groenenborgerlaan 171, 2020 Antwerp, Belgium
boris.bogaerts@uantwerpen.be
[2] Department of Mathematics, University of Antwerp, Antwerp, Belgium

Abstract. Range cameras suffer from both systematic and random errors. We present a procedure to evaluate both types of error separately in one test. To quantify the systematic errors, we use an industrial robot to provide a ground truth motion of the range sensor. We present an error metric that compares this ground truth motion with the calculated motion, using the range data of the range sensor. The only item present in the scene is a white plane that we move in different positions during the experiment. This plane is used to compute the range sensor motion for the purpose of systematic error measurement, as well as to quantify the random error of the range sensor. As opposed to other range camera evaluation experiments this method does not require any extrinsic system calibration, high quality ground truth test scene or complicated test objects. Finally, we performed the experiment for three common Time-of-flight (TOF) cameras: Kinect One, Mesa SR4500 and IFM 03D303 and compare their performance.

Keywords: Range camera · Hand-eye transformation · Time-of-flight · Error metric

1 Introduction

In this paper we present an easy procedure to quantify both the systematic and random errors of range sensors. Consequently, the presented method provides an evaluation tool to compare different range sensors. The proposed test delivers quantitative error values, that are easy to compare.

We distinguish between random and systematic errors, because different tasks are sensitive to different types of error. For example, the recognition of CAD objects in a scene is sensitive to random noise. Indeed, the presence of noise is a serious obstacle for segmentation [13]. On the other hand, applications of range sensors that make use of plane features, are sensitive to systematic errors. For example, in order to determine the eigenmotion of a Time-of-flight TOF camera by means of plane measurements [4,9], random noise can be handled by

© Springer International Publishing AG 2016
J. Blanc-Talon et al. (Eds.): ACIVS 2016, LNCS 10016, pp. 286–296, 2016.
DOI: 10.1007/978-3-319-48680-2_26

robust plane fitters [16], but the calculation of the transformation depends on the quality of the plane coordinates. Systematic errors induce inaccuracies in these determined plane coordinates, which in turn result in a deterioration in the quality of the determined camera motion.

Other experiments designed to evaluate various errors of range sensors rely on very strict manual placement [2] or calibration (relative to ground truth) of the range sensor [7,15]. Both these methods are cumbersome and affect the estimate of this error. Some experiments require detailed knowledge about the measurement scene [7,15], and require an extra highly accurate range scanner. Our method does not rely on extra system calibrations or ground truth scenes.

The presented test method comprises experiments with ToF cameras (as an example of range sensors) rigidly attached to a robot manipulator (Fig. 1). This choice was motivated by the reliability of the current robot controllers, such that the motion of the robot's end effector can be considered as an accurate ground truth. The ground truth motion of the robot manipulator will be compared with the motion determined by the range sensor to evaluate systematic errors of the sensor.

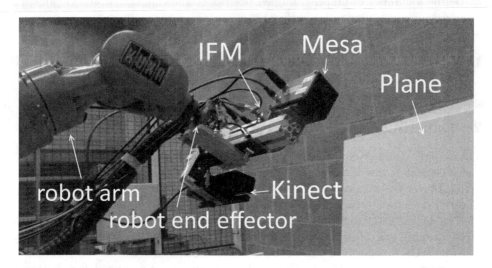

Fig. 1. Measurement setup. An industrial robot Kuka KR16W is holding the three ToF cameras we compared: Kinect One, Mesa SR4500 and IFM 03D303. The scene also contains a white plane.

However, it is a challenge to have access to this ground truth data, because of the famous hand-eye calibration problem [14]. This problem is caused by the fact that the relative motion between two positions of the camera is known in the robot basis instead of the camera basis. The transformation matrix between both reference frames, one at the camera center and the other at the robot tool center, is unknown. We can solve for this transformation matrix by doing the hand-eye calibration [8,14], but this is based on the availability of a reliable camera transformation. Therefore, using the hand-eye calibration for evaluating the systematic errors of a range sensor (camera motion) gives rise to a conceptual loop, and hence is not desirable. However, the quality of the system of equations that solves this hand-eye calibration will serve as an indication for the degree of systematic error: the *hand-eye error metric* (Sect. 3.2).

The second central element in our experiment is a planar object that is present in the scene. This plane has two functions. On one hand, the transformation of the range camera can be estimated using different orientations of this plane; the systematic error behaviour of the range sensor will be evaluated by means of the quality of the computed transformation. On the other hand, the noise of measurements on these planes is used to characterize random error. This approach yields a decoupled evaluation tool. Indeed, the plane based method for computing the motion of the sensor does not introduce random errors, while the effect of random errors on the estimated plane coordinates is very low.

The experiment consists of 4 steps:

1. Mount the range camera on the robot (no special pose is required).
2. Define a number of preprogrammed positions, allowing the attached camera to view a given plane (flat surface).
3. Capture a point cloud at each of the preprogrammed positions, corresponding to the viewed plane.
4. Repeat step 3 for at least three configurations of the measurement plane. It is important that the camera is rigidly attached to the robot, excluding relative motion of this camera with respect to the robot during the entire experiment.

2   Experimental Setup

The objective of our experiments is to measure both the systematic and random measurement errors of range cameras. We have tested and compared three common Time-of-flight cameras: **Kinect One**, **Mesa SR4500** and **IFM 03D303**. In order to compare the computed motion to a reliable ground truth, the TOF sensors are mounted rigidly on an articulated robotarm (KUKA KR16W, with a repeatibility error less than 0.1 mm) as shown in Fig. 1. In each single test we consider TOF images for a pair of robot positions, in which the attached camera observes a fixed plane. During the whole experiment we arranged five distinct positions of this plane, that could be viewed from twenty preprogrammed robot configurations, providing a supply of $\binom{20}{2}$ test pairs for each camera.

For the evaluation we need sets of 3-D points, generated by the TOF sensors, directly provided in (X, Y, Z) coordinates with respect to the camera frame. This means that we assumed a priori calibrated TOF cameras.

We only use points on the viewed planar object in the experimental setup. To this end we automatically selected the pixels in the white board that is visible in every TOF frame.

Next, we compute the best-fitting plane supporting the reconstructed 3-D points in all given range images of the fixed board. Working with plane coordinates provides following advantages over classical point based methods ([1,3,18]):

1. A fitted plane reduces error fluctuations compared to 3-D point measurements.
2. There is no need to detect point features and to establish correspondences between them.
3. It is easy to find a set of viewpoints from which a part of the plane is visible.
4. It is not necessary that the calibration object (in this case a board) is entirely visible in each used viewpoint.

This best-fitting plane can be computed by *principal component analysis*, but we prefer a more robust estimate based on Ransac [5]. More precisely, we applied the Matlab function **pcfitplane**, that implements the algorithm of [16]. Ransac eliminates pixels that exceed a predetermined treshold from the fitted model, even if they were selected inside the measured plane. To determine the random noise relative to the measured plane we use the fitted plane to determine the borders of the plane in the image, and calculate the total deviation of all pixels inside this segmented planar region with respect to the fitted plane.

3 Evaluation Metric for Systematic Error

The goal of this section is to devise an error metric that is a measure for the dimensional accuracy of a range sensor. There are two difficulties that need to be tackled:

1. The error metric should be independent of measurement noise. This is because we want to assess random error and systematic error independently.
2. The robot motion cannot be used directly as ground truth. This is because there is an unknown transformation between the robot tool center and the range sensor. This transformation is called the hand-eye transformation.

The first problem will be tackled by estimating the motion of the range camera by using planes. To get around the second problem we use an error metric we call the *hand-eye error metric*.

3.1 Plane-Based Method to Estimate the Motion of a Range Camera

A common way to describe mathematically the rigid motion of a TOF camera or any other 3-D object is by means of the coordinate transformation between the two positions of a rigidly attached reference frame before and after the motion. The rotational part of the rigid motion is represented by a 3×3 orthonormal matrix R ($R^{-1} = R^T$), and the translation part by a 3×1 vector t. If p and p' are the 3×1 coordinate vectors of a given spatial point w.r.t. the rigidly attached reference frame before and after the motion respectively, then

$$p = R \cdot p' + t. \tag{1}$$

Often, it is convenient to represent this transformation by one matrix multiplication $\bar{p} = B \cdot \bar{p'}$, using homogeneous coordinates $\bar{p} = (p^T, 1)^T$ with weight 1, and a 4×4 transformation matrix

$$B = \begin{pmatrix} R & t \\ \mathbf{0}^T & 1 \end{pmatrix} \tag{2}$$

with $\mathbf{0}$ the 3×1 zero vector.

If the rigid transformation of a depth camera is represented by a 4 by 4 transformation matrix B acting on homogeneous coordinates of 3-D points as given by Eq. 2, then the corresponding dual transformation acting on plane coordinates $(a, b, c, d)^T$ is represented by B^{-T} [11]:

$$\bar{p} = B \cdot \bar{p'} \Leftrightarrow \begin{pmatrix} a \\ b \\ c \\ d \end{pmatrix} \sim B^{-T} \begin{pmatrix} a' \\ b' \\ c' \\ d' \end{pmatrix} \Leftrightarrow \begin{pmatrix} a' \\ b' \\ c' \\ d' \end{pmatrix} \sim B^{T} \begin{pmatrix} a \\ b \\ c \\ d \end{pmatrix} \tag{3}$$

Because the homogeneous plane coordinates $(a, b, c, d)^T$ are determined up to a scale factor, it is convenient to normalize the plane normals $n = (a, b, c)^T$ to length 1. This leaves us with one more ambiguity, due to the two opposite directions for n. This can be resolved by some additional constraint, e.g. requiring that all plane normals point towards the 3D sensor. With these conventions the proportional similarity of Eq. 3 can be replaced by an equality. Due to the normalization of the plane coordinates, the transformation between planes can be computed analogous to the rigid transformation between points. For example, the least squares algorithm of [1] can be used. For more details on the implementation with planes, we refer to [4, 12, 17].

3.2   The Hand-Eye Error Metric

We evaluate the depth performance of a range sensor by the correctness of the reconstructed planes (white boards). On its turn, the reconstruction of the planes is validated by the accuracy of the computed motion between two camera positions. The estimated camera motion can be compared with the known motion of an articulated robot arm the camera was rigidly attached to (Fig. 1). However, the camera motion is *conjugated* to the known robot motion. This means that the motion is the same, but expressed in different bases. If the 4×4 transformation matrix A denotes the motion of the robot, and if B represents the camera motion matrix, then this conjugacy is algebraically expressed by *similarity* of matrices [6]:

$$A = XBX^{-1} \tag{4}$$

In the literature this issue is also known as the $AX = XB$ calibration problem [8]. This 4×4 matrix X is the so-called *hand-eye calibration* between robot and camera. In general, the transformation X between the robot coordinate frame and the camera frame is not a priori known. In our validation experiments, the robot transformation A is accurately known and considered as ground truth, while the computation of B has to be validated for the different types of TOF cameras. To this end, we compose a system of linear equations in the unknown entries of the hand-eye matrix X, following [8]. For the convenience of the reader we briefly explain how this system of equations is obtained.

If the exact camera transformation B matrix is available then we are guaranteed to have a solution X to the hand-eye calibration problem

$$AX - XB = 0 \tag{5}$$

These matrices are all 4×4 transformation matrices and can be expressed as in Eq. 2:

$$\begin{pmatrix} R_A & t_A \\ \mathbf{0}^T & 1 \end{pmatrix} \begin{pmatrix} R_X & t_X \\ \mathbf{0}^T & 1 \end{pmatrix} = \begin{pmatrix} R_X & t_X \\ \mathbf{0}^T & 1 \end{pmatrix} \begin{pmatrix} R_B & t_B \\ \mathbf{0}^T & 1 \end{pmatrix}. \tag{6}$$

After performing the matrix multiplication, the resulting block matrix can be decoupled into the following system of matrix equations:

$$\begin{cases} R_A R_X = R_X R_A \\ R_A t_X + t_A = R_X t_B + t_X \end{cases} \Leftrightarrow \begin{cases} R_A R_X - R_X R_A = 0 \\ R_X t_B + (I_3 - R_A) t_x = t_A \end{cases} \tag{7}$$

The *tensor product* $\otimes$ of matrices appears to be a convenient tool to rearrange the factors of a matrix product in order to separate the unknown matrix in a matrix equation [10]:

$$M \cdot P \cdot N = Q \Leftrightarrow (N^T \otimes M)\mathrm{vec}(P) = \mathrm{vec}(Q), \tag{8}$$

where $\mathrm{vec}(Q)$ denotes the *vectorization* of matrix Q: the vector obtained by concatenating the columns of Q. Consequently, using Eq. 8, we can reformulate Eq. 7 as follows:

$$\begin{cases} (I_3 \otimes R_A)\mathrm{vec}(R_X) = (R_B^T \otimes I_3)\mathrm{vec}(R_X) \\ (t_B^T \otimes I_3)\mathrm{vec}(R_X) + (I_3 - R_A)t_X = t_A \end{cases} \tag{9}$$

yielding a system of twelve linear equations in the nine unknowns $(\mathrm{vec}(R_X)^T, t_X^T)$:

$$M \cdot \begin{pmatrix} \mathrm{vec}(R_X) \\ t_X \end{pmatrix} = s \Leftrightarrow \begin{pmatrix} I_3 \otimes R_A - R_B^T \otimes I_3 & 0 \\ t_B^T \otimes I_3 & I_3 - R_A \end{pmatrix} \begin{pmatrix} \mathrm{vec}(R_X) \\ t_X \end{pmatrix} = \begin{pmatrix} \mathbf{0} \\ t_A \end{pmatrix} \tag{10}$$

Equation 10 was mentioned in the review paper [14] on hand-eye calibration. In order to determine (R_X, t_X) we need to know the robot motion A and the corresponding measured camera transformation B. To actually solve this system, at least three given transformation pairs (A, B) are necessary. Furthermore, to guarantee full rank for this system of equations the vectorized rotation matrices of the three given transformations must be linearly independent.

In practice, coping with noisy measurements, the camera motion B obtained from the plane-based method of Sect. 3.1 is not exact. Therefore, we combine Eq. 10 for multiple transformation pairs (A_i, B_i) $(1 \le i \le n, n \ge 3)$ as follows:

$$\begin{pmatrix} M_1 \\ \vdots \\ M_n \end{pmatrix} \begin{pmatrix} \text{vec}(R_X) \\ t_X \end{pmatrix} = \begin{pmatrix} s_1 \\ \vdots \\ s_n \end{pmatrix} \tag{11}$$

with

$$M_i = \begin{pmatrix} I_3 \otimes R_{A_i} - R_{B_i}^T \otimes I_3 & 0 \\ t_{B_i}^T \otimes I_3 & I_3 - R_{A_i} \end{pmatrix} \quad , \quad s_i = \begin{pmatrix} \mathbf{0} \\ t_{A_i} \end{pmatrix} \tag{12}$$

The hand-eye transformation X can be estimated by the least-squares approximation (LSA) of this overdetermined system of linear equation. In our context, the estimation of X in itself is less important than the least-squares error of the LSA, because this indicates the quality of the system of equations, and hence it validates the accuracy of B. This motivates us to define the mean least-squares solution error of the LSA of this systems as an error metric for the depth sensor that provided the reconstruction of the planes, called the *hand-eye error metric (HEE)*.

$$HEE = \sqrt{||s - M(M^T M)^{-1} M^T s||^2 / (12n)} \tag{13}$$

with $M = (M_1^T, \ldots, M_n^T)^T$ and $s = (s_1^T, \ldots, s_n^T)^T$. The error metric provided by Eq. 13 is motivated by the following arguments:

– The robot transformation A is known accurately (we can assume zero noise for A).
– The transformation matrix X necessarily exists and is fixed for a given robot-sensor system. Therefore, the hand-eye error would be zero if the rigid motion B of the depth sensor was computed correctly.
– HEE is able to assess the validity of a method over multiple measurements, yielding a growing system of equations (Eq. 11). The ability to combine multiple camera positions in one error metric enables us to cover the whole image space of the range sensor, such that the complete sensor is evaluated.

4   Evaluation Metric Random Error

The proposed experimental setup allows us to measure the random noise of the tested camera simultaneously. Different planes are measured in the scene in order to compute the transformation of the range sensor between different robot positions (Sect. 3.1). These planes are segmented by means of Ransac. With the computed plane coordinates it is possible to compute an expected depth measurement for each pixel inside the segmented rectangular image region representing the measured plane. The difference between the plane and the true depth measurements represents the measurement noise. The standard deviation of the Euclidean distances between the 3D-reconstructed pixel and the fitting, characterizes the random noise of the tested range sensor.

Furthermore, during the proposed procedure, the plane is viewed from different directions. This allows us to evaluate the measurement noise as a function of the measurement angle (Fig. 3).

5   Results

In the validation experiments described below, random transformations are sampled from our dataset. This dataset consists of measurements from twenty different robot positions. In each position, five images have been taken by a TOF sensor that was rigidly attached to the articulated robot arm. These TOF images contain 3-D point clouds from the scene. Finally, all these measurements have been repeated for three different commonly used Time-of-flight cameras: Kinect One, Mesa SR4500 and IFM O3D303. Both the systematic and random errors are evaluated separately:

1. For the systematic error, two random robot positions are chosen. The transformation of the range sensor between these positions is calculated using plane coordinates of the five planes measured in both positions. This random selection of positions is repeated fifteen times, avoiding to duplicate a previously chosen pair of transformations. Next the hand-eye error metric is calculated using these transformations (translations are in mm). The calculation of this error metric is repeated twenty times for different random positions. The distribution of this error metric is visualized for each TOF camera by means of a boxplot (Fig. 2).
2. For the evaluation of the random error, all measured planes are used. For each frame the standard deviation of the Euclidean distance between each measured point and the determined plane inside the segmented region represents the noise level. In addition, this noise level is plotted in Fig. 3 against the angle between the plane normal and the focal axis of the range sensor. The possible presence of a linear relation between the random error and the measurement angle is checked by the correlation coefficient.

5.1   Systematic Error

Figure 2 shows the boxplots representing the distribution of the hand-eye error metric (HEE) for multiple different systems of selected transformations for three different sensors. A small HEE indicates a low systematic error. Indeed, in this case the hand-eye calibration, found as solution of the system of Eq. (11), is stable and hardly affected by the choice of transformations that contribute to this system. Furthermore, if the 3D calibration of the range camera is accurate, we expect the HEE metric to be the same for every included transformation. A large spread of the hand-eye error metric points toward unreliable estimates for the transformation of the camera. This unreliability indicates a change of systematic error across the measurement volume of the considered range sensor.

The test shows that the systematic error of the Kinect One is the lowest, followed by the IFM O3D303 while the Mesa SR4500 performs worst. This test indicates that the dimensional accuracy is the most reliable for the Kinect One.

5.2   Random Error

Figure 3 shows a scatter plot of the spread of the measurement error against the measurement angle. A low spread indicates a low noise level of the sensor.

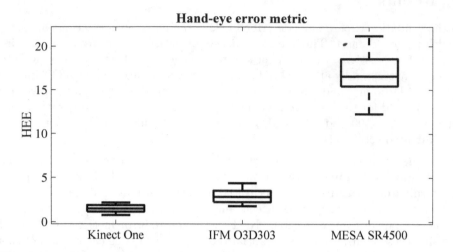

Fig. 2. Distribution of the hand-eye error metric for three different TOF cameras (transformations are in mm): Kinect One (mean: 0.92), IFM O3D303 (mean: 1.60) and Mesa SR4500 (mean: 5.59) represented as boxplot. This test shows that the systematic error of the Kinect One is low compared to the Mesa SR4500. The systematic error of the IFM O3D303 lies somewhere in between.

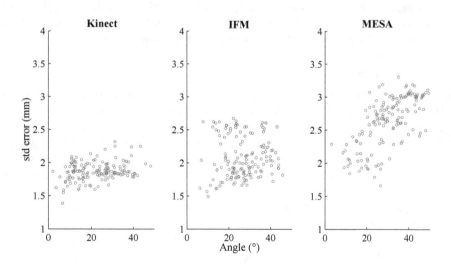

Fig. 3. Scatter of the standard error against measurement angle for the three considered TOF cameras. Lower noise is better, and independence between measurement angle and measurement noise is desired. The correlation coefficients between the measurement angle and the measurement error for Kinect One, IFM O3D303 and MESA SR4500 are respectively: 0.29, 0.03 and 0.67

A possible linear relationship between the measurement angle and the noise level is evaluated by means of the correlation coefficient, because this would indicate that noise levels depend on the measurement angle.

The boxplots in Fig. 3 show that the noise levels of Kinect One are the lowest. The noise levels of IFM O3D303 are the highest for small angles, but for larger angles (above 30 degrees) the noise level of MESA SR4500 becomes the highest. This is because there is a strong linear relationship between noise and angle for the MESA SR4500 (correlation coefficient of 0.67) but not for the IFM O3D303.

6   Conclusions

We presented a relatively simple experiment to compare different range sensors, both in terms of systematic and random measurement error. The experiment uses a robot and a plane. This robot is used to provide an accurate ground truth motion independent of the considered range sensor. Other methods to obtain an accurate ground truth motion are also allowed. This could for example be a coordinate measuring arm, infrared tracker, etc.

The data provided by this experiment contain useful characteristics of the considered range camera. The systematic error of the camera can be quantitatively assessed using the hand-eye metric. This error metric compares the ground truth motion with the motion assessed by the range camera. If both motions agree, this error metric is low. The noise levels can be assessed by computing the standard deviation of the difference between measured plane values and the plane fitted by a robust plane fitter. Because the measurement plane is viewed from different directions, we can determine the sensitivity of the measurement noise to the measurement angle, which is important in many applications.

This experiment can also be repeated to study different range sensor specific errors. For example, for a Time-of-flight camera the noise levels are dependent on the integration time. The test proposed in this paper can be repeated for different values of the integration time. The results provide insight in how the changed parameter affects both the systematic and random error.

Acknowledgements. The first author holds a PHD grant from the research Fund-Flanders (FWO Vlaanderen). This research has also been funded by the government agency Flanders Innovation & Entrepreneurship (VLAIO) by the support to the TETRA project Smart data clouds with project number 140336 and the Research Council of University of Antwerp (Stim-KP 31128 & the Research Committee of the Faculty of applied engineering fti-OZC).

References

1. Arun, K.S., Huang, T.S., Blostein, S.D.: Least-squares fitting of two 3-d point sets. IEEE Trans. Pattern Anal. Mach. Intell. **9**(5), 698–700 (1987)
2. Corti, A., Giancola, S., Mainetti, G., Sala, R.: A metrological characterization of the Kinect V2 time-of-flight camera. Robot. Auton. Syst. **75**, 584–594 (2016)

3. Eggert, D.W., Lorusso, A., Fisher, R.B.: Estimating 3-d rigid body transformations: a comparison of four major algorithms. Mach. Vis. Appl. **9**(5), 272–290 (1997)
4. Fernández-Moral, E., González-Jiménez, J., Rives, P., Arévalo, V.: Extrinsic calibration of a set of range cameras in 5 seconds without pattern. In: International Conference on Intelligent Robots and Systems. IEEE/RSJ, September 2014
5. Fischler, M., Bolles, R.: Random sampling consensus: a paradigm for model fitting with applications to image analysis and automated cartography. Commun. ACM **24**, 381–385 (1981)
6. Hoffman, K., Kunze, R.A.: Linear algebra. Prentice-Hall Mathematics Series. Prentice-Hall, Englewood Cliffs (1971)
7. Khoshelham, K., Elberink, S.O.: Accuracy and resolution of kinect depth data for indoor mapping applications. Sensors **12**(2), 1437–1454 (2012)
8. Mao, J., Huang, X., Jiang, L.: A flexible solution to AX=XB for robot hand-eye calibration. In: Proceedings of the 10th WSEAS International Conference on Robotics, Control and Manufacturing Technology, ROCOM 2010, pp. 118–122. World Scientific and Engineering Academy and Society (WSEAS), Stevens Point (2010)
9. Pathak, K., Birk, A., Vaškevičius, N., Poppinga, J.: Fast registration based on noisy planes with unknown correspondences for 3-d mapping. Trans. Rob. **26**(3), 424–441 (2010)
10. Petersen, K.B. Pedersen, M.S.: The Matrix Cookbook. Technical University of Denmark, Version 20121115, November 2012
11. Pottmann, H., Wallner, J.: Computational Line Geometry. Springer-Verlag New York, Inc., Secaucus (2001)
12. Raposo, C., Barreto, J.P., Nunes, U.: Fast and accurate calibration of a kinect sensor. In: International Conference on 3D Vision. IEEE (2013)
13. Sels, S., Ribbens, B., Bogaerts, B., Peeters, J., Vanlanduit, S.: 3d model assisted fully automated scanning laser doppler vibrometer measurements (Submitted)
14. Shah, M., Eastman, R.D., Hong, T.: An overview of robot-sensor calibration methods for evaluation of perception systems. In: Proceedings of the Workshop on Performance Metrics for Intelligent Systems, PerMIS 2012, pp. 15–20. ACM, New York (2012)
15. Stoyanov, T., Louloudi, A., Andreasson, H., Lilienthal, A.J.: Comparative evaluation of range sensor accuracy in indoor environments. In: Proceedings of the 5th European Conference on Mobile Robots, ECMR 2011, pp. 19–24 (2011)
16. Torr, P.H.S., Zisserman, A.: Mlesac: a new robust estimator with application to estimating image geometry. Comput. Vis. Image Underst. **78**(1), 138–156 (2000)
17. Vasconcelos, F., Barreto, J.P., Nunes, U.: A minimal solution for the extrinsic calibration of a camera and a laser-rangefinder. IEEE Trans. Pattern Anal. Mach. Intell. **34**(11), 2097–2107 (2012)
18. Zhang, Z.: Motion, structure from two perspective views: algorithms, error analysis, and error estimation. IEEE Trans. Pattern Anal. Mach. Intell. **11**(5), 451–476 (1989)

Accordion Representation Based Multi-scale Covariance Descriptor for Multi-shot Person Re-identification

Bassem Hadjkacem[(⊠)], Walid Ayedi, and Mohamed Abid

National Engineers School of Sfax, CES Research Unit,
Sfax University, Sfax, Tunisia
bassem.hadjkacem.tn@ieee.org, ayediwalid@yahoo.fr,
mohamed.abid@rnu.enis.tn

Abstract. Multi-shot person re-identification is a major challenge because of the large variations in a human's appearance caused by different types of noise such as occlusion, viewpoint and illumination variations. In this paper, we presented the accordion representation based multi-scale covariance descriptor, called AR-MSCOV descriptor, which considers in the first step an image sequence containing a walking human to convert it in one image with the accordion representation. To better exploit the spatial and temporal correlation of the video sequence and to deal with the different types of noise, it applies quadtree decomposition and extracts multi scale appearance features such as color, gradient and Gabor in a simple pass. This AR-MSCOV descriptor merges the static regions and captures the moving regions of interest. Therefore, it implicitly encodes the described human gait as a behavioral biometric with the appearance features through the accordion representation to reliably identify any person in motion. We evaluated the AR-MSCOV descriptor on the PRID 2011 multi-shot dataset and demonstrated a good performance in comparison with the current state-of-the-art.

Keywords: Multi-shot person re-identification · Accordion representation · Covariance descriptor · Multi-scale features · Gait

1 Introduction

Recently, the intelligent video surveillance starts responding to a security need that is increasingly growing in large public or private spaces. We consider an environment consisting of several disjoint cameras. With network cameras, there are several difficulties that can be faced when acquiring images as the variability of the angle of vision, the variable lighting conditions, the very noisy background, the difficulty of projection from 3D to 2D, the clutter in the background, occlusion etc. The major problem in video surveillance is located at the re-identification level. A learning step is to detect and track people in the sequence, to build descriptors of objects needed to build the model. A person's descriptor can be based on several cues such as the person's face, his appearance features etc. [1–7]. The image covariance descriptor, developed in [1], suffered a great success and it has been evolved in several research works like in [3, 5].

© Springer International Publishing AG 2016
J. Blanc-Talon et al. (Eds.): ACIVS 2016, LNCS 10016, pp. 297–310, 2016.
DOI: 10.1007/978-3-319-48680-2_27

Although the face is probably the most reliable, visually accessible biometric to a person's identity, it is not always useful in video surveillance scenarios due to the low resolution and pose variations of people in the-field-of-view. In several cases, the body features are more useful because they can be described at a lower resolution. Gait is a behavioral biometrics that describes the way a person walks and has long been studied for a person's identification [7–10, 12]. However, since gait is considered as behavioral biometrics, that is, not affected by the appearance of a person, the most state-of-the-art gait recognition approaches work with silhouettes, which are difficult to extract, especially from video sequence with cluttered background and occlusions [10].

In this work, we operate the spatio-temporal information with the appearance criteria and we propose a new Accordion- representation-based multi-scale covariance descriptor (AR-MSCOV). The main contribution is to apply the "Quadtree" decomposition in the "Accordion Representation", called ACREP, generated through the frames of a walking cycle, capture moving regions of interest, find the correlation between video frames and extract the relevant multi-scale features in a simple pass. The benefits of AR-MSCOV approach are: (1) It describes the appearance of people during a walking cycle and hence covers almost the entire variety of shapes and poses; (2) It aligns the appearance of any person both spatially and temporally using "Quadtree" decomposition; (3) It implicitly encodes the described human gait in the appearance features through the ACREP.

The remainder of this article is organized as follows. Section 2, describes the related work on multi-shot human re-identification and introduces the covariance descriptor. The AR-MSCOV descriptor approach is presented in Sect. 3. Finally, Sect. 4 details and discusses the obtained experimental results.

2   Related Works

Different multi-shot models for human re-identification have been proposed in literature. In fact, [13] proposed a space-time graph that uses different images to group the similar space-time regions. Space-time segmentation is applied to reject contours that are considered unstable information over time. Then, a triangulated model person is used to manage the correspondence between the body parts and adjust the image model person. In [14], the authors analyzed the video sequences to both encode the described human motion through the integration of time parameter and the appearance features and extract the covariance matrices. Then, they applied the Log-Euclidean Riemannian metric to the covariance matrices and compared the distances between the descriptors of the people. The appearance-based method, proposed in [4], condenses a set of frames of any person into a Histogram Plus Epitome (HPE) descriptor. It embeds global chromatic content via a histogram representation and local descriptions via an epitomic analysis. Then, the authors apply HPE at the asymmetry-based segmentation introduced in [2], giving rise to the Asymmetry-based Histogram Plus Epitome (AHPE) descriptor. Furthermore, [15] applied Local Fisher Discriminant Analysis method. Since the classification algorithms require vectors of fixed characteristics, the authors used « PCA » learning metric to reduce the vector size. Relying on the HOG space-time descriptor designed in [16] for action recognition, [17] presented a model capable of selecting and matching discriminative video fragments from unregulated pairs of image sequences. The model proposed in [18] is a part-based space-time appearance model which combines facial features and colors. We note that this approach is not valid due to the low resolution and pose changes.

Previously, we showed the variety of description methods adopted in these research works, such as KD-Tree of POI, local descriptors like SIFT and SURF, and region descriptors like HOG and covariance. We note that region descriptors generate fixed sizes of feature vectors from different images.

On the other hand, most gait approaches like in [9] are based on examining the silhouette of a person over time. The primary problem with silhouette based approaches is that they fundamentally entangle the body shape and gait. [10] introduced a gait representation that encodes the limb motions regardless of the body shape. To analyze the gait, [9] proposed an improved region-based kalman filter to estimate fine precise body joint trajectories. We note that several research studies, like [3, 5], applied the covariance descriptor in the mono-shot case, but did not integrated the space-time information for the multi-shot re-identification. The performance of the covariance descriptor is found to be superior to other methods, as rotation and illumination changes are absorbed by the covariance matrix [5].

The first covariance descriptor was introduced in [1] and applied to the person's detection, object tracking and face recognition. More recently, several research studies, like [19], have been developed in the action recognition. In fact, [1] proposed a covariance descriptor of d-features to characterize a region of any type of image through a compact representation. Let I be an image. Let F be the $W \times H \times d$ dimensional feature image extracted from I:

$$f(x, y) = \emptyset(I, x, y) \tag{1}$$

where the function $\emptyset$ can be any mapping multiple features such as color, intensity, filter responses, which might be correlated and located. For a given rectangular region $R \in F$, let $\{f_k\}_{k=1..n}$ be the d-dimensional feature points inside R. We represent the region R with the $d \times d$ covariance matrix of the feature points.

$$C_R = \frac{1}{N-1} \sum_{k=1}^{N} (f_k - m)(f_k - m)^T \tag{2}$$

where 'm' is the mean of the points. C_R is defined positive and symmetric. The diagonal entries of this covariance matrix represent the variance of each feature whereas the non diagonal entries represent the correlations. The noise corrupting individual samples are largely filtered out with an average filter during the covariance computation [1]. The covariance matrix does not lie on Euclidean space. Most of the common machines learning methods work on the Euclidean spaces. Thus, it is very necessary to find a proper distance metric to measure both covariance matrices.

Recently, a novel Log-Euclidean Riemannian metric [20] has been proposed on the SPD matrices. Under this metric, the distance measures between covariance matrices take a very simple form. Given an n x n covariance matrix C, the singular value decomposition (SVD) of C is denoted as $U \Sigma U^T$, where $\Sigma = diag(\lambda_1, \lambda_2, \ldots, \lambda_n)$ is the diagonal matrix of the eigenvalues, and U is an orthonormal matrix. By derivation, the matrix logarithm log(C) is defined in Eq. 3 where I_n is an n × n identity matrix.

$$\log(C) = \sum_{i=1}^{\infty} \frac{(-1)^{i+1}}{i}(C - I_n)^k = U.diag(\log(\lambda_1), \log(\lambda_2), \ldots, \log(\lambda_n)).U^T \quad (3)$$

Under the Log-Euclidean Riemannian metric, the distance between both covariance matrices A and B can be easily calculated by $\|\log(A) - \log(B)\|$.

Based on the-state-of-the-art, it seems that exploring space-time information from image sequences based on covariance function is appreciated. That is why the AR-MSCOV descriptor was proposed to encode the gait with the appearance features and solve the problem of multi-shot human re-identification.

3 The AR-MSCOV Descriptor

Generally, when monitoring an area covered with a network camera, the regions of interest of each human, which are extracted from video streams, have not the same dimensions. Our framework starts the re-identification process with pre-treatment step of the image sequences (e.g. applied the histogram equalization and resized the ROI of detected human). Then, to extract the spatial and temporal correlation between successive images, an accordion representation and quadtree decomposition are applied, which can give indirect modeling pedestrian gait. Therefore, the AR-MSCOV descriptor integrates several relevant parameters like color, gradient, LBP operator and Gabor banc and extracts signatures through the multi-scale features. Finally, the AR-MSCOV

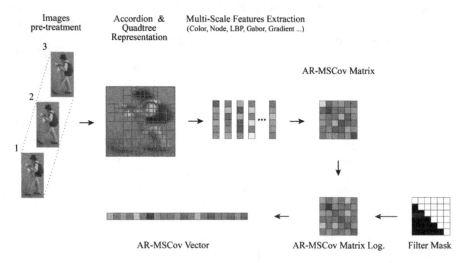

Fig. 1. Overview of a framework for multi-shot person re-identification based on AR-MSCOV descriptor

approach applies the Log-Euclidean Riemannian metric and a filter mask in covariance matrix to obtain a reduced AR-MSCOV vector. An overview of our approach is illustrated in Fig. 1.

At the beginning of this section, the accordion representation is introduced. Subsequently, the mathematical approach of the AR-MSCOV descriptor and its algorithm for their fast calculation will be detailed.

3.1 Accordion Representation

The Accordion representation (ACREP) tends to put in spatial adjacency the pixels having the same coordinates in the different frames of the image sequence. This representation turns the spatio-temporal correlation in video sequence source into a high spatial correlation in the 2D representation. The goal of turning over horizontally the event temporal frames is to better exploit the space correlation of the image sequence and focus on the moving regions of interest. In this way, ACREP also minimizes the distances between the pixels correlated in the source [11].

Let G denote the set of coordinates of all pixels belonging to an action segment (a group of picture or a short video clip) which is X pixels wide, Y pixels tall, and T frames long (Fig. 2).

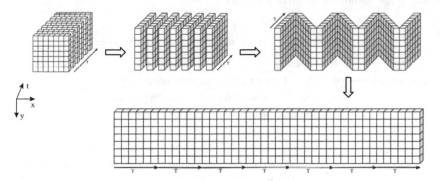

Fig. 2. Accordion representation of multiple images per person

$$G_{(X,Y,T)} := \{(x, y, t)^T : x \in [1, X], y \in [1, Y], t \in [1, T]\}.$$

The method of creating the ACREP is more described at the beginning of Algorithm 1.

3.2 Multi-scale Features Extraction

In the second step, we applied the quadtree structure [3] in the accordion representation of any image sequence. Table 1 shows the set of features used in this work. We can arrange these features into two groups: structure features which are related to the image data location, and content features which are derived from color information. The whole image has a root node and can be represented using a quadtree node by recursively dividing it into four equal descendant quadrants until a stopping condition is met. In this work, we store the covariance matrices and nominate this structure as 'Accordion Image Quadtree Features' or 'AIQF'. A node feature or a node signature in the AIQF characterizes its corresponding image quadrant. Let C be the set of nodes in the AIQF, a given node $c \in C$ has four child nodes c_i where $i \in \{0, 1, 2, 3\}$. F_c is the vector of features associated with the node c and Fc(k) is the kth node feature in F_c. We decompose the image based on luminance color component I only (i.e. k = 4). To compute $F_c(k)$, the relation between a parent node and its child can be defined as:

$$F_c(k) = \frac{1}{4} \sum_{i=0}^{3} F_{c_i}(k); k = 4 \tag{4}$$

A quadrant image is considered homogeneous when its corresponding node has similar descendant values. The considered homogeneity criterion is:

$$\|F_c(k) - F_{c_i}(k)\| < \varepsilon, c_i \text{ is leaf } \forall i; k = 4 \tag{5}$$

where ε is the homogeneity error tolerance.

Table 1. List of spatio-temporal covariance features

	K	Features
Structure features	0	The x location of the corresponding region
	1	The y location of the corresponding region
	2	The time of the corresponding region
	3	The Node Level
	4	I grayscale intensity value (the luminance component)
	5	Cr color component value (the red chrominance component)
	6	Cb color component value (the blue chrominance component)
	7	Ix the norm of the first order derivatives in x
	8	Iy the norm of the first order derivatives in y
	9	Gradient, $\theta(x, y) = tan^{-1}\left(\frac{I_y(x,y)}{I_x(x,y)}\right)$
Content features	10	Magnitude, $mag(x, y) = \sqrt{I_x^2(x, y) + I_y^2(x, y)}$
	11	LBP, R = 1, N = 8
	12	LBP, R = 2, N = 8
	13	LBP, R = 2, N = 16
	14	$Gabor_{00}$ O = 0, E = 0
	15	$Gabor_{01}$, O = 0, E = 1
	16	$Gabor_{02}$, O = 0, E = 2
	17	$Gabor_{03}$, O = 0, E = 3
	18	$Gabor_{04}$, O = 0, E = 4

For fast calculation of the covariance matrices, the integral image was used as an intermediate image representation. Using this representation, any rectangular region sum can be computed at a constant time. Therefore, the covariance matrix is rearranged to appear sum operators. Hence, the $(i, j)^{th}$ element of the covariance matrix is defined as:

$$C_R = \frac{1}{N-1} \left[\sum_{n=1}^{N} f_n(i) f_n(j) - \frac{1}{N} \sum_{n=1}^{N} f_n(i) \sum_{n=1}^{N} f_n(j) \right] \tag{6}$$

We compute the covariance matrices in each node using the relation between parent node and its children. Based on (Eq. 6), we compute the sum of each node feature as well as the multiplication of any two node features. Let be $P_c(k)$ the sum of each feature k of a node c, $Q_c(k,l)$ the multiplication of each of both features k and l of a node c. Three steps are required. First, P and Q of the nodes, whose children are leaves, were computed:

$$P_c(k) = \sum_{i=0}^{3} F_{c_i}(k); Q_c(k,l) = \sum_{i=0}^{3} F_{c_i}(k) \times F_{c_i}(l) \tag{7}$$

Second, P and Q of internal parent nodes were computed from the children's:

$$P_c(k) = \sum_{i=0}^{3} F_{c_i}(k); Q_c(k,l) = \sum_{i=0}^{3} F_{c_i}(k) \times F_{c_i}(l) \tag{8}$$

Third, the tree covariance matrix was computed:

$$C_c = \frac{1}{N_c} \left[Q_c(k,l) - \frac{1}{N_c} P_c(k) P_c(l) \right] \tag{9}$$

where Nc is the number of descendants nodes of c.

By defining relation between parent node and its child, we can easily compute covariance matrices of node features in a bottom-up traversal way and even by a single pass when building AIQF (see Algorithm 1) [3].

Algorithm 1: Recursive Bottom-up traversal algorithm of AR-MSCOV descriptor

---

Input: Image sequence
Output: Accordion Image Quadtree Features (AIQF node features)
Initialization:
  •Generate Accordion Representation (ACREP) :
    for (number of image (NI)= 0; NI < Total number of images(TNI) ; NI = NI +1)
      for (i = 0; i < Image.Width; i=i+2)
        for (j = 0; j < Image.Height; j=j+1)
          X = TNI * i + NI - 1;
          Y = TNI * i + (2 * TNI) - NI;
          Compute the values of X and Y elements of the ACREP
  • Define c as root node of an Accordion image
  •Set structure features of root node of an image sequence ; $F_c(k) = 0, k \in \{0,1,2,3\}$
  • Compute the number of the VTF levels; $v = log_2(\min(X * T, Y)) + 1$
Top-down pass. This downward recursion builds a full quadtree and store points features in last level nodes.
Recursion (Children node $c_i \in$ parent node c)
  • Set structures features of child nodes $F_{c_i,t}(k), k \in \{0,1,2,3\}$
  • When reaching last level ($F_c(3) = v - 1$)
    • Set node content features from corresponding point features ;
      $F_{c_i}(k), k \in \{4,5,..,13,18\}$
    • Initialize P et Q of node c_i (Eq.7))
    Buttom-up pass. This upward recursion computes internal node features and merges homogeneous quadrants.
    Recursion (parent node $c \in$ ancestor nodes of c)
      • Compute content features of internal nodes ;
        $(F_c(j) = \emptyset_j\left(F_{c_i}(j)\right), j \in \{4,5,..,13,18\}$
      • Compute P et Q of internal nodes (Eq.8)
      • If level of $c \leq \propto$
        Compute covariance matrix (Eq.9)
      • If homogeneity criterion is verified (Eq.5)
        • Remove child of c
        • Initialize P et Q of c

The covariance region can be computed in $O(d^2)$ time [1]. Although this algorithm is optimized, it is memory-intensive and its processing time also depends on local description degree $\propto$, d features, size of accordion representation. The computational complexity of constructing the integral image sequence is $O(d^2XYT/ \propto^2)$.

On the other hand, we integrated the Gabor bank and LBP operators with the other features detailed in Table 1 to reduce the impact of illumination and viewpoint changes. In fact, we can obtain Gabor features by convolving a 2-D Gabor wavelet with the image I(x, y) as follows:

$$G_{uv}(x,y) = |I(x,y) * \varphi_{u,v}(x,y)| \qquad (10)$$

The 2-D Gabor kernel is a product of an elliptical Gaussian and a complex plane wave. In a real scene of video surveillance, the distance between camera and people varies around a vertical axis. As a consequence, the vertical viewpoint change is smaller than the horizontal one. To form the Gabor bank, the orientation of Gabor kernel 'u' should be equals to 0. We take five different scales as [21] ($v \in \{0, .., 4\}$). Thus, the Gabor bank is equal to $\{G_{00}, G_{01}, G_{02}, G_{03}, G_{04}\}$.

The basic LBP operator, introduced by [22] as a texture descriptor, is used in several applications, such as in [23]. It encodes the relative intensity magnitude between each pixel and its neighboring pixels. LBP is extracted and the decimal code of each pixel is directly assigned to the mapping function instead of forming a histogram. We consider different neighborhood sizes of each pixel with two parameters; R means the region radius and N means the number of sampling points around the center. In our mapping function, we have chosen 3 cases of LBP operators; (First: R = 1, N = 8), (Second: R = 2, N = 8) and (Third: R = 2, N = 16).

As the covariance matrix is symmetric, we can apply a filter mask, as illustrated in Fig. 1. Consequently, the AR-MSCOV descriptor transforms any image sequence of size equal to X × Y × T into a compact vector of size equal to d × (d + 1)/2. In this case, the AR-MSCOV vector size of any sequence is equal to 171. It remains to prove by experiments that the multi-scale features extraction through the mapping function from the quadtree scheme of ACREP can find a spatial and temporal correlation integrating the pedestrian's gait models in the appearance models.

4 Experimental Results

In the research topic of our work, the databases which contain multiple shots for one person per camera can only be used to evaluate the proposed approach. In this section, an analysis of the performance of the AR-MSCOV on PRID 2011 database and a comparative study with several methods of the-state-of-the-art are presented.

4.1 Experimental Setup

As benchmark, the ≪ PRID 2011 ≫ database [24] is used to show the performance of the AR-MSCOV descriptor. This dataset consists of 400 image sequences for 200 people using two adjacent camera views captured in uncrowded outdoor scenes. These image sequences contain a clean background and rare occlusions but a color inconsistency does exist between the two camera views (i.e. variation of illumination) and viewpoint changes. Each image sequence has a variable length consisting of 5 to 675 image frames. The size of the images is fixed and equal to 64 × 128. Figure 3 shows a sample of two image sequences per person from the PRID2011 dataset with noise.

To evaluate the proposed approach, a biometric identification method was adopted: the Cumulative Matching Curve (CMC). It returns ranked lists of candidates to express the performance of any descriptor [25].

Fig. 3. A sample of two image sequences per person from PRID dataset [24]

4.2   Results

To evaluate the proposed AR-MSCOV descriptor, we conducted extensive experiments on the PRID2011 dataset. In our experimentation, we used all the features detailed in Table 1. First, we evaluated the recognition performances of this descriptor with different values of the descriptor parameters. Then, we studied the impact of the size of any image sequence on the recognition accuracy. Finally, we compared the proposed descriptor to some existing approaches.

Primary, we chose the size of image sequence of walking cycle equal to 15 frames. The AIQF of AR-MSCOV descriptor depends on two main parameters: the homogeneity error tolerance (ε) and the local description degree ($\propto$). We studied the recognition rate in four different ranks with different values of these parameters. A large number of experiments were executed. The recognition rates for some relevant combinations between (ε) and ($\propto$) are well described in Table 2.

In fact, the homogeneity error tolerance parameter depends on the background complexity. If a low intensity variation exists in the background of a video frame or between video frames, the AR-MSCOV method can discard it from the video sequence, using low ε values. Consequently, it allows reducing the weight of the color in people's description in the case of clothing similarity. If a high intensity change exists in the background of a video frame or between the video frames, we can use high ε values but MS-CV can discard some relevant information about the described human. Table 2. Illustrates that the recognition rate is better with average values for ε. The best rate is in the case of $\varepsilon = 8$. This explains that the complexity of the background in the « PRID2011 » dataset is average which is visually clear.

As a pedestrian is globally described with $\propto = 0$, the pedestrian is more locally described when increasing the value of $\propto$. Consequently, the processing time decreases. Table 2. shows the impact of $\propto$ on the recognition rate. The best rate is in the case of $\propto = 1$. In the rest of the experiment, we set $\varepsilon = 8$ and $\propto = 1$.

Table 2. A comparison between recognition rates of the AR-MSCOV on the PRID2011 dataset for different combinations between (ε) and (∝)

Homogeneity error tolerance: ε -	Local description degree: ∝	Recognition rate in different Rank (%)			
		R = 1	R = 5	R = 10	R = 20
3	1	22.6	47.2	58.2	63.2
5	1	28.1	54.0	64.4	70.3
6	1	30.0	55.6	66.2	73.5
7	1	33.8	58.9	69.8	76.8
8	**1**	**36.6**	**62.2**	71.4	**79.5**
8	2	20.9	45.5	56.8	66.8
9	1	34.2	57.1	**71.8**	79.0
10	1	31.6	54.1	63.1	74.1
16	1	27.3	49.3	58.7	68.9

On the other hand, our approach treats any image sequence with a various number of frames. We chose 7 cases for experimentation; the number of frames (T) is equal to 5, 7, 10, 15, 16, 17, 20. Table 3 illustrates the effect of the size on the PRID dataset in four recognition rates (R = 1, 5, 10, 20).

Table 3. A comparison between recognition rates of the AR-MSCOV on the PRID2011 dataset for various sizes of the image sequence

Size of image sequence (T)	Recognition rate in different Rank (%)			
	R = 1	R = 5	R = 10	R = 20
5	24.2	50.3	62.6	68.9
7	28.7	55.6	67.5	71.0
10	32.5	59.8	69.8	77.0
15	35.3	59.5	70.2	**80.5**
16	**36.6**	62.2	**71.4**	79.5
17	36.0	**62.8**	70.8	79.1
20	34.8	59.1	70.5	78.4

Based on this table, the recognition rates with various 'T' show that increasing the number of pictures is much better than the decreasing number. There are 2 reasons for this; (1) The gait models implicitly integrated in the AR-MSCOV descriptors are improved with a large number of images in the walking cycle. (2) The impact of noise integrated in one picture decreases when the size ratio of this picture in the image sequence decreases. However, the largest size does not automatically give the best rate because the noise like the occlusion, which is integrated in some added images to a large image sequence, allows changing the signatures of people and slightly decreasing the recognition rate.

Table 4. Comparison between the recognition rate in four different ranks of the AR-MSCOV descriptor and the existing approaches on the PRID2011 dataset

Approaches	Recognition rate in different Rank (%)			
	R = 1	R = 5	R = 10	R = 20
DVR [17]	28.9	55.3	65.5	82.8
Color&LBP [26] + RankSVM	34.3	56	65.5	77.3
SRID [27]	35.1	59.4	69.8	79.7
Color + LFDA [15]	43	73.1	82.9	90.3
AR-MSCov (proposed approach)	**36.6**	**62.2**	**71.4**	**79.5**

When comparing the pedestrian recognition rates given on our experimentation by the best existing results, Table 4 shows a good performance of the AR-MSCOV descriptor compared to the current methods of the-state-of-the-art.

5 Conclusion

In this work, we have introduced a framework which pre-treats and generates the accordion representation of image sequences to apply space-time approaches on multi-shot person re-identification process. Then we have developed the AR-MSCOV descriptor which decomposes the new representation in quadtree scheme (AIQF) and provides extracting spatial and temporal correlation between frames in a simple pass. To improve this descriptor against noises and to make it more robust, we have integrated some relevant features. We concluded that extracting the multi-scale features from accordion representation through quadtree scheme increases modeling capabilities of pedestrian's gaits integrated in the appearance model. In order to showcase the merits of the proposed approach, we have evaluated the AR-MSCOV descriptor on PRID2011 dataset and demonstrated a good performance when compared to the current state-of-the-art.

Acknowledgements. This 'Mobidoc' research was achieved through the partnership agreement 'Programme d'Appui au Système de Recherche et d'Innovation' (PASRI) between the Government of the Tunisian Republic (ANPR) and the European Union.

References

1. Tuzel, O., Porikli, F., Meer, P.: Region covariance: a fast descriptor for detection. In: Proceedings of 9th European Conference on Computer Vision (2006)
2. Farenzena, M., Bazzani, L., Perina, A., Murino, V., Cristani, M.: Person reidentification by symmetry-driven accumulation of local features. In: CVPR, pp. 2360–2367 (2010)
3. Ayedi, W., Snoussi, H., Abid, M.: A fast multi-scale covariance descriptor for object re-identification. Pattern Recogn. Lett. **13**(14), 1902–1907 (2012)

4. Bazzani, L., Cristani, M., Murino, V.: Symmetry-driven accumulation of local features for human characterization and re-identification. Comput. Vis. Image Underst. **117**, 130–144 (2013)
5. Bak, S., Bremond, F.: Re-identification by covariance descriptors. In: Gong, S., Cristani, M., Yan, S., Loy, C.C. (eds.) Person Re-identification. Advances in Computer Vision and Pattern Recognition, pp. 71–91. Springer, London (2014)
6. Ejaz, A., Michael, J., Tim K.M.: An improved deep learning architecture for person re-identification. In: IEEE Conference on Computer Vision and Pattern Recognition (CVPR), pp. 3908–3916 (2015)
7. Nair, B.M., Kendricks, K.D.: Improved region-based kalman filter for tracking body joints and evaluating gait in surveillance videos. In: Battiato, S., Blanc-Talon, J., Gallo, G., Philips, W., Popescu, D., Scheunders, P. (eds.) ACIVS 2015. LNCS, vol. 9386, pp. 311–322. Springer, Heidelberg (2015). doi:10.1007/978-3-319-25903-1_27
8. Boulgouris, N.V., Hatzinakos, D., Plataniotis, K.N.: Gait recognition: a challenging signal processing technology for biometric identification. IEEE Sig. Process. Mag. **22**(6), 78–90 (2005)
9. Wang, C., Zhang, J., Wang, L., Pu, J., Yuan, X.: Human identification using temporal information preserving gait template. IEEE TPAMI **34**(11), 2164–2176 (2012)
10. Lombardi, S., Nishino, K., Makihara, Y., Yagi, Y.: Two-point gait: decoupling gait from body shape. In: IEEE International Conference on Computer Vision (ICCV), pp. 1041–1048 (2013)
11. Ouni, T., Ayedi, W., Abid, M.: New low complexity DCT based video compression method. In: International Conference on Telecommunications, pp. 202–207 (2009)
12. Abdelhedi, S., Wali, A., Alimi, A.M.: Fuzzy logic based human activity recognition in video surveillance applications. In: Second International Afro-European Conference for Industrial Advancement (AECIA), pp. 227–235 (2015)
13. Gheissari, N., Sebastian, T., Hartley, R.: Person re-identification using spatiotemporal appearance. In: CVPR, vol. 2, pp. 1528–1535 (2006)
14. Hadjkacem, B., Ayedi, W., Snoussi, H., Abid, M.: A spatio-temporal covariance descriptor for person re-identification. In: Proceedings of the 15th International Conference on Intelligent Systems Design and Applications, pp. 618–622 (2015)
15. Pedagadi, S., Orwell, J., Velastin, S., Boghossian, B.: Local fisher discriminant analysis for pedestrian re-identification. In: CVPR, pp. 3318–3325 (2013)
16. Klaser, A., Marszalek, M.: A spatio-temporal descriptor based on 3D-gradients. In: BMVC (2008)
17. Wang, T., Gong, S., Zhu, X., Wang, S.: Person re-identification by video ranking. In: Fleet, D., Pajdla, T., Schiele, B., Tuytelaars, T. (eds.) ECCV 2014. LNCS, vol. 8692, pp. 688–703. Springer, Heidelberg (2014). doi:10.1007/978-3-319-10593-2_45
18. Bedagkar-Gala, A., Shah, S.K.: Part-based spatio-temporal model for multi-person re-identification. Pattern Recogn. Lett. **33**, 1908–1915 (2011)
19. Bilinski, P., Bremond, F.: Video covariance matrix logarithm for human action recognition in videos. In: International Joint Conference on Artificial Intelligence (2015)
20. Arsigny, V., Fillard, P., Pennec, X., Ayache, N.: Geometric means in a novel vector space structure on symmetric positive-definite matrices. SIAM J. Matrix Anal. Appl. **29**, 328–347 (2007)
21. Pang, Y., Yuan, Y., Li, X.: Gabor-based region covariance matrices for face recognition. IEEE Trans. Circuit Syst. Video Technol. **18**(7), 989–993 (2008)
22. Ojala, T., Pietikainen, M., Harwood, D.: A comparative study of texture measures with classification based on feature distributions. Pattern Recogn. **29**, 51–59 (1996)

23. Boudra, S., Yahiaoui, I., Behloul, A.: A comparison of multi-scale local binary pattern variants for bark image retrieval. In: Battiato, S., Blanc-Talon, J., Gallo, G., Philips, W., Popescu, D., Scheunders, P. (eds.) ACIVS 2015. LNCS, vol. 9386, pp. 764–775. Springer, Heidelberg (2015). doi:10.1007/978-3-319-25903-1_66
24. Hirzer, M., Beleznai, C., Roth, P.M., Bischof, H.: Person re-identification by descriptive and discriminative classification. In: Heyden, A., Kahl, F. (eds.) SCIA 2011. LNCS, vol. 6688, pp. 91–102. Springer, Heidelberg (2011). doi:10.1007/978-3-642-21227-7_9
25. Gray, D., Brennan, S., Tao, H.: Evaluating appearance models for recognition. In: Performance Evaluation of Tracking and Surveillance (2007)
26. Hirzer, M., Roth, P.M., Köstinger, M., Bischof, H.: Relaxed pairwise learned metric for person re-identification. In: Fitzgibbon, A., Lazebnik, S., Perona, P., Sato, Y., Schmid, C. (eds.) ECCV 2012. LNCS, vol. 7577, pp. 780–793. Springer, Heidelberg (2012). doi:10. 1007/978-3-642-33783-3_56
27. Karanam, S., Li, Y., Radke, R.J.: Sparse re-id: block sparsity for person re-identification. In: CVPR, pp. 33–40 (2015)

Jensen Shannon Divergence as Reduced Reference Measure for Image Denoising

Vittoria Bruni[1,2(✉)] and Domenico Vitulano[2]

[1] Department of SBAI, University of Rome La Sapienza, Rome, Italy
vittoria.bruni@sbai.uniroma1.it
[2] Istituto per le Applicazioni del Calcolo "M. Picone" — C.N.R., Rome, Italy
d.vitulano@iac.cnr.it

Abstract. This paper focuses on the use the Jensen Shannon divergence for guiding denoising. In particular, it aims at detecting those image regions where noise is masked; denoising is then inhibited where it is useless from the visual point of view. To this aim a reduced reference version of the Jensen Shannon divergence is introduced and it is used for determining a denoising map. The latter separates those image pixels that require to be denoised from those that have to be leaved unaltered. Experimental results show that the proposed method allows to improve denoising performance of some simple and conventional denoisers, in terms of both peak signal to noise ratio (PSNR) and structural similarity index (SSIM). In addition, it can contribute to reduce the computational effort of some performing denoisers, while preserving the visual quality of denoised images.

1 Introduction

Human perception is becoming fundamental in several applications involving image processing. In some cases it allows to make automatic some processes by simulating the action of a human observer [5,7,13]; in other cases, it is able to make some operations faster [4]. This paper focuses on image denoising and, in particular, on the use of human perception for inhibiting denoising where it is useless or destructive. Figure 1 clarifies this statement. It depicts an image corrupted by additive, zero-mean Gaussian noise. As it can be observed, noise is clearly visible in the sky, while it is hard to perceive it in correspondence to the rocks. The same figure depicts the image after denoising it with a conventional denoiser. As it can be observed, the sky is now more pleasant since noise has been removed. On the contrary, the rocks now attract human attention, since they have partially lost their typical texture. In other words, rocks seem degraded in the denoised image, while they look more natural in the noisy one. From the human perception point of view, this effect is a consequence of contrast masking [14]. Contrast masking is one of the main features of human perception. It mainly correlates with the visibility of an object having a given degree of disorder (structured or not structured textures) with respect to a textured background. In other words, it measures to what extent some frequencies

© Springer International Publishing AG 2016
J. Blanc-Talon et al. (Eds.): ACIVS 2016, LNCS 10016, pp. 311–323, 2016.
DOI: 10.1007/978-3-319-48680-2_28

are visible whenever embedded in a background having similar frequencies. Due to the random nature of noise, contrast masking often occurs in images corrupted by noise. As side effect, some artifacts can be introduced when denoising the image, especially if simple but less performing denoisers are employed. As a result smoothed textures can appear more annoying than noisy textures. This is not a trivial problem in the digital restoration of archive material (stamps, photos, movies, etc.) where not accurate denoising can alter the historical and artistic content of the artwork. On the other hand, more sophisticated denoisers require additional computational cost in terms of complexity, computing time and hardware implementation. In this case, it would be convenient to remove noise only where it is really necessary, while inhibiting denoiser where its effect will be not perceived. This would be useful in applications for mobile phones or for DSP equipped vehicles, such as UAV, often used in real time remote environmental monitoring, video surveillance, and so on.

In order to reach this goal, in this paper Jensen Shannon divergence (JSD) is used for discriminating pixels where denoising can be avoided. This measure has been selected since it has theoretical dependence on quantities directly related to human visual system [1,2]. In addition, it has also been tested as image quality assessment measure [2,3] with competitive results. From Information Theory point of view, the Jensen Shannon divergence is the information transmission rate [12]. Based on this evidence, the aim of this paper is to quantify the bits budget that can be saved in the presence of a distortion without side effects on the visual perception of the whole image. However, JSD requires the knowledge of the probability density function of the original image, that is unknown in real applications. That is why a simpler bound for JSD is derived in order to make it dependent on quantities that can be directly estimated from the analysed degraded image. In addition, the minimum value of such bound that guarantees invisible distortion is derived and it is used for determining the denoising map. This form is twofold advantageous. On the one hand, it allows to provide an estimate of the JSD from simple image quantities, like mean and standard deviations; on the other hand, it allows a fast computation of JSD. Hence, the additional cost required for determining the denoising map is moderate: it is comparable to the simplest denoisers, while it is negligible with respect to more sophisticated ones. Experimental results show that for low noise levels, the proposed method allows us to preserve the visual quality of denoised images. In addition, it allows to improve it, also in terms of PSNR, when applied to simple and conventional denoisers, like the spatially adaptive empirical Wiener filter [11].

The outline of the paper is the following. Next Section provides details concerning the denoising map, while Sect. 3 shows some experimental results on selected test images. Finally, Sect. 4 draws the conclusions.

2   Determining the Denoising Map

The perception of a given distortion in the vision process can be modeled as a problem of information transmission rate. Independently of the sent information (original image), the channel causes a distortion so that the received information is a degraded copy of the original one. In case of vision, the perceived distortion is not only due to the degradation process but it is also due to human vision that differently reacts to the presence of degradation, according to scene content. This is the capacity of the noisy channel and it can be measured by JSD between the two input sources [12]. In this paper, the two sources are an image and its noisy version. Let X be the original image, the noisy image is defined as $Y(\mathbf{i}) = X(\mathbf{i}) + \mathcal{N}(\mathbf{i})$ where $\mathbf{i}$ is the pixel location and $\mathcal{N}$ is the additive noise that is an i.i.d. random variable that is normally distributed with zero mean and standard deviation σ^2. The goal of denoising is to estimate X from its noisy version Y. The aim of this section is to determine the binary map M such that

$$M(\mathbf{i}) = \begin{cases} 1 & \text{if denoising is required} \\ 0 & \text{if denoising is useless.} \end{cases} \tag{1}$$

To this aim, the Jensen-Shannon divergence between the original and the degraded image in a block centered at each $\mathbf{i}$ is estimated and it is compared with the maximum value for the Jensen Shannon divergence that guarantees invisible noise in the same block. The latter will be indicated as just noticeable JSD (JN-JSD). The following subsections will give details concerning the estimation of both the Jensen Shannon divergence and the just noticeable detection threshold. They are valid in a neighborhood $\Omega_{\mathbf{i}}$ of an image pixel $\mathbf{i}$. The argument $\mathbf{i}$ will be then omitted for simplicity.

2.1   A Bound for Jensen Shannon Divergence of Noisy Images

The Jensen-Shannon divergence [12] measures the distance between two pdfs p and q and it is defined as follows

$$D_{JS}(p, q) = \frac{1}{2}(D_{KL}(p\|m) + D_{KL}(q\|m)), \tag{2}$$

where $D_{KL}(p\|q) = \int_{-\infty}^{-\infty} p(x) \log(\frac{p(x)}{q(x)}) dx$ is Kullback-Leibler divergence [6] of two random variables X and Y with distributions p and q and $m = \frac{p+q}{2}$. In particular, by denoting with S_p and S_q the supports of p and q, it is possible to prove the following Lemma (see [1] for the proof).

Lemma 1.   If p and q are two pdfs with supports S_p and S_q and $\overline{S} = S_p \cap S_q$, then

$$D_{JS}(p, q) \approx 1 - \frac{1}{2} \int_{\overline{S}} (q(x) + p(x)) \, dx. \tag{3}$$

Previous Lemma provides an explicit dependence of D_{JS} on the intersection of the involved pdfs. Hence, if p and q respectively are the pdfs of the original X and the degraded image Y, $D_{JS}(p, q)$ evaluates how much information the original and degraded image share. The more the common information, the smaller D_{JS} value, the more visually similar the compared images. D_{JS} is then the additional visual cost required in the presence of degradation for scene interpretation.

Fig. 1. *Top)* Lighthouse test image corrupted by additive Gaussian noise with variance $\sigma^2 = 64$. *Bottom)* Denoised image using a spatially adaptive Wiener filter.

However, even in this simpler form, the computation of D_{JS} requires the knowledge of the pdf of the original image, that is not usual in practical applications. The goal is then to provide a bound for D_{JS} in Eq. (3) that only depends on quantities that can be easily estimated from the noisy image. In particular, it is possible to prove that

Lemma 2.   If $X \sim p$, $Y \sim q$ and $Y = X + \mathcal{N}$, where $\mathcal{N} \sim N(0, \sigma^2)$, then

$$D_{JS} \leq \frac{1}{2}(E[e^{-t(M_X - y)}] + E[e^{-t(y - m_X)}]), \quad t \geq 0, \tag{4}$$

where $S_p = [m_X, M_X]$, with S_p the support of p.

Proof: $S_p \subseteq S_q$, with S_q the support of q. Hence, Eq. (3) can be rewritten as

$$D_{JS}(p,q) \approx \frac{1}{2}(1 - F_q(M_X) + F_q(m_X)) = \frac{1}{2}[\mathcal{P}(Y > M_X) + \mathcal{P}(Y \leq m_X)], \quad (5)$$

where F_q is the cumulative distribution function of q. Using Markov inequality, we have

$$\mathcal{P}(Y > M_X) = \mathcal{P}(e^{ty} > e^{M_X}) < e^{-tM_X} E[e^{ty}], \quad \forall t \geq 0,$$

$$\mathcal{P}(Y \leq m_X) = \mathcal{P}(e^{-ty} \geq e^{-tm_X}) \leq e^{tm_X} E[e^{-ty}], \quad \forall t \geq 0,$$

Using these relations in Eq. (5), we get Eq. (4). ∎

The bound in Eq. (4) depends on the real variable t; hence, we are interested in selecting the value of t that realizes the minimum of the function $G(t) = \frac{1}{2}(E[e^{-t(M_X-y)}] + E[e^{-t(y-m_X)}])$. $G(t)$ is convex and its minimum is attained at

$$\bar{t} \in I_t = \left[\frac{1}{6\sigma + M_X - m_X} log \frac{M_X - m_X + 3\sigma}{3\sigma}, +\infty \right]. \quad (6)$$

Since a closed form for $\bar{t}$ cannot be derived, we try to estimate a robust bound for D_{JS} by exploiting the following known result.

Proposition 1. If y is random variable distributed as $f(y)$, and z is a random variable such that $z = g(y)$, where g is a continuous function, under proper assumptions it holds

$$E[g(y)] \approx g(E[y]) + \frac{\sigma_y^2}{2} g''(E[y]), \quad (7)$$

where σ_y is the standard deviation of y.

Hence, $\bar{t}$ is approximated by the value of t such that the estimation error in (7) is sufficiently small. More precisely, it is possible to prove that

Proposition 2

$$D_{JS} \leq \frac{1}{2}(e^{-\bar{t}(M_X-E[y])} + e^{-\bar{t}(E[y]-m_X)})(1 + \frac{\sigma_y^2}{2}\bar{t}^2). \quad (8)$$

where

$$\bar{t} = \frac{1}{6\sigma + M_X - m_X} log \left(\frac{M_X - m_X + 3\sigma}{3\sigma} \right). \quad (9)$$

Proof. Let us set $g(y) = \frac{1}{2}(e^{-t(M_X-y)} + e^{-t(y-m_X)})$. Using (7) in (4) we have

$$D_{JS} \leq \frac{1}{2}(e^{-t(M_X-E[y])} + e^{-t(E[y]-m_X)})(1 + \frac{\sigma_y^2}{2}t^2), \quad \forall t \in I_t.$$

The estimation error in (7) is $R(y, E[y], t) = \frac{1}{6} \int g'''(\eta_y)(y - E[y])^3 q(y) dy$, with $g'''(\eta_y) = t^3(e^{-t(M_X-\eta_y)} - e^{-t(\eta_y-m_X)})$ and $\eta_y \in [y, E[y]]$. Since

$$|R(y, E[y], t)| \leq \frac{1}{6} \int \max_y |g'''(y)||y - E[y]|^3 |q(y)| dy = \frac{t^3}{6} M(t) C,$$

with $C = \int |y - E[y]|^3 |q(y)| dy$ and $M(t) = 2e^{3\sigma t}$, then the value of t which realizes the minimum of the second term of previous equation is

$$\bar{t} = argmin_{t \in I_t} 2C \frac{t^3}{6} e^{3\sigma t}.$$

The function $\frac{t^3}{6} e^{3\sigma t}$ increases as t increases, then it attains its minimum in correspondence to the lower bound of I_t, i.e. $\bar{t} = \frac{1}{6\sigma + M_X - m_X} \log\left(\frac{M_X - m_X + 3\sigma}{3\sigma}\right)$. ●

It is worth observing that Eq. (8) provides a bound for D_{JS} that depends on the mean and the standard deviation of the noisy image and the minimum and maximum value of the original image. In addition, the bound in Eq. (8) is not trivial. In fact, it can be proved that it is less than 1 for a wide range of signal to noise ratios. Details can be found in the Appendix. In this paper, the bound in Eq. (8) will be used as an estimation of the value for D_{JS}.

2.2 Just Noticeable Noise Standard Deviation

Let $C_X(\mathbf{i})$ be the Michelson contrast [14] of X at the point $\mathbf{i}$, i.e.

$$C_X(\mathbf{i}) = \frac{M_X(\mathbf{i}) - m_X(\mathbf{i})}{M_X(\mathbf{i}) + m_X(\mathbf{i})},$$

where $M_X(\mathbf{i})$ and $m_X(\mathbf{i})$ respectively are the maximum and the minimum value of X in a neighborhood $\Omega_{\mathbf{i}}$ of $\mathbf{i}$. By denoting with $C_Y(\mathbf{i})$ the Michelson contrast of Y at the point $\mathbf{i}$, then $Y(\mathbf{i})$ cannot be distinguished from $X(\mathbf{i})$ if

$$1 - \delta \leq \frac{C_Y(\mathbf{i})}{C_X(\mathbf{i})} \leq 1 + \delta,$$

where δ is the just noticeable contrast detection threshold [9]. Next Lemma derives an estimation of the just noticeable noise variance in dependence on δ.

Lemma 3. Let $X \sim p$, $Y \sim q$, with $Y = X + \mathcal{N}$ and $\mathcal{N} \sim N(0, \sigma^2)$. Let $S_p = [m_X, M_X]$ and $S_q = [m_Y, M_Y]$ be respectively the supports of p and q, while let $|S_p|$ be the size of S_p. If

$$\sigma \leq \sigma_\epsilon = \frac{|S_p|\delta}{6\left(1 + \frac{1+\delta}{2}C_X\right)} \qquad (10)$$

then $\mathcal{P}(1 - \delta \leq \frac{C_Y}{C_X} \leq 1 + \delta) \geq 0.997$.

Proof. From the 3σ rule of normal random variables we have

$$M_X - 3\sigma \leq M_Y \leq M_X + 3\sigma, \qquad m_X - 3\sigma \leq m_Y \leq m_X + 3\sigma.$$

Since $[m_X, M_X] \subseteq [m_Y, M_Y]$, it holds

$$M_X - m_X \leq M_Y - m_Y \leq M_X - m_X + 6\sigma \qquad (11)$$

$$M_X + m_X - 3\sigma \leq M_Y + m_Y \leq M_X + m_X + 3\sigma. \tag{12}$$

The rightmost inequality in (11) combined with the leftmost inequality in (12) gives $C_X \leq \frac{M_X - m_X + 6\sigma}{M_X + m_X - 3\sigma}$ and then $\frac{C_Y}{C_X} \leq \frac{(M_X + m_X)(|S_p| + 6\sigma)}{|S_p|(M_X + m_X - 3\sigma)}$. The latter is less than $1 + \delta$ if Eq. (10) holds, provided that $\sigma \leq \frac{2}{3}(M_X + m_X)$. On the other hand, since $M_X - 3\sigma \leq M_Y$ and $m_Y \leq m_X + 3\sigma$, we have $\frac{C_Y}{C_X} \geq \frac{M_X + m_X}{M_X + m_X + 3\sigma}$. By imposing the rightmost term greater than $1 - \delta$, we get

$$\sigma \leq \frac{M_X + m_X}{3} \frac{\delta}{1 - \delta} \tag{13}$$

The proof is complete after comparing Eqs. (10) and (13).   ●

σ_ϵ in Eq. (10) provides an estimation of the just noticeable noise standard deviation.

2.3   The Algorithm

Equation (8) provides a nearly no reference form of D_{JS} since it depends on quantities that can be computed directly in the noisy image except for M_X and m_X. The latter can be estimated by using a simple local regularization of the noisy image. If we put the just noticeable noise standard deviation σ_ϵ, as in Eq. (10), in Eq. (8) we get the just noticeable detection threshold in terms of the bits budget (Jensen Shannon divergence) required by an invisible distortion. Hence, the following algorithm can be applied to the noisy image Y.

Let σ be the noise standard deviation. For each pixel $\mathbf{i}$:

- Apply a regularization filter in a $l \times l$ block $\Omega_{\mathbf{i}}$ centered at $\mathbf{i}$ and let $\tilde{Y}(\Omega_{\mathbf{i}})$ the regularized block
- Compute the maximum $M_{\tilde{Y}}$ and minimum $m_{\tilde{Y}}$ value of $\tilde{Y}(\Omega_{\mathbf{i}})$
- Compute the mean $E[y]$ and the standard deviation σ_Y of $Y(\Omega_{\mathbf{i}})$
- Compute $D_{JS}(\mathbf{i})$ as in Eq. (8), using $E[y]$, σ_Y and setting $M_X = M_{\tilde{Y}}$ and $m_X = m_{\tilde{Y}}$
- Compute $\tilde{D}_{JS}(\mathbf{i})$ using Eq. (8), by setting $\sigma = \sigma_\epsilon$, as defined in Eq. (10)
- Define the denoising map $M(\mathbf{i}) = \begin{cases} 1 & \text{if} \quad D_{JS}(\mathbf{i}) \geq \tilde{D}_{JS}(\mathbf{i}) \\ 0 & \text{otherwise.} \end{cases}$

Only pixels having $M(\mathbf{i}) = 1$ have to be denoised.

The complexity of the denoising map M is $O(l^2 log(l^2)NL)$, where $N \times L$ is the image size. In fact, the complexity for $M_{\tilde{Y}}$ and $m_{\tilde{Y}}$ is $O(l^2 log(l^2))$, while $O(l^2)$ is the complexity for $E[y]$, σ_Y and the regularization filter. These operations are applied to each image pixel. It turns out that the proposed algorithm does not cost more than a simple point-wise regularization filter.

Table 1. PSNR and SSIM values for the noisy image (Y), the denoised image using a conventional spatially adaptive Wiener filter (D), the denoised image using Wiener filter and the proposed denoising map (SD). For each test image and noise standard deviation σ, the best results are in bold. The last column of each table provides the percentage of pixels that have not be denoised according to the proposed procedure.

		$\sigma = 2.5$			
Image		Y	D	SD	%
Barbara	PSNR	**39.840**	31.484	39.671	86
	SSIM	**0.993**	0.971	0.993	
Boat	PSNR	**40.152**	33.914	39.055	83
	SSIM	**0.992**	0.979	0.991	
Lighthouse	PSNR	40.166	33.383	**40.728**	59
	SSIM	0.989	0.979	**0.991**	
Flower	PSNR	40.148	25.024	**40.181**	93
	SSIM	0.978	0.807	**0.983**	

		$\sigma = 5$			
Image		N	D	SD	%
Barbara	PSNR	33.752	30.996	**33.897**	68
	SSIM	0.974	0.964	**0.976**	
Boat	PSNR	34.070	33.345	**34.421**	60
	SSIM	0.970	0.971	**0.976**	
Lighthouse	PSNR	34.091	32.802	**35.595**	47
	SSIM	0.957	0.968	**0.975**	
Flower	PSNR	**34.065**	24.921	33.745	82
	SSIM	0.927	0.801	**0.939**	

		$\sigma = 8$			
Image		N	D	SD	%
Barbara	PSNR	29.670	30.160	**30.730**	43
	SSIM	0.939	0.950	**0.954**	
Boat	PSNR	29.989	**32.388**	31.965	36
	SSIM	0.930	0.957	**0.957**	
Lighthouse	PSNR	30.018	31.832	**32.322**	33
	SSIM	0.904	0.948	**0.950**	
Flower	PSNR	**29.993**	24.713	29.360	69
	SSIM	0.857	0.789	**0.877**	

		$\sigma = 10$			
		N	D	SD	%
Barbara	PSNR	27.826	29.565	**29.714**	23
	SSIM	0.913	0.938	**0.941**	
Boat	PSNR	28.149	**31.719**	31.187	20
	SSIM	0.900	**0.945**	0.945	
Lighthouse	PSNR	28.177	**31.158**	31.068	22
	SSIM	0.862	0.931	**0.932**	
Flower	PSNR	**28.163**	24.542	27.7001	61
	SSIM	0.816	0.779	**0.844**	

3   Experimental Results

The proposed method has been tested on several test images. They have been corrupted with additive Gaussian noise with standard deviation from 2 to 10. Higher levels of noise have not been considered. In fact, in these cases noise is somewhat visible and denoising is required in the whole image. It is worth observing that the considered standard deviations are common in digital archive documents, where Gaussian noise is not severe, or in acquisitions from aircrafts. 16×16 blocks ($l = 16$) have been considered in the estimation of the local Jensen Shannon divergence for two main reasons. The first one is that it contains a suitable number of samples that can provide a robust estimation of local image statistics. The second one is that it corresponds to a viewing angle of 0.56 degrees, which is the angle that promotes the perception of the maximum perceivable frequency [10]. The parameter δ has been set equal to 0.66, since it is a consistent estimation of the slope of the contrast discrimination function [9]. The spatially adaptive Wiener filter has been considered as simple standard denoiser. Also hard and soft thresholding [11] in a wavelet domain have been tested. However, since the results are similar to those of Wiener filtering, they will be not reported in this paper. Table 1 provides the results achieved for the test images Barbara, Boats, Lighthouse and a frame of Flower-Garden video sequence for noise standard deviation $\sigma = 2.5, 5, 8, 10$. The results have been measured in terms of Peak Signal to Noise Ratio and Structural Similarity [13]. The percentage of not denoised pixels is also provided. As Table 1 clearly shows, for low levels of noise a conventional and/or not accurate denoiser can destroy informative image content (see, for example, the results for Barbara and Boat images at $\sigma = 2.5$). The use of the proposed denoising map allows us to preserve it and to limit either some destructive effects of the adopted denoiser or not accurate parameters estimation. For intermediate noise standard deviations, the proposed selective denoising allows us to improve denoising performance both in terms of objective measures (PSNR and SSIM) and subjective visual quality. An example is also shown in Figs. 2 and 3. The original and degraded Boat image with $\sigma = 5$ are shown as well as the estimated point-wise JSD and JN-JSD. The comparison of JSD and JN-JSD provides the denoising map at the bottom of the figure. As it can be observed, noise masking is measured in different areas of the image. Figure 3 compares the denoised image using Wiener filter and the one denoised according to the estimated denoising map. The textured region at the bottom of Boat image, for example, is better preserved in the second image, as better shown in the zoomed images. For higher levels of noise, it is more difficult to have wide areas with noise masking effect and then the denoising map is 1 almost everywhere. The level of noise at which $M \equiv 1$ obviously depends on the image content. More in general, the proposed method gives different results for distinct images and noise levels since the amount of noise masking strongly depends on single image content. Finally, Table 2 shows the results obtained by applying the proposed denoising mask to BM3D algorithm [8]. As it can be observed, the use of a powerful denoiser guarantees a better quality of the denoised image, even for small σs. However, the benefit of denoising cannot be perceived in the same way in the whole image. The use of a selective denoising allows to preserve the visual quality of denoised images (as SSIM values prove), while enabling a computational saving that can overexceed 50 % in case of small noise levels.

Table 2. PSNR and SSIM values for the noisy image (Y), the denoised image using BM3D (D), the denoised image using BM3D and the proposed denoising map (SD). The last column provides the percentage of not denoised pixels.

Image		$\sigma = 5$				$\sigma = 10$			
		Y	D	SD	$\%$	N	D	SD	$\%$
Barbara	PSNR	33.756	**37.958**	35.097	68	27.826	**34.646**	32.541	24
	SSIM	0.974	**0.989**	0.986		0.913	**0.977**	0.974	
Boat	PSNR	34.065	**37.252**	35.396	60	28.149	33.907	**34.411**	21
	SSIM	0.970	**0.986**	0.983		0.900	**0.966**	0.964	

Fig. 2. Boat image. *Top)* Original (*left*) and noisy image (*right*) with noise standard deviation $\sigma = 5$. *Middle)* Pointwise D_{JS} estimated using Eq. (8) (*left*); Pointwise $\tilde{D}_{JS}$ as in Eq. (8) with σ_ϵ in Eq. (10) (*right*). *Bottom)* Denoising map M as in Eq. (1).

Fig. 3. *Top)* Denoised image in Fig. 2 using the empirical Wiener filter (*left*); Denoised image in Fig. 2 using the empirical Wiener filter only in correspondence to pixels where the denoising map M (Fig. 2. bottom) is equal to 1 (*right*). *Bottom)* Zoomed images.

4   Conclusions

In this paper a method for determining a denoising map has been presented. Its aim is to promote denoising only where its benefits are perceived by a human observer. In addition, the creation of new artifacts, such as oversmoothed textures, is avoided where noise is masked. The Jensen Shannon divergence has been used for evaluating noise masking. In particular, a bound for JSD has been provided that depends on quantities that are directly estimated from the noisy image. The just noticeable JSD has been derived as the one that guarantees invisible noise in the analysed image. Experimental results show the benefits in adopting a selective denoising. On the one hand, performance of conventional and fast denoisers are improved; on the other, the computational complexity of powerful but more computationally demanding denoisers can be reduced up to more than 50 %, promoting their use in real time applications. Future research will be devoted to refine the bound for JSD and the estimation of the just noticeable JSD, also involving a wider class of image distortions and color images.

Appendix

Let us consider Eqs. (8) and (9). Since $\frac{2x}{2+x} \leq \log(1+x) \leq x$, then $\frac{2(a+b)}{(6\sigma+a+b)^2} \leq \bar{t} \leq \frac{1}{3\sigma}$ and then

$$D_{JS} \leq \frac{1}{2}\left(e^{-\frac{2a(a+b)}{(6\sigma+a+b)^2}} + e^{-\frac{2b(a+b)}{6\sigma+a+b)^2}}\right)\left(1 + \frac{\sigma_y^2}{2}\left(\frac{1}{3\sigma}\right)^2\right), \qquad (14)$$

where $a = M_X - E[y]$ e $b = E[y] - m_X$.

In general, for $x \in [0, \sim 1.59]$, it holds $e^{-x} \leq 1 - \frac{x}{2}$. Hence, by assuming that

$$\frac{2a(a+b)}{(6\sigma+a+b)^2} \leq \frac{3}{2}, \quad \frac{2b(a+b)}{(6\sigma+a+b)^2} \leq \frac{3}{2}, \qquad (15)$$

$a + b \sim 6\sigma_I$ and $6\sigma + a + b \sim 6\sigma_y$, we have

$$D_{JS} \leq \frac{1}{2}\left(1 - \frac{(a+b)^2}{2(6\sigma+a+b)^2}\right)\left(1 + \frac{\sigma_y^2}{18\sigma^2}\right).$$

Since $\sigma_Y^2 = \sigma_X^2 + \sigma^2$, then

$$\left(1 - \frac{36\sigma_X^2}{72\sigma_Y^2}\right)\left(1 + \frac{\sigma_Y^2}{18\sigma^2}\right) \leq 1 \Leftrightarrow -\frac{\sigma_X^2}{2\sigma_Y^2} + \frac{\sigma_Y^2}{18\sigma^2} - \frac{\sigma_X^2\sigma_Y^2}{36\sigma_X^2\sigma^2} \leq 0$$

$$\frac{17 - \sqrt{217}}{2}\sigma^2 \leq \sigma_Y^2 \leq \frac{17 + \sqrt{217}}{2}\sigma^2,$$

i.e. $0.14 \leq \frac{\sigma_X^2}{\sigma^2} \leq 14.87$,   with $\sigma^2 \geq 1$.

Observation.   If $\min(a, b) \leq \max(a, b) \leq 3\min(a, b)$, then constraints in Eq. (15) are satisfied. More in general, by setting $\sigma = k(a+b), k \in \mathbf{R}$, then

$$\frac{2a(a+b)}{(6\sigma+a+b)^2} \leq \frac{2(a+b)^2}{(a+b)(6k+1)^2} \leq \frac{3}{2} \Leftrightarrow k \geq \frac{2-\sqrt{3}}{6\sqrt{3}} \Rightarrow \frac{\sigma_X}{\sigma} \leq \frac{\sqrt{3}}{2-\sqrt{3}} \sim 5.6.$$

References

1. Bruni, V., Rossi, E., Vitulano, D.: On the equivalence between Jensen-Shannon divergence and Michelson contrast. IEEE Trans. Inf. Theory **58**(7), 4278–4288 (2012)
2. Bruni, V., Rossi, E., Vitulano, D.: Jensen-Shannon divergence for visual quality assessment. Sig. Image Video Process. **7**(3), 411–421 (2013)
3. Bruni, V., Vitulano, D.: Evaluation of degraded images using adaptive Jensen-Shannon divergence. In: Proceedings of ISPA, Trieste, Italy, September 2013
4. Bruni, V., De Canditiis, D., Vitulano, D.: Speed-up of video enhancement based on human perception. Sig. Image Video Process. **8**(7), 1199–1209 (2014)

5. Chandler, D.M., Hemami, S.S.: VSNR: a wavelet-based Visual Signal-to-Noise Ratio for natural images. IEEE Trans. Image Process. **16**(9), 2284–2298 (2007)
6. Cover, T.M., Thomas, J.A.: Elements of Information Theory. Wiley, Hoboken (1991)
7. Hontsch, I., Karam, L.: Adaptive image coding with perceptual distortion control. IEEE Trans. Image Process. **11**(3), 213–222 (2002)
8. Dabov, K., Foi, A., Katkovnik, V., Egiazarian, K.: Image denoising by sparse 3D transform-domain collaborative filtering. IEEE Trans. Image Process. **16**(8), 2080–2095 (2007)
9. Legge, G.E.: A power law for contrast discrimination. Vis. Res. **21**, 457–467 (1981)
10. Frazor, R.A., Geisler, W.S.: Local luminance and contrast in natural images. Vis. Res. **46**, 1585–1598 (2006)
11. Mallat, S.: A Wavelet Tour of Signal Processing. Academic Press, New York (1998)
12. Topsoe, F.: Some inequalities for information divergence and related measures of discrimination. IEEE Trans. Inf. Theory **46**(4), 1602–1609 (2000)
13. Wang, Z., Bovik, A.C., Sheikh, H.R., Simoncelli, E.P.: Image quality assessment: from error measurement to structural similarity. IEEE Trans. Image Process. **13**(4), 600–612 (2004)
14. Winkler, S.: Digital Video Quality. Wiley, Vision Models and Metrics, Hoboken (2005)

Visual Localization Using Sequence Matching Based on Multi-feature Combination

Yongliang Qiao$^{(\boxtimes)}$, Cindy Cappelle, and Yassine Ruichek

IRTES-SET, Université de Technology de Belfort-Montbéliard,
90010 Belfort Cedex, France
{yongliang.qiao,cindy.cappelle,yassine.ruichek}@utbm.fr

Abstract. Visual localization in changing environment is one of the most challenging topics in computer vision and robotic community. The difficulty of this task is related to the strong appearance changes that occur in scenes due to presence of dynamic objects, weather or season changes. In this paper, we propose a new method which operates by matching query image sequences to an image database acquired previously (video acquired when the vehicle was traveling the environment). In order to improve matching accuracy, multi-feature is constructed by combining global GIST descriptor and local LBP descriptor to represent image sequence. Then, similarity measurement according to Chi-square distance is used for effective sequences matching. For experimental evaluation, we conducted study of the relationship between image sequence length and sequences matching performance. To show its effectiveness, the proposed method is tested and evaluated in four seasons outdoor environments. The results have shown improved precision-recall performance against state-of-the-art SeqSLAM algorithm.

1 Introduction

Due to the visual sensor widely used in the robotic community, visual place localization plays a key role in visual Simultaneous Localization and Mappings (vSLAM) systems. In this context, identifying previously visited locations in long-term period under environment changes is a big challenge.

There has been lots of visual localization methods by regarding the problem as problem of matching a sensed image against a previously acquired image database in which locations are represented by images. One can cite FAB-MAP algorithm [3] which employs Bag-of-Words (BOW) image retrieval technique and a Bayesian frame-work [4] that achieves robust image matching.

Recently, sequence SLAM (SeqSLAM) [9] adopting sequence matching rather than single image matching for place recognition achieves significant performance improvements than FAB-MAP. The usage of sequences allows higher robustness to lighting or extreme perceptual changes. In SeqSLAM, image similarity is evaluated using the sum of absolute differences between contrast enhanced and low-resolution images without the need of image keypoint extraction.

© Springer International Publishing AG 2016
J. Blanc-Talon et al. (Eds.): ACIVS 2016, LNCS 10016, pp. 324–335, 2016.
DOI: 10.1007/978-3-319-48680-2_29

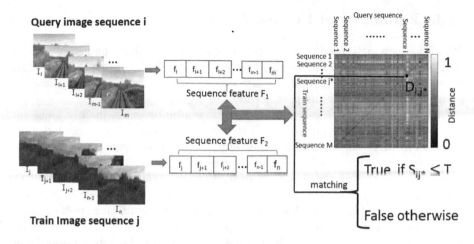

Fig. 1. General diagram of visual localization system using sequence matching. Here score value S_{ij*} is the ratio of the first (D_{ij*}) and second minimum distances of all the candidates to the query sequence i. T is a threshold (see Sect. 3.2 for more detail).

However, in [16] some weaknesses of SeqSLAM were reported, such as the field of view dependence and the complexity of parameters configuration.

Besides that, Local Binary Patterns (LBP) [11] as one of the widely used binary descriptors, which is invariant to monotonic changes in gray-scale and fast to calculate, has achieved good performance in image description and visual recognition. Nevertheless, as the author [5] noted, LBP lacks of spatial and shape information. To overcome this limitation, we propose to add GIST features [15] that focus more on the shape of scene itself and on the relationship between the outlines of the surfaces and their properties. GIST and LBP can be seen as complementary for image representation in the sense that GIST focuses more on global information while LBP emphasizes local texture information.

In this paper, we present a visual localization method using sequence matching based on multi-feature combination that is robust to extreme perceptual changes. Figure 1 illustrates the general diagram of our approach. Basing on features extracted from images, sequences are efficiently matched using Chi-square distance and the best candidate matching location is recognized according to coherent sequence matching. Image descriptor we use in this paper is a combination of LBP and GIST, which should improve image distinguishing ability by capturing local and global image information. We will demonstrate the algorithm performance using multi-season videos of 30000 Km long train ride in the northern Norway. For this, we conducted an extensive experimental study according to sequence matching length and compared the performance of the proposed approach with the state of the art method SeqSLAM.

The paper is organized as follows. Section 2 provides background and related works on visual place recognition. In Sect. 3 we describe the proposed visual localization approach. Experiments are presented with results shown in Sect. 4. Finally, Sect. 5 discusses the outcomes of this paper and presents future work.

2   Background and Related Works

With cameras widely used in many robot platforms, a large number of vision-based place recognition and localization algorithms have been proposed [13]. Here we briefly discuss some of the key vision-based mapping and localization algorithms proposed over the past decade.

The current state-of-the-art visual localization approaches mainly focus on image or sequence matching against a reference database of geotagged ground images. FAB-MAP [3] method matches appearance of the current scene image to a reference one by employing image retrieval system. The SIFT or SURF features used in this system allow invariance to scale and rotation, but lead to poor performance across large lighting variations and scene appearance changes.

Sequence SLAM (SeqSLAM) method achieves significant performance improvements over FAB-MAP under extreme lighting and atmospheric variations [10]. Image similarity is evaluated using the sum of absolute differences of the contrast enhanced images without relying on feature extraction. In paper [8], RatSLAM is proposed as a computational model based on competitive attractor networks. This method has been demonstrated in a number of experiments for mapping large environments or over long time periods [7]. Recently, RTAB-MAP [6], based on a long-term memory methodology has been also proposed. In [2], a multi-scale bio-inspired place recognition illustrates how to achieve better place recognition performance by recognizing places at multiple spatial scales.

Binary descriptors, with their high efficiency (low computational cost) and effectiveness, have been widely used in image description, fast image matching and visual place recognition. Paper [1] proposes a fast and more effective visual loop closure detection method (ABLE-S) which integrates disparity information into a binary descriptor to decrease the perceptual aliasing influence.

Nowadays, one of the most fashionable and challenging topics in life-long visual topological localization is to recognize previously visited places along different seasons. The method presented in [17] approaches visual topological localization over seasonal conditions by using SURF descriptors. Another very recent proposal is focused on the prediction of changes on places based on superpixel vocabularies [10], which has been tested using $3000\,km$ dataset across all four seasons.

3   Proposed Visual Localization Approach

In this section, we describe the key components of our approach: feature extraction and sequence matching.

3.1   Feature Extraction

As mentioned in paper [1], high resolution images are not needed to perform an effective visual recognition along time. Indeed, high resolution images increase computational cost without bringing significant visual recognition improvement.

For fast and efficient matching, in our work, we downsample the original images into 32×32 pixels before feature extraction.

(1) LBP feature: The generalized LBP definition is used with N sample points evenly distributed on a radius R around a center pixel located at (x_c, y_c). The position (x_p, y_p) of the neighbor points, where $p \in \{0, ..., N-1\}$, is given by:

$$(x_p, y_p) = (x_c + Rcos(2\pi/N), y_c - Rsin(2\pi/N)) \tag{1}$$

The local binary code for the position (x_c, y_c) can be computed by comparing the center pixel gray-scale value g_c and its neighbor pixel gray-scale values g_p. The value of the LBP at position (x_c, y_c) is given by:

$$LBP_{N,R}(x_c, y_c) = \sum_{p=0}^{N-1} s(g_p - g_c)2^p \tag{2}$$

where

$$s(x) = \begin{cases} 1, & x \geq 0 \\ 0, & othersize \end{cases} \tag{3}$$

One approach is to use the uniform patterns "U2" (U refers to the measure of uniformity, 2 is the number of 0/1 and 1/0 transitions in the circular binary code pattern) representing the statistically most common LBP codes. In our work, we use the uniform patterns and set N to 8 sampling points and radius R to 3 pixels around the center pixel to get a 59-dimensional LBP feature.

(2) GIST feature: It is a global image feature, which characterizes several important statistic about a scene [14]. A variety of experimental studies have demonstrated that humans perform rapid categorization of a scene by integrating only the coarse global information or "GIST" [15]. Using the model proposed by Oliva [12], GIST feature is computed by convolving an oriented filter with down-sampled images (32×32) at several different orientations and scales. The scores for the filter convolution at each orientation and scale are stored in an array and resulting in a 512-dimensional feature.

(3) Multi-feature combination: After getting the LBP f_{LBP} and GIST f_{GIST} features, we combine them into a new LBP-GIST feature f. The combination consists simply in concatenating $(++)$ the two features:

$$f = f_{LBP} + + f_{GIST} \tag{4}$$

Combining LBP and GIST features allows taking simultaneously advantage of local and global image information and thus allows representing the scene of each location more comprehensively.

(4) Sequence feature : Finally, the LBP-GIST features extracted from images of a sequence are concatenated $(++)$ to form the final sequence feature (F) representing the sequence of images:

$$F = f_{I_i} + + f_{I_{i+1}} + + f_{I_{i+2}} + + ... + + f_{I_{m-2}} + + f_{I_{m-1}} + + f_{I_m} \tag{5}$$

where, I_i, I_{i+1}, $\cdots$ I_m are the images composing the sequence and $L_{length} = m - i + 1$ is the length of the sequence.

3.2 Matching of Image Sequences

To perform sequence matching, we evaluate similarity between sequence features through chi-squared distance (cf. Eq. 6). The similarity values can be stored on a distance matrix (D) for evaluation purposes as follows:

$$D_{i,j} = \chi^2(F_i, F_j) = \sum_k \frac{((F_i)_k - (F_j)_k)^2}{|(F_i)_k + (F_j)_k|} \tag{6}$$

where F_i is the current feature vector sample (query sequence) and F_j is the feature vector of a train sequence (in the reference dataset). k is index of feature vector.

Given a current sequence i, to select a good sequence candidate from the reference database, a score S_{ij*} is calculated as follows:

$$S_{ij*} = \frac{D_{m1}}{D_{m2}} \tag{7}$$

where D_{m1} and D_{m2} are respectively the first and second minimum distances of all train sequences to the query sequence, i.e.:

$$\begin{cases} D_{m1} = \min_j \{D_{ij}\} = D_{ij*} \\ D_{m2} = \min_{j(j \neq j^*)} \{D_{ij}\} \end{cases} \tag{8}$$

Score value range is between 0 and 1. Lower the score value is, higher the similarity between the candidates is. A threshold is then applied to the score to determine if the sequence pair (i, j^*) is matched or not. True positives are obtained when score value is lower than the threshold.

4 Visual Localization Experiments and Results

4.1 Experimental Setup

In this section, we describe the dataset used, ground-truth and image pre-processing.

The dataset used in our work is an open dataset which called Nordland[1]. It is composed of footage videos of 728 Km long train ride in four seasons between two cities in north Norway [16]. Thus, the dataset can be considered as a single 728 Km long loop that is traversed four times. As illustrated in Fig. 2, there is an immense variation of the appearance of the landscape, reaching from green vegetation in spring and summer to colored foliage in autumn and a complete snow-cover in winter over fresh.

In addition to the seasonal changes, different local weather conditions like sunshine, overcast skies, rain and snowfall are experienced on the long trip. Most of the journey leads through natural scenery, but the train also passes through urban areas along the way and occasionally stops at train stations or signals.

---

[1] https://nrkbeta.no/2013/01/15/nordlandsbanen-minute-by-minute-season-by-season/.

(a) Spring (b) Summer

(c) Fall (d) Winter

Fig. 2. A typical four seasons images representing the same scene in spring, summer, fall and winter. It can be seen that the images show huge difference with season changing. Here, the images are original ones with their original resolution. In our experiment, we down-sampling the images into 32×32 pixels

The original videos have been recorded at 25 fps with a resolution of 1920×1080 using a SonyXDcam with a Canon image stabilizing lens. GPS readings were recorded in conjunction with the video at 1 Hz. The full-HD recordings have been time-synchronized such that the position of the train in an arbitrary frame from one video corresponds to the same frame in any of the other three videos. This was achieved by using the recorded GPS positions through interpolation of the GPS measurements to 25 Hz to match the video frame rate. The ground-truth was achieved by using the recorded GPS position.

For the experiments described in the following, we extracted image frames from the original videos at 1 fps, downsampling them to 32×32 pixels and converting them into gray-level images.

4.2 Evaluation Method

Precision-recall characteristics are widely used to evaluate image retrieval ability. Therefore, our evaluation methodology is based on precision-recall curves. These curves are determined by varying the threshold, used in the matching decision (see Sect. 3.2), between 0 and 1, and calculating precision and recall. Here 100 threshold values are considered to obtain well-defined precision-recall curves.

4.3   Feature Combination Analysis

In a first set of experiments, we evaluated how well does multi-feature combination perform for place recognition and also compared the results with those provided by the state-of-art SeqSLAM. The experiments were conducted using the videos presenting extreme situation in terms of appearance changes (Spring vs Winter). As shown in Fig. 3, the LBP and GIST features perform very well when they are used independently. Indeed, our method with LBP performs relatively well at high precision, while using GIST it outperforms SeqSLAM method. When using the multi-feature (LBP-GIST), the retrieval ability is increased significantly. The reason is that LBP-GIST takes advantage of local and global information to distinguish between images more accurately.

It can be seen that our method with LBP-GIST can reach around 65 % recall at 100 % precision, which outperforms the SeqSLAM method. It should be noted that the image size used in SeqSLAM is also 32×32 and the other parameters of SeqSLAM method correspond to default situation as used in [16].

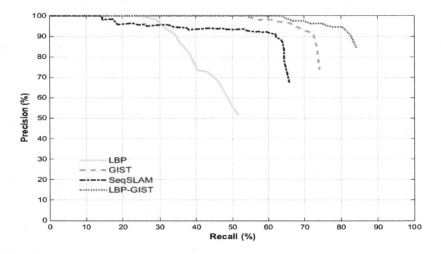

Fig. 3. Performance of the proposed method according different features and comparison with SeqSLAM method (Spring vs winter).

4.4   Sequence Length Selection

Traditionally visual localization has been performed by considering places represented by single images. Recently, several approaches such as SeqSLAM, have proved that recognizing places through sequences of images is more robust and effective.

In this paper, we also follow the idea of using sequences of images instead of single image for identifying places. This approach allows to achieve better results for visual localization in different seasons, as can be seen in Fig. 4.

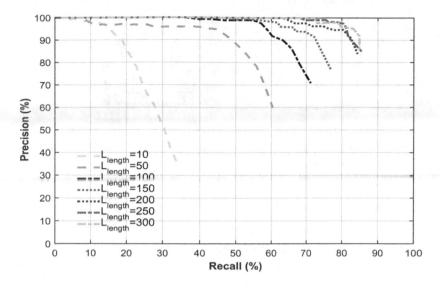

Fig. 4. Performance comparison of our proposed method with LBP-GIST feature combination, according to image sequence length (L_{length}) (spring vs winter).

Figure 4 shows the performance achieved when varying sequence length between 10 and 300 frames. Significant performance improvement was achieved by increasing the sequence length up to 200 frames, after which the improvement became modest.

According to the precision-recall curves demonstrated in Fig. 4, the influence of sequence length (L_{length}) is decisive for improving the performance of visual localization in different seasons. Moreover, we found a limit near to 200 frames, from which the results are not greatly enhanced. For this reason, we set L_{length} to 200 in the rest of the experiments.

4.5 Visual Recognition Results Under Different Season Couples

After feature performance evaluation and sequence length selection, visual place recognition using sequence matching based on multi-feature combination was compared under different season couples. Figure 5 (a) illustrates the ground-truth of the dataset. It should be noted that the position of the train in an arbitrary frame in one season corresponds to the same frame in any of the other three seasons thanks to time-synchronization. Figure 5 (b) shows an example of distance matrix obtained by our proposed method between fall and winter seasons.

Different matching results under different season couples are depicted in Fig. 6. As our objective is to correctly identify the place as much as possible at 100 % precision (along the diagonal), it can be seen that the result of "summer vs fall" is the best among the others. We can also notice that when the winter sequence is evaluated (Fig. 6 (b), (e) and (f)), the unrecognized places increase, that is because the snow in winter leads to scene featureless.

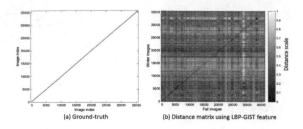

(a) Ground-truth   (b) Distance matrix using LBP-GIST feature

Fig. 5. Ground-truth and an example of distance matrix obtained by our proposed method between fall and winter seasons.

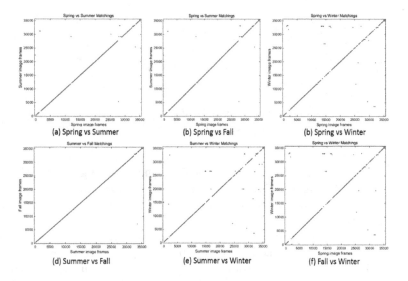

(a) Spring vs Summer   (b) Spring vs Fall   (b) Spring vs Winter

(d) Summer vs Fall   (e) Summer vs Winter   (f) Fall vs Winter

Fig. 6. Matching results under different season couples. The expected result is along the diagonal.

Figure 7 shows precision-recall curves of matching results under different season couples. It can be easily found that visual recognition performance of our method is better under (spring vs summer) and (spring vs fall), where we can reach above 85 % of recall at 100 % precision level. It can be seen also that our proposed multi-feature combination method can achieve recall rate above 60 % at 100 % precision under all the season couples. As expected, when winter sequence is evaluated, the effectiveness of our method decreases due to the extreme changes that this season causes in place appearance because of environmental conditions such as presence of snow, illumination, vegetation changes, etc.

The recall scores for high selected precision values of SeqSLAM method and our proposed approach are given in Table 1. For all the cases, our proposed place recognition algorithm achieves the better recall rate, which is the ratio of the number of true positive place recognition detections to the total number of

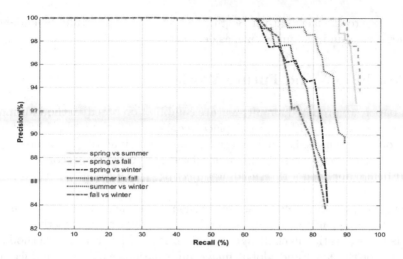

Fig. 7. Precision-recall curves comparing the performance of our proposed method under different season couples.

Table 1. The recall scores at selected high precision values

Different season couples	Method	Recall 100 % prec	Recall 99 % prec	Recall 90 % prec
Spring vs Summer	SeqSLAM	20.45	27.73	66.11
	Proposed	87.64	87.64	92.70
Spring vs Fall	SeqSLAM	15.41	27.45	63.87
	Proposed	88.20	89.89	93.82
Spring vs Winter	SeqSLAM	14.29	17.37	62.18
	Proposed	63.48	66.58	82.58
Summer vs Fall	SeqSLAM	9.80	23.81	65.27
	Proposed	71.35	76.97	87.64
Summer vs Winter	SeqSLAM	14.01	27.45	53.50
	Proposed	62.92	67.42	79.21
Fall vs Winter	SeqSLAM	2.24	2.35	44.82
	Proposed	64.40	66.29	77.53

possible true positives. Moreover, in "spring vs summer" and "spring vs fall" situations, the recall rates of our approach is higher than 85 % for all the high precision values recorded in Table 1.

For both SeqSLAM method and our approach, recall rate increases when precision is decreasing. The recall rate of the two methods increases drastically at 90 % precision. Besides that, the recall rate of SeqSLAM method is lower than the recall rate of the proposed method, and worst for all the high precision values. This is probably due to the fact that the SeqSLAM method has a certain dependence of the field of view and the image size, as demonstrated in [16].

5   Conclusions and Future Work

In this paper, we proposed a multi-feature combination based method for matching image sequences within visual place recognition framework. After feature extraction, Chi-square distance is used to measure similarity between a query sequence and the sequences of a reference database. A matching score is then calculated before applying a thresholding procedure to determine the good matching candidates.

Thanks to precision-recall based evaluation, experimental results showed that the proposed sequence matching method is more robust and effective for long-term visual localization in challenging environments. The proposed method takes advantage of the local and global image information, which can reduce aliasing problem. Sequence length analysis demonstrated that sequences as long as 200 frames could provide viable recognition results. Shorter sequences cannot achieve acceptable results, while longer ones cannot bring significant improvement. Compared to the state of the art SeqSLAM method, the proposed approach provided better recognition performances.

However, using multi-feature combination increases feature vector dimension and thus increases time computation. To overcome this limitation, we envision to deal with dimension reduction using space projection techniques or searching methods like local sensitive hashing.

References

1. Arroyo, R., Alcantarilla, P., Bergasa, L., Yebes, J., Bronte, S.: Fast and effective visual place recognition using binary codes and disparity information. In: 2014 IEEE/RSJ International Conference on Intelligent Robots and Systems (IROS 2014), pp. 3089–3094, September 2014
2. Chen, Z., Jacobson, A., Erdem, U., Hasselmo, M., Milford, M.: Multi-scale bio-inspired place recognition. In: 2014 IEEE International Conference on Robotics and Automation (ICRA), pp. 1895–1901, May 2014
3. Cummins, M., Newman, P.: Fab-map: probabilistic localization and mapping in the space of appearance. Int. J. Robot. Res. **27**(6), 647–665 (2008)
4. Cummins, M., Newman, P.: Appearance-only slam at large scale with fab-map 2.0. Int. J. Robot. Res. **30**(9), 1100–1123 (2011)
5. Kylberg, G., Sintorn, I.M.: Evaluation of noise robustness for local binary pattern descriptors in texture classification. EURASIP J. Image Video Process. **2013**(1), 1–20 (2013)
6. Labbe, M., Michaud, F.: Appearance-based loop closure detection for online large-scale and long-term operation. IEEE Trans. Robot. **29**(3), 734–745 (2013)
7. Milford, M., Wyeth, G.: Persistent navigation and mapping using a biologically inspired slam system. Int. J. Robot. Res. **29**(9), 1131–1153 (2010)

8. Milford, M.J., Wyeth, G.F., Prasser, D.: Ratslam: a hippocampal model for simultaneous localization and mapping. In: Proceedings of 2004 IEEE International Conference on Robotics and Automation, ICRA 2004, vol. 1, pp. 403–408. IEEE (2004)
9. Milford, M., Wyeth, G.: Seqslam: visual route-based navigation for sunny summer days and stormy winter nights. In: IEEE International Conference on Robotics and Automation (ICRA), pp. 1643–1649 (2012)
10. Neubert, P., Sunderhauf, N., Protzel, P.: Appearance change prediction for long-term navigation across seasons. In: 2013 European Conference on Mobile Robots (ECMR), pp. 198–203, September 2013
11. Ojala, T., Pietikäinen, M., Harwood, D.: A comparative study of texture measures with classification based on featured distributions. Pattern Recogn. **29**(1), 51–59 (1996)
12. Oliva, A., Torralba, A.: Modeling the shape of the scene: a holistic representation of the spatial envelope. Int. J. Comput. Vis. **42**(3), 145–175 (2001)
13. Pepperell, E., Corke, P.I., Milford, M.J.: All-environment visual place recognition with smart. In: 2014 IEEE International Conference on Robotics and Automation (ICRA), pp. 1612–1618. IEEE (2014)
14. Sikirić, I., Brkić, K., Šegvić, S.: Classifying traffic scenes using the gist image descriptor. arXiv preprint (2013). arXiv:1310.0316
15. Song, D., Tao, D.: Biologically inspired feature manifold for scene classification. IEEE Trans. Image Process. **19**(1), 174–184 (2010)
16. Sünderhauf, N., Neubert, P., Protzel, P.: Are we there yet? challenging seqslam on a 3000 km journey across all four seasons. In: Proceedings of Workshop on Long-Term Autonomy, IEEE International Conference on Robotics and Automation (ICRA), p. 2013. Citeseer (2013)
17. Valgren, C., Lilienthal, A.: Incremental spectral clustering and seasons: appearance-based localization in outdoor environments. In: IEEE International Conference on Robotics and automation, ICRA 2008, pp. 1856–1861. IEEE (2008)

Towards Automated Drone Surveillance in Railways: State-of-the-Art and Future Directions

Francesco Flammini[1](✉), Riccardo Naddei[2], Concetta Pragliola[1], and Giovanni Smarra[1]

[1] Ansaldo STS, Via Argine 425, Naples, Italy
{francesco.flammini,concetta.pragliola,
giovanni.smarra.ext}@ansaldo-sts.com
[2] 3F & EDIN Centro Direzionale Is. E/7, Naples, Italy
riccardo.naddei@3fedin.it

Abstract. The usage of UAV (Unmanned Aerial Vehicles) – widely known as 'drones' – is being increasingly investigated in a variety of surveillance scenarios. Being an emerging technology, several challenges still need to be tackled in order to make drones suitable in real applications with strict performance, dependability and privacy requirements. In particular, the monitoring of transit infrastructures represents one critical domain in which drones could be of huge help to reduce costs and possibly increase the granularity of surveillance. Furthermore, drones pave the way to the implementation of smart-sensing functionalities expanding current capabilities in railway monitoring, to support automation, safety of operations, prognostics and even forensic analyses. In this paper we provide a survey of current drone technology and their possible applications to automated railway surveillance, taking into account technical issues and environmental constraints. A current experimentation with drone intelligent video will be addressed, highlighting some preliminary results and future perspectives.

Keywords: UAV · Drones · Railways · Surveillance · Monitoring · Artificial vision · Smart-sensing

1 Introduction

Many transit systems can be spread through hundreds of kilometers and require thousands of employees for daily operations. A complete deployment of visual surveillance to cover a system of this magnitude requires thousands of cameras and hundreds of control room operators, which makes extensive traditional surveillance unfeasible in practice. This is the reason why automated surveillance through smart-sensors and video content analytics is being increasingly employed for railways and mass-transit systems (see e.g. [1–3, 19]).

In such a context, this position paper surveys drone technologies for automated railway surveillance, highlighting opportunities and current technical limits. The work addresses the main aspects of drone systems engineering (frame, payload organization, on-board sensors and computers, flying autonomy, etc.) and discusses some issues about

© Springer International Publishing AG 2016
J. Blanc-Talon et al. (Eds.): ACIVS 2016, LNCS 10016, pp. 336–348, 2016.
DOI: 10.1007/978-3-319-48680-2_30

computer vision algorithms running on drone cameras, also providing preliminary on-the-field experimentation results.

2   Railway Applications of Drone Surveillance

In the last years, the drones market has experienced a significant growth [22, 23]. Despite the several constraints such as the endurance (actually, drones can fly from 20 to 30 min and an operator should replace or recharge the battery after the flight [4]), weather conditions (strong wind and gust prevent drones from keeping the position and flying properly) and the look of harmonized standard regulation defined at international levels for drones with MTOW (maximum take-off weight) less than 150 kg [6, 7], nowadays, more and more civil applications require the usage of these unmanned vehicle as a support element [7]. In particular there is an increasing interest for vertical take-off UAVs (VTOL, *vertical take-off and landing*), rotor-wing, with MTOW less than 25 kg, commonly denoted like 'small drones' [12]. Those applications address several fields: agriculture, security surveillance, aerial photography, gas leak detection, fire detection, environmental monitoring, archeology, photovoltaic systems monitoring, monitoring of structures and buildings, inspections of power lines, just to name a few [7].

Despite more strict regulations rule the railway context to guarantee railway system safety and security, several companies are investigating in drones technology. For instance, the Dutch railway company named ProRail is already adopting drones equipped with infrared sensors to check the switch point heating systems on tracks [10]. If the switch points are frozen, trains are not allowed to move on the track, causing substantial delays. In Germany, the national railway company Deutsche Bahn is trialling micro drones to help combat graffiti on its property, that obliged the company to spend over 6 million Euros for their removal in 2012 [10]. Inspecting railway tracks by drones is one of the main challenge to be tackled in the future. The Mysuru division (India) recently completed an aerial survey of the ghat section between Sakleshpur and Subramanya using drones to inspect all the vulnerable areas close to the railway tracks in view of the monsoon. The drones survey was completed in two days respect to one week taken by maintenance operators with the advantage of saving time and cost but also with great quality of the aerial footage [18].

There are very interesting projects in urban contexts that could be applied to railways as well. In reference [4], a round-clock surveillance provided by drones has been proposed. An automated system which provides wireless charge through landing-pad mounted on the existing electrical facilities could be a strategy to overcome the problem of endurance.

In case of GSM-R equipped railways (standardized in the context of ERTMS, European Railway Traffic Management System), it would be possible to implement a drone-based automated monitoring system along railway tracks: by leveraging the GSM-R/GPRS WAN connection, drones could be remotely controlled to inspect an entire line (till hundreds of km) and receive wireless charge from landing-pads mounted on the existing infrastructure (e.g. Base Transceiver Stations, BTS) or from particular platforms like the DRONEBOX solution, developed by a Singaporean company named

H3Dynamics [8]. Trackside charging pads also represent points to download larger data (e.g. by Wi-Fi), overcoming the bandwidth limitations of cellular data transmission protocols.

Furthermore, drones could be used in short planned missions (fixed route patrolling) to automatically monitor railway depots against intrusions or damages/vandalism to trains/infrastructure. It would be also possible to control their route in case of detected threats and anomalies. On that regards, the engagement of the drone could be also triggered by the occurrence of events generated by fixed sensors like fence vibration detectors. More effectively than fixed CCTV surveillance, due to the freedom of movement implying precise positioning and lower hardware costs, drones can effectively support countermeasures and rescue operations.

Finally, railway drones could even support quicker post-disaster inspections and forensic analyses in critical points inaccessible to humans or in areas where a CBRN (Chemical Bacteriological Radiological Nuclear) contamination is suspected. Especially small sized and battery-powered chemical detectors, that can be currently found in the market, could be added to the payload to provide real-time data, or the drones can be used to pick-up a small sample and to bring it to the nearest fixed station for in-depth analyses. The synergic and concurrent operation of more drones featuring complimentary active infrared sensors (IR transmitter/receiver) also paves the way to the future usage of moving IR chemical detectors [9].

In conclusion, the possibility of using drones of a variety of current and future railway applications (summarized in Fig. 1) make them very appealing especially in terms of cost-effectiveness and flexibility.

Fig. 1. Possible railway applications of drones.

3   Intelligent Video in Railway Drone Surveillance

In order to fulfil automated railway surveillance requirements, drones must be equipped with cameras mounted on a two or three degrees of freedom gimbal, connected to a board device, to set the tracking actions with various levels of sophistication and with the possibility of automatically tracking a suitably selected target and maintaining it in the center of the observed scene; on-board devices of adequate computing power allow running the required computer vision algorithms and all the components dedicated to mission planning, collision detection and collision avoidance (see Fig. 2).

Fig. 2. Connection between the on-board computer and camera gimbal (left). On-the field testing of collision detection techniques (right).

Due to the aforementioned scenario requirements, railway monitoring drones need to be the result of an accurate process of design of a structured payload, including a computer and a set of sensors and other appropriate hardware components.

The heart of the payload is represented by a computer featuring reduced size and high computational power, in order to allow on-board processing of part of the algorithms. The most suitable Video Content Analytics (VCA) hardware boards are based on multi-core/multi-GPU (Graphics Processing Unit) architectures. The NVIDIA parallel computing architecture, 'CUDA', is currently widespread for VCA applications since it provides superior computing performances by leveraging the GPU power and by properly distributing the computational tasks between CPU and GPU. It includes a Streaming Multiprocessor (SM), designed to concurrently run a large number of threads by a SIMT (Single-Instruction, Multiple-Thread) architecture, that creates, manages and executes threads in groups of 32 (i.e. 'warps'). The individual threads of a warp start running with the same counter, but feature their own instruction addresses, registers and independent execution branches.

In order to better understand the computational requirements for the railway surveillance drone payload, the problems involved in the operation of the main software components, namely collision detection and tracking, need to be discussed.

3.1 Collision Detection

Collision Detection techniques are based on the estimation of the apparent motion of a body observed through the extrapolation of the motion field (also known as optical flow [11]) from a video stream generated by the drone on-board camera (forward looking, either gimbaled or strapdown). By the optical flow it is possible to locate the Focus of Expansion (FoE) [13, 20], that is the point on which there is a divergence of optical flow vectors: if it is not at infinity but resident in the image plane, this phenomenon is likely to be attributed to the vicinity of the camera (and thus of the drone) to an obstacle. Once the coordinates of the FoE and the camera speed in space are known, an estimate of the impact time (Time To Contact) can be derived and the information needed to implement a collision avoidance maneuver can be obtained. The logical structure of this strategy is shown in Fig. 3.

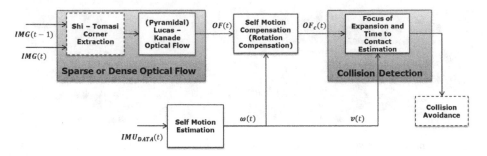

Fig. 3. Flow-chart of the railway drone collision detection process.

The algorithm employed for the optical flow estimation is known as Pyramidal Lucas-Kanade [15], that is by far the most widely used in the literature for the problem to be addressed. Depending on the performance of the on-board device, one of the following algorithms should be implemented:

- Dense Lucas – Kanade. It is robust but computationally intensive because the optical flow is calculated for each pixel. It does not require the extraction of salient features of the image.
- Sparse Lucas – Kanade. It is less robust, but extremely light-weight because the optical flow is calculated only for salient features of the image. It requires feature extraction.

The algorithm used for the estimation of the highlights (features or - in this case - corners) is known as Shi-Tomasi [21], that is quite reliable in this context since – due to the high correlation between consecutive frames – the geometric transformations (affine and projective) of what is represented on the image plane can be considered an adequate approach.

- Self-Motion Estimation. The aim is to estimate the proper motion of the camera and of the flying platform, in such a way to subtract the trim variations (rotations) to the apparent motion determined through the optical flow and to be able to determine the depth and the time until collision (Time to Contact). In order to obtain a reliable estimate, a low-pass filter must be applied to data.
- Focus of Expansion and Time to Contact Estimation. It estimates the points of largest divergence of the flow vectors, in order to identify the 'center of gravity' of the obstacle approaching. It calculates the time to impact according to own speed.
- Collision Avoidance. It is an evasive maneuver to avoid the collision and preserve the structural integrity of the flying platform.

The Focus of Expansion is ideally characterized by a flow vector of amplitude zero and therefore the motion field diverges radially from it (Fig. 4). In practice, the optical flow shows a greater width on the outskirts of the FoE and lesser extension in its vicinity.

The FoE, in the simplest case, is generated by a rectilinear motion parallel to the main axis of the camera, due to the motion of the observer, an object approaching in this direction, or both.

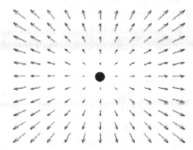

Fig. 4. Focus of expansion.

4   Tracking

The term tracking refers to the ability of a computer to recognize the position and orientation of the objects to be tracked. This ability can be implemented using a variety of sensors such as cameras, lasers, radar, GPS satellites, etc. Therefore, tracking is the ability of a computer, in our case mounted on the drone, to recognize the position and orientation of certain suitably identified/selected objects through the analysis of a continuous sequence of images. As part of a surveillance mission, the tracking is realized through the images captured by a camera accommodated on a gimbal so that it can rotate or tilt to give the most possible continuity to the tracking operation.

Tracking is one of the most difficult problems in computer vision as it is concerned with the task of generating an inference about the motion of a given object in a sequence of images [24]. Indeed, the tracking action can be defined as the analysis of video sequences in order to determine the position of the target on a sequence of frames starting from the bounding box selected in the first frame.

A first basic classification of trackers may be based on the techniques used and on the level of abstraction at which they operates. The categories are:

- Region based Tracking
- Active contour based Tracking
- Feature Based Tracking
- Model based Tracking
- Tracking model based

4.1   Part-Based Appearance Model-Based Tracking

One of the most innovative approaches to tracking is represented by part-based approach [5], a frame-to-frame tracking appearance-based model which is inspired by groups of organisms moving using simple common rules [14, 16]. The three rules at the basis of this behavior are: (i) alignment, (ii) cohesion, and (iii) separation.

To model the appearance of a target and estimate its motion, the motion is evaluated by target displacements or - more generically - by estimated transformation (i.e. by a statistically valid number of independent local trackers related to main features).

Typically, local trackers are not robust [14, 16]; they assume that the area is visible in all frames and that the apparent movement consists of translations. To make the estimate of the robust movement in terms of failure, the movements estimated by individual trackers are combined with the aid of online learning procedures taking into account both the positive and negative examples, suitably sampled at each frame.

The local trackers are positioned on a regular grid in a uniform manner, although not necessarily related to the same size of the sub-area. The object movement, well-modeled for the translation and scale invariance, is estimated using a combination of a stochastic subset (inlier) of the responses of local trackers. A filtering method of local tracker separates the positive examples (inlier) from the negative (outlier).

Hence, the approach includes:

– The initialization of a set of local trackers that cover the bounding box
– The association of each local tracker to a specific part
– The estimate of the part's movement for each tracker
– A procedure for a rugged design combining the estimates given by the tracker
– An online learning method to update the estimates
– A filtering method for identifying outlier, inlier and resampling of the tracker

From the operational viewpoint, the algorithm is structured in the following steps (Fig. 5):

- **Input**: capture of a stream of images from a camera and manual selection of a target defining the bounding box
- **Identification**: division of the bounding box in 4 or 8 parts per patch selection belonging to the tracking target; activation of a number equal to the patch tracker choices, each tracker managing a specific patch.
- **Feature extraction**: each tracker samples the patch associated with a polar grid made up of 16 segments. Each slice is selected in 5 radial positions getting so $5 \times 16 = 80$ positions, on each of which the characteristics are calculated.
- **Online learning**: each tracker estimates the next position of each patch/sample using the vector of characteristics calculated in the previous step.
- **Outlier detection**: after the estimation of patch/sample the algorithm checks for any outliers and endeavors to eliminate them.
- **Convex Hull:** finally 4 or 8 samples are obtained representing the best target classification from the extracted patch. The total bounding box, understood as the union of the best patch, represents the convex hull of the target. At this point the convex hull at step i is used as the target in step $(i + 1)$.

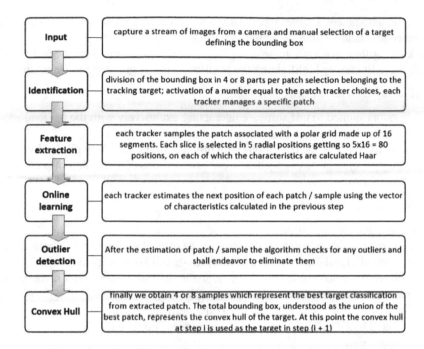

Fig. 5. Experimental tracking algorithm running on the prototype railway drone.

5 Preliminary Experimental Results

The professional drone used to test the proposed algorithms is made up of:

- DJI S900 frame with carbon fiber arms
- DJI A2 flight controller
- N° 2 custom interchangeable payloads equipped with a 4 K resolution camera on a 2-axis gimbal and a Laser Rangefinder which include the following on-board processors respectively:
    - ODROID-XU4 *(low-cost platform, including a quad core ARM Cortex- A15)*
    - NVIDIA JETSON TX1 *(including a quad core ARM Cortex-A57 and 256-core Maxwell GPU)*

The algorithms have been implemented and integrated into a mission software which was installed on both the payloads (ODROID XU4 based and NVIDIA TX1 based). Mission software includes an Android-based application, installed on tablet Samsung Tab S 10.5, enabling communication with payload to follow a mission, allowing:

- real-time video streaming from on-board camera with telemetry; during the mission, software displays in-flight data on tablet display too
- map preloading, to enable display drone's geographical position during the flight
- switching from streaming to map and viceversa
- selectively activate the 2 algorithms (collision detection or tracking)

- collision avoidance: a tablet vibration report collision detections for obstacles at a distance less than a value saved in the settings
- tracking: software allows to select a target inside the framed scene and to start tracking activities by highlighting the position of the target in video streaming

The following tests have been carried out:

- in laboratory, aimed to test software interacting exclusively with the payload and to verify the correct automatic handling of the gimbal during tracking
- on-the-field, to check the operations with drone in flight, remotely piloted by Futaba radio control system or engaged in a pre-planned mission (through a preliminary selection of waypoints)

The following results have been achieved:

- collision detection algorithm:
  - the software correctly detects the presence of obstacles with superior performance in terms of visual angle compared to the on-board laser rangefinder
  - it allows to detect obstacles from unpredictable directions within the camera observation range (80 % of the field of view)
  - it works properly on both the payloads, demonstrating that computing power provided by ODROID is enough for the process involved
- tracking algorithm:
  - the software was able to keep the selected target at the center of the scene through automatic handling of gimbal even in case of partial/total occlusions thanks to the Kalman filter
  - the results obtained embarking software on ODROID-based payload were unsatisfactory, highlighting a lack of computing power, missing the target after a few seconds after starting the tracking process and introducing unacceptable latency
  - the results obtained embarking software on TX1-based payload, by changing the algorithm implementation through the use of the GPU via CUDA, have yielded the expected results, allowing to correctly follow a target and to operate without affecting smooth streaming operations

A foremost aspect that has emerged during the experimentation is that though the TX1 platform has clearly superior hardware characteristics with respect to ODROID, the major advantages have been achieved by running the algorithm in parallel and by using CUDA. In fact, by comparing the serialized version of the algorithm with the concurrent one, it has been noted that the real performance improvement is related to the usage of CUDA combined with the fine grained computation that well suit GPU processing. Algorithm computing phases have been combined in a pipeline made-up by concurrent stages, distributing the workload by OpenMP (ODROID) and CUDA (TX1).

As reported in Table 1, thanks to CUDA it is possible to better exploit the on-board computing power, such to achieve an overall platform workload of 82 % with respect to the one available on TX1, against the 50 % of the one available on ODROID.

Table 1. Comparison between different versions of the algorithm

	Odroid UX-4 (8 core)	NVIDIA Jetson TX1 (4 core)	FPS
BST serialized	220 % out of 800 %	250 % out of 400 %	4–5
BST w Pipe + OpenMP	400 % out of 800 %	330 % out of 400 %	>10

The results demonstrated that NVIDIA TX1 can be considered the ideal platform for such applications. That is true not only for the Computer Vision related aspects, but also for the long-range Wi-Fi connectivity and video footage management. The experiments have shown a good streaming quality even when the distance from the base-station is several hundred meters. Those results have been achieved by using a video analytics strategy with variable frame-rate, till over 10 fps; such a frame-rate is certainly adequate for railway monitoring scenarios where target speeds are relatively low.

The experimentation has also paved the way to further improvements by leveraging computing power not only for image processing but also for other computations that are required during a mission. Those improvements are also related to the possibility of exploiting the H264 encoder that is provided on-board of the TX1. Even though ODROID also offers a H264 hardware encoding, so far it has not been possible to use that component for technical reasons (software encoding has been used). Tests performed on TX1 H264 encoder highlighted the possibility of effectively using the component, freeing the computing power presently required for encoding.

Those results are to be considered as preliminary since further testing is required in order to verify the performance and limits of drone VCA in railway scenarios where challenging conditions occur like targets entering tunnels, scene over-crowding, etc.

6 Conclusions and Future Developments

Automated railway surveillance by drones represents a very promising research and application field. While normative constraints still need to be extensively addressed to allow drone flying during railway operations, a number of attractive scenarios can be enabled, some of which (like train depot patrolling) seem to be viable in very short times using the state-of-the-art drone technologies addressed in this paper.

The experiments have shown that the prompt availability of professional drones represents an opportunity to design and implement new railway surveillance strategies due to their very light carbon-fiber frames and the housing capacity of payloads with adequate computing power. The results achieved in testing the collision avoidance and the tracking algorithms have shown that it is possible to take advantage of the on-board processing power to operate algorithms that a few years ago required workstation-class computing power.

Regarding drone-based object tracking in railway environments, the next development goals are listed in the following:

- ability of the on-board computer to interact with drone flight controller to automatically affect the navigation process, by carrying out actions to prevent collisions, like hovering or automatically changing waypoints. To achieve that, drones equipped with auto-pilots and with interaction capabilities through standard protocols (e.g. MAVLINK [17]) must be employed.
- introduce cooperation capabilities between drones with drone-to-drone or drone-ground-drone communication to carry out investigations and increasingly sophisticated missions.

Further progress is expected in terms of payload empowering for both streaming functionalities and light conditions required for the correct working of the algorithms. Regarding the first aspects, it is expected to use TX1 H264 hardware encoder to get extra CPU power for further on-board computations. That extra power can also be used to increase the frequency of video processing such to follow targets moving quicker or to provide smoother streaming.

Regarding the control over low-light conditions, it is scheduled to add an IR camera to drone payload. Current experiments have been performed using a GoPro Hero4 camera, allowing for effective operation in optimal light conditions. Lab and on-the-field testing have shown that the part-based approach (conversely to the features detection/extraction techniques) can be effective even on IR camera footage. Therefore, the idea is to include both cameras in drone payload, adding an automatic switching function between cameras depending on light conditions.

The results obtained so far confirm that the drones are a technically viable opportunity to be used in real applications in the field of monitoring and surveillance in the railway sector. One of the major issues to be solved is the flying autonomy since railway tracks cover huge distances; however, by equipping the track with an adequate number of wireless-rechargeable drones and charging pods (possible located in the existing and evenly distributed GSM-R BTS), the railway long-range data communication facilities allow drones to be controlled from remote centers. For real-time transmission of video and sensor data, larger bandwidth is provided by commercial mobile phone operators using more recent cellular data protocols (like UMTS and LTE). However, the possibility of on-board computation of VCA limits large data transmission to the cases of automatically detected anomalies; in addition, video footage download (e.g. for forensics) can be performed at the fixed charging pods where Wi-Fi will be made available. On that regard, a technology transfer from modern tramway on-board modems is envisaged, due to their capability of auto-detection and connection to the best available wireless network and subsequent adaptation of transmitted video quality (e.g. compression rate, resolution, frame-rate, etc.). Finally, it is to be taken into account that drones could be employed even in subways and metro-railway applications where Wi-Fi infrastructures covering the whole tracks are already employed for several communication requirements like CBTC (Communication Based Train Control), IP telephony for the staff, real-time on-board network cameras viewing from control rooms [1].

References

1. Bocchetti, G., Flammini, F., Pappalardo, A., Pragliola, C.: Dependable integrated surveillance systems for the physical security of metro railways. In: Proceedings of the 3rd ACM/IEEE International Conference on Distributed Smart Cameras, (ICDiSC 2009), 30 August – 2 September, 2009, Como (Italy), pp. 1–7
2. Candamo, J., Shreve, M., Goldgof, D.B., Sapper, D.B., Kasturi, R.: Understanding transit scenes: a survey on human behavior-recognition algorithms. IEEE Trans. Intell. Transp. Syst. **11**(1), 206–224 (2010)
3. Casola, V., Esposito, M., Flammini, F., Mazzocca, N., Pragliola, C.: Performance evaluation of video analytics for surveillance on-board traino. In: Blanc Talon, J., Kasinski, A., Phillps, W., Popescu, D., Scheunders, P. (eds.) ACIVS 2013. LNCS, vol. 8192, pp. 414–425. Springer, Heidelberg (2013). doi:10.1007/978-3-319-02895-8_37
4. Chae, H., Park, J., Song H., Kim Y., Jeong, H.: The IoT based Automate Landing System of a Drone for the Round-the-clock Surveillance Solution. In: IEEE International Conference on Advanced Intelligent Mechatronics (AIM), Busan, pp. 1575–1580 (2015)
5. Chang, W.Y., Chen, C.S., Hung, Y.P.: Tracking by parts: a Bayesian approach with component collaboration. IEEE Trans. Cybern. Syst. Man Cybern. **39**(2), 375–388 (2009)
6. Civil Drone in European Union (2015). http://www.europarl.europa.eu/RegData/etudes/BRIE/2015/571305/EPRS_BRI(2015)571305_EN.pdf. Accessed 8 Sept. 2016
7. Daponte, P., De Vito, L., Mazzilli, G., Picariello, F., Rapuano, S., Riccio, M.: Metrology for drone and drone for metrology: measurement systems on small civilian drones, pp. 306–311 (2015)
8. DRONEDOX solutions. http://www.h3dynamics.com/products/drone-box/. Accessed 9 June 2016
9. Flammini, F., Mazzocca, N., Pappalardo, A., Pragliola, C., Vittorini, V.: Augmenting surveillance system capabilities by exploiting event correlation and distributed attack detection. In: Tjoa, A.M., Quirchmayr, G., You, I., Xu, L. (eds.) CD-ARES 2011. LNCS, vol. 6908, pp. 191–204. Springer, Heidelberg (2011). doi:10.1007/978-3-642-23300-5_15
10. Future of Rail 2050. Arup (2015). http://www.arup.com/homepage_future_of_rail. Accessed 9 June 2016
11. Grabe, V., Bülthoff, H.H., Giordano, P.R.: Robust optical-flow based self-motion estimation for a Quadrotor UAV. In: IEEE/RSJ International Conference on Intelligent Robots and Systems, Vilamoura, pp. 2153–2159 (2012)
12. Valavanis, K.P., Vachtsevanos, G.J.: Handbook of Unmanned Aerial Vehicle. Springer, Netherlands (2015)
13. Harley, R., Zisserman, A.: Multiple View Geometry in Computer Vision. Cambridge University Press, Cambridge (2003)
14. Kristan, M., Pugfelder, R., Leonardis, A., et al.: The visual object tracking VOT2013 challenge results. In: ICCV Workshops, pp. 98–111 (2013)
15. Lucas, B.D., Kanade, T.: An iterative image registration technique with an application to stereo vision. In: International Joint Conference on Artificial Intelligence (1981)
16. Kristan, M., et al.: The visual object tracking VOT2014 challenge results. In: Agapito, L., Bronstein, M.M., Rother, C. (eds.) ECCV 2014. LNCS, vol. 8926, pp. 191–217. Springer, Heidelberg (2015). doi:10.1007/978-3-319-16181-5_14
17. MAVLINK Micro Air Vehicle Protocol, Common Message Set. https://pixhawk.ethz.ch/mavlink/. Accessed 9 June 2016

18. Krishna Kumar, R.: In a first, railways uses drones for survey of vulnerable sections, MYSURU, 16 August 2016. http://www.thehindu.com/todays-paper/in-a-first-railways-uses-drones-for-survey-of-vulnerable-sections/article8992379.ece. Accessed 9 June 2016
19. Räty, T.: Survey on contemporary remote surveillance systems for public safety. IEEE Trans. Syst. Man Cybern. Part C **40**(5), 493–515 (2010)
20. Sazbon, D., Rotstein, H., Rivlin, E.: Machine: finding the focus of expansion and estimating range using optical flow images and a matched filter. Vis. Appl. **15**, 229 (2004)
21. Shi, J., Tomasi, C.: Good Features to Track, Cornell University (1993)
22. Sumbesi, M.: Survey on the Drone industry, profile of sector company 2015. http://www.dronitaly.it/en/the-italian-drones-market-grows-fast/. Accessed 9 June 2016
23. UAV Global, unmanned systems and manufacturers. http://www.uavglobal.com/commercial-uav-manufacturers/. Accessed 9 June 2016
24. Xiang, W., Zhou, Y.: Part-based tracking with appearance learning and structural constrains. In: Loo, C.K., Yap, K.S., Wong, K.W., Teoh, A., Huang, K. (eds.) ICONIP 2014, Part I. LNCS, vol. 8834, pp. 594–601. Springer, Heidelberg (2014). doi:10.1007/978-3-319-12637-1_74

Combining Stacked Denoising Autoencoders and Random Forests for Face Detection

Jingjing Deng, Xianghua Xie$^{(\boxtimes)}$, and Michael Edwards

Department of Computer Science, Swansea University,
Singleton Park, Swansea SA2 8PP, UK
x.xie@swansea.ac.uk
http://csvision.swan.ac.uk

Abstract. Detecting faces in the wild is a challenging problem due to large visual variations introduced by uncontrolled facial expressions, head pose, illumination and so on. Employing strong classifier and designing more discriminative visual features are two main approaches to overcoming such difficulties. Notably, Deep Neural Network (DNN) based methods have been found to outperform most traditional detectors in a multitude of studies, employing deep network structures and complex training procedures. In this work, we propose a novel method that uses stacked denoising autoencoders (SdA) for feature extraction and random forests (RF) for object-background classification in a classical cascading framework. This architecture allows much simpler neural network structures, resulting in efficient training and detection. The proposed face detector was evaluated on two publicly available datasets and produced promising results.

1 Introduction

Face detection has been an active research topic in computer vision for decades. View-specific face detection methods, such as VJ detector (Viola-Jones object detection framework [37]), have achieved great success and are used in various commercial products. Recently, researchers are focusing on more challenging face detection problems under uncontrolled environment, i.e. so-called faces in the wild, where factors such as large pose and facial expression variations, severe occlusion and clutter, and poor lighting scenario are taken into consideration. Zhang et al. [43], and Zafeiriou et al. [42] provide a comprehensive review on recently proposed face detection methods. However, faces in the wild remain a challenging problem.

Cascade based methods with strong classifiers and discriminative features are popular in tackling multi-view detection problems, utilizing methods such as aggregating channel features [39], multi-scale block local binary pattern [27], and normalized pixel difference feature [26]. The features are designed specifically for certain detection problems, which may not be universally applicable. Deformable Part Model (DPM) [11,12,16] defines an object as a pictorial configuration of its parts. For example, an human pose can be estimated using a star-structured

© Springer International Publishing AG 2016
J. Blanc-Talon et al. (Eds.): ACIVS 2016, LNCS 10016, pp. 349–360, 2016.
DOI: 10.1007/978-3-319-48680-2_31

model by finding a confident configuration of torso root and its displaced limb parts [6]. The benefit of having flexible representation of an object can greatly help to tackle the challenges of occlusion, pose and appearance variations, at the cost of considerably more complex computation requirements. There are some works on accelerating DPM-based detection, such as cascade part pruning [38]. Exemplar-based face detection methods [24,33] formulate the problem as an image retrieval task, where a detection occurs when a successful matching is found in face exemplars for hypothesis by using visual feature descriptors, such as SIFT (Scale-Invariant Feature Transform). Matching with exemplars is time consuming, especially when a very large face dataset is required to cover huge amount of variations under uncontrolled environment, meaning that a sliding window method is not feasible. In these cases Hough voting based methods at multiple scales are used instead, to produce a confidence voting map to locate region candidates. The face can then be found by searching the peak regions on the ensemble confidence map. In order to achieve better performance, a large face exemplar dataset is critical in order to cover different variations in an uncontrolled environment. Meanwhile, detection speed will suffer due to exploring larger search space. Contour based object tracking method such as [5] can also be applied to face detection task.

The application of neural networks methods to detection problems goes back to 1980s [18,40], but its place was quickly taken by support vector machine and boosting based methods due to the limitations on computational cost. With the developments of better unsupervised initialization methods, availability of large amount of labeled data, and hardware improvements, especially the GPGPU (General-Purpose Graphics Processing Unit), training a deep neural network becomes a routine [17,23]. The success of Convolutionary Neural Networks (CNNs) on large scale object detection and recognition [15,22,32,34] shows that searching deep representative structures with a learned convolutionary feature space is vitally important for high-level visual recognition tasks, whereas it is indeed computationally expensive for relatively simple tasks. For instance, traditional object detection problem where over hundreds of thousands of subwindows are required to evaluate for just one image, is not affordable in real-time application. However, the power of representative feature learning of deep neural network should not be overlooked. Region-based CNNs (R-CNNs) [13,14,30] are a series of CNN-based methods for multi-object detection and semantic segmentation. In order to avoid densely scanning an image, R-CNN methods use selective search methods [35] to generate a relatively small amount of object region proposals. The features of the candidate regions are extracted by CNN, and a linear SVM is used to classify them into object categories. Its CNN consists of five convolutional layers and two fully connected layers, and it was pre-trained on a large image dataset, LSVRC2012 (Large Scale Visual Recognition Challenge [31]) discriminatively, and then followed by domain-specific fine tuning. Precisely locating an object is still a challenging problem to R-CNNs even with the help of bounding box refinement regressor. As R-CNN methods have been reported with relatively weak performance [10], Farfade et al. proposed DDFD

(Deep Dense Face Detector) by densely scanning through the image with sliding windows, and then performing a binary classification directly using the output of a fine-tuned AlexNet [22]. The idea of using CNN as a classifier component was further extended to DPM [29,41] for face detection. The most relevant work to our SdA-RF detector is [25], which constructed a 3-stages cascade detector using 3 detection nets, and 3 calibration nets. Within each stage, the detection net separates face and background, and then calibration net refines the locations of retained windows. The next stage processes the refined windows with the same procedure but using double resolution and deeper CNN models.

In this paper, we propose a general cascade object detection method, SdA-RF which embeds SdA and RF into a cascade framework. Two main differences compared to the deeper models make it unique. First, SdA-RF uses a rather simple neural network, 1-layer SdA, to extract the features, and RF to perform classification, which makes densely scanning an image possible for better localization without any refinement procedure. Second, SdA-RF does not rely on any pre-trained model. Unsupervised pre-training and supervised fine-tuning can all be done using the same dataset. The paper is organized as follows: In Sect. 2, we introduce SdA-RF model, and then present how an object detection cascade is built via combining individual SdA-RF stage classifiers; In Sect. 3, we show the experimental results on two public datasets, and discuss the findings; We conclude our work in Sect. 4.

2 Proposed Method

2.1 Stage Classifier

For detection problems, an ideal cascade detector requires individual stages trained with high recall rate and low fallout rate, which enable the cascade to eliminate negative sub-windows as early as possible, meanwhile preserve most of the positives. However, there is no free lunch to train such an ideal classifier. For example, Viola-Jones method [37] trained Adaboost classifiers via searching the feature space exhaustingly to meet the recall rate requirement. In that way, the classifiers constructed normally have very high recall but also have relatively high fallout, therefore increasing the number of stages is necessary to filter out most negatives. The upper bound of detection rate within a Viola-Jones cascade $Upper(R_c)$ depends on the number of stages N, and the recall rate of individual stage R_{s_i}, where $Upper(R_c) = \prod_i^N R_{s_i}$. Bourdev et al. [2] proposed a so-called soft cascade method, where the sub-windows are eliminated based on votes of multiple stages with importance weights, instead of one stage in a traditional cascade method. However, such an accumulative elimination scheme involves duplicative computational cost for each sub-windows. We seek to train each stage with a stronger classifier, which can greatly reduce the number of stages but also retain considerable high recall rate and low fallout rate.

Bengio et al. [1] proposed a deep representation learning method, namely Stacked Autoencoder (SA). Individual layer of SA is a latent model trained iteratively using two phases, encoding and decoding in an unsupervised fashion.

Given the observation $v \in \mathbb{R}^{D_v}$, where D_v is the number of dimensions of visible variable, firstly the encoder maps (upwards) v into latent representation $h \in \mathbb{R}^{D_h}$, where D_h is the number of dimensions of the latent variable. Between visible nodes and latent nodes, a fully connected network is constructed to represent the mapping functions, but intra-connection between the same type of node is not allowed in order to keep the complexity of the model itself relatively simple. The decoder works in an opposite way to the encoder, it maps (downwards) the latent representation v back to the so-called reconstructed observation $\bar{x}$. The mapping functions are rametrized using a continuous-value extension of Restricted Boltzmann Machine (RBM) [17] with $\theta = (W, W', b, b')$, where the upwards and downwards mappings are formulated as $h = \mathbb{S}(Wx + b)$, and $\bar{x} = \mathbb{S}(W'h + b')$ respectively. Typically, the sigmoid is used as activation function $\mathbb{S}$, and tied weights constrain, $W' = W^T$, is applied to the model. The estimator of the model can be obtained by minimising the squared reconstruction error, $Loss(\bar{x}, x) = ||\bar{x} - x||^2$. Greedy layer-wise training is applied, where the latent variable of the previous layer is fed into the current layer as input. Trained layers are stacked hierarchically and followed by a fine-tuning procedure, which also can be done in a supervised way by stacking a Softmax layer on the top. Furthermore, Vincent [36] proposed SdA model, which introduces an artificial input corruption scheme into the layer-wise training procedure in order to avoid identity learning and improve robustness. For an input x, SdA stochastically forces a certain amount of input channels to 0 in order to generate a corrupted version $\tilde{x}$, and then trains a normal autoencoder using $\tilde{x}$. This training strategy shows that sensibility to small irrelevant changes in input can be significantly reduced.

SdA offers a layer-wise unsupervised representation learning method, which can be used as a general feature extractor for various object detections. In the case that ground truth labels are available, supervised fine-tuning will help to improve classification performance even further. However, it is notable that the classification power of SdA with Softmax layer is relatively weak compared to the-state-of-art discriminative models. For example, random forests (RF) was used for human interaction recognition [7], which is one of challenge problems in computer vision field. In order to address such shortcomings, in this work, RF is trained using encoded representations learned by SdA to classify subwindows into positives and negatives. RF [4] grows a number of decision trees independently using the bagging subsets [3] which are randomly sampled from the complete training set with replacement. Individual decision tree consists of a set of tests (non-leaf node) and predictors (leaf node), where either Gini impurity or information gain is used to find the best split. During the prediction stage, the testing samples traverse through each decision tree by evaluating its properties at non-leaf node, and finally reaches a leaf node at the bottom, which votes the class with largest proposition of training samples it holds. The random forests combine all voting results from individual decision trees, and assigns the most voted class to the testing sample. The training procedure for stage classifier combining SdA feature learning, and RF classification is described in Algorithm 1.

Algorithm 1. Train a Stage Classifier for Binary Classification using SdA and RF.

1 function M = trainSdARF (I, L);

    Input : I is a set of training images containing positives and negatives.

    Input : L is a set of ground truth labels for I, where $L_i \in \{0, 1\}$, corresponding to negative and positive respectively.

    Output: M is stage classifier, which consists of one SdA model and one RF model.

2 $nLayers \leftarrow$ set the number of hidden layer used for training SdA;

3 $nHiddens \leftarrow$ set the numbers of hidden nodes of each layers;

4 $nTrees \leftarrow$ set the number of decision tree used for training RF;

5 $rLayers(0) \leftarrow$ initialise the encoded feature with original image I for the first layer training;

6 **for** $j \leftarrow 1$ **to** $nLayers$ **do**

7      $sdaLayers(j) \leftarrow$ train an SdA model using input feature $rLayers(j - 1)$ in an unsupervised fashion with $nHiddens(j)$ hidden nodes;

8      $rLayers(j) \leftarrow$ encode output feature using trained model $sdaLayers(j)$ and input feature $rLayers(j - 1)$;

9 **end**

10 $smLayer \leftarrow$ train a Softmax layer using encoded feature $rLayers(nLayers)$ given by the top level SdA model, and ground truth label L in a supervised fashion;

11 $Network \leftarrow$ stack the pre-trained $sdaLayers$ and $smLayer$ layer-wise to form a fully connected neural network;

12 $Network \leftarrow$ fine-tune $Network$ using input image I and label L in a supervised fashion;

13 $Representation \leftarrow$ collect the features encoded using $Network$;

14 $Forests \leftarrow$ train an RF model using $Representation$ and label L with $nTrees$ trees;

15 $M \leftarrow$ assemble the neural networks encoder $Network$ and RF $Forests$;

16 **return** M;

2.2   Detection Cascade

For object detection, as the number of positives is far less than negatives, cascade-based methods, which often bias towards negatives, are relatively more efficient. However, as discussed in Sect. 2.1, adding more stages is required to reduce false positive rate, at the expense of reducing true positive rates. The proposed stage classifier Algorithm 1 addresses this contradiction by introducing better feature learning methods and more discriminative models. To train each classifier stage a sliding window method is used to generate negative subwindows, which then pass through the previous stage's classifier. Only those predicted as positives are retained and used for training the current stage. It is notable that the classification problem becomes more challenging with increasing stage depth, as retained sub-windows are collected from more different images. With the number of stage growth, the number of tree in RF is progressively

---

Algorithm 2. Train an Object Detection Cascade.

---

1 function C = trainCascade (Pos, Neg);

    Input   : Pos is a set of positive training images all of which have the same size. h, w, $nPos$ are height, width, and total number of positive images respectively.

    Input   : Neg is a set of negative training images with no target object, where $nNeg$ is the total number of negative images.

    Output: C is object detection cascade, which consists of multiple stage classifiers.

2   $maxStages \leftarrow$ set the maximum number of stages;

3   $minRecall \leftarrow$ set the minimum overall recall rate;

4   $maxFallout \leftarrow$ set the maximum overall fallout rate;

5   $ratioNegPos \leftarrow$ set the number ratio of training samples, negatives over positives;

6   $nTrees \leftarrow$ set the number decision trees used for training stage classifier;

7   **for** $j \leftarrow 1$ **to** $maxStages$ **do**

8       $trnWindows \leftarrow$ create $nPos \times ratioNegPos$ negative samples of size (h, w) using sliding window methods from negative images Neg, where only those ones pass through $C(1 : j - 1)$ are retained, and then combine with positive sample Pos;

9       $trnLabels \leftarrow$ label the training windows as 0 for negative, and 1 for positive;

10     $Ctemp \leftarrow$ train a stage classifier with $nTrees$ using $trnWindows$ and $trnLabels$;

11     $nTrees \leftarrow$ increase the number of decision trees for next stage training;

12     $(oaRecall, oaFallout) \leftarrow$ compute the overall recall rate, and fallout rate;

13   **if** $(oaRecall < minRecall) \parallel (oaFallout > maxFallout)$ **then**

14 | break the stage training loop;

15   **end**

16     $C(j) \leftarrow Ctemp$ assign stage classifier to collection;

17 **end**

18 **return** C;

---

increased to overcome the difficulties introduced by the larger diversity present in the negative set. The cascade training procedure is described in Algorithm 2.

3 Experiments and Discussion

We used AFLW (Annotated Facial Landmarks in the Wild [21]) dataset to train a face detector. The dataset contains 22,712 labelled faces out of 21,123 images. The positive face windows were further augmented by applying 5 random perturbations to the location of face window within the range of 5 % of its size, and also collecting all flipped face windows. In total, 227,120 faces are used in the training procedure, and some examples of positive samples are shown in Fig. 1(a). The negative images should contain no face. To bootstrap non-face images the AFLW dataset was used, where the labeled face windows were replaced with

Fig. 1. Positive training face images (a), and negative images (b) from AFLW and PASCAL VOC datasets.

no face patches randomly cropped from PASCAL VOC dataset [8,9] (person subset was excluded). In total, 19,458 negative images were generated using this bootstrapping approach. As considerable amount of images of AFLW dataset are not well labeled with face bounding box, we further applied face detection on the negative images using Koestinger's VJ-LBP model (Viola-Jones detector with Local Binary Patterns feature) [20]. After removing those that have true positive response, the negative image set contains 18,089 images.

The size of the training image window is 24×24 pixels, to which all face windows were resized and converted into grey scale. There is no histogram equalization or any further image enhancement. To create negative training windows, we applied sliding window method to each negative image with scale factor $Sn = 1.2$, and stride $Sx = Sy = 2$ pixels. The generated negative windows were firstly sent to previous stage classifiers, only those ones passed through were retained for current training procedure. For SdA model, one hidden-layer with 12×12 nodes was used, which was trained in an unsupervised fashion with image intensity, this was then followed by a supervised fine-tuning. Figure 2 shows the visualization of the partial weights given by hidden nodes of the first and last stage classifier before and after supervised fine-tuning. The weights are shown as a set of basis for reconstructing original image signal using the output of encoder, which capture the characteristics of face rather well. It is notable that the reconstruction basis of the last stage classifier (2nd row) is more informative compared to the first stage (1st row). When the cascade goes deeper, training a stage classifier becomes more challenging, because easy negative windows are filtered out by the previous stages and hard ones are retained. Also we observed that fine-tuning SdA by back-propagating the prediction error given by the Softmax layer makes the basis more specific for face detection. For example, two red bounding boxes in Fig. 2 show the weights from the same hidden node before and after supervised fine-tuning. The same phenomenon can be observed across all stages. The output of the encoder was used as a high-level representation to train an RF classifier. The minimum number of samples in each leaf node was set to 3 in order to avoid over-fitting. The number of decision trees of the first stage was set to 25, and it was progressively increased with 5 more trees every one stage deeper. The whole cascade training finished with 5 stages as no more negative windows can be generated given 18,089 non-face images. This is

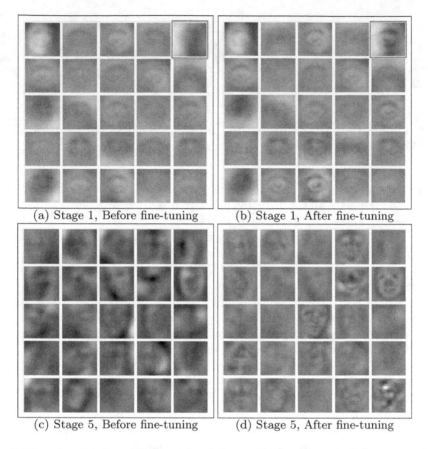

(a) Stage 1, Before fine-tuning   (b) Stage 1, After fine-tuning

(c) Stage 5, Before fine-tuning   (d) Stage 5, After fine-tuning

Fig. 2. The visualisation of SdA weights before and after supervised fine-tuning from the first and last stages.

a significant reduction in terms of number of stages compared to traditional VJ detectors (20 stages used in [21]).

The face detector was verified on two public datasets, GENKI [28] and FDDB (Face Detection Dataset and Benchmark [19]) and qualitative results are shown in Figs. 3 and 4 respectively. We evaluated our detector on SZSL, a subset of the GENKI database, which contain 3,500 images. Figure 3 shows our detector can handle different face expressions, view angles, illumination conditions. FDDB contains 2,845 images with a total of 5,171 faces. It is extremely challenging dataset, for example, Fig. 4 shows some representative detection results on images with severe occlusion and blurring (see 3rd and 4th images of 1st row), and over 90° rotation (see 3rd image of the 2nd and 3rd rows, and 2nd image of 4th row).

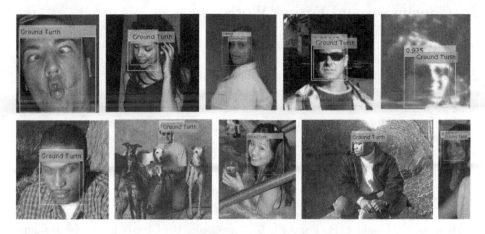

Fig. 3. Representative results of face detection on GENKI-SZSL dataset. Green bounding boxes are the ground truth, and yellow boxes are detection results given by SdA-RF detector. (Color figure online)

Fig. 4. Representative results of face detection on FDDB dataset.

4   Conclusion and Future Work

In this paper, we presents a general cascade-based object detection methods by employing SdA for feature extraction, and RF for object-background classification. It shows that by combining shallow neural networks and discriminative classifier it is possible to carry out binary object detection, and there is perhaps no need to introduce deeper models and complex training procedures. The preliminary results on two public datasets are promising. Quantitative analysis, code optimization with GPU implementation, and application on other detection problems such as pedestrian, are three main aspects for our future work.

References

1. Bengio, Y., Lamblin, P., Popovici, D., Larochelle, H.: Greedy layer-wise training of deep networks. Adv. Neural Inf. Process. Syst. **19**, 153–160 (2007)
2. Bourdev, L., Brandt, J.: Robust object detection via soft cascade. IEEE Comput. Soc. Conf. Comput. Vis. Pattern Recogn. **2**, 236–243 (2005)
3. Breiman, L.: Bagging predictors. Mach. Learn. **24**(2), 123–140 (1996)
4. Breiman, L.: Random forests. Mach. Learn. **45**(1), 5–32 (2001)
5. Chiverton, J., Xie, X., Mirmehdi, M.: Automatic bootstrapping and tracking of object contours. IEEE Trans. Image Process. **21**(3), 1231–1245 (2012)
6. Daubney, B., Xie, X., Deng, J., Parthalin, N.M., Zwiggelaar, R.: Fixing theroot node: efficient tracking and detection of 3d human pose through localsolutions. Image and Vis. Comput. **52**, 73–87 (2016)
7. Deng, J., Xie, X., Daubney, B.: A bag of words approach to subject specific 3d human pose interaction classification with random decision forests. Graph. Models **76**(3), 162–171 (2014)
8. Everingham, M., Eslami, S.M.A., Van Gool, L., Williams, C.K.I., Winn, J., Zisserman, A.: The pascal visual object classes challenge: a retrospective. Int. J. Comput. Vis. **111**(1), 98–136 (2015)
9. Everingham, M., Van Gool, L., Williams, C.K.I., Winn, J., Zisserman, A.: The PASCAL Visual Object Classes (VOC) challenge. Int. J. Comput. Vis. **88**(2), 303–338 (2010)
10. Farfade, S.S., Saberian, M.J., Li, L.J.: Multi-view face detection using deep convolutional neural networks. In: Proceedings of the ACM on International Conference on Multimedia Retrieval, pp. 643–650. ACM (2015)
11. Felzenszwalb, P.F., Girshick, R.B., McAllester, D.: Cascade object detection with deformable part models. In: Proceedings of the IEEE Conference on Computer Vision and Pattern Recognition, pp. 2241–2248 (2010)
12. Felzenszwalb, P.F., Girshick, R.B., McAllester, D., Ramanan, D.: Object detection with discriminatively trained part-based models. IEEE Trans. Pattern Anal. Mach. Intell. **32**(9), 1627–1645 (2010)
13. Girshick, R.: Fast R-CNN. In: Proceedings of the IEEE International Conference on Computer Vision, pp. 1440–1448 (2015)
14. Girshick, R., Donahue, J., Darrell, T., Malik, J.: Rich feature hierarchies for accurate object detection and semantic segmentation. In: Proceedings of the IEEE Conference on Computer Vision and Pattern Recognition, pp. 580–587 (2014)

15. He, K., Zhang, X., Ren, S., Sun, J.: Spatial pyramid pooling in deep convolutional networks for visual recognition. IEEE Trans. Pattern Anal. Mach. Intell. **37**(9), 1904–1916 (2015)
16. Heisele, B., Serre, T., Poggio, T.: A component-based framework for face detection and identification. Int. J. Comput. Vis. **74**(2), 167–181 (2007)
17. Hinton, G.E., Salakhutdinov, R.R.: Reducing the dimensionality of data with neural networks. Science **313**(5786), 504–507 (2006)
18. Hjelmås, E., Low, B.K.: Face detection: a survey. Comput. Vis. Image Underst. **83**(3), 236–274 (2001)
19. Jain, V., Learned-Miller, E.: FDDB: a benchmark for face detection in unconstrained settings. Technical report UM-CS-2010-009, University of Massachusetts, Amherst (2010)
20. Koestinger, M.: Efficient Metric Learning for Real-World Face Recognition. Ph.D. thesis, Graz University of Technology, Faculty of Computer Science (2013)
21. Koestinger, M., Wohlhart, P., Roth, P.M., Bischof, H.: Annotated facial landmarks in the wild: a large-scale, real-world database for facial landmark localization. In: IEEE International Workshop on Benchmarking Facial Image Analysis Technologies (2011)
22. Krizhevsky, A., Sutskever, I., Hinton, G.E.: Imagenet classification with deep convolutional neural networks. In: Advances in Neural Information Processing Systems, pp. 1097–1105 (2012)
23. LeCun, Y., Bengio, Y., Hinton, G.: Deep learning. Nature **521**(7553), 436–444 (2015)
24. Li, H., Lin, Z., Brandt, J., Shen, X., Hua, G.: Efficient boosted exemplar-based face detection. In: Proceedings of the IEEE Conference on Computer Vision and Pattern Recognition, pp. 1843–1850 (2014)
25. Li, H., Lin, Z., Shen, X., Brandt, J., Hua, G.: A convolutional neural network cascade for face detection. In: Proceedings of the IEEE Conference on Computer Vision and Pattern Recognition, pp. 5325–5334 (2015)
26. Liao, S., Jain, A.K., Li, S.Z.: A fast and accurate unconstrained face detector. IEEE Trans. Pattern Anal. Mach. Intell. **38**(2), 211–223 (2016)
27. Liao, S., Zhu, X., Lei, Z., Zhang, L., Li, S.Z.: Learning multi-scale block local binary patterns for face recognition. In: Lee, S.-W., Li, S.Z. (eds.) ICB 2007. LNCS, vol. 4642, pp. 828–837. Springer, Heidelberg (2007). doi:10.1007/978-3-540-74549-5_87
28. MPLab, University of California, S.D.: The MPLab GENKI Database, GENKI-SZSL Subset (2009). http://mplab.ucsd.edu. Accessed 12 May 2016
29. Ouyang, W., Luo, P., Zeng, X., Qiu, S., Tian, Y., Li, H., Yang, S., Wang, Z., Xiong, Y., Qian, C., et al.: Deepid-net: multi-stage and deformable deep convolutional neural networks for object detection. arXiv preprint arXiv:1409.3505 (2014)
30. Ren, S., He, K., Girshick, R., Sun, J.: Faster R-CNN: towards real-time object detection with region proposal networks. In: Advances in Neural Information Processing Systems, pp. 91–99 (2015)
31. Russakovsky, O., Deng, J., Su, H., Krause, J., Satheesh, S., Ma, S., Huang, Z., Karpathy, A., Khosla, A., Bernstein, M., Berg, A.C., Fei-Fei, L.: ImageNet large scale visual recognition challenge. Int. J. Comput. Vis. (IJCV) **115**(3), 211–252 (2015)
32. Sermanet, P., Eigen, D., Zhang, X., Mathieu, M., Fergus, R., LeCun, Y.: Overfeat: integrated recognition, localization and detection using convolutional networks. arXiv preprint arXiv:1312.6229 (2013)

33. Shen, X., Lin, Z., Brandt, J., Wu, Y.: Detecting and aligning faces by image retrieval. In: Proceedings of the IEEE Conference on Computer Vision and Pattern Recognition, pp. 3460–3467 (2013)
34. Szegedy, C., Toshev, A., Erhan, D.: Deep neural networks for object detection. In: Advances in Neural Information Processing Systems, pp. 2553–2561 (2013)
35. Uijlings, J.R., van de Sande, K.E., Gevers, T., Smeulders, A.W.: Selective search for object recognition. Int. J. Comput. Vis. **104**(2), 154–171 (2013)
36. Vincent, P., Larochelle, H., Bengio, Y., Manzagol, P.A.: Extracting and composing robust features with denoising autoencoders. In: Proceedings of International Conference on Machine Learning, pp. 1096–1103. ACM (2008)
37. Viola, P., Jones, M.J.: Robust real-time face detection. Int. J. Comput. Vis. **57**(2), 137–154 (2004)
38. Yan, J., Lei, Z., Wen, L., Li, S.: The fastest deformable part model for object detection. In: Proceedings of the IEEE Conference on Computer Vision and Pattern Recognition, pp. 2497–2504 (2014)
39. Yang, B., Yan, J., Lei, Z., Li, S.Z.: Aggregate channel features for multi-view face detection. In: IEEE International Joint Conference on Biometrics, pp. 1–8 (2014)
40. Yang, M.H., Kriegman, D.J., Ahuja, N.: Detecting faces in images: a survey. IEEE Trans. Pattern Anal. Mach. Intell. **24**(1), 34–58 (2002)
41. Yang, S., Luo, P., Loy, C.C., Tang, X.: From facial parts responses to face detection: a deep learning approach. In: Proceedings of the IEEE International Conference on Computer Vision, pp. 3676–3684 (2015)
42. Zafeiriou, S., Zhang, C., Zhang, Z.: A survey on face detection in the wild: past, present and future. Comput. Vis. Image Underst. **138**, 1–24 (2015)
43. Zhang, C., Zhang, Z.: A survey of recent advances in face detection. Technical report MSR-TR-2010-66, Microsoft Research, June 2010

Multimodal Registration of PET/MR Brain Images Based on Adaptive Mutual Information

Abir Baâzaoui$^{(\boxtimes)}$, Mouna Berrabah, Walid Barhoumi,
and Ezzeddine Zagrouba

Research Team on Intelligent Systems in Imaging and Artificial Vision (SIIVA),
Lim-Tic Laboratory, Institut Supérieur d'Informatique, Université de Tunis
El Manar, 2 Rue Abou Rayhane Bayrouni, 2080 Ariana, Tunisia
a.baazaoui@hotmail.fr, berrabah.mouna@gmail.com,
walid.barhoumi@enicarthage.rnu.tn, ezzeddine.zagrouba@fsm.rnu.tn

Abstract. Multimodal image registration remains a challenging task in medical image analysis, notably for PET/MR images since their combinations provide superior sensitivity and specificity, what improves the diagnosis quality. Mutual information (MI) is the commonly used multimodal image registration measure. Inasmuch as the traditional MI, based on Shannon entropy, does not integrate the spatial information such as edges and corners, an adaptation of MI is proposed in this work. The two main contributions are the incorporation of the spatial information through the curvelet transform and the avoiding of the binning problem using Gaussian probability density function. The objective behind this adaptation is to ignore the sensitivity to intensity permutations or pixel-to-pixel intensity transformations and to simultaneously handle the positive and negative intensity correlations. Realized experiments on PET/MR image datasets demonstrated the effectiveness of the proposed method for PET/MR image registration and showed its superiority over state-of-the-art methods.

Keywords: PET image · MRI · Multimodal registration · Adaptive Mutual Information · Gaussian Probability Density Function · Curvelet transform · Anisotropic Diffusion Filter

1 Introduction

Medical image registration aims to find the optimal transformation or spatial mapping that best aligns the anatomical or functional structures in the input images. It allows to overlay two or more images of the same organ acquired at different times, from distinct viewpoints or from different modalities [1]. In fact, multimodal registration helps to relate the complementary informations derived from different modalities. It allows to improve the diagnosis using these complementarity informations. Much of the research that has been developed for multimodal registration was devoted to register the anatomical brain images to

J. Blanc-Talon et al. (Eds.): ACIVS 2016, LNCS 10016, pp. 361–372, 2016.
DOI: 10.1007/978-3-319-48680-2_32

the functional ones. The anatomical brain images (e.g. computed tomography (CT), magnetic resonance (MR)) show the brain in its total structure, while functional brain images (e.g. positron emission tomography (PET), single photon emission computed tomography (SPECT)) expose the physiological activity of brain. In human brain studies, registration of brain PET image to MRI is a useful clinical application [2]. In the MRI case, a better contrast among soft tissues and functional-imaging capabilities were offered comparatively to CT images. PET images aim to measure vital functions (*e.g.* blood flow and glucose metabolism) to evaluate the effectiveness of a patient's treatment plan and to detect brain disorders such as brain tumors, memory disorders and seizures [3]. Nevertheless, brain PET images are limited by the low spatial resolution. For this reason, the registration that combines PET with MRI has a great interest and represents a challenging research area. Indeed, it plays an important role in many clinical applications, including PET segmentation [3], attenuation correction [4] and biopsy-guidance [5]. For this issue, several methods have been proposed. These methods can be classified into two main categories: feature-based methods and intensity-based methods [1]. The first category considers prominent features extracted from both images, which correspond to geometric primitives (points, lines, surfaces, invariant moments . . .), whereas the second one operates directly on intensities values. Despite that there is an amount of feature-based works [6,8] that aim to improve the robustness of the feature extraction and the accuracy of feature correspondences, and to decrease the frequent need of user interaction, the registration results in this category are still sensitive to feature point detection [8] and matching [7]. Therefore, if some correspondences or detected points are incorrect, the produced transformation function is incorrect and thus the results are totally wrong. In this work, we focus on intensity-based methods, which allow to optimize the similarity measure function of the images being registered without needing neither user intervention nor a segmentation.

Thanks to its first introduction as a similarity measure for multi-modal medical images both by Collignon et al. [9] and by Viola and Wells [10], mutual information (MI) is the most investigated measure for multi-modal medical image registration. Since then, several extensions of MI-based registration methods were proposed in the literature. For example, the maximization of mutual information (MMI) can be based on histogram, instead of intensity values, in order to evaluate accurately the correspondence between images [11,12]. Indeed, as image intensities are linearly rescaled, the joint intensity histogram (JIH) of the overlap regions of images is then used to estimate the joint probability density of corresponding voxel intensities in the moving and fixed images. Then, the MMI method is performed by estimating the joint probability density. To evaluate the MMI registration method, CT/MR as well as PET/MR images were registered within the framework of the retrospective registration evaluation project [13]. Although the result is satisfactory, it is not conclusive enough that this method is suitable for all types of medical images since the number of registration experiments is too small. In addition, the influence of histogram bin size is not taken into account. Differently, MI was extended to the spatial information by combining intensity and gradient information [14]. Therefore, the MI computation is performed using gradient values and intensity values. The quantitative performance of this method proved its superiority over the mutual information and the normalized mutual information (NMI). Recently, the impact of bin size selection on the registration result was demonstrated when constructing the histogram for probability estimation [15]. However, intensity-based histogram is unable to fully accommodate the spatial information. This makes MI-based registration methods under many criticisms in the last years. Furthermore, histogram-based density estimation methods suffer from binning problem, since there is no gold standard method to estimate the optimal number of bins in both marginal and joint histograms.

In this paper, an adaptive MI based on Gaussian probability density function (GPDF) curvelet transform is proposed. The proposed method makes use conjointly of curvelet transform and Gaussian probability density function. On the one hand, curvelet transform is able to detect accurately image edge information, and therefore it allows to integrate spatial information. Conditional entropy between the local neighboring curvelet coefficients of the two images was included to maximize the mutual information. This allows to overcome the main limit of the traditional MI, based on Shannon entropy, which does not investigate the spatial information. On the other hand, GPDF permits to avoid binning problem and it performs an accurate registration thanks to the Gaussian nature of each type of anatomical structure. Indeed, the proposed method is mainly composed of three modules in order to register the PET brain image, which is the moving image, with respect to the fixed MR brain image. Because of the low resolution and the signal-dependent noise distribution in PET images, PET denoising is firstly performed. The second module, which is based on GPDF and curvelet transform, allows to model the extracted features from the two images. The last module deals with the registration of PET/MRI based on adaptive mutual information (AMI).

The remaining of this paper is structured as follows. Section 2 describes the proposed method. Section 3 is devoted for the presentation of some experimental results to demonstrate the effectiveness of the proposed method. Finally, a conclusion and some future research directions are given in the last section.

2   Proposed Method

The proposed method for PET/MR brain image registration is composed of three modules: PET denoising, feature extraction and registration of the moving image according to the fixed one. Since the PET image is of high amount of noise, PET denoising has become a challenging and active step. Then, we extract the features using curvelet transform and we model them through GPDF. Lastly, the PET/MR image registration is carried out using the adaptive mutual information (AMI).

2.1 PET Denoising

PET images are limited by the low resolution and the high amount of noise resulting from the low number of detected photons, the time of acquisition and the electronic of scanners [3]. To circumvent these problems, PET denoising is performed in this work using anisotropic diffusion filtering (ADF) [16]. In addition to its edge preservation, the choice of this filter is justified by the comparative study presented in [17]. The qualitative and quantitative performances of nonlinear Anisotropic Diffusion (AD), Non-Local Means (NLM) and Linear Gaussian (LG) filters prove that AD and NLM filters outperformed LG filters for PET images. But, the NLM filters require a prior knowledge from CT images to determine similarities between neighboring PET voxels. Thus, AD filter is the most suitable to denoise PET images without requiring any prior knowledge. Indeed, the nonlinear AD filter (1) is based on a decreasing function $g()$ that varies according to the magnitude of the gradient vector $|\nabla I|$.

$$\frac{\partial I}{\partial t} = div(c(x,y,t)\nabla I) = g(\|\nabla I(x,y,t)\|) \triangle I + \nabla c \cdot \nabla I, \tag{1}$$

where, $\triangle$ denotes the Laplacian operator, $div()$ is the divergence operator, and $c(x,y,t)$ is the conduction coefficient. This coefficient allows to control the rate of diffusion and to preserve edges in the image I at a scale (or time) t. The application of AD filter on PET images allows to maximize the homogeneity of the images, to minimize the diffusion at the edges and to remove the blur introduced by the linear diffusion (Fig. 1).

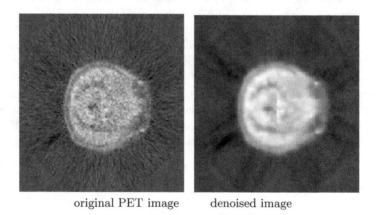

original PET image   denoised image

Fig. 1. PET image denoising using anisotropic diffusion filtering.

2.2 GPDF Curvelet-Based Feature Extraction

The feature extraction based on GPDF curvelet for the two input images consists on obtaining features from the moving and fixed images in terms of curvelet coefficients followed by modeling the probabilistic distribution of these coefficients.

We used a curvelet transform that decomposes the studied image into several subbands using a multiscale directional transform to generate the curvelet coefficients. In fact, the curvelet coefficients are obtained using fast discrete curvelet transform, which is implemented via wrapping with 4 subband decomposition levels and 16 angles. Wrapping-based fast curvelet transform is the most popular and widely studied implementation since it proved a high performance in capturing image edge information [18,19], which is important for PET/MR image registration. The obtained curvelet and the input image, which are transformed into Fourier domain, are convolved. The obtaining of curvelet coefficients is performed by applying inverse Fourier transform on the convolution product. Once the curvelet coefficients are defined, a GPDF is used to model the distribution of curvelet subband coefficients. The choice of GPDF is justified by many state-of-the-art medical registration methods [20–22]. In fact, contrary to the most popular nonparametric density-estimation technique, which is the Parzen-window density estimation [23,24], GPDF is insensitive to the selection of the σ parameter of the kernel and the kernel function itself. Besides, GPDF is the commonly used probability model for curvelet local neighboring coefficients [22] for images. Therefore, to estimate the probability of observing a given pair of curvelet coefficients at the corresponding point in the two images, we used the bivariate Gaussian PDF given by:

$$p_\Gamma(\Gamma) = \frac{1}{2\pi\sqrt{|\Sigma_2|}} e^{(-\frac{1}{2}(\Gamma-\mu)^T \Sigma_2^{-1}(\Gamma-\mu))} \tag{2}$$

where, $\Gamma = (\Gamma_f, \Gamma_m)$ are random variables of fixed and moving images, respectively, μ is the mean vector and $|\ |$ is the determinant of the covariance matrix Σ_2 (3).

$$\Sigma_2 = \begin{bmatrix} \sigma_f^2 & \rho_{fm}\sigma_f\sigma_m \\ \rho_{fm}\sigma_f\sigma_m & \sigma_m^2 \end{bmatrix} \tag{3}$$

where, σ_f σ_m are the standard deviations of the random variables and ρ_{fm} is the correlation coefficient between them.

Given a spatial index $(i,j)(1 \le i \le X, 1 \le j \le Y)$, where $X \times Y$ is the size of image, a local neighborhood $N(i, j)$ and the curvelet coefficient $cc(k,l)$, the mean, the variance and the covariance matrix can be estimated using the maximum likelihood method [25].

2.3 AMI-Based Registration

In order to register the PET moving image I_m with respect to the fixed MR image I_f, adaptive mutual information, based on conditional entropy $H(I_m|I_f)$ between the local neighboring curvelet coefficients of the two images, is used in this work to confine the optimization in the vicinity of an alignment. In fact, the relation between the mutual information MI (4) of I_m and I_f and the theoretic notion of entropy is expressed as follows:

$$MI(I_m, I_f) = H(I_m) + H(I_f) - H(I_m, I_f) = H(I_m) - H(I_m|I_f) \tag{4}$$

where, $H(I_m)$ and $H(I_f)$ (5) are the marginal entropies of I_m and I_f, respectively and $H(I_m, I_f)$ is their joint entropy.

$$H(\Gamma_{m/f}) = \frac{1}{2}[ln(2\pi\sigma^2_{m/f}) + 1]\tag{5}$$

Using the bivariate Gaussian probability density function, $H(\Gamma_m, \Gamma_f)$ (6) of the random variables Γ_m and Γ_f and the marginal entropies are defined by:

$$H(\Gamma_m, \Gamma_f) = \frac{1}{2}ln((2\pi e)^2|\Sigma_2|)\tag{6}$$

where, $\Gamma_{m/f}$ can be either Γ_m or Γ_f and $\sigma_{m/f}$ can be either σ_m or σ_f of Γ_m and Γ_f, respectively.

Then, in order to geometrically align the moving image with the fixed one using a transformation T_{β^*}, the mutual information is maximal (7) for this transformation. To do this, parameters, including mean $\mu_{m/f}$, variance $\sigma^2_{m/f}$, and covariance σ_{mf}, of the curvelet coefficients at the approximate subband of the fixed and moving images are determined for each index (i,j) using a local neighborhood $N(i,j)$ of size 7×7. The choice of the neighborhood size is justified by the quality of results, comparatively to other sizes, including 5×5 and 9×9.

$$\beta^* = \mathrm{argmax}_\beta \left(\frac{1}{2}([ln(2\pi\sigma^2_m) + 1] + [ln(2\pi\sigma^2_f) + 1] - [ln((2\pi e)^2|\Sigma_2|)]) \right)\tag{7}$$

3   Experimental Results

To evaluate the performance of the proposed PET/MR image registration method, we used two real clinical datasets of PET/MR brain images. The first one is obtained from the Centre for Addiction and Mental Health (CAMH) in Canada. The second one is the publicly available dataset from the Retrospective Image Registration Evaluation (RIRE) project [13]. The CAMH dataset consists on eight pair of PET and MR images of brain. The fixed image is the MR image of the subject, which has voxel dimensions in x, y, and z axes of 0.86, 0.86, and 3.00 mm, respectively. Two different modes, namely spin-echo sequence T1 and proton density-weighted images (PD), are captured by a General Electric Medical System Signa 1.5-T scanner. The moving image is the PET image of the same subject, which is obtained on a PET camera system Scanditronix GE 2048-15B with x, y, and z voxel dimensions of 2, 2, and 6.5 mm, respectively. In the RIRE dataset, the modalities MR and PET are utilized, and therefore it provides seven testing PET/MR images (i.e. patient 001, patient 002, patient 005, patient 006, patient 007, patient 008 and patient 009). The MR voxel size is $1.25 \times 1.25 \times 4\,\mathrm{mm}^3$, whilst it is $2.59 \times 2.59 \times 8\,\mathrm{mm}^3$ for PET images.

To quantify the accuracy of the proposed method, three commonly used performance metrics, including normalized cross-correlation coefficient (NCCC) (8),

NMI (9) and percent relative root mean square error (PRRMSE) (10), are used. PRRMSE measures the distortions between registered and fixed images. These distortions remain since the pixel intensities of these images are dissimilar even though a perfect registration. High accuracy of the registration entails a low value of PRRMSE. Contrary, higher values of NCCC and NMI, which measure the closeness of the fixed and registered images, show that the overlaying process has a higher accuracy.

$$NCCC = \frac{\sum_{i=1}^{X} \sum_{j=1}^{Y} (I_f(i,j) - \bar{I}_f)(I_r(i,j) - \bar{I}_r)}{\sqrt{\sum_{i=1}^{X} \sum_{j=1}^{Y} (I_f(i,j) - \bar{I}_f)^2 (I_r(i,j) - \bar{I}_r)^2}} \tag{8}$$

$$NMI = \frac{2[H(I_f) + H(I_r)]}{H(I_f) + H(I_r) + H(I_f|I_r) + H(I_r|I_f)} \tag{9}$$

$$PRRMSE = \sqrt{\frac{\sum_{i=1}^{X} \sum_{j=1}^{Y} (I_f(i,j) - I_r(i,j))^2}{XY \sum_{i=1}^{X} \sum_{j=1}^{Y} (I_f(i,j))}} \tag{10}$$

where, $\bar{I}_f(i,j)$ and $\bar{I}_r(i,j)$ are the mean values of pixel intensities, on a neighborhood of (i,j), of the fixed image and the registered one, respectively.

Figure 2 shows the result of the proposed method using the PD mode of the reference image, whereas the T1 mode of the reference image is shown in the next one (Fig. 3). It is clear that the PET image and the MR image are different in size and they present a translation distortion. In fact, in the first example, the first image shows the fixed T1 MR image, whereas the second one shows the moving

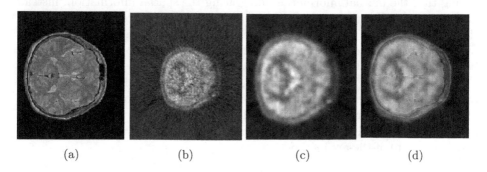

(a)   (b)   (c)   (d)

Fig. 2. Sample of PET/MRI registration results: (a) PD MR image, (b) PET image, (c) registred PET image, (d) superposed images.

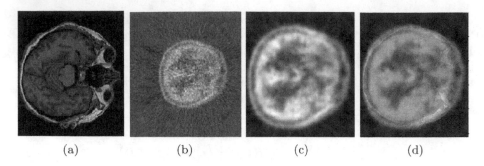

(a)   (b)   (c)   (d)

Fig. 3. Sample of PET/MRI registration results: (a) T1 MR image, (b) PET image, (c) registred PET image, (d) superposed images.

PET image that is distorted by a translation in x-axis ($t_x = -65$), a translation in y-axis ($t_y = -40$) as well as a scaling in x-axis ($s_x = 1.16$) and a scaling in y-axis ($s_y = 1.3$). The registered image, using the proposed method, is obtained from the translated and zoomed version of the moving image, whilst the last one in the two examples represents the superposition of the output image with respect to the fixed one. According to the fixed PD MR image, the PET image is distorted by $t_x = -50$, $t_y = -25$, $s_x = 2.5$ and $s_y = 2$. The visual assessments of the outputs show that the proposed adaptive mutual information method provides reliable registration results over the two PET/MR datasets. Besides, using the above two mentioned metrics, the proposed method achieves a good accuracy and outperforms two other relevant methods [22,26] using the CAMH dataset and the same parameters (Table 1). In fact, the herein reached outcomes are the highest values in all images according to the NCCC and NMI. The second best results are provided by traditional mutual information [26] except for the first image. The worst registration values are obtained by the entropy-based registration [22], which could be explained by the bit dependency between PET and MR images. Hence, entropy-based registration is convenient for monomodal images but less efficient for multimodal ones. Depending on this, it is worth noting that the mutual information integrating the spatial information, instead of traditional MI, is the most suitable for multimodal registration. Accordingly, the adaptive mutual information achieves the best results on the RIRE dataset (Table 2) as compared to the two other state-of-the-art methods either for mean, best and worst NCCC and NMI metric values.

Furthermore, the PRRMSE curves and bar graph, which measure the distortions between registered and fixed images, show that the proposed method "PM" (the blue color in the curve (Fig. 4) and the brown color with yellow edge in the bar graph (Fig. 5) achieves the low values of PRRMSE contrary to the two other state-of-the-art methods.

Table 1. Quantitative assessment of the proposed method (PM) against the presented methods in [22, 26].

Images	NCCC			NMI		
	[22]	[26]	PM	[22]	[26]	PM
1	0.2530	0.2199	**0.2548**	0.0509	0.0513	**0.0635**
2	0.1984	0.2445	**0.2817**	0.0558	0.0998	**0.1229**
3	0.1606	0.1946	**0.2364**	0.0070	0.0269	**0.0358**
4	0.1952	0.2236	**0.2676**	0.0657	0.0657	**0.0043**
5	0.1787	0.2060	**0.2669**	0.0365	0.0453	**0.0755**
6	0.1880	0.2374	**0.2795**	0.0415	0.0764	**0.1006**
7	0.1869	0.2419	**0.2795**	0.0449	0.0732	**0.0983**
8	0.1787	0.2155	**0.2551**	0.0487	0.0689	**0.0908**

Table 2. Summary of the results on RIRE dataset using PM against the presented methods in [22, 26].

Methods	NCCC			NMI		
	Mean	Best	Worst	Mean	Best	Worst
[22]	0.207	0.276	0.157	0.027	0.07	0.008
[26]	0.297	0.321	0.289	0.088	0.111	0.078
PM	0.333	0.361	0.315	0.103	0.123	0.091

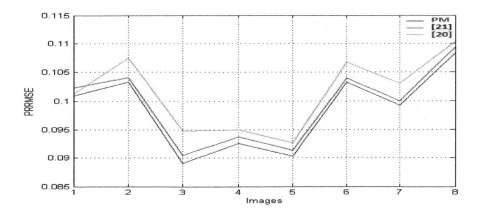

Fig. 4. PRRMSE curves (Color figure online).

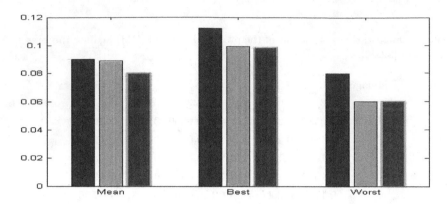

Fig. 5. Mean, best and worst PRRMSE metric values on the RIRE dataset (Color figure online).

4 Conclusion

As an intensity based similarity measure for PET/MR image registration, mutual information is adapted in this work using conditional entropy between the local neighboring curvelet coefficients. The goal is to improve the accuracy of the alignment process and to decrease the computational time since it gives a better result with a few similarity metrics, comparatively to other similarity measures [26]. In fact, the AMI was applied after modeling the extracted curvelet coefficients through a bivariate Gaussian PDF that well fits the data. The proposed method was evaluated for brain images on a dataset of PET/MRI pairs. The qualitative and quantitative assessments show that the proposed AMI-based registration is effective and more suitable for application in clinical practice. As future work, we will investigate the potential results of the proposed method on another type of images to confirm its suitability for all type of medical images and clinical scenarios as well as for synthetic data. Furthermore, we are trying to adopt the proposed method to be applied on non-rigid organs like the cardiac PET/MR images.

Acknowledgement. The authors would like to thank Dr. Rostom Mabrouk, Centre for Addiction and Mental Health (CAMH), University of Toronto, Toronto, Canada; who generously allowed us to use their set of PET/MRI benchmark test for our experimental study. The authors would like to thank also Dr. Md. Mushfiqul Alam, School of Electrical and Computer Engineering, Oklahoma State, Stillwater, USA; for providing us the permission to use their released comparison results.

References

1. Ayatollahi, F., Baradaran, S., Ayatollahi, A.: A new hybrid particle swarm optimization for multimodal brain image registration. J. Biomed. Sci. Eng. **5**, 153–161 (2012)

2. Schifter, T., Turkington, T.G., Berlangieri, S.U., et al.: Normal brain F-18 FDG-PET and MRI anatomy. Clin. Nucl. Med. **18**, 578–582 (1993)
3. Baâzaoui, A., Barhoumi, W., Zagrouba, E., Mabrouk, R.: A survey of PET image segmentation: applications in oncology, cardiology and neurology. Curr. Med. Imaging Rev. **12**, 13–27 (2016)
4. Hofmann, M., Steinke, F., Scheel, V., et al.: MRI-based attenuation correction for PET/MRI: a novel approach combining pattern recognition and atlas registration. J. Nucl. Med. **49**, 1875–1883 (2008)
5. Zettinig, O., Shah, A., Hennersperger, C., et al.: Multimodal image-guided prostate fusion biopsy based on automatic deformable registration. Int. J. Comput. Assist. Radiol. Surg. **10**, 1997–2007 (2015)
6. Xia, R., Zhao, J., Liu, Y.: A robust feature-based registration method of multimodal image using phase congruency and coherent point drift. In: SPIE 8919. MIPPR 2013: Pattern Recognition and Computer Vision, pp. 1–8. SPIE Press, China (2013)
7. Gholipour, A., Kehtarnavaz, A., Briggs, R., Devous, M., Gopinath, K.: Brain functional localization: a survey of image registration techniques. IEEE Trans. Med. Imaging **26**, 427–451 (2007)
8. Leng, C., Xiao, J., Li, M., Zhang, H.: Robust adaptive principal component analysis based on intergraph matrix for medical image registration. Comput. Intell. Neurosci. **2015**, 1–8 (2015)
9. Collignon, A., Maes, F., Delaere, D., Vandermeulen, D., Suetens, P., Marchal, G.: Automated multi-modality image registration based on information theory. In: Bizais, Y., Barillot, C., Di Paola, R. (eds.) Information Processing in Medical Imaging, pp. 263–274. Kluwer Academic Publishers, Dordrecht (1995)
10. Viola, P., Wells III, W.M.: Alignment by maximization of mutual information. Int. J. Comput. Vis. **24**(2), 137–154 (1997)
11. Maes, F., Collignon, A., Vandermeulen, D., Marchal, G., Suetens, P.: Multimodality image registration by maximization of mutual information. IEEE Trans. Med. Imaging **16**, 187–198 (1997)
12. Maes, F., Loeckx, D., Vandermeulen, D., Suetens, P.: Image registration using mutual information. In: Paragios, N., Duncan, J., Ayache, N. (eds.) Handbook of Biomedical Imaging, pp. 295–308. Springer, New York (2015)
13. West, J., Fitzpatrick, J.M., Wang, M.Y., et al.: Comparison and evaluation of retrospective intermodality brain image registration techniques. J. Comput. Assist. Tomogr. **21**, 554–566 (1997)
14. Pluim, J.P.W., Antoine Maintz, J.B., Viergever, M.A.: Image registration by maximization of combined mutual information and gradient information. IEEE Trans. Med. Imaging **19**, 1–6 (2000)
15. Legg, P., Rosin, P.: Improving accuracy and efficiency of mutual information for multi-modal retinal image registration using adaptive probability density estimation. Comput. Med. Imaging Graph. **37**, 597–606 (2013)
16. Perona, P., Malik, J.: Scale-space and edge detection using anisotropic diffusion. IEEE Trans. Pattern Anal. Mach. Intell. **12**, 629–639 (1990)
17. Xia, T., Qi, W., Niu, X., Asma, E., Winkler, M., Wang, W.: Quantitative comparison of anisotropic diffusion, non-local means and Gaussian post-filtering effects on FDG-PET lesions. J. Nucl. Med. **56**, 1797 (2015)
18. Candès, E., Demanet, L., Donoho, D., Ying, L.: Fast discrete curvelet transforms. Multiscale Model. Simul. **5**, 861–899 (2006)
19. Dhahbi, S., Barhoumi, W., Zagrouba, E.: Breast cancer diagnosis in digitized mammograms using curvelet moments. Comput. Biol. Med. **64**, 79–90 (2015)

20. Leventon, M.E., Grimson, W.E.L.: Multi-modal volume registration using joint intensity distributions. In: Wells, W.M., Colchester, A., Delp, S. (eds.) MICCAI 1998. LNCS, vol. 1496, pp. 1057–1066. Springer, Heidelberg (1998). doi:10.1007/BFb0056295
21. Rajwade, A., Banerjee, A., Rangarajan, A.: A new method of probability density estimation with application to mutual information based image registration. In: Proceedings of the IEEE Computer Society Conference Computer Vision Pattern Recognition, New York (2006)
22. Alam, M.M., Howlader, T., Rahman, S.M.M.: Entropy-based image registration method using the curvelet transform. Sig. Image Video **8**, 491–505 (2014)
23. Woo, J., Stone, M., Prince, J.L.: Multimodal registration via mutual information incorporating geometric and spatial context. IEEE Trans. Image Process. **24**, 757–769 (2015)
24. Li, B., Yang, G., Coatrieux, J.L., Li, B., Shu, H.: 3D nonrigid medical image registration using a new information theoretic measure. Phys. Med. Biol. **60**, 8767–8790 (2015)
25. Kline, R.B.: Principles and Practice of Structural Equation Modeling. The Guilford press, New York (2016)
26. Zhaoying, L., Fugen, Z., Xiangzhi, B., Hui, W., Dongjie, T.: Multimodal image registration by mutual information based on optimal region selection. In: Proceedings of the IEEE International Conference on Information Networking and Automation, pp. 249–253. Kunming (2010)

Aerial Detection in Maritime Scenarios Using Convolutional Neural Networks

Gonçalo Cruz[1]([⊠]) and Alexandre Bernardino[2]

[1] Portuguese Air Force, Sintra, Portugal
gccruz@academiafa.edu.pt
[2] Computer and Robot Vision Laboratory, Instituto de Sistemas e Robótica,
Instituto Superior Técnico, Lisboa, Portugal
alexandre.bernardino@tecnico.ulisboa.pt

Abstract. This paper presents a method to detect boats in a maritime surveillance scenario using a small aircraft. This method relies on Convolutional Neural Networks (CNNs) to perform robust detections even in the presence of distractors like wave crests and sun glare. The CNNs are pre-trained on large scale public datasets and then fine-tuned with domain specific images acquired in the maritime surveillance scenario. We study two variations of the method, with one being faster and the other one being more robust. The network's training procedure is described and the detection performance is evaluated in two different video sequences from UAV flights over the Atlantic ocean. The results are presented as precision-recall curves and computation time and are compared. We show experimentally that, as in many other domains of application, CNNs outperforms non-deep learning methods also in maritime surveillance scenarios.

Keywords: Convolutional neural network · Maritime detection · UAV · Aerial imagery

1 Introduction

In the last years, there has been a huge development on the use of Unmanned Aerial Vehicles (UAVs) both for recreational and business purposes. Although the gathering of information using these sensors is quite successful, transforming that data into information is more difficult. Often, a person is needed to inspect the data and, for instance, mark objects of interest in a surveillance mission. Although the flight duration of a UAV varies, an overwhelming amount of data can be gathered, making its analysis very tiresome.

Our work focuses on maritime surveillance scenarios, more specifically on the detection of vessels using an optical color sensor on-board a small UAV. This combination allows us to have a relatively simple and low cost system, especially when compared to systems that use radar technology. A typical surveillance flight is characterized by large intervals of time where nothing of interest is visible, interrupted by the appearance of objects of interest difficult to spot.

© Springer International Publishing AG 2016
J. Blanc-Talon et al. (Eds.): ACIVS 2016, LNCS 10016, pp. 373–384, 2016.
DOI: 10.1007/978-3-319-48680-2_33

To make it more challenging, a surveillance scenario may need an immediate action to be taken (send rescue assets, follow a target of interest, etc.) and therefore the monitoring must be done in near real-time.

Some approaches have been proposed to automatically process the data. Most of these approaches are based on a set of handcrafted features that are created by an expert and need to be adjusted if the scenario of application changes. Our work presents the application of convolutional neural networks to learn these features and reliably detect vessels in a maritime surveillance scenario. Our detection technique will be deployed aboard the UAV to avoid compression and transmission artifacts, though, this restrains the amount of computing power available. To address these issues, our work focuses on presenting a method capable of detecting vessels with a high degree of certainty, despite the variability of the vessel's appearance and the presence of sun glare or wave crests. We evaluate the performance of our method and compare it with a state-of-the-art approach based on handcrafted blob analysis rules, currently employed in our missions. We also measure the computation time and assess its ability to run on an embedded platform.

This paper is organized as follows. Section 2 presents a brief overview of related work about convolutional neural networks and detection on UAV imagery. In Sect. 3, we detail the process used to perform the detection. Section 4 provides more detail about the networks that and datasets used, the training and the deployment stages. Section 5 evaluates the performance of the system and finally Sect. 6 provides some concluding remarks.

2   Related Work

2.1   General Object Detection

Object detection is one of the most important tasks in computer vision but it is still challenging in many scenarios [13]. One of these scenarios is the analysis of aerial imagery where factors like the amount of clutter, the variability of the appearance of the objects in the image and the variable lighting conditions, still limit the accuracy of detection. Traditionally, the detection has been performed by engineering a set of features (texture, intensity, *etc.*) that are relevant, extract these features from the images and feed them to a classifier. Therefore, the performance was quite dependent on the quality of the features. Often, the process of choosing the adequate features is laborious, specially because the designer has to guarantee that these features provide a good separability between different classes.

In the last years, a different path has been tracked with the use of convolutional neural networks (CNN). Instead of using hand-crafted features, these networks learn which features to use. In particular, CNNs have established the top results in several competitions, like ILSVRC [13]. This technique not only has outperformed most algorithms in generic classification and detection benchmarks but also in problems like character recognition [7] and pedestrian detection [14].

2.2   Detection on Aerial Images

Following the developments on other fields of Computer Vision, there have been several approaches to detection using aerial images. One interesting approach uses a cascaded classifier to detect people on foot and land vehicles [3]. In [11], people detection on land is also accomplished but using Histograms of Oriented Gradients, though, it depends on the small appearance variability of human body. In a maritime scenario, the objects can vary from a castaway or small dinghies to large cargo ships. Approaches like [12] depend on the movement of the targets to perform detection but this is not very well suited for the maritime environment as some targets may be still and undesired events like wave crests and sun glare may have a significant movement. It is therefore difficult to characterize possible targets with respect to size, shape, colors or textures.

Even with the aforementioned peculiarities, several specialized maritime detectors have been proposed. In [1], a set of engineered features is created to distinguish nautical objects from the ocean. However, the authors use several other layers to discard clutter. Similar approach is followed in [9] to detect marine mammals, with the authors using color features on a first stage and shape features on a second stage. Another interesting application is the detection of castaways, which is presented in Westall *et al.* [19]. In this case the author use a Hidden Markov Model to detect the head of castaways, which is typically has a size of 3 pixels.

Like in many other applications, the first kind of neural networks used in the analysis of aerial imagery were shallow neural networks.

Shirvaikar and Trivedi, as early as 1995, have proposed a system for the detection in aerial images that used the image as input and convolved the image with the input layer of the network [15]. This operation produced a 2D map that indicated the possibility of having a given object of interest in the image. More recently, Maire *et al.* [8] have proposed convolutional neural networks for the detection of marine mammals in aerial images. The authors also provide a meta-algorithm to refine the dataset used for the training of the network.

In our work, we test two approaches. The first is a sliding window approach based on [8], where we perform an exhaustive search over the entire image. The other approach creates several candidate regions that are supplied to the classifier, based on [17].

We compare the results against [10], which is the specialized detector that is in use on-board our UAVs and verify if any of the two techniques may be used to process video on-board, in near real time.

3   Detection System

The detection system that we propose is composed of two main parts. The first part is responsible for generating patches of images to classify. For this task we present and test the use of a sliding window approach and a method to propose salient candidate regions. The second part consists of a convolutional neural network that classifies each of the aforementioned image patches. In the next two subsections, we detail the two different approaches to generate image patches and point their advantages and disadvantages.

3.1 Sliding Window

The first solution uses a sliding window approach to a given image captured by the camera, in a similar fashion to what was already described in other works as [18].

With a sliding window technique, overlapping image patches are extracted and fed to a classifier with the trained model, respectively represented in Fig. 1(a) and (b). Usually overlapping sliding windows are used and thus there is a significant possibility that a given object of interest is present on several patches. When a situation like Fig. 1(c) occurs, different patches may be correctly classified as belonging to the class *boat*, though there is only one boat on the image. Consequently, we merge the bounding boxes (BBs) that are near each other, into a single BB, obtaining a result similar to Fig. 1(d).

This approach is computationally expensive, as many regions are extracted and need to be classified. For instance, in our full resolution images (1920 × 1080 pixels), we use windows of 256 by 256 pixels with a overlap of 50 %, thus we get approximately 120 images patches to classify. With the classification of that many sub parts of the image, a lot of computational power is wasted, specially if we consider that many of these regions contain only ocean without any particular interest. This waste of resources could be even worse, if the search was done at several scales. In our procedure, we decided to search at only one scale. We allowed this simplification as the UAV has information of its position and parameters of the camera, therefore we may expect a typical size of the boat in the image.

3.2 Salient Candidate Regions

As we stated on the previous subsection, the sliding window approach performs an exhaustive search on captured image but wastes computational resources on

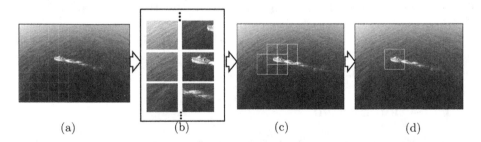

(a)　　　　　　(b)　　　　　　(c)　　　　　　(d)

Fig. 1. Detection pipeline using sliding window: (a) captured image with several versions of the sliding window overlayed, (b) Image patches that were extracted and fed to the classifier, (c) regions that are classified as containing a boat and (d) BB obtained by merging several positively classified regions.

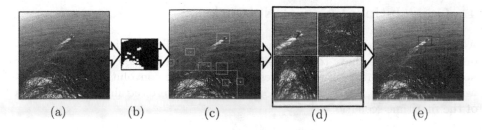

(a)   (b)   (c)   (d)   (e)

Fig. 2. Detection pipeline using candidate regions: (a) captured image, (b) binary image where white pixels correspond to salient regions, (c) candidate regions marked by green BBs, (d) image patches that are fed to the neural networks and (e) BB of the region that was validated by the neural network. (Color figure online)

areas that are easy to classify. We followed a strategy inspired in what is proposed in [17]. Instead of performing an exhaustive search over the complete image, we obtain candidate regions that are then classified as belonging to the class *boat* or *not boat*. We select regions that are salient, *i.e.* patches of the image that stand out from the background, and feed these patches to the neural network, which validates or discards these patches. This process is depicted in Fig. 2.

To create these candidate regions we first transform the image into the HSV colorspace and then threshold pixels with a hue between 105 and 240, considering that hue is represented by 8 bits. This threshold operation, which is similar to the first step of the method used on-board our UAVs [10], tries to isolate pixels that do not contain any shade of blue. After obtaining a binary image (represented in Fig. 2(b)), we perform a simple dilation and compute the connected components regions, which become the candidate regions (delimited in Fig. 2(c) by green BBs). Given that we want this step to be fast and we only want to identify regions of the image (not details), we used a reduced size version of the image. More specifically, we resize the image before the transformation to HSV colorspace and map the regions back to the original image size before extracting image patches.

Like in the sliding window approach, if several BBs are classified belonging to the class *boat*, the BBs are merged into one. Even though the computational complexity is a significant motivation behind the introduction of the candidate regions, it is not the only one. The other goal that we would like to achieve is to tailor the dimension of the BB to the object to detect. With the candidate regions approach, we allow each BB to have a variable size and aspect ratio, although some attention is needed as the input size of the convolutional neural network is fixed. To circumvent this limitation, we have followed three different paths. In case the candidate region is exactly the size of the input, we crop the image in that area. If the image region to classify is bigger than input of the network (256 by 256 pixels), then we shrink the image. If the image is smaller than 256×256, we use the area around the candidate region until the necessary dimension is attained.

4   Convolutional Neural Networks

After the extraction of image patches (either with sliding window or with candidate regions), these have to be classified as belonging to the class of interest or not. To perform this task we have tested two popular convolutional neural network architectures, AlexNet and GoogLeNet, which were retrained with samples of the maritime scenario.

4.1   Dataset Selection and Training

The training of the convolutional neural network was done using CAFFE [5] framework, using 36698 image patches with a resolution of 256 by 256 pixels. These were extracted from 6 video sequences acquired by a UAV on a maritime surveillance scenario, at slightly different altitudes[1]. This set contained 30209 negative examples and 6489 examples of boats and were divided into a training and validation subset according to a 75 and 25 % ratio. The validation subset was used to avoid overfitting the network to the training data.

One out every five labelled objects contained in the video sequences was included in the positive sample set. In order to improve robustness to rotation, the positive set was augmented by including rotated versions (90°, 180° and 270°) of the original images. The process of selection of negative samples started with the computation of the image signature [4] for a given video frame, that typically highlights areas of the image that stand out from the background, as represented in Fig. 3(a). Subsequently, areas with high saliency are assigned a higher probability of being chosen in a random selection process that picks samples for the training and validation set, as visible in Fig. 3(b).

After obtaining the dataset, we have used CAFFE [5] to train the different networks. In particular, we have used a GoogLeNet network [16] and an AlexNet network [6] previously trained on the ImageNet Large Scale Visual Recognition

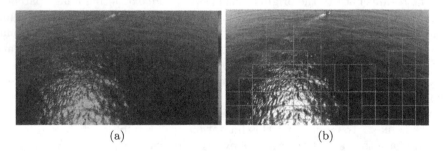

(a)   (b)

Fig. 3. Extraction of examples for the training and validation set: (a) Image Signature Map for a given image with areas of higher saliency represented in blue and purple; (b) patches of negative examples selected for the dataset represented with a green BB and the positive example represented with a red BB. (Color figure online)

---

[1] The scale variability of the observed ships due to altitude variations is rather small.

Challenge (ILSVRC) 2012[2], which contains approximately 1.2 million images belonging to 1000 classes. Additionally, we only considered two possible classes (*boat* and *not boat*) and we have used a lower learning rate in this case, as we would like the network to change slowly, to take advantage of the large scale training.

4.2 Deployment of the Network

After obtaining a trained network, the detection of a boat in an image was achieved by assigning a probability to each candidate region. This probability was computed by the last layer of the networks (a softmax layer), that converts networks scores into probabilities of image to belong to a given class. In our case, the straightforward approach would be to consider a detection if the probability of the class *boat* was bigger than 50 %. Because we wanted to control the trade-off between the false positives and missed detections, we made the decision dependent on a threshold that can be defined by an operator. If a given patch was considered to contain a boat, a BB was created and the probability computed by the network for that image patch was associated to this BB, as shown in Fig. 4(a) and (b). In Fig. 2, from all the candidate regions represented in Fig. 2(c) and (d), only one is considered as belonging to the class *boat*. The validated area is presented in Fig. 2(e).

The first results for this detection scheme were performed on a common desktop equipped with a GPU card, to improve the training and classification speed of the network. On a second step, the implementation of the detection algorithm was done on a Jetson TK1 board, which is specially suited for embedded applications due to small power consumption. In our case this is a serious requirement as the power on-board is very restricted.

5 Evaluation

To evaluate the performance of the proposed detection scheme, we have used two video sequences that were left out during the training process. These are representative of two different flight conditions, one where the aircraft is lower (50 m above sea) and closer to the object of interest and other where the aircraft is higher (300 m) and farther.

5.1 Setup Description

The used camera has a 1/2.3 in. RGB sensor and a wide angle lens, and was mounted on a fixed wing UAV, moving at approximately 15 m/s. The camera was pointing 90° to the left-hand side of the aircraft and approximately 45° downwards with respect to the horizontal plane. The first sequence (sequence A)

---

[2] The authors of each architecture provide the weights, resulting from training on the mentioned dataset, at https://github.com/BVLC/caffe/tree/master/models/.

(a)   (b)

Fig. 4. Typical video frame for (a) sequence A and (b) for sequence (b). Both images contain a correct detection with the respective probability associated to the BB.

contains 1400 frames with a resolution of 1920 × 1080 pixels and the object of interest is a boat with a length of 27 m and 6 m wide. The second sequence (sequence B) has the same resolution but contains 2250 frames, where a cargo ship is visible. Each sequence was labelled by an human operator and a Ground Truth (GT) corresponds to a rectangular BB. It is also worth noting that in sequence A, the object of interest has an average width of 111 pixels and an average height of 50 pixel. In sequence B the average dimension is 18 by 20 pixels.

As visible in Fig. 4(a) and (b), each classified image patch is given a probability of containing a boat, thus we have the ability of choosing the threshold, *i.e.*, the operating point of the detector.

5.2   Results

To quantify the performance of the algorithm, having in mind the already mentioned trade-off, we have used an evaluation approach similar to what is presented in [2] and display the results as precision and recall curves. Additionally, we have evaluated the computation time, to assess the ability of the proposed method to process a video feed in near real-time.

This evaluation method considers a detection as correct if there is any overlap between ground truth BB and the BB produced by the detection algorithm. In Fig. 5, we present the results obtained with the proposed methods in sequences A and B. Each of the plots contains four curves and these correspond to what was obtained using the sliding window (SW) and the candidate regions (CR) approach. We have used each of these approaches with two trained networks (GoogLeNet and AlexNet).

In the plots, there are also two points that correspond to the algorithm currently running in real-time time on-board our UAVs and presented in [10] applied to the same sequences, designated by *Blob Analysis* and used as baseline. *Blob Analysis* algorithm consists of three steps. In the first step, a set of blobs possibly containing a boat is extracted. The second step consists on the application of spacial constraints to reject blobs that contain sky or sun reflections. In the last

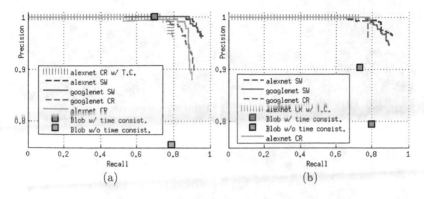

Fig. 5. Precision-Recall curves for (a) sequences A and (b) B.

step, the time consistency is checked by verifying if there are at least four detections in five consecutive frames. One of the points represents the results obtained by *Blob Analysis* applied to each frame individually (without time consistency), which is the closest comparison with the algorithm described in this paper. Nevertheless, we also present the results obtained with the entire *Blob Analysis'* detection pipeline and with time consistency applied to the candidate regions approach using AlexNet.

As visible on the plots, all approaches have a good performance, allowing a precision near 100 % for a recall of 50 %. The performance of our approach also outperforms what is achieved with *Blob Analysis* without the time consistency heuristic. When comparing with the results produced by the entire *Blob Analysis* pipeline, our technique (without the time consistency heuristic) produced slightly worse results in sequence A (for the same recall, our approach achieved 99.4 % precision instead of 100 %). On sequence B, our results are significantly better. The difference in performance is caused by the fact that *Blob Analysis* was originally tuned for boats with bigger apparent size, whereas the CNN was trained with boats of different dimensions. When comparing both tests that used the time consistency heuristic, we verify that the results obtained with the CNN were better.

Comparing convolutional neural networks' results, we can see that the sliding window approach, in general, produced better results, the only exception being a subtle difference on sequence B for recall between 0.7 and 0.8 (this is caused by the better fit of the candidate region to the boat with very small apparent size when compared to the fixed size sliding window). It is also possible to see that on sequence B, there is a rapid drop on the performance of the candidate regions approach around 80 % recall. This corresponds to more challenging conditions, where features like wave crests and sun glare are wrongly classified as belonging to the class *boat* (as depicted in Fig. 6(b)). In Fig. 6(a) is presented another challenging condition: a missed detection in an image where glare is present and the boat has a small apparent size. A correct detection in the presence of glare is also presented in Fig. 6(c). Finally in Fig. 6(d), we present the correct detection

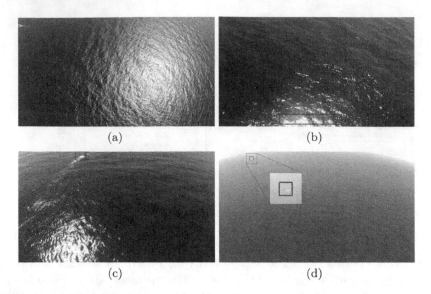

Fig. 6. Examples of challenging conditions present in the video sequences used in the evaluation: (a) missed detection of a ship with small apparent size in an image with the presence of glare, (b) false detection of ships in an image with significant presence of glare and correct detections of a ship in an image with significant glare and (d) ship with small apparent size very small contrast.

Table 1. Average computation time for each of the proposed approaches on a Nvidia Jetson TK1 board.

Approach	Average computation time (s)
AlexNet Sliding Window	10.58
GoogLeNet Sliding Window	15.11
AlexNet Candidate Regions	1.23
GoogLeNet Candidate Regions	1.86

of a boat with very small apparent size and very small contrast. It is also worth noting that in general, AlexNet yielded better results than GoogLeNet, even though in competitions like ILSVRC the opposite is true. We believe in our case, the amount of training samples is not enough to take full advantage of the deeper architecture of GoogLeNet.

When we consider real world application of any of these approaches, there is another important factor: the amount of time needed to process one image. The computation time for each of these techniques is summarized in Table 1. Despite the better results of sliding window approach, its computation time is not adequate to be used in a near real time application on the selected hardware platform. Even though the candidate regions approach cannot process video in real time, it can still detect objects of interest in a real world application since boats are typically visible for a interval greater than its computation time.

6 Conclusion

Our work has showed that the detection system based on neural networks achieves good performance when compared to other algorithms and is possible to use in our envisioned scenario, *i.e.* an embedded system on-board an UAV. The gains go beyond the measured precision-recall, since the output of the network provides a probability of the BB belonging to a given class.

One of the future tasks that we might carry out is to use the output of the network to integrate this algorithm with a tracker, that will run at a higher rate and allow the extraction of more information.

Another of the future tasks is to use a Recurrent Neural Network to explore the temporal correlation of successive frames in order to improve detection, instead of analysing each frame individually.

Acknowledgements. This work was partially supported by FCT project [UID/EEA/50009/2013]. The authors would like to thank the SEAGULL team and Computer Vision Lab team (VisLab) at ISR/IST, which were involved in obtaining the image dataset and annotating the ground truth.

References

1. Dawkins, M., Sun, Z., Basharat, A., Perera, A., Hoogs, A.: Tracking nautical objects in real-time via layered saliency detection. In: SPIE Defense + Security, p. 908903. International Society for Optics and Photonics (2014)
2. Dollar, P., Wojek, C., Schiele, B., Perona, P.: Pedestrian detection: an evaluation of the state of the art. IEEE Trans. Pattern Anal. Mach. Intell. **34**(4), 743–761 (2012)
3. Gaszczak, A., Breckon, T.P., Han, J.: Real-time people and vehicle detection from UAV imagery. In: IS&T/SPIE Electronic Imaging, p. 78780B. International Society for Optics and Photonics (2011)
4. Hou, X., Harel, J., Koch, C.: Image signature: highlighting sparse salient regions. IEEE Trans. Pattern Anal. Mach. Intell. **34**(1), 194–201 (2011)
5. Jia, Y., Shelhamer, E., Donahue, J., Karayev, S., Long, J., Girshick, R., Guadarrama, S., Darrell, T.: Caffe: convolutional architecture for fast feature embedding. arXiv:1408.5093 (2014)
6. Krizhevsky, A., Sutskever, I., Hinton, G.E.: ImageNet classification with deep convolutional neural networks. In: Advances in Neural Information Processing Systems, pp. 1097–1105 (2012)
7. LeCun, Y., Bottou, L., Bengio, Y., Haffner, P.: Gradient-based learning applied to document recognition. Proc. IEEE **86**(11), 2278–2324 (1998)
8. Maire, F., Mejias, L., Hodgson, A.: A convolutional neural network for automatic analysis of aerial imagery. In: 2014 International Conference on Digital Image Computing: Techniques and Applications (DICTA), pp. 1–8. IEEE (2014)

9. Maire, F., Mejias, L., Hodgson, A., Duclos, G.: Detection of dugongs from unmanned aerial vehicles. In: 2013 IEEE/RSJ International Conference on Intelligent Robots and Systems (IROS), pp. 2750–2756. IEEE (2013)
10. Marques, J.S., Bernardino, A., Cruz, G., Bento, M.: An algorithm for the detection of vessels in aerial images. In: 2014 11th IEEE International Conference on Advanced Video and Signal Based Surveillance (AVSS), pp. 295–300. IEEE (2014)
11. Oreifej, O., Mehran, R., Shah, M.: Human identity recognition in aerial images. In: 2010 IEEE Conference on Computer Vision and Pattern Recognition (CVPR), pp. 709–716. IEEE (2010)
12. Pollard, T., Antone, M.: Detecting and tracking all moving objects in wide-area aerial video. In: 2012 IEEE Computer Society Conference on Computer Vision and Pattern Recognition Workshops (CVPRW), pp. 15–22. IEEE (2012)
13. Russakovsky, O., Deng, J., Hao, S., Krause, J., Satheesh, S., Ma, S., Huang, Z., Karpathy, A., Khosla, A., Bernstein, M., Berg, A.C., Fei-Fei, L.: ImageNet large scale visual recognition challenge. Int. J. Comput. Vis. (IJCV) **115**(3), 211–252 (2015)
14. Sermanet, P., Kavukcuoglu, K., Chintala, S., LeCun, Y.: Pedestrian detection with unsupervised multi-stage feature learning. In: 2013 IEEE Conference on Computer Vision and Pattern Recognition (CVPR), pp. 3626–3633. IEEE (2013)
15. Shirvaikar, M.V., Trivedi, M.M.: A neural network filter to detect small targets in high clutter backgrounds. IEEE Trans. Neural Netw. **6**(1), 252–257 (1995)
16. Szegedy, C., Liu, W., Jia, Y., Sermanet, P., Reed, S., Anguelov, D., Erhan, D., Vanhoucke, V., Rabinovich, A.: Going deeper with convolutions. arXiv:1409.4842 (2014)
17. Szegedy, C., Toshev, A., Erhan, D.: Deep neural networks for object detection. In: Advances in Neural Information Processing Systems, pp. 2553–2561 (2013)
18. Vaillant, R., Monrocq, C., Le Cun, Y.: Original approach for the localisation of objects in images. IEEE Proc Vis. Image Signal Process. **141**(4), 245–250 (1994)
19. Westall, P., O'Shea, P., Ford, J.J., Hrabar, S.: Improved maritime target tracker using colour fusion. In: 2009 International Conference on High Performance Computing & Simulation, HPCS 2009, pp. 230–236. IEEE (2009)

R³P: Real-time RGB-D Registration Pipeline

Hani Javan Hemmat$^{(\boxtimes)}$, Egor Bondarev, and Peter H.N. de With

Eindhoven University of Technology, De Zaale 5, 5612 AZ Eindhoven, Netherlands
{h.javan.hemmat,e.bondarev,p.h.n.de.with}@tue.nl
http://vca.ele.tue.nl/

Abstract. Applications based on colored 3-D data sequences suffer from lack of efficient algorithms for transformation estimation and key points extraction to perform accurate registration and sensor localization either in the 2-D or 3-D domain. Therefore, we propose a real-time RGB-D registration pipeline, named R³P, presented in processing layers. In this paper, we present an evaluation of several algorithm combinations for each layer, to optimize the registration and sensor localization for specific applications. The resulting dynamic reconfigurability of R³P makes it suitable as a front-end system for any SLAM reconstruction algorithm. Evaluation results on several public datasets reveal that R³P delivers real-time registration with 59 fps and high accuracy with the relative pose error (for a time span of 40 frames) for rotation and translation of 0.5° and 8 mm, respectively. All the heterogeneous dataset and implementations are publicly available under an open-source license [21].

Keywords: RGB-D registration · Real-time · Heterogeneous 3-D Reconstruction · Simultaneously Localization and Mapping (SLAM)

1 Introduction

Nowadays a large amount of research is dedicated to 3-D image processing. Over the last decade, various 3-D sensors and devices have emerged based on a multitude of technologies, each coming with its own advantages, limitations and costs. On one end, low-cost depth sensors (e.g. the Kinect) and stereo cameras provide 3-D data in RGB-D format. Alternatively, there are relatively expensive laser scanners (e.g. for civil engineering) enabling extraction of RGB-D data from captured colored point-clouds. Processing RGB-D images in the 2-D domain requires dealing with a depth signal as grayscale images, while the conventional 2-D algorithms are not capable of efficiently handling depth data [1]. Using cameras as sensors, registration of 2-D images has been broadly investigated in literature and several mature algorithms are available for every aspect of the registration process, like motion estimation and visual SLAM approaches [2,3]. Despite this maturity, the 2-D registration methods cannot estimate 3-D transformation accurately, due to their intrinsic deficiency in extracting accurate depth information. In contrast to the 2-D domain, registration algorithms designed for 3-D point clouds are not mature and fast enough to

© Springer International Publishing AG 2016
J. Blanc-Talon et al. (Eds.): ACIVS 2016, LNCS 10016, pp. 385–397, 2016.
DOI: 10.1007/978-3-319-48680-2_34

be utilized in real-time applications, since they require an enormous amount of computation. However, when provided with well-corresponding point sets, the 3-D transformation-estimation algorithms performs more accurately, compared to the 2-D algorithms [4]. Accordingly, RGB-D SLAM systems [5–9] leverage depth data to enhance the pose estimation quality. However, these systems mostly utilize ICP-based computationally expensive algorithms to estimate the 3-D transformation, so that they do not offer real-time localization, when implemented on embedded systems.

Despite the multiple algorithms for RGB-D registration, there is no comprehensive survey to compare various combinations of interchangeable algorithms. Generally, these registration algorithms are based on a combination of specific methods (mostly, a 2-D matcher with an ICP-based pose-estimator) including: visual features combined with the Generalized-ICP [5], a combination of local visual features and geometric registration [10], a surfel-based SLAM method [11], an energy-based approach [12], a pairwise feature matching [13], minimizing the photometric error [14], a non-real-time RGB-D registration via edges [15], a non-real-time robust RGB-D odometry method using point and line features [16], a comparative survey for RGB-D videos [17], DeReEs as a real-time system for virtual reality applications [18], and switching between photometric and geometric information [19]. Several RGB-D registration systems perform only on a consecutive pair of images, which limits their application to camera-tracking [5,10–14,19,20]. In this paper, we aim at robotic and 3-D reconstruction applications, where the accuracy of registration affects the pose-estimator quality and sensor localization. Besides this, robotic applications require real-time performance (20–40 ms delay). We propose a scalable registration architecture that provides <20 ms processing delay and features relatively high accuracy of pose estimation with the relative pose error (for a time span of 40 frames) for rotation and translation of 0.5° and 8 mm, respectively.

The resulting registration processing consists of 3 main phases. In the first phase, it finds, describes and matches key points in pairs of the RGB images, followed by an outlier removal (the selection of pairs follows later). In the second phase, the process generates *key-point-clouds* by adding the depth information to the extracted key points. Finally, in the third phase, the process applies a RANSAC-based outlier removal and completes with estimating the transformation between the input RGB-D pairs based on the resulting corresponding inliers. To make this architecture scalable and flexible, we have deployed multiple exchangeable algorithms in each processing layer.

2   R³P Architecture

In this section, we describe the R³P pipeline for real-time transformation estimation of RGB-D image pairs. Any type of data presented in the form of RGB-D in any combination (e.g. the Kinect and a professional laser scanner[1]) can be

---

[1] The Kinect device is commercially available from Microsoft and the professional laser scanner is offered by FARO Corporation.

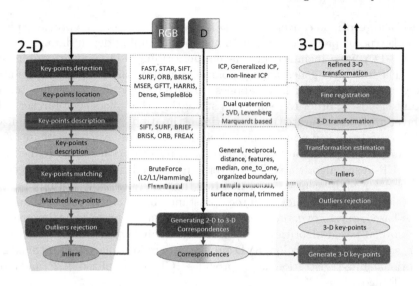

Fig. 1. R³P architecture: two main groups of the 2-D and 3-D algorithms.

supplied to the pipeline to obtain the corresponding rigid transformation. The aim is to exploit the beneficial aspects of both the 2-D and 3-D domains, in order to obtain a high-quality registration and a fast execution, compared to each of the individual domains. In terms of performance, the transformation estimation algorithms perform faster when applied to a smaller set of key points. Therefore, the core objective of the pipeline is to find an optimal number of high-confidence key point matches to enable real-time performance, while preserving high accuracy of the pose estimation by providing the strongest (dual-filtered inliers) key points to the algorithms.

Figure 1 demonstrates the R³P processing architecture. The pipeline consists of separate 2-D and 3-D phases, as shown at the left and right of the diagram, respectively. Besides this, there is a bridge phase in between, indicated at the bottom of the diagram. The following paragraphs describe these phases in detail.

The 2-D phase comprises four consecutive layers, where the registration process is performed in the 2-D domain with the color (RGB) image pairs. In the first three layers, the 2-D key points are detected, described and matched. The fourth layer performs an outlier removal to minimize and strengthen the 2-D key point pairs. The interchangeable algorithms for the key point detection layer include the FAST, STAR, SIFT, SURF, ORB, BRISK, MSER, GFTT, HARRIS, Dense, and SimpleBlob techniques [22]. The options for the key point description layer are the SIFT, SURF, BRIEF, BRISK, ORB, and FREAK algorithms [22]. For the key point matching layer, the BruteForce (L2/L1/Hamming) and Flann-based algorithms are provided. Finally, the outlier rejection layer operates based on source-to-target back-projection by choosing from rigid transformation, homography, fundamental, essential, affine, perspective matrices [22] as options.

The bridge phase converts the 2-D key point pairs from the previous phase into 3-D key point pairs, enriched with the corresponding depth data.

The 3-D phase includes three layers performing 3-D transformation estimation. The first layer generates key-point-clouds from the previously generated 3-D key points. The next layer applies an outlier-rejection algorithm to the key-point-clouds, in order to reduce and strengthen the inliers even further. The third layer provides accurate transformation estimation, based on the minimized and high-confidence key-point-clouds. Besides these main layers, the phase offers an optional fine-registration layer, where the transformation can be refined further by ICP-based algorithms. This layer can be used in case the architecture is deployed for high-accuracy and non-real-time systems. The options for the outlier rejection layer include reciprocal, distance-based, feature-based, median distance-based, one-to-one, organized boundary, sample consensus, trimmed and surface-normal based algorithms [23]. The transformation-estimation layer performs based on dual-quaternion, SVD and Levenberg Marquardt algorithms [23]. The optional fine-registration layer provides ICP, Generalized ICP and non-linear ICP algorithms [23].

Several conventional interchangeable algorithms are provided for each layer of the pipeline, varying significantly in terms of performance and accuracy, as shown in Fig. 1. This variety of algorithms allows the generic pipeline to be optimized for different applications. Later in this paper, we show that only a subset of the provided algorithms for each layer satisfying real-time constraints.

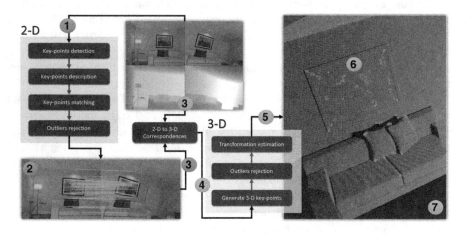

Fig. 2. R³P pipeline: (1) feeding color images to 2-D phase layers, (2) obtaining 2-D key points, (3) adding depth information to 2-D key points, (4) feeding 2-D key points with corresponding depth information to 3-D phase layers, (5) estimated transformation based on key-point-clouds, (6) key-point-clouds represented as bold dots, and (7) the complete point-clouds are well aligned based on the transformation obtained for key-point-clouds. The RGB-D pair is selected from the dataset collection (ICL [24]) with a distance of 40 skipped frames.

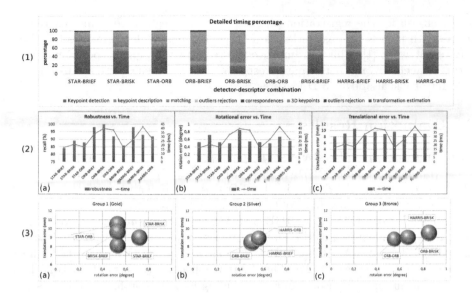

Fig. 3. (1): Time distribution among various layers of the R^{3}P architecture for the well-matched combinations. (2): Comparing (a) robustness, (b) rotation and (c) translation parts of the RPE to execution time of the 2-D detection and description algorithms combinations. (3): Intra-group comparison for the robustness, rotation and translation error metrics for the Groups 1, 2 and 3. The size of the bubbles indicates the robustness metric for each well-matched combination.

Figure 2 illustrates the registration process of the R^{3}P when applied to a pair of RGB-D images. The pipeline starts with feeding the color images to the 2-D layers (Fig. 2-1) in order to identify strong 2-D key points (Fig. 2-2). In the next step, the depth information is added to the 2-D key points based on the related depth images (Fig. 2-3). These 2-D key points with their corresponding depth information are sent to the next layer (Fig. 2-4) to generate key-point-clouds, reject outliers and estimate the transformation. Although the resulting transformation (Fig. 2-5) is merely based on a few key-point-clouds (Fig. 2-6), it is proven to be sufficiently accurate to register the full point-cloud pairs extracted from the depth images (Fig. 2-7). This is due to the selection process of the strongest inliers as indicated above.

The R^{3}P provides the following important benefits: high frame rate, dynamic tunability, robustness, and comparatively low error rate. The R^{3}P reaches upto 60 fps based on a CPU implementation, which is at least two times faster than the conventional (near) real-time [5, 10–12, 14, 18, 19] and non-real-time registration algorithms [13, 15, 15]. This makes it applicable to robotic applications with limited computation resources and for real-time constraints.

The architecture limitation is its poor performance for scenes with no visual and/or 3-D features, which can be suppressed by enriching the pipeline by adding efficient algorithms performing on depth images. Currently, we are working on an extension for the registration pipeline to utilize segmented planes extracted from depth images for pose estimation between a pair of depth images based on our recent work [1]. This can improve the registration pipeline performance in terms of accuracy and performance, especially for the scenes with an insufficient amount of visual and/or 3-D features.

3   Evaluation Results

Implementation and datasets: the proposed architecture is implemented in C++ (publicly available [21]). We have utilized the OpenCV [22] and PCL [23] libraries for several algorithms in the 2-D and 3-D domains, respectively. The experimental results have been obtained utilizing a workstation with a Xeon(R) W3550 @3.07 GHz CPU and 20 GB of RAM. For a comprehensive evaluation, we have applied the proposed architecture to several publicly available datasets including TUM [25], MSRC [26], ICL [24], as well as our own datasets (Kinect sequences and laser scans) [21]. The dataset collection consists of RGB-D data obtained from various sensors/sources including Kinect, a professional laser scanner, and virtual 3-D models.

Criteria: the experimental results are obtained based on three main basis of time, robustness, and relative pose error (RPE). The detailed timing information has been computed for evaluation of real-time behavior and also for identification of time share of each individual layer in the pipeline. Since we combine various key point detectors and descriptors in the registration pipeline, it is possible that some combinations cannot handle all the RGB-D pairs in a dataset collection. In order to address this issue, we define a *robustness* metric for a detector-descriptor combination, that indicates the percentage of the RGB-D pairs in a dataset collection, for which the combination is capable of estimating a transformation. The obtained transformations are compared to the ground truth based on the RPE metric in terms of both rotation and translation. The pipeline is tested on temporally subsampled sequences (every 40th frame deployed) to demonstrate the independence of the R^3P from the consecutive order of RGB-D frames.

3.1   Results of All Experiments

Combinatorially, the proposed architecture contains 388,080 ($= 11 \times 6 \times 5 \times 7 \times 4 \times 14 \times 3$) possible algorithm configurations to perform the registration pipeline. The following reasoning steps allow to select a representative subset of experimental configurations.

Step 1: since the most time-consuming layers of the pipeline are the 2-D algorithms (Table 4 and Fig. 3-1), we focus on variations for 2-D phase.

Step 2: we exclude any individual algorithm which behaves as an outlier in terms of time, robustness or RPE criteria.

Step 3: no significant effect emerges for the various combinations of the 3-D phase algorithms in terms of time, robustness and RPE metrics. Hence, we have selected a fixed configuration setting for the 3-D phase algorithms.

Table 1. Comparing various combinations of 2-D key point detection and description algorithms in terms of time (t) and robustness (r).

	SIFT		SURF		BRIEF		BRISK		ORB	
	t(ms)	r(%)	t(ms)	r(%)	t(ms)	r(%)	t(ms)	r(%)	t(ms)	r(%)
FAST	1050	100	345	36	578	95	1411	90	585	86
STAR	117	91	26	74	17	84	21	89	18	88
SIFT	346	88	179	25	190	94	285	81	-	-
SURF	1413	99	488	97	266	95	357	98	268	66
ORB	397	100	277	99	33	98	40	100	38	92
BRISK	113	99	29	11	17	86	25	59	17	16
MSER	703	98	249	69	197	81	202	82	197	67
GFTT	121	98	36	0	71	97	143	90	68	89
HARRIS	52	98	17	2	27	98	42	93	27	92

Table 2. Comparing various combinations of 2-D key-point detection and description algorithms regarding relative pose error for Rotation (degree) and Translation (mm).

	SIFT		SURF		BRIEF		BRISK		ORB	
	R	T	R	T	R	T	R	T	R	T
FAST	0.62	9.0	1.43	14.1	0.54	8.6	0.56	9.1	0.47	10.1
STAR	0.64	7.8	0.71	15.4	0.53	8.1	0.72	9.0	0.53	10.5
SIFT	0.64	9.8	1.36	9.7	0.53	8.3	0.49	13.4	-	-
SURF	0.57	8.5	0.50	8.4	0.52	8.4	0.61	8.2	0.92	13.3
ORB	0.59	9.6	0.58	8.7	0.50	8.4	0.85	9.5	0.55	8.8
BRISK	0.59	8.5	1.22	12.0	0.53	9.6	0.64	11.7	0.87	12.0
MSER	0.50	8.2	0.66	11.1	0.54	11.6	0.54	11.0	0.69	14.7
GFTT	0.50	8.7	0.43	6.3	0.51	8.7	0.57	9.4	0.50	9.9
HARRIS	0.60	9.0	0.39	7.3	0.50	8.5	0.67	9.0	0.56	8.9

As a result, the evaluated configuration consists of a variable combination of 2-D detector-descriptor algorithms and the following fixed algorithms for the remaining layers. We have chosen *BruteForce (L2)*, *rigid transformation*, *median distance* and *Singular Value Decomposition (SVD)* algorithms for the 2-D key-point matching, 2-D and 3-D outliers removal, and 3-D transformation-estimation layers, respectively. Our choices are motivated by selecting the algorithms with the lowest computing costs, due to the marginal performance differences.

Table 1 shows the timing and robustness metrics for various combinations of detector-descriptor algorithms. The rotation and translation RPE are demonstrated in Table 2 for the same combinations. Table 3 presents well-matched combinations, which show a real-time behavior ($\geq$25 fps) along with an acceptable robustness ($\geq$80 %). Detailed timing, robustness, error, and number of inliers (2-D and 3-D) metrics are provided in the table, enabling a detailed comparison. Figure 3-2 depicts robustness, rotation and translation errors for the well-matched combinations. Table 4 and Fig. 3-1 present the extracted detailed timing information for these combinations. Table 5 provides a comparison of the proposed R³P architecture to the conventional registration methods.

4   Discussion

We have evaluated the proposed R³P architecture in terms of two aspects: real-time performance and pose estimation accuracy. With respect to performance, the experimental results reveal that the R³P architecture enables real-time registration with a high frame rate of $\approx$60 fps for the well-matched combinations. Concerning the accuracy of the pose estimation, a large number of robotics applications can benefit from the R³P architecture due to its low average RPE translational error of 8 mm and rotational error of 0.5°. Table 1 shows that a large fraction of combinations do not satisfy real-time constraints, although these combinations deliver a high level of robustness. It also reveals a set of combinations with real-time behavior, at the expense of a poor performance in robustness. As presented in Table 2, most of the combinations result in a translation and rotation error between $8-10$ mm and $0.5-0.85$ degree, respectively. Table 3 describes the 10 well-matched combinations with real-time performance ($\approx \geq$25 fps) and an acceptable robustness ($\geq$80 %). Figure 3-2 compares the performance of the selected combinations to the corresponding robustness, rotation and translation error. Figure 3-2-a shows that the faster the combination executes, the lower the robustness becomes (with a few exceptions). In contrast, there is no correlation found between the performance and rotation error, as shown in Fig. 3-2-b. Besides this, most of the combinations, excluding a couple of outliers, result in a rotation error within 0.4–0.6 degree. Moreover, the combinations reveal identical results for translation error (8–10 mm), regardless of the provided performance, as demonstrated in Fig. 3-2-c.

Table 3. Detailed comparison of the well-matched combination performing in real-time ($\geq$25 fps) with a high-level of robustness ($\geq$80 %).

det.	STAR	STAR	STAR	ORB	ORB	ORB	BRISK	HARRIS	HARRIS	HARRIS
des.	BRIEF	BRISK	ORB	BRIEF	BRISK	ORB	BRIEF	BRIEF	BRISK	ORB
time	17	21	18	33	40	38	17	27	42	27
rob.	84	89	88	98	100	92	86	98	93	92
R	0.53	0.72	0.53	0.50	0.85	0.55	0.53	0.50	0.67	0.56
t	8.1	9.0	10.5	8.4	9.5	8.8	9.6	8.5	9.0	8.9
in. 2D	119	108	101	284	289	289	107	187	188	166
in. 3D	51	46	43	121	124	122	45	79	78	71

Table 4. Detailed information of execution time (in microseconds) among various 2-D and 3-D algorithms of the pipeline layers for the well-matched combinations.

det-des combination	2-D key points				3D key point			
	det	des	mat	rej	cor	gen	rej	est
STAR-BRIEF	11,635	1,650	3,833	67	56	15	504	16
STAR-BRISK	11,206	1,898	7,376	66	48	14	490	16
STAR-ORB	11,278	2,247	3,845	61	45	13	449	16
ORB-BRIEF	7,118	2,758	23,372	86	81	20	1,064	20
ORB-BRISK	7,132	3,227	28,379	72	82	19	1,085	21
ORB-ORB	6,971	7,374	23,248	76	87	19	1,080	22
BRISK-BRIEF	9,448	2,044	9,225	82	57	15	520	16
HARRIS-BRIEF	12,547	2,068	9,394	72	71	20	752	19
HARRIS-BRISK	12,626	2,646	22,097	79	77	17	706	18
HARRIS-ORB	11,922	2,578	8,960	69	65	17	665	18

With our main focus on real-time performance, we categorize the above-mentioned 10 detector-descriptor combinations into three groups: (1) STAR-BRIEF, STAR-BRISK, STAR-ORB, and BRISK-BRIEF combinations perform as the fastest couple with an average performance of 55 fps; (2) ORB-BRIEF, HARRIS-BRIEF and HARRIS-ORB combinations handle the transformation estimation with an average rate of 35 fps; and (3) ORB-ORB, HARRIS-BRIEF and HARRIS-BRISK couples are the slowest well-matched combinations with an average rate of 25 fps. Figure 3-3 demonstrates the target metrics of each combination in these groups in detail. In Group 1, the fastest STAR-BRIEF combination performs with the smallest rotation and translation error, while it exposes the lowest level of robustness. In Group 2, although the HARRIS-BRIEF and ORB-BRIEF perform equivalently in terms of the estimation error, the former (37 fps) outweighs the latter (30 fps) regarding performance. In Group 3, ORB-ORB combination outperforms others in terms of all criteria.

An interesting finding is the correlation between the number of 2-D and 3-D inliers as shown in Table 3. For all combinations, the number of 3-D inliers is ≈42 % of the number of 2-D inliers, revealing that not all 2-D inliers are sufficiently consistent with the corresponding depth information to be supplied into the 3-D phase. A reason for this is the lack of proper depth information for some of the 2-D inliers due to invalid data, noise and sensors distance-sensitivity [27,28].

According to Table 4 and Fig. 3-1, more than 97 % of the R³P execution time is spent on the 2-D phase algorithms. However, the obtained execution time varies considerably inside the 2-D domain for detection, description and matching algorithms. Therefore, investigation of more efficient 2-D algorithms can increase the time efficiency.

Table 5. Comparison of the proposed R^3P with several conventional algorithms/systems in terms of speed, RPE Rotation (degree) and Translation (mm).

System	SLAM	Speed	RPE		Dataset
			R	T	
R^3P	-	real-time	0.31	3	f1-room
			0.22	5	f2-desk
			0.10	1	f3-office
RGB-D SLAM [5]	✓	≈real-time	2.38	54	f1-room
			0.57	14	f2-desk
Surfel-based [11]	✓	≈real-time	0.009	5	f1-desk
			0.004	2	f2-desk
energy-based [12]	✓	real-time	0.005	7	f1-desk
			0.002	3	f2-desk
point and line [16]	-	non real-time	0.6	11	f2-desk
DeReEs [18]	-	real-time	2.68	13	own dataset
ranked order statistics [19]	✓	≈real-time	3.5	107	own dataset
combined RGB-D [20]	✓	≈real-time	2.7	51	f1-room
			0.94	19	f2-desk

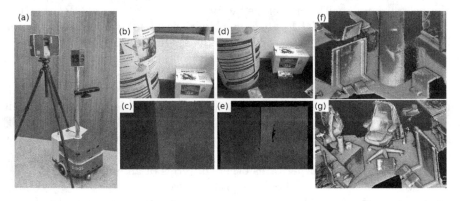

Fig. 4. R^3P architecture deployed for multi-modal 3-D reconstruction: (a) professional laser scanner (at the left) along with Kinect-equipped robot (at the right), (b-c) pair of RGB-D images extracted from a professional colored point-cloud, (d-e) corresponding Kinect RGB-D images for the same scene, but from a different pose, and (f) snapshots of aligned 3-D models, generated based on different sensor modalities (Kinect white clouds, and professional colored clouds) with an average distance error of <20 mm. (Color figure online)

Table 5 compares the R^3P architecture to several conventional registration algorithms. In terms of performance, the R^3P outperforms the conventional systems by at least a factor of two. This is due to the fact that most of the conventional systems utilize ICP-based algorithms in the 3-D domain, which increase computation complexity and execution time. Regarding RPE rotation, a couple of SLAM systems [11,12] deliver smaller error values, due to their pose-graph optimization phase and/or ICP-based pose-estimation algorithms. The R^{3}P performs with a (significantly) lower rotation error, when compared to remaining systems. Furthermore, the R^{3}P outperforms most of other tested systems with regards to the translation error (see Table 5).

The R^{3}P architecture has been designed and implemented as a generic framework, but we mainly deploy it for robotics applications for multi-modal 3-D reconstruction. We utilize a professional laser scanner (Fig. 4-a) to generate global 3-D models of large-scale environments. Besides this, we deploy our robot equipped with the Kinect depth-sensor (Fig. 4-a) to enrich the professional 3-D model. The R^{3}P enables us to address two challenges: (1) relocating the robot in real-time from a lost pose and (2) aligning various 3-D models (obtained from different sensors), as shown by Fig. 4-f.

5 Conclusions

In this paper, we have proposed a real-time RGB-D registration pipeline, called R^{3}P, as a generic processing architecture, that is applicable to any form of 3-D data presented in RGB-D format. The main focus of R^{3}P is on real-time robotic and 3-D reconstruction applications. One of the main attractive features of the proposed architecture is the reduction of the amount of corresponding key points between a pair of RGB-D images into a set of minimal, but the strongest corresponding key points. The minimal number of correspondents enables real-time performance, while their strength ensures the pose-estimation accuracy.

The R^{3}P processing architecture combines the 2-D and 3-D algorithms by utilizing the beneficial aspects of both domains in three steps. First, R^{3}P starts with color images to extract matched 2-D color key points. Second, the corresponding depth information is added to the resulting 2-D color key points to generate *key-point-clouds*. Third and finally, the transformation between the input pair of RGB-D frames is estimated based on the minimal strong key-point-clouds.

We have evaluated the performance of the R^{3}P by applying it to various public datasets, as well as our own dataset for various combinations of configuration settings. The evaluation has been performed based on time, robustness, and relative pose error (RPE) metrics. The results show that well-matched combinations deliver real-time performance upto 59 fps with the average rotation and translation RPE of 0.5° and 8 mm, respectively. Furthermore, we have demonstrated that the R^{3}P architecture enables robotic applications to register both homogeneous (e.g. Kinect to Kinect) and heterogeneous colored 3-D data (e.g. the Kinect and professional laser scanners). Our dataset and implementation codes are publicly available under an open-source license [21]

The dynamic reconfigurability of the R3P architecture makes it suitable to be utilized as a front-end system in any SLAM algorithm. Various robotic applications can benefit from the proposed architecture in terms of pose estimation, quick recovery of lost pose, navigation, multi-robot cooperation, multi-modal fusion and 3-D reconstruction. We plan to enrich the proposed pipeline by adding plane-based registration, according to our real-time planar-segmentation algorithm [1], which improves the quality of the results in case of insufficient features.

References

1. Javan Hemmat, H., et al.: Real-time planar segmentation of depth images: from 3D edges to segmented planes. J. Electron. Imaging **24**(5), 051008 (2015)
2. Mur-Artal, R., Montiel, J.M.M., Tards, J.D.: ORB-SLAM: a versatile and accurate monocular SLAM system. IEEE Trans. Robot. **31**(5), 1147–1163 (2015)
3. Lu, Y., Song, D.: Visual navigation using heterogeneous landmarks and unsupervised geometric constraints. IEEE Trans. Robot. **31**(3), 736–749 (2015)
4. Bouaziz, S., Pauly, M.: Dynamic 2D/3D registration for the kinect. In: ACM SIGGRAPH Courses, SIGGRAPH 2013, pp. 21:1–21:14. ACM, New York (2013)
5. Henry, P., et al.: RGB-D mapping: using kinect-style depth cameras for dense 3D modeling of indoor environments. Int. J. Robot. Res. **31**(5), 647–663 (2012)
6. Newcombe, R.A., Lovegrove, S., Davison, A.: DTAM: dense tracking and mapping in real-time. In: IEEE International Conference on Computer Vision, pp. 2320–2327 (2011)
7. Labbe, M., Michaud, F.: Appearance-based loop closure detection for online large-scale and long-term operation. IEEE Trans. Robot. **29**(3), 734–745 (2013)
8. Endres, F., Hess, J., Sturm, J., Cremers, D., Burgard, W.: 3-D mapping with an RGB-D camera. IEEE Trans. Robot. **30**(1), 177–187 (2014)
9. Hu, G., Huang, S., Zhao, L., Alempijevic, A., Dissanayake, G.: A robust RGB-D slam algorithm. In: International Conference on Intelligent Robots and Systems (IROS), pp. 1714–1719 (2012)
10. Andreasson, H., Stoyanov, T.: Real time registration of RGB-D data using local visual features and 3D-NDT registration. In: International Conference on Robotics and Automation (2012)
11. Stckler, J., Behnke, S.: Model learning and real-time tracking using multiresolution surfel maps. In: Proceedings of the AAAI Conference on Artificial Intelligence (2012)
12. Steinbrucker, F., Sturm, J., Cremers, D.: Real-time visual odometry from dense RGB-D images. In: ICCV Workshops, pp. 719–722. IEEE (2011)
13. Dib, A., et al.: A real time visual slam for RGB-D cameras based on chamfer distance and occupancy grid. In: International Conference on Advanced Intelligent Mechatronics, pp. 652–657 (2014)
14. Kerl, C., Sturm, J., Cremers, D.: Robust odometry estimation for RGB-D cameras. In: ICRA (2013)
15. Choi, C., Trevor, A.J.B., Christensen, H.I.: RGB-D edge detection and edge-based registration. In: IROS, pp. 1568–1575. IEEE (2013)
16. Lu, Y., Song, D.: Robust RGB-D odometry using point and line features. In: IEEE International Conference on Computer Vision, ICCV (2015)
17. Morell-Gimenez, V., et al.: A comparative study of registration methods for RGB-D video of static scenes. Sensors **14**(5), 8547 (2014)
18. Seifi, S., et al.: DeReEs: real-time registration of RGB-D images using image-based feature detection and robust 3D correspondence estimation and refinement. In: 29th International Conference on Image and Vision Computing, pp. 136–141 (2014)

19. Yousif, K., et al.: A real-time RGB-D registration and mapping approach by heuristically switching between photometric and geometric information. In: International Conference on Information Fusion (2014)
20. Figueroa, N., Dong, H., Saddik, A.E.: A combined approach toward consistent reconstructions of indoor spaces based on 6D RGB-D odometry and kinect fusion. ACM Trans. Intell. Syst. Technol. **6**(2), 14:1–14:10 (2015)
21. R3P-related codes, docs and dataset. https://gitlab.com/HaniJH/R3P/tree/master. Accessed 9 Sept 2016
22. Bradski, G.: OpenCV: an open source computer vision library. Dr. Dobbs Journal of Software Tools (2000)
23. Rusu, R., Cousins, S.: 3D is here: point cloud library (PCL). In: IEEE International Conference on Robotics and Automation (ICRA), pp. 1–4 (2011)
24. Handa, A., Whelan, T., McDonald, J., Davison, A.: A benchmark for RGB-D visual odometry, 3D reconstruction and SLAM. In: IEEE ICRA (2014)
25. Sturm, J., Engelhard, N., Endres, F., Burgard, W., Cremers, D.: A benchmark for the evaluation of RGB-D slam systems. In: Intelligent Robot Systems (IROS) (2012)
26. Shotton, J., et al.: Scene coordinate regression forests for camera relocalization in RGB-D images. In: Computer Vision and Pattern Recognition (IEEE CVPR) (2013)
27. Javan Hemmat, H., Bondarev, E., Dubbelman, G., de With, P.H.N.: Improved ICP-based pose estimation by distance-aware 3D mapping. In: 9th International Conference on Computer Vision Theory and Applications, pp. 360–367 (2014)
28. Javan Hemmat, H., Bondarev, E., de With, P.H.N.: Exploring distance-aware weighting strategies for accurate reconstruction of voxel-based 3D synthetic models. In: Gurrin, C., Hopfgartner, F., Hurst, W., Johansen, H., Lee, H., O'Connor, N. (eds.) MMM 2014. LNCS, vol. 8325, pp. 412–423. Springer, Heidelberg (2014). doi:10.1007/978-3-319-04114-8_35

Vector Quantization Enhancement
for Computer Vision Tasks

Remi Trichet[(⊠)] and Noel E. O'Connor

Insight Centre for Data Analytics, Dublin City University, Glasnevin, Ireland
remi.trichet@gmail.com, noel.oconnor@dcu.ie

Abstract. This paper augments the Bag-of-Word scheme in several respects: we incorporate a category label into the clustering process, build classifier-tailored codebooks, and weight codewords according to their probability to occur. A size-adaptive feature clustering algorithm is also proposed as an alternative to k-means. Experiments on the PASCAL VOC 2007 challenge validate the approach for classical hard-assignment as well as VLAD encoding.

1 Introduction

Many scientists claim that we are currently experiencing the golden age of computer vision. The introduction of machine learning techniques has played a major role in this ongoing evolution, facilitating the field to constantly break new ground.

Among all the discoveries contributing to this surge in progress, Bag-of Words (BoW) [9, 14] is one of the most renowned across computer vision and multimedia applications. The idea is to represent a large feature set with a much smaller *visual codebook* of vector-quantized features, called *codewords*. The analysed visual entities (i.e. image, video, object...) are then described with a distribution of their codewords. This technique has proved to increase classifier robustness due to its capacity to summarize information and has inspired many encoding techniques, either expressing feature descriptors as combinations of visual codewords [8, 27] or recording the difference between the features and the visual codeword [6, 11, 13].

However, little attention has been directed to the proper adjustment of this technique to computer vision tasks. Indeed, codebooks are built independently of classifier needs. Thus the resulting codewords do not necessarily discriminate the semantic classes that the user ultimately wants to distinguish. This should not be surprising given that the approach only focuses on feature value information.

We have identified 3 distinct sub-problems to this issue:

1- The construction of a visual codebook is unable to take categories into account. Indeed, the information provided by the codewords might overlap or describe the categories in an imbalanced way. As a result, there is no guarantee that the provided codebook will best suit the training needs of the corresponding classifier.
2- Codewords are assumed to be equiprobable. An erroneous assumption that leads to biased histogram representation.
3- Codebooks are not tailored to classifier purposes. Typically, when faced with an n-category classification task, n one-against-all classifiers are modelled to address the

© Springer International Publishing AG 2016
J. Blanc-Talon et al. (Eds.): ACIVS 2016, LNCS 10016, pp. 398–409, 2016.
DOI: 10.1007/978-3-319-48680-2_35

problem. Quantized histograms fed to these classifiers stem from a unique code-book with equal coverage of these n categories (and, eventually, negative examples). For best performance, half of the data fed to the one-against-all classifier should refer to that particular category of interest.

In this work, we intend to overcome the first drawback directly during the clustering process via the integration of prior knowledge. More specifically, during the training phase, we label features with their corresponding visual entity category, and utilize constrained clustering [3] to produce clusters including more features belonging to the same category. A modified version of the k-means algorithm [4], and a size-adaptive agglomerative clustering [2], harnessing the purity metric to assess a cluster's discriminative power, are introduced. We include the probability of a code-word to occur for an enhanced histogram representation as an answer to the second problem. Finally, we tackle the third problem with category-tailored codebooks that further enhance classifiers' performance.

Our method has the following advantages:

1. It provides, for each category, a specific codebook that enhances classifier performance.
2. It provides, for each codebook, a set of codewords that enhances classifier performance.
3. The only annotations needed are the entity category label.
4. We would like to emphasize the genericity of this work: all these modifications can be applied to any task that uses BoW and learns classifiers.

The remainder of this paper is organized as follows. After reviewing the related literature, Sect. 2 details the aforementioned BoW improvements, namely maximizing intra-cluster category similarity, size-adaptive clustering, and accounting for the probability of a codeword to occur during histogram generation. Section 3 covers experiments; Sect. 4 concludes this paper.

1.1 Related work

Two types of approaches can be associated with codebook generation: encoding techniques and semantically-oriented codebook construction.

Encoding methods precursors [9, 10] typically perform local descriptor hard quantization and describe the media of interest with a distribution of codewords. The soft assignment variant [8] represents each feature descriptor as a weighted combination of its n nearest codewords. Locally-constrained linear coding [26] (LLC) performs sparse coding [27] to code each point according to the k nearest neighbours. A recently breakthrough records the difference between features and codewords. Given a predefined vocabulary of size K in a feature space of D dimensions, Vector of Linearly Aggregated Descriptors (VLAD) [11] encodes features first order differences to each visual word, called residuals. These residuals are stacked together to form a KD-value vector for each descriptor. Many improvements exist such as the use of tensors (VLAT) [7], intra-normalization [29], or second order statistics and supervised labelling [33].

Similarly, Fisher vector (FV) [5] captures the average first and second order differences between the descriptors and GMM centres. A combination of VLAD and FV encodings [12], as well as the introduction of non-linear additive kernels and PCA normalization [6], further improve results. Super vector coding (SV) [13] represents descriptors with first order differences, and adds a cluster mass parameter. See [1] for a review on feature encoding methods.

Approaches building a semantically meaningful codebook often filter unreliable codewords by looking for co-occurring patterns. More specifically, [24] learn what they call co-location and co-activation. Context-constrained linear coding [25] (CLC) is a variation of LLC [26] that incorporates spatio-temporal context within the distance utilized to compare feature points. [23] build up the co-occurrence codebook on a video segmentation layout. Finally, [28] proposed contextual clustering, using feature co-occurrences to disambiguate the output of multi-view clustering. Despite the success of these approaches, the necessary pairing of codewords reduces their discriminative power and neighbourhood definitions are often arbitrary.

Alternate ways to extract a codebook in a semantic manner encompass diffusion maps [20], semantic aware distance metric [21], meaningful word pair counts [22], spatial pyramid matching kernel [10], or consensus clustering to minimize the disagreement between several clustering outputs [19]. These methods typically rely on cluster shape, density, or even repartition and thus are not tailored for category discrimination.

To address this, several semi-supervised approaches make use of the category labels prior knowledge to refine the codebook construction. [15] utilize extremely randomized clustering forest, [16] mutual information, and [17, 18] a unified vocabulary. But all these methods consider weighting or selecting codewords **after** they have been generated, therefore down-bounding the technique efficiency with the codebook discriminative power.

2   Encoding Enhancement

This section covers our various encoding enhancements. After justifying the need for similar clusters, we present two clustering algorithms using feature point purity. Then, we introduce category-tailored codebooks and incorporate the probability of a codeword to occur.

2.1   Maximizing Intra-cluster Category Similarity

A key requirement for any classification task to perform well is that histogram distributions are expected to be significantly different from one category to another. Hence, the idea is to have each bin characterizing as few categories as possible. At the clustering level, this idea translates to maximising the intra-cluster category similarity. In other words, having clusters that encompass feature points extracted from instances of the same category, to the extent possible. Figure 1 illustrates the principle.

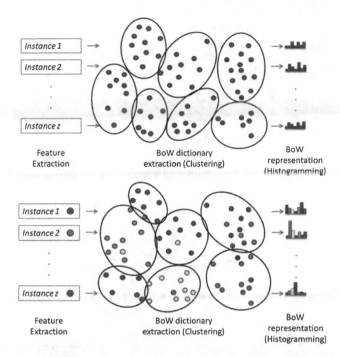

Fig. 1. Toy example demonstrating the impact of Maximizing intra-cluster category similarity. Each ellipse depicts one of the 7 clusters. Each colour represents one of the 5 categories. Top: Traditional codebook generation. Bottom: Codebook generation maximizing intra-cluster category similarity. Clusters better cover the categories, therefore leading to increased codeword discriminative power. Best viewed in colour.

Typically, a category label is associated to each training instance. We further extend this labelling process to the features extracted from a particular instance.

Consequently, each feature bears the category label of the instance to which it belongs. Let $C = \{C_0...C_k\}$ the set of k clusters, and $L = \{l_0, ..., l_n\}$ the set of n categories. Intra-cluster category similarity of a cluster p_i is assessed thanks to the purity evaluation measure:

$$purity(C_i, L) = max_j(|C_i \cap l_j|)/|C_i|, \qquad (1)$$

with |.| depicting the cardinality. Due to noise, extreme data variability, and outliers, optimal purity is rarely achievable. However, we will show through experiments that a codebook discriminative power is correlated to its global purity.

2.2   Purity k-means

This subsection extends the k-means algorithm [4] to incorporate feature point purity. The method is inspired from constrained clustering [3]. Constrained clustering is a type of semi-supervised clustering incorporating prior knowledge into algorithm by imposing grouping constraints.

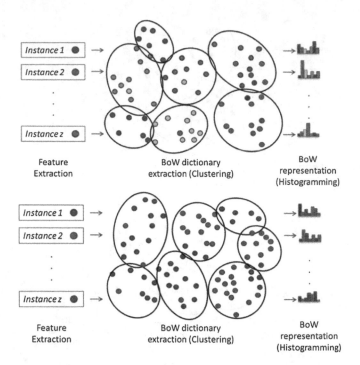

Fig. 2. Toy example demonstrating the impact of category-tailored codebooks. Each ellipse depicts one the 7 clusters. Each colour represents one of the 5 categories. Top: single codebook generation. Only one codeword/cluster represents the red category, leading to a discrepancy in the case of a one-versus-all classifier. Bottom: Codebook tailored for the red category (feature points are different). More codewords/clusters are dedicated to the red category, leading to increased discriminative power. Best viewed in colour.

Our algorithm is dubbed purity-k-means. It takes as input a set of feature points $X = \{x_j \mid j = 1,...,N\}$ and a desired numbered of clusters k. X should equally represent the n categories for best results. The only difference with k-means concerns the way cluster centres are updated. In order to maximize cluster purities, only features from the majority category are considered during this step. The algorithm is the following:

1. Randomly initialize the cluster centres C_i, $i = 1,...,k$
2. Assign feature vectors the same way as for typical k-means:

$$C_i = \{x_j | d(x_j, \mu(C_i)) \leq d(x_j, \mu(C_u)) \forall u \neq i, j = 1, \ldots, N\} \tag{2}$$

3. Update cluster centres.

$$A_i = C_i \cap l_{argmax_j(|C_i \cap l_j|)} \qquad \mu(C_i) = \frac{1}{|C_i|} \sum_{x_j \in A_i} x_j \tag{3}$$

4. Repeat step 2 and 3 until convergence.

2.3   Category-Tailored Codebooks Generation

Most applications that aim to discriminate n categories actually build n one-versus-all classifiers and eventually combine the classifier confidence values. For improved accuracy, it is then possible to further extend purity-based clustering by creating one codebook per category. Indeed, while constructing a one-versus-all classifier, feature points can be labelled as previously. In this case however, possible labels are "the category of interest" or "all other categories". Similarly, the set of feature points should equally represent the two categories. Therefore, the method builds up a range of n codebooks, each one of them specifically tailored for the classification of one particular type of instance. As a consequence, approximately the same number of codewords characterizes the category of interest and the remaining categories, leading to increased discriminative power. Figure 2 illustrates the principle.

2.4   Size-Adaptive Clustering

However, even with these extensions, k-means clustering [4], despite its advantages, still has one major drawback: Each cluster approximately covers the same portion of the feature space. Consequently, too many clusters are associated to regions with homogeneous feature labels and these arbitrary shaped clusters do not necessarily fit the configuration of feature groups in mixed label areas.

For better fit to the data, the cluster size should be driven by the data. More clusters would be dedicated to conflicting areas of the feature space, while fewer and bigger clusters would be associated to areas of high purity.

Hence, we present a clustering algorithm that frees clustering from the arbitrary cluster size, and better fits the data. This algorithm was designed bearing in mind 3 criteria:

1. The algorithm should maximize cluster purity.
2. Cluster size should adjust to the data.
3. New features falling into the cluster area should be easily associated to it.

This last criterion is paramount to keep further codeword encoding tractable. Either clusters should be compact enough to be approximated to k-means clusters, either an existing distance metric should be able to test the feature point association to arbitrarily shaped clusters. Figure 3 depicts the idea.

We employed agglomerative clustering [2] for this purpose, as it naturally fits the first two criteria. Agglomerative clustering is a hierarchical clustering algorithm that first initializes every data point as a cluster. The two closest clusters are then iteratively fused until a stopping criterion is met. The fusion distance typically considers the two closest points of each cluster for better fit to the data configuration. As this algorithm is renowned for creating clusters of complex shape, we modified the cluster distance assessment to enforce cluster compactness. More specifically, we use centroid-linkage, the centroid being defined by:

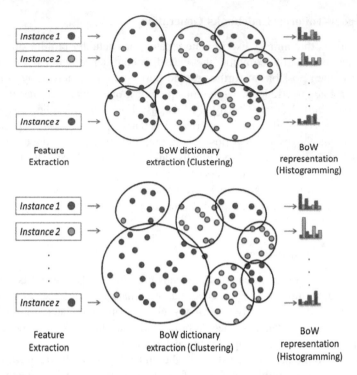

Fig. 3. Toy example showing the need of size-adaptive clusters. Each ellipse depicts one the 7 clusters. Each colour represents one of the 2 categories. Top: k-means clustering creating clusters of similar radius. Bottom: Size-adaptive clustering. More clusters are dedicated to conflicting areas of the feature space, while fewer and bigger clusters are associated to high purity areas. Best viewed in colour.

$$\mu(C_i) = \frac{1}{|C_i|} \sum_{x_j \in C_i} x_j \tag{4}$$

Also, to discourage extreme discrepancy between cluster sizes, we weight the distance between clusters according to the size of the smallest one:

$$W_{size} = \sqrt{\frac{k}{N} min(|C_i|, |C_j|)}, \tag{5}$$

where k is the desired number of clusters and N the feature points crdinality. Finally, we approximate the future purity of clusters to be fused C_i and C_j, named $purity(C_i, C_j, L)$, as the respective proportion of their majority label within the other cluster.

More formally:

$$purity(C_i, C_j, L) = \frac{\left| C_i \cap l_{argmax_u(|C_j \cap l_u|)} \right|}{2|C_i|} + \frac{\left| C_j \cap l_{argmax_v(|C_i \cap l_v|)} \right|}{2|C_j|} \tag{6}$$

Therefore, the similarity between 2 clusters C_i and C_j is a balance between their expected purity and their size-weighted distance:

$$S(C_i, C_j) = \left(1 + W_p\left(1 - purity(C_i, C_j, L)\right)\right) \times d\left(\mu(C_i), \mu(C_j)\right) \times W_{size}, \qquad (7)$$

with $d(.)$ a metric and W_p the weight assigned to purity. This parameter controls the purity of the clusters over their compactness. A high value will favour purity at the cost of eccentric cluster forms, and vice versa. We empirically set W_p to 0.5 for all our experiments, leading to a trade-off between these two factors.

As agglomerative clustering can be computationally expensive, we used dynamic programing to speed up its execution. More specifically, candidates for fusion are based on the (pre-computed) nn nearest neighbours of each feature point, the fusion list is only re-sorted if one of the updated similarities is lower than the current lowest one, and pruned from identical consecutive instances.

We deal with the variance in cluster sizes by computing the space coverage $\sigma(C_i)$ of each cluster C_i with a centroid $\mu(C_i)$ as follows:

$$\sigma^2(C_i) = max_{x_j \in C_i}\left(d\left(x_j, \mu(C_i)\right)\right) \qquad (8)$$

This differs from FV [5] priors or SV [13] posteriors as we aim to emphasise the coverage of the cluster. It is further utilized during feature encoding to weight the distance from a point to a cluster centroid:

$$C_i = \left\{ x_j \left| \begin{array}{c} \dfrac{d(x_j, \mu(C_i))}{\sigma(C_i)} \leq \dfrac{d(x_j, \mu(C_u))}{\sigma(C_u)} \\ \forall u \neq i; j = 1, \ldots, N \end{array} \right. \right\} \qquad (9)$$

The average purity loss caused by this approximation, with the aforementioned parameter setting, is 11 % for a single codebook, 6 % for category tailored ones.

2.5 Probability of a Codeword to Occur

Histogram construction is based on the underlying assumption that every single codeword is equiprobable. Consequently, each codeword occurrence increments the corresponding histogram bin by the same value. However, a simple experiment over 4000 k-means clusters determined from 1 million dense SIFT features on the PASCAL VOC 2007 dataset [30] invalidates this assumption: feature cardinality can vary by 113 % from cluster to cluster. This factor increases to 800 % when the same experiment is performed with the size-adaptive clustering described in Sect. 2.4. This biased cluster cardinality skews codeword occurrences, and therefore the entire histogram. For a fair distribution, the probability $p(C_i)$ of a codeword to occur within the database should be accounted while building up the histogram. We denote $p(C_i)$ of a codeword C_i, $i = 1, \ldots, n$, as:

$$p(C_i) = |C_i|/N, \tag{10}$$

with $|.|$ the cardinality of a cluster, k the codebook size, and N the total number of feature points used for clustering. Assuming all clusters to be equiprobable, $p(C_i) = 1/k \; \forall i$. Thus we simply increment a histogram codeword bin as follows:

$$h_i = h_i + \sqrt{k/p(C_i)} \tag{11}$$

Note that in the case of equiprobable clusters, this comes down to the traditional increment of h_i by 1.

Table 1. Results on the PASCAL VOC 2007 challenge. Baselines are in red, our runs in black. **KM:** k-means; **PKM:** Purity-kmeans; **PAC:** purity agglomerative clustering **GMM:** Gaussian mixture model.

Density correction	NO	NO	YES	YES	YES	NO	YES	NO	NO	NO	NO
Size (numbers) of codebooks	4000 (×1)	4000 (×1)	4000 (×1)	4000 (×20)	4000 (×20)	4000 (×1)	4000 (×20)	1024 (×1)	256 (×1)	256 (×1)	256 (×20)
Clustering	KM	PKM	PKM	PKM	PAC	KM	PAC	KM	GMM	KM	PAC
Encoding	BoW-hard [1]	BoW-hard	BoW-hard	BoW-hard	BoW-hard	BoW-soft [1]	BoW-soft	SV [1]	FV [1]	VLAD [34]	VLAD
Aeroplane	68.65%	74.59%	75.78%	76.96%	76.13%	69.82%	75.96%	74.32%	78.97%	75.90%	79.97%
Bicycle	57.04%	61.51%	60.08%	61.45%	63.32%	59.20%	63.24%	63.79%	67.43%	65.80%	67.53%
Bird	39.86%	46.04%	44.82%	46.41%	47.61%	41.97%	47.94%	47.02%	51.94%	51.10%	50.01%
Boat	64.59%	66.50%	68.08%	67.45%	67.21%	64.85%	67.31%	69.44%	70.92%	73.60%	74.95%
Bottle	21.96%	22.61%	25.00%	24.23%	24.40%	23.90%	25.48%	29.06%	30.79%	28.90%	27.64%
Bus	58.79%	54.46%	53.66%	57.74%	55.97%	59.02%	55.92%	66.46%	72.18%	63.60%	65.74%
Car	73.89%	76.61%	77.66%	77.81%	79.69%	74.98%	80.12%	77.31%	79.94%	80.30%	81.27%
Cat	53.77%	52.18%	53.24%	55.19%	53.02%	54.63%	53.05%	60.18%	61.35%	59.30%	60.57%
Chair	52.40%	45.61%	44.97%	46.57%	47.54%	52.49%	47.63%	50.19%	55.98%	52.10%	52.41%
Cow	38.57%	35.31%	36.45%	36.79%	37.30%	40.48%	36.74%	46.46%	49.61%	44.00%	45.24%
DiningTable	49.20%	51.31%	52.45%	54.06%	51.04%	50.53%	51.81%	51.86%	58.40%	50.50%	54.43%
Dog	36.85%	41.13%	42.72%	42.52%	43.92%	37.98%	43.68%	44.07%	44.77%	42.90%	42.33%
Horse	75.59%	77.23%	77.77%	76.65%	78.16%	76.03%	78.44%	77.85%	78.84%	78.80%	77.31%
Motorbike	61.59%	60.41%	61.65%	61.79%	64.50%	63.73%	64.46%	67.12%	70.81%	62.40%	65.29%
Person	81.63%	83.62%	83.91%	83.79%	84.31%	82.47%	84.60%	83.07%	84.96%	85.00%	85.94%
Potted Plant	20.47%	21.16%	21.34%	24.66%	24.05%	22.31%	24.52%	27.56%	31.72%	26.10%	28.35%
Sheep	40.05%	41.95%	40.09%	40.61%	42.93%	43.08%	42.61%	48.50%	51.00%	46.10%	47.56%
Sofa	50.92%	42.17%	46.03%	45.43%	49.32%	50.96%	50.58%	51.10%	56.41%	49.60%	49.17%
Train	73.39%	75.75%	76.03%	76.26%	76.66%	73.97%	76.36%	75.50%	80.24%	76.30%	79.02%
TV Monitor	49.21%	49.04%	49.31%	48.38%	52.26%	49.68%	51.22%	52.26%	57.46%	52.80%	55.02%
mAP	**53.42%**	**53.96%**	**54.55%**	**55.24%**	**55.97%**	**54.60%**	**56.08%**	**58.16%**	**61.69%**	**58.26%**	**59.49%**
Avg Purity	*30.90%*	*35.20%*	*35.20%*	*65.20%*	*71.90%*	*30.90%*	*71.90%*	*N. A.*	*N. A.*	*N. A.*	*64.30%*

3   Experiments

Our experiments are designed to compare results with the reference survey on feature encoding [1]. This paper comprehensively reviews existing encoding techniques on the PASCAL VOC 2007 object recognition dataset [30]. This dataset contains about 10000 images split into train, validation, and test sets, and labelled with 20 object classes. A one-vs-all SVM classifier is learned and evaluated independently for each category. The performance is measured as mean Average Precision (mAP) across all classes.

We compared our encoding methods with typical hard-[10], and soft-coding [8], as well as Fisher coding [5]. Each contribution is validated independently on the former; only the best run is provided for the latter.

We reproduced the same experimental conditions as in [1]. Dense SIFT (PHOW) features [32] are extracted with the publicly available VLFeat toolbox [31] for all runs. A pre-processing step reduces the feature dimensionality to 80 for all residual based methods. Moreover, VLAD encoding is also whitened to comply with the setup in [33]. The codebook size is 4000 for hard- and soft-coding, 1024 for SV, and 256 for Fisher and VLAD vectors. Hellinger's kernel is employed with Fisher encoding, a linear kernel for VLAD and SV, X^2 distance with all other encoding methods. VLAD histograms undergo power and intra-normalization, all others are L^2-normalized. See [1, 33] for details. Results are presented in Table 1.

Our first 4 runs (in black font) independently test the various improvements presented throughout this paper, demonstrating their gradual improvement over the traditional BoW scheme. Clearly, cluster purity is also correlated to discriminative power.

Our last 2 runs compare the full system with state-of the art encoding methods. The method boosts hard-coded BoW encoding by 2.55 %, 1.48 % for its soft-coding version and 1.26 % for the VLAD encoding. The soft coding experiment does not provide as much performance gain as its hard coding counterpart. This is sensible as soft-coding can be harmful in the case of neighbouring purity clusters with different dominant labels. As for the VLAD encoding, the reduced codebook cardinality explains its small improvement.

4   Conclusion

In this paper, we have enhanced the BoW scheme in several ways: maximizing intra-cluster category similarity, accounting for the probability of a codeword to occur and proposing a size-adaptive clustering algorithm.

As the cluster purity associated to each codeword offers a natural way to perform feature selection, we envision investigating this direction.

Acknowledgement. This publication has emanated from research conducted with the financial support of Science Foundation Ireland (SFI) under grant number SFI/12/RC/2289.

References

1. Chatfield, K., Lempitsky, V., Vedaldi, A., Zisserman, A.: The devil is in the details: an evaluation of recent feature encoding methods. In: BMVC (2011)
2. Kaufman, L., Rousseeuw, P.-J.: Finding Groups in Data: An Introduction to Cluster Analysis. Wiley, New York (1990)
3. Wagstaff, K., Cardie, C., Rogers, S., Schrödl, S.: Constrained K-means clustering with background knowledge. In: ICML (2001)
4. Hartigan, J., Wang, M.: A K-means clustering algorithm. Appl. Stat. **28**, 100–108 (1979)
5. Perronnin, F., Dance, C.: Fisher kenrels on visual vocabularies for image categorizaton. In: CVPR (2006)
6. Perronnin, F., Sánchez, J., Mensink, T.: Improving the fisher kernel for large-scale image classification. In: Daniilidis, K., Maragos, P., Paragios, N. (eds.) ECCV 2010, Part IV. LNCS, vol. 6314, pp. 143–156. Springer, Heidelberg (2010). doi:10.1007/978-3-642-15561-1_11
7. Negrel, R., Picard, D., Gosselin, P.H.: Compact tensor based image representation for similarity search. In: ICIP (2012)
8. Philbin, J., Chum, O., Isard, M., Sivic, J., Zisserman, A.: Lost in quantization: improving particular object retrieval in large scale image databases. In: CVPR (2008)
9. Csurka, G., Bray, C., Dance, C.R., Fan, L., Willamowski, J.: Visual categorization with bags of keypoints. In: ECCV (2004)
10. Lazebnik, S., Schmid, C., Ponce, J.: Beyond bags of features: spatial pyramid matching for recognizing natural scene categories. In: CVPR (2006)
11. Jegou, H., Douze, M., Schmid, C., Perez, P.: Aggregating local descriptors into a compact image representation. In: CVPR (2010)
12. Delhumeau, J., Gosselin, P.-H., Jégou, H., Pérez, P.: Revisiting the VLAD image representation. ACM Multimedia (2013)
13. Zhou, X., Yu, K., Zhang, T., Huang, T.S.: Image classification using super-vector coding of local image descriptors. In: Daniilidis, K., Maragos, P., Paragios, N. (eds.) ECCV 2010. LNCS, vol. 6315, pp. 141–154. Springer, Heidelberg (2010). doi:10.1007/978-3-642-15555-0_11
14. Sivic, J., Zisserman, A.: Video Google: a text retrieval approach to object matching in videos. In: ICCV (2003)
15. Moosmann, F., Nowak, E., Jurie, F.: Randomized clustering forests for image classification. PAMI **30**(9), 1632–1646 (2008)
16. Winn, J., Criminisi, A., Minka, A.: Object categorization by learned universal visual dictionary. In: ICCV (2005)
17. Yang, L., Jin, R., Sukthankar, R., Jurie, F.: Unifying discriminative visual codebook generation with classifier training for object category recognition. In: CVPR (2008)
18. Larlus, D., Jurie, F.: Latent mixture vocabularies for object categorization. In: BMVC (2006)
19. López-Sastre, R.J., Renes-Olalla, J., Gil-Jiménez, P., Maldonado-Bascón, S., Lafuente-Arroyo, S.: Heterogeneous visual codebook integration via consensus clustering for visual categorization. TCSVT **23**, 1358–1368 (2013)
20. Liu, J., Yang, Y., Shah, M.: Learning semantic visual vocabularies using diffusion distance. In: CVPR (2009)
21. Zhang, S., Tian, Q., Hua, G., Zhou, W., Huang, Q., Li, H., Gao, W.: Modeling spatial and semantic cues for large-scale near-duplicated image retrieval. CVIU **115**(3), 403–414 (2011)
22. Li, T., Mei, T., Kweon, I.-S., Hua, X.-S.: Contextual bag-of-words for visual categorization. TCSVT **21**(4), 381–392 (2011)

23. Trichet, R., Nevatia, R.: Video segmentation and feature co-occurrences for activity classification. In: WACV (2014)
24. Leibe, B., Ettlin, A., Schiele, B.: Learning semantic object parts for object categorization. Image Vis. Comput. **26**(1), 15–26 (2008)
25. Zhang, Z., Wang, C., Xiao, B., Zhou, W., Liu, S.: Action recognition using context-constrained linear coding. IEEE Sig. Process. Lett. **19**(7), 2112–2119 (2012)
26. Wang, J., Yang, J., Yu, K., Lv, F., Huang, T., Gong, Y.: Locality-constrained linear coding for image classification. In: CVPR (2010)
27. Kovashka, A., Grauman, K.: Learning a hierarchy of discriminative space-time neighborhood features for human action recognition. In: CVPR (2010)
28. Wang, H., Yuan, J., Tan, Y.-P.: Combining feature context and spatial context for image pattern discovery. In: ICDM (2011)
29. Arandjelovic, R., Zisserman, A.: All about vlad. In: CVPR (2013)
30. Everingham, M., Zisserman, A., Williams, C., Van Gool, L.: The PASCAL visual object classes challenge 2007 (VOC2007) results. Technical report, Pascal Challenge (2007)
31. Vedaldi, A., Fulkerson, B.: VLFeat-an open and portable library of computer vision algorithms. ACM Multimedia (2010)
32. Krystian, M., Schmid, C.: A performance evaluation of local descriptors. PAMI **27**(10), 1615–1630 (2005)
33. Peng, X., Wang, L., Qiao, Y., Peng, Q.: Boosting VLAD with supervised dictionary learning and high-order statistics. In: Fleet, D., Pajdla, T., Schiele, B., Tuytelaars, T. (eds.) ECCV 2014. LNCS, vol. 8691, pp. 660–674. Springer, Heidelberg (2014). doi:10.1007/978-3-319-10578-9_43

Learning Approaches for Parking Lots Classification

Daniele Di Mauro[1]([✉]), Sebastiano Battiato[1], Giuseppe Patanè[2],
Marco Leotta[2], Daniele Maio[2], and Giovanni M. Farinella[1]

[1] Image Processing Lab, University of Catania, Catania, Italy
{dimauro,battiato,farinella}@dmi.unict.it
[2] Parksmart s.r.l., Catania, Italy
{giuseppe.patane,marco.leotta,daniele.maio}@parksmart.it
http://iplab.dmi.unict.it, http://www.parksmart.it

Abstract. The paper exploits the problem of empty vs. non-empty parking lots classification from images acquired by public cameras through the comparison between a classic supervised learning method and a semi-supervised learning one. Both approaches are based on convolutional neural networks paradigm. Experimental results point out that the supervised method outperforms the semi-supervised approach already when few samples are used for training.

Keywords: Supervised learning · Semi-supervised learning · Convolutional Neural Networks

1 Introduction and Motivations

The social context where we live is changing rapidly. Recent studies show that more than half of global population lives in urban areas [10]. Cities are becoming more and more messy and disordered due to such huge number of inhabitants. These megacities are affected by new problems in different fields. The new concept of *Smart City* tries to solve such problems through innovative approaches by the massive use of ICT solutions in order to develop smart mobility systems, smart governance systems (also known as e-governance), as well as smart and share economy [3]. Focusing on the mobility, over the past few decades, the use of cars in large metropolitan areas has massively increased. On the other side parking lots have not. This causes more stressed drivers and an increasing of air pollution since people have to spend more time to find a free parking space. The industry is focusing on solving (or at least mitigate) this problem through different technologies that can be grouped in three major categories: *counter-based, sensor-based* and *image-based*. The first category is the oldest one. It is used in closed parking areas, to give informations about the number of free spaces giving no clue on where they are located. Sensor-based solutions adopt sensors installed at each parking space. Most of the time they are plunged in the asphalt. This solution is more expensive than the previous one. Moreover the sensors may be

© Springer International Publishing AG 2016
J. Blanc-Talon et al. (Eds.): ACIVS 2016, LNCS 10016, pp. 410–418, 2016.
DOI: 10.1007/978-3-319-48680-2_36

not reliable in some circumstances (e.g., in presence of ice). The third category is gaining interest in the last years due to the increasing of security cameras in our cities and because the advances of computer vision techniques. One of the first examples of image-based solutions in literature is described in [11]. The system consists of a pipeline composed by four modules. As first a preprocessing step is performed to rotate the raw input frames into the uniform axis and to segment them into small patches which include three parking spaces. The second module is devoted to the feature extraction (e.g., color distribution of patches). A classification stage is then performed with a Multi-class Support Vector Machine. Finally, a verification and conflict correction stage based on Markov Random Field model is applied to refine the results. The main objective in [1] was to build an annotated dataset to be exploited by the computer vision community to assess algorithms related to the free parking spaces detection problem. The images were taken in two different parking lots with three different views and different weather conditions (i.e. cloudy, sunny, rainy). In order to perform a benchmark on the dataset, the authors performed different tests using two different hand-crafted features: Local Binary Patterns [8] and Local Phase Quantization [9]. A Support Vector Machine with a Gaussian kernel has been employed for the classification stage. In a first experiment the authors used images sampled from a single parking lot to train and test their system. The main objective of this test was to evaluate the "goodness" of the used features. The second experiment was developed to evaluate the transfer learning property of the approach. Images from a single parking lot have been used as training set, whereas tests where performed with data from the others view/lots. In the third experiment training and testing data were built considering images of all lots and views in order to measure the learning ability of the system.

The aforementioned approaches used supervised learning algorithms to deal with the problem of classifying a parking space as empty or non-empty. The main drawback of this kind of approaches is the construction of a big dataset to train the classifier. Considering the needs of a company deploying an image-based parking monitoring system, the effort of manually labeling the images to build such big training dataset can became problematic since it is time consuming (i.e., it has high costs for the company). Moreover, it is difficult to build in advance a proper dataset for training by considering all the possible variabilities which can be observed in different parking spaces. Variabilities depend on the positioning of the cameras, shapes of the parking lots, as well as from the classic variabilities which can be considered in a standard image classification problem (e.g. appearence of vehicles, lighting conditions, presence of shadows, occlusions, etc. See Fig. 1). Moreover, most of the time the images to build the training set (and hence to include possible variabilities in the learning process) are only available after the deployment of the parking monitoring system. It is hence important to reduce the labeling time adopting learning methods able to propagate the previous learned model (i.e. models already working on others parking lots) to the new parking lot to be monitored.

The above considerations have motivated the study presented in this paper. In Supervised learning, the labeled datasets are fundamental for the training,

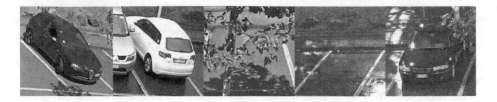

Fig. 1. Example of parking space variability in geometry, luminance, occlusions, shapes

but are "difficult" to create. On the other side, it is simple to create partly labeled sets. The main goal is how to propagate the labels from few labeled samples to the full dataset composed by both labeled and unlabeled data. Semi-supervised learning is usually proposed to deal with this kind of problem. In order to exploit unlabeled data, Semi-supervised approaches make some assumptions to the underlying data distribution. In particular, three assumptions are the most used in literature [12]:

- *The Smoothness assumption:* if two feature points x_1, x_2 in a high-density region are close, then they should have close corresponding outputs y_1, y_2.
- *The Cluster assumption:* if feature points are in the same cluster, they are likely to be of the same class.
- *The Manifold assumption:* high-dimensional data likely lie roughly on a low-dimensional manifold.

In this paper we evaluate the performances of a semi-supervised learning approach in comparison with respect to a classic supervised learning one in order to benchmark the problem of parking space monitoring. Specifically, considering the high interest of the community on the deep learning architectures, we compare the well-known supervised learning CNN architecture called Alexnet [5] with respect to the recent pseudo-label approach for semi-supervised learning of deep neural networks [7]. To perform this comparison we consider two different datasets; the recent introduced PKLot dataset [1] and a new dataset called Parksmart dataset (PSD) whose images have been collected in real scenarios by considering different variabilities.

Experiments have been done to evaluate the performances of Alexnet [5] and pseudo-label [7] with respect to different training settings. Results show that for the problem addressed in this paper (empty vs. non-empty space) Alexnet outperforms pseudo-label in all cases and independently from the number of training samples used as input. The lesson learned is that for the considered problem a supervised learning technique is to be preferred also in cases where only few labeled samples are available as training.

The remainder of the paper is organized as follows. Section 2 describes the deep learning approaches considered in the experiments. Section 3 gives details on the datasets used for evaluation purposes. In Sect. 4 the experiments are detailed and the results are presented. Finally, Sect. 5 concludes the paper.

2   Methods

To compare supervised vs semi-supervised methods we have exploited recent approaches presented in literature [5,7]. In the following we summarize the employed methods.

2.1   Deep Convolutional Neural Networks and Fine-Tuning

In recent years, Neural Networks have re-gained attentions in computer vision. In particular nowadays we talk about *Deep Convolutional Neural Networks (ConvNet)*. ConvNet architectures make the explicit assumption that the inputs are images. ConvNet allows to encode certain properties to be considered in the context of visual understanding into the Neural Network architecture, enabling also an efficient forward function implementation and reducing the amount of free parameters in the network [6].

In [5] was presented a ConvNet for the ILSVRC-2012 competition. The ConvNet proposed in [5] is known as *AlexNet* and in 2012 won the competition with a good margin of accuracy respect to other methods. AlexNet contains eight layers: the first five are convolutional layers and the remaining three are fully-connected. The last fully-connected layer is a 1000-way softmax which produces a distribution over 1000 object classes. AlexNet can be applied to problems different to the original one (i.e., discrimination among 1000 object classes) performing a fine-tuning. The fine-tuning method is a transfer learning mechanism. Usually researchers do not train the Convolutional Network from scratch but, most of the time, it is common to use a pre-trained ConvNet on a very large dataset (e.g., Alexnet over ImageNet) and only fine-tune (recalculate weights) some, or the very last, higher-level portion of the network. The rationale behind this choice comes from the observation that the earlier layers, because of their convolutional nature, extract low visual features that are useful to many general computer vision tasks. With fine-tuning the higher layers are trained for the specific task.

2.2   Pseudo-Label: The Simple and Efficient Semi-supervised Learning Method for Deep Neural Networks

In [7] is proposed a network trained in a semi-supervised fashion. The training is achieved using at the same time labeled and unlabeled data. To the unlabeled data is assigned the label that the network computed on the forward pass (this is why it is called "Pseudo Label"). During the training process the loss function calculated on labeled data and pseudo-labeled ones are summed using the following formula:

$$L = \frac{1}{n} \sum_{m=1}^{n} \sum_{i=1}^{C} L(y_i^m, f_i^m) + \alpha(t) \frac{1}{\tilde{n}} \sum_{m=1}^{\tilde{n}} \sum_{i=1}^{C} L(\tilde{y}_i^m, \tilde{f}_i^m) \tag{1}$$

where n is the number of labeled data, $\tilde{n}$ the number of unlabeled data, C the classes, t is the number of iterations, y and f are the labels and network result for labeled data, $\tilde{y}$ $\tilde{f}$ are pseudo-labels and network result for unlabeled data and $\alpha(t)$ is defined as

$$\alpha(t) = \begin{cases} 0 & \text{if } t < T_1 \\ 1 & \text{if } T_1 \leq t < T_2 \\ a_f & \text{if } T_2 \leq t \end{cases} \tag{2}$$

where $a_f = 3$ and $T_1 = 100$, $T_2 = 600$.

3 Dataset

In our experiments we used data sampled from the PKLot dataset [1] and a new dataset which is referred with the acronym PSD. Details on the dataset are given in the following.

3.1 PKLot Dataset

The dataset consists of 12,417 images resulting in 695,899 samples of parking spaces which have been manually labeled by the authors of [1]. The images were taken within a 5 min time interval, during a 30 days period, using a Full-HD camera (Microsoft LifeCam HD-5000) with resolution of 1280×720 pixels. The cameras were positioned at very high altitude to minimize occlusions (see Fig. 2). The images were stored in high quality JPEG (100 % quality). To crop and to label every space in the images as free or occupied, the authors of [1] developed a specific tool able to save information of each space in an Extensible Markup Language file (XML). To remove rotation variability every parking space patch has been rotated horizontally or vertically depending of their original rotation angle. The key features of this dataset are the following:

- images were taken with different weather conditions (sunny, rainy and overcast periods);
- images were taken from different parking lots;
- cameras were positioned at different heights;
- images have strong variability: such as the presence of shadows, low light, over-exposition, difference in perspective.

Fig. 2. Examples of images belonging to PKlot dataset

Fig. 3. Example of images belonging to PSD dataset

3.2 PSD Dataset

The proposed PSD dataset was acquired from August 2015 to November 2015 in a parking lot of the University of Catania. In order to capture variabilities we have considered three time slot during the day:

1. from 06:00 am to 09:00 am (3 h)
2. from 12:30 pm to 02:30 pm (2 h)
3. from 05:30 pm to 09:00 pm (3.5 h)

The monitored parking lot is composed by 46 parking spaces. To cover the whole parking lot the data have been acquired by four cameras with a resolution of 1920 × 1080 extracted from motion jpeg registration. The sampled images have been manually labeled. Specifically, for each image the different parking spaces have been manually labeled as free or occupied. For experimental purpose the final set of parking spaces is composed by 270796 crops. Examples of PSD parking lots are reported in Fig. 3.

4   Experiments and Results

To perform our experiments we used Caffe library [4]. All the code was developed using the Python api. We took advantage of GPU optimized code running the tests on a machine equiped with four *NVIDIA GeForce TITAN X with 12 Gb of DDR5 RAM*.

To test how the fine-tuned AlexNet and the pseudo-labeling method behave we have performed different experiments varying the number of training images. Following the rationale in [7], as training we selected a subset of images from PKLot and from PSD, equal to 0.16 %, 1 %, 1.6 %, 5 % of the entire dataset (see Table 1).

Table 1. Considered dataset and training images

Dataset	Images	Training			
		0.17 %	1 %	1.7 %	5 %
PKLot	72000	120	720	1200	3600
PSD	144000	240	1440	2400	7200
PSD*	42000	70	420	700	2100

Table 2. Results with training balanced per camera and class

Dataset	Method	Loss	0.17 %	1 %	1.7 %	5 %
PKLot	*finetuning*	*crossentropy*	97.35 % ± 2.17	99.40 % ± 0.04	99.54 % ± 0.04	99.76 % ± 0.02
	pseudolabel	*crossentropy*	94.85 % ± 1.81	98.90 % ± 0.13	99.35 % ± 0.17	99.77 % ± 0.04
	finetuning	*softmax*	97.35 % ± 2.17	99.40 % ± 0.04	99.54 % ± 0.04	99.76 % ± 0.02
	pseudolabel	*softmax*	97.03 % ± 0.79	99.07 % ± 0.17	99.32 % ± 0.37	99.81 % ± 0.06
PSD	*finetuning*	*crossentropy*	99.02 % ± 0.14	99.46 % ± 0.15	99.52 % ± 0.01	99.73 % ± 0.01
	pseudolabel	*crossentropy*	95.76 % ± 1.60	99.25 % ± 0.04	99.38 % ± 0.13	99.81 % ± 0.02
	finetuning	*softmax*	99.02 % ± 0.14	99.46 % ± 0.15	99.52 % ± 0.01	99.73 % ± 0.01
	pseudolabel	*softmax*	96.89 % ± 0.94	99.34 % ± 0.07	99.35 % ± 0.13	99.81 % ± 0.04
PSD*	*pseudolabel*	*crossentropy*	98.24 % ± 0.13	99.06 % ± 0.02	97.24 % ± 0.56	97.86 % ± 0.02
	pseudolabel	*softmax*	97.55 % ± 0.56	98.82 % ± 0.11	97.45 % ± 0.24	97.93 % ± 0.22

The network described in [7] is a neural network with 1 hidden layer. Rectified Linear Unit is used for hidden units, Sigmoid Unit is used for output units. The number of hidden units is 5000. Pseudo-label, is the method to feed a neural network with labeled and unlabeled data at the same time, thus we decided to implement such method using an augmented Alexnet able to behave in such way to proper compare the results. In particular we added an input layer and a concatenation layer on the front of the network to have two different entrances for labeled and unlabeled data and to concatenate them before feeding the network. At the end of the network, we added a slicing layer and a second loss layer in order to calculate different loss values considering the cases where the input belongs to the labeled set or to the unlabeled one. The losses calculated were summed using the loss weight defined by Eq. 1. We tested the methods using softmax and crossentropy loss functions in order to have a more complete comparison.

We performed two kind of experiments repeated three times with random labeled images for training purpose. In the first experiment (see results in Table 2) labeled images were balanced per camera and per class. We decided to balance labeled images per camera to give the possibility learn in equal way all the geometrical variabilities of parking spaces. In the second experiment (see results in Table 3) we balanced the labeled images only per class to verify the robustness of the classifier.

The networks were trained for 30 epochs calculated over the training set data. Pseudo-label approach takes more iterations than fine-tuning. The learning rate was set at 0.0005. As we can see in Tables 2 and 3 results of pseudo-label and

Table 3. Results with training balanced per class

Dataset	Method	Loss	0.17 %	1 %	1.7 %	5 %
PKLot	*finetuning*	*crossentropy*	96.46 % ± 0.49	98.36 % ± 0.33	98.70 % ± 0.01	99.02 % ± 0.04
	pseudolabel	*crossentropy*	15.24 % ± 0.67	17.13 % ± 0.91	20.65 % ± 6.00	14.65 % ± 0.00
	finetuning	*softmax*	96.39 % ± 0.26	98.25 % ± 0.33	98.47 % ± 0.08	99.00 % ± 0.15
	pseudolabel	*softmax*	15.24 % ± 0.67	17.13 % ± 0.91	20.65 % ± 6.00	14.65 % ± 0.00
PSD	*finetuning*	*crossentropy*	96.92 % ± 0.13	98.24 % ± 0.05	98.59 % ± 0.08	99.05 % ± 0.06
	pseudolabel	*crossentropy*	15.14 % ± 0.55	51.69 % ± 26.55	61.78 % ± 33.33	38.22 % ± 33.33
	finetuning	*softmax*	96.83 % ± 0.55	98.10 % ± 0.39	98.68 % ± 0.17	99.12 % ± 0.11
	pseudolabel	*softmax*	15.14 % ± 0.55	51.69 % ± 26.55	61.78 % ± 33.33	38.22 % ± 33.33
PSD*	*pseudolabel*	*crossentropy*	98.50 % ± 0.12	98.99 % ± 0.05	97.80 % ± 0.21	98.19 % ± 0.28
	pseudolabel	*softmax*	98.23 % ± 0.29	98.99 % ± 0.17	97.80 % ± 0.00	98.01 % ± 0.47

Fig. 4. Some example of misclassified images. From left to right they were classified as empty, empty, non-empty, empty

fine-tuned AlexNet are comparable over PKLot dataset. Fine-tuning works even better at lower training samples. On the other hand, our first experiment on the PSD dataset obtained results with a huge margin in favour of the fine-tuned AlexNet (see Tables 2 and 3). The standard deviation among different runs is really high. This suggested us that the result of Pseudo-label is highly depending on the input. The main difference between the experiments with the two dataset is related on the random choice of data to be labeled. In fact, PKLot unlabeled subset was balanced in terms of classes (i.c. 36000 Empty spaces, 36000 Non empty spaces), whereas the PSD unlabeled subset was not balanced (122903 empty vs. 21097 Non-empty spaces). To prove our intuition we then took a subset of PSD dataset balanced per class. In this case the dataset was composed by 42000 images (i.e. 21000 Empty spaces, 21000 Non empty spaces) and corresponding training data considered for the training were computed in percentage as before (see PSD* in Table 1). Results over PSD* in Tables 2 and 3 show that the behavior of pseudo-label changed obtaining results similar to the fine-tuned model. In sum, the experiments pointed out that the supervised method (AlexNet plus fine-tuning) outperforms the semi-supervised one (Pseudo-label) in all cases, obtaining very high accuracy (over 96 % with few images as training). Moreover good results can be obtained with Pseudo-label only when the dataset to be classified is balanced in terms of samples per classes, which is a prior knowledge too difficult have in real applications. In Fig. 4 are reported some challenging cases of images misclassified by the approaches.

5 Conclusion

In this paper we have compared supervised vs semi-supervised approaches on the problem of parking lots classification. Results shown that the supervised approach AlexNet with fine-tuning outperforms pseudo-label method. Moreover the pseudo-label suffers when the dataset to be classified is composed by samples unbalanced with respect to the classes. Future works will be devoted to consider the time dimension and tracking algorithms [2] in the monitoring of different spaces in order to improve the results.

References

1. de Almeida, P.R., Oliveira, L.S., Britto, A.S., Silva, E.J., Koerich, A.L.: PKLot-a robust dataset for parking Lot classification. Expert Syst. Appl. **42**(11), 4937–4949 (2015)
2. Battiato, S., Farinella, G.M., Furnari, A., Puglisi, G., Snijders, A., Spiekstra, J.: An integrated system for vehicle tracking and classification. Expert Syst. Appl. **42**(21), 7263–7275 (2015)
3. Chourabi, H., Nam, T., Walker, S., Gil-Garcia, J.R., Mellouli, S., Nahon, K., Pardo, T.A., Scholl, H.J.: Understanding smart cities: an integrative framework. In: 2012 45th Hawaii International Conference on System Science (HICSS), pp. 2289–2297. IEEE (2012)
4. Jia, Y., Shelhamer, E., Donahue, J., Karayev, S., Long, J., Girshick, R., Guadarrama, S., Darrell, T.: Caffe: convolutional architecture for fast feature embedding. arXiv preprint arXiv:1408.5093 (2014)
5. Krizhevsky, A., Sutskever, I., Hinton, G.E.: ImageNet classification with deep convolutional neural networks. In: Advances in Neural Information Processing Systems, pp. 1097–1105 (2012)
6. LeCun, Y., Bottou, L., Bengio, Y., Haffner, P.: Gradient-based learning applied to document recognition. Proc. IEEE **86**(11), 2278–2324 (1998)
7. Lee, D.H.: Pseudo-label: The simple and efficient semi-supervised learning method for deep neural networks. In: Workshop on Challenges in Representation Learning, ICML, vol. 3 (2013)
8. Ojala, T., Pietikäinen, M., Mäenpää, T.: Multiresolution gray-scale and rotation invariant texture classification with local binary patterns. IEEE Trans. Pattern Anal. Mach. Intell. **24**(7), 971–987 (2002)
9. Ojansivu, V., Heikkilä, J.: Blur insensitive texture classification using local phase quantization. In: Elmoataz, A., Lezoray, O., Nouboud, F., Mammass, D. (eds.) ICISP 2008. LNCS, vol. 5099, pp. 236–243. Springer, Heidelberg (2008). doi:10.1007/978-3-540-69905-7_27
10. Shapiro, J.M.: Smart cities: quality of life, productivity, and the growth effects of human capital. Rev. Econ. Stat. **88**(2), 324–335 (2006)
11. Wu, Q., Zhang, Y.: Parking Lots Space Detection. Machine Learning, Fall (2006)
12. Zhu, X., Goldberg, A.B.: Introduction to semi-supervised learning. Synth. Lect. Artif. Intell. Mach. Learn. **3**(1), 1–130 (2009)

Video Event Detection Based Non-stationary Bayesian Networks

Christophe Gonzales[2], Rim Romdhane[1], and Séverine Dubuisson[1(✉)]

[1] Sorbonne Universités, UPMC Univ Paris 06, UMR 7222, ISIR, Paris, France
severine.dubuisson@isir.upmc.fr
[2] Sorbonne Universités, UPMC Univ Paris 06, UMR 7606, LIP6, Paris, France

Abstract. In this paper, we propose an approach for detecting events online in video sequences. This one requires no prior knowledge, the events being defined as spatio-temporal breaks. For this purpose, we propose to combine non-stationary dynamic Bayesian networks (nsDBN) to model the scene and particle filter (PF) to track objects in the sequence. In this framework, an event corresponds to a significant difference between a new particle set provided by PF and the sampled density encoded by the nsDBN. Whenever an event is detected, the particle set is exploited to learn a new nsDBN representing the scene. Unfortunately, nsDBNs are designed for discrete random variables and particles are instantiations of continuous ones. We therefore propose to discretize them using a new discretization method well suited for nsDBNs. Our approach has been tested on real video sequences and allowed to detect two different events (forbidden stop and fight).

1 Event Understanding in Video Sequences

Event understanding is an important research topic which has attracted significant research interest in recent years. It includes many applications, such as visual surveillance, video annotation, video retrieval or video database indexing.

A lot of effort has been devoted to event-based video analysis. The latter may be classified into two main categories: explicit event *recognition* (normal or abnormal) and *detection* of abnormal/unusual/unknown events. In the first case, the events to recognize are explicitly known. The key events are initially modeled to be the most compact and representative of the dynamic scene. The recognition can be done in two main ways: (i) the semantic approaches [1,20] break down events into sub-events with a concept of order or spatio-temporal relationships and (ii) probabilistic approaches solve the problem of classification using methods such as k-NN, Random Forest or SVMs [13,24].

Event detection does not necessarily requires a prior event modeling. An event is seen as a "deviation" from examples of normal behaviors [10,19,26]. In this case we should have learned a number of normal events, which can limit applications. The event can also be seen as a change in behavior (speed, movement, *etc.*) between two instants or two time intervals. The goal is to detect

© Springer International Publishing AG 2016
J. Blanc-Talon et al. (Eds.): ACIVS 2016, LNCS 10016, pp. 419–430, 2016.
DOI: 10.1007/978-3-319-48680-2_37

rare [11], unusual [27,28] or abnormal [8,14,17,22] events. In [27] a HMM framework is used, in which usual event models are first learnt from a large amount of training data, while unusual event models are learned by a Bayesian adaptation in an unsupervised manner. The method in [9] selects normal event pattern groups based on clustering object trajectories, then an HMM training is performed on each normal group. Unusual events are detected by analyzing the likelihood of an unseen object trajectory in every model. In [10], a frequency-based analysis is performed to automatically discover regular rules of normal events and then events deviating from these rules are identified as anomalies. Wang *et al.* [25] use location and optical flow features along with a hierarchical Bayesian method to model activities and interactions. To detect unusual events, they use the likelihood measure calculated from the learnt model.

In recent years, the popularity of Bayesian networks for reasoning with uncertainties and their various extensions, in particular, dynamic Bayesian networks (DBN) [4], has stimulated the scientific community to apply them to video event detection. One advantage of Bayesian networks is the automatic learning of their structure and their parameters, a task for which many effective algorithms exist [2,4,5,23]. Quite naturally, as we have seen above, this type of model was used for the dynamic scene modeling in general and for event recognition in particular [11]. However, the structure and the parameters of a DBN are fixed over time, which is not suited to the case of video sequences in which objects (nodes) may appear or disappear over time, their probabilistic relationships (structure) or speed (parameters) may also change. For this reason, we use a non-stationary DBN (nsDBN), whose structure and parameters can change over time, thus enabling to better model the dynamic scene. To the best of our knowledge, this has never been used in computer vision for modeling spatio-temporal changes in a dynamic scene. In this paper, we propose a new variant of a learning algorithm (structure and parameters) which treats continuous data from the particle filter.

In this article, we focus on the detection of events for which we have no prior knowledge. We then take a very general definition for them: *an event is a spatio-temporal rupture in the dynamic scene.* Our approach combines particle filtering and nsDBNs. The particle filter (see Sect. 2) approximates at each time t the density of objects by a weighted sample, by using a succession of propagation, corrections, estimation and resampling steps. The nsDBN has at each time a structure and a set of parameters (which may of course change over time) and thus it encodes a probability density. The idea is to compare the density obtained at time t by the particle filter with the one encoded by the nsDBN. If these two densities are considered close, then the structure and parameters of the nsDBN are still appropriate to the current scene modeling and no event is detected. Otherwise, it is necessary to change the structure and/or the parameters for the nsDBN to fit well the scene changes: this means that there is a space-time break/rupture and thus an event. This paper is organized as follows. The particle filter is briefly described in Sect. 2. The nsDBNs, data discretization and event detection are discussed in Sect. 3. Experimental results on video sequences are presented in Sect. 4. Finally, Sect. 5 is devoted to a conclusion and some prospects.

2   Particle Filter for Object Tracking

Throughout the paper, we note with capital letters (X, Y) the random variables, with lowercase letters their instantiations (x, y). The indices represent a temporal dimension (x_t). Finally, we note in bold the sets $(\mathbf{x}_t)$ and in calligraphic letters the graphs or graphical models $(\mathcal{G}, \mathcal{B})$.

In this paper, object tracking consists of estimating a state sequence $\{\mathbf{x}_t\}_{t=1,...,T}$ from observations $\{\mathbf{y}_t\}_{t=1,...,T}$. From a probabilistic point of view, this problem consists to estimate, for each time t, the posterior density $p(\mathbf{x}_t|\mathbf{y}_{1:t})$ where $\mathbf{y}_{1:t}$ denotes a tuple $(\mathbf{y}_1, ..., \mathbf{y}_t)$. This can be computed iteratively using Eqs (1) and (2), which are referred to as a *prediction* step and a *correction* step respectively.

$$p(\mathbf{x}_{t+1}|\mathbf{y}_{1:t}) = \int p(\mathbf{x}_{t+1}|\mathbf{x}_t)p(\mathbf{x}_t|\mathbf{y}_{1:t})d\mathbf{x}_t \tag{1}$$

$$p(\mathbf{x}_{t+1}|\mathbf{y}_{1:t+1}) \propto p(\mathbf{y}_{t+1}|\mathbf{x}_{t+1})p(\mathbf{x}_{t+1}|\mathbf{y}_{1:t}) \tag{2}$$

Where $p(\mathbf{x}_{t+1}|\mathbf{x}_t)$ and $p(\mathbf{y}_{t+1}|\mathbf{x}_{t+1})$ represent the transition and the likelihood functions respectively.

The particle filter (PF) [7] aims at approaching a distribution by a set of N weighted samples or *particles*, $\mathbf{S}_{t+1} = \{\mathbf{x}_{t+1}^{(i)}, w_{t+1}^{(i)}\}_{i=1}^N$. Particles correspond to possible achievements of a hidden state (e.g., the position of objects in the scene) at time $t + 1$. As mentioned above, particle filtering is done in two steps:

(i) a *prediction* step (Eq. (1)) the particle filter (PF) propagates (using past observations): the particle set $\{\mathbf{x}_{t+1}^{(i)}, w_{t+1}^{(i)}\}_{i=1}^N$ according to an importance function

$$q(\mathbf{x}_{t+1}|\mathbf{x}_{0:t}^{(i)}, \mathbf{y}_{t+1})$$

(ii) a *correction* step (Eq. (2)): a correction of this prediction (using a new observation/image), where the particle weights are calculated using a likelihood function so that:

$$w_{t+1}^{(i)} \propto w_t^{(i)} p(\mathbf{y}_{t+1}|\mathbf{x}_{t+1}^{(i)}) \frac{p(\mathbf{x}_{t+1}^{(i)}|\mathbf{x}_t^{(i)})}{q(\mathbf{x}_{t+1}|\mathbf{x}_{0:t}^{(i)}, \mathbf{y}_{t+1})} \tag{3}$$

with $\sum_{i=1}^N w_{t+1}^{(i)} = 1$. The particles can then be resampled: those with the highest weights are duplicated, and those with the lowest weights are eliminated. The estimate of the posterior density is given by $\sum_{i=1}^N w_{t+1}^{(i)} \delta_{\mathbf{x}_{t+1}^{(i)}}(\mathbf{x}_{t+1})$ where $\delta_{\mathbf{x}_{t+1}^{(i)}}$ are Dirac masses centered on $\mathbf{x}_{t+1}^{(i)}$, the probable objects positions.

3   NsDBNs for Event Detection

In this section, we propose a new approach to detect events in video sequences based on an extension of Bayesian networks (BN). A Bayesian network is a compact probabilistic graphical model defined as:

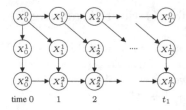

Fig. 1. A nsDBN $\langle(\mathcal{B}_0, 0), (\mathcal{B}_1, t_1)\rangle$ (left, shaded) and its grounded BN (right).

Definition 1 Bayesian Network (BN) [16]). *A BN is a pair $(\mathcal{G}, \Theta)$, where $\mathcal{G} = (\boldsymbol{V}, \boldsymbol{A})$ is a directed acyclic graph (DAG), $\boldsymbol{V}$ represents a set of discrete random variables[1], $\boldsymbol{A}$ is a set of arcs, and $\Theta = \{P(X|\boldsymbol{Pa}(X))\}_{X \in \boldsymbol{V}}$ is the set of the conditional probability distributions (CPT) of the node/random variables X in $\mathcal{G}$ given their parents $\boldsymbol{Pa}(X)$ in $\mathcal{G}$. The BN encodes the joint probability over $\boldsymbol{V}$ as:*

$$P(\boldsymbol{V}) = \prod_{X \in \boldsymbol{V}} P(X|\boldsymbol{Pa}(X)). \tag{4}$$

To detect events in video sequences, the BNs are inadequate because they lack a temporal dimension. Fortunately, time extensions have been proposed in the literature, including (stationary) DBNs [4] and nsDBNs [18]:

Definition 2 (Non-stationary Dynamic Bayesian Network (nsDBN)). *A nsDBN is a sequence of pairs $\langle(\mathcal{B}_h, t_h)\rangle_{h=0}^{m}$, where $t_0 = 0$ represents the first time slice, $\mathcal{B}_0$ is the BN representing the distribution over the random variables at time 0. Each $\mathcal{B}_h$, $h = 1, \ldots, m$, is a BN representing the conditional probability of the random variables (discrete) at time t given those at time $t - 1$, for all $t \in \mathbf{E}_h = \{t_{h-1}+1, \ldots, t_h\}$. t_h and $\mathbf{E}_h$ are called a transition time and an epoch respectively. By convention, $\mathbf{E}_0 = \{0\}$.*

A DBN is a nsDBN in which the sequence contains only two pairs. Figure 1 shows a nsDBN (left) and its grounded BN (right).

3.1   Detect Events with NsDBN

In this work, we consider that each transition time t_i corresponds to an event: it is indeed a rupture/break that may be due to:

(a) an addition or deletion of random variables. In our context, it corresponds to objects appearing or disappearing from the scene; and/or
(b) the observation of new values (never observed before) for some variables: this corresponds to new behaviors; and/or
(c) a change of the parameters of CPTs, which indicates a change in behavior of certain objects; and/or

---

[1] By abuse of notation, we use similarly $X \in \boldsymbol{V}$ to represent a node of the BN and the corresponding random variable.

(d) a structural change, which corresponds to a modification of the dependencies between objects in the scene.

All these situations correspond to an event in the sense that we have defined.

The idea of this work is therefore to dynamically learn the nsDBN underlying scene. For this purpose, whenever we observe that the set of variables in the particle set at time t differs from that at time $t - 1$, or if the observed values of the particles were never previously observed, this corresponds to causes (a) or (b) noted above and we deduce that an event has occurred. Otherwise, as suggested in [6], we determine using a goodness-of-fit test (either a χ^2 or G^2 test) whether it is more likely that the sample (particle set) at time t has been generated from the distribution of the last fragment of BN $\mathcal{B}_h$ or not. Unfortunately, performing such a test over the set of all the random variables is impossible due to the exponential size of the contingency tables required for the test. But, to detect ruptures, we just need to test whether at least one random variable X does not seem to be distributed w.r.t. the conditional probability $P(X|\mathbf{Pa}(X))$ of $\mathcal{B}_h$. Therefore, we perform a goodness-of-fit test for each random variable X conditionally to its parents $\mathbf{Pa}(X)$ in $\mathcal{B}_h$. The contingency tables thus created remain small and the tests can be significant. A transition/rupture is detected if and only if at least one of these tests indicates that a variable X has probably not been generated from $\mathcal{B}_h$. When no event is detected, our algorithm just updates the CPTs of $\mathcal{B}_h$, which may thus vary very marginally to reflect the scene at time t.

In the case of an event detection, we simply apply the learning algorithm proposed in [6] with, as a Dirichlet *a priori*, the BN parameters resulting from the application of Lemma 1 [6] on $\mathcal{B}_h$. The general method is described in Algorithm 1.

learn $\mathcal{B}_0$ from the sample image 0
learn $\mathcal{B}_1$ from the sample image 1
$h \leftarrow 1$
foreach *frame at time t* **do**
  construct the set of particles $\mathbf{S}_t$
  if *at least one variable of* $\mathbf{S}_t$ *differs from the variables in* $\mathbf{S}_{t-1}$ *or if some variables*
  have unknown values in $\mathcal{B}_h$ *or if a goodness-of-fit test indicates that* $\mathbf{S}_t$ *was not generated from* $\mathcal{B}_h$ **then**
    learn $\mathcal{B}_{h+1}$ from $\mathbf{S}_t$ with $\mathcal{B}_h$ as Dirichlet *a priori* (see Lemma 1 in [6])
    $h \leftarrow h + 1$
  else
    update the parameters of $\mathcal{B}_h$ to take into account $\mathbf{S}_t$

Algorithm 1. Detection of events and nsDBN learning.

Unfortunately, this algorithm has a major drawback: like BNs, nsDBNs are only defined over discrete random variables and it is assumed that the domain of these variables is very small (usually less than ten values). To be meaningful, goodness-of-fit tests also assume implicitly that this constraint is satisfied[2]. But particle sets contain continuous variables by definition. To exploit Algorithm 1, it is therefore needed to discretize the whole particle set. This task is not as trivial as it may be thought. Indeed, the results of the goodness-of-fit test are quite sensitive to the domain sizes of the variables after discretization and to the distribution of the continuous values inside discretization intervals (this corresponds to the well-known Simpson's paradox). Moreover, it is very difficult to determine *a priori* what is the good discretization to apply because it depends on the movement of the objects. It is therefore necessary to learn automatically the discretization to apply.

3.2   Automatic Discretization of the Particles

In the following, to distinguish discretized and continuous variables, we note $\mathring{X}$ the first ones and X the seconds. We note $\Omega_{\mathring{X}}$ the domain of variable $\mathring{X}$. The discretization of a continuous variable $\mathring{X}$ is defined as a function $d_{\mathring{X}} : \Omega_{\mathring{X}} \rightarrow \{0, \ldots, g\}$ specified by an increasing sequence of g cutpoints $\{t_1, t_2, \ldots, t_g\}$ such that:

$$d_{\mathring{X}}(\mathring{x}) = \begin{cases} 0 & \text{if } \mathring{x} < t_1, \\ k & \text{if } t_k \le \mathring{x} < t_{k+1}, \quad \text{for all } k \in \{1, \ldots, g-1\} \\ g & \text{if } \mathring{x} \ge t_g. \end{cases}$$

Thus the discrete variable X corresponding to $\mathring{X}$ has a (finite) domain $\{0, \ldots, g\}$. The simplest approach to learn a BN or a DBN from continuous data is to discretize all continuous variables and then to use a conventional learning algorithm. But this can be disastrous in terms of the quality of the learnt model. Actually, this highlights a problem similar to that of Simpson's paradox. For example, consider the following sample of 400 observations of two variables $A \in \{0, 1\}$ and $B \in [-4, 4]$:

$$\mathbf{S} = \{(a_i = 0, b_i = -4 + \tfrac{i}{100})\}_{i=0}^{99} \cup \{(a_i = 1, b_i = -3 + \tfrac{i}{100})\}_{i=0}^{99} \cup \\ \{(a_i = 1, b_i = 2 + \tfrac{i}{100})\}_{i=0}^{99} \cup \{(a_i = 0, b_i = 3 + \tfrac{i}{100})\}_{i=0}^{99}.$$

If we do not consider A, we can see that B is uniformly distributed on the intervals $[-4-2]$ and $[2,4]$. This suggests a discretization using cutpoints -2 and 2. In this case, it is easy to infer that B is independent of A. But in reality, B depends on A and this can be observed when using the following discretization cutpoints: $\{-3, -2, 2, 3\}$. This suggests that, when discretizing a random variable, we should also take into account its dependencies with the other random variables. This is precisely the approach we use, which is adapted from [3]. More precisely, we transform the DBN we want to learn into a DBN with truncated conditional densities, as defined below. The latter includes conditional truncated densities:

---

[2] Statistically, a χ^2 test is not considered as significant if some cells of the contingency table have a value less than 5.

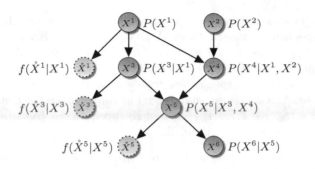

Fig. 2. A ctdBN.

Definition 3 (Conditional Truncated Density). *Let $\mathring{X}$ be a continuous random variable. Let $d_{\mathring{X}}$ be a discretization of $\mathring{X}$ with cutpoints $\{t_1, t_2, ..., t_g\}$. Finally, let X be a discrete variable whose domain is $\Omega_X = \{0, ..., g\}$. A conditional truncated density is a function $f(\mathring{X}|X) : \Omega_{\mathring{X}} \times \Omega_X \mapsto \mathbb{R}_0^+$ satisfying the following properties:*

1. *$f(\mathring{x}|x) = 0$ for all $x \in \Omega_X$ and $\mathring{x} \notin [t_x, t_{x+1}]$ with, by abuse of notation, $t_0 = \inf \Omega_{\mathring{X}}$ and $t_{g+1} = \sup \Omega_{\mathring{X}}$;*
2. *$\int_{t_x}^{t_{x+1}} f(\mathring{x}|x) \, d\mathring{x} = 1$, for all $x \in \Omega_X$.*

A non-stationary DBN with truncated conditional densities is an extension of a Bayesian network with conditional truncated densities [3]:

Definition 4 (Bayesian Network with Conditional Truncated Densities (ctdBN)). *Let $\mathbf{X^D} = \{X^1, ..., X^d\}$ and $\mathring{\mathbf{X}}^{\mathbf{C}} = \{\mathring{X}^{d+1}, ..., \mathring{X}^n\}$ be sets of discrete and continuous random variables respectively. Let $\mathbf{X^C} = \{X^{d+1}, ..., X^n\}$ be the variables resulting from the discretization of the variables of $\mathring{\mathbf{X}}^{\mathbf{C}}$. A ctdBN is a pair $(\mathcal{G}, \theta)$, where $\mathcal{G} = (\mathbf{X}, \mathbf{A})$ is a DAG, $\mathbf{X} = \mathbf{X^D} \cup \mathbf{X^C} \cup \mathring{\mathbf{X}}^{\mathbf{C}}$, and $\mathbf{A}$ is a set of arcs such that the nodes $\mathring{X}^i \in \mathring{\mathbf{X}}^{\mathbf{C}}$ have exactly one parent equal to X^i and no child. Finally, $\theta = \theta^{\mathbf{D}} \cup \theta^{\mathbf{C}}$, where $\theta^{\mathbf{D}} = \{P(X^i|\mathbf{Pa}(X^i))\}_{i=1}^n$ is the set of CPTs of the discrete variables X^i of $\mathcal{G}$ and where $\theta^{\mathbf{C}} = \{f(\mathring{X}^i|X^i)\}_{i=d+1}^n$ is the set of conditional truncated densities of the variables of $\mathring{\mathbf{X}}^{\mathbf{C}}$.*

Figure 2 illustrates the concept of a ctdBN. The nodes in solid circles represent the random variables in $\mathbf{X^D} \cup \mathbf{X^C}$ whereas those in dashed circles represent the random variables in $\mathring{\mathbf{X}}^{\mathbf{C}}$. More precisely, $\mathbf{X^D} = \{X^2, X^4, X^6\}$, $\mathring{\mathbf{X}}^{\mathbf{C}} = \{\mathring{X}^1, \mathring{X}^3, \mathring{X}^5\}$ and $\mathbf{X^C} = \{X^1, X^3, X^5\}$. One of the advantages of this graphical model is to combine continuous data (the $\mathring{X}^i$) with their discrete counterpart (X^i). As such, this graphical model is able to represent very faithfully very complex probability density functions.

Extending nsDBN to cope with continuous random variables is now simple: it is sufficient that each BN fragment of the nsDBN is a ctdBN. This leads to the definition of nsctdDBN:

Definition 5 (Non-stationary   Conditional   Truncated   Density Dynamic Bayesian Network (nsctdDBN)). *A nsctdDBN is a sequence of pairs* $\langle(\mathcal{B}_h, t_h)\rangle_{h=0}^m$, *where* $t_0 = 0$ *represents the first time slice,* $\mathcal{B}_0$ *is the ctdBN representing the distribution over the random variables at time 0. Each* $\mathcal{B}_h$, $h = 1, \ldots, m$, *is a ctdBN representing the conditional distribution of the random variables (both discrete and continuous) at time t given those at time* $t - 1$, *for all* $t \in \mathbf{E}_h = \{t_{h-1} + 1, \ldots, t_h\}$. t_h *and* $\mathbf{E}_h$ *are called a transition time and an epoch respectively. By convention,* $\mathbf{E}_0 = \{0\}$.

A ctdBN learning algorithm is described in [12] and we use it in this work. It allows us to learn a good discretization but also to learn the structure of a ctdBN and its parameters (both the CPTs and the conditional truncated densities). When performing the goodness-of-fit tests to detect events, we simply discretize the particles with the discretization learnt during the learning of the nsctdDBN. The weight of the particles are then multiplied by the values of conditional truncated densities to better reflect the continuous part of the model and, therefore, increase the quality of the test.

4   Experimental Results

We tested our approach on two video sequences. In these tests, we use the same settings for PF to estimate the positions of the objects (state vectors $\mathbf{x}_{t+1}$). The $N = 200$ particles $\mathbf{x}_{t+1}^{(i)}$ per object (positions in the image) between two

Fig. 3. Results on the sequence event from i-Lids dataset [21]: green box = no event, red box = event. (Color figure online)

time steps are propagated by using an auto-regressive model of the first order (constant speed associated with a Gaussian random walk centered on their former position and of variance $\sigma^2 = 10$). The weights of the particles are calculated from the current observation (image), and are given by $w_{t+1}^{(i)} \propto w_t^{(i)} e^{-\lambda d^2}$, with $\lambda = 20$ and d the Bhattacharyya distance between the target histogram (prior density) and the reference one (from a previous frame) of these regions. A multinomial resampling is performed at each instant.

4.1 Single Event Detection

The first sequence is from the i-Lids dataset (CLEAR 2007) [21]. It shows a car traveling on a road, slowing and stopping on the side. The event (the car stops) occurs on frame 130 of the sequence. We show in Fig. 3 the qualitative results

Fig. 4. Results on a sequence of VIRAT dataset [15]: green box = no event, red box = event. (Color figure online)

of the event detection, in which the tracked car is modeled by a rectangular region. When an event occurs, the rectangle is red, otherwise it is green. As we can see, the event is detected by our approach at frame 130. Here, the detected event corresponds to a change in the nsDBN parameters: the speed changes from positive to zero.

4.2   Multiple Event Detection

The second sequence belongs to the VIRAT dataset [15] and shows 6 people moving in a parking lot. In this sequence, a person attacks another one. This causes abrupt changes in the walking directions of several people: these changes are considered as events. We present some qualitative results in Fig. 4 (events are represented in red). We can see that on the first 100 frames, the 6 people follow a "normal" movement. From frames 120 to 150, the aggressor (person 8) catches the aggressed (person 1) and their trajectories become jerky: we have two events. At frame 170, the fight calms down but Person 2 and Person 7 turn around to help the aggressed person. The fight goes on between persons 1 and 8, while persons 2 and 3 come to interpose (frame 200). Calm returns gradually from frame 350 (only the aggressor still has an erratic trajectory) and the conflict stops at frame 410, and then no further event is detected.

5   Conclusion

We have presented in this paper a new approach to detect events in video sequences. The key idea is twofold: (i) to exploit non-stationary conditional truncated densities dynamic Bayesian networks (nsctdDBN) to model the scene and (ii) to estimate whether the particle sets provided by a particle filter used to track objects in the video sequence are likely to have been generated from the nsctdDBN which shall model the scene. If this appears to be unlikely, then an event is detected and a new nsctdDBN (both parameters and structure) is learnt from the particle set as well as from past data. By allowing probability distributions to evolve over time, nsctdDBNs can adapt themselves to the evolutions in the scene and this is precisely this feature which makes nsctdDBNs attractive for the task of event detection.

By exploiting goodness-of-fit tests to estimate whether the particle sets have been generated from the current nsctdDBN, we use no *a priori* knowledge about the events to be detected other than the fact that they correspond to a space-time rupture in the video. This flexible definition allows us to face different scenarios with the same model: detect a forbidden stop of a car on a road, or a fight in a parking lot. These first results open the path for many extensions of our work. We would like for example to ensure that the tracking algorithm, in particular the particle propagation, exploits the knowledge learned in the nsctdDBN. We also plan to test our method on other scenarios, notably some in which different groups of individuals gather and/or split during the video sequence. Similarly, the detection of abandoned luggages could be of interest.

References

1. Bhattacharya, S., Yu, F.X., Chang, S.: Minimally needed evidence for complex event recognition in unconstrained video. In: ICMR (2014)
2. Chickering, D.M.: Learning equivalence classes of Bayesian network structures. JMLR **2**, 445–498 (2002)
3. Cortijo, S., Gonzales, C.: Bayesian networks with conditional truncated densities. In: FLAIRS (2016)
4. Dean, T., Kanazawa, K.: A model for reasoning about persistence and causation. Comput. Intell. **5**, 142–152 (1989)
5. Geiger, D., Heckerman, D.: A characterization of the Dirichlet distribution with application to learning Bayesian networks. In: UAI, pp. 196–207 (1995)
6. Gonzales, C., Dubuisson, S., Manfredotti, C.: A new algorithm for learning non-stationary dynamic Bayesian networks with application to event detection. In: FLAIRS (2016)
7. Gordon, N., Salmond, D., Smith, A.: Novel approach to nonlinear/non-Gaussian Bayesian state estimation. IEE Proc. Radar Signal Process. **140**(2), 107–113 (1993)
8. Hung, Y.-X., Chiang, C.-Y., Hsu, S.J., Chan, C.-T.: Abnormality Detection for Improving Elder's Daily Life Independent. In: Lee, Y., et al. (eds.) ICOST 2010. LNCS, vol. 6159, pp. 186–194. Springer, Heidelberg (2010). doi:10.1007/978-3-642-13778-5_23
9. Jiang, F., Wu, Y., Katsaggelos, A.K.: Abnormal event detection from surveillance video by dynamic hierarchical clustering. In: ICIP, pp. 145–148 (2007)
10. Jiang, F., Yuan, J., Tsaftaris, S., Katsaggelos, A.: Anomalous video event detection using spatiotemporal context. CVIU **115**(3), 323–333 (2011)
11. Kwon, J., Lee, K.: A unified framework for event summarization and rare event detection. In: CVPR (2012)
12. Mabrouk, A., Gonzales, C., Jabet-Chevalier, K., Chojnaki, E.: Multivariate cluster-based discretization for Bayesian network structure learning. In: Beierle, C., Dekhtyar, A. (eds.) SUM 2015. LNCS (LNAI), vol. 9310, pp. 155–169. Springer, Heidelberg (2015). doi:10.1007/978-3-319-23540-0_11
13. Nevatia, R., Hongeng, S., Bremond, F.: Video-based event recognition : activity representation and probabilistic recognition methods. CVIU **2**, 129–162 (2004)
14. O'Gorman, L., Yin, Y., Ho, T.K.: Motion feature filtering for event detection in crowded scenes. PRL **44**, 80–87 (2014)
15. Oh, S., Hoogs, A., Perera, A.G.A., Cuntoor, N.P., Chen, C.C., Lee, J.T., Mukherjee, S., Aggarwal, J.K., Lee, H., Davis, L.S., Swears, E., Wang, X., Ji, Q., Reddy, K.K., Shah, M., Vondrick, C., Pirsiavash, H., Ramanan, D., Yuen, J., Torralba, A., Song, B., Fong, A., Chowdhury, A.K.R., Desai, M.: A large-scale benchmark dataset for event recognition in surveillance video. In: CVPR, pp. 3153–3160 (2011)
16. Pearl, J.: Probabilistic Reasoning in Intelligent Systems: Networks of Plausible Inference. Morgan Kaufman (1988)
17. Piciarelli, C., Micheloni, C., Foresti, G.: Trajectory-based anomalous event detection. IEEE. Trans. CSVT **18**(11), 1544–1554 (2008)
18. Robinson, J., Hartemink, A.J.: Learning non-stationary dynamic Bayesian networks. JMLR 3647–3680 (2010)
19. Roshtkhari, M., Levine, M.: An on-line real-time learning method for detecting anomalies in videos using spatio-temporal compositions. CVIU **117**(10), 1436–1452 (2013)

20. Ryoo, M.S., Aggarwal, J.K.: Stochastic representation and recognition of high-level group activities. In: CVPRW (2009)
21. Stiefelhagen, R., Bernardin, K., Bowers, R., Rose, R.T., Michel, M., Garofolo, J.: The CLEAR 2007 evaluation. In: Stiefelhagen, R., Bowers, R., Fiscus, J. (eds.) CLEAR/RT -2007. LNCS, vol. 4625, pp. 3–34. Springer, Heidelberg (2008). doi:10. 1007/978-3-540-68585-2_1
22. Tran, D., Yuan, J., Forsyth, D.: Video event detection: from subvolume localization to spatio-temporal path search. PAMI 36(2), 404–416 (2014)
23. Tsamardinos, I., Brown, L.E., Aliferis, C.F.: The max-min hill-climbing Bayesian network structure learning algorithm. ML 65(1), 31–78 (2006)
24. Wang, X., Ji, Q.: Context augmented dynamic Bayesian networks for event recognition. PRL 43(1), 62–70 (2013)
25. Wang, X., Ma, X., Grimson, E.: Unsupervised activity perception in crowded and complicated scenes using hierarchical Bayesian models. PAMI 31(3), 539–555 (2009)
26. Wu, S., Moore, B.E., Shah, M.: Chaotic invariants of lagrangian particle trajectories for anomaly detection in crowded scenes. In: CVPR (2010)
27. Zhang, D., Perez, D.G., Bengio, S., McCowan, I.: Semi-supervised adapted HMMs for unusual event detection. CVPR 1, 611–618 (2005)
28. Zhao, B., Fei-Fei, L., Xing, E.: Online detection of unusual events in videos via dynamic sparse coding. In: CVPR (2011)

Optimized Connected Components Labeling with Pixel Prediction

Costantino Grana$^{(\boxtimes)}$, Lorenzo Baraldi, and Federico Bolelli

Dipartimento di Ingegneria "Enzo Ferrari",
Università degli Studi di Modena e Reggio Emilia,
Via Vivarelli 10, 41125 Modena, MO, Italy
{costantino.grana,lorenzo.baraldi,federico.bolelli}@unimore.it

Abstract. In this paper we propose a new paradigm for connected components labeling, which employs a general approach to minimize the number of memory accesses, by exploiting the information provided by already seen pixels, removing the need to check them again. The scan phase of our proposed algorithm is ruled by a forest of decision trees connected into a single graph. Every tree derives from a reduction of the complete optimal decision tree. Experimental results demonstrated that on low density images our method is slightly faster than the fastest conventional labeling algorithms.

Keywords: Connected Components Labeling · Binary decision trees

1 Introduction

Connected Components Labeling (CCL) of binary images is an important and well-defined problem in image processing. With the labeling operation, a binary image is transformed into a symbolic image in which all pixels belonging to the same connected component are given the same label: this transformation is required whenever a computer program needs to identify independent components in an image, and is therefore a fundamental pre-processing task of many pattern analysis, computer vision and robot vision algorithms.

Given that an exact solution to the CCL problem exists, and should be provided as output, researchers have focused in the last years on optimizing existing CCL algorithms and on developing faster ones. The majority of existing algorithms scan the image and look at the neighborhood of a pixel through a mask (see Fig. 1 for an example), to assign provisional labels and collect label equivalences. This step, which can be expressed as a decision table [7], is done independently for each pixel, so that the pixels in the neighborhood are accessed multiple times during the scan phase.

In this work we propose a general paradigm to exploit already seen pixels during the scan phase, so to minimize the number of times a pixel is accessed. As shown in literature, the decision table which rules the scan step can be conveniently converted to an optimal binary decision tree [7], in which internal

© Springer International Publishing AG 2016
J. Blanc-Talon et al. (Eds.): ACIVS 2016, LNCS 10016, pp. 431–440, 2016.
DOI: 10.1007/978-3-319-48680-2_38

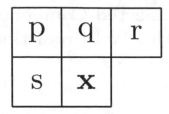

Fig. 1. The pixel mask used to compute the label of pixel x.

nodes represent conditions on mask's pixels, and leaves represents actions to be performed on the current pixel of the provisional image (x in Fig. 1), such as the creation of a new label, the assignment of an existing label to the pixel, or the merge of two existing labels. Usually, the same decision tree is traversed for each pixel of the input image, without exploiting values seen in the previous iteration, which, if considered, would result in a simplification of the decision tree for the pixel.

To go beyond this limitation, we compute a reduced decision tree for each possible set of known pixels; these reduced decision trees are then connected into a single graph, which rules the execution of the CCL algorithm on the whole image. This graph contains a starting tree, which should be accessed to process the first pixel of every row, and other trees, which are accessed to process the following pixels. Each leaf of a tree, which represent the action to be performed on a pixel, is connected to the root of a second tree which should be executed for the next pixel. The obtained graph can then be directly converted into running code.

The rest of this paper is organized as follows: in Sect. 2 we give an overview of existing Connected Components Labeling algorithms; Sect. 3 contains the description of the proposed strategy, which is then evaluated in Sect. 4. Finally, we draw the conclusions in Sect. 5.

2   Previous Works

The research efforts in labeling techniques have a very long story, where different strategies, improvements and results have been presented.

The algorithm described in [15, 16] is basically equivalent to the one in [9]. It uses a pixel based scanning with online equivalence resolution by means of a union find technique with path compression, plus a decision tree for accessing only the minimum number of already scanned labeled pixels.

In [7] it was proved that different versions of the decision tree are equivalent to the previous one and that, when performing 8-connected labeling, the scanning process can be extended to Block Based scanning, that is scanning the image in 2×2 blocks (we will refer to this algorithm as BBDT, for Block Based with Decision Tree). Building the decision tree for that case is much harder, because of the large number of possible combinations. In [8] a proved optimal strategy to build the decision tree has been proposed, by means of a dynamic programming approach. The final decision tree is generated automatically by another program.

Another variation of Block Based analysis was proposed in [4], which is reported to be faster than the previous one. We also include this algorithm thanks to the availability of the source code on the authors web pages, making the signature compliant with our testing standard.

He *et al.* [10] recently observed that BBDT still checks many pixels repeatedly, because after labeling one pixel, the mask moves to the next one, but many pixels in the current mask are overlapped to the previous ones, which may have already been checked. They thus propose a Configuration-Transition-Based (CTB) algorithm which uses a set of different configurations to represent the current *state* of the algorithm and employ it to make further decisions. This allows to save a number of accesses to pixels and thus to speed up the labeling process. The algorithm is specifically designed for the task and no provision to a general methodology is foreseen in the paper.

Recently, an open-source benchmark for CCL has been proposed by the authors of this paper: YACCLAB [6]. This project is intended to be a growing effort towards better reproducibility of CCL algorithms, and allows researchers to test new proposals and available implementations on standard datasets. Given that the source code of many CCL algorithms has not been released, YACCLAB also relies on implementations provided by the authors of the benchmark. In the following sections we will show that our variation is often faster than the algorithm from He [10], and even faster than [7] when tested on very low density images.

3   Method

We focus our analysis on 8-connected CCL and start by observing the neighborhood mask of Fig. 1, choosing one of the possible optimal decision trees we can obtain from it. Figure 2 provides a visual representation of such a tree: the first thing to do is to check whether current pixel x is background or foreground (0 or 1). If $x = 0$, than we don't need to do anything (action 1) and simply move to the next pixel, otherwise we start looking its neighborhood. We start from q because it is connected to all other pixels: if $q = 1$ its label will be equivalent to that of all others, so we simply *assign* its label to x (action 4). If instead $q = 0$ we are in the case of potential *merge* of different previously unconnected components through x. To this aim, we need to check pixels p, s and r basically in any order we like with the only saving of avoiding checking p if $s = 1$ or viceversa, since p is always connected to s. Finally, if no pixel is foreground, i.e. $p = r = s = 0$, we create a *new label* (action 2). In Fig. 2 actions 3, 5, and 6 are *assign p*, *r*, and *s* respectively, while actions 7 and 8 are *merge p + r* and *s + r* respectively.

Following [10], we observe that pixels x will be the next s, q will be the next p, pixels r will be the next q. So if during the tree traversal we made a choice on x, q or r we know the values of s, p and q at the next step. This means that the corresponding subtree may be substituted to the choice made on that pixel.

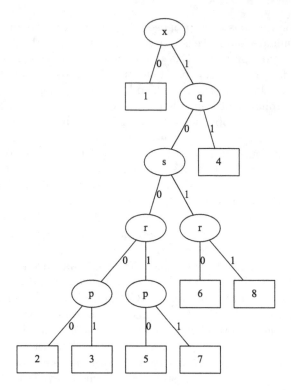

Fig. 2. One of the possible full decision trees obtainable from the mask of Fig. 1.

Let's start with the first thing we know for sure: at the beginning of a line pixels p and s are 0 (there is no foreground outside the image). So all choices do not need to check those, meaning that we can remove the right branch of s and use its left subtree instead. There $p = 0$, thus we remove that check and substitute it with actions 2 and 5. This gives reduced tree A of Fig. 3. Its meaning is very clear to understand: first check pixel x: if it is foreground check the previous line (q and r), otherwise move next.

If we had a background pixel x before, we know that $s = 0$ so, again, we can remove its right branch thus obtaining the reduced tree B. If instead x was foreground and q was too, both $p = s = 1$ and we can remove the left branch of s getting reduced tree C. We keep going in this way and in many cases we obtain the same information from every leaf. Overall just two more different reduced trees are obtained (D and E in Fig. 3). It is noteworthy that, if in any tree we observed that $r = 1$, we move to tree D, which is simply a check on x: if it is foreground we assign the label of q without even the need of checking if it is foreground.

At every leaf of every tree, we know which tree shall be used next, so we mark that edge with a dotted line, to stress the difference with respect to the choices within the trees: inside every tree we just check the pixels, after performing the

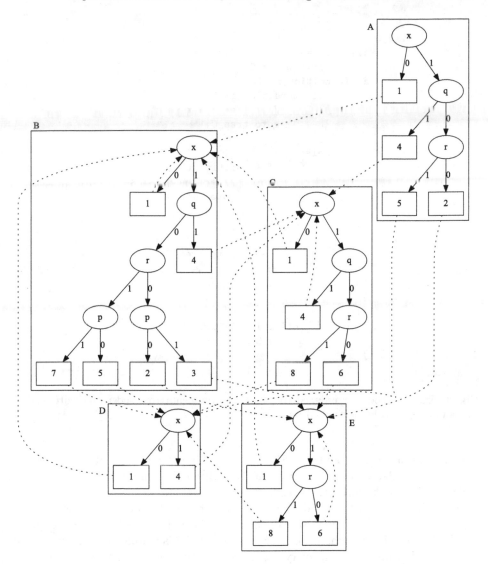

Fig. 3. The final graph of.decision trees, obtained from the full decision tree of Fig. 2.

action in a leaf we need to advance the mask, check if the image row is finished and then proceed or break out of the current line.

3.1 Implementation

Moving from theory to practice is just a matter of translating every branch with a conditional statement and every dotted link with an unconditional jump. At the beginning of every tree an increment of the current pixel position has to be made along with a check for the end of the row. A sample of the code in C

```
        ...
      tree_C:
            if (++c >= w - 1)
                    goto break_C;
            if (condition_x) {
                    if (condition_q) {
                            // action 4 - x <= q
                            goto tree_C;
                    }
                    else {
                            if (condition_r) {
                                    // action 8 - x <= r + s
                                    goto tree_D;
                            }
                            else {
                                    // action 6 - x <= s
                                    goto tree_E;
                            }
                    }
            }
            else {
                    // action 1 - do nothing
                    goto tree_B;
            }
        ...
```

Fig. 4. Example code for reduced tree C. Here comments are used to indicate where the actions should be performed.

language for tree C is provided in Fig. 4. The real implementation of the actions is omitted and substituted with comments. Conditions are indicated with a macro which shall be defined by the specific implementation.

One thing should be noted: the *end of row* check stops one pixel before the end of the row. In this way we can make specialized versions for all the trees for the last pixel case, where we know that $r = 0$. This simple trick allows us to save an end of line check at every use of pixel r, since we already know that we are at least one pixel inside the image.

4 Experimental Evaluation

Tests were performed on a Windows PC with an Intel Core i7-4790K CPU @ 4.00 GHz and Microsoft Visual Studio 2013. All algorithms reported in this Section were included in YACCLAB. Tests were repeated ten times: for each image only the minimum execution time was considered (in order to reduce/avoid the influence of other tasks on the final results). Charts and tables report average times for every dataset or density/size considering only the minimum execution time on every image.

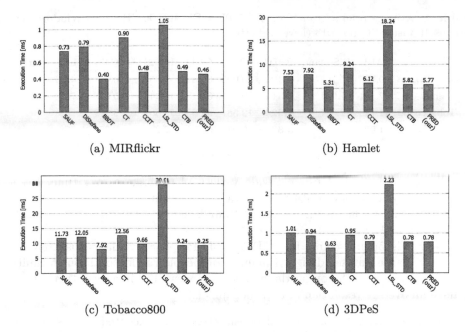

(a) MIRflickr

(b) Hamlet

(c) Tobacco800

(d) 3DPeS

Fig. 5. Average results on a i7-4790K CPU @ 4.00 GHz with Windows and Microsoft Visual Studio 2013 (lower is better).

In the following, we use acronyms to refer to the available algorithms: CT is the Contour Tracing approach by Chang *et al.* [3], CCIT is the algorithm by Chang *et al.* [4], Di Stefano is the algorithm in [5], BBDT is the Block Based with Decision Trees algorithm by Grana *et al.* [7], LSL_STD is the Light Speed Labeling algorithm by Lacassagne *et al.* [12], SAUF is the Scan Array Union Find algorithm by Wu *et al.* [16], which is the algorithm currently included in OpenCV, CTB is the Configuration-Transition-Based approach described in [10]. Our method is denoted as PRED.

Figure 5 and Table 1 report mean run-times for each dataset. As it can be noticed, YACCLAB provides an effective way to compare CCL algorithms on heterogeneous datasets:

- *MIRflickr*, Fig. 5(a): this dataset is composed by the Otsu-binarized version of the MIRflickr dataset [11]. It contains 25,000 standard resolution images taken from Flickr. These images have an average resolution of 0.18 megapixels, there are few connected components and are generally composed of not too complex patterns, so the labeling is quite easy and fast.
- *Hamlet*, Fig. 5(b): a set of 104 images scanned from a version of the Hamlet found on Project Gutenberg (http://www.gutenberg.org). Images have an average amount of 2.71 million of pixels to analyze and 1,447 components to label.
- *Tobacco800*, Fig. 5(c): it is composed of 1,290 document images and is a realistic database for document image analysis research as these documents were

Table 1. Average results in ms on a i7-4790K CPU @ 4.00 GHz with Windows and Microsoft Visual Studio 2013 (lower is better).

	SAUF	DiStefano	BBDT	CT	CCIT	LSL_STD	CTB	PRED (our)
MIRflickr	0.735	0.795	**0.403**	0.902	0.481	1.052	0.491	0.458
Hamlet	7.531	7.921	**5.314**	9.245	6.118	18.242	5.819	5.769
Tobacco800	11.728	12.047	**7.924**	12.561	9.663	29.608	9.237	9.252
3DPeS	1.014	0.945	**0.625**	0.953	0.791	2.234	0.778	0.778

collected and scanned using a wide variety of equipment over time. Resolutions of documents in Tobacco800 vary significantly from 150 to 300 DPI and the dimensions of images range from 1,200 by 1,600 to 2,500 by 3,200 pixels [1,13,14].

– *3DPeS*, Fig. 5(d): it comes from 3DPeS (3D People Surveillance Dataset [2]), a surveillance dataset designed mainly for people re-identification in multi-camera systems with non-overlapped fields of view. The images of this dataset have an average resolution of 0.41 megapixels.

Beside run-time tests, size and density test were executed on a synthetic dataset: random noise images with 9 different foreground densities (10 % up to 90 %), from a low resolution of 32×32 pixels to a maximum resolution of $4,096 \times 4,096$ pixels. For every combination of size and density, 10 images were provided for a total of 720 images.

– *Size*, Fig. 6(a): highlights a linear dependency of execution time with respect to the number of pixels. This is true for all algorithms except Di Stefano's one, which shows, as expected, a worse performance when the number of pixels is high.
– *Density*, Fig. 6(b): reports a series of density tests performed on the synthetic dataset. Like almost all others algorithms, PRED shows an increased execution time on middle densities, because the number of labels and merges between equivalence classes is higher and also branch prediction can affect negatively the execution times. Di Stefano's algorithm produces the worst performance in the middle densities instead LSL_STD is the only one that demonstrated a quasi-linear trend, probably due to the lower number of conditional statements.

It is important to underline that all numerical values reported in the graphs and tables also consider times needed to define and initialize data structures, except for the binary input matrix. Indeed, if an algorithm needs to save more information to compute correct labeling, these must be considered in the total amount of execution time.

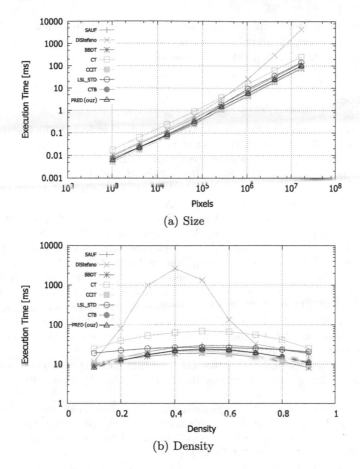

(a) Size

(b) Density

Fig. 6. Density and size tests on a i7-4790K CPU @ 4.00 GHz with Windows and Microsoft Visual Studio 2013 (lower is better).

5 Conclusions

In this paper we presented a novel approach for performing Connected Components Labeling, which employs a reproducible strategy able to avoid repeatedly checking the same pixels multiple times. Experimental results are very promising and even if the current algorithm is not able to beat BBDT algorithm on the real datasets, it was faster on the synthetic one for low density cases. Moreover, it was able to surpass the performance of CTB which is currently the second best accordingly to the YACCLAB benchmark. We plan to apply the same optimization strategy also to the BBDT algorithm, but in this case the tree reduction cannot be performed *by hand*, given the enormous size of the decision tree.

The source code of the described method has been included in the YACCLAB benchmark, so that it will be possible to check the real performance on different machines and compare it with future proposals. We strongly believe that given the maturity of the problem and the subtlety involved in the implementation, it should be mandatory to allow the community to reproduce the results without forcing everyone to reimplement every proposal.

References

1. Agam, G., Argamon, S., Frieder, O., Grossman, D., Lewis, D.: The Complex Document Image Processing (CDIP) Test Collection Project. Illinois Institute of Technology (2006). http://ir.iit.edu/projects/CDIP.html
2. Baltieri, D., Vezzani, R., Cucchiara, R.: 3DPeS: 3D people dataset for surveillance and forensics. In: Proceedings of the 2011 Joint ACM Workshop on Human Gesture and Behavior Understanding, pp. 59–64. ACM (2011)
3. Chang, F., Chen, C.J., Lu, C.J.: A linear-time component-labeling algorithm using contour tracing technique. Comput. Vis. Image Underst. **93**(2), 206–220 (2004)
4. Chang, W.Y., Chiu, C.C., Yang, J.H.: Block-based connected-component labeling algorithm using binary decision trees. Sensors **15**(9), 23763–23787 (2015)
5. Di Stefano, L., Bulgarelli, A.: A simple and efficient connected components labeling algorithm. In: International Conference on Image Analysis and Processing, pp. 322–327. IEEE (1999)
6. Grana, C., Bolelli, F., Baraldi, L., Vezzani, R.: YACCLAB - Yet another connected components labeling benchmark. In: 23rd International Conference on Pattern Recognition. ICPR (2016)
7. Grana, C., Borghesani, D., Cucchiara, R.: Optimized block-based connected components labeling with decision trees. IEEE Trans. Image Process. **19**(6), 1596–1609 (2010)
8. Grana, C., Montangero, M., Borghesani, D.: Optimal decision trees for local image processing algorithms. Pattern Recognit. Lett. **33**(16), 2302–2310 (2012)
9. He, L., Chao, Y., Suzuki, K.: A run-based two-scan labeling algorithm. IEEE Trans. Image Process. **17**(5), 749–756 (2008)
10. He, L., Zhao, X., Chao, Y., Suzuki, K.: Configuration-transition-based connected-component labeling. IEEE Trans. Image Process. **23**(2), 943–951 (2014)
11. Huiskes, M.J., Lew, M.S.: The MIR flickr retrieval evaluation. In: MIR 2008: Proceedings of the 2008 ACM International Conference on Multimedia Information Retrieval. ACM, New York (2008). http://press.liacs.nl/mirflickr/
12. Lacassagne, L., Zavidovique, B.: Light speed labeling: efficient connected component labeling on RISC architectures. J. Real-Time Image Process. **6**(2), 117–135 (2011)
13. Lewis, D., Agam, G., Argamon, S., Frieder, O., Grossman, D., Heard, J.: Building a test collection for complex document information processing. In: Proceedings of the 29th Annual International ACM SIGIR Conference on Research and Development in Information Retrieval, pp. 665–666. ACM (2006)
14. The Legacy Tobacco Document Library (LTDL). University of California, San Francisco (2007). http://legacy.library.ucsf.edu/
15. Wu, K., Otoo, E., Suzuki, K.: Two strategies to speed up connected component labeling algorithms. Technical report LBNL-59102, Lawrence Berkeley National Laboratory (2005)
16. Wu, K., Otoo, E., Suzuki, K.: Optimizing two-pass connected-component labeling algorithms. Pattern Anal. Appl. **12**(2), 117–135 (2009)

Hierarchical Fast Mean-Shift Segmentation in Depth Images

Milan Šurkala$^{(\boxtimes)}$, Radovan Fusek, Michael Holuša, and Eduard Sojka

Department of Computer Science, FEECS, Technical University of Ostrava,
17. listopadu 15, 708 33 Ostrava-Poruba, Czech Republic
{milan.surkala,radovan.fusek,michael.holusa,eduard.sojka}@vsb.cz

Abstract. Head position and head pose detection systems are very popular in recent times, especially with the rise of depth cameras like Microsoft Kinect and Intel RealSense. The goal is to recognize and segment a head in depth data. The systems could also detect the direction in which the head is pointing and we use these data to improve the gaze direction detection system and provide useful information to allow detectors to work properly. We present the Hierarchical Fast Blurring Mean Shift algorithm that is able to extract the data from depth images in real-time from above mentioned cameras. We also present some modifications for an effective reduction of the mean-shift dataset during the computation that allow us to increase the precision of the method. We use a hierarchical approach to reduce the dataset during the computation process and to improve the speed.

Keywords: Fast · Mean-shift · Tracking · Segmentation

1 Introduction

With the expansion of various depth systems and cameras, the need for segmenting depth data is also increasing. Depth cameras like Microsoft Kinect or Intel RealSense do not have to be used only for gaming purposes, but they are very popular in scientific world too. That applies especially for the Intel RealSense camera. In recent years, the processing of the depth images is an interesting research topic. Especially the segmentation of the depth images was used in many tasks over the past few years (e.g. human pose estimation, head pose estimation).

Depth images are very similar to classical images because the depth is given by the brightness of the pixel. In some cases, we may use common segmentation methods for processing depth images (e.g. watershed, classical mean-shift methods, graph cuts). Nevertheless, these classical methods are not optimized specifically for depth images. Therefore, we proposed the improvements of the mean-shift method that can be used for fast depth image segmentation which is the main contribution of this paper.

© Springer International Publishing AG 2016
J. Blanc-Talon et al. (Eds.): ACIVS 2016, LNCS 10016, pp. 441–452, 2016.
DOI: 10.1007/978-3-319-48680-2_39

The motivation to create our segmentation method comes from the fact that we are developing the software for an automotive industry which needs to recognize the gaze direction of a driver in real-time. This system consists of detection of the head, head center, eyes, eye centers, pupil, and iris. In this paper, we present the first part of this gaze detection system; recognition of head dimensions, position, and its center using our proposed Hierarchical Fast Mean-Shift method.

We are using the Intel RealSense camera during the development of the software. This camera provides RGB, IR, and depth images. The question is how to detect and recognize the real shape of the head. We may use classical Viola and Jones [10] algorithm for detecting the face or even the eyes in IR or RGB images. Nevertheless, the RGB images are sensitive to lighting conditions and it is important to note that the software has to work at night.

We can use IR images for face detection but the detector has to be trained specially for IR images that differ from RGB images. The output of the Viola and Jones detector is a rectangle that represents a position of the face. Position of this rectangle is often non very stable (the position of the rectangle is slightly different in every frame) and it represents the face location but not the real head dimensions. However, we would like to recognize the position of the head and especially the contours of the head precisely and quickly using the depth images only that are not deformed when they are recorded at night.

These shortcomings became the motivation for creating our novel method based on Blurring Mean Shift that is focused on depth image segmentation.

2   Related Work

We are using the method that is called Mean Shift [5] for segmenting the head in depth images. This method can be used for segmenting and filtering the images, nowadays it is also very popular for tracking objects. Whereas almost all versions of the Mean Shift (MS) are relatively slow for segmenting and filtering the images in real-time, versions used for tracking the objects are usually quite fast. Therefore, tracking versions of MS are the most developed mean-shift methods in recent years. The mean-shift method was developed in 1975 [5] but it was forgotten for almost 20 years. It was revisited in 1995 by Cheng [1] who studied its properties and developed the second version of this method. MS became very popular algorithm since then. In all cases, MS is iteratively seeking for the positions where the highest density of data points is.

The idea is relatively simple. For each data point (the pixel in the image, in our case), the position of the highest density is computed. We compute the density of data points in the neighbourhood of the computed pixel. This neighbourhood is given by the bandwidths in the spatial and the range (luminance) domain. These values limits the maximum x and y-axis spatial difference of the pixels and the maximum luminance difference. If the pixel belongs to the hypersphere with the dimensions according to the bandwidths (small spatial x, y and luminance differences), we compute the contribution of this pixel for finding the highest density position. First, we need the kernel density estimator

$$p(x) = \frac{1}{N} \sum_{n=1}^{N} K_H \left(x - x_n \right),$$

(1)

where $K(x)$ is the kernel function. It is a non negative number and works as a weighting function. If the pixel is closer and more similar in luminance, the kernel function will give a higher result. Less similar pixels give a smaller contribution or are not involved in the computation at all.

There are several types of kernel functions, for example the Gaussian, uniform, Epanechnikov, triangle and many others. We can distinguish between truncated and non-truncated kernels. If the kernel is truncated (Epanechnikov, uniform), the bandwidths completely limit the maximum difference. The bandwidths only change the shape of the weighting function when non-truncated kernels are used (the Gaussian). The index H is a symmetric positive definite $d \times d$ bandwidth matrix. The kernel function $K(x)$ can be written as follows

$$K(x) = k \left(\|x\|^2 \right).$$

(2)

K is the kernel when some conditions are met. There has to be its profile k that is non negative, non increasing ($k(a) \geq k(b)$ if $a < b$), piecewise continuous, and $\int_0^\infty k(r) dr < \infty$. The Epanechnikov kernel profile is denoted by

$$k(x) = \begin{cases} 1 - x, & \text{if } 0 \geq x \geq 1 \\ 0, & x > 1 \end{cases}$$

(3)

and the kernel itself may be written as

$$K(x) = \begin{cases} \frac{1}{2} c_d^{-1} (d + 2)(1 - \|x\|^2), & \text{if } \|x\| \leq 1 \\ 0, & \text{otherwise} \end{cases}.$$

(4)

If the contribution of all pixels in the neighbourhood is computed, we can specify the position of the highest density and the new position of the processed pixel. The point is moved to this position and the process is carried out again. The difference between the former position of the data point and the new one is called a *mean-shift vector*. The mean-shift algorithm is an iterative algorithm and its computation ends when there are no more moves or they are very small. The point where the points converge, is called an *attractor*. All the points that converge to one attractor, represent one segment from the dataset (the data points that have similar properties).

Because of the iterative nature of the algorithm, the speed is the biggest problem. It is highly influenced by the size of the input (number of data points) and the size of the neighbourhood (the bandwidth size). Therefore, if we want to make the mean-shift method faster, we need to reduce the dataset and/or to reduce the bandwidth size. If the bandwidth size is reduced, the algorithm tends to create smaller segments and that leads to an over-segmentation problem. There are many algorithms that are trying to solve this issue. Some MS methods use adaptive modification of the bandwidth size that reflects the nature of the data and increase or decrease the bandwidth size according to the needs [2,7,12].

The oversegmentation problem is also solved by hierarchical approaches that run several MS segmentation computations. In the first one, the entire dataset is used but the spatial bandwidths are very small. Therefore, the computation can be done very fast but the output is highly oversegmented. The output from the first one is used as an input for the second stage and the bandwidth is increased. Because the segments are considered as data points, we have the reduced dataset and this second stage can be also very fast because of this reduction even though the bandwidth is enlarged. In this case, we have several quite fast segmentation computations which causes that the hierarchical approaches usually save a lot of computational time. The hierarchical approaches emerge in 2002 [3] and were developed in the following years by Vatturi [9] and we have also brought few hierarchical methods - Hierarchical Blurring MS [11], Hierarchical Evolving MS [12], and Hierarchical Layered MS [8].

The reduction of the dataset can be also carried out by neglecting some points by utilizing the neighbourhood consistency. It is highly probable that the data point in the near neighbourhood has similar properties and we can take only samples (one representative). This method is called Fast Mean Shift (FMS) [6] and it was used also in other papers to improve the speed of algorithm [4]. Because of the omission of some points, we need to count with a lower precision of FMS method.

3   Proposed Method

Our algorithm improves the speed of the FMS algorithm because it is used in real environment in automotive industry where the real-time speed is crucial. We have used the blurring version of the mean-shift method and, therefore, we can say that our goal is to improve Fast Blurring Mean-Shift (FBMS). We have implemented several modification in order to improve the speed of the algorithm and we have incorporated hierarchical structure. Because the algorithm is used for segmenting the depth data images in cars, we are also providing the improvements that are exclusive for this type of data.

First of all, we can limit the amount of data according to the depth distances. If the driver needs to be observed only, we may use the depth data that correspond to the depth in the range of approximately 20–120 cm. All other points may be neglected and we can reduce the dataset quite a lot. Because of the nature of the FMS (or FBMS) method, we are skipping some data points (pixels in our case). For example, we can use only each 10th pixel in both spatial dimensions. That means we are using only 1/100th of the original data amount.

Using this reduction of dataset, the classic blurring mean-shift computation may take its place. As we have already stated, we need to estimate the position of the highest density for each data point. We examine the neighbourhood of

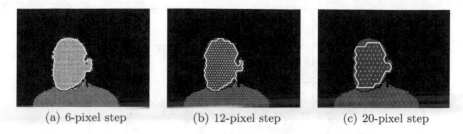

(a) 6-pixel step   (b) 12-pixel step   (c) 20-pixel step

Fig. 1. Comparison of segmentation results of fast blurring mean-shift method. If the step is 20 pixels (in x and y axis) then only each 400th pixel is involved in the computation. The white points represent the retained data points and the white line is the detected head.

the processed pixel and we compute the new position of the data point. The difference between the former and the new position is called *mean-shift vector* and it is computed using the following equation

$$
m_{\sigma,k}(pts) = \frac{\sum_{j=1}^{N} pts_j k\left(\left\|\frac{pts_i - pts_j}{\sigma}\right\|^2\right)}{\sum_{j=1}^{N} k\left(\left\|\frac{pts_i - pts_j}{\sigma}\right\|^2\right)} - pts_i. \tag{5}
$$

Such a computation is carried out for all the pixels and they are moved to their new positions. After that, the next iteration with modified positions of the data points is carried out until the movements stop. If there are no movements, all the data points are in their attractors and we have got the segments.

Our method is improved by a hierarchical approach and a special lattice that decreases the computational time. The lattice divides the image into several tiles. Therefore, we do not need to examine all the points in the dataset but we can search only through the data points that are covered by the tile of the lattice. For example, if the image has the 640 × 480 pixels size and the dimension of the tile is 20 × 20 pixels, the image would be divided into 768 tiles (areas). If the spatial bandwidth represents radius of 80 (the 160 × 160 pixels square), we need to examine pixels in 64 areas at maximum instead of 768. That can save a lot of time.

A simple lattice structure is presented in Fig. 2. The green tiles are the areas that are covered by the searching window (the kernel) of the black pixel (the pixel for which we are computing the mean-shift vector). Therefore, we need to examine only the pixels that are in lists represented as the green tiles here (9 lists of data points in this case) and there is no need to include pixels stored in other lists (white tiles). It is obvious that this lattice structure strictly limits the pixels that should be checked by the mean-shift computation or not.

As we can see in Table 1, the lattice structure can significantly improve the speed of the algorithm but it concurrently has some overheads. If the lattice structure is not used, the spatial bandwidth does not influence the result very much. It is caused by the fact that we need to check all the pixels if they are

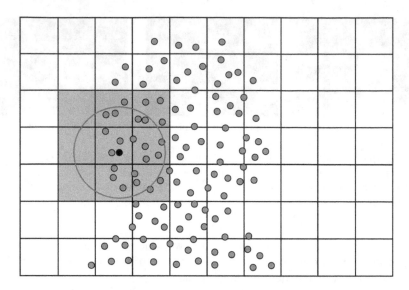

Fig. 2. A lattice structure. The black circle is the data point for which the mean-shift vector is computed. The red circle represents the kernel given by the σ_s parameter. In order to compute the mean-shift vector, we use only the points that are in lists of data points represented as green tiles in this image (these tiles are at least partially covered by the kernel). It is obvious that data points located under white tiles (stored in the lists) cannot be inside the red circle (the kernel) and, therefore, there is no need to include them in the computation. (Color figure online)

Table 1. Comparison of elapsed time with and without the lattice structure.

σ_s	No. of pixels	No. of iterations	Without tiles	Tile 10 × 10	Tile 20 × 20
20	1905	18.3	106.1 ms	27.5 ms	25.8 ms
40	1905	19.3	107.9 ms	50.6 ms	45.1 ms
80	1905	10.6	82.4 ms	74.4 ms	62.8 ms
20	680	17.1	19.0 ms	7.8 ms	6.2 ms
40	680	17.0	19.3 ms	12.3 ms	9.4 ms
80	680	10.0	14.0 ms	15.7 ms	11.6 ms
20	165	12.6	2.3 ms	2.0 ms	1.5 ms
40	165	13.3	2.3 ms	2.6 ms	1.6 ms
80	165	10.2	1.9 ms	3.2 ms	1.8 ms

in the neighbourhood of the processed pixel or not. Only if they are not close to each other, we can skip the following computation but the check operation is always there. On the other hand, a larger bandwidth usually lowers the required number of iterations and, therefore, bigger σ_s is paradoxically faster. It is better to keep the tile size reasonably large.

Table 2. The influence of the data point reduction check procedure.

Skipped iterations	0	1	2	3	4
Time	1.89 ms	1.81 ms	1.75 ms	1.78 ms	1.91 ms

There is an additional speed improvement using the merging rule. After few iterations of the mean-shift method, some of the data points are already in the same position. They form a moving attractor that is merging itself with other data points and other moving attractors until they create a very large one. The problem is that the algorithm considers these two or more points (with the same properties) as distinct ones. If we are able to check the equality, we can merge them together, increase their weight by one and the amount of data points in the dataset can be lowered. This can improve the speed of the algorithm in later stages of the MS method because it dynamically decreases the dataset.

This approach is beneficial and can be optimized twice. The first optimization is to use the above mentioned lattice structure. If it is not used, we need to examine all the pairs in the dataset and this operation can be very exhaustive. It can even decrease the speed of algorithm. On the other hand, if the lattice structure is used, we can check correspondence of the pixels under one tile only (check all the pixels in one list of data points). It is certain that there cannot be two pixels with the same values under two different tiles. See the Fig. 2. Instead of comparing the value of black pixel with more than hundred of pixels in the dataset, we can take only the tile where the black pixel was assigned. There are only four pixels under this tile (in this list of data points) and, therefore, the check need to be done with three pixels only.

The second optimization uses the fact that there are no attractors in few first iterations of the algorithm. Therefore, it is useless to check a correspondence when the probability of formation of two same pixels is very low and, moreover, this operation will be very demanding because of the full dataset. Because of that, this check can be postponed a little bit to the moment when there is a higher probability that there have been some attractors already created and the check makes sense (it actually lowers the dataset size and its overhead is overcame by the gains of the faster computations with the reduced dataset).

The results are presented in Table 2. All the measurements were carried out on a laptop with Intel Core M-5Y10 processor with 0.8 GHz frequency (2.0 GHz in turbo mode). Each of the following algorithms are single-thread only. These results can differ according to the used images but the idea is clear. If we skipped two iterations, the computational time was the best. If the iterations were not skipped, we have carried out these correspondence checks unnecessarily because they cannot reduce the dataset and have created the computational burden by themselves. On the other hand, if the check is carried out too late or not at all, we will achieve a worse speed because we are not using the speedup that could have been given by a dataset reduction.

Algorithm 1. Hierarchical Fast Blurring Mean Shift for depth images

---

Input: pts, step, tilesize, sigmas, eps

1 Keep only each *step*-th data point pts_i in x-axis and in y-axis.

2 Delete all data points pts_i, where their depth value is smaller than 20 or higher than 120.

3 Create lattice structure *tiles* of vectors (*width/tilesize* vectors in the first dimension and *height/tilesize* vectors in the second dimension).

4 *iteration* = 0; **while** *true* **do**

5   *iteration* + +; **foreach** pts_i **do**

6   Compute the location of the mean-shift kernel (from $x - sigmas$ to $x + sigmas$ and similarly for y-axis).

7   Carry out mean-shift computation and calculate the mean-shift vector m_i according to the Eq. 5 only with all pts_j data points that are stored in vectors *tiles* that spatially cover the mean-shift kernel computed in the previous step.

8   *movement* = 0;

9   **foreach** pts_i **do**

10   Set $pts_i+ = m_i$;

11   *movement*$+ = m_i$;

12   **if** *iteration* > 2 **then**

13   **foreach** pts_j in vectors *tiles* that spatially cover the kernel computed previously **do**

14   **if** $pts_i == pts_j$ **then**

15   Increase weight of pts_i by the weight of pts_j

16   Delete pts_j

17   **if** *movement* < *eps* **then**

18   break;

All these improvements can be used in ordinary Fast Mean Shift too (all our measurements of FMS are measured with these optimizations). Our method brings the hierarchical approach and utilizes above mentioned optimizations for further improvement of the results. As we have already mentioned, we use a small spatial bandwidth in the early stage of the algorithm. If the lattice structure is used, we will obtain the oversegmented result very quickly even though the dataset is large. When the first stage is finished, we enlarge the bandwidth and run the mean-shift segmentation algorithm again. Because the output from the first stage is used as an input in the second stage, the dataset is significantly reduced and the computation is very fast even though the larger bandwidth is used. Overall, the two computations are both carried out very quickly (the first one because of the small bandwidth and the second one because of the reduced dataset). The result is obtained much faster than if only the large bandwidth and one computation is used. Of course, the number of stages is not limited to two and we can use more stages.

Table 3. The comparison of various mean-shift methods with the final bandwidth set to 80. BMS-NL stands for Blurring MS without the lattice structure, BMS is the same with the lattice structure using the 20×20 tile size (this tile size is used for all tests). HBMS is Hierarchical Blurring MS using the lattice structure and the initial σ_s was set to 2–6. FBMS is Fast Blurring MS with skipped pixels and the lattice structure (the number of skipped pixels is given by the number - FBSM8 uses only each 8th pixel in each coordinate). HFBMS is Hierarchical Fast Blurring MS that skips pixels and uses the hierarchical approach (the initial σ_s was set to 1.5 times the distance of non-skipped pixels) and the lattice structure.

Method	σ_s		Latt.	No. of data points		Time
	First stage	Second stage		First stage	Second stage	
BMS-NL	80		–	68573		83842.4 ms
BMS	80		20	68573		62300.4 ms
HBMS	2	80	20	68573	3165	1908.8 ms
HBMS	4	80	20	68573	753	2203.5 ms
HBMS	6	80	20	68573	451	2868.2 ms
FBMS2	80		20	17362		4137.9 ms
FBMS4	80		20	4330		278.9 ms
FBMS8	80		20	1075		22.6 ms
FBMS16	80		20	260		2.8 ms
HFBMS2	3	80	20	17362	1346	236.3 ms
HFBMS4	6	80	20	4330	513	41.0 ms
HFBMS8	12	80	20	1075	160	9.0 ms
HFBMS16	24	80	20	260	39	2.4 ms

The graphical representation of the segmentation results is illustrated in Fig. 3. We present original BMS and our previous HBMS too. There are Fast Blurring MS results in the second row (with the above mentioned optimizations) and our new hierarchical version is in the third row. It is visible that both algorithms give almost the same segmentation results. The Table 3 shows the time differences. Original BMS needed more than one minute to segment the image whereas our previous hierarchical version took approximately 2–3 s depending on the bandwidth size. The results of HBMS can be improved by lowering the tile sizes but the measured minimum was about 0.5 s. It is a huge improvement but it is still not usable for real-time.

Fast Blurring Mean Shift with all above mentioned acceleration techniques (with the exception of the hierarchical approach) is not very fast if small skips are used. On the other hand, if we use only 1/64th of data points, we are able to segment the image in 22.6 ms but the precision starts to be a little bit low. It can be acceptable for our purposes but the new hierarchical approach further improves the speed with the same segmentation quality or provides better quality in the same amount of time. With the same amount of data points, the

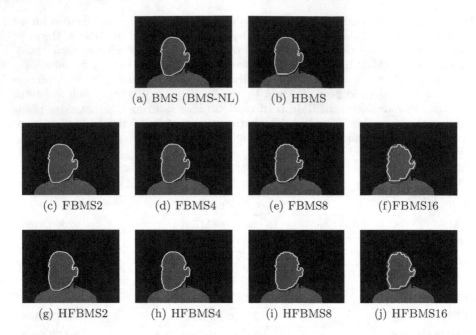

(a) BMS (BMS-NL)   (b) HBMS

(c) FBMS2   (d) FBMS4   (e) FBMS8   (f)FBMS16

(g) HFBMS2   (h) HFBMS4   (i) HFBMS8   (j) HFBMS16

Fig. 3. Comparison of segmentation results of fast blurring mean-shift method. If the step is 20 pixels (in x and y axis) then only each 400th pixel is involved in the computation. The white points represent the detected head.

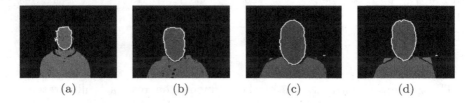

(a)   (b)   (c)   (d)

Fig. 4. Testing images segmented with our application.

hierarchical approach is able to segment the image in 9 ms only. If the Hierarchical Fast Blurring MS is used, we can improve the segmentation quality and the algorithm is able to run real-time even on slower CPUs. Because of real-time requirements, we consider to create a multi-core version of the algorithm to increase the speed further.

4   Conclusion

We have presented an improvement for well known mean-shift method. It is usually used for filtration, tracking or segmenting data but mostly it does not provide real-time performance when segmenting the data. The need for a new version emerged because of our project for the automotive industry where we need to solve the gaze direction problem in real-time. Gaze direction solves few smaller sub-tasks and our algorithm solves the first few tasks that are needed for further processing of the image. We have used the mean-shift segmentation method for finding the head boundaries, its location and center. These information can be used for limiting the area where to search for the eyes or for estimating the eye center that is needed for gaze direction estimation

There are hierarchical and so called fast versions of the algorithm that try to solve this speed problem but they are still relatively slow for a real-time use. In this paper, we have used the lattice structure that improves the speed of merging the corresponding data points. Hence, the dataset is dynamically reduced after each iteration. This structure also allows not to deal with data points that would not be needed for the computation and can avoid unnecessary steps. All these improvements are very useful for the hierarchical approach that carries out MS computation with a very small bandwidth to make an oversegmented image quickly and then this output is used once more with a larger bandwidth. Both stages are fast and it also solves the over-segmentation problem. We can use more than two stages in the hierarchical version of the algorithm. With all these improvements, we were able to create the algorithm that is able to segment the head in depth images in real-time and it is suitable for the industrial application. It can be incorporated into a pipeline application as one thread of the processing pipeline

References

1. Cheng, Y.: Mean shift, mode seeking, and clustering. IEEE Trans. Pattern Anal. Mach. Intell. **17**, 790–799 (1995)
2. Comaniciu, D., Ramesh, V., Meer, P.: The variable bandwidth mean shift and data-driven scale selection. IEEE Int. Conf. Comput. Vis. **1**, 438 (2001)
3. DeMenthon, D., Megret, R.: Spatio-temporal segmentation of video by hierarchical mean shift analysis. Technical Report LAMP-TR-090, CAR-TR-978, CS-TR-4388, UMIACS-TR-2002-68, University of Maryland, College Park (2002)
4. Freedman, D., Kisilev, P.: Fast mean shift by compact density representation. In: IEEE Conference on Computer Vision and Pattern Recognition, 2009. CVPR 2009, pp. 1818–1825, June 2009
5. Fukunaga, K., Hostetler, L.: The estimation of the gradient of a density function, with applications in pattern recognition. IEEE Trans. Inf. Theor. **21**(1), 32–40 (1975)
6. Guo, H., Guo, P., Lu, H.: A fast mean shift procedure with new iteration strategy and re-sampling. In: IEEE International Conference on Systems, Man and Cybernetics, 2006. SMC 2006, vol. 3, pp. 2385–2389 (2006)
7. Ren, Y., Domeniconi, C., Zhang, G., Yu, G.: A weighted adaptive mean shift clustering algorithm. In: Zaki, M.J., Obradovic, Z., Tan, P., Banerjee, A., Kamath, C., Parthasarathy, S. (eds.) Proceedings of the 2014 SIAM International Conference on Data Mining, Philadelphia, 24–26 April 2014, pp. 794–802. SIAM (2014)
8. Šurkala, M., Mozdřeň, K., Fusek, R., Sojka, E.: Hierarchical Layered Mean Shift Methods. In: Blanc-Talon, J., Kasinski, A., Philips, W., Popescu, D., Scheunders, P. (eds.) ACIVS 2013. LNCS, vol. 8192, pp. 538–545. Springer, Heidelberg (2013). doi:10.1007/978-3-319-02895-8_48

9. Vatturi, P., Wong, W.K.: Category detection using hierarchical mean shift. In: Proceedings of the 15th ACM SIGKDD International Conference on Knowledge Discovery and Data Mining. KDD 2009, pp. 847–856. ACM, New York (2009)
10. Viola, P., Jones, M.: Rapid object detection using a boosted cascade of simple features. In: Proceedings of the 2001 IEEE Computer Society Conference on Computer Vision and Pattern Recognition, 2001. CVPR 2001, vol. 1, pp. I-511–I-518 (2001)
11. Šurkala, M., Mozdřeň, K., Fusek, R., Sojka, E.: Hierarchical Blurring Mean-Shift. In: Blanc-Talon, J., Kleihorst, R., Philips, W., Popescu, D., Scheunders, P. (eds.) ACIVS 2011. LNCS, vol. 6915, pp. 228–238. Springer, Heidelberg (2011). doi:10. 1007/978-3-642-23687-7_21. http://dl.acm.org/citation.cfm?id=2034246.2034270
12. Šurkala, M., Mozdřeň, K., Fusek, R., Sojka, E.: Hierarchical blurring mean-shift. In: 2012 19th IEEE International Conference on Image Processing, pp. 1593–1596. IEEE (September 2012)

Robust Color Watermarking Method Based on Clifford Transform

Maroua Affes[✉], Malek Sellami Meziou, and Faouzi Ghorbel

CRISTAL Laboratory, GRIFT Research Group, Manouba, Tunisia
maroua.affes@ensi-uma.tn, malek.meziou@gmail.com,
Faouzi.ghorbel@ensi.run.tn

Abstract. In this paper, we propose a new watermarking scheme resistant to geometric attacks and JPEG compression. This method uses Fourier Clifford Transform and Harris interest points. First, we detect all circular Harris interest regions. Then, using the Delaunay-tessellation-based triangle matching method, we define robust interest region. Finally, the watermark is embedded into Clifford coefficients of robust interest region.

Keywords: Fourier Clifford Transform · Delaunay triangulation · Watermarking and geometric attacks

1 Introduction

Nowadays, many techniques are proposed to protect the intellectual property rights such as digital watermarking. These techniques transmit a message that is not interpretable by an unauthorized person and it must be invisible. In the literature, watermarking methods are categorized by processing domain, signal type of watermark, and hiding position. It is characterized by good visual fidelity and robustness of the watermark against common image processing and geometric attacks [1]. Several works treat the improved robustness against geometric transformations: the first approaches are based on embedding the mark into invariant domain [2, 3] such as the ordinary moments [4, 5], the Analytical Fourier Mellin Transform (AFMT) [6, 7] or the Fourier transform [8, 9] which define translation, rotation and scaling invariance. Also, they are based on a template which is a repeated structure embedded into the image to estimate the geometric distortions and to extract the watermark after reversing the geometric transformation [10]. The second approaches are based on feature-points [11, 12]. The main purpose for using the feature-points is to determine the interest areas where the watermark is embedded. This kind of methods resists against the geometric distortions since feature points present stable references for embedding and extraction process. The feature-points obtained by Harris corner detector are mixed with Delaunay to define the embedding regions [13, 14, 15]. In case of attacks, extracted feature-points may be lost. Other points may also appear. Tessellation can filter interest points and define an invariant subset.

In this paper, we are interested in studying feature based watermarking techniques. We propose to use Delaunay tessellation to identify a robust subset of feature-points.

© Springer International Publishing AG 2016
J. Blanc-Talon et al. (Eds.): ACIVS 2016, LNCS 10016, pp. 453–464, 2016.
DOI: 10.1007/978-3-319-48680-2_40

The watermark is embedded into the Clifford transform of interest regions in order to resist geometric distortions and compression attacks. In Sect. 2, Clifford Fourier Transform will be recalled. We will describe in Sect. 3, the old watermarked method based on CFT and its limits. In Sect. 4, Delaunay triangulation will be presented. Section 5 covers the details of our watermarking algorithm. Section 6 presents the experimental results in terms of robustness against geometric transformations and JPEG compression. We will finally conclude and give some possible perspectives for future works.

2 Clifford Fourier Transform

The classical Fourier transform has been used in grayscale images and 1D signal processing. However, on color images, many solutions have been proposed. The first one is to apply classical Fourier Transform on each channel. Sangwine and Ell proposed a more rigorous approach in [16]. They defined the Quaternion Fourier Transform (QFT) by considering two Fourier transforms for the luminance and chrominance. Recently, Batard et al. [17] defined another Fourier Transform, called Clifford Fourier transform (CFT).

The CFT is based on Clifford algebra that is noting $Cl(E, Q)$, also $\mathbb{R}_{p,q}$ and obtained from the pair: a finite-dimensional vector space E and a given quadratic form Q defined on E. The $Cl(E, Q)$ dimension is 2^n (when it considered as a vector space over the real line $\mathbb{R}$) and its base E is given by the set:

$$\{e_{i1}e_{i2}e_{i3}\ldots e_{ik}, i_1 < i_2 < i_k, k \in 1\ldots n\} \tag{1}$$

A color image f considered as a square integrated function from $\mathbb{R}^2$ to $\mathbb{R}^4$ (i.e. $f \in L^2(\mathbb{R}^2; \mathbb{R}^4)$) can be defined by:

$$f(x) = r(x)e_1 + g(x)e_2 + b(x)\ e_3 + 0\ e_4 \tag{2}$$

Where $x = (x_1, x_2)$ and r, g and b are respectively the red, green and blue channels pixel with coordinates (x_1, x_2)

Let $f \in L^2(\mathbb{R}^2; (\mathbb{R}^4, Q))$ be the embedded of f on $Cl(\mathbb{R}^4, Q)$ The clifford Fourier Transform of f is given by:

$$\begin{aligned}
\hat{f}(u_1, u_2, u_3, u_4) &= \int_{\mathbb{R}^4} f(x_1, x_2) \tilde{\phi}_{u_1,u_2,u_3,u_4,B}(-x_1, -x_2) dx_1 dx_2 \\
&= \int_{\mathbb{R}^4} \frac{e^{\frac{1}{2}(x_1(u_1+u_3)+x_2(u_2+u_4))B} e^{\frac{1}{2}(x_1(u_1-u_3)+x_2(u_2-u_4))I_4 B} f(x_1, x_2)}{e^{-\frac{1}{2}(x_1(u_1+u_3)+x_2(u_2+u_4))B} e^{-\frac{1}{2}(x_1(u_1-u_3)+x_2(u_2-u_4))I_4 B}} dx_1 dx_2
\end{aligned} \tag{3}$$

where $u_i \in \mathbb{R}$, I_4 is the pseudo scalar of $\mathbb{R}_{4,0}$, B is its unit bi-vector and $\tilde{\phi}_{u1,u2,u3,u4,B}$ is the morphisme of $\mathbb{R}^2$ in Spin(Q). Later, we denote Spin(4) the group representation of Spin(Q) in $Cl(\mathbb{R}^4, Q)$ [17, 18].

This equation gives a general formula of the Fourier transform for the 4D signals. Color images being values in $\mathbb{R}^3$, only a part of Spin(4) elements, those corresponding precisely to $\mathbb{R}^2$ morphism on Spin(3), is used. So, the color CFT is given by the following expression:

$$\hat{f}(u_1, u_2) = \int_{\mathbb{R}^2} f(x_1, x_2) \tilde{\Phi}_{u_1,u_2,0,0,B}(-x_1, -x_2) dx_1 dx_2$$
$$= \int_{\mathbb{R}^2} e^{\frac{1}{2}(x_1 u_1 + x_2 u_2)(B + I_4 B)} f(x_1, x_2) e^{-\frac{1}{2}(x_1 u_1 + x_2 u_2)(B + I_4 B)} dx_1 dx_2 \tag{4}$$

where I_4 is the scalar pseudo of $\mathbb{R}_{4,0}$ and B is its unit bi-vector. Within the Clifford algebras, a vector can be decomposed in a parallel part and an orthogonal part depending on the choice of the bi-vector B. The above equation can be rewritten by the decomposition described in [17, 19]:

$$\hat{f}_B(u) = \hat{f}_{\|B}(u) + \hat{f}_{\perp B}(u) \tag{5}$$

where

$$\hat{f}_{\|B}(u) = \int_{\mathbb{R}^2} e^{\frac{1}{2}(u1x1 + u2x2)B} f_{\|B}(x) e^{-\frac{1}{2}(u1x1 + u2x2)B} dx$$

is the CFT of $f_{\|B}$ the parallel projection of f on a bi-vector B and

$$\hat{f}_{\perp B}(u) = \int_{\mathbb{R}^2} e^{\frac{1}{2}(u1x1 + u2x2)I_4 B} f_{\perp B}(x) e^{-\frac{1}{2}(u1x1 + u2x2)I_4 B} dx$$

is the CFT of $f_{\perp B}$ which is the orthogonal projection of f on a bi-vector B.

We will use this decomposition in the proposed schema in order to embed the mark in the CFT coefficients of parallel projection of f.

3 Watermarking Method Based on CFT

In this section, we will recall the conventional embedding process of the watermarking method based on CFT [20] and after that we will present its limits.

First, Harris detector was employed to select robust interest points and to generate circular interest regions, denote $B(i)$. Each region was transformed into Clifford Fourier domain and the watermark was embedded into the Clifford transform coefficients magnitude of some valid regions. In fact, we chose the Clifford Fourier domain because it assures the invisibility and the robustness of the mark more than in spatial domain. Also, this domain enable us to avoid the marginal treatment of color image which can cause sometimes a false detection of the watermark.

So, we generate a bitmap, denoted ξ, which contains "1" if the region $B(i)$ of $f_{\|B}$ is valid i.e. $B(i)$ has a bit of the watermark. Its validity is computed as following:

- For each region, CFT is applied.

- Then, two mi-frequency coefficients are selected. To know the possible location of these two coefficients, in [20], we study the distribution of coefficients with bases magnitudes values. This study made us choose the support of potential coefficients of CFT where to embed the mark as illustrated in Fig. 1.

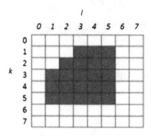

Fig. 1. Possible locations for embedding in 8×8 regions (shadowed area).

- Apply the following condition to fill the map ξ:

    If $\left|Q(k_i, l_j)\right| > \left|Q(k_n, l_m)\right| + p$,
    $\xi(i) \leftarrow 1$ then the region $B(i)$ is valid
        Else $\xi(i) \leftarrow 0$.
    where p is a marginal noise.

    After that, we generate a binary random watermark $W = \{w_i, \ i = 0\ldots M\}$. The size of the watermark equals to the number of "1" on bitmap ξ. Finally, we embed one bit of the watermark in each region. However, we integrate it in the CFT domain. So, for each valid region $B(i)$ (i.e. $\xi(i) = 1$) the following steps are applied:

- CFT is applied
- If W(i) = 1
    Permute $\left|Q(k_i, l_j)\right|$ and $\left|Q(k_n, l_m)\right|$:
    $\left|Q'(k_i, l_j)\right| = \left|Q(k_n, l_m)\right|$ and $\left|Q'(k_n, l_m)\right| = \left|Q(k_i, l_j)\right|$;
- If W(i) = 0
    $\left|Q'(k_i, l_j)\right| = \left|Q(k_i, l_j)\right|$ and $\left|Q'(k_n, l_m)\right| = \left|Q(k_n, l_m)\right|$
- Inverse CFT is applied

    The watermarked image f_w is then obtained by combining the watermarked regions.

    With the old method [20], all feature-points are used to embed the mark. But, we noted that this method was robust only to JPEG compression and not to geometric attacks, because there is an appearance/a disappearance of some feature-points.

    Figure 2 shows an example of set points which was modified after some geometric transformations.

    To overcome this problem, Delaunay triangulation will be used to detect only robust feature points and to identify the strong points which resist geometric attacks. In the next section, we will remind the principles of Delaunay triangulation and present how it is able to detect the points that do not disappear.

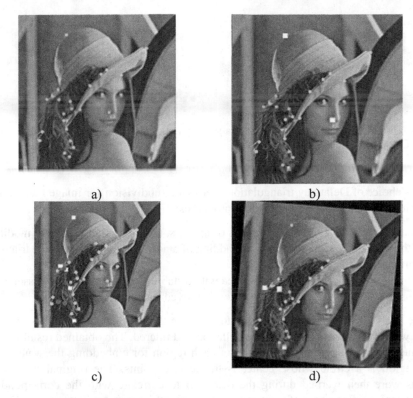

Fig. 2. An example of the appearance/disappearance of some feature-points: (a) the original image (b) scaling image 1.1 (c) scaling image 0.8 (d) rotated image 5°. The red circles (resp. white squares) points present the appeared (resp. disappeared) feature points (Color figure online).

4   Delaunay Triangulation

Delaunay triangulation is a process of partitioning a set of points E positioned in a space and composed triangles whose vertices are objects. We consider here a set of points belongs to the same plane because we are dealing with 2D points which are extracted using Harris detector. The Delaunay triangulation has many known properties that make it the most widely-used triangulation, among them:

- The criterion of the circle: A Delaunay triangle is a triangle that has three objects as a vertex, and such that its circumscribed circle has not in its inside any other object. All of them have to lie on a circumcircle with no point lying inside it.
- Delaunay triangulation maximizes the minimum angle triangles and minimizes the size of the circumcircle.

Delaunay triangulation of a discrete set of points E is the dual graph of the Voronoi tessellation associated with E. To construct the Delaunay tessellation, the nearest neighboring points, whose cells in the Voronoi tessellation sharing an edge are joined. Figure 3 illustrates the Voronoi and Delaunay tessellation of a set of points.

Fig. 3. Voronoi tessellation (blue color) of a set of points and their Delaunay tessellation (red color) (Color figure online).

Our choice of Delaunay triangulation as a space subdivision for image matching is motivated by the following remarkable properties:

- Local property. If a vertex disappears or appears, the triangulation is only modified on the connected triangles. Thus, the adding of a now point affects only the triangles connected to this point.
- Stability area. Each vertex is associated with a stability area in which the tessellation pattern is not changed when the vertex is moved inside this area.

We used the Harris corner detector to generate the set of points E. These feature points were mixed with a Delaunay tessellation and filtered. The obtained result is a set of feature points that mark the position of each region for embedding the watermark. This region is a circle whose center is the feature points. The original watermark regions were then warped during the detection to correlate with the corresponding marked regions. Examples of a set of feature points of images are illustrated in Fig. 4.

Fig. 4. Delaunay triangulation obtained by interest feature points.

5   The Proposed Algorithm

In this paper, watermark embedding algorithm uses Delaunay triangulation in order to get the same regions used in embedding process after some attacks.

The proposed method includes the following steps:

1. Transform the color image to grayscale in order to detect the interest points with Harris detector.
2. Construct the Delaunay triangulation of the original and the attacked image, several target triangles from the Delaunay of the original and corresponding triangles from attacked image are selected automatically. The selection of target triangles is obtained in order, to keep the strong triangles which resist geometric attacks such as:

$$T_{Strong} = T_{Original} \bigcap_{i=1}^{N} T_{Attack_i} \tag{6}$$

where T_{Strong} represents the set of strong triangles, $T_{Original}$ represents the set of original triangles which was described in the previous paragraph, $T_{Attacki}$ represents the set T after the ith best attack, which can be either pre-watermarking process and N represents the number of the attacks and it depends on the stability of the set of triangles

Figure 5 illustrates the effect of different pre-attacks on the resulting T_{Strong} and shows the relatively strong triangles obtained by intersecting the set triangles of the original and its pre-attacked images. We can easily observe the sensitivity of the triangulation to different attacks [21]. That is, some triangles may disappear, show up or shift a bit after attacks. Consequently, it is impossible to determine the robust triangles which remain unchangeable after various attacks. To address this challenging issue, we select a few geometric attacks to extract the strong triangles that are likely preserved under different attacks. The random pre-attacks are respectively applied on each image to obtain strong set triangles. The intersection of all triangles sets yields strong triangles to be saved for the detection process.

The matching criterion is based on the orientation angles, the sizes and the positions of vertices. That is, if two triangles are very similar, for example, if angle difference radian is less than 0.01 rad, that means these two triangles are claimed to be likely matched. With these pairs, we can determine the possible geometric distortion since the important feature points used to triangulation have the same transformation as the image itself.

3. Apply the remaining steps of the previously described embedding process in Sect. 2. These steps should be applied on points of the vertex of T_{Strong}.

The presence of T_{Strong}, in the extraction process, lets us restore the image after geometric attacks.

T_{Strong} presents the target triangles and the probe triangles are the triangles obtained from watermarked image after the flows steps:

- Detect the feature points with Harris detector
- Construct the Delaunay triangulation
- Find the similarity between the T_{Strong} and the triangles in the triangulation.

After obtained the target and probe triangles, we use the same method in [22] to determine three-element: rotation factor (RF), scaling factor (SF) and translation factor

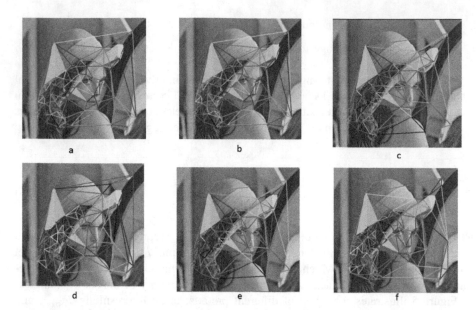

Fig. 5. An example of re-attacks used to obtain P_{Strong}: (a) The pre-watermarked image triangulation, (b) The pre-attacked set triangles translated image triangulation by (1,3) (c) The rotated image triangulation 5° (d) The scaling image triangulation 0.9 (e) The rotated image triangulation 1°. Final strong set triangles (color triangles) obtained after intersecting the original set (f) and its 5 common set triangles of pre-attacked images (Color figure online).

(TF). These factors are the average of distortions undergone by each triangle to present the geometric transformation. They are used to restore the image to its original form. Figure 6 illustrates the steps to restore the target triangle.

As it was presented in Fig. 6, the Scale Factor is calculated by resizing the probe triangle to the same size as the target matched triangle. Thus, we obtain this factor when we calculate the average of distances between vertices of probe triangle divided by distances between vertices of target matched triangle. The Translation Factor is obtained by registering one of the vertices of the matched triangle pair, for example, it can be the vertex's position of big angel radian. The last factor which is the rotation

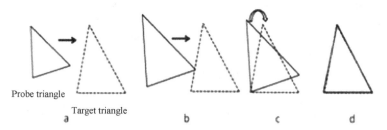

Fig. 6. Process of finding the geometric transformations: (a) The matched triangle pair, (b) The resizing result, (c) The translation result (d) The rotation result

factor is computed by aligning the other two unregistered vertices of the matched triangle pair. We compute the mean of the distortions of all triangles and use the averages as the rotation factor (RF), scaling factor (SF), translation factor (TF) and shear factor (SF) which are then used to restore the image to its original form. The factors are obtained using the formula given in Eq. 7.

$$F_{avg} = \frac{F_1 + F_2 + \ldots + F_N}{N} \tag{7}$$

Where F_{avg} is the mean of the distortions obtained from the probe triangles, F_N is the distortion obtained from the Nth probe triangle.

Once the image is restored, we apply the same steps to those in the embedding process. With the presence of ξ, we can specify which blocks are watermarked. So, for each block when $\xi(i) = 1$, it is transformed to CFT domain. The watermark is extracted by the flowing equation:

$$W' = \begin{cases} 1, |Q'(k_n, l_m)| > |Q'(k_i, l_j)| \\ 0, |Q'(k_n, l_m)| < |Q'(k_i, l_j)| \end{cases} \tag{8}$$

6 Experiment Results

To evaluate the performance of the proposed watermarking scheme, we conducted experiments on various color images the database of BSD300 and different kinds of attempting attacks. We first perform the watermark invisibility test using five color images from the data set. Then, we illustrate the robustness of the proposed method by testing it with some geometric attacks.

6.1 Watermark Invisibility Test

We evaluate watermark invisibility on five images: Lena image and four images from the BSD300 set with references: 61060, 46076, 78004 and 22090 respectively. The PSNRs of these four watermarked images are respectively 42, 48, 41.14, 45.89, and 44.79. These PSNR values are all greater than 35,00 dB, which is the empirical value for the image without any perceivable degradation.

6.2 Important Restoration Test

Image restoration is an important step in our watermarking scheme. In general, we apply the Delaunay triangulation to generate triangles and obtain from them the strong triangles, we use angle degrees to find the matched triangles between the original and probe image and to find the possible geometric attacks. Some random simulation results on the global geometric attacks are listed in Table 1.

Table 1. Watermark robustness to geometric attacks

Image/attacks	Lena	61060	46076	78004	22090
No attack	1	1	1	1	1
Rotation 1°	0,8	0,89	0,75	1	1
Rotation 5°	0,8	0,78	0,75	1	1
Rotation 10°	0,733	0,67	0,58	0,85	0,7
Translation 1 (5,5)	1	0,89	0,741	0,91	1
Translation 2 (1,3)	1	0,89	0,71	0,91	1
Scaling 0,7	0,8	0,78	1	1	1
Scaling 0,9	0,87	0,88	1	1	0,85
Scaling 1,1	0,733	0,89	1	1	1
Compression 80 %	1	1	1	1	1
Compression 70 %	0,71	0,92	1	1	1

To evaluate the robustness of the proposed algorithm, we compute the Normalized Hamming Similarity which is denoted by NHS:

$$NHS = 1 - \frac{HD(W, W')}{N} \tag{9}$$

Where W (resp. W') is the inserted watermark (resp. the extracted watermark) and N is its size.

It can be seen from Table 1 that when there are no attack occurs, te proposed method can extract the watermark accurately and therefore all NSH values are equal to one. Table 1 shows that the proposed scheme is robust to RST attacks. For rotation attacks, most of the similarities are higher than 0.58. The proposed scheme is robust to scaling, even when the watermarked image is scaled half the original size. When the image is scaled in, all the similarities are higher than 0.8. Also, it shows the robustness of our method against JPEG compression attacks, the NSH value reach one with quality factor 80 % for all tested images.

7   Conclusion and Perspectives

We have proposed here a novel robust content-based digital watermarking scheme against global geometric attacks, such as rotation, scaling, translation and also against JPEG compression. The mark is imperceptible as it is inserted into the parallel part $\widehat{f}_{\|B}$ of the Clifford Fourier Transform. We have proved that a watermark can be recovered after RST attacks on an image by employing Delaunay triangulation techniques and triangle matching. NSH values showed that our scheme is effective in watermark recovering. But, its payload depends on the number of valid regions and the vertex of the set of strong triangles. So, we think that the performances of the proposed method could be improved by increasing the payload capacity.

Acknowledgments. This research is part of a collaborative work between iTesLab company represented by its director, M. Mahfoudh and the CRISTAL Lab of ENSI.

This project was are performed in the device MOBIDOC program funded by the European Union under the PASRI program administered by the Agence Nationale de la Promotion de la recherche (ANPR) of Tunisia.

References

1. Potdar, V.M., Song, H., Chang, E.: A survey of digital image watermarking techniques. In: 3rd IEEE International Conference on Industrial Informatics, INDIN 2005, pp. 709–716 (2005)

2. Cox, I.J., Miller, M.L., Bloom, J.A., Honsinger, C.: Digital Watermarking, vol. 1558607145. Morgan Kaufmann, San Francisco (2002)

3. Zheng, D., Liu, Y., Zhao, J., Saddik, A.E.: A survey of RST invariant image watermarking algorithm. ACM Comp. Surv. **39**, 1–91 (2007)

4. Alghoniemy, M., Tewfik, A.H.: Image watermarking by moment invariant. In: Proceedings of IEEE International Conference Image Processing, pp. 73–76 (2000)

5. Kim, B.-S., Choi, J.-G., Park, K.-H.: RST-resistant image watermarking using invariant centroid and reordered Fourier-Mellin transform. In: Kalker, T., Cox, I., Ro, Y.M. (eds.) IWDW 2003. LNCS, vol. 2939, pp. 370–381. Springer, Heidelberg (2004)

6. Ghorbel, F.: A complete invariant description for gray level images by the harmonic analysis approach. Pattern Recogn. Lett. **15**(10), 1043–1051 (1994)

7. Guemir, O., Mhiri, S., Ghorbel, F.: Algorithme de tatouage basé sur le Prolongement Analytique de la Transformée de Fourier Mellin. CORESA 2005 Rennes France (2005)

8. Lin, C.Y., Wu, M., Bloom, J.A., Cox, I.J., Miller, M.L., Lui, Y.M.: Rotation, scale, and translation resilient watermarking for images. IEEE Trans. Image Process. **10**(5), 767–782 (2001)

9. Ruanaidh, J.J.O., Pun, T.: Rotation, scale and translation invariant spread spectrum digital image watermarking. Sig. Process. **66**(3), 303–317 (1998)

10. Herrigel, A., Voloshynovskiy, S.V., Rytsar, Y.B.: Watermark template attack. In: Proceedings of Photonics West 2001-Electronic Imaging, pp. 394–405. International Society for Optics and Photonics (2001)

11. Qi, X., Qi, J.: A robust content-based digital image watermarking scheme. Sig. Process. **87**(6), 1264–1280 (2007)

12. Kutter, M., Bhattacharjee, S.K., Ebrahimi, T.: Towards second generation watermarking schemes. In: Proceedings of 1999 International Conference on Image Processing, ICIP 1999, vol. 1, pp. 320–323. IEEE (1999)

13. Bas, P., Chassery, J.M., Macq, B.: Geometrically invariant watermarking using feature points. IEEE Trans. Image Process. **11**(9), 1014–1028 (2002)

14. Seo, J., Yoo, C.: Localized image watermarking based on feature points of scale-space representation. Pattern Recogn. **37**(7), 1365–1375 (2004)

15. Madhusudhan, K.N., Lalitha, S., Ashwini, V., Manjula, R.: Novel watermark recovery technique in various attack condition. Int. J. Innov. Eng. Technol. (IJIET) (2013). edn. 31st

16. Ell, T.A., Sangwine, S.J.: Hypercomplex Fourier transforms of color images. IEEE Trans. Image Process. **16**(1), 22–35 (2007)

17. Batard, T., Berthier, M., Saint-Jean, C.: Clifford-Fourier transform for color image processing. In: Bayro-Corrochano, E., Scheuermann, G. (eds.) Geometric Algebra Computing, pp. 135–162. Springer, London (2010)

18. Postnikov, M.: Leçons de géométrie. Groupes et algèbres de Lie. Mir 1985. Russian original, Nauka, Moskau (1982)

19. Porteous, I.R.: Clifford Algebras and the Classical Groups, vol. 50. Cambridge University Press, Cambridge (1995)

20. Affes, M., Sellami, M., Lehiani Y., Preda, M., Ghorbel, F.: A content-based watermarking scheme based on Clifford Fourier transform. In: Proceedings of the 12th International Joint Conference on Computer Vision, Imaging and Computer Graphics Theory and Applications, Rome, Italy, pp. 372–378 (2016)

21. Papakostas, G.A., Tsougenis, E.D., Koulouriotis, D.E., Tourassis, V.D.: On the robustness of Harris detector in image watermarking attacks. Optics Commun. **284**(19), 4394–4407 (2011)

22. Qi, X., Qi, J.: A desynchronization resilient watermarking scheme. In: Shi, Y.Q. (ed.) Transactions on Data Hiding and Multimedia Security IV. LNCS, vol. 5510, pp. 29–48. Springer, Heidelberg (2009)

Action-02MCF: A Robust Space-Time Correlation Filter for Action Recognition in Clutter and Adverse Lighting Conditions

Anwaar Ulhaq[1(✉)], Xiaoxia Yin[1], Yunchan Zhang[1], and Iqbal Gondal[2]

[1] Centre of Applied Informatics, Victoria University, Melbourne, VIC, Australia
anwaar.ulhaq@vu.edu.au
[2] Faculty of Science and Technology, Federation University, Ballarat, VIC, Australia

Abstract. Human actions are spatio-temporal visual events and recognizing human actions in different conditions is still a challenging computer vision problem. In this paper, we introduce a robust feature based space-time correlation filter, called Action-02MCF (0'zero-aliasing' 2M' Maximum Margin') for recognizing human actions in video sequences. This filter combines (i) the sparsity of spatio-temporal feature space, (ii) generalization of maximum margin criteria, (iii) enhanced aliasing free localization performance of correlation filtering using (iv) rich content of maximally stable space-time interest points into a single classifier. Its rich multi-objective function provides robustness, generalization and recognition as a single package. Action-02MCF can simultaneously localize and classify actions of interest even in clutter and adverse imaging conditions. We evaluate the performance of our proposed filter for challenging human action datasets. Experimental results verify the performance potential of our action-filter compared to other correlation filtering based action recognition approaches.

1 Introduction

A large number of potential applications in different areas (e.g. visual surveillance, video retrieval, sports video analysis, human computer interfaces, and smart rooms) have resulted the development of variety of automated action recognition approaches. Different challengiscenarios are considered like action in the wild (YouTube videos) [19], actions in group formations [10], actions in the crowd [22], actions in movies [17], actions across different viewpoints [13] and in the presence of occlusion [25]. However, majority of the above approaches discuss action recognition in high quality day-time videos or in the presence of good lighting conditions and do not consider adverse lighting conditions or the recognition of actions at night-time. Figure 1 illustrates a two-hand waving action in low light scenario. In this work, we present a new action-filer called Action-02MCF which can handle such variations in action datasets.

Space-time template matching has proved successful in action recognition. However, a major drawback of template based methods is their computational

© Springer International Publishing AG 2016
J. Blanc-Talon et al. (Eds.): ACIVS 2016, LNCS 10016, pp. 465–476, 2016.
DOI: 10.1007/978-3-319-48680-2_41

Fig. 1. A nighttime scenario of *waving* action captured by low light visible and infrared sensors which presents visual challenges for recognition due to poor visual quality and low light.

overhead during spatial template matching. Recently, a trend has emerged to use frequency domain filters instead of spatial domain template by analyzing response in the frequency domain which is faster than spatial template matching. Furthermore, use of frequency domain matching makes it useful for real-time action detection [8]. Our work is closely related to the development of frequency domain matching techniques for action recognition. Correlation filters are examples of such filters and have been used successfully for automatic target recognition [16]. Correlation filters were initially developed in the seminal work of [12], which is a way of learning a template/filter in the frequency domain that when correlated with a set of training signals, gives a desired response (correlation peak). A general correlation filter h can be expressed as:

$$h = \arg_h \min \sum_{i=1}^{N} ||h \otimes x_i - g_i||^2 \tag{1}$$

where $\otimes$ denotes the cross-correlation of the vector versions of the input signal x_i and the template h and g_i is the vector versions of the desired correlation output. The effectiveness of correlation filters has been explored by [2,9] for application such as target detection and tracking in (2D) images. As action recognition research community has greatly benefited from extending image recognition approaches to the temporal domain, the extension of correlation filters in spatio-temporal sense is worked out in a similar way.

Inspired from this approach, the Action MACH filter [21] is developed by extending traditional MACH filter in spatio-temporal sense. As the MACH filter is able to capture intra-class variability, Action MACH is synthesized for a given action class. Filters are then correlated with testing sequences in the frequency domain via 3D FFT transform. This filter has performed well in a variety of action datasets. However, the utility of Action MACH, has been questioned by [1] that proposes a linear SVM in the Fourier domain to improve intra-class variability. Despite improving intra-class variability, this approach fails to handle inter-class variability. Inter-class variability was addressed in [11] with a space-time distance classifier correlation filter. A multi-channel extension of 2D-MOSSE correlation filter [14] has proposed for action recognition based on multi-channel correlation filter [9]. However, these approaches are not aliasing-free as FFT based correlation operation produces circular correlation than linear correlation. Furthermore, these filters offer poor generalization.

To overcome these discrepancies, we propose (i) a new spatio-temporal correlation filter named Action-02MCF. This filter combines the design principles of support vector machines and zero-aliasing correlation filter by extending traditional 2D-MMCF [3,20] and 2D-zero-aliasing correlation filters [7] in spatio-temporal domain, (ii) in addition, rather using noisy intensity representation, it relies on sparsity of feature space by introducing maximally stable space-time interest points for action recognition. This proposed filter combines the sparsity of spatio-temporal feature space, generalization of maximum margin criteria, better localization performance of zero-aliasing correlation filtering and rich context of maximally stable interest points into a single classifier.

The rest of the paper is organized as follows: the proposed feature detectors and descriptors are presented in Sect. 2, the proposed Action-02MCF and action representation is presented in Sect. 3. Experimental results are discussed in Sect. 4. Finally, conclusion and references are presented.

2   Feature Extraction and Description

To capture salient information in video volumes, we introduce maximally stable 3D cuboid as spatio-temporal features and use HOG3D [15] as descriptor.

We extract maximally stable volumes [5] from each volume. The objective of finding maximally stable volume (MSV) is to compute stable connected region volumes from an input video sequence. A MSV volume is a connected component in (x,y,t) space which has homogeneous intensity distribution inside and high intensity difference at its boundary. By performing computation at various scales, both fine and large scale structures can be extracted. In addition, they can be computed automatically in real time with low computational complexity. We use MSV detection and their stability criteria following similar approach as [5]. The most stable volumes, i.e. the nodes with the highest stability values are returned as the detection result. The stability criterion ρ is defined by the area variation as:

$$\rho(V_i^I; \Delta) = \frac{|V_{j-\Delta}^I| - |V_{k+\Delta}^I|}{|V_i^I|}, \qquad (2)$$

where V_i^I is connected volume obtained by thresholding intensity value at intensity, I. Here operator $|.|$, is the cardinality and Δ is the importance parameter which sets the threshold range and the number of component tree levels for computation of stability. MSV volume is particularly attractive for the current problem as their computation does not require any elaborate contour tracking or object detection algorithms. They can handle topological changes in the region shape due to articulated body or camera motion. After extraction of maximally

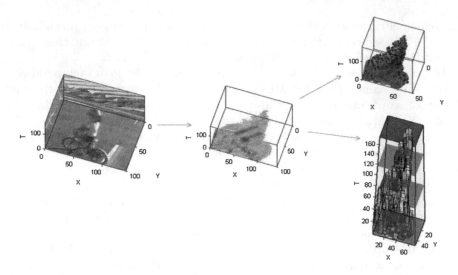

Fig. 2. Left to Right: Action volumes of cycling action: the respective maximally stable volume (MSV) and two different views of extracted spatio-temporal maximally stable cuboid We call these detectors as maximally stable cuboids

stable volumes from video sequences, we extract space-time cuboid features. The response function $\Re$ has the following form:

$$\Re = (V * G * h_{ev})^2 + (V * G * filter_{od})^2,$$
$$filter_{ev}(t; r, w) = -cos(2\pi tw)e^{-t^2/\tau^2},$$
$$filter_{od}(t; r, w) = -sin(2\pi tw)e^{-t^2/\tau^2}, \tag{3}$$

where $G(x, y; \sigma)$ is a 2D Gaussian smoothing kernel applied along spatial dimensions, and $filter_{ev}$ and $filter_{od}$ are the quadrature pair of 1D Gabor filter applied temporally. Response function $\Re$ has two important parameters, σ and τ, which correspond to spatial and temporal scales of the detector, respectively. HOG3D descriptor [15] f is used to describe each feature which comprises the histogram of 3D gradient directions. Figure 2 illustrates maximally stable interest point extraction process. Space-time cuboid in extracted maximally stable volume are shown in different colors.

3   Action-02MCF: Feature based 0 'zero aliasing' 2M' Maximum Margin Correlation Filter

In this sub-section, we describe our proposed feature based maximum margin correlation filter, named Action-02MCF.

Notation: Vectors are denoted by lower case letter f, matrices as upper case F, $\mathcal{F}^{-1}(\hat{f})$ is inverse Fourier transform of $\hat{f}$, where ˆ denotes variables in frequency

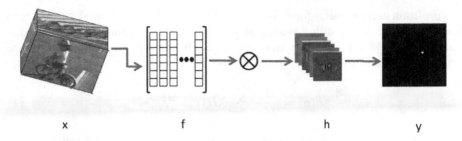

Fig. 3. An abstraction of feature based CF with multi-channel features f extracted from original video data x is correlated with multi-channel filter h to provide single-channel response y. The original data however, is colored.

domain, $'$ is transpose operation. Complex conjugate is shown by $*$ and $\dagger$ denotes the complex conjugate transpose (Fig. 3).

The filter design problem is posed as an optimization problem. Let us assume, we train a filter using N training feature vectors of length M. The multi-objective function of maximum margin correlation filter is given as:

The filter design problem is posed as an optimization problem. The multi-objective function of Action-02MCF is given as:

$$h = \min_{\hat{h}}\left(\frac{1}{N}\sum_{i=1}^{N}\sum_{k=1}^{M}||\hat{f}_i^k \otimes \hat{h}_i^k - \hat{g}_i||_2^2, \lambda\sum_{k=1}^{M}||h^k||_2^2 + C\sum_{i=1}^{N}\xi_i\right),$$

$$s.t. \qquad y_i\left(\sum_{k=1}^{M}.\hat{h}^{k^T}.\hat{f}_i^k\right) \geqslant u_i\xi_i \qquad (4)$$

where $\hat{h}$ and $\hat{f}$ are frequency domain filter and feature vectors respectively, ξ_i is the penalty term, a vector of slack variables and penalizes the training samples on wrong side of the margin, λ is the regularization parameter, $C > 0$ is trade-off parameter, y_i is the class label (1 for positive class, -1 for negative class), u_i is the minimum peak magnitude set to 1, N training videos and M is number of features. The above objective function can be reduced to a quadratic function:

$$\min_{\hat{h}} h^\dagger \hat{T}\hat{h} + C\sum_{i=1}^{N}\xi_i,$$

$$s.t. \qquad y_i(\hat{h}^\dagger\hat{f}_i + b) \geqslant u_i - \xi_i \qquad (5)$$

where $\hat{T} = \delta\mathcal{I} + (1-\lambda)\hat{D}$ with $\mathcal{I}$ is the identity matrix and cross power spectrum matrix $\hat{D}$ is given as:

$$\hat{D} = \begin{bmatrix} \frac{1}{N}\sum_{i=1}^{N}\hat{F}_i^{1\dagger}\hat{F}_i^1 & \cdots & \frac{1}{N}\sum_{i=1}^{N}\hat{F}_i^{1\dagger}\hat{F}_i^M \\ \vdots & \vdots & \vdots \\ \frac{1}{N}\sum_{i=1}^{N}\hat{F}_i^{M\dagger}\hat{F}_i^1 & \cdots & \frac{1}{N}\sum_{i=1}^{N}\hat{F}_i^{M\dagger}\hat{F}_i^M \end{bmatrix} \qquad (6)$$

To obtain zero aliasing formulation of the above filter, we need to add zero aliasing constraints according as suggested by [7]. Training signals are zero padded to size $M_{\mathcal{F}} \geqslant 2M - 1$. We know that time domain template $h(n)$ is related to the frequency domain filter $H(r)$ through inverse Fourier transform as:

$$h(n) = \frac{1}{M_{\mathcal{F}}} \sum_{i=1}^{M_{\mathcal{F}}-1} H(r)e^{\frac{j2\pi rn}{M_{\mathcal{F}}}} \tag{7}$$

To satisfy the zero aliasing constraints, we need to satisfy the following set of linear equations,

$$h(n) = \frac{1}{M_{\mathcal{F}}} \sum_{i=1}^{M_{\mathcal{F}}-1} H(r)e^{\frac{j2\pi rn}{M_{\mathcal{F}}}} = 0 \quad for \quad M \leq n < M_{\mathcal{F}} \tag{8}$$

or it can be summarized as $\hat{Z}^{\dagger}\hat{h} = 0$ where:

$$\hat{Z}^{\dagger} = \begin{bmatrix} 1 & e^{\frac{j2\pi(1)(M)}{M_{\mathcal{F}}}} & \cdots & e^{\frac{j2\pi(N_{\mathcal{F}}-1)(M)}{M_{\mathcal{F}}}} \\ 1 & e^{\frac{j2\pi(1)(M+1)}{M_{\mathcal{F}}}} & \cdots & e^{\frac{j2\pi(N_{\mathcal{F}}-1)(M+1)}{M_{\mathcal{F}}}} \\ \vdots & \vdots & \ddots & \vdots \\ 1 & e^{\frac{j2\pi(1)(M_{\mathcal{F}}-1)}{M_{\mathcal{F}}}} & \cdots & e^{\frac{j2\pi(M_{\mathcal{F}}-1)(M_{\mathcal{F}}-1)}{M_{\mathcal{F}}}} \end{bmatrix} \tag{9}$$

we can extend these constraints to N features as $\hat{A}^{\dagger}\hat{h} = 0$ where $\hat{A}^{\dagger} = I_N \otimes \hat{Z}^{\dagger}$ with $\otimes$ is the Kronecker product. Implementation of these constraints, however is not straightforward. We therefore, need a revised formulation of the objective function. By following approach of [7], we write the revised objective function of maximum margin correlation filter with zero aliasing constraints as:

$$\min_{\hat{h}} = \frac{1}{2C}h^{\dagger}\hat{T}\hat{h} + \frac{1}{2N}\sum_{i=1}^{N}(1 - y_i(\hat{h}^{\dagger}\hat{f}_i + b))^2, \quad s.t. \quad \hat{A}^{\dagger}\hat{h} = 0 \tag{10}$$

It can be solved using accelerated proximal gradient descent algorithm [7] in an iterative fashion.

3.1   Action Representation and Classification

We train our filter on maximally stable spatio-temporal interest points extracted from a series of spatio-temporal volumes. For the sake of representation, we denote each training volume in spatial domain by v and in frequency domain as $\hat{V}$ which can be produced by performing a 3D FFT operation as given below:

$$\hat{V}(u,v,w) = \sum_{t=0}^{R-1}\sum_{y=0}^{Q-1}\sum_{x=0}^{P-1} V(p,q,r)exp(-j2\pi(\frac{up}{P} + \frac{vq}{Q} + \frac{wr}{R}), \tag{11}$$

where $\hat{V}(u,v,w)$ is the resulting volume in frequency domain, P is the number of columns, Q is the number of rows and R is the number of frames of the volume.

We convert the original space-time volume and resulting 3D FFT matrix into $d \times 1$ column vectors with d as number of voxel, named s_i and S_i for training volume i for all N training videos respectively. If M is the number of features extracted from V_i, a feature vector x_i can be extracted as:

$$f_i = x^\dagger s_i \tag{12}$$

where $x = \{x_1, x_2, \ldots, x_M\}$ is $d \times M$ feature extraction matrix. Frequency domain representation of x_i is X_i can be denoted by $X = \{X_1, X_2, \ldots, X_M\}$ and frequency domain representation of f_i can be expressed as $F = \{F_1, F_2, \ldots, F_M\}$. If filter set is given as $h = \{h^1, h^1, \ldots, h^M\}$ with frequency domain representation H, the output correlation plane for a test volume V_t can be obtained as:

$$C_t(l, m, n) = \mathcal{F}^{-1}(< F_H, F_t >) \tag{13}$$

where $<,>$ denotes inner product of two vectors, F_t is frequency domain feature vector extracted from the test volume and F_h is frequency domain feature vector extracted from the template H.

4 Experimental Results and Discussion

We evaluate the performance of our proposed Action-02MCF filter using a comprehensive set of experiments on challenging human action datasets in both day-time and night-time settings. In this section, we describe dataset and experimental setup, action recognition accuracy and comparative performance of our work. The details about the performed experiments and used datasets are given below.

4.1 Dataset and Experimental Setup

Night Vision Action Dataset (NV): These videos were recorded using two separate cameras. The IR camera is Raytheon Thermal IR-2000B and the visual camera is Panasonic WV-CP470. Alignment of the thermal and visual videos is done by manually selecting corresponding points in both views and computing a least-squared error fitting homography for each sequence. The infrared video frames are warped to align with the visual pixels. It also includes 20 video sequences from TNO image fusion dataset [23], Eden project dataset [18] and Ohio-state University thermal dataset [4]. We used histogram equalization of individual frames to enhance contrast of low quality videos as pre-processing. Finally Action-02MCF filter is trained for representative actions. This dataset contains video sequences containing eight action categories: walking, wave1, wave2, stand-up, sit-down, clapping, pick-up and running by different actors.

UCF Dataset (UCF): This dataset contain low resolution (160×120, 25fps) video sequences containing six action categories: walking, running, jogging, boxing, clapping and waving. In total, there are 100 video sequences for each action

Fig. 4. Action instance shown in three used datasets, (A) UCF, (B)NV and (C) UAV with red bounding box as the actual ground truth action instance. (Color figure online)

performed by 25 different actors. Every actor performs each action four times in four different backgrounds.

Wide-area UAV Action Dataset (UAV): These video sequences are collected from different sources including Monash UAV research group and UAV research UCB which comprise both low and high altitude UAV. It includes 200 videos captured for the purpose of wide area surveillance and contain limited actions like walking and running. This data set is only used to test localization performance of our approach.

Figure 4 illustrates some action categories from given action datasets.

4.2   Recognition Accuracy

We train Action-02MCF filter for each action category from training videos and correlate the synthesized filter with test data in search of correlation peak. These filters are trained on extracted spatio-temporal features from original video sequences as described above. We use leave one out cross validation. For both UCF and NV dataset, confusion matrices are calculated and shown in Fig. 5. We observed that only diving, golf and pole-vaulting show a low performance because of messy noisy background context while all other action show high recognition performance. Comparison against the existing techniques, Action-MACH [21], Multi-channel-MOSSE [14], Action-DCCF [11] and Color-STIPS-BOF [6] is performed in terms of recognition accuracy. Performance comparison of different approaches is shown in Table 1. For NV dataset, All actions show good recognition except intermix between stand-up and pick-up actions. For this dataset, we achieved 95.77 % accuracy compared to 91.75 % of Action-context [24].

4.3   Action Detection and Localization

To evaluate localization performance, we use probability of detection against false alarms per second (FA/s). We define a performance metric P which is equal to the integration of an ROC curve from 0 to 5 FA/s. An ideal ROC curve corresponds to

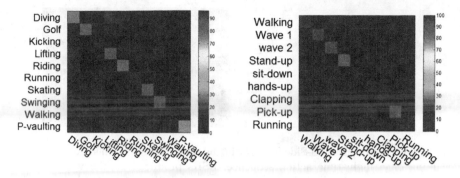

Fig. 5. (Left) Confusion matrix showing action recognition performance against UCF action dataset. Only diving, golf and pole-vaulting show a low performance because of messy noisy background context, (Right) Confusion matrix showing action recognition performance against NV action dataset. All actions show good recognition except intermix between stand-up and pick-up actions.

Table 1. Comparative Analysis in terms of recognition accuracy for UCF sports action dataset. Action-02MCF provides better recognition performance compared to other approaches.

Method	Recognition accuracy
Color-STIPS-BOF	78.6 %
Action-02MCF	85.78 %
Action-MACH	69.2 %
Multi-channel-MOSSE	82.6 %
Action-3DCCF	77.6 %

$P = 5$. We applied the correlation filters to each test video and varied the threshold of detection to generate receiver operating characteristic (ROC) curves. v A detection is labeled a true positive if the center of the bounding box and the ground truth (1) lie within 3 frames of each other and ≤ 9 pixels Euclidean distance in spacial domain to keep greater than 50 % bounding box overlap for every action. We then plot values of P against all actions and compare it with Action-DCCF filter [11]. This filter is chosen for comparison due to availability of code. A comparison graph is shown in Fig. 7 (A). To experiment with generalization of our filter, we use different number of videos for training and calculate the recognition rate. Figure 7 (B) shows our objective function achieves very good performance even if number of training videos is decreased considerably.

For quantitative evaluation, we use Peak-to-Side lobe-Ratio (PSR) described in [16] which calculated the ratio of peak response to the local surrounding response. Figure 6 plots PSRs for walking action present in test video sequence (sample frame displayed) using Action-02MCF for walking action trained on NV dataset.

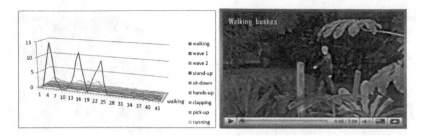

Fig. 6. Plot of PSR (Peak-to-Side lobe-Ratio) by applying the trained Action-02MCF of walking on a night-time action sequence. PSRs produced by the walking action filter are comparatively much higher than the action filters for other actions. One representative frame from respective video sequence is shown below.

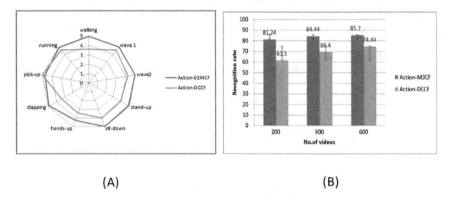

(A)   (B)

Fig. 7. (A) comparative analysis od detection performance of Action-02MCF and Action DCCF filter with plot of P vs Action categories of NV dataset, for every action Action-02MCF performance is near ideal P=5 (B) Recognition rate for UCF dataset vs no. of training videos action-02MCF and Action DCCF filter

5   Conclusion

In this paper, we discuss feature based spatio-temporal correlation filtering for action recognition. This filter combines the maximum margin property of SVMs, localization criteria of correlation filters and sparsity of spatio-temporal features in a combined framework. Furthermore, we introduce maximally stable cuboid detectors as interest points. We evaluate the performance of proposed filter against variety of human action datasets captured in different challenging condition and found that Action-02MCF provides better recognition performance. However, one limitation of our method is its lack of view- invariance. In future, we plan to extend our framework to be view-invariant while experimenting on large datasets.

References

1. Ali, S., Lucey, S.: Are correlation filters useful for human actionrecognition? In: 2010 20th InternationalConference on Pattern Recognition (ICPR), pp. 2608–2611, August 2010
2. Boddeti, V.N., Kanade, T., Kumar, B.: Correlation filters for object alignment. In: 2013 IEEE Conference on Computer Vision and Pattern Recognition, pp. 2291–2298 (2013)
3. Boddeti, V.N., Kumar, B.: Maximum margin vector correlation filter. arXiv preprint (2014). arXiv:1404.6031
4. Davis, J.W., Sharma, V.: Background-subtraction using contour-based fusion of thermal and visible imagery. Comput. Vis. Image Underst. 106(2), 162–182 (2007)
5. Donoser, M., Bischof, H.: 3d segmentation by maximally stable volumes (msvs). In: International Conference on Pattern Recognition, vol. 1, pp. 63–66. IEEE (2006)
6. Everts, I., Gemert, J., Gevers, T.: Evaluation of color stips for human action recognition. In: Proceedings of the IEEE Conference on Computer Vision and Pattern Recognition, pp. 2850–2857 (2013)
7. Fernandez, J.A., Boddeti, V.N., Rodriguez, A., Kumar, B.V.K.V.: Zero-aliasing correlation filters for object recognition. IEEE Trans. Pattern Anal. Mach. Intell. 37(8), 1702–1715 (2015)
8. Fernandez, J.A., Kumar, B.V.: Space-time correlation filters for human action detection. In: SPIE Electronic Imaging, pp. 866304–866304 (2013)
9. Galoogahi, H., Sim, T., Lucey, S.: Multi-channel correlation filters. In: Proceedings of the IEEE International Conference on Computer Vision, pp. 3072–3079 (2013)
10. Gong, S., Xiang, T.: Recognition of group activities using dynamic probabilistic networks. In: IEEE International Conference on Computer Vision, pp. 742–749 (2003)
11. Anwaar, G.I.H., Manzur, M.: Action recognition using spatio-temporal distance classifier correlation filter. In: International Conference on Digital Image Computing Techniques and Applications (DICTA), pp. 474–479 (2011)
12. Hester, C.F., Casasent, D.: Multivariant technique for multiclass pattern recognition. Appl. Optics 19(11), 1758–1761 (1980)
13. Junejo, I.N., Dexter, E., Laptev, I., Perez, P.: View-independent action recognition from temporal self-similarities. IEEE Trans. Pattern Anal. Mach. Intell. 33(1), 172–185 (2011)
14. Kiani, H., Sim, T., Lucey, S.: Multi-channel correlation filters for human action recognition. In: International Conference on Image Processing (ICIP), pp. 1485–1489. IEEE (2014)
15. Klaser, A., Marszałek, M., Schmid, C.: A spatio-temporal descriptor based on 3d-gradients. In: British Machine Vision Conference, pp. 275–281 (2008)
16. Kumar, B.V.K.V., Mahalanobis, A., Juday, R.D.: Correlation Pattern Recognition. Cambridge University Press, New York (2005)
17. Laptev, I., Marszałek, M., Schmid, C., Rozenfeld, B.: Learning realistic human actions from movies. In: IEEE Conference on Computer Vision and Pattern Recognition, pp. 1–8 (2008)
18. Lewis, J., Nikolov, S., Loza, A., Canga, E.F., Cvejic, N., Li, J., Cardinali, A., Canagarajah, C., Bull, D., Riley, T., et al.: The eden project multi-sensor data set. The Online Resource for Research in Image Fusion ImageFusion.org (2006)
19. Liu, J., Luo, J., Shah, M.: Recognizing realistic actions from videos in the wild. In: IEEE Conference on Computer Vision and Pattern Recognition, pp.1996–2003 (2009)

20. Rodriguez, A., Boddeti, V.N., Kumar, B., Mahalanobis, A.: Maximum margin correlation filter: a new approach for localization and classification. IEEE Trans. Image Process. **22**(2), 631–643 (2013)
21. Rodriguez, M.D., Ahmed, J., Shah, M.: Action mach a spatio-temporal maximum average correlation height filter for action recognition. In: IEEE Conference on Computer Vision and Pattern Recognition, CVPR 2008, pp. 1–8, June 2008
22. Siva, P., Xiang, T.: Action detection in crowd. In: British Machine Vision Conference, pp. 1–11 (2010)
23. Toet, A., de Jong, M.J., Hogervorst, M.A., Hooge, I.T.: Perceptual evaluation of colorized nighttime imagery. In: IS&T/SPIE Electronic Imaging, pp. 901412–901412 (2014)
24. Ulhaq, A., Iqbal, G., Murshed, M.: Contextual action recognition in multi-sensor nighttime video sequences. In: Digital Image Computing Techniques and Applications (DICTA), pp. 256–261 (2011)
25. Weinland, D., Özuysal, M., Fua, P.: Making action recognition robust to occlusions and viewpoint changes. In: Daniilidis, K., Maragos, P., Paragios, N. (eds.) ECCV 2010. LNCS, vol. 6313, pp. 635–648. Springer, Heidelberg (2010). doi:10.1007/978-3-642-15558-1_46

An Image Quality Metric with Reference for Multiply Distorted Image

Aladine Chetouani[(✉)]

University of Orleans, 12 rue de Blois, 45067 Orléans, France
aladine.chetouani@univ-orleans.fr

Abstract. In this paper, we propose a global framework to estimate the quality of multiply degraded images with reference (Full Reference approach). Our method is based on features fusion using a Support Vector Regression (SVR) model. The selected features are here some quality indexes obtained by comparing the reference image and its degraded version. Some of these features are based on Human Visual System (HVS), while some others are based on structural information or mutual information. The proposed method has been evaluated through the LIVE Multiply Distorted Image Quality Database, composed of 450 degraded images. The obtained results are compared to 12 recent image quality metrics.

Keywords: Image quality · Features fusion · Subjective judgments

1 Introduction

A lot of image quality metrics (more than 100) has been proposed in the literature [1]. Some of them require the reference image (Full-Reference approach) [16], while some others need only some characteristics of the reference image (Reduced-Reference approach) [9] or estimate the quality using just the degraded image (Blind or No-Reference approach) [8]. All these measures are often used to estimate the quality of an image distorted by one degradation type (JPEG, JPEG2000, Noise, Blur, Fast Fading, etc.). The obtained objective scores are then often compared to the subjective scores (MOS: Mean Opinion Score), which are achieved through some psycho-visual tests. Hence, the efficiency of most of the existing metrics is evaluated for a given degradation type.

Moreover, most of the proposed subjective image datasets are composed of degraded images with one type of degradation per image [2–4]. The LIVE database [2] is composed of 5 different degradation types (NOISE, JPEG and JPEG2000 compression, Gaussian Blur, Fast Fading) with one degradation per image. The TID 2013 database [3] proposes a large variety of distortions (24 degradation types) with one degradation type per image. A total of 3000 degraded images are available. The subjective tests have been here done in five countries (Finland, France, Italy, Ukraine and USA). The IVC database [4] contains 4 degradation types (JPEG, JPEG2000, LAR [Locally Adaptive Resolution] compression and Blur). Some others interesting datasets are also accessible CSIQ (Categorical Subjective Image Quality) [5], MICT [6], A57 [7].

© Springer International Publishing AG 2016
J. Blanc-Talon et al. (Eds.): ACIVS 2016, LNCS 10016, pp. 477–485, 2016.
DOI: 10.1007/978-3-319-48680-2_42

However, in some real cases, the perceptual quality of the image is impacted by several degradations at the same time (blur and noise during the capture step, blocking during the compression step and so on). To estimate the quality of multiply degraded images, the existing metrics can be used. However, the obtained results are not well correlated with the subjective judgments. In order to address this issue, the LIVE Multiply Distorted Image Quality Database has been proposed [8] where each image is distorted by two different degradation types (described is Sect. 4).

Some studies integrate this notion in the image quality estimation process. In [9], the authors propose a Reduced Reference Image Quality Measure based on a learning step using a Boltzmann machine. In [10], the author proposes to combine different metrics by associating a weight to each of them. Different combinations have been tested through 17 metrics with reference.

In this paper, we focus on multiply degraded images and we propose a full reference image quality measure based on a fusion step. Some selected features are first extracted from the original image and its degraded version. These features are then combined using a Support Vector Regression (SVR) model. The obtained performances have been compared in terms of correlation with the subjective judgments using the LIVE Multiply Distorted Image Quality Database [8].

This paper is organized as follows: Sect. 2 presents some common Full Reference measures. Our method is then described in Sect. 3. The evaluation and comparison parts are shown in Sect. 4. The conclusion is in Sect. 5.

2   Full Reference Image Quality Metrics: A Brief Review

This last decade, a lot of Full-Reference Image Quality Metrics have been proposed in the literature. In [1], more than 100 metrics have been listed and classified. Some of them are pixel-based such as the PSNR (Peak Signal to Noise Ratio) measure. However, this metric is not well correlated with the subjective judgments for most of the distortion types [11]. In order to improve its performance, several authors have proposed to integrate some Human Visual System (HVS) characteristics such as the WSNR (Weighted SNR) [12] measure where the Contrast Sensitivity Function (CSF), which models the sensitivity of our HVS to discern the contrast for different spatial-frequencies, has been added and used as a weight. The quality index is then obtained by the ratio of the CSF-weighted Fourier spectrum of the reference image over that of its degraded version. In [13], a perceptual version of the PSNR, called PSNR-HVS, has been proposed. The authors incorporated a CSF model in the DCT domain. An extended version where a masking model was considered has also been proposed in [14]. Other interesting metrics are also based on the SNR with some modifications [15].

Some other metrics are structural-based such as SSIM [16] (Structural SIMilarity image quality index), which is among the most used, have been proposed. Due to its simplicity and its relative performance (compared to the PSNR), this metric has a certain success. It has been taken up by several authors (a multi-scale version [17], an edge-based version [18], a gradient-based version [19] and a wavelet-based version [20]).

Some other studies are more interested by the perceptual aspects. In [21], the Visible Differences Predictor (VDP) has been proposed. The author focuses on the estimation of the perceptual differences between two images (reference images and its degraded version). The luminance adaptation, the CSF, the multichannel decomposition (Cortex transform [22]) and the masking effect have been considered in this method. An extended version for High Dynamic Range (HDR) Images has been also developed [23]. The C4 metric considers also all these characteristics, however the quality index is computed in a perceptual color space [24]. Hence, a lot of metrics with different approaches have been now available.

Some authors propose to optimize the utilization of this kind of metrics by integrating the degradation type in the quality estimation process [25]. Before computing the quality, the degradation type is first detected and the more adapted metric is then selected to estimate. In other words, the best metric for the detecting degradation type is thus used. Here, we propose also to optimize its utilization for multiply degraded images by combining some of them.

3   Proposed Method

Our method is described by the following flowchart (Fig. 1). The reference image and its degraded version have been first compared through different metrics. The computed indexes have been then combined using a SVR model in order to fit the computed indexes to the subjective scores.

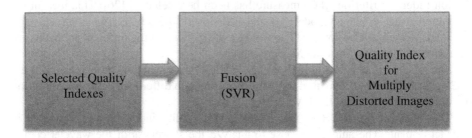

Fig. 1. Flowchart of the proposed method.

In this study, four features have been selected (see Table 1). Each of them is briefly described in this section. Note that these metrics have been selected experimentally by comparing different combinations ().

Table 1. Selected full reference image quality metrics.

FR-IQM	Based on
SSIM [16] *Structural SIMilarity image quality index*	Structural + Spatial
IFC [26] *Information Fidelity Criterion*	Entropy + Wavelet
VIF [27] *Visual Information Fidelity*	Entropy + HVS
WASH [28] *WAvelet based SHarp features*	Sharpness + Wavelet

The Structural SIMilarity image quality index (SSIM) [16] is an improved version of the Universal image Quality Index (UQI) [29] where the structural information are obtained by extracting some local statistical parameters from non-overlapping blocks. The quality index is given by three factors: luminance (l), contrast (c) and structure (s). The quality index between a given block of the reference image (x) and its corresponding block in the degraded version (y) is achieved by the following equation:

$$SSIM(x,y) = l(x,y).c(x,y).s(x,y)$$
$$= \frac{(2\mu_x\mu_y + C1)}{(\mu_x^2 + \mu_y^2 + C1)} \cdot \frac{2\sigma_x\sigma_y + C2}{(\sigma_x^2 + \sigma_y^2 + C2)} \cdot \frac{(2cov_{xy} + C3)}{(\sigma_x\sigma_y + C3)}$$

The final quality index is obtained by computing the mean of the SSIM values. C1, C2, C3 and C4 are small constants.

Based on some concepts from information theory (mutual information), the Information Fidelity Criterion (IFC) measure has been here selected [26]. This measure is computed using a source model (C) and a distortion model (D) for some selected subbands in the wavelet domain. The wavelet coefficients of the different subbands are here modeled using a Gaussian Mixture model.

The Visual Information Fidelity (VIF) [27] measure, which is an extension of the IFC measure, has been also used in this work. The main difference is the incorporation of some characteristics of the HVS.

The WAvelet based SHarp features (WASH) quality index [28] is computed in wavelet domain. The authors propose to analyze the sharpness of the wavelet coefficients of the image in order to derive a quality index that is correlated with subjective judgments.

Once these features are computed from the original image and its degraded version, a Support Vector Regression (SVR) model [30] is used to combine it. A Gaussian function has been here used as the kernel function. Note that some other regression methods based on neural approach (classical Multi Layer Perceptron) have been also explored. The best results have been obtained by the SVR.

A 5 fold cross-validation method has been applied to evaluate our method (80 % and 20 % for the learning and the testing steps, respectively). The parameters of our SVR model have been fixed experimentally. The final metric (after combination) is thus based on structural information, entropy, sharpness and HVS. So, the inputs of the final SVR model are the selected indexes, while its output corresponds to the predicted subjective score.

4 Evaluation and Performance

In order to evaluate our method, the LIVE Multiply Distorted Image Quality Database [8] has been used. This dataset is composed of 2 parts with 225 degraded images for each of them, obtained from 15 reference images. The Part 1 is composed of images that are blurred and then compressed using a JPEG encoder, while the Part 2 contains images that are also firstly blurred and then noise has been added. In our knowledge, there is not other database that includes several degradation types for each image.

Table 2. List of the compared measures.

Metric	Based on	Domain
PSNR *Peak Signal to Noise Rate*	Pixel to pixel difference	Spatial
MS-SSIM [17] *Multi Scale Structural SIMilarity*	Structural	Spatial
VIF [27] *Visual Information Fidelity*	Mutual information	Spatial
IFC [26] *Information Fidelity Criterion*	Mutual information	Spatial
NQM [31] *Noise Quality Measure*	Subjective model	Frequency
VSNR [15] *Visual Signal-to-Noise Ratio*	Perceptual	Wavelet
WSNR [12] *Weighted Signal to Noise Ratio*	Perceptual	Frequency
WASH [28] *WAvelet based SHarp features*	Sharpness	Wavelet
BRISQUE-2 [8] *Blind/Referenceless Image Spatial QUality Evaluator*	Natural scene statistic	Spatial
RBMSim [9] *Restricted Boltzmann Machine Similarity Measure*	Learning	Spatial
RR-IQM [32] *Reduced Reference Image Quality Metric*	Learning	Features extraction

Our method has been compared to the state-of-the-art (see Table 2). Some of them are based on structural information [17], while some others are based on mutual information [27] or based on Natural Scene Statistics (NSS) [32], performed in the spatial or in the frequency domains. We have also compared our method to some Learning-based methods [9, 32]. Note that metrics of the three existing approaches (with reference, without reference and reduced reference) have been selected. The Full-Reference metrics are represented in Tables 3 and 4 by a blue background, while the No-Reference and the Reduced-Reference measures are, respectively, represented by a green and white backgrounds. The obtained performances are likewise compared to the performance of each selected metric (without combination).

Table 3. Obtained Pearson correlation coefficients for each part.

Metric	Pearson Correlation Coefficient (PCC)	
	Part 1	Part 2
PSNR	0.8202	0.8031
SSIM	0.8231	0.7712
MS-SSIM	0.8395	0.8864
VIF	0.9499	0.8989
IFC	0.9349	0.9251
NQM	0.9035	0.8931
VSNR	0.8796	0.8391
WSNR	0.8707	0.8331
WASH	0.8563	0.6634
BRISQUE-2	0.9462	0.9262
RBMSim	**0.97**	0.91
RR-IQM	0.9479	0.9421
Our method	0.9476	**0.9493**

Table 4. Global performance in terms of Pearson correlation coefficients.

Metric	Pearson Correlation Coefficient (PCC)
PSNR	0.7985
SSIM	0.6680
MS-SSIM	0.8389
VIF	0.9221
IFC	0.9219
NQM	0.8991
VSNR	0.8598
WSNR	0.8534
WASH	0.7562
BRISQUE-2	0.9349
RBMSim	0.9300
RR-IQM	0.9420
Our metric	**0.9482**

The evaluation criterion used here is the Pearson Correlation Coefficient (PCC) which is computed between the subjective judgments (MOS: Mean Opinion Score) providing from the subjective database and the objective scores obtained by our method.

Table 3 presents the obtained correlation coefficients of different metrics for each part of the dataset. The best value is here represented in bold. The best performance for the Full-Reference approach for the part 1 and part 2 have been obtained, respectively, by the VIF and IFC metrics. The best performance whatever the approach has been obtained by the RBMSim metric for the part 1 (0.97), while our metric has obtained 0.9476. The best performance for the part 2 has been obtained by our metric (0.9493). About the selected metrics (SSIM, IFC, VIF and WASH), their performances are not higher than our method (except for the VIF metric for the part 1). The PCC values of SSIM, IFC, VIF and WASH metrics for the part 1 are, respectively, equal to 0.8231, 0.9349, 0.9499 and 0.8563, while for the part 2 their PCC values are, respectively, equal to 0.7712, 0.9251, 0.8989 and 0.6634.

Concerning the global evaluation of these metrics (whatever the part of the database), the best performance has been obtained by our metric with a PCC value equal to 0.9482, while the second and the third best metrics are equal, respectively, to 0.9420 and 0.9349 as PCC values. Note also that the global performance after the fusion step is better than the performance of each selected metrics (SSIM = 0.6680, IFC = 0.9219, VIF = 0.9221 and WASH = 0.7562). So, the combination step permits to improve the performance from 0.9221 to 0.9482.

In the Fig. 2, we show the scaled-MOS vs the objective scores (the data has been normalized between $[-1,1]$). The scatter of the data represents, visually, the correlation between the subjective scores and its predicted version (objective scores). Note that the red curve correspond to the logistic function obtained by interpolating the predicted MOS to the scaled MOS.

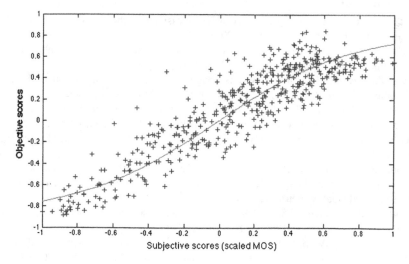

Fig. 2. Scaled-MOS vs Objective scores.

5 Conclusion

In this paper, we have proposed a quality measure with reference for multiply degraded images. The proposed fusion-based measure consists to first compute some quality indexes by comparing the reference image and its degraded version. The obtained values are then combined through a SVR model. Our metric has been also compared to the state-of-the-art and the obtained results show that our method is competitive.

References

1. Pedersen, M., Hardeberg, J.Y.: Survey of full-reference image quality metrics. Høgskolen i Gjøviks rapportserie, Gjøvik, Norway, Number 5 (2009). ISSN: 1890-520X
2. Sheikh, H.R., Wang, Z., Cormack, Z., Bovik, A.C.: Live image quality assessment database (2006). http://live.ece.utexas.eduesearch/quality
3. Ponomarenko, N., Jin, L., Ieremeiev, O., Lukin, V., Egiazarian, K., Astola, J., Vozel, B., Chehdi, K., Carli, M., Battisti, F., Jay Kuo, C.-C.: Image database TID2013: peculiarities, results and perspectives. Signal Process. Image Commun. **30**, 57–77 (2015)
4. Le Callet, P., Autrusseau, F.: Subjective quality assessment IRCCyN/IVC database (2005), http://www.irccyn.ec-nantes.fr/ivcdb/
5. Larson, E.C., Chandler, D.M.: Most apparent distortion: full-reference image quality assessment and the role of strategy. J. Electron. Imaging **19**, 1–21 (2010)
6. Tourancheau, S., Autrusseau, F., Sazzad, P., Horita,Y.: Impact of the subjective dataset on the performance of image quality metrics. In: IEEE International Conference on Image Processing (2008)
7. http://foulard.ece.cornell.edu/dmc27/vsnr/vsnr.html
8. Jayaraman, D., Mittal, A., Moorthy, A.K., Bovik, A.C.: Objective quality assessment of multiply distorted images. In: Asilomar Conference on Signals, Systems and Computers, pp. 1693–1697 (2012)
9. Dosselman, R., Yang, X.D.: A comprehensive assessment of the structural similarity index. Signal Image Video Process. **5**, 81–91 (2011)
10. Okarna, K.: Quality assessment of images with multiple distortions using combined metrics. Elektronika Ir Elektrotechnika **20**, 128–131 (2014)
11. Wang, Z., Bovik, A.C., Lu, L.: Why is image quality assessment so difficult? In: IEEE International Conference on Acoustics, Speech & Signal Processing (2002)
12. Cornsweet, T.N.: Visual Perception. Academic Press, New York (1970)
13. Egiazarian, K., Astola, J. Ponomarenko, N., Lukin, V., Battisti, F., Carli, M.: New full-reference quality metrics based on HVS. In: International Workshop on Video Processing and Quality Metrics (2006)
14. Ponomarenko, N., Silvestri, F., Egiazarian, K., Carli, M., Astola, J., Lukin, V.: On between-coefficient contrast masking of DCT basis functions. In: International Workshop on Video Processing and Quality Metrics (2007)
15. Chandler, D.M., Hemami, S.S.: VSNR: a wavelet-based visual signal-to-noise ratio for natural images. IEEE Trans. Image Process. **16**, 2284–2298 (2007)
16. Wang, Z., Bovik, A., Sheikh, H., Simoncelli, E.: Image quality assessment: from error visibility to structural similarity. IEEE Trans. Image Process. **13**(4), 600–612 (2004)
17. Wang, Z., Simoncelli, E.P., Bovik, A.C.: Multi-scale structural similarity for image quality assessment. In: Asilomar Conference on Signals, Systems and Computers, vol. 2, pp. 1398–1402 (2003)

18. Chen, G.H., Yang, C.L., Po, L.M., Xie, S.L.: Edge-based structural similarity for image quality assessment. In: IEEE International Conference in Acoustics, Speech and Signal Processing, vol. 2, pp. 933–936 (2006)
19. Chen, G., Yang, C., Xie, S.: Gradient-based structural similarity for image quality assessment. In: IEEE International Conference on Image Processing, pp. 2929–2932 (2006)
20. Wang, Z., Simoncelli, E.: Translation insensitive image similarity in complex wavelet domain. In: IEEE International Conference on Acoustics, Speech and Signal Processing, vol. 2, pp. 573–576 (2005)
21. Daly, S.: The visible differences predictor: an algorithm for the assessment of image fidelity. In: Digital Images and Human Vision, chap. 14, pp. 179–206. MIT Press (1993)
22. Watson, A.: The cortex transform: rapid computation of simulated neural images. Comput. Vis. Graph. Image Process. **39**, 311–327 (1987)
23. Mantiuk, R., Daly, S., Myszkowski, K., Seidel, H.P.: Predicting visible differences in high dynamic range images - model and its calibration. In: Human Vision and Electronic Imaging X, IS&T/SPIE's, pp. 204–214 (2005)
24. Carnec, M., Le Callet, P., Barba, D.: Objective quality assessment of color images based on a generic perceptual reduced reference. Signal Process. Image Commun. **23**(4), 239–256 (2008)
25. Chetouani, A., Beghdadi, A., Deriche, M.: A hybrid system for distortion classification and image quality evaluation. J. Signal Process. Image Commun. **9**, 948–960 (2012)
26. Shcikh, H.R., Bovik, A.C., de Veciana, G.: An information fidelity criterion for image quality assessment using natural scene statistics. IEEE Trans. Image Process. **14**, 2117–2128 (2005)
27. Sheikh, H.R., Bovik, A.C.: Image information and visual quality. IEEE Trans. Image Process. **15**, 430–444 (2006)
28. Reenu, M., David, D., Raj, S.S.A., Nair, M.S.: Wavelet based sharp features (WASH): an image quality assessment metric based on HVS. In: International Conference on Advanced Computing, Networking and Security, pp. 79–83 (2013)
29. Wang, Z., Bovik, A.C.: A universal image quality index. IEEE Signal Process. Lett. **9**, 81–84 (2002)
30. http://asi.insa-rouen.fr/enseignants/~arakoto/toolbox/
31. Damera-Venkata, N., Kite, T., Geisler, W., Evans, B., Bovik, A.C.: Image quality assessment based on a degradation model. IEEE Trans. Image Process. **9**, 636–650 (2000)
32. Chetouani, A.: A reduced reference image quality assessment for multiply distorted images. In: International Conference on Computer Systems and Applications (2015)

3D Planar RGB-D SLAM System

Hakim ElChaoui ElGhor[1,2]([✉]), David Roussel[1], Fakhreddine Ababsa[1], and El-Houssine Bouyakhf[2]

[1] IBISC Lab, Evry Val d'Essonne University, Évry, France
Hakim.ElChaoui@ibisc.univ-evry.fr
[2] LIMIARF Lab, Mohammed V University, Rabat, Morocco

Abstract. Applications such as Simultaneous Localization and Mapping (SLAM) can greatly benefit from RGB-D sensor data to produce 3D maps of the environment as well as sensor's trajectory estimation. However, the resulting 3D points map can be cumbersome, and since indoor environments are mainly composed of planar surfaces, the idea is to use planes as building blocks for a SLAM process. This paper describes an RGB-D SLAM system benefiting from planes segmentation to generate lightweight 3D plane-based maps. Our goal is to produce reduced 3D maps composed solely of planes sections that can be used on platforms with limited memory and computation resources. We present the introduction of planar regions in a regular RGB-D SLAM system and evaluate the benefits regarding both resulting map and estimated camera trajectory.

Keywords: RGB-D SLAM · Planar features · 3D Plane-based maps

1 Introduction

In recent years, mobile robots have received an increasing interest especially for indoor environment applications. In these environments RGB-D sensors offer an opportunity to significantly develop robotic navigation and interaction capabilities. Since they combine the advantages of RGB cameras with the ability to obtain geometric information, many works tend to exploit the potential of these novel sensors. For applications such as Simultaneous Localization and Mapping (SLAM), introducing RGB-D cameras allows to create three-dimensional maps in real time. Several RGB-D SLAM systems have been proposed. They can be placed in two large family: Sparse and Dense SLAM systems. Although the purpose is the same, the two approaches diverge in the modeling and processing. Sparse SLAM approaches are based on visual odometry. They use visual features correspondences with registration algorithms, as RANSAC [5] or ICP [16], to estimate and refine transformations between poses. The algorithm developed by Henry *et al.* [8] was one of the first RGB-D systems using features points to estimate camera poses and represent the environment by surfels [15]. It creates and optimizes a Graph-Based SLAM. This modeling [7] consists in constructing

© Springer International Publishing AG 2016
J. Blanc-Talon et al. (Eds.): ACIVS 2016, LNCS 10016, pp. 486–497, 2016.
DOI: 10.1007/978-3-319-48680-2_43

a graph which nodes are sensor poses and where an edge between two nodes represents the transformation (egomotion) between these poses. Such formulation enables the graph optimization step which aims to find the best nodes configuration that produces a correct topological trajectory and easier loop-closures detection when revisiting the same areas. Endres *et al.* [4] followed the same path and proposed a graph-based RGB-D SLAM which became very popular among Robotic Operating System (ROS) users due to its availability. The implementation and optimization of the pose-graph is performed by the G^2o framework [13]. To represent the environment, they used 3D occupancy grid maps generated by the OctoMapping approach [9]. This RGB-D SLAM system offers a good trade-off between the quality of pose estimation and computational cost. Indeed, sparse SLAM approaches are typically fast due to the sensor's egomotion estimation based on sparse points. In addition, such a lightweight implementation can be embedded easily on mobile robots and small devices. However, the reconstruction quality is limited to a sparse set of 3D points which leads to many redundant and repeated points in the map and lack of semantic description of the environment.

Instead, dense SLAM methods enable good pose estimation and high quality scene representation. However, they tend to drift over time and fail against scenes with poor geometric structure. To overcome high computational costs, these approaches use sophisticated equipments such as high performance graphics hardware GPU which may constrain the used platform. Dense RGB-D SLAM systems were introduced by Newcombe *et al.* in the well known Kinect Fusion [10,14]. It is a dense system integrating real-time depth measurements into a volumetric data structure to create highly detailed voxel-based maps. Camera poses are estimated by tracking only live depth data with a dense iterative closest point (ICP) algorithm. Despite the high quality maps, the algorithm fails in environments with poor structure and is restricted to small workspaces due to high memory consumption. Whelan *et al.* proposed a moving volume method [23] to overcome the restricted area problem. By moving the voxel grid with each current camera pose, real-time detailed mapping of unbounded areas became possible. Unlike voxel-based reconstruction, Keller *et al.* [12] proposed a more efficient solution. They proposed a point-based fusion representation supporting spatially extended reconstructions with a fused surfel-based model of the environment.

Recently, perceiving the geometry surrounding robots has become a research field of great interest in computer vision. For both robot planing and augmented reality applications as [1], using some geometric assumptions is a crucial prerequisite. Likewise, in current RGB-D SLAM systems researchers begin to pay a significant interest to geometric primitives in order to build three-dimensional (3D) structures. The observed geometry can be a good solution to better constrain the problem and help improve 3D reconstructions. For indoor environments, 3D planes can be relevant as they are extremely common and easily deduced from point clouds. Thus, they were introduced in several recent works. One of the earliest RGB-D SLAM approaches incorporating planes has been developed by

Trevor *et al.* [21]. They combined a Kinect sensor with a large 2D planar laser scanner to generate both lines and planes as features in a graph based representation. Data association is performed by evaluating the joint probability over a set of interpretation trees of the measurements seen by the robot at one pose. Taguchi *et al.* [20] presented a bundle adjustment system combining both 3D point-to-point and 3D plane-to-plane correspondences. Their system shows a compact representation but a slow camera tracking. This work was extended by Ataer-Cansizoglu *et al.* [2] to find point and plane correspondences using camera motion prediction. However, the constant velocity assumption used to predict the pose seems to be difficult to satisfy when using handheld camera. The RGB-D SLAM system [12] was extended by Salas-Moreno *et al.* [18] to enforce planarity on the dense reconstruction with application to augmented reality. In a recent work, Xiang and Zhang [6] proposed an RGB-D SLAM system based on planar features. From each detected 3D plane they generate a 2D image and try to extract its 2D visual features. These extracted features are back-projected on the depth image to generate 3D feature points used to estimate the egomotion with ICP. More recently, Whelan *et al.* [22] performed incremental planar segmentations on point clouds to generate a global mesh model consisting of planar and non-planar triangulated surfaces. In [11], the full representation of infinite planes is reduced to a point representation in the unit sphere $\mathbb{S}3$. This allowed to parameterize the plane as a unit quaternion and formulate the problem as a least-squares optimization of a graph of infinite planes.

In our works, we are also focused on searching alternative 3D primitives in structured indoor scenes. Especially, we use 3D planar regions to generate a reduced significant representation of the environment in sparse RGB-D SLAM systems. Indeed, an RGB-D point cloud contains 307200 points and requires 3.4 Megabytes in memory. Together with the sensor's characteristic noise, the large number of points lead to significantly redundant 3D maps when assembling several point clouds. Thus, using planar assumptions on the observed geometry can deal with sensor noise and redundant representation of the environment. This paper, based on our previous work [3], describes an RGB-D SLAM system benefiting from planes segmentation to generate lightweight 3D plane-based maps. Unlike previous work, we propose a new method for building low-cost 3D maps based on reliable estimations. As human living environments are mostly composed of planar features, such technique is suitable to overcome the sensor's weakness without using a dense approach.

Our contributions in this paper are three-fold: i. We detail our 3D plane-based SLAM system implementation. ii. We propose a 3D compact planar modeling for indoor environment representations. iii. We introduce a new protocol to evaluate the system performance over real world scenes.

In the reminder of this paper we give an overview of our system in the following section. In Sect. 3 we provide an evaluation of the qualitative and quantitative performance of our system using a handheld RGB-D sensor. Finally, we summarize and report future works in Sect. 4.

2   System Description

The schematic representation of our system is shown in Fig. 1. Our starting point was inspired by the RGB-D SLAM system introduced by Endres *et al.* [4]. Inputs are color images and depth maps (RGB-D data) provided by the Kinect sensor. Our system introduces 3D planes to estimate camera's transformations and generate a planar reconstruction of the environment by merging planes into a global map. We begin by extracting local 3D planar regions (planes models with their bounding boxes) π_l from Depth maps (See next subsection) and 2D feature points from RGB data concurrently. 2D features points belonging to detected planar regions are projected onto these planes as 3D planar feature points. These planar feature points are used to estimate the local transformation T_l between two camera poses and refine it with an iterative RANSAC. Let the global coordinates system be the first registered camera pose. In each pose addition we store the global transformation T_w leading to this coordinates system using current and previous local transformations. Then, global detected planar regions π_w can be obtained. The 3D planar map is updated either by merging detected planar regions to the existing ones (Planes set π), or by adding new planes.

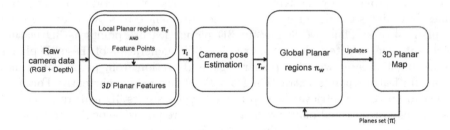

Fig. 1. Main system pipeline.

2.1   Planar Regions Detection and Representation

Planar regions detection is performed using the Point Cloud Library (PCL) [17]. We extract co-planar points sets into the full point cloud. To find the k most prominent planar regions, which contains the maximum number of 3D points (inlier points), we proceed to a multi-plane segmentation with an iterative RANSAC. At each stage, we detect the main planar region and remove its inliers from the point cloud. Then, we extract the next main planar region while the number N of its inliers is still significant (at least 700 points).

A detected planar region π is parameterized by its plane model $(n_x, n_y, n_z, d)^\top$ where $n^\top(n_x, n_y, n_z)$ is the normal vector and d the distance from the origin. A 3D point $\boldsymbol{p}(x, y, z)$ lying on this plane model satisfies the familiar equation $n_x x + n_y y + n_z z = -d$, otherwise written $n^\top \boldsymbol{p} = -d$.

This equation will be used to generate our 3D planar feature points detailed in the next subsection.

To represent a plane in the map, we also need its bounding box $\mathcal{B}$. When a planar region is detected in the local frame, the point cloud of its inlier points is stored and then projected into the world coordinates after the egomotion estimation. Then, we generate the matrix of the second central moments of this point cloud. Afterwards, we proceed to a Singular Value Decomposition (SVD) of this matrix in order to find the main axis vectors of the point cloud and therefore the bounding box according to these vectors.

In the sequel, each detected planar region will be formerly defined by $\pi[n, d, N, \mathcal{B}]$ encompassing the plane model (n, d), its inliers population N, and its bounding box $\mathcal{B}$. These parameters will be useful during the global planar map construction (Sect. 2.3).

2.2   3D Planar Feature Points

Studies conducted in [6,20] showed that planar primitives are safer and robust to noise which leads to more accurate pose estimation while making processing faster. Then, it is relevant to introduce planar feature points in our system since depth maps provided by the Kinect sensor are noisy and contain missing depth values. The aim is to minimize 3D points measurement errors by benefiting from 3D plane fitting. Thus, we define our 3D planar feature points as 3D feature points satisfying a detected 3D planar model. The generation of these 3D planar feature points begins with 3D planar regions detection from point clouds and visual 2D feature points extraction from RGB images concurrently. For each 2D feature point we retrieve the depth value, generate its 3D feature point and check it against detected planar regions. 3D feature points belonging to a planar region are kept and others are rejected. In addition, we perform a regularization step by projecting all remaining 3D planar feature points into their respective planar regions.

2.3   Planar-Maps Building

As mentioned before, our goal is to produce lightweight 3D planar maps which can be useful for indoor robot navigation and augmented reality applications. For low-cost applications such as small robots, this choice can be very efficient to avoid 3D point clouds representations which are highly redundant and require memory resources. Based on the detected planar regions and the estimated transformation in each added pose, our system adds and grows planar structures in the map over time. To construct the global map, planes must be represented in the same 3D coordinates system. As the planes detection is performed in local frames, registered planar regions can be transformed from the camera to world coordinates systems using the global egomotion estimation T_w. If the matrix M (Rotation R and Translation t) represents this global transformation, a 3D point $\boldsymbol{p}_w$ into the world coordinates can be found easily using its correspondent point in the camera $\boldsymbol{p}_c$ by the well known equation: $\boldsymbol{p}_w = R\boldsymbol{p}_c + t$ and conversely

$\boldsymbol{p}_c = R^\top \boldsymbol{p}_w - R^\top t$. Then, a plane in the world coordinates system is defined by its normal vector and distance $\pi_w(n_w, d_w)$ with $n_w = Rn_c$ and $d_w = d_c - n_c^\top R^\top t$. Once these parameters are defined, we proceed to a plane-to-plane comparison in order to update the global map. Whenever a new planar region matches to a registered one, we update the plane by merging their plane models. Correspondence between planar regions is examined in two stages (Fig. 2). Firstly, angle between two compared plane models must not exceed a threshold set to $10°$ and the distance limit between them is set to $5\,cm$. When this is satisfied, we check that the two planar regions overlap or are spatially close at least. This condition is added to avoid merging planes which have the same model but don't represent a continuous plane in the real world. An example of such situation can be a wall with an open door in the middle: the two parts of the wall have the same equation. Thus, using the bounding boxes of concerned planar regions we obtain the overlap between them if it exists. In case there is no overlap, we compare the minimum distance between the two bounding boxes to a distance threshold of $50\,cm$. When two planar regions match, they are merged together in a new resulting plane according to their inlier points populations. Their bounding boxes are compared and extrema are assigned to the merged planar region. If no correspondence can be found, the detected region is added to the map as a new plane. Even more than planes themselves, our map contains theoretical intersections between these planes. Planes intersections are generated using an adjacency criterion. We represent this intersection by lines and points when two or three planes intersect. This makes our map more significant and workable for other applications, and represents a first step towards a more semantic map.

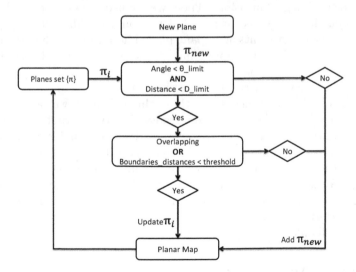

Fig. 2. Planar map building.

3   Evaluation and Results

In this section we evaluate our work with a series of experiments using RGB-D data acquired with a Kinect. We present real-time results obtained on a PC with an Intel Core i5-2400 CPU at 3.10 GHz × 4. Planes detection was performed within depth images with a plane thickness threshold set to 1.5 cm. We rejected all points exceeding this threshold. Also, only the first three main planes were considered during planar regions detection. Since planes detection produces larger planes first (in terms of population), adding further planes may introduce a lot of irrelevant small planar patches. These thresholds were chosen with preliminary experiments to provide accurate results. Experimental protocol and results concerning planes quality, map building and poses trajectory are shown in the following subsections. Unfortunately similar systems do not offer public softwares which makes comparisons impossible as we propose novel evaluations.

3.1   Planes Detection Process

In order to determine the overall performance of our system, we evaluated the influence of 3D data size on the detected planes quality. By default the Kinect images resolution is 640 × 480. Hence, a subsampling step seems essential to limit the plane detection process time. Also, this allows online data acquisition and processing with the Kinect 30 Hz update rate. Otherwise, the point cloud will contain 307200 points, which requires several seconds for planes detection. This is often used by sparse systems to overcome computational time. So we used a subsampling factor when creating a point cloud. This subsampling factor reduces the depth image dimensions. Then, we studied the impact of subsampled data on the quality and speed of planes detection over different distances. We performed specific experiments on a plane placed in front of the Kinect. For each distance we changed the subsampling factor and observed the detected planes. Table 1 (page 8) details results of these experiments. For each experiment, we considered planes detection runtimes, estimated distances and the number of erroneous detected extra planes. From these three columns we can deduce that the subsampling factor 4 gives a good trade-off between runtime and planes estimation quality. We can notice that planes detection quality decreases with the distance as the depth noise becomes greater than the planar region thickness threshold. As the depth noise increases with distance, planes detection over 3.5 m cannot be performed. Analysis of these results allowed us to choose subsampling data with factor 4 as it doesn't degrade the detected planes quality and enables real time processing. We also noticed that angle errors between detected planes from the same distance does not exceed 6 ° in any case.

3.2   3D Planar Maps

Here we show results of our planar SLAM system for a real time captured office scene. The Kinect was mounted on a movable support that enables it to be placed everywhere within the scene. The office scene contains several planes

Table 1. Impact of subsampled data on planes detection.

Real distance (m)	Subsampling factor	Estimation runtime (s)	Inliers points	Estimated distance (m)	Number of erroneous detected planes
1.5	1	2.37	234813	1.49	0
	2	0.23	58797	1.48	0
	4	**0.07**	14545	**1.49**	0
2.5	1	7.26	125107	2.44	1
	2	1.78	32320	2.41	2
	4	**0.4**	8619	2.41	0
3.5	1	7.57	62200	3.32	2
	2	1.72	14637	3.37	1
	4	**0.4**	1904	3.36	0

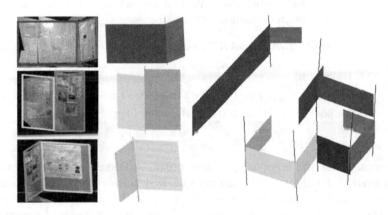

Fig. 3. Example of a 3D planar map resulting from our system. (**left**) Generated planes and their corresponding point cloud. (**right**) Our planar map with planes intersections.

with various sizes set in different locations and features several parallel and intersecting planes.

Figure 3 shows an example of our 3D plane-based map with computed intersections. Each plane in the map was generated progressively by the merging process described above. Theoretical intersections between adjacent planes was also updated whenever a plane model changed. Benefiting from this minimal representation, we generated a lightweight 3D global plane-based map unlike the usual heavyweight point-based maps.

Poses Estimation Error. In our previous work [3] we evaluated generated trajectories and runtimes of our approach against benchmark data (Sect. 4.1 Benchmark datasets). Evaluations have shown that we significantly reduced the egomotion run-time while keeping a good accuracy of the estimated trajectories over the compared approaches. Here we complet this study by introducing our novel evaluation protocol consisting in revisiting particular locations in the

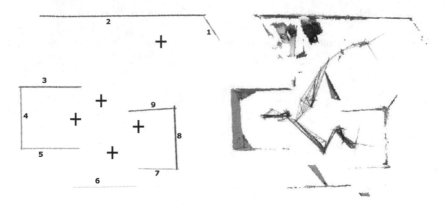

Fig. 4. Overhead view of (**right**) Point-based map with real trajectory inside and (**left**) Plane-based map with evaluation locations (crosses).

Table 2. ATE and RPE poses estimation errors.

ATE RMSE (m)	0.006 ± 0.003
Relative pose error (RPE) RMSE - Translation (m)	0.014 ± 0.002
Relative pose error (RPE) RMSE - Rotation (deg)	$1.30\,° \pm 0.54\,°$

scene several times and comparing stored poses. As we don't have an external tracking system, the idea is to consider the first passage at a location as the ground truth and to compare further visits poses. We chose five sparse locations in the scene (crosses in Fig. 4 **left**) and performed a series of experiments where we moved through these locations randomly. Such experiments are very appreciated as by evaluating the revisited areas we evaluate loop closures and thus the system's accuracy. Table 2 summarises the Absolute Trajectory Error (ATE) and the Relative Pose Error (RPE) proposed by Sturm *et al.* [19]. ATE computes the absolute difference between the ground truth and estimated poses after alignment and RPE measures the local accuracy of the trajectory over a fixed time interval Δ (equals 1 here). Results show poses estimation accuracy and consequently the robustness of our system. This confirms the 3D planar feature points reliability already shown in our previous work.

Evaluations of the Map. As our goal is to build planar maps which can be used in several contexts such as mobile navigation and augmented reality, it is very important to assess our map against real world scenes. Our evaluation, first time proposed, consists in comparing measurements of the generated maps with those of real scenes, namely distances and angles between planes. Tables 3 and 4 represent distances and angles estimations between numbered planes in Fig. 4 compared to the real ones in the office scene. Evaluations show that errors between real and estimated measurements do not exceeds 6 % for distances and

Table 3. Real and estimated distances between planes.

Plane i	Plane j	Real distance (Avg. $\pm$ Std. Dev.)	Estimation (Avg. $\pm$ Std. Dev.)
2	3	$1.50\,m \pm 0.02\,m$	$1.45\,m \pm 0.06\,m$
2	5	$2.82\,m \pm 0.02\,m$	$2.70\,m \pm 0.08\,m$
2	6	$3.42\,m \pm 0.02\,m$	$3.40\,m \pm 0.06\,m$
2	7	$3.20\,m \pm 0.02\,m$	$3.00\,m \pm 0.10\,m$
2	9	$1.95\,m \pm 0.02\,m$	$1.81\,m \pm 0.10\,m$
4	8	$2.95\,m \pm 0.02\,m$	$2.88\,m \pm 0.05\,m$

Table 4. Real and estimated angles between planes.

Plane i	Plane j	Real angle (Avg. $\pm$ Std. Dev.)	Estimation (Avg. $\pm$ Std. Dev.)
1	2	$56° \pm 2°$	$56.80° \pm 1.5°$
3	4	$90° \pm 2°$	$92.37° \pm 2.1°$
4	5	$90° \pm 2°$	$90.12° \pm 0.7°$
7	8	$90° \pm 2°$	$92.52° \pm 1.4°$
8	9	$90° \pm 2°$	$91.75° \pm 0.9°$

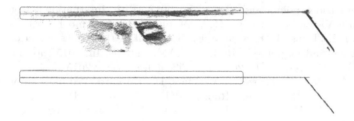

Fig. 5. Close overhead view of a planar region in the scene: **(top)** Raw point cloud representation and **(bottom)** 3D Plane-based map.

1 % for angles which is suitable for application requiring good accuracy. Hence, this lightweight map presents a good tradeoff between quality and memory consumption which is required by mobile robots and small devices.

3D Representations Comparison. Figure 5 shows a very close view of the second plane in Fig. 4 with two different 3D representations. The top row presents a point-based representation (Raw point cloud) and at the bottom we show our plane-based map which is a 3D planar representation. The point-based representation of this single plane already contains 340 thousand 3D points including many overlapping points due to assembling several point clouds. Such a representation would require a heavyweight process for the visualization of the entire map which leads to memory inefficiency. Our lightweight plane-based map is ready and much more usable for semantic labeling than raw 3D points based maps.

4   Conclusion

In this paper we proposed a simple 3D planar maps representation for RGB-D SLAM systems. We generated a 3D map based on detected 3D planes on the scene instead of the heavyweight point-based representation. During the reconstruction process, discovered planar areas are appended to the plane-based map. Moreover, all matched planes are progressively merged together in this map to give a compact representation and more information about the scene. Thus, we generated dense planar maps with significantly reduced sizes without relying on a dense approach. Besides, evaluations show that our system is able to build good quality maps while generating accurate trajectory. Also, the best tradeoff between precision and process time for planes detection have been evaluated. Once our plane-based map is available, the next step will consist in building the semantics associated to these planes such as floors or walls and planes structures such as desks or rooms which represents a first step towards semantic maps.

References

1. Ababsa, F., Mallem, M.: Robust camera pose tracking for augmented reality using particle filtering framework. Mach. Vis. Appl. **22**(1), 181–195 (2011)
2. Ataer-Cansizoglu, E., Taguchi, Y., Ramalingam, S., Garaas, T.: Tracking an rgb-d camera using points and planes. In: 2013 IEEE International Conference on Computer Vision Workshops (ICCVW), pp. 51–58, December 2013
3. Elghor, H.E., Roussel, D., Ababsa, F., Bouyakhf, E.H.: Planes detection for robust localization and mapping in RGB-D SLAM systems. In: 2015 International Conference on 3D Vision, 3DV 2015, pp. 452–459, October 2015
4. Endres, F., Hess, J., Sturm, J., Cremers, D., Burgard, W.: 3D mapping with an RGB-D camera. IEEE Trans. Robot. **30**(1), 177–187 (2014)
5. Fischler, M.A., Bolles, R.C.: Random sample consensus: a paradigm for model fitting with applications to image analysis and automated cartography. Commun. ACM **24**(6), 381–395 (1981)
6. Gao, X., Zhang, T.: Robust rgb-d simultaneous localization and mapping using planar point features. Robot. Auton. Syst. **72**, 1–14 (2015)
7. Grisetti, G., Kümmerle, R., Stachniss, C., Burgard, W.: A tutorial on graph-based SLAM. IEEE Intell. Transp. Syst. Mag. **2**(4), 31–43 (2010)
8. Henry, P., Krainin, M., Herbst, E., Ren, X., Fox, D.: RGB-D mapping: Using kinect-style depth cameras for dense 3D modeling of indoor environments. Int. J. Robot. Res. (IJRR) **31**(5), 647–663 (2012)
9. Hornung, A., Wurm, K.M., Bennewitz, M., Stachniss, C., Burgard, W.: Octomap: an efficient probabilistic 3d mapping framework based on octrees. Auton. Robots **34**(3), 189–206 (2013)
10. Izadi, S., Kim, D., Hilliges, O., Molyneaux, D., Newcombe, R., Kohli, P., Shotton, J., Hodges, S., Freeman, D., Davison, A., Fitzgibbon, A.: Kinectfusion: real-time 3d reconstruction and interaction using a moving depth camera. In: Proceedings of the 24th Annual ACM Symposium on User Interface Software and Technology, UIST 2011, pp. 559–568. ACM, New York, October 2011
11. Kaess, M.: Simultaneous localization and mapping with infinite planes. In: 2015 IEEE International Conference on Robotics and Automation (ICRA), pp. 4605–4611, May 2015

12. Keller, M., Lefloch, D., Lambers, M., Izadi, S., Weyrich, T., Kolb, A.: Real-time 3d reconstruction in dynamic scenes using point-based fusion. In: 2013 International Conference on 3D Vision - 3DV 2013, pp. 1–8. IEEE Computer Society, Washington (2013)
13. Kümmerle, R., Grisetti, G., Strasdat, H., Konolige, K., Burgard, W.: G2o: a general framework for graph optimization. In: IEEE International Conference on Robotics and Automation (ICRA 2011), pp. 3607–3613. IEEE, May 2011
14. Newcombe, R.A., Izadi, S., Hilliges, O., Molyneaux, D., Kim, D., Davison, A.J., Kohi, P., Shotton, J., Hodges, S., Fitzgibbon, A.: Kinectfusion: real-time dense surface mapping and tracking. In: 10th IEEE International Symposium on Mixed and Augmented Reality (ISMAR 2011), ISMAR 2011, pp. 127–136. IEEE Computer Society, October 2011
15. Pfister, H., Zwicker, M., van Baar, J., Gross, M.: Surfels: surface elements as rendering primitives. In: Proceedings of the 27th Annual Conference on Computer Graphics and Interactive Techniques, SIGGRAPH 2000, pp. 335–342 (2000)
16. Rusinkiewicz, S., Levoy, M.: Efficient variants of the ICP algorithm. In: Proceedings of the Third International Conference on 3-D Digital Imaging and Modeling, (3DIM 2001), pp. 145–152, May 2001
17. Rusu, R., Cousins, S.: 3d is here: point cloud library (PCL). In: IEEE International Conference on Robotics and Automation (ICRA 2011), pp. 1–4. IEEE, May 2011
18. Salas-Moreno, R.F., Glocken, B., Kelly, P.H.J., Davison, A.J.: Dense planar slam. In: 2014 IEEE International Symposium on Mixed and Augmented Reality (ISMAR), pp. 157–164, September 2014
19. Sturm, J., Engelhard, N., Endres, F., Burgard, W., Cremers, D.: A benchmark for the evaluation of RGB-D SLAM systems. In: IEEE/RSJ International Conference on Intelligent Robots and Systems (IROS 2012), pp. 573–580, October 2012
20. Taguchi, Y., Jian, Y.D., Ramalingam, S., Feng, C.: Point-plane SLAM for handheld 3D sensors. In: IEEE International Conference on Robotics and Automation (ICRA 2013), pp. 5182–5189, May 2013
21. Trevor, A.J.B., Rogers, J.G., Christensen, H.I.: Planar surface slam with 3d and 2d sensors. In: 2012 IEEE International Conference on Robotics and Automation (ICRA), pp. 3041–3048, May 2012
22. Whelan, T., Ma, L., Bondarev, E., de With, P., McDonald, J.: Incremental and batch planar simplification of dense point cloud maps. Robot. Auton. Syst. **69**(C), 3–14 (2015)
23. Whelan, T., Kaess, M., Johannsson, H., Fallon, M., Leonard, J.J., McDonald, J.: Real-time large-scale dense rgb-d slam with volumetric fusion. Int. J. Robot. Res. **34**(4–5), 598–626 (2015)

Towards a Generic M-SVM Parameters Estimation Using Overlapping Swarm Intelligence for Handwritten Characters Recognition

Marwa Amara[1]([⊠]), Kamel Zidi[2], and Khaled Ghedira[3]

[1] Northern Border University, Al-Awayqeelah, Saudi Arabia
amara1marwa@gmail.com
[2] Community College, Tabuk University, Tabuk, Saudi Arabia
[3] GR2IA Research Group, Tunis, Tunisia

Abstract. Support vector machines (SVM) is a statistical classification approach which has been successfully applied to solve various types of problems in pattern recognition. However, it has remained largely unexplored for Arabic recognition. It has been proved to be a good tool for multi-classification issues related to machine learning. But, the performance of the SVM depends solely upon the appropriate choice of parameters. Hence, particle swarm optimization (PSO) technique is employed in tuning SVM parameters. The proposed SVM-PSO model is used to solve the Arabic characters recognition problem. The selected models are compared in terms of the testing time and accuracy.

This study employs support vector machines in the Isolated Farsi/Arabic Character Database (IFHCDB) recognition. Experimental results have proven that PSO could be a good alternative for predicting SVM parameters.

Keywords: Arabic recognition · Support vector machines · Particle swarm optimization · SVM parameters

1 Introduction

The optical charters recognition (OCR) system goal is to convert a text image into an ASCII format that can be edited. To achieve this objective, OCR goes through pre-processing, segmentation, classification, recognition and post-processing steps.

First, a paper document is transferred into a digital le using a scanner. Some pre-processing techniques may be used depending on the quality of the text image [1,20]. For most documents, a binarization is necessary to remove the background. Then, lines in the binary image are segmented to extract the characters positions. Those characters will be used later to extract features. In the classification stage, the extracted features are compared with a prototype; if the

© Springer International Publishing AG 2016
J. Blanc-Talon et al. (Eds.): ACIVS 2016, LNCS 10016, pp. 498–509, 2016.
DOI: 10.1007/978-3-319-48680-2_44

features are matched, the input character is classified into the appropriate class. In this step, if a single classifier fails to yield high performance, several classifiers may be combined to give better rates [2]. Classification techniques utilized in recent research works are noticeably divers ed compared to those proposed before. In this paper, we mainly focus on character recognition methods based on SVM classifiers.

In 2007, Abd and Paschos [3] developed a multi-class classifier to recognize 58 Arabic character shapes. The classification phase takes place using one-against-all (OAA) technique with Gaussian RFB kernel. The obtained accuracy is in the range of 98–99 %. Later on, in 2008, Hamdi et al. [4] introduced an algorithm based on one-against-one(OAO) method, with a Gaussian RBF kernel, which recognizes only the shapes of the handwritten characters without dots. The proposed approach provided an accuracy of 96 %. In 2009, Alaei et al. used OAA method [5] in their approach. They experimented SVM with linear, Gaussian, and polynomial kernels for numeral recognition. They evaluated the performance of OAA on 80,000 handwritten Persian numerals. They obtained a 99.37 % accuracy using five-fold cross validation technique. The authors reported that SVM with Gaussian kernel gave the best results. In the same year, SVM with RBF kernel was used for Arabic numeral recognition in Mahmoud and Awaida work [6]. A two-stage exhaustive parameter estimation technique was used to estimate the best values for the SVM parameters. A database of 44 writers with 48 samples of each digit totaling 21, 120 samples were used to estimate parameters. The recognition results, given by SVM, were compared to those provided by the HMM classifier. The achieved average accuracy of the SVM and HMM classifiers were 99.83 % and 99.00 %, respectively. In 2010, Faouzi et al. [7] suggested a new handwriting character segmentation technique. Reported approach based on OAO Classifier with RBF kernel presented an accuracy of 94.11 % In 2012, Elzobi et al. [8] discussed an OAA Classifier with RBF kernel with an Arabic off-line handwritten database. Using this classifier, accuracy varied between 43 % and 93 %, with a median of 77 % and an average of 74.3 %. In 2012, Alalshekmubarak et al. introduced a novel approach to classify off-line handwritten Arabic words, applying SVM with normalized poly kernel [9]. Authors compared three different kernels; normalized, polynomial and linear. They proved that the first type is the best technique. The obtained accuracy rate was 95.27 % in a subset of 24 classes and 7, 971 entries. In 2014, Amara et al. provided a comprehensive survey about the recent developments in Arabic recognition based on SVM classifiers [10]. The paper discussed many MSVM methods and reported the recognition accuracy for each work. We note here that each work used a different database for testing. In 2015, the same authors tackled the problem of selecting a suitable multi-class SVM method to recognize Arabic script using the Arabic Printed Text Image Database-Multi-Font(APTID/MF) [11]. The different MSVM algorithms are compared in terms of training time, testing time and accuracy. Moreover, by analyzing the accuracy, they validated that the OAO SVM approach is the best method.

Regarding the state of the art, we can observe that the choice of SVM method was arbitrary except those of [11]. Although, an appropriate choice of SVM parameters should be made to ensure a better delimitation of classes. Thus, our objective is to determine a generic way to obtain the optimal parameters. In this study, particle swarm optimization (PSO) is adapted to nd out the better SVM parameters.

This paper is organized as follows: Sect. 2 reviews the multi-class SVM (MSVM) algorithms. Section 3 describes the efficiency of PSO algorithm in estimating the optimal SVM parameters. In Sect. 4, the PSO-SVM model is applied over the IFHCDB database, and the results are compared with those provided when using cross-validation. Finally, concluding remarks are presented in Sect. 5.

2   Multi-class Support Vector Machines

The objective of applying SVM is to nd an hyper plane that separates classes as accurately as possible. Given the labeled training data x_i and their classes y_i, a decision function ideal representation is that which ts best the training data without under-tting and over-tting. Determining such non-linear function is very difficult. Data is mapped to a space where this function becomes linear. To map data, Vapnik [12] suggested to directly choose a kernel function K that represents a dot product in some unspecified high dimensional space. The typical kernel functions are given below:

- Linear:

$$K(x_i, x_j) = (x_i x_j) \qquad (1)$$

- Polynomial:

$$K(x_i, x_j) = (\gamma x_i x_j + coef)^d \qquad (2)$$

- Gaussian radial basis function (RBF):

$$K(x_i, x_j) = \exp^{-\gamma ||x_i - x_j||^2} \qquad (3)$$

- Sigmoid :

$$tanh(\gamma x_i x_j + coef) \qquad (4)$$

where, γ, $coef$, and d are kernel parameters.

SVMs use a discriminant function to construct the decision boundary. It is given by the formula illustrated in (5).

$$\begin{cases} W(\alpha) = \sum_{i=1}^{n} \alpha_i - \frac{1}{2} \sum_{i,j=1}^{n} y_i y_j \alpha_i \alpha_j k(x_i, x_j) \\ \\ where \ 0 \leq \alpha_i \leq C \\ \\ Subject \quad to \sum_{i=1}^{n} \alpha_i y_i \end{cases} \qquad (5)$$

We note that the C regularization parameter controls the trade-off between maximizing the margin and minimizing the classification error.

Since SVMs were originally designed for binary problems, several methods have been proposed to extend binary SVMs in order to solve multi-classification problems. Some extensions are based on multiple binary SVM classifiers, while some others used "single step" SVM method.

We assume, hereafter, that $y_i \in \{1, ..., M\}$ are the class labels, $m \in \{1, ..., M\} \backslash y_i$ are class labels excluding y_i, Φ is the mapping function, and ζ_i^m is the gap between each two decision planes.

2.1   Binary Multi-class Support Vector Machines

The OAA approach is considered as the earliest extension of binary SVM [13]. In this approach, M binary SVM models are constructed where M is the number of classes. An SVM is constructed to discriminate each class against the $(M-1)$ others classes. The mth SVM is trained with all examples in the mth class with positive labels and all other examples with negative labels.

The desired class y_i for each training sample x_i is defined as follows:

$$\begin{cases} y_i = (+1) \ if \ c_i = k \\ y_i = (-1) \ if \ c_i \neq k \end{cases} \tag{6}$$

An optimal hyper plane is constructed to separate (N/M) positive examples $(y_i = +1)$ from $N(M-1)/M$ negative ones $(y_i = -1)$.

Later, the OAO method was introduced in [14]. In the OAO approach, an SVM is trained to discriminate each two classes (k, m). Thus, the number of SVMs used in this approach is $M(M-1)/2$. The class y_i for a training example x_i is defined as follows:

$$\begin{cases} y_i = (+1) \ if \ c_i = k \\ y_i = (-1) \ if \ c_i = m \end{cases} \tag{7}$$

The third SVM method proposed in [15] is based on the Directed Acyclic Graph (DAG). In the training phase, it works the same way as OAO method, solving $M(M-1)/2$ binary SVMs. However, it behaves differently in the test stage. It uses a binary DAG which has $M(M-1)/2$ internal nodes and M leaves.

Given a sample x, starting at the root node, a pairwise SVM decision is evaluated. Then, depending on the result, it moves to either left or right. Those tests continue to be carried on until reaching one of the leaves, indicating the predicted class.

2.2   Single Step Multi-class Support Vector Machines

The idea of Weston et al. [16] consists in constructing M two-class decision rules where the mth function $w_m^T(x) + b$ separates the training vectors of the class m from the others. Therefore, we obtained M decision boundaries by solving just one problem. The optimization problem is formulated as follows:

$$\begin{cases} min_{w,b,\zeta} \frac{1}{2} \sum_{m=1}^{M} w_m^t w_m + C \sum_{i=1}^{l} \sum_{m \neq y_i} \zeta_i^m \\ Subject\ to\ w_{y_i}^t \Phi(x_i) + b_{yi} \geq w_m^t \Phi(X_i) + b_m + 2 - \zeta_i^m \\ for\ i = 1, ..., l, m \in \{1, ..., M\} \setminus y_i\ where\ \zeta_i^m \geq 0 \end{cases} \tag{8}$$

The decision function used by the Weston SVM method is the same as in the equation used by OAA method. Crammer's multi-class approach [17], have extended the binary SVM classifier to classification problems with more than two classes. The training problem of the Crammer multi-class SVM can be expressed as:

$$\begin{cases} min_{w,\zeta} \frac{1}{2} \sum_{m=1}^{M} w_m^t w_m + c \sum_{i=1}^{l} \sum_{m=y_i} \zeta_i \\ Subject\ to\ w_{y_i}^t \Phi(x_i) - w_m^t \Phi(x_i) \geq e_m^i - \zeta_i \\ for\ i = 1, ..., l\ where\ e_i^m = 1 - \gamma_{y_i,m} \end{cases} \tag{9}$$

3 Overlapping Swarm Intelligence in the Selecting of SVM Parameters

The purpose of this research is to propose an efficient handwritten character recognition system. As described in Fig. 1, our system takes as input the image of the characters. It produces recognized characters.

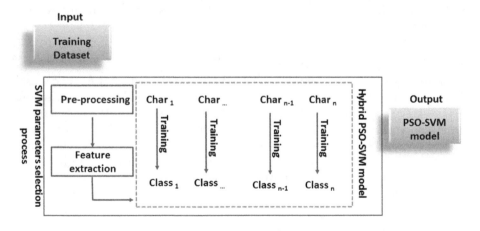

Fig. 1. Approach overview.

It is evident that the shift toward the recognition phase is preceded by the learning phase. In the latter, the character segments are binarized and normalized. These characters are then propagated to the feature extraction phase. After that, we pass to the learning stage. We use PSO algorithm to nd the best SVM parameters.

The parameters prediction process has several advantages. It improves the recognition process because the recognition rate depends essentially on the choice of the best SVM parameters. The produced model will be then used in the recognition stage. The PSO algorithm is applied in the learning step to produce the best SVM model. In fact, swarm optimization is an optimization technique based on the metaphor of social behavior. Particle swarm optimization is the member of a wide category of swarm intelligence-based methods, such as bird flocking, schooling and swarm theory. The general algorithm of PSO is shown in the Fig. 2.

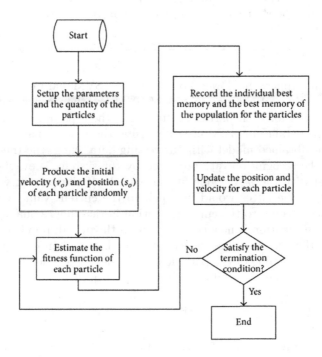

Fig. 2. Particle swarm optimization algorithm.

The PSO produces the particles of the initial population randomly through the evolutionary computation to find the optimal solution. In each evolution, the particle would change the individual search direction by two search memories. The first search is the optimal individual variable memory and the other is the optimal variable memory of the population. After the computation, the PSO would calculate the optimal solution according to the optimal variable memory. The purpose of this stage is to find the best (C, γ) SVM parameters using PSO intelligence. The Algorithm 1 describes the entire process of the hybrid PSO-SVM process.

Algorithm 1. Overlapping Swarm Intelligence

1: **while** Stopping criterion not met **do**
2:      Initialize the parameters (C_i, γ_i) randomly
3:      **for** Each particle (C_i, γ_i) of the PSO **do**
4:          Train the SVM classifier using (C_i, γ_i)
5:          Test the SVM model
6:          Evaluate the Fitness (C_i, γ_i)
7:          **if** Fitness (C_i, γ_i) is better than Fitness(p_i^t) **then**
8:              Update p_i^t
9:          **end if**
10:     **end for**
11:     Choose p_i^t with the best Fitness as p_{gbest}^t
12:     **for** Each particle (C_i, γ_i) of the PSO **do**
13:         Update the v_i^t and x_i^t of each particle (C_i, γ_i)
14:     **end for**
15: **end while**

Initially, the upper and lower bounds of the SVM parameters (C, γ) are specified. The values of the parameters of SVM are then generated randomly within the bounds for each particle. After that, these parameters are fed into SVM model. We train our SVM classifier using the (C_i, γ_i) parameters. Later on, we test the obtained model with our testing data. Next, the tness function, expressed by the recognition rate produced by the system, is evaluated. Then, it is compared with the p_{best} value of the particle. If the current value is best thought of p_{best}, the latter would be equal to the current value and the p_{best} location would be equal to the current location in the dimensional space.

The fitness evaluation is now compared with the overall previous *best* of the population. If the current value comes out to be better than g_{best}, the latter is reset to the current value of the particle array index. The velocity and position of the particle are then changed according to the Eq. 10.

$$\begin{cases} v_{ij}^t = wv_{ij}^{t-1} + c_1 r_1(p_{bestij}^{t-1} - x_{ij}^{t-1}) + c_2 r_2(g_{bestj}^{t-1} - x_{ij}^{t-1}) \\ x_{ij}^t = x_{ij}^{t-1} + v_{ij}^t \end{cases} \tag{10}$$

The c_1 and c_2 parameters are the acceleration constants and r_1 and r_2 are the random real numbers between 0 and 1.

Thus, the particle flies through a potential solution toward p_{best} and g_{best} in a navigated way while still exploring new areas through stochastic mechanism to escape from a local optimum. w represents the inertia weight calculated control the impact of the velocity history on the current one. The fitness function value is repeatedly determined until the criterion is met. This criterion is the maximum number of the allowed iterations.

4   Experiments and Results

In our study, have assessed the performance of our hybrid approach by showing its efficiency in enhancing the recognition rate. The proposed algorithm, deeply discussed in the previous section, has been tested with the Isolated Farsi/Arabic Character Database (IFHCDB) [19]. The latter is freely available for academic use. It includes 52,380 characters and 17,740 numerals.

Besides, for comparison purposes, each dataset has been properly divided into respective training and test sets. In all experiments, we use holistic representation as features extraction method. This method is based on lexicographic ordering of raw pixel values to yield one vector per image. After carrying some tests to choose the best size, each character was re-sized to a $21 * 15$ pixels. The classifier takes as input a vector of 315 attributes.

In what follows, we study two different methods for predicting SVM parameters. The first one consists of using the cross validation technique while the second is based on using of the swarm intelligence. Indeed, we have implemented our comparison tool using LIBSVM and BSVM software [18]. The experiments have been conducted on a computer embedding an Intel core I_3 processor and 4 Go of RAM.

4.1 Finding SVM Parameters Using Cross-Validation Technique

In this section, cross-validation was used to compare the performances of different predictive SVM models. We conducted a 10-folds cross validation on the training data to choose the best C and γ parameters. We find out the best model by performing multiple tests conducted on training data.

For each SVM method, the optimal regularization parameter C and the kernel parameter γ were estimated by repeating the classification process for $C = [2^{-2}, ..., 2^{12}]$ and $\gamma = [2^{-10}, ..., 2^4]$. The various SVMs classifiers were trained using $225 = 15 * 15$ combinations of C and γ. We repeated those tests using four different kernels.

Table 1 summarizes the comparison of accuracies of the five MSVM methods using the best (C, γ) values. Note that, if several (C, γ) values have the same accuracy, we choose values which report the shortest training time.

Table 1. A comparison in term of accuracies (%).

Classifiers kernel	OAA (C, γ) rate	OAO (C, γ) rate	DAG (C, γ) rate	Crammer (C, γ) rate	Weston (C, γ) rate
Linear	(2^4) 72.88	(2^{12}) 83.93	(2^{12}) 83.60	(2^{-1}) 84.76	(2^{-1}) 84.53
Polynomial	$(2^4, 2^0)$ 84.39	$(2^4, 2^1)$ 85.21	$(2^4, 2^1)$ 85.21	$(2^{-1}, 2^0)$ 84.56	$(2^{-1}, 2^0)$ 84.13
Rbf	$(2^4, 2^0)$ 87.08	$(2^4, 2^0)$ 88.47	$(2^4, 2^{-1})$ 87.74	$(2^1, 2^0)$ 81.57	$(2^{-1}, 2^0)$ 82.63
Sigmoid	$(2^4, 2^1)$ 73.96	$(2^0, 2^{-1})$ 79.66	$(2^0, 2^1)$ 78.44	$(2^1, 2^{-1})$ 88.66	$(2^1, 2^0)$ 84.63

From Table 1, we note that the values of C are high. Actually, they are the same for all methods except OAA using the linear kernel. The obtained results provided by the polynomial kernel show that optimal (C, γ) values are mostly in the same interval for different methods, except for OAA method. OAO and DAG gave the best results. Obviously, there are two parameters of polynomial kernel: the degree d and the coefficient $coef$. After some trials where $d \in \{1, 2, 3\}$, the degree was set to $d = 3$. The coefficient was set to the default values $coef = 0$. Using the rbf kernel, we also report the efficiency of MSVMs methods. We notice that the best kernel parameter (C, γ) varies from one method to another. Finally, we note that the accuracies obtained by using sigmoid kernel are lower than those given when applying linear, polynomial and RBF kernels.

In Table 2, we report the testing time based on the testing database using the best obtained model obtained from the above experiences.

Table 2. A comparison in term of testing time (s).

Kernel	OAA	OAO	DAG	Crammer	Weston
Linear	71.15	39.62	39.30	266.47	268.03
Polynomial	87.81	44.86	45.17	268.54	265.99
Rbf	101.95	50.46	50.85	264.86	311.07
Sigmoid	133.97	166.93	66.99	267.69	316.60

Overall, single step methods have huge testing times. Likewise, testing time, using polynomial kernel, are in most cases higher than those obtained using linear kernel. Nevertheless, we can observe a little difference in the term of testing time which are slightly higher applying RBF kernel. Moreover, using sigmoid testing times are higher.

To summarize, it may be said that a user should consider the accuracy requirement, the computational time, the resources available and the nature of the problem. Our purpose is the develop a generic SVM model. This objective is achieved using the hybrid SVM-PSO model. Obviously, the proposed approach is able to predict the best parameters in depending to the quality of data by maximizing the accuracies. This purpose will be the objective of the next section.

4.2   Finding SVM Parameters Using PSO Intelligence

After showing that the OAO is more efficient. In this section, we detail the experimentation and the results provided by the hybrid PSO-SVM algorithm to predict the OAO methods parameters. We come up with the best model by finding the best C and γ SVM parameters using PSO. Tests are conducted on the training data. The important parameters of PSO used in this model are given in Table 3.

The acceleration constant belongs to $[0, 2]$. And the performance of SVM-PSO is checked using a test data set in terms of its tness values. It is found that as acceleration coefficient increases, the fitness function increases till it reaches a maximum value. Thus, the value of c_1 and c_2 is taken respectively to be 1.5 and 1.6 for this case.

Table 3. Parameters used in the PSO algorithm.

Parameters	Values
Acceleration constants (c_1, c_2)	$(1.5, 1.6)$
Population size	40
Maximum number of iterations	300
Minimum error gradient	10^{-6}
Inertia weight w	Varied linearly
Fitness function	SVM accuracy

From experiments, we observe that, with an increase in the value of acceleration coefficient, the recognition rate, representing the fitness function value, decreases. Concerning the weight w, it was set to vary linearly from 1 to 0 during an iteration. OAO classifier was tested using the best (C, γ) obtained parameters. We repeated those tests using four different kernels. SVM parameters were estimated for the different models using the PSO technique as mentioned in Sect. 3. We report, in the Table 4, the resulting accuracies and the testing time obtained on the test dataset using the best values of (C, γ).

Table 4. A comparison in term of accuracies (%) and testing time (s).

kernel	(C, γ)	Rate (%)	Testing time
Linear	(16.3)	88.21	39.62
Polynomial	$(16.3, 1)$	89.21	45.86
Radial basis	$(16.3, 1)$	91.47	44.80
Sigmoid	$(16.3, 1.2)$	90.88	160.93

From the experiments, we can conclude that the hybrid approach gives better encouraging results to recognize 47 classes including handwritten numerals and Arabic characters. In fact, we note that both cross-validation and hybrid SVM PSO prediction methods have generally a similar recognition time. There is only a little difference in the recognition rate.

The major advantage of PSO is that it allows better exploration the research space than cross validation. Better accuracy is achieved using OAO multi-class SVM method with RBF kernel. Generally, we can conclude that the use of PSO algorithm can be a good alternative to predict SVM parameters.

5   Conclusions and Future Works

Because the classification task is necessary for any character recognition system, we have proposed a hybrid model based on the combination of SVM and PSO of Arabic character segmentation. The SVM-PSO model was obtained by combining the two methods of PSO and SVM.

Besides, PSO was employed to select the appropriate OAO-SVM parameters to enhance the character recognition accuracy. Experimental results about the Isolated Farsi/Arabic Character Database show that the One Against One method is more suitable for Arabic character recognition. The SVM-PSO model was proved to be a good alternative as it gave the best accuracy in a shorter time. Furthermore, its performance is better than that of cross validation methods.

As future work, we are planning to extend our approach in order to recognize words.

Acknowledgment. This research and innovation work is carried out within a MOBIDOC thesis, funded by the EU under the PASRI project.

References

1. Amara, M., Zidi, K.: Feature selection using a neuro-genetic approach for arabic text recognition. In: 4th International Conference on Meta Heuristics and Nature Inspired Computing (2012)
2. Amara, M., Zidi, K.: Arabic text recognition based on neuro-genetic feature selection approach. In: Hassanien, A.E., Tolba, M.F., Taher Azar, A. (eds.) AMLTA 2014. CCIS, vol. 488, pp. 3–10. Springer, Heidelberg (2014). doi:10.1007/978-3-319-13461-1_1
3. Abd, M.A., Paschos, G.: Effective Arabic character recognition using support vector machines. In: Sobh, T. (ed.) Innovations and Advanced Techniques in Computer and Information Sciences and Engineering, pp. 7–11. Springer, Dordrecht (2007)
4. Hamdi, R., Bouchareb, F., Bedda, M.: Handwritten Arabic character recognition based on SVM classifier. In: 3rd International Conference on Information, Communication Technologies: From Theory to Applications, pp. 1–4 (2008)
5. Alaei, A., Pal, U., Nagabhushan, P.: Using modified contour features and SVM based classifier for the recognition of Persian/Arabic handwritten numerals. In: 7th International Conference on Advances in Pattern Recognition, pp. 391–394 (2009)
6. Mahmoud, S.A., Awaida, S.M.: Recognition of off-line handwritten Arabic (Indian) numerals using multi-scale features and support vector machines vs. hidden Markov models. Arab. J. Sci. Eng. **34**, 429–444 (2009)
7. Faouzi, Z., Abdelhamid, D., Chaouki, B.M.: An approach based on structural segmentation for the recognition of arabic handwriting. Adv. Inf. Sci. Serv. Sci. **2**, 14–24 (2010)
8. Elzobi, M., Al-Hamadi, A., Saeed, A., Dings, L.: Arabic handwriting recognition using gabor wavelet transform and SVM. In: 11th IEEE International Conference on Signal Processing, pp. 2154–2158 (2012)
9. Alalshekmubarak, A., Hussain, A., Wang, Q.-F.: Off-line handwritten Arabic word recognition using SVMs with normalized poly kernel. In: Huang, T., Zeng, Z., Li, C., Leung, C.S. (eds.) ICONIP 2012. LNCS, vol. 7664, pp. 85–91. Springer, Heidelberg (2012). doi:10.1007/978-3-642-34481-7_11
10. Amara, M., Zidi, K., Zidi, S., Ghedira, K.: Arabic character recognition based M-SVM: review. In: Hassanien, A.E., Tolba, M.F., Taher Azar, A. (eds.) AMLTA 2014. CCIS, vol. 488, pp. 18–25. Springer, Heidelberg (2014). doi:10.1007/978-3-319-13461-1_3

11. Amara, M., Ghedira, K., Zidi, K., Zidi, S.: A comparative study of multi-class support vector machine methods for Arabic characters recognition. In: 12th ACS/IEEE Conference on Computer Systems and Applications, pp. 1–6 (2015)
12. Vapnik, V.N., Vapnik, V.: Statistical Learning Theory, vol. 1. Wiley, New York (1998)
13. Hsu, C.W., Lin, C.J.: A comparison of methods for multiclass support vector machines. IEEE Trans. Neural Netw. **13**, 415–425 (2002)
14. Knerr, S., Personnaz, L., Dreyfus, G.: Single-layer learning revisited: a stepwise procedure for building and training a neural network. Neurocomput. Algorithms Architectures Appl. **68**, 41 (2012)
15. Platt, J.C., Cristianini, N., Shawe-Taylor, J.: Large margin DAGs for multiclass classification. NIPS **12**, 547–553 (1999)
16. Weston, J., Watkins, C.: Support vector machines for multi-class pattern recognition. ESANN **99**, 219–224 (1999)
17. Crammer, K., Singer, Y.: On the algorithmic implementation of multiclass kernel-based vector machines. J. Mach. Learn. Res. **2**, 265–292 (2002)
18. Chang, C.C., Lin, C.J.: LIBSVM: a library for support vector machines. ACM Trans. Intell. Syst. Technol. **2**(3), 27 (2011). https://www.csie.ntu.edu.tw/~cjlin/libsvm/
19. Mozaffari, S., Faez, K., Faradji, F., Ziaratban, M., Golzan, S.M.: A comprehensive isolated Farsi/Arabic character database for handwritten OCR research. In: 10th International Workshop on Frontiers in Handwriting Recognition. Suvisoft. (2006)
20. Amara, M., Zidi, K., Ghedira, K., Zidi, S.: New rules to enhance the performances of Histogram projection for segmenting small-sized Arabic words. In: Abraham, A., Han, S.Y., Al-Sharhan, S.A., Liu, H. (eds.) Hybrid Intelligent Systems. AISC, vol. 420, pp. 167–176. Springer, Heidelberg (2016). doi:10.1007/978-3-319-27221-4_14

Human Action Recognition Based on Temporal Pyramid of Key Poses Using RGB-D Sensors

Enea Cippitelli[1]([✉]), Ennio Gambi[1], Susanna Spinsante[1],
and Francisco Florez-Revuelta[2]

[1] Dipartimento di Ingegneria dell'Informazione,
Universita' Politecnica delle Marche, 60131 Ancona, Italy
{e.cippitelli,e.gambi,s.spinsante}@univpm.it
[2] Department of Computer Technology, University of Alicante,
P.O. Box 99, 03080 Alicante, Spain
francisco.florez@ua.es

Abstract. Human action recognition is a hot research topic in computer vision, mainly due to the high number of related applications, such as surveillance, human computer interaction, or assisted living. Low cost RGB-D sensors have been extensively used in this field. They can provide skeleton joints, which represent a compact and effective representation of the human posture. This work proposes an algorithm for human action recognition where the features are computed from skeleton joints. A sequence of skeleton features is represented as a set of key poses, from which histograms are extracted. The temporal structure of the sequence is kept using a temporal pyramid of key poses. Finally, a multi-class SVM performs the classification task. The algorithm optimization through evolutionary computation allows to reach results comparable to the state-of-the-art on the MSR Action3D dataset.

Keywords: Kinect · Human action recognition · Bag of key poses · Temporal pyramid · Evolutionary computation

1 Introduction

Human Action Recognition (HAR) is an active research topic in computer vision, mainly because it may enable and facilitate different applications. Automatic action recognition algorithms can be, for example, applied in video-surveillance of public spaces, or in Active and Assisted Living (AAL) environments, to support ageing in place of older people [1,2]. Another interesting application is represented by Human-Computer Interaction (HCI), where gesture recognition in particular can provide an efficient way to interface a system [3].

In this scenario, the availability of inexpensive depth sensors, such as Microsoft Kinect, has fostered the research exploiting 3D data, which presents some advantages with respect to RGB cameras, such as less susceptibility to variations in light intensity [4]. Furthermore, depth data allow the extraction of skeleton joints [5], and enable the exploitation of different features for action

© Springer International Publishing AG 2016
J. Blanc-Talon et al. (Eds.): ACIVS 2016, LNCS 10016, pp. 510–521, 2016.
DOI: 10.1007/978-3-319-48680-2_45

recognition [6]. Many algorithms for action recognition exploiting 3D silhouettes have been proposed, since depth data make the process of silhouette extraction easier. Li et al. [7] developed a method that represents postures considering a bag of 3D points extracted from depth data. Only a small set of 3D points is considered, and a method has been developed to sample the representative 3D points by performing planar projections of the 3D depth map and extracting the points that are on the contours. Other interesting features are represented by local Spatio Temporal Interest Points (STIPs) applied to depth data [8]. Depth-based STIPs include a noise suppression scheme which can handle some characteristics of the depth images, such as the noise in the borders of an object, where the depth values show a big difference in the transition from foreground to background, or the noise given by errors in the depth estimation algorithm, which can result in some gaps in the depth map.

Despite the proposal of different depth-based descriptors, the skeleton joints extracted by depth data represent a compact and effective description of the human body, and many activity recognition algorithms rely only the joints as input. Considering joint coordinates, different feature extraction methods have been proposed. Some of them consider only spatial data, some others include also temporal information [6]. The HOJ3D representation [9] considers the partition of the 3D space into bins and the joints are associated to each bin using a Gaussian weight function. The histograms are clustered to obtain the salient postures and a discrete Hidden Markov Model (HMM) is employed to model the temporal evolution of the postures. In addition to k-means clustering, the use of sparse coding has been also proposed for the creation of the codebook. In particular, Luo et al. [10] proposed the DL-GSGC scheme, where the discriminative capacity of the dictionary is improved by adding group sparsity and geometry constraints to the sparse coding representation. A temporal pyramid is adopted to model the temporal information, and a linear Support Vector Machine (SVM) is chosen as the classification algorithm. Wang et al. [11] firstly considered relations among body joints in the spatial domain, by grouping joints into different body parts. Then, the temporal relations of the body parts are obtained, and actions are represented by histograms of the detected part-sets.

Feature selection methods or optimization strategies may be adopted to improve the performance of HAR algorithms. These methods may increase the recognition performance because they can select the relevant features for an efficient discrimination among the activities. Eweiwi et al. [12] proposed a HAR algorithm exploiting joints where the pose feature is a weighted sum of all joint features. The weights are estimated by Partial Least Squares (PLS). Wang et al. [13] proposed a data mining solution to discover discriminative actionlets, which are structures of base features built to be highly representative of one action and highly discriminative compared to other actions. Evolutionary computation has been successfully adopted in feature selection problems, and it has also been considered for the optimization of HAR algorithms [14]. Usually, two models are used to apply the evolutionary computation: the filter model and the wrapper model. The former determinates the features relevance considering their intrinsic properties, without including the learning method. The latter approach encloses the induction algorithm and, even if more computationally expensive, it is usually preferred because of better results [15]. Another model of evolutionary optimization is the coevolutionary algorithm, which considers several populations: individuals in a population are awarded fitness values based on their interactions with individuals from other populations. Interactions can be competitive, where individuals are rewarded at the expense of those with which they interact, or cooperative, where individual are rewarded if they work well with other individuals [16]. Cooperative coevolutionary algorithms have been also applied to address feature and parameter selection problems in HAR [17].

The HAR algorithm herein proposed considers skeleton joints and extracts features representing the person's posture. A bag of key poses model [18] is adopted, where the most informative postures are learned using the k-means clustering algorithm. Then, an action is modeled as histograms of key poses, and the temporal structure of the action is kept using a temporal pyramid. A multi-class SVM is finally exploited for classification. The algorithm parameters are optimized using evolutionary and cooperative coevolutionary algorithms proposed in [14,17], which detect the best configuration of joints, key poses, and training instances. The proposed algorithm reaches results comparable to the state-of-the-art on the well known MSR Action3D dataset [7].

The paper is organized as follows: Sect. 2 describes the proposed activity recognition algorithm, providing implementation details from the features computation procedure to the classification scheme. The optimization process by evolutionary computation is described in Sect. 3, and experimental results are presented and discussed in Sect. 4. Finally, Sect. 5 provides concluding remarks.

2 HAR Algorithm Based on Temporal Pyramid of Key Poses

The action recognition algorithm takes the 3D coordinates of the skeleton joints as input data and initially computes some position displacements between them, as the features representing a specific posture. All the feature vectors are then clustered to extract a set of key poses per action, which are then combined into a bag of key poses. Then, an action is represented as a sequence of key poses, from which histograms are computed. Histograms of key poses are then organized considering more levels of the temporal pyramid. The obtained histograms represent the input to a multi-class SVM, which performs the classification task. The entire process may be represented by 4 main steps, which are sketched in Fig. 1 and detailed in the following:

1. *Extraction of posture features*: in this step the 3D coordinates of the joints are considered and the features representing each posture are computed;
2. *Codebook generation and key poses substitution*: this phase consists of the codebook generation and the association of a key pose to each posture in the sequence;

3. *Histograms of key poses and temporal pyramid*: a sequence of key poses is represented as a set of histograms obtained at different levels of a temporal pyramid;
4. *Classification*: the histograms of key poses are classified using a multi-class SVM, implemented following the "one-versus-one" method.

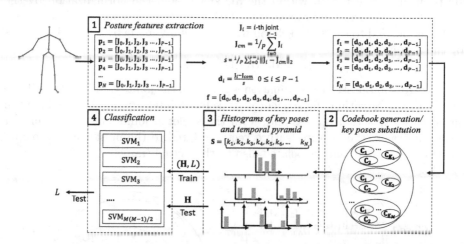

Fig. 1. Global scheme of the activity recognition algorithm. The first step consists in the extraction of the posture features vector, which are organized in a codebook to obtain the key poses. A sequence of key poses is then represented as a set of histograms obtained at each level of a temporal pyramid. Finally, the classification is performed using a multi-class SVM.

The extraction of features representing the posture consists of the calculation of the normalized position differences among the joints and their center-of-mass. Position differences are more robust features if compared to distances, with less ambiguity among different poses. Considering that the i-th joint of a skeleton is represented by a three-dimensional vector $\mathbf{J}_i$, a vector $\mathbf{p}_n$ stores all the coordinates for the n-th skeleton frame of an activity constituted by N frames. Each frame is represented by P joints, and the center-of-mass $\mathbf{J}_{cm}$ is represented by the average 3D position of all the P joints:

$$\mathbf{J}_{cm} = \frac{1}{P} \sum_{i=0}^{P-1} \mathbf{J}_i \tag{1}$$

The normalization factor s is computed based on the average ℓ_2-norm between each joint and the center-of-mass, according to (2):

$$s = \frac{1}{P} \sum_{i=0}^{P-1} \|\mathbf{J}_i - \mathbf{J}_{cm}\|_2 \tag{2}$$

The position difference $\mathbf{d}_i$ is represented by the displacement between the i-th joint and the center-of-mass, considering the scaling factor, and it is implemented according to (3):

$$\mathbf{d}_i = \frac{\mathbf{J}_i - \mathbf{J}_{cm}}{s} \tag{3}$$

Using the difference between two positions makes the feature vector invariant to the position of the person within the 3D space, and the normalization by the scaling factor ensures the invariance to the build of the person. The feature vector $\mathbf{f}_n$, associated to the n-th skeleton frame, is finally made by all the differences for the P joints:

$$\mathbf{f}_n = [\mathbf{d}_0, \mathbf{d}_1, \mathbf{d}_2, \ldots, \mathbf{d}_{P-1}] \tag{4}$$

Due to errors in the skeleton estimation algorithm, the joints could be unavailable for some frames within the sequence. A skeleton integrity check is included in the feature extraction process and, if all the skeleton joints are unavailable for a specific frame, the posture feature vector related to the most recent skeleton frame is considered, and associated also to the actual frame.

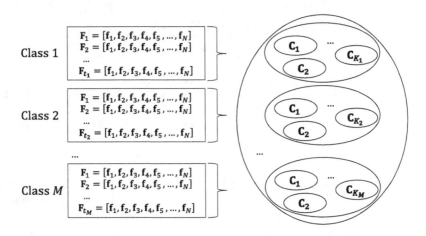

Fig. 2. Codebook generation and key poses extraction.

The second step concerns the generation of the codebook, which contains the key poses, i.e. the most informative feature vectors. This process is implemented according to the k-means algorithm, by a separated clustering process for each action of the dataset. This choice is motivated by the fact that different actions may be better represented by a different number of key poses [14]. Considering M classes, that are the M different actions of the dataset, it is necessary to define a vector $[K_1, K_2, \ldots, K_M]$ containing the number of key poses for each class. The clustering process is sketched in Fig. 2, where, for example, all the training instances of the first class $[\mathbf{F}_1, \mathbf{F}_2, \ldots, \mathbf{F}_{t_1}]$ are clustered in K_1 key poses, represented by the cluster centers $[\mathbf{C}_1, \mathbf{C}_2, \ldots, \mathbf{C}_{K_1}]$. The codebook is obtained by merging all the key poses obtained for each class. Each feature vector in an action is finally substituted with the corresponding key pose, by considering the closest one in terms of Euclidean distance. At the end of this step, an action, previously represented by a sequence of feature vectors $\mathbf{F} = [\mathbf{f}_1, \mathbf{f}_2, \ldots, \mathbf{f}_{n_1}]$, is encoded by a sequence of key poses $\mathbf{S} = [k_1, k_2, \ldots, k_{n_1}]$. Obviously, the codebook is generated during the training phase and exploited during testing, where unseen feature vectors are associated to learned key poses.

The third step regards the creation of the histograms of key poses obtained at each level of a temporal pyramid. The temporal pyramid is an effective representation to describe the temporal structure of a sequence representing an action. A sequence of key poses $\mathbf{S} = [k_1, k_2, \ldots, k_{n_1}]$ is split into 2^{l-1} segments, being l the level in the pyramid. For each segment, a histogram is obtained by counting the number of appearances of each key pose within the segment, and normalizing it to the segment length. The distribution of the key poses within the sequence is well represented by the temporal pyramid. Each segment is split into two parts, moving from the top to the bottom of the pyramid allows to have different descriptions of the same sequence, from the most general to the most detailed one. The final representation of the sequence is constituted by the histograms at each level of the pyramid. Considering a temporal pyramid of 3 levels, the whole sequence is represented by 7 histograms, denoted by the vector $\mathbf{H}$ in Fig. 1, containing the normalized number of occurrences for the 7 segments.

The last step aims to associate each set of histograms $\mathbf{H}$, which represents an action, to the corresponding class label, and it is based on a SVM. SVMs have been originally defined as binary classifiers, and the most common approach to have a multi-class SVM is to combine many binary SVMs, with two options: "one-versus-all" and "one-versus-one". Considering an M-classes classification task, the former considers the definition of M binary SVMs, each of which is trained to distinguish between one class and the rest. The winner class is the one with highest probability. The "one-versus-one" method considers a number of $M(M-1)/2$ binary classifiers, each of which has to deal with two classes. The classification is done through a voting strategy, where all the classifiers select one class and the one with more votes is the output class. The "one-versus-one" method implemented in LIBSVM [19] is the one used in this work.

3   Optimization

The algorithm detailed in the previous section requires several parameters in order to be executed. These parameters can be heuristically chosen, but the use of an optimization algorithm may lead to better results. In HAR, evolutionary computation has been successfully used for feature selection and parameters optimization [14,17]. The idea is to optimize three parameters of the HAR algorithm: the *features*, to select the optimal set of joints, the number of *clusters* to be used for each class in the bag of key poses model, and the set of training *instances*.

Considering the evolutionary optimization, the individual is constituted by three parts, each of them related to a different parameter. A detailed definition of the individual's structure can be found in [20], where the authors applied the evolutionary algorithm to have an evolving bag of key poses model. In this work, the same structure of the individual is exploited, where the *features* item is represented by a binary vector of length P, the *clusters* item is constituted by M integer values (one for each class), and the *instances* sub-individual is made up of I elements, each of them corresponding to a specific training sequence. Since the individual consists of three different parts, a 1-point crossover operator is applied to each part. A standard crossover is applied to *instances* and *clusters* vectors while a specific one, which is aware of the skeleton structure, is adopted for the *features* part. The mutation operator is also applied independently on the three parts of the individual with three probabilities mut_I (*instances* vector), mut_M (*clusters* vector) and mut_P (*features* vector). For the binary parts of the individual, each gene can change its value according to a mutation probability. Considering the *clusters* vector, the mutation is performed by considering a random value within an interval. The fitness value is represented by the accuracy of the HAR algorithm, and it is exploited to rank the individuals of the population.

In the cooperative coevolutionary algorithm, three different populations are defined: the *instances* population, the *clusters* population and the *features* one [17]. Each individual of the population has the same structure of the corresponding sub-individual considered in the evolutionary optimization, and the same choices about crossover and mutation operators can be adopted. In order to obtain a fitness value for a new individual of one population (i_1), it is necessary to consider also individuals from the two other populations (i_2 and i_3), and their selection is based on ranking. The obtained fitness value is updated for the individual i_1, but it is also updated for i_2 and i_3 if it improves their actual fitness value. Some techniques have been also adopted to give different priorities in the selection of individuals with the same fitness value. In *features* and *instances* populations, individuals with a lower number of selected values are preferred, while in the *clusters* population the individual with less accumulated sum is favored.

4   Experimental Results

The performance of the algorithm has been evaluated on the MSR Action3D dataset [7], which is one of the most used datasets for action recognition. It is constituted by 20 activities performed by 10 actors, 2 or 3 times. In total, 567 sequences of depth (320×240) and skeleton frames are collected using a structured-light depth camera at 15 fps. Considering the skeleton frames, there are 557 sequences effectively available because 10 instances are featured by missing skeletons or they are affected by too many errors. The following activities are included in the dataset: *high arm wave, horizontal arm wave, hammer, hand catch, forward punch, high throw, draw x, draw tick, draw circle, hand clap, two hand wave, side boxing, bend, forward kick, side kick, jogging, tennis swing, tennis serve, golf swing, pickup and throw.* Due to its complexity, the dataset is usually evaluated considering three different subsets, namely AS1, AS2, and AS3 [7].

Padilla-López et al. [21] reviewed the papers based on the MSR Action3D dataset for action recognition and found that the most used evaluation scheme is the cross-subject test defined by Li et al. [7], which considers actors 1-3-5-7-9 for training, and actors 2-4-6-8-10 for testing. This evaluation procedure has also been applied in this work.

Table 1. Results obtained considering Random selection, Evolutionary and Coevolutionary optimizations.

	AS1	AS2	AS3
Random selection			
Acc	95.24	86.61	95.5
clust.	[17 17 15 25 8 22 12 22]	[4 8 10 22 18 19 16 5]	[71 66 48 56 66 61 76 52]
Evolutionary optimization			
Acc	95.24	90.18	100
clust.	[10 26 12 10 17 22 10 10]	[7 13 10 5 9 16 23 17]	[68 69 60 62 55 48 75 60]
feat.	[11100001011110001000]	[11100111110110011111]	[10100101110010100011]
Coevolutionary optimization			
Acc	95.24	91.96	98.2
clust.	[15 7 9 12 12 13 5 10]	[10 10 10 5 13 4 10 16]	[51 15 16 34 29 56 55 43]
feat.	[10101001100010001100]	[00001001101110011110]	[11111001011110100011]
inst.	178/219	202/228	176/222

The selection of parameters for Radial Basis Function (RBF) kernel of SVM has been performed considering grid search and 5-fold cross-validation on training data, assuming the following intervals: $C = [2^{-5}, 2^{-3}, \ldots 2^{15}]$ and $\gamma = [2^{-15}, 2^{-13}, \ldots 2^{3}]$. The selection of parameters for the HAR algorithm has been performed using three different methods, all of them considering three levels of the temporal pyramid, with the following settings:

- *Random selection*: all the training instances and the features are considered, the clusters required by the bag of key poses model are selected randomly in the interval [4, 26] for the subsets AS1 and AS2, while the interval [44, 76] has been considered for AS3;
- *Evolutionary optimization*: all the training instances are considered, and the evolutionary algorithm is applied to select the features and the clusters, considering the same selection interval as the *Random* method. The population is constituted by 10 individuals, and the mutation probabilities have been randomly selected within the intervals [0, 0.15] for mut_P and [0, 0.25] for mut_C. The selection intervals for the clusters vector are the same as the *Random selection*, and the stop condition is reached after 100 generation without changing the best fitness value.

– *Coevolutionary optimization*: the optimization is applied to select instances, features and clusters, the mutation probability of instances vector mut_I is selected within the interval $[0, 0.025]$, and the clusters are randomly selected considering the interval $[4, 16]$ for AS1 and AS2, and $[4, 64]$ for AS3;

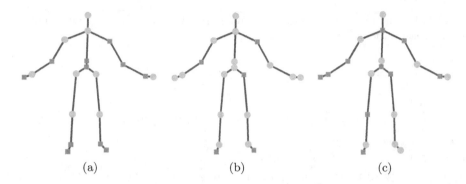

(a)   (b)   (c)

Fig. 3. Subsets of joints selected by the evolutionary algorithm for AS1 (a), AS2 (b) and AS3 (c). The selected joints are depicted as green circles, while the discarded ones are represented by red squares. (Color figure online)

Table 1 shows the results obtained with the evolutionary and coevolutionary algorithms as optimization methods. Considering the optimization with the evolutionary algorithm, the optimized parameters are the number of clusters per class, and the set of skeleton joints that have to be selected. The performance obtained confirms that AS3 is the easiest subset to be recognized, and the proposed method can reach 100 % score even if it requires a large number of key poses, which can be even 75 for the *golf swing* action. On the other hand, the set of selected features is rather limited, because only 10 joints out of 20 are required. AS2 is the most challenging subset, the best recognition accuracy is 90.18 %, it requires a set of 15 joints and a reduced number of clusters, which is 23 at most. The algorithm requires only 9 joints and a restricted number of clusters also for the AS1 subset, where the recognition accuracy is 95.24 %. Considering the joint representation in the *feature* vector, the selected subsets of joints by the evolutionary optimization is shown in Fig. 3. The coevolutionary optimization leads to the same average results. Considering AS1, the recognition accuracy is exactly the same, but only a number of 178 training instances are required out of the 219. Better results have been obtained considering AS2, the recognition accuracy of 91.96 % is achieved with only a number of 10 joints and 202 training instances. Regarding AS3, the best accuracy obtained is 98.2 %, and it is a suboptimal result that could be improved with a different stop condition, considering a greater number of iterations.

Table 2 shows the performance obtained by the proposed method, compared to the main HAR algorithms evaluated on the cross-subject test as well.

Table 2. Recognition accuracy (%) obtained by the proposed method, compared with other previously published works evaluated on the cross-subject test.

Method	AS1	AS2	AS3	avg
Li et al. [7]	72.9	71.9	79.2	74.67
Akkaladevi et al. [22]	84	62	80	75.3
Xia et al. [9]	87.98	85.48	63.46	78.97
Ghorbel et al. [23]	83.08	79.46	93.69	85.41
Evangelidis et al. [24]	88.39	86.61	94.59	89.86
Chen et al. [25]	96.2	83.2	92	90.47
Chaaraoui et al. [18]	92.38	86.61	96.4	91.8
Lo Presti et al. [26]	90.29	**95.15**	93.29	92.91
Tao and Vidal [27]	89.81	93.57	97.03	93.5
Du et al. [28]	93.3	94.64	95.5	94.49
Chen et al. [29]	98.1	92	94.6	94.9
This method	95.24	90.18	**100**	95.14
Xu et al. [30]	**99.1**	92.9	96.4	96.1
Shahroudy et al. [31]	–	–	–	**98.2**

The proposed method achieves results comparable to the state-of-the-art according to the accuracy averaged on AS1, AS2 and AS3 subsets. Shahroudy et al. [31], and Xu et al. [30] reach better average results but they exploit also depth data.

5   Conclusion

In this work, a HAR algorithm based on skeleton joints has been proposed. A feature extraction scheme, which is invariant to build and position of the human subject has been exploited, and key poses are extracted from posture feature vectors. An effective representation of the action is obtained considering histograms of key poses at different levels of a temporal pyramid. The parameters optimization based on the evolutionary computation allows to reach results comparable to the state-of-the-art on the challenging MSR Action3D dataset. Future works include the use of a class-aware algorithm to estimate the key poses.

Acknowledgment. This work was supported by a STSM Grant from COST Action IC1303 AAPELE - Architectures, Algorithms and Platforms for Enhanced Living Environments.

References

1. Poppe, R.: A survey on vision-based human action recognition. Image Vis. Comput. **28**(6), 976–990 (2010)
2. Chaaraoui, A.A., Climent-Pérez, P., Flórez-Revuelta, F.: A review on vision techniques applied to human behaviour analysis for ambient-assisted living. Expert Syst. Appl. **39**(12), 10873–10888 (2012)
3. Weinland, D., Ronfard, R., Boyer, E.: A survey of vision-based methods for action representation, segmentation and recognition. Comput. Vis. Image Underst. **115**(2), 224–241 (2011)
4. Gasparrini, S., Cippitelli, E., Spinsante, S., Gambi, E.: A depth-based fall detection system using a kinect $^{\circledR}$ sensor. Sensors **14**(2), 2756–2775 (2014)
5. Shotton, J., Fitzgibbon, A., Cook, M., Sharp, T., Finocchio, M., Moore, R., Kipman, A., Blake, A.: Real-time human pose recognition in parts from a single depth image. In: CVPR. IEEE, June 2011
6. Aggarwal, J., Xia, L.: Human activity recognition from 3D data: a review. Pattern Recogn. Lett. **48**, 70–80 (2014)
7. Li, W., Zhang, Z., Liu, Z.: Action recognition based on a bag of 3D points. In: 2010 IEEE Computer Society Conference on Computer Vision and Pattern Recognition Workshops (CVPRW), pp. 9–14, June 2010
8. Xia, L., Aggarwal, J.K.: Spatio-temporal depth cuboid similarity feature for activity recognition using depth camera. In: 2013 IEEE Conference on Computer Vision and Pattern Recognition (CVPR), pp. 2834–2841, June 2013
9. Xia, L., Chen, C.-C., Aggarwal, J.: View invariant human action recognition using histograms of 3D joints. In: 2012 IEEE Computer Society Conference on Computer Vision and Pattern Recognition Workshops (CVPRW), pp. 20–27 (2012)
10. Luo, J., Wang, W., Qi, H.: Group sparsity and geometry constrained dictionary learning for action recognition from depth maps. In: 2013 IEEE International Conference on Computer Vision, pp. 1809–1816, December 2013
11. Wang, C., Wang, Y., Yuille, A.L.: An approach to pose-based action recognition. In: 2013 IEEE Conference on Computer Vision and Pattern Recognition (CVPR), pp. 915–922, June 2013
12. Eweiwi, A., Cheema, M.S., Bauckhage, C., Gall, J.: Efficient pose-based action recognition. In: Cremers, D., Reid, I., Saito, H., Yang, M.-H. (eds.) ACCV 2014. LNCS, vol. 9007, pp. 428–443. Springer, Heidelberg (2015)
13. Wang, J., Liu, Z., Wu, Y., Yuan, J.: Mining actionlet ensemble for action recognition with depth cameras. In: 2012 IEEE Conference on Computer Vision and Pattern Recognition (CVPR), pp. 1290–1297 (2012)
14. Chaaraoui, A.A., Padilla-López, J.R., Climent-Pérez, P., Flórez-Revuelta, F.: Evolutionary joint selection to improve human action recognition with RGB-D devices. Expert Syst. Appl. **41**(3), 786–794 (2014)
15. Cantú-Paz, E.: Feature subset selection, class separability, and genetic algorithms. In: Deb, K., Tari, Z. (eds.) GECCO 2004. LNCS, vol. 3102, pp. 959–970. Springer, Heidelberg (2004)
16. Wiegand, R.P.: An analysis of cooperative coevolutionary algorithms. Ph.D. dissertation, Fairfax, VA, USA, aAI3108645 (2004)
17. Chaaraoui, A.A., Flórez-Revuelta, F.: Optimizing human action recognition based on a cooperative coevolutionary algorithm. Eng. Appl. Artif. Intell. **31**, 116–125 (2014)

18. Chaaraoui, A.A., Padilla-López, J.R., Flórez-Revuelta, F.: Fusion of skeletal and silhouette-based features for human action recognition with RGB-D devices. In: 2013 IEEE International Conference on Computer Vision Workshops (ICCVW), pp. 91–97, December 2013

19. Chang, C.-C., Lin, C.-J.: LIBSVM: a library for support vector machines. ACM Trans. Intell. Syst. Technol. **2**, 27:1–27:27 (2011)

20. Chaaraoui, A.A., Flórez-Revuelta, F.: Adaptive human action recognition with an evolving bag of key poses. IEEE Trans. Auton. Ment. Dev. **6**(2), 139–152 (2014)

21. Padilla-López, J.R., Chaaraoui, A.A., Flórez-Revuelta, F.: A discussion on the validation tests employed to compare human action recognition methods using the MSR Action3D dataset (2014). CoRR, abs/1407.7390

22. Akkaladevi, S.C., Heindl, C.: Action recognition for human robot interaction in industrial applications. In: 2015 IEEE International Conference on Computer Graphics, Vision and Information Security (CGVIS), pp. 94–99, November 2015

23. Ghorbel, E., Boutteau, R., Boonaert, J., Savatier, X., Lecoeuche, S.: 3D real-time human action recognition using a spline interpolation approach. In: 2015 International Conference on Image Processing Theory, Tools and Applications (IPTA), pp. 61–66, November 2015

24. Evangelidis, G., Singh, G., Horaud, R.: Skeletal quads: human action recognition using joint quadruples. In: 2014 22nd International Conference on Pattern Recognition (ICPR), pp. 4513–4518, August 2014

25. Chen, C., Liu, K., Kehtarnavaz, N.: Real-time human action recognition based on depth motion maps. J. Real-Time Image Process. **12**, 1–9 (2013)

26. Presti, L.L., Cascia, M.L., Sclaroff, S., Camps, O.: Hankelet-based dynamical systems modeling for 3D action recognition. Image Vis. Comput. **44**, 29–43 (2015)

27. Tao, L., Vidal, R.: Moving poselets: a discriminative and interpretable skeletal motion representation for action recognition. In: 2015 IEEE International Conference on Computer Vision Workshop (ICCVW), pp. 303–311, December 2015

28. Du, Y., Wang, W., Wang, L.: Hierarchical recurrent neural network for skeleton based action recognition. In: 2015 IEEE Conference on Computer Vision and Pattern Recognition (CVPR), pp. 1110–1118, June 2015

29. Chen, C., Jafari, R., Kehtarnavaz, N.: Action recognition from depth sequences using depth motion maps-based local binary patterns. In: Proceedings of the IEEE Winter Conference on Applications of Computer Vision (WACV), Waikoloa Beach, HI, pp. 1092–1099, January 2015

30. Xu, H., Chen, E., Liang, C., Qi, L., Guan, L.: Spatio-temporal pyramid model based on depth maps for action recognition. In: 2015 IEEE 17th International Workshop on Multimedia Signal Processing (MMSP), pp. 1–6, October 2015

31. Shahroudy, A., Ng, T.T., Yang, Q., Wang, G.: Multimodal multipart learning for action recognition in depth videos. IEEE Trans. Pattern Anal. Mach. Intell. **PP**(99), 1 (2015)

Multi-layer Dictionary Learning for Image Classification

Stefen Chan Wai Tim[✉], Michele Rombaut, and Denis Pellerin

GIPSA-Lab, University of Grenoble Alpes, 38000 Grenoble, France
Stefen.Chan-Wai-Tim@gipsa-lab.grenoble-inp.fr

Abstract. This paper presents a multi-layer dictionary learning method for classification tasks. The goal of the proposed multi-layer framework is to use the supervised dictionary learning approach locally on raw images in order to learn local features. This method starts by building a sparse representation at the patch-level and relies on a hierarchy of learned dictionaries to output a global sparse representation for the whole image. It relies on a succession of sparse coding and pooling steps in order to find an efficient representation of the data for classification. This method has been tested on a classification task with good results.

1 Introduction

Sparse coding is the approximation of an input signal by a linear combination of a few number of dictionary elements. Dictionary learning and sparse representations have received a lot of focus in the recent years because they have led to state-of-the-art results in many applications, in particular in image processing. One reason for its success is that it can efficiently learn the underlying patterns in the data, leading to good performances for example in denoising [6,12] or inpainting [1]. The sparse codes obtained can also be seen as a new representation of the input or as features in classification tasks [2,3,11,15,19]. In such cases, the dictionary is often learned in an unsupervised way. Then, the sparse codes obtained can either be used directly for classification [14], or as features fed to a classifier [3] (i.e. SVM).

Recent researches have emphasized the advantages of learning **discriminative** sparse models [2,11,20] instead of purely **reconstructive** ones. It is usually done by learning conjointly the sparse representation and the classifier. In practice, each input image is matched with a label and the dictionary is learned in a supervised setup.

Generally, in image processing applications, dictionary learning and sparse coding are computed on a small portion of an image (i.e. image patches) because learning a dictionary directly on high resolution images is computationally intensive. There is no particular problem doing so in denoising, however, in the case of classification, a mean to fuse efficiently the representation of the patches into an image-level descriptor is needed (i.e. pooling [20] or Bag of words [18]).

In this paper, we propose to learn discriminative dictionaries for classification (similarly as in [20]) while working at a patch-level in a supervised framework by

J. Blanc-Talon et al. (Eds.): ACIVS 2016, LNCS 10016, pp. 522–533, 2016.
DOI: 10.1007/978-3-319-48680-2_46

using an architecture which combines many layers of sparse coding and pooling in order to reduce the dimension of the problem.

Method Framework. In the proposed multi-layer architecture, the sparse codes obtained by encoding signals on a dictionary are used as inputs to a subsequent coding layer. Each additional layer of dictionary encoding changes the representation by projecting the features into a new space. The prospective objective is to increase the discriminability of the features by building a hierarchy of dictionaries.

In Sect. 2, we recall the dictionary learning framework going from the unsupervised setup to the supervised dictionary learning setup. In Sect. 3, we introduce our multi-layer dictionary learning setup. In Sect. 4, we present the experiments and their results.

2   Dictionary Learning

In this section, we recall various formulations of the dictionary learning problem, starting with an unsupervised method more suited to reconstruction and followed by the supervised method tailored around a specific task (here, classification).

2.1   Unsupervised Dictionary Learning

Dictionary learning has been widely used in reconstruction tasks. In its classical formulation, the goal is to learn a set of atoms directly from data. Let's consider a set of n signals $\mathbf{Y} = [\mathbf{y}_1, ..\mathbf{y}_n]$. A dictionary $\mathbf{D}$ can be learned by solving:

$$\min_{\mathbf{D}, \mathbf{x}_k} \quad \sum_{k=1}^{n} \|\mathbf{y}_k - \mathbf{D}\mathbf{x}_k\|_2^2 + \lambda \|\mathbf{x}_k\|_1 \tag{1}$$

with $\mathbf{D} = (d_{ij})_{i \in [1,m], j \in [1,K]}$ being a dictionary, K the number of dictionary atoms $\mathbf{d}_j$, m the dimension of $\mathbf{y}_k$, and $\mathbf{x}_k$ a sparse vector containing the coefficients to reconstruct $\mathbf{y}_k$. $\|\cdot\|_2$ and $\|\cdot\|_1$ denote ℓ_2-norm and ℓ_1-norm respectively. Once a sparse code $\mathbf{x}_k$ is obtained, the original signal can be approximated by computing $\hat{\mathbf{y}}_k \approx \mathbf{D}\mathbf{x}_k$.

This problem has been widely studied and many approaches exist in order to get both dictionary $\mathbf{D}$ and coefficients $\mathbf{x}_k$ [1,13,17].

In this formulation, the reconstruction error is minimized and the sparsity can be controlled with the value of the parameter λ (a higher λ increases sparsity). Using such unsupervised approach can yield good results in reconstruction problem and even in classification tasks [15,19], because it can often find the underlying patterns in the data. However, it has been shown that better results could be obtained by tuning the dictionaries for a specific task [2,11].

2.2 Supervised Dictionary Learning

Supervised dictionary learning methods began to be investigated [11,20] in order to take advantage of parsimony in classification tasks. Encoding a datum using a dictionary can be seen as a projection into another coordinate system. The objective is to obtain projected features that are discriminative in the new space.

Let's assume we know a set of pairs $(\mathbf{y}_k, l_k)$ where $\mathbf{y}_k$, $k \in [1,n]$ is a set of signals (i.e. images represented as column vectors) and l_k, $k \in [1,n]$ is the corresponding label for $\mathbf{y}_k$. We define $\mathcal{L}$, a differentiable classification loss function and $\mathbf{W}$, its set of parameters.

The supervised dictionary learning problem can be written as follows:

$$\hat{\mathbf{x}}_k = \underset{\mathbf{x}}{\text{argmin}} \quad \|\mathbf{y}_k - \mathbf{D}\mathbf{x}\|_2^2 + \lambda\|\mathbf{x}\|_1 \tag{2}$$

$$\underset{\mathbf{W},\mathbf{D}}{\min} \quad \sum_{k=1}^{n} \mathcal{L}(l_k, \hat{\mathbf{x}}_k, \mathbf{W}) \tag{3}$$

The objective here, is to minimize the suitable cost function $\mathcal{L}$ with respect to its parameters $\mathbf{W}$ and a dictionary $\mathbf{D}$ (Fig. 1) using gradient descent for example. The main difference between this formulation and the previous one (Eq. 1) is that the goal now is to minimize the classification loss instead of a reconstruction error term. To minimize the cost function $\mathcal{L}$ with respect to the parameters $\mathbf{D}$ and $\mathbf{W}$, it is possible to use a method similar to the backpropagation algorithm [10] used in neural networks.

Computing the gradient of $\mathcal{L}$ with respect to the parameters $\mathbf{W}$ is usually simple. The main difficulty when solving (Eq. 3) is the minimization of the cost function $\mathcal{L}$ with respect to dictionary $\mathbf{D}$ because it does not appear explicitly and involves another optimization problem (solving for $\hat{\mathbf{x}}_k$, (Eq. 2)). To overcome this problem, a way to compute the gradient of the cost function $\mathcal{L}(l_k, \hat{\mathbf{x}}_k, \mathbf{W})$ with respect to the dictionary $\mathbf{D}$ is needed. This problem has been tackled in [2,11].

In this paper, we follow the ideas of [11] which show the differentiability of $\mathcal{L}$ and give the steps to compute its gradient with respect to the parameters $\mathbf{W}$ and the dictionary $\mathbf{D}$. According to the paper, the desired gradient can be computed as follows:

$$\nabla_{\mathbf{D}}\mathcal{L}(l_k, \hat{\mathbf{x}}_k, \mathbf{W}) = \mathbf{D}\beta\hat{\mathbf{x}}_k^{\top} + (\mathbf{y} - \mathbf{D}\hat{\mathbf{x}}_k)\beta^{\top} \tag{4}$$

We define $\Lambda = \{i | x_i \neq 0\}$), the set of non-zero coefficients of the considered code $\mathbf{x}_k$.

Let's consider a vector $\beta \in \mathcal{R}^K$. β_Λ which is the vector β restricted to the indices in Λ is defined as follows:

$$\beta_\Lambda = (\mathbf{D}_\Lambda^{\top}\mathbf{D}_\Lambda)^{-1}\nabla_{\hat{\mathbf{x}}_{k\Lambda}}\mathcal{L}(l_k, \hat{\mathbf{x}}_k, \mathbf{W}) \tag{5}$$

where $\hat{\mathbf{x}}_{k\Lambda}$ corresponds to $\hat{\mathbf{x}}_k$ restricted to its non-zero coefficients and $\beta_j = 0$, if $j \notin \Lambda$.

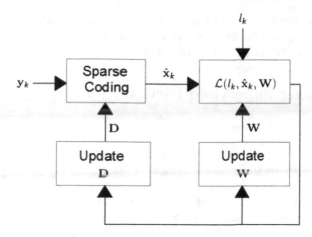

Fig. 1. A signal $\mathbf{y}_k$ associated to a label l_k is encoded by a dictionary $\mathbf{D}$, the resulting code $\hat{\mathbf{x}}_k$ is used as an input to a cost function with parameters $\mathbf{W}$. The cost $\mathcal{L}(l_k, \hat{\mathbf{x}}_k, \mathbf{W})$ is computed. Then, the dictionary $\mathbf{D}$ and the parameters $\mathbf{W}$ are updated to fit the classification problem.

2.3   Patch Decomposition and Pooling

Dictionary learning methods have been used for reconstructing or classifying either full image or image patches. It means that in practice, a signal $\mathbf{y}_k$ can be either an image (Sect. 2.2) or a patch reshaped as a column vector containing the pixel values (Sect. 3.2).

A supervised dictionary learning approach can successfully learn patterns for a classification task. However, in practice, some limitations can be observed: in particular, if we take the example of image classification, these methods are the most effective when the input images are relatively small and the object of interest homogeneously localized. Otherwise, the dictionary used would need a huge number of atoms in order to obtain an efficient sparse decomposition. Moreover, classifying a set of patches extracted from an image instead of the image itself is different, from the dictionary methods point of view. Indeed, when dealing with patches, a method to fuse the information of the set of patches is needed.

This particular problem has been studied by Yang et al. [20]. In the paper, the authors proposed to perform a single sparse coding step at patch level (with a patch size smaller than the input image) followed by numerous pooling steps in order to efficiently reduce the dimensions and obtain a multi-scale representation.

To be able to deal with large images, we recall the pooling function: the pooling operation is used to insert robustness and translation invariance to the features and are an effective way of reducing the dimensions. It is a mean of aggregating spatial local features in an image. Let's consider the classification of an image I. First, it can be decomposed into local overlapping patches $\mathbf{y}_k$ which are encoded on dictionary by computing the coefficients $\hat{\mathbf{x}}_k$. These patches can be spatially localized on a grid which gives the relative position of all patches. Then the codes $\hat{\mathbf{x}}_k$ obtained can be, for example, averaged over a small group of patches reducing the total number of patches.

3   Multi-layer Supervised Dictionary Learning

3.1   Multi-layer Framework

Intuitively, sparse coding can extract important characteristics for reconstruction in unsupervised frameworks and for classification in supervised methods.

The idea of the contribution is to reiterate the sparse coding layer in order to increase the discriminability of the features. The method is inspired by the convolutional networks [16]: the convolution by a filter is replaced by a sparse coding step.

The other goal of the proposed method is to control the dimension of the input patches by reducing the sparse coding of a large image, computationally intensive, to the sparse coding of small patches which can be processed more efficiently.

Encoding a vector on a dictionary is similar to projecting into a new space. The projection is non-linear and the resulting vector is sparse. The vector is then used as a new input for the following layer. So, adding another dictionary encoding step is akin to doing another projection in a new coordinate system.

Each dictionary is learned in a supervised manner. The process can be repeated many times, with as much dictionaries as the number of layers in the architecture.

The proposed multi-layer can be described as follows (Fig. 2):

1. An input image is decomposed into a set of overlapping patches ordered to retain their spatial localization.
2. Each patch $\mathbf{y}_k$ is encoded on a first dictionary $\mathbf{D}^{(1)}$. Since the spatial localization of the patches has been retained, the set of encoded sparse codes $\hat{\mathbf{x}}_k$ can be represented as a 3D volume $\mathbf{X}$ with a depth equal to the number of atoms in dictionary $\mathbf{D}^{(1)}$.
3. The resulting 3D volume is treated as a 3D image input for the next layer. (1) and (2) can be repeated for the chosen number of layers.

To complement (3), for example, if we consider the q-th layer, we can write: $\mathbf{Y}^{(q)} = \hat{\mathbf{X}}^{(q-1)}$, meaning that the stacked codes at layer $q-1$ are used as an input image $\mathbf{Y}^{(q)}$ in layer q (see Fig. 2). The image $\mathbf{Y}^{(q)}$ is then decomposed into 3D patches $\hat{\mathbf{y}}_k^{(q)}$ and $\hat{\mathbf{x}}_k^{(q)}$ are obtained by encoding $\mathbf{y}_k^{(q)}$ with $\mathbf{D}^{(q)}$. More generally, we can replace $\mathbf{Y}^{(q)} = \hat{\mathbf{X}}^{(q-1)}$ by $\mathbf{y}_k^{(q)} = f(\hat{\mathbf{X}}^{(q-1)})$ where f can denote a transformation on the codes coupled with the patch decomposition.

In order to optimize the multi-layer architecture for classification, it is needed to find the optimal dictionaries at each layer.

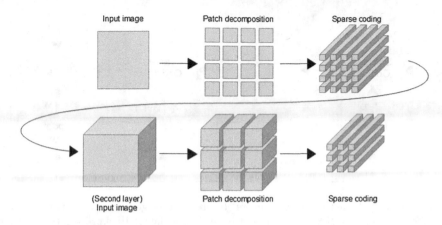

Fig. 2. Example of an architecture with 2 layers. An input image in presented to the first layer. The image is decomposed into patches $\mathbf{y}_k^{(1)}$ which are encoded by dictionnary $\mathbf{D}^{(1)}$. The codes $\mathbf{x}_k^{(1)}$ are processed and restructured into a 3D volume $\mathbf{X}^{(1)}$ and then decomposed again into 3D patches $\mathbf{y}_k^{(2)}$ in the second layer. These patches are encoded using the dictionary $\mathbf{D}^{(2)}$.

3.2   Formulation

Let's consider a set of input features $\mathbf{Y} = \{\mathbf{y}_1^{(1)}, \cdots, \mathbf{y}_p^{(1)}\}$ associated to a label l. This set is obtained by decomposing an input image into p patches. In the section, to simplify the notations, each subscript k used for denoting the index of patches or codes is tied to a specific layer q (it can be read as k_q). The upper index (q) denotes the q-th layer. Let's consider the proposed algorithm with Q layers, its formulation is as follows:

For $q \in [1, Q-1]$ (same as in (Eq. 2))

$$\hat{\mathbf{x}}_k^{(q)} = \underset{\mathbf{x}}{\text{argmin}} \qquad \|\mathbf{y}_k^{(q)} - \mathbf{D}^{(q)}\mathbf{x}\|_2^2 + \lambda_q \|\mathbf{x}\|_1 \tag{6}$$

$\mathbf{y}_k^{(q+1)}$ is obtained from the output of the previous layer $\hat{\mathbf{x}}_k^{(q)}$ by applying a transformation f (see [20] for an example with f being the max-pooling function) followed by a new patch decomposition step. In this paper, we propose to use the average-pooling function.

To optimize the classification cost function with respect to the dictionaries at each layer, we use the backpropagation algorithm. Therefore, we need to compute the gradients with respect to the various dictionaries $\mathbf{D}^{(1)}, \cdots, \mathbf{D}^{(Q)}$.

By extending the formulation given in (Eq. 3), we obtain:

$$\underset{\mathbf{W}, \mathbf{D}^{(1)}, \cdots, \mathbf{D}^{(Q)}}{\min} \qquad \sum_{k=1}^{n} \mathcal{L}(l_k, \hat{\mathbf{x}}_k^{(Q)}, \mathbf{W}) \tag{7}$$

We only use the output $\hat{\mathbf{x}}_k^{(Q)}$ of the last layer as features for the classification (Fig. 3) and the cost function is minimized over the entire training set of n images.

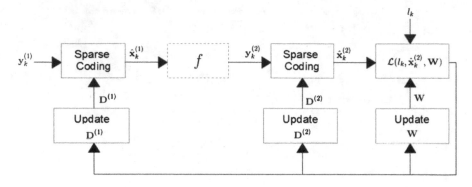

Fig. 3. Proposed structure with 2 layers. Input vectors go through a sparse coding step. We have $\mathbf{y}_k^{(2)} = f(\hat{\mathbf{X}}^{(1)})$ as input to the second layer. Backpropagation is then used to update both dictionaries simultaneously.

3.3 Computation of the Gradients

To use the backpropagation algorithm (i.e. computing each gradient using the chain rule, the gradient is computed the same way as presented in Sect. 2.2 by replacing $\hat{\mathbf{x}}_k$ by $\hat{\mathbf{x}}_k^{(q)}$ and $\mathbf{y}_k$ by $\mathbf{y}_k^{(q)}$.

For a pair $(\mathbf{Y}, l)$, the gradient of $\mathcal{L}$ with respect to dictionary $\mathbf{D}^{(Q)}$ (the dictionary of the last layer) is computed using Eqs. (4) and (6). If we introduce the notation using the layer number, the equation for the last layer becomes:

$$\nabla_{\mathbf{D}^{(Q)}} \mathcal{L}(l_k, \hat{\mathbf{x}}_k^{(Q)}, \mathbf{W}) = \mathbf{D}^{(Q)} \beta \hat{\mathbf{x}}_k^{(Q)\top} + (\mathbf{y}_k^{(Q)} - \mathbf{D}^{(Q)} \hat{\mathbf{x}}_k^{(Q)}) \beta^\top \tag{8}$$

with β defined as:

for the indexes contained in the set Λ,

$$\beta_\Lambda = (\mathbf{D}_\Lambda^{(Q)\top} \mathbf{D}_\Lambda^{(Q)})^{-1} \nabla_{\hat{\mathbf{x}}_{k\Lambda}^{(Q)}} \mathcal{L}(l_k, \hat{\mathbf{x}}_k^{(Q)}, \mathbf{W}) \tag{9}$$

and $\beta_j = 0$, if $j \notin \Lambda$.

To compute the gradient of the layer q, the computations for the dictionary become:

$$\nabla_{\mathbf{D}^{(q)}} \mathcal{L}(l_k, \hat{\mathbf{x}}_k^{(Q)}, \mathbf{W}) = \mathbf{D}^{(q)} \beta \hat{\mathbf{x}}_k^{(q)\top} + (\mathbf{y}_k^{(q)} - \mathbf{D}^{(q)} \hat{\mathbf{x}}_k^{(q)}) \beta^\top \tag{10}$$

$$\beta_\Lambda = (\mathbf{D}_\Lambda^{(q)\top} \mathbf{D}_\Lambda^{(q)})^{-1} \nabla_{\hat{\mathbf{x}}_{k\Lambda}^{(q)}} \mathcal{L}(l_k, \hat{\mathbf{x}}_k^{(Q)}, \mathbf{W}) \tag{11}$$

We underline that only the last layer Q intervenes in the classification step that is why the term is $\mathcal{L}(l_k, \hat{\mathbf{x}}_k^{(Q)}, \mathbf{W})$ and not $\mathcal{L}(l_k, \hat{\mathbf{x}}_k^{(q)}, \mathbf{W})$: by choice, the output of the last layer is a single code vector. To compute the gradient of the cost function $\mathcal{L}(l_k, \hat{\mathbf{x}}_k^{(Q)}, \mathbf{W})$ with respect to the dictionary $\mathbf{D}^{(q)}$ of the q-th layer using backpropagation, we need to compute $\nabla_{\hat{\mathbf{x}}_{k\Lambda}^{(q)}} \mathcal{L}(l_k, \hat{\mathbf{x}}_k^{(Q)}, \mathbf{W})$. The computation of this gradient can be decomposed as follows:

$$\frac{\partial \mathcal{L}}{\partial \hat{\mathbf{x}}^{(q)}} = \frac{\partial \mathcal{L}}{\partial \hat{\mathbf{x}}^{(q+1)}} \frac{\partial \hat{\mathbf{x}}^{(q+1)}}{\partial \mathbf{y}^{(q+1)}} \frac{\partial \mathbf{y}^{(q+1)}}{\partial \hat{\mathbf{x}}^{(q)}} \tag{12}$$

where $\frac{\partial \hat{\mathbf{x}}^{(q)}}{\partial \mathbf{y}^{(q)}}$:

$$\frac{\partial \hat{\mathbf{x}}_\Lambda^{(q)}}{\partial \mathbf{y}^{(q)}} = (\mathbf{D}_\Lambda^{(q)\top} \mathbf{D}_\Lambda^{(q)})^{-1} \mathbf{D}_\Lambda^{(q)} \tag{13}$$

and 0 elsewhere.

We remind that the transformation f between $\hat{\mathbf{x}}^{(q)}$ and $\mathbf{y}^{(q+1)}$ can be the identity, a pooling operation or a more general transformation (see Sect. 3.1) combined with a decomposition into patches, so the backpropagation includes a image "reconstruction" step to reverse the patch decomposition (Fig. 4).

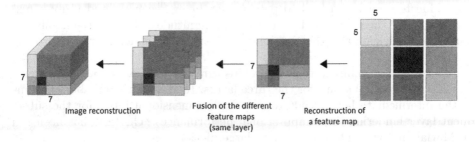

Image reconstruction   Fusion of the different feature maps (same layer)   Reconstruction of a feature map

Fig. 4. Example of the reconstruction step from 5×5 patches to $7 \times 7 \times K$ volume.

4   Experimentations

We tested the proposed algorithm on the MNIST [10] dataset and CIFAR-10 dataset [9]. The first well-known MNIST dataset used for classification regroups a set of handwritten digits divided in 10 classes (i.e. 0–9) and contains 60000 (28×28) pixels images for training and 10000 for testing. These images have been rescaled to (32×32) pixels to be able to fit the CIFAR-10 dataset.

We have chosen to use the cross-entropy function (Eq. 14) for the classification loss as it has proven to give good results in multiclass classification problems. The chosen classifier is a linear classifier coupled with softmax for the output. If we consider a classification problem with C classes, the cross-entropy loss is computed as follows:

$$\mathcal{L}(l_k, \hat{\mathbf{x}}_k^{(Q)}, \mathbf{W}) = - \sum_{i=1}^{C} l_{ik} log(p_{ik}) \tag{14}$$

where p_{ik} is defined by:

$$p_{ik} = \frac{\exp(\hat{\mathbf{x}}_k^{(Q)\top} \mathbf{w}_i)}{\sum_{j=1}^{C} \exp(\hat{\mathbf{x}}_k^{(Q)\top} \mathbf{w}_j)}$$

To demonstrate the proposed method, we choose to use an architecture with $Q = 3$ layers. For the first layer, we decompose the input image into patches of (5 × 5) pixels with a stride of 1 pixels. The second layer use patches of size (5×5). Then, a pooling step is done on a 2×2 region without overlap. We follow last layer with size (5 × 5). After the last layer, only one code remains for the whole image and this code is used as input for the classification.

The optimization method used is the stochastic gradient descent with a batch size of 10. The training set is shuffled randomly and the training samples for each batch are used in order. The learning step is initially fixed at 0.3 and divided by 2 every 3 passes on the full dataset.

For parameter λ (Eq. 1), we choose $\lambda = 0.1$ for all three layers. Empirically, this value leads to good reconstruction while giving very sparse codes. Increasing this value too much can lead to patches not being reconstructed (only zeros) while reducing the value (i.e. by an order of magnitude) increases the number of non-zero coefficients and the computation costs without necessarily improving the performances.

We tested two configurations of architecture: we used $K = 25, 25, 50$ atoms and $K = 50, 50, 100$ atoms for the three layers. Increasing the number of atoms in the intermediate layers leads to very high dimensional input for the subsequent layer hindering the computational performances. The tests has been run on Matlab and we could not test very large dictionaries.

The results in Table 1 are obtained with the classifier directly learned by the algorithm. We used the original training and test sets with no data augmentation. Supervised learning greatly improves the performances for the tested configurations. Moreover, the gain in performances between the two choices of the number of atoms is small even though the number of atoms is doubled. It may be explained by the fact that the images in the MNIST dataset are not really complex so additional atoms are not needed to describe more features.

Table 2 regroups some performances of state of the art methods on the MNIST dataset. The results for the proposed method are obtained with no data augmentation as opposed to [11,20].

Table 1. Performance comparison between supervised and unsupervised learning with a linear classifier on the MNIST dataset.

Methods	Dictionary size K	Error rate
1 layer (unsupervised)	700	3.71 %
3 layers (unsupervised)	25, 25, 50 (5 × 5), (5 × 5), (5 × 5)	4.93 %
3 layers (unsupervised)	25, 25, 50 (5 × 5), (5 × 5), (5 × 5)	2.2 %
3 layers (supervised)	25, 25, 50 (5 × 5), (5 × 5), (5 × 5)	0.46 %
3 layers (supervised)	50, 50, 100 (5 × 5), (5 × 5), (5 × 5)	0.41 %

We also tested our method on the CIFAR-10 dataset [9] which is constructed with 60000 real images (50000 images for learning and 10000 images for testing) of size (32 × 32) pixels, separated into 10 classes. This dataset is more challenging than the MNIST dataset because the variance of view points, poses and

Table 2. Performance comparison on the MNIST dataset.

Methods	Error rate
Yang et al. [20]	0.84 %
Mairal et al. [11]	0.54 %
Proposed method	0.41 %

localizations of the object of interest is much higher. In particular, the dictionary learning methods which process the whole image at once usually have some difficulties to learn the features efficiently. For this test, we used the same structure as the one used for the MNIST dataset (3 layers) with the same parameters (Table 3).

Table 3. Performance comparison between supervised and unsupervised learning with a linear classifier on the CIFAR-10 dataset.

Methods	Dictionary size K	Accuracy
3 layers (unsupervised)	25, 25, 50 (5×5), (5×5), (5×5)	34.98 %
3 layers (unsupervised)	25, 25, 50 (5×5), (5×5), (5×5)	42.39 %
3 layers (supervised)	25, 25, 50 (5×5), (5×5), (5×5)	78.86 %
3 layers (supervised)	50, 50, 100 (5×5), (5×5), (5×5)	83.03 %

Only a few works present classification results on the CIFAR-10 dataset using a dictionary learning method only. However, other methods exist (i.e. Convolutional neural networks) [8] to deal with this kind of dataset.

Table 4. Performance comparison on the CIFAR-10 dataset.

Methods	Accuracy
Fawzi et al. [7]	53.44 %
Coates et al. [4]	79.6 %
Coates et al. [5]	81.5 %
Proposed method	83.03 %

Table 4 shows some results on the CIFAR-10 dataset without data augmentation. Fawzi et al. [7] use a single layer dictionary learning method for comparison. Coates et al. [4,5] used unsupervised multi-layer sparse coding with large dictionaries (up to 4k atoms). The proposed method performs better using a few number of atoms (undercomplete dictionaries) showing the capability of learning discriminative dictionaries. Better performances may be obtained by increasing the number of atoms in the layers, however at the moment, the MATLAB implementation used is too slow.

During our experiments, we noticed that the number of atoms in the first layer (image layer) is important, for example choosing $K = 15, 25, 50$ (15 instead of 25 in the first layer) could leave to a drop of about 10% in performances. The same can also be said of the number of atoms of the last layer (size of the features) but with a lesser extent.

5   Conclusion

In this paper, we have presented a multi-layer dictionary learning framework. It can potentially handle an image of any size as input and performs the learning of features at the patch level. Its goal is to allow the use of supervised dictionary learning methods on images while evading the computational issues that arise when dealing with large dictionary atoms.

We still have not fully investigated this method and we will continue to work on the proposed structure in order to study the effects of the choices of the different parameters (dictionary size, sparsity, number of layers). For future work, we will confront this method with more complex datasets, containing larger images, to challenge the limit of this approach.

Acknowledgement. This work has been partially supported by the LabEx PERSYVAL-Lab (ANR-11-LABX-0025-01).

References

1. Aharon, M., Elad, M., Bruckstein, A.: K-SVD: an algorithm for designing overcomplete dictionaries for sparse representation. IEEE Trans. Signal Process. **54**, 4311–4322 (2006)
2. Bradley, D.M., Bagnell, J.A.: Differential sparse coding. In: NIPS (2008)
3. Tim, C.W.S., Rombaut, M., Pellerin, D.: Rejection-based classification for action recognition using a spatio-temporal dictionary. In: EUSIPCO (2015)
4. Coates, A., Lee, H., Ng, A.: An analysis of single-layer networks in unsupervised feature learning. In: AISTATS (2011)
5. Coates, A., Ng, A.: The importance of encoding versus training with sparse coding and vector quantization. In: ICML (2011)
6. Elad, M., Aharon, M.: Image denoising via sparse and redundant representations over learned dictionaries. IEEE Trans. Image Process. **15**, 3736–3745 (2006)
7. Fawzi, A., Davies, M., Frossard, P.: Dictionary learning for fast classification based on soft-thresholding. Int. J. Comput. Vis. **114**, 306–321 (2015)
8. Hinton, G.E., Srivastava, N., Krizhevsky, A., Sutskever, I., Salakhutdinov, R.R.: Improving neural networks by preventing co-adaptation of feature detector. https://arxiv.org/pdf/1207.0580.pdf (2012)
9. Krizhevsky, A., Hinton, G.: Learning multiple layers of features from tiny images. Technical report, University of Toronto (2009)
10. LeCun, Y., Bottou, L., Bengio, Y., Haffner, P.: Gradient-based learning applied to document recognition. Proc. IEEE **86**, 2278–2324 (1998)

11. Mairal, J., Bach, F., Ponce, J.: Task-driven dictionary learning. IEEE Trans. Pattern Anal. Mach. Intell. **34**, 791–804 (2012)
12. Mairal, J., Elad, M., Sapiro, G.: Sparse representation for color image restauration. IEEE Trans. Image Process. **17**, 53–69 (2008)
13. Olshausen, B.A., Field, D.J.: Emergence of simple-cell receptive field properties by learning a sparse code for natural images. Nature **381**, 607–609 (1996)
14. Qiu, Q., Jiang, Z., Chellappa, R.: Sparse dictionary-based representation and recognition of action attributes. In: ICCV (2011)
15. Raina, R., Battle, A., Lee, H., packer, B., Ng, A.Y.: Self-taught learning: transfer learning from unlabeled data. In: ICML (2008)
16. Springenberg, J.T., Dosovitskiy, A., Brox, T., Riedmiller, M.: Striving for simplicity: the all convolutional net. In: ICLR (2015)
17. Tibshirani, R.: Regression shrinkage and selection via the lasso. J. R. Stat. Soc. **58**, 267–288 (1996)
18. Wang, H., Ullah, M.M., Klaser, A., Laptev, I., Schmid, C.: Evaluation of local spatio-temporal features for action recognition. British Machine Vision Conference (2009)
19. Wright, J., Yang, A.Y., Ganesh, A., Sastry, S.S., Ma, Y.: Robust face recognition via sparse representation. IEEE Trans. Pattern Anal. Mach. Intell. **31**, 210–227 (2009)
20. Yang, J., Yu, K., Huang, T.: Supervised translation-invariant sparse coding. In: CVPR (2010)

Intelligent Vision System for ASD Diagnosis and Assessment

Marco Leo$^{(\boxtimes)}$, Marco Del Coco, Pierluigi Carcagnì, Pier Luigi Mazzeo, Paolo Spagnolo, and Cosimo Distante

Institute of Applied Sciences and Intelligent Sistems,
National Research Council of Italy, Via Monteroni, 73100 Lecce, Italy
m.leo@isasi.cnr.it
http://www.isasi.cnr.it

Abstract. ASD diagnose and assessment make use of medical protocol validated by the scientific community that is still reluctant to new protocols introducing invasive technologies, as robots or wearable devices, whose influence on the theraphy has not been deeply investigated. This work attempts to undertake the difficult challenge of embedding a technological level into the standardized ASD protocol known as *Autism Diagnostic Observation Schedule* (ADOS-2). An intelligent video system is introduced to compute, in an objective and automatic way, the evaluation scores for some of the tasks involved in the protocol. It make use of a hidden RGB-D device for scene acquisition the data of which feed a cascade of algorithmic steps by which people and objects are detected and temporally tracked and then extracted information is exploited by fitting a spatial and temporal model described by means of an ontology approach. The ontology metadata are finally processed to find a mapping between them and the behavioral tasks described in the protocol.

Keywords: Autism spectrum disorders · ADOS · RGB-D device · People and object tracking · Ontology

1 Introduction

Autism spectrum disorders affect three different areas of a child's life: Social interaction, Communication (both verbal and nonverbal) and Behaviors and interests. Diagnosis and assessment of ASD can be difficult since children with ASD vary considerably in their individual strengths and difficulties. Detailed assessment of communication, neuropsychological functioning, motor and sensory skills, and adaptive functioning has to be carried out and to do that different scheduled methods have been introduced. These methods provide standard contexts to elicit relevant social and communicative behaviours. Healthcare professionals should directly observe and assess the child or young persons social

M. Leo—We would like to thank the NPO 'Amici of Nico' and in particular the founder and President Dr. Maria Antonietta Bove, and the caregivers Dr. Giovanna Di Carlo and Dr. Annachiara Rosato who have guided us in setting up the technological framework as well as to experience it during actual sessions of assessment.

© Springer International Publishing AG 2016
J. Blanc-Talon et al. (Eds.): ACIVS 2016, LNCS 10016, pp. 534–546, 2016.
DOI: 10.1007/978-3-319-48680-2_47

and communication skills and behaviour. ICT applications, already in use to deliver educational and behavioral services to individuals with ASD [9], have been recently also exploited to develop advanced tools that allow an early identification and assessment of the disorder during its evolution. In particular technologies have enabled the introduction of interactive and virtual environments [4,13], serious games [1] and telerehabilitation [12]. The crucial point is that the technological trend in place requires the abandonment of standardized traditional protocols to allow the introduction of new ones built around the available technologies. However, many improvements are still needed to attain significant success in treating individuals with autism using ICT: in particular practical and clinical issues have yet to be addressed [2]. From the practical perspective, the adoption of ICT based protocols requires the medical staff training (which in turn can be successful only if there is a caregivers' strong willingness and conviction), acceptance by parents and an evaluation phase on the individual child to check his inclination towards new diagnostic methods and therapies that use technologies. Besides, many of the existing technologies have limited capabilities in their performance and this limit the success in the therapeutic approach of children with ASD. Clinically, most of the ICT proposals have not been validated outside the context of proof of concept studies [5]. As a consequence more studies should be performed to assess whether ICT architectures and devices are clinically relevant. It's clear that the development of ICT based protocols have to be more and more investigated and this process it is not straightforward since it necessitates a multidisciplinary collaborative effort between engineers, psychologists, neuropsychiatrics and cognitive scientists. A different way to exploit the proliferation of inexpensive technology also for diagnose and assessment of ASD, could be to hold standardized protocols and to embed in them a technological level (that the subject under evaluation does not perceive) which support the care-givers by the mining of objective evaluation scores from the observation of the subject during scheduled sessions. The main advantage of this approach is its peculiarity to work without any intervention in the standardized assessment protocols and in the environment (preserving ecological validity). This makes it very attracting for caregivers but, unfortunately, it requires additional efforts from the technological side since involved algorithms have to deal with unconstrained environments and non-collaborative subjects. Most likely, these are the reasons why there are no work in the literature for this applicative context. To partially fill this gap, in this work a first attempt to undertake this difficult challenge is introduced: in particular the standardized Autism Diagnostic Observation Schedule (ADOS-2) is taken under consideration and a technological framework is introduced to compute, in an objective and automatic way, numerical information that can be used by the therapist in order to assign the scores for some of the involved tasks. In particular the module 1 of the protocol (see Sect. 2 for details) has been explored and the 4 tasks involved in the phase 1 (free play) have been analyzed by the proposed technological framework that makes use of an RGB-D device for scene acquisition. Acquired data then feed a cascade of algorithmic steps by which people and objects are detected and temporally tracked and then extracted information is exploited by fitting a spatial and temporal model described by means of an ontology approach. The ontology metadata are finally processed to find a mapping between them and the behavioral tasks described in the protocol. The validity of the proposed approach was proved during preliminary experiments carried out in the lab and by the exploitation of the framework during two actual ASD assessment sessions. In the rest of the paper Sect. 2 gives a short overview of the ADOS-2 protocol, Sect. 3 describes the technological component of the proposed framework and, finally, Sect. 4 reports experimental outcomes. Section 5 will conclude the paper.

2   Autism Diagnostic Observation Schedule (ADOS-2)

The Autism Diagnostic Observation Schedule (ADOS-2) [10] is one of the few standardized diagnostic and assessment measures that involves scoring direct observations of the childs communication, social interaction, play, and restricted and repetitive behaviours. The ADOS-2 includes five modules, each requiring just 40 to 60 min to administer. The individual being evaluated is given only one module, selected on the basis of his or her expressive language level and chronological age. Each module engages the individual in a series of activities involving interactive stimulus materials. In particular Module 1 (aimed to children 31 months and older who do not consistently use phrase speech on which this paper focuses) includes ten activities (free play, response to name, response to joint attention, bubble play, anticipation of a routine with objects, responsive social smile, anticipation of social routine, functional and symbolic imitation, birthday party, snack) that are appropriate for children who have an expressive language level of less than three years of age. Activities within this module focus on a childs ability to interact playfully with toys and other items appropriate for use with very young children. The technological framework presented in this paper maps into objective numerical data the behavioral observations carried out during the free play activity. In particular behavioral observations focus on the propensity of the child to parental/caregiver involvement, child's way to explore materials (both symbolic and functional), dwell time (time performing the same activity) and interactions that display affection.

3   The Proposed Technological Framework

The proposed framework, schematized in Fig. 1, makes use of an RGB-D acquisition device and a cascade of algorithmic steps by which objective numerical outcomes are extracted and linked to some of the behavioral tasks described in the ADOS-2 protocol.

The algorithmic core consists of three processing modules: the first one perfoInterpreting images by propagating Bayesian beliefs, Yair Weissrms the *Detection, Localization and Tracking of People and Objects* in the scene; the second one combines the extracted spatial information and then, trough an *Ontology*, it maps thcm into different semantic states; the last step processes the temporal

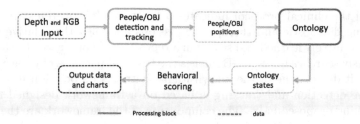

Fig. 1. Pipeline of the framework: RGBD input data are processed in order to track people and objects in the scene and successively work out them through an ontological approach and a behavioral module.

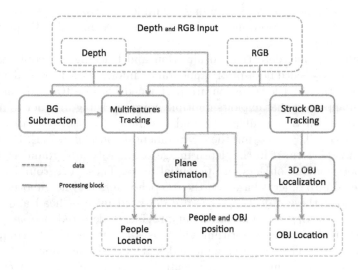

Fig. 2. People and object tracking scheme: the data provided by the RGB-D sensor are exploited by two separate tracking algorithms for people and objects respectively; the 3D positions are finally mapped in a common 2D plane (floor) reference system previously estimated

sequences of semantic states in order to get numerical scores associated to each behavioral tasks (*Behavioral Scoring*).

In the following the aforementioned modules will be detailed.

3.1   Detection, Localization and Tracking of People and Objects

This module is mainly aimed to compute, frame by frame, the positions of both people and toys of interest by means of an algorithmic scheme, illustrated in Fig. 2, exploiting a joint analysis of RGB and depth data. As shown in the scheme, two different approaches have been used for people and toys respectively due to the different logic with which to they relate to the context.

Indeed the clinical protocol indicates a finite number of items (toys) to be used during diagnostic and therapeutic sessions and then the relative patterns can be preventively learned and stored in a repository. In other words, the system continuously searches in the RGB images the textural patterns of expected items and, once it detects one of the known items, it tracks its position in the image plane. The detection and tracking is based on a framework designed for long-term tracking proposed in [8]. The components of the framework are the *Tracker* that estimates the objects motion between consecutive frames, the *Detector* that treats every frame as independent and performs full scanning of the image to localize all appearances that have been observed and learned in the past and the *Learning* that observes performance of tracker and detector and it estimates detectors errors and generates training examples to avoid these errors in the future. The 2D object coordinates are finally mapped into the 3D point cloud coordinate system.

On the other side, detection, localization and tracking of people has to be treated differently since no a-priori appearance information is available. In this case the detection and localization are performed by an advanced background subtraction approach that exploits multiple noise modeling in order to make the background subtraction available beyond the limit of 4, 5 m (constraint of the standard Kinect SDK) relaxing the environmental constraints [11]. Background subtraction is performed in the depth image to identify foreground region that contains both moving objects and potential noise. These foreground pixels are then clustered into objects based on their depth values and neighborhood information. Among these objects, people are detected using a head and shoulder detector and tracking information about previously detected people. Detected persons are tracked by an algorithm which uses a feature pool to compute the matching score [3]. This feature pool includes 2D, 3D displacement distances, 2D sizes, color histogram, histogram of oriented gradient (HOG), color covariance and dominant color At this point, the available positions of objects and people in the scene are expressed into the 3-dimensional reference system of the acquisition device. Since, as will be detailed in the next session, the proposed ontology defines semantic occupancy areas then the positions of objects and people onto the floor plain have to be recovered. To do that the floor plane has to be preventively estimated and this is done by an evolution of the classical RANSAC ("RANdom SAmple Consensus") algorithm named RANSAC-LEL and proposed in [7] Once the plane coordinates are available the positions onto the floor plain of objects and people can be computed by projection. In particular this allows the systems to match (in an unsupervised manner) the generic labels used by the tracker with the semantic entities given by the ontology (child, caregiver and parents). This is done by counting the occurrences of a given label into a specific semantic area.

3.2 Ontology

In computer science, an ontology is a formal naming and definition of the types, properties, and interrelationships of entities of a specific context. In other words, an ontology models a set of rules defining semantic states and events that represent a generic baseline for a subsequent processing.

The proposed ontology is inspired by the structure proposed in [6], a declarative constraint based ontology that defines state/event models based on *prior* knowledge about the context, the scene and the real-world objects involved. A state/event model can be composed of three main key elements:

- Physical objects refer to real-world objects involved in the realization of the event (e.g., person, toys, areas).
- Components refer to sub-events of which the model is composed of.
- Constraints are conditions that the physical objects and/or the components should satisfy.

Going into detail three kinds of physical objects have been considered in this work: person, toy and area. Person is a class of physical object characterized by two main properties: the people role (child, caregiver, parent) and the position (coordinate on the floor coordinate system). Toy represents a class that has properties similar to the previous one. It is characterized by an ID (opportunely mapped on a known repository) and a position on the floor coordinate system. Area represents a specific space zone of the scene that is aimed to a specific purpose characterized in a semantic way (i.e. *play area* is the area where the child is free to play and to move, *parental area* is aimed to host the parents and *caregiver area* is the area where the caregiver use to stay). Constraints are defined in terms of space location of a subject/toy (relation with an area), temporal persistence of a specific state or as the simultaneous occur of two states/events. Given the elements cited above, state and events hierarchy can be defined as:

- Primitive State models a value of property of a physical object constant in a time interval.
- Composite State refers to a composition of two or more primitive states.
- Primitive Event models a change in value of a physical objects property (e.g., posture), and
- Composite Event defines a temporal relationship between two sub-events (components).

Following the above mentioned structure, a specific ontology has been defined. More specifically each state/event (primitive or composite) is made up by the involved physical objects (`PsyOby`), the components representing the state or event (if necessary), of the same hierarchy level or lower, involved in the definition (`Comp`) and the constraints defining the condition that physical objects or components must respect (`Const`). Moreover, in order to simplify the ontology managing, two assumptions have been made: both the caregiver and the parents have to stay in their respective areas. Due to the space restriction, only 2 examples of state/event definition (a primitive state and a composite event) are fully presented; the other ones are listed by their label and description.

$$PS1 : \begin{cases} \text{PsyOby} = \text{CH}, Z_{PY} \\ \text{Const} = \text{CH} \rightarrow \text{pos} \in Z_{PY} \\ \text{Child is in play area} \end{cases}$$

$$CE8_i : \begin{cases} \text{PsyOby} = \text{CH}, \text{CG} \\ \text{Comp} = PS6 \\ \text{Const} = PS6 > 3\,\text{sec} \\ \text{Child shows affect for caregiver} \end{cases} \tag{1}$$

where t is the current frame, CH is the child, CG the caregiver, Z_{PY} the play area and i refers to the i-th toys.

Concerning the **Primitive states** the following cases have been defined:

- $PS1$: Child is in play area
- $PS2$: Child is in parental area
- $PS3$: Child is in caregiver area
- $PS4_i$: Toy i is moving
- $PS5$: Child is close to parents
- $PS6$: Child is close to caregiver

Concerning the **Composite states** the following cases have been defined

- $CS1_i$: Child is playing with object i
- $CS2_i$: Child is interacting with object i and parents
- $CS3_i$: Child is interacting with object i and caregiver

Concerning the **Primitive events** the following cases have been defined

- $PE1_i$: Toy i starts moving

Concerning the **Composite events** the following cases have been defined

- $CE1_i$: Child starts interacting with toy i
- $CE2$: Child starts interacting with parents
- $CE3$: Child starts interacting with caregiver
- $CE4_i$: Child starts interacting with parents with toy i
- $CE5_i$: Child starts interacting with caregiver with toy i
- $CE7$: Child shows affect for parents
- $CE8$: Child shows affect for caregiver

3.3 Behavioral Scoring

Once the ontology states (i.e. active states at each sample time) are available, the information useful to the therapist can be obtained. In this work, the attention has been focused on the *free play* phase of the second module of ADOS 2 evaluation protocol. It considers some aspects, some of which are most oriented to a subjective evaluation, whereas, others, would be widely treated by means of a numerical evaluation. This phase of the protocol tries to understand fundamental child behaviors in some specific scenarios. Some of these have been here accounted, whereas others have been scheduled as future works. More precisely the knowledge of the approach adopted by the child in order to interact with other people when objects (toys) are available is observed. Some points of the protocol section under exam can be summarized in the following questions. Does the child use the object in the room as an interaction instrument? Does the child focus his attention on a single toy or does he move his attention among toys quickly? Does the child expresses love?

As first aspect, the way the child use to interact with parents and caregiver (by means of the toys or just look for affection interactions) is treated. The proposed ontology makes the answer quite easy; two possible situation have been considered:

TI *Time spent interacting by means toys*: the child use the toys available in the room during the communication with parents or caregiver; this time is computed counting the consecutive occurrences of $CS2_i$ and $CS3_i$ ($\forall i$) respectively triggered by the composite events $CE4_i$ and $CE5_i$.

FI *Time spent on free interaction*: the child interact with parents or caregiver overlooking the toys; this time is computed counting the consecutive occurrences of $PS2_i$ and $PS3_i$ ($\forall i$) respectively triggered by the composite events $CE2_i$ and $CE3_i$.

It is important to stress as the use of events (including temporal restriction to the event recognition) as a trigger for counting the consecutive occurrences of a specific state allows to avoid the counting of spurious state occurrences. It is straightforward as the a comparison between the total time under the condition TI and the total time under the condition FI represents a quantitative answer to the protocol question. This first case is sufficient to highlight as the availability of a precise numerical quantification of these temporal scoring allow to track the evolution of the child throughout sessions.

A second aspect of interest is about the approach of the child toward the toys. More precisely the protocol asks how quickly the child move his attention from an object to another one. Moreover, a meeting with the staff of the NPO *Amici di Nico* has brought out as the selection of a favorite toy would be useful. With this in mind the following parameters have modeled and computed.

Let I be the number of object under exam, T_{i_s} the duration of the s-th interaction of child with the i-th object computed as the number of consecutive occurrences of the composite state $CS1_i$ between the s-th composite event $CE1_i$ and the next one whereas S_i is the number of interaction of the child with the i-th object computed as the number of occurrence of composite event $CE1_i$,

The total number of times that the child move his attention among different object is defined as

$$T_C = \sum_{i=1}^{I} S_i \tag{2}$$

The total time spent playing with object i is:

$$T_i = \sum_{s=1}^{S_i} T_{i_s} \tag{3}$$

The total time spent playing with objects is:

$$T_{CO} = \sum_{i=1}^{I} \sum_{s=1}^{S_i} T_{i_s} \tag{4}$$

The variance of the usage time of the object i is defined as

$$V_i = \frac{1}{S_i} \sum_{s=1}^{S_i} [T_{i_s} - \overline{T_i}]^2 \tag{5}$$

where $\overline{T_i}$ is the average time spent on the object i.

As a last aspect an evaluation of the display of affection has been studied. In this case the specific kind of interaction with the parents and the caregiver has been evaluated. To this aim the following definitions are mandatory

T_{AP}: it is time spent on affection interaction with parents; it is computed counting the number of consecutive occurrences of the state $PS5$ triggered by the event $CE7$

T_{AT}: it is time spent on affection interaction with therapist; it is computed counting the number of consecutive occurrences of the state $PS6$ triggered by the event $CE8$

T_P: it is time spent on the s-th interaction with parents; it is computed counting the number of consecutive occurrences of the state $PS2$ triggered by the event $CE3$

T_T: it is time spent on the s-th interaction with therapist; it is computed counting the number of consecutive occurrences of the state $PS3$ triggered by the event $CE4$

S_{AP}: is the number of affection interaction with the parents, corresponding to the occurrences of the event $CE7$

S_{AT}: is the number of affection interaction with the therapist, corresponding to the occurrences of the event $CE8$

S_P: is the number of interaction with the parents, corresponding to the occurrences of the event $CE3$

S_T: is the number of interaction with the therapist, corresponding to the occurrences of the event $CE4$

4 Experimental Outcomes

The validity of the proposed framework was proved by two different experimental phases performed by placing the acquisition device on a closet (to make it invisible for children). The first experimental phase, performed in the ISASI-CNR Computer Vision Lab, was aimed to set some system parameters and, at the same time, to give a qualitative evaluation of the reliability of algorithmic steps. In particular, this was carried out by reproducing in the lab a typical therapeutic room (with the play, parental and caregiver area) and then running the algorithms on the data acquired while two adults and a child (without ASD) moved in the scene performing a specific list of activities (walking around, taking and leaving a specific toy, carrying the toy to the caregiver or the parents and so on). At the end of this phase the predefined list of activities was compared with the list of those automatically estimated by the cascade of involved algorithms. In Fig. 4 a graphical comparison between actual (leftmost) and estimated (rightmost) activities is reported. In particular Y-axis represents the floor area in which the child was detected (0 for play area, 1 for parental area e 2 for caregiver area) whereas line colours are associated to the manipulated object (black for no object, red blue and green for object 1 2 and 3 i.e. doll, puppet and toy car). Finally, the marker 'x' is associated to affective occurrences, i.e. when the distance between the child and the adults was under the proximity thresholds. The similarity between the two plots indicates that persons and objects were properly detected and tracked and then the ontology was successfully applied to determine the semantic states that are the input of the subsequent behavioral scoring phase. For a better comprehension, one of the frame acquired during this phase is reported in Fig. 3. The figure contains the superimposed information about floor areas (with relative identification number) as well as the color assigned to the object manipulated by the child.

The second experimental phase was carried out at the NPO "Amici di Nico" by acquiring two ADOS-2 sessions. The first session was scheduled to asses a 5 years old child with ASD whereas the second one was scheduled for diagnosing if the language delay of a 3 year old child was associated to ASD (fortunately it was not).

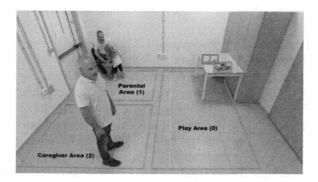

Fig. 3. One frame extracted from the preliminary experimental phase carried out in the ISASI-CNR Computer Vision Lab.

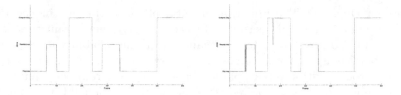

Fig. 4. Comparison between actual (leftmost) and estimated (rightmost) activity states during preliminary experimental sessions performed in our lab

Table 1. Statistics carried out for the two children under exam: the two tables show the results for Child 1 and child 2 respectively. Each report is divided in 3 parts referred to different focuses of the ADOS 2 protocol.

Child 1	
Part 1	
TI	21 min
FI	24 min
Part 2	
T_{CO}	37 min
T_C	12
T_i	(1) 7 min; (2) 18 min; (3) 12 min;
S_i	(1) 4; (2) 2; (3) 6;
V_i	(1) 0.92; (2) 32; (3) 0.8;
Part 3	
T_{AP}	5 min
T_{AT}	1 min
T_P	27 min
T_T	12 min
TT	63 min

Child 2	
Part 1	
TI	26 min
FI	14 min
Part 2	
T_{CO}	42 min
T_C	7
T_i	(1) 21 min; (2) 10 min; (3) 11 min;
S_i	(1) 2; (2) 2; (3) 3;
V_i	(1) 40; (2) 2; (3) 1.3;
Part 3	
T_{AP}	6 min
T_{AT}	3 min
T_P	26 min
T_T	5 min
TT	54 min

In Table 1 the outcomes of the proposed framework at the end of the sessions are reported. In particular, according to Subsect. 3.3 the following behavioral scores were extracted: TI = Time of interaction by means toys, FI = Time of free interaction, T_CO = The total time spent playing with objects, T_C = Toys changes, T_i = The total time spent playing with object i, S_i = Number of interaction with the i-th toy, V_i = variance on the time of interaction with the i-th toy through sessions, T_{AP} =, Total time on affection interaction with parents, T_{AT} =, Total time on affection interaction with therapist, T_P = Total time on interaction with parents, T_T = Total time on interaction with therapist, TT = total session time. The clinical evaluation of the data is out of the scope of this paper. However what we think is important to highlight here is the capability of the framework to provide the caregiver with objective data extracted from the scene allowing him to achieve a fair assessment of the child.

Both reports are divided in 3 part corresponding to the three aspects/questions described in Subsect. 3.3 respectively. As widely discussed, these results would be highly useful in the diagnosis process. As an instance, looking to the part 1 it is clear that the child 2 is more oriented to an interaction via toys compared with the child 1 that shows a more balanced attitude for both toys/non toys interaction. Concerning the second part many information about the attitude to play with object are provided. More precisely it would be interesting to observe as the second child is highly interested in objects and that he is capable to pay more attention in each of them avoiding frequent changes. Moreover S_i and V_i are useful data in order to take awareness of a preference on a specific toys or how the child rise out an interest for one of them. The last part highlight the time spent with parents or therapist and if this interaction is oriented to a affection interaction or a most standard interaction.

5 Conclusions and Future Works

In this work a first attempt to undertake the difficult challenge of embedding a technological level into a standardized protocol for ASD diagnose and assessment has been introduced. Experimental proofs demonstrated the huge potentiality of this research trend since, by this technological tools, objective data can be provided to the caregivers in order to get a more accurate diagnose and assessment of ASD. In this work only the module 1 of the ADOS-2 protocol has been explored and the 4 tasks involved in the phase 1 (free play) have been analyzed by the proposed technological framework. Future works will deal with the extension of the framework to other phases and modules of the ADOS-2 protocol: this will be done by including new functionalities facing emotions recognition, gesture analysis for symbolic and functional manipulation of objects and a deeper analysis of interactions between children and adults.

References

1. Bernardini, S., Porayska-Pomsta, K., Smith, T.J.: Echoes: an intelligent serious game for fostering social communication in children with autism. Inf. Sci. **264**, 41–60 (2014). http://www.sciencedirect.com/science/article/pii/S0020025513007548, serious Games
2. Boucenna, S., Narzisi, A., Tilmont, E., Muratori, F., Pioggia, G., Cohen, D., Chetouani, M.: Interactive technologies for autistic children: a review. Cogn. Comput. **6**(4), 722–740 (2014). http://dx.doi.org/10.1007/s12559-014-9276-x
3. Chau, D.P., Bremond, F., Thonnat, M.: A multi-feature tracking algorithm enabling adaptation to context variations. In: 4th International Conference on Imaging for Crime Detection and Prevention 2011 (ICDP 2011), pp. 1–6, November 2011
4. Cheung, S.C.S.: Integrating multimedia into autism intervention. IEEE MultiMedia **22**, 4–10 (2015)
5. Crippa, A., Salvatore, C., Perego, P., Forti, S., Nobile, M., Molteni, M., Castiglioni, I.: Use of machine learning to identify children with autism and their motor abnormalities. J. Autism Dev. Disord. **45**(7), 2146–2156 (2015)

6. Crispim, C.F., Bathrinarayanan, V., Fosty, B., Konig, A., Romdhane, R., Thonnat, M., Bremond, F.: Evaluation of a monitoring system for event recognition of older people. In: 2013 10th IEEE International Conference on Advanced Video and Signal Based Surveillance (AVSS), pp. 165–170, August 2013

7. Distante, C., Indiveri, G.: RANSAC-LEL: an optimized version with least entropy like estimators. In: 18th IEEE International Conference on Image Processing, pp. 1425–1428, September 2011

8. Kalal, Z., Mikolajczyk, K., Matas, J.: Tracking-learning-detection. IEEE Trans. Pattern Anal. Mach. Intell. **34**(7), 1409–1422 (2012)

9. Lofland, K.B.: The use of technology in the treatment of autism. In: Cardon, T.A. (ed.) Technology and the Treatment of Children with Autism Spectrum Disorder, pp. 27–35. Springer International Publishing, Cham (2016). doi:10.1007/978-3-319-20872-5_3

10. Lord, C., Rutter, M., DiLavore, P.C., Risi, S., Gotham, K., Bishop, S.: Autism Diagnostic Observation Schedule: ADOS-2. Western Psychological Services, Los Angeles (2012)

11. Nghiem, A.T., Bremond, F.: Background subtraction in people detection framework for RGB-D cameras. In: 2014 11th IEEE International Conference on Advanced Video and Signal Based Surveillance (AVSS), pp. 241–246, August 2014

12. Shamsuddin, S., Yussof, H., Mohamed, S., Hanapiah, F.A., Ainudin, H.A.: Telerehabilitation service with a robot for autism intervention. Procedia Comput. Sci. **76**, 349–354 (2015). http://www.sciencedirect.com/science/article/pii/S1877050915038077, 2015 IEEE International Symposium on Robotics and Intelligent Sensors (IEEE IRIS2015)

13. Warren, Z., Zheng, Z., Das, S., Young, E.M., Swanson, A., Weitlauf, A., Sarkar, N.: Brief report: development of a robotic intervention platform for young children with ASD. J. Autism Dev. Disord. **45**(12), 3870–3876 (2015)

Visual Target Detection and Tracking in UAV EO/IR Videos by Moving Background Subtraction

Francesco Tufano, Cesario Vincenzo Angelino, and Luca Cicala$^{(\boxtimes)}$

CIRA, The Italian Aerospace Research Center, 81043 Capua, Italy
{f.tufano,c.angelino,l.cicala}@cira.it

Abstract. In the last years the Italian Aerospace Research Center (CIRA) designed many versions of on-board payload management software for Unmanned Aerial Vehicles (UAVs), to be used in ISTAR (Intelligence, Surveillance, Target Acquisition and Reconnaissance) missions. A typical required function in these software suites is detection and tracking of moving ground vehicles.

In this work, we propose a detection and tracking approach to moving objects that is suitable when the background is static in the real world and appears to be affected of global motion in the image plane. Each object is described as a set of SURF points enhanced with a related appearance model. Experiments on real world video sequences confirm the effectiveness of the proposed approach.

1 Introduction

Nowadays, Medium Altitude Long Endurance (MALE) class Unmanned Aerial Vehicles (UAVs), are commonly used by military forces for Intelligence, Surveillance, Target Acquisition and Reconnaissance (ISTAR) missions. For this purpose, UAVs are usually equipped with gyrostabilized electro-optical (EO) and thermal infrared (IR) cameras. These payloads, however, are suitable not only for military tasks but also for civilian applications (borders security, environmental persistence surveillance, search and rescue, emergency response, *etc.*). The potential of such applications will be evident in the next years, when UAVs will be share the civilian air space with manned air vehicles.

The Italian Aerospace Research Center (CIRA), in the years, developed an experience in design of mission sensor management software [1] at TRL (Technology Readiness Level) 4–6 [2]. This software handles the imaging sensors of the mission payload for data acquisition, synchronization, sensor fusion [3], on-board processing and communication [4]. Furthermore, it is able to position the point of view and to modify the zoom level of the cameras in order to frame the targets at the required Interpretability Rating Scale (IRS) [5].

Low level and high level video processing functions are typically implemented in order to reduce the amount of information that has to be sent to the ground control station and to extract information that can be used by the on-board

© Springer International Publishing AG 2016
J. Blanc-Talon et al. (Eds.): ACIVS 2016, LNCS 10016, pp. 547–558, 2016.
DOI: 10.1007/978-3-319-48680-2_48

mission control software. The latter, in the next future, will be able to automatically and quickly re-plan the flight route, in order to accomplish the mission tasks (*i.e.*: anomalies detection, target acquisition, target tracking, *etc.*). In particular, autonomous target following technologies have been studied in the last years using one [6] or more UAVs [7]. The target of interest must be quickly selected by the human mission operator in the ground control station, using a graphical user interface. For this reason also a detecting function must be implemented in order to reduce the regions of interest in the image and ease the manual target selection.

In this paper, we present a solution for aided target detection and automatic target tracking of ground vehicles from MALE class UAVs, using either an EO or IR camera. The proposed solution, hereafter named VTT (Visual Target Tracking), is suited for the following user requirements:

- detecting and tracking objects on solid terrain (not water surfaces), using UAV's on-board cameras;
- working with either visible or thermal infrared cameras;
- aiding the mission operator to quickly select the target, limiting the region of interest to the moving objects;
- tracking of the selected objects;
- obtaining high detection and tracking performance, under the computational resource constraints (see the Sect. 4.3 for details).

The paper is organized as follows. Section 2 describes some related works and in Sect. 3, the design of the system and, in particular, the detection and tracking algorithms are discussed. In Sect. 4 experimental results on real video sequences, both in the visible and in the infrared spectrum, are reported and commented. Conclusions are drawn in Sect. 5.

2   Related Works

VTT implements moving background subtraction and a mixed feature and appearance based description of the moving foreground objects. The solution has elements of originality with respect to other proposed approaches and is suitable for real world applications.

In [8] a detection and tracking approach is proposed. For the detection purpose, the background is modeled with some statistics and dynamically updated. A coregistration step, based on an homography model, is needed, in order to match the pixels belonging to two consecutive frames and to generate the current foreground mask. The detected objects are described with their color histograms. The detection algorithm is repeated, every time, before the tracking phase, in order to extract the foreground moving objects from the current video frame. In the tracking phase the detected objects are matched with that extracted in the previous frame by means of position and histograms comparison. In particular the position of the detected objects is compared with that predicted by a Kalman filter. Respect to the above approach our background subtraction strategy is simpler and faster, because is based only on the difference between the current and the reference frame, without generating a statistical model of the background. Our design choice is motivated by the fact that quick light changes do not occur during the background update time. With aim to avoid repeating the execution of the detection routine before every tracking step and then strongly reduce the computational complexity, our objects descriptors, as discussed in Sect. 3.2, are sets of sparse feature points. Such descriptors are used also in [9], but for matching with reference object templates belonging to a reference database.

In [10] the background subtraction is performed creating an artificial optical flow field that is estimated by the camera motion between two subsequent video frames and is compared with the real optical flow directly calculated from the video frames. By comparing the two optical flows, a list of moving objects can be extracted. The method is based on the hypothesis that the optical flow can be appropriately estimated on all the moving objects and no moving objects are neglected. In our approach, instead, we can force the system to describe every detected object with at least a certain number of feature points in order to have appropriate objects descriptors.

In [11] the detection problem is specifically addressed to vehicle detection. Trained cascaded Haar classifiers are used to detect moving and static targets. The reported method can be followed to implement functions that are complementary to that proposed in this paper.

3 Design of the Visual Target Detection and Tracking System

A software system for aided target selection and automatic tracking, due to the many functions that work together and the needed interaction between the air and the ground segment, is difficult to characterize in terms of performance. In this paper, we propose an architecture for the detection and tracking functions and, after its implementation, we characterize it respect to state of the art reference alternatives, using an open test data set. For this purpose we artificially separate the detection and tracking functions by others that are strongly related (*i.e.*, manual target selection, target geographic localization, data communication, communication delay handling), simplifying the behavior of the described system and making possible clear performance comparisons.

3.1 Detection Module

The aim of this module is the detection of moving vehicles. This processing step is obtained by separating the set of moving foreground points of interest from the terrain background and assembling them in sets corresponding to moving objects of interest.

Usually, in visual target tracking applications, this task is accomplished separating the foreground moving objects from the static background. Since the camera is installed on board of an air vehicle, the point of view is always moving and the background cannot be considered static, as in many on-ground video surveillance applications. Because the background consists in the overflown terrain, it can be considered subject to global motion in the image plane. Such global motion can be approximated by means of an homography [12]. This hypothesis holds for typical MALE class UAVs missions because the "roughness" of the terrain, due to the non planar shape of the ground surface and to the presence of 3D objects on the terrain (like trees, building,...), is usually negligible with respect to the distance of the point of view from the ground. With aim to distinguish the background from the foreground in the current video frame, a previous reference video frame is considered. In order to estimate the global motion of the background, between a previous reference $I(t - dt)$ and the current video frame $I(t)$, the following steps have been implemented:

- gaussian filtering $G(t)$ of the current video frame $I(t)$;
- detection of a sparse set of feature points $F(t)$ in the current filtered video frame $G(t)$, in particular SURF (Speed Up Robust Features) are considered because invariant to rotations [13];
- point features matching, between the current and the reference frames, by means of a FANN (Fast Approximate Nearest Neighbor) algorithm [14];
- robust model estimation of the homography, in particular using Random Sample Consensus (RANSAC) [15].

After that, the perspective warping $W(t)$ of the reference video frame $I(t - dt)$ is performed in order to coregister the reference frame with the current frame. A background mask $M(t)$ is then built by subtracting to the current video frame $I(t)$ the warped reference image $W(t)$ and applying a threshold to the result. In the masks, some blobs represents areas that are correctly detected as pieces of moving objects in the images. These pieces of objects are clustered together using information inherent to their relative positions and their velocity in the image plane.

   After the detection phase, a bounding box is showed to the ground operator in correspondence of any of the detected moving objects. By means of an interactive user interface the operator can rapidly select the object of interest in order to activate the tracking function on it. In order to facilitate the choice of the moving objects a characterization of them (size, velocity, type) can be optionally activated. This function however is not computationally negligible and is not included in the processing cycle for the purpose of the performance evaluation of the detection and tracking system.

   The structure of the proposed detection module is shown in Fig. 1. In Fig. 2 the coordinates of the detected SURF points in an IR video frame are overlayed as red dots. In Fig. 3 the features selected by the FANN algorithm are displayed as colored dots and connected with yellow segments. The green points are selected as part of the background by the RANSAC algorithm. The blue points belong to the foreground. Red points are unmatched.

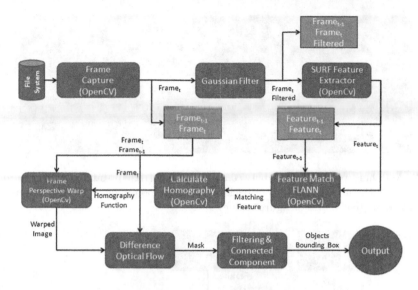

Fig. 1. Detection module scheme.

Fig. 2. The coordinate of the SURF features detected in the IR video frame under analysis. (Color figure online)

3.2 Tracking Module

After the detected moving objects have been selected, they are tracked by means of the tracking function. For the purpose of the evaluation of the tracking performance and of the processing frame rate in the Sect. 4, only one moving object at time is selected.

In the initialization phase, the set of the K SURF points $F = \{f_1, ..., f_K\}$ extracted by the detection module is associated to each selected object. To each

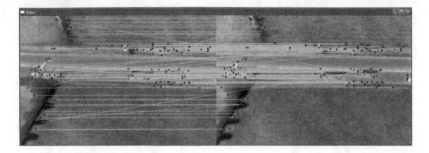

Fig. 3. Matching point features between the current (right) and the reference video (left) frames. Green points represent background. Blue points belong to the foreground. Red dots unmatched. (Color figure online)

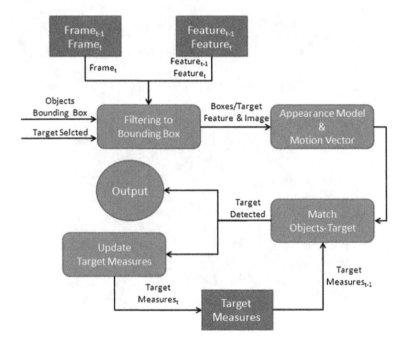

Fig. 4. Tracking module scheme.

feature point belonging to the object, an active appearance model [16] is further associated. The model is calculated on the 5×5 pixels window around the feature point and considers the patch histograms of all the available color channels (three for RGB video sequences and only one for the IR video sequences). The resulting histograms are also rotation invariant. The full information associated to a feature point, hereafter is named "descriptor".

After the initialization phase, the tracking function works in the following steps, for each new video frame:

- the position $x_i(t)$ of each feature point $f_i(t)$ in the current video frame is estimated, predicting it from the position $x_i(t - dt)$ in the reference frame and velocity $v_i(t - dt)$ of the point in the image plane (if available);
- in the neighborhood of the predicted coordinates $\hat{x}_i(t)$ (a window), new feature points $F(t)$ are found in the current frame;
- the new feature points $F(t)$ are matched to that belonging to the reference frame $F(t - dt)$, using a FANN algorithm;
- the velocity $v_i(t)$ is updated for each tracked point;
- the descriptor $f_i(t)$ is updated for each tracked point, replacing it with its moving average;

The update of the descriptor $f_i(t)$ is performed only if it is similar enough to the reference $f_i(t - dt)$, in order to avoid the influence of false matches. The structure of the proposed tracking module is shown in Fig. 4.

4   Experimental Results

In the following experimental results on real aerial video sequences are reported. The test videos are both in the visible and in the thermal infrared spectrum, are captured by aerial platforms, show moving vehicles that follow more or less complex trajectories in more or less occluded scenarios.

4.1   Test Data

The test data reported in this paper belong to a dataset produced within the VIVID (VIdeo Verification of IDentity) project [17][1]. The dataset has been prepared by the DARPA (Defense Advanced Research Projects Agency) and it comes with associated ground truth data. The ground truth in the image plane are represented as bounding boxes that include the moving targets.

Experiments have been performed on four video sequences: two RGB video sequence and two thermal infrared video sequence as reported in Table 1. EGtest01, the first RGB video sequence, shows six cars, not always all together present in the scene, on a airport runway. The digital definition of the video is 640×480 and it contains 1820 frames. In this video sequence, it is easy to loose the identity of the tracked target because vehicles are very close to each other. EGtest02, the second RGB video sequence, has the same definition and it lasts 1301 frames. The scene is the same but, this time, the trajectories of vehicles intersect each other. PKtest01, the first thermal infrared video, of definition 320×256 and length 1460 frames, shows up to three vehicles moving on a road in an open area. The vehicles moves with simple maneuvers according the road rules. However some trees or buildings sometimes partially or totally occlude

---

[1] Data can be downloaded at http://vision.cse.psu.edu/data/vividEval.

Table 1. Aerial video sequences characteristics.

Video seq.	UAV altitude [meters]	Definition [pix × pix]	Sensor EO/IR	Num of objects	Occlusions
EGtest01	≈ 400	640 × 480	RGB	6	NO
EGtest02	≈ 400	640 × 480	RGB	6	NO
PKtest01	≈ 100	320 × 256	IR	3	YES
PKtest02	≈ 100	320 × 256	IR	5	YES

the moving vehicles. PKtest02, the second IR video, of the same definition and length of 1565 frames, shows up to five vehicles in a urban zone. With respect the first IR video, the partial occlusion has an higher occurrence while the total occlusions are approximately the same.

4.2   Performance Measures

Measuring the performance of a detection system is not a simple task, because many aspects have to be taken in account:

1. the presence of an intersection I_{ij} between the detector D_i and the ground truth bounding box G_j (is a necessary but not sufficient condition to a right detection, as discussed below);
2. the extension $A(I_{ij})$ of such overlap respect to the extension $A(G_j)$ of the bounding box (enough points of the detected object must be included in the area covered by the detector, in order to obtain a robust description);
3. the extension $A(I_{ij})$ of such overlap respect to the extension $A(D_j)$ of the detector (the size of the detector must be comparable with that of the detected object in order to separate the foreground from the background);
4. the presence of multiple overlaps among one detector and many bounding boxes (many objects erroneously can be merged together);
5. the presence of multiple overlaps among one bounding box and many detectors (a single object can erroneously separated in many parts).

In order to consider all these issues, the following approach has been used. Two $N \times M$ matrices $\Gamma = \{\gamma_{ij}\}$ and $\Delta = \{\delta_{ij}\}$ have been introduced, where

$$\gamma_{ij} = \frac{A(I_{ij})}{A(G_j)},$$

and

$$\delta_{ij} = \frac{A(I_{ij})}{A(D_i)}.$$

Then, we considered the following conventions:

1. D_i detects G_j if $\gamma_{ij} > 0.65$ and $\delta_{ij} > 0.65$.

2. D_i is a multiple detector if this condition exists for more than one G_j.
3. G_j has many detectors if this condition exists for more than one D_i.
4. The detection score d_i of D_i is positive if D_i is a detector, is 0 otherwise. In particular the score is 0.85 if D_i is a multiple detector and 1.0 if it is a single detector. The same for the detection score g_j of G_j.

We can then define:

$$\text{Recall} = \frac{1}{M} \sum_{j=1}^{M} g_j$$

and

$$\text{Precision} = \frac{1}{N} \sum_{i=1}^{N} d_i,$$

where M is the number of boxes in the ground truth and N the number of detectors.

For the tracking performance, instead, we can define a tracking performance index. We define the tracking score τ_i as 1 if there is an intersection between the tracked blob $\hat{D}_i$ and the corresponding tracked object G_j and 0 otherwise. The tracking performance index can be then defined as:

$$\text{Tracking} = \frac{1}{T} \sum_{t=1}^{T} \tau_i(t),$$

where the sum is on all the T video frames in which the target is present.

4.3   Results Discussion

In order to assess the performance of the proposed system, it has been compared to the following state of the art algorithms:

1. Template Matching by Correlation;
2. Basic Meanshift;
3. Histogram Ratio Shift;
4. Variance Ratio Feature Shift.

The reference implementation of the above algorithms is that of the software "Open Source Tracking Testbed" [18], developed by the Robotic Institute of the Carnegie Mellon University within the program VIVID. It is worth to notice that the algorithm Basic Meanshift works only in the detection phase, so that the tracking performance is not reported.

The results have been obtained on an embedded computer, with 2 I7 Intel Processors, each with clock frequency 2.1 GHz, and 8 RAM cores, each with capacity of 3.4 Gbytes). In the experiments, the video frames have been grabbed from file, as showed in Fig. 1.

In general, the proposed approach results more computational demanding than the state of the art reference algorithms. In particular the processing frame rate is reduced from two up to four times.

Table 2. Experimental results for the RGB video sequence EGtest01.

Video seq. algorithm	Proc. FR [fps]	Precision [%]	Recall [%]	Tracking [%]
VTT	19.7	72.4	**89.3**	**89.7**
Template matching	49.1	**74.1**	71.4	84.2
Basic meanshift	34.6	66.1	83.8	-
Histogram ratio shift	**56.9**	56.0	78.6	80.4
Variance ratio feature shift	39.4	62.6	88.4	80.8

Table 3. Experimental results for the RGB video sequence EGetest02.

Video seq. algorithm	Proc. FR [fps]	Precision [%]	Recall [%]	Tracking [%]
VTT	19.0	**75.1**	**90.5**	**88.4**
Template matching	50.5	71.6	76.6	81.3
Basic meanshift	36.3	60.7	88.2	-
Histogram ratio shift	**52.2**	58.4	74.2	77.9
Variance ratio feature shift	36.8	63.5	87.3	81.7

Table 4. Experimental results for the IR video sequence PKtest01.

Video seq. algorithm	Proc. FR [fps]	Precision [%]	Recall [%]	Tracking [%]
VTT	26.4	**84.3**	**69.5**	**72.2**
Template matching	104.3	74.9	60.4	70.3
Basic meanshift	95.4	66.3	59.1	-
Histogram ratio shift	108.1	60.1	64.1	**59.3**
Variance ratio feature shift	71.8	69.7	65.5	68.6

In Table 2 the test results on the RGB video sequence EGtest01 are reported. The proposed solutions outperforms all the references except for the precision. In terms of precision the results, in fact, are similar to that of the Basic Meanshift method, that however is not used for the tracking task.

As reported in Table 3, the proposed solution significantly outperforms all the references on the RGB video sequence EGtest02.

Also on the IR video sequence PKtest01, the proposed detection and tracking system reaches always better performance than the references (Table 4).

In Table 5 the test results on the IR video sequence PKtest02 are reported. All the algorithms have worse performance than on the other video sequences. The proposed solutions outperforms all the other methods in precision and tracking performance, but does not distinguish for the recall.

Table 5. Experimental results for the IR video sequence PKtest02.

Video seq. algorithm	Proc. FR [fps]	Precision [%]	Recall [%]	Tracking [%]
VTT	22.6	**74.3**	64.4	**80.1**
Template matching	102.7	43.0	63.8	61.6
Basic meanshift	97.1	41.1	72.9	-
Histogram ratio shift	99.4	50.2	59.5	58.8
Variance ratio feature shift	70.4	62.4	75.4	73.6

5 Conclusions

In this work we proposed a customized detection and tracking scheme for EO/IR cameras mounted on UAVs that is suitable for tracking of ground vehicles. The complexity of the approach was limited by overall system design constraints. The proposed system uses global motion estimation to separate the moving objects from the terrain background. The detected objects are modeled as a set of SURF features. The feature point descriptors are completed with an appearance model for each. The experimental results on a public available test set show the effectiveness of the proposed solution and the significantly improved performance with respect to simpler state of the art algorithms.

References

1. Garibotto, G., et al.: White paper on industrial applications of computer vision and pattern recognition. In: Petrosino, A. (ed.) ICIAP 2013. LNCS, vol. 8157, pp. 721–730. Springer, Heidelberg (2013). doi:10.1007/978-3-642-41184-7_73
2. EARTO: The TRL scale as a research & innovation policy tool, April 2014. http://www.earto.eu/fileadmin/content/03_Publications/The_TRL_Scale_as_a_R-1_Policy_Tool_-_EARTO_Recommendations_-_Final.pdf
3. Angelino, C.V., Baraniello, V.R., Cicala, L.: High altitude UAV navigation using IMU, GPS and camera. In: Proceedings of the 16th International Conference onInformation Fusion (FUSION), Istanbul, Turkey, pp. 647–654, July 2013
4. Cicala, L., Angelino, C.V., Raimondo, N., Baccaglini, E., Gavelli, M.: An H.264 sensor aided encoder for aerial video sequences with in-the-loop metadata enhancement. In: Battiato, S., Blanc-Talon, J., Gallo, G., Philips, W., Popescu, D., Scheunders, P. (eds.) ACIVS 2015. LNCS, vol. 9386, pp. 853–863. Springer, Heidelberg (2015). doi:10.1007/978-3-319-25903-1_73
5. Irvine, J.M.: National imagery interpretability rating scales (NIIRS): overview and methodology. In: Optical Science, Engineering and Instrumentation 1997. International Society for Optics and Photonics, pp. 93–103 (1997)
6. Rafi, F., Khan, S., Shafiq, K., Shah, M.: Autonomous target following by unmanned aerial vehicles. In: Defense and Security Symposium. International Society for Optics and Photonics, p. 623010 (2006)

7. Shaferman, V., Shima, T.: Unmanned aerial vehicles cooperative tracking of moving ground target in urban environments. J. Guidance Control Dyn. **31**(5), 1360–1371 (2008)
8. Symington, A., Waharte, S., Julier, S., Trigoni, N.: Multi target tracking on aerial videos. In: ISPRS Istanbul Workshop 2010 on Modeling of Optical Airborne and Spaceborne Sensors, Istambul, Turkey, October 2010
9. Gelertm, M., Csaba, B., Tamas, S.: Probabilistic target detection by camera-equipped UAVs. In: IEEE International Conference on Robotics and Automation, Anchorage, Alaska, USA, October 2010
10. Rodríguez-Canosa, G., Thomas, S., del Cerro, J., Barrientos, A., MacDonald, B.: A real-time method to detect and track moving objects (DATMO) from unmanned aerial vehicles (UAVs) using a single camera. Remote Sens. **4**(4), 1090–1111 (2012)
11. Breckon, T.P., Barnes, S.E., Eichner, M.L., Wahren, K.: Autonomous real-time vehicle detection from a medium-level UAV. In: Proceedings of the 24th International Conference on Unmanned Air Vehicle Systems, p. 29:1–29:9 (2009)
12. Hartley, R.I., Zisserman, A.: Multiple View Geometry in Computer Vision, 2nd edn. Cambridge University Press, Cambridge (2004). ISBN: 0521540518
13. Bay, H., Tuytelaars, T., Gool, L.: SURF: speeded up robust features. In: Leonardis, A., Bischof, H., Pinz, A. (eds.) ECCV 2006. LNCS, vol. 3951, pp. 404–417. Springer, Heidelberg (2006). doi:10.1007/11744023_32
14. Muja, M., Lowe, D.G.: Fast approximate nearest neighbors with automatic algorithm configuration. VISApp (1) **2**(331–340), 2 (2009)
15. Fischler, M.A., Bolles, R.C.: Random sample consensus: a paradigm for model fitting with applications to image analysis and automated cartography. Commun. ACM **24**(6), 381–395 (1981)
16. Cootes, T.F., Edwards, G.J., Taylor, C.J.: Active appearance models. IEEE Trans. Pattern Anal. Mach. Intell. **6**, 681–685 (2001)
17. Laboratory of Perception Action and Cognition of the Penn State Univesity: vivid video dataset and tracker testbed program (2005). http://vision.cse.psu.edu/data/vividEval/
18. Collins, R., Zhou, X., Teh, S.K.: An open source tracking testbed and evaluation web site. In: IEEE International Workshop on Performance Evaluation of Tracking and Surveillance (PETS), January 2005

A Multiphase Level Set Method on Graphs for Hyperspectral Image Segmentation

Kaouther Tabia$^{(\boxtimes)}$, Xavier Desquesnes, Yves Lucas, and Sylvie Treuillet

Université d'Orléans, 12 rue de Bois, 45067 Orléans, France
kaouthesr.tabia@univ-orleans.fr

Abstract. In this paper, we propose a new multiphase level set method for hyperspectral image segmentation. Our approach generalize the partial differential equation based front propagation concept initially introduced for gray image segmentation to images with huge wavelength dimension. Experimental results demonstrate the effectiveness of our method.

1 Introduction

HyperSpectral Images (HSI), which were initially introduced for remote sensing during the 1970s, have recently emerged as an important and powerful tool for many areas including food quality [14], geological monitoring [7], and medical diagnosis [9,16]. Unlike human vision system which is restricted to some wavelengths, hyperspectral sensors are able to capture a set of images representing the information in a wide electromagnetic spectrum, ranging from ultraviolet to infrared. An HSI can be considered as a three dimensional cube containing two spatial and one wavelength dimensions. Compared to conventional RGB images, limited to three large channels, hyperspectral images exhibit improved spectral differentiation on several hundreds of narrow channels which make them more informative. However high amount of information implies further complications when applying conventional image processing techniques such as segmentation algorithms.

Due to the wide number of bands, several approaches consider HSI segmentation as a pure classification problem, where pixels spectrum are reduced to feature vectors and the image to a list of unorganised pixels. In this case, the spatial information (pixel position and neighborhood) is lost and the clustering is performed in spectrum space only [12]. Nevertheless, the spatial information can be added to the feature vector by computing spatial descriptors for each pixel. In a previous study [10] the combined use of spatial and spectral information, coupled with a SVM classifier, has been used and has demonstrated its effectiveness.

A third way to perform HSI segmentation is to consider HSI images as weighted graphs, where pixels are represented by vertices that are connected one to the other by edges. By nature, the graph includes both spatial and spectral information. Moreover, the graph construction is not constrained to usual regular-grid topologies (where each pixel is connected to its adjacent neighbors) but can be adapted to each particular application. One can mention large or

© Springer International Publishing AG 2016
J. Blanc-Talon et al. (Eds.): ACIVS 2016, LNCS 10016, pp. 559–569, 2016.
DOI: 10.1007/978-3-319-48680-2_49

complete neighborhood for textured images or Region Adjacency Graphs (RAG) where pixels are replaced by regions or superpixels, and so on. On the last decade, several graph-based methods have been applied to HSI for dimensionality reduction, anomaly detection, classification and segmentation. In a recent study [6] the spatial-spectral structure of weighted graphs has shown its potential for HSI segmentation with the graph-cut method, and we feel that this approach should be deeply investigated with novel graph-based segmentation techniques.

In this paper, we propose to focus on a different approach of graph-based segmentation, starting from the recent adaptation of the level set method for active contour on weighted graphs and investigate its potential for HSI segmentation. The level set method has been proposed and popularized by Osher and Sethian [11] to describe the evolution of a given parametrized curve. This formulation is the basis of the well known Chan and Vese active contour model [1,2] where the curve splits the image domain in two regions: background and foreground, according to a function that minimizes curve length and maximizes intra-regions homogeneity. This active contour model has been widely used for grayscale and multispectral images and has been adapted to weighted graphs in [4]. It can then be applied to any data that can be represented by a weighted graph, such as images, meshes or unorganized data.

For more than two regions, Chan and Vese introduced a multiphase version of their model that splits image in 2^n regions with n level set functions [18]. This multiphase version inherits all advantages of the initial two-phase model as detection of edges or automatic change of topology and generalises it with a few algorithmic changes. It has been widely used in grayscale and multispectral segmentation [3] but, to our knowledge, never applied to HSI segmentation neither adapted to weighted graphs.

1.1   Contributions

Two contributions are presented in this paper. First, a novel application of the two-phase level set graph-based method to HSI segmentation. Secondly, an extension of the graph-based model to multiphase active contour. In the following section, we review some basic definitions and operators on weighted graphs. We briefly present the level set method and its transcription on weighted graphs, with two phase and multiphase Chan-Vese model. Then, Sect. 3 introduces the new formulation of multiphase active contour on weighted graphs and its evaluation on HSI benchmark images.

2   Theoretical Background

In this section, we introduce the concepts implied in the elaboration of this work.

2.1   Weighted Graphs

Let $G = (V, E, \omega)$ be a weighted graph composed of a set of vertices $V = (v_1, ..., v_n)$ and a set of weighted edges $E = \{(u, v) \in V \times V | u \sim v\}$ where $\sim$ means that u and

v are adjacent vertices and ω represents the weights on each edge in G. The weight ω defined by ω_{uv} can be considered as a function $\omega : V \times V \rightarrow \mathbb{R}^+$ for $u \sim v$ and 0 otherwise. We denote by $N(u)$ the neighborhood of a vertex u, defined as the subset of vertices connected with u i.e. $\{v \in V | u \sim v\}$.

We also review some operators on weighted graphs from [5]. For a given discrete function f which assigns a real value $f(u)$ to each vertex $u \in V$, the weighted discrete partial derivative operator of f applied on an edge $(u, v) \in E$ is:

$$\partial_v f(u) = \sqrt{\omega_{uv}} \left(f(v) - f(u) \right). \tag{1}$$

Based on this definition, two weighted directional difference operators are defined. The external and internal operators are respectively:
$\partial_v^+ f(u) = \sqrt{\omega_{uv}} \left(f(v) - f(u) \right)^+$ and $\partial_v^- f(u) = -\sqrt{\omega_{uv}} \left(f(v) - f(u) \right)^-$, with $(x)^+ = \max(0, x)$ and $(x)^- = \min(0, x)$. The weighted gradient of f at vertex u, denoted ∇_w is the vector of all edge directional derivatives:

$$(\nabla_w f)(u) = (\partial_v f(u))_{(u,v) \in E}^T. \tag{2}$$

The external and the internal weighted gradient operators of f, denoted respectively ∇_w^+ and ∇_w^- are:

$$(\nabla_w^\pm f)(u) = \left(\partial_v^\pm f(u) \right)_{(u,v) \in E}^T. \tag{3}$$

2.2   Level Set Method

The level set formulation introduced in [11] describes the evolution of a given parametrized curve $\Gamma : [0, 1] \rightarrow \Omega$. The level set method aims to find a function $\phi(x, y, t)$ such that at each time t the evolving curve Γ_t can be provided by the zero-level of ϕ. That means $\Gamma_t = \{(x, y) | \phi(x, y, t) = 0\}$ and the curve evolution can be done solving

$$\frac{\partial \phi(x, y, t)}{\partial t} = F \|\nabla \phi(x, y, t)\|, \tag{4}$$

where $F : \Omega \rightarrow \mathbb{R}$ is a scalar field that controls the direction of the evolution of the Γ curve.

2.3   Transcription on Graphs

This transcription of level set method from the continuous domain to the discrete domain over a weighted graph was previously introduced in [17].

By analogy with the continuous case, we represent the curve Γ evolving on a weighted graph $G = (V, E, \omega)$ as a subset Ω_t defined by the zero-level of function ϕ:

$$\phi(u, t) \begin{cases} < 0 \ if \ u \notin \Omega_t \\ > 0 \ if \ u \in \Omega_t \end{cases} \tag{5}$$

The curve Γ is defined as the hyperplane between the two subsets $\Omega_t \subset V$ and $\bar{\Omega}_t \subset V$, which represent respectively the vertices inside and outside Γ at the time t.

The evolution of the curve Γ is controlled by a velocity function F. The curve extends when F is positive (vertices are added to Ω_t) and shrinks when F is negative (vertices are removed from Ω_t):

The equation of the curve evolution [4] can be expressed as a combination of morphological processes that recovers unary dilation if $F > 0$ and unary erosion if $F < 0$

$$\frac{\partial\phi(u,t)}{\partial t} \begin{cases} F(u,t)||(\nabla_\omega^+\phi)(u,t)||, \ if \ F(u,t) > 0 \\ F(u,t)||(\nabla_\omega^-\phi)(u,t)||, \ if \ F(u,t) < 0 \\ 0, \ otherwise \end{cases} \tag{6}$$

Where $(\nabla_\omega^+\phi)(u,t)$ and $(\nabla_\omega^-\phi)(u,t)$ are the external and internal weighted gradient operators given in (3).

2.4   Two-Phase Chan-Vese Model

The two-phase Chan-Vese model [2] segments an image I in two regions or phases by solving the PDE below:

$$\frac{\partial\phi}{\partial t} = \delta_\epsilon(\phi)[\mu.div(\frac{\nabla\phi}{|\nabla\phi|}) - (I - c_1)^2 + (I - c_2)^2], \tag{7}$$

Where $div(\frac{\nabla\phi}{|\nabla\phi|})$ represents the curvature of the evolving curve Γ, $\delta_\epsilon(\phi)$ is a Delta function defined by $\delta_\epsilon(\phi) = \frac{\epsilon}{\pi(\epsilon^2+\phi^2)}$ which ϵ is a positive constant. c_1 and c_2 are the average values of pixels respectively inside and outside of Γ.

The region term given by $-(I - c_1)^2 + (I - c_2)^2$ is considered as the velocity of the curve evolution. The curvature term regularizes Γ to be smooth.

A recent adaptation of the two-phase level set method for active contour on graphs has been presented in [4]. This adaptation is based on the graph-based level set Eq. (6), with a velocity function inspired of (7) and expressed using discrete operators on graphs. In (6), $F(u,t) = \kappa_w(u,t) + (I(u) - c_1)^2 + (I(u) - c_2)^2$ where $\kappa_w(u,t)$ is the curvature on weigthed graphs.

2.5   Multiphase Chan-Vese Model

The multiphase Chan-Vese model [18] is a generalisation of the previous two-phase model. Given n curves Γ_n, represented by n level set functions ϕ_n, this model aims to split an image to $m = 2^n$ regions or phases. As an example, let consider the case of a four-phase Chan-Vese model, in which we have $n = 2$ level set functions ϕ_1 and ϕ_2 evolving simultaneously, and split the image I into four regions.

Figure 1 shows how this two level set functions split the domain into four regions.

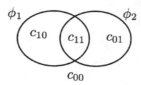

Fig. 1. 2 curves split the domain into 4 regions: $\{\phi_1 > 0, \phi_2 > 0\}, \{\phi_1 > 0, \phi_2 < 0\}, \{\phi_1 < 0, \phi_2 > 0\}, \{\phi_1 < 0, \phi_2 < 0\}$

The evolution of ϕ_1 and ϕ_2 are defined as follow:

$$\frac{\partial \phi_1}{\partial t} = \delta_\epsilon(\phi_1)\{\mu div(\frac{\nabla \phi_1}{|\nabla \phi_1|}) - [((I - c_{11})^2 - (I - c_{01})^2)H(\phi_2)$$
$$+((I - c_{10})^2 - (I - c_{00})^2)(1 - H(\phi_2))]\}$$
$$\frac{\partial \phi_2}{\partial t} = \delta_\epsilon(\phi_2)\{\mu div(\frac{\nabla \phi_2}{|\nabla \phi_2|}) - [((I - c_{11})^2 - (I - c_{10})^2)H(\phi_1)$$
$$+((I - c_{01})^2 - (I - c_{00})^2)(1 - H(\phi_1))]\} \qquad (8)$$

where $div(\frac{\nabla \phi_1}{|\nabla \phi_1|})$ and $div(\frac{\nabla \phi_2}{|\nabla \phi_2|})$ represent the curvatures of the evolving curves ϕ_1 and ϕ_2. H represents the Heaviside function defined by $H(x) = 1$ when $x > 0$ and $H(x) = 0$ when $x < 0$ and c_{00}, c_{01},c_{11},c_{10} are averaged pixel values inside the respective four regions.

Unlike the two-phase model, the multiphase model has not yet been applied on weighted graphs.

3   Experiments for HSI

Inspired by existing works for the adaptation of the two-phase Chan and Vese's model on graphs [4], we generalize this formulation to multiphase model and study its potential on HSI. In that case, each level set is independantly driven by the graph-based level set Eq. (6) with a specific velocity function. To illustrate we take the example of $n = 2$ level set functions, the above PdE in Eq. (6) becomes:

$$\frac{\partial \phi_1(u,t)}{\partial t} \begin{cases} \delta_\epsilon(\phi_1)[F_1(u,t)||(\nabla_\omega^+ \phi_1)(u,t)||], \ if \ F_1(u,t) > 0 \\ \delta_{\epsilon_1}(\phi_1)[F_1(u,t)||(\nabla_\omega^- \phi_1)(u,t)||], \ if \ F_1(u,t) < 0 \\ 0, \ otherwise \end{cases} \qquad (9)$$

$$\frac{\partial \phi_2(u,t)}{\partial t} \begin{cases} \delta_\epsilon(\phi_2)[F_2(u,t)||(\nabla_\omega^+ \phi_2)(u,t)||], \ if \ F_2(u,t) > 0 \\ \delta_\epsilon(\phi_2)[F_2(u,t)||(\nabla_\omega^- \phi_2)(u,t)||], \ if \ F_2(u,t) < 0 \\ 0, \ otherwise \end{cases} \qquad (10)$$

The velocity F_1 and F_2 (respectively for ϕ_1 and ϕ_2) are defined as:

$$F_1(u,t) = \mu.\kappa_1 - ((I(u) - c_{11})^2 - (I(u) - c_{01})^2)H(\phi_2) \qquad (11)$$
$$+((I(u) - c_{10})^2 - (I(u) - c_{00})^2)(1 - H(\phi_2)),$$

and

$$F_2(u,t) = \mu.\kappa_2 - ((I(u) - c_{11})^2 - (I(u) - c_{10})^2)H(\phi_1) \qquad (12)$$
$$+((I(u) - c_{01})^2 - (I(u) - c_{00})^2)(1 - H(\phi_1)),$$

Where $I(u)$ is the spectral vector at the vertex u, c_{11} is the mean value when $\{\phi_1(u,t) > 0, \phi_2(u,t) > 0\}$, c_{10} is the mean value when $\{\phi_1(u,t) > 0, \phi_2(u,t) < 0\}$, c_{01} is the mean value when $\{\phi_1(u,t) < 0, \phi_2(u,t) > 0\}$, and c_{00} is the mean value when $\{\phi_1(u,t) < 0, \phi_2(u,t) < 0\}$.

3.1   Graph Construction

The first step of the proposed approach is the construction of the weighted graph $G(V,E,\omega)$ from the HSI. Each pixel within the image corresponds to a vertex $v \in V$. Each pair of spatially neighbor vertices u and v are connected with an edge $(u,v) \in E$. A weight $w(u,v)$ is assigned to each edge in G according to the spectral similarity between the vertices u and v. This spectral similarity is measured by Gillis-Bowles's approach [6]:

$$\omega(u,v) = e^{-\theta(u,v)} \times \begin{cases} e^{\frac{-d^2(u,v)}{\sigma^2}} \; if \; d^2(u,v) < r^2 \\ 0 \; otherwise \end{cases} \qquad (13)$$

Where $\theta(u,v) = cos^{-1}(\frac{<u,v>}{||u||.||v||})$ is the spectral angle (measured in degrees) between the spectrum of u and v, and $d(u,v)$ is the Euclidean distance between the spatial position of u and v. The parameters r and σ are have to be adjusted.

3.2   Evaluation

The experiments have been realized on two different HSI samples commonly used for benchmarking. The first image from the university of Pavia, Italy, was acquired by the ROSIS-03 optical sensor acquired (Fig. 2). This image is 610×340 pixels with a spatial resolution of $1.3\,\mathrm{m/pixel}$ and 103 wavelength spectral bands. The second image is the AVIRIS Indian Pine image which was recorded by the AVIRIS sensor (Fig. 3). This image contains 145×145 pixels with 200 spectral reflectance bands.

Figures 2 and 3 show the segmentation results with two-phase, multiphase, with 2 and 3 level sets respectively. These results have been performed with $\sigma^2 = 50$ and $r^2 = 2$.

As it can be seen, increasing the number of level sets produces a finer segmentation.

Which facilitates the spectrum classification. The segmentation results implicitly handle spatial and spectral information, by using the graph.

We compare our method with the graph-cut method proposed in [6]. Figure 4 shows a zoom of segmentation results of a part of Pavia image. The two upper parts of Fig. 4, shows the RGB image and the ground truth of this part of Pavia

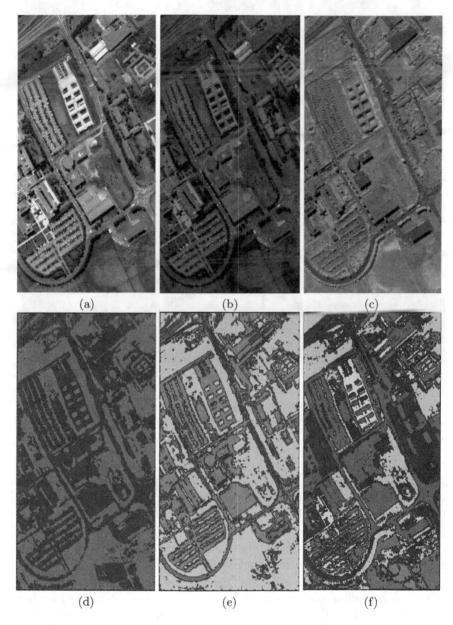

Fig. 2. Pavia university image: (a) RGB Image, (b) 30th band (c) 100th band, (d) Two-phase segmentation, (e) Multiphase segmentation (2 level sets), (f) Multiphase segmentation (3 level sets)

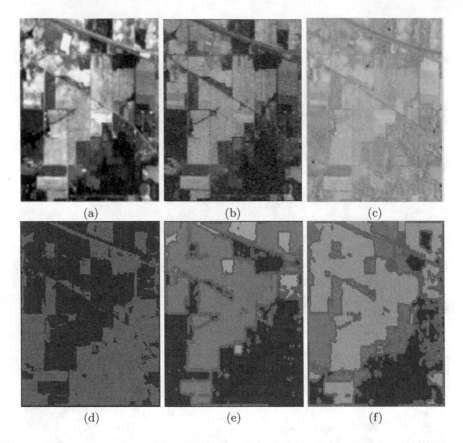

Fig. 3. Indian Pine image: (a) RGB Image, (b) 30th band (c) 100th band, (d) Two-phase segmentation, (e) Multiphase segmentation (2 level sets), (f) Multiphase segmentation (3 level sets)

image. Figures 4c, d, e and f present the results obtained when using our two-phase method with ($r^2 = 2$), our two-phase method with ($r^2 = 25$), graph-cut method with complete graph and our two-phase method with complete graph, respectively.

We use four metrics to evaluate these results with ground truth: the overlap score (OS) that compares two segmentations S and G by $\frac{|S \cap G|}{min(|S|,|G|)}$, Pratt criterion [13], Roman-Roldan criterion [15] and Hausdorff criterion [8].

The Roman-Roldan and the Hausdorff criterions give small values for a better segmentation. On the other hand Pratt and OS criterions consider higher values close to 1 as the better segmentation.

It is clearly noticeable that the results obtained with the two-phase method with complete graph are far superior than all the aforementioned methods.

Evaluation of segmentation results is given in Table 1.

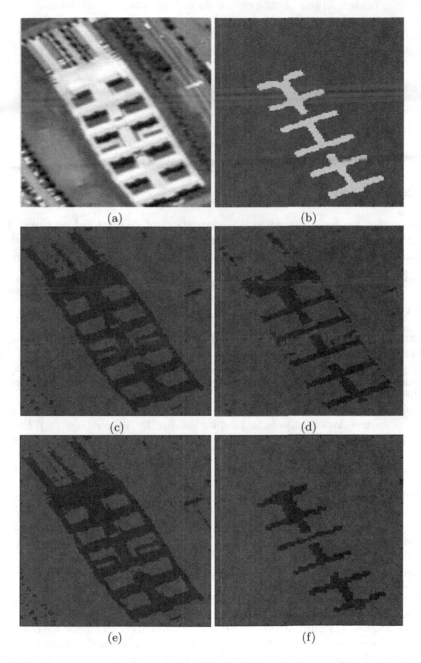

Fig. 4. Zoom on segmentation result of Pavia University image: (a) Original image, (b) Ground truth, (c) Two-phase segmentation ($r^2 = 2$), (d) Two-phase segmentation ($r^2 = 25$), (e) Graph-cut (complete graph), (f) Two-phase segmentation (complete graph)

Table 1. Table of different results of segmentation evaluation

Evaluation criterion	Two-phase method 4-order neighbor graph ($r^2 = 2$)	Graph-cut method complete graph	Two-phase method complete graph
OS	0.8209	0.8131	**0.9566**
Roman-Roldan	6751	6716	**3135**
Hausdorff	3170	5365	**2612**
Pratt	0.3679	0.3858	**0.7739**

4   Conclusion

In this paper, we have presented an adaptation of PDEs level sets over HSIs using a front propagation on weighted graphs. Experimental results have shown the potential of our proposed formulation of PdEs level sets and its efficiency in both two-phase and multiphase models.

References

1. Chan, T., Vese, L.: An active contour model without edges. In: Nielsen, M., Johansen, P., Olsen, O.F., Weickert, J. (eds.) Scale-Space 1999. LNCS, vol. 1682, pp. 141–151. Springer, Heidelberg (1999). doi:10.1007/3-540-48236-9_13
2. Chan, T.F., Vese, L.A.: Active contours without edges. IEEE Trans. Image Process. **10**(2), 266–277 (2001)
3. Dell'Acqua, F., Gamba, P., Prevedini, P.: Level-set based extraction and tracking of meteorological objects in satellite images. In: Proceedings of IEEE 2000 International Geoscience and Remote Sensing Symposium, IGARSS 2000, vol. 2, pp. 627–629. IEEE (2000)
4. Desquesnes, X., Elmoataz, A., Lezoray, O.: PDEs level sets on weighted graphs. In: 2011 18th IEEE International Conference on Image Processing (ICIP), pp. 3377–3380. IEEE (2011)
5. Desquesnes, X., Elmoataz, A., Lézoray, O.: Eikonal equation adaptation on weighted graphs: fast geometric diffusion process for local and non-local image and data processing. J. Math. Imaging Vis. **46**(2), 238–257 (2013)
6. Gillis, D.B., Bowles, J.H.: Hyperspectral image segmentation using spatial-spectral graphs. In: SPIE Defense, Security, and Sensing, p. 83901Q. International Society for Optics and Photonics (2012)
7. Goetz, A.F.: Three decades of hyperspectral remote sensing of the earth: a personal view. Remote Sens. Environ. **113**, S5–S16 (2009)
8. Huttenlocher, D.P., Rucklidge, W.J.: A multi-resolution technique for comparing images using the Hausdorff distance. Technical report, Cornell University (1992)
9. Jakovels, D., Spigulis, J., Saknite, I.: Multi-spectral mapping of in vivo skin hemoglobin and melanin. In: SPIE Photonics Europe, p. 77152Z. International Society for Optics and Photonics (2010)
10. Melgani, F., Bruzzone, L.: Classification of hyperspectral remote sensing images with support vector machines. IEEE Trans. Geosci. Remote Sens. **42**(8), 1778–1790 (2004)

11. Osher, S., Sethian, J.A.: Fronts propagating with curvature-dependent speed: algorithms based on Hamilton-Jacobi formulations. J. Comput. Phys. **79**(1), 12–49 (1988)
12. Paoli, A., Melgani, F., Pasolli, E.: Clustering of hyperspectral images based on multiobjective particle swarm optimization. IEEE Trans. Geosci. Remote Sens. **47**(12), 4175–4188 (2009)
13. Pratt, W.K., Faugeras, O.D., Gagalowicz, A.: Visual discrimination of stochastic texture fields. IEEE Trans. Syst. Man Cybern. **8**(11), 796–804 (1978)
14. Qin, J., Chao, K., Kim, M.S., Lu, R., Burks, T.F.: Hyperspectral and multispectral imaging for evaluating food safety and quality. J. Food Eng. **118**(2), 157–171 (2013)
15. Román-Roldán, R., Gómez-Lopera, J.F., Atae-Allah, C., Martínez-Aroza, J., Luque-Escamilla, P.L.: A measure of quality for evaluating methods of segmentation and edge detection. Pattern Recogn. **34**(5), 969–980 (2001)
16. Schweizer, J., Hollmach, J., Steiner, G., Knels, L., Funk, R.H., Koch, E.: Hyperspectral imaging-a new modality for eye diagnostics. Biomedical Engineering/Biomedizinische Technik 57(SI-1 Track-P), pp. 293–296 (2012)
17. Ta, V.-T., Elmoataz, A., Lézoray, O.: Adaptation of Eikonal equation over weighted graph. In: Tai, X.-C., Mørken, K., Lysaker, M., Lie, K.-A. (eds.) SSVM 2009. LNCS, vol. 5567, pp. 187–199. Springer, Heidelberg (2009). doi:10.1007/978-3-642-02256-2_16
18. Vese, L.A., Chan, T.F.: A multiphase level set framework for image segmentation using the Mumford and Shah model. Int. J. Comput. Vis. **50**(3), 271–293 (2002)

A Mobile Application for Leaf Detection in Complex Background Using Saliency Maps

Lorenzo Putzu$^{(\boxtimes)}$, Cecilia Di Ruberto, and Gianni Fenu

Department of Mathematics and Computer Science, University of Cagliari,
via Ospedale 72, 09124 Cagliari, Italy
lorenzo.putzu@gmail.com, {dirubert,fenu}@unica.it

Abstract. Plants are fundamental for human beings, so it's very important to catalogue and preserve all the plants species. Identifying an unknown plant species is not a simple task. The leaf analysis is one of the approach used for the plant species identification. This task can be completed also automatically by image processing techniques, able to analyse the leaf images and provide a classification based on prior information. Many methods have been proposed in literature in order to complete the whole cataloguing task, providing excellent classification results. Nevertheless, many of the proposed methods work only on images acquired in controlled lighting conditions and with uniform background. In this work we propose a mobile application for leaf analysis for the automatic identification of plant species. The application is mainly devoted to the identification and segmentation steps, resolving the main issues created by uncontrolled lighting conditions with very accurate results.

Keywords: Image analysis · Leaf recognition · Saliency maps · Segmentation

1 Introduction

Hundreds of thousands of plants exist on earth, which share a very close relationship to human beings and play a very important role for human life in many areas, such as food, medical science, industry and environment. For this reason it is very important to catalogue and preserve all species of existing plants. Plant cataloguing is a very complex task, since it requires the collection of a sample of the plant, to be analysed and processed by specialists in laboratories. Another approach consists on the analysis of the leaf, that can be completed directly in the habitat of the plant, but it requires accurate observations and prior knowledge or the ability to navigate through complex databases. The analysis of the leaf can be completed also automatically by image processing techniques, able to process the leaf images and provide a classification based on prior information about other leaves of the same plant species. Many methods have been proposed in literature in order to complete the whole cataloguing task providing excellent classification results [3]. However, many of the best approaches have been

© Springer International Publishing AG 2016
J. Blanc-Talon et al. (Eds.): ACIVS 2016, LNCS 10016, pp. 570–581, 2016.
DOI: 10.1007/978-3-319-48680-2_50

developed to work on non-mobile device, thus they do not provide the opportunity to catalogue the plants directly in their habitat. Instead, most of the mobile application present in literature perform well only on images acquired in controlled lighting conditions and with uniform background. In this work we propose a mobile application for the automatic identification of plant species through the analysis of leaf images acquired directly in their habitat and so presenting uncontrolled lighting conditions and complex backgrounds. The main goal of this work is to provide a system able to automatically detect the leaf of interest and provide an accurate segmentation. We focused on the segmentation task since it's the most important step of the whole cataloguing process, from which depends the accuracy of the whole system. The proposed method is based on saliency map extraction, in order to detect the leaf of interest discarding the other objects and the background of the acquired scene. In order to find the most suitable approach we compare different saliency extraction approaches. The best saliency extraction approach is then used to compute the final saliency map, that represents the starting point for a Region Growing segmentation. The paper is organized as follows. In Sect. 2 we discuss the related works. In Sect. 3 our problem is detailed and our approach presented. In Sect. 4 we evaluate the performance of the proposed algorithm with real images. Finally, in Sect. 5, we present our conclusions and some directions for future work.

2 Related Works

Segmentation is a basic pre-processing task in many image processing applications and fundamental in agriculture computer vision. In the recent years many algorithms to separate plant leaves from the background have been proposed. But most of them have been tested on simple or uniform background. Usually the leaf is put on a constant sheet before segmentation. In [18] two parallelisation strategies (fine-grain and coarse-grain approach) are proposed for segmenting leaf image. The Canny edge detector and Otsu thresholding methods are used and experimental results present only uniform backgrounds. In [22] the authors have proposed a system where a user in the field can take a picture of an unknown plant, feed it to the system carried on a portable computer for classification of different plants. The segmentation has achieved on fuzzy threshold and clustering. Before applying the proposed method pre-processing techniques like image conversion, noise reduction by median filter, morphological operation and finally wavelet transformation, have to be processed. The performance of the segmentation is analysed by Jaccard, dice, variation of index and global consistency error method. The proposed approach is verified with real time plant leaf database, giving good accuracy results, but still on uniform background. In [24] an effective method for image segmentation of cucumber leaf images is proposed. First, the colour space model is analysed. Then a kind of color feature is applied to obtain the feature map, which combines RGB and HSI models. Finally, a morphological method is used to accomplish the image segmentation. This method has been shown effective through experiments on samples on uniform background.

In [2] the authors propose a robust and accurate method for segmenting specular objects acquired under loosely controlled conditions. Many techniques are based on expectation-maximization (EM) and estimate the colour distributions of the background and foreground pixels of the input image. The authors show they can improve the EM-based and classification-based methods by first segmenting the pixels around the leaf boundary and use them to initialize the colour distributions of an EM optimization. They show that this simple approach results in a robust and accurate method if the leaves are not on complex background. Currently, every mobile phone running the Android operating system is equipped with a high-quality digital camera with support for auto-focus and flash photography. Since the importance of cataloguing leaf from an unknown plant species, many systems for automated plant leaf classification on mobile device have been proposed. The input to the recognition algorithm is a photograph of a leaf of unknown species taken with the mobile phone's camera. One of the firsts mobile application for plant cataloguing using automatic visual recognition is Leafsnap [10]. This application extract from the leaf images the features representing the curvature over multiple scales, and identifying the species from a dataset of 184 trees. Unfortunately it is able to segment the leaf only with the presence of an untextured background. In [20], after capturing the leaf image, preprocessing is executed. Preprocessing includes grey scale conversion, image segmentation, binary conversion and image smoothing. Its aim is to improve extracted features that are used for further processing. This paper introduces a neural network approach for plant leaf identification. In the paper no details about segmentation step have been reported. In the Android mobile application proposed in [9] the picture must be taken at a reasonable distance, in decent lighting, roughly normal to the surface, and against a background which provides sufficient contrast. The method is proved quite robust under reasonable conditions. MedLeaf [17] is a new mobile application for medicinal plants identification based on leaf image. The application runs on the Android operating system. The authors use Local Binary Pattern to extract leaf texture and Probabilistic Neural Network to classify the image. The evaluation result shows that MedLeaf is promising for medicinal plants identification. However all the analysed plants are on uniform background. In [15] the user captures a leaf image with an Android device. The image must contain a centred single leaf on a uniform background. Before launching the identification, the user has to select a leaf character that will be the basis of the identification (margin, venation points). Then, the leaf image is sent to a primary intermediate server with a degraded quality to save bandwidth. The role of the primary server is to store the image in order to broaden the knowledge about plant species. The identification step is performed on the second server using the descriptor previously selected by the user. Finally, a ranked list of leaf species is returned and displayed on the Android device. In [16] a solution to unsupervised L*a*b* colour texture based image segmentation in which K-means algorithm with minor change is used to find homogeneously textured clusters is proposed. The developed algorithm performs very well in segmenting leaf diseases from constant background. In [11] a method using client-server

Fig. 1. Comparison of the state-of-the-art mobile application for leaf identification. From left to right: Leafsnap [9,10,20], MedLeaf [11,15–17].

architecture has been proposed. The client is an Android mobile device. In the client side, the authors implemented the interactive image segmentation. The user can take a picture of the plant or can use an existing picture in the album to do plant identification. In the server side, the authors implemented the kernel descriptor. The proposed method is proved to be robust, however it is still limited to the simple leaf images with no complex background. To better highlight the standard condition for which the mobile application just mentioned are targeted, in Fig. 1 we have illustrated some screenshots of their main activity. As can be noted just two application are targeted for leaf that present a non uniform background, but as said previously in [20] none details about leaf detection and segmentation are reported while in [11] the segmentation is aided by the users interactions, that should draw different markers on the screen. In this work we propose a mobile application for leaf detection in more realistic condition, able to achieve robust segmentation results also in complex background without asking for the users interactions.

3   System Overview

Of course, the acquisition of images in the outdoors with uncontrolled lighting conditions introduces several problems. The main problem, however, is the detection of the object of interest in a complex background and the subsequent segmentation step. When we talk about complex background we mean all that scene presenting a leaf on its foreground and different other objects on its foreground. Obviously in most cases the objects in the image background will be other leaves, thus among all the images showed in Fig. 2 the last is the one that most likely will be captured by a user who intends to catalogue a plant species. Therefore, a further problem could be caused by the presence of two or more close leaves on the same image which can greatly affect the segmentation algorithm. Furthermore, leaves do not preserve the same pigmentation during the whole year or they could present small colour defect caused by the presence of pests or diseases. For all these reasons we have decided to create a system that could be as more general as possible, able to handle all these different situations. The proposed leaf detection system, differently from all the other state-of-the-art system, before the segmentation uses a preliminary step devoted to the detection of the leaf of interest and also capable of discriminating it against other

Fig. 2. Different kind of complex background taken from MSRA dataset [13].

objects and the background. We have decided to address these issues by proposing the application of saliency algorithms to the original images to detect the leaf, since saliency algorithms always highlight salient points in the image, even in the absence of targets.

3.1 On Saliency

Saliency algorithms are inspired to the ability of humans to easily segment image regions that are distinct from their neighbourhood for brightness, colour, shape and movement and therefore are defined salient. Therefore, the purpose of saliency detection is to identify the most important and informative part of a scene. Saliency methods have been applied to numerous vision problems included image segmentation. They can be based on prior information or assumptions about the image, or based on a supervised learning using class labels to fit with the information, the expectations or the tasks. In this work we test four different approaches. The first method for the saliency extraction is the algorithm of Itti, Koch and Niebur [8], based on the extraction of the Gaussian pyramids [6]. These pyramids are composed by nine spatial scales that are realised filtering by a low-pass filter and sub-sampling the original image, producing a vertical and horizontal reduction in the image factors from 1:1 to 1:256. The images at different scales are used to perform some centre-surround operations, simply by calculating the differences between the images with fine scales and images with rough scales. The first set of feature map is extracted from the intensity image, created by averaging the values of the three colour components. A second set of maps is extracted from the colour channels called double-opponent that are red/green and yellow/blue. The last set of feature map is extracted from the local information on the orientation obtained by the Gabor filters performed at 4 orientations with intervals of 45°. The three different sets of feature maps are first normalized individually, in order to flatten the map values? where the local features are almost homogeneous and at the same time emphasizing the local features that have large variations. Finally, the 3 feature maps are averaged between them in order to extract the final saliency map. The second method for the saliency extraction is the Visual Saliency Feature (VSF) method [14]. The main difference with the previous one lies in the features extraction step, that is not based on a pyramidal decomposition mechanism, but starting from the original image it calculates the so-called Integral image or Summed Area Table (SAT). The SAT image is used to extract the differences on-centre and off-centre using rectangles of different sizes, as proposed also in the VOCUS System [5], with dimensions 12, 24, 28, 48, 56, 112. Finally, the on-centre and off-centre maps are calculated by adding up pixel by pixel the 6 sub-maps on-centre and off-centre. The next two algorithms for saliency maps extraction make use of superpixels, an image representation that provides a primitive able to capture the local characteristics and redundancy of the image [19]. There are several algorithms for extracting superpixels [4,12,21,23], but in this work the Simple Linear Iterative Clustering (SLIC) algorithm [1] has been chosen, as it produces high quality superpixels, compact and almost uniform very efficiently. It creates a local grouping of pixels on the *5-D* space according to their colour, defined by the *Lab* values of the CIELAB colour space, and their proximity, defined by the coordinates x, y. To speed up the subsequent steps the value of K, that define the number of clusters and the coarseness of the regions, has been set to *300*, generating superpixels approximately equal to *1024* pixels. The third approach for the calculation of saliency makes is called Flash No-Flash [7] and comes from the observation that only the objects in the foreground, being closest to the camera, are significantly illuminated by the flash. Therefore, assuming that all the salient objects are placed in the foreground they can be easily distinguished from the objects in the background computing the difference between the captured images with and without flash, that generates a rough distance map. This information is combined with the information given by the colour and orientation of the surfaces, which can be extracted thanks to the brightness variations introduced by the flash. Finally, the spatial information is used to asses that the salient pixels are compact both in the image plane and both in the 3D space. These different maps are then combined with each other to form the final saliency map, by normalizing the values of the individual maps and then multiplying their values between them. The fourth and last method used for the saliency extraction instead is based on the observation that the objects of interest, and therefore with high saliency, are in the foreground and then next to the centre of the image, while the background often presents a local or global appearance connectivity with each of the 4 edges of the image. In this approach, these clues are exploited to compute the saliency of pixels based on the classification or ranking of the superpixels. Once the superpixels have been calculated from the original image, it builds a closed cycle graph where each node represents a superpixel. This method is called saliency detection via Graph-Based Manifold Ranking (GMR) [25]. The identification of the salience is modelled as a multiple classification problems based on graphs, where each node is used as a query and the remaining nodes are classified according to their relevance to the given query. The salience of each node is defined by its classification score calculated at the end of all queries.

3.2   Saliency Guided Segmentation

Although the information contained in the saliency map clearly defines the object of interest, a trivial segmentation algorithm based on threshold could be greatly influenced by the presence of too close leaves or objects with an orientation not perpendicular to the camera. For a more accurate segmentation of the leaf a Region Growing algorithm has been used, with the aim to also exploit the colour information for the growth of the initial region. The initial region obviously corresponds to the region or regions of the saliency map with maximum value. The growth makes use of the Euclidean distance between the starting region and the neighbours, considering not only the values of the saliency map s but also the colour information. This information has been extracted from the channels a and b of the CIELAB colour space, which represent the pixels chromaticity, while the brightness channel L is excluded from the calculation, in order to neglect sudden changes of brightness that can be present acquiring images in open spaces or generated by the flash. Thus a pixel is represented as $[s\ a\ b]^T$. At each iteration the Region Growing algorithm computes the mean value of the pixels already included in the growing region s_μ, a_μ and b_μ and the distance with all its neighbouring pixels as in (1).

$$d = \sqrt{(s_\mu - s_{x,y}^2) + (a_\mu - a_{x,y}^2) + (b_\mu - b_{x,y}^2)} \tag{1}$$

A neighbouring pixel is included in the growing region if the distance value is less than a prefixed value D, that is automatically extracted from the maximum distance between pairs of pixels of the starting region. The region growing stops when an iteration doesn't include any pixel in the growing region.

4   Implementation and Experimental Evaluation

The leaf detection application has been developed for Android systems with the use of OpenCV libraries which provide the basic tools for computer vision, whose main programming language is C++, but can also be used with other languages such as C, Python and Java, and consequently also in the Android environment. Image acquisition makes use of the OpenCV classes for an optimal capture of the scene, using the camera embedded in the device. For practical reasons, the image can be acquired only from the back camera of the device, allowing the user to view the leaf during the acquisition process, keeping it completely inside the screen border. Another implementative choice has been to decrease the resolution of the acquired images at 640×480 pixels, not only to make the application accessible to older devices, and then with a low-level acquisition system, but also because a higher resolution would have increased the computational time, not acceptable for a mobile device and for the purposes of the application itself. Given the importance of having a sharp image and to avoid as much as possible blurring due to the movement of the device, the image acquisition occurs automatically at the end of the autofocus process. Therefore, the acquisition process is actually initiated by pushing a button, which after 5 s starts the autofocus process and only when the object of interest, namely the centre of the image, is completely in focus, the scene is captured. This expedient is particularly crucial for the calculation of the saliency via Flash/No-Flash, as in this case two images are required, whose spatial differences should be as minor as possible. All the four saliency extraction methods described in the previous section have been implemented and tested. A qualitative evaluation of all the methods is shown in Fig. 3, where the four different approaches for saliency extraction have been computed with three different images acquired with our smartphones in different lighting conditions. As it can be seen the outputs of the various approaches are very different between them. The results obtained through the first two algorithms are very rough, in fact they tend to recognise as more salient just few points of the images. In particular it can be observed how the salient point are scattered thought the images instead of being concentrated in the centre where the object of interest is supposed to be. The other two approaches instead are able to detect the central leaf as the most salient object. However, we observed in these and other images that, while the GMR algorithm has proved more solid, being able to produce a very precise map of salience in different lighting conditions, instead the results obtained with the algorithm via Flash/No-Flash are too variable, since this method depends excessively from the environment and from the used instrumentation. In fact, in conditions of very intense light and with a direction almost perpendicular to the leaf, the two images, acquired with and without Flash, do not differ significantly, while in low light conditions, in covered spaces or indoors, as shown in the third image of the Fig. 3, the image acquired without the flash looks too dark so the two images differ too greatly, producing an imprecise saliency. In order to asses if the GMR approach could be definitively the most suitable for our purposes we made a quantitative evaluation we performed two different experiment. The first one make use of one of the most used image database for saliency comparison that is the MSRA dataset [13], from which we have selected 100 images containing leaves, such as that ones showed in Fig. 2. But since these images cannot be used to test the Flash/No-flash approach, and since they are not representative of a real use case, we performed a second experiment using 100 images acquired directly with our smartphones. Both experiments are devoted to evaluate the performances of the saliency methods by measuring the *F-score*. In order to assess also the segmentation performances of the Region Growing algorithm we made a further comparison, by computing the binary image using a fixed threshold and an image dependent adaptive threshold [1], which is computed as twice the mean value of the saliency map (Fig. 4).

As it can be seen, the results are much better with the GMR saliency, in particular if combined with the segmentation based on Region Growing algorithm, able to preserve the whole leaf shape without neglecting the parts in which the saliency has lower values, as it occurs with the threshold based segmentation, that can be observed in detail in Fig. 5. In that figure we qualitative compared the segmentation based on thresholds and the Region Growing algorithm. As it can be observed with the Region Growing algorithm the leaf of interest is

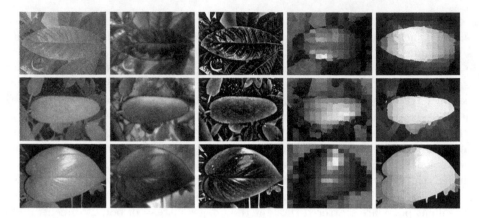

Fig. 3. Comparison between the four different saliency extraction approaches. From left to right: original images, saliency maps extracted with Itti, Koch e Niebur, VSF, Flash/No-Flash e GMR approaches.

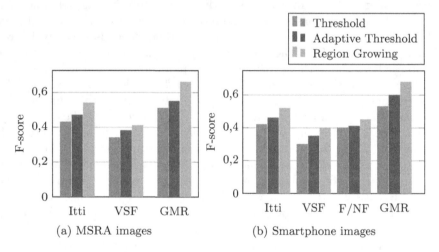

Fig. 4. Comparison between the different saliency extraction approaches using the MSRA dataset [13] and the images acquired directly with our application.

almost always preserved in its integrity and the contours are more defined, with very few inaccuracies or connections with other objects that are not of interest, which can be effectively removed with some simple post-processing operations. It is also important to note how the algorithm behaves well even in cases when the chromaticity of the leaf of interest differs from the green colour or in cases where there are more leaves in the same plane with the same orientation, as showed in the last two rows of Fig. 5.

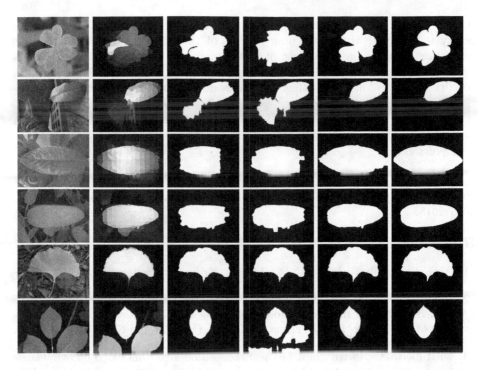

Fig. 5. Comparison of the different segmentation approaches. From left to right: original images, GMR saliency, threshold, adaptive threshold, Region Growing and Ground Truth.

5   Conclusion

In this work we have proposed a mobile application for the automatic identification of plant species through the analysis of leaf images acquired directly in their habitat and so presenting different lighting conditions and complex backgrounds. The main goal of this work has been to design and develop a system able to automatically detect the leaf of interest and provide an accurate segmentation. It is based on saliency extraction to detect the leaf of interest and segmentation by Region Growing algorithm, which exploits both the information contained in the saliency map and both the colour information of the individual pixels. A comparison among different saliency extraction approaches has helped us to identify the GMR as the most suitable approach for our application, able to facilitate not only the segmentation task but demonstrating excellent performance, suitable for a mobile application. Unfortunately we cannot make any comparison with the other mobile application or the state-of-the-art approaches for leaf segmentation. Indeed, as said previously, just few authors developed an approach targeted to images presenting a complex background, which moreover have not provided any results on the segmentation accuracy. The next efforts to improve and complete the application will be definitely devoted to the realization of the subsequent steps of feature extraction and classification, necessary to complete the cataloguing process of the plants. Therefore, it will be important to define a robust set of features, independent from variable characteristics such as brightness, since images are acquired with different lighting conditions and colour, given that the leaves do not present the same pigmentation throughout the whole year or because of the presence of pests or diseases. It will also be very important to identify a classification model able to obtain very precise cataloguing results, but at the same time able to complete the task very efficiently.

Acknowledgements. This work was supported by the Research Program "Natura 2000", funded by the Autonomous Region of Sardinia (Legge Regionale 7/2007) 2015–2018.

References

1. Achanta, R., Shaji, A., Smith, K., Lucchi, A., Fua, P., Ssstrunk, S.: SLIC Superpixels. Technical report, EPFL (2010)
2. Buoncompagni, S., Maio, D., Lepetit, V.: Leaf segmentation under loosely controlled conditions. In: Xie, X., Jones, M.W., Gary, K.L., Tam, E. (eds.) Proceedings of the British Machine Vision Conference (BMVC), pp. 133.1–133.12. BMVA Press, September 2015
3. Di Ruberto, C., Putzu, L.: A fast leaf recognition algorithm based on svm classifierand high dimensional feature vector. In: 2014 International Conference on Computer Vision Theory and Applications (VISAPP), vol. 1, pp. 601–609, January 2014
4. Felzenszwalb, P.F., Huttenlocher, D.P.: Efficient graph-based image segmentation. Int. J. Comput. Vis. **59**(2), 167–181 (2004)
5. Frintrop, S.: VOCUS: A Visual Attention System for Object Detection and Goaldirected Search. LNCS (LNAI), vol. 3899. Springer, Heidelberg (2006). doi:10. 1007/11682110
6. Greenspan, H., Belongie, S., Goodman, R., Perona, P., Rakshit, S., Anderson, C.H.: Overcomplete steerable pyramid filters and rotation invariance. In: 1994 IEEE Computer Society Conference on Computer Vision and Pattern Recognition, Proceedings CVPR 1994, pp. 222–228, June 1994
7. He, S., Lau, R.W.H.: Saliency detection with flash and no-flash image pairs. In: Fleet, D., Pajdla, T., Schiele, B., Tuytelaars, T. (eds.) ECCV 2014, Part III. LNCS, vol. 8691, pp. 110–124. Springer, Heidelberg (2014)
8. Itti, L., Koch, C., Niebur, E.: A model of saliency-based visual attention for rapid scene analysis. IEEE Trans. Pattern Anal. Mach. Intell. **20**(11), 1254–1259 (1998)
9. Knight, D., Painter, J., Potter, M.: Automatic plant leaf classification for a mobile field guide: an android application. Technical report, Stanford University (2010)
10. Kumar, N., Belhumeur, P.N., Biswas, A., Kress, D., Lopez, I.C., Soares, J.V.B.: Leafsnap: a computer vision system for automatic plant species identification. In: Fitzgibbon, A., Lazebnik, S., Perona, P., Sato, Y., Schmid, C. (eds.) ECCV 2012. LNCS, vol. 7573, pp. 502–516. Springer, Berlin (2012)
11. Le, T.L., Duong, D.N., Nguyen, V.T., Vu, H., Hoang, V.N., Nguyen, T.T.N.: Complex background leaf-based plant identification method based on interactive segmentation and kernel descriptor. In: EMR 2015 Proceedings of the 2nd International Workshop on Environmental Multimedia Retrieval, pp. 3–8. ACM, New York (2015)

12. Levinshtein, A., Sminchisescu, C., Dickinson, S.: Multiscale symmetric part detection and grouping. Int. J. Comput. Vis. **104**(2), 117–134 (2013)
13. Liu, T., Sun, J., Zheng, N.N., Tang, X., Shum, H.Y.: Learning to detect a salient object. In: 2007 IEEE Conference on Computer Vision and Pattern Recognition, pp. 1–8, June 2007
14. Montabone, S., Soto, A.: Human detection using a mobile platform and novel features derived from a visual saliency mechanism. Image Vis. Comput. **28**(3), 391–402 (2010)
15. Mouine, S., Yahiaoui, I., Verroust-Blondet, A., Joyeux, L., Selmi, S.: Goau, H.: An android application for leaf-based plant identification. In: ICMR 2013 - Proceedings of the 3rd ACM International Conference on Multimedia Retrieval, (ICMR 2013), pp. 309–310. ACM, New York (2013)
16. Prasad, S., Peddoju, S.K., Ghosh, D.: Unsupervised resolution independent based natural plant leaf disease segmentation approach for mobile devices. In: I-CARE 2013 Proceedings of the 5th IBM Collaborative Academia Research Exchange Workshop. No. 11 in I-CARE 2013. ACM, New York (2013)
17. Prasvita, D.S., Herdiyeni, Y.: Medleaf: mobile application for medicinal plant identification based on leaf image. Int. J. Adv. Sci. Eng. Inf. Technol. **3**(2), 5–9 (2013)
18. Rahman, M.N.A., Nasir, A.F.A., Mat, N., Mamat, A.R.: Image segmentation using openmp and its application in plant species classification. Int. J. Softw. Eng. Appl. **9**(5), 135–144 (2015)
19. Ren, X., Malik, J.: Learning a classification model for segmentation. In: Ninth IEEE International Conference on Computer Vision, Proceedings, vol. 1, pp. 10–17, October 2003
20. Shejwal, S., Nikale, P., Datir, A., Kadus, A., Bhade, P., Pawar, R.: Automatic plant leaf classification on mobile field guide. Int. J. Comput. Sci. Technol. **6**(2), 93–97 (2015)
21. Shi, J., Malik, J.: Normalized cuts and image segmentation. IEEE Trans. Pattern Anal. Mach. Intell. **22**(8), 888–905 (2000)
22. Valliammal, N., Geethalakshmi, S.N.: A novel approach for plant leaf image segmentation using fuzzy clustering. Int. J. Comput. Appl. **44**(13), 10–20 (2012)
23. Vedaldi, A., Soatto, S.: Quick shift and kernel methods for mode seeking. In: Forsyth, D., Torr, P., Zisserman, A. (eds.) ECCV 2008, Part IV. LNCS, vol. 5305, pp. 705–718. Springer, Heidelberg (2008)
24. Wang, L., Yang, T., Tian, Y.: Crop disease leaf image segmentation method based on color features. In: Li, D. (ed.) Computer and Computing Technologies in Agriculture, vol. 1. Springer, Heidelberg (2008)
25. Yang, C., Zhang, L., Lu, H., Ruan, X., Yang, M.H.: Saliency detection via graph-based manifold ranking. In: 2013 IEEE Conference on Computer Vision and Pattern Recognition (CVPR), pp. 3166–3173, June 2013

Content-Based Mammogram Retrieval Using Mixed Kernel PCA and Curvelet Transform

Sami Dhahbi$^{(\boxtimes)}$, Walid Barhoumi, and Ezzeddine Zagrouba

Research Team on Intelligent Systems in Imaging and Artificial Vision (SIIVA),
LimTic Laboratory, Institut Supérieur d'Informatique (ISI),
Université de Tunis El Manar, 2 Rue Abou Rayhane Bayrouni, 2080 Ariana, Tunisia
sami.dhahbi@laposte.net, walid.barhoumi@enicarthage.rnu.tn,
ezzeddine.zagrouba@fsm.rnu.tn
http://www.isi.rnu.tn

Abstract. Content-based image retrieval (CBIR) has recently emerged as a promising method to assist radiologists in diagnosing mammographic masses by displaying pathologically similar cases. In this paper, a CBIR system using curvelet transform and kernel principal component analysis (KPCA) is proposed. Thanks to its improved direction and edge representation abilities, curvelet transform first provides desirable mammographic features. Once the region of interest (ROI) is curvelet transformed, the KPCA is then applied and the first components are used as descriptors. Bearing in mind that neighbor points are the most important but faraway points may contain useful information in mammogram retrieval, we propose a new mixed kernel that overcomes the shortcoming of Gaussian kernels and emphasis neighbor points without neglecting faraway ones. The proposed mixed kernel is a mixture of two gaussian kernels with high and low sigma values. Experiments performed on a large dataset of mammograms showed the superiority of the proposed kernel over single gaussian kernels.

Keywords: Mammography · CBIR · Kernel PCA · Curvelet transform · Mixed gaussian kernel

1 Introduction

According to worldwide statistics in 2012 [1], it is estimated that 1.7 million new cases were diagnosed with breast cancer which is the most common female cancer (25 % of all cancers). It is also the leading cause of cancer deaths among women (14.71 % of total cancer deaths). Early detection of breast cancer plays an important role in increasing treatment options and thus decreasing mortality rates [2]. Even though screening mammography is the most cost-effective tool to detect breast cancer at early stages, nationwide mammogram screening programs result in high false-positive and false-negative rates. Indeed, because of the difficulty of mammogram interpretation even for skilled radiologists, cancer cases could be missed and non-cancerous lesions could be misinterpreted. Besides, even though

J. Blanc-Talon et al. (Eds.): ACIVS 2016, LNCS 10016, pp. 582–590, 2016.
DOI: 10.1007/978-3-319-48680-2_51

double reading is effective clinically, it is not a likely solution due to the huge amount of mammograms to be analyzed and the limited number of radiologists [3]. A more efficient solution is to rely on computer-aided diagnosis (CAD) systems [4]. These systems could replace the second reader by analyzing a given mammogram and returning a decision about its malignancy. The CAD could be used also to assist radiologists in their interpretation. However, a major concern with these black-box CAD systems is the doubt of radiologists about their output, which prevents their widespread. To cope with this problem, a promising alternative to traditional CAD systems is to use content-based image retrieval (CBIR) techniques that display similar mammograms with their corresponding ground truth. Indeed, radiologists will have much more confidence in the output of the CBIR because they know the cases used to make the decision. Many content-based image retrieval systems have been proposed in order to cope with different issues of mammogram retrieval such as relevance feedback [5], similarity measure [6], scalability [7], multi-view information fusion [8] and feature extraction [9,10].

In this work, we focus on the feature extraction step, which is a key step for effective content-based mammogram retrieval. Hence, curvelet transform provides several desirable properties related to its improved direction and edge representation abilities, which makes it a good performer in multi-resolution texture analysis. Thus, several curvelet-based feature extraction methods have been proposed in recent years in order to characterize mammogram masses [9,11]. In Gedik et al. [11], a principal component analysis (PCA) on curvelet subbands were performed and the first principal components were used to describe lesion masses. Hence, the use of the traditional PCA requires a normal distribution, which is not the case of the distributions of curvelet coefficients computed from mammograms [9]. To overcome the shortcoming of PCA and to cope with the non-gaussianity of curvelet coefficients, we have proposed in a previous work [9] to use higher order curvelet moments. Experiments showed that curvelet moments outperformed state-of-the-art curvelet-based mammogram description methods, including PCA analysis. Even though, the obtained results were not satisfactory, mainly in distinguishing between the malignant masses and the benign ones.

The main motivation of this work is to extract a set of curvelet descriptors for mammogram retrieval that could discriminate between malignant masses and benign ones. To overcome the shortcoming of PCA and to cope with the non-gaussianity of curvelet coefficient distributions, we propose to use kernel principal component analysis (KPCA). Besides, to further improve the performance of our CBIR system, we propose to use the mixture of gaussian kernels as a kernel for KPCA. Bearing in mind that, in the context of mammogram retrieval, faraway points are not as important as neighbor ones but they may contain valuable information, our goal is to have a kernel that emphasizes neighbor points and takes into consideration faraway points. According to the used sigma values for Gaussian kernels, higher values take into consideration faraway but fail to emphasize neighborhood, whereas lower values emphasize neighbor points but ignore faraway ones. To take advantage of higher sigma values as well as of lower sigma values, we propose to use as a kernel a mixture of gaussian obtained through the combination of two gaussian kernels having high and low sigma values. In this way, the proposed mixture of gaussian kernel emphasizes neighbor points without neglecting faraway ones. Experiments performed on the DDSM database showed that KPCA with the proposed kernel outperforms not only KPCA with gaussian kernels but also state-of-the-art curvelet-based feature extraction methods including PCA.

The rest of this paper is organized as follows. The proposed method is presented in Sect. 2. Section 3 is devoted for experimental results. Conclusion and future works are given in the last section.

2   Proposed Method

In this section, we describe the proposed method. After reviewing the curvelet transform and the kernel PCA, we present the proposed mixture of gaussian kernels.

2.1   Curvelet Transform

Curvelet transform is a multiscale and multidirectional geometric transform. It was introduced in [12] to overcome the inherent limitations of wavelet-like transforms. Compared with wavelet, curvelet exhibits desirable properties of directionality, anisotropy, efficient representation of smooth objects with discontinuities along curves, and optimally sparse representation. Being an extension of wavelets, curvelet-based methods have not only becoming popular in similar fields, but also outperformed wavelet-based methods, namely in image denoising [13] and feature extraction [14]. Figure 1 illustrates the difference between curvelet and wavelet transforms.

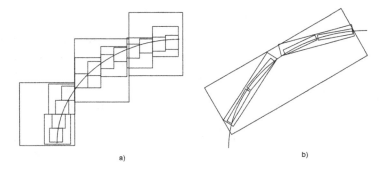

a)   b)

Fig. 1. Comparison between approximation using (a) wavelet and (b) curvelet [12].

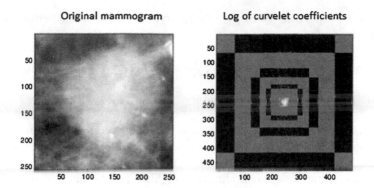

Fig. 2. Example of a mammogram image and its curvelet transform.

Given an image $f(x,y)$, the discret curvelet coefficient is defined as follows:

$$c(j,l,k) = \sum_{x=0}^{N}\sum_{y=0}^{N} f(x,y)\overline{\varphi_{j,l,k}(x,y)} \tag{1}$$

where, $\varphi_{j,l,k}(x,y)$ is the discrete mother curvelet; and j, l, and k are the parameters of scale, orientation and translation, respectively.

There exist two implementations to perform fast discrete curvelet transform. They differ in the way curvelets at a given scale and angle are translated with respect to each other. The first implementation is based on unequally spaced fast fourier transforms (USFFT), whereas the second one is based on the wrapping of specially selected fourier samples. In this study, we used the USFFT implementation since it is used in similar studies on curvelet-based mammogram analysis [9,11,14]. Figure 2 displays an example of mammogram image and its curvelet transform.

2.2 Kernel PCA

Principal components analysis (PCA) is a classical multivariate statistical method commonly used for feature reduction with successful application in several areas. The main drawback of PCA is that it allows only linear dimension reduction. In the context of mammogram characterization, this method was used in [11] to extract a set of features from curvelet coefficients. However, PCA-based curvelet feature extraction yields poor results in the case of mammogram analysis, mainly because of the non-gaussianity of the distribution of curvelet coefficients [9]. Hence, the kernel PCA is proposed to cope with the non-linearity of curvelet coefficient distributions. Several kernels can be used to perform KPCA. Indeed, the appropriate choice of the kernel functions and their parameters seriously affect the performance of the KPCA. Commonly used kernels include polynomial kernels, gaussian kernels and sigmoid kernels. In particular, gaussian kernel (2) is the most commonly used kernel because it exhibits several good properties (isotropy, stationary, ...) and it outperforms all the other kernels.

$$k_G^\sigma(x, y) = exp(-\frac{\|x - y\|^2}{2\sigma^2}),$$ (2)

where σ (sigma) is the width parameter.

The choice of the optimal value of σ is application dependent, and it is typically selected using the cross-validation approaches. A large sigma value allows to take into consideration faraway points but it does not emphasize neighbors, whereas a low value of sigma emphasizes neighbor points but it neglects faraway points.

2.3 Mixture of Gaussian Kernels

The aim of this section is the definition of a kernel that is more suited for mammogram retrieval than (single) gaussian kernel. In fact, in image retrieval, the kernel function must emphasize the neighborhood without neglecting faraway points. Indeed, the neighbors of a point are more likely to be similar to this point. Therefore, the kernel function must emphasize the neighborhood. For faraway points, even though they are most likely to be dissimilar to the point in question, they could contain useful information about this point. Thus, they must not be omitted. We assume that weighting data points is better than simply discarding some of them. In gaussian kernels, the value of sigma defines how the kernel will handle neighbor and faraway points. A low value of sigma emphasizes the neighborhood and discards faraway points, whereas a high value of sigma takes into account all points but does not emphasize neighborhood. To take advantage of both low and high sigma values, we propose a new kernel as a mixture of two gaussian kernels having high and low sigma values. The proposed mixed kernel $k_{Mixed}(x, y)$ is defined as follows:

$$k_{Mixed}(x, y) = \lambda_H . k_G^{\sigma_H}(x, y) + \lambda_L . k_G^{\sigma_L}(x, y);$$ (3)

where, $k_G^{\sigma_H}$ is a gaussian kernel with high sigma value, $k_G^{\sigma_L}$ is a gaussian kernel with low sigma value, and λ_H and λ_L are the weighting parameter of $k_G^{\sigma_H}$ and $k_G^{\sigma_L}$, respectively. The mixed gaussian kernel is a positive definite kernel because it is a linear combination of positive definite kernels.

3 Experimental Results

The mammograms used in the realized experiments are extracted from the Digital Database for Screening Mammography (DDSM) [15]. DDSM is currently the largest publicly available dataset of mammograms. This dataset includes 2604 cases, and each case is composed of 4 mammograms. The database includes the ground truth of each mammogram, mainly its diagnostic result (benign or

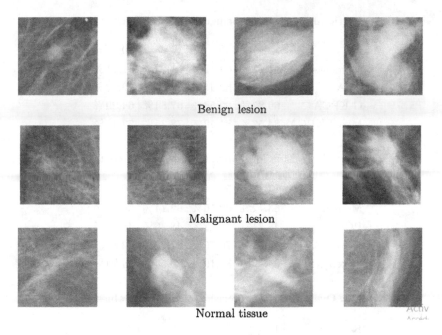

Benign lesion

Malignant lesion

Normal tissue

Fig. 3. A sample of the used ROIs from the DDSM database.

malignant) and the location of the lesions. It is not possible to perform curvelet transform directly in the whole mammographic image because it comprises the pectoral muscle and the background with a lot of noise. Therefore, we removed the unwanted parts and we computed features on a limited Region of Interest (ROI) that contains the prospective abnormality. This step is crucial to extract and focus on the appropriate part of the mammography. In fact, we performed a manual cropping based on the information provided in the ground truth. Thus, the dataset consists of 1914 ROIs (862 benign and 1052 malignant). Figure 3 illustrates some examples of the ROIs from the DDSM database used in the experiments.

For comparison purposes, we have implemented and tested several curvelet-based feature extraction methods, including moments, PCA, KPCA with gaussian kernel and KPCA with the proposed mixed gaussian kernel. Evaluation was performed using the 5-fold cross validation method and the Euclidean distance was used to estimate the similarity between cases. For all the compared methods, we have computed the retrieval precision values for different number K of returned images (1, 5, 10 and 20). Tables 1, 2 and 3 illustrate the retrieval precision for benign cases, for malignant cases, and the overall precision, respectively.

We can conclude that in all tested cases, the proposed mixed kernel records the highest precision values for benign cases (=84.57 %), malignant cases (=84.29 %) and overall images (=84.43 %). Besides, the gaussian KPCA yields the second better results, whereas the lowest precision values were recorded for

Table 1. Retrieval precision for benign cases at different values of K.

K	1	5	10	20
Moments	61.17 %	64.12 %	61.23 %	61.11 %
PCA	52.29 %	52.4 %7	52.04 %	52.16 %
G-KPCA	69.87 %	69.54 %	67.84 %	64.29 %
Mixed KPCA	84.57 %	81.42 %	78.35 %	73.47 %

Table 2. Retrieval precision for malignant cases at different values of K.

K	1	5	10	20
Moments	63.12 %	62.76 %	62.14 %	60.99 %
PCA	48.7 %	47.52 %	48.36 %	48.69 %
G-KPCA	73.67 %	70.76 %	67.76 %	62.6 %
Mixed KPCA	84.29 %	82.19 %	80.54 %	74.24 %

Table 3. Overall retrieval precision at different values of K.

K	1	5	10	20
Moments	62.15 %	63.44 %	61.69 %	61.05 %
PCA	50.5 %	50.0 %	50.42 %	50.43 %
G-KPCA	71.77 %	70.15 %	67.8 %	63.45 %
Mixed KPCA	84.43 %	81.8 %	79.44 %	73.86 %

Table 4. Classification accuracy at different values of K.

K	1	5	10	20
Moments	62.15 %	65.12 %	63.29 %	61.14 %
PCA	50.5 %	49.92 %	51.99 %	53.4 %
G-KPCA	71.77 %	73.38 %	73.5 %	72.52 %
Mixed KPCA	84.43 %	85.71 %	85.93 %	84.75 %

PCA. In addition, we have evaluated the classification performance via the accuracy (Table 4), false positive (Table 5) and false negative values (Table 6).

Once again, the mixed gaussien kernel achieves the highest accuracy (=85.93 %) and the lowest false-positive (=15.16 %) and false-negative values (=12.99 %). The obtained results show that KPCA (gaussian and mixed) yield better results than curvelet moments. This indicates that kernel PCA is more suited than moments to cope with non-linear dimension reduction. The poor results gathered with the PCA confirm its inability to handle non-linear dimension reduction problems. Finally, the superiority of the mixed gaussian kernel

Table 5. False positive values at different values of K.

K	1	5	10	20
Moments	36.88 %	34.89 %	37.63 %	39.11 %
PCA	51.3 %	54.24 %	52.88 %	51.31 %
G-KPCA	26.33 %	25.54 %	25.2 %	28.14 %
Mixed KPCA	15.71 %	13.33 %	12.99 %	14.8 %

Table 6. False negative values at different values of K.

K	1	5	10	20
Moments	38.83 %	34.87 %	35.79 %	38.61 %
PCA	47.71 %	45.92 %	43.14 %	41.88 %
G-KPCA	30.13 %	27.71 %	27.8 %	26.82 %
Mixed KPCA	15.43 %	15.25 %	15.26 %	15.7 %

PCA over single gaussian kernel PCA confirms our assumption that a better kernel for mammogram retrieval must emphasize neighbor points without neglecting faraway ones.

4 Conclusion

In this paper, we have proposed a content-based mammogram retrieval system designed to assist radiologists in analyzing mammogram lesions by displaying pathologically similar cases. The proposed framework used the curvelet transform and kernel PCA to extract a set of multiresolution texture features. More importantly, we proposed a new kernel that is more suited for mammogram retrieval. By taking advantage of gaussian kernels with low and high sigma values, the mixed gaussian kernel emphasizes the neighbor points without neglecting the faraway ones. Experimental results on the challenging DDSM dataset showed that KPCA with the proposed mixed kernel outperforms KPCA with gaussian kernels as well as state-of-the-art methods that used PCA [11] and moment theory [9] in curvelet-based mammogram retrieval. Our future work will focus on adapting the proposed mixed gaussian kernel in other kernel-based methods such as support vector machine (SVM) and kernel canonical correlation analysis (CCA).

References

1. Ferlay, J., Soerjomataram, I., Dikshit, R., Eser, S., Mathers, C., Rebelo, M., Parkin, D.M., Forman, D., Bray, F.: Cancer incidence and mortality worldwide: sources, methods and major patterns in GLOBOCAN 2012. Int. J. Cancer **136**(5), E359–E386 (2015)

2. Nelson, H.D., Tyne, K., Naik, A., Bougatsos, C., Chan, B.K., Humphrey, L.: Screening for breast cancer: an update for the US Preventive Services Task Force. Ann. Intern. Med. **151**(10), 727–737 (2009)
3. Dinnes, J., Moss, S., Melia, J., Blanks, R., Song, F., Kleijnen, J.: Effectiveness and cost-effectiveness of double reading of mammograms in breast cancer screening: findings of a systematic review. Breast **10**(6), 455–463 (2001)
4. Astley, S.M., Gilbert, F.J.: Computer-aided detection in mammography. Clin. Radiol. **59**(5), 390–399 (2004)
5. Wei, C.-H., Li, C.-T.: Calcification descriptor and relevance feedback learning algorithms for content-based mammogram retrieval. In: Astley, S.M., Brady, M., Rose, C., Zwiggelaar, R. (eds.) IWDM 2006. LNCS, vol. 4046, pp. 307–314. Springer, Heidelberg (2006)
6. Bedo, M., dos Santos, D., Ponciano, M., de Azevedo, P., Traina, C.: Endowing a content-based medical image retrieval system with perceptual similarity using ensemble strategy. J. Digit. Imaging **29**(1), 22–37 (2016)
7. Jiang, M., Zhang, S., Li, H., Metaxas, D.N.: Computer-aided diagnosis of mammographic masses using scalable image retrieval. IEEE Trans. Biomed. Eng. **62**(2), 783–792 (2015)
8. Dhahbi, S., Barhoumi, W., Zagrouba, E. Multi-view score fusion for content-based mammogram retrieval. In: 8th International Conference on Machine Vision, pp. 987515-1–987515-6 (2015)
9. Dhahbi, S., Barhoumi, W., Zagrouba, E.: Breast cancer diagnosis in digitized mammograms using curvelet moments. Comput. Biol. Med. **64**, 79–90 (2015)
10. Gardezi, S., Faye, I., Eltoukhy, M.: Analysis of mammogram images based on texture features of curvelet Sub-bands. In: 5th International Conference on Graphic and Image Processing (2014)
11. Gedik, N., Atasoy, A.: A computer-aided diagnosis system for breast cancer detection by using a curvelet transform. Turkish J. Electr. Eng. Comput. Sci. **21**(4), 1002–1014 (2013)
12. Candes, E.J., Donoho, D.L.: Curvelets: a surprisingly effective nonadaptive representation for objects with edges. Stanford University, Dept of Statistics, California, pp. 1–10 (2000)
13. Starck, J.L., Cands, E.J., Donoho, D.L.: The curvelet transform for image denoising. IEEE Trans. Image Process. **11**(6), 670–684 (2002)
14. Eltoukhy, M.M., Faye, I., Samir, B.B.: A comparison of wavelet and curvelet for breast cancer diagnosis in digital mammogram. Comput. Biol. Med. **40**(4), 384–391 (2010)
15. Heath, M., Bowyer, K., Kopans, D., Kegelmeyer, W., Moore, R., Chang, K., Munishku-maran, S.: Current status of the digital database for screening mammography. In: Karssemeijer, N., Thijssen, M., Hendriks, J., van Erning, L. (eds.) Digital Mammography. Computational Imaging and Vision, pp. 457–460. Springer, New York (1998)

Combination of RGB-D Features for Head and Upper Body Orientation Classification

Laurent Fitte-Duval, Alhayat Ali Mekonnen[✉], and Frédéric Lerasle

LAAS-CNRS, Université de Toulouse, CNRS, UPS, Toulouse, France
{lfittedu,aamekonn,lerasle}@laas.fr

Abstract. In Human-Robot Interaction (HRI), the intention of a person to interact with another agent (robot or human) can be inferred from his/her head and upper body orientation. Furthermore, additional information on the person's overall intention and motion direction can be determined with the knowledge of both orientations. This work presents an exhaustive evaluation of various combinations of RGB and depth image features with different classifiers. These evaluations intend to highlight the best feature representation for the body part orientation to classify, i.e., the person's head or upper body. Our experiments demonstrate that high classification performances can be achieved by combining only three families of RGB and depth features and using a multiclass SVM classifier.

Keywords: Head pose estimation · Upper body pose estimation · Multiclass classification · Feature combination

1 Introduction

A person's head and body orientations convey important cues about the intention of the person. Whether the person is trying to interact with an intelligent machine or another person, orienting ones head and body towards the agent is a natural way to establish engagement. As a result, automated perception of people's head and body orientation has attracted a lot of attention in computer vision, human-machine interaction (HMI), and robotics disciplines. Possible applications are many: relevant examples include, user's intention characterization in human-robot interaction (HRI) [15], social interaction trends analysis [2], automated sport video analysis [9], human attention understanding for business and perceptual interface, etc. It can also be used to improve people tracking [2], body pose estimation [9], and action recognition [14] functionalities.

Nevertheless, correct estimation of people's head and body orientation is very challenging due to low image resolution, poor lighting conditions, frequent partial occlusions, and articulated body poses. In the past, the majority of approaches relied on RGB cameras [2,9,16]. But, their performance has been hampered because of their sensitivity to lighting condition, resolution, and lack of 3D information. With the advent of commercially available consumer RGB-D cameras

© Springer International Publishing AG 2016
J. Blanc-Talon et al. (Eds.): ACIVS 2016, LNCS 10016, pp. 591–603, 2016.
DOI: 10.1007/978-3-319-48680-2_52

like the Kinect and Asus Xtion, improved performance has been recorded, primarily as a result of the added depth information and its insensitivity to lighting conditions [5, 7, 13].

RGB-D based head pose estimation has been popularly addressed as a regression problem with approaches that provide continuous head pose angular estimates [5, 19]. But, these approaches require high resolution data and hence work only in very close range (<2 m). For applications entailing further operating ranges, a classification approach with coarse discrete orientation classes is privileged [10] (referred here as orientation classification than pose estimation). This alleviates the need to obtain precise ground truth for head pose, which is difficult, and is reasonably sufficient for user intention understanding applications. On the other hand, to determine body orientation, the trend is to extract discriminant features from a coarsely segmented full person (usually obtained by employing a pedestrian or people detector) and apply a trained classifier [7, 13]. These approaches, however, deteriorate in presence of partial occlusions, for instance, partial occlusions of the legs, which is a common occurrence in close human-machine interaction. Estimating body orientation based on upper body data (pertaining to shoulder orientation) helps alleviate this shortcoming. Similar to head orientation, by using both RGB and depth data and considering discrete orientation classes rather than continuous estimation, overall performance over a wide operating range can be improved [7].

In this work, we investigate head and upper body orientation classification (discrete classes) based on RGB and depth image features, and linear and nonlinear classifiers. Our aim is to classify the orientation of a person's head (yaw angle) and body (horizontal shoulder anterior orientation) independently into eight discrete classes. The upper body consideration enables body orientation classification in all ranges (especially in close range where full body based approach severely deteriorates). In both cases, the depth information robustifies performance in close and medium range operation, and the added RGB compensates the deficit in depth data in far range. Our work relies on popular RGB and depth features: local binary patterns (LBP) [18], histogram of oriented gradients (HOG) [3], depth local binary patterns (LBP$_D$), and histogram of depth difference (HDD) [24]. Additionally, multiscale variants of HOG and HDD features are also considered. For orientation classification, three different multiclass classifiers are considered: Random forest (RF), linear support vector machine (SVM), and sparse based classifier (SBC). This kind of systematic RGB-D feature combinations evaluation for head and upper body orientation classification is lacking in the literature. All evaluations are based on a recently released RGB-D public dataset [13]. The work is presented organized as follows: The rest of this section discusses related work and contributions. Section 2 addresses the adopted head and upper body representation with emphasis on the feature sets considered. It is then followed by a description of the different classifiers used in Sect. 3. Experiments and comparative results are presented in Sect. 4 and finally, the paper finishes with concluding remarks in Sect. 5.

1.1   Related Work

The majority of works in head orientation estimation are presented as head pose regression, predicting the continuous 2D or 3D head orientation, e.g., [5,16]. Though very useful and informative, these approaches obtain acceptable performance in close range. For medium and far range applications, a classification approach with discrete orientation classes is preferred [9,10]. Depending on the intended application, as is the case in this work, the coarse orientation estimate provided could be sufficient. Another point on head orientation estimation is the data used. RGB data has been extensively used (see survey [16]), but the recent advent of consumer RGB-D sensors have shifted the focus from RGB based approaches to mainly depth based approaches [5,19]. Furthermore, though demonstrated in close range, improved performance can be obtained by using both RGB and depth image data [8].

On the other hand, in human body orientation classification, the objective is to determine a person's body orientation angle (yaw angle). This is a relatively simplified problem than 3D human pose estimation, and yet conveys invaluable information about the heading direction of a person and his/her intention. Human body orientation classification can be achieved based on either full body [2,7,22] or upper body [6,9] image data analysis. Most works are based on RGB images in video-surveillance contexts, e.g., [2,22], though recent trends in RGB-D sensors made it possible for more improved full body orientation classification [7,13]. Full body approaches do not work well in presence of partial occlusions, either due to close human-camera distance or intra-person occlusions when multiple persons are in view. This shortcoming is better alleviated with upper body approaches, e.g., [6,9]. These works are based on RGB images. As shown in this work, further improvement can be obtained by adding depth information. Our work investigates RGB-D data for both head and upper body orientation classification which, though evident, is lacking in the literature.

A popular paradigm for orientation classification is to first extract relevant features from a bounding box encapsulating a body part (head or upper body), usually provided by a detector, then to utilize a trained multiclass classifier to determine orientation class. Although some approaches have tried a coupled detection-orientation classification paradigm that detects and determines orientation in one go, e.g., [22], the former is preferred as it dissociates the tackled problem. Furthermore, detector performance has improved significantly [4] so more focus can be dedicated to orientation classification. In the literature, relevant features considered include HOG [2,9,22], LBP [18], and HDD [7]. The trend seems to pick a specific family of feature set and use it without any systematic feature combination evaluation. For classification, popular choices are multiclass SVM (one-vs-all configuration) [7], sparse representation based classifier [2,6], and random forest [9,22]. This non-comparative feature-classifier trends, added with the lack of benchmarking in RGB-D approaches using public dataset makes feature-classifier choices difficult. Even though Liu *et al.* [13] introduced a public RGB-D dataset, called MCG-RGBD dataset, it has not been extensively used by the community yet. In light of these challenges, our work presents evaluation of several RGB and depth feature combinations for head and upper body orientation classification. All experiments are carried on MCG-RGBD to facilitate future benchmarking.

1.2 Contributions

The main contribution of this work is a comprehensive evaluation of several RGB and depth features, and their combinations, on a public dataset for head and upper body pose estimation. It also reports classification results based on three multi-class classifiers, capturing the essence of existing approaches and making future benchmarking easy.

2   Head and Upper Body Representation

We start with the premise that the position of the head and upper body of people in an image are known (in the form of a bounding box). Typically, this can easily be obtained using an upper body detector and a head region segmentation technique [6,12]. The next steps for orientation classification are relevant feature set extraction and classification, bearing in mind an underlying discrete orientation class representation. This section presents orientation class representation aspects and the adopted heterogeneous feature sets.

2.1   Discrete Orientation Classes

The head pose representation is usually defined by its pitch, yaw and roll angles [16]. Considering our problematic, we focus on the yaw angle which is discretized into eight orientation classes equally distant at 45° [9,20]. Similar to previous works on body orientation classification [1,2], we also quantize the upper body orientation into the same eight discrete orientations.

These eight orientations (Fig. 1) analogically denotes the four cardinal directions with the four intercardinal directions where E, NE, N, NW, W, SW, S, NE corresponds to these directions considered around the yaw rotation axis. In order to determine the actual pose of the body part, a multi-instances classification problem is considered where the classes are the eight possible directions of the considered body part. The predicted direction computed as an output of the classifier will give essential cues that indicate a user's intention.

Fig. 1. Illustration of the head (top row) and upper body (bottom row) eight discrete orientation classes.

2.2   Feature Sets

The choice of the features for our work has been inspired from previous work in orientation classification and person detection.

HOG [3]. The HOG features is the most widely used feature for person detection and full body pose classification in the literature [1]. The computation of the feature is based on a division of the considered window in cells of equal sizes which will be efficiently associated in order to gather the gradient orientations computed in a histogram. The variations of values in this histogram are characteristics of local shape of the classified object. The final feature is obtained by concatenating all block histogram with a dimensionality function of the number of bins used to divide the gradient orientation range and the number of subdivisions in the windows.

HDD [21,24]. This feature set is extracted by applying similar procedure as in the original HOG feature on the depth data. It tries to compute a histogram of depth difference based on the disparity of depth variations, and extending the orientation space and scaling the depth information in a suitable way to improve its representation.

Multiscale HOG and HDD [2,22]. These feature sets generally compute the features (HOG or HDD) at three scales which are multiples of each other by a factor of two before concatenating the generated feature vectors into a final multilevel feature. M-HOG and M-HDD denote these multiscale variants.

LBP and Its Depth Variant LBP$_D$ [11,17]. LBP is a robust texture descriptor because of its invariance to gray-scale and rotation. It mainly consists to label a pixel after testing a threshold on its neighborhood. The simplicity of this image analysis allows a fast computation in addition to its ability to underline patterns while being immune to contrast changes. In the vein of [11] which proposes a new LBP-based feature for gender recognition, we decide to apply the LBP pattern to depth images in order to enrich our set of features with depth-based texture information.

3   Multiclass Classification

For classification, both head and upper body orientation classification is treated as a multiclass classification problem with as many classes as number of considered discrete orientations. In this work, this results in an eight class multiclass classification problem. The classifiers are trained and tested based on the set of features described in Sect. 2.2. The three classifier types considered are presented below.

Random Forest (RF). Random forest is an ensemble methods that uses N randomly trained decision trees (separately trained in parallel) of depth D to create a strong classifier. It uses the average of each tree output to define the final classification. There are several variants of random forest learning strategies. In this work, each decision tree is learned using random samples drawn with replacement from the training set. In addition, when splitting a decision tree node during the construction of the tree, the split that is chosen is no longer the best split among all features. Instead, the split that is picked is the best split among a random subset of the features.

SVM One-vs-All. Support vector machines (SVMs) are statistical supervised learning methods used for classification and regression [23]. Linear SVM (used here) specifically, uses a hyperplane to define the decision boundary that separates the two classes. To extend it as a multiclass classifier, the one-vs-all strategy is adopted which involves fitting one classifier per class. For each classifier, the class is fitted against all the other classes. In addition to its computational efficiency, it is easily interpretable. Since each class is represented by one and one classifier only, it is possible to gain knowledge about the class by inspecting its corresponding classifier. The final classification label is determined as the one that maximizes the classification score.

Sparse Representation Based Classification (SBC). In [2], a sparse representation approach for multi-instances classification with proven efficiency in face recognition was introduced. The objective is to project the feature vector in a base of the considered classes by approximating the feature vector as a linear combination of the training features. The reconstruction weights of this decomposition are subject to a non-negative constraint and obtained using an L_1 regularization. These weights will have non-zero values if they corresponds to the data associated to the same class. Summing all the values of this sparse decomposition, it is possible to calculate the probability of each class. Then the maximal probability gives the output label.

4   Experiments

We carry out an exhaustive evaluation of different feature combinations in order to emphasize a trade-off between feature representation, classification effectiveness, and CPU cost.

4.1   Evaluation Metrics

The classification is evaluated based on standard confusion matrices where the columns corresponded to the predicted classes while each row corresponds to the ground truth classes. Concentrated detections along the diagonal indicate good performance. We can extract the classification accuracy per class considering the exact instances of the class normalized by all the classified instances for this same class. Then we can average the accuracy for all the classes which is our first performance criteria, accuracy 1 (acc1). We consider a second criteria, accuracy 2 (acc2), where the predictions to one of the two adjacent classes are considered as correct as in [1].

4.2 Dataset

In order to evaluate our approach and make future benchmarking easy, the MCG-RGBD public dataset [13] is used. The dataset contains 10 RGB-D video sequences of 11 people acting indoors in three different scenes (meeting room, corridor, and entrance) with a 640×480 resolution. It includes a wide variety of situations as walking, standing, jumping, running rotating, etc. The sensor limits the field of the acquisition allowing to observe people between 2.5 and 10 m. As it focuses on people's global body orientation in a similar way as [1], the yaw angle of each person is provided as ground truth. The dataset contains a total of 4000 images. Head and upper body bounding boxes have been manually annotated for evaluation.

We divide the dataset into training and testing sampled in a 2/3 and 1/3 proportion, respectively. The training set is doubled by adding reflections of each annotated data. It is then filtered to discard occluded samples. In our experiments, we observed that using equal number of samples in each class for training improved overall performance. Hence, the final training set consisted of an equal sample of 116 instances in each class, resulting in a total of 928 samples for training. The final test set consists of 2256 annotated samples.

4.3 Implementation Details

Before generating the different features, we extracted head and upper body windows from the dataset which are normalized to a fixed size of 64×64 pixels. When computing HOG, an 8×8 pixels cell size, a 2×2 cells block size, and a 9 bins gradient orientation quantization (same parameters as in [3]). As in [2], HOG features and the derived HDD features are computed using non-overlapping blocks, meaning a block stride of 8 pixels or more generally equal to the cell length. The multiple scale variants of HOG and HDD features (M-HOG and M-HDD) use respectively one and two additional cells with sizes of 16×16 and 32×32 pixels for head and upper body feature computation. The difference between RGB and depth based features is with the spacing of the bins which extends from 180° in the first case and 360° in the second case. The additional texture information from the LBP is computed on both RGB and depth channels (LBP$_D$) using an efficient implementation inspired by the works in [17] and integrated in a channel way as in [6]. The six base features presented in Sect. 2.2 (LBP, LBP$_D$, HOG, M-HOG, HDD, M-HDD) are all combined in every possible way leading to 63 features sets which are all evaluated. The dimensions of our six base features vary from 336 to 1512 while the dimensions of their combinations vary from 672 to 4668.

Regarding the multiclass classifiers, the random forest (RF) parameters, number of trees and the maximum depth of tree, are obtained by cross validation varying the values from 5 to 60 and from 5 to 30, respectively. The SVM classifier is used with default parameters and a unitary penalty parameter C. The sparse-based classifier (SBC) does not require any mandatory parameters but requires the same necessary parameters than any classification approaches: matrices of training and testing data associated to a ground truth associating a class to each of the considered sample. During our experiments, the sparse-based approach proposed in [2] reveals to be compelling to tune. A tolerance depending to the features dimension has to be set up in the L_1 solver used and computation of its value for the wide variety of feature combination has revealed to be constraining. Relaxing non-negative constraint and using a L_2 norm for the regularization, the approach remains time consuming although slightly faster and presenting better performances. The L_2 regularization is easily computed using the pseudo-inverse of the feature matrix. The sparse based classifier used for our evaluation differs of the original approach but presents more pertinent results for our evaluation.

4.4   Results

In this section, we will present the main results of our analysis but an extensive comparison of the feature combination is developed in the supplementary material[1]. The results observed allow to retrieve and compare some approaches of the literature with the combination of features and classifiers evaluated. The main works dealing with orientation classification in the literature are using the HOG features associated with SVM [7] or random forest [9] or the multiscale variant of HOG associated with random forest [22] and sparse-based classifier [2]. Figure 2a and b depict the $acc1$ results obtained for head orientation and upper body orientation classification, respectively.

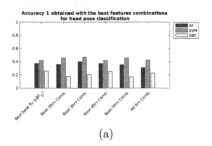
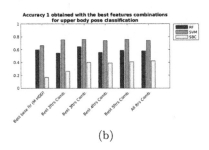

(a)   (b)

Fig. 2. Classification performance result, $acc1$, for: (a) head orientation classification, and (b) upper body classification by classifier. See text for description.

---

[1] For extensive evaluation results, please refer to the supplemental material at http://homepages.laas.fr/aamekonn/acivs16/supplement.pdf.

For brevity[2], of all combinations evaluated, we present the best single feature (base ftr), and two (2fts comb.), three (2fts comb.), four (2fts comb.), and five (2fts comb.) features combinations. Additionally, we also present the results obtained with all combined features (all ftrs comb.). The results are reported for each multiclass classifier. The best features for head orientation classification are (considering single, two, three, four, and five combinations): LBP_D, LBP_D+M-HOG, LBP_D+M-HOG+M-HDD, LBP+LBP_D+HOG+M-HOG, and LBP_D+HOG+M-HOG + HDD+M-HDD. For that of upper body, they are: M-HDD, HOG+HDD, LBP_D+M-HOG+HDD, LBP+LBP_D+HOG+HDD, and LBP_D+HOG+M-HOG+HDD+M-HDD. As observed, in the two histograms in Fig. 2, the first two classifiers (SVM and RF) are in the same order of performance whereas the sparse-based approach achieve lower performances. This observation is easily explained by the use of the entirety of data available without selection or optimization of its parameters in this approach used whereas the two first are trained to keep the most pertinent features or parameters during the classification process.

For computation time aspect, Fig. 3 presents the CPU cost of the best feature combinations determined during evaluation on the test set. Regardless of the number of features combined, which might directly affect the CPU cost, the random forest runs in times of the range of the tenth of a second whereas the SVM classifier runs in tens of seconds. This difference is due to the features selection realized during the random forest training whereas the SVM compute an optimal separation hyperplane using all the features available. This gap in scale would be a decision factor when integrating these functionalities, head and upper body orientation classification, in a wider application framework.

Regarding the classification accuracy and more precisely $acc1$, common approach in the literature are superseded seeing that the best scores obtained using one feature easily exceed them (Table 1). We can notice that in both problem, the best score classifying the orientation with unique features are obtained by

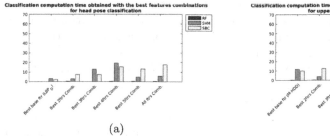
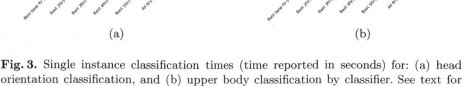

(a)   (b)

Fig. 3. Single instance classification times (time reported in seconds) for: (a) head orientation classification, and (b) upper body classification by classifier. See text for description.

---

[2] For extensive evaluation results, please refer to the supplemental material at http:// homepages.laas.fr/aamekonn/acivs16/supplement.pdf.

Table 1. Comparison of our best results and common approaches in the literature.

Approach	Classifier	Head			Upper body		
		Feature	acc1	acc2	Feature	acc1	acc2
Hayashi et al. [9]	RF	HOG	0.32	0.66	HOG	0.21	0.52
Tao et al. [22]	RF	M-HOG	0.32	0.64	M-HOG	0.21	0.51
Fumito et al. [7]	SVM	HOG	0.38	0.74	HOG	0.30	0.69
Chen et al. [2]	SBC	M-HOG	0.29	0.68	M-HOG	0.24	0.63
Ours best base ftr	SVM	LBP_D	0.42	0.83	M-HDD	0.66	0.88
Ours best 3ftrs comb.	SVM	LBP_D+M-HOG+M-HDD	**0.47**	**0.92**	LBP_D+M-HOG+HDD	**0.76**	**0.98**

depth based feature. The LBP_D feature in the head case and the M-HDD for the upper body. The use of RGB-based features from the literature approaches appears insufficiently informative on our dataset. Globally, the scores obtained combining from two up to six heterogeneous features mixing depth and RGB information and using the SVM classifier features are of the same range (Fig. 2). The maximum acc1 scores are obtained combining three features. A score of 47 % acc1 is obtained mixing LBP_D, M-HOG and M-HDD for head orientation classification, whereas a 76 % acc1 is achieved mixing LBP_D, M-HOG and HDD for upper body orientation classification. Upper body based classification demonstrates a significantly better accuracy, nearly 30 %, than head orientation. This gap is due to the extension of the analyzed area which reduce the ambiguity between classes. Considering the second performance criteria, acc2, scores of 92 and 98 % are observed. This means that, on average, there is a 47 % confidence to correctly classify a head orientation and there is a 45 % possibility that it is misclassified for a neighboring orientation. An average error score of 8 % for head orientation and 2 % for upper body (considering neighboring classes as correct) on our orientation classifications is an outstanding performance with regards to the literature.

To further illustrate the classification performance in each discrete class, Figs. 4a and b show the confusion matrices for the best head and upper body orientation classification results respectively. The best results pertain to the three feature combinations highlighted in Table 1. From the confusion matrices, we can observe a matrix presenting some full lines for the head case whereas the upper body one present a sparser structure. On the first case, we have concentrated scores for the lateral classes (W and E) and spread estimations with imprecision on the orientation classification for the frontal and dorsal class (N and S). However, there is a global concentration of the estimations around the diagonal explaining the high score of 92 % acc2. On the second case, we have a sparse matrix presenting a light cross shape. This low score symmetrically to the high score are due to the front/rear ambiguity. Nevertheless, high scores are reached all along the diagonal leading to the high scores for the two performance criteria. These differences confirm the complexity rising according to the size of the body part considered but an overlap would easily be established if these analysis were realized jointly.

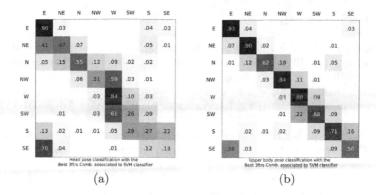

(a)   (b)

Fig. 4. Confusion matrix for (a) head and (b) upper body orientation classification obtained using the best approaches – best three features combined with SVM classifier.

5 Conclusion

In this work, we presented an extensive evaluation of several RGB and depth feature set combinations for head and upper body orientation classification. We showed the interest of adding the depth information. Using the heterogeneity of this information, we obtain a 47 % and a 92 % accuracies ($acc1$ and $acc2$ respectively) for head orientation classification. For upper body orientation classification, accuracy scores of 76 % and 98 % are obtained. Our results also attest that by using a combined feature set composed of a single variant of each LBP, HOG, and HDD features, it is possible to obtain the best classification performance. The preferred variants are LBP_D and M-HOG, with M-HDD for head orientation and with HDD for upper body orientation classification. The best results are indeed obtained by using both RGB and depth based feature sets. In addition, our experimental results indicate that better results are obtained with the SVM classifier. But, this should be considered in light of the intended application, as the improvement obtained using SVM over RF based approach might not justify the incurred CPU cost (which is at least higher by an order of magnitude).

Future prospects include integration of the best trained model in human-robot interaction context and using the classification output as percepts for user's intention estimation. We also believe further improvements on head and upper body orientation estimation can be obtained using probabilistic filtering approaches, possibly with underlying head-should physiological models.

Acknowledgment. This work is funded by the ROMEO2 project (http://www.projetromeo.com/) in the framework of the Structuring Projects of Competitiveness Clusters (PSPC).

References

1. Andriluka, M., Roth, S., Schiele, B.: Monocular 3d pose estimation and tracking by detection. In: IEEE Conference on Computer Vision and Pattern Recognition (CVPR 2010), pp. 623–630, June 2010
2. Chen, C., Heili, A., Odobez, J.: Combined estimation of location and body pose in surveillance video. In: IEEE International Conference on Advanced Video and Signal-Based Surveillance (AVSS 2011), pp. 5–10 (2011)
3. Dalal, N., Triggs, B.: Histograms of oriented gradients for human detection. In: IEEE Conference on Computer Vision and Pattern Recognition (CVPR 2005), vol. 1, pp. 886–893, June 2005
4. Dollar, P., Appel, R., Belongie, S., Perona, P.: Fast Feature Pyramids for Object Detection. IEEE Trans. Pattern Anal. Mach. Intell. $36(8)$, 1532–1545 (2014). 00127
5. Fanelli, G., Gall, J., Van Gool, L.: Real time head pose estimation with random regression forests. In: IEEE Conference on Computer Vision and Pattern Recognition (CVPR 2011), pp. 617–624, June 2011
6. Fitte-Duval, L., Mekonnen, A.A., Lerasle, F.: Upper body detection and feature set evaluation for body pose classification. In: International Conference on Computer Vision Theory and Applications (VISAPP 2015), pp. 439–446 (2015)
7. Fumito, S., Daisuke, D., Ichiro, I., Hiroshi, M., Hironobu, F.: Estimation of human orientation using coaxial RGB-depth images. In: International Conference on Computer Vision Theory and Applications (VISAPP 2015), pp. 113–120 (2015)
8. Ghiass, R.-S., Arandjelović, O., Laurendeau, D.: Highly accurate, fully automatic head pose estimation from a low quality consumer-level rgb-d sensor. In: Workshop on Computational Models of Social Interactions: Human-Computer-Media Communication, pp. 25–34 (2015)
9. Hayashi, M., Yamamoto, T., Aoki, Y., Ohshima, K., Tanabiki, M.: Head and upper body pose estimation in team sport videos. In: IAPR Asian Conference on Pattern Recognition (ACPR 2013), pp. 754–759, November 2013
10. Huang, C., Ding, X., Fang, C.: Head pose estimation based on random forests for multiclass classification. In: International Conference on Pattern Recognition (ICPR 2010), pp. 934–937, August 2010
11. Huynh, T., Min, R., Dugelay, J.-L.: An efficient LBP-based descriptor for facial depth images applied to gender recognition using RGB-D face data. In: Park, J.-I., Kim, J. (eds.) ACCV 2012. LNCS, vol. 7728, pp. 133–145. Springer, Heidelberg (2013). doi:10.1007/978-3-642-37410-4_12
12. Jafari, O.H., Mitzel, D., Leibe, B.: Real-time RGB-D based people detection and tracking for mobile robots and head-worn cameras. In: IEEE International Conference on Robotics and Automation (ICRA 2014), pp. 5636–5643, May 2014
13. Liu, W., Zhang, Y., Tang, S., Tang, J., Hong, R., Li, J.: Accurate estimation of human body orientation from RGB-D sensors. IEEE Trans. Cybern. $43(5)$, 1442–1452 (2013)
14. Maji, S., Bourdev, L., Malik, J.: Action recognition from a distributed representation of pose and appearance. In: 2011 IEEE Conference on Computer Vision and Pattern Recognition (CVPR), pp. 3177–3184, June 2011. 00124
15. Mollaret, C., Mekonnen, A.A., Ferrane, I., Pinquier, J., Lerasle, F.: Perceiving user's intention-for-interaction: a probabilistic multimodal data fusion scheme. In: IEEE International Conference on Multimedia and Expo (ICME 2015), pp. 1–6, June 2015

16. Murphy-Chutorian, E., Trivedi, M.M.: Head pose estimation computer vision: a survey. IEEE Trans. Pattern Anal. Mach. Intell. **31**(4), 607–626 (2009). 00859
17. Ojala, T., Pietikäinen, M., Mäenpää, T.: Gray scale and rotation invariant texture classification with local binary patterns. In: Vernon, D. (ed.) ECCV 2000. LNCS, vol. 1842, pp. 404–420. Springer, Heidelberg (2000). doi:10.1007/3-540-45054-8_27
18. Ojala, T., Pietikinen, M., Harwood, D.: A comparative study of texture measures with classification based on featured distributions. Pattern Recogn. **29**(1), 51–59 (1996)
19. Papazov, C., Marks, T.K., Jones, M.: Real-time 3d head pose and facial landmark estimation from depth images using triangular surface patch features. In: IEEE Conference on Computer Vision and Pattern Recognition (CVPR 2015), pp. 4722–4730, June 2015
20. Siriteerakul, T.: Advance in head pose estimation from low resolution images: a review. Int. J. Comput. Sci. Issues **9**(3), 442–449 (2012)
21. Spinello, L., Arras, K.O.: People detection in RGB-D data. In: IEEE/RSJ International Conference on Intelligent Robots and Systems (IROS 2011), pp. 3838–3843, September 2011
22. Tao, J., Klette, R.: Integrated pedestrian and direction classification using a random decision forest. In: IEEE International Conference on Computer Vision Workshops (ICCVW'13), pp. 230–237, December 2013
23. Vapnik, V.N.: The Nature of Statistical Learning Theory. Springer, New York (1999)
24. Wu, S., Yu, S., Chen, W.: An attempt to pedestrian detection in depth images. In: Chinese Conference on Intelligent Visual Surveillance (IVS 2011), pp. 1–3 (2011)

A Parametric Algorithm for Skyline Extraction

Mehdi Ayadi[1,2(✉)], Loreta Suta[1], Mihaela Scuturici[1], Serge Miguet[1], and Chokri Ben Amar[2]

[1] University of Lyon, CNRS University Lyon 2 LIRIS, UMR 5205, 69676 Lyon, France
{Mehdi.Ayadi,Mihaela.Scuturici,Serge.Miguet}@univ-lyon2.fr, loradrian@gmail.com
[2] REGIM-Lab: REsearch Groups in Intelligent Machines, University of Sfax, ENIS, BP 1173, 3038 Sfax, Tunisia
chokri.benamar@ieee.org

Abstract. This paper is dedicated to the problem of automatic skyline extraction in digital images. The study is motivated by the needs, expressed by urbanists, to describe in terms of geometrical features, the global shape created by man-made buildings in urban areas. Skyline extraction has been widely studied for navigation of Unmanned Aerial Vehicles (drones) or for geolocalization, both in natural and urban contexts. In most of these studies, the skyline is defined by the limit between sky and ground objects, and can thus be resumed to the sky segmentation problem in images. In our context, we need a more generic definition of skyline, which makes its extraction more complex and even variable. The skyline can be extracted for different depths, depending on the interest of the user (far horizon, intermediate buildings, near constructions, ...), and thus requires a human interaction. The main steps of our method are as follows: we use a Canny filter to extract edges and allow the user to interact with filter's parameters. With a high sensitivity, all the edges will be detected, whereas with lower values, only most contrasted contours will be kept by the filter. From the obtained edge map, an upper envelope is extracted, which is a disconnected approximation of the skyline. A graph is then constructed and a shortest path algorithm is used to link discontinuities. Our approach has been tested on several public domain urban and natural databases, and have proven to give better results that previously published methods.

1 Introduction

This work is part of interdisciplinary projects funded by the French National Research Agency (ANR-12-VBDU-008-Skyline) and by the Excellence Laboratory "Urban World Intelligence" (Labex IMU). These projects are dedicated to the study, in a very interdisciplinary way, of the immaterial "skyline" object. As mentioned in [2], a city's skyline is defined as *the unique fingerprint of a city* and it *abstracts a city's identity in terms of its spatial, historical, social, cultural and economic structures over time.* One of the tasks of the projects is devoted

© Springer International Publishing AG 2016
J. Blanc-Talon et al. (Eds.): ACIVS 2016, LNCS 10016, pp. 604–615, 2016.
DOI: 10.1007/978-3-319-48680-2_53

to the subjective evaluation of the reception of the urban landscape by human subjects. Several pictures of the city are presented to people, that are then asked to evaluate the perceived skyline by marks ranging between 0 and 10, for different continuous variables: ugly-beautiful, disturbing-reassuring, messy-ordered,... The objective of our work is to measure the geometrical information from the skyline and to extract objective variables, that can be related to those subjective evaluations. The tool could be used for example to help urban planners to predict the most likely perception of different possible city's evolutions or construction scenarios. We therefore need a tool for automatically extracting the skyline in images, which is the main topic of this paper.

We found two possible operational definitions of the skyline:

1. The one-dimensional contour that represents the boundary between the sky and the ground objects [1]
2. The artificial horizon that a city's overall structure creates[1]

As will be illustrated in Sect. 2, several papers are related to this problem of automatic skyline extraction. Most of them use the first definition, that resumes the problem of skyline extraction to the problem of sky segmentation: the skyline can be defined as the frontier of the sky region. Skyline extraction can be used in several applications: from geo-localization, path planning and obstacle detection to aerial and ground vehicles guiding.

In our work, we will rather use the second definition, which is more general, but also more versatile: As illustrated in Fig. 1a, we want our algorithm to be able to extract both the background skyline, including mountains, but also the foreground skyline, delimiting the silhouette of man-made buildings. We need thus a parametric, semi-automatic algorithm that allows the user to extract his own desired skyline, or a set of different users to define a range of valid skylines.

The paper is organized as follows: Sect. 2 presents the state of the art on skyline detection methods, which, according to definition 1, are considered as an image segmentation problem. They can be divided into region-based and edge-based approaches. Section 3 describes then our parametric skyline extraction algorithm based on low level image processing that allows to extract the upper envelope, which is a disconnected approximation of the skyline, and a graph-based modelization of the picture which allows to connect the skyline help to the execution of a shortest path algorithm.

We tested our algorithm on several databases of real images in various weather conditions and for several kinds of urban and natural landscapes dominated by man made buildings or including natural objects. Detailed steps and experimental results are explained in Sect. 4. Finally, Sect. 5 concludes our paper and presents our future works.

2   State of the Art on Skyline Detection

In the last few years, there has been an increasing interest for finding algorithms and techniques to automatically extract the skyline in digital pictures. Skyline

---

[1] See Wikipedia: https://en.wikipedia.org/wiki/Skyline.

extraction is only a first step in a whole chain where the specific shape of the horizon can act as a signature for geo-spatial localization. In this paper, we focus on the first step of skyline extraction. Further works, using this skyline for augmented reality purposes are in progress (see Sect. 5). For this extraction task, previous works are clearly classified as image segmentation problems that can be handled with common: *region-based* or *contour-based* approaches.

2.1 Region Based Methods

In [3], a region based method is proposed where the algorithm first tries to automatically extract the sky region using a region growing method based on the luminosity's gradient. From the input image, 10 sub-windows are chosen at the top region of a video image. For each of these sub-windows, the average of intensity is computed. The minimum of the 10 obtained values is then be used as a threshold. Starting from the top of image, and for each column, first pixels whose intensities are lower than this threshold are considered as skyline's pixels. Otherwise, skyline extraction might fail due to the presence of clouds or noise in the image. Added to that, the extracted skyline is non continuous, as in [4], due to the non connection of skyline pixels in neighboring columns.

In another approach, [5], a neural network is used to assign a score in [0..1], to each pixel. Pixels that belong to the sky must have high score. However, in some cases, where clouds are present, the algorithm fails and increases the ratio of false positives.

In [6] or [7], authors propose to use machine learning, namely Support Vector Machine (SVM), to segment the image and extract the skyline. Used descriptors are essentially based on the color, static features and location information of edges. This step is followed by a dynamic programming step to link discontinuities. However, this approach allows to extract only the background skyline. In fact, as illustrated in Fig. 1, images can present multi-level depth skylines. Added to that, such methods require a lot of computing power and memory resources

2.2 Edge Based Methods

In [8], an edge detection step is applied on the luminance component to detect edge pixels and construct an edge map. This step is followed by an edge map construction stage where a dynamic programming algorithm allows to find paths between two horizontally consecutive disconnected vertices. First, exploration is permitted only on pixel's right area. This means that concavities or convexities, due to perspective problems when taking a photo or to original architectures, are not taken into consideration. Second, when a path cannot be found between two consecutive edge points separated with a vertical distance greater than a predefined threshold, a linear interpolation is done. This does not reflect in all cases the real shape of the scene. Finally, cost of links between two vertices is calculated using the pixel's to reach position. This cost affects the capability of the algorithm to detect steep skyline curves, especially present in an urban images (formed by buildings).

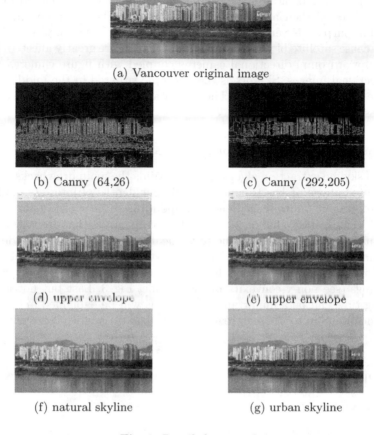

(a) Vancouver original image

(b) Canny (64,26)

(c) Canny (292,205)

(d) upper envelope

(e) upper envelope

(f) natural skyline

(g) urban skyline

Fig. 1. Detailed approach

In [9], an edge detection using Canny filter is applied with high and low scales. Using the topological information, a seed selection step is performed on Canny images allowing to detect the break point at the top of mountains. This seed is detected by searching the maximum point (highest y position) and two local minimum points on its left and right side. The joint angle between the two lines, formed by maximum point and the two local minimums, validate the seed point. This assumption, that a break point is present, may be verified in some mountainous areas, but not always in suburb scenario. Finally, the choice of a threshold for joint angle affects the seed point selection and prohibit steep curves to be taken into consideration.

In [10], catadioptric infra-red images are used to detect the skyline for UAV navigation. This method relies on infra-red images which adds robustness to brightness conditions and overcome the sensibility of catadioptric images to luminosity but are not always available, especially in outdoor environments or for a general public application.

In [11–13], authors situate the work in the context of geolocation in urban canyon, and tested their approach in Fujisawa City. The skyline extraction for geo-location purpose is very useful especially in urban canyons, where high-rise buildings cause satellite blockages, GPS measurement are greatly affected. In this method, upward omni-directional cameras coupled with figure cameras deliver omni-directional images. Sky pixels then become situated in the middle part of the image and not in its uppers. The advantage of using IR-camera is to add robustness to light disturbance.

2.3   Limitations and Needs for a New Skyline Extraction Method

We need a skyline extraction algorithm that avoids the main drawbacks of methods presented above: it has to adapt to different depths of interests, making it possible to extract multiple skylines corresponding to near objects or to background objects. It has to handle correctly the steep curves that are very likely to be present in urban landscapes, due to vertical structures of home-made buildings. It has to take into account the fact that the skyline might have several intersections with a single vertical line, in the case of arches, perspective views or overhangs (see non-v-convexity of the skyline, Fig. 3. Last but not least, its processing time can be a important criterion, as will be explained in our future works, since we plan to use it in real time for a mobile augmented reality application.

3   Proposed Algorithm

3.1   Overview

For the rest of the paper, as in the literature, we assume that the skyline is an imaginary curve composed of edge points separating the ground objects and the sky. Added to that, the sky has to be located in the upper part of the image.

Figure 1 shows the steps of our algorithm: we transform the original image to gray scale color space and perform on an edge detection by applying a Canny filter. Manual adjustment of the two Canny filter parameters allows targeting different skylines, according to the subjective definition of each user. Canny edge detection results in many interrupted lines or curves which is followed by a connecting discontinuities step.

In the subsequent sub-sections, we explain detailed procedures.

3.2   Edge Detection and Upper Envelope

In this step, input images are converted to a gray scale color space, then in the domain of the Canny Edge. The user interacts with two sliders to choose its parameters. The choice has to be made so we keep only the most possible pixels that are part of the skyline.

Fig. 2. Image with noise

In Fig. 1b and c, depending on the chosen Hysteresis threshold values, we can make two-scale Canny edge images. When choosing low scale values, some pixels (from noisy clutters) which are part of the edge image are taken as skyline's pixels. These edge segment cause later algorithm failure. In Fig. 2, we give an example where low scales are chosen, and cloud's pixels are taken as skyline's ones.

This parameter choice step allows us to extract what we call an *upper envelope*. In fact, for each column, we keep the highest point in the gradient image. An initial set of points is then obtained. This upper envelope doesn't really define the skyline, but rather a cloud points that, in some cases, reflects the shape of the scene. In this upper envelope, based on human's perception system, we can still recognize the shape of the scene and the skyline due to our ability to link some separated edges pixels. This step of upper envelope extraction is done in real-time and users see it overlapped on the real image.

3.3   V-Convexity

After upper envelope extraction step, we obtain a set of points that has the disadvantage of being disconnected since two neighboring columns in the image may define points that are vertically very distant (example of steep curve).

A first naive approach would leads us to connect them by segments of straight lines to obtain a continuous curve. This approach is obviously unsatisfactory: In fact, the extracted skyline does not always reflect the real shape of the objects in the image as illustrated in Fig. 3a. To formalize this problem, we introduced the concept of *v-convexity*.

A skyline that defines the two region *sky* and *non-sky*, is said v-convex if and only if the intersection of any vertical line with the region *non-sky* is limited to a single line segment.

These cases where the skyline is non v-convex is due to perspective problems, where image present distortion, or image orientation where user take image with non-zero tilt angle. Finally, images can contain artificial objects that are architecturally original (Fig. 3). The skyline is then called <u>non v-convex</u>. This is also

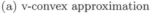

(a) v-convex approximation   (b) non v-convex skyline

Fig. 3. Pearl TV tower in Shanghai

applicable for natural objects, where our algorithm follows the concavities and convexities described by trees, as illustrated in Fig. 4a and b.

We explain in next Sect. 3.4 the proposes method where the previously taken highest points are linked using a shortest path algorithm based on a well-known dynamic programming method, namely *Dijkstra*.

3.4 Connecting Discontinuities

In Fig. 4a or b, green points represents the upper envelope pixels, which have to be connected to obtain a continuous curve defining the skyline. Red line segments represent the followed path after connecting upper envelope points. Figure 3b illustrates an example of our results for the *Oriental Pearl TV Tower* in Shanghai.

Actually, we treat each discontinuity as a weighted graph. First, we use the binary edge map obtained from upper envelope extraction and convert it to a map. In this map, we denote:
w = map's width, h=map's height and each pixel is noted "$p_{i,j}$" where $p_{i,j} = 1$ or 0, with i=$\in$[1..w] and j=$\in$[1..h]. Wee then construct a graph G = {V, E, ψ}, where its components are:

(a) result1   (b) result2

Fig. 4. Results

1. **V = Vertex:** Each point p_i, j in the map (green pixels in Fig. 4a or b) corresponds to one vertex v_i, j in V;

$$V(i,j) = \begin{cases} Edge\ vertex, & if\ b(i,j)=1 \\ Non\ edge\ vertex, & if\ b(i,j)=0 \end{cases} \tag{1}$$

2. <u>**E = Edge points:**</u> At adjacent stages, (i) and (i+1), having the two vertices <u>V(i,j) and V(i+1,k)</u>, a link has to be established. Thus, depending on a certain criteria, defined below, two cases are possible:
   $|k - j| < 2$: The vertical gap between the two edge vertices is lower than two <u>pixels. In this case, no costs are calculated but a simple line between them is</u> drawn.
   $|k - j| \geq 2$: The vertical gap is larger than two pixels. We use a shortest <u>path-searching</u> algorithm using a *cost function* detailed below, allowing to find a path between the front and the rear end of this sub-graph.
3. ψ = **Cost function**: Costs are calculated using the gradient's magnitude from the filtered original image with *Sobel* filter, as illustrated in Fig. 5a. In fact, each pixel is connected to its 8 closest neighbors. For each one, we associate a cost value depending on its level's contrast: Lower cost to those with high contrast. A graph is then obtained, allowing to find this shortest path. Using an Excel sheet, we give an example (Fig. 5b) where red cells are source and destination pixels and green ones correspond to the followed path. In this case, we have a path with 52 pixels size, a source image pixel's coordinate at (184,457) and destination at (185,417).

3.5   Interacting with the Given Skyline

In some cases, the algorithm fails due to the presence of heavy grey clouds in the image. in fact, some isolated points that have a strong gradient are taken as part of the upper envelope. Thus, the shortest path algorithm tries to link them to next and previous skyline's pixels.

(a) Sobel filtering

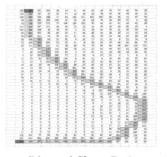

(b) excel Sheet Path

Fig. 5. Cost function

For this, inspired by the *magnetic lasso* in Photoshop or path's modification in *Google Maps* (adding a checkpoint to a path), we give users the ability to interact with our Graphical User Interface and change one pixel's ordinate in the proposed skyline (up or down). At the same time, while moving the cursor on the interface, the algorithm tries to calculate *two new sub-paths* using the same dynamic programming function: the first, from user's new chosen point previous's area to this last. The second from it (new chosen point) to its next's area. The more and more ordinate amplitude changes increases, neighbouring area expands.

Mobile prototype: Our algorithm runs on desktop in real time. We used and adapted our codes and developed a mobile prototype for extracting the skyline on the move. This prototype allows users to extract the skyline in live video stream while strolling through the city.

4   Results

In our experiments, different databases were used. Firstly, two databases (namely CH1 and CH2) from [7] containing especially natural images taken in the Alpes. Ground truth images are given only for the first one (CH1). However, for some of them, we found that the segmentation doesn't really correspond to the real shape of the scene. We give an example in Fig. 6 illustrating the difference between our new ground truth image and the original one. In fact, the ground truth doesn't take into consideration the concavities and convexities of image elements.

(a) original image   (b) ground truth   (c) new ground truth

Fig. 6. CH1 ground truth

Secondly, we used database from [16], where original and ground truth images are available. Result of the proposed algorithm is also furnished. These images are especially taken in urban areas in the city of *Barcelona*. We could extract skylines accurately in this dataset and compared our result to [16].

All of these images (3 databases 320 images) are taken in various conditions (weather, luminosity, noise..). Only some of them are show in Fig. 4.

4.1   Assessment of the Extracted Skyline

First, we define a *discontinuity indice*, giving the distance of the extracted skyline to its ground truth using formula below:

$$\mathtt{dist} = \frac{1}{w} \sum_{i=0}^{w} |Sg(k) - Se(k)|$$

where: w = image's width, Sg is the ground-truth Skyline and Se is the extracted one.

We then calculate, for each dataset, the average and the maximum indice. An overview of our results is given in the Table 1, giving number of images of each data set, average and maximum CPU-time calculation, average and minimum of Precision and Recall and finally Hamming distance. We compare our method to result of [16] in Table 1.

Table 1. Results

		CH1 [our]	CH2 [our]	Barcelona [16]	Barcelona [our]
images		175	80	52	52
Processing time	average	0,98	0,7 s		0,71
	max	19 s	10 s		5 s
Precision	average	0,999	0,988	0,959	0,977
	min	0,97	0,293	0,32	0,36
Recall	average	0,99	0,989	0,95	0,55
	min	0,94	0,56	0,95	0,67
Hamming distance	average	2,54	12,59	25,75	23,85
	min	8,31	0,59	143	195

We conducted our experiments on a desktop machine. Step of extracting the upper envelop is done in real time. Depending on the complexity of the scene, the CPU time needed for the connecting discontinuities step goes from 0,4 to 19 seconds. We also conducted our experiments on a smartphone. Algorithm runs in real-time and allows extracting the upper envelop without latency. As for desktop GUI, connecting discontinuities take more time, and depends also of the smartphone's performance. The developed prototype is ready to be used in an Augmented Reality context.

5   Conclusion and Future Work

Developed algorithms allow us to extract skyline in real-time on mobile device. This one, called *real skyline* will be compared to a *theoretical* one generated from a 3D City's model. For augmented reality purposes, this comparison will help us correcting the user's pose to more accurate insertion of 3D objects in real-time video stream. We used Lyon's 3D model and are able to extract the theoretical skyline corresponding to user's GPS position. Similar works were done, as in [14], where the image gives pose estimation with panorama's skyline matched with real one, or in [15] where only embedded instruments (GPS, Gyroscope and magnetic compass) were used for the same purpose.

In this paper we have proposed a new interactive system for practical skyline extraction from real images. First, we integrated edge based image segmentation algorithm based on parametric low level image processing. This approach is robust to noise and weather variation. Then, we integrated our approach in a GUI to compare our algorithm's results with user's ones. Finally, we demonstrated that our approach is feasible and adapted it for mobile uses, especially on smartphone, with the intention to use it later for Augmented Reality purpose. Further work are in progress integrating the skyline as a maker for an AR system, which will be later compared with other methodologies and existing approaches as [8] or [15].

Acknowledgments. This work was part of the "ANR-12-VBDU-0008 - Skyline" project, funded by the "Agence Nationale de la Recherche (ANR)" and the Labex (Laboratoire d'Excellence) "Intelligence des mondes Urbains (IMU)".

References

1. Johns, D., Dudek, G.: Urban position estimation from one dimensional visual cues. In: 3rd Canadian Conference on Computer and Robot Vision (CRV 2006), pp. 22–22. IEEE (2006)
2. Yusoff, N.A.H., Noor, A.M., Ghazali, R.: City skyline conservation: sustaining the premier image of Kuala Lumpur. Procedia Environ. Sci. **20**, 583–592 (2014). Elsevier B.V
3. Fang, M., Chiu, M.-Y., Liang, C.-C., Singh, A.: Skyline for video-based virtual rail for vehicle navigation. In: Proceedings of the Intelligent Vehicles 1993 Symposium, pp. 207–212. IEEE (1993)
4. Byung-Ju, K., Jong-Jin, S., Hwa-Jin, N., Jin-Soo, K.: Skyline extraction using a multistage edge filtering. Int. J. Electr. Comput. Energ. Electron. Commun. Eng. **5**, 10–14 (2011)
5. Jiebo, L., Etz, S.P.: A physical model-based approach to detecting sky in photographic images. IEEE Trans. Image Process. **11**, 201–212 (2002)
6. Saurer, O., Baatz, G., Köser, K., Ladický, U., Pollefeys, M.: Image based geo-localization in the Alps. Int. J. Comput. Vis. **116**, 213–225 (2016)
7. Baatz, G., Saurer, O., Koser, K., Pollefeys, M.: Large scale visual geo-localization of images in mountainous terrain. In: Fitzgibbon, A., Lazebnik, S., Perona, P., Sato, Y., Schmid, C. (eds.) ECCV 2012. LNCS, vol. 7573, pp. 517–530. Springer, Heidelberg (2012)
8. Lie, W., Lin, T.C.-I., Lin, T., Hung, K.-S.: A robust dynamic programming algorithm to extract skyline in images for navigation. Pattern Recogn. Lett. **26**, 221–230 (2005)

9. Yang, S.W., Kim, I.C., Kim, J.S.: Robust skyline extraction algorithm for mountainous images. In: Proceedings of the Second International Conference on Computer Vision Theory and Applications, pp. 253–257. SciTePress - Science and and Technology Publications (2007)

10. Bazin, J.-C., Kweon, I., Demonceaux, C., Vasseur, P.: Dynamic programming and skyline extraction in catadioptric infrared images. In: IEEE International Conference on Robotics and Automation, pp. 409–416. IEEE (2009)

11. Meguro, H.-I., Murata, T., Amano, Y., Hasizume, T., Takiguchi, J.-I.: Development of a positioning technique for an urban area using omnidirectional infrared camera and aerial survey data. Adv. Robot. **22**, 731–747 (2008)

12. Ramalingam, S., Bouaziz, S., Sturm, P., Brand, M.: SKYLINE2GPS: localization in urban canyons using omni-skylines. In International Conference on Intelligent Robots and Systems, pp. 3816–3823. IEEE (2010)

13. Ramalingam, S., Bouaziz, S., Sturm, P., Brand, M.: Geolocalization using skylines from omni-images. In: the 12th International Conference on Computer Vision Workshops, ICCV Workshops, pp. 23–30. IEEE (2009)

14. Zhu, S., Morin, L., Pressigout, M., Moreau, G., Servieres, M.: Video/GIS registration system based on skyline matching method. In: International Conference on Image Processing, pp. 3632–3636. IEEE (2013)

15. Fukuda, T., Zhang, T., Yabuki, N.: Improvement of registration accuracy of a handheld augmented reality system for urban landscape simulation. Front. Architectural Res. **3**, 386–397 (2014)

16. Tighe, J., Lazebnik, S.: SuperParsing: scalable nonparametric image parsing with superpixels. In: Daniilidis, K., Maragos, P., Paragios, N. (eds.) ECCV 2010. LNCS, vol. 6315, pp. 352–365. Springer, Heidelberg (2010). doi:10.1007/978-3-642-15555-0_26

Quaternion Linear Color Edge-Glowing Filter Using Genetic Algorithm

Shagufta Yasmin$^{(\boxtimes)}$ and Stephen J. Sangwine

School of Computer Science and Electronic Engineering, University of Essex,
Wivenhoe, Colchester CO4 3SQ, UK
{syasmi,sjs}@essex.ac.uk

Abstract. This paper presents a quaternion linear color edge-glowing filter, based on a zooming technique using a genetic algorithm (GA) and quaternion (hypercomplex) convolution, to create a mask of the proposed filter. The zooming technique helps to produce the glowing color edges in all directions, with only one mask, and the GA helps to find the coefficients of the filter mask. This was a challenge with previous mathematical frameworks. The proposed filter employs linear color vector filtering operations on images. This converts the areas of smoothly-varying colors into black and generates glowing color edges in regions where color (but not intensity) edges occur in the image. The filter has been tested on different types of color images; the experimental results show that the proposed filter is a great advance towards the development of linear color vector image filtering. The computation time for the GA is about 1 h, which is very reasonable. The novelty of this filter is that one mask is enough for producing glowing color edges in all directions.

1 Introduction

The motivation for this research was to design a linear color vector image filter mask using a GA and zooming techniques: the design of such a mask is hard to do, even with the mathematical framework described in [11]. We have successfully done this and found a single filter mask which gives glowing color edges in all directions.

The process of edge detection both in gray and color images, in the spatial (or image) domain, has until now been needed separate masks for each direction of edges (i.e. vertical, horizontal or diagonal). This greatly limits the type of filters that may be realized. Vector image filtering based on a hypercomplex convolution scheme was first introduced by Sangwine [5]. He designed a quaternion based color edge detector, which could detect edges both in horizontal or vertical mask separately with two different masks (horizontal and vertical). Further development in the design of such linear color image filters by mathematical methods was difficult: Sangwine [11] suggested the use of a GA approach for the design of linear vector color image filters. This problem has been successfully resolved by the new approach described in this paper.

© Springer International Publishing AG 2016
J. Blanc-Talon et al. (Eds.): ACIVS 2016, LNCS 10016, pp. 616–625, 2016.
DOI: 10.1007/978-3-319-48680-2_54

2   Representation of Color Image Pixels in Terms of Quaternions

The quaternions are a four-space generalization of the complex numbers consisting one real part and three imaginary parts with imaginary operators i, j and k, which satisfy $i^2 - j^2 - k^2 = 1$ and $ij = -ji, ki = -ik, jk = -kj, ijk = -1$.

RGB colour images can be represented using quaternion-valued pixels. Where, the values of the red, green and blue components are stored in the three imaginary parts while the real part is zero, as a pure quaternion. Generally, image filtering may be employed by convolving a filter 'mask' with an image and it is generally a convolution with a quaternion-valued mask [5].

However, vector filtering based on a hypercomplex convolution scheme was first reported in Sangwine [5] and according to him, the definition of hypercomplex convolution can be described as:

$$\bar{g}(n,m) = \sum_{x=-X}^{X} \sum_{y=-Y}^{Y} h_L(x,y)g(n-x \bmod N, m-y \bmod M)h_R(x,y),$$

where

$\bar{g}(n,m)$ = Filtered image in a quaternion array $(N + 2 \times M + 2)$.
$g(\cdot)$ = Original image in a quaternion array $(N \times M))$.
$h_L(x,y)$ = Quaternion left mask $((2X+1) \times (2Y+1))$.
$h_R(x,y)$ = Quaternion right mask $((2X+1) \times (2Y+1))$.

Due to the non-commutative nature of quaternions, two masks with quaternion coefficients are needed, one on the left of each pixel and one on the right. These coefficients permit masks to implement linear operations on the pixel values, such as rotation in RGB color space.

3   Genetic Algorithm

Genetic algorithms are based on the theory of natural selection, first described by Charles Darwin, and they belong to the set of evolutionary algorithms used to generate solutions for optimization problems. A genetic algorithm optimization process starts with an initial random population and basically consists of three major operations: selection, crossover and mutation. The selection evaluates each individual and keeps only the fittest ones in the population. In addition to those fittest individuals, some less fit ones would be chosen according to a small probability. The others are discarded from the current population. Crossover recombines two individuals to create new ones which may be fitter. The mutation operator introduces alteration in a small number of individuals. Its purpose is to maintain the population diversity during the optimization process in order to provide a wider search space required for finding a good solution. The process of selection, crossover and mutation continues for a fixed number of generations or until a termination condition is satisfied [1].

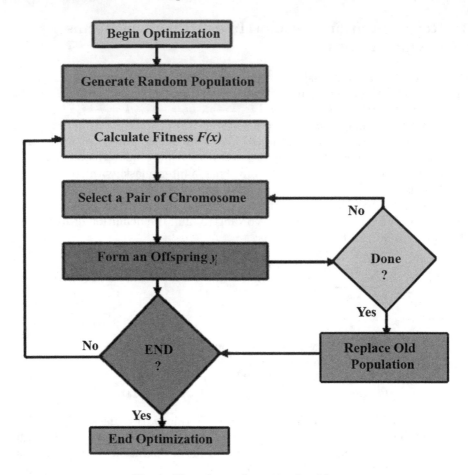

Fig. 1. Flow chart of genetic algorithm

There are five simple steps as shown in Fig. 1 of a genetic algorithm technique [4].

1. Start with a randomly generated population of N chromosomes, where N is the size of population.
2. Measure the fitness value $F(x)$ of each chromosome x in the population.
3. Repeat until N offspring are created:
   (a) Probabilistically choose a pair of chromosomes from the current population using the values of the fitness function.
   (b) Create an offspring y_i using crossover and mutation operators, where $i = 1, \ldots, N$.
4. Replace the current population with the newly generated one.
5. Terminate when a stopping criterion is satisfied.

For the work reported in this new scheme, we need floating-point values to be computed as qaternion mask that are totally based on quaternion arithmetic and the more advanced form of genetic algorithms in Matlab provides floating point numbers.

Bhandarkar *et al.* [2] reported edge detection using genetic algorithm, in which the process of edge detection is designed as selecting a minimum cost edge configuration. The adaptation of mutation and crossover rates helps a rapid convergence. The experimental results showed the effective convergence rate and noise immunity.

Zhang *et al.* [8] proposed a combined approach of Sobel detector and a GA for edge detection. The experimental results showed a better performance as compared to Otsu thresholding method.

Yutang and Lulu [7] presented a new scheme for enhancing the convergence rate of edge detection using genetic optimization technique. In this method, the theory of good point a set for redesigning the crossover operation is used. The image is filtered to remove the non-edge pixels prior to edge detection which increases the convergence rate with effective and efficient edge detection and noise-immunity.

Rahebi *et al.* [9] proposed Ant Colony Optimization based on GA to increase the processing speed of search algorithms. In this scheme, a series of answers made by artificial ants is considered initially then GA is employed to produce the next population. Experimental results showed this method was efficient in edge detection with increase in speed and answers optimum.

Sheta *et al.* [10] proposed a scheme in which they combined traditional edge detection methods and genetic algorithm approach. The results showed better performance when compared with K-means clustering.

Preeti and Rajesh [12] presented an overview of Sobel and Canny operators and the experiment results showed that the genetic algorithm that works with improved Sobel operator generated much better results in comparison to them with limited to gray scale images. However, the novel approach that maximizes the objective function had been reviewed and found better outputs.

4   History of Linear Color Vector Image Filters

Until recently, no mathematical framework of edge detection filters to gray or color had been reported that could find edges in vertical, horizontal or diagonal direction with only one mask simultaneously. In 1998 Sangwine [5] published the first example of a color image filter based on convolution with hypercomplex or quaternion masks, detecting edges horizontally or vertically with different masks. Further development of linear vector image filtering was hard wth any present mathematical framework [11]. In this paper we rectify this problem by a very general approach with the convolution of hypercomplex coefficients inspired by Sangwine [5] based on the zooming technique using a genetic algorithm.

5   Designing Methodology of the New Filter

5.1   Zooming Technique

We applied the zooming technique to produce glowing color edges in all directions. The technique is as follows.

We begin by making a target image in Adobe Photoshop editor using its glowing edges filter, which gives the original image an artistic effect as shown in the left-hand image of Fig. 4. The target image is used by the GA, which attempts to produce a filter (represented to the GA as an array of floating-point numbers) such that, if convolved with the original image, will produce the target image exactly. The fitness function used by the GA has to produce a numeric measure that reduces to zero, if the target image and filtered image (filtered by the proposed filter) are identical. Thus the GA attempts to minimize the fitness measure for each element of the population. The fitness function therefore computes the difference between the target and filtered image (filtered by the proposed filter) and sums the absolute value of the difference across the image.

To glow the color edges in all directions and also to speed up the GA, a 'zooming' technique is employed in which the GA initially works with a small portion of the image (a 'zoomed-in' view). Let us take an example to describe the zooming technique. Eleven sizes of the original Lena image and eleven sizes of target images are used. The eleven original Lena images are cropped from the full-size one. A 17×17 pixels section of the Lena image (around the eye) as shown in Fig. 2 and a low resolution 19×19 pixels target image of full size as shown in Fig. 3 are used in the first optimization stage. The GA computes an initial population using these images.

This computation is relatively fast because of the small number of pixels. It enhances the initial random population but it will not produce a good result,

Fig. 2. Original Lena images used in each fitness function from (left) 17×17, 28×28, 40×40, 53×53, 66×66, 99×99, 153×153, 233×233, 330×330, 409×409, 514×514 to (right)

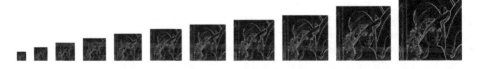

Fig. 3. Target Lena images (Photoshopped images) used in each fitness function from (left) 19×19, 30×30, 42×42, 55×55, 68×68, 101×101, 155×155, 235×235, 332×332, 411×411, 516×516 to (right)

because it is operating only on a small part of the original image and a low resolution target image with small generation and population size. Next, a 28×28 pixels part-image of the original Lena and a 30×30 pixels low resolution full-size target image are used in the next optimization stage, producing a better population, but it will again computing somewhat more slowly.

The sizes of original Lena image to be filtered (40×40, 53×53, 66×66, 99×99, 153×153, 233×233, 330×330, 409×409, 514×514 pixels) and target image (42×42, 55×55, 68×68, 101×101, 155×155, 235×235, 332×332, 411×411, 516×516 pixels) are increased in each optimization stage, step by step. At each stage of optimization, the already converged population from the previous one is moved as the initial population in the next one.

5.2 Benefits of the Zooming Technique

There are four benefits of using the zooming technique.

1. First and the most powerful aspect of using the zooming technique is that it guides GA to glow color edges in all directions with only one mask. The filtered results using our new filter are much better than the target image.
2. Second, the image sizes increase step by step, and because most of the computation time is taken up with convolution, so the total computation time is reduced by approximately 90 %, compared to working with the full-size image from the start.
3. Third benefit is that the already converged population towards the best fitness values is moved to the next stage of the optimization as the initial population, which makes the fitness functions more effective to find the best result.

Initially, a function '*qmask*' is made for a 3×3 Quaternion matrix from a 1×36 real vector. In edge detection the number of variables is the number of filter coefficients. For the 3×3 mask, the number of coefficients is 36. The genetic algorithm helps to find the coefficients of the proposed filter that was difficult manually.

The generations used here are 935 and population size is double of generations size; that is 1870 (85 generations and a population size of 170 are used in each optimization stage). The time consumption is approximately 1 h, crossover and mutation are selected heuristic and gaussian respectively while the elite children used here are 10.

The *fitness function* (*errror*) is designed as follows:

$fitness\ function = mean(mean(abs(conv2(\{qmask, conj(qmask)\}, qp) - qt)))$.

where

qp = Original Lena image (to be filtered by the proposed filter), in a quaternion array.

qt = Target image (Photoshopped Lena image), in a quaternion array.

$conv2(\{qmask, conj(qmask)\}, qp) =$ Filtered Lena image by the proposed filter, in a quaternion array.

$qmask =$ Quaternion left mask (3×3) generated by GA.

$cqmask =$ Quaternion right mask (3×3) generated by GA.

6   Experimental Results

We used our filter on a color Lena image. It produced glowing color edges in all directions, i.e. a sudden change of color, with the remaining parts of the image convert to black as shown in the right-hand image of Fig. 4. The Lena image as filtered by the proposed filter is much better than the actual target image, because it has more detail, fine and thin color edges in all directions. Although the quality of the GA is measured by the closeness of the proposed filter and the target image, the use of the zooming technique produces the better result than

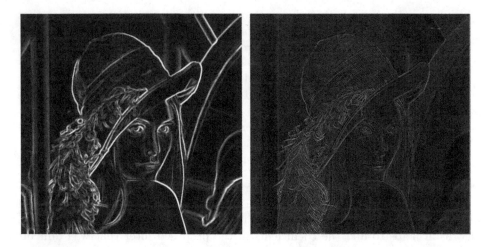

Fig. 4. Target Lena image (left) and filtered Lena image by the proposed filter (right)

Fig. 5. Original Tulips image (left) and filtered Tulips image by the proposed filter (right)

the target image. The filter has been tested on different types of color images and the results show that the performance of the new filter is outstanding.

Table 1 shows the coefficients of the Quaternion left mask (*qmask*) of the proposed filter. Quaternion right mask (*cqmask*) is created by negating the vector parts of the *qmask* (taking the conjugate of the Quaternion left mask), where *qmask.s* represents the scalar part and *qmask.x*, *qmask.y* and *qmask.z* represent the vector parts of the proposed filter mask (Figs. 5, 6 and 7).

Fig. 6. Original Monarch image (left) and filtered Monarch image by the proposed filter (right)

Fig. 7. Original Peppers image (left) and filtered Peppers image by the proposed filter (right)

Table 1. Quaternion left mask ($qmask$) of the proposed filter

qmask of the Proposed filter generated by GA					
qmask.s			qmask.y		
0.6686	0.3723	−1.4099	0.4307	1.1371	0.0912
1.3286	0.0135	0.0977	−0.4921	−1.0957	−0.5378
−0.3206	0.7164	0.2499	−0.9979	0.7224	−0.0650
qmask.x			qmask.z		
−0.2231	−0.5688	−0.1375	0.7438	−0.9727	−0.1082
−0.0436	−1.1117	0.6252	−0.7934	0.3882	−1.1099
1.0987	0.7940	−1.0956	−0.0579	1.2914	0.1682

7   Conclusion

We can see from the experimental results that the proposed filter not only produces glowing color edges, but also finer detail than the target image due to the use of the zooming technique. Further advances after [5] in the design of linear vector image filters now becomes possible: this was a challenge using any mathematical approach as suggested in Sangwine [11]. We used zooming and GA techniques for the design of a linear color vector image filter. This new filter uses only one mask and produces color glowing edges in all directions. The proposed filter has been tested on different kind of color images and the experimental results show that the new filter is real need for glowing color edges in all directions with only one mask.

References

1. Goldberg, D.E.: Genetic Algorithms in Search, Optimization and Machine Learning. Addison-Wesley, New York (1989)
2. Bhandarkar, S.M., Zhang, Y., Potter, W.D.: An edge detection using genetic algorithm based optimization. Pattern Recogn. **27**(9), 1159–1180 (1994)
3. Sangwine, S.J.: Fourier transforms of colour images using quaternion, or hypercomplex, numbers. Electron. Lett. **32**, 1979–1980 (1996)
4. Falkenauer, E.: Genetic Algorithms and Grouping Problems. Wiley, Boston (1998)
5. Sangwine, S.J.: Colour image edge detector based on quaternion convolution. Electron. Lett. **34**(10), 969–971 (1998)
6. Sangwine, S.J., Ell, T.A.: Colour image filters based on hypercomplex convolution. IEE Proc. Vis. Image Sig. Process. **147**(2), 89–93 (2000). doi:10.1049/ip-vis: 20000211
7. Yutang, G., Lulu, L.: An edge detection method based on good point set genetic algorithm. In: IEEE Conference on CCC 2008 (2008)
8. Yu, Z.J., Yang, C., Xiang, H.X.: Edge detection of images based on improved sobel operator and genetic algorithm. In: IEEE International Conference on ISAP (2009)

9. Rahebi, J., Elmi, Z., Nia, A.F., Shyam, K.: Digital image edge detection using an ant colony optimization based on genetic algorithm. In: IEEE Conference on Cybernetics and Intelligent Systems (2010)
10. Sheta, A., Braik, M.S., Aljahadli, S., Algorithm, G.: A tool for image segmentation. In: IEEE International Conference on ICMS (2012)
11. Sangwine, S.J.: Perspectives on color image processing by linear vector methods using projective geometric transformations. In: Hawkes, P.W. (ed.) Advances in Imaging and Electron Physics, vol. 175, pp. 283–307. Academic Press: Elsevier Inc., Amsterdam (2013). ISBN: 9780124076709
12. Adhana, P., Singh, R.K.: The review paper comparing sobel, canny with genetic algorithm, novel approach. Int. J. Sci. Res. Educ. 2(5), 727–734 (2014). ISSN (o): 2321-7545

Scalable Vision System for Mouse Homecage Ethology

Ghadi Salem[1]($\boxtimes$), Jonathan Krynitsky[1], Brett Kirkland[1], Eugene Lin[1],
Aaron Chan[1], Simeon Anfinrud[1], Sarah Anderson[1],
Marcial Garmendia-Cedillos[1], Rhamy Belayachi[1], Juan Alonso-Cruz[1],
Joshua Yu[1], Anthony Iano-Fletcher[1], George Dold[1], Tom Talbot[1],
Alexxai V. Kravitz[1], James B. Mitchell[1], Guanhang Wu[2], John U. Dennis[2],
Monson Hayes[3], Kristin Branson[4], and Thomas Pohida[1]

[1] National Institutes of Health, Bethesda, MD, USA
ghadi.salem@nih.gov
[2] Food and Drug Administration, Silver Spring, MD, USA
[3] George Mason University, Fairfax, VA, USA
[4] Howard Hughes Medical Institute (JFRC), Ashburn, VA, USA

Abstract. In recent years, researchers and laboratory support companies have recognized the utility of automated profiling of laboratory
mouse activity and behavior in the home-cage. Video-based systems
have emerged as a viable solution for non-invasive mouse monitoring.
Wider use of vision systems for ethology studies requires the development of scalable hardware seamlessly integrated with vivarium ventilated racks. Compact hardware combined with automated video analysis
would greatly impact animal science and animal-based research. Automated vision systems, free of bias and intensive labor, can accurately
assess rodent activity (e.g., well-being) and behavior 24-7 during research
studies within primary home-cages. Scalable compact hardware designs
impose constraints, such as use of fisheye lenses, placing greater burden (e.g., distorted image) on downstream video analysis algorithms. We
present novel methods for analysis of video acquired through such specialized hardware. Our algorithms estimate the 3D pose of mouse from
monocular images. We present a thorough examination of the algorithm
training parameters' influence on system accuracy. Overall, the methods
presented offer novel approaches for accurate activity and behavior estimation practical for large-scale use of vision systems in animal facilities.

1 Introduction

The application of vision systems' technologies could have a huge impact on
animal-based medical research, including corresponding animal care. During
recent decades, the use of laboratory mice in biomedical research increased considerably [1]. Laboratory animals including mice are used to gain new knowledge
for improving the health and well-being of both humans and other animals [2].

© Springer International Publishing AG 2016
J. Blanc-Talon et al. (Eds.): ACIVS 2016, LNCS 10016, pp. 626–637, 2016.
DOI: 10.1007/978-3-319-48680-2_55

However, mice are the most frequently characterized and used mammals in biomedical research because of their small size and ease of use, including relative ease for sophisticated genetic manipulation [1]. To achieve high-density housing while maintaining consistent, controlled microenvironments, animal facility managers frequently utilize individually ventilated cages that mate with specialized racks. These ventilated cage environments have become the standard in laboratory facilities as they provide protection for personnel (e.g., infectious agent and allergen containment) and maintain low levels of ammonia and CO_2 allowing an increased number of cages in animal holding rooms. When there are hundreds or thousands of cages in one institution, monitoring of animal health and activity is infrequent, of limited measures, and rather subjective. The use of vision systems could significantly reduce the workload and more appropriately focus the efforts of trained animal care staff by providing continual automated monitoring. This would increase efficiency and reduce bias (e.g., due to fatigue or drift [3]). For example, abnormalities in behavior patterns can be automatically identified leading to early detection of illness, which can be quickly treated or managed. The activity measures are of use to researchers conducting phenotyping, drug-efficacy, and animal model characterization studies. While many commercial and academic systems have been developed to automate home-cage ethology, the wide use of vision systems is contingent on availability of minimal footprint hardware with seamless integration in ventilated racks. Salem et al. [4] reported on the first video-based hardware design specifically targeted for use in cage-racks. This system integrates into the ventilated rack without modification to the cages or racks, nor alteration to animal husbandry procedures. The resulting video poses processing challenges as mouse appearance exhibits large variations induced by the nonlinearity of fisheye lenses, which is exacerbated by lens placement in very close proximity to the cage. The position estimation presented by the authors is limited to predicting the mouse 2D physical centroid projected to the cage-floor, and only in cases when the mouse has all its limbs on the cage-floor.

In this work, we begin addressing the task of mouse pose estimation using the challenging video output from the system described in [4]. We present a novel approach to producing accurate 3D pose estimates from monocular images. The approach utilizes a rich dataset with mouse posterior/anterior annotations from two orthogonal views. We describe slight modifications to the hardware system that enable gathering of a unique training set. We investigate estimation accuracy as a function of training parameters. The prototype example output images and pose estimation results are shown in Fig. 1. The datasets are made publicly available (scorhe.nih.gov) to encourage further development in field.

2   Related Work

Automated analysis of mice activity and behavior has attracted commercial and academic interest over the past two decades [3,5,6]. Desired analysis output measures range from pose estimation to detection of predefined behaviors [6–8].

We limit our review to video-based systems for mice home-cage monitoring. We explore hardware systems as well as pose estimation methods.

2.1   Hardware Systems

Hardware systems employed in academic works are typically simple prototypes and ad hoc setups [6] that use cameras fitted with standard lenses, positioned a sufficient distance from the cage ensuring the field-of-view encompasses the cage volume. Some setups rely on overhead cameras [8,9]. However, as noted by many [7,10], such placement is not well-suited for scalability due to cage and rack obstructions in high-density housing. Commercial hardware systems are reviewed in [4].

2.2   Pose Estimation Methods

One sought output of automated video analysis is a per-frame pose estimate, which can be subsequently used for motion analysis. Two defining components of pose estimation are the pose model (i.e., pose parameters) and pose detection method. For pose model, ellipses are used by [11–13]. Oriented ellipses (i.e.,

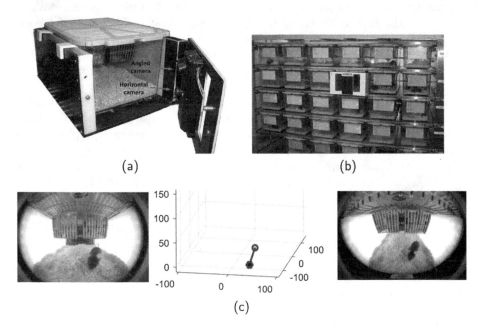

(a)

(b)

(c)

Fig. 1. (a) The video acquisition system used for this work. (b) The system is designed to seamlessly integrate into vivarium cage racks. (c) Example images from the horizontal (leftmost image) and angled (rightmost image) cameras acquired at the same time instance, along with the corresponding 3D position (in mm) of posterior (lighter circle) and anterior (darker circle) estimated by our algorithm.

with an ellipse axis end-point identified as the anterior of the mouse) are used in [8] and the commercial Ethovision package by Noldus [14]. Twelve deformable contour templates are used as the pose model by Branson and Belongie [7]. A lower dimensional ellipse pose model is used to localize the detection area for the more elaborate deformable template model. de Chaumont et al. [15] model the mouse as a head, belly, and neck, with corresponding constrained displacements between each part. Each part is represented by a 2D articulated rigid body model. The parts are linked together through a physics model that defines the motion constraints between the parts. For pose detection, [11–13] simply fit an ellipse to the observed foreground. During occlusion, Pistori et al. [11] employ a particle filter to predict pose, while Branson et al. [12] generate the poses acausally once occlusion ends. A more elaborate cascaded pose regression method [16] is used in [17]. Branson and Belongie [7] use a mutliblob tracker for the ellipse detection and particle-filter contour tracker for contour detection. de Chaumont et al. [15] use the foreground binary mask and edges for initial alignment and mean-shift processes drive the physics engine for refinements.

The hardware setups for all the described methods make it straightforward to define pose parameters in 2D image domain. Given the geometry and optics, physical correspondence is easily established by scaling. Scaled orthography, however, does not apply for the hardware system used for the work presented in this paper for two reasons: (1) the use of a fisheye lens, and (2) the very close proximity of the lens to the monitoring arena. Instead of defining pose parameters in image domain, which might well be uninformative, we instead define pose parameters as the 3D physical coordinates of the mouse posterior and anterior.

3   Method

In what follows, we describe the pose estimation methods employed for solitary home-cage housed mice. Since the ingenuity of the approach is motivated by the uniqueness of the hardware configuration, we start with a quick overview of the hardware system. We then describe the segmentation and pose estimation processing modules.

3.1   Hardware System

The original hardware design is thoroughly described in [4]. A quick overview is herein presented to make this paper self-contained. The video acquisition system is designed to operate in the near-infrared (NIR) spectrum, hence producing monochromatic video. The design employs two cameras fitted with fisheye lenses that are positioned very close to the cage (i.e., < 5 mm). The lenses are mounted near the top of the cage front and rear walls with a downwards tilt of 25°. We have enhanced the NIR illumination uniformity of the prototype by replacing the NIR LED strips within each side assembly with custom designed LED array. The LED array spans the majority of surface of each side assembly. Translucent acrylic is used to diffuse the LED sources resulting in uniform illumination.

We also augmented the prototype with two additional cameras, one at each end of the cage. The cameras were positioned at mid-height and pointed horizontally (i.e., no tilt) into the cage. Lastly, we've designed an overhead camera system to synchronously capture top-down view of the cage. The overhead system is strictly used for video acquisition related to building training sets, and is not utilized at runtime. The additional cameras proved instrumental in both generating the unique datasets and enabling the novel development and validation presented in this paper. Figure 1a shows an image of the prototype. The front cameras are labeled in the figure, whereas the rear cameras are not seen. Due to cage obstructions (e.g., water and food baskets), each camera view is mainly limited to its side of the cage (e.g., rear or front). The algorithms are coded such that if the mouse is closer to the front of the cage, the estimation is done through a front camera image, and vice-versa. It is also noted that despite our augmented hardware system having two cameras at each end (i.e., horizontal and angled), the algorithms are trained on a pre-chosen camera, and subsequently run strictly on images from the camera on which they are trained. In other words, the addition of the horizontal camera to the original system was not with the intent of making the system a binocular vision system, but rather to facilitate construction of training sets. However, we do take advantage of the availability of the horizontal camera to compare the estimation accuracy between it and the angled camera. While using both tilted and horizontal views at once would likely lead to more accurate results, using a single camera for each end of the cage would be desirable if one is concerned about video storage requirements, processing expense (e.g., future real-time processing), and hardware cost and simplicity.

3.2 Segmentation

Segmentation identifies mouse pixels in the image. Although the mouse is generally darker than background, segmentation based simple intensity thresholding produces poor results due to four main factors: (1) the large disparity in pixel intensity values between the backside of the mouse and its underside, (2) the presence of dark regions in the cage with pixel intensity ranges overlapping those of the mouse (e.g., between food and water baskets), (3) the variability in background intensity patterns in and around the cage-floor region resulting from frequent bedding changes, and (4) the significant shadows cast by the mouse on the bedding. Figure 4 shows example frames highlighting the challenges of segmentation. Our segmentation method capitalizes on the constrained environment and the constant camera position. We build a segmentation model for each camera (i.e., horizontal and angled at both front and rear). Mouse pixels were manually annotated in a set of 250 images from each camera. The images were selected to account for the varied mouse appearance in different positions and poses within the cage. Approximately 350,000 foreground and 350,000 background pixels are chosen randomly from the images and used to train each tree of an 8-tree decision forest classifier to predict a binary label (foreground vs background) for each image pixel. To derive discriminative features, a set of information channels registered to the image are obtained through linear and nonlinear transformations of the image as per [18]. Namely, we use the intensity gradient magnitude and the 4-bin histogram of orientation of the gradients (HOG). The feature vector for each labeled pixel includes its intensity value along with the values of the feature channels at the pixel position. Additionally, to exploit the stationary camera placement, the pixel's (x, y) location in the image are included in the feature set. Using the pixel image location as a feature results in region-specific classification rules and more robust thresholds (e.g., a more robust intensity threshold against the bright panels, etc.). To segment an incoming image during run-time, the feature channels are first computed for the whole image. The feature vectors for each pixel are formed by concatenating its intensity value, x and y image locations, and feature channel values (i.e., gradient magnitude and HOG as used in training). The decision forest is evaluated for each pixel's feature vector. The returned result is a value representing the probability that the pixel is foreground. A segmentation probability image map, which is pixel-to-pixel registered to the intensity image, is formed by setting the value of location (x, y) to the returned foreground probability value. The foreground probability map is converted to a binary image by thresholding. The threshold level can be selected empirically based on visualizing segmentation results. Alternatively, a more systematic method of tuning a threshold to achieve a desired precision or recall can be employed. Connected component analysis is run on the binary segmentation mask. Size-based filtering is employed to discard small connected components deemed as noise. The largest connected component is regarded as the mouse. Statistics of the binary silhouette such as ellipse fit parameters, ellipse axes end points, bounding box, and area are computed. The area is used to decide which camera will be used for pose estimation. Namely, if the mouse area in the front camera's image is bigger than the area in the rear camera's image, then the front camera image is used and vice-versa.

3.3   Pose Estimation

Pose estimation recovers the three dimensional physical coordinates of the mouse anterior and posterior from a monocular image. The motivation behind 3D posterior/anterior position estimation is to obtain a meaningful measure of mouse activity and behavior. Motion analysis relying on 2D image positions could be non-informative due to the significant distortions resulting from the fisheye lens and its close proximity to the cage. The pose estimation problem is formulated as a non-parametric regression supervised learning task. Hence the objective is to find a mapping $f(\cdot)$ from feature space $\mathcal{X}$ to continuous pose parameters space $\mathcal{Y} \in \mathbb{R}^D$ given a training set $\mathcal{S} \subset \mathcal{X} \times \mathcal{Y}$. Each pose parameter entry $y \in \mathcal{Y}$ in the training set constitutes six parameters denoting 3D coordinates of the mouse posterior (p) and anterior (a). Namely, $y = [p, a], p = [p_i, p_j, p_k], a = [a_i, a_j, a_k]$, where i, j, k are the three axes of the Cartesian coordinates system. Corresponding to each y is a vector $x \in \mathcal{X}$ of features drawn from the image of the mouse having pose y. The challenge in learning $f(\cdot)$, however, is to construct the ground truth set for the pose 3D coordinates, i.e. $y's$. The mouse is highly deformable and the fisheye lens placed close to the cage rules out the assumption of scaled orthography. Both factors impede recovery of 3D coordinates from a single image. Hence, as described in Sect. 3.1, we augmented the system with an overhead camera with acquisition synchronized to the side-view cameras. All cameras are calibrated such that each image point maps to a line in 3D space. The same mouse key point (e.g., anterior or posterior) is manually marked in two views, namely the horizontal view and the overhead view as shown in Fig. 2. For each view, the 3D line corresponding to the marked image point is computed. The 3D point at which distance between the two resulting lines in minimum is regarded as the ground truth 3D position for the key point. The full training set comprises approximately 200,000 annotations (e.g., two points on side view image and two points on top-down image). To aid the human annotators and speed up the task, the frames were segmented to isolate the mouse and posterior/anterior were pre-annotated as the fitting ellipse major axis end points. Since the end points were arbitrarily designated as posterior/anterior, in most of the cases the annotator's task was to reverse the designation. In some cases, where the major axis end points did not align well with posterior/anterior of the mouse, the annotator would displace the pre-annotated points to more suitable locations in the image.

The vector x is populated with two sets of features. The first set is statistics drawn from the binary silhouette returned by the segmentation module. The features include silhouette area, ellipse fit parameters (e.g., orientation, centroid, length of major and minor axes), and bounding box parameters. The second set is pixel intensity value lookups for randomly chosen locations within the detection window. To compute N such features, a set of positions $\{\phi_n\}, n \in \{1, ..., N\}$ is randomly chosen at training time. Each position ϕ_i is specified as relative offsets from the binary silhouette bounding box, i.e. $\phi_i = (o_x, o_y), o \in [0, 1]$. To compute the feature value, the offsets are scaled to the size of the bounding box, i.e., $\phi_i^s = (o_x \cdot b_w, o_y \cdot b_h)$, where b_w and b_h are the bounding box width and height respectively and the superscript s denotes the scaled ϕ. The feature is then simply computed as $I_b(\phi_i^s)$, where I_b denotes the subset of the whole image I enclosed by the binary silhouette bounding box. The feature extraction concept is illustrated in the cartoon shown in Fig. 3 for $N = 6$. Our implementation uses $N = 125$.

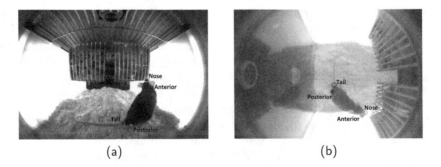

(a)   (b)

Fig. 2. Mouse in different camera views at the same time instance, shown with example posterior/anterior as well as tail/nose manual annotations. (a) horizontal camera view (b) overhead mounted camera view.

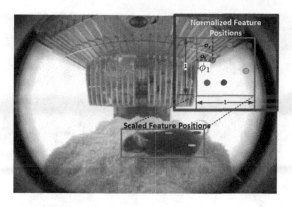

Fig. 3. Cartoon demonstrating the scaling of normalized feature positions to compute the ferns-like features.

The set of discriminative feature vectors each paired with the corresponding ground truth pose are used to train regression forests to act as the mapping function $f(\cdot)$. We treat the parameters (e.g., coordinates) as uncorrelated, and for each of the six parameters of y, a regression forest $f_i(\cdot), i \in \{1, \ldots, 6\}$ is trained to estimate parameter y_i separately. Regression forests constitute an effective non-parameteric regression technique and are well described in literature, e.g. [19].

4 Results

We have built four segmentation models, one for each camera (cage-front angled camera, cage-front horizontal camera, cage-rear angled camera, and cage-rear horizontal camera). Since the decision forests for segmentation yield a probability map for foreground, we use 0.7 as a threshold to convert the map to a binary image. The threshold was selected empirically such that the foreground pixels are well matched to the mouse pixels in the image. We used 60 images with ground truth annotations that were set aside for testing purposes (i.e., not included in segmentation classifier training) to compute the precision/recall for the chosen threshold. The computed values achieved 94 % precision with 85 % recall. Figure 4 shows example segmentation results.

To establish a basis for assessing key point estimation performance, a set R of approximately 6,000 frames was redundantly annotated to provide a range of acceptable deviation between annotations. The chosen frames account for a wide variety of mouse posture in different positions within the cage. Noting that posterior and anterior do not correspond to a single well-defined point on the mouse, but are rather proximity designations (mainly corresponding to the ellipse endpoints as explained in Sect. 3.3), the redundant annotations aimed to establish a Euclidean distance range for 3D posterior position deviation relative to the mouse tail and 3D anterior position deviation relative to mouse nose (refer to Fig. 2). Hence, for the frames in R having posterior/anterior annotations, an

(a)   (b)

Fig. 4. Example segmentation output for challenging frames highlighting the method's (a) robustness to shadows and dark background regions (i.e., center of image) (b) detection of lighter underside of the mouse.

annotator carefully labeled the tail and nose. For each frame in the redundantly annotated set, the 3D points for posterior/anterior $y = [p_i, p_j, p_k, a_i, a_j, a_k]$ and the 3D points for tail/nose $\bar{y} = [t_i, t_j, t_k, n_i, n_j, n_k]$ were reconstructed via the calibration mappings. The variance, σ_i^2 of each coordinate in $y(i)$ around the corresponding coordinate in $\bar{y}(i)$ was computed as the variance of the distance $\|y(i) - \bar{y}(i)\|$, $i \in \{1, \cdots, 6\}$, where $\| \cdot \|$ is defined as Euclidean distance. We define a distance measure similar to that proposed in [16] utilizing the observed variances σ_i for all six coordinates to equally weigh the estimation errors for each coordinate. The distance, $d(\hat{y}, \bar{y})$, is computed between the regression models output $\hat{y} = [\hat{p}, \hat{a}]$ and the earlier defined $\bar{y} = [t, n]$ which is regarded as ground truth. Namely,

$$d(\hat{y}, \bar{y}) = \sqrt{\frac{1}{6} \sum_{i=1}^{6} \frac{1}{\sigma_i^2} (\hat{y}(i) - \bar{y}(i))^2} \tag{1}$$

In addition to the distance measure, we define a metric to deem an estimation output $\hat{y}$ as either a success or a failure, as is done in [16]. The metric is based on the normalized distance measure of Eq. (1) and an unweighted overall distance measure defined as $\tilde{d}(\hat{y}, \bar{y}) = \|p - t\| + \|a - n\|$. We let d_{thr} be the normalized distance (1) such that 99 % of R, the redundantly annotated frames, are within d_{thr} of each other. We let $\tilde{d}_{thr}$ be the unweighted overall distance such that 99 % of R are within $\tilde{d}_{thr}$ of each other. Our metric for success is if $d(\hat{y}, \bar{y}) < d_{thr}$ and $\tilde{d}(\hat{y}, \bar{y}) < \tilde{d}_{thr}$. The computed thresholds for R where $d_{thr} = 2.73$ and $\tilde{d}_{thr} = 69$ mm.

To evaluate the accuracy of the regression models, the models were applied to the frames in set R, which was held out of training. For each frame, the feature vector is formed as described in Sect. 3.3. The vector is then fed to all regression forests $f_i(\cdot)$ to separately estimate each parameter in $\hat{y}$. The output $\hat{y}$ is compared to $\bar{y}$, the reconstructed 3D points for the tail/nose annotations, which are regarded as ground truth. Namely, we compute both distance measures, $d(\hat{y}, \bar{y})$ and $\tilde{d}(\hat{y}, \bar{y})$. The computed distance measures are then compared to the thresholds to set the failure rates. For successful estimates, a mean d and $\tilde{d}$ are computed as well. To analyze the influence of training parameters on accuracy, different regression models were built by varying training parameters including number of trees, image resolution, and training set size. Another variation was to compare taking the median versus the mean of the leaf-node predictions from the trees. Additionally, the hardware system equipped with a horizontal and angled camera offers a unique opportunity to assess accuracy as a function of camera view-point. Recall that the horizontal cameras were added, as stated in Sect. 3.1, to aid in generating training sets. While having a system with two cameras (i.e., horizontal and angled) might lead to greater accuracy, it is desirable to limit the number of cameras per system. Having multiple cameras for each end of the cage would increase the storage requirements for the output video and increase the processing load. To compare the accuracy of estimates as a function of camera view-point, one set of regression models was built to estimate pose from horizontal camera images, and another set of models was built to estimate pose from angled camera images. The result of the comparison between horizontal and angled cameras helps with design choices for such compact systems (i.e., if results are more accurate using horizontal versus angled camera). The base model was chosen to be the horizontal camera, using 50 trees, taking the median of the leaf-node predictions, with features drawn from $\frac{1}{2}$ scale image. Table 1 shows the failure rates. The table also shows the mean distance

Table 1. Results of algorithm training parameters sweeps for horizontal and angled cameras

Parameters	Horizontal			Angled		
	% fail	d mean	$\tilde{d}$ mean	% fail	d mean	$\tilde{d}$ mean
Trees = 25	0.91	0.84	23.2	0.96	0.87	23.6
Trees = 50	**0.83**	**0.84**	**23.2**	0.86	0.87	23.6
Trees = 75	0.81	0.84	23.2	0.98	0.86	23.6
Trees = 100	0.83	0.84	23.2	0.93	0.86	23.6
Image Scale = 1	0.88	0.85	23.3	0.11	0.87	23.6
Image Scale = 0.25	0.91	0.84	23.2	0.10	0.87	23.6
Mean of leaf-nodes	0.78	0.88	23.9	0.88	0.90	24.1
70 % of Training Set	6.73	1.05	28.1	6.88	1.06	28.3
52 % of Training Set	7.49	1.09	28.9	7.37	1.10	29.3
45 % of Training Set	8.30	1.11	29.6	8.61	1.10	29.4

measures for successful estimates. Each entry in the table shows the results of varying a single training parameter relative to the base model. It is clear that the estimation is not sensitive to any of the parameter changes except for the training set size.

5 Discussion

We have demonstrated a viable algorithmic path for accurately estimating 3D posterior/anterior positions of a mouse from monocular fisheye distorted images. These or similar types of images will likely arise in specialized compact systems designed for large scale use in animal vivaria. Our methods capitalize on the constrained environment and known tracking subject to overcome challenges caused by the unusual camera configuration and the highly deformable tracking target. We experimented with algorithm training parameters and demonstrated, as per Table 1 that the accuracy is robust to changes in training parameters. We also experimented with two camera orientations: the horizontal view and angled view. Table 1 suggests that both camera views produce similar results. While an algorithm relying on both cameras horizontal and angled cameras (at both the cage front and rear) to estimate pose would likely be more accurate, some users may wish to decide, for practicaly reasons such as goals aimed at real-time processing, to limit the amount of video data stored and/or processed. The training and testing sets utilized for this study are for a limited mouse size range. Encompassing a larger mouse weight range would simply involve generating additional annotations for the desired mouse sizes. The uniqueness of the hardware system and the specificity of the algorithms to the custom hardware percludes direct comparison with existing state of the art. The per-frame 3D pose estimates produced by our algorithm, however, provide meaningful position information. The 3D position information can be subsequently used for accurate motion analysis. Burgos-Artizzu et al. [8] have shown that trajectory features derived from pose estimates are discriminant for behavior detection. Overall, the algorithm should provide researchers and animal care professionals accurate measures to assess well-being and phenotypical changes.

The training set and the videos are available online (scorhe.nih.gov).

References

1. Jacoby, R., Fox, J., Davisson, M.: Biology and diseases of mice. Lab. Anim. Med. **2**, 35–120 (2002)
2. Conn, P.M.: Animal Models for the Study of Human Disease. Academic Press, London (2013)
3. Noldus, L.P., Spink, A.J., Tegelenbosch, R.A.: Ethovision: a versatile video tracking system for automation of behavioral experiments. Behav. Res. Meth. Instrum. Comput. **33**(3), 398–414 (2001)
4. Salem, G.H., Dennis, J.U., Krynitsky, J., Garmendia-Cedillos, M., Swaroop, K., Malley, J.D., Pajevic, S., Abuhatzira, L., Bustin, M., Gillet, J.-P., et al.: Scorhe: a novel and practical approach to video monitoring of laboratory mice housed in vivarium cage racks. Behav. Res. Meth. **47**(1), 235–250 (2015)

5. Steele, A.D., Jackson, W.S., King, O.D., Lindquist, S.: The power of automated high-resolution behavior analysis revealed by its application to mouse models of huntington's and prion diseases. Proc. Natl. Acad. Sci. **104**(6), 1983–1988 (2007)
6. Jhuang, H., Garrote, E., Yu, X., Khilnani, V., Poggio, T., Steele, A.D., Serre, T.: Automated home-cage behavioural phenotyping of mice. Nat. Commun. **1**, 68 (2010)
7. Branson, K., Belongie, S.: Tracking multiple mouse contours (without too many samples). In: 2005 IEEE Computer Society Conference on Computer Vision and Pattern Recognition (CVPR 2005), vol. 1, pp. 1039–1046, June 2005
8. Burgos-Artizzu, X.P., Dollár, P., Lin, D., Anderson, D.J., Perona, P.: Social behavior recognition in continuous video. In: IEEE Conference on Computer Vision and Pattern Recognition (CVPR), pp. 1322–1329. IEEE (2012)
9. Ohayon, S., Avni, O., Taylor, A.L., Perona, P., Egnor, S.R.: Automated multi-day tracking of marked mice for the analysis of social behaviour. J. Neurosci. Meth. **219**(1), 10–19 (2013)
10. Farah, R., Langlois, J., Bilodeau, G.-A.: Catching a rat by its edglets. IEEE Trans. Image Process. **22**(2), 668–678 (2013)
11. Pistori, H., Odakura, V.V.V.A., Monteiro, J.B.O., Gonçalves, W.N., Roel, A.R., de Andrade Silva, J., Machado, B.B.: Mice and larvae tracking using a particle filter with an auto-adjustable observation model. Pattern Recognit. Lett. **31**(4), 337–346 (2010)
12. Branson, K., Rabaud, V., Belongie, S.J.: Three brown mice: See how they run. In: VS-PETS Workshop at ICCV (2003)
13. Zarringhalam, K., Ka, M., Kook, Y.-H., Terranova, J.I., Suh, Y., King, O.D., Um, M.: An open system for automatic home-cage behavioral analysis and its application to male and female mouse models of huntington's disease. Behav. Brain Res. **229**(1), 216–225 (2012)
14. Noldus EthoVision-XT (2016). http://www.noldus.com/animal-behavior-research/products/ethovision-xt
15. de Chaumont, F., Coura, R.D.-S., Serreau, P., Cressant, A., Chabout, J., Granon, S., Olivo-Marin, J.-C.: Computerized video analysis of social interactions in mice. Nat. Meth. **9**(4), 410–417 (2012)
16. Dollár, P., Welinder, P., Perona, P.: Cascaded pose regression. In: 2010 IEEE Conference on Computer Vision and Pattern Recognition (CVPR), pp. 1078–1085, June 2010
17. Burgos-Artizzu, X.P., Hall, D.C., Perona, P., Dollár, P.: Merging pose estimates across space and time. In: BMVC (2013)
18. Dollár, P., Tu, Z., Perona, P., Belongie, S.: Integral channel features. In: BMVC (2009)
19. Criminisi, A., Shotton, J., Konukoglu, E.: Decision forests: a unified framework for classification, regression, density estimation, manifold learning and semi-supervised learning. Found. Trends Comput. Graph. Vis. **7**(2–3), 81–227 (2012)

Spatiotemporal Features Learning with 3DPyraNet

Ihsan Ullah[1,2(✉)] and Alfredo Petrosino[1]

[1] CVPR Lab, University of Napoli Parthenope, Napoli, Italy
{ihsan.ullah,alfredo.petrosino}@uniparthenope.it
[2] Department of Computer Science, University of Milan, Milan, Italy

Abstract. A discriminative approach based on the 3DPyraNet model for spatiotemporal feature learning is proposed. In combination with a linear SVM classifier, our model outperform state-of-the-art methods on two datasets (KTH, Weizmann). Whereas, shows comparable result with current best methods on third dataset (YUPENN). The features are compact, achieving 94.08 %, 99.13 %, and 94.67 % accuracy on KTH, Weizmann, and YUPENN, respectively. The proposed model appears more suitable for spatiotemporal feature learning compared to traditional feature learning techniques; also, the number of parameters is far less than other 3DConvNets.

Keywords: Action recognition · Dynamic scene understanding · Pyramidal neural network · Deep learning

1 Introduction

In real-world, with the passage of time, people in a video and their surrounding change dramatically, resulting in varying pose, occlusion, illumination in each frame, or subject interactions with some object/subject in the surrounding. Local space-time features have been shown useful for recognition tasks such as object and scene recognition (SR) [1–8]. These aforementioned techniques have captured peculiar shape and motion in video and provide a representation of events that is relatively independent from their spatiotemporal shifts and scales. For instance, in case of action recognition (AR), 2D hand-crafted features concerning gradient information, optical flow, and brightness information are substituted in video from spatiotemporal extensions of image descriptors, such as 3D-SIFT [9], HOG3D [10], extended SURF [11], or Local Trinary Patterns [12]. These extracted features are anticipated to translate information which is useful for recognition of an action in a numerical form, namely a vector. Additionally, these vectors are trained to form a representation, such as a histogram of most frequent motions of a video, which captures actions that occur at a specific time in a video clip. Definitely, a general representation is learned using the derived representation of a set of labeled training videos. Subsequently, a classifier models a test sample to its closest action class. Therefore, despite the huge variety

© Springer International Publishing AG 2016
J. Blanc-Talon et al. (Eds.): ACIVS 2016, LNCS 10016, pp. 638–647, 2016.
DOI: 10.1007/978-3-319-48680-2_56

of descriptors, it is still intuitive to handle them in a special manner. Classifiers will result in achieving optimal results on specific datasets.

However, video frames contain complex, redundant, and highly variable information. Thus, it is necessary to discover useful features from raw data. Traditional hand-crafted features often require expensive human labor and expert knowledge. Normally they do not generalize well. This motivates the design of an efficient general 'feature learning' technique that can work on different application and datasets. Recently, deep models such as Convolutional-RBM [13], ST-DBN [14], 3DConvNet [15], 3DPyraNet [16], and C3D [8] have been explored to learn and extract spatiotemporal features. These approaches, automatically learn low-to-high level discriminative representations directly from raw videos. Further, feature extraction process is motivated by the fact that classifier require input that is mathematically and computationally convenient to process.

An important aspect of convolutional DL models [7,8,13,14,17,18] is the weight learning and sharing concept. Sharing reduces large number of parameters as opposed to conventional NN models. Learning parameters in the convolutional models mean learning a kernel shape which is not specific to any neuron as it is slided and shared over the whole image. This reduces the number of parameters, but increases the chance to put burden on those parameters while considering huge amounts of data from videos [16,19]. In addition, most of these models did not follow a biological pyramidal structure, i.e. in these models, while resolution is reduced, kernels and maps actually increase together with the number of layers which violates the biological pyramidal structure, which might be helpful in enhancing the model interpret-ability.

Recently, other models like [20,21] were studied with the common aim to model artificial neural networks for recognition capable to catch the typical biological structure of cortical neural networks. For instance, Phung et al. [21] proposed a pyramidal model *(PyraNet)* where each neuron has a unique kernel obtained from a weight matrix. This weight matrix has the same size as the image/feature map at lower layer. The model is quite similar to CNN, however, the difference is in the weight sharing concept and processing i.e. it performs a correlation operation *(Corr)* instead of a convolution to get an output neuron.

This idea was extended to the three dimensional domain in [16] i.e. *3DPyraNet*. It extracts features from both spatial and temporal domain while maintaining pyramid structure for refinement. Thereby it is capable to capture the motion information encoded in multiple adjacent frames. Analyzing traditional CV and deep models, we are motivated to propose a generalized model that consists of a new descriptor that replaces local hand-crafted descriptors and histogram generation steps by deep learned representation. Here, we use the *3DPyraNet* model to learn features from raw data and classify them with a linear SVM for AR and scene understanding *(SU)*.

The paper is further organized as follows. Section 2 will start with motivational background followed by description of our proposed models for feature extraction. In Sect. 3 we discuss results as well as additional benefits of the proposed model. In the end, Sect. 4 will conclude the paper.

2   Feature Extraction with 3DPyraNet

A short review of *3DPyraNet* will be given in the following section. Subsequently, we will explain the proposed models in coming Subsects. 2.2 and 2.3.

2.1   3DPyraNet

3DPyraNet [16] is inspired from *3DCNN* and *PyraNet*. The key factors that make it different from *3DCNN* is its pyramid structure and the adaptation of weighting scheme that results in correlation. These characteristics are adopted and extended from *PyraNet*. *3DPyraNet* model consist of 5 main layers i.e. (1) input layer, (2) followed by 3-D Correlation (*3D-WeightedSum* or *3DCORR*) layer to learn similar features among input frames/features maps, (3) a 3-D Pooling (*3DPOOL*) layer to reduce resolution for faster processing and to obtain a translation and scale invariant features, (4) another *3DCORR* layer, (5) and finally a fully connected (*FC*) layer for classification as shown in Fig. 1 (without

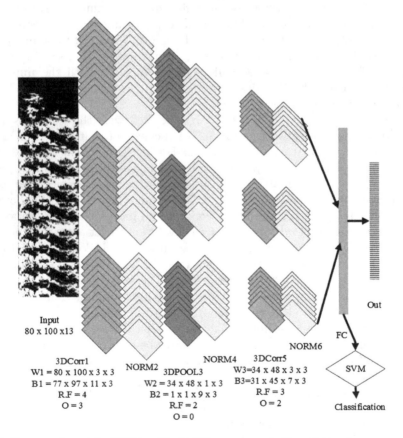

Fig. 1. Proposed model of 3DPyraNet-F. Blue represents Correlation layers, gray represents normalization, and brown represents pooling (Color figure online)

SVM step). Leaky rectified linear unit (*LReLu*) and Sigmoid (*Sig*) are used as activation functions in pyramidal and fully connected layers, respectively. Normalization (zero mean unit variance) is done after every layer to achieve faster convergence and better performance. No sophisticated pre-processing is done as compared to existing *DL* models [17]. However, the given input in case of *AR* was in silhouettes/binary form extracted using [22].

3DPyraNet uses a weight matrix of equal size to the input image/feature map. They have a fixed unique kernel $RF \times RF \times D$ for each output neuron. These kernels have low sharing i.e. in the worst case 1 otherwise depends on overlap (*O*) and receptive field (*RF*). Overlap '*O*' represents the number of columns or rows reused in a new adjacent *RF*. Whereas, *RF* can also be considered as the size of the kernel. *3DPyraNet* uses depth of size '$D = 3$' at each step to incorporate the spatial as well as temporal information from the given input frames. To extract more variant and discriminative features, multiple sets of 3-D weight matrices are used. Even in this case, the number of parameters are less than other deep models. This model generates sparse features as compared to convolutional kernel. The training process is performed using same back-propagation with stochastic mini-batch gradient descent approach [16].

A variety of deep architectures can be designed from *3DPyraNet* based on its application area and performance can be enhanced using different input image size, complexity of model, or combination of multiple models. However, we discuss and elaborate mainly two types of models to advere feature extraction, i.e. Late fusion (local) and early fusion (global) an inspiration from work done in [23].

2.2 3DPyraNet-F

Selection of optimal architecture for problem is challenging, since it depends on the specific application. A generalized model was shown in Fig. 1 due to limited space. Mainly, it consists of two *3DCORR* layers, a *3DPOOL*, a *FC* layer, and a linear-SVM classifier layer. Once the convergence is advered, learned features from the last *Norm4* layer are extracted and fused in a single column feature vector. This global/early fusion model is a balanced mix between the spatial and temporal information. These are incorporated in such a way that global information in both spatial and temporal dimensions are progressively accessed by *SVM*. Finally, the trained *SVM* model is used to classify the feature vectors extracted using *3DPyraNet*. One-vs-all criteria is used for classification.

The depth and width of a network and the resulting size of the feature vector depends on the input size, receptive field (*RF*) and overlap (*O*) parameters in each layer. (*RF*) size and (*O*) are the two main tune-able parameters for handling the performance. We used (*RF*) size of 4, 2, and 3 with 3, 0, 2 for (*O*) in layer 1, 2, and 3 of models for *AR*, respectively. Whereas, model for *SR* uses (*RF*) size of 4, 2, and 4 with (*O*) as 3, 0, 3 in layer 1, 2, and 3, respectively.

2.3 3DPyraNet-F_M

The difference between *3DPyraNet-F* and *3DPyraNet-F_M* is in the construction of feature vectors. After *3DPyraNet* converges, rather than just concatenating all the feature in one column vector, this model first converts feature maps of same set in one single column vector. Then, the resultant feature vectors are summed together and divided by the number of weight sets to derive their mean vector. This results in a smaller feature vector compared to previous model resulting in faster processing. These features behave as local due to local addition with other features maps. The rest of the model and network architecture is similar to *3DPyraNet-F*.

Third variation of *3DPyraNet-F* can be the size of the network. This difference exists due to different size input image of *AR* and *SR* datasets. Network structures for all models are given in Table 1.

Table 1. Network Structure used for Action (Weizmann(10) and KTH(6)) and Scene (YUPENN(14)) datasets. Feature map size at main Layers

Model	3DCORR1	3DPOOL3	3DCORR5	FC	Output
3DPyraNet-F	$61 \times 45 \times 11 \times 3$	$30 \times 22 \times 9 \times 3$	$27 \times 19 \times 7 \times 3$	10773	6/10
3DPyraNet-F_M	$61 \times 45 \times 11 \times 3$	$30 \times 22 \times 9 \times 3$	$27 \times 19 \times 7 \times 3$	3591	6/10
3DPyraNet-F	$77 \times 97 \times 11 \times 3$	$38 \times 48 \times 9 \times 3$	$35 \times 45 \times 7 \times 3$	33075	14

3   Experiments

3DPyraNet-F has been evaluated for recognition tasks. Firstly, we analyze action recognition on the *Weizmann* and *KTH* datasets [4,24]. We will show *3DPyraNet-F* and *3DPyraNet-F_M* enhancement over plain *3DPyraNet* for *AR* datasets. Further, we will compare our model with state-of-the-art hand-crafted feature descriptors as well as feature learners. In second experiment, we examined our models for *SR* on *YUPENN* dataset. In the end, beside its accuracy, another key advantage of our proposed model will be discussed i.e. it's fewer trainable parameters.

Training: Each model is trained on its respective dataset. Table 1 shows feature map size in the form of $w \times h \times m \times s$. Where 'w', 'h', 'm' and 's' represents width, height, number of maps, and weight sets, respectively. *KTH* and *Weizmann* have similar input size i.e. $64 \times 48 \times 13$. Whereas, *YUPENN* has $80 \times 100 \times 13$ with an overlap of 7 images for each clip. Training is done by SGD with mini batch size of 100 clips. We start with a small learning rate i.e. 0.000015 and than decrease it after every 20 epochs by multiplying it with 0.9. The training stops when the testing accuracy stops improving. The *RF* and *O* size are shown in Fig. 1 as well mentioned in Sect. 2.2. A linear-*SVM* is used to analyze discriminative power of the learned features for recognition of action or scene. The *SVM* is trained with Sequential Minimal Optimization (SMO) method of Matlab-2014b Statistical and Machine Learning toolbox [25].

3.1 Action Recognition

KTH and *Weizmann* datasets are relatively small in number, allowing for a more in-depth study. However, they are still challenging to train a deep model as we have to deal with a small training set. *KTH*, an *AR* dataset include 6 classes i.e. Walking, Running, Jogging, Hand clapping, Hand waving, and Boxing. It is a challenging dataset due to outdoor environment and camera movement. We used the same setting and protocol as used in [16]. 3DSOBS [22] is used to extract person from the clip. But due to camera movement very few consecutive clips can be collected, especially in the running case. Therefore, reasonable subsets of random clips of size $64 \times 48 \times 13$ are considered. Features from the *Norm4* layer are extracted and fed to the linear-*SVM*. It classifies each class similar to [4,8,28]. However, we did two types of extraction, i.e. local and global fusion of features as in [23].

In the first case *3DPyraNet-F_M*, vectors consist of 3591 features. Whereas, in the second case *3DPyraNet-F* feature vectors are longer (10733). We achieved mean accuracy of 93.42 % from the binary classifications of one vs all scenarios. Further, (*3DPyraNet-F_M*) enhances the overall performance by 0.67 %. Similarly to [4,17,28], despite fewer training examples, the global fusion (*3DPyraNet-F*) achieved optimal accuracy. In comparison to hand crafted features, our learned feature classified with *SVM* gets better results than *3DHOG*, *Cuboids*, and *Gabor3D + HOG3D*, whereas, almost equal performance are achieved when compared to combination of *HOG*, *HOF*, *MBH*, and *Trajectories* descriptors [3], highlighting more discriminative power of our learned features.

Weizmann is a 10 class *AR* dataset that includes walking, running, jumping, gallop sideways, bend, one-hand wave, two-hands wave, jump in place, jumping jack, and skip. We considered full *Weizmann* dataset and pre-processed it similarly to *KTH*. The same *3DPyraNet-F* and *3DPyraNet-F_M* models were applied. In this case, despite more classes, optimal results were achieved compared to state-of-the-art as shown in Table 2. *3DPyraNet-F* enhances previous results by 8.09 % whereas, *3DPyraNet-F_M* enhanced it further with additional 0.14 %. Only in the case of combination of $HOG + HOF + MBH + Trajectories$, *3DPyraNet-F_M* have a lower accuracy of 0.87 %.

3.2 Scene Understanding

YUPENN is a dynamic scene recognition *(SR)* benchmark. It consists of 420 videos of 14 scene categories i.e. beach, city street, elevator, forest fire, fountain, highway, lighting storm, ocean, railway, rushing river, sky-clouds, snowing, waterfall, and windmill farm. In *SR*, a model has to learn the whole mask rather than a specific portion of the image. As discussed in Sect. 2, *3DPyraNet-F* weight matrix is of equal size of the input image/feature map. Therefore, it could be

Table 2. Accuracies for Action (Weizmann and KTH) and Scene (YUPENN) datasets, Layers represents main layers

Model(classifier)	Weizmann	KTH	YUPENN	Layers
3D-ConvNet [15]	88.26	89.40	-	7
3DCNN [17]	-	90.2	-	6
3DHOG [10]	84.3	91.4	-	-
Cuboids [2]	-	90	-	-
Gabor3D + HOG3D (SVM) [26]	-	93.5	-	-
3DSIFT (SVM) [9]	82.6	-	-	-
HOG + HOF + MBH + Trajectories (SVM) [3]	-	94.2	-	-
C3D (SVM) [8]	-	-	98.1	15
ImageNet [8]	-	-	96.7	8
ST-DBN [27]	-	85.2	-	4
Schuldt (SVM) [4]	-	71.7	-	-
Dollar (SVM) [28]	-	81.2	-	-
3DHOG + Local weighted SVM [29]	100	92.4	-	-
3DPyraNet	90.9	72	-	4
3DPyraNet-F	98.99	93.42	**94.67**	4
3DPyraNet-F_M	**99.13**	**94.083**	-	4
Christoph's [30]	-	-	86.0	-
Theriault's (SVM) [31]	-	-	85.0	-

an ideal case for scene recognition in videos which can also be used as a hint in other recognition tasks.

Model used in this dataset has bigger input size compared to the previous one, i.e. $80 \times 100 \times 13$ hence, resulting in large feature vector of size 33075. We considered an overlap of 7, considering a small number of frames compared to previous models [5,8,32] - for instance, [8] uses $128 \times 171 \times 16$ frames in a clip from which $112 \times 112 \times 16$ random crops were extracted for data augmentation purpose.

Our model achieved best accuracy of 96.2134 % after 25 epochs. However, it achieves mean accuracy of 94.67 % for one-vs-rest classification. Although, it is better than [5,30,31] at huge margin, it does not achieve state-of-the-art performance by 3.43 % fewer accuracy. This could be caused by several reasons; possibly, one resides in the fact that *C3D* [8] is trained on Sports 1-Million videos dataset [23], whereas we trained on the same smaller dataset. In addition, they have high resolution and use augmentation. Although our model is less competitive compared to *C3D* and Imagenet, *3DPyraNet-F* still achieves comparable results, i.e. 94.67 %; a good starting point for future work to test *3DPyraNet-F* on very large scale datasets. Christoph's et al. [32] shows better accuracy than ours by 1.5 % i.e. 96.2 %. However, as opposed to our model where we classify each clip individually, their model uses several complex feature encoding such as FV, LLC, and dynamic pooling to achieve that result on majority voting for video classification.

3.3 Parameters Reduction

After strong success of ImageNet [8,33], models became deeper and deeper. Beside accuracy, their trainable parameters also increased. A separate consideration should be made about the reduction of parameters. The number of parameters is unarguably a substantial issue in application space and the memory cost increases due to the large size of trained models on the disk [8,33–35].

Network in Network (*NIN*) [35] highlighted the issue of reducing parameters, but they achieved it at greater computation cost. As most of the parameters are in fully connected (*FC*) layers, Szegedy et al. [36] uses sparsity reduction complex methodologies for refining those trained models. Han et al. [34] tries to learn connections in each layer instead of weights and then the network is trained again to reduce the number of parameters. *C3D* has about 17.5 M parameters, whereas our model have less than a million parameters (specifically 0.83 M parameters in case for *YUPENN* dataset). Disk occupancy is almost negligible compared to the model trained by C3D; this is of help in embedded systems and mobile devices where the memory usage is a problem.

4   Conclusion

We address the difficulty in learning spatiotemporal features from videos, proposing to adopt the *3DPyraNet* model for feature learning. We show that despite less deeper than state-of-the-art models, our fusion models are capable of learning powerful features by refining the sparse features provided by *3DPyraNet*, achieving competitive results with respect to current best methods on several video analysis benchmarks.

References

1. Laptev, I., Marszaek, M., Schmid, C., Rozenfeld, B.: Learning realistic human actions from movies. In: 26th IEEE Conference on Computer Vision and Pattern Recognition, CVPR (2008)
2. Wang, H., Ullah, M.M., Klaser, A., Laptev, I., Schmid, C.: Evaluation of local spatiotemporal features for action recognition. In: BMVC 2009 - British Machine Vision Conference, pp. 124.1–124.11 (2009)
3. Wang, H., Kläser, A., Schmid, C., Cheng-Lin, L.: Action recognition by dense trajectories. In: CVPR 2011 - IEEE Conference on Computer Vision & Pattern Recognition, Colorado Springs, United States, pp. 3169–3176. IEEE, June 2011
4. Schüldt, C., Laptev, I., Caputo, B.: Recognizing human actions: a local SVM approach. In: Proceedings - International Conference on Pattern Recognition, vol. 3, pp. 32–36 (2004)

5. Derpanis, K.G., Lecce, M., Daniilidis, K., Wildes, R.P.: Dynamic scene understanding: the role of orientation features in space and time in scene classification. In: 2012 IEEE Conference on Computer Vision and Pattern Recognition, pp. 1306–1313 (2012)
6. Soomro, K., Zamir, A.R., Shah, M.: UCF101: a dataset of 101 human actions classes from videos in the wild. CoRR abs/1212.0402 (2012)
7. Le, Q.V., Zou, W.Y., Yeung, S.Y., Ng, A.Y.: Learning hierarchical invariant spatiotemporal features for action recognition with independent subspace analysis. In: Proceedings of the IEEE Computer Society Conference on Computer Vision and Pattern Recognition, pp. 3361–3368 (2011)
8. Tran, D., Bourdev, L., Fergus, R., Torresani, L., Paluri, M.: Learning spatiotemporal features with 3D convolutional networks. In: ICCV, pp. 1725–1732. IEEE, June 2015
9. Scovanner, P., Ali, S., Shah, M.: A 3-dimensional sift descriptor and its application to action recognition. In: Proceedings of the ACM International Conference on Multimedia (MM 2007), pp. 357–360 (2007)
10. Klaser, A., Marszalek, M., Schmid, C.: A spatiotemporal descriptor based on 3D-gradients. In: Proceedings of the British Machine Conference, pp. 99.1–99.10 (2008)
11. Willems, G., Tuytelaars, T., Gool, L.: An efficient dense and scale-invariant spatiotemporal interest point detector. In: Forsyth, D., Torr, P., Zisserman, A. (eds.) ECCV 2008. LNCS, vol. 5303, pp. 650–663. Springer, Heidelberg (2008). doi:10.1007/978-3-540-88688-4_48
12. Yeffet, L., Wolf, L.: Local trinary patterns for human action recognition. In: IEEE 12th International Conference on Computer Vision, pp. 492–497, September 2009
13. Taylor, G.W., Fergus, R., LeCun, Y., Bregler, C.: Convolutional learning of spatiotemporal features. In: Daniilidis, K., Maragos, P., Paragios, N. (eds.) ECCV 2010. LNCS, vol. 6316, pp. 140–153. Springer, Heidelberg (2010). doi:10.1007/978-3-642-15567-3_11
14. Freitas, N.D.: Deep learning of invariant spatiotemporal features from video. In: Workshop on Deep Learning and Unsupervised Feature Learning in NIPS, pp. 1–9 (2010)
15. Baccouche, M., Mamalet, F., Wolf, C., Garcia, C., Baskurt, A.: Sequential deep learning for human action recognition. In: Salah, A.A., Lepri, B. (eds.) HBU 2011. LNCS, vol. 7065, pp. 29–39. Springer, Heidelberg (2011). doi:10.1007/978-3-642-25446-8_4
16. Ullah, I., Petrosino, A.: A strict pyramidal deep neural network for action recognition. In: Murino, V., Puppo, E. (eds.) ICIAP 2015. LNCS, vol. 9279, pp. 236–245. Springer, Heidelberg (2015)
17. Ji, S., Yang, M., Yu, K.: 3D convolutional neural networks for human action recognition. IEEE Trans. Pattern Anal. Mach. Intell. 35(1), 221–231 (2013)
18. Simonyan, K., Zisserman, A.: Two-Stream Convolutional Networks for Action Recognition in Videos. arXiv preprint arXiv:1406.2199, pp. 1–11, June 2014
19. Uetz, R., Behnke, S.: Locally-connected hierarchical neural networks for gpu-accelerated object recognition. In: NIPS: Workshop on Large-Scale Machine Learning: Parallelism and Massive Datasets, Whistler, Canada, pp. 10–13, December 2009
20. Cantoni, V., Petrosino, A.: Neural recognition in a pyramidal structure. IEEE Trans. Neural Netw. 13(2), 472–480 (2002)
21. Phung, S.L., Bouzerdoum, A.: A pyramidal neural network for visual pattern recognition. IEEE Trans. Neural Netw. Publ. IEEE Neural Netw. Counc. 18(2), 329–343 (2007)

22. Maddalena, L., Petrosino, A.: The 3dsobs+ algorithm for moving object detection. Comput. Vis. Image Underst. **122**, 65–73 (2014)
23. Karpathy, A., Leung, T.: Large-scale video classification with convolutional neural networks. In: Proceedings of 2014 IEEE Conference on Computer Vision and Pattern Recognition, pp. 1725–1732 (2014)
24. Blank, M., Gorelick, L., Shechtman, E., Irani, M., Basri, R.: Actions as space time shapes. In: Tenth IEEE International Conference on Computer Vision (ICCV 2005), vol. 1, pp. 1395–1402 (2005). Vol. 2
25. MATLAB: Matlab version 8.4.0.150421 (R2014b). The MathWorks Inc., Natick, Massachusetts (2014)
26. Maninis, K., Koutras, P., Maragos, P.: Advances on action recognition in videos using an interest point detector based on multiband spatiotemporal energies. In: 2014 IEEE International Conference on Image Processing, ICIP 2014, Paris, France, October 27–30, 2014, pp. 1490–1494 (2014)
27. Chen, B., Ting, J.A., Marlin, B., de Freitas, N.: Deep learning of invariant spatiotemporal features from video. In: NIPS 2010 Deep Learning and Unsupervised Feature Learning Workshop (2010)
28. Dollár, P., Rabaud, V., Cottrell, G., Belongie, S.: Behavior recognition via sparse spatiotemporal features. In: Proceedings - 2nd Joint IEEE International Workshop on Visual Surveillance and Performance Evaluation of Tracking and Surveillance, VS-PETS 2005, pp. 65–72 (2005)
29. Weinland, D., Özuysal, M., Fua, P.: Making action recognition robust to occlusions and viewpoint changes. In: Daniilidis, K., Maragos, P., Paragios, N. (eds.) ECCV 2010. LNCS, vol. 6313, pp. 635–648. Springer, Heidelberg (2010). doi:10.1007/978-3-642-15558-1_46
30. Feichtenhofer, C., Pinz, A., Wildes, R.P.: Spacetime forests with complementary features for dynamic scene recognition. In: BMVC (2013)
31. Theriault, C., Thome, N., Cord, M.: Dynamic scene classification: Learning motion descriptors with slow features analysis. In: 2013 IEEE Conference on Computer Vision and Pattern Recognition (CVPR), pp. 2603–2610, June 2013
32. Feichtenhofer, C., Pinz, A., Wildes, R.: Bags of spacetime energies for dynamic scene recognition. In: Proceedings of the IEEE Conference on Computer Vision and Pattern Recognition, pp. 2681–2688 (2014)
33. Krizhevsky, A., Sutskever, I., Hinton, G.E.: Imagenet classification with deep convolutional neural networks. In: Advances in Neural Information Processing Systems, pp. 1097–1105 (2012)
34. Han, S., Pool, J., Tran, J., Dally, W.J.: Learning both weights and connections for efficient neural networks. CoRR abs/1506.02626 (2015)
35. Lin, M., Chen, Q., Yan, S.: Network in network. CoRR abs/1312.4400 (2013)
36. Szegedy, C., Liu, W., Jia, Y., Sermanet, P., Reed, S., Anguelov, D., Erhan, D., Vanhoucke, V., Rabinovich, A.: Going deeper with convolutions. In: CVPR, USA, June 7–12, pp. 1–9 (2015)

Automatic Segmentation of TV News into Stories Using Visual and Temporal Information

Bogdan Mocanu[1,2], Ruxandra Tapu[1,2(✉)], and Titus Zaharia[1]

[1] ARTEMIS, Institut Mines-Telecom/TelecomSudParis,
CNRS MAP5, 8145 Paris, France
{bogdan.mocanu,ruxandra.tapu,titus.zaharia}@telecom-sudparis.eu
[2] Telecommunication, Faculty of ETTI, University Politehnica of Bucharest,
Bucharest, Romania

Abstract. In this paper we propose a new method for automatic storyboard segmentation of TV news using image retrieval techniques and content manipulation. Our framework performs: shot boundary detection, global key-frame representation, image re-ranking based on neighborhood relations and temporal variance of image locations in order to construct a unimodal cluster for anchor person detection and differentiation. Finally, anchor shots are used to form video scenes. The entire technique is unsupervised being able to learn semantic models and extract natural patterns from the current video data. The experimental evaluation performed on a dataset of 50 videos, totalizing more than 30 h, demonstrates the pertinence of the proposed method, with gains in terms of recall and precision rates with more than 5–7% when compared with state of the art techniques.

Keywords: News video story segmentation · Relevant interest points · Anchor person extraction · Temporal and visual constrained clustering

1 Introduction

Nowadays, with the development of the video on demand capabilities, large collection of video archives dating back decades can be accessed over the Internet by regular users. Furthermore, most of the TV chains broadcast and publish the video content on-line. In this context, the efficient retrieval of images clips, and notably in the case of television news, is not always feasible, because of the poor or incomplete video indexation available.

In the last years, the semantic segmentation of news videos has captured the attention of the scientific community. The main focus is to efficiently structure the video information so that the system can be able to retrieve only a particular segment or a specific topic of interest rather than the complete broadcasted video stream. The challenge is to temporally segment the multimedia information into meaningful and manageable high-level semantic parts (*i.e.* coherent news stories)

© Springer International Publishing AG 2016
J. Blanc-Talon et al. (Eds.): ACIVS 2016, LNCS 10016, pp. 648–660, 2016.
DOI: 10.1007/978-3-319-48680-2_57

that can be automatically indexed and then retrieved to users. Such video units need to be defined at a higher level of abstraction, superior to the one of video shots, satisfying the user needs at an increased level of granularity. In the case of movies a video scene needs to respect three rules of continuity: in space, time and in action. However, in the case of TV journals the definition of a scene is highly difficult, most of the underlying hypotheses that are made within the context of scene identification being violated. In this context, we argue that the shots included in a story segment need to satisfy the following proprieties: temporal continuity and semantic coherence. Based on the above considerations, this paper tackles the issue of TV news segmentation into scenes from the perspective of visual similarities and semantic content. More specifically, we aim at identifying the boundaries between different news stories in order to facilitate the navigation.

The rest of the paper is organized as follows. Section 2 reviews the state of the art in the field. In Sect. 3 we introduce and describe in detail the proposed video temporal segmentation method. Section 4 presents the experimental results obtained on a set of videos from the French national television broadcast, NBC and CNN TV stations. Finally, Sect. 5 concludes the paper and opens some perspectives of future work.

2   Related Work

In the last couple of years, the increase volume of video news has lead to the development of various systems dedicated to TV journal management and understanding. The structure of news magazines was studied in [1] where authors conclude that news typically begin with a highlight, the main body is organized in subjects and each story begins with an anchorperson corresponding to the presenter. Thus, two categories of shots are identified [2]: (1) anchorperson shots and (2) news reports. A novel subject usually starts with an anchor shot and therefore, for content-based news understanding, it is important to identify the location of the presenters within the video stream. Anchor shots can be characterized as containing a certain percentage of similar visual features, static/dynamic camera movement and one or two news presenters.

Existing content-based approaches for structuring the video news [3] aim of automatically determining the temporal interval of each story, without any human intervention. One of the first methods in the field has been proposed in [4]. Here, a trained classifier is used to categorize shots into a set of 9 predefined classes (intro, anchor, people, interview, sports, text scenes, special and logos). The story boundaries are finally detected using a Hidden Markov Model (HMM). Although the proposed method seems to return good results, the results are highly dependent on the quality of the annotated data. In order to avoid training a Support Vector Machine (SVM), in [5] the stories are extracted with the help of an anchorperson shots detection technique. In addition, the text associated to each subtitle is assigned to a story by using the Latent Dirichlet Allocation (LDA) method.

A different anchor person identification method is proposed in [6]. The system uses low level image descriptors and text transcripts within a split and merge algorithm in order to identify different subject boundaries. In [7], different sources of information are considered (*i.e.* features extracted from audio tracks with an automatic speech recognition system, concepts selected from large scale ontology of images) and combined within a discriminative fusion scheme.

In [8], the anchor person identification system is based on a spatio-temporal analysis dedicated to news magazine with dynamic studio background motion or multiple presenters. The method starts by extracting two diagonal spatio-temporal slices that are further divided into three parts. Then, a sequential clustering method is applied to determine a set of candidate anchor shots. The actual presenter shots are established by applying a structural tensor.

The authors in [9] introduce a cost-effective anchor shot detection method that performs search space reduction. The method combines a skin color detector, a face detector and support vector data descriptions in order to localize the presenter within the video stream. More recently, in [10] an automatic method for news video segmentation into stories is proposed based on visual features as: face and anchor person detection, junk frames removal, motion activity and TV logo extraction. Both approaches in [9,10] outperform the state-of the art methods, but still require the availability of a large amount of manually annotated data.

Although there are many works addressing the problem of effectively and efficiently extraction of relevant subjects from news video, the robust identification of subject boundaries remains very challenging because of the camera or object movement, cropping, illumination changes, clutter or important background variation. In addition, nowadays most of the news videos contain interviews where different invited persons appear in the presence of the news presenter.

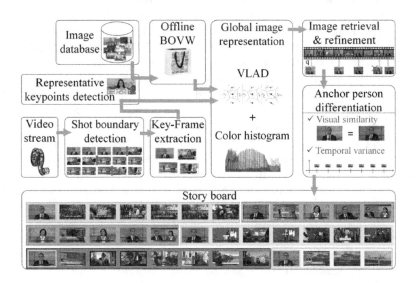

Fig. 1. The proposed news video segmentation framework

In order to overcome such limitations, in this paper we propose a novel segmentation method of TV news videos, which is fully unsupervised and able to automatically learn semantic models from video data. The main contributions presented in this paper concern:

1. An anchor person identification technique based on relevant interest point extraction, global image representation using a fusion of VLAD (Vector of Locally Aggregated Descriptors) and color histograms, confident image retrieval using neighborhood relations and Jaccard similarity coefficient.
2. A dedicated method that differentiates between news presenters and invited guests, by analyzing the temporal location of candidate anchor images within the video streams.

Figure 1 presents the pipeline of the proposed news video segmentation method. The following section describes in detail the proposed approach.

3   Proposed Approach

In a first stage we perform a temporal structuring of the video stream into shots. For each shot, we then identify a set of representative key-frames. Finally, we select a set of candidate anchor key-frames, corresponding to potential anchor persons.

3.1   Temporal Video Segmentation

In order to perform temporal video segmentation into shots, we considered our method firstly introduced in [11], which includes both an enhanced shot boundary detection algorithm and a key-frame extraction technique, briefly recalled here. Each frame of the video stream is represented as a vertex in a graph spanning structure, connected with others by edges expressing the visual similarity between two nodes. The analysis is performed by using a temporal sliding window that selects a fixed number of frames for analyses. Then, for each position of the sliding window a graph partition is computed. In order to detect a transition we perform the analysis within the scale space of derivatives of the local minimum vector. The computational complexity is reduced by applying the two-pass approach. Then, for each detected shot a set of representative key-frames are extracted.

Two additional features to the baseline method introduced in [11] are here introduced. The first one concerns the quality of the selected key-frames. In order to avoid blurry images that can occur in current videos, we perform an edge sharpness analysis. Thus, the image edges are detected with a Canny edge detector [12]. A vote is associated to each contour point, depending on its gradient magnitude, in order to construct a global sharpness measure for each considered frame. Between the candidate frames, solely the one with the maximum global sharpness coefficient is finally retained. The second feature corresponds to the detection of key-frames including faces, that are candidates for anchor images. To this purpose, we apply the face detection method introduced in [13] that shows high detection performances. In this way, we obtain a set of candidate key-frames (S_{key-fr}), corresponding to possible anchor persons. This set of images is further analyzed, as described in the following section.

3.2 Anchor Shot Identification System

Representative Key-Point Selection. For each key-frame, we first extract interest points using the pyramidal FAST algorithm [14] that are further described using SIFT descriptor [15]. However, in the case of anchor shot identification we have observed that relevant objects (*i.e.* the news presenter) returns a significantly lower number of interest points than the one corresponding to textured objects appearing during the TV news (*e.g.* background information, trees, grass, buildings). For this reason, in order to jointly reduce the computational time and to ensure a sufficient number of interest points we have privileged a simple, semi-dense sampling approach. A regular rectangular grid is overlapped on each key-frame. The sets of interest points included in each grid cell is then determined. Then, for each cell we retain only the most relevant point, *i.e.* the one with the highest value of the Harris-Laplacian operator [16]. The size of the grid cell is defined as: $P = (H * W)/T$, where W and H are the width and height of the image, while T is the maximum total number of interest points we retain for an image. In our work, we have restricted T to 1000 interest points.

Figure 2 illustrates three different strategies of selecting relevant points from a key-frame. Figure 2a shows the key-points extracted using the classical FAST algorithm. The key-points obtained using FAST and refined using the Harris-Laplacian operator (*i.e.* the points are ranked based on the magnitude of their interest strength and the first T are kept) as proposed in [17] are presented in Fig. 2b. The results obtained with our method are illustrated in Fig. 2c. Let us underline that the examples illustrated in Fig. 2b and c contain the same number of interest points.

We can observe that the proposed method yields more evenly distributed key-points and avoids over-accumulations of points in certain textured areas.

a.   b.   c.

Fig. 2. Three different strategies for interest point extraction: (a). FAST extractor; (b). FAST extractor with Harris-Laplacian filtering; (c). our method based on regular grid filtering.

In order to obtain a robust representation of the key-frame, each SIFT descriptor is transformed into a normalized RootSIFT [18] and projected on 128 principal directions using PCA basis learned off-line [19].

Global Key-Frame Description. In order to characterize the informational content of a key-frame I, we develop a global image representation using the PCA-VLAD (Vector of Locally Aggregated Descriptors) representation [20], which encodes descriptors using the locality of feature space. The size of the vocabulary used for VLAD is set to 256 visual words.

The VLAD image representation proves to be invariant to rotation and illumination changes. However, in the case of anchor shot identification the color information is a useful parameter that needs to be taken into account. In order to capture the color information present in every key-frame we retain also for each image a color histogram, computed in the HSV color space. Several histogram sizes have been evaluated, with equivalent performances between 128 and 256 bins (corresponding to a uniform quantization of the HSV color space).

Representative Anchor Image Retrieval. Based on the observation that the news video content is highly structured in a regular and repetitive manner, we focused on identifying recursive patterns that can correspond with the anchor person. In [1], the authors conclude that key-frames containing news readers have an occurrence rate superior to any other image appearing during the video. However, for TV news with invited guests where the camera switches between them and the visual content has low variation (*i.e.* constant background), the previous assumption may not hold. In order to deal with all type of video news and extract, with high confidence, the most relevant key-frame showing the presenter, we propose the following strategy that transforms the anchor image identification problem into an image retrieval task.

Each image from the key-frame set (S_{key-fr}) is considered as query (q) to S_{key-fr}. The retrieved results are presented as a sorted list of candidate images with respect to a similarity measure that takes into account the two global image descriptors considered (*i.e.* VLAD and HSV color histogram).

$$Score(q, x) = \alpha \cdot Score_{VLAD}(q, x) + (1 - \alpha) \cdot Score_{Hist}(q, x); \qquad (1)$$

where $q \neq x$, x is an image from the static summary associated to the video stream $(x \in S_{key-fr})$, α is a weighting parameter that controls the influence of each descriptor, while $Score_{VLAD}$ and $Score_{Hist}$ are the cosine distances between VLAD and the color HSV histogram image representation, respectively. In our experiments, we have considered relatively high values of the α parameter (*i.e.*, within the range 0.8–0.9). Such a strategy makes it possible to privilege the similarity score provided by the VLAD representation, which is highly discriminative, while taking into account a rather minimal amount of color information, yielded from the global HSV histograms.

After analyzing the top-k ranked candidate images we observed that the similarity curve returns good results at the beginning, but after a period it starts flattening. This behavior signifies that relevant, but also false positive images can have equivalent scores with the query image. To refine the results and determine the outliers (that can correspond to spurious faces) we propose first to remove from the retrieved list the key-frames not satisfying the following reciprocal neighborhood relation:

$$R_k(q, d) = q \in N_k(x) \cap x \in N_k(q);$$

(2)

where $N_k(x)$ and $N_k(q)$ denotes the sets of top-k retrieved key-frames for queries x and q, respectively.

Then, a query image q is considered to be similar with a key-frame if the associated Jaccard similarity coefficient $J(d, x)$ is superior to a pre-establish threshold:

$$J(q, x) = \frac{\mid N_k(q) \cap N_k(x) \mid}{\mid N_k(q) \cup N_k(x) \mid} \geq Th_1;$$

(3)

where $\mid \cdots \mid$ denotes the cardinality of the corresponding sets. The values of $J(q, x)$ range from 0 to 1, where 0 corresponds to no overlap and 1 signify that x and q share exactly the same list of neighbors. In our experiments, we have considered a value of $Th_1 = 0.5$ which means x and q are considered as belonging to the same class if they share at least half of their corresponding neighbors.

Each query image and its associated top-k ranked results forms a cluster for which we compute an intra-cluster similarity score as:

$$SimScore_{q-class} = \sum_{d=0}^{N_k} Score(q, d); d \in S_{key-fr}.$$

(4)

The value of $SimScore_{q-class}$ can be interpreted as a measure that determines the degree of resemblance between different members of the considered cluster. The class with the maximum value of $SimScore_{q-class}$ is considered as the one containing the reference anchor shots.

The proposed strategy is effective in detecting the presence of anchor persons, but it is insufficient to help us differentiate between actual news presenters and invited guests. This is illustrated in Fig. 3. Here, the background variation of frames corresponding to news presenters is relatively high (images marked with green), while the key-frames showing the invited guest are very similar (images marked with magenta), thus boosting up the $SimScore_{q-class}$ of the corresponding class.

Anchor Person Differentiation. In order to distinguish between multiple anchor persons and differentiate various occurrence patterns we analyze the time component of each key-frame (temporal location within the video stream).

We propose to characterize a cluster of images not only based on the visual similarity, but also by the temporal position of the key-frames included in the class. For each cluster, we compute the temporal variance of all key-frames positions:

$$VarScore_{q-class} = \frac{1}{N_k} \sum_{i=1}^{N_k} (t_i - \mu_{q-class})^2;$$

(5)

Fig. 3. Different classes of anchor persons: news presents (green box); invited guest (magenta box). (Color figure online)

where N_k is the list of images belonging to the current class, t_i is the key-frame timestamp and $\mu_{q-class}$ is the average temporal position of all images within the class q. The $VarScore_{q-class}$ value can help to automatically understand the role of each character within the video stream. Thus, the temporal variance corresponding to the news presenter tends to take more important values, since the presenter occurrences are spread out over the entire video. On the contrary, the occurrences of invited guests are much more localized in time and the corresponding variance is significantly lower. Finally, the score of each image class is given by:

$$Score_{q-class} = SimScore_{q-class} \cdot VarScore_{q-class}; \tag{6}$$

where $SimScore_{q-class}$ and $VarScore_{q-class}$ are normalized ($SimScore_{q-class}$ to the maximum visual similarity score retrieved from all the considered classes, while $VarScore_{q-class}$ to the highest variance of all clusters). The class with the highest value for $Score_{q-class}$ will contain the relevant anchor person. We need to highlight that, after this step, the anchor person class will not incorporate an exhaustive set of key-frames where the presenter appears, but instead just a model which corresponds to a sub-set of visual appearances of the presenter, characterized by the most represented visual and temporal characteristics.

For segmenting the news video into stories we compare each key-frame from the static summary to the set of all images included in the reference anchor shots class. If the similarity measure (*cf.* eq. 1) is above a threshold (Th_2) then the present key-frame is considered as the first shot of a news story. The value of Th_2 is adaptively establish as half of the average similarity scores of all images included in anchor shot class.

However, the semantic content of video news is extremely diverse. Solely the correct identification of the anchor person is insufficient for obtaining a correct and comprehensive segmentation into stories of all type of video streams. Most TV news contain conversational scenes that are characterized as a collection of shots that exhibit a high similarity of the visual content, where the camera switches back and forth between different personages. For the conversation scenes the occurrence rate of the news presenter shots is significantly higher than the actual change within the addressed subject. Because the conversation scenes are characterized by continuity in time and space we propose using our scene grouping method, based on temporally constrained clustering, firstly introduced in [11]. The method consists of iteratively merging shots falling into a temporal analysis window and satisfying similarity clustering criteria. The influence of outlier shots which might correspond to some punctual digressions from the main action within the considered scene is reduced based on a shot neutralization process.

4   Experimental Evaluation

To evaluate the accuracy of the proposed framework we have performed an extensive testing on a database of 50 videos, with a total of more than 30 h of broadcast. The dataset is composed of two types of video clips: the first one selected from the broadcasted news of the French national television (30 videos with the average duration of 35 min denoted: JT13 France2, JT20 France2, Grand Soir, JT12, JT19 edition national, JT19 edition regional from France3), and corresponding to various programs of France Television (FTV) broadcast programs. The second has been acquired from YouTube and includes 20 video from NBC and CNN TV stations. The FTV videos are at a resolution of 1280×720 pixels, while the YouTube videos present a lower, 704×396 pixels resolution.

The shot boundary detection method [11] produces an average number of 375 shots per video; with the associated key-frames. Here, we selected a unique key-frame. After the face detection method [13], an average of 150 images per video was identified as possible candidates as anchor persons. In order to determine the performances of the anchor person detection system we used as evaluation metrics the traditional precision, recall and F-score defined as:

$$Recall = \frac{N_{CDA}}{N_{GT}}; Precision = \frac{N_{CDA}}{N_{ES}}; F-score = \frac{2 \cdot Recall \cdot Precision}{Recall + Precision}; \quad (7)$$

where N_{CDA} represent the number of correctly detected anchors shots, N_{GT} number of anchor shots in the ground truth and N_{ES} is the number of shots extracted as anchor elements.

Figure 4 presents the average results obtained for the anchor person identification. The average precision combining all the broadcasted channels exceeds 92 % with about 95 % of recall.

As it can be observed the video selected from YouTube return the lowest results in term of $F - score$. This behavior can be explained by the reduced quality of the video stream and the continuous presence of a scroll bar.

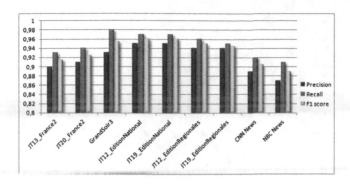

Fig. 4. Precision, Recall and F-scores obtained of the anchor person identification method

Table 1. Comparative evaluation of the proposed method

Analyzed method	$Precision$ [%]	$Recall$ [%]	$F-score$ [%]
Chen *et al.* [21]	79	84	81
Broilo *et al.* [22]	81	88	84
Ji *et al.* [2]	85	90	87
Proposed method	**92**	**95**	**93**

In order to provide a comprehensive evaluation of our framework we have compared our results with different state of the art techniques: Chen *et al.* [21], Broilo *et al.* [22] and Ji *et al.* [2]. In Table 1 we present the synthesized results of all methods.

The experimental evaluation clearly demonstrates the superiority of our proposed framework, with gains in terms of recall and precision rates with more than 5 % and 7 %, respectively. The results can be explained by the fact that our method is designed to be robust to important geometric and photometric distortion. Moreover, the use of VLAD image representation combined with color histograms allows the representation of key-frames in a global manner tolerating large changes in the appearance. Because, our method is entirely unsupervised, the system is not depended on a training phase and can naturally extract patterns from the considered video data. The increase in the precision rate can be explained by the use of the temporal location variance in extracting the most relevant cluster, which allows us to differentiate between anchor persons and invited guests. Finally, we evaluated the quality of the story segmentation method on the considered TV news videos dataset. The results are presented in Fig. 5. As it can observed, we obtain an average $F-score$ for the story segmentation of 88 %. A story is considered as correctly identified if the scene automatically obtained covers more than 80 % of the ground truth scene. The results can be explained by use of the temporal scene cluttering methods and by ability of our system to differentiate between news presents and invited guest.

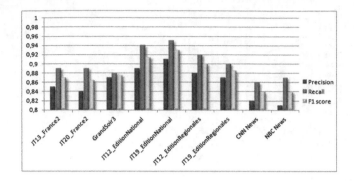

Fig. 5. Precision, Recall and F-scores obtained for the story segmentation

5   Conclusion and Perspectives

In this paper we have introduced a complete framework from automatic story-board segmentation of TV news. The method is based on a novel anchor person identification system that uses relevant interest point extraction, global image representation and image retrieval based on neighborhood relations. Then, the system is able to differentiate between news readers and invited guests, by taking advantage of visual similarity between key-frames and the temporal variance of candidates anchor images.

The experimental evaluation clearly demonstrates the superiority of our proposed framework, with gains in terms of recall and precision rates with more than 5 % and 7 %, respectively. The entire system proves to be robust to important geometric and photometric distortion allowing large variation on the object appearance. In our future work we will consider including within the framework more high-level functionalities as: identification and clustering of news stories addressing the same subject, face and location recognition capabilities. In addition, the textual data available in subtitles can be considered within a multi-modal semantic, approach.

Acknowledgments. This work has been partially accomplished within the framework of the FUI 19 Media4D project, supported by BPI (Banque Publique d'investissement) France and DGE (Direction Generale des Entreprises).

This work was supported by a grant of the Romanian National Authority for Scientific Research and Innovation, CNCS - UEFISCDI, project number: PN-II-RU-TE-2014-4-0202.

References

1. Chaisorn, L., Chua, T.S., Lee, C.H.: A multi-modal approach to story segmentation for news video. World Wide Web **6**(2), 187–208 (2003)
2. Ji, P., Cao, L.J., Zhang, X.G.: News videos anchor person detection by shot clustering. Neurocomputing **123**, 86–99 (2014)

3. Dumont, E., Quenot, G.: A local temporal context-based approach for TV news story segmentation. In: IEEE ICME, pp. 973–978 (2012)
4. Chaisorn, L., Chua, T.S.: Story boundary detection in news video using global rule induction technique. In: IEEE ICME, pp. 2101–2104 (2006)
5. Misra, H., Hopfgartner, F., Goyal, A., Punitha, P., Jose, J.M.: TV news story segmentation based on semantic coherence and content similarity. In: Boll, S., Tian, Q., Zhang, L., Zhang, Z., Chen, Y.-P.P. (eds.) MMM 2010. LNCS, vol. 5916, pp. 347–357. Springer, Heidelberg (2010)
6. Goyal, A., Punitha, P., Hopfgartner, F., Jose, J.M.: Split and merge based story segmentation in news videos. In: Boughanem, M., Berrut, C., Mothe, J., Soule-Dupuy, C. (eds.) ECIR 2009. LNCS, vol. 5478, pp. 766–770. Springer, Heidelberg (2009)
7. Ma, C., Byun, B., Kim, I., Lee, C.H.: A detection-based approach to broadcast news video story segmentation. In: IEEE ICASSP, pp. 1957–1960 (2009)
8. Zheng, F., Li, S., Wu, H., Feng, J.: Anchor shot detection with diverse style backgrounds based on spatial-temporal slice analysis. In: Boll, S., Tian, Q., Zhang, L., Zhang, Z., Chen, Y.-P.P. (eds.) MMM 2010. LNCS, vol. 5916, pp. 676–682. Springer, Heidelberg (2010). doi:10.1007/978-3-642-11301-7_68
9. Lee, H., Yu, J., Im, Y., Gil, J.M., Park, D.: A unified scheme of shot boundary detection and anchor shot detection in news video story parsing. Multimedia Tools Appl. 51(3), 1127–1145 (2011)
10. Dumont, E., Quénot, G.: Automatic story segmentation for TV news video using multiple modalities. Int. J. Digit. Multimedia Broadcast. 2012, 11 (2012). doi:10.1155/2012/732514
11. Tapu, R., Zaharia, T.: High level video temporal segmentation. In: Bebis, G., et al. (eds.) ISVC 2011. LNCS, vol. 6938, pp. 224–235. Springer, Heidelberg (2011). doi:10.1007/978-3-642-24028-7_21
12. Canny, J.: A computational approach to edge detection. IEEE Trans. Pattern Anal. Mach. Intell. PAMI–8(6), 679–698 (1986)
13. Zhu, X., Ramanan, D.: Face detection, pose estimation, and landmark localization in the wild. In: CVPR, pp. 2879–2886 (2012)
14. Tuzel, O., Porikli, F., Meer, P.: Region covariance: a fast descriptor for detection and classification. In: Leonardis, A., Bischof, H., Pinz, A. (eds.) ECCV 2006. LNCS, vol. 3952, pp. 589–600. Springer, Heidelberg (2006)
15. Lowe, D.: Distinctive image features from scale-invariant keypoints. IJCV 60(2), 91–110 (2004)
16. Harris, C., Stephens, M.: A combined corner and edge detector. In: Alvey Vision Conference, pp. 147–151 (1988)
17. Mikolajczyk, K., Schmid, C.: Scale and affine invariant interest point detectors. IJCV 60(1), 63–86 (2004)
18. Arandjelovic, R., Zisserman, A.: Three things everyone should know to improve object retrieval. In: CVPR (2012)
19. Zou, H., Hastie, T., Tibshirani, R.: Sparse principal component analysis. J. Comput. Graph. Stat. 15(2), 265–286 (2006)
20. Delhumeau, J., Gosselin, P.H., Jegou, H., Perez, P.: Revisiting the VLAD image representation. In: ACM Multimedia, pp. 653–656 (2013)

21. Chen, D.M., Vajda, P., Tsai, S., Daneshi, M., Yu, M., Chen, H., Araujo, A., Girod, B.: Analysis of visual similarity in news videos with robust and memory-efficient image retrieval. In: IEEE ICME Workshops, pp. 1–6 (2013)
22. Broilo, M., Basso, A., De Natale, F.G.B.: Unsupervised anchor persons differentiation in news video. In: 9th International Workshop on Content-Based Multimedia Indexing, pp. 115–120 (2011)

Wavelet Neural Network Initialization Using LTS for DNA Sequence Classification

Abdesselem Dakhli[1(✉)], Wajdi Bellil[2], and Chokri Ben Amar[2]

[1] Department of Computer Science, REGIM,
University of Gabes, 6002 Gabes, Tunisia
abdesselemdakhli@gmail.com
[2] Department of Computer Science, REGIM,
University of Sfax, 3018 Sfax, Tunisia
{wajdi.bellil, chokri.benamar}@ieee.org

Abstract. In this paper, we present a new approach for DNA sequence classification. The proposed approach is based on using the Wavelet Neural Network (WNN) and the k-means algorithm. The satisfying performance of the Wavelet Neural Networks (WNN) depends on an appropriate determination of the WNN structure. Our approach uses the Least Trimmed Square (LTS) and the Gradient Algorithm (GA) to solve the architecture of the WNN. The initialization of the Wavelet Neural Network is solved by using the Least Trimmed Square (LTS) method, which is applied for selecting the wavelet candidates from the Multi Library of the Wavelet Neural Networks (MLWNN) for constructing the WNN. Besides, the Gradient Algorithm (GA) is implemented for training the WNN in our method. The GA is used to solve the structure and learning of the WNN. This algorithm is applied to adjust the parameters of WNN. The performance of the WNN is investigated by detecting the simulating and real signals in white noise. The proposed method has been able to optimize the wavelet neural network and classify the DNA sequences. In this study, the LTS model is compared to the two initialization algorithms: Residual Based Regressor Selection (RBRS) and Stepwise Regressor Selection by Orthogonalization (SRSO). The LTS algorithm is to find the regressors, which provide the most significant contribution to the approximation of error reduction. The advantage of the LTS algorithm is to select the candidate wavelet from the MLWNN. This wavelet can reduce the approximation error. Our aim is to construct classifier method that gives highly accurate results. This classifier permits to classify the DNA sequence of organisms. The classification results are compared to other classifiers. The experimental results have shown that the WNN-LTS model outperformed the other classifier in terms of both the running time and clustering. In this paper, our system consists of three phases. The first one, which is called transformation, is composed of three sub steps; binary codification of DNA sequences, Fourier Transform and Power Spectrum Signal Processing. The second section is the approximation; it is empowered by the use of Multi Library Wavelet Neural Networks (MLWNN). Finally, the third section, which is called the classification of the DNA sequences.

Keywords: LTS · Wavelet neural networks · DNA sequences · MLWNN · RBRS · SRSO

© Springer International Publishing AG 2016
J. Blanc-Talon et al. (Eds.): ACIVS 2016, LNCS 10016, pp. 661–673, 2016.
DOI: 10.1007/978-3-319-48680-2_58

1 Introduction

The construction of the neural networks structure suffers from some deficiencies: the local minima, the lack of efficient constructive methods, and the convergent efficiency, when using ANNs. As a result, the researchers discovered that the WNN, is a new class of neural networks which joins the wavelet transform approach. The WNN were presented by Benveniste and Zhang. This approach is used to approximate the complex functions with a high rate of convergence [1]. This model has recently attracted extensive attention for its ability to effectively identify nonlinear dynamic systems with incomplete information [1–5]. The satisfying performance of the WNN depends on an appropriate determination of the WNN structure. To solve this task many methods are proposed to optimize the WNN parameters. These methods are applied for training the WNN such as the least-square which is used to train the WNN when outliers are present. These training methods are applied to reduce some function costs and improve performed the approximation quality of the wavelet neural network. On the other hand, the WNN has often been used on a small dimension [6]. The reason is that the complexity of the network structure will exponentially increase with the input dimension. The WNN structure has been studied by several researchers. Moreover, the research effort has been made to deal with this problem over the last decades [6–9]. The application of WNN is usually limited to problem of small dimension. The number of wavelet functions in hidden layer increases with the dimension. Therefore, building and saving WNN of large dimension are of prohibitive cost. Many methods are used to reduce the size of the wavelet neural networks to solve large dimensional task. Such as, magnitude approach is applied to eliminate of wavelets function with small coefficients [3]. The method, referred as Matching Pursuit (MP), was first introduced by Mallat. This method is used to determine a good wavelet basis in a dictionary [10]. Following this line of works, the Residual Based Regressor Selection (RBRS) algorithm is proposed for the synthesis of WNN. The Stepwise Regressor Selection by Orthogonalization (SRSO) and the Orthogonal Least Square (OLS) suggested are both the popular approaches [8]. These methods are used to reduce the complexity of the selected subset models. The number of regressors is smaller than that of the inputs [27, 28]. In addition, Bellil et al. applied a new initialization by selecting the method of the library WNN training. This approach is used to approximate a small number of inputs [22]. In this study, we use the Least Trimmed Square (LTS) method to select a little subset of wavelet candidates from MLWNN constructing the WNN structure in order to build a method to classify a collection containing a dataset of DNA sequences. This method is used to optimize an important number of inputs of DNA sequences. The Beta wavelet function is used to build the WNN. This wavelet makes the WNN training very efficient a reason of adjustable parameters of this function. Various approaches are used for clustering the DNA sequences such as the WNN, which is applied to construct a classification system. Wu et al. usedii an artificial neural network to classify the DNA sequences [11]. Moreover, Jach and Marín are proposed a method to classify the mitochondrial DNA Sequences. This approach joins the WNN and a Self-organizing map method. The feature vector sequences constructed by using the WNN [12]. Yang et al. used a Wavelet packet analysis to extract features of DNA sequences, which are applied to recognize the types of other sequences [13]. Wu et al. applied the neural network to classify the nucleic acid sequence. This classifier used three-layer and feed-forward networks that employ back-propagation learning algorithm [14]. Since a DNA sequence can be converted into a sequence of digital signals, the feature vector can be built in time or frequency domains. However, most traditional methods, such as k-tuple and DMK,... models build their feature vectors only in the time domain, i.e., they use direct word sequences. This paper contains three sections: in Sect. 2, we present our proposed approach. Section 3 presents the wavelet theory used to construct the WNN of our method. Section 4 shows the simulation results of our approach and Sect. 5 ends up with a conclusion.

2 Methods

This paper presents a new approach based on the wavelet neural network, which is constructed by using the Multi-library Wavelet Neural Networks (MLWNN). The WNN structure is solved by using the LTS method. Our approach is divided into two stages: approximation of the input signal sequence and clustering of feature extraction of the DNA sequences using the WNN and k-means algorithm.

2.1 Conversion of the DNA Sequence into a Genomic Signal

The species are classified in class by using the DNA sequence, which is composed of four basic nucleotides A(Adenine), G(Guanine), C(Cytosine) and T(Thymine), where each organism is identified by its DNA sequence [21, 22]. The feature extraction vector presents the DNA sequence. This vector is used to classify the species [23]. In this study, this vector coded by using a digital format, which can be used for DNA signal spectrum indicates 1 or 0 for the existence or not of a specific nucleotide at the DNA sequence level [24, 25]. For example, if x[n] = [A A A T...], we obtain: x[n] = [1000 1000 1000 0001...]

The indicator sequence is manipulated with mathematical methods. The sequence of complex numbers, called f (x) (1), is obtained by using the discrete Fourier Transform:

$$f(x) = \sum_{n=0}^{N-1} X_e(n)\, e^{-j\pi k/N}, k = 0, 1, 2, \cdots N - 1 \tag{1}$$

The Power Spectrum is applied to compute the Se[k] (2) for frequencies k = 0, 1, 2, ..., N−1 is defined as,

$$Se[k] = |f(x)|^2 \tag{2}$$

2.2 Wavelet Neural Network

The wavelet neural network is defined by the combination of the wavelet transform and the artificial neuron networks [33, 34]. It is composed of three layers. The salaries of the weighted outputs are added. Each neuron is connected to the other following layer.

The WNN (Fig. 1) is defined by pondering a set of wavelets dilated and translated from one wavelet candidate with weight values to approximate a given signal f. The response of the WNN is:

$$\hat{y} = \sum_{i=1}^{N_w} w_i \Psi \left(\frac{x - b_i}{a_i} \right) + \sum_{k=0}^{N_i} a_k x_k \tag{3}$$

where $(x_1, x_2, \ldots, x_{Ni})$ is the vector of the input, Nw is the number of wavelets and y is the output of the network. The output can have a component refine in relation to the variables of coefficients a k (k = 0, 1... N_i) (Fig. 1). The wavelet mother is selected from the MLWNN, which is defined by dilation (a_i) which controls the scaling parameter and translation (b_i) which controls the position of a single function $(\Psi(x))$. A WNN is used to approximate an unknown function:

$$y = f(x) + \varepsilon, \tag{4}$$

Where f is the regression function and ε is the error term.

2.3   Multi Library Wavelet Neural Network (MLWNN)

Many methods are used to construct the Wavelet Neural Network. Zhang applied two stages to construct the Wavelet neural Network [2, 3]. First, the discretely dilated and translated version of the wavelet mother function Ψ is used to build the MLWNN.

$$W = \left\{ \psi_i : \psi_i(x) = \alpha_i \psi \left(\frac{(x_k - b_i)}{a_i} \right), \ \alpha_i = \left(\sum_{k=1}^{n} \left[\psi \left(\frac{(x_k - b_i)}{a_i} \right) \right]^2 \right)^{\frac{1}{2}}, \ i = 1, \ldots L \right\}, \tag{5}$$

Where L is the number of wavelets in W and x_k is the sampled input. Then the best M wavelet mother function is selected based on the training sets from the wavelet library W, in order to construct the regression:

$$f_M(x) = \hat{y} = \sum_{i \in I} w_i \psi_i(x), \tag{6}$$

Where $M \leq L$ and I is a subset wavelet from the wavelet library.
Secondly, the minimized cost function:

$$j(I) = \min_{w_i, i \in I} \frac{1}{n} \sum_{k=1}^{n} \left(y_k - \sum_{i \in I} w_i \psi_i(x_k) \right)^2, \tag{7}$$

The stepwise selection by orthogonalization and the backward elimination are used by Zhang; the first is applied to select the appropriate wavelet in the hidden units while the second is used to choose the number of the hidden units, and of wavelets M, which are selected as the minimum of the so-called Akaike's final prediction error criterion (FPE) [2, 3]:

$$j_{FPE}\left(\hat{f}\right) = \frac{1 + n_{pa}/n}{1 - n_{pa}/n} \frac{1}{2n} \sum_{k=1}^{n} \left(\hat{f}(x_k) - y_k\right)^2 \qquad (8)$$

Where the estimator have n_{pa} parameters.

The gradient algorithms used to train the WNN, like least mean squares to reduce the mean-squared error:

$$j(w) = \frac{1}{n} \sum_{i=1}^{n} (y_i - \hat{y}(w))^2, \qquad (9)$$

Where $j(w)$ is the output of the Wavelet neural networks. The time-frequency locality property of the wavelet is used to give a signal f, a candidate library w of wavelet basis can be constructed.

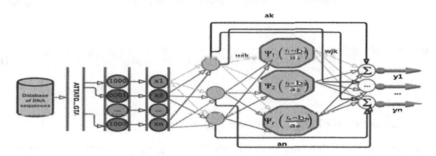

Fig. 1. The three layer wavelet network

2.4   Wavelet Network Construction Using the LTS Method

The set of training data $TN = \{x_1, x_2, \ldots, x_k, f(x_k)\}_{k=1}^{N}$ is used to adjust the weights and the WNN parameters, and the output of the three layers of the WNN in Fig. 2 can be expressed via (7). The model selection is used to select the wavelet candidates from the Multi Library Wavelet Neural Networks (MLWNN). These wavelet mothers are used to construct the wavelet neural network structure. In this study, the Least Trimmed Squares estimator (LTS) is proposed to select a little subset of wavelet candidates from the MLWNN. These wavelet candidates are applied to construct the hidden layer of the WNN [35]. Furthermore, the Gradient Algorithm is proposed to optimize the wavelet neural networks parameter. The residual (or error) e_i at the ith output of the WNN due to the ith example is defined by:

$$e_i = y_i - \hat{y}_i, \ i \in n \qquad (10)$$

The Least Trimmed Square estimator is used to select the WNN weights that minimize the total sum of trimmed squared errors:

$$E_{total} = \frac{1}{2}\sum_{k=1}^{p}\sum_{i=1}^{l} e_{ik}^2 \tag{11}$$

The Gradient Algorithm used to optimize the parameters (a_i, b_i, w_i) of the WNN is as follows:

$$\frac{\partial c}{\partial \hat{y}} = e_k \tag{12}$$

$$\frac{\partial c}{\partial w_i} = e_k \psi(\frac{x_i - b_i}{a_i}) \tag{13}$$

$$\frac{\partial c}{\partial b_i} = -e_k w_i \frac{1}{a_i} \psi'\left(\frac{x_i - b_i}{a_i}\right) \tag{14}$$

$$\frac{\partial c}{\partial a_i} = -e_k w_i \left(\frac{x_k - b_i}{a_i^2}\right) \psi'\left(\frac{x_k - b_i}{a_i}\right) \tag{15}$$

where

$$e = \hat{y}(x_k) - f(x_k) \tag{16}$$

2.5   Approximation of DNA Sequence Signal

The classification of DNA sequences is an NP-complete problem; the alignment is outside the range of two sequence of DNA, the problem rapidly becomes very complex because the space of alignment becomes very important. The recent advance of the sequence technology has brought about a consequent number of DNA sequences that can be analyzed. This analysis is used to determine the structure of the sequences in homogeneous groups using a criterion to be determined. In this paper, the Power Spectrum is used to process the signal of the DNA sequence. These signals are used by the wavelet neural networks (WNN) to extract the signatures of DNA sequences, which are used to match the DNA test with all the sequences in the training set [29]. Initially, the signatures of DNA sequences developed by the 1D wavelet network during the learning stage gave the wavelet coefficients which are used to adapt the DNA sequences test with all the sequences in the training set. Then, the DNA test sequence is transmitted onto the wavelet neural networks of the learning DNA sequences and the coefficients specific to this sequence are computed. Finally, the coefficients of the learning DNA sequences compared to the coefficients of the DNA test sequences by computing the Correlation Coefficient. In this stage, the k-means clustering is used to classify the signatures of the DNA sequences [27].

2.6 Learning Wavelet Network Using Gradient Algorithm and LTS Methods

In this section, we show how the library wavelet is used to learn a wavelet neural network [15, 16, 26, 27].

- **Learning approach**

  Step 1: The data set of DNA sequence is divided into two groups: training and testing dataset. These groups are applied to train and test the wavelet neural network.

  Step 2: Conversion of DNA sequence to a genomic signal using a binary indicator and Power Spectrum Signal Processing

  Step 3: the discretely dilated and translated version are used to construct the library W. The training data are proposed to create this library wavelet, apply the Least Trimmed Square (LTS) algorithm to select the optimal mother wavelet function (10), (11) and choose, from the library, the N wavelet candidate that best matches an output vector.

  Step 3.1: Initializing of the mother wavelet function library

  Step 3.2: Randomly initialize w_{jk} and v_{ij}.

  Step 3.3: For $k = 1,\ldots, m$

  (a) Calculate the predicted output $\hat{y}_i$ via (3).
  (b) Compute the residuals $e_{ik} = y_i - \hat{y}_i$ via (10).
  (c) the algorithm is stopped when the criteria diverged, then stop; otherwise, go to the next step
  (d) Find the arranged values $e_{ik}^2 \leq \ldots \leq e_{im}^2$. Choosing the N best mother wavelet function to initialize the WNN.

  Step 4: The values of w_{ij}^{opt}, a_i^{opt} and b_i^{opt} are computed using the Gradient algorithm via (13), (15), (14) and (16) go to step 3.3.

- **Clustering using K-means**

  Step 1: Generate a matrix M_signature of DNA sequences $\left(\left(w_{ij}^{opt}, a_i^{opt} \text{ and } b_i^{opt} \right) \right)$.

  Step 2: Let M_signature $s_i = \left\{ w_{ij}^{opt}, a_i^{opt}, b_i^{opt} \right\}$ be the set of data points and $V = \{v1, v2,\ldots, vc\}$ be the set of centers.

  Step 3: choose the Number of groups (k)

  Step 4: Assume the k training instance of signature of DNA as lonely-unit groups.

  Step 5: Affect each of (n-k) training instance of signature of DNA to the group with the proximate centroid and Recalculate the centroid of the winning group.

  Step 6: Compute the distance of each signature of DNA from the centroid of each group, switch the instance if it is not in the group and update the centroid of the winning and losing group.

  Step 7: Go to Step 6 if the convergence is not achieved

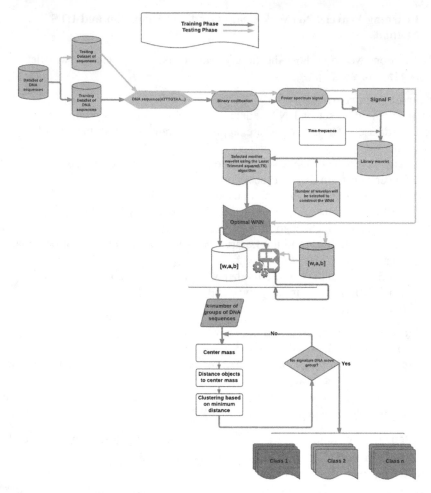

Fig. 2. Proposed approach

3   The Bêta Wavelet Family

The function beta is defined by β(x) = βx$_0$, x$_1$, p, q(x) [21, 22, 32, 33], x$_0$ and x$_1$ are real parameters.

$$\beta(x, p, q, x_0, x_1) = \begin{cases} \left(\dfrac{x - x_0}{x_c - x_0}\right)^p \left(\dfrac{x - x_1}{x_1 - x_c}\right)^q & if \ \ x \in [x_0, x_1] \\ 0 & otherwise \end{cases} \tag{17}$$

The derivatives of this function $\in$ L2($\Re$) are of class C∞. The general form of the nth derivative of Beta function is:

$$\psi_n(x) = \frac{d^n \beta(x)}{dx^n} = \left[(-1)^n \frac{n!p}{(x-x_0)^{n+1}} + \frac{n!q}{(x_1-x)^{n+1}}\right] \beta(x) + P_n(x) P_1(x)\beta(x) +$$

$$\sum_{i=1}^{n} C_n^i \left[(-1)^n \frac{(n-i)!p}{(x-x_0)^{n+1-i}} + \frac{(n-i)!q}{(x_1-x)^{n+1-i}}\right] \times P_1(x)\beta(x) \qquad (18)$$

where:

$$P_1(x) = \frac{p}{x-x_0} - \frac{q}{x_1-x} \qquad (19)$$

$$P_n(x) = (-1)^n \frac{n!p}{(x-x_0)^{n+1}} - \frac{n!q}{(x_1-x)^{n+1}} \qquad (20)$$

$$x_c = \frac{(px_1 + qx_0)}{(p+q)} \qquad (21)$$

4 Results and Discussion

This paper used three datasets HOG100, HOG200, and HOG300 selected from microbial organisms [23]. In this study, different experiments are used to evaluate the performance of our approach. The data set of DNA sequences are divided into test and train data. The published empirical and synthetic datasets are selected to perform the clustering comparative analysis [23] (Table 1).

Table 1. Distribution of available data into training and testing set of DNA sequence

Dataset	Total	Training	Test
HOG100	500	300	200
HOG200	600	400	200
HOG300	700	600	100

4.1 Selecting the Mother Wavelet

To evaluate the performance of our method, the NSRMSE and the training time serve. The LTS has a better performance to select the wavelet candidates from the Multi Library Wavelet Neural Networks (MLWNN). In the beginning, during the phase of approximation our approach tried to decompose the input signal for every DNA sequence and in the end, it tried to reconstruct the input signal of DNA. The estimation of the performance of this phase is measured by the NSRMSE. (Table 4) shows that obtained NSRMSE are low (0.000869) and the run time increases relatively with size of the DNA sequence. The result shows that the size of DNA sequence increases the time of the training phase. This time depends in the length of a DNA sequence. The training time increases (12.213 s) when the size is equal to 700. The complexity of the WNN structure increases exponentially with the input dimension. To solve the approximation problem we applied the library wavelet which incorporates a family wavelet. This library is called the Multi Library Wavelet Neural Network Model (MLWNN) (Tables 2 and 3).

Table 2. Selected mother wavelets and normalized square root of mean square error using residual based regressor selection (RBRS)

Dataset	Size	Beta 1	Beta 2	Beta 3	Mexhat4	Slog5	NSRMSE	Training time
HOG100	500	0	1	3	2	2	3.68777	43.337
HOG200	600	1	2	2	3	1	3.7984	47.654
HOG300	700	2	1	3	1	1	3.9523	52.654

Table 3. Selected mother wavelets and normalized root mean sequare using stepwise regressor selection by orthogonalization (SRSO)

Dataset	Size	Beta 1	Beta 2	Beta 3	Mexhat4	Slog5	NSRMSE	Training time
HOG100	500	2	2	1	1	2	0.675238	13.584
HOG200	600	0	3	2	1	2	0.78235	16.213
HOG300	700	1	1	2	2	2	0.79856	17.654

Table 4. Selected mother wavelets and normalized root mean sequare using the least trimmed square (LTS).

Dataset	Size	Beta 1	Beta 2	Beta 3	Mexhat4	Slog5	NSRMSE	Training time
HOG100	500	2	2	1	3	1	0.000869	9.869
HOG200	600	3	1	2	1	2	0.00543	10.542
HOG300	700	2	1	1	1	3	0.00896	12.213

4.2 Classification Results

Experiment results were performed to prove the effectiveness of our proposed approach. Evaluation metrics namely Precision, Recall and F-measures are used to compare our approach with other competitive methods. The F-measure combines the precision and the recall metric. We then calculate the recall and the precision of that cluster for each given class. More specifically, for cluster j and class i. The F-measure of the class j and the group i is the given by

$$F(j,i) = (2 * Recall(i,j) * Precision(i,j)) / ((Precision(i,j) + Recall(i,j)) \qquad (22)$$

Table 5. The classification results of WNN- LTS (Our Method) and other models (WFV, K-tuple, DMK) on different datasets of DNA sequences

Dataset	Our method		WFV		K-tuple		DMK	
	F-Score	# class	F-Score	#class	F-Score	# class	F-Score	# class
HOG100	**0.68**	**330**	0.58	854	0.52	451	0.55	658
HOG200	**0.7**	**468**	0.57	845	0.53	566	0.55	754
HOG300	**0.78**	**232**	0.58	185	0.52	654	0.54	256

Table 5 shows that WNN-LTS (our method) is better than other models(WFV, K-tuple and DMK) in terms of the classification results and optimal settings. The number of classes obtained by our approach is little less than in the other methods. The F-score (F-measure) proves the efficiency of our method. The F-measure is increased using WNN and LTS method. The LTS is applied to optimize the WNN structure.

4.3 Running Time

Tables 5 and 6 show that the WNN can produce very good the prediction accuracy. The results of our approach WNN-LTS tested on datasets show that accuracy outperforms the other techniques in terms of percentage of the correct species identification. Tables 5 and 6 show the distribution of the good classifications by class as well as the rate of global classification for all the DNA sequences of the validation phase. The WNN-LTS (our approach) is faster than the other methods. This speed is due to the use of the Least Trimmed Square (LTS) algorithm.

Table 6. Running time in seconds of each method on all datasets.

Dataset	Model	Length of feature vector	Time of building feature vector	Time of k-means	Total running time
HOG100	**Our method**	**128**	**5.3569**	**75.645**	**81.0019**
	WFV	32	8.4857	102.2634	110.7491
	K-tuple	64	7.9544	763.5223	771.4767
HOG200	**Our method**	**128**	**16.758**	**350.664**	**367.422**
	WFV	32	20.5239	645.8376	666.3615
	K-tuple	64	19.6306	3010.5426	3030.1732

5 Conclusions

In this study, we have used the LTS method to select a subset of wavelet function from the Library Wavelet Neural Network Model. This subset wavelet is applied to build Wavelet Neural Network (WNN). The WNN is used to approximate function f (x) of a DNA sequence signal. Firstly, the binary codification and Power Spectrum are used to process the DNA sequence signal. Secondly, the Library Wavelet is constructed. The LTS method is used to select the best wavelet from library. These wavelets are applied to construct the WNN. Thirdly, the k-means classification is used to classify the similar DNA sequences according to some criteria. This clustering aims at distributing DNA sequences characterized by p variables X1, X2...Xp in a number m of subgroups which are homogeneous as much as possible while every group is well differentiated from the others. The proposed approach helps to classify DNA sequences of organisms into many classes. These clusters can be used to extract significant biological knowledge.

Acknowledgment. We would like to acknowledge the financial support, under the form of grant, from the General Direction of Scientific Research (DGRST), Tunisia.

References

1. Zhang, Q., Benveniste, A.: Wavelet networks. IEEE Trans. Neural Netw. **3**(6), 889–898 (1992)
2. Zhang, J., Walter, G., Miao, Y., et al.: Wavelet neural networks for function learning. IEEE Trans. Signal Process. **43**(6), 1485–1497 (1995)
3. Zhang, Q.: Using wavelet network in nonparametric estimation. IEEE Trans. Signal Process. **8**, 227–236 (1997)
4. Pati, Y.C., Krishnaprasad, P.S.: Analysis and synthesis of feed-forward neural networks using discrete affine wavelet transformations. IEEE Trans. Neural Netw. **4**, 73–85 (1993)
5. Billings, S.A., Wei, H.L.: A new class of wavelet networks for nonlinear system identification. IEEE Trans. Neural Netw. **16**, 862–874 (2005)
6. Xu, J.H., Ho, D.W.C.: A basis selection algorithm for wavelet neural networks. Neurocomputing **48**, 681–689 (2002)
7. Mallat, S.G., Zhifeng, Z.: Matching pursuits with time-frequency dictionaries. IEEE Trans. Signal Process. **41**, 3397–3415 (1993)
8. Chen, S., Wigger, J.: Fast orthogonal least squares algorithm for efficient subset model selection. IEEE Trans. Signal Process. **43**, 1713–1715 (1995)
9. Han, M., Yin, J.: The hidden neurons selection of the wavelet networks using support vector machines and ridge regression. Neurocomputing **72**, 471–479 (2008)
10. Wu, C.H.: Artificial neural networks for molecular sequence analysis. Comput. Chem. **21**(4), 231–256 (1997)
11. Jach, A.E., Marín, J.M.: Classification of genomic sequences via wavelet variance and a self-organizing map with an application to mitochondrial DNA. Stat. Appl. Genet. Mol. Biol. **9**, 1544–6115 (2010)
12. Zhao, J., Yang, X.W., Li, J.P., Tang, Y.Y.: DNA sequences classification based on wavelet packet analysis. In: Tang, Y.T., Wickershauser, V., Yuen, P.C., Li, C.-H. (eds.) WAA 2001. LNCS, vol. 2251, pp. 424–429. Springer, Heidelberg (2001)
13. Wu, C., Berry, M., Fung, Y.-S., McLarty, J.: Neural networks for molecular sequence classification. Proc. Int. Conf. Intell. Syst. Mol. Biol. **1**, 429–437 (1993)
14. Vinga, S., Almeida, J.: Alignment-free sequence comparison-a review. Bioinformatics **19**, 513–523 (2003)
15. Wei, D., Jiang, Q. A.: DNA sequence distance measure approach for phylogenetic tree construction. In: Proceedings of the IEEE Fifth International Conference on Bio-Inspired Computing: Theories and Applications (BIC-TA), pp. 204–212. IEEE (2010)
16. Shi, L., Huang, H.: DNA sequences analysis based on classifications of nucleotide bases. In: Luo, J. (ed.) Affective Computing and Intelligent Interaction. AISC, vol. 137, pp. 379–384. Springer, Heidelberg (2012)

17. Bauer, M., Schuster, S.M., Sayood, K.: The average mutual information profile as a genomic signature. BMC Bioinf. **9**, 48 (2008)
18. Qi, J., Wang, B., Hao, B.I.: Whole proteome prokaryote phylogeny without sequence alignment: a K-string composition approach. J. Mol. Evol. **58**, 1–11 (2004)
19. Carter, O.B., et al.: Alignment-free genetic sequence comparisons: a review of recent approaches by word analysis. Briefings Bioinf. **15**(6), 800 805 (2012)
20. Bao, J.P., Yuan, R.Y.: A wavelet-based feature vector model for DNA clustering. Genet. Mol. Res. **14**, 19163–19172 (2015)
21. Ben Amar, C., Bellil, W., Adel Alimi, M.: Beta function and its derivatives: a new wavelet family. Trans. Syst. Signals Devices **1**, 275–293 (2006)
22. Bellil, W., Othmani, M., Ben Amar, C.: Initiazation by selection for multi-library wavelet neural network training. In: Conference: Artificial Neural Networks and Intelligent Information Processing (ANNIIP), Angers, France (2007)
23. http://doua.prabi.fr/databases/hogenom/
24. Mejdoub, M., Ben Amar, C.: Classification improvement of local feature vectors over the KNN algorithm. Multimedia Tools Appl. **64**(1), 197–218 (2013)
25. Zaied, M., Said, S., Jemai, O., Amar, C.: A novel approach for face recognition based on fast learning algorithm and wavelet network theory. Int. J. Wavelets Multiresolut. Inf. Process. World Sci. **19**, 923–945 (2011)
26. Said, S., Ben Amor, B., Zaied, M., Ben Amar, C., Daoudi, M.: Fast and efficient 3D face recognition using wavelet networks. In: 16th IEEE International Conference on Image Processing, Cairo, Egypt, pp. 4153–4156 (2009)
27. Jemai, O., Zaied, M., Ben Amar, C.: Fast learning algorithm of wavelet network based on fast wavelet transform. Int. J. Pattern Recognit. Artif. Intell. **25**(8), 1297–1319 (2011)
28. Jemai, O., Zaied, M., Ben Amar, C., Alimi, A.: Pyramidal hybrid approach: wavelet network with OLS algorithm- based image classification. Int. J. Wavelets Multiresolut. Inf. Process. **9**, 111–130 (2011). World Scientific Publishing Company
29. Ejbali, R., Benayed, Y., Zaied, M., Alimi, A.: Wavelet networks for phonemes recognition. In: International Conference on Systems and Information Processing (2009)
30. Ejbali, R., Zaied, M., Ben Amar, C.: Multi-input multi-output beta wavelet network modeling of acoustic units for speech recognition. In: International Journal of Advanced Computer Science and Applications (IJACSA). The Science and Information Organization (SAI), vol. 3 (2012)
31. Ejbali, R., Zaied, M., Ben Amar, C.: Wavelet network for recognition system of Arabic word. Int. J. Speech Technol. **13**, 163–174 (2010). Springer edition
32. Bouchrika, T., Zaied, M., Jemai, O., Ben Amar, C.: Ordering computers by hand gestures recognition based on wavelet networks. In: International Conference on Communications, Computing and Control Applications (CCCA), Marseilles, France, pp. 36–41 (2012)
33. Mejdoub, M., Fonteles, L., Ben Amar, C., Antonini, M.: Embedded lattices tree: an efficient indexing scheme for content based retrieval on image databases. J. Vis. Commun. Image Represent. **20**(2), 145–156 (2009)
34. Dammak, M., Mejdoub, M., Zaied, M., Amar, C.B.: Feature vector approximation based on wavelet network. In: ICAART 2012 - Proceedings of the 4th International Conference on Agents and Artificial Intelligence, vol. 1, pp. 394–399 (2012)
35. Ben Aoun, N., Mejdoub, M., Ben Amar, C.: Graph-based approach for human action recognition using spatio-temporal features. J. Vis. Commun. Image Represent. **25**(2), 329–338 (2014)

Collection of Visual Data in Climbing Experiments for Addressing the Role of Multi-modal Exploration in Motor Learning Efficiency

Adam Schmidt[✉], Dominic Orth, and Ludovic Seifert

University of Rouen, Mont-Saint-Aignan, France
Adam.Schmidt@univ-rouen.fr

Abstract. Understanding how skilled performance in human endeavor is acquired through practice has benefited markedly from technologies that can track movements of the limb, body and eyes with reference to the environment. A significant challenge within this context is to develop time efficient methods for observing multiple levels of motor system activity throughout practice. Whilst, activity can be recorded using video based systems, crossing multiple levels of analysis is a substantive problematic within the computer vision and human movement domains. The goal of this work is to develop a registration system to collect movement activity in an environment typical to those that individuals normally seek to participate (sports and physical activities). Detailed are the registration system and procedure to collect data necessary for studying skill acquisition processes during difficult indoor climbing tasks, practiced by skilled climbers. Of particular interest are the problems addressed in trajectory reconstruction when faced with limitations of the registration process and equipment in such unconstrained setups. These include: abrupt movements that violate the common assumption of the smoothness of the camera trajectory; significant motion blur and rolling shutter effects; highly repetitive environment consisting of many similar objects.

Keywords: Visual scene understanding · Data collection · Registration system · Motor learning · Gaze tracking · Rock climbing

1 Introduction

Understanding of skilled performance in human endeavor, such as sport, has benefited markedly from technologies that can track movements of the limb, body and eyes with reference to key surfaces, objects, events and significant others [5]. Indeed, ongoing technological advances continues to increase capacities of researchers to test their assumptions in the actual conditions, under which the relevant expertise is expressed [11]. In conjunction, image processing approaches for automatic detection of movement relative to environmental reference frames have also extended the timescales over which the evolution of

© Springer International Publishing AG 2016
J. Blanc-Talon et al. (Eds.): ACIVS 2016, LNCS 10016, pp. 674–684, 2016.
DOI: 10.1007/978-3-319-48680-2_59

expertise can be observed (such as learning and development) [1]. Within this context, a remaining challenge to overcome is to develop time efficient methods for behavioral analysis at multiple levels relative to the environmental reference (e.g., body-gaze-environment coordination). Thus, the current work presents automatic image processing methods for combining limb, body and gaze movements as they evolve through practice in a sport performance task relative to a three dimensional environmental reference.

A general purpose of observing practice dynamics is to address the efficiency of motor learning (the stabilization of new actions) under a given set of constraints (i.e., the combined task, environmental and individual boundary condition) [12]. Indeed, the efficiency of learning is highly influenced by the individuals level of experience under similar task and environmental constraint [4]. For example, different sub-systems (such as the visual or muscular systems), limited in their rate of adaptation to practice, strongly influence the learning efficiency [3,23]. Whilst efficiency provides an estimate of skilled performance [12], criteria for quantifying the novel (or exploration) component in motor learning is an ongoing problematic [15]. One approach, taken in this study, is to establish the degree of novelty in performer-environment interactions across trials and determine co-related levels of efficiency [10].

For example, in climbing tasks, the purpose of exploratory activity is to assist the individual to adapt to a more or less vertical and ever changing structure of a climbing surface to complete the route [14]. In climbing, exploration is functional (supports the individuals goals) across multiple levels as related to constraints that emerge though learning [8], such as determining postural stability to avoid falling or efficient progress to further optimize performance [14]. For example, it has been shown that visual search (non-physical exploration of a route), is used by experienced climbers to identify rest locations [18]. Haptic exploration of holds reduces uncertainty in reach-ability and grasp-ability of supports [13,17] and a key skill is to support exploration whilst maintaining an efficient climbing trajectory [22]. Finally, emergence of new climbing actions, through exploration, may also be observed over practice [20]. For example, from one trial to the next, different visual search patterns, route pathways, body orientations or grasping patterns can be developed and potentially stabilized [20].

Thus, during practice the nature of motor learning may be better understood by evaluating the levels at which exploration emerges. The challenge, therefore, in this study was to assess exploration across gaze, limb and postural levels of analysis. Through observing the evolution of exploration over practice, we aimed to determine its relative importance in supporting performance efficiency. The additional interest in recording exploration across multiple levels, was to determine in what ways gaze, limb and hip levels of exploration might evolve at different rates.

2   Methods

2.1   Variables of Interest

The goal of this work was to develop a registration system and procedure to collect data necessary for studies of the skill acquisition and exploration of the climbing wall by skilled climbers. As there are different ways of exploring the following data needed to be recorded:

– the gaze direction and head pose required for the analysis of the visual exploration;
– the positions of the limbs on the climbing wall for the analysis of the haptic exploration;
– the position of the hips relative to the limbs for the analysis of the postural exploration.

Traditionally, determining exploratory behavior in climbing requires that a given level of analysis is assessed with respect to motion detected at the hip (i.e., hip displacement being the overall objective of the climber). For example, visual fixations and limb actions in climbing are considered exploratory' when they are not associated to hip motion and performatory when they are associated to hip motion [13,17]. The main limitation in current work for determining hip mobility is operator involvement. For example, criteria for mobility have included manual frame-by-frame video notation using criteria statements like: "progress of the hips was observed" [2] whereas, criteria for immobility have included: "no discernible movement in pelvic girdle" [24]. Since hip mobility is determined as an acceptable level of displacement over time, one solution is directly using the hip velocity and applying an appropriate threshold (for example [21]). Finally, qualitative assessment of kinks or knots in hip trajectories over trials of practice, are suggestive of exploration at the hip level, often referred to as 'route finding' [4]. In this case, assessment of the hip path, from one trial to the next, provides the area explored by the hip.

2.2   Constraints

The conditions present at the climbing wall, the characteristics of the climbing task, and the required data imposed several constraints on the selection of the equipment used for the experiment. Wall climbing at advanced levels of difficulty is an activity requiring performing at the limits of strength, agility and endurance. Therefore, any additional equipment worn by the climbers increases the difficulty of the approach and alters their behavior due to limited field of view, restricted movement or even subtle shifts in the center of balance. Therefore, the amount, size and weight of the wearable equipment needed to be kept light and unobtrusive.

The artificial climbing wall is a very demanding environment for a motion tracking system due to the amount of dust in the air and high presence of metal components in the walls (e.g. hold screws and mounting holes). Moreover, due to the organizational and safety reasons, the cameras could not be installed permanently, their possible mounting locations were limited to certain areas of the opposing wall, and preferably no wired connection were to be used. Finally, the deployment, calibration and dissembling of the registration system had to be performed repeatedly and thus the procedure had to be as efficient and effortless as possible.

2.3 Instrumentation

After considering the requirements and constraints it was decided, that the system comprise of static external cameras for the reconstruction of the climbing wall and tracking of the LED markers attached to the climbers body. For detecting gaze positioning, the climber would wear eye-tracking glasses with a portable recording unit.

The GoPro Hero cameras were used in the registration system due to their robustness and reliability. Moreover, they can be controlled remotely, operate for prolonged periods on battery power supply and can record high-resolution (1920×1080) videos at 25 fps. The cameras were mounted on the opposing wall (i.e., 5 m away from the climbing surface) (Fig. 1) in a way making sure, that regardless of the climber's position, the markers could be visible from at least two cameras at the same time.

The biggest limitations of the GoPro cameras is that the manufacturer does not provide an SDK allowing users to directly control the cameras through

Fig. 1. The external cameras placement on the opposing wall.

Fig. 2. The equipment of the climbers: the LED markers - left, the SMI-ETG - right.

custom software. As a result, a wireless controller had to be used, which caused slight de-synchronization of the cameras. To solve that issue an additional procedure for synchronization of the video streams was proposed (Sect. 3.2).

The SensoMotoric Instruments Eye-Tracking Glasses (SMI-ETG) were used to record the video sequences of the scene observed by the climbers during their ascent approaches as well as to track the gaze direction during the experiments. The scene camera of the glasses records videos at 1280×960 pixels with the frequency of 24 fps. The binocular gaze direction data is recorded with a frequency of 60 Hz. The glasses provide automatic parallax compensation and track the gaze with the accuracy of $0.5°$. The glasses weigh 68 g and are used with the recording unit weighing additional 246 g. Their main drawback is that the scene camera uses a rolling shutter which unfortunately results in presence of distortions such as wobble, skew and smear during fast head movements. Additionally, the climbers were equipped with LED stripes attached to their forearms and ankles and a LED lamp placed on their back at the hip level. All the LED elements can be easily detected on the video frames and used to triangulate the positions of limbs and hips. Figure 2 shows the placement of the equipment on the climber's body. The system also supports 3-point, non-colinear, calibration prior to data collections and can be updated in post processing if needed.

2.4   Participants

A group of 20 experienced climbers were recruited on the basis of self-reported after practice ability levels between 6b–7a on the French rating scale of difficulty [6]. All participants provided informed consent and the study was conducted with local university ethical committee approval and in accordance with the Geneva Convention. Additionally, age, anthropometric characteristics (standing height, arm-span, hip-leg distance, neck-hip distance) and climbing histories (climbing age, best on-sight and after practice ability level on boulder routes) were recorded. Finally, body weight was recorded using a portable electronic scale whilst fully equipped (climbing gear and instrumentation).

2.5   Routes and Experimental Design

Participants were required to climb two different routes repeatedly and in succession over six trials. Each route was designed at a 6b F-RSD level. The level was confirmed by consensus between two qualified route-setters [6]. The routes were designed to be relatively challenging for participants in order to promote a learning effect [7] (Fig. 3).

Participants were assigned into one of two different conditions of treatment (i.e., 10 participants per condition) by random allocation. That is, the list of 20 participants were randomly sorted to an order of position in a list from 1–20 and every odd numbered participant climbed under condition 1 and every even ordered participant climbed in condition 2. In the first condition participants were afforded a two minutes period prior to each climb to non-physically practice the route from the ground (referred to as 'route preview' and is a typical feature of a climbers pre-ascent preparation [16]). The purpose of this manipulation was to allow the group to visually explore the route prior to attempting to climb it. It was anticipated that this would allow the 'with-preview' group of participants to plan their ascent before climbing, thus reducing the degree of haptic, postural and visual exploration required during the climb and throughout practice. The group of climbers assigned to condition 2, were not afforded a preview prior to climbing. In this case it was anticipated that a greater degree of exploration would be evident in the, 'no-preview', group during climbing and throughout practice. The route that was practiced first was counterbalanced across participants to control for any order of treatment effects. That is, five participants from each group carried out their first six trials of practice on

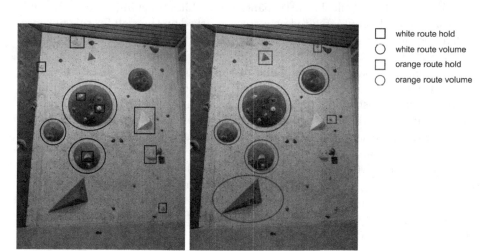

Fig. 3. The climbing routes used in the experiments

Route 1, before carrying out six trials of practice on Route 2, and, the remaining participants started on Route 2 and ended on Route 1.

2.6   Procedure

Across all testing sessions participants upon arrival were immediately fitted with recording apparatus and materials (gaze recording unit and glasses and LED markers). All participants used their personal climbing shoes. They were then required to undertake a 10-min climbing specific warm-up in order to habituate to the equipment and warm-up their hands, feet and body. Their anthropemtric details, climbing histories and informed consent were then recorded. Prior to undertaking experimental climbs they were instructed as to the general procedures and given the global task goal to: climb the route to end and through practice attempt to climb as fluently as possible. In the condition where participants were given a preview, they were instructed that they would have up to two minutes to visually inspect the route from the ground. They were also informed they were not allowed to physically touch the holds during preview, but were free to move around as they wished. All participants, prior to the commencement of recording, were shown the location of each hold and volume in the route. During this they were explicitly requested not to simulate the climb.

Prior to each trial the calibration of the glasses were updated using 3-, non-co-linear, points. Accuracy was verified using the portable recording unit interface. The recording unit was then activated to begin data collection. The four GoPro cameras were then initiated to begin recording using the wi-fi remote. The participants, who standing 3 m from the wall, were then required to look directly at a red LED that was flashed 5 times to act as a synchronization for the GoPros and SMI scene camera. In conditions 'with-preview', to help locate the end of preview in post-processing the participants, after completing their preview looked at a single LED flash. Participants then whilst touching with both hands the first hold of the route, fixated on a cross, marked on the wall for this purpose, for five seconds (this allowed for a final fail safe to make any offset corrections to the gaze tracking during post-processing). They were then instructed to begin to climb when they liked. The beginning of the climb was marked as when both feet had left the ground and the end was marked as when both hands made contact with the last hold. In cases where the climbers fell, the moment of last contact with either hand with the route was taken as the end of the trial. All recording equipment was then stopped. Between each climb, a seated 4-min rest was enforced to minimize effects of fatigue on performance. Participants were also required to solve a hand-held physics game during each rest. The purpose of this activity was to prevent them mentally simulating/practicing the route during the rest periods. They were also explicitly told not to mentally practice during rest periods and especially just after finishing each climb (since this is when climbers also tend to visually inspect).

3   Data Processing

3.1   Calibration

All the cameras used in the system (the GoPros and the scene camera of the SMI-ETG) were calibrated according to the Heikkila and Silvén camera model [9] using the freely available OpenCV library. As the external cameras were reassembled before each experiment their pose regarding the climbing wall had to be reestablished every time. In order to do that the multi-camera calibration method proposed by Schmidt et al. [19] was adapted. The images used for the calibration contain both the calibration marker of known size held in different pose while being observed by all the cameras and the empty scene containing flat surfaces of known structure (the climbing wall with regularly spaced mounting points). Moreover, the images of the climbing wall itself, with the mounting holes defining the coordinate system were used for the calibration (Fig. 4).

Fig. 4. Exemplary image used for the calibration of the camera poses

3.2   Synchronization

Despite being triggered with the same remote controller the GoPro cameras recorded video sequences are de-synchronized. To synchronize all the videos (including the scene camera of the SMI-ETG) each trial started with a red

Fig. 5. The detection of the blinks - two consecutive frames and the thresholded differential image

Fig. 6. Exemplary, synchronized images from the GoPro cameras (top) and the scene camera of the SMI-ETG (bottom) (Color figure online)

LED light being blinked 5 times. Such a signal is easily detectable on all the videos through the thresholding of the differential images. The time-shifts for the GoPro recordings relative to the SMI-ETG glasses recording are found by maximizing the correlation between the detected time series of blinking. The exemplary, synchronized images from all five cameras are presented in Fig. 6.

4   Conclusions

The paper presents the experimental setup and the procedure for registration of the visual data during climbing on an artificial, indoor climbing wall. The further work will focus on developing methods for estimating the trajectories of the climbers' heads, limbs and hips as well as tracking the gaze fixations projected onto the climbing wall (and particular holds) (Fig. 5).

The results of this will be used in further research on human skill acquisition including the understanding of the exploration across tactile, visual and postural forms. However, the visual data may be also of interest to the wider computer vision community (especially in the field of SLAM and visual odometry). The data recorded using the scene camera comprise images observed by humans involved in a physical activity. The main difficulty of the trajectory reconstruction lie in the limitations of the registration process and equipment in such unconstrained setups:

- abrupt movement of the head clearly violating the common assumption of the smoothness of the camera trajectory;
- significant motion blur and rolling shutter effect caused by the limitations of the SMI-ETG;
- highly repetitive environment consisting of many similar objects.

In order to facilitate research in both computer vision and human movement science the data will be made publicly available according to the open science paradigm.

References

1. Barris, S., Button, C.: A review of vision-based motion analysis in sport. Sports Med. **38**(12), 1025–1043 (2008)
2. Billat, V., Palleja, P., Charlaix, T., Rizzardo, P., Janel, N.: Energy specificity of rock climbing and aerobic capacity in competitive sport rock climbers. J. Sports Med. Phys. Fitness **35**(1), 20–24 (1995)
3. Cordier, P., Dietrich, G., Pailhous, J.: Harmonic analysis of a complex motor behavior. Hum. Mov. Sci. **15**(6), 789–807 (1996)
4. Cordier, P., France, M.M., Pailhous, J., Bolon, P.: Entropy as a global variable of the learning process. Hum. Mov. Sci. **13**(6), 745–763 (1994)
5. Davids, K., Button, C., Araújo, D., Renshaw, I., Hristovski, R.: Movement models from sports provide representative task constraints for studying adaptive behavior in human movement systems. Adapt. behav. **14**(1), 73–95 (2006)

6. Draper, N., Dickson, T., Blackwell, G., Fryer, S., Priestley, S., Winter, D., Ellis, G.: Self-reported ability assessment in rock climbing. J. Sports Sci. **29**(8), 851–858 (2011)
7. Guadagnoli, M.A., Lee, T.D.: Challenge point: a framework for conceptualizing the effects of various practice conditions in motor learning. J. Motor Behav. **36**(2), 212–224 (2004)
8. Guerin, S., Kunkle, D.: Emergence of constraint in self-organizing systems. Nonlinear Dyn. Psychol. Life Sci. **8**(2), 131–146 (2004)
9. Heikkila, J., Silvén, O.: A four-step camera calibration procedure with implicit image correction. In: 1997 IEEE Computer Society Conference on Computer Vision and Pattern Recognition, 1997. Proceedings, pp. 1106–1112. IEEE (1997)
10. Hristovski, R., Davids, K., Araujo, D., Passos, P.: Constraints-induced emergence of functional novelty in complex neurobiological systems: a basis for creativity in sport. Nonlinear Dyn.-Psychol. Life Sci. **15**(2), 175–206 (2011)
11. Mann, D.T., Williams, A.M., Ward, P., Janelle, C.M., et al.: Perceptual-cognitive expertise in sport: a meta-analysis. J. Sport Exerc. Psychol. **29**(4), 457–478 (2007)
12. Newell, K.M., Latash, M., Turvey, M.: Change in movement and skill: learning, retention, and transfer. In: Dexterity and Its Development, pp. 393–429 (1996)
13. Nieuwenhuys, A., Pijpers, J.R., Oudejans, R.R., Bakker, F.C., et al.: The influence of anxiety on visual attention in climbing. J. Sport Exerc. Psychol. **30**(2), 171–185 (2008)
14. Orth, D., Davids, K., Seifert, L.: Coordination in climbing: effect of skill, practice and constraints manipulation. Sports Med. **24**(2), 255–268 (2015)
15. Pacheco, M.M., Newell, K.M.: Transfer as a function of exploration and stabilization in original practice. Hum. Mov. Sci. **44**, 258–269 (2015)
16. Pezzulo, G., Barca, L., Bocconi, A.L., Borghi, A.M.: When affordances climb into your mind: advantages of motor simulation in a memory task performed by novice and expert rock climbers. Brain Cogn. **73**(1), 68–73 (2010)
17. Pijpers, J., Oudejans, R.R., Bakker, F.C., Beek, P.J.: The role of anxiety in perceiving and realizing affordances. Ecol. Psychol. **18**(3), 131–161 (2006)
18. Sanchez, X., Boschker, M., Llewellyn, D.: Pre-performance psychological states and performance in an elite climbing competition. Scand. J. Med. Sci. Sports **20**(2), 356–363 (2010)
19. Schmidt, A., Kasinski, A., Kraft, M., Fularz, M., Domagala, Z.: Calibration of the multi-camera registration system for visual navigation benchmarking. Int. J. Adv. Robot. Syst. **11**, 1–12 (2014)
20. Seifert, L., Orth, D., Hérault, R., Davids, K., Davis, T., Passos, P., Dicks, M., Weast-Knapp, J.: Affordances and graspingpatterns variability during rock climbing. In: Davis, T., Passos, P., Dicks, M., Weast-Knapp, J. (eds.) Studies in Perceptionand Action XII: Seventeenth International Conference on Perceptionand Action, pp. 114–118. Psychology Press, Taylor & Francis, Estori (2013)
21. Seifert, L., Wattebled, L., Herault, R., Poizat, G., Adé, D., Gal-Petitfaux, N., Davids, K.: Neurobiological degeneracy and affordance perception support functional intra-individual variability of inter-limb coordination during ice climbing. PloS ONE **9**(2), e89865 (2014)
22. Seifert, L., Wattebled, L., Orth, D., LHermette, M., Boulanger, J., Davids, K.: Skill transfer specificity shapes perception and action under varying environmental constraints. Hum. Mov. Sci. **48**, 132–141 (2016)
23. Thelen, E.: Motor development: a new synthesis. Am. Psychol. **50**(2), 79–95 (1995)
24. White, D.J., Olsen, P.D.: A time motion analysis of bouldering style competitive rock climbing. J. Strength Conditioning Res. **24**(5), 1356–1360 (2010)

Fog Augmentation of Road Images for Performance Analysis of Traffic Sign Detection Algorithms

Thomas Wiesemann and Xiaoyi Jiang[✉]

Department of Mathematics and Computer Science,
University of Münster, Münster, Germany
xjiang@uni-muenster.de

Abstract. This paper studies the influence of fog on traffic sign detection algorithms used in intelligent driver assistance systems. Previous studies are all based on synthetic images. In this work we use instead real-life photos of different road situations for fog augmentation to investigate the performance of five detection methods. To obtain depth information about the scene a depth map is first estimated for every source image of the dataset. Different visibility distances are then simulated with Koschmieder's fog model and the implemented algorithms are applied on the resulting images. Among others, the analysis of the results shows that in foggy situations the performance of a HSI-based algorithm is not always better than that of a RGB-based method.

1 Introduction

Traffic sign detection methods play an important role for driving assistance systems. In the last decades many approaches have been presented and evaluated [2,4,10]. Usually, traffic sign detection systems consist of three stages: segmentation, detection, and recognition [3,20,22]. In the segmentation stage an algorithm tries to identify all relevant pixels that might belong to a sign. Then, the detection stage examines the shape of all pixel regions. For instance, only circular or triangular regions are considered as possible traffic sign components and all other pixel regions are discarded. Finally, the recognition stage identifies the sign type of the remaining components.

Fog Augmentation for Performance Analysis. Recently, researchers addressed the problem of bad visibility conditions caused by fog. Enhancement and dehazing methods are introduced [7,12,17]. For performance analysis fog simulation using synthetic road images is presented in [1], which is applied to examine the impact on a traffic sign detection method.

The presence of fog in a road image directly effects the segmentation stage. The light scattering blurs the colors of traffic signs and lowers the contrast of the image. As a result, the segmentation stage misses more relevant pixels. The following stages thus receive worse input data and are possibly not able to detect

© Springer International Publishing AG 2016
J. Blanc-Talon et al. (Eds.): ACIVS 2016, LNCS 10016, pp. 685–697, 2016.
DOI: 10.1007/978-3-319-48680-2_60

and recognize all signs. Not surprisingly, the study [1] showed that the detection rate decreases with increasing fog density.

The previous studies [1,12,17] are all based on synthetic images. The main advantage of using synthetic images is the direct availability of depth information from scene modeling, which is essential, because the influence of fog depends on the distance of an object to the camera. However, such synthetic images differ from reality in a way that can have a huge impact on performance analysis. Generally, it is hard to completely and accurately model the world in a geometric manner. Also the other image formation factors are far too complex to be well simulated. For instance, the lighting conditions of photos can vary even in clear weather depending on daytime, clouds or light reflection. Indeed, the synthetic images used in [1] represent a simplistic world of very low complexity only (road, traffic signs, green area, sky). Consequently, the performance comparison presented there is not fully conclusive.

Contributions and Paper Organization. In this work we use real-life road photos for performance analysis of traffic sign detection algorithms. The contributions are twofold. The main challenge is clearly an efficient and reliable depth estimation of real images. We propose a semi-automatic approach for this purpose. It is applied to establish a database of images with estimated depth and augmented fog. In addition, a performance analysis for five traffic sign detection algorithms is conducted using this database. We plan to provide all related materials (dataset of depth images, software, etc.) in the Internet for public usage.

The remainder of the paper is organized as follows. In Sect. 2 we describe the details of the established database. The depth estimation approach is detailed in Sect. 3. In the next step fog is augmented into the images based on the Koschmieder's fog model in Sect. 4. The following Sect. 5 explains the common scheme for traffic sign detection together with five variants for color detection, which is used in our performance study. Section 6 presents the performed experiments and discusses the experimental results. Finally, Sect. 7 concludes this paper.

2   Test Database

For all experiments performed in the context of this work images from The German Traffic Sign Detection Benchmark [16] are used. It contains 900 still images (1360 × 800 pixels) of roads in Germany with traffic situations in city centers as well as on country roads and highways. The images were shot during different daytimes and different weather conditions, which results in a wide range of lighting situations. The varying distances of the signs to the observer cause different traffic sign sizes.

Currently, our test database contains 110 images with 147 traffic signs, which were selected from the benchmark, see Fig. 1 for some examples. The images cover different daytimes and traffic situations in cities and on highways. Because

Fig. 1. Example images from the database

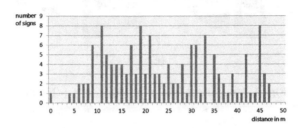

Fig. 2. Number of signs in certain distances

fog will be augmented later in the images, the focus of selection lies on source images with clear visibility. The signs appear in various distances. A related statistics is shown in Fig. 2, where the depth value is taken from the depth map generation described later.

Ground truth is available for the test database. It includes the location, the size, and the type of all traffic signs and can be used as reference for comparisons with the results of a detection algorithm. However, the database does not provide depth information. Therefore, the distance from the camera to the traffic signs is unknown.

3   Depth Map Generation

Adding fog into an image requires depth information of every pixel. This information can be stored in an extra depth map, whose different shades of gray represent the distance of every pixel to the observer. The lighter the shade the closer the object is located to the camera. Black pixels define the farthest distance and are used for the sky. Because the test database does not provide the depth maps, a depth map has to be generated for every test image.

2D-to-3D conversion has been studied in the literature. One popular application is to convert single-view footage for creating 3D film materials [13,21]. We apply a semi-automatic approach to generate the depth maps. A sparse depth map (predefined regions with known depth) is manually generated first. It is then expanded to a complete depth map by means of a random walker method.

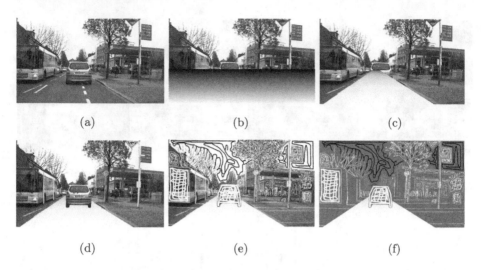

Fig. 3. Manual generation of a sparse depth map

Manual Generation of Sparse Depth Map. An image editing software (in our case GIMP 2) can be used to generate a sparse depth map. First of all, the depth of the ground plane has to be marked. This is done by creating a rectangle with a gradient from white to black as shown in Fig. 3 (b). Then, the rectangle is deformed by a perspective warp so that the edges are aligned to the road boundaries and markings (c). The result are perspective depth values for the road. Since some vertical objects, e.g. cars, on the road are now covered by the plane as well, the related areas have to be erased (d). In the next step all vertical objects, e.g. trees, can be marked by picking the corresponding depth from the road plane. The correct depth can be found by following an imaginary horizontal line from the base of the object to the road plane (d). Finally, the whole object can be roughly marked with the same depth (e). Planes located in line with the camera view only get some straight vertical or horizontal markings. The depth of the space in between these markings is calculated automatically by the algorithm. In the end the unmarked part of the image is removed, which is shown as red in (f), for automatic depth generation.

An important issue of manual depth initialization is to achieve depth genuineness as much as possible. In our work this relationship was obtained by experimenting with the warp tool in the photo editing software and by estimating distances in the images with the help of traffic sign sizes and road markings.

Random Walker Based Generation of Depth Map. The random walker algorithm was proposed in [5] and has been successfully applied to ensemble segmentation [19] and semi-automatic 2D-3D conversion [15]. It works as follows. All pixels in the image are considered as a graph, in which every pixel is connected to its neighboring pixels with a weighted edge. The weight represents

Fig. 4. Result of the depth map generation

the color similarity of two connected pixels. For each pixel the probability is calculated that a random walker starting at this pixel will reach a pixel, which is already associated to a region with known depth. The weights guide the random walker to take more likely a path with similar pixels. After the probabilities to different regions with known depth are calculated, the one with the highest probability gets associated with the current pixel.

Our current work is based on semi-automatic 2D-3D conversion [15] and we used the random walk implementation provided by the software Depth Map Automatic Generator 4[1]. To obtain the best possible result the number of iterations is set to the maximum of 10000. All other parameters are left at their default values. Figure 4 shows the final result of depth generation. In this way depth maps are created for all 110 test images used in the following experiments. It is possible to set different visibility distances for every single image and compare the effects on the traffic sign detection algorithms.

4   Fog Augmentation by Koschmieder's Model

The fog augmentation is done for each color channel of every pixel in the image using a model introduced by Koschmieder, which describes how an object covered by fog blends in with the sky [9] and is still widely used today [1,12,17]. Koschmieder's model calculates a new value L for every pixel in the image by:

$$L = L_0 e^{-kd} + L_\infty (1 - e^{-kd}) \tag{1}$$

L_0 is defined as the initial value of the current pixel in the source image, while L_∞ equals to the luminance of the sky. The coefficient d represents the distance from the observer to the pixel and k describes the extinction of the fog. It is inversely proportional to the visibility range d_m.

$$k = \frac{\ln(20)}{d_m} \tag{2}$$

In this way it is possible to set a new value for every pixel in the image only depending on its distance to the observer and the predefined visibility range. Results with homogeneous fog can be seen in Fig. 5.

---

[1] http://3dstereophoto.blogspot.de/2014/02/depth-map-automatic-generator-4-dmag4.html

Fig. 5. Result of fog augmentation with homogeneous fog. (a) Original image. (b) 400 m visibility. (c) 100 m visibility

Fig. 6. Result of fog augmentation with 200 m visibility. (a) Heterogeneous fog. (b) Cloudy homogeneous fog. (c) Cloudy heterogeneous fog

Similar to [17] random cloudy noise maps can be used to give the fog a more natural look by manipulating the extinction coefficient and the luminance value of the sky. To create heterogeneous fog, k is changed in a range from 50–150% of its original value while L_∞ is changed in a range from 80–100% of its original value to create a cloudy sky. Thus, fog can be slightly lighter or denser in front of planes, which results in a more realistic look. Results are shown in Fig. 6.

5   Traffic Sign Detection

We also conduct a preliminary study to compare different traffic sign detection algorithms in this work. The study is based on a simple sign detection method. An essential element of this method, namely color detection, is realized in five different ways, thus resulting in five algorithm variants in total for the performance analysis study. It is import to remark that it is not the intention here to conduct a comprehensive study including the most advanced traffic sign detection algorithms. Instead, the focus is to demonstrate the potential of the proposed fog augmentation.

Brief Description of Sign Detection Algorithm. First we try to identify all red pixels in the current image. Usually this is done by examining color values in a certain color space. Five variants of red color detection will be detailed later. The result is an image with black and white areas. Then, a connected component algorithm is applied to merge red pixels into pixel regions. The resulting components have to fulfill two conditions, otherwise they will be discarded: (1) A component has to be larger than 200 pixels. This corresponds to a circular speed limit sign with a height around 22 pixels and guarantees that small regions are discarded but far traffic signs are still detected. (2) The width-to-height ratio has to be higher than 0.7. Because a bounding box around a traffic sign has almost the ratio of a square, the region of interest must have approximately the same ratio. The threshold of 0.7 guarantees that rotated or tilted signs up to an angle of 45° are still detected. All remaining components are then considered as possible traffic signs.

The ground truth data contains the location and the size of all traffic signs in an image. Because the implemented algorithms focus only on red signs, the data of blue and white signs is ignored. For the remaining red signs the center of the bounding box is calculated and compared with the centers of all remaining components of the detection algorithm. A match occurs if the center coordinates of the ground truth sign equal the center coordinates of a detected region with a tolerance of 10 % of the traffic signs height and width. If a match is found, the traffic sign is marked as detected. Any other signs of the ground-truth without a corresponding detected component of the algorithm are marked as missed.

Color Detection Variants. Some of the implemented red color detection methods are based on the RGB color model while others use the HSI space. Generally, it is believed that a color detection algorithm based on hue and saturation values is less sensitive to illumination changes than a RGB-based algorithm [6,11]. Therefore, the HSI-based algorithms are expected to provide better results because they are able to compensate different daytimes or bad weather conditions.

De la Escalera et al. The traffic sign recognition system [3] works with HSI color classification followed by a shape-based algorithm. The intensity component gets ignored to avoid different results under different lighting conditions. The basic idea of the algorithm is that the hue and the saturation component can compensate wrong values of each other. If one of them is low, the other one can help out and the pixel can still be detected. To achieve this the hue and the saturation component are first transformed to a range from 0 to 255 and then replaced by a new value.

$$H_{\text{new}} = \begin{cases} 255\frac{H_{min}-H}{H_{min}} & \text{if } 0 \le H \le H_{min} \\ 0 & \text{if } H_{min} \le H \le H_{max} \\ 255\frac{H-H_{max}}{H_{max}} & \text{if } H_{max} \le H \le 255 \end{cases} ; \quad S_{\text{new}} = \begin{cases} S & \text{if } 0 \le S \le S_{min} \\ 255 & \text{if } S_{min} \le S \le 255 \end{cases}$$

For the detection of red color H_{min} is set to 40 while H_{max} is set to 140. S_{min} is defined as 190. The new hue value increases the closer the original hue value was to color red. The new saturation component increases together with the original value. If the original value reaches a certain threshold, the new one is set to the maximum.

Afterwards the results are multiplied to achieve the idea of the two components helping each other. After all values are calculated they are normalized to the maximum level of 255. If the result is larger than a predefined threshold, the pixel is marked as red. After some experiments in this implementation the threshold is set to 50.

Kuo and Lin. In [8] the HSI color model is used. Before applying a shape-based method to find circular and triangular contours, a threshold on the hue, saturation and intensity values of each pixel is applied.

$$\text{IF } ((0 \leq Hi < 0.111\pi) \text{ OR } (1.8\pi \leq Hi < 2\pi)) \text{ AND } (0.1 < Si \leq 1.0)$$
$$\text{AND } (0.12 < Ii < 0.8) \text{ THEN Pixel i is red}$$

First the algorithm checks if the hue value has the right angle. In addition, the values of the saturation and the intensity have to be in a proper range.

Varun et al. A two-stage roadsign detection and recognition system based on a tree classifier is proposed in [18]. In the first step the algorithm tries to find all red pixels in the image by using the RGB color model. The red component is first multiplied by a factor of 1.5. If the result is larger than the sum of the green and blue component, the pixel is marked as red.

$$\text{IF } (1.5 * Ri > Gi + Bi) \text{ THEN Pixel i is red}$$

Xu et al. The method from [20] is based on the HSI color model. After transforming the RGB values into HSI space a color segmentation is performed.

$$\text{IF } ((Hi < 0.05) \text{ OR } (Hi > 0.94)) \text{ AND } (0.18 < Si < 0.71)$$
$$\text{THEN Pixel i is red}$$

While a threshold is used for the hue and saturation value, the intensity component is completely ignored. The result is then passed to the next stage, which performs a circle detection based on the symmetry of the found components.

Zaklouta and Stanciulescu. In [22] the color detection is based on an approach from [14] and uses the RGB color model. All pixels with a dominant red color are extracted and all others are set to zero.

$$f_R(x) = \max\left(0, \frac{\min(Ri - Gi, Ri - Bi)}{Ri + Gi + Bi}\right)$$

All red pixels of the remaining filtered image are then checked for a certain threshold:

$$\theta = \mu + 4 \cdot \sigma$$

where μ represents the mean deviation and σ the standard deviation of all pixels in the filtered image. In this way the global illumination of the image is considered. Afterwards all remaining pixels are marked as red. The result is then passed to the shape detection stage.

6 Experiments

The realized software allows the user to adjust the visibility distance as desired and to run the traffic sign detection with different color detection variants. The results are then compared with the ground truth. The code is written in C# with usage of the Emgu Open CV library.

Experiment Design. The four types of fog are simulated in every of the 110 source images with four different visibility distances (400m, 300m, 200m, and 100m). The result is a dataset of 1,700 foggy road images. To guarantee consistent results in the following experiments, the random component of the noise maps is eliminated by only using the source images and the images with homogeneous fog. The traffic sign detection algorithm is applied to the 550 remaining images using the five different color detection variants. The results are presented in a chart analog to the performance analysis using synthetic foggy road images [1]. The x-axis represents the distance of the traffic sign to the observer while the y-axis shows the correct detection rate. For every visibility distance one graph is drawn into the chart. In this way it is possible to see how the detection rate decreases with greater distances of the traffic signs. Additionally, the position of the different graphs shows how the visibility distance effects the detection rate. The resulting charts for every algorithm are presented in Fig. 7. Analog to [1] the road sign distances with a detection rate of 80 % are observed related to the different visibility distances. In this way it is possible to see how the fog density effects the detection range of the algorithms.

It is important to point out one detail of Fig. 7. The distributions there are drawn for a small number of bins of distance values and all effective distances of signs are rounded to one of the bins. Because of the perspective view the effect of a standard rounding process has a higher influence on near traffic signs. For instance, if the position of a near traffic sign is changed by 5 meters, the effect on its size and location in the image is higher than if the same change is applied to a far traffic sign. Therefore, nonlinear values are used for the rounding process, which guarantees that the distances of near signs are less changed than the distances of far signs. The used values are the triangular numbers 3, 6, 10, 15, 21, 28, 36, and 45.

Experimental Results. The different levels of the graphs for the RGB-based algorithm of Varun et al. vary a lot, which means that it is highly influenced by the presence of fog. The gap between the graph for no fog and the graphs for the different fog densities in the charts for the HSI-based algorithms of XU QINGSONG ET AL. and KUO AND LIN is quite high. This means that on the one hand they are robust to different lighting conditions in the images, but on the other hand they get difficulties once fog is there. Even though ZAKLOUTA AND STANCIULESCU's approach is based on RGB values the detection rate with different fog densities is surprisingly high. Also the level of the graphs for different fog densities does not vary much, which means that fog has only low influence

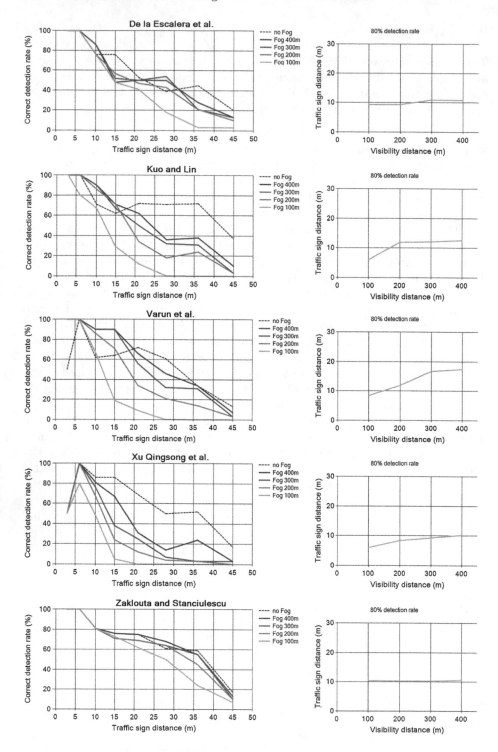

Fig. 7. Results of the traffic sign detection

on the detection. This results from the fact that the global illumination of the image is taken into account. The idea of DE LA ESCALERA ET AL. of the hue and saturation value helping each other out results in a stable behavior under different visibility conditions. However, the algorithm provides overall only average detection rates.

In the performance analysis using synthetic images [1] the detection rate is constantly falling with decreasing the visibility range. In addition, the lines for the different visibility ranges are always in the same order. The lower the visibility the lower the graph is located in the chart. However, in our work some analyzed algorithms show an increasing detection rate at some points. This behavior occurs even without fog being added into the image. The reason for that are the previously mentioned lighting conditions in real-life photos. Because traffic signs in the same distance do not always appear in the same color or shape, the detection rate of the algorithm can vary a lot from image to image.

In [1] the second graph showed that the detection distance decreases linearly with the fog density. While the decreasing behavior could be confirmed, the algorithms analyzed in this work do not give linear results. Different fog densities have almost no effect on the detection distance with 80 % detection rate for the algorithms of DE LA ESCALERA ET AL. or ZAKLOUTA AND STANCIULESCU. In contrast, the detection distance of the algorithm of VARUN ET AL. decreases stronger with the fog density. This means that some algorithms are more robust to the presence of fog than others when focusing on a detection rate of 80 %.

7   Conclusion

A database of foggy road images with different visibility distances was successfully created from a set of real life photos. The semi-automatic depth map generation lead to convincing results using Koschmieder's fog model. In this way, an authentic test environment for the performance analysis of traffic sign detection algorithms was realized.

After testing the different algorithms on foggy images it became clear that HSI-based algorithms are not always the better choice. While they might work better in clear weather they start to fail when fog is added into the image. It seems that an RGB-based algorithm delivers good results as well, but only if the global illumination of the images is taken into account.

In addition, it stands out that the detection rate of an algorithm can vary much instead of being monotonically decreasing. Further research should therefore focus more on real-life images than on synthetic images. The generated depth maps can be used to simulate and analyze other weather conditions like dust, rain or snow.

Acknowledgment. This research has received funding from the FP7 for Research, Technological Development and Demonstration of European Union under grant agreement HAZCEPT (318907).

References

1. Belaroussi, R., Gruyer, D.: Impact of reduced visibility from fog on traffic sign detection. In: Proceedings of IEEE Intelligent Vehicles Symposium, pp. 1302–1306 (2014)
2. Brkic, K.: An overview of traffic sign detection methods. Comput. Intell. Syst. (2010)
3. de la Escalera, A., Armingol, J., Mata, M.: Traffic sign recognition and analysis for intelligent vehicles. Image Vis. Comput. 21(3), 247–258 (2003)
4. Gomez-Moreno, H., Maldonado-Bascon, S., Gil-Jimenez, P., Lafuente-Arroyo, S.: Goal evaluation of segmentation algorithms for traffic sign recognition. IEEE Trans. Intell. Transp. Syst. 11(4), 917–930 (2010)
5. Grady, L.: Random walks for image segmentation. IEEE Trans. Pattern Anal. Mach. Intell. 28(11), 1768–1783 (2006)
6. Jau, U.L., Chee, S.T., Giap, W.N.: A comparison of RGB and HSI color segmentation in real - time video images: a preliminary study on road sign detection. In: Proceedings of International Symposium on Information Technology (2008)
7. Kim, J.H., Jang, W.D., Sim, J.Y., Kim, C.S.: Optimized contrast enhancement for real-time image and video dehazing. J. Vis. Commun. Image Represent. 24(3), 410–425 (2013)
8. Kuo, W.J., Lin, C.C.: Two-stage road sign detection and recognition. In: Proceedings of IEEE International Conference on Multimedia and Expo, pp. 1427–1430 (2007)
9. Middleton, W.E.K.: Vision Through the Atmosphere. University of Toronto Press, Toronto (1952)
10. Møgelmose, A., Trivedi, M.M., Moeslund, T.B.: Vision-based traffic sign detection and analysis for intelligent driver assistance systems: perspectives and survey. IEEE Trans. Intell. Transp. Syst. 13(4), 1484–1497 (2012)
11. Ali Mohd, N., Md Rashid, N.K.A., Mustafah, Y.M.: Performance comparison between RGB and HSV color segmentations for road signs detection. Appl. Mech. Mater. 393, 550–555 (2013)
12. Negru, M., Nedevschi, S.: Assisting navigation in homogenous fog. In: Proceedings of International Conference on Computer Vision Theory and Applications, vol. 2, 619–626 (2014)
13. Phan, R., Androutsos, D.: Robust semi-automatic depth map generation in unconstrained images and video sequences for 2D to stereoscopic 3D conversion. IEEE Trans. Multimedia 16(1), 122–136 (2014)
14. Ruta, A., Li, Y., Liu, X.: Real-time traffic sign recognition from video by class-specific discriminative features. Pattern Recogn. 43(1), 416–430 (2010)
15. Rzeszutek, R., Phan, R., Androutsos, D.: Semi-automatic synthetic depth map generation for video using random walks. In: Proceedings of IEEE International Conference on Multimedia and Expo, pp. 1–6 (2011)
16. Stallkamp, J., Schlipsing, M., Salmen, J., Igel, C.: The German traffic sign recognition benchmark: a multi-class classification competition. In: Proceedings of International Joint Conference on Neural Networks, pp. 1453–1460 (2011)
17. Tarel, J.P., Hautiere, N., Caraffa, L., Cord, A., Halmaoui, H., Gruyer, D.: Vision enhancement in homogeneous and heterogeneous fog. IEEE Intell. Transp. Syst. Mag. 4(2), 6–20 (2012)

18. Varun, S., Singh, S., Kunte, R.S., Samuel, R.D.S., Philip, B.: A road traffic signal recognition system based on template matching employing tree classifier. In: Proceedings of International Conference on Computational Intelligence and Multimedia Applications, pp. 360–365 (2007)
19. Wattuya, P., Rothaus, K., Praßni, J., Jiang, X.: A random walker based approach to combining multiple segmentations. In: Proceedings of International Conference on Pattern Recognition, pp. 1–4 (2008)
20. Xu, Q., Su, J., Liu, T.: A detection and recognition method for prohibition traffic signs. In: Proceedings of International Conference on Image Analysis and Signal Processing, pp. 583–586 (2010)
21. Yuan, H., Wu, S., Cheng, P., An, P., Bao, S.: Nonlocal random walks algorithm for semi-automatic 2D-to-3D image conversion. IEEE Signal Process. Lett. **22**(3), 371–374 (2015)
22. Zaklouta, F., Stanciulescu, B.: Real-time traffic sign recognition in three stages. Robot. Auton. Syst. **62**(1), 16–24 (2014)

Statistical Modeling Based Adaptive Parameter Setting for Random Walk Segmentation

Ang Bian and Xiaoyi Jiang[(✉)]

Department of Mathematics and Computer Science,
University of Münster, Münster, Germany
{bian,xjiang}@uni-muenster.de

Abstract. Segmentation algorithms typically require some parameters and their optimal values are not easy to find. Training methods have been proposed to tune the optimal parameter values. In this work we follow an alternative goal of adaptive parameter setting. Considering the popular random walk segmentation algorithm it is demonstrated that the parameter used for the weighting function has a strong influence on the segmentation quality. We propose a statistical model based approach to automatically setting this parameter, thus adapting the segmentation algorithm to the statistic properties of an image. Experimental results are presented to demonstrate the usefulness of the proposed approach.

1 Introduction

Image segmentation is one of the mostly studied and challenging problems in image analysis. Semi-automatic segmentation methods have been introduced to overcome the complexity of understanding image patterns by user interaction. This kind of algorithms are very helpful in providing targeted segments by roughly labeling scribbles by users. The popular random walk algorithm [1] belongs to this category of segmentation methods. In addition to image segmentation the random walk approach has meanwhile been applied to solve other tasks like ensemble segmentation [2], clustering [3], and semi-automatic 2D-to-3D conversion [4].

Random walk segmentation is a graph-based method that maximizes the image entropy satisfying the Markov property [5]. In [1] a Gaussian weighting function as proposed in [6] was introduced to measure the correspondence of connected nodes by normalizing the difference of intensities with a manually set parameter β. For random walk based data classification it is already shown that only suitable parameter β can yield good results [7]. In this paper we propose a data-driven weighting function based on a piecewise Gaussian image model as prior to solve the parameter setting problem for image segmentation.

The remainder of this paper is organized as follows. In Sect. 2 we give a brief overview of the random walk segmentation method [1]. Then, we motivate our work by demonstrating the influence of parameter β on segmentation quality in Sect. 3. Section 4 presents the theory and implementation of our adaptive

J. Blanc-Talon et al. (Eds.): ACIVS 2016, LNCS 10016, pp. 698–710, 2016.
DOI: 10.1007/978-3-319-48680-2_61

weighting function. The usefulness of our approach is shown in Sect. 5 on both synthetic data and real (CT slice) images. Finally, some discussions conclude this paper.

2   Random Walk Image Segmentation

The fundamental idea of random walk segmentation is to assign an unlabeled pixel to the label of the highest probability that a random walker starting from that pixel reaches the user provided scribbles (seeds).

An image is defined as a connected and undirected graph $G(V, E)$, where V is the set of all nodes v_i and E is the set of all edges e_{ij} connecting nodes v_i and v_j. Denoting by x_i^s the probability that a node v_i reaches seeds of label $s = 1, \dots, l$, for each unseeded node it holds:

$$x_i^s = \frac{1}{d_i} \sum_{e_{ij}} \omega_{ij} x_j^s \qquad (1)$$

where ω_{ij} is the weight of edge e_{ij} and $d_i = \sum_{e_{ij}} \omega_{ij}$ is the degree of node v_i. In [1] the weight is defined as Gaussian in a way typical to the dissimilarity measure as used in many other works:

$$\omega_{ij} = exp(-\beta(f_i - f_j)^2) \qquad (2)$$

where f_i, f_j are the intensities of two connected nodes v_i, v_j, and β is a manually set parameter.

The constrained probabilities (1) can be solved as a combinatorial Dirichlet problem with boundary conditions by its Laplace equation. Define the combinatorial Laplacian matrix L as:

$$L_{ij} = \begin{cases} d_i & \text{if } i = j \\ -\omega_{ij} & \text{if } v_i \text{ and } v_j \text{ are adjacent nodes} \\ 0 & \text{otherwise} \end{cases}$$

By partitioning the nodes into two sets V_M (marked seed nodes, regardless of their label) and V_U (unseeded nodes) and rearranging the probability vector of vertices (for a particular label s, which is skipped to simplify the notation) and matrix L, we can depose the Dirichlet integral into:

$$D[x_U] = \frac{1}{2} \begin{bmatrix} x_M^T & x_U^T \end{bmatrix} \begin{bmatrix} L_M & B \\ B^T & L_U \end{bmatrix} \begin{bmatrix} x_M \\ x_U \end{bmatrix} = \frac{1}{2}(x_M^T L_M x_M + 2x_U^T B^T x_M + x_U^T L_U x_U)$$

where x_M and x_U correspond to the probabilities of seeded and unseeded nodes, respectively. Since L is positive semidefinite, the minimal solution of $D[x_U]$ would be the only solution of the following system of linear equations:

$$L_U x_U = -B^T x_M$$

This computation is repeated for all labels. Given the probabilities x_i^s of an unseeded node v_i reaching seeds of label $s = 1, \dots, l$ determined this way, v_i is assigned the label with the highest probability.

3 Influence of Parameter β on Segmentation Quality

The segmentation result critically relies on how the edge weights ω_{ij} in (2) are defined and indirectly the parameter β. In this section we use two groups of synthetic images to demonstrate this influence.

The first group of images (256×256 pixels) contains one circle as foreground. The background intensity is set to 12. The contrast ratio r_{fb} of foreground to background intensity varies from 1.2 to 2.4 with step 0.2. Gaussian noise of σ from 1 to 5 with step 1 is added. For each of these 35 settings we randomly generate 10 images, thus resulting in a total of 350 test images. For each of these test images we run the random walk method with β varying from 1 to 1001 with step 10 and calculate the Dice index ($\frac{2|A \cap B|}{|A|+|B|}$ for set A and B) of the segmented foreground object according to the ground truth. Then, we pick up the β that achieves the best Dice index. Figure 1 shows the distribution of the optimal β values. As a concrete example, five results for one of the 350 test images (corresponding to $\sigma = 2$, $r_{fb} = 1.6$, $\beta = 51, 201, 401, 701, 1001$) are shown in Fig. 1 as well.

The second group of images (256×256 pixels) contains multiple foreground objects of various intensities while the background intensity is set to 12. The contrast ratio of foreground to background intensity depends on the foreground object (circle: 1.7–2.9, ellipse: 1.3–2.5, triangle: 1.5–2.7, irregular shape: 1.4 to 2.6, all with step 0.2). Gaussian noise of σ from 1 to 5 with step 1 is added. Again, 350 test images are collected by randomly generating 10 images for each of these 35 settings. The same test procedure (β varying from 1 to 1001 with step 10) results in the distribution of the optimal β values shown in Fig. 2.

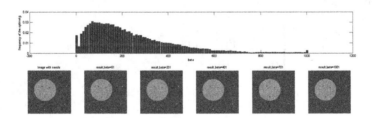

Fig. 1. Test image group 1: distribution of the optimal β (top). Segmentation results with five different β values for one particular image of this group (bottom).

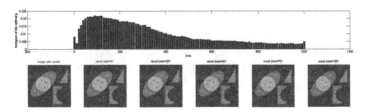

Fig. 2. Test image group 2: distribution of the optimal β (top). Segmentation results with five different β values for one particular image of this group (bottom).

As a concrete example, five results for one of the 350 test images (corresponding to $\sigma = 2$, $r_{fb} = 1.9, 1.5, 1.7, 1.6$ for circle, ellipse, triangle, and irregular shape respectively, $\beta = 51, 201, 401, 701, 1001$) are shown in Fig. 1 as well.

It is easy to see that the optimal β substantially varies for different images. In fact, the test images in each of the two groups are very similar. Even under this rather favorable testing condition it is not possible to fix the optimal β value. This motivates us to develop an approach to automatically setting this parameter, thus adapting the segmentation algorithm to the statistic properties of an image.

Dealing with parameters is an important task of image segmentation in general. Traditionally, supervised training approaches have been applied [8]. The critical disadvantage there is the need of ground truth segmentation for the training. Recently, unsupervised parameter learning has been studied, e.g. by means of ensemble consensus learning [9]. This work follows this unsupervised line and will develop a statistical modeling based approach for the task at hand.

4   Adaptive Parameter Setting

In this section we present our adaptive weighting function based on a Gaussian piecewise image model. To ease the reading Table 1 provides a list of the most important symbols.

4.1   Image Model

We assume a piecewise constant image $G = (V, E)$:

$$V = \cup_{s=1}^{l} V^s, \quad V^i \cap V^j = \emptyset, \quad \forall i \neq j$$

where l is the number of regions and V^s is the set of all the nodes in an image region with label s. The intensity f_i of any node $v_i \in V^s$ is an independently

Table 1. Definition of symbols.

V^s	Set of image nodes in an image region labeled s
u^s	Mean intensity of V^s
f_i	Intensity of node v_i
$\hat{u}_i$	Estimated mean for f_i
x_i^s	Probability that unseeded node v_i reaches seeds of label s
$\hat{f}_i$	Transformed image intensity of node v_i
σ^2	Global variance according to our image model
σ_e^2	Estimation of global variance $\sigma_e^2 = var(\hat{u}_i)$
σ_d^2	Global variance of difference of estimations at connected nodes $\sigma_d^2 = var(\hat{u}_i - \hat{u}_j)$

and identically realization of a Gaussian distribution with a global variance parameter σ^2 (identical for all regions) and a regional mean parameter u^s. The corresponding probability density function is:

$$p(f_i; u^s, \sigma^2) = \frac{1}{\sqrt{2\pi\sigma^2}} \exp \frac{-(f_i - u^s)^2}{2\sigma^2}$$

An interactive image segmentation should achieve a partition of homogeneous regions by their *hidden* regional parameters $u^s, s = 1, \cdots, l$, identified by the user labeled seeds.

4.2   Adaptive Weighting Function

Based on our image model we consider the intensity of each node as a random variable. Then, we redefine the probability that node v_i reaches seeds of label s as the probability that its intensity f_i shares the same mean of seeds with label s:

$$x_i^s = P(u^s | f_i)$$

that shall be solved by random walks with the following Markov constraint [10]:

$$x_i^s = P(u^s | f_i) = \frac{\sum_{e_{ij}} w_{ij} P(u^s | f_j)}{\sum_{e_{ij}} w_{ij}}$$

Here w_{ij} is defined by a weighting function measuring the probability that the connected nodes v_i and v_j belong to the same region.

Without loss of generality, we assume that node v_i belongs to V^s of regional mean u^s and v_j is an arbitrary neighbor node of v_i. By defining $\hat{u}_j$ as the estimated mean of intensity at v_j, a mixture Gaussian distribution can be obtained as follows:

$$pdf(\hat{u}_j | e_{ij} \in E) = \frac{r^s}{\sqrt{2\pi\sigma_e^2}} \exp \frac{-(\hat{u}_j - u^s)^2}{2\sigma_e^2} + \sum_{t \neq s} \frac{r^t}{\sqrt{2\pi\sigma_e^2}} \exp \frac{-(\hat{u}_j - u^t)^2}{2\sigma_e^2}$$

where r^s is the proportion of v_i's neighborhood that belongs to the region with regional mean u^s. The same proportion can also be defined for all other regions with regional mean u^t, $t \neq s$. Obviously, it holds $r^s + \sum_{t \neq s} r^t = 1$. In addition, $\sigma_e^2 = var(\hat{u}_i)$ is the global estimation variance. An example probability density curve is shown in Fig. 3, where the neighborhood of v_i is a mixture of nodes belonging to three regions with label s, $t1$, and $t2$, respectively.

Based on the discussion above we can postulate the conditional probability density:

$$pdf\left(\hat{u}_j | v_i, v_j \in V^s\right) = pdf\left(\hat{u}_j; u^s, \sigma_e^2\right) = \frac{1}{\sqrt{2\pi\sigma_e^2}} \exp \frac{-(\hat{u}_j - u^s)^2}{2\sigma_e^2}, \quad \forall e_{ij} \in E$$

as a measure of the probability whether v_j falls in the same region of v_i. However, we cannot calculate the accurate value of $\hat{u}_j - u^s$ directly as we do not have the

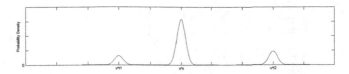

Fig. 3. Probability density curve for the estimations $\hat{u}_j$ of the neighbor nodes of v_i. Here we set $u^s = 30$, $u^{t1} = 10$, $u^{t2} = 60$, $r^s = \frac{10}{15}$, $r^{t1} = \frac{2}{15}$, $u^{t2} = \frac{3}{15}$, $\sigma_e^2 = 4$.

prior u^s. For this reason we take the estimation $\hat{u}_i$ as a substitute to achieve the approximate result $\hat{u}_j - \hat{u}_i$. Consequently, the estimation of variance $\sigma_e^2 = var(\hat{u}_j) = var(\hat{u}_j - u^s)$ [because u^s is a constant, although unknown] also has to be replaced by $\sigma_d^2 = var(\hat{u}_j - \hat{u}_i)$ [11], which is the variance of difference of two estimations at connected nodes. This leads to the weighting function:

$$\omega_{ij} = pdf(\hat{u}_j; \hat{u}_i, \sigma_d^2) = \frac{1}{\sqrt{2\pi\sigma_d^2}} \exp \frac{-(\hat{u}_j - \hat{u}_i)^2}{2\sigma_d^2}, \quad \forall e_{ij} \in E$$

Since σ_d^2 is a global variance parameter for $\forall v_i, v_j \in V$, $e_{ij} \in E$, we can simplify our weighting function:

$$\omega_{ij} = \exp \frac{(\hat{u}_j - \hat{u}_i)^2}{2\sigma_d^2} \propto pdf(\hat{u}_j; \hat{u}_i, \sigma_d^2), \quad \forall e_{ij} \in E \tag{3}$$

Clearly, this weighting function is positive and symmetrical. Its computation needs $\hat{u}_i$ for all pixels and σ_d^2. We discuss the related details in the following.

Mean Estimator. An unbiased mean estimation for Gaussian distribution is:

$$\hat{u}_i = \frac{1}{(2k+1)^2} \sum_{k \in N_i} f_k$$

where N_i contains the index of all pixels from the $(2k+1) \times (2k+1)$ neighborhood of node v_i.

For any 4-connected neighbor nodes $v_i, v_j \in V$, their $(2k+1) \times (2k+1)$ neighborhoods N_i and N_j have only $2k+1$ non-overlapping nodes with each other. Therefore, $\hat{u}_i - \hat{u}_j$ is a linear combination of $2(2k+1)$ i.i.d. variables and the estimation of its variance σ_d^2 is:

$$\sigma_d^2 = var\left(\frac{1}{(2k+1)^2} \sum_{k \in N_i} f_k - \frac{1}{(2k+1)^2} \sum_{k \in N_j} f_k\right)$$

$$= var\left(\frac{1}{(2k+1)^2} \sum_{k \in N_i \backslash N_j} f_k - \frac{1}{(2k+1)^2} \sum_{k \in N_j \backslash N_i} f_k\right)$$

$$= \frac{1}{(2k+1)^4}\left(\sum_{k \in N_i \backslash N_j} var(f_k) + \sum_{k \in N_j \backslash N_i} var(f_k)\right)$$

$$= \frac{1}{(2k+1)^4}\left(\sum_{k\in N_i\setminus N_j}\sigma^2 + \sum_{k\in N_j\setminus N_i}\sigma^2\right)$$

$$= \frac{2(2k+1)}{(2k+1)^4}\sigma^2 = \frac{2}{(2k+1)^3}\sigma^2 \tag{4}$$

Note that the rule of computing weighted sum of independent variables $var(ax + by) = a^2 \cdot var(x) + b^2 \cdot var(y)$ is applied here, after we have removed the overlapping nodes. Then, the variables in $N_i \setminus N_j$ and $N_j \setminus N_i$ are all independent.

The determination of σ_d^2 depends on σ^2, the global variance according to our image model. Given n image pixels, it can be computed by:

$$\sigma^2 = \frac{1}{n}\sum_{i=1}^n \frac{(2k+1)^2}{(2k+1)^2 - 1}(f_i - \hat{u}_i)^2$$

as

$$var(f_i - \hat{u}_i) = var\left(f_i - \frac{1}{(2k+1)^2}\sum_{k\in N_i}f_k\right)$$

$$= var\left(\frac{2k+1)^2 - 1}{(2k+1)^2}f_i - \frac{1}{(2k+1)^2}\sum_{k\in N_i\setminus\{i\}}f_k\right)$$

$$= \left(\frac{(2k+1)^2 - 1}{(2k+1)^2}\right)^2 var(f_i) + \left(\frac{1}{(2k+1)^2}\right)^2 \sum_{k\in N_i\setminus\{i\}}var(f_k)$$

$$= \left(\frac{(2k+1)^2 - 1}{(2k+1)^2}\right)^2 \sigma^2 + \left(\frac{1}{(2k+1)^2}\right)^2 \sum_{k\in N_i\setminus\{i\}}\sigma^2$$

$$= \frac{(2k+1)^2 - 1}{(2k+1)^2}\sigma^2$$

Again, the rule of computing weighted sum of independent variables is used in a similar way here.

Median Estimator. For better edge preservation we can also use the more robust median estimator:

$$\hat{u}_i = \text{median}_{k\in N_i}(f_k)$$

However, it is way more complicated to give an expression of σ_d^2 by σ^2 for median estimator than for the mean estimator. For this reason we conducted a numerical simulation to estimate their linear relationship. For each window size $(2k+1) \times (2k+1)$, we randomly generate 10000 groups of data. Each group contains three $N(0,1)$ Gaussian random trails $T_1 \in R^{(2k+1)\times(2k-1)}, T_2, T_3 \in R^{(2k+1)}$ to simulate the neighborhoods of two connected nodes. By defining $z_i = \text{median}(T1\cup T2) - \text{median}(T1\cup T3), i = 1, \cdots, 10000$, the computation in Eq. (4) corresponds to calculating the variance of z_i. This way we have $\sigma_d^2 \approx var(z_i)$. The numerical simulation led to $\sigma_d^2 = 0.142$ for $k = 1$ and $\sigma_d^2 = 0.030$ for $k = 2$. This result can be generalized for Gaussian model $N(\mu, \sigma^2)$ in the following way.

The simulation is independent of μ. In addition, a linear dependence $\sigma_d^2 = c \cdot \sigma^2$ with constant c is assumed, see Eq. (4). Thus, we use $\sigma_d^2 = 0.142\sigma^2$ for window size 3×3 and $\sigma_d^2 = 0.030\sigma^2$ for window size 5×5 for our experiments.

Implementation. Our approach can be easily implemented in two steps:

- In order to determine the weights ω_{ij} in Eq. (3) we calculate $\hat{u}_i$ at each node by the mean or median estimator and σ_d^2 by Eq. (4).
- Run the random walker algorithm using these adaptive weights.

By defining the transformation:

$$\hat{f}_i = \hat{u}_i / \sigma_d \qquad (5)$$

it turns out:

$$\omega_{ij} = exp\frac{-(\hat{u}_i - \hat{u}_j)^2}{2\sigma_d^2} = exp\frac{-(\hat{u}_i/\sigma_d - \hat{u}_j/\sigma_d)^2}{2} = exp\frac{-(\hat{f}_i - \hat{f}_j)^2}{2}$$

Therefore, an equivalent implementation is simply to run the random walk algorithm on the transformed image $\hat{f}_i$ using $\beta = 1/2$.

Fig. 4. Probability maps of original random walk algorithm (top) vs. our method using mean estimator (bottom).

The transformation (5) is basically a normalization. Compared to the normalization method suggested in [1] that rescales $(f_i - f_j)^2$ to $[0, 1]$, our data-driven method rescaling data by its global parameter σ_d is more robust and more sensitive to the image statistics.

Taking the image in Fig. 2 as an example, Fig. 4 shows the computed probability maps and the final segmentation. For comparison purpose the original random walk algorithm is run with $\beta = 91$, which is among the highest frequencies in Fig. 2.

5   Experimental Results

In this section we assess the performance of our adaptive weighting method on both synthetic and real data. The window size for mean or median estimator is set to 5×5.

Synthetic Data. On the two groups from Sect. 3 with 350 test images each we run the random walk algorithm using β varying from 1 to 1001 with step 10. The performance comparison with our adaptive weighting is done in two different ways:

– For each β value the difference $D_{\mathrm{ours}} - D_\beta$ is averaged over all test images, where D_x denotes the Dice index of method x, see Fig. 5. No matter which β value is used, our adaptive weighting method consistently has superior performance.
– For each test image we study $D_{\mathrm{ours}} - D_{opt\_\beta}$, where D_{opt_β} is the Dice index achieved using the optimal β value for each individual image, which is in fact *unknown*. The distributions over all images are shown in Fig. 6. Even when challenging the unknown optimal opt_β, our method is very favorable and achieves better Dice index for 90.29 % (86.43 %) of the test images from image group 1 using the mean (median) estimator. For the test image group 2 the behavior is very similar.

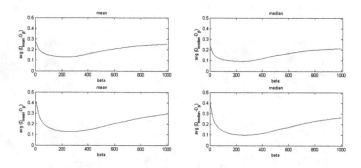

Fig. 5. Average of $D_{\mathrm{ours}} - D_\beta$ over all test images for each β value. Top: test image group 1. Bottom: test image group 2.

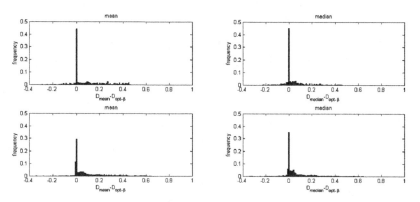

Fig. 6. Distribution of $D_{\mathrm{ours}} - D_{opt\_\beta}$ over all test images. Top: test image group 1. Bottom: test image group 2.

Note that for the second test image group the Dice index is computed for all detected objects and the averaged Dice index is taken for comparison.

Using the second test image group we now study the algorithm behavior for the different shapes therein. Breaking the global statistics in Fig. 6 into that of individual shapes, Fig. 7 displays the distribution of $D_{\text{ours}} - D_{opt\_\beta}$ over all test images for each shape. The overall good performance of our adaptive approach is clearly reflected by each individual object in the scene.

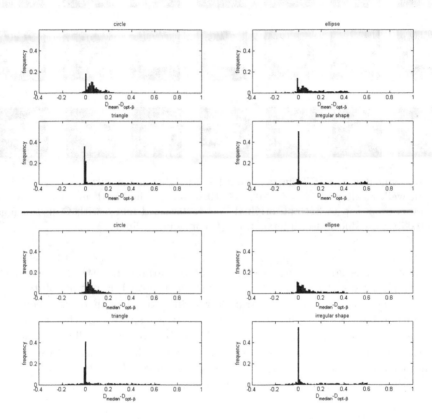

Fig. 7. Distribution of $D_{\text{ours}} - D_{opt\_\beta}$ over all test images (from test image group 2) using mean (top) and median (bottom) estimator.

Real Data. We take a CT (computed tomography) slice from [1]. Figure 8 shows the segmentation results for four cases: original image, distorted image with Gaussian noise ($\sigma = 0.05, 0.1$), reduced user intervention. Note that the value domain of this image is $[0, 1]$. We tried to mark similar scribbles as in [1]. Four results with $\beta = 50, 200, 500, 1000$ are contrasted with our results using the mean and median estimator. While in all four cases our method achieves good results, none of these β values works consistently well.

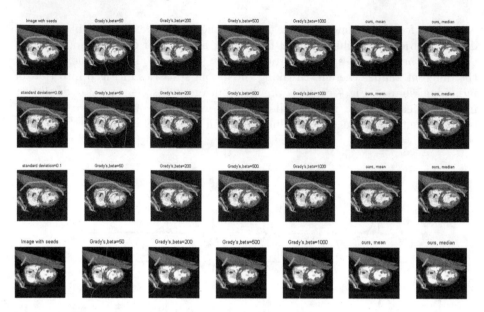

Fig. 8. Segmentation of CT image. From left to right: image with colored scribbles, random walk result with $\beta = 50, 200, 500, 1000$, our method with mean and median estimator. From top to bottom: original image, distorted image with Gaussian noise ($\sigma = 0.05, 0.1$), reduced user intervention. (Color figure online)

Discussion. The goal of this work is adaptive parameter setting to avoid the need of manually setting the parameter β. Our approach is not absolutely free of parameter; the window size parameter k has to be defined to specify the neighborhood for local estimation. However, it is easy to fix this parameter in practice. A reasonable value of k should enable to catch sufficient statistics for local estimation on the one hand and avoid multiple distributions in the neighborhood on the other hand. In our experiments $k = 2$, i.e. 5×5 local neighborhood, turned out to be a good choice.

6   Conclusion

In this work it is demonstrated that the parameter used for the weighting function has a strong influence on the segmentation quality of the popular random walk algorithm. This motivated us to propose an adaptive parameter setting method. A statistical model based approach has been developed to automatically set this parameter, thus adapting the segmentation algorithm to the statistic properties of an image. Experimental results on both sythetic and real data have been presented to demonstrate the usefulness of the proposed approach.

There are several issues for future research. Evaluating semi-automatic segmentation methods is not an easy task [12]. Although being the most effective way, user experiments are often prohibitively time-consuming to run.

The current experimental validation is still preliminary and needs further study. In applications fields like remote sensing and medical imaging many important imaging sensors deliver data with non-Gaussian noise models. There are relatively few segmentation methods incorporating physical noise models [13,14]. We are working on adaptive random walk segmentation that can cope with such noise models. In the current work we have studied the adaptive weighting function in the context of image segmentation. The question arises if this method (idea) can be used for other applications of random walk algorithms like ensemble segmentation [2], clustering [3], and semi-automatic 2D-to-3D conversion [4].

Acknowledgments. Ang Bian was supported by the China Scholarship Council (CSC). Xiaoyi Jiang was supported by the Deutsche Forschungsgemeinschaft (DFG): SFB656 MoBil (project B3) and EXC 1003 Cells in Motion – Cluster of Excellence.

References

1. Grady, L.: Random walks for image segmentation. IEEE Trans. Pattern Anal. Mach. Intell. **28**, 1768–1783 (2006)
2. Wattuya, P., Rothaus, K., Praßni, J., Jiang, X.: A random walker based approach to combining multiple segmentations. In: Proceedings of the International Conference on Pattern Recognition, pp. 1–4 (2008)
3. Abdala, D.D., Wattuya, P., Jiang, X.: Ensemble clustering via random walker consensus strategy. In: International Conference on Pattern Recognition, pp. 1433–1436 (2010)
4. Phan, R., Androutsos, D.: Robust semi-automatic depth map generation in unconstrained images and video sequences for 2D to stereoscopic 3D conversion. IEEE Trans. Multimedia **16**, 122–136 (2014)
5. Zhang, J.: The mean field theory in EM procedures for Markov random fields. IEEE Trans. Signal Process. **40**, 2570–2583 (1992)
6. Zhu, X., Lafferty, J., Ghahramani, Z.: Combining active learning and semi-supervised learning using gaussian fields and harmonic functions. In: ICML 2003 Workshop on the Continuum from Labeled to Unlabeled Data in Machine Learning and Data Mining (2003)
7. Zhu, X., Ghahramani, Z., Lafferty, J., et al.: Semi-supervised learning using Gaussian fields and harmonic functions. In: Proceedings of the International Conference on Machine Learning, pp. 912–919 (2003)
8. Pignalberi, G., Cucchiara, R., Cinque, L., Levialdi, S.: Tuning range image segmentation by genetic algorithm. EURASIP J. Adv. Signal Process. **8**, 780–790 (2003)
9. Wu, Z., Jiang, X., Zheng, N., Liu, Y., Cheng, D.: Exact solution to median surface problem using 3D graph search and application to parameter space exploration. Pattern Recogn. **48**, 380–390 (2015)
10. Geman, S., Graffigne, C.: Markov random field image models and their applications to computer vision. In: Proceedings of the International Congress of Mathematicians, pp. 1496–1517 (1986)
11. Gilboa, G., Osher, S.: Nonlocal linear image regularization and supervised segmentation. Multiscale Model. Simul. **6**, 595–630 (2007)
12. McGuinness, K., O'Connor, N.E.: Toward automated evaluation of interactive segmentation. Comput. Vis. Image Underst. **115**, 868–884 (2011)

13. Sawatzky, A., Tenbrinck, D., Jiang, X., Burger, M.: A variational framework for region-based segmentation incorporating physical noise models. J. Math. Imaging Vis. **47**, 179–209 (2013)
14. Tenbrinck, D., Jiang, X.: Image segmentation with arbitrary noise models by solving minimal surface problems. Pattern Recogn. **48**, 3293–3309 (2015)

On-the-Fly Architecture Design and Implementation of a Real-Time Stereovision System

Mohamed B.M. Masmoudi[1,2(✉)], Chadlia Jerad[1,2], and Rabah Attia[1]

[1] Sercom Laboratory, EPT, University of Carthage, Tunis, Tunisia
rabah_attia@yahoo.fr
[2] ENSI, University of Manouba, Manouba, Tunisia
{mohamed.masmoudi,chadlia.jerad}@ensi-uma.tn

Abstract. Stereovision is a way to reconstruct 3D information that is inspired from the basic mechanism of human eyes. When dealing with real-time stereo computation, the use of specialized hardware architecture becomes mandatory. Consequently, many research work dealt with the implementation of this process using FPGA platforms, each one with a particular emphasis. This paper describes a novel architecture that optimizes the memory size to be used in a pipelined, pixel clock synchronized, stereo vision system. Consequently, this last provides the disparity map in real-time. The resulting work is a tiny architecture capable of processing stereo video streams on-the-fly, without external memory storage for stereo pairs. This implementation is fully pipelined and covers the entire stereovision process. In addition, the hardware implementation of the Hamming distance as well as the index computation were enhanced. The design is generic as the disparity window, the image size, and the matching algorithm can be selected (Census or SAD). The hardware implementation shows better performance over previous studies.

Keywords: Stereovision · Real-time · FPGA implementation · Optimization

1 Introduction

Driver assistance, autonomous space exploration robots [12], mini- and micro-unmanned vehicles, precision radars, etc. are all examples of emerging applications of real-time stereovision. Indeed, this technique represents a good way to reconstruct the 3D scene by calculating the depth information. It is based on the use of two (or more) images taken from two (or several) cameras separated by already known distances. Although real-time depth estimation was achieved by purely software implementations [21], the performance revealed the limitation of such solution, particularly for embedded applications. With the high complexity and computation demands of this process, constrains such as time, size, energy and memory demands make the problem even harder.

© Springer International Publishing AG 2016
J. Blanc-Talon et al. (Eds.): ACIVS 2016, LNCS 10016, pp. 711–722, 2016.
DOI: 10.1007/978-3-319-48680-2_62

In the last decades, several architectures were deployed to solve this problem, and several targets were used, i.e. Digital Signal Processors (DSPs), GPUs (Graphics Processing Units) and Fields Programmable Gate Arrays (FPGAs). Chang et al. proposed in [4] a real-time and low-power embedded stereovision system that is implemented on DSP processors. In [20], authors took benefit from GPU's computation capability over CPU to build real time Stereovision systems. Nevertheless, the computation power of DSP based solutions is not high enough to support real-time dense processing, while GPU based solutions suffer from high power and large size demands compared to FPGAs [10]. Thanks to its high achievable speed, parallelization potential and its low power consumption, FPGA-based solutions were revealed to be the most attractive in literature.

This work is a contribution to answer the challenges raised by real time stereovision processing for embedded systems. Compared to previous FPGA-based solutions [1,2,7–9,11,13,15,17,19] (selected according to their relevance and date of publication), our designed architecture improves the overall performance while answering scalability issues. In a similar approach to [9], we opted for a pixel clocked synchronized system, dubbed "on-the-fly" frames processing, which rises the number of frames per second to 550 (based on the ISE synthesis tool report). This implementation is fully pipelined and covers the entire stereovision process: rectification, pre-processing, stereo correspondence (using either SAD or Census algorithms), and depth calculation. In addition, we perform edge detection using Sobel algorithm is order to improve results accuracy and we optimize the hardware implementation of the Hamming distance as well as the index computation. The design is generic since we can vary the disparity window (up to 128), the image size (up to 2048), and the matching algorithm (Census or SAD). The hardware implementation shows better performance compared to previous studies.

The rest of this paper is organized as follows: After this introductory section, Sect. 2 presents an overview of passive stereovision in addition to the algorithmic background of the selected process. Thereafter, a detailed description of the hardware implementation of the real time stereovision process is given in Sect. 3. The following section illustrates an experimental validation, while Sect. 5 exhibits the related work and shows how this work gives better performance compared to previous studies. Finally we conclude this work in Sect. 6 and announce future directions.

2   Overview on Passive Stereovision

2.1   Stereovision Process

Binocular stereovision consists on determining depth information from two images taken at the same time from distinct viewpoints. The 3D model is estimated by finding matching pixels in the images, using calibration information. These information are performed offline and obtained from the cameras properties (intrinsic parameters) and positions (extrinsic parameters) [6], based on assumptions about epipolar geometry [16].

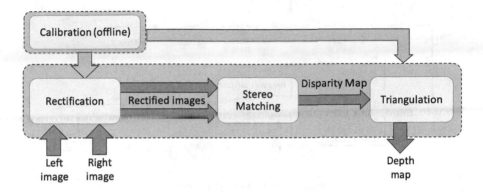

Fig. 1. Stereovision process.

As depicted in Fig. 1, Binocular stereovison is an online performed 3-stages process. The first stage is the rectification. It aims at using the information from the calibration, made offline, in order to remove lens distortions and turn the stereo pairs in standard form. For this purpose, an image transformation is applied in order to obtain a pair of rectified images from the original ones. It is worth-mentioning that a pre-processing step, consisting in a mere filtering operation, can be inserted between rectification and stereo matching to give more accurate rectified images to the following stage.

The second stage is stereo correspondence, also called stereo matching or disparity estimation. The aim is to find homologous points in the stereo pair in order to construct the disparity map. Using rectified images reduces the search operation to the epipolar line, which is sufficient to evaluate the disparity. In the letterature, several stereo matching algorithms were proposed based on different correspondence methods: local and global. In [3], authors claim that eventhough global methods provide better estimation quality, local methods can also lead to efficient results. Since we target in this work embedded applications with speed, power, size and resource constrains, we opted for local stereo matching. According to [14], most stereo algorithms perform a subset of these steps: (1) matching cost computation, (2) cost aggregation, (3) disparity computation/optimization, and (4) disparity refinement with the strategy Winner Takes All (WTA).

The final step, which is the triangulation, computes the position of the correspondence in the 3D space from the disparity map and calibration information.

2.2 Algorithmic Background of the Selected Process

In this subsection, we expose the different steps of our process to be implemented in this work. The flowchart of this process is illustrated in Fig. 2. Furthermore, we exhibit the algorithmic/mathematical background for each of the main steps in the following items.

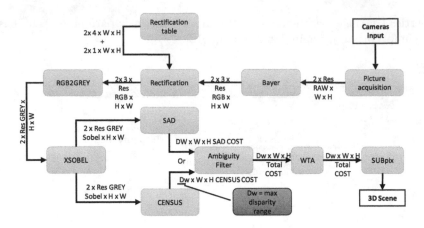

Fig. 2. Implemented process.

Rectification: consider the xth pixel in line y of an input image seen as a $I_w \times I_h$ matrix. We say that this pixel is of coordinates (x, y). The rectification phase attributes to a pixel of coordinates (x, y) new coordinates (x', y'), such that $x' = x$ and $y' = y + max\_distortion$, where $max\_distortion$ is the maximum adjustment range calculated as described in Eq. (1). In this equation, $R_r(j)$ and $R_l(j)$ are the calculated rectified destination for the pixel with j vertical coordinate.

$$max\_distortion = \max_{i=0}^{I_w} \left(\max_{j=0}^{I_h} |j - R_r(j)|, \max_{j=0}^{I_h} |j - R_l(j)| \right) \tag{1}$$

Pre-processing: Sobel: In the pre-processing module we aim to reduce the complexity of the matching algorithm by removing all unneeded and confusing information contained in the stereo pair. Since the purpose is matching pixels from one image to the other, all flat areas may be considered as a good matching for all pixels in the same area of reference. Removing this information makes the entire process much easier, which may be done using the Sobel filter. The appropriateness of this filter is due to its ability to detect object's edges. Consequently, the intensity of these edges will be the only information used for the rest of this work. Many other stereovision processes use X-Sobel instead of the full Sobel transform, since that rectification ensures the epipolar conditions which makes all transformation around the Y-axis non-useful.

Stereo Matching: Census and SAD: In this work, we focus on the local stereo method as a cost function. We particularly implement Census and SAD to estimate the correlation between the left and right images. For page limitation reasons, we give only the description of Census. The census transform maps the window surrounding a given pixel p to a bit vector representing the relationship between this pixel p and its neighbors. If the intensity value of a neighboring pixel is less than the intensity value of pixel p, then the corresponding bit is set to 1, otherwise it is set to 0. The dissimilarity between two bit strings can be measured through the hamming distance, which determines the number of bits that differ between these two bit strings.

Post-processing: The post processing step consists of applying filters aiming at further eliminating superfluous information. In the case of this work, filters are applied in order to delimit matching operation on edges and resolve ambiguities that could be resultant from horizontal edges and repetitive textures. In those two cases we opt for a very simple approach which considers a pixel-based decision as confusing and thus, it will be ignored at this stage of our research work.

Disparity: Based on census results the disparity step consists on calculating the Hamming distance between the reference pixel p and all other candidates in order to find the best matching one. The resulting pixel will be the one that has the least hamming distance with respect to p.

3 Hardware Implementation

The complexity of the implemented process described above can be easily determined. It depends on various parameters such as the correlation algorithm (SAD, Census), Matching window size as well as the stereo pair size. The scaling issue will be resolved by the deployment of a fully parallelized architecture that handles each pixel as soon as received. Given that processing may need several information (pixels) in the same time, we provide minimal sized buffers.

3.1 High Level Hardware Architecture

Figure 3 describes the high level hardware architecture. The overall process goes through 4 distinct pipeline stages. These stages are chosen according to the selected algorithms. Each stage performs the needed operation in highly parallel way and is implemented in a distinct module. The hole pipeline chain consist of the rectification, Sobel, Census, ambiguity filter and WTA stages.

For the in-depth implementation of the dedicated datapath, the following design decisions were made: intensive use of parallelism and pipelining, single pixel clock synchronization, and elimination of the use of an external image buffer. Because parallelism and pipelining are intrinsic resources of an FPGA, it is important to fully utilize these resources to improve computational performance.

In addition, an external image buffer is excluded, because it requires more than one clock cycle when fetching data from external memory devices. Even though this intensive pipelining causes additional use of routing resources, it helps the overall throughput. After the initial pipeline latency, the disparity for the corresponding input is generated in real-time and synchronized with the pixel clock. A detailed description of each module is given below.

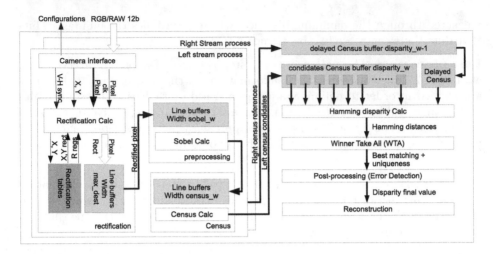

Fig. 3. High level hardware architecture.

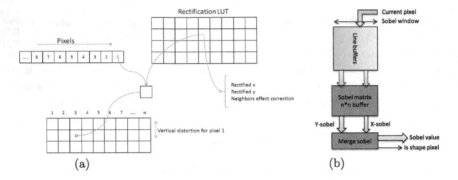

Fig. 4. Hardware architecture implementation for (a) rectification LUT and (b) Sobel filter.

3.2 Detailed Hardware Architecture Main Modules

In this subsection, we give further details about the implementation of the main architectural modules.

Implementation of the rectification: Following the equations processing the rectification (given in the previous section), correspondence matrices are computed offline. Consequently, obtaining the pair of rectified images is done using two Look-Up-Tables (LUTs). The rectification LUT contains in addition to the coordinate transformation further information that describes the neighbors effects on the current pixel. These information are used in order to correct edge variation on both images. The rectification is performed as illustrated in Fig. 4-(a). The needed hardware modules for this operation are:

– a memory controller allowing the access to rectification LUT which are loaded in an external memory,

- a rectification module that indicate the destination and the transformation of a given pixel,
- and *max_destortion* line buffer that acts as a simple shift register. This latter delays pixels in order to ensure that all those preceding are already rectified.

Implementation of the pre-processing stage: Many implementations of the Sobel filter were proposed in literature. However, most of them use line buffer to bufferize the Sobel window and then execute the Sobel transform. In this work we use the same architecture as in [9] and enhance it by the saving of binary information that determines whether the current pixel belongs to an edge or not. Figure 4-(b) shows the hardware architecture of Sobel filter implementation.

Algorithmic transformation implementation: The Cencus transform implementation is done almost in a similar way to previous works. The output of the first Census calculation will be delayed while waiting for candidates to be collected. Once all candidates are ready, the Hamming calculation will be lunched. Figure 5-(a) shows the hardware architecture of the algorithmic transformation implementation.

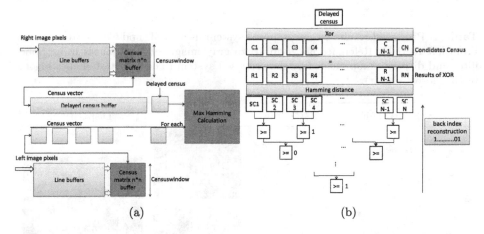

(a)   (b)

Fig. 5. Hardware architecture implementation of (a) Census transform and (b) Hamming distance calculation.

Disparity map computation implementation: As already said, census results are the entry of the disparity map computation, that consist on Hamming distance computation. The aim is to find, for a given reference pixel, the best matching one. Hamming distance calculation process typically needs large hardware resources since it needs several mathematical processing for each candidate and several iterations to elect the best score. In this work, we use the back index reconstruction mechanism in order to eliminate superfluous iterations. Hence, we changed the basic iterative calculation of scores by Wenger method [18]. Figure 5-(b) shows the hardware architecture of the Hamming distance calculation implementation.

4   Experimental Results

The used FPGA is the Xilinx Zynq-z7030 and we used a custom-built stereo camera system consisting of two video cameras configured to output 640 × 480 images at 30 fps. Obviously, given cameras with higher rates and higher resolution, this hardware implementation can be fitted on feature-rich FPGA that provides more processing power than the one experimented within this work. Although the proposed disparity estimation architecture is scalable and can support parallel computation of all disparity levels in a single clock cycle, the FPGA implementation of the architecture was configured taking into account the available FPGA resources and frame rate of the cameras. The present work can be fully customized by changing one of these parameters: the image width, pixel resolution, Sobel window, Census window, or Disparity window. FPGA reports were generated from the Xilinx ISE Synthesis Tool 14.7. Table 1 shows the processed results by the proposed and implemented system. The well known Cones and TSU stereo pairs were used for this purpose to validate our work. The last column represent our resulting disparity map, we can see that The brightest shapes belong to the closest object. We can clearly notice that the quality of

Table 1. Processed results by the proposed system using TSU and Cones Stereo pairs. From left to right: Reference image, RGB to gray image, edge emphasis using Sobel filter and disparity map yielded by the proposed system (The brightest shapes belong to the closest object).

the resulting disparity map is not too high but it still acceptable considering real-time constraints.

5   Performances Evaluation

A simulation based and synthesis based analysis were done in order to evaluate the performance of this architecture and its implementation.

5.1   Related Work and Performances Comparison

In [9], authors use the same steps as the proposed solution except for the Sobel transformation which makes the proposed work faster since it handles only edges. They also use multiple blocs to perform census transform, in this research, the census transform is performed on-the-fly and only results of the whole matching window is saved is a small line buffer.

Table 2. Performance comparison

Ref.	Hardware	Rectif.	Pre-processing	Matching algorithm	Disparity range	Window size	Image size	Frames per second	LUT Nbr
[9]	FPGA	Hard wired	No	Census /Local	64	11x11	640x480	up to 230 pixel clock	N/A
[1]	FPGA	Hard wired	No	Census /SGM	128	N/A	640x480	30 pixel clock	68.427
[11]	FPGA	No	No	Census /Local	var.	var.	640x480	45	296.578
[2]	FPGA	No	No	Census /Profile shape matching	60	N/A	450x375	30	9.637
[7]	FPGA +CPU	Hard wired	No	Census /SGM	N/A	8x6	752x480	60	N/A
[8]	FPGA	No	No	Local (CA and FLC)	N/A	15x15	640x480 1920x1080	507.9 76.0	N/A
[5]	FPGA +CPU +GPU	Hard wired	Bayer demosaicing Noise correct.	ZSAD/ Local	64	N/A	2048x2048	30	100.916
[13]	FPGA	No	Linear filter	SAD /Local	70	5x5	640x480	114	N/A
[15]	FPGA	No	No	Mini -Census	256 128	N/A	1920x1080 1024x768	47.6 129	N/A
[19]	FPGA	No	No	SGM /Local	N/A	N/A	1920x1080	30	70.745
[17]	FPGA	Hard wired	No	ADSW	64	N/A	640x480	60	135.292
This work	FPGA	Hard wired matrix	Sobel	Census/Local SAD/Local	128 Limit: Image width	Census(9x9) Sobel(3x3) Limit: Census(15x15) Sobel(3x3)	640x480 Limit: 2048x2048	30 (25 MHz cp) clock pixel Limit: 550 MHz cp (Xilinx ISE Rep.)	25.640 Limit: see Fig. 6

Some other works like [1,7] supply the stereo system with pixels from external memory which makes the rectification faster. The proposed solution allows buffering for several lines of pixels in order to wait for the first line to be rectified; this will cause the longest latency.

Table 2 provides performance comparison details of the referenced implementations listed above. It is obvious that the FPGA device used in each work influences the resource utilization considerably, in addition to the effectiveness of the synthesis tool and the quality of the place and route software. However, we can have an overall idea about the different implementations.

In this table, we give for each cited work the used hardware, the rectification implementation, the used pre-processing filter (if applicable), the matching algorithm, the disparity range, the considered window and image sizes, the reached number of frames per second, and the used number of LUTs. The last line in the table shows the performed results of our work. We note that we reached the highest number of frames per second, while keeping a reasonable size (LUT number) and increasing the image size. In addition, more flexibility is provided since one can choose the matching algorithm to use.

5.2   Scalability Analysis

The scalability of the proposed real-time stereovision process is explored by illustrating how the number of used LUTs reacts regarding to selected parameters. Rectification table utilization are neglected since the targeting FPGA contains RAM block. Table 3 summarizes this evolution in term of LUTs numbers, while

Table 3. Scalabilty analysis results: default image width = 320, default disparity window = 128

Disparity Window	Rectification #LUT	Sobel #LUT	Census #LUT	Hamming #LUT	Total #LUT	Image width	Rectification #LUT	Sobel #LUT	Census #LUT	Hamming #LUT	Total #LUT
16	561	317	950	1440	3268	320	561	316	950	23116	24944
32	561	317	950	5644	7472	450	742	445	1336	23116	25640
64	561	317	950	11468	13296	640	1005	633	1900	23116	26655
128	561	317	950	23116	24944	1280	1892	1267	3801	23116	30076
256	561	317	950	46412	48240						

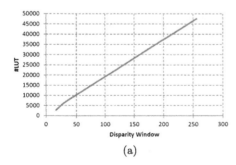

(a)

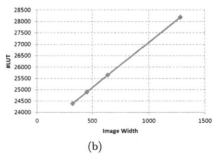

(b)

Fig. 6. Scalability analysis: impact of the disparity window and image size on the number of LUT.

Fig. 6 shows how this scalability scales linearly either with disparity window (Fig. 6-a) or the image size (Fig. 6-b).

6   Conclusion

In this paper, we presented an FPGA implementation of a selected stereovision process. This latter uses census transform, for providing disparity information. The rectification step is performed using a hard wired fixed matrix that could be computed offline. A pre-processing phase consisting in Sobel filtering, and a post-processing phase, thus enhancing quality by removing ambiguities, were also implemented.

This implementation enables real-time performance thanks to an intensive parallelization, pipelining, and optimized use of memory buffers. In addition, all elements are synchronized with a single pixel clock, allowing us to reach 550 MHz as a pixel clock. Experimental results validated the appropriateness of the implementation, and the scalability analysis announces a linear increase of used FPGA size with image width or disparity window increase.

In the future, we plan to integrate the system parts as IPs within a Multi-Processor System on Chip (MPSoC) architecture.

References

1. Banz, C., Hesselbarth, S., Flatt, H., Blume, H., Pirsch, P.: Real-time stereo vision system using semi-global matching disparity estimation: architecture and FPGA-implementation. In: International Conference on Embedded Computer Systems (SAMOS), pp. 93–101, July 2010
2. Tippetts, B., Lee, D.J., Lillywhite, K., Archibald, J.K.: Hardware-efficient design of real-time profile shape matching stereo vision algorithm on FPGA. Int. J. Reconfigurable Comput. **2014**, Article No. 2 (2014)
3. Brown, M., Burschka, D., Hager, G.: Advances in computational stereo. IEEE Trans. Pattern Anal. Mach. Intell. **25**(8), 993–1008 (2003)
4. Chang, N., Lin, T.M., Tsai, T.H., Tseng, Y.C., Chang, T.S.: Real-time DSP implementation on local stereo matching. In: 2007 IEEE International Conference on Multimedia and Expo, pp. 2090–2093, July 2007
5. Greisen, P., Heinzle, S., Gross, M., Burg, A.: An FPGA-based processing pipeline for high-definition stereo video. EURASIP J. Image Video Process. **2011**(1), 18 (2011)
6. Hartley, R.I., Zisserman, A.: Multiple View Geometry in Computer Vision, 2nd edn. Cambridge University Press, Cambridge (2004). ISBN: 0521540518
7. Honegger, D., Oleynikova, H., Pollefeys, M.: Real-time and low latency embedded computer vision hardware based on a combination of FPGA and mobile CPU. In: IEEE/RSJ International Conference on Intelligent Robots and Systems (IROS), pp. 4930–4935, September 2014
8. Jin, M., Maruyama, T.: Fast and accurate stereo vision system on FPGA. ACM Trans. Reconfigurable Technol. Syst. **7**(1), 3:1–3:24 (2014)
9. Jin, S., Cho, J., Pham, X.D., Lee, K.M., Park, S.K., Kim, M., Jeon, J.: FPGA design and implementation of a real-time stereo vision system. IEEE Trans. Circ. Syst. Video Technol. **20**(1), 15–26 (2010)

10. Kalarot, R., Morris, J.: Comparison of FPGA and GPU implementations of real-time stereo vision. In: 2010 IEEE Computer Society Conference on Computer Vision and Pattern Recognition Workshops (CVPRW), pp. 9–15, June 2010

11. Kim, J.H., Park, C.O., Kim, J.H., Cho, J.D.: Hardware implementation for census 3D disparity map with dynamic search range estimation. In: Signal Processing Algorithms, Architectures, Arrangements, and Applications Conference Proceedings (SPA), pp. 1–4, September 2011

12. Kostavelis, I., Nalpantidis, L., Boukas, E., Rodrigalvarez, M.A., Stamoulias, I., Lentaris, G., Diamantopoulos, D., Siozios, K., Soudris, D., Gasteratos, A.: SPARTAN: developing a vision system for future autonomous space exploration robots. J. Field Robot. **31**(1), 107–140 (2014)

13. Michailidis, G.T., Pajarola, R., Andreadis, I.: High performance stereo system for dense 3-D reconstruction. IEEE Trans. Circ. Syst. Video Technol. **24**(6), 929–941 (2014)

14. Scharstein, D., Szeliski, R.: A taxonomy and evaluation of dense two-frame stereo correspondence algorithms. Int. J. Comput. Vis. **47**(1–3), 7–42 (2002)

15. Shan, Y., Hao, Y., Wang, W., Wang, Y., Chen, X., Yang, H., Luk, W.: Hardware acceleration for an accurate stereo vision system using mini-census adaptive support region. ACM Trans. Embed. Comput. Syst. **13**(4s), 132:1–132:24 (2014)

16. Szeliski, R.: Computer Vision: Algorithms and Applications. Texts in Computer Science, 1st edn. Springer, London (2011)

17. Ttofis, C., Kyrkou, C., Theocharides, T.: A hardware-efficient architecture for accurate real-time disparity map estimation. ACM Trans. Embed. Comput. Syst. **14**(2), 36:1–36:26 (2015)

18. Wegner, P.: A technique for counting ones in a binary computer. Commun. ACM **3**(5), 322, May 1960. http://doi.acm.org/10.1145/367236.367286

19. Werner, M., Stabernack, B., Riechert, C.: Hardware implementation of a full HD real-time disparity estimation algorithm. IEEE Trans. Consum. Electron. **60**(1), 66–73 (2014)

20. Xiang, X., Zhang, M., Li, G., He, Y., Pan, Z.: Real-time stereo matching based on fast belief propagation. Mach. Vis. Appl. **23**(6), 1219–1227 (2012)

21. Zinner, C., Humenberger, M., Ambrosch, K., Kubinger, W.: An optimized software-based implementation of a census-based stereo matching algorithm. In: Bebis, G., et al. (eds.) ISVC 2008, Part I. LNCS, vol. 5358, pp. 216–227. Springer, Heidelberg (2008)

Complex Image Processing Using Correlated Color Information

Dan Popescu[(⊠)], Loretta Ichim, Diana Gornea, and Florin Stoican

Faculty of Automatic Control and Computers,
University Politehnica of Bucharest, Bucharest, Romania
dan.popescu@upb.ro, loretta.ichim@aii.pub.ro,
diana.gornea@yahoo.com, florin.stoican@gmail.com

Abstract. The paper presents a method for patch classification and remote image segmentation based on correlated color information. During the training phase, a supervised learning algorithm is considered. In the testing phase, we used the classifier built a priori to predict which class an input image sample belongs to. The tests showed that the most relevant features are contrast, energy and homogeneity extracted from the co-occurrence matrix between H and S components. Compared to gray-level, the chromatic matrices improve the process of texture classification. For experimental results, the images were acquired by the aid of an unmanned aerial vehicle and represent various types of terrain. Two case studies have shown that the proposed method is more effective than considering separate color channels: flooded area and road segmentation. Also it is shown that the new algorithm provides a faster execution time than the similar one proposed.

Keywords: Color decomposition · Co-occurrence matrix · Image recognition · Image segmentation · Remote images · Texture features

1 Introduction

As the name suggests, image segmentation represents the process of dividing a digital image into multiple parts that have a specific meaning for the applications/people that use/interpret the output of this process. Image segmentation is often used in conjunction with the procedure of classification.

Lately, numerous articles have introduced image segmentation methods and techniques, but few were focused on color images. For textured image segmentation, Haralicks' features [1] are the most efficient (like contrast, correlation, energy and homogeneity). Traditionally, texture analysis is based on features extracted from gray-level co-occurrence matrix (GLCM), but more recent work [2, 3] is directed towards the so-called color co-occurrence matrix (CCM), which takes into consideration inter-spectral dependencies as well. It was expected that the involvement of the color information in this features to give better results. Thus, recently, Khelifi et al. [2] used an extension of classical gray level co-occurrence matrix (GLCM) to multispectral images, named spatial and spectral gray level dependence method (SSGLDM). The authors applied their method on 624 medical images, aiming in prostate cancer

© Springer International Publishing AG 2016
J. Blanc-Talon et al. (Eds.): ACIVS 2016, LNCS 10016, pp. 723–734, 2016.
DOI: 10.1007/978-3-319-48680-2_63

diagnosis and observed an improvement from the classical GLCM, as far as the accuracy was concerned. However, authors chose to represent the RGB image, which is a third order tensor, meaning a three dimensional array $\chi \in R^{I_1 \times I_2 \times I_3}$ with $I_3 = 3$ in this particular case (the spectral bands), into a n-flattened matrix $X_n \in R^{I_n \times M_n}$ with $M_n = I_p \times I_q, p, q \neq n$. In this way, their intended SSGLDM can be computed in a similar manner as the classical co-occurrence matrix.

Losson et al. [3] use to determine descriptors for, which are another version of taken by the majority of cameras that do not have an optical sensor for each color component, but instead characterize each pixel by only one of the three components. The authors in [3] introduced the chromatic co-occurrence matrices to color filter array (CFA) images, but considered 'flattened' images, in the form of mosaic pictures. They tested the method on two benchmark texture datasets: Outex and VisTex with positive results, but since CFA images are not of three-dimensional type, the computation of this CCM is not actually very different from the computation of a co-occurrence matrix for any gray-scale image. Also, there is room for extending their technique to other color spaces, since they only applied it on RGB images.

On the other hand, extracting constantly reliable information from aerial imagery is a complicated problem, but it has numerous useful utilizations [4–8]. Some of them are related to flood monitoring [4, 5, 7]. Others deal with road detection [9–11]. Mnih et al. [9] also suggests a supervised learning approach using a priori labeled data from aerial images, but adopting a neural network to detect road textures.

In this paper we proposed a method and algorithm to classify patches from aerial images in order to segment the region of interest in different applications. Two case studies are presented in order to prove the benefit of the method: flooded area and road segmentation from UAV images. Compared to the algorithms presented in literature, ours has the advantage of simplicity and accuracy.

2 Proposed Methods

GLCM $C_{d,\theta} \in M_{g \times g}(N)$ can be computed for a gray level image, $f(x,y)$, with $x = \overline{1,n}$ and $y = \overline{1,m}$, which can take g integer values $\{0, 1, 2,..., g-1\}$. This is a square matrix $C_{d,\theta} \in M_{g \times g}(N)$ with g^2 elements and parameters d (distance) and θ (direction-angle). The elements of the co-occurrence matrix are (1):

$$C_{d,\theta}(i,j) = \sum_{x=1}^{n} \sum_{y=1}^{m} \left\{ \begin{array}{ll} 1, & if f(x,y) = i \quad and \quad f(x+d \cdot \cos\theta, y+d \cdot \sin\theta) = j \\ 0, & otherwise \end{array} \right\} \quad (1)$$

Starting from this, the authors in [2] made segmentation of textured images based on CCM, but they consider the color image as flat, similarly with a gray scale image not as a tensor (3D). Therefore there are not differences between the CCM calculus and GLCM.

In our approach, the image I is considered in a three-dimensional configuration (Fig. 1): $I = (I_1, I_2, I_3), I \in N^{n \times m \times 3}$. Each $I_j, j = 1, 2, 3$ has n rows and m columns (the proper dimension of image) and can take g positive integers $\{0, 1, 2,..., g - 1\}$.

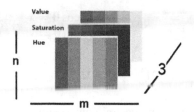

Fig. 1. Three dimensional representation of an image in HSV space

Let A and B two components of a color space. So, CCM is considered as a square matrix, $CCM \in N^{g \times g}$, having $g \times g$ elements in N. It has three parameters: the distance d, the direction θ (the co-occurrence is the same as in GLCM case), and the component-pair (A, B) between which it is calculated:

$$CCM_{d,\theta}^{AB}(i,j) = \sum_{x=1}^{n} \sum_{y=1}^{m} \left\{ \begin{array}{l} 1, \; if \; I_A(x,y) = i \quad and \quad I_B(x+d \cdot \cos \theta, y+d \cdot \sin \theta) = j \\ 0, \qquad\qquad\qquad\qquad otherwise \end{array} \right\} \quad (2)$$

A better illustration is given in Fig. 2. So, we consider two image components $A, B \in N^{3 \times 4}$ having 4 levels of pixel intensity and the CCM computed between these two components, along a distance $d = 1$ and orientation $\theta = 0°$ (e.g. because there are two (0,0) pairs of pixels with this orientation between A and B, the first element of the CCM will be 2).

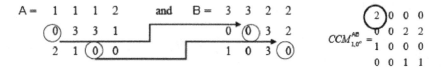

Fig. 2. Example of a proposed CCM

From Eqs. (3), (4) and (5) it can be observed that the co-occurrence matrices of mirrored pair combinations are transposed of each other (6).

$$CCM_{d,\theta}^{AB}(i,j) = \sum_{x=0}^{n-1} \sum_{y=0}^{m-1} \left\{ \begin{array}{l} 1, \; if \; A(x,y) = i \quad and \; B(x+d \cdot \cos \theta, y+d \cdot \sin \theta) = j \\ 0, \qquad\qquad\qquad\qquad otherwise \end{array} \right\} \quad (3)$$

$$[CCM_{d,\theta+180°}^{BA}(i,j)]^T = CCM_{d,\theta+180°}^{BA}(j,i) =$$

$$\sum_{p=0}^{n-1}\sum_{q=0}^{m-1}\begin{cases} 1, & \text{if } B(p,q)=j \quad \text{and } A(p+d\cdot\cos(\theta+180°), q+d\cdot\sin(\theta+180°))=i \\ 0, & \text{otherwise} \end{cases} \quad (4)$$

$$\begin{cases} p+d\cdot\cos(\theta+180°) \overset{denote}{=} x \\ q+d\cdot\sin(\theta+180°) \overset{denote}{=} y \end{cases} \Leftrightarrow \begin{cases} p-d\cdot\cos\theta = x \\ q-d\cdot\sin\theta = y \end{cases} \Rightarrow \begin{cases} p = x+d\cdot\cos\theta \\ q = y+d\cdot\sin\theta \end{cases} \quad (5)$$

$$CCM_{d,\theta}^{AB} = \left[CCM_{d,\theta+180°}^{BA}\right]^T \quad (6)$$

Therefore only one of pairs of spectral components will be considered.

The proposed algorithm for computing the co-occurrence matrix between spectral components was implemented in Matlab software [12]. Because the components H and S are less sensitive to lighting variations we choose the HSV color space.

In the learning phase we tested different pair combinations of color components for feature selection in two applications: flooded area and road detection and segmentation. In order to increase the performance of image segmentation we used the non-overlapping small boxes in a grid covering the image. Considering HSV space, the following attempts have been made:

(i) Calculate *CCM* for the following pairs: HS, HV, SV, HH, SS and VV.
(ii) Calculate a mean matrix of *CCMs* for each of the 8 main direction $(\theta = 0°, 45°, 90°, 135°, 180°, 225°, 270°, 315°)$ on different distance d [13].
(iii) Extract features (contrast, correlation, energy, entropy and homogeneity) from each of the computed *CCM*.
(iv) Establish a representative (reference) feature for the classes of interest.
(v) Calculate some important distances between current extracted features $f(k,k')$ and the texture class reference features $f_r(k,k')$ [14].

- Euclidian distance (7):

$$dist = \sqrt{\sum_{k,k'\in\{1,2,3\}} [f_r(k,k')-f(k,k')]^2} \quad (7)$$

- Minkowski (1-norm) distance (8):

$$dist = \sum_{k,k'\in\{1,2,3\}} |f_r(k,k')-f(k,k')| \quad (8)$$

- Chebyshev distance (9):

$$dist = \max_{k,k' \in \{1,2,3\}} \{|f_r(k,k') - f(k,k')|\} \qquad (9)$$

(vi) Assign the input texture to the nearest class of textures, in terms of *dist* and verify the accuracy.

(vii) Select the most efficient features (minimal number) and distance in terms of accuracy.

(viii) Establish the representatives of the classes by the mean of the selected features on a training set of patches from flooded area and asphalt road.

As it can be observed, there are numerous possible combinations to choose for the classification problem. For the particular cases of flood recognition and road recognition the conclusions were the following:

- **Features selected**. Since the input images were affected by lightning conditions (some parts were shadowed), we decided to remove the V component to improve the classification results, as it only propagated useless information. Therefore, we compute CCM_{HH}, CCM_{SS} and CCM_{HS} and extract from each of them Contrast, Correlation, Energy and Homogeneity features, which will become our predictors (thus, a total of 12 predictors per sample).
- **Distance type** for classifier: Chebyshev.
- **Number of patches** to calculate the representatives of classes: 100.

Taking into account the above considerations, the block diagram for the learning phase (training) is presented in Fig. 3 where A represents the texture class corresponding to region of interest (flood or road).

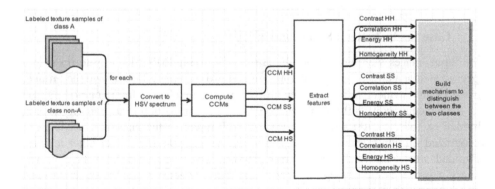

Fig. 3. Block diagram for the learning phase (training)

In the testing phase (Fig. 4) the train data are the representative of the class and the classifier is based on the distance between benchmark feature values and current feature values.

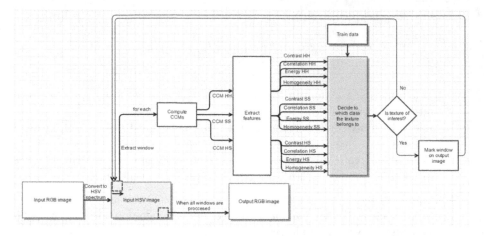

Fig. 4. Block diagram for the testing phase

3   Experimental Results

Considering that co-occurrence matrix calculation implies rather high computational costs and that the primary goal is proposing a new form of co-occurrence distribution, it was decided a constraint relaxation regarding the real time execution. Therefore, the implementation was started from the next simplifying assumption: the image acquisition task is not immediately followed by the image processing task. Moreover, the latter is performed separately, on a central computer system and not ad-hoc, on the aerial platform that captures the images. For this reason, no wireless data communication is necessary between the two.

3.1   Case Study 1: Road Segmentation

The input images were taken from the Hirrus UAV (Fig. 5) [15] set up to fly over a specific area at a cruise velocity of 100 km/h, approximately 300 m above the ground, using a photo camera with a resolution of 24.3 megapixels and frame rate of 10 fps.

After acquisition, 500 texture samples were chosen to build the training dataset, divided as follows: 100 samples of textures belonging to the class that needs to be recognized (in our case – Road samples – Fig. 6) and 400 samples of other textures (Flooded area, Non-flooded area, Grass, Forest, Houses etc. samples – Fig. 7). The binary classifier is built based on a predictors feature vector X (discussed above) and output Y, which represents the labels 1 (wanted texture) or 0 (not-wanted texture), using Matlab's implementation of the AdaBoost (adaptive boosting) algorithm [16]. During the testing phase, we slide a 64 × 64 pixels window across the input image by five pixels at a time and apply the classifier built a priori to predict whether each sliding window from the input image belongs to the desired class or not and mark it accordingly in the output image.

Fig. 5. Hirrus UAV being launched

Fig. 6. Road texture samples

Fig. 7. Non-road texture samples

In Table 1 it is presented a fragment of the training dataset and in Fig. 8 an example of an output image. All results discussed were obtained computing the CCM as a mean matrix of CCMs for each of the 8 main directions.

3.2   Case Study 2: Flooded Area Segmentation

In our application, we considered to have two classes of textures: flooded and non-flooded land. For the training phase of the classification task, a number of samples were chosen to be representative for each of the two classes that we considered (similarly as in Case study 1). The benchmark feature values for "flooded land" texture class are presented in Table 2 and in Fig. 9 an example of an output image for flooded area segmentation is done. The Matlab GUI application screen shot is presented in Fig. 10.

Fig. 8. Output for asphaltic road segmentation

Table 1. Fragment of the training dataset for road detection.

Sample	Con HH	Con SS	Con HS	Cor HH	Cor SS	Cor HS
asphalt1.jpg	0.067	0.114	3.684	0.811	0.768	0.525
asphalt2.jpg	0.103	0.100	3.590	0.793	0.746	0.534
asphalt3.jpg	0.076	0.093	4.022	0.846	0.689	0.511
asphalt4.jpg	0.033	0.147	4.472	0.934	0.711	0.605
non-asphalt1.jpg	0.047	0.073	16.023	0.656	0.179	4.70E-15
non-asphalt2.jpg	0.044	0.045	15.972	0.700	0.293	1.10E-14
non-asphalt3.jpg	0.069	0.036	16.028	0.581	0.307	2.42E-15
non-asphalt4.jpg	0.063	0.022	16.105	0.463	0.045	8.18E-15
Sample	En HH	En SS	En HS	Hom HH	Hom SS	Hom HS
asphalt1.jpg	0.590	0.426	0.728	0.967	0.943	0.351
asphalt2.jpg	0.409	0.551	0.504	0.949	0.950	0.362
asphalt3.jpg	0.438	0.616	0.935	0.962	0.953	0.334
asphalt4.jpg	0.476	0.377	0.466	0.984	0.927	0.331
non-asphalt1.jpg	0.819	0.844	0.995	0.976	0.963	0.19991
non-asphalt2.jpg	0.813	0.893	0.986	0.978	0.977	0.20024
non-asphalt3.jpg	0.772	0.914	0.985	0.966	0.982	0.19996
non-asphalt4.jpg	0.824	0.957	0.975	0.968	0.989	0.19962

Table 2. Benchmark feature values for flooded area class.

	Contrast	Correlation	Energy	Homogeneity
HS	18.7001	−0.0001	0.9106	0.1906
HV	53.4737	−0.0016	0.7673	0.121
SV	9.771	0.0368	0.6953	0.2656
HH	0.0003	0.0239	0.9994	0.9999
SS	0.0926	0.3184	0.7672	0.9537
VV	0.1596	0.1845	0.6571	0.9204

Fig. 9. Output image for flooded area segmentation

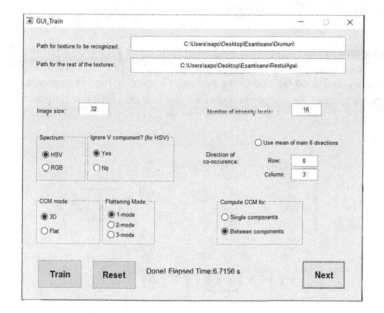

Fig. 10. Matlab GUI application screen shot

3.3 Performance Analysis

The performances were analysed in terms of accuracy and execution time. Thus, the accuracy A is given by (10) taken into account the false positive rate (11) and the false negative rate (12):

$$A = 1 - FPR - FNR \tag{10}$$

$$FPR = \frac{number \quad of \quad false \quad positive}{total \quad number \quad of \quad tested \quad textures} \tag{11}$$

$$FNR = \frac{number \quad of \quad false \quad negative}{total \quad number \quad of \quad tested \quad textures} \tag{12}$$

For the both both types of segmentation, the values are presented in Table 3. It can be seen that in the case of correlated components (like HS) the results are better that in the case of non-correlated components (like HH and SS).

Table 3. Accuracy for correlated color information.

	Non correlated components	Correlated components
Total no. of evaluations	5766	5766
False Positive Rate	0.69 %	0.09 %
False Negative Rate	0.12 %	0.12 %
Accuracy	99.18 %	99.79 %

With regards to execution time, compared to [2], our proposed algorithm for CCM is shorter. Tests were performed on PC, having 2.40 GHz quad-core processor, 8 GB RAM memory and a 64-bit operating system. Graphs in Fig. 11 represent comparatively execution times for segmentation of 15 test images, with our proposed algorithm

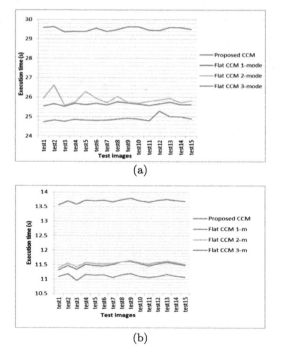

(a)

(b)

Fig. 11. (a) Execution times (s) – using a sliding step of 64 pixels, (b) Execution times (s) – using a sliding step of 128 pixels

and the algorithms proposed in [2] (for all three flattening modes), using either a sliding step of 64 pixels (Fig. 11a), or a step of 128 pixels (Fig. 11b).

4 Conclusions

In this paper, a new co-occurrence matrix was computed from images represented as three-dimensional tensors, taking into consideration the occurrences between color components of the image (H, S and V).

The proposed algorithm is better, in terms of accuracy, than the classical method of GLCM, and in terms of execution times, than the method described in [2].

The applications can be developed on remote sensing for detection and segmentation different regions of interest (in the presented work: flooded area and road detection).

A sufficiently robust method for ROI detection through texture analysis using the proposed CCM was designed and implemented with satisfactory results meaning good discrimination rates were obtained (low false positive rate and tending to zero false negative rates).

Moreover, we compute estimates of predictors' importance and repeated tests showed that most relevant features for road recognition are: Contrast, Homogeneity and Energy extracted from CCM_{SS} and CCM_{HS}, and Correlation from CCM_{HH}, which sustains the idea that the there is a certain gain using the inter-spectral co-occurrence matrices, comparing to the classical approach of GLCM.

Practical implementation can be used to provide roads monitoring or mapping services for traffic related purposes.

Throughout the practical implementation, concepts of image segmentation (co-occurrence matrix, texture features and texture classification), technologies (MATLAB) and devices (UAV) were integrated in a single functional application, managing their operation together.

Acknowledgements. The work has been funded by Romanian National Authority for Scientific Research and Innovation, CNCS-UEFISCDI, project number PN-II-RU-TE-2014-4-2713.

References

1. Haralick, R., Shanmugam, K., Dinstein, I.: Textural features for image classification. IEEE Trans. Syst. Man Cybern. **SMC-3**, 610–620 (1973)
2. Khelifi, R., Adel, M., Bourennane, S.: Multispectral texture characterization: application to computer aided diagnosis on prostatic tissue images. EURASIP J. Adv. Signal Process. **2012**, 118 (2012)
3. Losson, O., Porebski, A., Vandenbroucke, N., Macaire, L.: Color texture analysis using CFA chromatic co-occurrence matrices. Comput. Vis. Image Underst. **117**, 747–763 (2013)
4. Lai, C.L., Yang, J.C., Chen, Y.H.: A real time video processing based surveillance system for early fire and flood detection. In: Instrumentation and Measurement Technology Conference, Warsaw, Poland, pp. 1–6 (2007)

5. Lo, S.W., Wu, J.H., Lin, F.P., Hsu, C.H.: Cyber surveillance for flood disasters. Sensors **15**, 2369–2387 (2015)
6. Khurshid, H., Khan, M.F.: Segmentation and classification using logistic regression in remote sensing imagery. IEEE J. Sel. Top. Appl. Earth Obs. Remote Sens. **8**, 224–232 (2015)
7. Scarsi, A., Emery, W., Moser, G., Pacifici, F., Serpico, S.: An automated flood detection framework for very high spatial resolution imagery. In: Geoscience and Remote Sensing Symposium (IGARSS), pp. 4954–4957 (2014)
8. Ahmad, A., Tahar, K.N., Udin, W.S., Hashim, K.A., Darwin, N., Hafis, M., Room, M., Hamid, N.F.A., Azhar, N.A.M., Azmi, S.M.: Digital aerial imagery of unmanned aerial vehicle for various applications. In: IEEE International Conference on Control System, Computing and Engineering (ICCSCE 2013), pp. 535–540 (2013)
9. Mnih, V., Hinton, G.E.: Learning to detect roads in high-resolution aerial images. In: Daniilidis, K., Maragos, P., Paragios, N. (eds.) ECCV 2010. LNCS, vol. 6316, pp. 210–223. Springer, Heidelberg (2010). doi:10.1007/978-3-642-15567-3_16
10. Kong, H., Audibert, J.Y., Ponce, J.: General road detection from a single image. IEEE Trans. Image Process. **19**, 2211–2220 (2010)
11. He, Y., Wang, H., Zhang, B.: Color-based road detection in urban traffic scenes. IEEE Trans. Intell. Transp. Syst. **5**, 309–318 (2004)
12. Matlab documentation. http://www.mathworks.com/products/matlab/
13. Popescu, D., Ichim, L.: Image recognition in UAV application based on texture analysis. In: Battiato, S., Blanc-Talon, J., Gallo, G., Philips, W., Popescu, D., Scheunders, P. (eds.) ACIVS 2015. LNCS, vol. 9386, pp. 693–704. Springer, Heidelberg (2015). doi:10.1007/978-3-319-25903-1_60
14. Deza, E., Deza, M.: Dictionary of Distances. Elsevier, Amsterdam (2006)
15. UAV Hirrus documentation. www.aft.ro/bro.pdf
16. http://www.mathworks.com/discovery/adaboost.html

Using PNU-Based Techniques to Detect Alien Frames in Videos

Giuseppe Cattaneo, Gianluca Roscigno[(✉)], and Andrea Bruno

Dipartimento di Informatica, Università degli Studi di Salerno,
84084 Fisciano, SA, Italy
{cattaneo,giroscigno,andbruno}@unisa.it

Abstract. In this paper we discuss about video integrity problem and specifically we analyze whether the method proposed by Fridrich *et al.* [16] can be exploited for forensic purposes. In particular Fridrich *et al.* proposed a solution to identify the source camera given an input image. The method relies on the Pixel Non-Uniformity (PNU) noise produced by the sensor and existing in any digital image.

We first present a wider scenario related to video integrity. Then we focus on a particular case of video forgery where sequences of frames, recorded by a different camera (in short, *alien frames*), could be added to the original video.

By means of experimental evaluation in specific real world forensic scenarios we analyzed the accuracy degree that this method can achieve and we evaluated the critical conditions where the results are not enough reliable to be considered in courts.

The results show that the method is robust, and alien frames can be reliably detected provided that the source device (or its faithful fingerprint) is available. Nevertheless the discussed method applies to a rather limited concept of video integrity (alien frames detection) and more extensive solutions, able to cover a wider range of application scenarios, would be required as well.

Keywords: Digital image forensics · Pixel non-uniformity noise · Source camera identification · Video forgery detection · Video integrity

1 Introduction

Nowadays we are surrounded by digital cameras for video surveillance purposes which record any kind of activity. The resulting digital videos are often extremely useful as digital evidence for the investigations and law courts. As consequence courts, before considering such evidence, must assess their integrity and reliability and, in many cases, digital forensic analysts are invited to certify the collected evidence. Therefore it would be worth to provide the experts with well known methodologies or tools whose reliability and robustness have already been approved.

© Springer International Publishing AG 2016
J. Blanc-Talon et al. (Eds.): ACIVS 2016, LNCS 10016, pp. 735–746, 2016.
DOI: 10.1007/978-3-319-48680-2_64

In order to be considered as forensic evidence, experts first have to prove the integrity of the whole file containing the video. Digital signature is normally used to prove the integrity and the ownership of the file, but this approach cannot be applied to live data streams because digital signature can only be applied to static files. Another issue arises when the stream is saved on a digital media and it is not possible to prove that its content has not been altered by human intervention before saving it. In fact, video can be readily modified using popular software solutions which enable the user to both remove, add or change one or more frames in the existing video. Specifically added frames could be recorded by a different source device.

The *Image Forensics* research area is very active for digital images, but less results has been produced for videos. For instance, for digital images many well established results are available to verify: the integrity of the image (i.e., *Image Integrity*) (e.g., [5–7,13,14,22,24]), the presence of hidden data (i.e., *Image Steganography*) (e.g., [9,17]) or the compliance with a target source camera that has been used to capture that image (i.e., *Source Camera Identification*) (e.g., [2–4,8,16,18]). However these results cannot be straightly extended to videos due to a higher compression ratio and a different encoding schema.

In this paper we present the result of the experimental evaluation of the method proposed by Fridrich *et al.* [16], based on the *Pixel Non-Uniformity* (PNU) noise, when used to detect the presence of one or more *alien* frames inside a video. We define as alien a frame that has been acquired by a certain camera (or device) and then injected in a video recorded using a different camera. The Fridrich *et al.* technique has been originally proposed to identify the device used to take a picture through the extraction of a sort of *camera fingerprint* introduced by the PNU noise. In a few words, we adapted this technique to the problem of detecting alien frames in videos, by considering these as sequences of images.

The trial has been conducted to clearly state the accuracy and the robustness of this method when used in specific real world forensic scenarios like, for instances, video surveillance. More specifically two different scenarios have been evaluated: (a) the camera itself or an original video (i.e., not containing alien frames) recorded with that camera is available to calculate its fingerprint; (b) the camera is not available but only a forged video, originally recorded with that camera but containing a variable percentage of alien frames, is available. In both cases, we considered as input a full-HD video $(1,920 \times 1,080$ pixels) encoded in the H.264 standard [21,23].

Organization of the paper. The rest of the paper is organized as follows. In Sect. 2 we briefly discuss the state of the art both in the field of image and video forgery detection. In Sect. 3 we first present the original Fridrich *et al.* technique, then we propose our adaptation of it for solving the problem of identifying the alien frames. In Sect. 4 we present the results of an experimental analysis where we measure the performance of this technique in some application scenarios. Finally, in Sect. 5 we outline some future directions for our work.

2   Digital Video Forgery Detection

The digital video forgery detection research field is concerned with the development of automatic or semi-automatic techniques able to determine any forgery in a digital video. The particular case of forgery that is discussed in this paper is about the possibility to modify a digital video, recorded using a certain device, by including video sequences recorded using a different device. We will refer to these additional frames as to *alien frames*.

As observed by Fridrich *et al.* in [11], the sensors used by digital camcorders are the same used by digital cameras. Thus, one possible approach to this problem is to adapt the techniques already used to detect forgeries in digital images. In this particular case, the most relevant contribution is indeed the detection technique presented by Fridrich *et al.* in [22]. It uses the *Sensor Pattern Noise* (SPN), i.e., the characteristic noise left by a digital camera sensor while taking a picture, to determine if an input image has been forged by means of the copy-move technique. In a few words, their method works by looking for regions in an image under inspection whose pattern noise does not match the one of the camera sensor supposedly used to take that image. This comparison is done by correlating the pattern noise existing in a region of the input image with the pattern noise of the camera sensor corresponding to that region. If the correlation value is below a calculated significance level, that region is assumed to be forged. The proposed method is available in two variants, the first requiring the user to manually select the region that is suspected to be forged whereas the second is able to determine automatically which region has been forged (if any). This method works under the assumption that a forged region will not contain the SPN from the camera for that region, which is certainly true if the region was pasted from another image from a different camera. This is also true if the region is from an image coming from the same camera as long as its spatial alignment in the image is different than in the forged image. This approach has been explored and improved in several other contributions (see, e.g., [5,10,12,13]).

The image forgery detection technique by Fridrich *et al.* has first been applied to the video forgery problem in [11]. Here, the authors used this technique to determine if two videos are taken from the same camera. In particular, the authors estimate the sensor noise from an input video using the maximum likelihood estimator and, then, a normalized cross-correlation.

A refinement of this idea has been proposed by Hsu *et al.* in [19]. In a few words, they introduce the concept of temporal sensor pattern noise existing in a video, with respect to a reference camera, and whose correlation is modeled using a *Gaussian Mixture Model* (GMM). Another copy detection scheme has been presented by Bayram *et al.* in [1]. Their idea is that all visual media possess unique characteristics that links the media with its source. In particular, their proposal attempts to detect duplicate and modified copies of a specific video by using only the characteristic of the image sensor and not the content of the video. The SPN signature is a weighted combination of the signature of the devices used to generate video. Finally, the authors in [20] present a forgery detection specifically designed system for surveillance videos. They analyze the peculiar characteristic of these videos and then they propose to transform the SPN for each video by applying a *Minimum Average Correlation Energy* (MACE) filter to identify both RGB and infrared video. The manipulation are detected by estimating the scaling factor and calculating the correlation coefficient.

3 Video Forgery Detection Using the Technique by Fridrich *et al.*

In this section, we present an adaptation of the Source Camera Identification (SCI) technique by Fridrich *et al.* [16] to the problem of assessing the integrity of a video file. We restrict our attention to the particular case of a video that has been forged through the addition of sequences of frames recorded using a different device. We will refer to these frames as to *alien frames*. The adaptation we present has been experimented on video files encoded using the H.264 standard [21,23].

3.1 The Source Camera Identification Technique by Fridrich *et al.*

This technique allows to establish if an input image I has been taken by a camera (or device) C by looking at the Pixel Non-Uniformity (PNU) noise existing in I. The PNU noise is caused by the imperfections existing in the imaging sensor of any digital camera. It is unique for any sensor, so it can be used as a fingerprint to identify the source camera used to take an image. An estimation of this noise, called *Residual Noise* (RN), can be derived from an image I using a PNU denoising filter F_{PNU}, in the following way:

$$RN_I = I - F_{PNU}(I) \,. \tag{1}$$

The identification technique by Fridrich *et al.* works in three steps.

Step 1: Initialization. The first step is the calculation of a *Reference Pattern* (RP) for the camera C, i.e., its fingerprint. This can be done by averaging the RNs from a set of images taken using C. Formally, given a camera C and a set $\{RN_1^C, \ldots, RN_m^C\}$ of RNs from images taken by C, RP_C can be computed as:

$$RP_C = \frac{\sum_{i=1}^{m} RN_i^C}{m} \,. \tag{2}$$

Step 2: Training. The second step requires the calculation of a set of acceptance thresholds to be associated to each of the cameras (i.e., RPs) under scrutiny. This is done by using a set of training images.

In particular, let T be a training image, RN_T is correlated with RP_C using the Bravais-Pearson correlation index as defined in the following formula:

$$corr(RN_T, RP_C) = \frac{(RN_T - \overline{RN_T})(RP_C - \overline{RP_C})}{\|(RN_T - \overline{RN_T})(RP_C - \overline{RP_C})\|} \,. \tag{3}$$

The outcoming value is in the range $[-1, 1]$, where higher values implies an higher confidence that T comes from camera C. After evaluating all these correlations, the thresholds for each camera C are computed using the Neyman-Pearson approach. This allows to design the detection function from the statistical description of two distributions: correlation indices for images taken by camera C and correlation indices for images that were not taken by camera C. In particular, the outcoming thresholds are chosen so to minimize the *False Rejection Rate* (FRR) for images taken by using C, given an upper bound on the *False Acceptance Rate* (FAR) for images taken by using a camera different than C (see [16] for details).

Step 3: Detection. The third step is the identification step and it requires the extraction of the residual noise of an unknown image I, i.e., RN_I. In particular, if the correlation between the residual noise of an image I and the Reference Pattern of a camera C exceeds the corresponding acceptance threshold, then C is assumed to be the camera that originated I.

3.2   The H.264 Standard

The *H.264* [21,23] is a popular standard format for encoding videos. It works by organizing a video track as a sequence of frames, i.e., images taken from a camera with a specific frequency, where each frame is of one of three types. The first type is the *intra-frame* (in short, I-frame). It refers to the first frame of a new sequence, where this frame is not directly linked with previous frames. It is encoded as a static image, typically using the JPEG format. The second type is the *predictive-frame* (in short, P-frame). It reports the delta, in terms colors or contents, with respect to the previous frame. The third type is the *bidirectional predictive frame* (in short, B-frame). It reports the delta, in terms of color or contents, with respect to the previous or to the next frame.

If an I-frame is lost, then all P-frames and B-frames linked to this frame are lost as well. For this reason, I-frames are also called *Key Frames*.

The *Group Of Pictures* (GOP) size indicates the length between two near I-frames, i.e., the distance between two full images.

3.3   Using the Fridrich *et al.* Technique to Detect Alien Frames

Given an input video v, that has supposed to be recorded using a device C, we are interested in establishing if it contains frames recorded using a different device. This problem can be solved by resorting to the Fridrich *et al.* technique, as in the following description.

Step 1: Initialization. We calculate the Reference Pattern of C, i.e., RP_C. This can be done following the original technique by Fridrich *et al.* and using, as input images, the image frames extracted from a (non-forged) video recorded with C.

Step 2: Training. We calculate a decision threshold that will be later used to establish if a frame is taken by C. This threshold will represent the minimum correlation value between the RN of an input frame f, RN_f, and RP_C, for f to be recognized as a frame recorded by C. This value is chosen by using the Neyman-Pearson method on a correlations set built by comparing RP_C with the RNs extracted from a training set of 100 frames recorded using C as well as 100 frames recorded using a different device C'. The threshold thr is calculated so as to minimize the FRR of frames extracted from video taken with C, given an upper bound on FAR.

Step 3: Detection. We extract all the frames from v. Then, we calculate the RN for each of these frames. If the correlation between the residual noise of a frame f and RP_C is below the threshold thr, f is marked as *"Alien"*, otherwise as *"Original"*.

There is however one detail that should be taken into account when applying this algorithm to a H.264 video. As seen in Sect. 3.2, most of the frames existing in a H.264 video are encoded using a differential compression scheme, whereas the Fridrich *et al.* algorithm requires to work on full content images. This problem could be solved by considering only on the I-frames existing in a video.

4   Experimental Analysis

In this section we present the results of an experimental analysis we conducted to assess the performance of our adaptation of the Fridrich *et al.* technique when used to find alien frames in a H.264 video. We considered two application scenarios. In the first scenario (see Sect. 4.2), a non-forged video recorded with a device C (or the camera C itself) is available to the investigator. In the second scenario (see Sect. 4.3), the investigator has only a video originally recorded with C and then forged with the addition of alien frames. Two different datasets have been assembled for conducting these experiments. Finally, in Sect. 4.4 we discuss about comparing the PNU noises extracted from JPEG images and video frames using the same camera C. The performance of the method in the considered application scenarios is evaluated according to the indicators introduced in Sect. 4.1.

4.1   Key Performance Indicators

We measured the performance of the Fridrich *et al.* technique when used to detect alien frames in a video using four of the classical binary classifier statistics [15]: *True Positive Rate* (TPR), *True Negative Rate* (TNR), *False Positive Rate* (FPR) and *False Negative Rate* (FNR), where by positive we refer to a frame identified as alien.

In addition, we also considered the following measures:

- *Accuracy (ACC)*. It describes the efficiency and goodness of the classification, that is: higher is this value then lower are the error rates. It can be calculated with the following equation:

$$ACC = \frac{TP + TN}{TP + FP + FN + TN}.$$

(4)

- *Balanced Accuracy (BAC)*. A measure alternative to the ACC and useful when the size of the two classes is unbalanced, for example when the number of alien frames is very different than the number of original frames.

$$BAC = \frac{TPR + TNR}{2}.$$

(5)

4.2   Experiment 1: Analysis of Forged Videos Using an Accurate Reference Pattern

In our first experiment, given a video file v supposedly recorded using a certain device A, we measured the ability of the proposed technique to correctly identify the I-frames existing in v but recorded using a different device. In this case, we are assuming that either the device A or a (relatively) long non-forged video recorded by A is available to the investigator. This allows to correctly evaluate the Reference Pattern of A (i.e., RP_A).

As first step, we extracted the RP_A by applying the technique described in Sect. 3.3 to a non-forged video recorded with device A. Here we have used an original video lasting about 60 s with the following features: GOP size equal to 30, 30 *frames per second* (fps), rotation 90°, and containing outdoor and indoor scenes. As next step, we forged three videos, each assembled by merging a video recorded by A with a video recorded by a different device, i.e., B. These videos represent three application scenarios varying according to the severity of the alteration of an original video. All the original videos recorded by A and B last no less than 20 s and have the following features: GOP size equal to 30, 30 fps, rotation 90°, and contain outdoor and indoor scenes. In the first scenario (Video 1), a relatively long video recorded with A is altered by the addition of a relatively short sequence recorded with B. In the second scenario (Video 2), a relatively long video recorded with A is altered by the addition of a video recorded with B and having approximately a similar duration. In the third scenario (Video 3), a relatively short video recorded with A is altered by the addition of a video recorded with B and having approximately a similar duration. The structure of these videos is summarized in Table 1, where it is reported only the number of I-frames per each video.

The outcoming results, available in Table 2, show that the considered technique is robust in correctly classifying the origin of each I-frame, provided that the video recorded with A is long enough.

Table 1. Number of I-frames existing in the considered forged videos, classified according to their originating device.

Name	Device A	Device B
Video 1	61	11
Video 2	61	73
Video 3	17	21

Table 2. Key performance indicators in percentage of the considered technique in the identification of I-frames that have been recorded using a device different than A.

Experiment	TPR	FPR	TNR	FNR	ACC	BAC
Video 1	100	0	100	0	100	100
Video 2	100	0	100	0	100	100
Video 3	95	24	76	5	87	86

4.3 Experiment 2: Analysis of Forged Videos Using an Inaccurate Reference Pattern

In our second experiment we assume that neither the device A nor a (relatively) long non-forged video recorded by A is available to the investigator. Instead, we experimented with the extraction of the RP of A by using the I-frames available in a video originally recorded by A and then forged. The purpose of this experiment was to assess the performance of the technique when used with an inaccurate RP, i.e., a RP calculated using also the pattern noise existing in some alien frames.

As first step, we extracted RP_A by applying the technique described in Sect. 3.3 to a set of five forged videos (see Table 3). Each video was obtained by merging a video recorded by A with a sequence of frames of increasing duration recorded by a different device B. The original videos recorded by A and B last approximately 60 s and have the following features: GOP size equal to 30, 30 fps, rotation 90°, and contain outdoor and indoor scenes. In the next step, we used the five RPs obtained during the previous step to classify the I-frames

Table 3. Number of I-frames, per device, existing in forged videos used to compute RP_A.

Name	Device A	Device B
Video RP 1	60	0
Video RP 2	60	1
Video RP 3	60	6
Video RP 4	60	12
Video RP 5	60	30

existing in a video v created by merging 30 I-frames from device A with 30 I-frames from a device B and 30 more I-frames from a third device. The corresponding original videos last about 30 s and have the following features: GOP size equal to 30, 30 fps, rotation 90°, and contain outdoor and indoor scenes. As we can see in Table 4, the usage of a forged video to extract the RP_A does not prevent the technique from successfully identifying always all the I-frames that have been recorded by this device. Instead, increasing the duration of the forged part of the video used to extract RP_A, implies an increase of the number of alien frames classified as being recorded with A. A closer inspection revealed that the frame to be misclassified originate all from D. This phenomenon could be expected as the I-frames existing in the forged part of the videos used to extract RP_A come from B as well.

Table 4. Key performance indicators in percentage of the considered technique in the identification of I-frames that have been recorded using a device different than A exploiting RPs for device A computed on forged video (see Table 3).

Experiment	TPR	FPR	TNR	FNR	ACC	BAC
Corruption Test 1	100	0	100	0	100	100
Corruption Test 2	100	0	100	0	100	100
Corruption Test 3	78	0	100	22	86	89
Corruption Test 4	57	0	100	43	71	78
Corruption Test 5	50	0	100	50	67	75

4.4   Comparing the PNU Noises Extracted from Images and Video Frames

During the experimental evaluation of the technique of Fridrich *et al.*, an interesting operating scenario arose: *Given a set of images and a video, is it possible to state if they have been produced by the same device?* In other words: *In which conditions the two RPs extracted from the set of images and from the video frames can be compared?*

Nowadays almost all digital cameras produce both images and videos using the same digital sensor. While images can have a number of pixels close to the sensor physical resolution, videos have always a lower resolution. For example, full-HD videos have $1,920 \times 1,080$ pixels as frame resolution, while JPEG images taken by the same camera can have much higher resolutions. For this reason, video frames are recorded after applying a number of operations on the source image acquired by the sensor. These transformations are implemented by the software installed on the camera, often they are undocumented and may vary from model to model. Obviously these post-processing operations affect the PNU noise extracted from the frames of a video making hard to compare it with the one extracted by the JPEG images.

We have experimentally evaluated this scenario using the following setup: a set S of 100 JPEG images (with resolution of $4,608 \times 3,456$) and a H.264 video v (with resolution of $1,920 \times 1,080$), both recorded using a device C (i.e., a Olympus OM-D E-M5 Mark II digital camera). Due to the mismatch existing between the two resolutions, in order to make comparable the two Reference Patterns, we had to figure out which transformations have been applied by the camera on the source frames before recording the video. Then the equivalent operations are applied on the JPEG images before comparing the resulting Reference Patterns. The following procedure has been empirically discovered: before applying the PNU filter, each image from S is shrunk to $1,920 \times 1,440$ pixels and, then, the top and the bottom bands (with heights of 180 pixels) are removed.

The RP_C calculated from the JPEG images after applying this procedure and the RNs extracted by the I-frames of v gave high correlation indices, confirming that the PNU noise can provide valuable information even in this new scenario.

However, we have experimented that these transformations are device-based, and, therefore, there are many cameras that use different post-processing operations.

5   Conclusions and Future Works

In this paper we have experimentally evaluated the technique proposed by Fridrich *et al.* [16] to verify if it is suitable for assessing the integrity of video files. In particular, the method has been used to detect alien frames of a video, i.e., if it contains frames that have been recorded using a different sensor than the one used to produce the original video.

On one hand, the experimental results confirmed that a good accuracy can be achieved by the adopted technique proving that the PNU is preserved by the video encoding process. On the other hand, as reported in Sect. 4, this accuracy decreases when the input video contains many alien frames and/or the source camera is not available.

Moreover, the technique does not work when the video has been forged by removing some frames or adding external frames produced by the same source camera.

As far the live data streams, the method has been conceived to work only on off-line videos. This means that first a fingerprint should be computed and, thereafter, it can be used to validate the next frames.

Therefore, the method is suitable for forensic purposes, but it represents only a partial solution to the problems of video integrity and does not eliminate the need for a more extensive method. In fact, we are currently working on a different approach able to provide a reliable and complete solution to the problem of video integrity delegating the source camera (or a proxy) to embed integrity check information into the video stream.

References

1. Bayram, S., Sencar, H.T., Memon, N.: Video copy detection based on source device characteristics: a complementary approach to content-based methods. In: Proceedings of the 1st ACM International Conference on Multimedia Information Retrieval, pp. 435–442. ACM (2008)
2. Bayram, S., Sencar, H.T., Memon, N.: Efficient techniques for sensor fingerprint matching in large image and video databases. In: IS&T/SPIE Electronic Imaging, vol. 7541, pp. 1–8. International Society for Optics and Photonics (2010)
3. Castiglione, A., Cattaneo, G., Cembalo, M., Ferraro Petrillo, U.: Experimentations with source camera identification and online social networks. J. Ambient Intell. Humaniz. Comput. 4(2), 265–274 (2013)
4. Cattaneo, G., Faruolo, P., Ferraro Petrillo, U.: Experiments on improving sensor pattern noise extraction for source camera identification. In: Sixth International Conference on Innovative Mobile and Internet Services in Ubiquitous Computing (IMIS), pp. 609–616 (2012)
5. Cattaneo, G., Ferraro Petrillo, U., Roscigno, G., De Fusco, C.: A PNU-based technique to detect forged regions in digital images. ACIVS 2015. LNCS, vol. 9386, pp. 486–498. Springer, Heidelberg (2015). doi:10.1007/978-3-319-25903-1_42
6. Cattaneo, G., Roscigno, G.: A possible pitfall in the experimental analysis of tampering detection algorithms. In: 17th International Conference on Network-Based Information Systems (NBiS 2014), pp. 279–286 (2014)
7. Cattaneo, G., Roscigno, G., Ferraro Petrillo, U.: Experimental evaluation of an algorithm for the detection of tampered JPEG images. In: Linawati, Mahendra, M.S., Neuhold, E.J., Tjoa, A.M., You, I. (eds.) ICT-EurAsia 2014. LNCS, vol. 8407, pp. 643–652. Springer, Heidelberg (2014)
8. Cattaneo, G., Roscigno, G., Ferraro Petrillo, U.: A scalable approach to source camera identification over Hadoop. In: IEEE 28th International Conference on Advanced Information Networking and Applications (AINA), pp. 366–373. IEEE (2014)
9. Cheddad, A., Condell, J., Curran, K., McKevitt, P.: Digital image steganography: survey and analysis of current methods. Signal Process. 90(3), 727–752 (2010)
10. Chen, M., Fridrich, J., Lukáš, J., Goljan, M.: Imaging sensor noise as digital X-ray for revealing forgeries. In: Furon, T., Cayre, F., Doërr, G., Bas, P. (eds.) IH 2007. LNCS, vol. 4567, pp. 342–358. Springer, Heidelberg (2008)
11. Chen, M., Fridrich, J., Goljan, M., Lukáš, J.: Source digital camcorder identification using sensor photo response non-uniformity. In: Electronic Imaging 2007, p. 65051G. International Society for Optics and Photonics (2007)
12. Chen, M., Fridrich, J., Goljan, M., Lukáš, J.: Determining image origin and integrity using sensor noise. IEEE Trans. Inf. Forensics Secur. 3(1), 74–90 (2008)
13. Chierchia, G., Cozzolino, D., Poggi, G., Sansone, C., Verdoliva, L.: Guided filtering for PRNU-based localization of small-size image forgeries. In: International Conference on Acoustics, Speech and Signal Processing (ICASSP) 2014, pp. 6231–6235. IEEE (2014)
14. Farid, H.: Exposing digital forgeries from JPEG ghosts. IEEE Trans. Inf. Forensics Secur. 4(1), 154–160 (2009)
15. Fawcett, T.: An introduction to ROC analysis. Pattern Recogn. Lett. 27(8), 861–874 (2006)
16. Fridrich, J., Lukáš, J., Goljan, M.: Digital camera identification from sensor noise. IEEE Trans. Inf. Secur. Forensics 1(2), 205–214 (2006)

17. Fridrich, J., Goljan, M., Du, R.: Steganalysis based on JPEG compatibility. In: International Symposium on the Convergence of IT and Communications (ITCom), vol. 4518, pp. 275–280. International Society for Optics and Photonics (2001)
18. Goljan, M., Fridrich, J., Filler, T.: Large scale test of sensor fingerprint camera identification. In: IS&T/SPIE, Electronic Imaging, Security and Forensics of Multimedia Contents XI, vol. 7254, pp. 1–12. International Society for Optics and Photonics (2009)
19. Hsu, C.C., Hung, T.Y., Lin, C.W., Hsu, C.T.: Video forgery detection using correlation of noise residue. In: IEEE 10th Workshop on Multimedia Signal Processing, 2008, pp. 170–174. IEEE (2008)
20. Hyun, D.K., Lee, M.J., Ryu, S.J., Lee, H.Y., Lee, H.K.: Forgery detection for surveillance video. In: Hyun, D.-K., Lee, M.-J., Ryu, S.-J., Lee, H.-Y., Lee, H.-K. (eds.) The Era of Interactive Media, pp. 25–36. Springer, Heidelberg (2013)
21. ITU Telecommunication Standardization Sector: H.264: advanced video coding for generic audiovisual services, February 2016. http://www.itu.int/rec/T-REC-H.264. Accessed 30 Apr 2016
22. Lukáš, J., Fridrich, J., Goljan, M.: Detecting digital image forgeries using sensor pattern noise. In: Electronic Imaging 2006, p. 60720Y. International Society for Optics and Photonics (2006)
23. Richardson, I.E.: H.264 and MPEG-4 Video Compression: Video Coding for Next-Generation Multimedia. Wiley, Hoboken (2004)
24. Ye, S., Sun, Q., Chang, E.C.: Detecting digital image forgeries by measuring inconsistencies of blocking artifact. In: IEEE International Conference on Multimedia and Expo 2007, pp. 12–15. IEEE, July 2007

Author Index

Printed in the United States
By Bookmasters